M.L. Jhingan is an alumnus of the University of Delhi who after his M.A., worked as Research Assistant on a project of Dr.V.K.R.V. Rao, the then Director, Delhi School of Economics. Dr. Jhingan taught economics to postgraduate classes for over three decades and had been contributing to academic journals.

He is the author and co-author of a number of widely acclaimed textbooks on Economics and Management that sell in India and abroad. His books combine theoretical rigour and lucid exposition of the various concepts and theories of economics.

His most popular and the best selling text, The Economics of Development and Planning, was published 50 years ago in 1966 . Dr.Jhingan also guided Ph.Ds in India and abroad. Prof. Jhingan was Head of Economics Department and Principal, Government Post Graduate Evening College, Bhiwani and retired as Deputy Director, Higher Education, Haryana.

MONEY, BANKING, INTERNATIONAL TRADE AND PUBLIC FINANCE

8TH REVISED AND ENLARGED EDITION

M.L. JHINGAN

Retired Deputy Director,
Higher Education, Haryana

B.K. JHINGAN

B.A.(Hons.)Economics,M.A.(Economics)
Contributing Editor

VRINDA

SIMPLY THE TEXT !

VRINDA PUBLICATIONS (P) LTD.

VRINDA PUBLICATIONS (P) LTD.
B-5, Ashish Complex (opp. Ahlcon Public School),
Mayur Vihar, Phase-I, Delhi-110 091
Tel. : +91(11) 22755315, 22755316
WhatsApp : (+91) 9953003795
E-mail—info@vrindaindia.com
http://www.vrindaindia.com

First Edition 1984
Fifth Revised & Enlarged Edition : 1997
Sixth Revised & Enlarged Edition : 2001
Seventh Revised & Enlarged Edition : 2004
Eighth& Revised Enlarged Edition :2011
Reprinted : 8 Times

Reprint: 2024

e Textbook Available

ISBN 978-81-8281-384-7
(Money,Banking,International Trade & Public Finance-8th Edition)

Typeset by : Kumud Printographics, Delhi-53
Printed at : Nisha Enterprises

Preface to the Eighth Edition

This is a substantially revised edition in a new get-up. Many diagrams have been redrawn. Besides the following chapters have been rewritten :

- **Part One :** The Demand for Money
- **Part Two :** Central Banking
  Monetary Policy
- **Part Three :** The Concept of Multiplier
  National Income
- **Part Four :** The Terms of Trade
- **Part Five :** The World Trade Organisation
- **Part Seven :** Public Debt

I hope the present edition will prove more helpful to students.
Suggestions to improve the book are solicited.

M.L. JHINGAN

E-mail : vrinda@ndf.vsnl.net.in

PREFACE TO THE FIRST EDITION

This is an introductory textbook on Money, Banking and International Trade meant for B.A. and B. Com. (Pass and Hons.) students. It presents the subject matter in a simple, coherent and critical manner. It takes the reader from an introductory to a higher level gradually. Since monetary economics is a part of macroeconomics, the book also deals with the Keynesian economics at an elementary level. Bibliography and footnotes reveal my indebtedness to different writers. Exercises at the end of each chapter are meant to acquaint the student with the type of questions on every topic.

I am thankful to my students for their views during the writing of the book. Above all, I am indebted to my wife for her immense and varied help

Suggestions for the improvement of the book are most welcome from students and teachers.

ML. JHINGAN

PREFACE TO THE SEVENTH EDITION

This is a thoroughly revised and substantially enlarged edition in keeping with the latest UGC syllabus. Besides revising and updating part six relating to *Money and Banking in India. The* following eight chapters have been added:

- Keynes' Fundamental Equations
- Foreign Trade Multiplier
- Mill's Theory of Reciprocal Demand
- International Monetary System
- New International Economic Order (NIEO)
- Public Goods, Private Goods and Market Failure
- Theories of Taxation
- Trends in Revenue and Expenditure of Centre and State Governments in India

I hope the present edition will be more useful to students preparing for B.A. / B.Com. (Pass and Hons.) and similar courses.

Suggestions for further improvement of the book are welcome.

M.L JHINGAN

E-mail: vrinda@ndf.vsnl.net.in

Brief Contents

PART ONE
MONEY

PART TWO
BANKING

PART THREE
KEYNESIAN THEORY OF INCOME, OUTPUT AND EMPLOYMENT

PART FOUR
INTERNATIONAL TRADE

PART FIVE
INTERNATIONAL MONETARY SYSTEM

PART SIX
MONEY AND BANKING IN INDIA

PART SEVEN
PUBLIC FINANCE

Contents

PART ONE
MONEY

PART THREE
KEYNESIAN THEORY OF INCOME, OUTPUT AND EMPLOYMENT

PART FOUR
INTERNATIONAL TRADE

PART FIVE
INTERNATIONAL MONETARY SYSTEM

PART SIX

MONEY AND BANKING IN INDIA

PART SEVEN
PUBLIC FINANCE

PART ONE

MONEY

Chapter 1

Evolution and Functions of Money

1. THE BARTER SYSTEM

Before the evolution of money, exchange was done on the basis of direct exchange of goods and services. This is known as barter. Barter involves the *direct exchange of one good for some quantity of another good.* For example, a horse may be exchanged for a cow, or 3 sheep or 4 goats. For a transaction to take place, there must be a *double coincidence of wants.* For instance, if the horse-owner wants a cow, he has to find out a person who not only possesses the cow but wants to exchange it with the horse. In other cases, goods are exchanged for services. A doctor may be paid in kind as payment for his services. For example, he may be paid a cock, or some wheat or rice or fruit. Thus, a barter economy is a *moneyless economy.* It is also a *simple economy* where people produce goods either for self-consumption or for exchange with other goods which they want. Bartering was found in *primitive societies.* But it is still practised at places where the use of money has not spread much. Such non-monetised areas are to be found in many rural areas of underdeveloped countries.

Difficulties of Barter

But the barter system is the most inconvenient method of exchange. It involves loss of much time and effort on the part of people in trying to exchange goods and services. As a method of exchange, the barter system has the following difficulties and disadvantages :

1. *Lack of Double Coincidence of Wants.* The functioning of the barter system requires a double coincidence of wants on the part of those who want to exchange goods or services. It is necessary for a person who wishes to trade his good or service to find some other person who is not only willing to buy his good or service, but also possesses that good which the former wants. For example, suppose a person possesses a horse and wants to exchange it for a cow. In the barter system, he has to find out a person who not only possesses a cow but also wants a horse. The existence of such a double coincidence of wants is a remote probability. For, it is a very *laborious and time-consuming* process to find out persons who want each other's goods. Often the horse-owner would have to carry through a number of intermediary transactions. He might have to trade his horse for

some sheep, sheep for some goats and goats for the cow he wants. To be successful, the barter system involves *multilateral* transactions which are not possible practically. Consequently, if the double coincidence of wants is not matched exactly, no trade is possible under barter. Thus a barter system is time-consuming and is a great hindrance to the development and expansion of trade.

2. *Lack of a Common Measure of Value.* Another difficulty under the barter system relates to the lack of a common unit in which the value of goods and services should be measured. Even if the two persons who want each other's goods meet by coincidence, the problem arises as to the proportion in which the two goods should be exchanged. There being no common measure of value, the rate of exchange will be arbitrarily fixed according to the intensity of demand for each other's goods. Consequently, one party is at a disadvantage in the terms of trade[1] between the two goods.

Moreover, under the a barter system the value of each good is required to be stated in as many quantities as there are types and qualities of other goods and services. The exchange rate formula given by Prof. Culbertson[2] is $n(n-1)/2$. For example, if there are 100 different types of goods in a barter economy, then there would be 4950 exchange rates for it to function smoothly, i.e. 100(100 –1)/2=100×99/2 or 9900/2=4950. This makes accounting an impossibility because a balance sheet would consist of a long physical inventory of the various types and qualities of goods owned and owed. Similarly, it is difficult to draw and interpret the profit and loss accounts of even a small shop. That is why the existence of the barter system is associated with a small primitive society confined to a local market.

3. *Indivisibility of Certain Goods.* The barter system is based on the exchange of goods with other goods. It is difficult to fix exchange rates for certain goods which are indivisible. Such indivisible goods pose a real problem under barter. A person may desire a horse and the other a sheep and both may be willing to trade. The former may demand more than four sheep for a horse but the other is not prepared to give five sheep and thus there is no exchange. If a sheep had been divisible, a payment of four and a half sheep for a horse might have been mutually satisfactory. Similarly, if the man with the horse wants only two sheep, then how will he exchange his horse for two sheep. As it is not possible to divide his horse, no trade will be possible between the two persons. Thus indivisibility of certain goods makes the barter system inoperative.

4. *Difficulty in Storing Value.* Under the barter system, it is difficult to store value. Anyone wanting to save real capital over a long period would be faced with the difficulty that during the intervening period, the stored commodity may become obsolete or deteriorate in value. As people trade in cattle, grains, and other such perishable commodities, it is very expensive and often difficult to store and to prevent their deterioration and loss over the long period.

5. *Difficulty in Making Deferred Payments.* In a barter economy, it is difficult to make payments in future. As payments are made in goods and services, debt contracts are not possible due to disagreements on the part of the two parties on the following grounds:"[1] . It would often invite controversy as to the quality of the goods or services to be repaid.[2] The two parties would often be unable to agree on the specific commodity to be used for repayment.[3] Both parties would run the risk that the commodity to be repaid would increase or decrease seriously in value over the duration of the contract. For example, wheat might rise markedly in value in terms of other commodities, to the debtor's regret, or decrease markedly in value, to the creditor's regret."[3] Thus, it is not possible to make just payments involving future contracts under the barter system.

6. *Lack of Specialisation.* Another difficulty of the barter system is that it is associated with a production system where each person is a jack-of-all trades. In other words, a high degree of specialisation is difficult to achieve under the barter system. Specialisation and interdependence in production is only possible in an expanded market system based on the money economy. Thus no economic progress is possible in a barter economy due to lack of specialisation.

The above mentioned difficulties of barter have led to the evolution of money.

---

1. The terms of trade refer to the rate at which one good exchanges for another good.
2. John M. Culbertson, *Money and Banking,* 1972.
3. L.V. Chandler and S.M. Goldfield, *The Economics of Money and Banking,* 7/e, 1977.

2. THE EVOLUTION OF MONEY

The word "money" is derived from the Latin word "Moneta" which was the surname of the Roman Goddess of Juno in whose temple at Rome, money was coined. The origin of money is lost in antiquity. Even the primitive man had some sort of money. The type of money in every age depended on the nature of its livelihood. In a hunting society, the skins of wild animals were used as money. The pastoral society used livestock, whereas the agricultural society used grains and foodstuffs as money. The Greeks used coins as money.

STAGES IN THE EVOLUTION OF MONEY

The evolution of money has passed through the following five stages depending upon the progress of human civilisation at different times and places.

1. *Commodity Money.* Various types of commodities have been used as money from the beginning of human civilisation. Stones, spears, skins, bows and arrows, and axes were used as money in the hunting society. The pastoral society used cattle as money. The agricultural society used grains as money. The Romans used cattle and salt as money at different times. The Mongolians used squirrel skins as money. Precious stones, tobacco, tea, shells, fishhooks, and many other commodities served as money depending upon time, place and economic standard of the society.

The use of commodities as money had the following defects: (1) All commodities were not uniform in quality, such as cattle, grains, etc. Thus, lack of standardisation made pricing difficult. (2) Difficult to store and prevent loss of value in the case of perishable commodities. (3) Supplies of such commodities were uncertain. (4) They lacked in portability and hence were difficult to transfer from one place to another. (5) There was the problem of indivisibility in the case of such commodities as cattle.

2. *Metallic Money.* With the spread of civilisation and trade relations by land and sea, metallic money took the place of commodity money. Many nations started using silver, gold, copper, tin, etc. as money.

But metal was an inconvenient thing to accept, weigh, divide and assess in quality. Accordingly, metal was made into coins of predetermined weight. This innovation is attributed to King Midas of Lydia in the eighth century B.C. But gold coins were in use in India many centuries earlier than in Lydia. Thus coins came to be accepted as a convenient method of exchange.

But some ingenious persons started debasing the coins by clipping a thin slice off the edge of coins. This led to the hoarding of full-bodied coins with the result that debased coins were found in circulation. This led to the minting of coins with a rough edge.

As the price of gold began to rise, gold coins were melted in order to earn more by selling them as metal. This led the governments to mix copper or silver in gold coins so that their intrinsic value might be more than their face value. As gold became dearer and scarce, silver coins were used, first in their pure form and later on mixed with alloy or some other metal.

But metallic money had the following *defects:* (1) It was not possible to change its supply according to the requirements of the nation both for internal and external use. (2) Being heavy, it was not possible to carry large sums of money in the form of coins from one place to another by merchants. (3) It was unsafe and inconvenient to carry precious metals for trade purposes over long distances. (4) Metallic money was very expensive because the use of coins led to their debasement, and their minting and exchange at the mint cost a lot to the government.

3. *Paper Money.* The development of paper money started with goldsmiths who kept strong safes to store their gold. As goldsmiths were thought to be honest merchants, people started keeping their gold with them for safe custody. In return, the goldsmiths gave the depositors a receipt promising to return the gold on demand. These receipts of the goldsmiths were given to the sellers of commodities by the buyers. Thus, the receipts of the goldsmiths were a substitute for money. Such paper money was backed by gold and was convertible on demand into gold. This ultimately led to the development of bank notes.

The bank notes are issued by the central bank of the country. As the demand for gold and silver increased with the rise in their prices, the convertibility of bank notes into gold and silver was gradually given up during the beginning and after the First World War in all the countries of the world. Since then the bank money has ceased to be representative money and is simply fiat money which is inconvertible and is accepted as money because it is backed by law.

4. *Credit Money.* Another stage in the evolution of money in the modern world is the use of the cheque as money. The cheque is like a bank note in that it performs the same function. It is a means of transferring money or obligations from one person to another. But a cheque is different from a bank note. A cheque is made for a specific sum, and it expires with a single transaction. But a cheque is not money. It is simply a written order to transfer money. However, large transactions are made through cheques these days and bank notes are used only for small transactions.

5. *Near Money.* The final stage in the evolution of money has been the use of bills of exchange, treasury bills, bonds, debentures, savings certificates, etc. They are known as "near money". They are close substitutes for money and are liquid assets. Thus in the final stage of its evolution, money has become intangible. Its ownership is now transferable simply by book entry.

Thus, the origin of money has been through various stages: from commodity money to metallic money, and to paper money, and from credit money to near money.

3. CLASSIFICATION OF MONEY

Money can be classified on the following different basis: (1) the physical characteristics of the materials of which money is made, or the monetary system criterion; (2) the nature of the issuer such as a government, central bank, commercial bank, or other bank or the acceptability criterion; and (3) the relationship between the value of money as money and the value of money as commodity or what Keynes called Money of Account and Money Proper. We shall follow this classification while explaining the various *kinds of money.*

1. Monetary System Criterion

The monetary system criterion classifies money into : (1) metallic money, (2) paper money, and (3) credit money which we discuss below:

(1) Metallic Money

Money made of any metal such as gold, silver, nickel, copper, etc. is called metallic money. Metallic money is further classified into standard money, token money and subsidiary money.

(i) Standard Money. Standard money "is money whose value as a commodity for non-monetary purposes is as great as its value as money." Such money is made of coins whose face value equals their intrinsic or metallic value. The holder of such coins may use them as metal by melting them or as money, because the value of the metal in the coins is the same as their monetary value. Standard money is, therefore, known *as full-bodied money.* Between 1835-93 the Indian Rupee-coin made of silver was a full-bodied coin. Further, standard money is unlimited legal tender in which any amount of payment can be made.

(ii) Token Money. Token money is representative money whose intrinsic value of the metal is less than its face value. The rupee coin in circulation in India is a token coin. If it is melted, its metal will not be sold worth one rupee.

(iii) Subsidiary Money. Subsidiary money is to assist the token money. All coins of the denominations 50 paise in India are subsidiary money. Such coins are limited legal tender in which payments can be made only up to Rs. 25 in India.

(2) Paper Money

Paper money refers to notes of different denominations made of paper and issued by the central bank and/or the government of the country. Paper money can be classified into (i) representative paper money, (ii) convertible paper money, (iii) inconvertible paper money, and (iv) fiat money.

(i) Representative Paper Money. Representative paper money is "in effect a circulating warehouse receipt for full-bodied coins or their equivalent in bullion." It is also known as representative full-bodied money because it is fully backed by gold coins or gold bullion held by the treasury. They are fully convertible into gold

coins or bullion. The gold certificates which circulated in the United States prior to 1933 were representative paper money.

(ii) Convertible Paper Money. Convertible paper money is that which does not have 100 per cent backing in the form of standard coins. But the holder of paper money can get it converted into coins on demand. The only difference between representative and convertible paper money is that the former is fully backed by standard coins while the latter is not fully backed by them. But both types of paper money are convertible.

(iii) Inconvertible Paper Money. The paper money which does not have any backing of standard coins and is also not convertible into them is known as inconvertible paper money. Notes issued by central banks of all countries represent inconvertible paper money. They are also known as *fiduciary money*.

(iv) Fiat Money. Paper money which circulates on the authority (i.e. fiat) of the government is fiat money. Fiat money is created and issued by the state. But it is not convertible by law and is legal tender. Fiat money is thus representative or token money. One rupee note issued by the Ministry of Finance and token coins issued by the Government of India are fiat money. Practically, there is no difference between fiat money and inconvertible paper money these days.

(3) Credit Money

Credit money or bank money is transferred by a commercial bank in the form of a cheque or draft. But a cheque or draft is not money. Demand deposits in a bank is money which is withdrawable by a holder of the deposit through a cheque or draft. Thus, it is demand deposit which is credit or bank money that is transferable from one person to another through a cheque or draft. But a cheque or draft is not legal tender and may not be accepted as a means of payment or medium of exchange. However, in advanced countries bank money is as important as the paper notes issued by the government or the central bank of the country.

2. Acceptability Criterion

On the basis of acceptability criterion, money is classified into legal tender money and non-legal tender money.

(1) *Legal Tender Money.* Legal tender money is that which the state and the people accept as the means of payment and in discharge of debts. Since it has the authority of the government, such money is accepted compulsorily by the people. All notes and coins issued by the government and the central bank of a country are compulsory legal tender in that country. Legal tender money is further divided into limited and unlimited legal tender money.

(i) Limited Legal Tender Money. Limited legal tender money is that in which payments can be made legally upto a certain limit. All coins of the denominations of 50 paise are limited legal tender in India. Payments in them can be made up to a limit of Rs. 25.

(ii) Unlimited Legal Tender Money. A money is unlimited legal tender when payments can be made in it legally in unlimited quantities. All paper notes and coins of 1 Rupee are unlimited legal tender in India. People have to accept payments in unlimited quantities in notes and these coins.

(2) *Non-legal Tender or Optional Money.* Money which does not possess any legal authority of the state or the central bank is non-legal tender money. Robertson called it "optional money". Bank money in the form of cheques, drafts, etc. is non-legal tender money. People are not bound to accept such money because there is no legal sanction behind their issue.

Besides cheques and drafts, there are many other forms of optional money such as time deposits, bonds, securities, debentures, bills of exchange, treasury bills, postal certificates, insurance policies, etc. They are known as "near money" or "money substitutes". They are almost perfect substitutes for money as a store of value. They possess moneyness or liquidity. They also yield income. They economise in the use of currency. But they do not have any legal status.

3 Money of Account and Money Proper

Keynes distinguished between money of account and money proper. According to him, "Money of account is that in which Debts and Prices and General Purchasing Power are expressed." On the other hand, money proper is the actual money in which contracts or debts are settled, such as the Indian Rupee, the British

Pound, the American Dollar, the French Franc, the German Mark, the Japanese Yen, the Italian Lira, etc. Usually, there is no difference between money of account and money proper when the accounts in a country are maintained in money proper. But if accounts are kept in some other currency, money of account differs from money proper, as happened in Germany after World War I when the money of account was the American Dollar and the money proper was the German Mark. However, the two may differ when the value of money as money and the value of money as commodity are different. For example, value of Indian rupee as money of account has remained the same but the value of Indian rupee as commodity or money proper has been changing overtime, that is, it is an unlimited legal tender. It is a token coin or money whose present intrinsic value is negligible in relation to its face value as compared to 1939.

4. MONEY AND NEAR MONEY

Money consists of currency and bank deposits. Coins and currency notes issued by the central bank of a country and cheques of commercial banks of a country are liquid assets. In fact, cheques and bank drafts are almost perfect substitutes for money. This is because they perform the medium of exchange function of money, but cheques and drafts can be issued at a short notice only in the case of *demand deposits.* This is not the case with time deposits which can be withdrawn either at the end of the fixed period or by giving a prior notice to the bank and incurring a penalty. Thus time deposits are not 'real' money and for them to become money, they must be converted into cash or demand deposits. However, they are near money for they can be converted into real money in a short period without any loss. For example, a time deposit of Rs. 10,000 for three years can always be converted into demand deposit or Rs. 10,000 in cash at any time before the completion of three years. They also fetch a fixed rate of interest which may be reduced if the deposit is converted into cash or demand deposit before the expiry of the fixed period. Thus, near money assets serve the store of value function of money temporarily and are convertible into a medium of exchange in a short time without loss in their face value.

Besides time deposits, other near money assets are bonds, securities, debentures, bills of exchange, treasury bills, insurance policies, etc. All these types of assets have a market and are negotiable so that they can be converted into real money within a short time. We discuss how these negotiable instruments are near moneys.

Bonds, securities and debentures fall in the same category. *Bonds* and *securities* are issued by the government, while debentures are issued by companies. They are the means to borrow funds for short, medium or long periods and carry a fixed rate of interest. They are near money assets because they are convertible into cash at a short notice in the money market.

A *bill of exchange* is another form of money. It is an IOU (I Owe You). It is drawn by an individual or firm to pay a stated sum of money on a specified date which is never more than 90 days. A bill of exchange is not money by itself but is certainly money on the due date. It is, however, near money if its owner wishes to turn it into cash. It can be easily converted into money at a discount or by receiving less money than its face value.

Treasury bills issued by the government also fall in the category of near money. A treasury bill is a promise by the government to pay a stated sum in the near future usually 30, 60 or 90 days. A treasury bill is also like a bill of exchange which is convertible into money at a discount within a short period.

Life insurance policy is another example of near money. The holder of a life insurance policy can obtain cash in the form of loan on his policy at a short notice. Thus, a life insurance policy is a form of liquid asset which can be regarded as near money.

Besides these recognised instruments of near money, some intermediaries have come into existence to provide a market for certain assets. Such intermediaries are *financial companies* which provide funds on the security of some assets, and *brokers* who buy and sell property, bonds, debentures, shares, etc. They help in increasing the liquidity of such assets thereby converting them into near money.

Money and near money can now be distinguished. Money is a legal-tender and gives the possessor liquidity in hand. It performs the medium of exchange function. On the other hand, near money assets do not have any legal status. They possess moneyness or liquidity but not ready liquidity like money. They are almost perfect substitutes for money as a store of value. They are superior to money because they yield income. They also economise in the use of money proper and tend to reduce the quantity of money used by the people as a medium of exchange, as a medium of deferred payments and as a store of value.

Despite the fact that near money assets do not possess ready liquidity, they are preferred by individuals. According to Professor A.G. Hart, near money is preferred to cash by individuals because it serves as a margin of safety motive. Prof. Dean points out that 80 per cent of near money in the USA is held by individuals. The tremendous growth of near money assets in the United States is due to the fact that the yield from them is higher than that from demand deposits and that they are safer than cash. Moreover, savings in the near money assets have been encouraged by such special techniques as pay roll saving plan, and commercial bank plans covering automatic regular transfer of specified sums from the demand to time deposits of the customers.

5. CHARACTERISTICS OF MONEY

Economists have pointed towards the following characteristics or qualities for a thing to be money :

1. *General Acceptability.* For anything to be money, it should be acceptable by everybody. People accept a thing as money which is used by everybody as a medium of exchange. Gold and silver are considered good money materials because they have alternative uses and are generally accepted. Paper notes are accepted as money when they are issued by the central bank and/or the government and are legal tender. Cheques and bills of exchange are not accepted generally. Hence they are not money.

2. *Durability.* For a thing to be money, it must possess durability. It should be storable and last long without losing its value over a period of time. Animals and perishable commodities are not good money materials because they do not possess durability. In this sense, gold, silver, alloy, brass, etc. are the best materials which are used as money. Paper notes are less durable than these metals. But they are money because they are legal tender.

3. *Portability.* The material used as money should be easily carried and transferred from one place to another. It should contain large value in small bulk. Gold and silver possess this quality. Hence, they are good money materials. But they involve risk in carrying or transferring them from one place to another. Therefore, paper is considered as a better material and is used in the form of notes.

4. *Cognisability.* The material with which money is made should be easily recognised by sight or touch. Coins and currency notes of different denominations in different designs and sizes meet this quality of good money.

5. *Homogeneity.* The material with which money is made should be of the same quality. All coins of one denomination must be of the same metal, weight, shape and size. Similarly, paper notes of one denomination must have the same quality of paper, design and size.

6. *Divisibility.* The money material should be capable of being divided into smaller parts without losing value. Gold, silver, and other such materials possess this quality. Gold has the same value in whatever number of parts it may be divided. The same is the case with paper when notes of small and large denominations are issued which facilitate the operation of small and large transactions.

7. *Stability.* Money should be stable in value because it has to serve as a measure of value. Gold and silver possess this quality because they are not available in abundance. They are neither very scarce because being durable, they can be easily stocked. Their supplies can thus be increased or decreased when required. So they act as a store of value because their value is stable. But governments prefer paper money to gold and silver because it is cheap and easily available. Its value is kept stable by keeping control over its issue. It is another thing that the central bank of a country is seldom able to exercise complete control over its issue which makes paper money unstable in value.

6. NATURE AND DEFINITION OF MONEY

There has been lot of controversy and confusion over the meaning and nature of money. As pointed out by Scitovsky, "Money is a difficult concept to define, partly because it fulfils not one but three functions, each of them providing a criterion of moneyness ... those of (i) a unit of account,(ii) a medium of exchange, and (iii) a store of value."[4] Though Scitovsky points toward the difficulty of defining money due to moneyness[5], yet he gives a wide definition of money. Professor Coulborn defines money as "the means of valuation and of payment; as both the unit of account and the generally acceptable medium of exchange." Coulborn's definition is very wide. He includes in it the 'concrete' money such as gold, cheques, coins, currency notes, bank draft, etc. and also abstract money which "is the vehicle of our thoughts of value, price and worth." Such wide definitions have led Sir John Hicks to say that "money is defined by its functions: anything is money which is used as money: "money is what money does." [6] These are the functional definitions of money because they define money in terms of the functions it performs.

Some economists define money in legal terms saying that "anything which the state declares as money is money." Such money possesses general acceptability and has the legal power to discharge debts. But people may not accept legal money by refusing to sell goods and services against the payment of legal tender money. On the other hand, they may accept some other things as money which are not legally defined as money in discharge of debts which may circulate freely. Such things are cheques and notes issued by commercial banks. Thus besides legality, there are other determinants which go to make a thing to serve as money.

7. THEORETICAL AND EMPIRICAL DEFINITIONS OF MONEY

There being no unanimity over the definition of money, Prof. Johnson[7] distinguishes four main schools of thought in this regard which are discussed below:

1. *The Traditional Definition of Money.* According to the traditional view, also known as the view of the Currency School, money is defined as currency and demand deposits, and its most important function is to act as a medium of exchange. Keynes in his *General Theory* followed the traditional view and defined money as currency and demand deposits. Hicks in his *Critical Essays in Monetary Theory* points towards a threefold traditional classification of the nature of money: "to act as a unit of account (or measure of value), as a means of payment, and as a store of value." The Banking School criticised the traditional definition of money as arbitrary. This view about the meaning of money is very narrow because there are other assets which are equally acceptable as media of exchange. These include time deposits of commercial banks, commercial bills of exchange, etc. By ignoring these assets, the traditional view is not in a position to analyse their influence in increasing their velocity.

2. *Friedman's Definition of Money.* The monetarist (or Chicago) view is associated with Prof. Friedman and his followers at the University of Chicago. By money Friedman means "literally the number of dollars people are carrying around in their pockets, the number of dollars they have to their credit at banks in the form of demand deposits and commercial bank time deposits".[8] Thus he defines money as "the sum of currency plus all adjusted deposits in commercial banks". This is the "working definition" of money which Friedman uses for the empirical study of the monetary trends of the US for selected years 1929, 1935, 1950, 1955 and 1960. This was a narrower definition of money and the adjustment in both demand and time deposits of commercial banks was devised to take into account the increasing financial sophistication of the commercial banks and the community. But he could not establish a single index of this sophistication. Even with this adjustment, cash and deposit monies were not strictly comparable over long periods. He also suggested a broader definition of money as "any asset capable of serving as a temporary abode of purchasing power". So Friedman gives two types of definitions of money. One on theoretical basis and the other on empirical basis. This led to a lot of controversy. However, he takes a broader view in his definition of money which includes bank deposits, non-

---

4. T. Scitovsky, *Money and the Balance of Payments,* 1969.
5. Moneyness means liquidity. All things which possess liquidity have moneyness. For its detailed discussion refer to Sections 1 and 5 of Chapter "The Supply of Money".
6. John Hicks, *Critical Essay in Monetary Theory,* 1967.
7. H.G. Johnson, "Monetary Theory and Policy", *A.E.R.,* Vol. 52, June 1962.
8. M. Friedman, *Employment, Growth and Price Level,* 1959.

bank deposits and any other type of assets through which the monetary authority influences the future level of income, prices, employment or any other important macro variable.

3. *The Radcliffe Definition.* The Radcliffe Committee[9] defined money as "note plus bank deposits". It includes as money only those assets which are commonly used as media of exchange. Assets refer to liquid assets by which it means the monetary quantity influencing total effective demand for goods and services. This is interpreted widely to include credit. Thus the whole liquidity position is relevant to spending decisions. Spending is not limited to cash or money in the bank but to the amount of money people think they can get hold of either by selling an asset or by borrowing or by receipts of income from, say, sales.

4. *The Gurley-Shaw Definition.* Gurley and Shaw[10] regard a substantial volume of liquid assets held by financial intermediaries and the liabilities of non-bank intermediaries as close substitutes for money. Intermediaries provide substitutes for money as a store of value. Money proper which is defined as equal to currency plus demand deposits is only one liquid asset. They have thus formulated a wider definition of money based upon liquidity which includes bonds, insurance reserves, pension funds, savings and loan shares. They believe in the velocity of the money stock which is influenced by non-bank intermediaries. Their views on the definition of money are based on their own and Goldsmith's empirical findings.

8. FUNCTIONS OF MONEY

Money performs a number of primary, secondary, contingent and other functions which not only remove the difficulties of barter but also oils the wheels of trade and industry in the present day world.[11] We discuss these functions one by one.

1. Primary Functions

The two primary functions of money are to act as a medium of exchange and as a unit of value.

(i) Money as a Medium of Exchange. This is the primary function of money because it is out of this function that its other functions developed. By serving as a medium of exchange, money removes the need for double coincidence of wants and the inconveniences and difficulties associated with barter. The introduction of money as a medium of exchange decomposes the single transaction of barter into separate transactions of sale and purchase, thereby eliminating the double coincidence of wants.[12] This function of money also separates the tran-sactions in time and place because the sellers and buyers of a commodity are not required to perform the transactions at the same time and place. This is because the seller of a commodity buys some money and money, in turn, buys the commodity over time and place.

When money acts as a medium of exchange, it means that it is generally acceptable. It, therefore, affords the freedom of choice. With money, we can buy an assorted bundle of goods and services. At the same time, we can purchase the best and also bargain in the market. Thus money gives us a good deal of economic independence and also perfects the market mechanism by increasing competition and widening the market.

As a medium of exchange, money acts as an intermediary. It facilitates exchange. It helps production indirectly through specialisation and division of labour which, in turn, increase efficiency and output. According to Prof. Walters, money, therefore, serves as a factor of production,' enabling output to increase and diversify.

In the last analysis, money facilitates trade. When acting as the intermediary, it helps one good or service to be traded indirectly for others.

(ii) Money as Unit of Value.[13] The second primary function of money is to act as a unit of value. Under barter one would have to resort to some standard of measurement, such as a length of string or a piece of wood. Since one would have to use a standard to measure the length or height of any object, it is only sensible

9. *Report of the Committee on the Working of the Monetary System,* 1959.
10. J.G. Gurley and E.S. Shaw, *Money in a Theory of Finance,* 1960.
11. For the "Static and Dynamic Functions of Money", refer to section 2 of the next chapter.
12. W.T. Newlyn, *op. cit.,* p. 1.
13. This function is known by various other names such as unit of account, standard of value, common measure of value or common denominator of value.

that one particular standard should be accepted as the standard. Money is the standard for measuring value just as the yard or metre is the standard for measuring length.[14] The monetary unit measures and expresses the values of all goods and services. In fact, the monetary unit expresses the value of each good or service in terms of price. Money is the common denominator which determines the rate of exchange between goods and services which are priced in terms of the monetary unit. There can be no pricing process without a measure of value.

The use of money as a standard of value eliminates the necessity of quoting the price of apples in terms of oranges, the price of oranges in terms of nuts, and so on. Unlike barter, the prices of such commodities are expressed in terms of so many units of dollars, rupees, francs, pounds, etc., depending on the nature of the monetary unit in a country. As a matter of fact, measuring the values of goods and services in the monetary unit facilitates the problem of measuring the exchange value of goods in the market. When values are expressed in terms of money, the number of prices are reduced from $n(n—1)$ in barter economy to (n—1) in monetary economy.

Money as a unit of value also facilitates accounting. "Assets of all kinds, liabilities of all kinds, income of all kinds, and expenses of all kinds can be stated in terms of common monetary units to be added or substracted."[15]

Further, money as a unit of account helps in calculation of economic importance such as the estimation of the costs and revenues of business firms, the relative costs and profitability of various public enterprises and projects under a planned economy, and the gross national product. As pointed out by Culbertson, "Prices quoted in terms of money become the focus of people's behaviour. Their calculations, plans, expectations, and contracts focus on money prices."[16]

2. Secondary Functions

Money performs three secondary functions: (i) as a standard of deferred payments, (ii) as a store of value, and (iii) as a transfer of value. They are discussed below:

(i) Money as a Standard of Deferred Payments. The third function of money is that it acts as a standard of deferred or postponed payments. All debts are taken in money. It was easy under barter to take loans in goats or grains but difficult to make repayments in such perishable articles in the future. Money has simplified both the taking and repayment of loans because the unit of account is durable. Money links the present values with those of the future. It simplifies credit transactions. It makes possible contracts for the supply of goods in future for an agreed payment of money. It simplifies borrowing by consumers on hire-purchase and from house-building and co-operative societies. Money facilitates borrowing by firms and businessmen from banks and other non-bank financial institutions. The buying and selling of shares, debentures and securities is made possible by money. By acting as a standard of deferred payments, money helps in capital formation both by the government and business enterprises. In fine, this function of money develops financial and capital markets and helps in the growth of the economy.

But there is the danger of changes in the value of money over time which harms or benefits the creditors and debtors. If the value of money increases over time, the creditors gain and debtors lose. On the other hand, a fall in the value of money over time brings losses to creditors and windfalls to debtors. To overcome this difficulty, some of the countries have fixed debt contracts in terms of a price index which measures changes in the value of money. Such a contract over time guarantees the future payment of debt by compensating the loser by the same amount of purchasing power when the contract was entered into.

(ii) Money as a Store of Value. Another important function of money is that it acts as a store of value. "The good chosen as money is always something which can be kept for long periods without deterioration or wastage. It is a form in which wealth can be kept intact from one year to the next. Money is a bridge from the present to the future. It is, therefore, essential that the money commodity should always be one which can be

14. A.W. Stonier and D.C. Hague, *A Textbook of Economic Theory*, 4/e, 1972.
15. Lester V. Chandler and S.M. Goldfield, *The Economics of Money and Banking*, 7/e. 1977.
16. J.M. Culbertson, *Money and Banking*, 1972.

easily and safely stored."[17] Money as a store of value is meant to meet unforeseen emergencies and to pay debts. Newlyn calls this *the asset function of money*. "Money is not, of course, the only store of value. This function can be served by any valuable asset. One can store value for the future by holding short-term promissory notes, bonds, mortgages, preferred stocks, household furniture, houses, land, or any other kind of valuable goods. The principal advantages of these other assets as a store of value are that they, unlike money, ordinarily yield an income in the form of interest, profits, rent or usefulness ..., and they sometimes rise in value in terms of money. On the other hand, they have certain disadvantages as a store of value, among which are the following: (1) They sometimes involve storage costs; (2) they may depreciate in terms of money; and (3) they are "illiquid" in varying degrees, for they are not generally acceptable as money and it may be possible to convert them into money quickly only by suffering a loss of value."[18]

Keynes placed much emphasis on this function of money. According to him, to hold money is to keep it as a reserve of liquid assets which can be converted into real goods. It is a matter of comparative indifference whether wealth is in money, money claims, or goods. In fact, money and money claims have certain advantages of security, convenience and adaptability over real goods. But the store of value function of money also suffers from changes in the value of money. This introduces considerable hazard in using money or assets as a store of value.

(iii) Money as a Transfer of Value. Since money is a generally acceptable means of payment and acts as a store of value, it keeps on transferring values from person to person and place to place. A person who holds money in cash or assets can transfer that to any other person. Moreover, he can sell his assets at Delhi and purchase fresh assets at Bangalore. Thus money facilitates transfer of value between persons and places.

3. Contingent Functions

Money also performs certain contingent or incidental functions, according to Prof. David Kinley. They are:

(i) Money as the Most Liquid of all Liquid Assets. Money is the most liquid of all liquid assets in which wealth is held. Individuals and firms may hold wealth in infinitely varied forms. They may, for example, choose between holding wealth in currency, demand deposits, time deposits, savings, bonds, Treasury Bills, short-term government securities, long-term government securities, debentures, preference shares, ordinary shares, stocks of consumer goods, and productive equipment."[19] All these are liquid forms of wealth which can be convened into money, and vice-versa.

(ii) Basis of the Credit System. Money is the basis of credit system. Business transactions are either in cash or on credit. Credit economises the use of money. But money is at the back of all credit. A commercial bank cannot create credit without having sufficient money in reserve. The credit instruments drawn by businessmen have always a cash guarantee supported by their bankers.

(iii) Equaliser of Marginal Utilities and Productivities. Money acts as an equaliser of marginal utilities for the consumer. The main aim of a consumer is to maximise his satisfaction by spending a given sum of money on various goods which he wants to purchase. Since prices of goods indicate their marginal utilities and are expressed in money, money helps in equalising the marginal utilities of various goods. This happens when the ratios of the marginal utilities and prices of the various goods are equal. Similarly, money helps in equalising the marginal productivities of the various factors. The main aim of the producer is to maximise his profits. For this, he equalises the marginal productivity of each factor with its price. The price of each factor is nothing but the money he receives for his work.

(iv) Measurement of National Income. It was not possible to measure the national income under the barter system. Money helps in measuring national income. This is done when the various goods and services produced in a country are assessed in money terms.

(v) Distribution of National Income. Money also helps in the distribution of national income. Rewards of factors of production in the form of wages, rent, interest and profit are determined and paid in terms of money.

---

17. A.W. Stonier and D.C. Hague, *op. cit.*, p. 406.
18. W.T. Newlyn, *Loc. cit.*
19. *Ibid.*

4. Other Functions

(i) Helpful in Making Decisions. Money is a means of store of value and the consumer meets his daily requirements on the basis of money held by him. If the consumer has a scooter and in the near future he needs a car, he can buy a car by selling his scooter and money accumulated by him. In this way, money helps in taking decisions.

(ii) Money as a Basis of Adjustment. To carry on trade in a proper manner, the adjustment between money market and capital market is done through money.

Similarly, adjustments in foreign exchange are also made through money. Further, international payments of various types are also adjusted and made through money.

It is on the basis of these functions that money guarantees the solvency of the payer and provides options to the holder of money to use it any way, he likes.

EXERCISES

1. Discuss the principal difficulties faced by a barter economy.
2. What led to the emergence of money in the modern world?
3. Describe the various stages in the evolution of money.
4. Discuss the nature and functions of money.
5. Define money and discuss its main functions.
6. "Money is what money does." Explain this statement and define money.
7. Distinguish between (a) money proper and money-of-account, *(b)* money and near money.
8. Discuss the theoretical and empirical definitions of money.
9. Explain the primary and secondary functions of money.
10. Explain the contingent functions of money.
11. How money overcomes the difficulties of barter?

Chapter 2

Role of Money

1. INTRODUCTION

Money is of vital importance to the operation of the national and international economy. Money plays an important role in the daily life of a person whether he is a consumer, a producer, a businessman, an academician, a politician or an administrator. "An individual need not be an economicst to be actually aware that money plays an important role in odern life; he need think only of his own experience."[1] We study below the importance of money in a modern economy.

2. SIGNIFICANCE OR ROLE OF MONEY

Money is of vital importance to an economy due to its static and dynamic roles.[2] Its static role emerges from its static or traditional functions. In its dynamic role, money plays an mportant part in the life of every citizen and in the economic system as a whole.

Static Role of Money

In its static role, the importance of money lies in removing the dificulties of barter in the following ways :

(i) By serving as a medium of exchange, money removes the need for double conicidence of wants and the inconveniences and difficulties associated with barter. The introduction of money as a medium of exchange breaks up the single transactions of barter into separate transactions of sales and purchases, thereby eliminating the double coincidence of wants. Instead of exchanging commodities directly with commodities *i.e.* $C \leftrightarrow C$, commodities are exchanged for money and money, in turn, buys other commodities as $C \rightarrow M \rightarrow C$,, where C refers to commodities and M to money.

(ii) By acting as a unit of account, money becomes a common measure of value. The use of money as a standard of value eliminates the necessity of quoting the price of apples in terms of oranges, the price of oranges in terms of nuts, and so on. Money is the standard of measuring value and value expressed in money

1. Lester V.Chandler and S.M. Goldfield, *op. cit.*
2. The explanation in this section also relates to the "Static and Dynamic Functions of Money."

is price. The prices of different commodities are expressed in terms of so many units of dollars, rupees, pounds, etc. depending on the nature of monetary unit in a country. The measurement of the values of goods and services in the monetary unit facilitates the problem of measuring the exchange values of goods in the market.

(iii) Money acts as a standard of deferred payments. Under barter, it was easy to take loans in goats or grains but difficult to make repayments in such perishable articles in the future. Money has simplified both taking and repayment of loans because the unit of account is durable. It also overcomes the difficulty of indivisibility of commodities.

(iv) By acting as a store of value, money removes the problem of storing of commodities under barter. Money being the most liquid asset can be kept for long periods without deterioration or wastage.

(v) Under barter, it was difficult to transfer value in the form of animals, grains, etc. from one place to another. Money removes this difficulty of barter by facilitating the transfer of value from one place to another. A person can transfer his money through draft, bill of exchange, etc. and his assets by selling them for cash at one place and buying them at another place.

Dynamic Role of Money

In its dynamic role, money plays an important part in the daily life of a person whether he is a consumer, a producer, a businessman, an academician, a politician or an administrator. Besides, it influences the economy in a number of ways.

(1) *To the Consumer.* Money possesses much significance for the consumer. The consumer receives his income in the form of money rather than in goods and services. With money in hands, he can get any commodity and service he likes, in whatever equaliser of marginal utilities for the consumer. The main aim of a consumer is to maximise his satisfaction by spending his limited income on different goods which he wants to purchase. Since prices of goods indicate their marginal utilities and are expressed in money, money helps in equalising the marginal utilities of goods. This is done by substituting goods with higher utilities for others having lower utilities. Thus money enables a consumer to make a rational distribution of his income on various commodities of his choice.

(2) *To the Producer.* Money is of equal importance to the producer. He keeps his account of the values of inputs and outputs in money. The raw materials purchased, the wages paid to workers, the capital borrowed, the rent paid, the expenses on advertisements, etc. are all expenses of production which are entered in his account books. The sale of products in money terms are his sale proceeds. The difference between the two gives him profit. Thus a producer easily calculates not only his costs of production and receipts but also profit with the help of money. Further, money helps in the general flow of goods and services from agricultural, industrial and tertiary sectors of the economy because all these activities are performed in terms of money.

(3) *In Specialisation and Divisions of Labour.* Money plays an important role in large scale specialisation and division of labour in modern production. Money helps the capitalist to pay wages to a large number of workers engaged in specialised jobs on the basis of division of labour. Each worker is paid money wages in accordance with the nature of work done by him. Thus money facilitates specialisation and division of labour in modern production. These, in turn, help in the growth of industries. It is, in fact, through money that production on a large scale is possible. All inputs like raw materials, labour, machinery, etc. are purchased with money and all output is sold in exchange for money. As rightly pointed out by Prof. Pigou, "In the modern world industry is closely enfolded in a garment of money.".

(4) *As the Basis of Credit.* The entire modern business is based on credit and credit is based on money. All monetary transactions consist of cheques, drafts, bills of exchange etc. These are credit instruments which are not money. It is the bank deposits that are money. Banks issue such credit instruments and create credit. Credit creation, in turn, plays a major role in transferring funds from depositors to investors. Thus credit expands investment on the basis of public saving lying in bank deposits and helps in maintaining a circular flow of income within the economy.

(5) *As a Means to Capital Formation.* By transforming savings into investment, money acts as a means to capital formation. Money is a liquid asset which can be stored and storing of money implies savings, and

savings are kept in bank deposits to earn interest on them. Banks, in turn, lend these savings to businessmen for investment in capital equipment, buying of raw materials, labour, etc. from different sources and places. This makes capital mobile and leads to capital formation and economic growth.

(6) *As an Index of Economic Growth.* Money is also an index of economic growth. The various indicators of growth are national income, per capita income and economic welfare. These are calculated and measured in money terms. Changes in the value of money or prices also reflect the growth of an economy. Fall in the value of money (or rise in prices) means that the economy is not progressing in real terms. On the other hand, a continuous rise in the value of money (or fall in prices) reflects retardation of the economy. Somewhat stable prices imply a growing economy. Thus money is an index of economic growth.

(7) *In the Distribution and Calculation of Income.* The rewards to the various factors of production in a modern economy are paid in money. A worker gets his wages, capitalist his interest, a landlord his rent, and an entrepreneur his profit. But all are paid their rewards in money. An organiser is able to calculate the marginal productivity of each factor in terms of money and pay it accordingly. For this, he equalises the marginal productivity of each factor with its price. Its price is, in fact, its marginal productivity expressed in terms of money. As payments are made to various factors of production in money, the calculation of national income becomes easy.

(8) *In National and International Trade.* Money facilitates both national and international trade. The use of money as a medium of exchange, as a store of value and as a transfer of value has made it possible to sell commodities not only within a country but also internationally. To facilitate trade, money has helped in establishing money and capital markets. There are banks, financial institutions, stock exchanges, produce exchanges, international financial institutions, etc. which operate on the basis of the money economy and they help in both national and international trade.

Further, trade relations among different countries have led to international cooperation. As a result, the developed countries have been helping the growth of underdeveloped countries by giving them loans and technical assistance. This has been made possible because the value of foreign aid received and its repayment by the developing countries is measured in money.

(9) *In Solving the Central Problems of an Economy.* Money helps in solving the central problems of an economy; what to produce, for whom to produce, how to produce and in what quantities. This is because on the basis of its functions, money facilitates the flow of goods and services among consumers, producers and the government.

(10) *To the Government.* Money is of immense importance to the government. Money facilitates the buying and collection of taxes, fines, fees and prices of services rendered by the government to the people. It simplifies the floating and management of public debt and government expenditure on development and non-developmental activities. It would be impossible for modern governments to carry on their functions without the use of money. Not only this, modern governments are welfare states which aim at improving the standard of living of the people by removing poverty, inequalities and unemployment, and achieving growth with stability. Money helps in achieving these goals of economic policy through its various instruments.

(11) *To the Society.* Money confers many social advantages. It is on the basis of money that the superstructure of credit is built in the society which simplifies consumption, production, exchange and distribution. It promotes national unity when people use the same currency in every nook and corner of the country. It acts as a lubricant for the social life of the people, and oils the wheels of material progress. Money is at the back of social prestige and political power.

Thus money is the pivot around which the whole science of economics clusters.

3. DEFECTS OF MONEY

The Bible says, "The love of money is the root of all evil." Rightly so. Perhaps acting on this saying of the Bible the classical economists did not attach much importance to money. They regarded it as a veil or garment or wrapper for goods and services. According to them, money is simply a tool of convenience to facilitate the exchange of goods and services, but it is not a determinant of the quantities produced. The evils of money are shrouded behind a monetary veil, and what really happens behind the veil is sometimes quite different from what appears to take place on the surface. This extreme view has ben discarded. Now economists regard money not merely as veil but also as an extremely valuable social instrument promoting wealth and welfare.

But money which is a useful servant, often misbehaves when it tries to act like a master. This leads to a number of economic and non-economic defects of money.

ECONOMIC DEFECTS

The economic defects are as under :

(1) *Instability in the Value of Money.* The first drawback about money is that its value does not remain stable over time. When the value of money falls, it means rise in the price level or inflation. On the contrary, rise in the value of money means fall in the price levels or deflation. These changes are brought about by increase or decrease in the supply for money. Large changes in the value of money are disastrous and even moderate changes have certain disadvantages.

Inflation or fall in the value of money causes direct and immediate damage to creditors and consumers. On the contrary, deflation or rise in the value of money brings down the level of output, employment and income. Thus instability in the value of money adversely affects consumers, producers and other sections of the society.

(2) *Unequal Distribution of Wealth and Income.* The second defect of money is that changes in the value of money lead to unequal distribution of wealth and income. Inflation or deflation which brings benefits to some and damages to others leads to redistribution of wealth and income not only between social and industrial classes, but between different persons in the same class. Such changes in the structure of the society widen the differences between the rich and the poor and lead to class conflict.

(3) *Growth of Monopolies.* Too much of money leas to the concentration of capital in the hands of a few capitalists. This leads to growth of monopolies which exploit both consumers and workers.

(4) *Wastage of Resources.* Money is the basis of credit. When banks create too much of credit, it may be used for productive and unproductive purposes. If much credit is used for production, it leads to over capitalisation and overproduction, and consequently to wastage of resources. Similarly, if liberal credit facilities are given for unproductive uses, they also lead to wastage of resources.

(5) *Black Money.* Money being the store of value lures people to hoard it. The tendency to hoard money and become rich is the root cause of the evil of black money. When people evade taxes and conceal their income and hoard it, it is black money. This leads to a "parallel" economy within the country which encourages conspicuous consumption, black marketing, speculation, etc.

(6) *Cyclical Fluctuations.* Another defect of the institution of money is that it leads to cyclical fluctuations in the economy. When the supply of money increases it leads to a boom and when it contracts there is a slump. In a boom, output, employment and income increase which lead to overproduction. On the contrary, they decline during a depression, thereby leading to under consumption. Such cyclical fluctuations bring untold miseries to the people.

NON-ECONOMIC DEFECTS

Money has the following non-economic defects :

(1) Besides the above noted economic drawbacks of money the institution of money has brought down the moral, social and political fibre of the society. It leads to corruption, turpitude, political bankruptcy and artificiality in religion based on materialism. In fact, money is "the cause of theft and murder, of deception and betrayal. Money is blamed when the prostitute sells her body and when the bribed judge perverts the law. Significantly enough avarice is called the love of money; all evil is attributed to it."[3]

(2) *Political Instability.* Overissue of money leading to hyper-inflation leads to political instability and downfall of government. This has happened in many Latin American countries.

(3) *Tendency to Exploit.* People who want to amass money and wealth, adopt underhand methods and have tendency to exploit others. Even nations are not far behind in this. As pointed out by Davenport, "Money

3. L. Von Mises, *The Theory of Money and Credit,* p. 93.

has enabled strong nations to destroy backward communities to win them on their side with the help of financial aid."

Conclusion

All these defect are not due to money but are the result of the attribute of man towards the use of money. It is of immense importance to every type of society whether it be capitalist or socialist. It is impossible to imagine this world without money. Money is an indispensable lubricant, a tool of convenience, for a continuous and smooth functioning of the economic machine. But its uncontrolled use, instead of solving, creates many complicated problems. It is these complex problems that led Disraeli to remark. "Money has made more people mad than love." So the best way is to keep money under control like a faithful and obedient servant and not to let it to take the role of a master. The controlling authority over money is the government which can achieve this by a judicious monetary policy.

4. ROLE OF MONEY IN A CAPITALIST ECONOMY

A capitalist economy is one in which each individual in his capacity as a consumer, producer and resource owner is engaged in economic activity with a large measure of economic freedom. Individual economic actions are governed by the instruction of private property, profit motive, freedom of enterprise and consumers's sovereignty. All factors of production are privately owned and managed by individuals who are at liberty to dispose them of within the prevalent laws. Individuals have the freedom to choose any occupation, and to buy and sell any number of goods and services.

Such an economy is essentially a money economy where money plays an important role in its functioning. Consumers and producers receive income in money. Consumers receive money income in the form of wages, rents, interest an dividends by selling the services of the factors of production which they own in the form of labour, land, and capital respectively. They are free to spend their money income on whichever goods and services they wish to buy. They may partly spend their money income and partly save in the form of money.

Big and small firms, in turn, buy the services of the factors of production for producing commodities. These services are purchased in money terms. The entire productive process ina capitalist economy is determined by the profit motive. Profit is the difference between outlay and receipt. All these—profit, outlay and receipt—are calculated in terms of money.

In fact, there is a circular flow of money in such an economy. Allirms demand the services of the factors of production to produce consumer goods. All factors of production are paid for their services in money, who buy consumer goods with it. Thus money flows back to firms which again make monetary payments to consumers for the services rendered by them in the further production of goods of varied types.

Money and the Price Mechanism in a Capitalist Economy

The most significant role of money lies in the functioning of the price mechanism. The price system functions through prices of goods and services. Prices determine the production of innumerable goods and services. They organise production and help in the distribution of goods and services. Since prices are expressed in money, the price mechanism under capitalism cannot function without money.

In a capitalist economy where means of production are owned privately and production is also carried out by private enterprise, money performs the important function of solving the central problems of such an economy. This is done through the price mechanism. The price mechanism operates automatically without any direction and control by the government.

The central problems of a capitalist economy as to what, how much, and how and for whom to produce are solved through the price mechanism. We discuss them as under.

This problem of what, how much and how to produce are solved by the price mechanism on the basis of the profit motive. Profit is the difference between expenditure and receipt of a firm. The size of profit depends upon prices of commodities. The larger the difference between price and costs, the higher is the profit. Again the higher the prices, the greater are the efforts of the producers to produce the different types of commodities in different quantities. On the other hand, prices depend upon consumers' choices of the various commodities. It is also the consumer's choices which determine what to produce, how much to produce, how to produce and for what type of consumers.

It is, in fact, competition between consumers and producers which equalises the demand and supply of both goods and services in a capitalist economy. There being sufficient flexibility under capitalism, prices adjust themselves to changes in demand, in production techniques, and in the supply of factors of production. Changes imprecise, in turn, bring adjustments in production, factor demand and consumer incomes. Money is, therefore, the basis of the price mechanism under capitalism. It is a pivot around which the entire capitalist economy revolves. Since such an economy functions without any government interference, money plays a crucial role in maximising the wants of consumers and profits of producers.

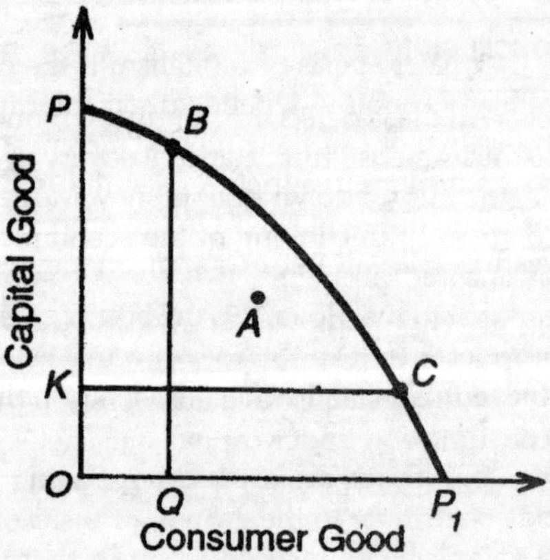

FIG. 1

For the Consumer. Under capitalism, the consumer is the king who buys only those commodities which give him the maximum satisfaction with a given money income. This he does by equalising the marginal utilities of different goods he wishes to buy. When the price of each commodity expressed in money equals its marginal utility, the consumer gets maximum satisfaction. Thus money enables a consumer to make a rational choice out of the various commodities he wants to buy with his given money income. Figure 1 illustrates this argument. Suppose only two commodities are produced in a capitalist economy. They are capital goods and consumer goods taken on the vertical and horizontal axes respectively. The production possibility curve PP_1 represents the area of choice for the consumer. It is for the producer to decide whether to produce capital goods or consumer goods depending on consumer's rational choice. The consumer will choose either combination *B* or *C* which gives him the maximum satisfaction with a given money income. At combination *A* he will be buying lesser quantities of the two goods and will be at a lower level of satisfaction than at any point on the PP_1 curve.

For the Producer. Money is equally important for the producer who buys and sells inputs and outputs in money. His aim being to maximise profits, he calculates the marginal cost and marginal revenue in money. Profits appear when marginal revenue exceeds marginal cost, and they lead to further production. When marginal cost exceeds marginal revenue, losses appear and production is curtailed. But these situations do not continue for long. The price mechanism restores the equilibrium between marginal revenue and marginal cost at prices which do not need further adjustments. Thus producers earn normal profit which they receive in the form of money.

Basis of Capitalist Production

In fact, money is the very basis of the capitalist production. By facilitating the purchase of inputs, and by increasing specialisation and division of labour, money helps in the growth of research in the agricultural, industrial and tertiary sectors of a capitalist economy. Since all these sectors are mutually dependent and are based on mutual exchanges through money, capitalist production tends to increase. In other words, money help in capitalist production through a circular flow of goods and services from these sectors.

Basis of Credit

The entire capitalist system of production is based on credit. Credit instruments are a form of money which are issued by banks to facilitate trade, commerce, agriculture, industry, transport, etc. under capitalism. It is on the basis of credit instruments that banks advance loans to the different sectors of a capitalist economy. The amount of credit is determined by the interest rate which expresses the price of loanable funds, and loans find their expression in money.

Means of Capital Formation

The very basis of capitalism is the capital and money is the most liquid form of capital. The growth of a capitalist economy depends upon the capital accumulation. And capital accumulation is a process whereby people save out of their money incomes, deposit them with banks and other financial institutions which, in turn, lend them to agriculturists, industrialists, transporters and other businessmen for investment in capital assets. The different stages in the process of capital formation under capitalism—receiving income, saving and investing—are all performed in money terms.

Link between the Present and the Future

Money establishes a link between the present and future through the freedom of enterprise and freedom of consumption under capitalism. The freedom of consumption the part of the consumer leads to freedom to save a part of his money income. Saving leads to the production of capital goods via investment and capital goods contribute to the growth of the economy. Thus it is through money that consumers save in the present and saving helps in production in the future. Similarly, freedom of enterprise under capitalism helps the businessman and the trader to make payments in the future for bargains made in the present. This is possible through money when the goods are stored in the present and sold in the future. It is in these ways that money helps to establish a link between the present and the future.

Leads to Business Cycles

Besides these apparent merits of money in a capitalist economy, it has one serious defect in that an excess of money leads to inflation and its shortage leads to deflation. These changes in the quantity of money result in cyclical fluctuations with their attendant consequences on the economy. In fact, an excess of money supply creates more demand which, in turn, leads to overproduction, to glut of commodities in the market and finally to depression and mass unemployment. There is thus wastage of resources and loss in productivity when there are business cycles in a capitalist economy. But Schumpeter regarded business cycles as the cost of economic development, a permanent feature of the dynamic path of a capitalist economy which takes it to a higher level of development every time a cycle takes place.

In fine money plays a crucial role in the functioning of a capitalist economy.

5. ROLE OF MONEY IN A SOCIALIST ECONOMY

In a socialist economy, the central authority owns and controls the means of production and distribution. All mines, farms, factories, financial institutions, distributing agencies (such as internal and external trade, shops, stores, etc.) means of transport and communications, etc., are owned, controlled and regulated by government departments and state corporations. Therefore, the pricing process in a socialist economy does not operate freely but works under the control and regulation of the central planning authority.

Marx believed that money had no role to play in a socialist economy because it led to the exploitation of labour at the hands of capitalists. He, therefore, advocated the abolition of money and exchange by bartering goods measured in terms of labour value.

In keeping with the Marxi an ideas, the Bolshevik Government in Russia eliminated money as a medium of exchange in 1917. Money payments for the use of various services and goods were abolished. "But barter transactions proved to be too clumsy. Although some communist writers had prematurely hailed the dying out of money, it became obvious that the socialist economy needed a stable currency nearly as much as a private enterprise economy." Accordingly, market exchanges, money and monetary incentives were reintroduced in the New Economic Policy (1921-27) in the USSR. Since then the Soviet economy has been using money in production, distribution and exchange such that money acts as a medium of exchange, a store of value, and a unit of account.

We have given above a brief description of the role of money in the Soviet economy which is the finest variant of a socialist economy in action.

Theoretically, the role of money in a socialist economy is different from that in a capitalist economy.

Money and Price Mechanism in a Socialist Economy

The price mechanism has little relevance in a socialist economy because it is regarded as a distinguishing feature of a free market economy. In a socialist economy the various elements of the price mechanism—costs, profits and prices—are all planned and calculated by the planning authority in accordance with the objectives and targets of the plan. Thus rational economic calculation or allocation of resources is not possible in a socialist economy. Let us find out how a socialist society solves the central problems of an economy, what, how and for whom to produce.

In a socialist state, it is the central planning authority that performs the functions of the market. Since all the material means of production are owned, controlled and directed by the government, the decisions about *what* to produce are taken within the framework of a central plan. The decisions, as to the nature of goods to be produced and their quantities, depend upon the objectives, targets and priorities laid down by the central planning authority. The prices of the various commodities are also fixed by this authority. Prices reflect the social preferences of the common man. Consumers choice is limited only to the commodities that the planners decide to produce and offer.

The problem of *how* to produce is also decided by the central planning authority. "It establishes the rules for combining factors of production and choosing the scale of output of a plant, for determining the output of an industry, for the allocation of resources, and for the parametric use of prices in accounting." The central planning authority lays down two rules for the guidance of plant managers. *One,* that each manager should combine productive goods and services in such a manner that the average cost of producing a given output is the minimum. *Two,* that each manager should choose that scale of output which equalises marginal cost to price. Since all resources in the economy are owned and regulated by the government, the raw materials, machines and other inputs are also sold at prices which are equal to their marginal cost of production. If the price of a commodity happens to be above its average cost, the plant managers will earn profits, and if it is below the average cost of production, they will incur losses. In the former case, the industry would expand and in the latter case it would cut down production, and ultimately a position of equilibrium will be reached by the *process of trial and error*. The process of trial and error would, however, proceed on the basis of *historically* given prices which would necessitate relatively small adjustments in prices from time to time. Thus "all decisions of the managers of production and of the productive resources in public ownership and also all decisions of individuals as consumers and as suppliers of labour are made on the basis of these prices. As a result of these decisions the quantity demanded and supplied of each commodity is determined. If the quantity demanded of a commodity is not equal to the quantity supplied, the price of that commodity has to be changed. It has to be raised if demand exceeds supply and lowered if the reverse is the case. Thus the central planning board fixes a new set of prices which serves as a basis for new decisions, and which results in a new set of quantities demanded and supplied."

The problem of *for whom to produce* is also solved by the state in a socialist economy. The central planning authority takes this decisions at the time of deciding what and how much to produce in accordance with the overall objectives of the plan. In making this decision, social preferences are given weightage. In other words, higher weightage is given to the production of those goods and services which are needed by the majority of the people over luxury items. They are based on the minimum needs of the people, and are sold at fixed prices through government stores. Since goods are produced in anticipation of demand, an increase in demand brings about shortages and this leads to rationing.

Thus in a socialist society the problem of income distribution is automatically solved because all resources are owned by the state and their rewards are also fixed and paid by the state. Economic surpluses are deliberately created and utilised for capital accumulation and growth.

Capital Accumulation

Besides, capital accumulation is possible through money. It is money that provides liquidity and mobility required for capital accumulation. In a socialist economy the sources of investment funds are basically the same as under a capitalist economy. The turnover tax, planned profits of public enterprises, amortisation quotas and taxation of agricultural produce in kind or in low procurement prices are all expressed in money and help in capital accumulation.

Foreign Trade

Moreover, socialist economies do not enter into foreign trade on bilateral trade relations based on commodity transactions. Rather, being members of the World Bank and the IMF, they make payments in monetary terms in their international trade relations.

Circular Flow of Money

There is also circular flow of money in a socialist economy. The producing units receive funds for investment from the state budget as grants or as loans from the state bank to purchase the necessary inputs and for making payments to workers. The workers spend their wages on consumer goods. The producing units receive revenues from sales, which, in turn, go into tax payments and profit earnings and as repayments of loans to the state bank. These funds again flow from the state budget and the state bank to the producing units. Thus money helps in the circular flow of goods and services in a socialist economy.

To conclude, the role of money in a socialist economy may be less important as compared to a capitalist economy due to state regulation and control. Nevertheless, it helps in fixing prices, wages, incomes and profits. It guides a socialist economy in determining the allocation of its resources equitably, in capital accumulation and flow of resources within and outside the economy.

EXERCISES

1. Define money. What is its social significance?
2. "The institution of money is an extremely valuable social instrument making a large contribution to economic welfare. Money is not merely a veil or a garment or a wrapper." Discuss this statement.
3. "Money is a good servant, but a bad master." Examine this statement.
4. Discuss the role of money in a modern capitalist economy.
5. What role does money play in a socialist economy?
6. Discuss the static and dynamic role of money.

CHAPTER 3

The Circular Flow of Money

1 MEANING

The circular flow of money refers to the process whereby money payments and receipts of an economy flow in a circular manner continuously through time. The various components of money payments and receipts are saving, investment, taxation, loans, government purchases exports, imports, etc. These are shown on diagrams in the form of currents and cross- currents in such a manner that the total money payments equal the total money receipts in the economy.

2. CIRCULAR FLOW OF MONEY BETWEEN HOUSEHOLD AND BUSINESS SECTORS

We begin with a simple hypothetical economy where there are only two sectors, the household and business. The household sector owns all the factors of production, that is land, labor, capital and enterprise. This sector receives income in the form of rent, wages, interest and profit, by selling the services of these factors to the business sector. The business sector consists of producers who produce commodities and sell them to the household sector. The household sector consists of consumers who buy commodities produced by the business sector

Thus in the first instance, money flows in the form of such income payments as rent, wages, intersest and profits from the business sector to the household sector when the former buys the services of the factors of production to produce good. Money so received is, in turn, spent by the household sector to by goods produced by the business sector. In this way, money flows in a circular manner from the business sector to the household sector and from the household sector to the business sector in the economy.

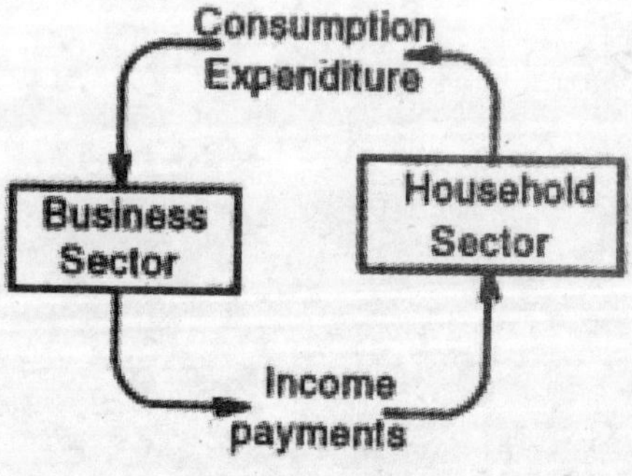

FIG. 1

The circular flow in a two-sector economy is depicted in

Figure 1 where the flow of money as income payments from the business sector to the household sector is shown in the form of an arrow in the lower portion of the diagram. On the other hand, the flow of money as consumption expenditure on the purchase of goods and services by the household sector is shown to go to the business sector by an arrow in the upper portion of the diagram. As long as income payments by the business sector for factor services are returned by the household sector to purchase goods, the circular flow of income payments and consumption expenditure tends to continue indefinitely. Production equals sales or supply equals demand, and the economy will continue to operate at this level in a circular flow of money.

Assumptions. The above analysis of the circular flow of money is based on a number of assumptions.

1. It is assumed that the household sector spends the entire income received from the business sector on buying goods and services produced by the latter.

2. The business firms keep their production exactly equal to their sales, and there are no changes in their inventories.

3. The business sector does not keep any undistributed money as reserve. The money it receives by selling goods and services to the household sector is fully spent in making payments as rent, wages, interest and profits to the household sector.

It is these assumptions that keep the flow of money to move in a circular manner in the economy. But these assumptions are unrealistic and do not fit in the actual working of the economy.

The fact is that there are regular withdrawals and injections from the circular flow of money in the economy. A withdrawal or leakage is any income that does not enter into the circular flow of money, and an injection is an addition to the circular flow of money. A leakage occurs in the income flow and an injection in the expenditure flow.

3. CIRCULAR FLOW OF MONEY WITH SAVING AND INVESTMENT

In the circular flow of money, saving is one of the leakages and investment is an injection. In fact, the household and business sectors do not spend their entire money income. The consumers who represent the household sector do not spend their income wholly in purchasing goods and services. Rather, they save a part of their income for a variety of motives. Similarly, business firms do not spend their entire income from the sale of goods. But they keep a part of it in the form of undistributed profit. Such savings of consumers and firms are not hoarded but are invested in bonds, shares, debentures, etc. in the capital market. They flow in to the capital market.

On the other hand, business firms borrow funds from the capital market for making investment. Thus savings which flow into the capital market are taken away by the business sector for investment and the ircular flow of money is maintained in the economy.

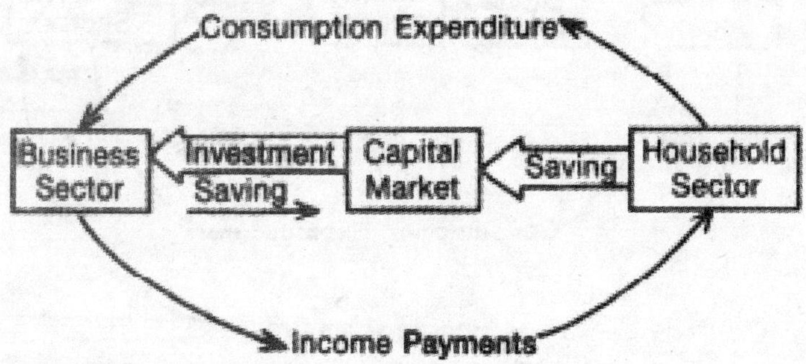

FIG. 2

Figure 2 shows how the circular flow of money is altered by the inclusion of saving and investment. Expenditure has now two paths: (*i*) directly via consumption from the households to the business sector, and (*ii*) indirectly via investment expenditure by the business sector.

In the centre of Figure 2, there is the capital (or credit or financial) maarket which shows the inflow of savings from the household sector and the business sector into the capital market, and the *outflow* of investment into the business sector from the capital market. The capital market coordinates the saving and investment activities of the household and business sectors and maintains the circular flow of money in the economy.

4. CIRCULAR FLOW OF MONEY WITH GOVERNMENT SECTOR

So far we have been working on the circular flow of a two-sector model of an economy. To this we add the government sector so as to make it a three-sector closed model. For this, we add taxation and government purchases (or expenditure) in our presentation. Taxation is a leakage from the circular flow and government purchases are injections into the circular flow of money.

First, take the circular flow between the household sector and the government sector. Taxes in the form of personal income tax and commodity taxes paid by the household sector are outflows or leakages from the circular flow. But the government purchases the services of the households, makes transfer payments in the form of old age pensions, unemployment relief, sickness benefit, etc., and also spends on them to provide certain social services like education, health, housing, water, parks and other facilities. All such expenditures by the government are injections into the circular flow of money.

Next take the circular flow between the business sector and the government sector. All types of taxes paid by the business sector to the government are leakages from the circular flow. On the other hand, the government purchases all its requirements of goods of all types from the business sector, gives subsidies and makes transfer payments to firms in order to encourage their production. These government expenditures are injections into the circular flow of money.

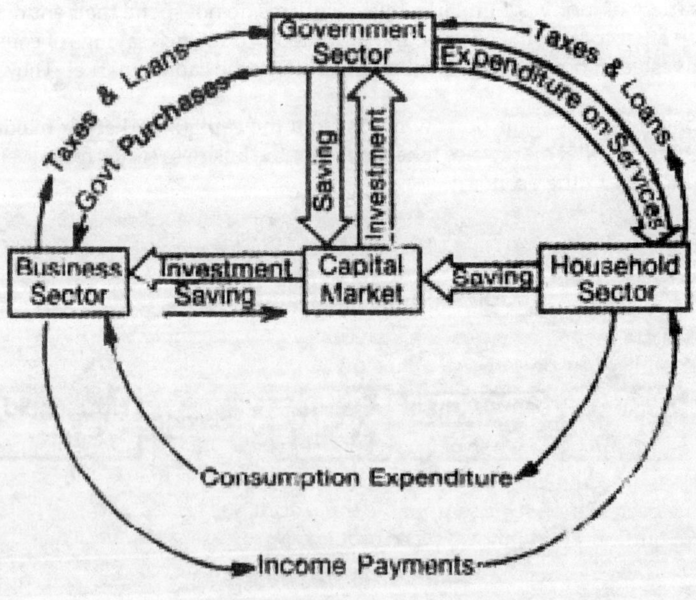

FIG. 3

Now we take the household, business and government sectors together to show their inflows and outflows in the circular flow. As already noted, taxation is a leakage from the circular flow. It tends to reduce consumption and saving of the household sector. Reduced consumption, in turn, reduces the sales and incomes of the firms. On the other hand, taxes on business firms tend to reduce their investment and production. The government offsets these leakages by making purchases from the business sector and buying services of the household sector equal to the amount of taxes. Thus total sales again equal production of firms. In this way, the circular flows of income and expenditure remain in equilibrium.

Figure 3 shows that taxes flow out of the household and business sectors and go to the government. Now the government makes investment and for this purchases goods from the household. Thus government purchases of goods and services are an injection in the circular flow of income and taxes are leakages.

If government purchases exceed net taxes then the government will incur a deficit equal to the difference between the two, i.e., government expenditure and taxes. The government finances its deficit by borrowing from the capital market which receives funds from household sector in the form of saving. On the other hand, if net taxes exceed government purchases the government will have a budget surplus. In this case, the government reduces the public debt and supplies funds to the capital market which are received by the business sector.

5. CIRCULAR FLOW OF MONEY WITH THE FOREIGN SECTOR

So far the circular flow of income and expenditure has been shown in the case of a closed economy. But the actual economy is an open one where foreign trade plays an important role. Exports are an injection or inflows into the economy. They create incomes for the domestic firms. When foreigners buy goods and services produced by domestic firms, they are exports in the circular flow of income. On the other hand, imports are leakages from the circular flow. They are expenditures incurred by the household sector to purchase goods from foreign countries. These exports and imports in the circular flow are shown in Figure 4.

Take the inflows and outflows of the household, business and government sectors in relation to the foreign sector. The household sector buys goods imported from abroad and makes payment for them of money. The householder may receive transfer payments from the foreign sector for the services rendered by them in foreign countries.

On the other hand, the business sector exports goods to foreign countries and its receipts are an injection in the circular flow. Similarly, there are many services rendered by business firms to foreign countries such as shipping, insurance, banking, etc. for which they receive payments from abroad. They also receive royalties, interests, dividends, profits, etc. for investments made in foreign countries. On the other hand, the business sector makes payments to the foreign sector for imports of capital goods, machinery, raw materials, consumer goods, and services from abroad. These are the leakages from the circular flow.

Like the business sector, modern governments also export and import goods and services, and lend to and borrow from foreign countries. For all exports of goods, the government receives payments from abroad. Similarly, the government receives payments from foreigners when they visit the country as tourists and for receiving education, etc. and also when the government provides shipping, insurance and banking services to foreigners through the state-owned agencies. It also receives royalities, interest, dividends etc. for investments made abroad. These are injections into the circular flow. On other hand, the leakages are payments made for the purchase of goods and services to foreigners.

Figur 4 shows the circular flow of the four-sector open economy with saving, taxes and imports shown as leakages from the circular flow on the right hand side of the figure, and investment, government purchases and exports as injections into the circular flow on the left side of the figure. Further, imports, exports and transfer payments have been shown to arise from the three domestic sectors—the household, the business and the government. These outflows and inflows pass through the foreign sector which is also called the "Balance of Payments Sector."

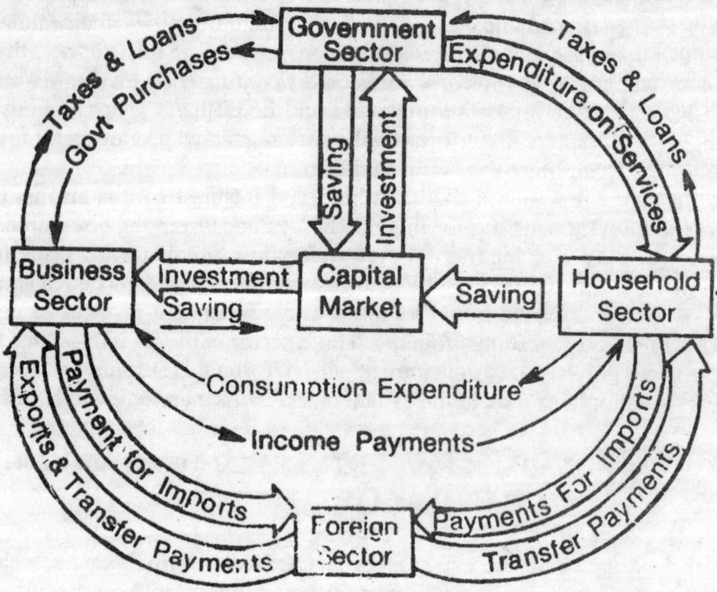

FIG. 4

Thus Figure 4 shows the circular flow of money where there are inflows and outflows of money, receipts and payments among the business sector, the household sector, the government sector and the foreign sector in currents and cross-currents.

6. IMPORTANCE OF THE CIRCULAR FLOW OF MONEY

Money being the life blood of a modern economy, its circular flow gives a clear picture of the economy. We can know from its study whether the economy is working smoothly or there is any disturbance in its smooth functioning. As such, the circular flow of money is of immense significance for studying the functioning of the economy and for helping the government in formulating policy measures.

1. Link between Producers and Consumers. The circular flow of money establishes a link between producers and consumers. It is through money that producers buy the services of the factors of production with which the latter, in turn, purchase goods from the producers.

2. Creates a Network of Markets. As a corollary to the above point, the linking of producers and consumers through the circular flow of money ahs created a network of markets for different goods and services where problems relating to their sale and purchase are automatically solved.

3. Inflationary and Deflationary Tendencies. Leakages or injections in the circular flow of money disturb the smooth functioning of the economy. For example, saving is a leakage out of the expenditure stream. If saving increases, this depresses the circular flow of money. Given the supply of money in the economy, this tends to reduce employment, income and prices, thereby leading to a deflationary process in the economy. On the other hand, consumption expenditure and investment are injections in the circular flow of money wihci tend to increase employment, income, output and prices, and thus lead to inflationary tendencies.

4. Basis of the Multirplier. Again, if leakages exceed injections in the circular flow of money, the total money supply becomes less than the total output. This leads to a cumulative decline in employment, income, outpur,and prices over time. On the other hand, if injections into the circular flow of money exceed leakages, the money supply is increased in the economy, This leads to a cumulative rise in employment, income, output, and prices over a period of time. In fact, the basis of the Keynesian multiplier is the cumulative movements in the circular flow of money.

5. *Importance of Monetary Policy.* The study of the circular flow of money also highlights the importance of monetary policy in bringing about the equality of saving and investment. Figure 2 shows that the equality between saving and investment comes about through the capital market. The capital market is controlled by the government through its monetary policy. When saving exceeds investment or investment exceeds saving, there is deflation or inflation. It is through monetary policy that investment is encouraged or retarded to control deflationary or inflationary situations.

6. *Importance of Fiscal Policy.* The circular flow of money also points towards the importance of fiscal policy. For the circular flow of money to be in equilibrium, saving plus taxes ($S+T$) must equal investment plus government expenditure ($I+G$). $S+T$ represent leakages from the money stream which must be offset by injections of $I+G$ into the money stream. So if $S+T$ exceed $I+G$, deflationary tendencies develop in the economy which can be removed by adopting such fiscal measures as reduction in taxes and by increase in government expenditure. On the other hand, If $I + G$ exceed $S + T$, there are inflationary tendencies in the economy which can be checked by encouraging saving and increaing government revenues through taxation. Thus the circular flow of money highlights the importance of adopting compensatory fiscal policy.

7 *Importance of Trade Policies.* Similarly, imports are leakages in the circular flow of money because they are payments made to a foreign country. To stop it, the government adopts such measures as to increase exports and decrease imports. Thus the circular flow of money points towards the importance of adopting export promotion and import control policies.

8 *Basis of Flow of Funds Accounts*. The circular flow of money helps in calculating national income on the basis of the flow of funds accounts. The flow of funds accounts are concerned with all transactions in the economy that are accomplished by money transfers. They show the financial transactions among different sectors of the economy, and the link between saving and investment, and lending and borrowing by them.

To conclude, the circular flow of money possesses much theoretical and practical significance in an economy.

EXERCISES

1. What do you mean by the circular flow of money? Explain the circular flow of money in an economy. Use diagram to illustrate your answer.
2. What is meant by the circular flow of money? Explain the significance of circular flow of money in an economy.
3. Explain the circular flow of money in an economy including the foreign sector. Use diagrams to illustrate your answer.

Chapter 4

Monetary Standards

1. MEANING AND TYPES OF MONETARY STANDARD

Monetary standard refers to the overall set of laws and practices which control the quality and quantity of money in a country. It is, in fact, the standard money of the country which determines and regulates the exchange value of goods and services. Thus the monetary standard of a nation is its standard monetary unit. If, for instance, the standard monetary unit is made of silver, the country is said to be on the silver standard. A monetary standard aims at maintaining stability in the internal as well as external value of the currency.

There have been different types of monetary standards in the evolution of money. But only two types of monetary standards have been popular with nations in the recent past. They are metallic or commodity standard and paper or fiat standard. The metallic standard refers to a monetary system in which the value of the monetary unit is expressed in terms of a fixed quantity of some metal. If the monetary system is related to only one metal, it is known as *monometallism.* Monometallism may refer to the gold standard, if the metal is gold, and to silver standard, if the metal is silver. If the monetary unit is made of two metals, the monetary standard is called *bimetallism.* In the paper standard, paper notes circulate as legal tender money. They may be convertible into metal, such as gold or silver, of a fixed weight, or inconvertible.

In this chapter, we shall study the gold standard, bimetallism and paper standard.

2. THE GOLD STANDARD

Meaning. The gold standard is a monometallic standard in which the value of the monetary unit is fixed in terms of a specified weight and purity. As pointed out by Robertson, "Gold standard is a state of affairs in which a country keeps the value of its monetary and the value of a defined weight of gold at an equality with one another."[1] Coulborn's definition is simple. He writes, "The gold standard is an arrangement whereby the chief piece of money of a country is exchangeable with a fixed quantity of gold of a specified quality."[2]

---

1. D.H. Robertson, *op. cit.,* p. 64.
2. W.A.L. Coulborn. *op. cit.,* p. 117.

TYPES OF THE GOLD STANDARD

The meaning of the gold standard, as given above, relates to its general form. But different countries at different times adopted different types of gold standard which are explained as under.

1. *Gold Currency Standard.* This standard prevailed prior to 1914 in the UK, USA and certain other countries. It was also known as the gold coin standard, gold circulation standard or full or pure gold standard. It had six main features: (i) Gold coins of a definite weight and fineness circulated within the country. For instance, in England the sovereign was the gold coin which contained 123.2744 grams of gold of 11/12th purity. (ii) The gold coin (i.e. sovereign in Britain) was full and unlimited legal tender. (iii) Non-gold metallic coins and paper currency notes also circulated side by side but they were convertible on demand into gold coins at fixed rates. (iv) There was free coinage in gold. Any body could take gold or jewellery to the mint for coinage. (v) Gold coins could be freely minted for other purposes. (vi) Export and import of gold was free and unrestricted. Since this standard was costly to operate, it was given up after the First World War in favour of the gold bullion standard.

2. *Gold Bullion Standard.* This standard was in operation in the UK between 1925-31 and in India between 1927-31. This monetary system had five distinguishing features: (1) Gold coins did not circulate within the country. The legal tender currency in circulation consisted of paper currency notes and token coins of silver and other metals. (ii) These were convertible at fixed rates into gold bars or bullion. For instance, in England currency notes were convertible into gold bars containing 400 oz. of gold at the fixed price of £3-17s-10d per oz. of 11/12th fineness. When India adopted this system in 1927, rupee was convertible into gold bars containing 40 tolas at the price of Rs. 27–7 annas – 10 pies per tola.[3] (iii) For converting currency into gold, the monetary authority was required to keep gold bars in reserve. (iv) The monetary authority also bought gold from the public at a fixed price. (v) Gold was freely exported and imported.

3. *Gold Exchange Standard.* This system was in operation in India between 1898 to 1913 and in a number of eastern countries which were poor and did not possess sufficient gold. But mostly such countries were under the colonial rule and their currencies were linked with the currency of the ruling country. The principal features of this monetary system were: (i) Gold coins did not circulate within the country. (ii) The currency consisted of paper notes and token coins of silver and other metals. (iii) These were not convertible into gold coins or bullion. (iv) But the local currency was linked with some foreign currency which was on gold currency standard. (v) It was convertible into such foreign currency at a fixed rate. For instance, the Indian rupee coins were convertible into British sterling at the ratio of 1s-4d per rupee. (vi) Since the currency was indirectly linked with gold, prices of goods and services were consequently determined by the price of gold. (vii) Gold could not be exported and imported freely. Only the monetary authority was authorised to export or import gold. But actually payments were made in the securities of the two countries. For instance, rupee and sterling securities were bought and sold by England and India respectively at the fixed exchange rate of 1s-4d per rupee.

4. *Gold Reserve Standard.* England was the first country to abandon the gold standard in 1931, followed by the USA in 1933 and France in 1936. This led to instability in their exchange rates. To maintain exchange stability, they entered into Tripartite Monetary Agreement in September 1936 and they were joined by the Netherlands, Belgium and Switzerland in the same year. This Agreement came to be known as the Gold Reserve Standard and worked successfully till the outbreak of the Second World War in September 1939. The main features of this system were: *(a)* There were no gold coins within the country. *(b)* The currency consisted of paper notes and token coins of cheap metals, *(c)* This currency was incovertible into bullion. *(d)* Under the Agreement, each country maintained an Exchange Equalisation Fund which kept gold, local currency and foreign exchange. The exchange rate was stabilised by purchase and sale of foreign exchange or gold from the fund. *(e)* There was no free export or import of gold except by the Fund authority for maintaining stability in the exchange rate. Such gold was meant to be kept in the Fund. *(f)* There was strict secrecy about the reserves of gold and foreign exchange kept in the Fund.

5. *Gold Parity Standard.* This system has emerged with the establishment of the International Monetary

---

3. These weights and currency were prevalent in those times.

Fund in 1944. It does not possess any feature of the various gold standards explained above. Under this system, every country has to declare the par value of its monetary unit in terms of a fixed quantity of gold. So, this is not gold standard in the real sense of the term, except that it aims at keeping the exchange rate of the currency stable in terms of gold.

"But whatever form the gold standard may take, its essential characteristic is that the currency is, either directly or at one move, either in volume or in value, linked to gold."[4]

Crowther has distinguished between *domestic and international gold standard.* According to him, "The domestic gold standard is mainly concerned with the *volume* of money and with its influence on the domestic price level. The international gold standard is concerned with the external *value* of the currency and with problem of maintaining the stability of foreign exchange." All the variants of the gold standard discussed above differ with regard to the operation of the domestic gold standard in one respect or the other. But they have one feature in common relating to the maintenance of exchange stability under international gold standard. We shall, therefore, be concerned with the discussion of the working of the international gold standard which was abandoned by the countries of the world in 1930s.

Rules of the Gold Standard

The gold standard functioned smoothly before the First World War. In order to study its working, it is essential to analyse the conditions for its success. These conditions have come to be known as the "*rules of the game*". The Macmillan Committee pointed out in this connection, "It is difficult to define in precise terms what is implied by the rules of the game." The management of an international standard is an art and not a science, and no one would suggest that it is possible to draw up a formal code of action. Much must be left to time and circumstances."[5] But it recommended the following general principles for the successful working of the international gold standard.

1. It should involve a common agreement among nations as to the objectives for which it existed.
2. It should bring stability of prices and guarantee stability of exchange.
3. Individual central banks should avoid such actions which might endanger stability of prices through their effects on the policy of other central banks.

Given these three principles the countries on the gold standard were expected to observe the following rules or conditions for its smooth working.

1. There should be free and unrestricted export and import of gold between countries.
2. The country receiving (importing) gold should expand credit within the country and the gold-exporting country should contract credit.
3. There should be a high degree of price, wages, income and cash flexibility in countries on the gold standard so that these change with gold movements. For instance, when gold flows into the country, money supply should increase which should lead to rise in prices, wages and income, and costs would be adjusted accordingly. The opposite would be the case in the event of the outflow of gold to other countries. It would lead to decrease in money supply, fall in prices, wages, income and costs. Thus, the success of the gold standard depends upon flexibility in the economic set-up of the economy.
4. The successful working of the gold standard presupposed the existence of free trade among nations. The gold standard was essentially a laissez-faire standard.
5. The country on the gold standard should strictly adhere to the policy of maintaining exchange stability and other objectives should be subservient to it.
6. There should be no disturbing large capital movements based on speculative activities. In fact, the smooth working of the gold standard depended to a large extent upon the degree to which the movement of short-term funds could be influenced by changes in the bank rate.
7. Another condition was that the gold value of the domestic currency was to be kept stable. It should not be overvalued or undervalued.
8. Last but not the least, the success of the gold standard required normal times. That is why, it broke

---

4. G. Crowther, *op. cit.,* p. 280.
5. *Report of the Committee on Finance and Industry,* 1913.

down during the First World War and the disturbed conditions following the War.

9. The gold standard worked smoothly so long as the countries followed these rules to the letter. As pointed out by Crowther, "The gold standard is a jealous god. It will work provided it is given exclusive devotion."[6] This continued upto 1914 and after that when they started breaking these rules gradually, the gold standard broke down.

WORKING OF THE GOLD STANDARD

The question arises: how did the gold standard work or what was the mechanism of the gold standard? The answer to this question is related to the functioning of the gold standard before 1914.

All countries which were on the gold standard in the late 19th and early 20th century were interrelated and interdependent. A country having a favourable balance of trade received gold from other country, because it had excess of exports over imports. On the contrary, a country having an unfavourable trade suffered from the loss of gold on account of the excess of imports over exports. This movement of gold affected both the countries, the country with the inflow of gold and that having an outflow of gold.

The monetary reserves of the country with the gold inflow would increase. It would lead to an increase in the internal money supply of the country. The increased money supply was reflected in increased expenditures on goods and services. This led to rise in prices, wages, income, and costs. Consequently, the increase in the cost-price structure of the economy's domestically produced goods became relatively dearer in comparison with foreign goods. This tended to reduce exports and increase imports. Thus a surplus in the balance of payment of a country caused by a favourable balance of trade would be automatically corrected in the country with the gold inflow.

On the other hand, the reverse process would be repeated in the country with the gold outflow. The outflow of gold would lead to decline in its monetary reserves. This would decrease the internal money supply of the country. As a result, prices declined along with wages, income, and costs. This made the domestically produced goods relatively cheaper than foreign goods. So exports increased and imports declined. Thus, a deficit in the balance of payments of a country caused by an unfavourable balance of trade was automatically corrected in the country with gold outflow.

Was it Automatic? From the above analysis of the working of the gold standard, it seems that there was some visible hand which helped the attainment of "automatic equilibrium" in the balance of payments of both gold inflow and gold outflow countries. But this is not a correct view about the actual working of the gold standard. In reality, there was a large degree of management in its working even during its hey days before the First World War. Powerful central banks, like the Bank of England managed the internal policies of the government in each country for the gold standard to function the way the economists thought it should function.

One of the principal objectives of the central bank policy was to maintain stable exchange rates for a country on the gold standard. The adjustment in the domestic price level as a result of gold movements was not automatic. Rather, it was modified by the bank rate policy of the central bank.

Moreover, the total currency in a country was connected to gold reserves which increased or decreased with the rise or fall in the latter. It was the total volume of currency which affected the price level in turn. So, the central bank operated the bank rate policy to undertake corrective measures within the economy for keeping exchange rates stable with gold outflows or inflows.

When there was an outflow of gold, the gold reserves of the country declined. Consequently, the total volume of currency also declined and prices fell. But in order to protect the monetary reserves of the country, the central bank raised the bank rate. Higher interest rates induced the indigenous capitalists to invest funds internally and also attracted foreign investment to the country. These tendencies led to the reduction of gold outflow and also to an inflow of gold. In either case, the monetary reserves of the country were protected. Similarly, the bank rate was lowered and prices increased when there was an inflow of gold. As a matter of practice, the central bank seldom adopted corrective measures in the event of gold inflow. The increase in the

6. G. Crowther, *op. cit.,* p. 306.

monetary reserves of the country was welcomed. So, it was left to the gold losing country to undertake corrective measures.

The Deflationary Bias. Whenever a country lost gold, it experienced falling prices, In fact, it was in the interest of the gold losing country to deflate prices. But it became difficult to bring revival once deflation started. If the country lost much gold during a short period of time, the deflating pressures along with the rise in the bank rate would bring a financial crisis. Since wages are rigid in the downward direction, it would lead to large scale unemployment. Once the economy was in deep depression, it was difficult to bring a revival with the efforts of the central bank. Considering all this, Mrs. Joan Robinson pointed out that the gold standard had an "inherent bias towards deflation".

There were two more reasons for the deflationary bias of the gold standard mechanism. First, trade took place between countries of unequal size. But gold standard presupposed trade relations between homogeneous countries of approximately equal size." Second, for some countries balance of payments were more important relative to their internal economy, while for others balance of payments had less importance. Naturally, countries which depended more on imports having large gold outflows tended to have deflationary bias.

Despite this deflationary bias, the gold standard functioned smoothly prior to 1914. This is because "the gold standard mechanism was ... never put to a really severe test. Major international interruptions were absent, the price-cost structures of the different countries were in conformity with the. exchange rates and internati6nal capital movements served mainly to put sufficient reserves at the disposal of those countries which were, at the moment in need of it."[7]

The Decline and Fall of the Gold Standard

The gold standard could work only if the "rules of the game" were observed which could be observed under normal conditions. But when the First World War broke out in 1914, the belligerent countries went off the gold standard because they had to suspend convertibility of currency into gold. They withdrew gold coins from circulation and replaced them by paper currency. England prohibited the melting of gold coins and the export of gold though it did not stop conversion of notes into gold coins. Some of the countries did make payments to the neutral countries in gold. During the war the belligerent countries suffered from inflation of varying degrees. But they could not be controlled because the countries could not observe the rules of the game. So the gold standard virtually broke down during the war period.

After the War, most countries suffered from inflation of varying degrees which made it difficult to fix gold value of domestic currency at pre-war rates. Prestige led Great Britain to return to the gold standard at the pre-war parity and it was commonly estimated that the pound was overvalued by 10 per cent. This was because the price level in Britain was higher than in America by this percentage. The actual exchange rate was fixed at \$4.866=£1 but the equilibrium rate was \$4.38=£1. So England's goods were overpriced and of America's under-priced. This adversely affected British exports and favoured imports from America. But Italy overvalued its Lira and France undervalued its Franc. By 1928 the restoration of the gold standard was complete.

But it was not the same gold standard which existed before the 1914 war. Rather, it was a truncated gold standard with failure of the governments to follow the golden rules of the gold standard game. Consequently, with the beginning of the Great Depression in 1929, the final collapse of the gold standard began. Four South American countries were the first to go off the gold standard by the end of 1930. England, alongwith twenty-two other countries, abandoned the gold standard in 1931. By the end of 1936, practically all cou‵tries had left the gold standard.

Causes of the Breakdown of the Gold Standard. Economists have pointed to a number of causes which led to the breakdown of the gold standard. *First,* the monetary authorities in the different countries were no longer exclusively devoted to the aims of the gold standard as they had been before the war. As put by Crowther, "Gold standard is a jealous god. It will work provided it is given exclusive devotion." They were not prepared to follow the rules of the gold standard. After the restoration of the gold standard in 1920s, every country wanted to have price stability. But the primary objective of the gold standard was to have exchange stability.

7. G.N. Halm, *Monetary Theory,* 2/e.

So price stability was not compatible with the maintenance of the gold standard. Hence, it broke down for failure to observe this golden rule of the game.

Second, the technical task of maintaining exchange stability was more difficult than before the First World War. Exchange stability could be maintained by making adjustment in the internal price level of countries. But it was difficult to make constant readjustment in prices due to three reasons: (i) The domestic currencies were either overvalued or undervalued; *(ii)* there was downward rigidity in the wage-cost structure in case of downward readjustment of prices; and *(iii)* readjustments were also difficult because the short-term funds of banks could not be influenced by changes in the rate of interest. The short-term funds were affected more by speculation or fear.than by the interest rate.

Third, the imposition of Reparations and the insistence on the repayment of war debts from Germany made it difficult for the foreign market to be controlled by the weapons of the gold standard. To pay Reparations and War Debts, Germany had to buy dollars irrespective of its gold reserve position and the bank rate, and the countries which received such payments could not make adjustments accordingly.

Fourth, almost every country imposed high tariffs. Imposition of high tariffs especially by the creditor countries restricted imports from debtor countries. This was a clear violation of the rule of the gold standard. When a debtor country was losing gold, it was essential for it to lower internal prices in order to expand exports. But high tariffs by the creditor countries prevented the expansion of exports and thus made adjustments in foreign exchange difficult. This led many countries to abandon the gold standard.

Fifth, the central banks failed to observe the golden rule: "expand credit when gold is coming in; contract credit when gold is going out." The United States and France, which were receiving gold did not expand credit sufficiently. On the other hand, Germany and Great Britain which were losing gold tried to make adjustments by borrowing from the gold-receiving countries. This meant the non-observance of the rule of the gold standard. There were, however, some *immediate causes* which led to the breakdown of the gold standard beginning from 1930.

(i) The first cause was the steep fall in the price levels of a number of countries. This brought a fall in the demand for exports and reduced the foreign exchange earnings of exporting countries. These were the countries which depended on exports of raw materials whose prices fell sharply. Their export earnings declined considerably but they could not protect their gold reserves from falling as they continued to make gold payments for their international obligations.

(ii) The second immediate cause of the abandonment of the gold standard was the virtual cessation of international lending from 1929. We saw above that many debtor countries had been borrowing from the United States to meet their international payment and protect their gold reserves during 1920-27. But with the coming in of the Great Depression, such countries stopped borrowings and found it difficult to make repayments of interest and principal because their export earnings were declining.

(iii) The last immediate cause was the presence of large short-term international debts against London and New York financial markets. These were payable on demand at short notice. A wave of fear caused the lenders of these short-term funds or "Hot Money" to ask for their repayments. It all started with the failure of the largest bank in Austria, the Credit Anstalt in May 1931. This led to international banking panic in Germany, France, United States and Great Britain, where there were run on banks by creditors with the result that they stopped payments and froze credits in terms of gold. And the gold standard had finally ended. Hawtrey observes, "The immediate cause of the crisis, it is true, was the withdrawal of foreign money, first from Austria and Germany and then from England, But this was the result of distrust, and the distrust was directly due to the appreciation of gold."

Merits of the Gold Standard

The international gold standard which operated for more than three decades in different forms had certain merits.

1. *Inspired Public Confidence.* The gold standard inspired public confidence because the domestic currency was linked with gold. People knew that gold was an internationally accepted medium of payment, and a standard and a store of value. Therefore, they had full confidence in the paper currency which was convertible into gold bullion or coins or securities.

2. *No Outside Interference.* The international gold standard had the merit of working without any outside interference by any other country or international authority.

3. *Automatic Operation.* The gold standard functioned smoothly provided "the rules of the game" were observed. These rules were not complex but easy to understand and follow for the countries. Thus, the gold standard provided a simple and automatic monetary system to the countries of the world.

4. *Stable Exchange Rates.* Another merit of the gold standard was that it maintained stable exchange rates between countries. The exchange rate of every country was fixed in terms of its mint par or the gold value of its currency. The actual exchange rate between gold export and gold import points which took account of the cost of transporting gold from one country to the other. Thus the exchange rate was stable and fluctuations occurred only between the two gold points.[8]

5. *Stable Internal Prices.* The gold standard secured relative stability of internal prices. When there was an inflow of gold, prices rose. And they fell with gold outflow. But when prices rose, exports diminished and imports increased. On the other hand, fall in prices led to expansion of exports and decline in imports. These opposite tendencies started gold outflow in the former case and gold inflow in the latter case. Ultimately, price stability was maintained in the trading countries.

6. *Check on Inflation.* Under the gold standard the currency of a country was linked with gold and was convertible into it. As the issuing of currency was backed by specified quantity of gold, there was a limit up to which the authorities could issue currency. For every increase in the amount of currency, gold reserves were also required to be increased to a given extent. There was thus an automatic check on the issuing of paper currency by a country. There was also no fear of inflation, because the country could not increase the quantity of money in unlimited quantity. As against this, the present system of managed paper standard, having a fixed gold backing, leads the authorities to issue paper money in unlimited quantities thereby leading to inflation.

7. *Expansion of International Trade.* The gold standard helped in the expansion of international trade. This was made possible by stable exchange rate and stable value of gold in countries. These led to the expansion of international trade and capital movements.

Demerits of the Gold Standard

Despite these merits, the actual working of the gold standard revealed a number of disadvantages which the countries of the world had to experience. Some of them were as under:

1. *Fair Weather Standard.* Critics pointed out that the gold standard acted like a fair weather friend. It worked smoothly in normal or peace times but failed during war or economic crises. Its actual working shows that it had to be suspended during the First World War and finally abandoned during the Great Depression. So it was a fair weather standard.

2. *Not Automatic.* It is a misnomer to say that the gold standard worked automatically. In fact, all varieties of it had to be managed by the monetary authority or the central bank. The gold standard did not work automatically. The central bank had to change the bank rate in accordance with gold movements in order to affect the price level.

3. *Exchange Stability at the Cost of Economic Stability.* One of the principal objectives of the gold standard was to maintain exchange stability. But this was always attained at the cost of economic stability. When every time there were gold movement, the internal price level had to be adjusted accordingly in order to maintain exchange stability. These price fluctuations led to internal economic instability which ultimately harmed the country. It is for this reason that now a days all countries prefer internal price stability to exchange stability.

4. *Anarchy in World Credit Control.* Hawtrey characterised the gold standard as state of anarchy in world credit control.[9] Since the gold standard was a laissezfaire standard and operated only under normal times, it failed miserably in conditions of severe inflation or deflation. During the First World War, inflation spread to all countries of the world. On the other hand, when depression started in 1929 it became a worldwide phenomenon. Thus the gold standard by itself was unable to control either inflation or deflation. Rather, it had

---

8. For the understanding of this mechanism refer to the chapter on "Foreign Exchange".
9. R.G. Hawtrey, *The Gold Standard: Theory and Practice*, 5/e, 1947.

to sacrifice itself at the altars of inflation and deflation.

5. *Deflationary Bias.* According to Mrs. Joan Robinson, the gold standard had an inherent bias towards deflation. It was in the interest of the gold losing country to deflate prices, But once deflation started it became very difficult to bring revival even with the best efforts of the central bank. The long drawn depression of 1930s proved this fact without any shadow of doubt.

6. *No Independent Policy. A* country on the gold standard could not follow an independent policy of its own. It had to follow that policy which was adopted by all other countries. Failure to follow a common policy alongwith other countries mean; abandoning the gold standard. This implied breaking of all trade relations with countries on the gold standard which could be harmful for the country.

7. *Costly Standard.* The gold standard was a costly standard because it was based on gold. Every country had to circulate gold coins or keep gold reserves. As against this the paper standard is much cheaper and also economises the use of gold.

8.. *Rigid Standard.* The gold standard was a rigid standard because for its success the rules of the game had to be observed in letter and spirit. A country could not increase the money supply to finance a war or development activities or any financial emergency without increasing the gold reserves with its central bank. If it had to export gold to import the necessary equipment, raw materials and other goods it needed for war or development purposes. It was expected to reduce the internal price level by force in keeping with the rules of the gold standard game. Thus it was a highly rigid standard.

9. *Adverse Effects of Interest Rate Changes.* Under one of the rules of the gold standard, the central bank of the country was required to affect changes in the bank rate in keeping with gold movements. When there was an infl6w of gold, the bank rate was lowered, while it was raised with the outflow of gold. Such changes in interest rates were forced upon trade and industry simply to expand or reduce money income within the country. They, therefore, adversely affected trade and industry.

Taking into account the various disadvantages of the gold standard enumerated above, it can be concluded that the gold standard was an unnecessary standard. The managed paper standard can secure on all the advantages enjoyed by the gold standard minus its disadvantages. That is why the gold standard is now a thing of the past and is only of academic interest, never to be restored again.

What Led to the Non-restoration of the Gold Standard?

After the collapse of the gold standard, no country was willing to restore the gold standard for the following reasons: *First,* the supply of gold could not be increased to meet its increasing demand. So no country was willing to export it to observe the rules of the game. *Secondly,* more so because the majority of gold reserves flowed into the United States. *Thirdly,* no country was willing to bring instability to its economy for the sake of maintaining exchange stability. *Fourthly,* development of nationalism motivated every country to formulate economic policies in keeping with its self-interest. *Lastly,* every country felt that it could manage its monetary affairs in a far better way by adopting a managed paper standard than the gold standard.

3. BIMETALLISM

Bimetallism, also known as bimetallic standard, is a monetary system under which the monetary unit of the country is expressed by law in terms of two metals, usually gold and silver, in a specific ratio. In other words, under bimetallism both silver and gold coins circulate simultaneously within the country. They are unlimited legal tender. They are minted freely and in unlimited quantities free or with some charge. Both metals are imported and exported freely. Both types of coins are exchanged for each other at a fixed mint par ratio.

Bimetallism was in vogue in England throughout the 18th century. The United States adopted it in 1792, when the mint ratio between silver and gold was fixed at 15 :1. France adopted it in 1803 followed by Belgium, Switzerland and Italy in 1865. With the growing popularity of the gold standard, it was abandoned by these European countries in 1874.

MERITS OF BIMETALLISM

Bimetallism as monetary system had the following advantages:

1. *Adequate Supply of Currency.* One of the merits of bimetallism was that it ensured an adequate supply of currency within the country. As both gold and silver coins were in circulation and freely minted, there was no likelihood of both becoming short in supply simultaneously.

2. *Price Stability.* It was also argued that flexibility of money supply assured price stability. The internal price level was linked with the prices of gold and silver. And the prices of gold and silver depended upon their supply and demand. If the output of silver rose, that of gold fell and vice versa. It meant that fall in the price of silver was compensated by rise in the price of gold and vice versa. So there was greater stability in the prices of gold and silver taken together than in the case of one metal. It was like two drunken men walking hand in hand steadily than apart.

3. *Stable Price of Silver.* The proponents of bimetallism argued in the last quarter of the 19th century and twenties of the 20th century that bimetallism would stop the fall in the price of silver. In those days, the price of silver was falling and the silver producing countries were at a disadvantage in trading with gold standard countries. It was, therefore, felt that the adoption of bimetallism would increase the demand for silver and raise its price. This would increase the purchasing power of silver-producing countries and also help in overcoming depression in them.

4. *Stable Exchange Rates.* It was further argued that bimetallism helped to maintain stable exchange rates between countries. This was because the ratio of exchange between gold and silver was fixed, being determined by the gold value of silver. Therefore, there was no possibility of the market rate of exchange to deviate from the mint par rate of exchange.

5. *Encouragement to Foreign Trade.* As a corollary to the above, bimetallism encouraged foreign trade in two ways. First, due to exchange stability between countries, and second, a country on bimetallism could have trade relations with any country on bimetallism and on silver or gold standard.

6. *Easy to Keep Cash Reserves.* As both gold and silver coins were unlimited legal tender under bimetallism, it was convenient and easy for commercial banks to keep minimum cash reserves against their liabilities either in gold or silver coins. Similarly, it was also argued that it was more easy for the government to meet its cash requirements with two types of coins than with either silver or gold coins.

7. *Encouragement to Production.* The advocates of bimetallism contended that bimetallism as a monetary system was superior to the silver or gold standard because it encouraged production. As money consisted of gold and silver coins under bimetallism, the total money supply was greater than its demand. As a result, the rate of interest declined which encouraged investment and production.

DEMERITS OF BIMETALLISM

The opponents of bimetallism give the following arguments against this monetary system.

1. *Inequality of Market Ratio and Mint Ratio.* The success of the bimetallic standard depended upon the maintenance of equality between the market ratio and mint ratio of gold and silver. But it was not possible to maintain this equality because of a strong tendency towards the continuous increase in the supply of one metal. This would bring a fall in its value thereby creating divergence between the two ratios. The metal whose value increased was hoarded by the people. Speculation would start thereby creating confusion within the economy.

2. *Operation of Gresham's Law.* As a corollary to the above, when there was divergence between the mint ratio and the market ratio the Gresham's law would operate and bimetallism would breakdown. According to this law, cheap money drives out dear money, or bad money drives out good money. If silver became cheaper, people used this as medium of exchange and hoarded or melted gold coins with the result that gold coins disappeared from the market. This would happen when the market rate of gold exceeded its mint rate. When Gresham's law operated the country would be on monometallism.

3. *Not Successful Internationally.* It was argued that if bimetallism was adopted by many countries, it would be successful. But this presupposed the adoption of the *same* mint ratio between the gold and silver by all countries. But it was not possible to expect international cooperation on maintaining a uniform ratio in every country. Even if the countries agreed on this question, no government could prevent its citizens to hoard or

melt the costly metal when its price increased within the country.

4. *No Price Stability.* The opponents of bimetallism dispute that flexibility of money led to price stability. According to them, there was no set rule that when the supply of one metal rose that of the other metal would fall. There was every likelihood for the supplies of both metals to fall, as has happened in the case of gold and silver.

Thus on all counts, Bimetallism was never favoured by the nations of the world. For it was a complex and costly standard which could not work smoothly. They found that a constant supply of money could be ensured in a much better way by the managed paper standard. So the study of bimetallism is of historical and academic interest only.

4. GRESHAM'S LAW

During the reign of Queen Elizabeth I, it was found that debased coins continued to circulate while full-bodied coins were hoarded or melted for their specie content. The Chancellor of the Exchequer under Elizabeth I, Sir Thomas Gresham enquired about this phenomenon in 1558 and came to the conclusion that "bad money drives out good money." This has come to be known as Gresham's Law. Marshall defined this law more explicitly thus, "whenever the specie value of a certain class of coins exceeds their currency value, the coins will begin to go into the melting pot or be exported." Thus "bad money" refers to debased or clipped or worn out legal tender money such as coins and paper notes.

When full-bodied and debased coins circulate together, people have a tendency to hoard the good and try to pass on the bad ones as medium of exchange. They may even melt the full-bodied coins for bullion in order to export it or use it for jewellery. This actually happened in countries which were on silver or gold standard.

This law also operates under the bimetallic standard when gold and silver coins circulate simultaneously and one metal becomes overvalued relative to the other metal. The metal which is overvalued drives out the undervalued metal out of circulation. Suppose the mint ratio between gold and silver is 1 oz of gold coin= 15 ozs. of silver coin (1: I5). Suppose silver coins become overvalued which means that their money (face) value exceeds their metallic (intrinsic) value. On the other hand, gold coins become undervalued which means their metallic value exceeds their money value. As a result, let us say the market ratio becomes 1:17. People will thus find it profitable to melt gold coins to exchange 1 oz of gold for 17 ozs of silver in the market, and thereby gain 2 ozs of silver. It is in this way that the overvalued (bad) currency drives out the undervalued (good) currency out of circulation under bimetallism.

Further, Gresham's law operates when paper currency notes circulate alongwith gold and or silver coins. In this case paper notes are bad money and gold and or silver coins are good money. This actually happened during the Revolutionary War in the United States of America when the bad paper money drove all gold and silver coins out of circulation between 1775-79.

Limitations of the Law

There are, however, certain limitations of this law so that it will operate only if the following conditions are fulfilled:

1. If the total money in circulation, including, both good and bad money, exceeds the actual monetary demand of the public.
2. If the public is prepared to accept and circulate bad money.
3. If the good money is full-bodied legal tender whose face value equals its intrinsic value.
4. If the total supply of bad money is sufficient to meet the total monetary demand of the public.

With managed paper standard in circulation alongwith token coins, Gresham's law is only of limited validity in modern times. Still we find the tendency among people to pass on worn out notes and debased coins first. But this is not Gresham's law proper because neither fresh notes nor good coins go out of circulation but their use is suspended for a while.

5. PAPER CURRENCY STANDARD

Paper currency standard consists of paper money which is unlimited legal tender and token coins of cheap metals. Paper money may be either convertible or inconvertible. Convertible paper money is convertible into gold or silver coins or bullion of specified weight on demand. Paper money is not convertible into coins of a precious metal of bullion now a days. Therefore, it is inconvertible. People accept it because it is legal tender. Since it has the command of the government, people have to accept it. That is why it is also known as *fiat* money or standard. It is also referred to as managed standard because the issue of paper money and token coins is managed by the central bank of the country.

MERITS OF THE PAPER STANDARD

The paper standard, which is universally used, has a number of merits :

1. *Economical.* The paper standard is cheaper than gold or silver standard. There is no need to waste gold or silver for coinage purposes. Rather precious metals can be used for productive purposes and for making payments to foreign countries. As paper money is not convertible, there is no need to keep gold in the form of reserves. The monetary authorities keep only a fixed quantity of gold in reserve for reasons of security. Thus the paper standard is cheap and economical and even a poor country can easily adopt it.

2. *Elastic.* The paper standard is a highly useful monetary system because it possesses great elasticity. The monetary authority can easily adjust the money supply in accordance with the requirements of the economy. This was not possible under the gold standard. The supply of money can be increased by printing more notes in times of financial emergency, war, and for economic development. It can also be reduced when the economic situation so demands. Thus there is also freedom in the management of the money supply in the economy.

3. *Price Stability.* As a corollary to the above, the paper standard ensures price stability in the country. The monetary authority can stabilise the price level by maintaining equilibrium between demand and supply of money by an appropriate monetary policy.

4. *Free from Cyclical Effects.* The paper standard is free from the effects of business cycles arising in other countries. This merit was not available to other monetary standards, especially the gold standard, where cyclical movements in one country were automatically passed on to other countries through gold movements.

5. *Full Utilisation of Resources.* The gold standard had a deflationary bias whereby the resources of the country remained unutilised. Whenever there was gold outflow prices fell and resources became unemployed. But this is not the case under the paper standard in which the monetary authority can manipulate the monetary policy in order to ensure full utilisation of the country's resources.

6. *Equilibrium in Exchange Rate.* One of the merits of the paper standard is that it immediately restores equilibrium in the exchange rate of a country whenever disequilibrium occurs in the demand and supply of its currency in the foreign exchange market.

7. *Portable.* It is very convenient to carry large sums of paper money from one place to another.

8. *Easy to count.* It is easier to count paper money than metallic money.

9. *Easy to store.* It is easier to store large sums of paper money in a small space.

10. *Cognisable.* It is easy to recognise paper notes of different denominations.

11. *Replaceable.* Paper notes of one type and denomination can be easily replaced by printing notes of different types of the same denomination.

DEMERITS OF THE PAPER STANDARD

Despite these merits, the paper standard has certain disadvantages:

1. *Inflationary Bias.* One of the serious defect of the paper standard is that it has an inflationary bias. As paper notes are inconvertible, there is every likelihood of the government printing notes in excess of the requirements. Or, the government may deliberately resort to the printing press to meet a financial emergency or war or even to meet ordinary budget deficits. This leads to excess of money supply and to inflation in the country.

2. *Price Stability a Myth.* It has been pointed out in the merits of the paper standard that it leads to price

stability. In actuality, price stability is a myth as has been the experience of the majority of countries on the paper standard.

3. *Exchange Instability.* Another disadvantage of this system is that it leads to instability in exchange rates whenever there are large fluctuations in external prices as against internal prices. Such wide and violent fluctuations in exchange rates are harmful for the growth of international trade and capital movements among countries. These have led governments to adopt exchange control measures.

4. *Lacks Confidence.* Paper money lacks confidence as it is not backed by gold reserves.

5. *Lacks Durability.* Paper money has less durability than metallic coins. It can be easily destroyed by fire or insects.

6. *Unstable.* Paper money lacks stability because its supply can be changed easily.

7. *Uncertainty.* Instability in the value of paper money leads to uncertainty in the economy which adversely affects business and economic progress.

8. *Token Money.* Paper money is token money and in the event of demonetisation of notes, they have no intrinsic value and are simply like waste paper.

9. *Not Automatic.* The paper currency standard does not operate automatically. It is a highly managed standard which requires much care and caution on the part of the monetary authority. A little carelessness may bring disaster to the economy.

6. STANDARD SYSTEMS OF NOTE ISSUE

Over the years, different countries have evolved various methods of note issue and adopted them from time to time. They are discussed below:

1. *Simple Deposit System.* Under this system, the monetary authority is required to keep 100% of the bullion (gold or silver) for every note issued. That is why it is also known as the Full Reserve System.

This system has certain merits. It is safe and enjoys public confidence because there is full backing of the bullion for every note issued. The monetary authority cannot take any arbitrary decision in issuing notes. So, there is no possibility of over issue of notes. There is also the saving of precious metals through debasement because metal coins are not circulated.

However, this system lacks in elasticity *firstly,* because the money supply cannot be increased without the full backing of bullion reserves. This may be harmful during war or emergency or for development. It may also adversely affect trade and currency. *Second,* this system is especially unsuited for poor countries lacking insufficient quantities of gold or silver. *Third,* it is uneconomical for it does not make a profitable use of bullion reserves lying idle with the monetary authority. Thus this system is highly impracticable in modern times. Perhaps this is the reason for its being not put into practice in any country of the world.

2. *Fixed Fiduciary System.* Under this system, a fixed amount of notes is issued by the central bank against reserves of government securities. Such amount is issued on the faith or fiduciary of the central bank and is called the fiduciary limit. The central bank is required to keep 100% gold reserves beyond the fiduciary limit. The fiduciary limit is raised from time to time with the expansion of trade and industry. This system was introduced in England in 1844, in India in 1860, followed by Japan and Norway.

This system ensures security, inspires public confidence, and is without any danger of mismanaging the currency through overissue of notes by the central bank.

But it has also certain disadvantages. *First,* it is a rigid and inelastic system because in times of a financial emergency, notes cannot be issued without keeping cent per cent gold in reserves. *Second,* the system is inconvenient because in the event of a fall in gold reserves, the central bank has to withdraw notes from circulation with the result that the quantity of money is reduced in the country with its adverse effects on prices, trade and industry. Third, this system is uneconomical because gold reserves are blocked up with the central bank. It was, therefore, abandoned by all countries after World War I when they faced these problems.

3. *Maximum Fiduciary System.* Under this system, there is a maximum limit up to which the central bank is authorised to issue notes without any gold reserves. But there has to be full backing of gold reserves beyond this limit. The central bank is, however, authorised to raise or lower the maximum fiduciary limit and to fix the quantity of gold reserves. Thus, this system is not rigid but is elastic. It is also economical because the gold

reserves can be kept to the minimum to meet the requirements of trade and industry. In case the central bank fixes the fiduciary limit very high, there may be excess of notes in circulation thereby leading to inflation. This system was in operation in France, Japan, Russia, Norway, Finland and England. This system has one major defect that there is the possibility of inflation through over issue when the maximum limit may be raised by the government.

4. *Proportional Reserve System.* In this system, a certain percentage of the total notes issued by the central bank has to be in gold reserves and the remaining in the form of government securities. This percentage varied between 25 to 40 per cent in countries like Switzerland, Holland, Belgium, USA and India. This system is simple and elastic. The money supply can be changed with changes in the percentage of gold reserves. It provides sufficient security because a certain percentage of note issue is supported by gold.

Still, this system has certain *drawbacks. Firstly,* It is uneconomical because large quantities of gold reserves have to be kept which cannot be issued for productive purposes. *Second,* if the gold reserves fall, the reduction in currency in circulation may be more than in proportion to the fall in reserves. This may lead to deflationary tendencies. The opposite may happen when gold reserves increase. This system was in vogue in India between 1927 to 1956.

5. *Minimum Reserve System.* Under the minimum reserve system, the central bank is authorised to issue notes up to any extent but it must keep a statutory minimum reserve of gold and foreign securities. India adopted this system of note issue in 1956 after discarding the proportional reserve system. Accordingly, the Reserve Bank of India is required to keep a minimum reserve of Rs 200 crores. Of this, Rs. 115 crores must be in gold and Rs 85 crores in foreign securities.

This system is highly useful for'developing countries because they can meet their financial requirements by printing more notes. They can also reduce the money supply to check inflation. It is, therefore, an elastic system. Further, it is very economical because only a small and fixed amount of gold is required to be kept in reserve.

Despite these merits, the minimum reserve system is a dangerous tool in the hands of the monetary authority. It can print any number of notes, thereby creating inflationary pressure within the economy. A corrupt and inefficient government can bring disaster to the economy by excessive printing of notes and thus lose confidence of the people. On the other hand, an efficient and honest administration can transform the economy by a judicious use of this system.

Conclusion. It can be concluded from the discussion of the various systems of note issue that an ideal system should fulfil the criteria of elasticity, economy, stability, convenience and safety. Every country tries to adopt that system which is flexible enough to meet its needs of growth and development. On this criterion, the minimum reserve system stands out unique among all the systems of note issue.

EXERCISES

1. When is a country said to be on gold standard? Explain the types of gold standards.
2. Discuss the merits and demerits of the gold standard.
3. What are the main features of gold standard? Distinguish between gold exchange standard and gold currency standard.
4. What were the causes of the failure of the gold standard during the inter-war period? Can the gold standard be restored?
5. Describe the mechanism of the gold standard. Why was the gold standard abandoned in 1930s?
6. What is paper currency standard? Give its merits and demerits.
7. Discuss the standard system of note issue. Which is the present system of note issue in India?

CHAPTER 5

Measurement of Changes in the Value of Money : Index Numbers

1. MEANING OF INDEX NUMBERS

An index number is a statistical device to measure *changes* in the value of money. It is a number which represents the average price of a group of commodities at a particular time in relation to the average price of the *same* group of commodities at another time. Professor Chandler defines it thus: "An index number of prices is a figure showing the height of average prices at one time relative to their height at some other time that is taken at the base period." To understand the meaning of the term index number, three points are to be noted. *First,* an average figure relates to a single group of commodities. But the various items in the group are expressed in different units. For example, a consumer price index contains such diverse items as food, clothing, fuel and lighting, house rent, and miscellaneous things. Food consists of wheat, ghee, etc. expressed in kgs. cloth is expressed in metres, and lighting in kws. An index number expresses the average of all such diverse items in different units. *Second,* an index number measures the net increase or decrease of the average prices for the group under study. For instance, if the consumer price index has increased from 150 in 1982 as compared to 100 in 1980, it shows a net increase of 50 per cent in the prices of commodities included in the index. *Third,* an index number measures the extent of changes in the value of money (or price level) over a period of time, given a base period. If the base period is the year 1970, we can measure change in the average price level for the preceding and succeeding years.

2. METHODS OF CONSTRUCTION OF INDEX NUMBER

In constructing an index number, the following steps should be noted :

1. *Purpose of the Index Number.* Before constructing an index number, it should be decided the purpose for which it is needed. An index number constructed for one category or purpose cannot be used for others. A cost of living index of working classes cannot be used for farmers because the items entering into their consumption will be different.

2. *Selection of Commodities.* Commodities to be selected depend upon the purpose or objective of the index number to be constructed. But the number of commodities should neither be too large nor too small. Moreover, commodities to be selected must be broadly representative of the group of commodities. They should also be comparable in the sense that standard or graded items should be taken.

3. *Selection of Prices.* The next step is to select the prices of these commodities. For this purpose, care should be taken to select prices from representative persons, places or journals or other sources. But they must be reliable. Prices may be quoted in money terms i.e. Rs. 100 per quantal or in quantity terms. i.e. 2 kg. per rupee. Care should be taken not to mix these prices. Then the problem is to select wholesale or retail prices. This depends on the type of index number. For a consumer price index, wholesale prices are required, while for a cost of living index, retail prices are needed. But different prices should not be mixed up.

4. *Selection of an Average.* Since index numbers are averages, the problem is how to select an appropriate average. The two important averages are the arithmetic mean and geometric mean. The arithmetic mean is the simpler of the two. But geometric mean is more accurate. However, the average prices should be reduced to price relatives (percentages) either on the basis of the fixed base method or the chain base method.

5. *Selection of Weights.* While constructing an index number due weightage or importance should be given to the various commodities. Commodities which are more important in the consumption of consumers should be given higher weightage than other commodities. The weights are determined with reference to the relative amounts of income spent on commodities by consumers. Weights may be given in terms of value or quantity.

6. *Selection of the Base Period.* The selection of the base period is the most important step in the construction of an index number. It is a period against which comparisons are made. The base period should be normal and free from any unusual events such as war, famine, earthquake, drought, boom, etc. It should not be either very recent or remote.

7. *Selection of Formula.* A number of formulas have been devised to construct an index number. But the selection of an appropriate formula depends upon the availability of data and purpose of the index number. No single formula may be used for all types of index numbers.

We give below an example each of the simple price index and the weighted price index.

Simple Price Index

To construct a simple price index, compute the price relatives and average them. Add the price relatives and divide them by the number of items. Table 1 illustrates the construction of a simple index of wholesale prices.

TABLE 1

Commodity	*Prices in 1970(P_0)*	*Base 1970=100*	*Prices in 1980(P_1) = $P_1/P_0 \times 100$*	*Price Relatives (R)*
A	Rs. 20 per kg	100	Rs. 25	125
B	5 per kg	100	10	200
C	15 per metre	100	30	200
D	25 per kg	100	30	120
E	200 per quantal	100	450	225
N = 5		500		$\Sigma R = 870$

$$\text{Price index in 1980} = \frac{\text{Prices in 1980}}{\text{Prices in 1970}} \times 100 \text{ or } \frac{\Sigma P_1}{\Sigma P_0} \times 100 = \frac{870}{500} \times 100 = 174$$

$$\text{Using arithmetic mean, price index in 1980} = \frac{\Sigma R}{N} = \frac{870}{5} = 174$$

The preceding table shows that 1970 is the base period and 1980 is the year for which the price index has been constructed on the basis of price relatives. The index of wholesale prices in 1980 comes to 174. This means that the price level rose by 74 per cent in 1980 over 1970.

WEIGHTED PRICE INDEX

Taking the example of Table 1 already given, we assign high weights to commodities of greater importance to consumers and low weights to commodities of lesser importance.

TABLE 2

Commodity	*Weight* (W)	*Prices in 1970* Rs	*Base 1970 = 100*	*Prices in 1980* Rs	*Price Relatives* (R)	*W×R*
A	6	20	100	25	125	750
B	4	5	100	10	200	800
C	2	15	100	30	200	400
D	4	25	100	30	120	480
E	10	200	100	450	225	2250
	Σ26					Σ*WR* = 4680

Using arithmetic mean, the weighted price index in 1980 = $\frac{4680}{26}$ = 180.

The weighted price index is more accurate than the simple price index. In the example given above, the weighted price index shows an increase of 80 per cent in the price level in 1980 over 1970 as against the increase of 74 per cent according to the simple price index.

3. DIFFICULTIES IN THE CONSTRUCTION OF INDEX NUMBERS

There are many difficulties in the construction of index numbers. They are discussed as under :

1. *Difficulties in the Selection of the Base Period.* The first difficulty relates to the selection of the base year. The base year should be normal. But it is difficult to determine a truly normal year. Moreover, what may be the normal year today may become an abnormal year after some period. Therefore, it is not advisable to have the same year as the base period for a number of years. Rather, it should be changed after ten years or so. But there is no fixed rule for this.

2. *Difficulties in the Selection of Commodities.* The selection of representative commodities for the index number is another difficulty. The choice of representative commodities is not an easy matter. They have to be selected from a wide range of commodities which the majority of people consume. Again, what were representative commodities some ten years ago may not be representative today. The consumption pattern of consumers might change and thereby make the index number useless. So the choice of representative commodities presents real difficulties.

3. *Difficulties in the Collection of Prices.* Another difficulty is that of collecting adequate and accurate prices. It is often not possible to get them from the same source or place. Further, the problem of choice between wholesale and retail prices arises. There are much variations in the retail prices. Therefore, index numbers are based on wholesale prices.

4. *Arbitrary Assigning of Weights.* In calculating weighted price index, a number of difficulties arise. The problem is to give different weights to commodities. The selection of higher weight for one commodity and a lower weight for another is simply arbitrary. There is no set rule and it entirely depends on the investigator.

Moreover, the same commodity may have different importance for different consumers. The importance of commodities also changes with the change in the tastes and incomes of consumers and also with the passage of time. Therefore, weights are to be revised from time to time and not fixed arbitrarily.

5. *Difficulty of Selecting the Method of Averaging.* Another difficulty is to select an appropriate method of calculating averages. There are a number of methods which can be used for this purpose. But all methods give different results from one another. It is, therefore, difficult to decide which method to choose.

6. *Difficulties Arising from Changes Overtime.* In the present times, changes in the nature of commodities are taking place continuously overtime due to technological changes. As a result, new commodities are introduced and people start consuming them in place of the old ones. Moreover, prices of commodities might also change with technical changes. They may fall. But new commodities are not entered into the list of commodities in preparing the index numbers. This makes the index numbers based on old commodities unreal.

7. *Not All Purpose.* An index number constructed for a particular purpose cannot be used for some other purpose. For instance, a cost of living index number for industrial workers cannot be used to measure the cost of living of agricultural workers. Thus there are no all purpose index numbers.

8. *International Comparisons not Possible.* International price comparisons are not possible with index numbers. The commodities consumed and included in the construction of an index number differ from country to country. For instance, meat, eggs, cars, and electrical appliance are included in the price index of advanced countries whereas they are not included in that of backward countries. Similarly, weights assigned to commodities are also different. Thus international comparisons of index numbers are not possible.

9. *Comparisons of Different Places not Possible.* Even if different places within a country are taken, it is not possible to apply the same index number to them. This is because of differences in the consumption habits of people. People living in the northern region consume different commodities than those consumed by the people in the south of India. It is, therefore, not right to apply the same index number to both.

10. *Not Applicable to an Individual.* An index number is not applicable to an individual belonging to a group for which it is constructed. If an index number shows a rise in the price level, an individual may not be affected by it. This is because an index number reflects averages.

CONCLUSION

It may be concluded from the difficulties and limitations of index numbers that index numbers are at best approximations to measure changes in the value of money. However, these difficulties become less significant if index numbers are constructed for short intervals. This is because habits, tastes, techniques of production and the qualities of commodities entering into a price index number do not change during the short period.

4. USES OF INDEX NUMBERS

Index numbers possess much practical importance in measuring changes in the cost of living, production trends, trade, income variations, etc. Some of the uses of index numbers are discussed below :

1. *In Measuring Changes in the Value of Money.* Index number are used to measure changes in the value of money. A study of the rise or fall in the value of money is essential for determining the direction of production and employment to facilitate future payments and to know changes in the real income of different groups of people at different places and times. As pointed out by Crowther, "By using the technical device of an index number, it is thus possible to measure changes in different aspects of the value of money, each particular aspect being relevant to a different purpose."

2. *In Cost of Living.* Cost of living index numbers in the case of different groups of workers throw light on the rise or fall in the real income of workers. It is on the basis of the study of the cost of living index that money wages are determined and dearness and other allowances are granted to workers. The cost of living index is also the basis of wage negotiations and wage contracts.

3. *In Analysing Markets for Goods and Services.* Consumer price index numbers are used in analysing markets for particular kinds of goods and services. The weights assigned to different commodities like food, clothing, fuel, and lighting, house rent, etc., govern the market for such goods and services.

4. *In Measuring Changes in Industrial Production.* Index numbers of industrial production measure increase or decrease in industrial production in a given year as compared to the base year. We can know from such as index number the actual condition of different industries, whether production is increasing or decreasing in them, for an industrial index number measures changes in the quantity of production.

5. *In Internal Trade.* The study of indices of the wholesale prices of consumer and industrial goods and of industrial production help commerce and industry in expanding or decreasing internal trade.

6. *In External Trade.* The foreign trade position of a country can be assessed on the basis of its export and import indices. These indices reveal whether the external trade of the country is increasing or decreasing.

7. *In Economic Policies.* Index numbers are helpful to the state in formulating and adopting appropriate economic policies. Index numbers measure changes in such magnitudes as prices, incomes, wages, production, employment, products, exports, imports, etc. By comparing the index numbers of these magnitudes for different periods, the government can know the present trend of economic activity and accordingly adopt price policy, foreign trade policy and general economic policies.

8. *In Determining the Foreign Exchange Rate.* Index numbers of wholesale price of two countries are used to determine their rate of foreign exchange. They are the basis of the purchasing power parity theory which determines the exchange rate between two countries on inconvertible paper standard.

CONCLUSION

Thus index numbers are used to measures all types of quantitative changes in the agricultural, industrial, and commercial fields, as also in such economic magnitudes as income, employment, exports, imports, prices, etc. A close study of such changes helps the government to adopt appropriate monetary and fiscal measures in order to achieve growth with stability.

EXERCISES

1. How are changes in the value of money measured? What are the limitations of this measurement?
2. What are index numbers? How are they constructed? Briefly discuss the difficulties faced in constructing them.
3. How would you construct an index number of wholesale prices? What are the uses of the index numbers?

CHAPTER 6

The Quantity Theory of Money and Its Variants

1. MEANING OF VALUE OF MONEY

By value of money is meant the purchasing power of money over goods and services in a country. What a rupee can buy in India represents the value of money of the rupee. Thus the phrase, "value of money" is a relative concept which expresses the relationship between a unit of money and the goods and services which can be purchased with it. This shows that the value of money is related to the price level because goods and services are purchased with a money unit at given prices. But the relation between the value of money and price level is an inverse one. If V presents the value of money and P the price level, then, $V = 1/P$. When the price level rises, the value of money falls, and vice versa. Thus in order to measure the value of money, we have to find out the general price level.

The value of money is of two types: The internal value of money and the external value of money. The internal value of money refers to the purchasing power of money over domestic goods and services. The external value of money refers to the purchasing power of money over foreign goods and services.

2. FISHER'S QUANTITY THEORY OF MONEY: THE CASH TRANSACTIONS APPROACH

The quantity theory of money states that the quantity of money is the main determinant of the price level or the value of money. Any change in the quantity of money produces an exactly proportionate change in the price level. In the words of Irving Fisher, "Other things remaining unchanged, as the quantity of money in circulation increases, the price level also increases in direct proportion and the value of money decreases and vice versa."[1] If the quantity of money is doubled, the price level will also double and the value of money will be one half. On the other hand, if the quantity of money is reduced by one half, the price level will also be reduced by one half and the value of money will be twice.

Fisher has explained his theory in terms of his equation of exchange:

---

1. Iwing Fisher, *The Purchasing Power of Money,* (Revised Ed.), 1926.

$PT = MV + M'V'$

where P = price level, or $1/P$ = the value of money;
M = the total quantity of legal tender money;
V = the velocity of circulation of M;
M' = the total quantity of credit money;
V' = the velocity of circulation of M';
T = the total amount of goods and services exchanged for money or transactions performed by money.

This equation equates the demand for money (PT) to supply of money (MV=$M'V'$). The total volume of transactions multiplied by the price level (PT) represent the demand for money. According to Fisher, PT is SPQ. In other words, price level (P) multiplied by quantity bought (Q) by the community (S) gives the total demand for money. This equals the total supply of money in the community consisting of the quantity of actual money M and its velocity of circulation V *plus* the total quantity of credit money M' and its velocity of circulation V'. Thus the total value of purchases (PT) in a year is measured by MV+$M'V'$. Thus the equation of exchange is PT=MV+$M'V'$. In order to find out the effect of the quantity of money on the price level or the value of money, we write the equation as

$$P = \frac{MV + M'V'}{T}$$

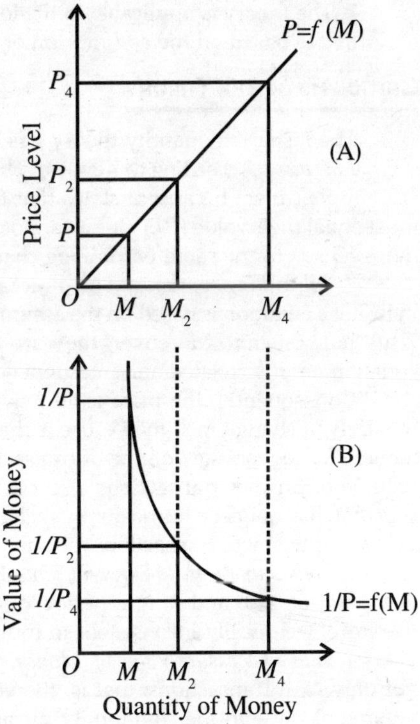

Fig. 1.

Fisher points out the price level (P) (M+M') provided the volume of tra remain unchanged. The truth of this proposition is evident from the fact that if M and M' are doubled, while V, V' and T remain constant, P is also doubled, but the value of money ($1/P$) is reduced to half.

Fisher's quantity theory of money is explained with the help of Figure 1. (A) and (B). Panel A of the figure shows the effect of changes in the quantity of money on the price level. To begin with, when the quantity of money is M, the price level is P.

When the quantity of money is doubled to M_2, the price level is also doubled to P_2. Further, when the quantity of money is increased four-fold to M_4, the price level also increases by four times to P_4. This realtionship is expressed by the curve P=f (M) from the origin at 45^0.

In panel B of the figure, the inverse relation between the quantity of money and the value of money is depicted where the value of money is taken on the vertical axis. When the quantity of money is M_1, the value of money is $1/P$. But with the doubling of the quantity of money to M_2, the value of money becomes one-half of what it was before, $1/P_2$. And with the quantity of money increasing by four-fold to M_4, the value of money is reduced by $1/P_4$. This inverse relationship between the quantity of money and the value of money is shown by downward sloping curve $1/P$=f (M).

Assumptions of the Theory

Fisher's theory is based on the following assumptions:

1. P is passive factor in the equation of exchange which is affected by the other factors.
2. The proportion of M' to M remains constant.
3. V and V' are assumed to be constant and are independent of changes in M and M'.
4. T also remains constant and is independent of other factors such as M, M', V and V'.
5. It is assumed that the demand for money is proportional to the value of transactions.
6. The supply of money is assumed as an exogenously determined constant.

7. The theory is applicable in the long run.
8. It is based on the assumption of the existence of full employment in the economy.

Criticisms of the Theory

The Fisherian quantity theory has been subjected to severe criticisms by economists.

1. *Truism.* According to Keynes, "The quantity theory of money is a truism." Fisher's equation of exchange is a simple truism because it states that the total quantity of money ($MV+M'V'$) paid for goods and services must equal their value (PT). But it cannot be accepted today that a certain percentage change in the quantity of money leads to the same percentage change in the price level.

2. *Other things not equal.* The direct and proportionate relation between quantity of money and price level in Fisher's equation is based on the assumption that "other things remain unchanged". But in real life, V, V' and T are not constant. Moreover, they are not independent of M, M' and P. Rather, all elements in Fisher's equation are interrelated and interdependent. For instance, a change in M may cause a change in V.

Consequently, the price level may change more in proportion to a change in the quantity of money. Similarly, a change in P may cause a change in M. Rise in the price level may necessitate the issue of more money. Moreover, the volume of transactions T is also affected by changes in P. When prices rise or fall, the volume of busines transactions also rises or falls. Further, the assumptions that the proportion M' to M is constant, has not been borne out by facts. Not only this, M and M' are not independent of T. An increase in the volume of business transactions requires an increase in the supply of money (M and M').

3. *Constants Relate to Different Time.* Prof. Halm criticises Fisher for multiplying M and V because M relates to a point ot time and V to a period of time . The former is a static concept and the latter a dynamic. It is therefore, technically inconsistent to multiply two non-comparable factors.[2]

4. *Fails to Measure Value of Money.* Fisher's equation does not measure the purchasing power of money but only cash transactions, that is, the volume of business transactions of all kinds or what Fisher calls the volume of trade in the community during a year. But the purchasing power of money (or value of money) relates to transactions for the purchase of goods and services for consumption. Thus the quantity theory fails to measure the vlaue of money.

5. *Weak Theory.* According to Crowther,[3] the quantity theory is weak in many respects. First, it cannot explain 'why' there are fluctutations in the price level in the short run. Second, it gives undue importance to the price level as if changes in prices were the most critical and important phenomenon of the economic system. Third, it places a misleading emphasis on the quantity of money as the principal cause of changes in the price level during the trade cycle. Prices may not rise despite increase in the quantity of money during depression; and they may not decline with reduction in the quantity of money during boom. Further, low prices during depression are not caused by shortage of quantity of money, and high prices during prosperity are not caused by abundance of quantity of money. Thus, "the quantity theory is at best an imperfect guide to the causes of the trade cycle *in the short period*," according to Crowther.

6. *Neglects Interest Rate.* One of the main weaknesses of Fisher's quantity theory of money is that it neglects the role of the rate of interest as one of the causative factors between money and prices. Fisher's equation of exchange is related to an equilibrium situation in which rate of interest is independent of the quantity of money.

7. *Unrealistic Assumptions.* Keynes in his *General Theory* severely criticised the Fisherian quantity theory of money for its unrealistic assumptions. *Firts,* the quantity theory of money for its unrealistic assumptions. First, the quantity theory of money is unrealistic because it analyses the relation between M and P in the long run. Thus it neglects the short run factors which influence this relationship. Second, Fisher's equation holds good under the assumption of full employment. But Keynes regards full employment as a special situation. The general situation is one of the under-employment equilibrium. Third, Keynes does not believe that the relationship between the quantity of money and the price level is direct and proportional. Rather, it is an indirect one via the rate of interest and the level of output. According to Keynes, "So long as there is

2. G.N. Halm, *Monetary Theory,* 2/e,p. 22.
3. Crowther, *An Outline of Money, Ch. V,* 1958.

unemployment, *output* and employment will change in the same proportion as the quantity of money, and when there is full employment, prices will change in the same proportion as the quantity of money." Thus Keynes integrated the theory of output with value theory and monetary theory and criticised Fisher for dividing economics "into two compartments with no doors and windows between *the theory of value and theory of money and prices*."

8. V not Constant. Further, Keynes pointed out that when there is underemployment equilibrium, the velocity of circulation of moeny V is highly unstable and would change with changes in the stock of money or money income. Thus it was unrealistic for Fisher to assume V to be constant and independent of M.

9. Neglects Store of Value Function. Another weakness of the quantity theory of money is that it concentrates on the supply of money and assumes the demand for money to be constant. In order words, it neglects the store-of-value function of moeny and considers only the medium-of-exchange function of money. Thus the theory is one-sided.

10. Neglects Real Balance Effect. Don Patinkin[4] has critcised Fisher for failure to make use of the real balance effect, that is, the real value of cash balances. A fall in the price level raises the real value of cash balances which leads to increased spending and hence to rise in income, output and employment in the economy. According to Patinkin, Fisher gives undue importance to the quantity of money and neglects the role of real money balances.

11. Static. Fisher's theory is static in nature because of its such unrealistic assumptions as long run, full employment, etc. It is, therefore, not applicable to a modern dynamic economy.

3. THE CAMBRIDGE EQUATIONS : THE CASH BALANCES APPROACH

As an alternative to Fisher's quantity theory of money, Cambridge economists Marshall, Pigou, Robertson and Keynes formulated the cash balances approach. Like value theory, they regarded the determination of value of money in terms of supply and demand. Robertson wrote in this connection: "Money is only one of the many economic things. Its value, therefore, is primarily determined by exactly nomic things. Its value, therefore, is primarily determined by exactly the same two factors as determine the value of any other thing, namely, the conditions of demand for it, and the quantity of it available."[5]

The supply of money is exogenously determined at a point of time by the banking system. Therefore, the concept of velocity of circulation is altogether discarded in the cash balances approach because it 'obscures the motives and decisions of people behind it'. On the other hand, the concept of demand for money plays the major role in determining the value of money. The demand for money is the demand to hold cash balance for transactions and precautionary motives. Marshall wrote with regard to the demand for money. "To give definiteness to this notion, let us suppose that the inhabitants of a country...find it just worthwhile to keep by them on the average ready purchasing power to the extent of a tenth part of their annual income, together with a fiftieth part of their property, then the aggregate value of the currency of the country will tend to be equal to the sum of these amounts."[6]

Thus the cash balances approach considers the demand for money not as a medium of exchange but as a store of value. Robertson expressed this distinction as money "on the wings" and money "sitting". It is "money sitting" that reflects the demand for money in the Cambridge equations. The Cambridge equations show that given the supply of money at a point of time, the value of money is determined by the demand for cash balances. When the demand for money increases, people will reduce their expenditures on goods and services in order to have larger cash holdings. Reduced demand for goods and services will bring down the price level and raise the value of money. On the contrary, fall in the demand for money will raise the price level and lower the value of money.

---

4. Don Patinkin, *Money Interest andPrices*, 2/e, 1965.
5. Denis H. Robertson, *Money*, 1959.
6. AlfredMarshall, *Money Credit and Commerce*, 1923.

The Cambridge cash balances equations of Marshall, Pigou, Robertson and Keynes are discussed as under:

Marshall's Equation. Marshall did not put his theory in equation form and it was for his followers to explain it algebraically. Friedman has explained Marshall's views thus: "As a first approximation, we may suppose that the amount one wants to hold bears some relation to one's income, since that determines the volume of purchases and sales in which one is engaged. We then add up the cash balances held by all holders of money in the community and express the total as a fraction of their total income."[7] Thus we can write:

$M = kPY$

where M stands for the exogenously determined supply of money, k is the fraction of the real money income (PY) which people wish to hold in cash and demand deposits, P is the price level, and Y is the aggregate real income of the community.[8] Thus the price level $P = \frac{M}{kY}$ or the value of money (the reciprocal of price level) is $\frac{1}{P} = \frac{kY}{M}$

Pigou's Equation. Pigou was the first Cambridge economist to express the cash balances approach in the form of an equation:

$$P = \frac{kR}{M}$$

where P is the purchasing power of money or the value of money (the reciprocal of the price level), k is the proportion of total real resources or income (R) which people wish to hold in the form of titles to legal tender, R is the total resources (expressed in terms of wheat), or real income, and M refers to the number of actual units of legal tender money.[9]

The demand for money, according to Pigou, consists not only of legal money or cash but also bank notes and bank balances. In order to include bank notes and bank balances in the demand for money, Pigou modifies his equation as

$$P = \frac{kR}{M}\{c + R(1-c)\}$$

where c is the proportion of total real income actually held by people in legal tender including token coins, (1-c) is the proportion kept in bank notes and bank balances, and h is the proportion of actual legal tender that bankers keep against the notes and balances held by their customers.[10]

Pigou points out that when k and R in the equation $P=kR/M$ and k, R, c and h are taken as constants then the two equations give the demand curve for legal tender as a rectangular hyperbola. This implies that the demand curve for money has a uniform unitary elasticity. This is shown in Figure 2 where DD_1 is the demand curve for money and Q_1M_1, Q_2M_2, and Q_3M_3 are the supply curves of money drawn on the assumption that the supply of money is fixed at a point of time. The value of money or Pirou's purchasing power of money P is taken on the vertical axis. The figure shows that when the supply of money increases from OM_1 to OM_2, the value of money is reduced from OP_1 to OP_2. The fall in the value of money by P_1P_2 exactly equals the increase in the supply of money by M_1M_2. If the supply of money increases three times from OM_1 to OM_3, the value of money is reduced by exactly one-third from OP_1 to OP_3. Thus the demand curve for money DD_1 is a rectangular

7. Miltion Friedman, 'Money : Quantity Theory.' *in International Encyclopedia of the Social Sciences,* 1968.
8. Marshall's equation is also written as $M = kPO$ or $M + kPT$ or $M = kpy$ or $M = KpY$ or $M=kPT$. But all these equations are identical because $k = K$, $p = P$, and $O = T = y = Y$.
9. In the February 1918 issue of the *QJE*. Pigou issued a modification with regard to M that it should be regarded as "the number of titles to units of legal tender."
10. A.C. Pigou 'Value of Money', *QJ.E.* Vol. XXXII, November 1917.

hyperbola because it shows changes in the value of money exactly in reverse proportion to the supply of money.

Robertson's Equation. To determine the value of money or its reciprocal the price level, Robertson formulated an equation similar to that of Pigou. The only difference between the two being that instead of Pigou's total real resources R, Robertson gave the volume of total transactions T. The Robertsonian equation is $M = PkT$ or

$$P = \frac{M}{kT}$$

where P is the price level, M is the total quantity of money, k is the proportion of the total amount of goods and services (T) which people wish to hold in the form of cash balances, and T is the total volume of goods and services purchased during a year by the community.

If we take P as the value of money instead of the price level as in Pigou's equation, then Robertson's equation exactly resembles Pigou's $P = kT/M$.

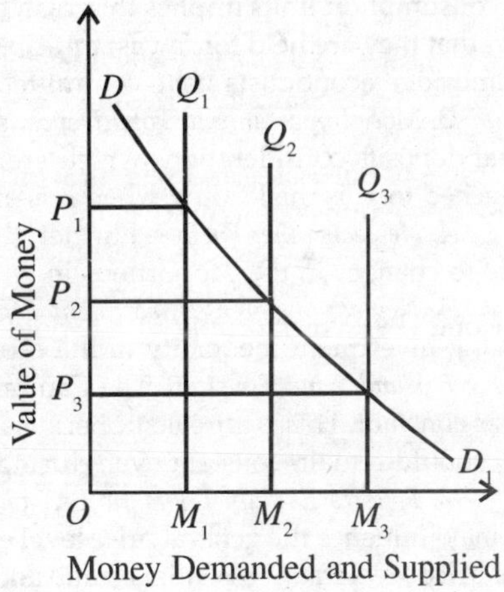

Fig. 2

Keynes's Equation. Keynes in his *A Tract on Monetary Reform* (1923) gave his Real Balances Quantity Equation as an improvement over the other Cambridge equations. According to him, people always want to have some purchasing power to finance their day to day transactions. The amount of purchasing power (or demand for money) depends partly on their tastes and habits, and partly on their wealth. Given the tastes, habits, and wealth of the people, their desire to hold money is given. This demand for money is measured by consumption units. A consumption unit is expressed as a basket of standard articles of consumption or other objects of expenditure.

If k is the number of consumption units in the form of cash, n is the total currency in circulation, and p is the price for consumption unit, then the equation is

$$n = pk$$

If k is constant, a proportionate increase in n (quantity of money) will lead to a proportionate increase in p (price level).

This equation can be expanded by taking into account bank deposits. Let k be the number of consumption units in the form of bank deposits, and r the cash reserve ratio of banks, then the expanded equation is

$$n = p\,(k + rk')$$

Again, if k, k' and r are constant, p will change in exact proportion to the change in n.

Keynes regards his equation superior to other cash balances equations. The other equations fail to point how the price level (p) can be regulated. Since the cash balances (k) held by the people are outside the control of the monetary authority, p can be regulated by controlling n and r. It is also possible to regulate bank deposits k' by appropriate changes in the bank rate. So p can be controlled by making appropriate changes in n, r and k' so as to offset changes in k.

Criticisms of the Cash Balance Approach

The cash balances approach to the quantity theory of money has been criticised on the following counts:

1. *Truisms.* Like the transactions equation, the cash balances equations are truisms. Take any Cambridge equation: Marshall's $P=M/kY$ or Pigou's $P=kR/M$ or Robertson's $P=M/kT$ or Keynes's $p=n/k$, it establishes a proportionate relation between quantity of money and price level.[11]

2. *Price Level Does not Measure the Purchasing Power.* Keynes in his *A Treatise on Money* (1930) criticised Pigou's cash balances equation and also his own real balances equation. He pointed out that measuring the price level in wheat, as Piogu did or in terms of consumption units, as Keynes himself did, was a serious defect.

11. Here all equations have been changed in terms of the price level.

The price level in both equations does not measure the purchasing power of money. Measuring the price level in consumption units implies that cash deposits are used only for expenditure on current consumption. But in fact that they are held for "a vast multiplicity of business and personal purposes." By ignoring these aspects the Cambridge economists have committed a serious mistake.

3. More Importance to Total Deposits. Another defect of the Cambridge equation "lies in its applying to the total deposits considerations which are primarily relevant only to the income-deposits." And the importance attached to *k* "is misleading when it is extended beyond the income deposits."

4. Neglects other Factors. Further, the cash balances equation does not tell about changes in the price level due to changes in the proportions in which deposits are held for income, business and savings purposes.

5. Neglect of Saving Investment Effect. Moreover, it fails to analyse variations in the price level due to saving-investment inequality in the economy.

6. k and Y not Constant. The Cambridge equation, like the transactions equation, assumes *k* and *Y* (or R or T) as constant. This is unrealistic because it is not essential that the cash balances (*k*) and the income of the people (*Y*) should remain constant even during short period.

7. Fails to Explain Dynamic Behaviour of Prices. The theory argues that changes in the total quantity of money influence the general price level equiproportionally. But the fact is that the quantity of money influences the price level in an "essential erratic and unpredictable way." Further, it fails to point out the extent of change in the price level as a result of a given change in the quantity of money in the short period. Thus it fails to explain the dynamic behaviour of prices.

8. Neglects Interest Rate. The cash balances approach is also weak in that it ignores other influences, such as the rate of interest which exerts a decisive and significant influence upon the price level. As pointed out by Keynes in his *General Theory*, the relation between quantity of money and price level is not direct but indirect via the rate of interest, investment, output, employment and income. This is what the Cambridge equation ignores and hence fails to integrate monetary theory with the theory of value and output.

9. Demand for Money not Interest Inelastic. The neglect of the rate of interest as a causative factor between the quantity of money and the price level led to the assumption that the demand for money is interest inelastic. It means that money performs only the function of medium of exchange and does not possess any utility of its own, such as store of value.

10. Neglect of Goods Market. Further, the omission of the influence of the rate of interest in the cash balance approach led to the failure of neoclassical economists to recognise the interdependence between the commodity and money markets. According to Patinkin, they laid an undue concentration on the money market a corresponding neglect of the commodity markets, and a resulting 'dehumanising' of the analysis of the effects of monetary changes."

11. Neglects Real Balance Effect. Patinkin has criticised the Cambridge economists for their failure to integrate the goods market and the money market. This is borne out by the dichotomy which they maintain between the two markets. The dichotomisation implies that the absolute price level in the economy is determined by the demand and supply of money, and the relative price level is determined by the demand and supply of goods. The cash balances approach keeps the two markets rigidly apart. For instance, this approach tells that an increase in the quantity of money leads to an increase in the absolute price level but exercises no influence on the market for goods. This is because of the failure of Cambridge economists to recognise "the real balance effect." The real balance effect shows that a change in the absolute price level does influence the demand and supply of goods. The weakness of cash balances approach lies in ignoring this.

12. Elasticity of Demand for Money not Unity. The cash balances theory establishes that the elasticity of demand for money is unity which implies that the increase in the demand for money leads to a proportionate decrease in the price level. Patinkin holds that "the Cambridge function does not imply uniform elasticity." According to him, this is because of the failure of Cambridge economists to recognise the full implications of the "real balance effect". Patinkin argues that a change in the price level will cause a real balance effect. For instance, a fall in the price level will increase the real value of cash balances held by the people. So when there is excess demand for money, the demand for goods and services is reduced. In this case, the real balance effect will not cause a proportionate but non-proportionate change in the demand for money. Thus the elasticity of demand for money will not be unity.

13. Neglects Speculative Demand for Money. Another serious weakness of cash balances approach is its failure to consider the speculative demand for money. The neglect of the speculative demand for cash balances makes the demand for money exclusively dependent on money income thereby again neglecting the role of the rate of interest and the store of value function of money.

4. TRANSACTIONS APPROACH VS. CASH BALANCES APPROACH

There are certain points of similarities between Fisher's transaction approach and the Cambridge cash balances approach. These are discussed as under:

1. SIMILARITIES

The two approaches have the following similarities:

1. Same Conclusion. The Fisherian and Cambridge versions lead to the same conclusion that there is a direct and proportional relationship between the quantity of money and the price level and an inverse proportionate relationship between the quantity of money and the value of money.

2. Similar Equations. The two approaches use almost similar equations. Fisher's equation $P=\frac{MV}{T}$ is similar to Robertson's equation $P=\frac{M}{kT}$ However, the only difference is between the two symbols V and k which are reciprocal to each other. Whereas $V=\left|\frac{1}{k}\right|$ $k=\left|\frac{1}{V}\right|$ Here V refers to the rate of spending and k the amount of money which people wish to hold in the form of cash balances or do not want to spend. As these two symbols are reciprocal to each other, the differences in the two equations can be reconciled by substituting $\frac{1}{V}$ for k in Robertson's equation and $\frac{1}{k}$ for V in Fisher's equation.

3. Money as the Same Phenomenon. The different symbols given to the total quantity of money in the two approaches refer to the same phenomenon. As such $MV+M'V'$ of Fisher's equation, M of the equations of Pigou and Robertson, and n of Keynes' equation refer to the total quantity of money.

2. DISSIMILARITIES

Despite these similarities the two approaches have many dissimilarities:

1. Functions of Money. The two versions emphasize on different functions of money. The Fisherian approach lays emphasis on the medium of exchange function while the Cambridge approach emphasises the store of value of function of money.

2. Flow and Stock. In Fisher's approach money is a flow concept while in the Cambridge approach it is a stock concept. The former relates to a period of time and the latter to a point of time.

3. V and k Different. The meaning given to the two symbols V and k in the two versions is different. In Fisher's equation V refers to the rate of spending and in Robertson's equation k refers to the cash balances which people wish to hold. The former emphasises the transactions velocity of circulation and the latter the income velocity.

4. Nature of Price Level. In Fisher's equation, P refers to the average price level of all goods and services.

But in the cambridge equation *P* refers to the prices of final or consumer goods.

5. *Nature of T.* In Fisher's version, *T* refers to the total amount of goods and services exchanged for money, whereas in the Cambridge version, it refers to the final or consumer goods exchanged for money.

6. *Emphasis on Supply and Demand for Money.* Fisher's approach emphasises the supply of money, whereas the Cambridge approach emphasises both the demand for money and the supply of money.

7. Different in Nature. The two approaches are different in nature. The Fisherian version is mechanistic because it does not explain how changes in *V* bring about changes in *P*. On the other hand, the Cambridge version is realistic because it studies the psychological factors which influence *k*.

It is on account of these differences that Hansen wrote: "It is not true as is often alleged that the cash balance equation is merely the quantity theory in new algebraic dress."

5. SUPERIORITY OF CASH BALANCES APPROACH OVER TRANSACTIONS APPROACH

The Cambridge cash balances approach to the quantity theory of money is superior to Fisher's transaction approach in many respects. They are discussed as under:

1. *Basis of Liquidity Preference Theory of Interest.* The cash balances approach emphasises the importance of holding cash balances rather than the supply of money which is given at a point of time. It thus led Keynes to propound his theory of liquidity preference and of the rate of interest, and to the integration of monetary theory of value and output.

2. *Complete Theory.* The cash balances version of quantity theory is superior to the transactions version because the former determines the value of money in terms of the demand and supply of money. Thus it is a complete theory. But in the transactions approach, the determination of value of money is artificially divorced from the theory of value.

3. *Discards the Concept of Velocity of Circulation.* The cash balances approach is superior to the transactions approach because it altogether discards the concept of the velocity of circulation of money which 'obscures the motives and decisions of people behind it.'

4. *Related to the Short Period.* Again the cash balances version is more realistic than the transactions version of the quantity theory, because it is related to the short period while the latter is related to the long period. As pointed out by Keynes, "In the long run we may all be dead." So the study of the relationship between quantity of money and price level during the long run is unrealistic.

5. *Simple Equations.* In the cash balances equations, transactions relating to final goods only are included where *P* refers to the level of final goods. On the other hand, in the transactions equation *P* includes all types of transactions. This creates difficulties in determining the true price level. Thus the former equations are simpler and realistic than the latter.

6. *New Formulation in the Monetary Theory.* Further, the Cambridge equation regards the cash balances held by the people as a function of the level of income. The introduction of income (*Y* or *R* or *T* or *O*) in this equation as against *V* (the velocity of circulation of money) in the transaction equation has made the cash balances equation realistic and led to new formulations in monetary theory. "It points out that changes in the level of money income can come about through changes in the price level, through changes in real output or through both at once."

7. *Explains Trade Cycles.* Hansen[12] regards *k* in the Cambridge equation superior to *V* in Fisher's equation for understanding cyclical fluctuations. According to him, "Drastic and sudden shifts in the desire to hold money, reflected in a change in *k*, may produce large and quickly moving changes in the level of income and prices. Shifts in the public psychology, in expectations must be taken into account not less than changes in the money supply. In the Cambridge analysis, a shift in *k* may start an upward or downward movement." For instance, when *k* (the fraction of total real income that people wish to hold in cash balances) increases because

12. A.H. Hansen, *Monetary Theory and Fiscal Policy,* 1949, pp. 49-50, Italics mine.

of low business expectation, the price level falls, and vice versa.

8. Study of Subjective Factors. As a corollary to the above, V in Fisher's equation is mechanistic while k in the Cambridge equation is realistic. The subjective factors behind variations in k have led to the study of such factors as expectations, uncertainty, motives for liquidity, and the rate of interest in modern monetary theory. In this sense, it can be justifiably said that, "the Cambridge equation moves us on from the tautology represented by the equation of exchange to a study of economic behaviour."

9. Applicable under All Circumstances. Fisher's transactions approach holds true only under full employment. But the cash balances approach holds under all circumstances whether there is full employment or less than full employment.

10. Based on Micro Factors. The Cambridge version is superior to the Fisherian version because it is based on micro factors like individual decisions and behaviours. On the other hand, the Fisherian version is based on macro factors like T, total velocity of circulation, etc.

EXERCISES

1. Critically examine Fisher's Quantity Theory of Money.
2. Discuss the Cambridge Cash Balances Approach to the Quantity Theory of Money. How far is it superior to the Cash Transactions Approach ?
3. Give the similarities and dissimilarities of the Quantity Theory of Money and Cambridge cash balances theory.
4. Write notes on.
   (a) Fisher's Equation of Exchange.
   (b) Keynes' Real Balance Equation.
5. What do you mean by value of money ? What determines value of money, according to Fisher ?

CHAPTER 7

Keynes' Income and Expenditure Theory

1. INTRODUCTION

The old quantity theory of money is weak in that it establishes a direct relationship between the money supply and the aggregate demand. According to the quantity theorists, an increase in the money supply leads to an increase in the aggregate demand for goods and services, and vice versa. It is the increase in the quantity of money which by increasing the aggregate demand for goods and services leads to rise in prices, and vice versa. But the experience during the Great Depression has shown that increase in the money supply failed to increase the aggregate demand.

The income theory was gradually developed by Tooke, Wicksell and Aftalion and finally by Keynes. According to them, it is changes in income rather than in the money supply which cause changes in the agggregate demand. When income increases, aggregate demand for goods and services also increases. People spend more and the price level rises. On the contrary, with the decline in income, the aggregate demand falls. People spend less and the price level falls. Therefore, changes in the price level depend upon the volume of expenditure in the economy which in turn is determined by changes in the level of income. And the level of income depends upon the volume of saving and investment in the economy. Thus changes in the price level or value of money are caused by the income and expenditure of the community or by the volume of saving and investment. Thus income and expenditure, and saving investment are the two approaches to the income theory which we discuss below.

2. INCOME-EXPENDITURE APPROACH**

The income theory of prices involves on the one side an analysis of income and aggregate demand, and on the other, an analysis of costs and aggregate supply. Prices are determined by money income and real income.

The total *money* income (Y) is the value of goods and services produced in any period of time and

* It is also known as the Income Theory or the Saving and Investment Theory of the Value of Money.

** Students should give only that approach which is asked.

expressed in terms of money. It is determined by the remuneration paid in terms of money to the factors of production. Thus it also refers to the sum of total expenditure (*E*) incurred on goods and services pricing a period. On the other hand, the 'real' income is the total value of *real* money value of goods and services expressed in terms of a general price level of a particular year taken as the base. Thus the money value of real income is the money income which is determined by the prices of goods and services or output. Symbolically,

$$Y = P.O$$

Where *Y* is Money income or money expenditure which produces a flow of income, *P* is the general level of prices, and *O* is the physical volume of goods and services produced. It follows that

$$P = \frac{Y}{O}$$

It means that prices are determined by the ratio of money income to total output. When money income (*Y*) rises more rapidly than output (*O*) prices (*P*) will tend to increase. If, on the other hand, output (*O*) increases more rapidly than money income (*Y*), prices (*P*) will tend to fall.

It is clear from the above that total money income equals total expenditure which, in turn, is equal to consumption expenditure (*C*) plus investment expenditure (*I*). Therefore, symbolically, $Y = E = C + I$.

According to Keynes, it is the total money income which determines the total expenditure of the community. An increase in the money income means increase investment expenditure, the propensity to consume being stable in the short run. The increased investment will raise effective demand which will, inturn, raise output and employment. But what about prices? So long as there is unemployment, prices do not rise with the increase in output. This is because the supply of factors is perfectly elastic. Therefore, output will change in the same proportion as the quantity of money, and there will be no change in prices. When the supply of factors becomes somewhat inelastic (or factor are in short supply), this may lead to increase in marginal costs and prices. As full employment is reached, the elasticity of supply of output falls to zero (perfectly inelastic), and prices rise in proportion to the increase in the quantity of money. Thus the income theory states that the increase in the quantity of money depends upon increase in money income and aggregate expenditure, and prices start rising when the full employment level is being reached. Once the full employment level is reached, prices rise in the same proportion as the increase in money income and aggregate expenditure.

3. SAVING-INVESTMENT APPROACH

INTRODUCTION

An alternative to the Keynesian income-expenditure theory is the saving investment approach to income theory. In fact the income-expenditure approach ($Y = C + I$) is the same thing as the saving-investment approach. Both saving (*S*) and investment (*I*) are defined as the excess of income over consumption (*Y–C*) so that they are necessarily equal. Symbolically

$$S = Y - C$$
$$I = Y - C$$
$$\therefore S = I$$

Keynes also established this equality in another way. He defined income as equal to consumption plus investment ($Y = C + I$), and saving as the excess of income over consumption ($S = Y - C$). Thus

$$Y = C + I \qquad \text{or } I = Y - C$$
$$S = Y - C$$
$$\therefore S = I$$

THE THEORY

We have seen above that the equality between saving and investment is brought about by the mechanism of income. On the other hand, income depends upon relation between saving and investment. So long as saving and investment are equal, there will be the equilibrium level of income and the price level will be stable.

If saving and investment are disturbed, the price-level also changes via the change in expenditure.

If saving exceeds investment, it means that people reduce their expenditure on goods and services. They are hoarding more money and spending less. This reduces the velocity of circulation of money. This leads to a reduction in the income of the producers of goods and services. Reduced expenditure and income lead to a fall in the price level. As prices fall, investment also declines due to a fall in the marginal efficiency of capital which leads to further falling income, output, employment, and prices. This process will continue till prices reach the bottom of the depression.

If investment exceeds saving, people increase their expenditure on goods and services. They are spending more and saving less. This causes the velocity of circulation to increase. This increases the income of the producers of goods and services. Increase in expenditure and income lead to a rise in the price level.

This will increase the profit expectations or marginal efficiency of capital. As a result, investment will increase further which will, in turn, raise employment, income, expenditure, output and prices to still higher levels. But the increase in investment leading to an increase in aggregate expenditure, demand, and income do not lead to a rise in the price level immediately. So long as the output of goods and services rises proportionately with the increase in the demand for goods and services, there would not be a general rise in the price level. If output does not increase proportionately, increase in investment will increase income and the price level. But increase in output is possible only if there are unemployed resources in the economy. When the economy reaches the full employment level, further increase in income will not raises output to the level of increase in aggregate expenditure. But it will to an upward rise in the price levelling the same proportion as the increase in income.

To conclude, it is the inequality in saving and investment that brings about changes in the price level, and changes in the price level are due to changes in income rather than in the quantity of money.[1]

Superiority of Income-Expenditure (or Saving-Investment) Theory Over the Quantity Theory

The income-expenditure theory of money is considered superior to the quantity theory of money on the following grounds:

1. *Explains Business Cycles.* The quantity theory cannot explain changes in prices during the upswing and downswing of a business cycle. It does not explain why an abundance of money during a depression fails to bring about a revival, and shortage of money stops a boom. The income theory is superior to the quantity theory because it explains them. According to the saving investment theory, when investment exceeds saving rival starts from a depression. More increase in the supply of money is not enough to bring about a revival. It is the rise in business expectations of profit (or the marginal efficiency of capital) that encourage investment and the revival starts. On the other hand, a boom does not stop due to decrease in the money supply alone. Rather it stops because saving exceeds investment due to the falling the expectations of profit. Thus it is changes in investment due to changes in business expectations of profit that lead to cyclical upswing and downswing. Crowther has apathy said, "The Quantity Theory of Money explains, as it were, the average level of the sea; the Saving and Investment Theory explains the violence of the tides."[2]

2. *Explains Changes in Velocity of Circulation of Money.* The quantity theory of money does not explain the causes of changes in the velocity of circulation of money. The saving-investment theory is superior in that it gives an adequate explanation of such changes. When saving exceeds investment, it means that people are hoarding more money and spending less. This reduces the velocity of circulation of money. On the contrary, when investment exceeds saving, people are spending more which causes the velocity of circulation of money to increase. Thus changes in the velocity of circulation of money are caused by the relationship between saving and investment.

3. *Explains Causal Relationship between Quantity of Money and Price Level.* The quantity theory of money fails to explain the causal relationship between the quantity of money and the price level. It simply explains that the relationship between the two is direct and proportional. The saving-investment theory is superior in that

1. Students are not expected to give figures of saving and investment as they do not explain changes in the price level when there is inequality between the two.
2. G. Crowther, *op.cit.*, p. 147.

it shows that the actual relationship between the money supply and price level is neither direct nor proportional. It is disequilibrium between saving and investment that leads to changes in the spent. If investment exceeds saving, income will increase which will raise aggregate expenditure, output, employment and prices. The inverse will be the case when saving exceeds investment. Thus thee is no direct relationship between the quantity of money and price level. As pointed out by Crowther, "The effect of a given change in *M* (*quantity of money*) on the price level is not a simple cause-and-effect relationship as the Quantity Theory supposed, but a most complex chain reaction."

Moreover, when the quantity of money increases, the price level does not rise proportionately. So long as there are unemployed resources in the economy, an increase in money income will not lead to a rise in the price-level if output increases proportionately to the increase in aggregate demand. It is only when the resources are fully employed that the price level will increase proportionately to the increase in the quantity of money.

4. *Applicable in the Full Employment and Unemployment.* The quantity theory of money is based on the assumption of full employment that is why it establishes a direct and proportional relationship between the quantity of money and price level. The saving-investment theory is superior to it because it analyses the effect of money on the price level when there is unemployment in the economy.

5. *Explains Short Run Changes.* The saving-investment theory is more realistic than the quantity theory of money because it explains short run changes in the value of money (or price level), whereas the quantity theory of money explain the longrun changes. This is unrealistic because in the long run we are all dead.

6. *Considers both Monetary and Real Factors. Again,* the saving-investment theory is superior to the quantity theory of money in that it takes into consideration both the monetary and real factors in determining the value of money. Such factors as saving, investment, aggregate output are taken alongwith the quantity of money and aggregate expenditure. This makes the income theory better than the quantity theory of money.

7. *Policy Implications.* The policy implications of the saving-investment theory are more realistic than the quaintly theory of money. The quantity theory of money concentrates exclusively on monetary policy. On the other hand, the saving-investment theory lays more emphasis on expenditure and income that affect economic activity more than the quantity of money. This fact has been proved by the dominance of income (fiscal) policy over the monetary policy since 1950s.

We may conclude with Crowther that the saving-investment theory "goes considerably nearer to the reality of things than the quantity theory. It reveals the fundamental tendencies of which the behaviour of money and prices is merely the surface of the symptom."

EXERCISES

1. Discuss the view that price changes are better explained by savings and investment Theory than by the Traditional Quantity Theory of Money.
2. The value of money, in fact, is a consequence of the total income rather than of the quantity of money." Discuss.
3. What are the shortcomings of the quantity theory of money? How does the income-expenditure approach is an improvement over it?
4. "The saving-investment theory can explain a number of things about the behaviour of money that the quantity theory cannot." Discuss.

Chapter 8

The Keynesian Theory of Money and Prices

1. INTRODUCTION

In Chapter 21 of his *General Theory*, Keynes attacked the classical quantity theorists for keeping separate monetary theory and value theory. He then presented a reformulated quantity theory of money which brought about a transition from a monetary theory of prices to a monetary theory of output. In doing this, Keynes made an attempt to intergrate monetary theory with value theory and also linked the theory of interest into monetary theory. But "it is through the theory of output that value theory and monetary theory are brought into just a position with each other."[1]

Keynes does not agree with the older quantity theorists that there is a direct and proportional relationship between quantity of money and prices. According to him, the effect of a change in the quantity of money on prices is indirect and non-proportional.

Keynes complains "that economics has been divided into two compartments with no doors or windows between the theory of value and the theory of money and prices."[2] This dichotomy between the relative price level (as determined by demand and supply of goods) and the *absolute price level* (as determined by demand and supply of money) arises from the failure of the classical monetary economists to integrate value theory with monetary theory. Consequently, changes in the money supply affect only the absolute price level but exercise no influence on the relative price level.

Further, Keynes criticises the classical theory of static equilibrium in which money is regarded as neutral and does not influence the economy's real equilibrium relating to relative prices. According to him, the problems of the real world are related to the theory of shifting equilibrium whereas money enters as a "link between the present and future".

2. KEYNES'S REFORMULATED QUANTITY THEORY OF MONEY

The Keynesian reformulated quantity theory of money is based on the following

1. D.Dillard, *op. cit.*, pp. 224-225
2. A.H. Hansen, *op. cit.*, p. 184

Assumptions

1. All factors of production are in perfectly elastic supply so long as there is any unemployment.
2. All unemployed factors are homogeneous, perfectly divisible and interchangeable.
3. There are constant returns to scale so that prices do not rise or fall as output increases.
4. Effective demand and quantity of money change in the same proportion so long as there are any unemployed resources.

Given these assumptions, the Keynesian chain of causation between changes in the quantity of money and in prices is an indirect one through the rate of interest. So when the quantity of money is increased, its first impact is on the rate of interest which tends to fall. Given the marginal efficiency of capital, a fall in the rate of interest will increase the volume of investment. The increased investment will raise effective demand through the multiplier effect thereby increasing income, output and employment. Since the supply curve of factors of production is perfectly elastic in a situation of unemployment, wage and non-wage factors are available at constant rate of remuneration. There being constant returns to scale, prices do not rise with the increase in output so long as there is any unemployment. Under the circumstances, output and employment will increase in the same proportion as effective demand, and the effective demand will increase in the same proportion as the quantity of money. But "once full employment is reached, output ceases to respond *at all* to changes in the supply of money and so in effective demand. The elasticity of supply of output in response to changes in the supply, which was infinite as long as there was unemployment falls to zero. The entire effect of changes in the supply of money is exerted on prices, which rise in exact proportion with the increase in effective demand." Thus so long as there is unemployment, output will change in the same proportion as the quantity of money, and there will be no change in prices; and when there is full employment, prices will change in the same proportion as the quantity of money. Therefore, the reformulated quantity theory of money stresses the point that with increase in the quantity of money prices rise only when the level of full employment is reached, and not before this.

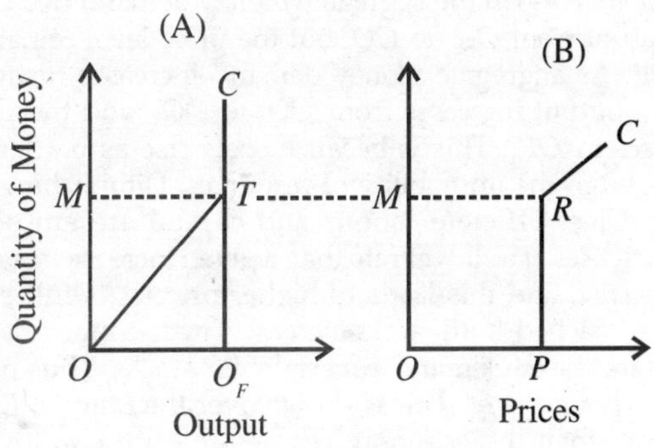

Fig. 1

This reformulated quantity theory of money is illustrated in Figure 1 (A) and (B) where *OTC* is the output curve relating to the quantity of money and *PRC* is the price curve relating to the quantity of money. Panel A of the figure shows that as the quantity of money increases from *O* to *M*, the level of output also rises along the *OT* portion of the *OTC* curve. As the quantity of money reaches *OM* level, full employment output OQ_F is being produced. But after point *T* the output curve becomes vertical because any further increase in the quantity of money cannot raise output beyond the full employment level OQ_F.

Panel B of the figure shows the relationship between quantity of money and prices. So long as there is unemployment, prices remain constant whatever the increase in the quantity of money. Prices start rising only after the full employment level is reached. In the figure, the price level *OP* remains constant at the *OM* quantity of money corresponding to the full employment level of output OQ_T. But an increase in the quantity of money above *OM* raises prices in the same proportion as the quantity of money. This is shown by the *RC* portion of the price curve *PRC*.

Keynes himself pointed out that the real world is so complicated that the simplifying assumptions upon which the reformulated quantity theory of money is based, will not hold. According to him, the following possible complications would qualify the statement that so long as there is unemployment, employment will change in the same proportion as the quantity of money, and when there is full employment, *prices* will change in the same proportion as the quantity of money."

(1) "Effective demand will not change in exact proportion to the quantity of money.

(2) Since resources are homogenous, there will be diminishing, and not constant returns as employment

gradually increases.

(3) Since resources are not interchangeable, some commodities will reach a condition of inelastic supply while there are still unemployed resources available for the production of other commodities.

(4) The wage-unit will tend to rise, before full employment has been reached.

(5) The remunerations of factors entering into marginal cost will not all change in the same proportion."[3]

Taking into account these complications, it is clear that the reformulated quantity theory of money does not hold. An increase in effective demand will not change in exact proportion to the quantity of money, but it will partly spend itself in increasing output and partly in increasing the price level. So long as there are unemployed resources, the general price level will not rise much as output increases. But a sudden large increase in aggregate demand will encounter bottlenecks when resources are still unemployed. It may be that the supply of some factors becomes inelastic or others may be in short supply and are not interchangeable. This may lead to increase in marginal cost and price. Price would accordingly rise above average unit cost and profits would increase rapidly which, in turn, tend to raise money wages owing to trade union pressures. Diminishing returns may also set in. As full employment is reached, the elasticity of supply of output falls to zero and prices rise in proportion to the increase in the quantity of money.

The complicated model of the Keynesian theory of money and prices is shown diagrammatically in Figure 2 in terms of aggregate supply (*S*) and aggregate demand (*D*) curves. The price level is measured on the vertical axis and output on the horizontal axis.

According to Keynes, an increase in the quantity of money increases aggregate money demand on investment as a result of the fall in the rate of interest. This increases output and employment in the beginning but not the price level. In the figure, the increase in the aggregate money demand from D_1 to D_2 raises output from OQ_1 to OQ_2 but the price level remains constant at *OP*. As aggregate money demand increases further from D_2 to D_3, output increases from OQ_2 to OQ_3, and the price level also rises to OP_3. This is because costs rise as bottlenecks develop through the immobility of resources. Diminishing returns set in and less efficient labour and capital are employed. Output increases at a slower rate than a given increase in aggregate *money demand*, and this leads to higher prices. As full employment is approached, bottlenecks increase. Further-more, rising prices lead to increased demand, especially for stocks. Thus prices rise at an increasing rate." This is shown over the range E_3E_5 in the figure. But when the economy reaches the full employment level of output, any further increase in aggregate money demand brings about a proportionate increase in the price level but output remains unchanged at that level. This is shown in the figure when the demand curve D_5 shifts upward to D_6 and the price level increases from OP_5 to OP_6 while the level of output remains constant at OQ_F.

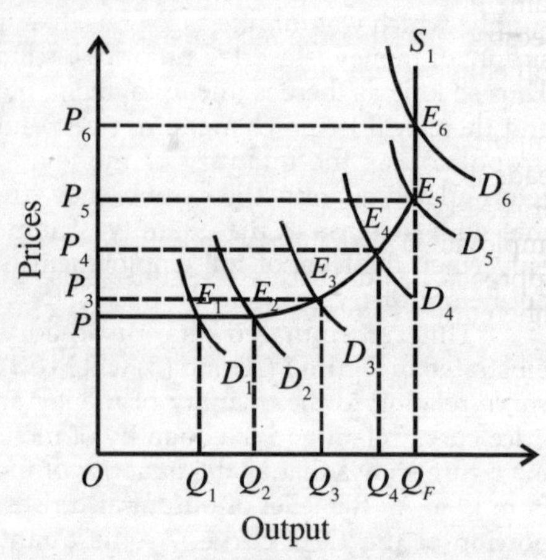

Fig. 2

3. SUPERIORITY OF THE KEYNESIAN THEORY OVER THE TRADITIONAL QUANTITY THEORY OF MONEY

The Keynesian theory of money and prices is surperior to the traditional quantity theory of money for the following reasons.

Keynes's reformulated quantity theory of money is superior to the traditional approach in that he discards the old view that the relationship between the quantity of money and prices is direct and proportional. Instead, he establishes an indirect and non-proportional relationship between quantity of money and prices.

In establishing such a relationship, Keynes brought about a transition from a pure monetary theory of

3. J.M. Keynes, *op. cit.,* pp. 296-97.

prices to a monetary theory of output and employment. In so doing, he integrates monetary theory with value theory. He integrates monetary theory with value theroy and also with the theory of output and employment through the rate of interest. In fact, the integration between monetary theory and value theory is done through the theory of output in which the rate of interest plays the crucial role. When the quantity of money increases the rate of interest falls which increases the volume of investment and aggregate demand thereby raising output and employment. In this way, monetary theory is integrated with the theory of output and employment. As output and employment increase they further raise the demand for factors of production. Consequently, certain bottlenecks appear which raise the marginal cost including money wage rates. Thus prices start rising. Monetary theory is integrated with value theory in this way. The Keynesain theory is, therefore, superior to the traditional quantity theory of money because it does not keep the real and monetary sectors of the economy into two separate compartments with 'no doors or windows between the theory of value and the theory of money and prices.'

Again, the traditional quantity theory is based on the unrealistic asumption of full employment of resources. Under this assumption, a given increase in the quantity of money always leads to a proportionate increase in the price level. Keynes, on the other hand, believes that full employment is an exception. Therefore, so long as there is unemployment, output and employment will change in the same proportion as the quantity of money, but there willl be no change in prices; and when there is full employment, prices will change in the same proportion as the quantity of money. Thus the Keynesian analysis is superior to the traditional analysis because it studies the relationship between the quantity of money and prices both under unemployment and full employment situations.

Further, the Keynesian theory is superior to the traditional quantity theory of money in that it emphasises important policy implications. The traditional theory believes that every increase in the quantity of money leads to inflation. Keynes, on the other hand, establishes that so long as there is unemployment, the rise in prices is gradual and there is no danger of inflation. It is only when the economy reaches the level of full employment that the rise in prices is inflationary with every increase in the quantity of money. Thus "this approach has the virtue of emphasising that the objectives of full employment and price stability may be inherently irreconcilable."

4. CRITICISMS OF KEYNES' THEORY OF MONEY AND PRICES

Keynes' views on money and prices have been criticised by the monetarists on the following grounds.

1. *Direct Relation.* Keynes mistakenly took prices as fixed so that the effect of money appears in his analysis in terms of quantity of goods traded rathere than their average prices. That is why Keynes adopted an indirect mechanism through bond prices, interest rates and investment of the effects of monetary changes on economic activity. But the actual effects of monetary changes are direct rather than indirect.

2. *Stable Demand for Money.* Keynes assumed that monetary changes were largely absorbed by changes in the demand for money. But Friedman has shown on the basis of his empirical studies that the demand for money is highly stable.

3. *Nature of Money.* Keynes failed to understand the true nature of money. He believed that money could be exchanged for bonds only. In fact, money can be exchanged for many different types of assets like bonds, securities, physical assets, human wealth, etc.

4. *Effect of Money.* Since Keynes wrote for a depression period, this led him to conclude that money had little effect on income. According to Friedman, it was the contraction of money that precipitated the depression. It was, therefore, wrong on the part of Keynes to argue that money had little effect on income. Money does affect national income.

EXERCISES

1. Show how the Theory of Value has been integrated with the Theory of Money by Keynes.
2. How has Keynes correlated money and rate of interest on the one hand and rate of interest, employment and prices on the other hand ?

Chapter 9

Friedman's Restatement of the Quantity Theory of Money

1. INTORDUCTION

Following the publication of Keynes's the *General Theory of Employment, Interest and Money* in 1936, economists discarded the traditional quantity theory of money. But at the University of Chicago "the quantity theory continued to be a central and vigorous part of the oral tradition throughout the 1930s and 1940s." At Chicago, Milton Friedman, Henry Simons, Lloyd Mints, Frank Knight and Jacob Viner taught and developed 'a more subtle and relevant version' of the quantity theory of money in its theoretical form "in which the quantity theory was connected and integrated with general price theory." The foremost exponent of the Chicago version of the quantity theory of money who led to the so-called "Monetarist Revolution" is Professor Friedman. He, in his essay "The Quantity Theory of Money—A Restatement" published in 1956', set down a particular model of quantity theory of money. This is discussed below.

2. FRIEDMAN'S THEORY

In his reformulation of the quantity theory, Friedman asserts that "the quantity theory is in the first instance a theory of the demand for money. It is not a theory of output, or of money income, or of the price level." The demand for money on the part of ultimate wealth holders is formally identical with that of the demand for a consumption service. He regards the amount of real cash balances (M/P) as a commodity which is demanded because it yields services to the person who holds it. Thus money is an asset or capital good. Hence the demand for money forms part of capital or wealth theory.

For ultimate wealth holders, the demand for money, in real terms, may be expected to be a function primarily of the following variables:

1. *Total Wealth.* The total wealth is the analogue of the budget constraint. It is the total that must be divided among various forms of assets. In practice, estimates of total wealth are seldom available. Instead, income may serve as an index of wealth. Thus, according to Friedman, income is a surrogate of wealth.

2. *The Division of Wealth between Human and Non-Human Forms.* The major source of wealth is the productive

1. Milton Friedman (ed.), *Studies in the Quantity Theory of Money*, 1956, pp. 3-21.

capacity of human beings which is human wealth. But the conversion of human wealth into non-human wealth or the reverse is subject to institutional constraints. This can be done by using current earnings to purchase non-human wealth or by using non-human wealth to finance the acquisition of skills. Thus the fraction of total wealth in the form of non-human wealth is an additional important variable. Friedman calls the ratio of non-human to human wealth or the ratio of wealth to income as w.

3. *The Expected Rates of Return on Money and Other Assets.* These rates of return are the counterparts of the prices of a commodity and its substitutes and complements in the theory of consumer demand. The nominal rate of return may be zero as it generally is on currency, or negative as it sometimes is on demand deposits, subject to net service charges, or positive as it is on demand deposits on which interest is paid, and generally on time deposits. The nominal rate of return on other assets consists of two parts: first, any currently paid yield or cost, such as interest on bonds, dividends on equities, and costs of storage on physical assets, and second, changes in the prices of these assets which become especially important under conditions of inflation or deflation.

4. *Other Variables.* Variables other than income may affect the utility attached to the services of money which determine liquidity proper. Besides liquidity, variables are the tastes and preferences of wealth holders. Another variable is trading in existing capital goods by ultimate wealth holders. These variable also determine the demand function for money alongwith other forms of wealth. Such variables are noted as u by Friedman.

Broadly, total wealth includes all sources of income or consumable services. It is capitalised income. By income, Friedman means "permanent income" which is the average expected yield on wealth during its life time.

Wealth can be held in five different forms: money, bonds, equities, physical goods, and human capital. Each form of wealth has a unique characteristic of its own and a different yield.

1. *Money* is taken in the broadest sense to include currency, demand deposits and time deposits which yield interest on deposits. Thus money is luxury good. It also yields real return in the form of convenience, security, etc. to the holder which is measured in terms of the general price level (P).
2. *Bonds* are defined as claim to a time stream of payments that are fixed in *nomianl units*.
3. *Equities* are defined as a claim to a time stream of payments that are fixed in *real* units.
4. *Physical goods or non-human goods* are inventories of producer and consumer durable.
5. *Human capital* is the productive capacity of human beings. Thus each form of wealth has a unique characteristic of its own and a different yield either explicitly in the form of interest, dividends, labour income, etc., or implicitly in the form of services of money measured in terms of P, and inventories. The present discounted value of these expected income flows from these five forms of wealth constitutes the current value of wealth which can be expressed as:

$$W = \frac{y}{r}$$

where W is the current value of total wealth, Y is the total flow of expected income from the five forms of wealth, and r is the interest rate. This equation shows that wealth is capitalised income. Friedman in his latest empirical study *Monetary Trends in the United States and the United Kingdom* (1982) gives the following demand function for money for an individual wealth holder with slightly different notations from his original study of 1956 as:

$$M/P = f(y, w; R_m, R_b, R_e, g_p, u)$$

where M is the total stock of money demanded; P is the price level; y is the real income; w is the fraction of wealth in non-human form: R_m is the expected nominal rate of return on money; R_b is the expected rate of return on bonds, including expected changes in their prices; R_e is the expected nominal rate of return on equities, including expected changes in their prices; $g_p = (1/P)(dP/dt)$ is the expected rate of change of prices of goods and hence the expected nominal rate of return on physical assets; and u stands for variables other than income that may affect the utility attached to the services of money.

The demand function for business is roughly similar, although the division of total wealth and human wealth is not very useful since a firm can buy and sell in the market place and hire its human wealth at will. But the othere factors are important.

The aggregate demand function for money is the summation of individual demand functions with M and y referring to per capita money holdings and per capita real income respectivley, and w to the fraction of aggregate wealth in non-human form.

The demand function for money leads to the conclusion that a rise in expected yields on different assets (R_b, R_e and g_p) reduces the amount of money demanded by a wealth holder, and that an increase in wealth raises the demand for money. The income to which cash balances (M/P) are adjusted is the expected long term level of income rather than current income being received. Empirical evidence suggests that the income elasticity of demand for money is greater than unity which means that income velocity is falling over the long run. This means that the long-run demand for money function is stable and is relatively interest inelastic, as shown in Fig. 1, where M_D is the demand for money curve. If there is change in the interest rate, the long-run demand for money is neligible.

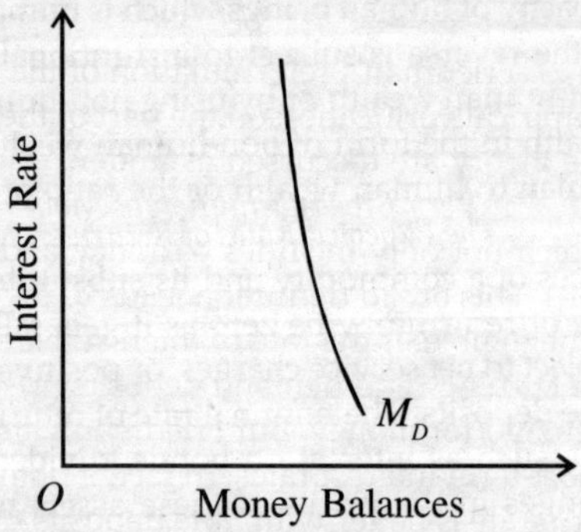

Fig. 1

In Friedman's restatement of the quantity theory of money, the supply of money is independent of the demand for money. The supply of money is unstable due to the actions of monetary authorities. On the other hand, the demand for money is stable. It means that money which people want to hold in cash or bank deposits is related in a fixed way to their permanent income. If the central bank increases the supply of money by purchasing securities, people who sell securities will find their holdings of money have increased in relation to their permanent income. They will, therefore, spend their excess holdings of money partly on assets and partly on consumer goods and services. This spending will reduce their money balances and at the same time raise the nominal income. On the contrary, a reduction in the money supply by selling securities on the part of the central bank will reduce the holdings of money of the buyers of securities in relation to their permanent income. They will, therefore, raise their money holdings partly by selling their assets and partly by reducing their consumption expenditure on goods and services. This will tend to reduce nominal income. Thus, on both counts, the demand for money remains stable. According to Friedman, a change in the supply of money causes a proportionate change in the price level or income or in both. Given the demand for money, it is possible to predict the effects of changes in the supply of money on total expenditure and income. If the economy is operating at less than full employment level, an increase in the supply of money will raise output and employment with a rise in total expenditure. But this is only possible in the short run. Friedman's quantity theory of moeny is explained in terms of Figure 2, where income (Y) is measured on the vertical axis and the demand for the supply of money are measured on the horizontal axis. M_D is the demand for money curve which varies with income. MS is the money supply curve which is perfectly inelalstic to changes in income. The two curves intersect at E and determine the equilibrium income OY. If the money supply rise, the MS curve shifts to the right to M_1S_1. As a result, the money supply is greater than the demand for money which raises total expenditure until new equilibrium is established at E_1 between M_D and M_1S_1 cirves. The income rises to OY_1.

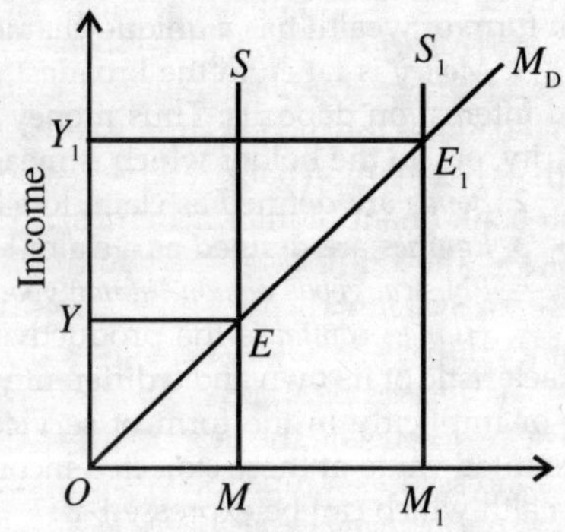

Demand and Supply of Money

Fig. 2

Thus Friedman presents the quantity theory as the theory of the demand for money and the demand for money is assumed to depend on asset prices or relative returns and wealth or income. He shows how a theory of the stable demand for money becomes a theory of prices and output. A discrepancy between the nominal quantity of money demanded and the nominal quantity of money supplied will be evident primarily in attempted spending. As the demand for money changes in response to changes in its determinants, it follows that substantial changes in prices or nominal income are almost invariably the result of changes in the nominal supply of money.

Its Criticisms

Friedman's reformulation of the quantity theory of money has evoked much controversy and has led to empirical verification on the part of the Keynesians and the Monetarists. Some of the criticisms levelled against the theory are discussed as under.

1. *Very Broad Definition of Money.* Friedman has been criticised for using the broad definition of money which not only includes currency and demand deposits (M_1) but also time deposits with commercial banks (M_2). This broad definition leads to the obvious conclusion that the interest elasticity of the demand for money is negligible. If the rate of interest increases on time deposits, the demand for them (M_2) rises. But the demand for currency and demand deposits (M_1) falls. So the overall effect of the rate of interest will be negligible on the demand for money. But Friedman's analysis is weak in that he does not make a choice between long-term and short-term interest rates. In fact, if demand deposits (M_1) are used a short-term rate is preferable, while a long-term rate is better with time deposits (M_2). Such an interest rate structure is bound to influence the demand for money.

2. *Money not a Luxury Good.* Friedman regards money as a luxury good because of the inclusion of time deposits in money. This is based on his finding that there is higher trend rate of the money supply than income in the United States. But no such 'luxury effect' has been found in the case of England.

3. *More Importance to Wealth Variables.* In Friedman's demand for money function, wealth variables are preferable to income and the operation of wealth and income variables simultaneously does not seem to be justified. As pointed out by Johnson, income is the return on wealth, and wealth is the present value of income. The presence of the rate of interest and one of these variables in the demand for money function would appear to make the other superfluous.

4. *Money Supply not Exogenous.* Friedman takes the supply of money to be unstable. The supply of money is varied by the monetary authorities in an exogenous manner in Friedman's system. But the fact is that in the United States the money supply consists of bank deposits created by changes in bank lending. Bank lending, in turn, is based upon bank reserves which expand and contract with (a) deposits and withdrawals of currency by non-bank financial intermediaries; (b) borrowings by commercial banks from the Federal Reserve System; (c) inflows and outflows of money from and to abroad: and (d) purchase and sale of securities by the Federal Reserve System. The first three items definitely impart an endogenous element to the money supply. Thus the money supply is not exclusively exogenous, as assumed by Friedman. It is mostly endogenous.

5. *Ignores the Effect of Other Variables on Money Supply.* Friedman also ignores the effect of prices, output or interest rates on the money supply. But there is considerable empirical evidence that the money supply can be expressed as a function of the above variables.

6. *Does not consider Time Factor*. Friedman does not tell about the timing and speed of adjustment or the length of time to which his theory applies.

7. No Positive Correlation between Money Supply and Money GNP. Money supply and money GNP have been found to be positively correlated in Friedman's findings. But, according to Kaldor,[2] in Britain the best correlation is to be found between the quarterly variations in the amount of cash held in the form of notes and coins by the public and corresponding variations in personal consumption at market prices, and not between money supply and the GNP.

8. *Conclusion.* Despite these criticisms, "Friedman's application to monetary theory of the basic principle of capital theory—that is the yield on capital, and capital the present value of income—is probably the most important development in monetary theory since Keynes's *General Theory*. Its theoretical significance lies in the conceptual integration of wealth and income as influences on behaviour."[3]

3. FRIEDMAN VS KEYNES

Friedman's demand for money function differs from that of Keynes's in many ways which are discussed as under.

2. N. Kaldor, 'The New Monetarism,' L.B.R., July 1970
3. H.G. Johnson, *op. cit.*

First, Friedman uses a broader definition of money than that of Keynes in order to explain his demand for money function. He treats money as an asset or capital good capable of serving as a temporary abode of purchasing power. It is held for the stream of income or consumable services which it renders. On the other hand, the Keynesian definition of money consists of demand deposits and non-interest bearing debt of the government.

Second, Friedman postulates a demand for money function quite different from that of Keynes. The demand for money on the part of wealth holders is a function of many variables. These are R_m, the yield on money; R_b, the yield on bonds; R_e, the yield on securities; g_p, the yield on physical assets; and u referring to other variables. In the Keynesian theory, the demand for money as an asset is confined to just bonds where interest rates are the relevant cost of holding money.

Third, there is also the difference between the monetary mechanisms of Keynes and Friedman as to how changes in the quantity of money affect economic activity. According to Keynes, monetary changes affect economic activity *indirectly* through bond prices and interest rates. The monetary authorities increase the money supply by purchasing bonds which raises their prices and reduces the yield on them. Lower yield on bonds induces people to put their money elsewhere, such as investment in new productive capital that will increase output and income. On the other hand, in Friedman's theory, monetary disturbances will *directly* affect prices and production of all types of goods since people will buy or sell any asset held by them. Friedman emphasises that the market interest rates play only a small part of the total spectrum of rates that are relevant.

Fourth, there is the difference between the two approaches with regard to the motives for holding money balances. Keynes divides money balances into "active" and "idle" categories. The former consist of transactions and precautionary motives, and the latter consist of the speculative motive for holding money. On the other hand, Friedman makes no such division of money balances. According to him, money is held for a variety of different purposes which determine the total volume of assets held such as money, physical assets, total wealth, human wealth, and general preferrences, tastes and anticipations.

Fifth, in his analysis, Friedman introduces permanent income and nominal income to explain his theory. Permanent income is the amount a wealth holder can consume while maintaining his wealth intact. Nominal income is measured in the prevailing units of currency. It depends on both prices and quantities of goods traded. Keynes, on the other hand, does not make such a distinction.

EXERCISES

1. Explain the contribution of Milton Friedman to the Quantity Theory of Money.
2. Critically examine the statement that the revised version of the quantity theory of money is that there exists a stable demand function for real money holdings.
3. Explain Friedman's reformulation of the Quantity Theory of Money. How does if differ from that of Keynes ?
4. Comment on the following statements:
   (a) The Quantity Theory of Money is a Theory of Demand for Money.
   (b) The Quantity Theory of Money is a Theory of Money-Income Determination.

CHAPTER 10

The Supply of Money

1. DEFINITIONS OF MONEY SUPPLY

The supply of money is a stock at a particular point of time, though it conveys the idea of a flow over time. The term 'the supply of money' is synonymous with such terms as 'money stock', 'stock of money', 'money supply' and 'quantity of money'. The supply of money at any moment is the total amount of money in the economy. There are three alternative views regarding the definition or measures of money supply. The most common view is associated with the traditional and Keynesian thinking which stresses the medium of exchange function of money. According to this view, money supply is defined as currency with the public and demand deposits with commercial banks. Demand deposits are savings and current accounts of depositors in a commercial bank. They are the liquid form of money because depositors can draw cheques for any amount lying in their accounts and the bank has to make immediate payment on demand. Demand deposits with commercial banks plus currency with the public are together denoted as M_1, the money supply. This is regarded as a narrower definition of the money supply.

The second definition is broader and is associated with the modern quantity theorists headed by Friedman. Professor Friedman defines the money supply at any moment of time as "literally the number of dollars people are carrying around in their pockets, the number of dollars they have to their credit at banks or dollars they have to their credit at banks in the form of demand deposits, and also commercial bank time deposits." Time deposits are fixed deposits of customers in a commercial bank. Such deposits earn a fixed rate of interest varying with the time period for which the amount is deposited. Money can be withdrawn before the expiry of that period by paying a penal rate of interest to the bank. So time deposits possess liquidity and are included in the money supply by Friedman. Thus this definition includes M_1 plus time deposits of commercial banks in the supply of money. This wider definition is characterised as M_2 in America and M_3 in Britain and India. It stresses the store of value function of money or what Friedman says, 'a temporary abode of purchasing power'.

The third definition is the broadest and is associated with Gurley and Shaw.[1] They include in the supply of money, M_2 plus deposits of savings banks, building societies, loan associations, and deposits of other credit and financial institutions.

The choice between these alternative definitions of the money supply depends on two considerations: One "a particular choice of definition may facilitate or blur the analysis of the various motives for holding

1. J.G. Gurley and E.S. Shaw, *Money in a Theory of Finance*, 2/e, 1965.

cash;"[2] and *two* from the point of view of monetary policy an appropriate definition should include the area over which the monetary authorities can have direct influence. If these two criteria are applied, none of the three definitions is wholly satisfactory.

The first definition of money supply may be analytically better because M_1 is a sure medium of exchange. But M_1 is an inferior store of value because it earns no rate of interest, as is earned by time deposits. Further, the central bank can have control over a narrower area if only demand deposits are included in the money supply.

The second definition that includes time deposits (M_2) in the supply of money is less satisfactory analytically because "in a highly developed financial structure, it is important to consider separately the motives for holding means of payment and time deposits." Unlike demand deposits, time deposits are not a prefect liquid form of money. This is because the amount lying in them can be withdrawn immediately by cheques. Normally, it cannot be withdrawn before the due date of expiry of deposit. In case a depositor wants his money earlier, he has to give a notice to the bank which allows the withdrawal after charging a penal interest rate from the depositor. Thus time deposits lack perfect liquidity and cannot be included in the money supply. But this definition is more appropriate from the point of view of monetary policy because the central bank can exercise control over a wider area that includes both demand and time deposits held by commercial banks.

The third definition of money supply that includes M_2 plus deposits of non-bank financial institutions is unsatisfactory on both the criteria. Firstly, they do not serve the medium of exchange function of money. Secondly, they almost remain outside the area of control of the central bank. The only advantage they possess is that they are highly liquid store of value. Despite this merit, deposits of non-bank financial institutions are not included in the definition of money supply.

2. DETERMINANTS OF MONEY SUPPLY

There are two theories of the determination of the money supply. According to the first view, the money supply is determined exogenously by the central bank. The second view holds that the money supply is determined endogenously by changes in the economic activity which affect people's desire to hold currency relative to deposits, the rate of interest, etc.

Thus the determinants of money supply are both exogenous and endogenous which can be described broadly as: the minimum cash reserve ratio, the level of bank reserves, and the desire of the people to hold currency relative to deposits. The last two determinants together are called the monetary base or the high powered money.

1. The Required Reserve Ratio

The required reserve ratio (or the minimum cash reserve ratio or the reserve deposit ratio) is an important determinant of the money supply. An increase in the required reserve ratio reduces the supply of money with commercial banks and a decrease in required reserve ratio increases the money supply. The RR_1 is the ratio of cash to current and time deposit liabilities which is determined by law. Every commercial bank is required to keep a certain percentage of these liabilities in the form of deposits with the central bank of the country. But notes or cash held by commercial banks in their tills are not included in the minimum required reserve ratio.

But the short-term assets along with the cash are regarded as the liquid assets of a commercial bank. In India the statutory liquidity ratio (SLR) has been fixed by law as an additional measure to determine the money supply. The SLR is called secondary reserve ratio in other countries while the required reserve ratio is referred to as the primary ratio. The raising of the SLR has the effect of reducing the money supply with commercial banks for lending purposes, and the lowering of the SLR tends in increase the money supply with banks for advances.

---

2. R.J. Ball, *Inflation and the Theory of Money*, 1964.

2. The Level of Bank Reserves

The level of bank reserves is another determinant of the money supply. Commercial bank reserves consist of reserves on deposits with the central bank and currency in their tills or vaults. It is the central bank of the country that influences the reserves of commercial banks in order to determine the supply of money. The central bank requires all commercial banks to hold reserves equal to a fixed percentage of both time and demand deposits. These are legal minimum or required reserves. Required reserves (*RR*) are determined by the required reserve ratio (*RRr*) and the level of deposits (D) of a commercial bank: *RR=RRr D*. If deposits amount of Rs 80 lakhs and required reserve ratio is 20 percent, then the required reserves will be 20% x 80=Rs 16 lakhs. If the reserve ratio is reduced to 10 per cent, the required reserves will also be reduced to Rs 8 lakhs. Thus the higher the reserve ratio, the higher the required reserves to be kept by a bank, and vice versa. But it is the excess reserves (*ER*) which are important for the determination of the money supply. Excess reserves are the difference between total reserves (*TR*) and required reserves (*RR*): ER=TR-RR. If total reserves are Rs 80 lakhs and required reserves are Rs 16 lakhs, then the excess reserves are Rs 64 lakhs (Rs 80 - 16 lakhs). When required reserves are reduced to Rs 8 lakhs, the excess reserves increase to Rs 72 lakhs. It is the excess reserves of a commercial bank which influence the size of its deposit liabilities. A commercial bank advances loans equal to its excess reserves which are an important component of the money supply. To determine the supply of money with a commercial bank, the central bank influences its reserves by adopting open market operations and discount rate policy.

Open market operations refer to the purchase and sale of government securities and other types of assets like bills, securities, bonds, etc., both government and private in the open market. When the central bank buys or sells securities in the open market, the level of bank reserves expands or contracts. The purchase of securities by the central bank is paid for with cheques to the holders of securities who, in turn, deposit them in commercial banks thereby increasing the level of bank reserves. The opposite is the case when the central bank sells securities to the public and banks who make payments to the central bank through cash and cheques thereby reducing the level of bank reserves.

The discount rate policy affects the money supply by influencing the cost and supply of bank credit to commercial banks. The discount rate, known as the bank rate in India, is the interest rate at which commercial banks borrow from the central bank. A high discount rate means that commercial banks get less amount by selling securities to the central bank. The commercial banks, in turn, raise their lending rates to the public thereby making advances dearer for them. Thus there will be contraction of credit and the level of commercial bank reserves. Opposite is the case when the bank rate is lowered. It tends to expand credit and the consequent bank reserves.

It should be noted that commercial bank reserves are affected significantly only when open market operations and discount rate policy supplement each other. Otherwise, their effectiveness as determinants of bank reserves and consequently of money supply is limited.

3. Public's Desire to Hold Currency and Deposits

People's desire to hold currency (or cash) relative to deposits in commercial banks also determines the money supply. If people are in the habit of keeping less in cash and more in deposits with the commercial banks, the money supply will be large. This is because banks can create more money with larger deposits. On the contrary, if people do not have banking habits and prefer to keep their money holdings in cash, credit creation by banks will be less and the money supply will be at a low level.

4. High Powered Money

The current practice is to explain the determinants of the money supply in terms of the monetary base or high-powered money. High-powered money is the sum of commercial bank reserves and currency (notes and coins) held by the public. High-powered money is the base for the expansion of bank deposits and creation of the money supply. The supply of money varies directly with changes in the monetary base, and inversely with the currency and reserve ratios.

4. Other Factors

The money supply is a function not only of the high-powered money determined by the monetary authorities, but of interest rates, income and other factors. The latter factors change the proportion of money balances that the public holds as cash. Changes in business activity can change the behaviour of banks and the public and thus affect the money supply. Hence the money supply is not only an exogenous controllable item but also an endogenously determined item.

Conclusion

We have discussed above the factors which determine money supply through the creation of bank credit. But money supply and bank credit are indirectly related to each other. When the money supply increases, a part of it is saved in banks depending upon the depositors' propensity to save. These savings become deposits of commercial banks who, in turn, lend after meeting the statutory reserve requirements. Thus with every increase in the money supply, the bank credit goes up. But it may not happen in exactly the same proportion due to the following factors:

(a) The marginal propensity to save does not remain constant. It varies from time to time depending on changes in income levels, prices, and subjective factors.

(b) Banks may also create more or less credit due to the operation of leakages in the credit creation process.

(c) The velocity of circulation of money also affects the money supply. If the velocity of money circulation increases, the bank credit may nor fall even after a decrease in the money supply. The central bank has little control over the velocity of money which may adversely affect bank credit.

3. MEASURES OF MONEY SUPPLY IN INDIA

There are four measures of money supply in India which are denoted by M_1, M_2, M_3, and M_4. This classification was introduced by the Reserve Bank of India (RBI) in April 1977. Prior to this till March 1968, the RBI published only one measure of the money supply, M or M_1, defined as currency and demand deposits with the public. This was in keeping with the traditional and Keynesian views of the narrow measure of the money supply. From April 1968, the RBI also started publishing another measure of the money supply which it called Aggregate Monetary Resources (AMR). This included M_1 *plus* time deposits of banks held by the public. This was a broad measure of money supply which was in line with Friedman's view. But since April 1977, the RBI has been publishing data on four measures of the money supply which are discussed as under.

M_1. The first measure of money supply, M_1 consists of :

(*i*) Currency with the public which includes notes and coins of all denominations in circulation excluding cash on hand with banks:

(*ii*) demand deposits with commercial and cooperative banks, excluding inter-bank deposits; and

(*iii*) 'other deposits' with RBI which include current deposits of foreign central banks, financial institutions and quasi-financial institutions such as IDBI, IFCI, etc, other than of banks, IMF, IBRD, etc. The RBI characterises M_1 as narrow money.

M_2. The second measure of money supply is M_2 which consists of M_1 *plus* post office savings bank deposits. Since savings bank deposits of commercial and cooperative banks are included in the money supply, it is essential to include post office savings bank deposits. The majority of people in rural and urban India have preference for post office deposits from the safety viewpoint than bank deposits.

M_3. The third measure of money supply in India is M_3 which consists of M_1 plus time deposits with commercial and cooperative banks, excluding interbank time deposits. The RBI calls M_3 as broad money.

M_4. The fourth measure of money supply is M_4 which consists of M_3 plus total post office deposits comprising time deposits and demand deposits as well. This is the broadest measure of money supply.

Of the four inter-related measures of money supply for which the RBI publishes data, it is M_3 which is of special significance. It is M_3 which is taken into account in formulating macroeconomic objectives of the economy every year. Since M_1 is narrow money and includes only demand deposits of banks alongwith currency held by the public, it overlooks the importance of time deposits in policy making. That is why, the RBI prefers M_3 which includes total deposits of banks and currency with the public in credit budgeting for its credit policy. It is on the estimates of increase in M_3 that the effects of money supply on prices and growth of national income are estimated. In fact M_3 is an empirical measure of money supply in India, as is the practice in developed countries. The Chakravarty Committee also recommended the use of M_3 for monetary targeting without any reason.

EXERCISES

1. Explain the various components of the money supply.
2. Discuss the determinants of the money supply. Should time deposits be included under the supply of money?
3. Discuss the various measures of the money supply adopted by the Reserve Bank of India. How do they differ from those adopted by developed countries?

Chapter 11

The Demand for Money

1. INTRODUCTION

The demand for money arises from two important functions of money. The first is that money acts as a medium of exchange and the second is that it is a store of value. Thus individuals and businesses wish to hold money partly in cash and partly in the form of assets.

What explains changes in the demand for money ? There are two views on this issue. The first is the "scale" view which is related to the impact of the income or wealth level upon the demand for money. The demand for money is directly related to the income level. The higher the income level, the greater will be the demand for money. The second is the "substitution" view which is related to relative attractiveness of assets that can be substituted for money. According to this view, when alternative assets like bonds become unattractive due to fall in interest rates, people prefer to keep their assets in cash, and the demand for money increases, and vice versa. The scale and substitution view combined together have been used to explain the nature of the demand for money which has been split into the transactions demand, the precautionary demand and the speculative demand. There are three approaches to the demand for money: the classical, the Keynesian, and the post-Keynesian. We discuss the first two approaches and in the last approach only Friedman's view.

2. THE CLASSICAL APPROACH

The classical economists did not explicitly formulate demand for money theory but their views are inherent in the quantity theory of money. They emphasized the transactions demand for money in terms of the velocity of circulation of money. This is because money acts as a medium of exchange and facilitates the exchange of goods and services. In Fisher's "Equation of Exchnage".

$$MV = PT$$

where M is the total quantity of money, V is its velocity of circulation, P is the price level, and T is the total amount of goods and services exchanged for money.

The right hand side of this equation PT represents the demand for money which, in fact, "depends upon the value of the transactions to be undertaken in the economy, and is equal to a constant fraction of those transactions." MV represents the supply of money which is given and in equilibrium equals the demand for money. Thus the equation becomes

$$Md = PT$$

This transactions demand for money, in turn, is determined by the level of full employment income. This is because the classicists believed in Say's Law whereby supply created its own demand, assuming the full employment level of income. Thus the demand for money in Fisher's approach is a constant proportion of the level of transactions, which in turn, bears a constant relationship to the level of national income. Further, the demand for money is linked to the volume of trade going on in an economy at any time.

Thus its underlying assumption is that people hold money to buy goods.

But people also hold money for other reasons, such as to earn interest and to provide against unforeseen events. It is, therefore, not possible to say that V will remain constant when M is changed. The most important thing about money in Fisher's theory is that it is transferable. But it does not explain fully why people hold money. It does not clarify whether to include as money such items as time deposits or savings deposits that are not immediately available to pay debts without first being converted into currency.

It was the Cambridge cash balance approach which raised a further question: Why do people actually want to hold their assets in the form of money ? With larger incomes, people want to make larger volumes of transactions and that larger cash balances will, therefore, be demanded.

The Cambridge demand equation for money is

$$Md = kPY$$

where Md is the demand for money which must equal the supply to money ($Md=Ms$) in equilibrium in the economy. k is the fraction of the real money income (PY) which people wish to hold in cash and demand deposits or the ratio of money stock to income, P is the price level, and Y is the aggregate real income. This equation tells us that "other things being equal, the demand for money in normal terms would be proportional to the nominal level of income for each individual, and hence for the aggregate economy as well."

Its Critical Evaluation

This approach includes time and saving deposits and other convertible funds in the demand for money. It also stresses the importance of factors that make money more or less useful, such as the costs of holding it, uncertainty about the future and so on. But it says little about the nature of the relationship that one expects to prevail between its variables, and it does not say too much about which ones might be important.

One of its major criticisms arises from the neglect of store of value function of money. The classicists emphasized only the medium of exchange function of money which simply acted as a go-between to facilitate buying and selling. For them, money performed a neutral role in the economy. It was barren and would not multiply, if stored in the form of wealth. This was an erroneous view because money performed the "asset" function when it is transformed into other forms of assets like bills, equities, debentures, real assets (houses, cars, TVs, and so on), etc. Thus the neglect of the asset function of money was the major weakness of classical approach to the demand for money which Keynes remedied.

3. THE KEYNESIAN APPROACH : LIQUIDITY PREFERENCE

Keynes in his *General Theory* used a new term "liquidity preference" for the demand for money. Keynes suggested three motives which led to the demand for money in an economy:(1) the transactions demand, (2) the precautionary demand, and (3) the speculative demand.

The Transactions Demand for Money

The transactions demand for money arises from the medium of exchange function of money in making regular payments for goods and services. According to Keynes, it relates to "the need of cash for the current transactions of personal and business exchange" It is further divided into income and business motives. The income motive is meant "to bridge the interval between the receipt of income and its disbursement." Similarly, the business motive is meant "to bridge the interval between the time of incurring business costs and that of the receipt of the sale proceeds." If the time between the incurring of expenditure and receipt of income is small, less cash will be held by the people for current transactions, and vice versa. There will, however, be changes in the transactions demand for money depending upon the expectations of income recipients and businessmen.

They depend upon the level of income, the interest rate, the business turnover, the normal period between the receipt and disbursement of income, etc.

Given these factors, the transactions demand for money is a direct proportional and positive function of the level of income, and is expressed as

$$L_T = kY$$

where L_T is the transactions demand for money, k is the proportion of income which is kept for transactions purposes, and Y is the income.

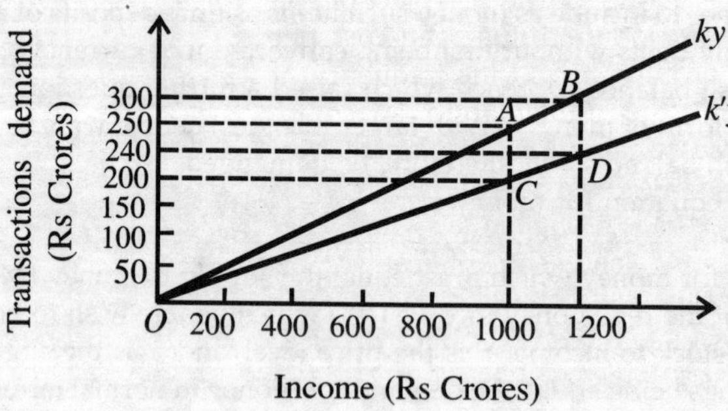

Fig. 1

This equation is illustrated in Figure 1 where the line kY represents a linear and proportional relation between transactions demand and the level of income. Assuming k=1/4 and income Rs 1000 crores, the demand for transactions balances would be Rs 250 crores, at point A. With the increase in income to Rs 1200 crores, the transactions demand would be Rs 300 crores at point B on the curve kY. If the transactions demand falls due to a change in the institutional and structural conditions of the economy, the value of k is reduced to say, 1/5, and the new transactions demand curve is $k'Y$. It shows that for income of Rs 1000 and 1200 crores, transactions balances would Rs 200 and 240 crores at points C and D respectively in the figure. "Thus we conclude that the chief determinant of changes in the actual amount of the transactions balances held is changes in income. Changes in the transactions balances are the result of movements along a line like kY rather than changes in the slope of the line. In the equation, changes in transactions balances are the result of changes in Y rather than changes in k."[1]

Interest Rate and Transactions Demand. Regarding the rate of interest as the determinant of the transactions demand for money Keynes made the L_T function interest inelastic. But the pointed out that the "demand for money in the active circulation is also the some extent a function of the rate of interest, since a higher rate of interest may lead to a more economical use of active balances."[2] "However, he did not stress the role of the rate of interest in this part of his analysis, and many of his popularizers ignored it altogether."[3] In recent years, two post-Keynesian economists William J. Baumol[4] and James Tobin[5] have shown that the rate of interst is an important determinant of transactios demand for money. The have also pointed out the the relationship between transactions demand for money and income is not linear and proportional. Rather, changes in income lead to proportionatley smaller changes in transactions demand.

Transactions balances are held because income received once a month is not spent on the same day. In fact, an individual spreads his expenditure evenly over the month. Thus a portion of money meant for

1. Edward Shapiro, *op. cit.*, pp. 367-68.
2. J.M.Keynes in A.D. Gayer (ed.), *The Lessons of Monetary Experience*, 1937, p. 149.
3. David E.W.Laidler, *op. cit.*, p. 52.
4. William J.Baumol, "Transactions Demand for Cash--An Inventory Theoretic Approach", *Quarterly Journal of Economics*, November 1952.
5. James Tobin, "The Interest Elasticity of the Transactions Demand for Cash", *Review of Economics and Statistics*, August 1956.

transactions purposes can be spent on short-term interest-yielding securities. It is possible to "put funds to work for a matter of days, weeks, or months in interest-bearing securities such as U.S. Treasury bills or commercial paper and other short-term money market insturments. The problem here is that there is a cost involved in buying and selling. One must weigh the financial cost and inconvenience of frequent entry to and exit from the market for securities against the apparent advantage of holding interest-bearing securities in place of idle transactions balances. Among other things, the cost per purchase and sale, the rate of interest, and the frequency of purchases and sales determine the profitability of switching from ideal transactions balances to earning assets. Nonetheless, with the cost per purchase and sale given, there is clearly some rate of interest at which it becomes profitable to switch what otherwise would be transactions balances into interest-bearing securities, even if the period for which these funds may be spared from transactions needs is measured only in weeks. The higher the interest rate, the larger will be the fraction of any given amount of transactions balances that can be profitably diverted into securities."

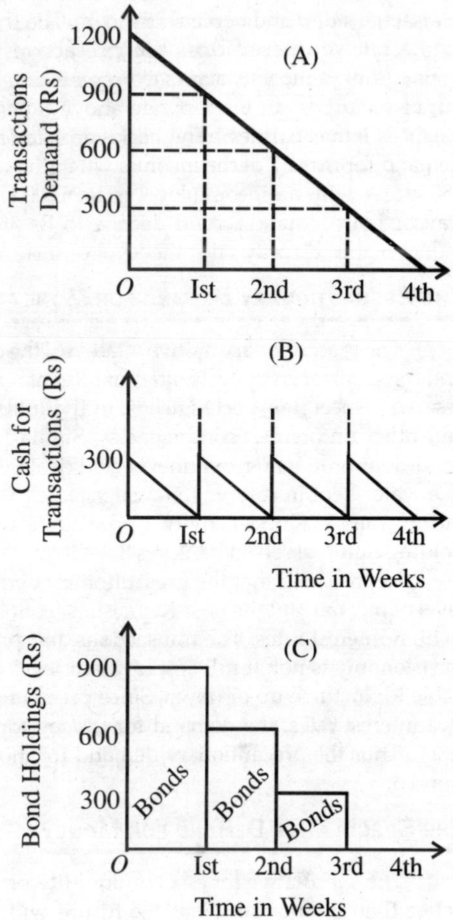

Fig. 2

The structure of cash and short-term bond holdings is shown in Figure 2 (A), (B) and (C). Suppose an individual receives Rs 1200 as income on the first of every month and spends it evenly over the month. The month has four weeks. His saving is zero. Accordingly, his transactions demand for money in each week is Rs 300. So he has Rs 900 idle money in the first week, Rs 600 in the second week, and Rs 300 in the third week. He will, therefore, convert this idle money into interest bearing bonds, as illustrated in Panel (B) and (C) of Figure 2. He keeps and speds Rs 300 during the first week (shown in Panel B), and invests Rs 900 in interest-bearing bonds (shown in Panel C). On the first day of the second week he sells bonds worth Rs. 300 to cover cash transactions of the second week and his bond holdings are reduced to Rs 600. Similarly, he will sell bonds worth Rs 300 in the beginning of the third and keep the remaining bonds amounting to Rs 300 which he will sell on the first day of the fourth week to meet his expenses for the last week of the month. The amount of cash held for transactions purposes by the individual during each week is shown in saw-tooth pattern in Panel (B), and the bond holdings in each week are shown in blocks in Panel (C) of Figure 2.

The modern view is that the transactions demand for money is a function of both income and interest rates which can be expressed as

$$L_T = f(Y, r).$$

This relationship between income and interest rate and the transactions demand for money for the economy as a whole is illustrated in Figure 3. We saw above that $L_T = kY$. If Y=Rs 1200 crores and k=1/4, then L_T=Rs 300 crores.

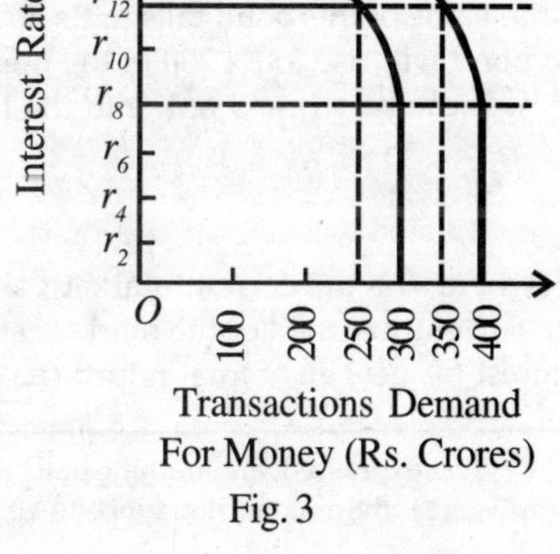

Fig. 3

This is shown as Y_1 curve in Figure 3. If the income level rises to Rs 1600 crores, the transactions demand also increases to Rs 400 crores, given k=1/4. Consequently, the transactions demand curve shifts to Y_2. The transactions demand curves Y_1 and Y_2 are interest-inelastic so long as the rate of interest does not rise above r_8 per cent. As the rate of interest starts rising above r_8, the transactions demand for money becomes interest elastic. It indicates that "given the cost of switching into and out of securities, an interest rate above 8 per cent is sufficiently high to attract some amount of transaction balances into securities." The backward slope of the Y_1 curve shows that at still higher rates, the transaction demand for money declines. Thus when the rate of interest rises to r_{12}, the transactions demand declines to Rs 250 crores with an income level of Rs 1200 crores. Similarly, when the national income is Rs 1600 crores the transactions demand would decline to Rs 350 crores at r_{12} interest rate. Thus the transactions demand for money varies directly with the level of income and inversely with the rate of interest.

THE PRECAUTIONARY DEMAND FOR MONEY

The Precautionary motive relates to "the desire to provide for contingencies requiring sudden expenditures and for unforeseen opportunities of advantageous purchases." Both individuals and businessmen keep cash in reserve to meet unexpected needs. Individuals hold some cash to provide for illness, accidents, unemployment and other unforeseen contingencies. Similarly, businessmen keep cash in reserve to tide over unfavourable conditions or to gain from unexpected deals. Therefore, "money held under the precautionary motive is rather like water kept in reserve in a water tank." The precautionary demand for money depends upon the level of income, and business activity, opportunities for unexpected profitable deals, availability of cash, the cost of holding liquid assets in bank reserves, etc.

Keynes held that the precautionary demand for money, like transactions demand, was a function of the level of income. But the post-Keynesian economists believe that like transactinos demand, it is inversely related to high interest rates. The transactions and precautionary demand for money will be unstable, particularly if the economy is not at full employment level and transactions are, therefore, less than the maximum, and are liable to fluctuate up or down. Since precuationary demand, like transactions demand is a function of income and interest rates, the demand for money for these two purposes is expressed in the single equation $LT = f(Y,r)$[6]. Thus the precautionary demand for money can also be explained diagrammatically in terms of Figures 2 and 3.

THE SPECULATIVE DEMAND FOR MONEY

The speculative (or asset or liquidity preference) demand for money is for securing profit from knowing better than the market what the future will bring forth".Individuals and businessmen having funds, after keeping enough for transactions and precautionary purposes, like to make a speculative gain by investing in bonds. Money held for speculative purposes is a liquid store of value which can be invested at an opportune moment in interest-bearing bonds or securities.

Bond prices and the rate of interest are inversely related to each other. Low bond prices are indicative of high interest rates, and high bond prices reflect low interest rates. A bond carries a fixed rate of interest. For instance, if a bond of the value of Rs 100 carries 4 per cent interest and the market rate of interest rises to 8 per cent, the value of this bond falls to Rs 50 in the market. If the market rate of interest falls to 2 per cent, the value of the bond will rise to Rs 200 in the market.

This can be worked out with the help of the equation

$$V = \frac{R}{r}$$

where V is the current market value of a bond, R is the annual return on the bond, and r is the rate of return currently earned or the market rate of interest. So a bond worth Rs 100 (V) and carrying a 4 per cent rate of interest (r), gets an annual return (R) of Rs 4, that is, V=Rs 4/0.04=Rs100. When the market rate of interest

6. Keynes expressed the amount held under these two motives (M_1) as a function (L_1) of the level of income (Y), M_1=L_1(Y). By making it a function of interest rate (r), it can be written as $M_1 = L_1(Y,r)$.

rises to 8 per cent, then V=Rs 4/0.08=Rs50; when it fall to 2 per cent, then V=Rs 4/0.02=Rs 200.

Thus individuals and businessmen can gain by buying bonds worth Rs 100 each at the market price of Rs 50 each when the rate of interest is high (8 per cent), and sell them again when they are dearer (Rs 200 each when the rate of interest falls (to 2 per cent).

According to Keynes, it is expectations about changes in bond prices or in the current market rate of interest that determine the speculative demand for money. In explaining the speculative demand for money, Keynes had a normal or critical rate of interest (r_c) in mind. If the current rate of interest (r) is above the "critical" rate of interest, businessmen expect it to fall and bond price to rise. They will, therefore, buy bonds to sell them in future when their prices rise in order to gain thereby. At such times, the speculative demand for money would fall. Conversely, if the current rate of interest happens to be below the critical rate, businessmen expect it to rise and bond prices to fall. They will, therefore, sell bonds in the present if they have any, and the speculative demand for money would increase. Thus when $r>r_0$, an investor holds all his liquid assets in bonds, and when $r<r_0$ his entire holdings go into money. But when $r=r_0$, he becomes indifferent to hold bonds or money.

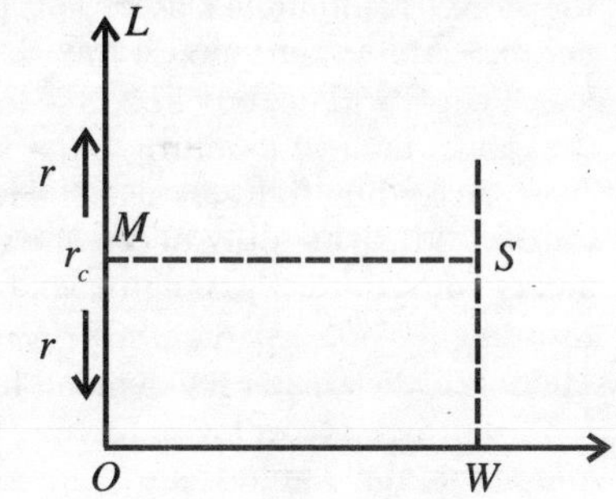

Speculative Demand for Money

Fig. 4

Thus relationship between an individual's demand for money and the rate of interest is shown in Figure 4 where the horizontal axis shows the individual's demand for money for speculative purposes and the current and critical interest rates on the vertical axis. The figure shows that when r is greater than r_0, the asset holder puts all his cash balances in bonds and his demand for money is zero. This is illustrated by the LM portion of the vertical axis. When r falls below r_0, the individual expects more capital losses on bonds as against the interest yield. He, therefore, converts his entire holdings into money, as shown by OW in the figure. This relationship between an individual asset holder's demand for money and the current rate of interest gives the discontinuous step demand for money curve $LMSW$.

For the economy as a whole the individual demand curve can be aggregated on this presumption that individual asset-holders differ in their critical rates r_0. It is smooth curve which slopes downward from left to right, as shown in Figure 5.

Thus the speculative demand for money is a decreasing function of the rate of interest. The higher the rate of interest, the lower the speculative demand for money, and the lower the rate of interest, the higher the speculative demand for money. It can be expressed algebraically as $Ls = f(r)$, where Ls is the speculative demand for money and r is the rate of interest. Geometrically, it is shows in Figure 5. The figure shows that at a very high rate of interest r_{12}, the speculative demand for money is zero and businessmen invest their cash holdings in bonds because they believe that the interest rate cannot rise further. As the rate of interest falls to say, r_8 the speculative demand for money is OS. With a further fall in the interest rate to r_6, it rises to OS'. Thus the shape of the Ls curve shows that as the interest rate rises, the speculative demand for money declines; and with the fall in the interest raet, it increases. Thus the Keynesian speculative demand for money function is highly volatile, depending upon the behaviour of interest rates.

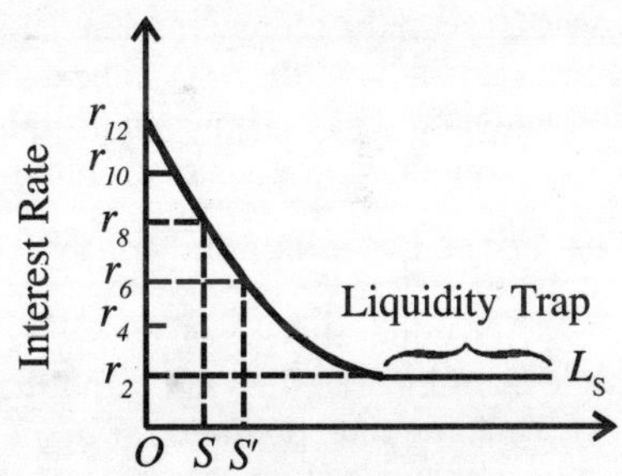

Speculative Demand for Money

Fig. 5

Liquidity Trap

Keynes visualised conditions in which the speculative demand for money would be highly or even totally elastic so that changes in the quantity of money would be fully absorbed into speculative balances. This is the famous Keynesian *liquidity trap.* In this case, changes in the quantity of money have no effects at all on prices or income. According to Keynes, this is likely to happen when the market interest rate is very low so that yields on bond, equities and other securities will also be low.

At a very low rate of interest, such as r_2, the *Ls* curve becomes *perfectly elastic* and the speculative demand for money is infinitely elastic. This portion of the *Ls* curve is known as the liquidity trap. At such a low rate, people prefer to keep money in cash rather than invest in bonds because purchasing bonds will mean a definite loss. People will not buy bonds so long as the interest rate remain at the low level and they will be waiting for the rate of interest to return to the "normal" level and bond prices to fall.[7]

According to Keynes, as the rate of interest approaches zero, the risk of loss in holding bonds becomes greater. "When the price of bonds has been bid up so high that the rate of interest is, say, only 2 per cent or less, a very small decline in the price of bonds will wipe out the yield entirely and a slightly further decline would result in loss of the part of the principal." Thus the lower the interest rate, the smaller the earnings from bonds. Therefore, the greater the demand for cash holdings. Consequently, the *Ls* curve will become perfectly elastic.

Further, according to Keynes, "a long-term rate of interest of 2 per cent leaves more to fear than to hope, and offers, at the same time, a running yield which is only sufficient to offset a very small measure of fear." This makes the Ls curve "virtually absolute in the sense that almost everybody prefers cash to holding a debt which yields so low a rate of interest."

Prof. Modigliani believes that an infinitely elastic *Ls* curve is possible in a period of great uncertainty when price reductions are anticipated and the tendency to invest in bonds decreases, or if there prevails "a real scarcity of investment outlets that are profitable at rates of interest higher than the institutional minimum."[8]

Its Implications

The phenomenon of liquidity trap possesses certain important implications.

First, the monetary authority cannot influence the rate of interest even by following a cheap money policy. An increase in the quantity of money cannot lead to a further decline in the rate of interest in a liquidity-trap situation. *Second,* the rate of interest cannot fall to zero. *Third,* the policy of a general wage cut cannot be efficacious in the face of a perfectly elastic liquidity preference curve, such as Ls in Figure 5. No doubt, a policy of general wage cut would lower wages and prices, and thus release money from transactions to speculative purpose, the rate of interest would remain unaffected because people would hold money due to the prevalent uncertainty in the money market. *Last,* if new money is created, it instantly goes into speculative balances and is put into bank vaults or cash boxes instead of being invested. Thus there is no effect on income. Income can change without any change in the quantity of money. Thus monetary changes have a weak effect on economic activity under conditions of absolute liquidity preference.

The Total Demand for Money

According to Keynes, money held for transactions and precautionary purposes is primarily a function of the level of income, $L_T = f(Y)$, and the speculative demand for money is a function of the rate of interest, $Ls = f(r)$. Thus the total demand for money is a function of both income and the interest rate :

$$L_T + L_S = f(Y) + f(r)$$

or

$$L = f(Y) + f(r)$$

or

$$L = f(Y, r)$$

where *L* represents the total demand for money.

Thus the total demand for money can be derived by the lateral summation of the demand function for transactions and precautionary purposes and the demand function for speculative purposes, as illustrated in Figure 6 (A), (B) and (C). Panel (A) of the Figure shows *OT*, the transactions and precautionary demand for money at Y level of income and different rates of interest. Panel (B) shows the speculative demand for money

7. The remaining portion of this section can be left out safely except for a note on the Liquidity Trap.
8. F. Modigliani, "Liquidity Preference and the Theory of Interest and Money," *Economica* January 1944.

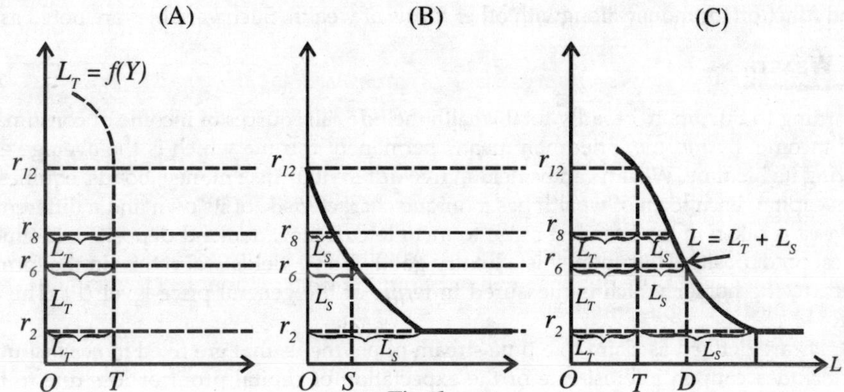

Fig. 6

at various rates of interest. It is an inverse function of the rate of interest. For instance, at r_6 rate of interest it is *OS* and as the rate of interest falls to r_2, the Ls curve becomes perfectly elastic. Panel (C) shows the total demand cuve for money *L* which is a lateral summation of *LT* and *Ls* curves : $L=L_T+L_S$. For example, at r_6 rate of interest, the total demand for money is *OD* which is the sum of transactinos and precautionary demand *OT plus* the speculative demand *TD*, *OD=OT+TD*. At r_2 interest rate, the total demand for money curve also becomes perfectly elastic, showing the position of liquidity trap.

3 FRIEDMAN'S THEORY OF DEMAND FOR MONEY

Friedman's theory of demand for money is a capital or wealth theory, because he regards money as an asset or capital good.

For ultimate wealth holders, the demand for money, in real terms, may be expected to be a function primarily of the following variables :

1. *Total Wealth.* The total-wealth is the analogue of the budget constraint. It is the total that must be divided among various forms of assets. In practice, estimates of total wealth are seldom available. Instead, income may serve as an index of wealth. Thus, according to Friedman, income is a surrogate of wealth.

2. *The Division of Wealth between Human and Non-Human Forms.* The major source of wealth is the productive capacity of human beings which is human wealth. But the conversion of human wealth into non-human wealth or the reverse is subject to institutional constraints. This can be done by using current earnings to purchase non-human wealth or by using non-human wealth to finance the acquisition of skills. Thus the fraction of total wealth in the form of non-human wealth is an additional important variable. Friedman calls the ratio of non-human to human wealth or the ratio of wealth to income as *W*.

3. *The Expected Rates of Return on Money and Other Assets.* These rates of return are the counterparts of the prices of a commodity and its substitutes and complements in the theory of consumer demand. The nominal rate of return may be zero as it generally is on currency, or negative as it sometimes is on demand deposits, subject to net service charges, or positive as it is on demand deposits on which interest is paid, and generally on time deposits. The nominal rate of return on other assets consits of two parts : *first,* any currently paid yield or cost, such as interest on bonds, dividends on equities, and costs of storage on physical assets, and *second,* changes in the prices of these assets which become especially important under conditions of inflation or deflation.

4. *Other Variables.* Variables other than income may affect" the utility attached to the services of money which determine liquidity proper. Besides liquidity, variables are the tastes and preferences of wealth holders. Another variables is trading in existing capital goods by ultimate wealth holders. These variables also determine

the demand function for money alongwith other forms of wealth. Such variables are noted as μ by Friedman.

FORMS OF WEALTH

According to Friedman, broadly total wealth includes all sources of income or consumable services. It is capitalised income. By income, Friedman means permanent income which is the average expected yield on wealth during its life time. Wealth can be held in five different forms : money, bonds, equities, physical goods, and human capital. Each form of wealth has a unique characteristic of its own and a different yield..

1. *Money* is taken in the broadest sense to include currency, demand deposits and time deposits which yield interest on deposits. Thus money is a luxury good. It also yields real return in the form of convenience, security, etc. to the holder which is measured in terms of the general price level *(P)*. The expected rate on money is R_m.

2. *Bonds* are defined as claim to a time stream of payments that are fixed in *nominal* units. The yield on bonds, R_b includes coupon interest rate or the expectation of capital profit or loss due to fall or rise in the expected market rate of interest.

3. *Equities* are defined as a claim to a time stream of payments that are fixed in *real* units. The yield on equities, R_e includes return on dividend rate, expected profit or loss due to changes in interest rate.

4. *Physical goods or non-human goods* are inventories of producer and consumer durables. Their returns are affected by expected rate of changes in prices.

5. *Human capital* is the productive capacity of human beings

Thus each form of wealth has a unique characteristic of its own and a different yield either explicitly in the form of interest, dividends, labour income, etc., or implicitly in the form of services of lyoney measures in terms of price level, *P*, and inventories. The present discounted value of these expected income flows from these five forms of wealth constitutes the current value of wealth which can be expressed as:

$$W=Y/r$$

where *W* is the current value of total wealth, *Y* is the total flow of expected income from the five forms of wealth, and *r* is the interest rate. This equation shows that *wealth is capitalised income.*

DEMAND FUNCTION FOR MONEY

Friedman in his latest empirical study *Monetary Trends in the United States and the United Kingdom* (1982) gives the following demand function for money for an individual wealth holder with slightly different notations from his original study of 1956 as :

$$M/P=f(Y,W;R_m,R_b,R_e,g_p,\mu)$$

where *M* is the total stock of money demanded; *P* is the price level; *Y* is the real income; *W* is the fraction of wealth in non-human form; R_m is the expected nominal rate of return on money; R_e is the expected nominal rate of return on bonds, including expected changes in their prices; R_e is the expected nominal rate of return on equities, including expected changes in their prices; $g_p = (1/P)\ (dP/dt)$ is the expected rate of change of prices of goods and hence the expected nominal rate of return on physical assets; and μ stands for variables other than income that may affect the utility attached to the services of money.

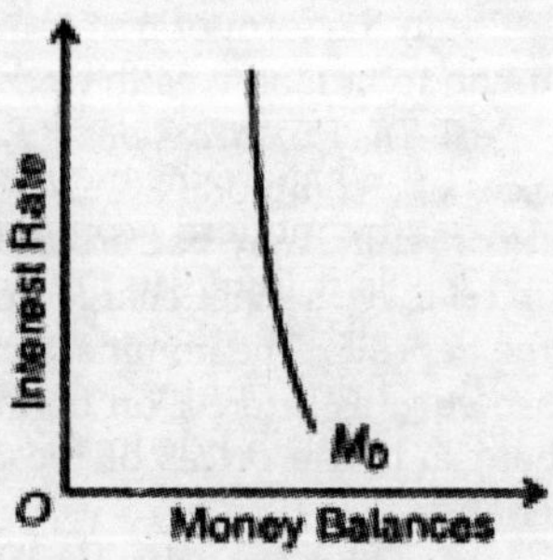

Fig. 7

The demand function for business is roughly similar, although the division of total wealth and human wealth is not very useful since a firm can buy and sell in the market place and hire ils human wealth at will. But the other factors are important.

The aggregate demand function for money is the summation of individual demand functions with *M* and *Y* referring to per capital money holdings and per capita real income respectively, and *W* to the fraction of aggregate wealth in non-human form.

The demand function for money leads to the conclusion that a rise in expected yields on different assets (R_b, R_e, and g_p) reduces the amount of money demanded by a wealth holder, and than an increase in wealth raises the demand for money. But the relation of demand for money with wealth is positive. When wealth increases, the demand for money also increases because people hold more wealth. Empirical evidence suggests that the income elasticity of demand for money is greater than unity which means that income velocity is falling over the long-run. This means that the long-run demand for money function is stable and is relatively interest inelastic, as shown in Fig. 7 where M_D is the demand for money curve. If there is change in the interest rate, the change in assets will be negligible.

Its Superiority over Keynesian Theory

Friedman's theory of demand for money is superior to Keynes' Theory in the following ways:

First, Friedman uses a broader definition of money than that of Keynes in order to explain his demand for money function. He treats money as as asset or capital good capable of serving as a temporary abode of purchasing power. It is held for the stream of income or consumable services which it renders. On the other hand, the keynesian definition of money consists of demand deposits and non-interest bearing debt of the government.

Second, Friedman postulates a demand for money function quite different from that of Keynes. The demand for money on the part of wealth holders is a function of many variables. These are R_m, the yield on money; R_b, the yield on bonds; R_e, the yield on securities; g_p, the yield on physical assets; and *u* referring to other variables. In the Keynesian theory, the demand for money as an asset is confined to just bonds where interest rates are the relevant cost of holding money.

Third, there is also the difference between the monetary mechanisms of Keynes and Friedman as to how changes in the quantity of money affect economic activity. According to Keynes, monetary changes affect economic activity *indirectly* through bond prices and interest rates. The monetary authorities increase the money supply by purchasing bonds which raises their prices and reduces the yield on them. Lower yield *oa* bonds induces people to put their money elsewhere, such as investment in new productive capital that will increase output and income. On the other hand, in Friedman's theory monetary distrubances will *directly* affect prices and production of all types of goods since people will buy or sell any asset held by them. Friedman emphasises that the market interest rates play only a small part of the total spectrum of rates that are relevant.

Fourth, there is the difference between the two approaches with regard to the motive for holding money balances. Keynes divides money balances into "active" and "idle" categories. The former consist of transactions and precautionary motives, and the latter consist of the speculative motive for holding money. On the other hand, Friedman makes no such division of money balances. According to him, money is held for a variety of different purposes which determine the total volume of assets held such as money, physical assets, total wealth, human wealth, and general preferences, tastes and anticipations.

Fifth, in his analysis, Friedman introduces permanent income and nominal income to explain his theory. Permanent income is the amount a wealth holder can consume while maintaining his wealth intact. Nominal income is measured in the prevailing units of currency. It depends on both prices and quantities of goods traded. Keynes, on the other hand, does not make such a distinction.

EXERCISES

1. What are the motives for holding cash balances according to Keynes? Give the modifications made by modern economists.
2. Is it liquidity preference satisfying the speculatyive demand for money alone which is interest elastic, or other liquidity preference also? Give reasons for your answer.
3. Bring out the relationship between money and interest.
4. Explain Friedman's demand for money theory. How is it superior to Keynes' Theory?

Chapter 12

Keynes' Fundamental Equations

Keynes formulated his "Fundamental Equations" through which he explains the factors that affect the general price level and price fluctuations in terms of saving and investment. He introduces two fundamental equations. The *First* equation explains the factors determining the price-level of consumption goods and the *second* explains the price level of output as a whole.

The first fundamental equation is :

$$P = \frac{E}{O} + \frac{I'-S}{R} \qquad \text{...(i)}$$

where P = price level of consumption goods; E = total factor income of a community in a certain time period; O = total output; I' = the part of E which is earned by the production of cost of new investment goods or by the production of investment goods; S = aggregate savings; and R = physical quantity of consumption goods.

This equation indicates the following relations :

(1) $E - S$ (or $P \times R$) = current expenditure on consumption goods; and (2) $E - I'$ = production cost of current output of consumption goods. By deducting (2) from (1), we find

$$\begin{aligned} &(E-S)-(E-I') \\ &= E - S - E + I' \\ &= I' - S \end{aligned}$$

which is profit from the sale of consumption goods.

Thus the first fundamental equation shows that the price of a unit of consumption goods is determined by two or all factors, such as $E/O, I', S$ and R or price level of consumption goods E/O (total output and the ratio of total factor income) plus $(I'-S)/R$ (the number of consumption goods and the ratio of profit from the sale of consumption goods)

In his second fundamental equation, Keynes presents a summary of the factors that affect the general price level. He calls it the Fundamental Equation of Price and expresses it in this way :

$$Y = \pi O = E + Q \qquad \text{...(2)}$$

Where Y = aggregate real income of a community; π = the general price level; E = nominal income level (factor income) of a community; and Q = windfall profits. Keynes assumes Q as the difference between value of output and cost of production of investment and savings. Thus

$$Q = I - S \qquad \text{...(3)}$$

Equilibrium requires that Q should be zero. In other words, the equilibrium income is $Y = \pi O = E$. The fundamental equation of price can be written as follows:

$$\pi = \frac{Y}{O} = \frac{E+Q}{O} = \frac{E}{O} + \frac{I-S}{O} \quad ...(4)$$

This equation shows that the price level (π) is determined by the total real income of the community (Y) and the ratio of total output. Or, the price level (π) changes with the change in E/O and Q (windfall profits). Keynes holds that E/O remains constant under full employment. Therefore, windfall profits (Q) bring changes in the price level. Windfall profits depends upon changes in the natural and market rates of interest. The market rate of interest is the rate at which money is borrowed in the market. The natural rate of interest is the windfall profit on new capital investments (or the rate at which the demand for loans is just equal to the supply of savings). Since $Q = I - S$, the difference between savings and investment brings changes in the price level. If the natural rate of interest is more than the market rate of interest, the investment on capital goods will increase, because people expect more profit. Thus, the investment demand is more than savings. In a situation of full employment, the demand for goods increases which raises prices. On the contrary, when the natural rate of interest is less than the market rate of interest, investment is less than savings and people expect less profit. The demand for goods falls which reduces prices. If the natural rate of interest is equal to the market rate of interest, $I = S$, the price-level is constant and Q is zero. In equilibrium, according to Keynes, "when the quantum of savings is equal to the costs (I') and the value of new investment goods (I), the relation between the quantity of money and the price-level of consumption goods as well as total production is such strange that if the quantity of money is double, the price-level will also be double."

Keynes combines his fundamental equation (2) with Fisher's transactions equation. He Writes :

$$E = M_1V_1$$

where, M_1 = income deposits and V_1 = velocity of M_1. Thus the fundamental equation can be written as under :

$$Y = \pi O = M_1V_1 + Q$$

Keynes regards V_1 as constant and in equilibrium Q as zero, the fundamental equation becomes as

$$\pi O = M_1V_1$$

This equation is closely related to Fisher's transaction equation $PT = MV$ except that Q represents current output while T is not the output but the quantity of transactions and M_1V_1 indicates income-deposits and their velocity while MV represents cash-deposits and their velocity. Thus Keynes' fundamental equation of price is not much different from Fisher's transaction equation.

Criticisms

Keynes himself points out certain defects of his fundamental equations in his **Treatise of Money** and the **General Theory** and some other economists also eriticise them on the following grounds :

1. *Mere Indentities.* Keynes' fundamental equations are mere identities. As Keynes himself says," They are purely formal; they are mere identities, truisms which tell us nothing themselves."

2. *Not Different from other Versions.* Keynes' fundamental equations are not different from the other version of the quantity theory of money. As Keynes himself writes in this context, "The Fundamental Equations are themselves not more than identities. In this respect, they resemble all other versions of the Quantity Theory of Money."

3. Not Possible to determine Elements Statistically. It is not possible to determine such elements as E, O, R, Q, etc. statistically.

4. *Unrealistic Assumption of Full Employment.* Keynes' fundamental equation of price is based on the unrealistic assumption of full employment. In reality, when he wrote his **A Treatise on Money**, he had no conception of an underemployment equilibrium.

5. *Variable E not explained properly.* According to Prof. Klein, the variable E which represents the income paid out to the factors of production not been properly explained by Keynes. This is the main defect of his

fundamental equations. This variable represents the effective demand and the failure to explain the principle of effective demand was the main weakness of Keynes' analysis at that time.

6. *Output not Fixed.* Keynes assumes the variable *O* (output) as given and fixed. This is unrealistic. As Keynes himself wrote in his *General Theory,* "Assuming the given output, forces could develop which involved a profit disequilibrium and thus required a change in the level of output."

7. *Price Level not determined by I and S alone.* Keynes tells the relation between saving and investment depends upon the price level and brings about cyclical fluctuations. This is not correct because there are other factors that bring changes in prices. According to Prof. Klein, Keynes could not realise at that time that saving and investment can be in equilibrium at various levels of employment.

8. *Static.* Keynes regards his fundamental equations as dynamic. But their nature is static because such variables as *E, Q* and π are related to 'a unit of time.'

Conclusion

Despite these weaknesses, Keynes regards his fundamental equations superior to the earlier quantity theory equations in that he explains changes in prices in the form of differences between investment and saving.

EXERCISES

1. Explain critically Keynes' Fundamental Equations.
2. Explain Keynes' Fundamental equations. How are they similar to Fisher's Exchange Equation?

Chapter 13

Inflation and Deflation

1. MEANING OF INFLATION

Inflation is a highly controversial term which has undergone modification since it was first defined by the neo-classical economists. They meant by it a galloping rise in prices as a result of the excessive increase in the quantity of money.

To the neo-classicals and their followers at the University of Chicago, inflation is fundamentally a monetary phenomenon. In the words of Friedman, *"Inflation is always and everywhere a monetary phenomenon...and can be produced only by a more rapid increase in the quantity of money than output."*[1] But economists do not agree that money supply alone is the cause of inflation. As pointed out by Hicks, *"Our present troubles are not of a monetary character."* Economists, therefore, define inflation in terms of a continuous rise in prices. Johnson defines "inflation as a sustained rise"[2] in prices. Brooman defines it as "a continuing increase in the general price level."[3] Shapiro also defines inflation in a similar vein "as a *persistent and appreciable rise in the general level of prices.*"[4] Dernberg and McDougall are more explicit when they write that "the term usually refers to a continuing rise in prices as measured by an index such as the consumer price index (CPI) or by the implicit price deflator for gross national product."[5]

2. TYPES OF INFLATION

Inflation is of various types. We discuss below some of its important types.

1. Creeping Inflation. When the rise in prices is very slow like that of a snail or creeper, it is called creeping inflation. In terms of speed, a sustained rise in prices of annual increase of less than 3 per cent per annum is characterised as creeping inflation. Such an increase in prices is regarded safe and essential for economic growth.

2.Walking or Trotting Inflation. When prices rise moderately and the annual inflation rate is a single digit.

---

1. M. Friedman, *The Conter-Revolution in Monetary Theory,* 1970.
2. Harry W. Johnson, *Essays in Monetary Economics,* p. 104.
3. F.S. Brooman, *Macroeconomics,*p. 285.
4. Edward Shapiro, *Macroeconomic Analysis,* p. 502.
5. *Macroeconomics,* p. 288.

In other words, the rate of rise in prices is in the intermediate range of 3 to 6 per cent per annum or less than 10 per cent. Inflation at this rate is a warning signal for the government to control it before it turns into running inflation.

3. *Running Inflation.* When prices rise rapidly like the running of a horse at a rate or speed of 10 to 20 per cent per annum, it is called running inflation. Such an inflation affects the poor and middle classes adversely. Its control requires strong monetary and fiscal measures, otherwise it leads to hyperinflation.

4. *Hyperinflation.* When prices rise very fast at double or triple digit rates from more than 20 to 100 per cent per annum or more, it is usually called *runaway* or *galloping* inflation. It is also characterised as hyperinflation by certain economists. In reality, hyperinflation is a situation when the rate of inflation becomes immeasurable and absolutely uncontrollable. Prices rise many times every day. Such a situation brings a total collapse of monetary system because of the continuous fall in the purchasing power of money.

The speed with which prices tend to rise is illustrated in Figure 1. The curve C shows creeping inflation when within a period of ten years the price level has been shown to have risen by about 30 per cent. The curve W depicts walking inflation when the price level rises by more than 50 per cent during ten years. The curve *R* illustrates running inflation showing a rise of about 100 per cent in ten years. The steep curve *H* shows the path of hyperinflation when prices rise by more than 120 per cent in less than one year.

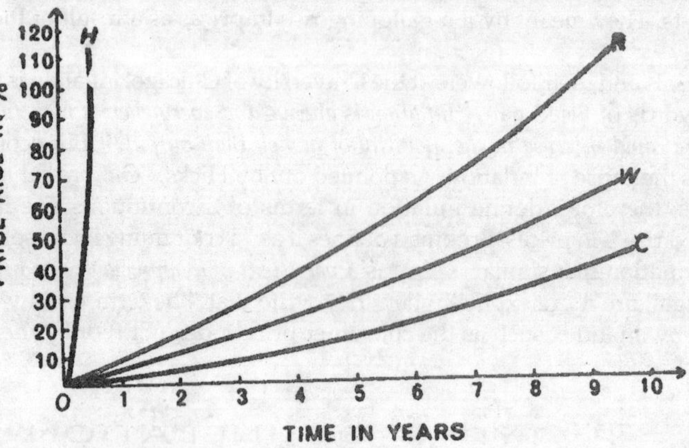

Fig. 1

5. *Semi-Inflation.* According to Keynes, so long as there are unemployed resources, the general price level will not rise as output increases. But a large increase in aggregate expenditure will face shortages of supplies of some factors which may not be substitutable. This may lead to increase in costs, and prices start rising. This is known as semi-inflation or *bottleneck* inflation because of the bottlenecks in supplies of some factors.

6. *True Inflation.* According to Keynes, when the economy reaches the level of full employment, any increase in aggregate expenditure will raise the price level in the same proportion. This is because it is not possible to increase the supply of factors of production and hence of output after the level of full employment. This is called true inflation.

The Keynesian semi-inflation and true inflation situations are illustrated in Figure.2.

Employment and price level are taken on vertical axis and aggregate expenditure on horizontal axis. *FE* is the full employment curve. When with the increase in aggregate expenditure, the price level rises slowly from *A* to the full employment level *B*, this is semi-inflation. But when the aggregate expenditure increases beyond point *B* the price level rises from *B* to *T* in proportion to the increase in aggregate expenditure. This is true inflation.

7. *Open Inflation.* Inflation is open when "markets for goods or factors of production are allowed to function freely, setting prices of goods and factors without normal interference by the authorities." Thus open

inflation is the result of the uninterrupted operation of the market mechanism. There are no checks or controls on the distribution of commodities by the government. Increase in demand and shortage of supplies persist which tend to lead to open inflation. Unchecked open inflation ultimately leads to hyperinflation.

8. Suppressed Inflation. When the government imposes physical and monetary controls to check open inflation, it is known as repressed or suppressed inflation. The market mechanism is not allowed to function normally by the use of licensing, price controls and rationing in order to suppress extensive rise in prices. So long as such controls exist, the present demand is postponed and there is diversion of demand from controlled to uncontrolled commodities. But as soon as these controls are removed, there is open inflation. Moreover, suppressed inflation adversely affects the economy. When the distribution of commodities is controlled, the prices of uncontrolled commodities rise very high. Suppressed inflation reduces the incentive to work because people do not get the commodities which they want to have. Controlled distribution of goods also leads to mal-allocation of resources. This results in the diversion of productive resources from essential to non-essential industries. Lastly, suppressed inflation leads to black marketing, corruption, hoarding and profiteering.

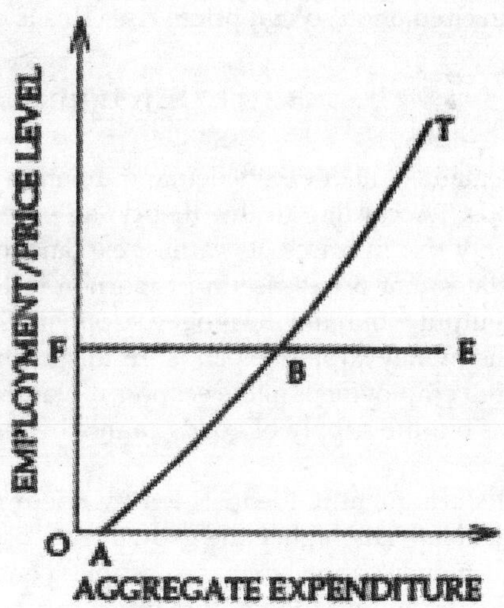

Fig. 2

9. Stagflation. Stagflation is a new term which has been added to economic literature in the 1970s. It is a paradoxical phenomenon where the economy experiences stagnation as well as inflation. The word stagflation is the combination of 'stag' plus 'flation' taking 'stag' from stagnation and 'flation' from inflation.

Stagflation is a situation when recession is accompanied by a high rate of inflation. It is, therefore, also called inflationary recession. The principal cause of this phenomenon has been excessive demand in commodity markets, thereby causing prices to rise, and at the same time the demand for labour is deficient, thereby creating unemployment in the economy.

Three factors have been responsible for the existence of stagflation in the advanced countries since 1972. *First,* rise in oil prices and other commodity prices along with adverse changes in the terms of trade; *second,* the steady and substantial growth of the labour force; and *third,* rigidities in the wage structure due to strong trade unions.

10. Mark-up Inflation. The concept of mark-up inflation is closely related to the price-push problem. Modern labour organisations possess substantial monopoly power. They, therefore, set prices and wages on the basis of mark-up over costs and relative incomes. Firms possessing monopoly power have control over the prices charged by them. So they have administered prices which increase their profit margin. This sets off an inflationary rise in prices. Similarly, when strong trade unions are successful in raising the wages of workers, this contributes to inflation.

11. Ratchet Inflation. A ratchet is a toothed wheel provided with a catch that prevents the ratchet wheel from moving backward. The same is the case under ratchet inflation when despite donwward pressures in the economy, prices do not fall. In an economy having price, wage and cost inflations, aggregate demand falls below full employment level due to the deficiency of demand in some sectors of the economy. But wage, cost and price structures are inflexible downward because large business firms and labour organisations possess monopoly power. Consequently, the fall in demand may not lower prices significantly. In such a situation, prices will have an upward ratchet effect, and this is known as "ratchet inflation."

12. Sectoral Inflation. Sectoral inflation arises initially out of excess demand in particular industries. But it leads to a general price rise because prices do not fall in the deficient demand sectors.

13. *Reflation* is a situation when prices are raised deliberately in order to encourage economic activity.

When there is depression and prices fall abnormally low, the monetary authority adopts measures to put more money in circulation so that prices rise. This is called reflation.

3. DEMAND-PULL INFLATION

Demand-Pull or excess demand inflation is a situation often described as "too much money chasing too few goods." According to this theory, an excess of aggregate demand over aggregate supply will generate inflationary rise in prices. Its earliest explanation is to be found in the simple quantity theory of money. The theory states that prices rise in proportion to the increase in the money supply. Given the full employment level of output, doubling the money supply will double the price level. So inflation proceeds at the same rate at which the money supply expands. In this analysis, the aggregate supply is assumed to be fixed and there is always full employment in the economy. Naturally, when the money supply increases it creates more demand for goods but the supply of goods cannot be increased due to the full employment of resources. This leads to rise in prices.

Modern quantity theorists led by Friedman hold that "inflation is always and everywhere a monetary phenomenon." The higher the growth rate of the nominal money supply, the higher the rate of inflation. When the money supply increases, people spend more in relation to the available supply of goods and services. This bids prices up. Modern quantity theorists neither assume full employment as a normal situation nor a stable velocity of money. Still they regard inflation as the result of excessive increase in the money supply.

The quantity theory version of the demand-pull inflation is illustrated in Figure 3. Suppose the money supply is increased at a given price level *OP* as determined by the demand and supply curves *D* and $S\ S_1$ respectively. The initial full employment situation OY_F at this price level is shown by the interaction of these curves at point *E*. Now with the increase in the quantity of money, the aggregate demand increases which shifts the demand curve *D* to D_1 to the right. The aggregate supply being fixed, as shown by the vertical portion of the supply curve $S\ S_1$, the D_1 curve intersects it at point E_1. This raises the price level to OP_1.

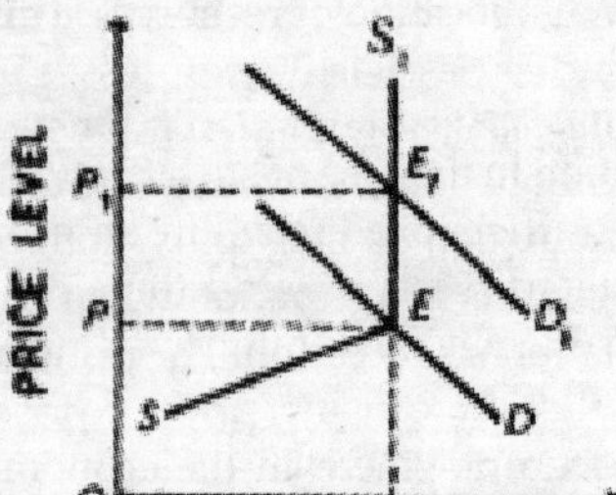

Fig. 3

The Keynesian theory on demand-pull inflation is based on the argument that so long as there are unemployed resources in the economy, an increase in investment expenditure will lead to increase in employment, income and output. Once full employment is reached and bottlenecks appear, further increase in expenditure will lead to excess demand because output ceases to rise, thereby leading to inflation.

The Keynesian theory of demand-pull inflation is explained diagrammatically in Figure 3. Suppose the economy is in equilibrium at *E* where the SS_1 and *D* curves intersect with full employment income level OY_F. The price level is *OP*. Now the government increases its expenditure. The increase in government expenditure implies an increase in aggregate demand which is shown by the upward shift of the *D* curve to D_1 in the figure. This tends to raise the price level to OP_1, as aggregate supply of output cannot be increased after the full employment level.[6]

4. COST-PUSH INFLATION

Cost-push inflation is caused by wage increases enforced by unions and profit increases by employers. This type of inflation has not been a new phenomenon and was found even during the medieval period. But it was revived in the 1950s and again in the 1970s as the principal cause of inflation. It also came to be known as

6. There are many causes leading to Demand-Pull Inflation which are discussed under Factors Affecting Demand in the section, "Causes of Inflation".

the "*New Inflation.*" Cost-push inflation is caused by wage-push and profit-push to prices for the following reasons:

1. *Rise in Wages.* The basis cause of cost-push inflation is the rise in money wages more rapidly than the productivity of labour. In advanced countries, trade unions are very powerful. They press employers to grant wage increases considerably in excess of increases in the productivity of labour, thereby raising the cost of production of commodities. Employers, in turn, raise prices of their products. Higher wages enable workers to buy as much as before, in spite of higher prices. On the other hand, the increase in prices induces unions to demand still higher wages. In this way, the wage-cost spiral continues, thereby leading to cost-push or wage-push inflation. Cost-push inflation may be further aggravated by upward adjustment of wages to compensate for rise in the cost of living index.

2. *Sectoral Rise in Prices.* Again, a few sectors of the economy may be affected by money wage increases and prices of their products may be rising. In many cases, their production such as steel, raw materials, etc. are used as inputs for the production of commodities in other sectors. As a result, the production cost of other sectors will rise and thereby push up the prices of their products. Thus wage-push inflation in a few sectors of the economy may soon lead to inflationary rise in prices in the entire economy.

3. *Rise in Prices of Imported Raw Materials.* An increase in the prices of imported raw materials may lead to cost-push inflation. Since raw materials are used as inputs by the manufacturers of the finished goods, they enter into the cost of production of the latter. Thus a continuous rise in the prices of raw materials tends to sets off a cost-price-wage spiral.

4. *Profit-Push Inflation.* Oligopolist and monopolist firms raise the prices of their products to offset the rise in labour and production costs so as to earn higher profits. There being imperfect competition in the case of such firms, they are able to "administer prices" of their products. "In an economy in which so called administered prices abound there is at least the possibility that these prices may be administered upward faster than cost in an attempt to earn greater profits. To the extent such a process is wide-spread profit-push inflation will result."[7] Profit-push inflation is, therefore, also called administered-price theory of inflation or price-push inflation or sellers' inflation or market-power inflation.*

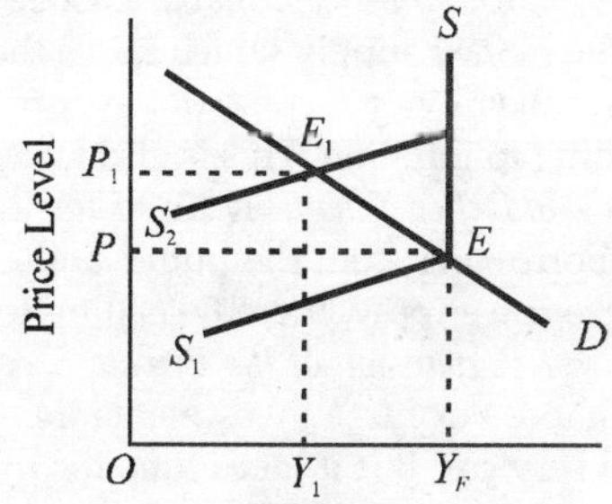

Fig. 4

Cost-push inflation is illustrated in Figure 4. where S_1S is the supply curve and D is the demand curve. Both intersect at E which is the full employment level OY_F, and the price level OP is determined. Given the demand, as shown by the D curve, the supply curve S_1 is shown to shift to S_2 as a result of cost-push factors. Consequently, it intersects the D curve at E_1 showing rise in the price level from OP to OP_1 and fall in aggregate output from OY_F to OY_1 level. Any further shift in the supply curve will shift and tend to raise the price level and decrease aggregate output further.

5. CAUSES OF INFLATION

Inflation is caused when the aggregate demand exceeds the aggregate supply of goods and services. We analyse the factors which lead to increase in demand and the shortage of supply.

FACTORS AFFECTING DEMAND

Both Keynesians and monetarists believe that inflation is caused by increase in the aggregate demand.

7. Edward Shapiro, *op.cit.*, p. 522.

* For other causes refer to Factors Affecting Supply under "Causes of Inflation."

They point towards the following factors which raise it.

1. *Increase in Money Supply.* Inflation is caused by an increase in the supply of money which leads to increase in aggregate demand. The higher the growth rate of the nominal money supply, the higher is the rate of inflation. Modern quantity theorists do not believe that true inflation starts after the full employment level. This view is realistic because all advanced countries are faced with high levels of unemployment and high rates of inflation.

2. *Increase in Disposable Income.* When the disposable income of the people increases, it raises their demand for goods and services. Disposable income may increase with the rise in national income or reduction in taxes or reduction in the saving of the people.

3. *Increase in Public Expenditure.* Government activities have been expanding much with the result that government expenditure has also been increasing at a phenomenal rate, thereby raising aggregate demand for goods and services. Governments of both developed and developing countries are providing more facilities under public utilities and social services, and also nationalising industries and starting public enterprises with the result that they help in increasing aggregate demand.

4. *Increase in Consumer Spending.* The demand for goods and services increases when consumer expenditure increases. Consumers may spend more due to conspicuous consumption or demonstration effect. They may also spend more whey they are given credit facilities to buy goods on hire-purchase and instalment basis.

5. *Cheap Monetary Policy.* Cheap monetary policy or the policy of credit expansion also leads to increase in the money supply which raises the demand for goods and services in the economy. When credit expands, it raises the money income of the borrowers which, in turn, raises aggregate demand relative to supply, thereby leading to inflation. This is also known as *credit-induced* inflation.

6. *Deficit Financing.* In order to meet its mounting expenses, the government resorts to deficit financing by borrowing from the public and even by printing more notes. This raises aggregate demand in relation to aggregate supply, thereby leading to inflationary rise in prices. This is also known as *deficit-induced* inflation.

7. *Expansion of the Private Sector.* The expansion of the private sector also tends to raise the aggregate demand. For huge investments increase employment and income, thereby creating more demand for goods and services. But it takes time for the output to enter the market.

8. *Black Money.* The existence of black money in all countries due to corruption, tax evasion etc. increases the aggregate demand. People spend such unearned money extravagantly, thereby creating unnecessary demand for commodities. This tends to raise the price level further.

9. *Repayment of Public Debt.* Whenever the government repays its past internal debt to the public, it leads to increase in the money supply with the public. This tends to raise the aggregate demand for goods and services.

10. *Increase in Exports.* When the demand for domestically produced goods increases in foreign countries, this raises the earnings of industries producing export commodities. These, in turn, create more demand for goods and services within the economy.

Factors Affecting Supply

There are also certain factors which operate on the opposite side and tend to reduce the aggregate supply. Some of the factors are as follows :

1. *Shortage of Factors of Production.* One of the important causes affecting the supplies of goods is the shortage of such factors as labour, raw materials, power supply, capital, etc. They lead to excess capacity and reduction in industrial production.

2. *Industrial Disputes.* In countries where trade unions are powerful, they also help in curtailing production. Trade unions resort to strikes and if they happen to be unreasonable from the employers' viewpoint and are prolonged, they force the employers to declare lock-outs. In both cases, industrial production falls, thereby reducing supplies of goods. If the unions succeed in raising money wages of their members to a very high level than the productivity of labour, this also tends to reduce production and supplies of goods.

3. *Natural Calamities.* Drought or floods is a factor which adversely affects the supplies of agricultural products. The latter, in turn, create shortages of food products and raw materials, thereby helping inflationary pressures.

4. *Artificial Scarcities.* Artificial scarcities are created by hoarders and speculators who indulge in black marketing. Thus they are instrumental in reducing supplies of goods and raising their prices.

5. *Increase in Exports.* When the country produces more goods for export than for domestic consumption, this creates shortages of goods in the domestic market. This leads to inflation in the economy.

6. *Lop-sided Production.* If the stress is on the production of comforts, luxuries, or basic products to the neglect of essential consumer goods in the country, this creates shortages of consumer goods. This again causes inflation.

7. *Law of Diminishing Returns.* If industries in the country are using old machines and outmoded methods of production, the law of diminshing returns operates. This raises cost per unit of production, thereby raising the prices of products.

8. *International Factors.* In modern times, inflation is a worldwide phenomenon. When prices rise in major industrial countries, their effects spread to almost all countries with which they have trade relations. Often the rise in the price of a basic raw material like petrol in the international market leads to rise in the price of all related commodities in a country.

6. MEASURES TO CONTROL INFLATION

We have studied above that inflation is caused by the failure of aggregate supply to equal the increase in aggregate demand. Inflation can, therefore, be controlled by increasing the supplies and reducing money incomes in order to control aggregate demand. The various methods are usually grouped under three heads: monetary measures, fiscal measures and other measures.

1. Monetary Measures

Monetary measures aim at reducing money incomes.

(a) Credit Control. One of the important monetary measures is monetary policy. The central bank of the country adopts a number of methods to control the quantity and quality of credit. For this purpose, it raises the bank rates, sells securities in the open market, raises the reserved ratio, and adopts a number of selective credit control measures, such as raising margin requirements and regulating consumer credit.

Monetary policy may not be effective in controlling inflation, if inflation is due to cost-push factors. Monetary policy can only be helpful in controlling inflation due to demand-pull factors.

(b) Demonetisation of Currency. However, one of the monetary measures is to demonetise currency of higher denominations. Such a measure is usually adopted when there is abundance of black money in the country.

(c) Issue of New Currency. The most extreme monetary measure is the issue of new currency in place of the old currency. Under this system, one new note is exchanged for a number of notes of the old currency. The value of bank deposits is also fixed accordingly. Such a measure is adopted when there is an excessive issue of notes and there is hyperinflation in the country. It is a very effective measure. But is inequitable for it hurts the small depositors the most.

2. Fiscal Measures

Monetary policy alone is incapable of controlling inflation. It should, therefore, be supplemented by fiscal measures. Fiscal measures are highly effective for controlling government expenditure, personal consumption expenditure, and private and public investment. The principal fiscal measures are the following :

(a) Reduction in Unnecessary Expenditure. The government should reduce unnecessary expenditure on non-development activities in order to curb inflation. This will also put a check on private expenditure which is dependent upon government demand for goods and services. But it is not easy to cut government expenditure. Though economy measures are always welcome but it becomes difficult to distinguish between essential and non-essential expenditure. Therefore, this measure should be supplemented by taxation.

(b) Increase in Taxes. To cut personal consumption expenditure, the rates of personal, corporate and

commodity taxes should be raised and even new taxes should be levied, but the rates of taxes should not be so high as to discourage saving, investment and production. Rather, the tax system should provide larger incentives to those who save, invest and produce more. Further, to bring more revenue into the tax-net, the government should penalise the tax evaders by imposing heavy fines. Such measures are bound to be effective in controlling inflation. To increase the supply of goods within the country, the government should reduce import duties and increase export duties.

(c) Increase in Savings. Another measure is to increase savings on the part of the people. This will tend to reduce disposable income with the people, and hence personal consumption expenditure. But due to the rising cost of living, people are not in a position to save much voluntarily. Keynes, therefore, advocated compulsory savings or what he called 'deferred payment' where the saver gets his money back after some years. For this purpose, the government should float public loans carrying high rates of interest, start saving schemes with prize money, or lottery for long periods, etc. It should also introduce compulsory provident fund, provident fund-cum-pension schemes, etc. compulsorily. All such measures to increase savings are likely to be effective in controlling inflation.

(d) Surplus Budgets. An important measure is to adopt anti-inflationary budgetary policy. For this purpose, the government should give up deficit financing and instead have surplus budgets. It means collecting more in reve-nues and spending less.

(e) Public Debt. At the same time, it should stop repayment of public debt and postpone it to some future date till inflationary pressures are controlled within the economy. Instead, the government should borrow more to reduce money supply with the public.

Like the monetary measures, fiscal measures alone cannot help in controlling inflation. They should be supplemented by monetary, non-monetary and non-fiscal measures.

3. Other Measures

The other types of measures are those which aim at increasing aggregate supply and reducing aggregate demand directly.

(a) To Increase Production. The following measures should be adopted to increase production: (*i*) One of the foremost measures to control inflation is to increase the prodution of essential consumer goods like food, clothing, kerosene oil, sugar, vegetable oils, etc. (*ii*) If there is need, raw materials for such products may be imported on preferential basis to increase the production of essential commodities. (*iii*) Efforts should also be made to increase productivity. For this purpose, industrial peace should be maintained through agreements with trade unions, binding them not to resort to strikes for some time. (*iv*) The policy of rationalisation of industries should be adopted as a long-term measure. Rationalisation increases productivity and production of industries through the use of brain, brawn and bullion. (*v*) All possible help in the form of latest technology, raw materials, financial help, subsidies, etc. should be provided to different consumer goods sectors to increase production.

(b) Rational Wage Policy. Another important measure is to adopt a rational wage and income policy. Under hyperinflation, there is a wage-price spiral. To control this, the government should freeze wages, incomes, profits, dividends, bonus, etc. But such a drastic measure can only be adopted for a short period and by antagonising both workers and industrialists. Therefore, the best course is to link increase in wages to increase in productivity. This will have a dual effect. It will control wages and at the same time increase productivity, and hence increase production of goods in the economy.

(c) Price Control. Price control and rationing is another measure of direct control to check inflation. Price control means fixing an upper limit for the prices of essential consumer goods. They are the maximum prices fixed by law and anybody charging more than these prices is punished by law. But it is difficult to administer price control.

(d) Rationing. Rationing aims at distributing consumption of scarce goods so as to make them available to a large number of consumers. It is applied to essential consumer goods such as wheat, rice, sugar, kerosene oil, etc. It is meant to stabilise the prices of necessaries and assure distributive justice. But it is very inconvenient for consumers because it leads to queues, artificial shortages, corruption and black marketing. Keynes did not

favour rationing for it "involves a great deal of waste, both of resources and of employment."

Conclusion. From the various monetary, fiscal and other measures discussed above, it becomes clear that to control inflation, the government should adopt all measures simultaneously. Inflation is like a hydra-headed monster which should be fought by using all the weapons at the command of the government.

7. EFFECTS OF INFLATION[8]

Inflation affects different people differently. This is because of the fall in the value of money. When prices rise or the value of money falls, some groups of the society gain, some lose and some stand in between. Broadly speaking, there are two economic groups in every society, the fixed income group and the flexible income group. People belonging to the first group lose and those belonging to the second group gain. The reason is that price movements in the case of different goods, services, assets, etc. are not uniform. When there is inflation, most prices are rising, but the rates of increase of individual prices differ much. Prices of some goods and services rise faster, of others slowly, and of still others remain unchanged. We discuss below the effects of inflation on redistribution of income and wealth, production, and on the society as a whole.

1. On Distribution of Income and Wealth

Inflation tends to increase inequalities in the distribution of income and wealth. The poor and middle classes suffer because their wages and salaries are more or less fixed but the prices of commodities continue to rise. They become more impoverished. On the other hand, businessmen, industrialists, traders, real estate holders, speculators, and others with variable incomes gain during rising prices. The latter category of persons become rich at the cost of the former group. There is an unjustified transfer of income and wealth from the poor to the rich. As a result, the rich roll in wealth and indulge in conspicuous consumption, while the poor and the middle classes live in abject misery and poverty. The effects of inflation on different groups of society are discussed below.

(1) *Debtors and Creditors.* During periods of rising prices, debtors gain, creditors lose. When prices rise, the value of money falls. Though debtors return the same amount of money but they pay less in terms of goods and services. This is because the value of money is less than when they borrowed the money. Thus the burden of the debt is reduced and debtors gain. On the other hand, creditors lose. Although they get back the same amount of money which they lent, they receive less in real terms, because the value of money falls. Thus there is transfer of wealth from creditors to debtors.

(2) *Salaried Persons.* Salaried workers such as clerks, teachers, and other white collar persons lose when there is inflation. The reason is that their salaries are slow to adjust when prices are rising.

(3) *Wage Earners.* Wage earners may gain or lose depending upon the speed with which their wages adjust to rising prices. If their unions are strong, they may get their wages linked to the cost of living index. In this way, they may be able to protect themselves from the bad effects of inflation. But the problem is that there is often a time-lag between the raising of wages by employers and the rise in prices. So workers lose because by the time wages are raised, the cost of living index may have increased further. But where the

unions have entered into contractual wages for a fixed period, the workers lose when prices continue to rise during the period of contract. On the whole, the wage earners are in the same position as the white collar persons.

(4) *Fixed Income Group.* Pensioners, recipients of interest and rent belong to the fixed income group. Pensioners get fixed pensions. Similarly, the rentier class consisting of interest and rent receivers get fixed payments. The same is the case with the holders of fixed interest-bearing securities, debentures and deposits. All such persons lose because they receive fixed payments, while the value of money continues to fall with rising prices.

(5) *Equity Holders or Investors.* Persons who hold shares or stocks of companies gain during inflation. For when prices are rising, business activities expand which increase profits of companies. As profits increase, dividends on equities also increase at a faster rate than prices. But those who invest in debentures, securities,

8. It is also known as effects of changes in the value of money.

bonds, etc. which carry a fixed interest rate lose during inflation because they receive a fixed sum while the purchasing power is falling.

(6) *Businessmen*. Businessmen of all types, such as producers, traders and real estate holders gain during periods of rising prices. Take producers first. When prices are rising, the value of their inventories (goods in stock) rise in the same proportion. So they profit more when they sell their stocked commodities. The same is the case with traders in the short-run. But producers profit more in another way. Their costs do not rise to the extent of the rise in the prices of their goods. This is because prices of raw materials and other inputs and wages do not rise immediately to the level of the price rise. The holders of real estates also profit during inflation because the prices of landed property increase much faster than the general price level.

(7) *Agriculturists*. Agriculturists are of three types : landlords, peasant proprietors, and landless agricultural workers. Landlords lose during rising prices because they get fixed rents. But peasant proprietors who own and cultivate their farms gain. Prices of farm products increase more than the cost of production. For prices of inputs and land revenue do not rise to the same extent as the rise in the prices of farm products. On the other hand, the landless agricultural workers are hit hard by rising prices. Their wages are not raisedby the farm owners, because trade unionism is absent among them. But the prices of consumer goods rise rapidly. So landless agricultural workers are losers.

Conclusion. Thus inflation redistributes income from wage earners and fixed income groups to profit recipients, and from creditors to debtors. In so far as wealth redistributions are concerned, the very poor and the very rich are more likely to lose than middle income groups. This is because the poor hold what little wealth they have in monetary forms and have few debts, whereas the very rich hold a substantial part of their wealth in bonds and have relatively few debts. On the other hand, the middle income groups are likely to be heavily in debt and hold some wealth in common stock as well as in real assets.

2. Effects on Production

When prices start rising production is encouraged. Producers earn windfall profits in the future. They invest more in anticipation of higher profits in the future. This tends to increase employment, production and income. But this is only possible up to the full employment level. Further increase in investment beyond this level will lead to severe inflationary pressure within the economy because prices rise more than production as the resources are fully employed. So inflation adversely affects production after the level of full employment. The adverse effects of inflation on production are discussed below.

(1) *Misallocation of Resources*. Inflation causes misallocation of resources when producers divert resources from the production of essential to non- essential goods from which they expect higher profits.

(2) *Change in the System of Transactions*. Inflation leads to change in the transactions pattern of producers. They hold a smaller stock of real money holdings against unexpected contingencies than before. They devote more time and attention to converting money into inventories or other financial or real assets. It means that time and energy are diverted from the production of goods and services and some resources are used wastefully.

(3) *Reduction in Production*. Inflation adversely affects the volume of production because the expectation of rising prices alongwith rising costs of inputs bring uncertainty. This reduces production.

(4) *Fall in Quality*. Continuous rise in prices creates a sellers' market. In such a situation, producers produce and sell sub-standard commodities in order to gain higher profits. They also indulge in adulteration of commodities.

(5) *Hoarding and Blackmarketing*. To profit more from rising prices, producers hoard stocks of their commodities. Consequently, an artificial scarcity of commodities is created in the market. The producers sell their products in the black market which increases inflationary pressures.

(6) *Reduction in Saving*. When prices rise rapidly, the propensity to save declines because more money is needed to buy goods and services than before. Reduced saving adversely affects investment and capital formation. As a result, production is hindered.

(7) *Hinders Foreign Capital*. Inflation hinders the inflow of foreign capital because the rising costs of materials and other inputs make foreign investments less profitable.

(8) *Encourage Speculation*. Rapidly rising prices create uncertainty among producers who indulge in

speculative activities in order to make quick profits. Instead of engaging themselves in productive activities, they speculate in every types of raw materials required in production.

3. Other Effects

Inflation leads to a number of other effects which are discussed as under.

(1) *Government*. Inflation affects the government in various ways. It helps the government in financing its activities through inflationary finance. As the money income of the people increases, government collects that in the form of taxes on incomes and commodities. So the revenues of the government increase during rising prices. Moreover, the real burden of the public debt decreases when prices are rising. But the government expenses also increase with rising production costs of public projects and enterprises. There is also increase in administrative expenses as prices and wages rise. On the whole, the government gains under inflation for rising wages and profits spread an illusion of prosperity within the country.

(2) *Balance of Payments*. Inflation affects adversely the balance of payments of a country. When prices rise more rapidly in the home country than in foreign countries, domestic products become costly compared to foreign products. This tends to increase imports and reduce exports, thereby making the balance of payments unfavourable for country.

(3) *Exchange Rate*. When prices rise more rapidly in the home country than in foreign countries, it lowers the exchange rate in relation to foreign currencies.

(4) *Collapse of the Monetary System*. If hyper-inflation persists and the value of money continues to fall many times in a day, it ultimately leads to the collapse of the monetary system, as happened in Germany after World War I.

(5) *Social*. Inflation is socially harmful. By widening the gulf between the rich and the poor, rising prices create discontentment among the masses. Pressed by the rising cost of living, workers resort to strikes which lead to loss in production. Lured by profit, people resort to hoarding, blackmarketing, adulteration, manufacture of substandard commodities, speculation, etc. Corruption spreads in every walk of life. All this reduces the efficiency of the economy.

(6) *Political*. Rising prices also encourage agitations and protests by political parties opposed to the government. And if they gather momentum and become unhandy they may bring the downfall of the government. Many governments have been sacrificed at the alter of inflation.

8. THE INFLATIONARY GAP

In his pamphlet *How to Pay for the War* published in 1940, Keynes explained the concept of the inflationary gap. It differs from his views on inflation given in his *General Theory*. In the *General Theory*, he started with underemployment equilibrium. But in *How to Pay for the War*, he began with a situation of full employment in the economy. He defined an inflationary gap as an excess of planned expenditure over the available output at pre-inflation or base prices. According to Lipsey, "The inflationary gap is the amount by which aggregate expenditure would exceed aggregate output at the full employment level of income." The classical economists explained inflation as mainly due to increase in the quantity of money, given the level of full employment. Keynes, on the other hand, ascribed it to the excess of expenditure over income at the full employment level. The larger the aggregate expenditure, the larger the gap and the more rapid the inflation. Given a constant average propensity to save, rising money incomes at full employment level would lead to an excess of demand over supply and to a consequent inflationary gap. Thus Keynes used the concept of the inflationary gap to show the main determinants that cause an inflationary rise of prices.

The inflationary gap is explained with the help of the following example:

Suppose the gross national product at pre-inflation prices is Rs. 200 crores.Of this Rs. 80 crores is spent by the government. Thus Rs. 120 (Rs. 200–80) crores worth of output is available to the public for consumption at pre-inflation prices. But the gross national income at current prices at full employment level is Rs. 250 crores. Suppose the government taxes away Rs. 60 crores, leaving Rs. 190 crores as disposable income. Thus Rs. 190 crores is the amount to be spent on the available output worth Rs. 120 crores, thereby creating an inflationary gap of Rs. 70 crores.

This inflationary gap model is illustrated as under :

1.	Gross national income at current prices	=	Rs. 250 Cr.
2.	Taxes	=	Rs. 60 Cr.
3.	Disposable income	=	Rs. 190 Cr.
4.	GNP at pre-inflation prices	=	Rs. 200 Cr.
5.	Government expenditure	=	Rs. 80 Cr.
6.	Output available for consumption at pre-inflation prices	=	Rs. 120 Cr.
	Inflationary gap (Item 3–6)	=	Rs. 70 Cr.

In reality, the enitre disposable income of Rs. 190 crores is not spent and a part of it is saved. If, say 20 per cent (Rs. 38 croes) of it is saved, then Rs. 152 crores (Rs. 190–Rs. 38 crores) would be left to create demand for goods worth Rs. 120 crores. Thus the actual inflationary gap would be Rs. 32 (Rs. 152–120) crores instead of Rs. 70 crores.

The inflationary gap is shown diagrammatically in Figure 5 where OY_F is the full employment level of income, 45^0 ine represents aggregate supply *AS* and $C + 1 + G$ line the desired level of consumption, investment and government expenditure (or aggregate demand curve). The economy's aggregate demand curve $(C+1+G) = AD$ intersects the 45^0 line (*AS*) at point *E* at the income level OY_1 which is greater than the full employment income level OY_F. The amount by which aggregate demand (Y_FA) exceeds the aggregate supply ($Y_F B$) at the full employment income level is the inflationary gap. This is *AB* in the figure. The excess volume of total spending when resources are fully employed creates inflationary pressures. Thus the inflationary gap leads to inflationary pressures in the economy which are the result of excess aggregate demand.[9]

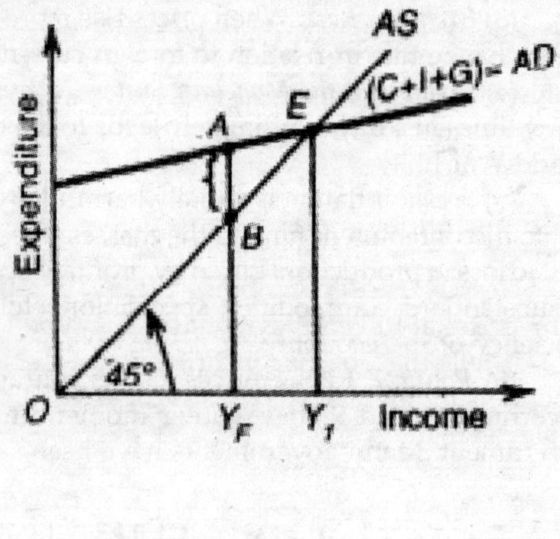

Fig. 5

HOW CAN THE INFLATIONARY GAP BE WIPED OUT ?

The inflationary gap can be wiped out by increase in savings so that the aggregate demand is reduced. But this may lead to deflationary tendencies.

Another solution is to raise the value of available output to match the disposable income. As aggregate demand increases, businessmen hire more labour to expand output. But there being full employment at the current money wage, they offer higher money wages to induce more workers to work for them. As there is already full employment, the increase in money wages leads to proportionate rise in prices. Moreover, output cannot be increased during the short run because factors are already fully emplcyed. So the inflationary gap can be closed by increasing taxes and reducing expenditure. Monetary policy can also be used to decrease the money stock. But Keynes was not in favour of monetary measures to control inflationary pressures within the economy.

ITS CRITICISMS

The concept of the inflationary gap has been severely criticised by economists.

9. For detailed causes of the inflationary gap, refer to section 5 in the present chapter.

The analysis of inflationary gap is based on the assumption that full employment prices are flexible upward. In other words, they respond to excess demand in the market for goods. It also assumes that money wages are sticky when prices are rising, but the share of profits in GNP increases. So this concept is related to excess demand inflation in which there is profit inflation. This has led to the mixing up of demand and cost inflations.

Bent Hansen also criticises Keynes for confining the infationary gap to the goods market only and neglecting the role of the factor market.

According to him, an inflationary gap is the result of excess demand in the goods market as well as in the factor market.The inflationary gap is a static analysis. But the inflationary phenomena are dynamic. To make them dynamic, Keynes himself suggested the introduction of time lags concerning receipts and expenditures of income. Koopmans has developed relationships between lags and the rate of price increase per unit of time. He has shown with the help of spending lags and wage-adjustment lags that the speed of inflation becomes smaller, that is the inflationary gap is narrowed.Holzman has criticised Keynes for applying the multiplier technique to a full employment situation. According to him, the multiplier technique is not adequate in periods of full employment and inflation. It abstracts from changes in the distribution of income. In a full employment situation, the share of one group in the national output can only be increased at the expense of another.

Another weakness of the inflationary-gap analysis is that it is related to flow concepts, such as current income, expenditure, consumption, and saving. In fact, the increase in prices at the full employment level is not confined to prices of current goods alone. But they also affect the prices of goods already produced. Further, the disposable income which is the difference between current income and taxes, may include idle balances from the income of previous periods.[10]

Its Importance

Despite these criticisms the concept of inflationary gap has proved to be of much importance in explaining rising prices at full employment level and policy measures in controlling inflation.

It tells that the rise in prices, once the level of full employment is attained, is due to excess demand generated by increased expenditures. But the output cannot be increased because all resources are fully employed in the economy. This leads to inflation. The larger the expenditure, the larger the gap and more rapid the inflation.

As a policy measure, it suggests reduction in aggregate demand to control inflation. For this, the best course is to have a surplus budget by raising taxes. It also favours saving incentives to reduce consumption expenditure. "The analysis of the inflationary gap in terms of such aggregates as national income, investment outlays and consumption expenditures clearly reveals what determines public policy with respect to taxes, public expenditures, savings campaigns, credit control, wage adjustment—in short, all the concievable anti-inflationary measures affecting the propensities to consume, to save and to invest which together determine the general price level."

9. DEFLATION

The opposite of inflation is deflation. It is "a state in which the value of money is rising i.e. prices are falling." It is usually associated with falling activity and employment. As pointed out by Coulborn, "Involuntary unemployment is the hall- mark of deflation." Deflation is caused when prices are falling more than proportionately to the output of goods and services in the economy as a result of decrease in the money supply.

Sometimes, deflation is confused with *disinflation*. Deflation is a situation when prices fall along with reduction in output and employment. Disinflation, on the other hand, is a situation when prices are reduced deliberately but output and employment remain unaffected. According to Coulborn, "A lowering of prices, incomes, and expenditures, when they would be beneficial, would be disinflation."

10. R.N. Mitra and H. Roy, *A Tract on Money*, 1958, p. 56.

Effects of Deflation. The effects of deflation are the reverse of inflation.[11]

Deflation affects different groups differently. Persons with fixed incomes such as workers, white collar salaried workers, pensioners, the rentier class, etc. gain because the value of money rises with falling prices. On the other hand, all types of producers such as industrialists and farmers lose with falling prices. Traders and equity holders also lose. Thus deflation affects adversely the distribution of income and wealth. When prices are falling, the purchasing power is increasing. So the lower, middle, and other classes with low incomes gain. On the other hand, businessmen, industrialists, traders, real estate holders, and others with variable incomes are hit hard and their profits decline with deflation. But this does not mean that there is improvement in income distribution. Rather, the low income groups suffer more because of the fall in employment and income. So both the better off and the worse off feel discontented under deflation.

Deflation also affects production adversely. With falling prices, production falls because income and employment are also declining and the aggregate demand is on the decline. Commodities start accumulating. Profits fall. Small firms close down. Unemployment spreads. This vicious circle of fall in demand, production, employment, income and aggregate demand leads to a depression.

The government also suffers under deflation. Revenues from direct and indirect taxes decline. The real burden of public debt increases. Development of the economy suffers because the government is unable to increase public expenditure.

Comparison between Inflation and Deflation

Of the two—inflation and deflation—which is better than the other? Of course, both are equally bad in their effects on the society. But inflation is the lesser evil. As pointed out by Keynes, "Inflation is unjust, deflation is inexpedient. Of the two deflation is worse."[12] Inflation brings about rising prices and redistribution of income in favour of the better-off classes. On the other hand, deflation leads to fall in output, employment and income. Of all the evils in a capitalist society, unemployment leading to poverty is the worst. We discuss below why Keynes regarded inflation as unjust and deflation inexpedient.

Inflation is unjust because it widens the gulf between the rich and the poor. It makes the rich richer at the cost of the poor. On the other hand, the poor are made poorer. The poor and low income classes suffer because their wages and salaries do not rise to the extent prices rise. It becomes difficult for them to make both ends meet with rising prices of consumer goods. On the other hand, businessmen, traders, industrialists, real estate holders, speculators, etc. gain because their profits and incomes increase much more than the rise in prices. So they are not affected by the fall in purchasing power when prices are rising. Thus it leads to inequalities of income and wealth.

When the government resorts to deficit financing to meet its rising expenditure during inflationary pressures, it increases the demand for goods and services. This deprives the people of the use of essential goods, thereby creating shortages and hardships for the common man.

Again, inflation is unjust because persons who save are losers in the long-run. When prices are rising, the value of money is falling. Since savers are mostly the low and middle income groups who save for a variety of reasons, they are the losers. Their savings lying in deposits are reduced automatically in real terms as inflationary pressures increase.

Inflation is unjust because it is socially harmful. People are lured to amass wealth by unscrupulous means. They, therefore, resort to hoarding, black-marketing, adulteration, manufacture of sub-standard commodities, speculation, etc. Corruption spreads in every walk of life. All this reduces the efficiency of the economy.

Deflation, on the other hand, *is inexpedient* because it reduces national income, output and employment. While inflation takes away half the bread of the poor, deflation impoverishes them by taking away the whole of it.

Deflation leads to mass unemployment because fall in production, prices and profits force producers and businessmen to close down their enterprises. Deflation is also inexpedient because falling prices lead to depression.

---

11. For a detailed account, write just on the basis of arguments *opposite* to that given under "Effects of Inflation."
13. J.M. Keynes, *A Tract on Monetary Reforms*, p. 45

All economic activities are stagnant. Factories are locked out. Trade and business are at a standstill. There is glut of commodities in all types of markets for goods and services. Even a bumper agricultural crop brings poverty to the peasantry. It is a situation of poverty in the midst of plenty.

Again, once the downward movement of prices begins, the economy plunges into a depression. But the downward movement of the economy is much faster as compared to the upward movement in a cycle. This makes the depression for longer period. Consequently, people suffer a lot and the economy also remains in a state of stagnation for long.

It is on these grounds that inflation is unjust and deflation is inexpedient. Keynes pointed out that "It is not necessary that we weigh one evil against the other. It is easier to agree that both are evils to be shunned." Still he preferred inflation as the lesser of the two evils. This is because inflation increases national output, employment and income, whereas deflation reduces national income and brings the economy backwards to a state of depression. Again, inflation is better than deflation because when it occurs the economy is already in a situation of full employment. On the other hand, there is always unemployment under deflation. And unemployment leading to poverty are the two scourges of mankind. Again inflation is a lesser evil than deflation. It redistributes income and wealth in favour of the rich. But deflation is a greater evil. Though it redistributes income in favour of the low income groups, yet it fails to benefit them because they are unemployed and have little income during deflation. In fact, they are reduced to paupers. It is also easier to control inflation than deflation through appropriate monetary, fiscal, and direct control measures. But to control deflation is a very difficult thing because of the presence of pessimism among producers and businessmen. So far as the increase in inequalities of income and wealth under inflation is concerned, it can be reduced by larger expenditure on social services by the government. The government is in a better position to improve the conditions of the masses under inflation than under deflation due to its larger spending capacity. Moreover, so long as inflation is mild, it helps the economy to grow. It is only when inflation takes the shape of hyper-inflation that it is dangerous. Still its effects on the economy may not be so injurious as under deflation.

10. CONTROL OF DEFLATION

Deflation can be controlled by adopting monetary and fiscal measures in just the opposite manner to control inflation. However, we discuss these measures in brief.

Monetary Policy. To control deflation, the central bank can increase the reserves of commercial banks through a cheap money policy. They can do so by buying securities and reducing the interest rate. As a result, their ability to extend credit facilities to borrowers increases. But the experience of the Great Depression tells us that in a serious depression when there is pessimism among businessmen, the success of such a policy is practically nil. In such a situation, banks are helpless in bringing about a revival. Since business activity is almost at a standstill, businessmen do not have any inclination to borrow to build up inventories even when the rate of interest is very low. Rather, they want to reduce their inventories by repaying loans already drawn from the banks. Moreover, the question of borrowing for long-term capital needs does not arise during deflation when the business activity is already at a very low level. The same is the case with consumers who faced with unemployment and reduced incomes do not like to purchase any durable goods through bank loans. Thus all that the banks can do is to make credit available but they cannot force businessmen and consumers to accept it. In the 1930s, very low interest rates and the piling up of unused reserves with the banks did not have any significant impact on the depressed economies of the world. Thus the success of monetary policy in controlling deflation is severely limited.

Fiscal Policy. Fiscal policy through increase in public expenditure and reduction in taxes tends to raise national income, employment, output, and prices. An increase in public expenditure during deflation increases the aggregate demand for goods and services and leads to a large increase in income via the multiplier process. While a reduction in taxes has the effect of raising disposable income thereby, increasing consumption and investment expenditures of the people. The government should increase its expenditure through deficit budgeting and reduction in taxes. The public expenditure includes expenditure on such public works as roads, canals, dams, parks, schools, hospitals and other buildings, etc. and on such relief measures as unemployment insurance, pensions, etc. Expenditure on public works creates demand for the products of private construction industries and helps in reviving them, while expenditure on relief measures stimulates the demand for consumer goods industries. Reduction in such taxes as corporate profits tax, income tax, and excise taxes tends to leave more income for spending and investment. Borrowing by the government to finance budget deficits utilises idle money lying with banks and financial institutions for investment purposes. But the effectiveness of public expenditure primarily depends upon the public works programme, its importance in the economic system, the volume and nature of public works and their planning and timing.

EXERCISES

1. What is inflation? Explain its economic effects on different people.
2. Discuss the causes of inflation. How can it be controlled?
3. Explain the inflationary gap. How can it be removed?
4. "Inflation is unjust and deflation is expedient." Discuss.
5. Distinguish between demand-pull inflation and cost-push inflation.
6. Write notes on: open and suppressed inflation, stagflation, hyper-inflation, true inflation, open inflation, sectoral inflation, disinflation and reflation.
7. Is inflation a purely monetary or non-monetary phenomenon? Give reasons in support of your answer.
8. Discuss the causes of inflation. How can it be controlled?

PART TWO

BANKING

CHAPTER 14

Commercial Banking

1. EVOLUTION, ORIGIN AND GROWTH OF BANKING

The word 'bank' is used in the sense of a commercial bank. It is of Germanic origin though some persons trace its origin to the French word 'Banqui' and the Italian word 'Banca'. It referred to a bench for keeping, lending, and exchanging of money or coins in the market place by money lenders and money changers.

There was no such word as 'banking' before 1640, although the practice of safe-keeping and savings flourished in the temple of Babylon as early as 2000 B.C. Chanakya in his *Arthashastra* written in about 300 B.C.mentioned about the existence of powerful guilds of merchant bankers who received deposits, and vanced loans and issued *hundis* (letters of transfer). The Jain scriptures mention the names of two bankers who built the famous Dilware Temples of Mount Abu during 1197 and 1247 A.D.

The first bank called the 'Bank of Venice' was established in Venice, Italy in 1157 to finance the monarch in his wars. The bankers of Lombardy were famous in England. But modern banking began with the English goldsmiths only after 1640. The first bank in India was the 'Bank of Hindustan' started in 1770 by Alexander & Co., an English agency house in Calcutta which failed in 1782 with the closure of the agency house. But the first bank in the modern sense was established in the Bengal Presidency as the Bank of Bengal in 1806.

History apart, it was the 'merchant banker' who first evolved the system of banking by trading in commodities than money. Their trading activities required the remittances of money from one place to another. For this, they issued 'hundis' to remit funds. In India, such merchant bankers were known as 'Seths'.

The next stage in the growth of banking was the goldsmith. The business of goldsmith was such that he had to take special precautions against theft of gold and jewellery. If he seemed to be an honest person, merchants in the neighbourhood started leaving their bullion, money and ornaments in his care. As this practice spread, the goldsmith started charging something for taking care of the money and bullion. As evidence for receiving valuables, he issues a receipt. Since gold and silver coins had no marks of the owner, the goldsmith started lending them. As the goldsmith was prepared to give the holder of the receipt and equal amount of money on demand, the goldsmith receipt became like cheques as a medium of exchange and a means of payment.

The next stage in the growth of banking is the moneylender. The goldsmith found that on an average the withdrawals of coins were much less than the deposits with him. So he started advancing the coins on loan by charging interest. As a safeguard, he kept some money in the reserve. Thus the goldsmith-money-lender became a banker who started performing the two functions of modern banking, that of accepting deposits and advancing loans.

2. MEANING OF BANK

Chamber's Twentieth Century Dictionary defines a bank as an "institution of the keeping, lending and exchanging, etc. of money." Economists have also defined a bank highlighting its various functions. According to Crowther, "The banker's business is to take the debts of other people to offer his own in exchange, and thereby create money."[1] A similar definition has been given by Kent who defines a bank as "an organisation whose principal operations are concerned with the accumulation of the temporarily idle money of the general public for the purpose of advancing to others for expenditure.[2] Sayers, on the other hand, gives a still more detailed definition of a bank thus: "Ordinary banking business consists of changing cash for bank deposits and bank deposits for cash; transferring bank deposits from one person or corporation (one 'depositor') to another; giving bank deposits in exchange for bills of exchange, government bonds, the secured or unsecured promises of businessmen to repay, etc."[3] Thus a bank is an institution which accepts deposits from the public and in turn advances loans by creating credit. It is different from other financial institutions in that they cannot create credit though they may be accepting deposits and making advances.

3. TYPES OF BANKS

Banks are of various types which are explained as under :

1. *Commercial Banks.* Commercial banks are those banks which perform all kinds of banking functions such as accepting deposits, advancing loans, credit creation, and agency functions. They are also called joint stock banks because they are organised in the same manner as joint stock companies. They usually advance shorty-term loans to customers. Of late, they have started giving medium term and long-term loans also. In India 20 major commercial banks have been nationalised, whereas in developed countries they are run like joint stock companies in the private sector. Some of the commercial banks in India are Andhra Bank, Canara Bank, Indian Bank, Punjab National Bank, etc.

2. *Exchange Banks.* Exchange banks are those banks which deal in foreign exchange and specialise in financing foreign trade. They are also called foreign exchange banks. In India, these exchange banks have their head offices located outside India. The Chartered Bank, and the Brindlays Bank have their head officers in England, whereas the American Express Bank, and Citi Bank have their head offices in the USA. These banks also render other services such as collecting and supplying information about the foreign customers, providing remittance facilities etc.

3. *Industrial Banks.* Industrial banks are those banks which provide medium term and long-term finance to industries for the purchase of land, machinery etc. They underwrite the debentures and shares of industries and also subscribe to them. In India, there are a number of financial institutions which perform the functions of industrial banks such as Industrial Development Bank of India, Industrial Finance Corporation of India, Industrial Credit and Investment Corporation of India, etc. Each State in India has its own State Financial Corporation. These institutions are also known as Development Banks.

4. *Agricultural Banks.* Agricultural banks are those banks which provide credit to farmers for short-term, medium-term and long-term needs. In India, commercial banks, regional rural banks and Agricultural Cooperative Banks provide short-term loans to farmers. Land Development Bank give medium-term and long-term loans to farmers on the mortgage of their land. The National Bank for Agriculture and Rural Development (NABARD) provides refinance facilities to all types of banks which give loans to agriculturists.

---

1. G. Crowther, *An Outline of Money,* p. 81.
2. R.P. Kent, *Money and Banking,* p. 76.
3. R.S. Sayers, *Modern Banking,* 7th edn., p. 22.

5. *Cooperative Banks.* Cooperative banks are those financial institutions which are organised on the principle of cooperation. They provide short-term and medium-term loans to their members. In rural areas, there are agricultural cooperative banks which accept deposits and give loans to agriculturists, rural artisans, etc. In urban areas, there are also cooperative banks which perform the functions of ordinary commercial banks but give loans to their members only. There is a State Cooperative Bank in every state of India with its branches at the district level known as the Central Cooperative Bank. The Central Cooperative Bank, in turn, has is branches both in urban and rural areas. Every State Cooperative bank is an apex bank which provides credit facilities to the Central Cooperative Banks. It mobilises financial resources from the richer sections of the urban population by accepting deposits and creating credit like commercial banks and borrowing from the money market. It also gets funds from the Reserve Bank of India.

6. *Savings Banks.* Savings banks help promote small savings, and mobilise them. They have been very successful in Japan and Germany. In India, post offices act as savings bank.

7. *Central Bank.* The central bank is the apex bank in a country which controls its monetary and banking structure. It is owned by the government of the country and operates in national interest. It regulates and issues currency, performs banking and a agency services for the state, keeps cash reserves of commercial banks, keeps and manages international currency, acts as the lender of the last resort, acts as a clearing house, and controls of credit. The Reserve Bank of India is the Central bank in India.

4. FUNCTIONS OF COMMERCIAL BANKS

Commercial banks perform a variety of functions which can be divided as : (1) accepting deposits; (2) advancing loans; (3) Credit creation; (4) financing foreign trade; (5) agency services; and (6) miscellaneous services to customers. These functions are discussed as follows :

(1) Accepting Deposits

This is the oldest function of a bank and the banker used to charge a commission for keeping the money in its custody when banking was developing as an institution. Nowadays a bank accepts three kinds of deposits from its customers. The first is the *savings* deposits on which the bank pays small interest to the depositors who are usually small savers. The depositors are allowed to draw their money by cheques up to a limited amount during a week or year. Businessmen keep their deposits in current accounts. They can withdraw any amount standing to their credit in current deposits by cheques without notice. The bank does not pay interest on such accounts but instead charges a nominal sum for services rendered to its customers. Current accounts are known as demand deposits. Deposits are also accepted by a bank in *fixed* or *time* deposits. Savers who do not need money for a stipulated period from 6 months to longer periods ranging up to 10 years or more are encouraged to keep it in fixed deposit accounts. The bank pays a higher rate of interest on such deposits. The rate of interest increases with the length of the time period of the fixed deposit. But there is always the maximum limit of the interest rate which can be paid. For instance, the interest rate on fixed deposits over five years is 11 per cent in India.

2. Advancing Loans

One of primary functions of a commercial banks is to advance loans to its customers. A bank lends a certain percentage of the cash lying in deposits on a higher interest rate than it pay on such deposits. This is how it earns profits and carries on its business. The bank advances loans in the following ways:

(a) Cash Credit. The bank advances loan to businessmen against certains specified securities. The amount of the loan is credited to the current account of the borrower. In cash of a new customer a loan account for the sum is opened. The borrower can withdraw money through cheques according to his requirements buy pays interest on the full amount.

(b) Call Loans. These are very short-term loans advanced to the bill brokers for not more than fifteen days. They are advance against first class bill or securities. Such loans can be recalled at a very short notice. In normal times they can also be renewed.

(c) Overdraft. A bank often permits a businessman to draw cheques for a sum greater than the balance lying in his current account. This is done by providing the overdraft facility up to a specific amount to the businessman. But he is charged interest only on the amount by which his current account is actually overdrawn and not by the full amount of the overdraft sanctioned to him by the banks.

(d) Discounting Bills of Exchange. If a creditor holding a bill of exchange wants money immediately, the bank provides him the money by discounting the bill of exchange. It deposits the amount of the bill in the current account of the bill-holder after deducting its rate of interest for the period of the loan which is not more than 90 days. When the bill of exchange matures, the bank gets its payment from the banker of the debater who accepted the bill.

3. Credit Creation

Credit creation is one of the most important functions of the commercial banks. Like other financial institutions, they aim at earning profits. For this purpose, they accept deposits and advance loans by keeping a small cash in reserve for day-to-day transactions. When a bank advances a loan, it opens and account in the name of the customer and does not pay him in cash but allows him to draw the money by cheque according to his needs. By granting a loan, the bank creates credit or deposit.

4. Financing Foreign Trade

A commercial bank finances foreign trade of its customers by accepting foreign bills of exchange and collecting them from foreign banks. It also transacts other foreign exchange business and buys and sells foreign currency.

5. Agency Services

A bank acts as an agent of its customers in collecting and paying cheques, bills of exchange, drafts, dividends, etc. It also buys and sells shares, securities, debentures, etc. for its customers. Further, it pays subscriptions, insurance premia, rent, electric and water bills, and other similar charges on behalf of its clients. It also acts as a trustee and executor of the property and will of its customers. Moreover, the bank acts as an income tax consultant to its clients. For some of these services, the bank charges a normal fee while it renders others free of charge.

6. Miscellaneous Services

Besides the above noted services, the commercial bank performs a number of other services. It acts as the custodian of the valuables of its customers by providing them lockers where they can keep their jewellery and valuable documents. It issues various forms of credit instruments, such as cheques, drafts, travellers' cheques, etc. which facilitate transactions. The bank also issues letter of credit and acts as a referee to its clients. It underwrites shares and debentures of companies and helps in the collection of funds from the public. Some commercial banks also publish journal which provide statistical information about the money market and business trends of the economy.

5. THE BALANCE SHEET OF A COMMERCIAL BANK

The balance sheet of a commercial bank provides a picture of its functioning. It is a statement which shows its assets and liabilities on a particular date at the end of one year. The assets are shown on the right-hand side and the liabilities on the left-hand side of the balance sheet. As in the case of a company, the assets and liabilities of a bank must balance. The balance sheet which every commercial bank in India is required to publish once in a year is shown as under :

TABLE 1. FORM OF BALANCE SHEET

Liabilities	Assets
1. Share Capital	1. Cash
2. Reserve Fund	2. Balances with the Central Bank and other banks.
3. Deposits	3. Money at call and Short-Notice
4. Borrowings from other banks	4. Bills Discounted and Purchased.
5. Bills Payable	5. Investments
6. Bills for collection	6. Loans, Advances, Cash Credits and Overdrafts.
7. Acceptances, Endorsements and other obligations	7. Liabilities of Customer for Acceptances. Endorsements and other Obligations.
8. Contingent Liabilities	8. Property, Furniture, Fixtures less Depreciation
9. Profit and Loss	9. Profit and Loss.

We analyse the distribution of assets and liabilities of a commercial bank on the basis of the division given in the above Table.

The Distribution of Assets

The assets of a bank are those items from which it receives income and profit. The *first* item on the assets side is the cash in liquid form consisting of coins and currency notes lying in reserve with it and in its branches. This is a certain percentage of its total liabilities which it is required to keep by law. Cash reserves do not yield income to the bank but are essential to satisfy the claims of its depositors. The *second* item is in the form of balances with the central bank and other banks. The commercial banks are required to keep a certain percentage of their time and demand deposits with the central bank. They are the assets of the bank because it can withdraw from them in cash in case of emergency or when the seasonal demand for cash is high. The *third* item, money at call and short notice, relates to very short-term loans advanced to bill brokers, discount houses and acceptance houses. They are repayable on demand within fifteen days. The banks charge low rate of interest on these loans. The *fourth* item of assets relates to bills discounted and purchased. The bank earns profit by discounting bills of exchange and treasury bills of 90 days duration. Some bills of exchange are accepted by a commercial bank on behalf of its customers which i ultimately purchases. They are a liability but they are included under assets because the bank can get them rediscounted from the central bank in case of need. The *fifth* item, investments by the bank in government securities, state bonds and industrial shares, yields a fixed income to the banks. The bank can sell its securities when there is need for more cash. The *sixth* item relating to loans and advances is the most profitable source of bank assets as the bank changes interest at a rate higher than the bank rate. The bank makes advances on the basis of cash credits and overdrafts and loans on the basis of recognised securities. In the *seventh* item are included liabilities of the bank's customers which the bank has accepted and endorsed on their behalf. They are the assets of the bank because the liabilities of customers remain in the custody of the bank. The bank charges a nominal commission for all acceptances and endorsements which is a source of income. The *eighth* item relates to the value of permanent assets of the bank in the form of property, furniture, fixtures, etc. They are shown in the balance sheet after allowing for depreciation every year. The *last* item includes profits retained by the bank after paying corporation tax and profits to shareholders.

The Distribution of Liabilities

The liabilities of a commercial banks are claims on it. These are the items which form the sources of its funds. Of the liabilities, the share capital of the bank is the *first* item which is contributed by its shareholders and is a liability to them. The *second* item is the reserve fund. It consists of accumulated resources which are meant to meet contiguencies such as losses in any year. The bank is required to keep a certain percentage of its annual profits in the reserve fund. The reserve fund is also a liability to the shareholders. The *third* item compresses both the time and demand deposits. Deposits are the debts of the bank to its customers. They are the main source from which the bank gets funds for investment and are indirectly the source of its income. By keeping a certain percentage of its time and demand deposits in cash the bank lends the remaining amount on interest.

Borrowings from other banks is the *fourth* item. The bank usually borrows secured and unsecured loans from the central bank. Secured loans are on the basis of some recognised securities, and unsecured loans out of its reserve funds lying with the central bank. The *fifth* item bills payable refer to the bills which the bank pays out of its resources. The *sixth* items relates to bills for collection. These are the bills of exchange which the bank collects on behalf of its customers and credits the amount to their accounts. Hence it is a liability to the bank. The *seventh* item is the acceptance and endorsement of bills of exchange by the bank on behalf of its customers. These are the claims on the bank which it has to meet when the bills mature. The *eighth* item contingent liabilities relates to those claims on the bank which are unforeseen such as outstanding forward exchange contracts, claims on acknowledge debts, etc. In the *last* item, profit and loss, are shown profits payable to the shareholders which are a liability on the bank.

The various items of the balance sheet shown in Table 1 are a rough indicator of the assets and liabilities of commercial banks. The balance sheet of a particular bank shown its financial soundness. By studying the balance sheets of the major commercial banks of a country, one can also know the trend of the monetary market. "The bank balance sheet reflects bank credit extension on its asset side in loans and investments, and on the liabilities side reflects the bank's operations as an intermediary in time deposits and its role as an element in the nation's monetary system in demand deposits."

6. ROLE OF COMMERCIAL BANKS IN A DEVELOPING COUNTRY

Besides performing the usual commercial banking functions, banks in developing countries play an effective role in their economic development. The majority of people in such countries are poor, unemployed and engaged in traditional agriculture. There is acute shortage of capital. People lack initiative and enterprise. Means of transport are undeveloped. Industry is depressed. The commercial banks help in overcoming these obstacles and promoting economic development. The role of a commercial bank in a developing country is discussed as under.

1. *Mobilising Saving for Capital Formation.* The commercial banks help in mobilising savings through network of branch banking. People in developing countries have low incomes but the banks induce them to save by introducing variety of deposit schemes to suit the needs of individual depositors. They also mobilise idle savings of the few rich. By mobilising savings, the banks channelise them into productive investments. Thus they help in the capital formation of a developing country.

2. *Financing Industry.* The commercial banks finance the industrial sector in a number of ways. They provide short-term, medium-term and long-term loans to industry. In India they provide short-term loans. Income of the Latin American countries like Guatemala, they advance medium-term loans for one to three years. But in Korea, the commercial banks also advance long-term loans to industry. In India, the commercial banks undertake short-term and medium-term financing of small scale industries, and also provide hire-purchase finance. Besides, they underwrite the shares and debentures of large scale industries. Thus they not only provide finance for industry but also help in developing the capital market which is undeveloped in such countries.

3. *Financing Trade.* The commercial banks help in financing both internal and external trade. The banks provide loans to retailers and wholesalers to stock goods in which they deal. They also help in the movement of goods from one place to another by providing all types of facilities such as discounting and accepting bills of exchange, providing overdraft facilities, issuing drafts, etc. Moreover, they finance both exports and imports of developing countries by providing foreign exchange facilities to importers and exporters of goods.

4. *Financing Agriculture.* The commercial banks help the large agricultural sector in developing countries in a number of ways. They provide loans to traders in agricultural commodities. They open a network of branches in rural areas to provide agricultural credit. They provide finance directly to agriculturists for the marketing of their produce, for the modernisation and mechanisation of their farms, for providing irrigation facilities, for developing land, etc. They also provide financial assistance for animal husbandry, dairy farming, sheep breeding, poultry farming, pisciculture and horticulture. The small and marginal farmers and landless agricultural workers, artisans and petty shopkeepers in rural areas are provided financial assistance through

the regional rural banks in India. These regional rural banks operate under a commercial bank. Thus the commercial banks meet the credit requirements of all types of rural people.

5. *Financing Consumer Activities.* People in underdeveloped countries being poor and having low incomes do not possess sufficient financial resources to buy durable consumer goods. The commercial banks advance loans to consumers for the purchase of such items as houses, scooters, fans, refrigerators, etc. In this way, they also help in raising the standard of living of the people in developing countries by providing loans for consumptive activities.

6. *Financing Employment Generating Activities.* The commercial banks finance employment generating activities in developing countries. They provide loans for the education of young persons studying in engineering, medical and other vocational institutes of higher learning. They advance loans to young entrepreneurs, medical and engineering graduates, and other technically trained persons in establishing their own business. Such loan facilities are being provided by a number of commercial banks in India. Thus the banks not only help inhuman capital formation but also in increasing entrepreneurial activities in developing countries.

7. *Help in Monetary Policy.* The commercial banks help the economic development of a country by faithfully following the monetary policy of the central bank. In fact, the central bank depends upon the commercial banks for the success of its policy of monetary management in keeping with requirements of a developing economy.

Thus the commercial banks contribute much to the growth of a developing economy by granting loans to agriculture, trade and industry, by helping in physical and human capital formation and by following the monetary policy of the country.

EXERCISES

1. What is a commercial bank? Discuss the various functions performed by a bank.
2. Draw an imaginary balance sheet of a commercial bank and explain the items mentioned therein.
3. Discuss the role of a commercial bank in promoting economic development.

Chapter 15

Organisation and Structure of Commercial Banks

1. INTRODUCTION

Commercial banks differ in their organisation and structure from country to country. The two principal banking systems are the unit banking and the branch banking. The unit banking is peculiar to the USA. Branch banking, on the other hand, is found in the majority of countries such as England, Australia, Canada, New Zealand, etc. Two other important types are the group banking and the chain banking which are also found in the USA. We discuss below these different systems of banking.

2. UNIT BANKING

Unit banks are independent, one-office banks. Their operations are confined in general to a single office. The existence of unit banking in the USA is due to legal restrictions which prevent the growth of monopoly in banking. Some unit banks have grown to large sizes but they operate under severe restrictions which limit or prohibit the establishment of branches. The unit banks operate in small towns and cities and are called country banks and city banks respectively. All unit banks are linked together by a correspondent bank relationship. A country bank has deposits in city banks, and city banks have deposits in branch banks in the same and other big cities like New York and Chicago.

MERITS OF UNIT BANKING

The unit banks, being independent and one-office banks, possess certain advantages :

1. *Efficient Working.* A unit bank works very efficiently and provides prompt service to its customers. For like a departmental store in a locality, it has competitors in other unit banks.

2. *Personal Relations.* Since its organisers and other staff are generally local people, they have personal relations which help in mobilising larger resources for the bank.

3. *Quick Decisions.* They are able to meet the financial requirements of the people promptly and efficiently. There is always on-the-spot decision-making by the bank management.

4. *Less Irregularities.* There are less chances of fraud and irregularities under the unit banking because of the close supervision and control of the management.

5. *Local Utilisation of Deposits.* Local deposits are utilised by a unit bank on the development of the same locality and they are not to be transferred to other towns as is done under branch banking.

6. *Economies.* The unit banking operations being on a small scale, they are free from the diseconomies which arise in large scale banking operations.

7. *Prevention of Monopoly.* Unit banking helps in the prevention of monopoly banking.

8. *Enjoy Merits of Branch Banking.* The unit banks also enjoy the advantages of branch banking as they are connected with big banks through correspondent banking system in the USA.

Demerits of Unit Banking

Despite these merits, unit banking suffers from certain disadvantages :

1. *Failure to Spread Risks.* The unit banking system suffers from its failure to spread risks. As the unit banking operations are localised in a particular area, the failure of a big party to repay the loan in time may bring disaster to the bank.

2. *Limited Resources.* Unit bank has another disadvantage that it has limited resources at its disposal. So, in the event of a financial or economic crisis, if its depositors start withdrawing their money, the bank fails. This is what actually happened in the USA during the Great Depression of 1930s when 5000 banks failed and an additional 1200 were absorbed by larger banks.

3. *Non-diversified Services.* The unit bank cannot provide diversified banking services to its customers because of its inability to establish branches and higher costs. For example, businessmen may prefer a branch of their city bank in the local business centre to facilitate their business transactions

4. *No Economies of Large Operations.* The unit banking system cannot have the advantages of a large scale banking in that it cannot recruit more efficient and highly paid staff, and cannot enjoy the economies of large scale and intensive specialisation and division of labour.

5. *Lack of Fund Mobility.* An important argument against the unit banking system is that there is lack of mobility of funds within the country. The unit banks do not attract funds from outside their areas. On the other hand, there is every likelihood of local funds flowing out to the large money markets in pursuit of higher interest rates. This is because the unit banks are unable to pay high interest rates.

6. *Non-Economic Considerations.* A unit bank may not advance loans strictly on economic considerations thereby jeopardising the interests of its depositors. It may be pressurised to give loans to a few local businessmen who may not be creditworthy.

7. *Backward Areas.* Since a unit bank has limited resources at its disposal, it cannot be opened in backward towns. As a result, such areas continue to remain backward.

8. *Unhealthy Competition.* As every company starts a unit bank in a large town, it leads to unhealthy competition among different unit banks with the result that very few survive in the long run.

9. *Remittance of Funds.* As a unit bank has no branches at other towns, it has to depend upon the correspondent banks for remittance of funds. This is very expensive.

These demerits have led to modification of the banking laws in the USA whereby branch banking has been permitted in a number of states, though branch banking across state boundaries is still prohibited.

3. BRANCH BANKING

Branch banking is the most prevalent banking system in the majority of countries. Under this system, a big bank has a number of branches in different parts of the country and even many branches within a cosmopolitan city like Mumbai, Kolkata, Chennai or New Delhi. Small commercial banks also carry on branch banking operations within a state or region. In the USA, branch banking is confined to the states. Accordingly, a number of banks have merged under a holding company to carry on branch banking business efficiently and profitably.

Merits of Branch Banking

The branch banking system has many advantages which make this system superior to the unit banking system.

1. *Spreading of Risks.* The branch banking has the advantage of spreading risks geographically and industrially. If branches in a particular area suffer losses due to recession in industries located there, these losses can be offset by profits from prosperous areas.

2. *Large Scale Organisation.* The branch banking system has the advantages of large scale organisation because a large bank is able to recruit efficient and trained staff and pay better than the unit banks. It can thus realise the advantages of intensive specialisation and division of labour by carrying out separate banking operations under different staff.

3. *Economy in Reserves.* The branch banking system helps in economising the use of cash reserves. It can move cash reserves from one branch where they are less needed to the other where they are more required in times of necessity.

4. *Advances on Merits.* Under this system, loans are advanced on merits than on personal or local considerations. There are set rules under which loans are advanced to customers.

5. *Diversification of Operations.* Under the branch banking system, there is diversification of banking operations. Big banks can provide banking facilities to trade, industry, businessmen and the common man at cheaper rates and more efficiently than unit banks because they possess larger financial resources.

6. *Equitable Distribution of Funds.* As a corollary to the above, big banks can provide banking facilities throughout the length and breadth of the country, whether it is a small village or a big city, and a backward or a prosperous area. It is in this way that branch banking also helps in the equitable distribution of funds within the country.

7. *Proper Utilization of Funds.* A big bank with large number of bank branches is able to utilise its funds most profitably. It can carry out its banking operations with lower cash reserves in each branch and lend the remaining amount to its customers. In case the need arises for excess cash in one branch, it can be met by transferring funds from some other branch. Thus, the commercial banks earn larger profits under branch banking than under unit banking.

8. *Remittance Facilities.* With its network of branches spread in all parts of the country, a big bank can provide cheaper and better remittance facilities to its clients than under the unit banking system having correspondent banking relations.

9. *Large Investments.* Under the branch banking system a big bank with large financial resources is in a better position to choose securities and make large investment in keeping with the principles of safety and liquidity.

10. *Effective Central Bank Control.* The central bank of the country can control the banks more effectively under the branch banking system than under the unit banking. It is easier to control the credit policies of a few large banks than those of numerous unit banks.

Demerits of Branch Banking

The branch banking has its critics who point towards a number of disadvantages of this system. They are discussed as under :

1. *Bureaucratisation.* Under the branch banking system, there is bureaucratisation and the management of all the branches is under the control of the head office, this leads to delay in taking, prompt decisions by the branch managers. They have to refer all cases above a certain limit for advances to the head office.

2. *Do not Meet Local Needs.* The branch managers are not able to meet the borrowing needs of the local business community as efficiently and sympathetically as the unit banks. This is because the branch bank managers stay in one locality only temporarily and have to operate under rules set by the head office.

3. *Monopoly Banking.* The branch banking system leads to the establishment of nonopoly banking in the country. When a few big banks open branches in all parts of the country, they limit competition in banking and ultimately lead to the establishment of monopoly in the banking industry. Funds tend to concentrate in a few banks. It may further lead to concentration of economic power in industry and even to political power by such financially powerful banks.

4. *Lax Supervision.* As big bank has a number of branches spread throughout the country, it is dlfficult to manage and supervise them efficiently. Control becomes lax, the banking services suffer and the clients are hit

hard.

5. *Transfer of Funds.* Another disadvantage of branch banking is that deposits of one area may be used for financing business and industry in other areas where the banks expect to earn more by lending. This may adversely affect the former area if it is already backward.

6. *Fear of Loss.* If branch banking spreads on a large scale, some of the branches may run under losses due to bad debts and low mobilisation of deposits. Such a situation may lead to huge loss to the bank thereby leading to its failure.

7. *Unhealthy Competition.* Branch banking leads to competition among different banks in establishing branches at various places. This tendency leads to unnecessary increase in expenses. The usual practice is for the different commercial banks to open branches in the same locality in big towns and cities. This leads to concentration of branches, thereby resulting in unhealthy competition and rivalry. Sometimes, the banks give inducements in the form of gifts and provide free outstation services to attract customers. Such devices increase bank expenses and lead to wastage of national resources.

Conclusion. Despite demerits, the branch banking system is preferred to the unit banking in developing countries like India. In poor countries, the unit banking cannot be successful. There is need to develop agriculture, industry and trade which is only possible through the branch banking system with its large financial resources. Further, for a balanced regional development, it is through branch banking that funds can be utilised from branches in developed regions to backward regions. However, the disadvantages of the. branch banking can be avoided through their proper regulation by the central bank of the country. If the banks fail to follow the central bank, they can be nationalised by the government. This is what has been done in India and a few other developing countries.

4. GROUP BANKING

Group banking is part of the USA banking system. It is a type of multiple office banking consisting of two or more banks under the control of a holding company, which itself may or may not be a bank. The term "bank holding Company" is based on 25 per cent ownership or control of two or more banks. The holding company is called the parent company and the banks under the parent company are called operating companies. The parent company controls and manages the operating banks under the group but each bank continues to keep its separate entity or name. The parent company may also be an operating bank.

MERITS OF GROUP BANKING

The group banking system has certain advantages :

1. *Pooling of Resources.* The parent company pools the resources of the group and helps the group banks to provide large loans and advances.

2. *Do not need large Cash Reserves.* The banks in the group need not keep large cash reserves for they can transfer funds to each other when the need arises.

3. *Increase in Efficiency.* The efficiency of the group increases when the parent company provides such specialised services as research, advice on investments, loans and legal matters to all the banks in the group.

4. *Economies of Large Operations.* The group also gains from the economies of large scale banking operations when the parent company advertises, makes bulk purchases, and hires the services of experts on behalf of the banks in the group.

5. *No Mergers.* As already noted above, under the group banking system the operating companies do not merge with the parent company and continue to keep their separate entities but benefit from all the advantages of a large scale organisation.

6. *No Unhealthy Competition.* Group banking avoids unhealthy competition among banks when they are under one holding company.

DEMERITS OF GROUP BANKING

Despite the above merits, the group banking system suffers from certain disadvantages:

1. *Monopoly Banking.* The group banking system is a step towards monopoly banking which is not healthy from the economic view point.

2. *Inefficient System.* The operating banks may not follow the guidelines and policies laid down by the parent company from time to time. This may lead to inefficiency.

3. *Chain Reaction.* If the business of one member declines, it may adversely affect the business of other members of the group.

4. *Diversion of Funds.* If the parent company is not an operating banking company, it may divert the funds of the group in furthering its own interests. This may prove harmful for the entire operating group which may be starved of funds and ultimately bring disaster to the group.

5. CHAIN BANKING

Chain banking is also a USA banking system. It is a banking system where the same individual or group of individuals controls two or more banks, as against control by a holding company under group banking. This is done by stock ownership in two or more banks. Stockholders directly or through their nominees exercise control of competing banks. The chain banking system possesses almost the same advantages and disadvantages as that of the group banking discussed above.

6. MIXED BANKING

The mixed banking system is one in which the commercial banks advance both short-term and long-term loans to commerce and industry. Under the British banking system, the commercial banks give short-term loans to commerce and industry. But in other European countries like Germany, the Netherlands, Hungary and Belgium, the mixed banking system operates whereby the commercial banks lend money to meet the short-term and long-term requirements of industry and commerce. Mixed banks perform the usual banking functions and also provide industrial finance.

Merits of Mixed Banking

The mixed banking system has some *advantages* which the British type "pure" banking system lacks. They are as follows :

1. *Provide Initial Capital.* The mixed banks help the establishment of industries by providing them initial capital for long-term.

2. *Underwrite Shares and Debentures.* They undertake to underwrite the equity shares and debentures of industries and thus help them in mobilising public savings for capital formation.

3. *Higher Profits.* The profits of the commercial banks increase when they themselves invest in the long-term securities of industries. For they earn high interest rates on them.

4. *Help in Feasibility Reports.* The industries stand to gain when such banks render expert advice in preparing feasibility reports and in financial matters.

5. *Help in Industrialisation.* The granting of long-term loans to industries by the mixed banks helps in the rapid industrial development of the economy.

6. *Advice to Customers.* Mixed banks help customers by giving valuable advice on investments in shares and debentures of industrial concerns.

Demerits of Mixed Banking

The mixed banking system has the following disadvantages that is why it is not practised in England, the USA and some of the other developed countries :

1. *Against the Liquidity Principle.* It is against the banking principle of liquidity of bank assets. When the bank advances long-term loans to industries, its large funds are locked up which prevent the bank to meet the short-term requirements of trade and commerce.

2. *Heavy Losses.* If there is depression in economy it is not possible for industries to repay the loans. This leads to failure of the banks if they have lent vast sums to industries. This actually happened during the Great Depression of 1930s. Even a recession in industries which have borrowed capital will adversely affect the mixed banks leading to heavy losses.

3. *Fear of Overinvestment.* During a boom mixed banks overinvest their funds in industries in order to earn more profits. They may also indulge in trade in securities and do speculation. Such operations may lead to huge losses if prices of securities fall suddenly.

Despite many advantages and few disadvantages of mixed banking, many banks failed in America, France, Germany and other European countries because they operated as mixed banks and industries failed to repay the loans.

7. CORRESPONDENT BANKING

Correspondent banking is again an important feature of USA banking system. The USA is geographically a very big country where there are thousands of banks which operate in restricted areas. The various types of banks are able to operate efficiently through a correspondent relationship with one-another. The country banks have deposits with city banks and city banks have deposits in state banks in the same and other cities. The centre of correspondent banking is New York city, followed by Chicago and other regional centres in big American cities. Many banks have deposits fn more than one centre and correspondent banks in one centre have correspondent relations with banks in other centres.

When a small bank maintains its deposits with a big correspondent bank having a network of branches, the latter provides such services to the former as extending large credit facilities, facilitating foreign exchange transactions, cheque clearing and collection, purchase and sale of securities, etc. It also provides a wide range of other services to small banks which include reports on the state of the economy, advice on portfolio management, borrowing from FRS in small lots, sharing computer facilities, etc.

MERITS OF CORRESPONDENT BANKING

This unique American banking system has certain advantages for the country (unit) banks, the city (branch) banks and for the economy. They are as follows :

1. *Rapid Movement of Funds.* Under correspondent banking, cheques of country banks are cleared and collected without much delay. Thus there is a rapid movement of funds from one area to the other. This system facilitates trade and industry.

2. *Help in Dealing in Securities.* Correspondent city banks help the country banks in the buying and selling of securities.

3. *Help in Providing Finance.* Such banks also help the country banks in financing loans and advances by providing them funds.

4. *Help in Transfer of Funds.* They also accept or draw drafts on the country banks and thus help in transferring funds.

5. *Help in Foreign Exchange Transactions.* They facilitate foreign exchange transactions of their correspondent banks.

6. *Increase in Mobility of Credit.* They increase the geographical mobility of credit when business is transacted from one area to the other through these banks.

7. *Render Technical Advice.* City banks also render technical advice to the country banks in installing new machines, providing legal advice, and in making investments in securities and advancing loans.

8. *Provide Information.* They also provide information about the general and economic conditions of the country to the unit banks regularly.

9. *Gain in Deposits and Business.* The correspondent city banks themselves gain in deposits and new business by entering into correspondent relations with the country banks. On the basis of the deposits, the city banks are able to profit more.

10. *Increase in Balances.* Balances in correspondent banks tend to increase manifold which provide liquid

assets with the result that they can be utilised as a ready source of funds for all banks engaged in corresponding relations. They can also be used as legal reserves with the Federal Reserve Banks and can be withdrawn in case of need.

11. *Gains to the Economy.* The whole economy benefits from the correspondent banking system. There is no fear of monopoly banking. The general public can easily transfer funds from one part of the country to the other. People can use travellers' cheques issued even by a small unit bank throughout the country. Foreign exchange business can easily be transacted and investments in stocks, shares etc. can be made even from the remotest corner of the vast American mainland through a tiny village bank. Thus the correspondent banking system facilitates ail types of transactions and helps trade and industry.

Its Demerits

The only *dement* of this system is that the correspondent city banks may make excess advances on the basis of the deposits of their correspondent country banks. They may thus operate against the principles of safety and liquidity and harm not only the country banks but also the entire banking structure in the economy.

EXERCISES

1. Distinguish between unit and branch banking. Which one would you suggest for a country like India? Give reasons.
2. Discuss the relative merits and demerits of unit and branch banking systems.
3. What is the difference between group and chain banking? Give the merits and demerits of group banking.
4. Explain the mixed banking system. Why is it preferred to 'pure' banking system?
5. What is the correspondent banking? Explain its role in the American banking system.

CHAPTER 16

Commercial Bank Policies and Principles

1. INTRODUCTION

The main aim of a commercial bank is to seek profit like any other institution. Its capacity to earn profit depends upon its investment policy. Its investment policy, in turn, depends on the manner in which it manages its investment portfolio. Thus "commercial bank investment policy emerges from a straight froward application of the theory of portfolio management to the particular circumstances of commercial bank."[1] Portfolio management refers to the prudent management of a bank's assets and liabilities in order to seek some optimum combination of income or profit, liquidity, and safety.

When a bank operates, it acquires and disposes of income-earning assets. These assets *plus* the bank's cash make up what is known as it *portfolio. A* bank's *earning assets* consist of (*a*) securities issued by the central and state governments, local bodies and government institutions, and (*b*) financial obligations, such as promissory notes, bills of exchange, etc. issues by firms. There earning assets constitute between one-fourth and one-third of a commercial bank's total assets. Thus a bank's earning assets are an important source of its income. The manner in which banks manage their portfolios, that is acquiring and disposing of their earning assets, can have important affects on the financial markets, on the borrowing and spending practices of households and businesses, and on the economy as a whole.

In this chapter, we study the objective, principles and theories of portfolio management and essentials of a sound banking system.

2. OBJECTIVES OF PORTFOLIO MANAGEMENT

There are three main objectives of potfolio management which a wise bank follows: liquidity, safety and income. The three objectives are opposed to each other. To achieve on the bank will have to sacrifice the other objectives. For example, if the banks seeks high profit, it may have to sacrifice some safety and liquidity. If it seeks more safety and liquidity it may have to give up some income. We analyse these objectives one by one in relation to the other objectives.

1. J.M. Culbertson, *op.cit.*,p. 144.

1. Liquidity

A commercial bank needs a higher degree of liquidity in its assets. The liquidity of an assets refers to the ease and certainty with which it can be turned into cash. The liabilities of a bank are large in relation to its assets because it holds a small proportion of its assets in cash. But its liabilities are payable on demand at a short notice. Therefore, the bank must hold a sufficiently large proportion of its assets in the form of cash and liquid assets for the purpose of profitability. If the bank keeps liquidity the uppermost, its profit will below. On the other hands, if it ignores liquidity and aims at earning more, it will be disastrous for it. Thus in managing its investment portfolio a bank must strike a balance between the objectives of liquidity and profitability. The balance must be achieved with a relatively high degree of safety. This is because banks are subject to a number of restrictions that limit the size of earning assets they can acquire.

The nature of conflict between liquidity and profitability is illustrated in Figure 1 where earning assets are taken on the horizontal axis and cash on the vertical axis. *CE* is the *investment possibility line* which shows all combinations of cash and earning assets. For instance, point *A* denotes a combination of *OM* of cash and *OS* of earning assets; and point *B* shows *ON* of cash and *OT* of earning assets. Each bank seeks to obtain its optimum point along the line *CE* which will be a combination of cash and earning assets so as to achieve the highest possible level of earnings consistent with its liquidity and safety.

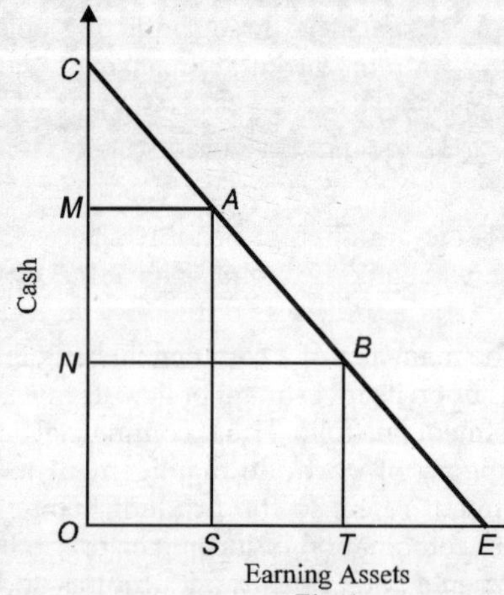

Fig. 1

Many types of assets are available to a commercial bank with varying degrees of liquidity. The most liquid of assets is money in cash. The next most liquid assets are deposits with the central bank, treasury bills and other short-term bills issues by the central and state governments and large firms, and call loans to other banks, firms, dealers and brokers in government securities. The less liquid assets are the various types of loans to customers and investments in long term bonds and mortgages. Thus the principle sources of liquidity of a bank are its borrowings from the other banks and the central bank and from the sales of the assets.

But the amount of liquidity which the bank can have depends on the availability and cost of borrowings. If it can borrow large amounts at any time without difficulty at a low cost (interest rate), it willhod very little liquid assets. But if it is uncertain to borrow funds or the cost of borrowing is high, the bank will keep more liquid assets in its portfolio.

2. Safety

A commercial bank always operates under conditions of uncertainty and risk. It is uncertain about the amount and cost of funds it can acquire and about its income in the future. Moreover, it face two types of risks. The first is the market risk which results from the decline in the prices of debt obligations when the market rate of interest rises. The second is the risk by default where the bank fears that the debtors are not likely to repay the principle and pay the interest in time. "This risk is largely concentrated in customer loans, where banks have a special function to perform, and bank loans to businesses and bank mortgage loans are among the high grade loans of these typs."[2]

In the light of these risks, a commercial bank has to maintain the safety of its assets. It is also prohibited by law to assume large risks because it is required to keep a high ration of its fixed liabilities to its total assets with itself and also with the central bank in the form of cash. But if the bank follows the safety principle strictly by holding only the safest assets it will not be able to create more credit. It will thus lose customers to other banks and its income will also be very low. One the other hand, if the bank takes too much risk, it may be highly

2. J.M. Culbertson, *op.cit.*

harmful for it. Therefore, a commercial bank "must estimate the amount of risks attached to the various types of available assets, compare estimated risk differentials, consider both long-turn and short-run consequences, and strike a balance."

3. Profitability

One of the principle objectives of a bank is to earn more profit. It is essential for the purpose of paying interest to depositors, wage to the staff, dividend to shareholders and meeting other expenses. It cannot afford to hold a large amount of funds in cash for that will mean forgoing income. But the conflict between profitability and liquidity is not very sharp. Liquidity and safety are primary considerations while profitability is subsidiary for the very existence of a bank depends on the first two.

Conclusion. The three conflicting objectives of portfolio management lead to the conclusion that for a bank to earn more profit, it must strike a judicious balance between liquidity and safety.

3. THEORIES OF PORTFOLIO MANAGEMENT

There are apparent conflicts between the objectives of liquidity, safety and profitability relating to a commercial bank. Economists have tried to resolve these conflicts by laying down certain theories from time to time. These principles or theories, in fact, govern the *distribution of assets* keeping in views these objectives. They have also come to be known as the theories of liquidity management which are discussed as under.

1. The Real Bills Doctrine

The real bills doctrine or the commercial loan theory states that a commercial bank should advance only short-term self-liquidating productive loans to business firms. Self-liquidating loans are those which are meant to finance the production, and movement of goods through the successive stages of production, storage, transportation, and distribution. When such goods are ultimately sold, the loans are considered to liquidate themselves automatically. For instance, a loan give by the bank to a businessman to finance inventories would be repaid out of the receipts from the sale of those very inventories, and the loan would be automatically self-liquidated.

The theory states that when commercial banks make only short term self-liquidating productive loans, the central bank, in turn, should only land to the banks on the security of such short-term loans. This principle would ensure the proper degree of liquidity for each bank and the proper money supply for the whole economy. The central bank was expected to increase or diminish bank reserves by rediscounting approved loans. When business expanded and the needs of trade increased, banks were able to acquire additional reserves by rediscounting bills with the central banks. When business fell and the needs of trade declined, the volume of rediscounting of bills would fall, the supply of bank reserves and the amount of bank credit and money would also contract.

Its Merits. Such short-term self-liquidating productive loans possess three advantages. *First,* they possess liquidity that is why they liquidate themselves automatically. *Second,* since they mature in the short run and are for productive purposes, there is no risk of their running to bad debts. *Third,* being productive such loans earn income for the banks.

Its Demerits. Despite these merits, the real bills doctrine suffers from certain defects.

First, if a bank refuses to grant a fresh loan till the old loan is repaid, the disappointed borrower will have to reduce production which will adversely affect business activity. If all the banks follow the same rule, this may lead to reduction in the money supply and price in the community. This may, in turn, make it impossible for existing debtors to repay their loans in time.

Second, the doctrine assumes that loans are self-liquidating under normal economic conditions. If there is depression, production and trade suffer and the debtor will not be able to repay the debt at maturity.

Third, this doctrine neglects the fact that the liquidity of a bank depends on the saleability of its liquid assets and not on real trade bills. If a bank possesses a variety of assets like bills and securities which can be readily should in the money and capital markets, it can ensure safety, liquidity and profitability. Then the bank need not rely on maturities in time of trouble.

Fourth, the basic defect of the theory is that no loan is in itself automatically self-liquidating. A loan to a retailer to purchase inventor is is not self-liquidating if the inventories are not sold to consumers and remain with the retailer. Thus a loan to be successful involves a third party, the consumers in this case, besides the lender and the borrower.

Fifth, this theory is based on the "needs of trade" which is no longer accepted as an adequate criterion for regulating this type of bank credit. If bank credit and money supply fluctuate on the basis of the needs of trade, the central bank cannot prevent either spiralling recession or inflation.

2. The Shiftability Theory

The shiftability theory of bank liquidity was propounded by H.G. Moulton who asserted that if the commercial banks maintain a substantial amount of assets that can be shifted on to the other banks for cash without material loss in case of necessity, then there is no need to rely on maturities. According to this view, an asset to be perfectly shiftable must be immediately transferable without capital loss when the need for liquidity arises. This is particularly applicable to short term market investments, such as treasury bills and bills of exchange which can be immediately sold whenever it is necessary to raise funds by banks. But in a general crisis when all banks are in need of liquidity, the shiftability theory requires that all banks should possess such assets which can be shifted on to the central bank which is the lender of the last resort.

This theory has certain elements of truth. Banks now accept sound assets which can be shifted on to other banks. Shares and debentures of large companies are accepted as liquid assets along with treasury bills and bills of exchange. This has encouraged term lending by banks.

Its Demerits. But it has its weaknesses. *First,* mere shiftability of assets does not provide liquidity to the banking system. It entirely depends upon the economic circumstances. *Second,* the shiftability theory ignores the fact that in times of acute depression, the shares and debentures cannot be shifted on to others by the banks. In such a situation, there are no buyers and all who possess them want to sell them. *Third,* a single bank may have shiftable assets in sufficient quantities but if it tries to sell them when thee is a run on the bank, it may adversely affect the entire banking system. *Fourth,* If all the banks simultaneously start shifting their assets, it would have disastrous effects on both the lenders and borrowers.

3. The Anticipated Income Theory

The anticipated income theory was developed by H.V. Prochanow in 1944 on the basis of the practice of extending term loans by the US commercial banks. According to this theory, regardless of the nature and character of a borrower's business, the bank plans the liquidation of the term-loan from the anticipated income of the borrower. A term-loan is for a period exceeding one year and extending to less than five years. It is granted against the hypothecation of machinery, stock and even immovable property. The bank puts restrictions on the financial activities of the borrower while granting this loan. At the time of granting a loan, the bank takes into consideration not only the security but the anticipated earnings of the borrower. Thus a loan by the bank gets repaid out of the future income of the borrower in instalments, instead of in a lump sum at the maturity of the loan.

Its Merits. This theory is superior to the real bills doctrine and the shiftability theory because it fulfils the three objectives of liquidity, safety and profitability. Liquidity is assured to the bank when the borrower saves and repays the loan regularly in instalments. It satisfies the safety principle because the bank grants a loan not only on the basis of a good security but also on the ability of the borrower to repay the loan. The bank can utilise its excess reserves in granting term-loan and is assured of a regular income. Lastly, the term-loan is highly beneficial for the business community which gets funds for medium-terms.

Its Demerits. The theory of anticipated income is not free from a few defects.

1. *Analyses Creditworthiness.* It is not a theory but simply a method to analyse a borrower's creditworthiness. It gives the bank criteria for evaluating the potential of a borrower to successfully repay a loan on time.

2. *Fails to Meet Emergency Cash Needs.* Repayment of loans in instalments to the bank no doubt provide a

regular stream of liquidity, but they fail to meet emergency cash needs of the lender bank.

4. The Liabilities Management Theory

This theory was developed in the 1960s. According to this theory, there is no need for banks to grant self-liquidating loans and keep liquid assets because they can borrow reserve money in the money market in case of need. A bank can acquire reserves by creating additional liabilities against itself from different sources. These sources include the issuing of time certificates of deposit, borrowing from other commercial banks, borrowing from the central banks, raising of capital funds by issuing shares, and by ploughing back of profits. We discuss these sources of bank funds briefly.

(a) Time Certificates of Deposits. These are the principle source of reserve money for a commercial bank in the USA. Time certificates of deposits are of different maturities ranging from 90 days to less than 12 months. They are negotiable in the money market. So a bank can have access to liquidity by selling them in the money market. But there are two limitations. First, if during a boom, the interest rate structure in the money market is higher than the ceiling rate set by the central bank, time deposit certificates cannot be sold in the market. *Second,* they are not a dependable source of funds for the commercial banks. Bigger commercial banks are at an advantage in selling these certificates because they have large certificates which they can afford to sell at even low interest rates. So the smaller banks are at a disadvantage in this respect.

(b) Borrowing from other Commercial Banks. A bank may create additional liabilities by borrowing from other banks having excess reserves. But such borrowings are only for a very short duration, for a day or week at the most. The interest rate of such borrowings depends upon the prevailing rate in the money market. But borrowings from other banks are only possible during normal economic conditions. In abnormal times, no bank can afford to lend to others.

(c) Borrowing from the Central Bank. Banks also create liabilities on themselves by borrowing form the central bank of the country. They borrow to met their liquidity needs for short term and by discounting bills from the central bank. But such borrowings are relatively costlier than borrowings from other sources.

(d) Raising Capital Funds. Commercial banks acquire funds by issuing fresh shares or debentures. But the availability of funds through this sources depends on the amount of dividend or interest rate which the bank is prepared to pay. Usually the banks are not in a position to pay rates higher than paid by manufacturing and trading companies. So they are not able to get sufficient funds from this sources.

(e) Ploughing Back Profits. Another source of liquid funds for a commercial bank is the ploughing back of its profits. But how much it can get from this source will depend upon its rate of profit and its dividend policy. It is the larger banks that can depend on this source rather than the smaller banks.

4. INVESTMENT POLICY OF A COMMERCIAL BANK

A bank makes investments for the purpose of earning profits. First it keeps primary and secondary reserves to meet its liquidity requirements. This is essential to satisfy the credit needs of the society by granting short-term loans to its customers. Whatever is left with the bank after making advances is invested for long period to improve its earning capacity.

Before discussing the investment policy of a commercial bank, it is instructive to distinguish between a loan and an investment because the usual practice is to regard the two as synonymous. The bank gives a loan to a customer for a short period on condition of repayment. It is the customer who asks for the loan. By advancing a loan, the bank creates credit which is a temporary source of fund for the bank. An investment by the bank, on the other hand, is the outlay of its funds for a long period without creating any credit. A bank makes investments in government securities and in the stocks of large reputed industrial concerns, while in the case of a loan the bank advances money against recognised securities and bills. However, the goal of both is to increase its earnings.

The investment policy of a bank consists of earning high returns on its unloaned resources. But it has to keep in view the safety and liquidity of its resources so as to meet the potential demand of its customers. Since the objective of profitability conflicts with those of safety and liquidity, the wise investment policy is to strike a judicious balance among them. Therefore, a bank should lay down its investment policy in such a manner so as to ensure the safety and liquidity of its funds and at the same time maximise its profits. This requires adherence to certain principles.

PRINCIPLES OF BANK LENDING POLICIES

Banks follow the following principles of lending :

1. Liquidity

Liquidity is an important principle of bank lending. Bank lend for short periods only because they lend public money which can be withdrawn at any time by depositors. They, therefore, advance loans on the security of such assets which are easily marketable and convertible into cash at a short notice.

A bank chooses such securities in its investment portfolio which possess sufficient liquidity. It is essential because if the bank needs cash to meet the urgent requirements of its customers, it should be in a position to sell some of the securities at a very short notice without disturbing their market prices much. There are certain securities such as central, state and local government bonds which are easily saleable without affecting their market prices. The shares and debentures of large industrial concerns also fall in this category. But the shares and debentures of ordinary firms are not easily marketable without bringing down their market prices. So the banks should make investments in government securities and shares and debentures of reputed industrial houses.

2. Safety

The safety of funds lent is another principle of lending. Safety means that the borrower should be able to repay the loan and interest in time at regular intervals without default. The repayment of the loan depends upon the nature of security, the character of the borrower, his capacity to repay and his financial standing.

Like other investments, bank investments involve risk. But the degree of risk varies with the type of security. Securities of the central government are safer than those of the state governments and local bodies. And the securities of state government and local bodies are safer than those of the industrial concerns. This is because the resources of the central government are much higher than the state and local governments and of the latter higher than the industrial concerns. In fact, the share and debentures of industrial concerns are tied to their earnings which may fluctuate with the business activity in the country. The bank should also take into consideration the debt repaying ability of the governments while investing in their securities. Political stability and peace and security are the prerequisites for this. It is very safe to invest in the securities of a government having large tax revenue and high borrowing capacity. The same is the case with the securities of a rich municipality or local body and state government of a prosperous region. So in making investments the bank should choose securities, shares and debentures of such governments, local bodies and industrial concerns which satisfy the principle of safety.

Thus from the bank's viewpoint, the nature of security is the most important consideration while giving a loan. Even then, it has to take into consideration the creditworthiness of the borrower which is governed by his character, capacity to repay, and his financial standing. Above all, the safety of bank funds depends upon the technical feasibility and economic viability of the project for which the loan is advanced.

3. Diversity

In choosing its investment portfolio, a commercial bank should follow the principle of diversity. It should not invest its surplus funds in a particular type of security but in different types of securities. It should choose the shares and debentures of different types of industries situated in different regions of the country. The same principle should be followed in the case of state governments and local bodies. Diversification aims at minimising risk of the investment portfolio of a bank.

The principle of diversity also applies to the advancing of loans to varied types of firms, industries, businesses and trades. A bank should follows the maxim: "Do not keep all eggs in one basket." It should spread it risks by giving loans to various trades and industries in different parts of the country.

4. Stability

Another important principle of a bank's investment policy should be to invest in those stocks and securities which possess a high degree of stability in their prices. The bank cannot afford any loss on the value of its securities. It should, therefore, invest it funds in the shares of reputed companies where the possibility of decline in their prices is remote. Government bonds and debentures of companies carry fixed rates of interest. Their value changes with changes in the market rate of interest. But the bank is forced to liquidate a portion of them to meet its requirements of cash in cash of financial crisis. Otherwise, they run to their full term of 10 years or more and changes in the market rate of interest do not affect them much. Thus bank investments in debentures and bonds are more stable than in the shares of companies.

5. Profitability

This is the cardinal principle for making investment by a bank. It must earn sufficient profits. It should, therefore, invest in such securities which was sure a fair and stable return on the funds invested. The earning capacity of securities and shares depends upon the interest rate and the dividend rate and the tax benefits they carry. It is largely the government securities of the centre, state and local bodies that largely carry the exemption of their interest from taxes. The bank should invest more in such securities rather than in the shares of new companies which also carry tax exemption. This is because shares of new companies are not safe investments.

5. ESSENTIALS OF A SOUND BANKING SYSTEM

The essentials of a sound banking system are usually regarded as liquidity and profitability. As pointed out by Crowther, "The secret of successful banking is to distribute resources between the various forms of assets in such a way as to get a sound balance between liquidity and profitability, so that their is cash (on hand or quickly realizable) to meet every claim, and at the same time enough income for the bank to pay it way and earn profits for its shareholders."[3] But modern bankers also consider a few other essentials which are discussed below.

1. Liquidity

One of the essentials of a sound banking system is to have a higher degree of liquidity. The bank holds a small proportion of its assets in cash. Therefore, its other assets must possess the criterion of liquidity so that they may be turned into such easily. A commercial bank is under an obligation to pay its depositors cash on demand. This is only possible if the bank possesses such securities which can be easily liquidated. Central banks have made it obligatory on the commercial banks to keep a certain proportion of their assets in cash to ensure liquidity.

2. Safety

Another essential of a sound banking system is that it must be safe. Since the bank keeps the deposits of the people, it must ensure the safety of their money. So it should make safe loans and investments and avoid unnecessary risks. If the debtors of the banks donot repay the loans in time and it loses on its investments, the bank shall become insolvent. As a result, its depositors lose money and suffer hardships. Thus the bank must ensure the safety of its deposits.

3. Stability

A sound banking system must be stable. It should operate rationally. There should neither be undue contraction nor expansion of credit. If the bank restricts the creation of credit when trade and industry need it the most, it will harm the interests of the business community. On the other hand, if it expands credit when the

3. G. Crowther, *op. cit.*, p. 3.

economic conditions do not permit, it will lead to boom and inflation. So the banking system should follow a stable lending policy. The central bank of the country can help in achieving stability in the banking operations of the commercial banks by a judicious credit control policy.

4. Elasticity

But the stability of banking operations should not be interpreted as rigidity. Rather, the banking system should have sufficient elasticity in its lending operations. It should be in a position to expand and contract the supply of loanable funds with ease in accordance with the directives of the central bank of the country.

5. Profitability

A sound banking system should be able to earn sufficient profits. Profits are essential for it to be viable. It has to pay the corporation tax like any other company, pay interest to its depositors, dividend to shareholders, salaries to the staff and meet other expenses. So unless the bank earns, it cannot operate soundly. For this purpose, it must adopted judicious loan and investment policies.

6. Reserve Management

Sound banking system must follow the principle of efficient reserve management. A bank keeps some amount of money in reserve for meeting the demand of its customers in case of emergency. Though the money kept in reserve is idle money, yet the bank cannot afford the risk of keeping a small amount in reserve. There are, however, some statutory limits laid down by the central bank in maintaining minimum reserves with itself and with the bank. But how much reserve money should a bank maintain is governed by its own wisdom, experience and the size of the bank. The bank should manage its reserve policy effectively and efficiently without keeping too much or too little cash. It has to balance between profitability and safety.

7. Expansion

A sound banking system must be spread throughout the country. It should not be concentrated only in big towns and cities but in rural areas and backward regions. It is only by widespread expansion of the banking system that the deposits can be mobilised and credit facilities can be made available to trade, industry, agriculture, etc. This is especially the case in a developing country where the banking system must provide these facilities through its expansion in all areas. This is essential for capital formation and economic growth.

EXERCISES

1. Discuss the principles governing the distribution of bank assets.
2. Critically examine the liquidity management theories of commercial banks.
3. Discuss and reconcile the conflicts among the objectives of liquidity, profitability and safety of commercial banks.
4. Explain the main features of an investment policy which a commercial bank should follow.
5. Discuss the essentials of a sound banking system.

CHAPTER 17

Credit Creation by Commercial Banks

1. DO BANKS CREATE CREDIT ?

The creation of credit or deposits is one of the most important functions of commercial banks. Like other corporations, banks aim at earning profits. For this purpose, they accept cash in demand deposits and advance loans on credit to customers. When a bank advances a loan, it does not pay the amount in cash. But it opens a current account in his name and allows him to withdraw the required sum by cheques. In this way, the bank creates credit or deposits.

Demand deposits arise in two ways: *one*, when customers deposit currency with commercial banks, and *two*, when banks advance loans, discount bills, provide overdraft facilities, and make investments through bonds and securities. The first type of demand deposits are called "primary deposits". Banks play a passive role in opening them. The second type of demand deposits are called "derivative deposits". Banks actively create such deposits.

Do banks really create credit or deposits ?

There have been two views on this subject: one held by certain economists like Hartley Withers, and the other held by practical bankers like Walter Leaf.

According to Withers, banks can create credit by opening a deposit, every time they advance a loan. This is because every time a loan is sanctioned, payment is made through cheques by the customers. All such payments are adjusted through the clearing house. So long as a loan is due, a deposit of that amount remains outstanding in the books of the bank. Thus every loan creates a deposit. But this is an exaggerated and extreme view.

Dr Leaf[1] and practical bankers do not agree with this view. They go to the opposite extreme. They hold that banks cannot create money out of thin air. They can lend only what they have in cash. Therefore, they cannot and do not create money.

---

1. Water Leaf, *Banking*, 1928, pp. 101-4.

This view is also wrong becuase it is based on arguments relating to a single bank. As pointed out by Prof Samuelson, "The banking system as a whole can do what each small bank cannot do: it can expand its loans and investments many times the new reserves of cash created for it, even though each small bank is lending out only a fraction of its deposits."[2]

In fact, a bank is not a cloak room where one can keep currency notes and claim those very notes when one desires. Banks know by experience that all depositors do not withdraw their money simultaneously. Some withdraw while others deposit on the same day. So by keeping a small cash in reserve for day-to-day transactions, the bank is able to advance loans on the basis of excess reserves. When the bank advances a loan it opens an account in the name of the customer. The bank knows by experience that the customer will withdraw money by cheques which will be deposited by his creditors in this bank or some other bank, where they have their accounts. Settlements of all such cheques are made in the clearing house. The same procedure is followed in other banks. The banks are able to create credit or deposits by keeping a small cash in reserves and lending the remaining amount.

In granting a loan, a bank actively creates a claim against itself in favour of the borrower. "The claims the bank takes from its customers, in exchange for the deposits entered in the books, are the bank's assets. The standard assets of a commercial bank are overdrafts and loans, bills discounted, investments and cash."[3]

The bank provides overdraft facility to a customer on the basis of some security. It enters the amount of the overdraft in the existing account of the customer and allows him to draw cheques for the overdraft amount agreed upon. It thus creates a deposit.

When a bank discounts a bill of exchange, it in fact, buys the bill from the customer for a short period of 90 days or less. The amount of the bill is credited in the account of the customer who withdraws it through a cheque. Or, it pays the sum through a cheque on itself. In both cases, the bank creates a deposit equal to the amount of the bill of exchange less the discount charges.

A commercial bank also creates a deposit by making investments by buying government bonds and securities. The bank pays for the bond through a cheque on itself to the central bank. If it buys a bond from the stock exchange, it credits the amount in the account of the seller, if he happens to be its customer. Otherwise, it pays a cheque on itself which is deposited in some other bank. In any case, a deposit is created either in this bank or some other bank. In all such cases, liabilities and assets in the banking system on the whole are increased. Thus loans by banks create deposits. It is in this sense that credit is created by commercial banks.

2. THE PROCESS OF CREDIT CREATION

Let us explain tha actual process of credit creation. We have seen above that the ability of banks to create credit depends on the fact that banks need only a small percentage of cash to deposits. If banks kept 100 per cent cash against deposits, there would be no credit creation. Modern banks do not keep 100 per cent cash reserves. They are legally required to keep a fixed percentage of their deposits in cash, say 10, 15 or 20 per cent. They lend and/or invest the remaining amount which is called *excess reserves*. A bank can lend equal to its excess reserves. But the entire banking system can lend and create credit (or deposits) upto a multiple of its original excess reserves. The deposit multiplier depends upon the required reserve which is the basis of credit creation. Symbolically, the required reserve ratio:

$$RRr = \frac{RR}{D}$$

or $RR = RRr \times D$

where RR are the required cash reserves with banks, RRr is the required reserve ratio and D is the demand deposits of banks. To show that D depends on RR and RRr, divide both sides of the above equation by RRr:

2. Paul A. Samuelson, *Economics*, 10th edn., 1976, p. 301.
3. R.S. Sayers, *Modern Banking*, 7th edn,. 1967, pp. 7-8.

$$\frac{RR}{RRr}=\frac{RRr\times D}{RRr}$$

or $$\frac{RR}{RRr}=D$$

or $$\frac{1}{RRr}=\frac{D}{RR}$$

or $$D=\frac{1}{RRr}\times RR$$

where $1/RRr$, the reciprocal of the percentage reserve ratio, is called the *deposit (or credit) expansion multiplier*. It determines the limits of the deposit expansion of a bank. The maximum amount of demand deposits which the banking system can support with any given amount of *RR* is by applying the multiplier to *RR*. Taking the initial change in the volume of deposits (D*D*) and in cash reserves (D*RR*), it follows from any given percentage of *RRr* that

$$\Delta D = RR\times\frac{1}{RRr}$$

To understand it, suppose the *RRr* for the banks is fixed at 10 per cent and the initial change in cash reserves is Rs 1000. By applying the above formula, the maximum increase in demand deposits will be

$$\Delta D = 1000\times\frac{1}{0.10}=\text{Rs } 10000.$$

This is the extent to which the banking system can create credit. The above equation can also be expressed as follows:

$DD = RR[1+(1-RRr) + (1-RRr)^2+...+(1-RRr)^n]$

The sum of the geometric progression within brackets gives:

$$\frac{1}{1-(1-RRr)}=\frac{1}{RRr}$$

$$\Delta D=\Delta RR\times\frac{1}{RRr}$$

The deposit expansion multiplier rests on the assumptions that banks lend out all their excess reserves and *RRr* remains constant.

To explain the process of credit creation, we make the following assumptions:

1. There are many banks, say A, B, C, etc. in the banking system.

2. Each bank has to keep 10 per cent of its deposits in reserves. In other words, 10 per cent is the required ratio fixed by law.

3. The first bank has Rs. 1000 as deposits.

4. The loan amount drawn by the customer of one bank is deposited in full in the second bank, and that of the second bank into the third bank, and so on.

5. Each bank starts with the initial deposit which is deposited by the debtor of the other bank.

Given these assumptions suppose that Bank A receives a cash deposits of Rs. 1000 to begin with. This is the cash in hand with the bank which is its asset and this amount is also the liability of the bank by way of deposits it holds. Given the reserve ratio of 10 per cent, the bank keeps Rs. 100 in reserves and lends Rs 900 to one of its customers who, in turn, gives a cheque to some person from whom he borrows or buys something. The net changes in Bank A' is balance sheet are +Rs 100 in reserves and +Rs 900 in loans on the assets side and Rs 1000 in demand deposits on the liabilities side as shown in Table I. Before these changes Bank A had zero excess reserves.

Table I. Balance Sheet of Bank A

Assets		Liabilities	
Reserves	Rs 1000	Deposits	Rs 1000
	net changes		*net changes*
Reserves	Rs 100	Deposits	Rs 1000
Loans	Rs 900		

This loan of Rs 900 is deposited by the customer in Bank *B* whose balance sheet is shown in Table II Bank *B* starts with a deposit of Rs 900, keeps 10 per cent of it or Rs 90 as cash in reserve. Bank *B* has Rs 810 as excess reserves which it lends thereby creating new deposits.

Table II Balance Sheet of Bank B

Assets		Liabilities	
Reserves	Rs 900	Deposits	Rs 900
net changes		*net changes*	
Reserves	Rs 90	Deposits	Rs 900
Loans	Rs 810		

This loan of Rs 810 is deposited by the customer of Bank *B* into Bank *C*. The balance sheet of Bank *C* is shown in Table III Bank *C* keeps Rs 81 or 10 per cent of Rs 810 in cash reserves and lends Rs 729.

Table III Balance Sheet of Bank C

Assets		Liabilities	
Reserves	Rs 810	Deposits	Rs 810
net changes		*net changes*	
Reserves	Rs 81	Deposits	Rs 810
Loans	Rs 729		

This process goes on to other banks. Each bank in the sequence gets excess reserves, lends and creates new demand deposits equal to 90% of the preceding bank's. In this way, new deposits are created to the tune of Rs 10000 in the banking system, as shown in Table IV.

Table IV Multiple Credit Creation

Bank	Required Reserves	New Loans	New Deposits
A	Rs 100	Rs 900	Rs 1000
B	Rs 90	Rs 810	Rs 900
C	Rs 81	Rs 729	Rs 810
All other Banks	Rs 729	Rs 6561	Rs 7290
Total for the Banking System	Rs 1000	Rs 9000	Rs 10000

The multiple credit creation shown in the last column of the above table can also be worked out algebraically as:

Rs 1000 $[1+(9/10)+(9/10)^2+(9/10)^3+...+(9/10)^n]$

=Rs 1000 (1/1-9/10)= Rs 1000 (1/1/10)= Rs 1000×10 = Rs 10000.

3. LIMITATIONS ON THE POWER OF BANKS TO CREATE CREDIT

We have seen above how the banking system as a whole can create credit. But it does not mean that banks have unlimited powers to create credit. In fact, they have to function under certain restrictions. The following are the limitations on the power of commercial banks to create credit.

1. *Amount of Cash.* The credit creation power of banks depends upon the amount of cash they possess. The larger the cash, the larger the amount of credit that can be created by banks. The amount of cash that a bank has in its vaults cannot be determined by it. It depends upon the primary deposits with the bank. The bank's power of creating credit is thus limited by the cash it possesses.

2. *Proper Securities.* An important factor that limits the power of a bank to create credit is the availability of adequate securities. A bank advances loans to its customers on the basis of a security, or a bill, or a share, or a stock or a building, or some other type of asset. It turns ill-liquid form of wealth into liquid wealth and thus creates credit. If proper securities are not available with the public, a bank cannot create credit. As pointed out by Crowther, "Thus the bank does not create money out of thin air, it transmutes other forms of wealth into money."

3. *Banking Habits of the People.* The banking habits of the people also govern the power of credit creation on the part of banks. If people are not in the habit of using cheques, the grant of loans will lead to the withdrawal of cash from the credit creation stream of the banking system. This reduces the power of banks to create credit to the desired level.

4. *Minimum Legal Reserve Ratio.* The minimum legal reserve ratio of cash to deposits fixed by the central bank is an important factor which determines the power of banks of create credit. The higher this ratio (RRr), the lower the power of banks to create credit; and the lower the ratio, the higher the power of banks to create credit.

5. *Excess Reserves.* The process of credit creation is based on the assumption that banks stick to the required reserve ratio fixed by the central bank. If banks keep more cash in reserves than the legal reserve requirements, their power to create credit is limited to that extent. If Bank A of our example keeps 25 per cent of Rs 1000 instead of 20 per cent, it will lend Rs 750 instead of Rs 800. Consequently, the amount of credit creation will be reduced even if the other banks in the system stick to the legal reserve ratio of 20 per cent.

6. *Leakages.* If there are leakages in the credit creation stream of the banking system, credit expansion will not reach the required level, given the legal reserve ratio. It is possible that some persons who receive cheques do not deposit them in their bank accounts, but withdraw the money in cash for spending or for hoarding at home. The extent to which the amount of cash is withdrawn from the chain of credit expansion, the power of the banking system to create credit is limited.

7. *Cheque Clearances.* The process of credit expansion is based on the assumption that cheques drawn by commercial banks are cleared immediately and reserves of commercial banks expand and contract uniformly by cheque transactions. But it is not possible for banks to receive and draw cheques of exactly equal amount. Often some banks have their reserves increased and others reduced through cheque clearances. This expands and contracts credit creation on the part of banks. Accordingly, the credit creation stream is disturbed.

8. *Behaviour of other Banks.* The power of credit creation is further limited by the behaviour of other banks. If some of the banks do not advance loans to the extent required of the banking system, the chain of credit expansion will be broken. Consequently, the banking system will not be "loaned up".

9. *Economic Climate.* Banks cannot continue to create credit limitlessly. Their power to create credit depends upon the economic climate in the country. If there are boom times, there is optimism. Investment opportunities increase and businessmen take more loans from banks. So credit expands. But in depressed times when the business activity is at a low level, banks cannot force the business community to take loans

from them. Thus the economic climate in a country determines the power of banks to create credit.

10. *Credit Control Policy of the Central Bank.* The power of commercial banks to create credit is also limited by the credit control policy of the central bank. The central bank influences the amount of cash reserves with banks by open market operations, discount rate policy and varying margin requirements. Accordingly, it affects the credit expansion or contraction by commercial banks.

We may conclude that commercial banks do not possess unlimited powers to create credit.

EXERCISES

1. Explain the statement that "loans create deposits."
2. Explain how "loans make deposits". What are the limitations to such credit creation by banks ?
3. Describe the process of credit creation by commercial banks.
4. How do banks create credit ? What are the limitations on the power of banks to create credit ?

CHAPTER 18

Credit and Credit Instruments

1. MEANING OF CREDIT

The word "credit" is derived from the Latin word *creditum* which means to believe or trust. In economics, the term credit refers to a promise by one party to pay another for money borrowed or goods or services received. It is a medium of exchange to receive money or goods on demand at some future date. R.P. Kent defines credit "as the right to receive payments or the obligation to make payment on demand at some future time on account of the immediate transfer of goods."

2. FEATURES OR ESSENTIALS OF CREDIT

The following are the essential features of credit :

1. *Trust and Confidence.* Trust is the fundamental element of credit. The lender will lend his money or goods on the trust and confidence that the borrower or buyer will payback the money or price in time.

2. *Time Element.* All credit transactions involve time element. Money is borrowed or goods are bought with a promise to repay the money or pay the price on some future date.

3. *Transfer of Goods and Services.* Credit involves transfer of goods and services by the seller to the buyer on the pay-back promise of the buyer on some future date.

4. *Willingness and Ability.* Credit depends in a person's willingness and ability to pay the borrowed money. In fact, credit of a person depends on his character, capacity and capital. It is these three C's on which a man's credit depends. A person who is honest and fair in his dealings possesses the capacity of making his business a success. Such a person can get credit easily.

5. *Purpose of Credit.* Banks and financial institutions give large amounts of credit for productive purposes rather than for consumption purposes.

6. *Security.* Security in the form of property, gold, silver, bonds or shares is an important element for raising credit.

3. CREDIT INSTRUMENTS

Credit plays a significant role in modern business and that part is represented by credit instruments. These are written or printed or typed financial documents that serve either as promises to pay or as orders to pay. They provide the means by which funds are transferred from one party to another. Some of the important credit instruments are explained below:

1. *Promissory Note.* Promissory note is the earliest type of credit instrument. It is an "I.O.U." (I Owe You)—a written promise by a debtor to pay to another person a specified sum of money by an agreed given date, usually within a year with three days of grace. Such notes are issued by individuals, corporations and government agencies. A promissory note is drawn by the debtor and has to be *accepted* by the bank in which the debtor has his account for it to be valid. The creditor can get it discounted from his bank at a premium by paying interest till the date of recovery. The usual form of a promissory note is:

Rs. 10,000/-   Chennai
12 July, 2010

Three months after date, I promise to pay Bhanu Kant Bearer/Order the sum of Rs. Ten Thousand only for value received.

R. Vasudevan

A promissory note can also be for a longer period.

2. *Bill of Exchange or Commercial Bill.* A bill of exchange is an order drawn by the creditor to the debtor instructing the latter to pay a specified sum of money to the former, or to the bearer, or to his nominee. The payment is to be made after some fixed date, usually 90 days with three days of grace. The following steps are involved in the bill of exchange.

The bill is drawn by the drawer (creditor) and sent to the drawee (debtor) for acceptance. The bill is accepted when the drawee puts his signature on the bill. If it is a firm, then the stamp of the accepting firm is put on which an authorised person signs. Now the creditor can discount the bill either with a broker or a bank. Suppose he presents it to his bank which calculates interest on its face value for the period for which he wants credit on the bill, deducts it from the face value and credits the balance in the account of the creditor.

The bill of exchange is a negotiable instrument which can be bought and sold by the holder of the bill till the time of its maturity at the prevailing rate of discount (interest). The discount rate is the market price of the bill. The higher the discount rate, the lower the price of the bill at the time of discounting, and vice versa. After the date of maturity, the holder of the bill presents it to the drawee who pays the amount written on the bill.

The bill of exchange usually takes the form as below.

Rs. 10,000/-   New Delhi
6 July, 2006

Three months after date pay to the person or bearer/order a sum of Rs. Ten Thousand only for value received.

N.K. Sharma

To
P. Ram & Sons,
Sector 17-C, Chandigarh.

There is also the foreign bill of exchange which becomes due for payment vfrom the date of acceptance. The rest of the procedure is the same as for the internal bill of exchange.

The difference between a promissory note and a bill of exchange should be noted. A promissory note is drawn by a debtor and accepted by his bank, whereas a bill of exchange is drawn by a creditor and is accepted by the debtor.

3. *Bank Notes.* The central bank of a country issues currency notes. All notes carry the promise of the governor of the central bank (R.B.I. in India) to pay on demand to the bearer of the note an amount mentioned on it. Strictly speaking, a bank note is a currency and not a credit instrument.

4. *Credit Cards.* A recent addition to credit instruments is the issue of credit cards by banks. Credit card holders are allowed credit facilities by the concerned bank for a specified period of time without any security from them. They can also purchase commodities from cloth and shoes to T.V. and air conditioners and pay for such services as hotel bills, railways and airways tickets, etc. without making cash payments. There are national and international credit cards.

5. *Cheque.* A cheque is an order on the bank, written by the drawer who has his deposit with that bank, to pay on demand the stated sum of money to the person named in the cheque. A cheque may be a "bearer cheque" or an "order cheque" or "crossed cheque". The "bearer cheque" can be cashed by the payee (whose name appears on the cheque) or by any other person who holds it. The responsibility of making payment does not rest with the bank. If it is an "order cheque", the responsibility of payment to the payee is on the bank. In the case of a "crossed cheque", the amount of the cheque must be credited to the account of the payee in his bank. The cheque is crossed on the left hand side upper corner and the words "Payee's A/c only" are written there.

The usual form of a cheque is:

_______19______

Pay..or Bearer

Rupees .... Rs. ....

A/c No. | L.F.

BANK OF INDIA
Ansari Road Br., New Delhi-110002

"104312"

6. *Draft.* A draft, also called demand draft, is in the form of a cheque and is an order of a bank to its branch in some other city for making payment of the amount specified in it to the person or firm or organisation.

Besides receiving the amount of the draft, the bank charges a commission for preparing the draft. The draft is handed over to the person who sends it to the payee. The payee, in turn, presents it to his bank in that city to be deposited in his account. This is the procedure in the case of a "crossed draft". If it is not crossed, the payee presents it to the bank on which it is drawn and receives the money after identification.

The usual form of a draft is as under:

State Bank of India
Kalkaji, New Delhi
On Demand Pay.. _______19____
....OR ORDER
RUPEES.. Rs.............................
....VALUE RECEIVED.

STATE BANK OF INDIA
Nariman Point, Goa. No.

FOR STATE BANK OF INDIA
Br. Manager

7. *Hundi.* A Hundi is an internal bill of exchange which has been in use in India from ancient times. It is written in an Indian language by a creditor to the debtor to pay the amount mentioned in the Hundi on the date noted in it. A Hundi is of two types: (a) *Darshani* or Sight Hundi which is payable on demand by the debtor, *(b) Muddati* or Time Hundi which is payable after the period mentioned on the face of the Hundi.

Discounting of Hundis is an important function of indigenous bankers. They write, buy and sell Hundis for trade purposes.

4. FACTORS INFLUENCING THE VOLUME OF CREDIT

Sometimes credit expands when borrowing and lending go on briskly. At other times, credit contracts when borrowing and lending take place slowly. We discuss below the factors on which the volume of credit depends in a country.

1. *Boom and Recession.* Under boom conditions when industry and trade are expanding, the demand for credit increases. The creditors lend more because the interest rate is rising. They also know that the money will be returned due to high rate of profit in the industry. But when there is recession, the quantity of credit contracts. Businessmen are not prepared to borrow even though the interest rate is low.

2. *Political Conditions.* Credit expands when there is political stability in the country. It encourages investment which increases the demand for credit. On the other hand, political instability and insecurity of life and property, business and investment are discouraged. Consequently, the quantity of credit contracts.

3. *Currency Conditions.* The volume of credit expands or contracts depending upon the currency condition of the country. If the currency system is stable, the quantity of credit will increase. On the other hand, an unstable currency system which leads to depreciation or hyper inflation will bring uncertainty. This leads to contraction of credit.

4. *Banking System.* If the banking system is fully developed with a large number of commercial, cooperative and non-banking financial institutions in the country, the quantity of credit expands. Such banking institutions provide large credit facilities to trade and industry. On the contrary, an undeveloped banking system keeps the quantity of credit at a low level.

5. *Speculation.* Speculation and credit expansion or contraction go together. When speculative activity is high, credit expands. When speculators lose, credit contracts.

6. *Credit Policy of the Central Bank.* When the central bank follows a cheap credit policy, it lowers the interest rate and the demand for credit increases. On the contrary, a dear credit policy by raising the interest rate contracts the quantity of credit in the country.

7. *Economic Development.* Credit expands in a developing country in which new banks and financial institutions are being set up. Such institutions provide credit to tiny, small, medium and large industries, to agriculture, etc. In a poor country which lacks financial institutions, the volume of credit is low because trade, business, industry, agriculture, etc. are backward.

5. SIGNIFICANCE OF CREDIT*

Modern economy is said to be a credit economy. Credit is of vital importance for the working of an economy. It is the oil of the wheel of trade and industry and helps in the economic prosperity of a country in the following ways:

1. *Economical.* Credit instruments economise the use of metallic currency. They are cheaper than coinage. The metal used in coins can be used for other productive purposes.

2. *Increases Productivity of Capital.* Credit increases the productivity of capital. People having idle money deposit it in banks and with non-banking financial institutions which is lent to trade and industry for productive uses.

---

* This also relates to the role of credit in the economic development of a country.

3. *Convenient.* Credit instruments are a convenient mode of national and international payments. They help in transferring payments with little cost and without the use of actual money from one place to another quickly.

4. *Internal and External Trade.* As a corollary to the above by facilitating payments quickly, credit helps in the expansion of internal and external trade of a country.

5. *Encourages Investment.* According to Keynes, credit is the payment along which production travels and that bankers provide facilities to manufacturers to produce to full capacity. Credit encourages investment in the economy. Financial institutions help mobilising savings of the people through deposits, bonds, etc. These are, in turn, given as credit to trade, industry, agriculture, etc. which lead to more production and employment.

6. *Increases Demand.* Availability of cheap and easy credit increases the demand for goods and services in the country. This leads to increase in the production of such durable consumer goods as motor vehicles, refrigerators, T.Vs. etc. They raise the standard of living of the people when they consume more goods and services. Consumption loans by banking and non-banking financial institutions coupled with the use of credit cards have made these possible.

7. *Utilises Resources.* Credit helps in the proper utilisation of a country's manpower and other resources. Cheap and easy credit encourages people to start their own businesses which provide them employment. Agriculture develops when farmers get seeds, fertilisers, pumping sets, tractors, etc. on credit. Similarly, transport, communications, industry, mines, plantations, power, etc. develop with the help of credit.

8. *Price Stability.* Credit helps in maintaining price stability in the country. The central bank controls price fluctuations through its credit control policy. It reduces the credit supply to control inflation and increases the supply of credit to control deflation.

9. *Helpful to Government.* Credit helps the government in meeting exigencies or emergencies when the usual fiscal measures fail to fill the financial needs of the government. Government resorts to deficit financing for economic development by creating excess credit.

Conclusion. Thus credit helps in mobilising savings, increasing investment and the rate of capital formation by raising production and employment. Credit is essential for the overall economic development of the country.

6. DEFECTS OF CREDIT

Credit is a dangerous tool if it is not properly controlled and managed. The following are some of the defects of credit.

1. *Too Much and Too Little Credit Harmful.* Too much and too little of credit are harmful for the economy. Too much of credit leads to inflation which causes direct and immediate damage to creditors and consumers. On the contrary, too little of credit leads to deflation which brings down the level of output, employment and income.

2. *Growth of Monopolies.* Too much of credit leads to concentration of capital and wealth in the hands of a few capitalists. This leads to growth of monopolies which exploit both consumers and workers.

3. *Wastage of Resources.* When banks create excessive credit, it may be used for productive and unproductive purposes. If too much of credit is used for production, it leads to over-capitalisation and over-production, and consequently to wastage of resources. 'Similarly, if credit is given liberally for unproductive purposes, it also leads to wastage of resources.

4. *Cyclical Fluctuations.* When there is an excess supply of credit, it leads to boom. When it contracts, there is a slump. In a boom, output, employment and income increases which leads to over-production. On the contrary, they decline during a depression, thereby leading to under-consumption. Such cyclical fluctuations bring about untold miseries to the people.

5. *Extravagance.* Easy availability of credit leads to extravagance on the part of people. People indulge in conspicuous consumption. They buy those goods which they do not need even. With borrowed money, they spend recklessly on luxury articles. The same is the case with businessmen and even governments who invest

in unproductive enterprises and schemes.

6. *Speculation and Uncertainty.* Over issue of credit encourages speculation which leads to abnormal rise in prices. The rise in prices, in turn, brings an element of uncertainty into trade and business. Uncertainty hinders economic progress.

7. *Black Money.* Excessive supply of credit encourages people to amass money and wealth. For this they tend to adopt underhand means and exploit others. To become rich, they evade taxes, conceal income and wealth and thus hoard black money.

8. *Political Instability.* Over issue of credit leading to hyper-inflation leads to political instability and even the downfall of government. This has happened in many Latin American countries.

Conclusion

Despite these defects, credit is of utmost importance to a country. It is impossible to think of the present day economies without the use of credit. Credit is an indispensable lubricant and a tool of convenience for the economic progress of a country. But its uncontrolled, use brings untold problems for an economy.

7. BANKERS' CLEARING HOUSE

A clearing house is an office or institution where bankers make cheque and draft collections among themselves and clear them rapidly and conveniently. It should be noted that banks also draw drafts against other banks at places where they do not have their branches. Each day member banks present to the clearing house all cheques and drafts deposited with them by their customersfor collection but drawn against other banks. The clearing house adopts the following procedure for changing cheques and drafts in order to arrange the differences against each other.

(1) It calculates the total amount of all cheques and drafts presented for collection both *by* and *against* each bank.

(2) For each bank, it enters the first total against the second.

(3) It *demands from or pays to* each bank equal to its *net* debit or credit collections on that day.

(4) The payments of such balances are made by the concerned banks through cheques drawn on the clearing house.

The principal merit of a clearing house is that most cheques presented to the clearing house for collection cancel out each other. As a result, the interbank payments that are made in connection with cheque clearing is reduced. After each day's clearing, the clearing house returns every cheque presented to it to the bank against which it was drawn so that the cheque writer's account can be debited.

In India, the Reserve Bank of India acts as a clearing house for banks. It has clearing houses at its 14 branches and offices, and at other places the State Bank of India and its associate banks provide clearing facilities on its behalf. In recents times the clearing house procedure has changed. Some banks take 24 hours to credit your account. Banks charge between Rs. 100 to Rs. 200 from the customer if his cheque is dishonoured for short balance.

EXERCISES

1. Define credit. What are its essential features? Explain five credit instruments.
2. What is the role of credit in the economic development of a country? Explain the factors which govern the quantity of credit.
3. What do you mean by credit? Describe the various types of credit instruments.
4. Write a short note on: (1) Clearing house; (2) Bills of Exchange; (3) Promissory Note; (4) Credit Card.

Chapter 19

Central Banking : Functions and Credit Control

1. INTRODUCTION

The central bank is the apex bank in a country. It is called by different names in different countries. It is the Reserve Bank of India in India, the Bank of England in England, the Federal Reserve System in America, the Bank of France in France, the Riksbank in Sweden, etc.

2. DIFFERENCE BETWEEN CENTRAL BANK AND COMMERCIAL BANK

A central bank is basically different from a commercial bank in the following ways :

1. The central bank is the apex institution of the monetary and banking structure of the country. The commercial bank is one of the organs of the money market.

2. The central bank is a no-profit institution which implements the economic policies of the government. But the commercial bank is a profit-making institution.

3. The central bank is owned by the government, whereas the commercial bank is owned by shareholders.

4. The central bank is a banker to the government and does not engage itself in ordinary banking activities. The commercial bank is a banker to the general public.

5. The central bank has the monopoly of note issue, while the commercial bank can issue only cheques. The notes are legal tender. But the cheques are in the nature of near-money.

6. The central bank is the banker's bank. As such, it grants accommodation to commercial banks in the form of rediscount facilities, keeps their cash reserves, and clears their balances. On the other hand, the commercial bank advances loans to and accepts deposits from the public.

7. The central bank controls credit in accordance with the needs of business and economy. The commercial bank creates credit to meet the requirements of business.

8. The central bank helps in establishing financial institutions so as to strengthen money and capital markets in a country. On the other hand, the commercial bank helps industry by underwriting shares and debentures, and agriculture by meeting its financial requirements through cooperative or individually.

9. Every country has only one central bank with its offices at important centres of the country. On the

other hand, there are many commercial banks with hundreds of branches within and outside the country.

10. The central bank is the custodian of the foreign currency reserves of the country while the commercial bank is the dealer of foreign currencies.

11. The chief executive of the central bank is designated as "Governor", whereas the chief executive of a commercial bank is called 'Chairman'.

3. DEFINITION OF A CENTRAL BANK

A central bank has been defined in terms of its functions. According to Vera Smith, "The primary definition of central banking is a banking system in which a single bank has either complete control or a residuary monopoly of note issue." W.A. Shaw defines a central bank as a bank which control credit. To Hawtrey, a central bank is that which is the lender of the last resort. According to A.C.L. Day, a central bank is "to help control and stabilise the monetary and banking system." According to Sayers, the central bank "is the organ of government that undertakes the major financial operations of the government and by its conduct of these operations and by other means, influences the behaviour of financial institutions so as to support the economic policy of the Government." Sayers refers only to the nature of the central bank as the government's bank. All these definitions are narrow because they refer only to one particular function of a central bank.

On the other hand, Samuelson's definition is wide. According to him, a central bank "is a bank of bankers. Its duty is to control the monetary base.... and through control of this 'high-powered money' to control the community's supply of money." But the broadest definition has been given by De Kock. In his words, a central bank is "a bank which constitutes the apex of the monetary and banking structure of its country and which performs as best as it can in the national economic interest, the following functions: (i) The regulation of currency in accordance with the requirements of business and the general public for which purpose it is granted either the sole right of note issue or at least a partial monopoly thereof. (ii) The performance of general banking and agency for the state. (iii) The custody of the cash reserves of the commercial banks. (iv) The custody and management of the nation's reserves of international currency. (v) The granting of accommodation in the form of re-discounts and collateral advances to commercial banks, bill brokers and dealers, or other financial institutions and the general acceptance of the responsibility of lender of the last resort. (vi) The settlement of clearance balances between the banks. (vii) The control of credit in accordance with the needs of business and with a view to carrying out the broad monetary policy adopted by the state." De Kock's definition is too long to be called a definition. For, a definition must be brief.

4. FUNCTIONS OF A CENTRAL BANK

A central bank performs the following functions, as given by De Kock and accepted by the majority of economists.

1. Regulator of Currency

The central bank is the bank of issue. It has the monopoly of note issue. Notes issued by it circulate as legal tender money. It has its issue department which issues notes and coins to commercial banks. Coins are manufactured in the government mint but they are put into circulation through the central bank.

Central banks have been following different methods of note issue in different countries. The central bank is required by law to keep a certain amount of gold and foreign securities against the issue of notes. In some countries, the amount of gold and foreign securities bears a fixed proportion, between 25 to 40 per cent of the total notes issued. In other countries, a minimum fixed amount of gold and foreign currencies is required to be kept against note issue by the central bank. This system is operative in India whereby the Reserve Bank of India is required to keep Rs 115 crores in gold and Rs 85 crores in foregin securities. There is no limit to the issue of notes after keeping this minimum amount of Rs 200 crores in gold and foreign securities.

The monopoly of issuing notes vested in the central bank ensures uniformity in the notes issued which helps in facilitating exchange and trade within the country. It brings stability in the monetary system and creates confidence among the public. The central bank can restrict or expand the supply of cash according to the requirements of the economy. Thus it provides elasticity to the monetary system. By having a monopoly of note issue, the central bank also controls the banking system by being the ultimate source of cash. Last but not the least, by entrusting the monopoly of note issue to the central bank, the government is able to earn profits from printing notes whose cost is very low as compared with their face value.

2. Banker, Fiscal Agent and Adviser to the Governement

Central banks everywhere act as bankers, fiscal agents and advisers to their respective governments. As banker to the government, the central bank keeps the deposits of the central and state governments and makes payments on behalf of governments. But it does not pay interest on governments depostis. It buys and sells foreign currencies on behalf of the government., It keeps the stock of gold of the government. Thus it is the custodian of government money and wealth. As a fiscal agent, the central bank makes short-term loans to the government for a period not exceeding 90 days. It floats loans, pays interest on them, and finally repays them on behalf of the government. Thus it manages the entire public debt. The central bank also advises the government on such economic and money matters as controlling inflation or deflation, devaluetion or revaluation of the currency, deflicit financing, balance of payments, etc. As pointed out by De Kock, "Central banks everywhere operate as bankers to the state not only because it may be more convenient and economical to the state, but also because of the intimate connection between public finance and monetary affairs."

3. Custodian of Cash Reserves of Commercial Banks

Commercial banks are required by law to keep reserves equal to a certain percentage of both time and demand desposits liabilities with the central banks. It is on the basis of these reserves that the central bank transfers funds from one bank to another to facilitate the clearing of cheques. Thus the central bank acts as the custodian of the cash reserves of commercial banks and helps in facilitating their transactions. There are many advantages of keeping the cash reserves of the commercial banks with the central bank, according to De Kock. In the first place, the centralisation of cash reserves in the central bank is a source of great strength to the banking system of a country. *Secondly*, centralised cash reserves can serve as the basis of a large and more elastic credit structure than if the same amount were scattered among the individual banks. *Thirdly*, centralised cash reserves can be utilised fully and most effectively during periods of seasonal strains and in financial crises or emergencies. *Fourthly*, by varying these cash reserves the central bank can control the credit creation by commercial banks. *Lastly*, the central bank can provide additional funds on a temporary and short term basis to commercial banks to overcome their financial difficulties.

4. Custody and Management of Foreign Exchange Reserves

The central bank keeps and manages the foreign exchange reserves of the country. It is an official reservoir of gold and foreign currencies. It sells gold at fixed prices to the monetary authorities of other countries. It also buys and sells foreign currencies at international prices. Further, it fixes the exchange rates of the domestic currency in terms of foreign currencies. It holds these rates within narrow limits in keeping with its obligations as a member of the International Monetary Fund and tries to bring stability in foreign exchange rates. Further, it manages exchange control operations by supplying foreign currencies to importers and persons visiting foreign countries on business, studies, etc. in keeping with the rules laid down by the government.

5. Lender of the Last Resort

De Kock regards this function as a *sine qua non* of central banking. By granting accommodation in the form of re-discounts and collateral advances to commercial banks, bill brokers and dealers, or other financial institutions, the central bank acts as the lender of the last resort. The central bank lends to such institutions in order to help them in times of stress so as to save the financial structure of the country from collapse. It acts as lender of the last resort through discount house on the basis of treasury bills, government securities and bonds at "the front door". The other method is to give temporary accommodation to the commercial banks or discount houses directly through the "back door". The difference between the two methods is that lending at the front door is at the bank rate and in the second case at the market rate. Thus the central bank as lender of the last resort is a big source of cash and also influences prices and market rates.

6. Clearing House for Transfer and Settlement

As bankers' bank, the central bank acts as a clearing house for transfer and settlement of mutual claims of commercial banks. Since the central bank holds reserves of commercial banks, it transfers funds from one bank to other banks to facilitate clearing of cheques. This is done by making transfer entries in their accounts on the principle of book-keeping. To transfer and settle claims of one bank upon others, the central bank operates a seperate department in big cities and trade centres. This department is known as the "clearing house" and it renders the service free to commercial banks.

When the central bank acts as a clearing agency, it is time-saving and convenient for the commercial banks to settle their claims at one place. It also economises the use of money. "It is not only a means of economising cash and capital but is also a means of testing at any time the degree of liquidity which the community is maintaining."[1]

7. Controller of Credit

The most important function of the central bank is to control the credit creation power of commercial bank in order to control inflationary and deflationary pressures within this economy. For this purpose, it adopts quantitative methods and qualitative methods. Quantitative methods aim at controlling the cost and quantity of credit by adopting bank rate policy, open market operations, and by variations in reserve ratios of commercial banks. Qualitative methods control the use and direction of credit. These involve selective credit controls and direct action. By adopting such methods, the central bank tries to influence and control credit creation by commercial banks in order to stabilise economic activity in the country.

Besides the above noted functions, the central banks in a number of developing countries have been entrusted with the responsibility of developing a strong banking system to meet the expanding requirements of agriculture, industry, trade and commerce. Accordingly, the central banks possess some additional powers of supervision and control over the commercial banks. They are the issuing of licences; the regulation of branch expansion; to see that every bank maintains the minimum paid up capital and reserves as provided by law; inspecting or auditing the accounts of banks; to approve the appointment of chairmen and directors of such banks in accordance with the rules and qualifications; to control and recommend merger of weak banks in order to avoid their failures and to protect the interest of depositors; to recommend nationalisation of certain banks to the government in public interest; to publish periodical reports relating to different aspects of monetary and economic policies for the benefit of banks and the public; and to engage in research and train banking personnel etc.

5. CENTRAL BANK AS THE CONTROLLER OF CREDIT

Objectives of Credit Control

Credit control is the means to control the lending policy of commercial banks by the central bank. The central bank controls credit to achieve the following objectives:

1. To Stabilise the Internal Price Level. One of the objective of controlling credit is to stabilise the price level in the country. Frequent changes in prices adversely affect the economy. Inflationary or deflationary trends need to be prevented. This can be achieved by adopting a judicious policy of credit control.

2. To Stabilise the Rate of Foreign Exchange. With the change in the internal prices level, exports and imports

1. H.P. Willis, *Theory and Practice of Central Banking*, p. 313.

of the country are affected. When prices fall, exports increase and imports decline. Consequently, the demand for domestic currency increases in the foreign market and its exchange rate rises. On the contrary, a rise in domestic prices leads to a decline in exports and an increase in imports. As a result, the demand for foreign currency increases and that of domestic currency falls, thereby lowering the exchange rate of the domestic currency. Since it is the volume of credit money that affects prices, the central bank can stabilise the rate of foreign exchange by controlling bank credit.

3. To Protect the Outflow of Gold. The central bank holds the gold reserves of the country in its vaults. Expansion of bank credit leads to rise in prices which reduce exports and increase imports, thereby creating an unfavourable balance of payments. This necessitates the export of gold to other countries. The central bank has to control credit in order to prevent such outflows of gold to other countries.

4. To Control Business Cycles. Business cycles are a common phenomenon of capitalist countries which lead to periodic fluctuations in production, employment and prices. They are characterised by alternating periods of prosperity and depression. During prosperity, there is large expansion in the volume of credit, and production, employment and prices rise. During depression, credit contracts, and production, employment and prices fall. The central bank can counteract such cyclical fluctuations through contraction of bank credit during boom periods, and expansion of bank credit during depression.

5. To Meet Business Needs. According to Burgess, one of the important objectives of credit control is the "adjustment of the volume of credit to the volume of business." Credit is needed to meet the requirements of trade and industry. As business expands, larger quantity of credit is needed, and when business contracts less credit is needed. Therefore, it is the central bank which can meet the requirements of business by controlling credit.

6. To Have Growth with Stability. In recent years, the principal objective of credit control is to have growth with stability. The other objectives, such as price stability, foreign exchange rate stability, etc., are regarded as secondary. The aim of credit control is to help in achieving full employment and accelerated growth with stability in the economy without inflationary pressures and balance of payments deficits.

Methods of Credit Control

The central bank adopts two types of methods of credit control. They are the quantitative and qualitative methods. *Quantitative* methods aim at controlling the cost and quantity of credit by adopting such techniques as variations in the bank rate, open market operations, and variations in the reserve ratios of commercial banks. On the other hand, *qualitative* methods control the use and direction of credit. These involve selective credit controls and direct action.

1. Bank Rate or Discount Rate Policy

The bank rate or the discount rate is the rate fixed by the central bank at which it rediscounts first class bills of exchange and government securities held by the commercial banks. The bank rate is the interest rate charged by the central bank at which it provides rediscount to banks through the *discount window.* The central bank controls credit by making variations in the bank rate. If the need of the economy is to expand credit, the central bank lowers the bank rate. Borrowing from the central bank becomes cheap and easy. So the commercial banks will borrow more. They will, in turn, advance loans to customers at a lower rate. The market rate of interest will be reduced. This encourages business activity, and expansion of credit follows which encourages the rise in prices. The opposite happens when credit is to be contracted in the economy. The central bank raises the bank rate which makes borrowing costly from it. So the banks borrow less. They, in turn, raise their lending rates to customers. The market rate of interest also rises because of the tight money market. This discourages fresh loans and puts pressure on borrowers to pay their past debts. This discourages business activity. There is contraction of credit which depresses the rise in price. Thus lowering the bank rate offsets deflationary tendencies and raising the bank rate controls inflation.

But how do changes in the bank rate affect prices and production ? There are two views which explain this process. One held by R.G. Hawtrey and the other by Keynes.

Hawtrey's View. According to Hawtrey, changes in the bank rate affect changes in the short-term rates of interest which, in turn, affect the behaviour of dealers and producers in holding short of finished and semi-finished goods. Suppose the bank rate rises. It raises the stock-term interest rates. Consequently, the cost of borrowing and of holding stocks of goods increases. The dealers will, therefore, try to reduce their stocks of goods, and place less orders to the producers of goods. The sales of producers will start declining. So they will lower prices to induce dealers to buy more of their goods. Or, they will reduce output. As they curtail output, some of the factors of production become unemployed. Money incomes fall due to unemployment. This further reduces the sale of goods, and the dealers reduce their orders to the producers further who, in turn, reduce their production. So ultimately there will be a fall in prices, production and employment in the economy. The converse will be the case when the bank rate falls which will reduce the short-term interest rates, and encourage prices, production and employment through the encouraging behaviour of traders and producers.

Keynes's View. Keynes in his *Treatise on Money* gives an alternative view based upon changes in the volume of fixed capital following a change in the long-term rate of interest. According to him, when the bank rate changes, the long-term interest rates also change in the same direction and will affect investment, prices and employment in the following manner.

Suppose the bank rate is increased. It will raise the short-term interest rates in the money market, while the long-term interest rates remain unchanged. As a result, short-term securities become more attractive because they carry high rates of interest. But the value of long-term securities declines because they now carry low rates of interest than at which they were purchased in the past. The holders of long-term securities will, therefore, sell their securities and invest in short-term securities. This will adversely affect long-term investments in the economy. Consequently, long-term rates of interest will also rise. With the rise in the long-term interest rates, businessmen and producers will reduce investment on fixed capital assets. Employment falls in the capital goods industries. Money income declines. Expenditure on consumption goods is reduced. This leads to fall in their prices and production. Conversely, a fall in the bank rate will lower the long-term interest rates, investment, employment, income, prices and production.

It is not possible to verify empirically these two views. They presuppose that businessmen and producers are very sensitive to interest rate changes and interest charges form a considerable part of the cost of holding and production of goods. Both the assumptions are unrealistic. *First,* prices and production are not so sensitive to changes in interest rates. *Second,* interest rates form an insignificant part of the total cost of holding and production of goods. Interest rate is only one of the factors which determines the volume of investment in stocks of goods and in fixed capital goods. Further, the two views are neither contrary nor mutually exclusive. Hawtrey lays emphasis on changes in the short-term interest rates and Keynes on the long-term interest rates, as a result of changes in the bank rate. But ultimately both lead to the same results, though the process of causation is a little different in each case. For instance, a change in the bank rate may affect the holdings of stocks of goods as well as the volume of fixed capital goods whether the short-term or the long-term interest rates change.

Views of Radcliffe Committee. The Radcliffe Committee appointed by the British Government in 1959 analysed two effects of the bank rate policy upon business activity. The first is the interest-incentive effect. When the bank rate changes, it brings changes in the market rates of interest, thereby inducing a change in the incentive of investment expenditures of business firms. A rise in the bank rate raises interest rates. The cost of holding capital goods increases which causes a disincentive for investors and business firms to borrow funds. Thus with the increase in the cost of borrowing funds, there will be a disincentive for investors and business firms to borrow from the commercial banks. The opposite will be the case when the bank rate falls. It reduces market interest rates, thereby reducing the cost of borrowing from the banks. This provides an incentive to investors and businessmen to get more advances from the banks. But the Committee ruled out the interest-incentive effect because business decisions are primarily independent of changes in interest rates. Moreover, interest-payments form an insignificant proportion of total costs of business firms.

The Committee analysed a more important effect of the bank rate changes, known as the 'general liquidity effect'. According to the Committee, the interest-incentive effect of a change in the bank rate being small, there may take place a 'valuation effect' or general liquidity effect. Bank rate changes affect the capital values of the assets of business firms, and consequently, their balance sheets and their ability to lend. A rise in the bank rates raises the market rates, thereby reducing the value of capital assets of financial institutions. Thus they are willing to lend less. On the other hand, a fall in the bank rate lowers the market rates, and the value of capital assets increases. It encourages lenders to seek new business. The real force of changes in the bank rate lies in its effects on the liquidity of the various groups of financial institutions through market interest rates which (i.e. liquidity), in turn, affects the liquidity of others. This is the general liquidity effect of changes in the bank rate. While analysing this effect, the Committee takes into view the interrelationship of short, medium and long-term interest rates.

Limitations of Bank Rate Policy

The efficacy of the bank rate policy as an instrument of controlling credit is limited by the following factors:

1. *Market Rates do not change with Bank Rate.* The success of the bank rate policy depends upon the extent to which other market rates of interest change along with the bank rate. The theory of bank rate policy presupposes that other rates of interest prevailing in the money market change in the direction of the change in the bank rate. If this condition is not satisfied, the bank rate policy will be totally ineffective as an instrument of credit control.

2. *Wages, Costs and Prices not Elastic.* The success of the bank rate policy requires elasticity not only in interest rates but also in wages, costs and prices. It implies that when suppose the bank rate is raised, wages, costs and prices should automatically adjust themselves to a lower level. But this was possible only under gold standard. Now-a-days the emergence of strong trade unions have made wages rigid during deflationary trends. And they also lag behind when there are inflationary tendencies because it takes time for unions to get a wage rise from employers. So the bank rate policy cannot be a success in a rigid society.

3. *Banks do not approach Central Bank.* The effectiveness of the bank rate policy as a tool of credit control is also limited by the behaviour of the commercial banks. It is only if the commercial banks approach the central bank for rediscounting facilities that this policy can be a success. But the banks keep with them large amounts of liquid assets and do not find it necessary to approach the central bank for financial help.

4. *Bills of Exchange not used.* As a corollary to the above, the effectiveness of the bank rate policy depends on the existence of eligible bills of exchange. In recent years, the bill of exchange as an instrument of financing commerce and trade has fallen into disuse. Businessmen and banks prefer cash credit and overdrafts. This makes the bank rate policy less effective for controlling credit in the country.

5. *Pessimism or Optimism.* The efficacy of the bank rate policy also depends on waves of pessimism or optimism among businessmen. If the bank rate is raised, they will continue to borrow even at a higher rate of interest if there are boom conditions in the economy, and prices are expected to rise further. On the other hand, a reduction in the bank rate will not induce them to borrow during periods of falling prices. Thus businessmen are not very sensitive to changes in interest rates and they are influenced more by business expectations.

6. *Power to Control Deflation Limited.* Another limitation of the bank rate policy is that the power of a central bank to force a reduction in the market rates of interest is limited. For instance, a lowering of bank rate below 3 per cent will not lead to a decline in the market rates of interest below 3 per cent. So the bank rate policy is ineffective in controlling deflation. It may, however, control inflationary tendencies by forcing an increase in the market rates of interest.

7. *Level of Bank Rate in relation to Market Rate.* The efficacy of the discount rate policy as an instrument of credit control depends upon its level in relation to the market rate. If in a boom the bank rate is not raised to such an extent as to make borrowing costly from the central bank, and it is not lowered during a recession so as to make borrowing cheaper from it, it would have a destabilising effect on economic activity.

8. *Non-Discriminatory.* The bank rate policy is non-discriminatory because it does not distinguish between productive and unproductive activities in the country.

9. *Not Successful in Controlling BOP Disequilibrium.* The bank rate policy is not effective in controlling balance of payments disequilibrium in a country because it requires the removal of all restrictions on foreign exchange and movements of international capital.

Conclusion. The above points have led the majority of economists to conclude that the power to alter the bank rate is an extremely weak weapon of monetary management. Friedman even went to the extent of proposing outright elimination of the "discount window" itself.

2. Open Market Operations

Open market operations are another method of quantitative credit control used by a central bank. This method refers to the sale and purchase of securities, bills and bonds of government as well as private financial institutions by the central bank. But in its narrow sense, it simply means dealing only in government securities and bonds.

There are two principal motives of open market operations. *One,* to influence the reserves of commercial banks in order to control their power of credit creation. *Two,* to affect the market rates of interest so as to control the commercial bank credit.

Its method of operation is as follows. Suppose the central bank of a country wants to control expansion of credit by the commercial banks for the purpose of controlling inflationary pressures within the economy. It sells government securities in the money market amounting to, say, Rs 10 crores. The latter give the central bank cheques for this amount drawn against the commercial banks in which the public have their accounts. The central bank reduces this amount in their accounts with it. This applies equally if the commmercial banks have also purchased securities from the central bank. The sale of securities in the open market has thus reduced their cash holdings with the central bank. This tends to reduce the actual cash ratio of the commercial banks by Rs. 10 crores. So the banks are forced to curtail their lending.

Suppose that initially the commercial banks have assets worth Rs 1000 crores and the cash-deposit ratio is 10. This means that Rs 1000 crores are divided between Rs 100 crores cash and Rs 900 crores as deposits or loans. As a result of the sale of securities by the central bank worth Rs 10 crores, the cash is reduced by Rs 100 crores. So the total cash with banks remains Rs 900 crores and loans are also reduced by the same percentage, that is, to Rs 810 crores. This reduction in the cash holding of the commercial banks causes a decrease in the supply of bank money, as shown in Figure 1. In this figure, S is the supply curve of bank money which shifts to the left as S_1 showing a decrease in the supply of bank money from B to A, given the level of interest rate r.

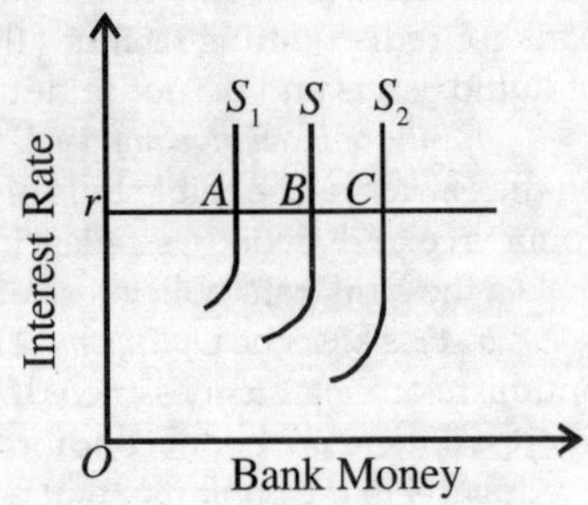

Fig. 1

On the other hand, when the central bank aims at an expansionary policy during a recessionary period, it purchases government securities from the commercial banks and institution dealing with such securities. The central bank pays the sellers its cheques drawn against itself which are deposited into their accounts with the commercial banks. The reserves of the latter increase with the central bank which are just like cash. As a result the supply curve of bank money shifts to the right from S to S_2 showing an increase in the supply of bank money from B to C, as shown in Figure 2. The banks will now lend more at the given rate of interest, r.

Another aspect of the open market policy is that when the supply of money changes as a result of open market operations, the market rates of interest also change. A decrease in the supply of bank money through the sale of securities will have the effect of raising the market interest rates. On the other hand, an increase in the supply of bank money through the purchase of securities will reduce the market interest rates. Thus open market operations have a direct influence on the market rates of interest also.

Limitations of Open Market Operations. The effectiveness of open market operations as a method of credit control is dependent upon the existence of a number of conditions, the absence of which limits the full working of this policy.

1. *Lack of Securities Market.* The first condition is the existence of a large and well-organised security market. This condition is very essential for open market operations because without a well developed security market the central bank will not be able to buy and sell securities on a large scale, and thereby influence the reserves of the commercial banks. Further, the central bank must have enough saleable securities with it.

2. *Cash Reserve Ratio not Stable.* The success of open market operations also requires the maintenance of a stable cash-reserve ratio by the commercial bank. It implies that when the central bank sells or buys securities, the reserves of the commercial banks decrease or increase accordingly to maintain the fixed ratio. But usually the banks do not stick to the legal minimum reserve ratio and keep a higher ratio than this. This makes open market operations less effective in controlling the volume of credit.

3. Penal Bank Rate. According to Prof. Aschheim, one of the necessary conditions for the success of open market operations is a penal bank rate. If there is no penal discount rate fixed by the central bank, the commercial banks can increase their borrowings from it when the demand for credit is strong on the part of the latter. In this situation, the scale of securities by the central bank to restrict monetary expansion will be unsuccessful. But if there is a penal rate of discount, which is a rate higher than the market rates of interest, the banks will be reluctant to approach the central bank for additional financial help easily.

4. Banks Act Differently. Open market operations are successful only if the people also act the way the central bank expects them. When the central bank sells securities, it expects the business community and financial institutions to restrict the use of credit. If they simultaneously start dishoarding money, the act of selling securities by the central banks will not be a success in restricting credit. Similarly, the purchase of securities by the central bank will not be effective if people start hoarding money.

5. Pessimistic or Optimistic Attitude. Pessimistic or optimistic attitude of the business community also limits the operation of open market policy. When the central bank purchases securities and increases the supply of bank money, businessmen may be unwilling to take loans during a depression because of the prevailing pessimism among them. As aptly put by Crowther, banks may place plenty of water before the public horse, but the horse cannot be forced to drink, if it is afraid of loss through drinking water. On the other hand, if businessmen are optimistic during a boom, the sale of securities by the central bank to contract the supply of bank money and even the rise in market rates cannot discourage them from getting loans from the banks. On the whole, this policy is more successful in controlling booms than depressions.

6. Velocity of Credit Money not Constant. The success of open market operations depends upon a constant velocity of circulation of bank money. But the velocity of credit money is not constant. It increases during periods of brisk business activity and decreases in periods of falling prices. Thus a policy of contracting credit by the sale of securities by the central bank may not be successful by increased velocity of circulation of bank credit.

Despite these limitations, open market operations are more effective than the other instruments of credit control available with the central bank. This method is being successfully used for controlling credit in developed countries where the securities market is highly developed.

Open Market Operations vs Bank Rate Policy

The question arises whether the bank rate is more effective as an instrument of credit control or open market operations. The bank rate policy influences the cost and supply of commercial bank credit, while open market operations affect the cash reserves of the commercial banks. Changes in the bank rate affect the credit creation power of the commercial bank only if they rediscount their bills with the central bank. If the banks do not feel the necessity of availing rediscounting facilities of the central bank, a rise in the bank rate will have no effect on the commercial banks. On the other hand, the lending power of the commercial banks is directly related to their cash reserves, and open market operations influence their cash reserves directly and immediately thereby affecting their credit creation power.

Further, "from the standpoint of their strategic value to the central bank, open market operations possess a degree of superiority over rediscount policy because of the fact that initiative is in the hands of the monetary authority in the case of the former, whereas bank rate policy is passive in the sense that its effectiveness depends on the responses of commercial banks and their customers to changes in bank rates."[2]

Again, open market operations are flexible with respect to timing and magnitude as compared with the bank rate policy. They are carried on continuously and do not have any destablilising effects on the economy that accompany changes in the bank rate.

It is further argued that since bank rate changes have destabilising effects on the economy, this policy should be used to correct permanent maladjustments in the money market rather than temporary maladjustments. On the other hand, open market policy can be used for correcting both temporary and permanent maladjustments in the money market.

But the experience of developed countries like the USA and the UK tells us that these two policies are not

---

2. G.N. Halm, *Monetary Theory*, p.59.

competitive but complementary to each other. If they are supplemented, they can control credit more effectively than individually. For instance, if the central bank raises the discount rate for the purpose of contracting credit, it will not be effective when the commercial bank have large excess reserves with them. They will continue to expand credit irrespective of the rise in the bank rate. But if the central bank first draws away to itself the excess reserves of the commercial banks by the sale of securities and then raises the bank rate, it will have the effect of contracting credit. Similarly, the sale of securities alone will not be so effective in contracting credit unless the bank rate is also raised. The sale of securities by the central bank will reduce the cash reserves of commercial banks but if the discount rate is low, the latter will get funds from the "discount window" of the central bank. So for an effective policy credit control, bank rate policy and open market operations should be judiciously supplemented.

3. Variable Reserve Ratio

Variable reserve ratio (or required reserve ratio or legal minimum requirements), as a method of credit control was first suggested by Keynes in his *Treatise on Money* (1930) and was adopted by the Federal Reserve System of the United States in 1935.

Every commercial bank is required by law to maintain a minimum percentage of its deposits with the central bank. The minimum amount of reserve with the central bank may be either a percentage of its time and demand deposits separately or of total deposits. Whatever the amount of money remains with the commercial bank over and above these minimum reserves is known as the excess reserves. It is on the basis of these excess reserves that the commercial bank is able to create credit. The larger the size of the excess reserves, the greater is the power of a bank to create credit, and vice versa. It can also be said that the larger the required reserve ratio, the lower the power of a bank to create credit, and vice versa.

When the central bank raises the reserve ratio of the commercial banks, it means that the latter are required to keep more money with the former. Consequently, the excess reserves with the commercial banks are reduced and they can lend less than before.

This can be explained with the help of the deposit multiplier formula. If a commercial bank has Rs 100 crores as deposits and 10 per cent is the required reserve ratio, then it will have to keep Rs 10 crores with the central bank. Its excess reserves will be Rs 90 crores. It can thus create credit to the extent of Rs 900 crores in this way ER/RRr where ER is the excess reserves, and RRr the required reserve ratio... 90x1/10% = 90 x 100/10 = Rs 900 crores. When the central bank raises the required reserve ratio to 20 per cent, the bank's power to create credit will be reduced to Rs 400 crores = 80 x 100/20.

On the contrary, if the central bank wants to expand credit, it lowers the reserve ratio so as to increase the credit creation power of the commercial banks. Thus by varying the reserve ratio of the commercial banks the central bank influences their power of credit creation and thereby controls credit in the economy.

Limitations of Variable Reserve Ratio. The variable reserve ratio as a method of credit control has a number of limitations.

1. Excess Reserves. The commercial banks usually possess large excessive reserves which make the policy of variable reserve ratio ineffective. When the banks keep excessive reserves, an increase in the reserve ratio will not affect their lending operations. They will stick to the legal minimum requirements of cash to deposits and at the same time continue to create credit on the strength of the excessive reserves.

2. Clumsy Method. It is a clumsy method of credit control as compared with open market operations. This is because it lacks definiteness in the sense that it is inexact and uncertain as regards changes not only in the amounts of reserves but also the place where these changes can be made effective. It is not possible to tell "how much of active or potential reserve base" has been affected by changes in the reserve ratio. Moreover, the changes in reserves involve far larger sums than in the case of open market operations.[3]

3. Discriminatory. It is discriminatory and affects different banks differently. A rise in the required reserve ratio will not affect those banks which have large excess reserves. On the other hand, it will hit hard the banks with little or no excess reserves. This policy is also discriminatory in the sense that non-banking financial intermediaries like co-operative societies, insurance companies, building societies, development banks, etc. are

3. K. Basu, *A Review of Current Banking Theory and Practice*, 1971.

not affected by variations in reserve requirements, though they compete with the commercial banks for lending purposes.

4. Inflexible. This policy is inflexible because the minimum reserve ratio fixed by the central banks is applicable to banks located in all regions of the country. More credit may be needed in one region where there is monetary stringency, and it may be superfluous in the other region. Raising the reserve ratio for all banks is not justified in the former region though it is appropriate for the latter region.

5. Business Climate. The success of the method of credit control also depends on the business climate in the economy. If the businessmen are pessimistic about the future, as under a depression, even a sizable lowering of the reserve ratio will not encourage them to ask for loan. Similarly, if they are optimistic about profit expectations, a considerable rise in the variable ratio will not prevent them from asking for more loans from the banks.

6. Stability of Reserve Ratio. The effectiveness of this technique depends upon the degree of stability of the reserve ratio. If the commercial banks are authorised to keep widely fluctuating ratio, say between 10 per cent to 17 per cent, and change in the upper or lower limit will have no effect on the credit creation power of the banks.

7. Other Factors. The reserve ratio held by the commercial banks is determined not only by legal requirements but also by how much they want to hold in relation to their deposits in addition to such requirements. This, in turn, will depend upon their expectations about future developments, their competition with other banks, and so on.[4]

8. Depressive Effect. The variable reserve ratio has been criticised for exercising a depressive effect on the securities market. When the central bank suddenly directs the commercial banks to increase their reserve ratios, they may be forced to sell securities to maintain that ratio. This widespread selling of securities will bring down the prices of securities and may even lead to an utter collapse of the bond market.[5]

9. Rigid. It is rigid in its operations because it does not distinguish between desired and undesired credit flows and can affect them equally.

10. Not for Small Changes. This method is more like an axe than a scalpel. It cannot be used for day-to-day and week-to-week adjustments but can be used to bring about large changes in the reserve positions of the commercial banks. Thus it cannot help in 'fine tuning' of the money and credit systems by making small changes.

Conclusion. The variable reserve ratios as a method of credit control is a very delicate and sensitive tool which not only produces a state of uncertainty among the banks but also adversely affects their liquidity and profitability. Therefore, according to De Kock, "it should be used with moderation and discretion and only under obvious abnormal conditions."[6]

Variable Reserve Ratio vs Open Market Operations

There are divergent views about the superiority of variable reserve ratio over open market operations. To those who consider the former as a superior instrument of credit control, it is "a battery of the most improved type that a central bank can add to its armoury."[7] They give the following arguments.

The variable reserve ratio affects the power of credit creation of the commercial banks more directly, immediately, and simultaneously than open market operations. The central bank has simply to make a declaration for changing the reserve requirements of the banks and they have to implement it immediately. But open market operations require sale or purchase of securities which is a time consuming process.

When the central bank sells securities to the banks to control inflation, they are forced to buy them. They are, therefore, prevented from giving more loans to the private credit market. On the other hand, if the reserve ratio is raised, the banks will be required to keep larger balances with the central bank. They will also be faced with reduced earnings. They will, therefore, be induced to sell government securities and give more loans to the private credit market. Thus open market operations are more effective for controlling inflation than the change in reserve ratio.

---

4. H.G. Johnson, 'Recent Development in Monetary Theory', I.E.R., Feb. 1963.
5. S.K. Basu, *op.cit.*, p. 122.
6. De Kock, *op.cit.*, p. 251.
7. S.K. Basu, *op.cit.*, p. 120.

In another sense, open market operations are more effective as an instrument of credit control than variations in the reserve ratio. In every country there are non-banking financial intermediaries which deal in securities, bonds, etc. and also advance loans and accept deposits from the public. But they are outside the legal control of the central bank. Since they also deal in government securities, open market sale and purchase of such securities by the central bank also affect their liquidity position. But they are not required to keep any reserves with the central bank, unlike the commercial banks.

Again, variations in the reserve ratio are meant for making major and long-run adjustments in the liquidity position of the commercial banks. They are, therefore, not suited for making short-run adjustments in the volume of available bank reserves, as are done under open market operations.

The effectiveness of open market operations depends upon the existence of a broad and well-organised market for securities. Thus this instrument of credit control cannot be operative in countries which lack such a market. On the other hand, the method of variable reserve ratio does not require any such market for its operation and is applicable equally in developed and underdeveloped markets, and is thus superior to open market operations.

Further, since open market operations involve the sale and purchase of securities on a day-to-day and week-to-week basis, the commercial banks and the central bank which deal in them are likely to incur losses. But variations in the reserve ratio do not involve any losses.

Despite the superiority of variable reserve ratio over open market operations, economists like Prof. Aschheim[8] have argued that open market operations are more effective as a tool in controlling credit than variable reserve ratio. Therefore, changes in the reserve ratio do not have any effect on their lending power. Thus open market operations are superior to variable ratio because they also influence non-banking financial institutions.

Further, as a technique, reserve ratio can only influence the volume of reserves of the commercial banks. On the other hand, open market operations can influence not only the reserves of the commercial banks but also the pattern of the interest rate structure. Thus open market operations are more effective in influencing the reserves and the credit creation power of the banks than variations in reserve ratio.

Last but not the least, the technique of variations in reserve ratio is clumsy, inflexible, and discriminatory whereas that of open market operations is simple, flexible and non-discriminatory in its effects.

It can be concluded from the above discussion of the relative merits and demerits of the two techniques that in order to have the best of the two, they should be used jointly rather than independently. If the central bank raises the reserve ratio, it should simultaneously start purchasing, and not selling, securities in those areas of the country where there is monetary stringency. On the contrary, when the central bank lowers the reserve requirments of the banks, it should also sell securities to those banks which already have excess reserves with them, and have been engaged in excessive lending. The joint application of the two policies will not be contradictory but complementary to each other.

4. Selective Credit Controls

Selective or qualitative methods of credit control are meant to regulate and control the supply of credit among its possible users and uses. They are different from quantitative or general methods which aim at controlling the cost and quantity of credit. Unlike the general instruments, selective instruments do not affect the total amount of credit but the amount that is put to use in a particular sector of the economy. The aim of selective credit control is to channelise the flow of bank credit from speculative and other undesirable purposes to socially desirable and economically useful uses. They also restrict the demand for money by laying down certain conditions for borrowers. They therefore, embody the view that the monopoly of credit should in fact become a discriminating monopoly.[9] Prof. Chandler defines selective credit controls as those measures "that would influence the allocation of credit, at least to the point of decreasing the volume of credit used for selected purposes without the necessity of decreasing the supply and raising the cost of credit for all purposes."[10] We discuss below the main types of selective credit controls generally used by the central banks in different countries.

---

8. J. Aschheim, *Theory of Monetary Control*, Ch. 2.
9. S.K. Basu, *op.cit.*, pp. 144-45.
10. L.V. Chandler, *op.cit.*, p. 247.

(A) Regulation of Margin Requirements

This method is employed to prevent excessive use of credit to purchase or carry securities by speculators. The central bank fixes minimum margin requirements on loans for purchasing or carrying securities. They are, in fact, the percentage of the value of the security that cannot be borrowed or lent. In other words, it is the maximum value of loan which a borrower can have from the banks on the basis of the security (or collateral). For example, if the central bank fixes a 10 per cent margin on the value of a security worth Rs 1,000, then the commercial bank can lend only Rs 900 to the holder of the security and keep Rs 100 with it. If the central bank raises the margin to 25 per cent, the bank can lend only Rs 750 against a security of Rs 1,000. If the central bank wants to curb speculative activities, it will raise the margin requirements. On the other hand, if it wants to expand credit, it reduces the margin requirements.

Its Merits. This method of selective credit control has certain merits which make it unique.

1. It is non-discriminatory because it applies equally to borrowers and lenders. Thus it limits both the supply and demand for credit simultaneously.

2. It is equally applicable to commercial banks and non-banking financial intermediaries.

3. It increases the supply of credit for more productive uses.

4. It is a very effective anti-inflationary device because it controls the expansion of credit in those sectors of the economy which breed inflation.

5. It is simple and easy to administer since this device is meant to regulate the use of credit for specific purposes.

But the success of this technique requires that there are no leakages of bank credit for non-purpose loans to speculators.

Its Weaknesses. However, a number of leakages have appeared in this method over the years.

1. A borrower may not show any intention of purchasing stocks with his borrowed funds and pledge other assets as security for the loan. But it may purchase stocks through some other source.

2. The borrower may purchase stocks with cash which he would normally use to purchase materials and supplies and then borrow money to finance the materials and supplies already purchased, pledging the stocks he already has as security for the loan.

3. Lenders, other than commercial banks and brokers, who are not subject to margin requirements, may increase their security loans when commercial banks and brokers are being controlled by high margin requirements. Further, some of these nonregulated lenders may be getting the funds they lent to finance the purchase of securities from commercial banks themselves.

Despite these weaknesses in practice, margin requirements are a useful device of credit control.

(B) Regulation of Consumer Credit

This is another method of selective credit control which aims at the regulation of consumer instalment credit or hire-purchase finance. The main objective of this instrument is to regulate the demand for durable consumer goods in the interest of economic stability. The central bank regulates the use of bank credit by consumers in order to buy durable consumer goods on instalments and hire-purchase. For this purpose, it employs two devices: minimum down payments, and maximum periods of repayment. Suppose a bicycle costs Rs 500 and credit is available from the commercial bank for its purchase. The central bank may fix the mimimum down payment to 50 per cent of the price, and the maximum period of repayment to 10 months. So Rs 250 will be the minimum which the consumer will have to pay to the bank at the time of purchase of the bicycle and the remaining amount in ten equal instalments of Rs 25 each. This facility will create demand for bicycles. The bicycle industry would expand along with the related industries such as tyres, tubes, spare parts, etc. and thus lead to inflationary situation in this and other sectors of the economy. To control it, the central bank raises the minimum down payment to 70 per cent and the maximum period of repayment to three instalements. So the buyer of a bicycle will have to pay Rs 350 in the beginning and remaining amount in three instalments of Rs 50 each. Thus if the central bank finds slump in particular industries of the economy, it reduces the amount of down payments and increases the maximum periods of repayment. Reducing the down payments tends to increase the demand for credit for particular durable consumer goods on which the central bank regulation is applied. Increasing the maximum period of repayment, which reduces monthly payments, tends to increase the demand for loans, thereby encouraging consumer credit. On the other hand, the central bank raises the amount of down payments and reduces the maximum periods of repayment in boom.

The regulation of consumer credit is more effective in controlling credit in the case of durable consumer goods during both booms and slumps, whereas general credit controls fail in this area. The reason is that the latter operate with a time lag. Moreover, the demand for consumer credit in the case of durable consumer goods is interest inelastic. Consumers are motivated to buy such goods under the influence of the demonstration effect and the rate of interest has little consideration for them.

But this instrument has its *drawbacks*.

It is cumbersome, technically defective and difficult to administer because it has a narrow base. In other words, it is applicable to a particular class of borrowers whose demand for credit forms an insignificant part of the total credit requirements. It, therefore, discriminates between different types of borrowers. This method affects only persons with limited incomes and leaves out higher income groups. Finally, it tends to malallocate resources by shifting them away from industries which are covered by credit regulations and lead to the expansion of other industries which do not have any credit restrictions.

(C) Rationing of Credit

Rationing of credit is another selective method of controlling and regulating the purpose for which credit is granted by the commercial banks. It is generally of four types. The first is the variable portfolio ceiling. According to this method, the central bank fixes a ceiling on the aggregate portfolios of the commercial banks and they cannot advance loans beyond this ceiling. The second method is known as the variable capital assets ratio. This is the ratio which the central bank fixes in relation to the capital of a commercial bank to its total assets. In keeping with the economic exigencies, the central bank may raise or lower the portfolio ceiling, and also vary the capital assets ratio.

Rationing of credit has been used very effectively in Russia and Mexico. It is, therefore, 'a logical concomitant of the intensive and extensive planning adopted in regimented economies.' The technique also involves discrimination against larger banks because it restricts their lending power more than the smaller banks. Lastly, by rationing of credit for selective purposes, the central bank ceases to be the lender of the last resort. Therefore, central banks in mixed economies do not use this technique except under extreme inflationary situations and emergencies.

(D) Direct Action

Central banks in all countries frequently resort to direction action against commercial banks. Direction action is in the form of "directives" issued from time to time to the commercial banks to follow a particular policy which the central bank wants to enforce immediately. This policy may not be used against all banks but against erring banks. For example, the centrl bank refuses rediscounting facilities to certain banks which may be granting too much credit for speculative purposes, or in excess of their capital and reserves, or restrains them from granting advances against the collateral of certain commodities, etc. It may also charge a penal rate of interest from those banks which want to borrow from it beyond the prescribed limit. The central bank may even threaten a commercial bank to be taken over by it in case it fails to follow its policies and instructions.

But this method of credit suffers from several limitations which have been enumerated by De Kock as "the difficulty for both central and commercial bank to make clear-cut distinctions at all times and in all cases between essential and non-essential industries, productive and unproductive activities, investment and speculation, or between legitimate and excessive speculation or consumption; the further difficulty of controlling the ultimate use of credit by second, third or fourth parties; the dangers involved in the division of responsibility between the central bank and commercial bank for the soundness of the lending operations of the latter; and the possibility of forfeiting the whole-hearted and active co-operations of the commercial banks as a result of undue control and intervention."[11]

(E) Moral Suasion

Moral suasion in the method of persuasion, of request, of informal suggestion, and of advice to the

11. De Kock, *op.cit.*, pp. 228-29.

commercial bank usually adopted by the central bank. The executive head of the central bank calls a meeting of the heads of the commercial banks wherein he explains them the need for the adoption of a particular monetary policy in the context of the current economic situation, and then appeals to them to follow it. This "jawbone control" or "slaps on the wrist" method has been found to be highly effective as a selective method of credit control in India, New Zealand, Canada and Australia, though it failed in the USA.

Its Limitations. Moral suasion is a method "without any teeth" and hence its effectiveness is limited.

1. Its success depends upon the extent to which the commercial banks accept the central bank as their leader and need accommodation from it.

2. If the banks possess excessive reserves they may not follow the adivce of the central bank, as is the case with the commercial banks in the USA.

3. Further, moral suasion may not be successful during booms and depressions when the economy is passing through waves of optimism and pessimism respectively. The bank may not heed to the advice of the central bank in such a situation.

4. In fact, moral suasion is not a control device at all, as it involves cooperation by the commercial banks rather than their coercion.

It may, however, be a success where the central bank commands prestige on the strength of the wide statutory powers vested in it by the government of the country.

(F) Publicity

The central bank also uses publicity as an instrument of credit control. It publishes weekly or monthly statements of the assets and liabilities of the commercial bank for the information of the public. It also publishes statistical data relating to money supply, prices, production and employment, and of capital and money market, etc. This is another way of exerting moral pressure on the commercial bank. The aim is to make the public aware of the policies being adopted by the commercial bank vis-a-vis the central bank in the light of the prevailing economic conditions in the country.

It cannot be said with definiteness about the success of this method. It presupposes the existence of an educated and knowledgeable public about the monetary phenomena. But even in advanced countries, the percentage of such persons is negligible. It is, therefore, highly doubtful if they can exert any moral pressure on the banks to strictly follow the policies of the central bank. Hence, publicity as an instrument of selective credit control is only of academic interest.

Limitations of Selective Credit Controls. Though regarded superior to quantitative credit controls, yet selective credit controls are not free from certain limitations.

1. *Limited Coverage.* Like general credit controls, selective credit controls have a limited coverage. They are only applicable to the commercial banks but not to non-banking financial institutions. But in the case of the regulation of consumer credit which is applicable both to banking and non-banking institutions, it becomes cumbersome to administer this technique.

2. *No Specificity.* Selective credit controls fail to fulfil the specificity function. There is no guarantee that the bank loans would be used for the specific purpose for which they are sanctioned.

3. *Difficult to distinguish between Essential and Non-essential Factors.* It may be difficult for the central bank to distinguish precisely between essential and non-essential sectors and between speculative and productive investment for the purpose of enforcing selective credit controls. The same reasoning applies to the commercial banks for the purpose of advancing loans unless they are specifically laid down by the central bank.

4. *Require Large Staff.* The commercial banks, for the purpose of earning large profits, may advance loans for purposes other than laid down by the central bank. This is particularly so if the central bank does not have a large staff to check minutely the accounts of the commercial banks. As a matter of fact, no central bank can afford to check their accounts. Hence selective credit controls are liable to be ineffective in the case of unscrupulous banks.

5. *Discriminatory.* Selective controls unnecessarily restrict the freedom of borrowers and lenders. They also discriminate between different types of borrowers and banks. Often small borrowers and small banks are hit harder by selective control than big borrowers and large banks.

6. *Malallocation of Resources.* Selective credit controls also lead to malallocation of resources when they are

applied to selected sectors, areas and industries while leaving others to operate freely. They place undue restrictions on the freedom of the former and affect their production.

7. Not Successful in Unit Banking. Unit banks being independent one-office banks in the USA operate on a small scale in small towns and meet the financial needs of the local people. Such banks are not affected by the selective credit controls of the FRS (central bank of the USA) because they are able to finance their activities by borrowing from big banks. So this policy is not effective in unit banking.

Conclusion. From the above discussion, it should not be concluded that selective credit controls are used to the total exclusion of general credit controls. Their demerits primarily arise from this thinking. In fact, they are an adjunct to general quantitative controls. They are meant to supplement the latter and are regarded only as a "second-line instrument". "The vital point is not the question of general vs. selective credit control the assessment of the pros and cons as between the two mehtods, but that of integrating them. Indeed the coordination of selective and general controls appears to have been more effective than the use of any one of them singly and by itself."[12]

6. ROLE OF CENTRAL BANK IN A DEVELOPING ECONOMY

The central bank in a developing economy performs both traditional and non-traditional functions. The principal traditional functions performed by it are the monopoly of note issue, banker to the government, bankers' bank, lender of the last resort, controller of credit and maintaining stable exchange rate.[13] But all these functions are related to the foremost function of helping in the economic development of the country.

ROLE OF CENTRAL BANK IN ECONOMIC DEVELOPMENT

The central bank in a developing country aims at the promotion and maintenance of a rising level of production, employment and real income in the country. The central banks in the majority of underdeveloped countries have been given wide powers to promote the growth of such economies. They, therefore, perform the following functions towards this end.

Creation and Expansion of Financial Institutions. One of the aims of a central bank in an underdeveloped country is to improve its currency and credit system. More banks and financial institutions are requried to be set up to provide larger credit facilities and to divert voluntary savings into productive channels. Financial institutions are localised in big cities in underdeveloped countries and provide credit facilities to estates, plantations, big industrial and commercial houses. In order to remedy this, the central bank should extend branch banking to rural areas to make credit available to peasants, small businessmen and traders. In underdeveloped countries, the commercial banks provide only short-term loans. Credit factilites in rural areas are mostly non-existent. The only source is the village moneylender who charges exorbitant interest rates. The hold of the village moneylender in rural areas can be slackened if new institutional arrangementss are made by the central bank in providing short-term, medium term and long-term credit at lower interest rates to the cultivators. A network of co-operative credit societies with apex banks financed by the central bank can help solve the problem. Similarly, it can help the establishment of lead banks and through them regional rural banks for providing credit facilities to marginal farmers, landless agricultural workers and other weaker sections. With the vast resources at its command, the central bank can also help in establishing industrial banks and financial corporations in order to finance large and small industries.

Proper Adjustment between Demand for and Supply of Money. The central bank plays an important role in bringing about a proper adjustment between demand for and supply of money. An imbalance between the two is reflected in the price level. A shortage of money supply will inhibit growth while an excess of it will lead to inflation. As the economy develops, the demand for money is likely to go up due to gradual monetization of the non-monetized sector and the increase in agricultural and industrial production and prices. The demand for money for transactions and speculative motives will also rise. So the increase in money supply will have to

12. S.K. Basu, *op.cit.*, p. 155.
13. These functions of a central bank in an LDC may be explained briefly.

be more than proportionate to the increase in the demand for money in order to avoid inflation. There is, however, the likelihood of increased money supply being used for speculative purposes, thereby inhibiting growth and causing inflation. The central bank controls the uses of money and credit by an appropriate monetary policy. Thus in an underdeveloped economy, the central bank should control the supply of money in such a way that the price level is prevented from rising without affecting investment and production adversely.

A Suitable Interest Rate Policy. In an underdeveloped country the interest rate structure stands at a very high level. There are also vast disparities between long-term and short-term interest rates and between interest rates in different sectors of the economy. The existence of high interest rates acts as an obstacle to the growth of both private and public investment, in an underdeveloped economy. A low interest rate is, therefore, essential for encouraging private investment in agriculture and industry. Since in an underdeveloped country businessmen have little savings out of undistributed profits, they have to borrow from the banks or from the capital market for purposes of investment and they would borrow only if the interest rate is low. A low interest rate policy is also essential for encouraging public investment. A low interest rate policy is a cheap money policy. It makes public borrowing cheap, keeps the cost of servicing public debt low, and thus helps in financing economic development.

In order to discourage the flow of resources into speculative borrowing and investment, the central bank should follow a policy of discriminatory interest rates, charging *high* rates for non-essential and unproductive loans and *low* rates for productive loans. But this does not imply that savings are interest-elastic in an underdeveloped economy. Since the level of income is low in such economies, a high rate of interest is not likely to raise the propensity to save. In the context of economic growth, as the economy develops, a progressive rise in the price level is inevitable. The value of money falls and the propensity to save declines further. Money conditions become tight and there is a tendency for the rate of interest to rise automatically. This would result in inflation. In such a situation any effort to control inflation by raising the rate of interest would be disastrous. A *stable price* level is, therefore, essential for the success of a low interest rate policy which can be maintained by following a judicious monetary policy by the central benk.

Debt Management. Debt management is one of the important functions of the central bank in an underdeveloped country. It should aim at proper timing and issuing of governnment bonds, stabilizing their prices and minimizing the cost of servicing public debt. It is the central bank which undertakes the selling and buying of government bonds and making timely changes in the structure and composition of public debt. In order to strengthen and stabilize the market for government bonds, the policy of low interest rates is essential. For, a low rate of interest raises the price of government bonds, thereby making them more attractive to the public and giving an impetus to the public borrowing programmes of the government. The maintenance of structure of low interest rates is also called for minimizing the cost of servicing the national debt. Further, it encourages funding of debt by private firms. However, the success of debt management would depend upon the existence of well-developed money and capital markets in which wide range of securities exist both for short and long periods. It is the central bank which can help in the development of these markets.

Credit Control. Central Bank should also aim at controlling credit in order to influence the patterns of investment and production in a developing economy. Its main objective is to control inflationary pressures arising in the process of development. This requires the use of both quantitative and qualitative methods of credit control.

Open market operations are not successful in controlling inflation in underdeveloped countries because the bill market is small and undeveloped. Commercial banks keep an elastic cash-deposit ratio because the central bank's control over them is not complete. They are also reluctant to invest in government securities due to their relatively low interest rates. Moreover, instead of investing in government securities, they prefer to keep their reserves in liquid form such as gold, foreign exchange and cash. Commercial banks are also not in the habit of rediscounting or borrowing from the central bank.

The *bank rate policy* is also not so effective in controlling credit in LDCs due to: (a) the lack of bills of discount; (b) the narrow size of the bill market; (c) a large non-monetised sector where barter transactions take place; (d) the existence of a large unorganised money market; (e) the existence of indigenous banks which do not discount bills with the central baks; and (f) the habit of commercial banks to keep large cash reserves.

The use of *variable reserve ratio* as method of credit control is more effective than open market operations and bank rate policy in LDCs. Since the market for securities is very small, open market operations are not successful. But a rise or fall in the reserve ratio by the central bank reduces or increases the cash available with the commercial banks without affecting adversely the prices of securities. Again, the commercial banks keep large cash reserves which cannot be reduced by a raise in the bank rate or sale of securities by the central bank. But raising the cash-reserve ratio reduces liquidity with the banks. However, the use of variable reserve ratio has certain *limitations* in LDCs. First, the non-banking financial intermediaries do not keep deposits with the central bank so they are not affected by it. Second, banks which do not maintain excess liquidity are not affected than those who maintain it.

The qualitative credit control measures are, however, more effective than the quantitative measures in influencing the allocation of credit, and thereby the pattern of investment. In underdeveloped countries, there is a strong tendency to invest in gold, jewellery, inventories, real estate, etc., instead of in alternative productive channels available in agriculture, mining, plantations and industry. The selective credit controls are more appropriate for controlling and limiting credit facilitates for such unproductive purposes. They are beneficial in controlling speculative activities in foodgrains and raw materials. They prove more useful in controlling 'sectional inflations' in the economy. They curtail the demand for imports by making it obligatory on importers to deposit in advance an amount equal to the value of foreign currency. This has also the effect of reducing the reserves of the banks in so far as their deposits are transferred to the central banks in the process. The selective credit control measures may take the form of changing the margin requirements against certain types of collateral, the regulation of consumer credit and the rationing of credit.

Solving the Balance of Payments Problem. The central bank should also aim at preventing and solving the balance of payments problem in a developing economy. Such economies face serious balance of payments difficulties to fulfil the targets of development plans. An imbalance is created between imports and exports which continues to widen with development. The central bank manages and controls the foreign exchange of the country and also acts as the technical adviser to the government on foreign exchange policy. It is the function of the central bak to avoid fluctuations in the foreign exchange rates and to maintain stability. It does so through exchange controls and variations in the bank rate. For instance, if the value of the national currency continues to fall, it may raise tha bank rate and thus encourage the inflow of foreign currencies.

Conclusion. Thus the central bank plays an important role in achieving economic growth of a developing country through the various measures discussed above. It should promote economic growth with stability, help in attaining full employment of resources, in overcoming balance of payments disequilibrium, and in stabilising exchange rates.

EXERCISES

1. Discuss the essential functions of a central bank.
2. Distinguish between quantitative and qualitative methods of credit control. Which are more effective in an inflationary situation ?
3. Account for the recent shift from conventional quantitative control to qualitative control.
4. Between Bank Rate and Open Market Operations which is more effective as an instrument of credit control ? Give reasons.
5. Explain the significance of selective credit controls. How do they operate and with what success ?
6. Discuss the role of a central bank in promoting economic growth in a developing country.

Chapter 20

Money and Capital Markets

The study of money and capital markets in all their facets is so exhaustive that it is not possible to discuss them in one chapter. We shall, therefore, confine our analysis to the nature and scope of money and capital markets. The Indian money market and capital market are studies separately in the last part of the book.

1. THE MONEY MARKET

Meaning and Features

The money market is a market for short-term instruments that are close substitutes for money. The short term instruments are highly liquid, easily marketable, with little change of loss. It provides for the quick and dependable transfer of short term debt instruments maturing in one year or less, which are used to finance the needs of consumers, business agriculture and the government. The money market is not one market but is "a collective name given to the various form and institutions that deal with the various grades of near-money."[1] In other words, "it is a network of market that are grouped together because they deal in financial instruments that have a similar function in the economy and are to some degree substitutes from the point of view of holders."[2] Thus the money market consists of call and notice market, commercial bills market, commercial paper market, treasury bills market, inter-bank market and certificates of deposit market. All these markets are closely interrelated so as to make the money market. It is a wholesale market where large number of financial assets or instruments are traded.

The money market is divided into direct, negotiated, or customers' money market and the open or impersonal money market. In the former, banks and financial firms supply funds to local customers and also to larger centres such as London for direct lending. In the open money market, idle funds drawn from all-over the country are transferred through intermediaries to the New York City market or the London market. These intermediaries comprise the Federal Reserve Banks in the USA or the Bank of England in England, commercial banks, insurance companies, business corporations, brokerage houses, finance companies, state and local government securities' dealers.[3] The money market is a dynamic market in which new money market instruments are evolved and traded and more participants are permitted to deal in the money market.

---

1. G. Crowther, *op.cit.*, p. 66.
2. J.M. Culbertson, *Money and Banking*, 1972.
3. In underdeveloped Countries, the money market is divided into organised and unoganised categories. These are discussed in the chapter "The Indian Money Market". Also refer to the chapter on "Financial Dualism".

Institutions of the Money Market

The various financial institutions which deal in short term loans in the money market are its members. They comprise the following types of institutions :

1. *Central Bank.* The central bank of the country is the pivot around which the entire money market revolves. It acts as the guardian of the money market and increases or decreases the supply of money and credit in the interest of stability of the economy. It does not itself enter into direct transactions. But controls the money market through variations in the bank rate and open market operations.

2. *Commercial Banks.* Commercial banks also deal in short-term loans which they lend to business and trade. They discount bills of exchange and treasury bills, and lend against promissory notes and through advances and overdrafts.

3. *Non-bank Financial Intermediaries.* Besides the commercial banks, there are non-bank financial intermediaries which lend short-term funds to borrowers in the money market. Such financial intermediaries are savings banks, investment houses, insurance companies, provident funds, and other financial corporations.

4. *Discount Houses and Bill Brokers.* In developed money markets, private companies operate discount houses. The primary function of discount houses is to discount bills on behalf of other. They, in turn, form the commercial banks and acceptance houses. Alongwith discount houses, there are bill brokers in the money market who act as intermediaries between borrowers and lenders by discounting bills of exchange at a nominal commission. In underdeveloped money markets, only bill brokers operate.

5. *Acceptance Houses.* The institution of acceptance houses developed from the merchange bankers who transferred their headquarters to the London Money Market in the 19th and the early 20 the century. They act as agents between exporters and importers and between lender and borrower traders. They accept bills drawn on merchants whose financial standing is not known in order to make the bills negotiable in the London Money Market. By accepting a trade bill they guarantee the payment of bill at maturity. However, their importance has declined because the commercial banks have undertaken the acceptance business.

All these institutions which comprise the money market do not work in isolation but are interdependent and interrelated with each other.

Instruments of the Money Market

The money market operates through a number of instruments.

1. *Promissory Note.* The promissory note is the earliest types of bill. It is a written promise on the part of a businessman today to another a certain sum of money at an agreed future data. Usually, a promissory note falls due for payment after 90 days with three days of grace. A promissory note is drawn by the debtor and has to be accepted by the bank in which the debtor has his account, to be valid. The creditor can get it discounted from his bank till the date of recovery. Promissory notes are rarely used in business these days, except in the USA.

2. *Bill of Exchange or Commercial Bills.* Another instrument of the money, market is the bill of exchange which is similar to the promissory note, except in that it is drawn by the creditor and is accepted by the bank of the debater. The creditor can discount the bill of exchange either with a broker or a bank. There is also the foreign bill of exchange which becomes due for payment from the date of acceptance. The rest of the procedure is the same as for the internal bill of exchange. Promissory notes and bills of exchange are known as trade bills.

3. *Treasury Bill.* But the major instrument of the money markets is the treasury bill which is issued for varying periods of less than one year. They are issued by the Secretary to the Treasury in England and are payable at the Bank of England. There are also the short-term government securities in the USA which are traded by commercial banks and dealers in securities. In India, the treasury bills are issued by the Government of India at a discount generally between 91 days and 364 days. There are three types of treasury bills in India—91 days, 182 days and 364 days.

4. *Call and Notice Money.* There is the call money market in which funds are borrowed and lent for one day. In the notice market, they are borrowed and lent upto 14 days without any collateral security. But deposit receipt is issued to the lender by the borrower who repays the borrowed amount with interest on call. In India, commercial banks and cooperative banks borrow and lend funds in this market but mutual funds and all-India

financial institutions participate only as lenders of funds.

5. *Inter-bank Term Market.* This market is exclusively for commercial and cooperative banks in India, which borrow and lend funds for a period of over 14 days and upto 90 days without any collateral security at market-determined rates.

6. *Certificates of Deposits (CD).* Certificates of deposits are issued by commercial banks at a discount on face value. The discount rate is determined by the market. In India the minimum size of the issue is Rs. 25 lakhs with the minimum subscription of Rs. 5 lakhs. The maturity period is between 3 months and 12 months.

7. *Commercial Paper (CP). Commercial* papers are issued by highly rate companies to raise short-term working capital requirements directly from the market instead of borrowing from the banks. CP is a promise by the borrowing company to repay the load at a specified date, normally for a period of 3 months to 6 months. This instrument is very popular in the USA, UK, Japan, Australia and a number of other countries. It has been introduced in India in January 1990.

WORKING OF THE MONEY MARKET

The money market consisting of commercial banks, discount houses, bill brokers, acceptance houses, non-bank financial houses and the central bank operates through the bills, securities, treasury bills, government securities and call loans of various types. As the money market consists of varied types of institutions dealing in different types of instruments, it operates through a number of sub-markets.

First, the money market operates through the call loan market. It has been defined as "a market for marginal funds, for temporarily unemployed or unemployable funds." In this market the commercial banks use their unsued funds to lend for very short periods to bill brokers and dealers in stock exchange. In developed countries, even big corporations lend their dividends before distribution to earn interest for a very short period. The central bank also lends to commercial bank is for very short periods. Such loans are mostly for a week even for a day or a night and can be recalled at a very short notice. That is why a short period loan is known as call loan or call money market. Bill brokers and stock brokers who borrow such funds use them to discount or purchase bills or stocks. Such funds are borrowed at the "call rate" which is generally one per cent below the bank rate. But this rate varies with the volume of funds lent by the bank. If the brokers are asked to pay off loans immediately, then they are forced to get funds from large corporations and even from the central bank at high interest rate.

Second, the money market also operates through the bill market. The bill market is the short-period loan market. In this market, loans are made available to businessmen and the government by the commercial banks, discount houses and brokers. The instruments of credit are the promissory notes. Internal bills of exchange and treasury bills. The commercial banks discount bills o exchange, lend against promissory notes or through advances or overdrafts to the business community. Similarly, the discount houses and bills brokers lend to businessmen by discounting their bills of exchange before they mature within 90 days. On the other hand, government borrows through the treasury bills from the commercial banks and non-bank financial institutions. Third, the money market operater through the collateral loan market fora short period. The commercial banks lend to brokers and discount houses against collateral bonds, stock, securities, etc. In case of need, commercial banks themselves borrower from the large banks and the central bank on the basis of collateral securities.

Finally, the other important sub-market through which the money market operates is the acceptance market. The merchant bankers accept bills drawn on domestic and foreign traders whose financial standing is not known. When they accept a domestic or foreign trade bill, they guarantee its payment at maturity. In recent years, the commercial banks have also started the acceptance business.

FUNCTIONS OF A MONEY MARKET*

A money market performs a number of functions in an economy.

1. *Provides Funds.* It provides short-term funds to the public and private institutions needing such financing

* This also relates to the importance of money market.

for their working capital requirements. It is done by discounting trade bills through commercial banks, discount houses, brokers and acceptance houses. Thus the money market helps the development of commerce, industry and trade within and outside the country.

2. *Use of Surplus Funds.* It provides and opportunity to banks and other institutions to use their surplus funds profitably for a short period. These institutions include not only commercial banks and other financial institutions but also large non-financial business corporations, states and local governments.

3. *No Need to Borrow from Banks.* The existence of a developed money market removes the necessity of borrowing by the commercial banks from the central bank. If the former find their reserves short of cash requirements they can call in some of their loans from the money market. The commercial banks prefer to recall their loans rather than borrow from the central banks at a higher rate of interests.

4. *Helps Government.* The money market helps the government in borrowing short-term funds at low interest rates on the basis of treasury bills. On the other hand, if the government were to issue paper money or borrow from the central bank. It would lead to inflationary pressures in the economy.

5. *Helps in Monetary Policy.* A well developed money market helps in the successful implementation of the monetary policies of the central bank. It is through the money market that the central banks is in a position to control the banking system and thereby influence commerce and industry.

6. *Helps in Financial Mobility. By* facilitating the transfer for funds from one sector to another, the money market helps in financial mobility. Mobility in the flow of funds is essential for the development of commerce and industry in an economy.

7. *Promotes Liquidity and Safety.* One of the important functions of the money market is that it promotes liquidity and safety of financial assets. It thus encourages savings and investments.

8. *Equilibrium between Demand and Supply of Funds.* The money market brings equilibrium between the demand and supply of loanable funds. This it does by allocating saving into investment channels. In this way, it also helps in rational allocation of resources.

9. *Economy in Use of Cash.* As the money market deals in near-money assets and not money proper, it helps in economising the use of cash. It thus provides a convenient and safe way of transferring funds from one place to another, thereby immensely helping commerce and industry.

CHARACTERISTICS OF AN UNDEVELOPED MONEY MARKET

The money markets in the majority of underdeveloped countries are mostly undeveloped or unorganised. In fact, they are dualistics, both developed and undeveloped money markets exist side by side. The developed money market consists of the central bank, the commercial banks, bill broker; discount houses, acceptance houses, etc. On the other hand, the undeveloped money market consists of the moneylenders, the indigenous bankers, traders, merchants, landlords, pawnbrokers, etc. Since the majority of the people in underdeveloped countries live in rural areas and are poor, the undeveloped market controls a major portion of the money market. The main characteristics of such a market are :

1. *Personal Touch.* The lenders have a personal touch with the borrowers. The lender knows every borrower personally in the village because the latter sides there.

2. *Flexibility in Loans.* There is no rigidity in loan transactions. The borrower can have more or less amount of loan according to his requirements depending upon the nature of security or his goodwill with the moneylender.

3. *Multiplicity of Lending Activities.* Mostly people do not specialise is moneylending alone. They combine moneylending with other economic activities. A merchant may supply goods on loan instead or money in cash.

4. *Varied Interest Rates.* There is multiplicity of interest rates. Interest rates are much higher than rates in the developed sector of the money market. The interest rate are not even uniform. The rate depends on the need of the borrower, the amount of loan, the time for which it is required and the nature of security. The greater the urgency, the higher will be the interest rate.

5. *Defective System of Accounting.* In the unorganised sector of the money market, the system of maintaining accounts is highly defecate. Proper accounts are never maintained. Formal receipts are not issued for interest and the principal repaid by the borrowers. Besides, there is utmost secrecy in maintaining accounts and lending

procedures in the undeveloped money market. The accounts of the moneylenders are not liable to checking by any higher authority.

6. *Absence of Link with the Developed Money Market.* The undeveloped sector is not linked with the developed sector of the money market in such countries. The former works independently of the latter and is also not under the control of the developed market. This has the effect of reducing the volume of monetary transactions and savings, and prevent their use in productive investments.

Characteristics of a Development Money Market

The developed money market is a well organised market which has the following main features :

1. *A Central Bank. A* developed money market has a central banks at the top which is the most powerful authority in monetary and banking matter. I controls, regulates and guides the entire money market. It provides liquidity to the money market, as it is the lender of the last resort to the various constituents of the money market.

2. *Organised Banking System.* An organised and integrated banking system is the second feature of a developed money market. In fact, it is the pivot around which the whole money market revolves. It is the commercial banks which supply short-term loans, and discount bills of exchange. They form an important link between the borrowers, brokers, discount houses and acceptance houses and the central bank in the money market.

3. *Specialised Sub-Markets.* A developed money market consists of a number of specialised sub-markets dealing in various types of credit instruments. There is the call loan market, the bill market, the treasury bill market, the collateral loan market and the acceptance market, and the foreign exchange market. The larger the number of sub-markets, the more developed is the money market. But the mere number of sub-markets is not enough. What is required is that the various sub-markets should have a number of dealers in each market and the sub-markets should be properly integrated with each other.

4. *Existence of Large Near-Money Assets.* A developed money market has a large number of near-money assets of various types such a bills of exchange, promissory notes, treasury bills, securities, bonds, etc. The larger the number of near-money assets, the more developed is the money market.

5. *Integrated Interest-Rate Structure.* Another important characteristic of a developed money market is that it has an integrated interest-rate structure. The interest rates prevailing in the various sub-markets are integrated to each other. A change in the bank rate leads to proportional changes in the interest rate prevailing in the sub-markets.

6. *Adequate Financial Resources.* A developed money market has easy access to financial sources from both within and outside the country. In fact, such a market attracts adequate funds from both sources, as is the case with the London Money Market.

7. *Remittance Facilities.* A developed money market provides cash and cheap emittance facilities for transferring funds from one market to the other. The London Money Market provides such remittance facilities throughout the world.

8. *Miscellaneous Factors.* Besides the above noted features, a developed money market is highly influenced by such factors as restrictions on international transactions, crisis, boom, depression, war, political instability, etc.

2. THE CAPITAL MARKET

Meaning and Features

The capital market is a market which deals in long-term loans. It supplies industry with fixed and working capital and finances medium-term and long-term borrowings of the central, state and local governments. The capital market deals in ordinary stock is, shares and debentures of corporations, and bonds and securities of governments.

The funds which flow into the capital market come from individuals who have savings to invest, the merchant banks, the commercial banks and non-bank financial intermediaries, such as insurance companies, finance houses, unit trusts, investment trusts, venture capital, leasing finance, mutual funds, building societies, etc. Further, there are the issuing houses which do not provide capital but underwrite the shares and debentures of companies and help in selling their new issues of shares and debentures. The demand for funds comes from joint stock companies for working and fixed capital assets and inventories and from local, state and central governments, improvement trusts, port trusts, etc. to finance a variety of expenditures and assets.

The capital market functions through the stock exchange market. A stock exchange is a market which facilitates buying and selling of shares, stocks, bonds, securities and debentures. It is not only a market for old securities and shares but also for new issues shares and securities. In fact, the capital market is related to the supply and demand for new capital, and the stock exchange facilitates such transactions. Thus the capital market comprises the complex of institutions and mechanisms through which medium-term funds and long-term funds are pooled and made available to individuals, business and governments. It also encompasses the process by which securities already outstanding are transferred.[4]

Importance or Functions of Capital Market

The capital market plays an important role immobilising saving and channel is in them into productive investments for the development of commerce and industry. As such, the capital market helps in capital formation and economic growth of the country. We discuss below the importance of capital market.

The capital market acts as an important link between savers and investors. The savers are lenders of funds while investors are borrowers of funds. The savers who do not spend all their income are called. "Surplus units" and the borrowers are known as "deficit units". The capital market is the transmission mechanism between surplus units and deficit units. It is a conduit through which surplus units lend their surplus funds to deficit units. Funds flow into the capital market from individuals and financial intermediaries which are absorbed by commerce, industry and government. It thus facilitates the movement of stream of capital to be used more productively and profitability to increases the national income. Surplus units buy securities with their surplus funds and deficit units sells securities to raise the funds they need. Funds flow from lenders to borrowers either directly or indirectly through financial institutions such as banks, unit trusts, mutual funds, etc. The borrowers issue primary securities which are purchased by lenders either directly or indirectly through financial institutions.

The capital market prides incentives to savers in the form of interest or dividend and transfers funds to investors. Thus it leads to capital formation. In fact, the capital market provides a market mechanism for those who have savings and to those who need funds for productive investments. It diverts resources from wasteful and unproductive channels such as gold, jewellery, real estate, conspicuous consumption, etc. to productive investments.

A well-developed capital market comprising expert banking and non-banking intermediaries brings stability in the value of stocks and securities. It does so by providing capital to the needy at reasonable interest rates and helps in minimising speculative activities.

The capital market encourages economic growth. The various institutions which operate in the capital market give quantities and qualitative direction to the flow of funds and bring rational allocation of resources. They do so by converting financial assets into productive physical assets. This leads to the development of commerce and industry through the private and public sector, thereby inducing economic growth.

In an underdeveloped country where capital is scarce, the absence of a developed capital market is a greater hindrance to capital formation and economic growth. Even though the people are poor, yet they do not have any inducements to save. Others who save, they invest their savings in wasteful and unproductive channels, such as gold, jewellery, real estate, conspicuous consumption, etc. Such countries can induce people to save more by establishing banking and non-banking financial institutions for the existence of a developed capital market. Such a market can go a long way in providing a link between savers and investors, thereby leading to capital formation and economic growth.

---

4. For a detailed study of the features of the Capital Market refer to the chapter "Indian Capital Market."

3. DISTINCTION BETWEEN MONEY AND CAPITAL MARKETS

The money market differs from the capital market on several grounds.

1. The money market deals in short-term funds which are used for financing current business operations and short-term needs of the government. On the other hand, the capital market deals in long-term funds required by industry and government.

2. Short-term funds in the money market refer to a period of less than a year, while in the capital market long-term funds refer to a period up to 25 years.

3. The money market uses such instruments as promissory notes, bills of exchange, treasury bills, certificates of deposits, commercial papers, etc. On the other hand, the capital market uses long-term securities such as shares, debentures and bonds of industrial concerns, and bonds and securities of the government.

4. The institutions operating in the money market and the capital market also differ from each other. The central bank, commercial banks, non bank financial intermediaries and bill brokers deal in money market instruments. On the other hand, stock exchanges, mutual funds, leasing companies, investment banks, investment trusts, insurance companies, etc. dealing capital market instrument.

4. INTERRELATIONS BETWEEN MONEY AND CAPITAL MARKETS

The money market and capital market are closely interrelated because most corporations and financial institutions are active in both. Firms may borrow funds from the money market for a short period or for a loan period from the capital market. A number of factors may prompt borrowers and lenders to resort to either the money market or the capital market which reflect the interdependence of the two markets. They are discussed below.

1. Lenders may choose to direct their funds to either or both markets depending on the availability of funds, the rates of return, and their investment policies.

2. Borrowers may obtain their funds from either or both markets according to their requirements. A firm may borrow short-term funds by selling commercial paper or it may float additional shares or bonds.

3. Some corporations and financial institutions serve both markets by buying and selling short-term and long-term securities.

4. All long-term securities become short-term instruments at the time of maturity. So some capital market instruments also become money market instruments.

5. Funds flow back and forth between the two market s whenever the treasury finances maturing bills with treasury securities or whenever a bank lends the proceeds of a maturing loan to a firm on a short-term basis.

6. Yields in the money market are related to those of the capital market. A fall in the short-term interest rates in the money market shows a condition of essay credit which is likely to be followed or accompanied by a more moderate fall in the long-term interest rates in the capital market. However, money market interest rates are more sensitive than are long-term interest rates in the capital market.

EXERCISES

1. What is a money market? Describe the working of a money market.
2. Describe the working of money market. Why is the money market important?
3. Define money market. Explain its functions.
4. What do you understand by the capital market? Explain its importance.
5. Distinguish between money and capital markets. How are they interrelated?

Chapter 21

Non-Bank Financial Intermediaries (NBFIs)

1. MEANING

Non-bank financial intermediaries are such institutions as savings and loan associations, life insurance companies, mutual savings banks, common trust funds, pension funds, and government lending agencies. These intermediaries pool funds from net savers and lend them to finance expenditured of business firms and local bodies. To obtain funds from net savers, the intermediaries issue and sell indirect securities such as time deposits, common fund stocks, saving and loan shares, and insurance policies. They purchase primary securities to lend funds to ultimate borrowers. Primary securities include government securities, mortgages, common and preferred stocks, and consumer and other short-term debts. Thus, NBFIs are financial firms that buy one kind of financial asset and sell another. For instance, savings and loan associations and mutual savings banks mainly buy mortgages and sell saving deposits; insurance companies buy mainly bonds and sell insurance policies and finance companies buy instalment loans and sell commercial papers.

2. ROLE OF NON-BANK FINANCIAL INTERMEDIARIES*

Non-bank financial intermediaries have been playing an important role in the following directions.

Reduce Hoarding. By bringing the ultimate lenders (or savers) and ultimate borrowers together, NBFIs reduce hoarding of cash by the people under the "mattress", as is commonly said.

Help the Household Sector. The household sector relies on NBFIs for making profitable use of its surplus funds and also to provide consumer credit loans, mortgage loans, etc. Thus they promote saving and investment habits among ordinary people.

Help the Business Sector. NBFIs also help the non-financial business sector by financing it through loans, mortgages, purchase of bonds, shares, etc. Thus they facilitate investment in plant, equipment and inventories.

Help the State and Local Government. NBFIs help the state and local bodies financially by purchasing their bonds.

*This section also relates to functions of NBFIs.

Help the Central Government. Similarly, they buy and sell central government securities and thus they help the central government.

Lenders and NBFIs both Earn. When savers deposit their funds with NBFIs, they earn interest. When NBFIs lend to ultimate borrowers, they earn profits. In fact, the reward of intermediation arises from the difference between the rate of return on primary securities held by NBFIs and the interest or dividend rate they pay on their indirect debt.

Provide Liquidity. NBFIs provide liquidity when they convert an asset into cash easily and quickly without loss of value in terms of money. When NBFIs issue claims against themselves and supply funds they, especially banks, always try to maintain their liquidity. This they do by following two rules: *first,* they make short-term loans and finance them by issuing claims against themselves for longer periods; and second, they diversify loans among different types of borrowers.

Help in Lowering Interest Rate. Competition among NBFIs leads to the lowering of interest rates. NBFIs prefer to keep their saving with NBFIs rather than in cash. The NBFIs, in turn, invest them in primary securities. Consequently, prices of securities are bid up and interest rates fall. Moreover, when people keep their cash holdings with NBFIs which are safe and liquid, the demand for money falls thereby lowering interest rates.

Low Interest Rates Benefit both Savers and Investors. When interest rates decline, both savers and investors benefit. *First,* the real cost of lending to borrowers is reduced. These, in turn, tend to reduce costs and prices of goods and services. With reduction in interest rated, the return on time deposits is also reduced which induces savers to deposit their funds with NBFIs, even though the latter pay lower interest rates. Still the savers benefit because NBFIs provide greater safety, convenience and other related services to them thereby increasing the savers' real return and income.

Brokers of Loanable Funds. NBFIs play an important role as brokers of loanable funds. They act as intermediaries between ultimate saver and ultimate investor. They sell indirect securities to savers and purchase primary securities from investors. Indirect securities are the short-term liabilities of financial intermediaries. On the other hand, primary securities are their earning assets but they are the debts of the borrowers. Thus NBFIs act as brokers of loanable funds by changing debt into credit.

Reduce Risks. When the non-bank financial intermediaries convert debt into credit, they reduce the risk to the ultimate lender. *First,* they create tiabilities on themselves by selling indirect securities to the lenders. Then they buy primary securities from borrowers of funds. So by acting as intermediaries between the lenders and borowers of funds, NBFIs take the risk on themselves and reduce it on the ultimate lenders. Moreover, by holding varied types of financial assets, they decrease their own risks. Low returns on some assets can be offset by high returns on others.

Mobilising Savings. NBFIs raise funds in the capital market and supply credit to investors. Expert financial services provided by them have been attracting larger share of public savings. Such services include easy liquidity, safety of principal, and ready divisibility of savings into direct securities of different values. They have been able to mobilise more funds due to development of two types of non-bank financial intermediaries. The first are the depository intermediaries which include savings and loan associations, credit unions, and mutual savings banks. There is high liquidity of savings in such institutions which attract small savers. Moreover, they issue fixed price assets whose value does not change like the market price of other types of assets. The second are the contractual intermediaries which enter into contract with savers and provide them various types of benefits over the long run. Such institutions are pension funds, life insurance companies and public provident funds. These two types of financial intermediaries in particular help in mobilising public savings.

Investment of Funds. NBFIs exist because they want to earn profit by investing the mobilised savings. Different financial intermediaries follow different investment policies. For instance, savings and loan associations and mutual savings banks invest in mortgages, and insurance companies invest in bonds and securities. Thus intermediaries mobilise public savings, invest them and thereby help in capital formation and economic growth.

Create New Assets and Liabilities. Gardner Ackley has shown that in intermediating between ultimate lenders and direct investors, NBFIs add greatly to the stock of financial assets available to savers and for every extra asset, they also create an equal new financial liability. But intermediation does not affect total net worth. He concludes that although intermediation does not increase total wealth or income, it can be assumed that it increases welfare.

Economies of Scale. NBFIs reap a number of economies of specialisation and scale in mobilising savings and making investments. It would be costly and cumbersome for individual savers to lend their funds to individual borrowers. NBFIs make larger transactions with ultimate lenders and borrowers. They specialise in trading large financial assets and thus have lower costs in buying and selling securities. They employ expert staff and efficient machinery and equipment, thereby increasing productivity in the transfer of funds.

Bring Stability in the Capital Market. NBFIs deal in a variety of assets and liabilities which are mostly traded in the capital market. If there were no NBFIs, there would be frequent changes in the demand and supply of financial assets and their relative yields, thereby bringing instability in the capital market. As NBFIs function within a legal framework and set rules, they provide stability to the capital market and benefit savers and firms through diversified financial services.

Benefit to the Economy. NBFIs are of immense help in the working of financial markets, in executing monetary and credit policies of the central bank and hence in promoting the growth of an economy. By transferring funds from surplus to deficit units, NBFIs create large financial assets and liabilities. They provide the economy with money supply and with near money assets. Thus they help in the working of financial markets. Since the financial markets govern the working of the economy; the monetary and credit policies of the central bank are changed in such a manner from time to time that the financial markets function smoothly in the country. In fact, the growth of the economy is dependent upon the proper functioning of the financial system which, in turn, depends to a large extent upon the NBFIs.

In Economic Growth. NBFIs help in the growth process of the economy. They intermediate between ultimate lenders who are savers and ultimate borrowers who are investors. By performing this function, they discourage hoarding bythe people, mobilise their savings and lend them to investors. Thus, NBFIs encourage saving and investments which are essential for promoting economic growth. Goldsmith's study has shown that the growth of NBFIs has been responsible for economic growth of developed countries in a significant way.

Conclusion : NBFIs provide liquidity and safety to financial assets and help in transferring funds from ultimate lenders to ultimate borrowers for productive purposes. They increase capital formation and consequently lead to economic growth.

3. NON-BANK FINANCIAL INTERMEDIARIES AND MONETARY POLICY: THE GURLEY-SHAW THESIS

There has been considerable discussion from the mid-1950s about the role of financial intermediaries in influencing monetary policy. The Radcliffe Committee in Britain studied the growth of financial intermediaries since World War II and came to the conclusion that they adversely affected the power of Bank of England to control credit. Gurley and Shaw also came to the same conclusion.

According to Gurley and Shaw, NBFIs perform the intermediary role of purchasing primary securities such as government securities, mortgages, common and preferred stocks, consumer and other short-term debt. On the other hand, they issue and sell indirect securities such as time deposits, common funds stocks, saving and loan-shares, and insurance policies to the ultimate lenders. By buying primary securities from the ultimate borrowers and selling indirect securities to the ultimate lenders, the intermediaries influence the availability of credit and the structure and level of interest rates. They create credit different from commercial banks. But they create new assets and liabilities which tend to influence the supply of money and thus hinder the operation of an effective monetary policy.

According to them, the savings deposits of NBFIs resemble the demand deposits of commercial banks because it is not difficult for NBFIs to convert their savings deposits into cash. These savings deposits, whether of commercial bank or of NBFIs, are for all practical purposes as liquid as demand deposits. Such savings deposits held by NBFIs are known as near-monies. Since the demand deposits are not controlled by the central bank, it follows that the savings deposits held by NBFIs will hinder the successful operation of a successful monetary policy.

If the central bank wishes to control excess liquidity in the economy only through reduction in money supply, it will not be successful because the savings deposits of NBFIs can be converted into cash. Similarly, if the central bank tries to control lending by commercial banks, it wil not be successful if the lending of all other NBFIs are not under its control, as is the case. According to Gurley and Shaw, this problem arises especially when the central bank adopts an anti-inflationary monetary policy. Suppose the central bank reduces the money supply in order to control inflation. Among other effects, the interest rates on market securities rise. In anticipation of higher yields and profits, NBFIs will raise the interest rates on their savings deposits to attract more funds in order to invest them in higher yielding securities.

Persons already holding securities find that their prices have fallen because of the rise in interest rates on present securities. They will, therefore, sell them and deposit their funds with intermediaries in order to earn higher interest rates on saving deposits. In the meantime, attracted by higher interest rates, others holding idle cash balances will also deposit them with intermediaries. So when NBFIs raise interest rates on their savings deposits, the public reduces its demand for money which, in turn, reduces the market rate of interest. Thus, NBFIs make tight monetary policy less successful or effective. This is explained in Fig. 1 where the demand and supply of money are taken on the horizontal axis and the rate of interest on the vertical axis. *MS* is the money supply curve and *MD* the money demand curve. Both intersect at *E* where *r*, rate of interest is determined. Suppose there is an inflationary situation and the central bank reduces the money supply by a certain amount to control it. The reduction in money supply is shown by the shifting of the *MS* curve to the left as M_1S_1 so that the new equilibrium point is established at E_1 and the rate of interest rises to r_2. The NBFIs also raise interest rate of their deposits which, in turn, reduces the demand for money by the public. The *MD* curve shifts to the left to M_1D_1 and intersects the M_1S_1 curve at E_2. The interest rate is now reduced from r_2 to r_1. Thus the NBFIs are able to counteract tight money policy.

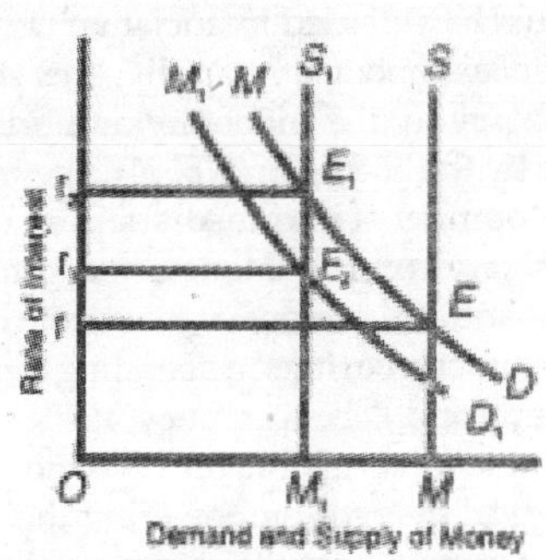

Fig. 1

Credit Creation. NBFIs make monetary policy ineffective even when the central bank adopts a restrictive monetary policy by selling securities in the open market and raising requirements of commercial banks. As a result, money supply with the bank is reduced and interest rates tend to rise. Non-bank financial intermediaries also find a rise in the interest rates of their primary securities. They, therefore, raise the interest rate on indirect securities in order to attract more funds from individual savers. This increase in interest rates, in turn, encourages savers to shift their savings from commercial bank demand deposits into time deposits, saving and loan shares, and other indirect securities of non-bank financial intermediaries. This tends to increase funds with the intermediaries for lending purposes and they are able to purchase more primary securities. Thus the supply of available credit is increased in the economy even though the money supply remains unchanged. "When this happens, the intermediary, in effect, acts as an agent facilitating the process of dishoarding cash balances."[1] Ultimately, the purchase of primary securities by intermediaries causes money to flow back into the commercial banks which end up with the same amount of deposits which they had before the operation of intermediaries. Thus when money supply is reduced by a restrictive monetary policy, the non-bank financial intermediaries are able to increase velocity of money and total spending by turning primary securities into indirect securities for the portfolios of ultimate lenders.

Similarly, non-bank financial intermediaries can make an expansionary monetary policy ineffective by reducing the velocity of money.

The question arises as to what extent non-bank financial intermediaries have actually been instrumental in offsetting the monetary policy. If they have been doing so on a large scale, then it is advisable to extend the control of the central bank over them.

There has been a hot controversy over the issue. But the consensus is that the role played by intermediaries

1. Warren L. Smith, *Staff Report on Employment, Growth and Price Level*, 1959.

in under-cutting monetary policy is minimal. As the United States Commission on Money and Credit noted: "The evidence, for either the cyclical or the secular periods, does not support a case for an extension of the direct monetary control over non-bank financial intermediaries. Their contribution to cyclical changes in velocity appears to be too small to warrant such an extension."

The Radcliffe Committee of Britain rejected the idea of controlling the intermediaries because it was not politically feasible in England. It further observed: "Such a prospect would be unwelcome except as a last resort, not mainly because of its administrative burdens, but because the further growth of new financial institutions would allow the situation continually to slip from under the grip of the authorities."

But unlike the Radcliffe view, Gurley and Shaw have argued that the central bank's control over the non-bank financial intermediaries should be extended. In the absence of control over NBFIs, the central bank would behave in a discriminatory manner against the commercial banks. If NBFIs remain outside its control, they would expand very rapidly, thereby making monetary policy less effective. Gurley and Shaw opine that consequently the monetary authorities "crack down" on the good boys (commercial banks) for the mischief done by the bad boys (NBFIs). They, therefore, opine: "The lag of regulatory techniques behind the institutional development of intermediaries can be overcome when it is appreciated that 'financial control' should supplant 'monetary control.' Monetary control limits the supply of one financial asset money. Financial control, as the successor to the monetary control would regulate creation of financial assets in all forms that are competitive with direct securities in spending units' portfolios. "Tight finance" and "cheap finance" are the sequels of "tight money" and "cheap money".

However, Johnson does not agree with Gurley and Shaw. He observes that there seems to be no empirical case for empowering the central bank to extend its control over financial intermediaries similar to that exercised over the commercial banks. According to him, there is little reason for believing that the central bank's control is weakened by the presence of financial intermediaries. Moreover, so long as the public does not switch easily from bank deposits into indirect securities of intermediaries, the presence of intermediaries may increase the leverage of the central bank on economic activity. It implies that it is not possible for the interest rates to settle back at their old levels even by the operation of non-bank financial intermediaries. Rather, interest rates would tend to rise further. The money supply will remain tight and its influence on spending would be restrictive.

4. DISTINCTION BETWEEN BANKS AND NON-BANK FINANCIAL INTERMEDIARIES

Before we discuss how far commercial banks differ from NBFIs, let us study their similarities.

SIMILARITIES BETWEEN BANKS AND NBFIs

From a functional viewpoint the operations of commercial banks are similar to those of NBFIs on the following counts:

1. Like NBFIs, commercial banks acquire the primary securities of borrowers, loans and deposits, and in turn, they provide their own indirect securities and demand deposits to the lenders. Commercial banks resemble NBFIs in that both create secondary securities in their role as borrowers.

2. Commercial banks create demand deposits when they borrow from the central bank, and NBFIs create various forms of indirect debt when they borrow from commercial banks.

3. Both commercial banks and NBFIs act as intermediaries in bringing ultimate borrowers and ultimate lenders together and facilitate the transfer of currency balances from non-financial lenders to non-financial borrowers for the purpose of earning profits.

4. Both commercial banks and NBFIs provide liquid funds. The bank deposits and other assets of commercial banks and the assets provided by NBFIs are liquid assets. Of course, the degree of liquidity varies in accordance with the nature and the activity of the concerned financial intermediaries.

5. Both banks and NBFIs are important creators of loanable funds. The commercial banks by net creation of money and the NBFIs by mobilising existing money balance in exchange for their own newly issued

financial liabilities.

HOW ARE COMMERCIAL BANKS DIFFERENT FROM NBFIs?

Commercial banks are different from NBFIs following respects:

1. *Credit Creation.* Prof. J. Tobin[2] has shown that the existence of NBFIs significantly modifies the conventional view of commercial banks as creators of money because they can directly issue their own new liabilities to acquire other assets. On the other hand, NBFIs do not create money.

Like all other financial intermediaries (FIs), commercial banks lend to borrowers only currency deposited with them and make profit by charging borrowers a high rate than they pay to lenders. But both differ in the effects of their operations so far as secondary securities are concerned. The two main financial assets that serve as money are currency, known as high powered money, and demand deposits of commercial banks. Demand deposits are the secondary securities issued by commercial banks which are substitutes for currency. They represent a promise to pay currency on demand and are transferred direct by cheque without encashment in settlement of debt. Banks offer convenient safe-keeping, book-keeping and a large number of other services to depositors that are not available by holding currency. Consequently, depositors who lend their money to commercial banks receive in return a secondary security that itself serves as a medium of payment. Loans made or deposits created by any bank through the issue of cheques will ultimately be deposited by the borrowers or by other persons to whom they made cheque payments in the commercial banking system. Thus cheques help in creating credit by the bank credit multiplier. Money lent by an individual bank is retained as cash reserves by the banking system minus only a small leakage in money used by the borrower. The bank credit multiplier implies that banks if uncontrolled would have an unlimited power to expand deposits, since the latter are determined only by the amount of primary securities that the banking system purchases. "Bank money, once created in the process of bank lending, lives on as a virtually permanent part of the money supply. Thus, banks do manufacture money; and once manufactured, it is relatively immortal." It is in this sense that commercial banks are unique among FIs in their ability to create money. But in the case of NBFIs, the amount of primary securities they can buy is limited by the amount of indirect securities they can sell to lenders. Since they do not possess the bank credit multiplier power of commercial banks, they perform the brokerage function of simply transferring to borrowers the funds entrusted to them by lenders. Moreover, government regulations prevent NBFIs from offering chequing facilities on their liabilities and convertibility into currency on demand. But a number of secondary securities, such as commercial bank time and demand deposits and deposits in some thrift institutions while directly not transferable by cheque can be turned into cash quickly, easily, conveniently and without cost. Therefore, they are a close substitute of money than other assets, are called near money assets. Thus NBFIs can create liquidity and not money. Since the majority of NBFIs are small, the banking system multiplier does not operate fully in their case because of the leakages to banks of the money lent. Suppose a small non-banking financial institution lends and issues a cheque on its bank as payment. This will lead to a drain on its resources unless an equal amount is redeposited by some other borrower. In the case of small NBFIs, the redeposit ratio is low which makes it difficult for them to continue in business unless they have sufficient assets. But a commercial bank faces no problem of the type and can create money as well as liquidity to meet its lending requirements.

2. *Cash Reserve Requirements.* Commercial banks, like other FIs, have to earn a higher rate on their total assets than they pay on their total liabilities. They have to keep cash reserves. But cash reserves do not earn income. So banks wish to maintain their cash reserves as low as possible. But, unlike NBFIs, they are legally required to maintain a minimum cash reserve ratio. This ratio is always more than what the banks would wish to maintain. As a result, banks do not normally hold cash reserves in excess of those legally required and invest all excess cash in earning assets. With a reduction of required cash reserve ratio, the volume of bank intermediation would expand and vice versa.

As deposits are preferred to currency, an increase in the stock of high powered money results in an increase in the public demand for bank deposits. This leads to an increase in deposits with the banking system. So long as the average cost of providing and servicing demand deposits is low, relative to the interest rate earned on primary securities, banks have a profit incentive to lend all excess cash by buying securities and

---

2. J. Tobin, 'Commercial Banks as Creators of "Money", in D. Carson (Ed), *Banking and Monetary Studies*, 1963.

granting loans. Consequently, the volume of bank intermediation expands. This process will continue until bank assets and deposits have risen to a level where the required cash reserves and actual reserves are equal. It should, however, be noted that the foreign exchange liabilities of commercial banks are not required to meet cash reserve requirements. So this part of the bank business can be regarded like an NBFI.

On the other hand, NBFIs are not subject to any such restrictions. They are thus in an advantageous position over the banks. But this regulatory distinction between banks and NBFIs does not apply now in almost all the developed and developing countries of the world because reserve requirements have been enforced in one form or another on NBFIs with the exception of insurance companies, pension funds, and investment and unit trusts.

3. *Portfolio Structure.* Commercial banks differ from NBFIs in their portfolio structure. Bank liabilities are very liquid. The liabilities of a bank are large in relation to its assets, because it holds a small proportion of its assets in cash. But its liabilities are payable on demand at a short notice. Many types of assets are available to a bank with varying degree of liquidity. The most liquid is cash. The next most liquid assets are deposits with the central bank, treasury bills and other short-term bills issued by the centre and state governments and large firms, and call loans to other banks, firms, dealers and brokers in government securities. The less liquid assets are the various types of loans to customers and investment in longer-term bonds and mortgages. Thus banks have a large and varied portfolio on the basis of which they create liquidity.

NBFIs also create liquidity but in the form of savings and time deposits, which are not used as a means of payment. They are limited in the choice of their assets and are also prohibited from holding certain assets. Thus the size of their portfolio is very small as compared with banks. They generally issue claims against themselves that are fixed in money terms and have maturities shorter than the direct securities they hold. They borrow for short period, and lend for long period. This is because of the small size of their portfolio and they hold less liquid assets than banks.

4. *Risk.* Banks have to follow certain norms at the time of advancing loans. These are detailed appraisals of projects and hence delays in sanctioning loans. On the other hand, NBFIs do not enter into detailed appraisal of projects, they have to follow less stringent rules for advances. There are no time delays in granting loans. Thus NBFIs are able to take greater risk and lesser supervision as compared to banks.

5. *Security.* NBFIs insist on greater security than banks before lending. Normally, it is in the form of shares and post-dated cheques. This is to ensure that if one project goes bad, they can recover from the others.

6. *Recovery.* NBFIs are very innovative in their methods of recovery and calculation of interest rates. They combine a good security with other factors such as upfront fee and higher lending rates.

Consequently, their recovery rates are good and the percentage of bad debts to their assets is very low. Banks, on the other hand, have to follow specific norms in making loans. Their prime lending rates are much lower than the NBFIs. Since banks advance huge loans to corporates, the rate of default is very high in their case.

Conclusion

The entire discussion can be summarised as follows: (*a*) The distinction between commercial banks and NBFIs has been too sharply drawn. The differences are of degree rather than of kind, (*b*) The differences which do exist have little intrinsically to do with the monetary nature of bank liabilities, (*c*) The differences are more importantly related to the special reserve requirements. If NBFIs are subject to the same kind of regulations they would behave in much the same way. (*d*) Commercial banks do not possess a 'widow's cruse' which means that any expansion of assets will generate a corresponding expansion of deposit liabilities.

Despite these differences, commercial banks are unique among financial intermediaries.

EXERCISES

1. "Non-bank financial intermediaries are said to reduce the effectiveness of monetary policy." Examine the statement.
2. What are non-bank financial intermediaries? How do they differ from banks?
3. Explain the main functions of non-bank financial intermediaries. How do they create credit?

CHAPTER 22

Monetary Policy

1. MEANING OF MONETARY POLICY

Monetary policy refers to the credit control measures adopted by the central bank of a country. Johnson defines monetary policy "as policy employing central bank's control of the supply of money as an instrument for achieving the objectives of general economic policy."[1] G.K. Shaw defines it as "any conscious action undertaken by the monetary authorities to change the quantity, availability or cost... of money."[2]

2. OBJECTIVES OR GOALS OF MONETARY POLICY

The following are the principal objectives of monetary policy.

1. Full Employment

Full employment has been ranked among the foremost objectives of monetary policy. It is an important goal not only because unemployment leads to wastage of potential output, but also because of the loss of social standing and self-respect. Moreover, it breeds poverty.

According to Keynes, full employment means the absence of involuntary unemployment. It other words, full employment is a situation in which everybody who wants to work, gets work. Full employment so defined is consistent with frictional and voluntary unemployment. To achieve full employment, Keynes advocated increase in effective demand to bring about reduction in real wages. Thus the problem of full employment is one of maintaining adequate effective demand. Keynes gave an alternative definition of full employment at another place in his *General Theory* thus: "It is a situation in which aggregate employment is inelastic in response to an increase in which aggregate employment is inelastic in response to an increase in the effective demand for its output." It means that the test of full employment is when any further increase in effective demand is not accompanied by any increase in output. Since the supply of output becomes inelastic at the full employment level, any further increase in effective demand will lead to inflation in the economy. Thus

---

1. H.G. Johnson, *op.cit.*, p. 53.
2. G.K. Shaw, *An Introduction to the Theory of Macroeconomic Policy*, p. 65.

the Keynesian concept of full employment involves three conditions: (*i*) reduction in the real wage rate; (*ii*) increase in effective demand; and (*iii*) inelastic supply of output at the level of full employment.

According to Professor W.W. Hart attempting to define full employment raises many people's blood pressure. Rightly so, because there is hardly any economist who does not define it in his own way. Lord Beveridge in his book *Full Employment in a Free Society* defined it as a situation where there were more vacant jobs than unemployed men so that the normal lag between losing one job and finding another will be very short. By full employment he does not mean zero unemployment which means that full employment is not always full. There is always a certain amount of frictional unemployment in the economy even when there is full employment. He estimated frictional unemployment of 3% in a full employment situation for England. But his pleading for more vacant jobs than the unemployed cannot be accepted as the full employment level.

According to the American Economic Association Committee, "Full employment is a situation where all qualified persons who want jobs at current wage rate find full time jobs." It does not mean unemployment is zero. Here again, like Beveridge, the Committee considered full employment to be consistent with some amount of unemployment.

Individual economists may, however, continue to differ over the definition of full employment, but the majority has veered round the view expressed by the U.N. Experts on *National and International Measures for Full Employment* that "full employment may be considered as a situation in which employment cannot be increased by an increase in effective demand and unemployment does not exceed the minimum allowances that must be made for the effects of frictional and seasonal factors." This definition is in keeping with the Keynesian and Beveridgian views on full employment. It is now agreed that full employment stands for 96 to 97 per cent employment, with 3 to 4 per cent unemployment existing in the economy due to frictional factors. Full employment can be achieved in an economy by following an expansionary monetary policy.

2. Price Stability

One of the policy objectives of monetary policy is to stabilise the price level. Both economists and laymen favour this policy because fluctuations in prices bring uncertainty and instability to the economy. Rising and falling prices are both bad because they bring unnecessary loss to some and undue advantage to others. Again, they are associated with business cycles. So a policy of price stability keeps the value of money stable, eliminates cyclical fluctuations, brings economic stability, helps in reducing inequalities of income and wealth, secures social justice and promotes economic welfare.

However, there are certain difficulties in pursuing a policy of stable price level. The first problem relates to the type of price level to be stabilised. Should the relative or general price level be stabilised, the wholesale or retail, of consumer goods or producer goods? There is no specific criteria with regard to the choice of a price level. Halm suggests, "The compromise solution would be to try to stabilise a price level which would include consumers' goods prices as well as wages." But this will necessitate increase in the quantity of money but not by as much as is implied in the stabilisation of consumers goods price.[3] Second, innovations may reduce the cost of production but a policy of stable prices may bring larger profits to producers at the cost of consumers and wage earners. Again, in an open economy which imports raw materials and other intermediate products at high prices, the cost of production of domestic goods will rise. But a policy of stable prices will reduce profits and retard further investment. Under the circumstances, a policy of stable prices is not only inequitable but also conflicts with economic progress.

Despite these drawbacks, the majority of economists favour a policy of stable prices. But the problem is one of defining price stability. Price stability does not mean that prices remain unchanged indefinitely. "Comparative prices will change as fluctuating tastes alter the composition of demand, as new products are developed and as cost reducing technologies are introduced. Differential price changes are essential for allocating resources in the market economy. Since modern economies tend to exhibit fairly rigid downward inflexibility of prices, differential price changes can only be attained by gradual increases in the aggregate price level over the long-run. Further, prices may have to be changed if costs of imported goods increase or if taxation policy

3. G.N. Halm, *op. cit.*

leads to the rise in the domestic cost of production. As pointed out by Dasgupta and Hagger, price stability means *"stability of some appropriate price index in the sense that we can detect no definite upward trend in the index after making proper allowance for the upward bias inherent in all price indexes."*[4]

Price stability can be maintained by following a counter-cyclical monetary policy, that is easy monetary policy during a recession and dear monetary policy during a boom.

3. Economic Growth

One of the most important objectives of monetary policy in recent years has been the rapid economic growth of an economy. Economic growth is defined as *"the process whereby the real per capita income of a country increases over a long period of time."*[5] Economic growth is measured by the increase in the amount of goods and services produced in a country. A growing economy produces more goods and services in each successive time period. Thus, growth occurs when an economy's productive capacity increases which, in turn, is used to produce more goods and services. In its wider aspect, economic growth implies raising the standard of living of the people, and reducing inequalities of income distribution. All agree that economic growth is a desirable goal for a country. But there is no agreement over "the magic number," viz., the annual growth rate which an economy should attain.

Generally, economists believe in the possibility of continual growth. This belief is based on the presumption that innovations tend to increase productive technologies of both capital and labour over time. But there is very likelihood that an economy might not grow despite technological innovations. Production might not increase further due to the lack of demand which may retard the growth of the productive capacity of the economy. The economy may not grow further if there is no improvement in the quality of labour in keeping with the new technologies.

However, policy makers do not take into consideration the costs of growth. Growth is not limitless because resources are scarce in every economy. All factors have opportunity cost. To produce more of one particular product will mean reduction in that of the other. New technologies lead to the replacement of old machines which become useless. Workers are also displaced because they cannot be fitted in the new technological set up immediately. Moreover, rapid growth leads to urbanisation and industrialisation with their adverse effects on the pattern of living and environment. People have to live in squalor and slums. The environment becomes polluted. Social tensions develop. "But growth has other more basic effect on our environment, and, today, people are not so sure that unrestricted growth is worth all its costs, since the price in terms of change in, deterioration of, or even destruction of the environment is not yet fully known. What does seem clear, however, is that growth is not going to be halted because of environmental problems and that mankind must learn to cope with the problem or face the consequences."

The main problem is to what extent monetary policy can lead to the growth of the economy? It is difficult to say anything definite on this issue. The monetary authority may influence growth by controlling the real interest rate through its effect on the level of investment. By following an easy credit policy and lowering interest rates, the level of investment can be raised which promotes economic growth. Monetary policy may also contribute towards growth by helping to maintain stability of income and prices. By moderating economic fluctuations and avoiding deep depressions, monetary policy helps in achieving the growth objective. Since rapid and variable rates of inflation discourage investment and adversely affect growth, monetary policy helps in controlling hyper-inflation. Similarly, by a judicious monetary policy which encourages investment, growth can be promoted. For example, tight monetary policy affects small firms more than large firms, and higher interest rates have a greater impact on small investments than on large industrial investments. So monetary policy should be such that encourages investment and at the same time controls hyper-inflation so as to promote growth and control economic fluctuations.*

---

4 A.K. Dasgupta and A.J. Hagger, *The Objectives of Macroeconomic Policy,* 1971.

5 T.M. Meier. *Leading Issues in Development Economics,* p. 20.

* Other objectives may also be discussed on similar lines.

4. Balance of Payments

Another objective of monetary policy since the 1950s has been to maintain equilibrium in the balance of payments. The achievement of this goal has been necessitated by the phenomenal growth in the world trade as against the growth of international liquidity. It is also recognised that deficit in the balance of payments will retard the attainment of other objectives. This is because a deficit in the balance of payments leads to a sizeable outflow of gold. But "it is not clear what constitutes a satisfactory balance of payments position. Clearly a country with a net debt must be at a surplus to repay the debt over a reasonably short period of time. Once any debt has been repaid and an adequate reserve attained, a zero balance maintained over time would meet the policy objective. But how is this satisfactory balance to be achieved on the trading account or on the capital account? .... The capital account must be looked upon as fulfilling merely a short-term emergency role in times of crises."[6]

Again, another problem relates to the question: What is the balance of payments target of a country? It is where imports equal exports. But, in practice, a country whose current' reserves of foreign exchange are inadequate will have a mild export surplus as its balance of payments target. But when its reserves become satisfactory, it will aim at the equality of imports and exports. This is because an export surplus means that the country is accumulating foreign exchange and it is producing more than it is consuming. This will lead to low standard of living of the people. But this cannot last long because some other country must be having import surplus and in order to avoid it, it would impose trade restrictions on the export surplus country. So the attainment of a balance of payments equilibrium becomes an imperative goal of monetary policy in a country. How can monetary policy achieve it? A balance of payments deficit is defined as equal to the excess of money supply through domestic credit creation over extra money demand based on increased demand for cash balances. Thus a balance of payments deficit reflects excessive money supply in the economy. As a result, people exchange their excess money holdings for foreign goods and securities. Under a system of fixed exchange rates, the central bank will have to sell foreign exchange reserves and buy the domestic currency for eliminating excess supply of domestic currency. This is how equilibrium will be restored in the balance of payments.

On the other hand, if the money supply is below the existing demand for money at the given exchange rate, there will be a surplus in the balance of payments. Consequently, people acquire the domestic currency by selling goods and securities to foreigners. They will also seek to acquire additional money balances by restricting their expenditure relatively to their income. The central bank, on its part, will buy excess foreign currency in exchange for domestic currency in order to eliminate the shortage of domestic currency.

3. INSTRUMENTS OF MONETARY POLICY

The instruments of monetary policy are of two types: *first*, quantitative, general or indirect; and *second*, qualitative, selective or direct. They affect the level of aggregate demand through the supply of money, cost of money and availability of credit. Of the two types of instruments, the first category includes bank rate variations, open market operations and changing reserve requirements. They are meant to regulate the overall level of credit in the economy through commercial banks. The selective credit controls aim at controlling specific types of credit. They include changing margin requirements and regulation of consumer credit. We discuss them as under.[7]

Bank Rate Policy. The bank rate is the minimum lending rate of the central bank at which it rediscounts first class bills of exchange and government securities held by the commercial banks. When the central bank finds that inflationary pressures have started emerging within the economy, it raises the bank rate. Borrowing from the central bank becomes costly and commercial banks borrow less from it. The commercial banks, in turn, raise their lending rates to the busniess community and borrowers borrow less from the commercial

6. G.K. Shaw, *op. cit.*, p. 9.
7. For a detailed study of these instruments of monetary policy, refer to 'Credit Control' in Chapter of Central Banking.

banks. There is contraction of credit and prices are checked from rising further. On the contrary, when prices are depressed, the central bank lowers the bank rate. It is cheap to borrow from the central bank on the part of commercial banks. The latter also lower their lending rates. Businessmen are encouraged to borrow more. Investment is encouraged. Output, employment, income and demand start rising and the downward movement of prices is checked.

Open Market Operations. Open market operations refer to sale and purchase of securities in the money market by the central bank. When prices are rising and there is need to control them, the central bank sells securities. The reserves of commercial banks are reduced and they are not in a position to lend more to the business community. Further investment is discouraged and the rise in prices is checked. Contrariwise, when recessionary forces start in the economy, the central bank buys securities. The reserves of commercial banks are raised. They lend more. Investment, output, employment, income and demand rise and fall in price is checked.

Changes in Reserve Ratios. This weapon was suggested by Keynes in his *Treatise on Money* and the USA was the first to adopt it as a monetary device. Every bank is required by law to keep a certain percentage of its total deposits in the form of a reserve fund in its vaults and also a certain percentage with the central bank. When prices are rising, the central bank raises the reserve ratio. Banks are required to keep more with the central bank. Their reserves are reduced and they lend less. The volume of investment, output and employment are adversely affected. In the opposite case, when the reserve ratio is lowered, the reserves of commercial banks are raised. They lend more and the economic activity is favourably affected.

Selective Credit Controls. Selective credit controls are used to influence specific types of credit for particular purposes. They usually take the form of changing margin requirements to control speculative activities within the economy. When there is brisk speculative activity in the economy or in particular sectors in certain commodities, and prices start rising, the central bank raises the margin requirement on them. The result is that the borrowers are given less money in loans against specified securities. For instance, raising the margin requirement to 60% means that the pledger of securities of the value of Rs 10,000 will be given 40% of their value, i.e. Rs 4,000 as loan. In case of recession in a particular sector, the central bank encourages borrowing by lowering margin requirements.

Conclusion. For an effective anticyclical monetary policy, bank rate, open market operations, reserve ratio and selective control measures are required to be adopted simultaneously. But it has been accepted by all monetary theorists that (*i*) the success of monetary policy is nil in a depression when business confidence is at its lowest ebb; and (*ii*) it is successful against inflation. The monetarists contend that as against fiscal policy, monetary policy possesses greater flexibility and it can be implemented rapidly.[8]

4. EXPANSIONARY MONETARY POLICY

An expansionary (or easy) monetary policy is used to overcome a recession or a depression or a deflationary gap. When there is a fall in consumer demand for goods and services, and in business demand for investment goods, a deflationary gap emerges. The central bank starts an expansionary monetary policy that eases the credit market conditions and leads to an upward shift in aggregate demand. For this purpose, the central bank purchases government securities in the open market, lowers the reserve requirements of member banks, lowers the discount rate and encourages consumer and busniess credit through selective credit measures. By such measures, it decreases the cost and availability of credit in the money market, and improves the economy.

The expansionary monetary policy is explained in terms of Figure 1 (A) and (B) where the initial recession equilibrium is at *R*, *Y*, *P* and *Q*. At the interest rate *R* in Panel (A) of the figure, there is already an excess money supply in the economy. Suppose the central bank credit policy results in an increase in the money supply in the

8. For limitations of Monetary Policy, refer to the limitations given under the Scope of Monetary Policy in Depression and Inflation discussed below.
9. This and the next section also relate to the effectiveness of monetary policy.

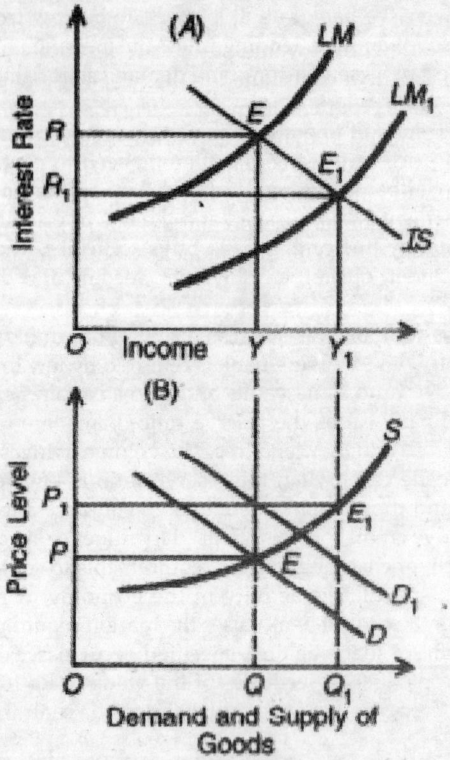

Fig. 1

economy. This leads to a rightwards shift of the *LM* curve to LM_1. This increases income from *OY* to OY_1 and aggregate demand expands and the demand curve *D* shifts upwards to D_1 in panel (B). With the increase in the demand for goods and services, output increases from *OQ* to OQ_1 at a higher price level P_1. If the expansionary monetary policy operates smoothly, the equilibrium at E_1 can be at the full employment level. But this is not likely to be attained because of the following limitations.

Its Scope and Limitations. During the 1930s and 1940s, it was believed that the success of monetary policy in stimulating recovery from a depression was severely limited than in controlling a boom and inflation. This view emerged from the experiences of the Great Depression and the appearance of Keynes's *General Theory*.

The monetarists hold that during a depression the central bank can increase the reserves of commercial banks through a cheap money policy. They can do so by buying securities and reducing the interest rate. As a result, their ability to extend credit facilities to borrowers increases. But the experience of the Great Depression tells us that in a serious depression when there is pessimism among businessmen, the success of such a policy is practically nil. In such a situation, banks are helpless in bringing about a revival. Since business activity is almost at a stand still, businessmen do not have any inclination to borrow to build up inventories even when the rate of interest is very low. Rather, they want to reduce their inventories by repaying loans already drawn from the banks. Moreover, the question of borrowing for long-term capital needs does not arise in a depression when the business activity is already at a very low level. The same is the case with consumers who faced with unemployment and reduced incomes do not like to purchase any durable goods through bank loans. Thus all that the banks can do is to make credit available but they cannot force businessmen and consumers to accept it. In the 1930s, very low interest rates and the piling up of unused reserves with the banks did not have any significant impact on the depressed economies of the world.

"This is not to say that an easy monetary policy in times of severe contraction will be without beneficial effect, its effect will be largely that of preventing a bad situation from getting worse. *But* a restrictive monetary policy combined with a business downturn would surely aggravate the downturn—the classical example of this was the monetary policy in 1931 that contributed to the deepening of the Great Depression...On the other hand, if credit is readily available on favourable terms, it clearly has a stabilising effect. By meeting the liquidity requirments of business, it can slow and perhaps reduce the extent of the downturn."

But what led to the decline of monetary policy in the 1930s and 1940s ? In addition to the sad and disillusioning experiences during and after the Great Depression, it was Keynes's *General Theory* that led to a decline in monetary policy as an instrument of economic stabilisation. Keynes pointed out that a highly elastic liquidity preference schedule (*liquidity trap*) renders monetary policy impotent in time of severe depression.

5. RESTRICTIVE MONETARY POLICY

A monetary policy designed to curtail aggregate demand is called restrictive (or dear) monetary policy. It is used to overcome an inflationary gap. The economy experiences inflationary pressures due to rising consumers' demand for goods and services and there is also boom in business investment. The central bank starts a restrictive monetary policy in order to lower aggregate consumption and investment by increasing the cost and availability of bank credit. It might do so by selling government securities in the open market, by raising reserve requirements of member banks, by raising the discount rate, and controlling consumer and business credit through selective measures. By such measures, the central bank increases the cost and availability of credit in the money market and thereby controls inflationary pressures.[9]

Its Scope and Limitations. But the scope of monetary policy is severly limited in controlling inflation. The following are its *limitations.*

1. *Increase in the Velocity of Money.* One of the important limitations on the effectiveness of monetary policy in controlling inflation is the increase in the velocity of money held by the public. The central bank can control the money supply and the cost of money by a tight monetary policy but it does not possess any power to control the velocity of money. The public can make an effective use of the money supply held by them thereby making a restrictive monetary policy ineffective. This can be done in a number of ways.

(a) Commercial Bank Portfolio Adjustments. In the face of a restrictive monetary policy, commercial banks meet the borrowers' demand for loans by selling government securities to the central bank. Such a policy simply converts idle deposits held by the banks in the form of securities into active deposits. Government securities lying in the bank's portfolios are substituted for loans. But there is no change in either the total deposits or the money supply with the banks. However, this leads to increase in total spending when the banks lend money to borrowers. Thus the restrictive monetary policy of the central bank becomes ineffective.

Moreover, when the banks sell government securities to the central bank, their prices fall and the interest on them rises in the market. This will raise the general interest rate structure in the market. But the fall in the prices of securities brings capital losses to the banks and they may be reluctant to bear them. This depends upon whether they expect the fall in security prices (or rise in interest rate) to be short-lived or continue overtime. If the fall in security prices is expected to be short-lived, the banks will prefer to keep securities rather than sell them at a capital loss. On the other hand, if they expect it to continue for some time, they will sell securities for giving loans to customers at higher interest rates, thereby recouping the capital loss on the sale of securities through higher interest rates on loans. But once the demand for loans subsides, the banks can buy back government securities now at prices lower than at which they sold, and again gain in the transaction. Thus the commercial banks' policy of portfolio adjustment raises the velocity of total money supply even in the face of a tight monetary policy thereby making the latter ineffective.

(b) The Role of Non-Bank Financial Intermediaries. NBFIs act as a restraint on the effectiveness of monetary policy to restrict the money supply in two ways. *First,* they sell securities for advancing loans, and thus increase velocity in the same manner as commercial banks do, as explained above. *Second,* as interest rates on securities

---

9. It may be explained diagrammatically by starting with the initial equilibrium at R_1, Y_1, Q_1 and P_1 in Figure 1 and reversing the arguments.

rise in a tight monetary policy, financial intermediaries raise the interest rates on deposits with them to attract more funds from savers. This induces savers to shift more idle money to the intermediaries which increases their lending power further. In this way, they are able to raise the velocity of money thereby making tight restrictive monetary policy ineffective.

(c) Methods to Make Better Use of Available Money Supply. The private sector has evolved many ways to make better use of available supply of money which make a restrictive monetary policy ineffective. Some of the methods are the evolvement of improved methods of collecting funds by sales finance companies, borrowing funds by companies from the public at higher rates than offered by commercial banks, etc. By getting funds from sources other than the commercial banks, such institutions are able to increase the velocity of the available supply of money even under restrictive monetary policy.

2. *Discriminatory.* A restrictive monetary policy is discriminatory in its effects on particular sectors of the economy. It is argued that firms that depend upon internal source of financing are not affected by a restrictive monetary policy. On the other hand, only those firms are affected that depend for funds on the banking system. In particular, a tight monetary policy *"is thought to work against small businessmen, becuase they are poorer credit risks, and against residential construction and some types of state and local government spending, because they are most sensitive to changes in credit cost."* It may slow down or even halt spending by them.

3. *Threat to Credit Market.* If the central bank rigorously tightens the credit market and investors expect continued increases in interest rates, this may lead to the drying up of loanable funds to the credit market. As a result, securities may not be sold and the credit market may cease to function.

4. *Threatens Solvency of NBFIs.* A vigorous monetary policy by swiftly raising interest rates may threaten the solvency of such NBFIs as savings banks, and savings and loan associations. This is because unlike the commercial banks, they are not in a position to adjust themselves to rapidly increasing interest rates.

5. *Alter Expectations of Borrowers and Lenders.* A very tight monetary policy may alter the expectations of borrowers and lenders. So they bring irreversible changes in credit market conditions. A rapid rise in interest rates may so change expectations that even when this policy is abandoned and an expansionary policy is started, lenders may be reluctant to make long-term loans in anticipation of rise in interest rates again. On the other hand, borrowers may borrow long-term funds even if they do not need them immediately in anticipation of rise in interest rates in the future.

6. *Time Lags.* Another important limitation of a tight monetary policy is the existence of time lags which are related to the need of action, its recognition, and the decision and operation of actions in time. As the monetary authority is not able to adopt restrictive monetary measures in time due to these time lags, monetary policy works very slowly and hence it is not very effective in controlling inflation.

6. ROLE OF MONETARY POLICY IN A DEVELOPING ECONOMY

Monetary policy in an underdeveloped country plays an important role in increasing the growth rate of the economy by influencing the cost and availability of credit, by controlling inflation and maintaining equilibrium the balance of payments. So the principal objectives of monetary policy in such a country are to control credit for controlling inflation and to stabilise the price level, to stabilise the exchange rate, to achieve equilibrium in the balance of payments and to promote economic development.

To Control Inflationary Pressures. To control inflationary pressures arising in the process of development, monetary policy requires the sue of both quantitative and qualitative methods of credit control. Of the instruments of monetary policy, the open market operations are not successful in controlling inflation in underdevelopment countries because the bill market is small and undeveloped. Commercial banks keep an elastic cash-deposit ratio because the central bank's control over them is not complete. They are also reluctant to invest in government securities due to their relatively low interest rates. Moreover, instead of investing in government securities, they prefer to keep their reserves in liquid form such as gold, foreign exchange and cash. Commercial banks are also not in the habit of redics counting or borrowing from the central bank.

The *bank rate policy* is also not so effective in such countries due to : *(i)* the lack of bills of discount; *(ii)* the narrow size of the bill market; *(iii)* a large non-monetised sector where barter transactions take place; *(iv)* the existence of indisgenous banks which do not discount bills with the central bank; *(v)* the habit of the commercial banks to keep large cash reserves; and *(vi)* the existence of a large unorganised money market.

The use of *variable reserve ratio* as an instrument of monetary policy is more effective than open market operations and bank rate policy in LDCs. Since the market for securities is very small, open market operations are not successful. But a rise or fall in the variable reserve ratio by the central bank reduces or increases the cash available with the commercial banks without affecting adversely the prices of securities. Again, the commercial banks keep large cash reserves which cannot be reduced by an increase in bank rate or sale of securities by the central bank. But raising the cash reserve ratio reduces liquidity with the banks. The use of variable reserve ratio has certain *limitations* in LDCs. The non-banking financial intermediaries do not keep deposits with the central bank so they are not affected by it. Second, banks which do not maintain excess liquidity are more affected than those who maintain it.

The *qualitative credit control* measures are, however, more effective than the quantitative measures in influencing the allocation of credit, and thereby the pattern of investment. In LDCs, there is a strong tendency to invest in gold, jewellery, inventories, real estate, etc., instead of in alternative productive changels available in agriculture, mining, plantations and industry. The selective credit controls are more appropriate for controlling and limiting credit facilities for such unproductive purposes. They are beneficial in controlling speculative activities in foodgrains and raw materials. They prove more useful in controlling 'sectional inflations' in the economy. They curtail the demand for imports by making it obligatory on importers to deposit in advance an amount equal to the value of foreign currency. This has also the effect of reducing the reserves of the banks in so far as their deposits are transferred to the central bank in the process. The selective credit control measures may take the form of changing the margin requirements against certain types of collateral, the regulation of consumer credit and the rationing of credit.

To Achieve Price Stability. Monetary policy is an important instrument for achieving price stability. It brings a proper adjustment between the demand for and supply of money. An imbalance between the two will be reflected in the price level. A shortage of money supply will retard growth while an excess of it will lead to inflation. As the economy develops, the demand for money increases due to the gradual monetization of the non-monetized sector, and the increase in agricultural and industrial production. These will lead to increase in the demand for transactions and speculative motives. So the monetary authority will have to raise the money supply more than proportionate to the demand for money in order to avoid inflation.

To Bridge BOP Deficit. Monetary policy in the form of interest rate policy plays an important role in bridging the balance of payments deficit. Underdeveloped countries develop serious balance of payments difficulties to fulfil the planned targets of development. To establish infrastructure like power, irrigation, transport, etc. and directly productive activities like iron and steel, chemicals, electricals, fertilisers, etc., underdeveloped countries have to import capital equipment, machinery, raw materials, spares and components thereby raising their imports. But exports are almost stagnant. They are high priced due to inflation. As a result, an imbalance is created between imports and exports which leads to disequilibrium in the balance in payments. Monetary policy can help in narrowing the balance of payments deficit through high rate of interest. A high interest rate attracts the inflow of foreign investments and helps in bridging the balance of payments gap.

Interest Rate Policy. A policy of high interest rate in an underdeveloped country also acts as an incentive to higher savings, develops banking habits and speeds up the monetization of the economy which are essential for capital formation and economic growth. A high interest rate policy is also anti-inflationary in nature, for it discourages borrowing and investment for speculative purposes, and in foreign currencies. Further, it promotes the allocation of scarce capital resources in more productive channels. Certain economists favour a low interest rate policy in such countries because high interest rates discourage investment. But empirical evidence suggests that investment in business and industry is interest-inelastic in underdeveloped countries because interest forms a very low proportion of the total cost of investment. Despite these opposite views, it is advisable for the monetary authority to follow a policy of discriminatory interest rate, charging high interest rates for non-essential and unproductive uses and low interest rates for productive uses.

To Create Banking and Financial Institutions. One of the objectives of monetary policy in an underdeveloped country is to create and develop banking and financial institutions in order to encourage, mobilise and channelise savings for capital formation. The monetary authority should encourage the establishment of branch banking in rural and urban areas. Such a policy will help in monetizing the non-monetized sector and encourage saving and investment for capital formation. It should also organise and develop money an capital market. These are essential for the success of a development oriented monetary policy which also includes debt management.

Debt Management. Debt management is one of the important functions of monetary policy in an underdeveloped country. It aims at proper timing and issuing of government bonds, stabilising their prices and minimising the cost of servicing the public debt. The primary aim of debt management is to create conditions in which public borrowing can increase from year to year. Public borrowing is essential in such countries in order to finance development programmes and to control the money supply. But public borrowing must be at cheap rates. Low interest rates raise the price of government bonds and make them more attractive to the public. They also keep the burden of the debt low.

Thus an appropriate monetary policy, as outlined above, helps in controlling inflation, bridging balance of payments gap, encouraging capital formation and promoting economic growth.

LIMITATIONS OF MONETARY POLICY IN LDCs.

The experience of underdeveloped countries reveal that monetary policy plays a limited role in such countries. The following arguments are given in support of this view.

1. *Large Non-monetized Sector.* There is a large non-monetized sector which hinders the success of monetary policy in such countries. People mostly live in rural areas where barter is practised. Consequently, monetary policy fails to influence this large segment of the economy.

2. *Undeveloped Money and Capital Markets.* The money and capital markets are undeveloped. These markets lack in bills, stocks and shares which limit the success of monetary policy.

3. *Large Number of NBFLs.* Non-bank financial intermediaries like the indigenous bankers operate on a large scale in such countries but they are not under the control of the monetary authority. The factor limits the effectiveness of monetary policy in such countries.

4. *High Liquidity.* The majority of commercial banks possess high liquidity so that they are not influenced by the credit policy of the central bank. This also makes monetary policy less effective.

5. *Foreign Banks.* In almost every underdeveloped country foreign owned commercial banks exist. They also render monetary policy less effective by selling foreign assets and drawing money from their head officers when the central bank of the country is following a tight monetary policy.

6. *Small Bank Money.* Monetary policy is also not successful in such countries because bank money comprises a small proportion of the total money supply in the country. As a result, the central bank is not in a position to control credit effectively.

7. *Money not Deposited with Banks.* The well-to-do people do not deposit money with banks but use it in buying jewellery, gold, real estate, in speculation, in conspicuous consumption, etc. Such activities encourage inflationary pressures because they lie outside the control of the monetary authority.

On account of these limitations of monetary policy in an under-developed country, economists advocate the use of fiscal policy alongwith it.

EXERCISES

1. Explain the principal instruments of monetary policy. What are their limitations?
2. Critically discuss the effectiveness of monetary policy in controlling inflation.
3. Discuss the role of monetary policy in a developing economy.
4. Distinguish between cheap and dear monetary policy. Explain their relative effectiveness.
5. Define monetary policy. Discuss its objectives.

CHAPTER 23

The Liquidity Theory of Money

1. INTRODUCTION

The liquidity theory is a new approach to monetary policy which has been propounded by the Radcliffe Report and Gurley and Shaw. This theory highlights the role of liquid assets in influencing aggregate demand and economic activity. According to this theory, it is non-bank financial intermediaries (NBFIs) which provide a link between liquidity and monetary policy.

Broadly speaking, liquidity means *moneyness.* Liquidity is characterised by the ease of converting an asset into money at little cost. A liquid asset is one which is easily spendable, marketable (transferable) and has capital certainty.

Depending on these properties, different assets differ in the degree of liquidity. Money is the most important liquid asset which consists of coins, currency and bank deposits. This is because they perform the medium of exchange function of money. In the case of bank deposits only *demand deposits* are money because cheques can be issued on their basis. Thus cheques are perfect substitutes for money. But time deposits are *not real* money but are *near money* because they cannot be *withdrawn before* the expiry of a fixed period.

Besides time deposits, other near money assets are bonds, securities, debentures, bills of exchange, treasury bills, insurance policies, etc. All these types of assets are *less* liquid because they involve cost for converting them into real money.

Liquidity is created by the central bank by issuing coins and notes and by commercial banks by creating demand deposits. A change in the supply of money by the central bank affects liquidity by bringing changes or readjustments in the portfolio assets of the people. This depends on the effect of money supply on aggregate spending. For instance, if people decide to spend the increased money supply in purchasing such assets as shares and debentures, there will be less money available in liquid form with the public. If the stock market is bullish, people may buy shares and the liquidity is reduced. On the other hand, if there is uncertainty in the stock market, people may hold the increased money supply in bank deposits or invest in property if they expect property prices to rise. But it is the central bank that influences money supply in the economy by following "easy" or "tight" monetary policy. It does so by controlling aggregate spending and thereby influencing business activity, output and employment. But it is not always successful in controlling spending by increasing or decreasing the money supply and hence liquidity. This is because the central bank has little control over the velocity of circulation of money, non-bank financial intermediaries, business expectations, time lags in monetary policy, etc. It is, therefore, very difficult to predict the effects of changes in money supply on liquidity.

The Radcliffe Report and Gurley and Shaw have shown separately that the existence of NBFIs weaken the effect of monetary policy in increasing the money supply in the economy because they control a large portion of liquidity in the economy. Therefore, the role of NBFIs in increasing liquidity is equally important. We explain their views as under.

2. THE RADCLIFFE COMMITTEE VIEW : RADCLIFFE - SAYERS THESIS

The Radcliffe Committee in its report did not accept the monetarist view that there was any direct link between money supply and national income. This is because money is a close substitute for other financial assets, particularly those issued by non-bank financial institutions. If the central bank wanted to follow a contractional monetary policy by selling securities in the open market, non-bank financial intermediaries would be able to release idle demand deposits and currency. In this way, they would offset the restriction of money supply, and leave aggregate demand unchanged. Thus it held the view that "changes in rates of interest only very exceptionally have direct effects on the level of demand." It also did not find any indirect relation between money supply and national income.

According to the Radcliffe Committee, it is liquidity that influences total effective demand for goods and services rather than the supply of money The Committee pointed out that the "decisions to spend on goods and services, the decisions that determine the level of total demand, are influenced by the liquidity of the spenders. The spending is not limited by the amount of money in existence; but it is related to the amount of money people think they can get hold of, whether by receipt of income (for instance, from sales), by disposal of capital assets or by borrowing". Thus liquidity consists of the amount of money people can get hold of from income, sales, disposal of capital assets or borrowing. Suppose if liquidity is reduced, expenditures would decline to the extent they exceed current income and vice versa.

The second element by which the monetary authority can influence the level of overall liquidity and hence the level of aggregate expenditures is the *interest rate*. It is by manipulating the structure of interest rates which affects the overall liquidity structure. A movement of interest rates means significant changes in the capital values of many assets held by individuals and financial institutions. When interest rates rise, they reduce liquidity because they reduce the capital value of assets held by the latter. Financial institutions, in turn, reduce the supply of loanable funds. Since individuals and businesses cannot procure funds, they reduce their expenditures. On the other hand, a fall in the interest rate "strengthens balance sheets and encourages lenders to seek new business". In this monetary mechanism, the commercial banks hold a special position in the Committee's view, because they are the most convenient institutional source of funds for most borrowers for short-term purposes.

On the basis of this transmission mechanism, the Committee concluded that monetary policy performed a "background function". It thought that business investment was insensitive to changes in short-term interest rates. But it was influenced by long-term interest rates. Therefore, it was undesirable to cause long-term interest rates to fluctuate sharply because sharp fluctuations would undermine the strength and stability of financial institutions. In fact, financial institutions are accustomed to stable interest rates and they plan their lending policies accordingly. The monetary authority should, therefore, try to hold long-term interest rates at the level which maintained approximate balance between saving and investment in the economy.

The Committee did not favour reliance on *monetary policy* alone in severe deflationary or severe inflationary conditions. Apart from the removal of credit control and a possible effect of lower long-term interest rates on house-building activity during a slump, monetary policy was thought to be of not much help. Rather, the use of monetary measures to raise the economy from a slump carried the danger of flooding the financial system with liquidity. It would be difficult to control it later on when business activity expanded during the upswing. Thus in the Committee's view, "in general, the potentialities of monetary policy alone in the face of a severe slump are well represented by the proverb that you can take a horse to water but you cannot make him drink." Similarly, it was against any restriction on the money supply during severe inflation. It advocated measures to strike directly and rapidly at the liquidity of spenders through control of capital issues, bank advances and consumer credit. But it did not favour control over the lending power of the non-bank financial intermediaries because it entailed additional administrative burdens. More so because new financial institutions would be coming up which would make it difficult for the monetary authority to control the situation. Thus the Radcliffe Committee suggested "liquidity controls" through changes in long-term interest rates. According to it, "monetary measures cannot alone be relied upon to keep in nice balance an economy subject to major strains from without and within. Monetary measures can help but that is all". It, therefore, recommended reliance on fiscal policy in normal times which should be supplemented with monetary policy during severe inflations.

Its Criticisms

The views of the Radcliffe Committee have been severely criticised on the following grounds:

1. Economists have criticised it for advocating the control of overall liquidity of the economy rather than the money supply.

2. It did not precisely define liquidity or liquid assets. This makes the whole approach to liquidity as haphazard.

3. Prof. Gurley in his review of the Radcliffe Report found "confusion every where in the role of money supply, in the concept of liquidity, and in money to satisfy the liquidity desire of the public."

4. Other economists characterised the Report as "an utterly muddled one, indicating a stock-flow muddle, a liquidity muddle, and an interest rate muddle."

3. THE GURLEY-SHAW VIEW

According to Gurley and Shaw, it is the NBFIs that provide liquidity and safety to financial assets and help in transferring funds from ultimate lenders to ultimate borrowers for productive purposes. They increase capital formation and consequently lead to economic growth.

By buying primary securities from the ultimate borrowers and selling indirect securities to the ultimate lenders, the intermediaries influence the availability of credit and the structure and level of interest rates. They create credit different from commercial banks. But they create new assets and liabilities which tend to influence the supply of money and thus hinder the operation of an effective monetary policy.

According to them, the savings deposits of NBFIs resemble the demand deposits of commercial banks because it is not difficult for NBFIs to convert their savings deposits into cash. These savings deposits, whether of commercial banks or of NBFIs, are for all practical purposes as liquid as demand deposits. Such savings deposits held by NBFIs are known as near moneys. Since the demand deposits are not controlled by the central bank, it follows that the savings deposits held by NBFIs will hinder the successful operation of a successful monetary policy.

If the central bank wishes to control excess liquidity in the economy only through the reduction in money supply, it will not be successful because the savings deposits of NBFIs can be converted into cash. Similarly, if the central bank tries to control lending by commercial banks, it will not be successful if the lending of all other FIs are not under its control, as is the case. According to Gurley and Shaw, this problem arises especially when the central bank adopts an anti-inflationary monetary policy. Suppose the central bank reduces the money supply in order to control inflation. Among other effects, the interest rates on market securities rise in anticipation of higher yields and profits. NBFIs will raise the interest rates on their savings deposits to attract more funds in order to invest them in higher yielding securities.

Persons already holding securities find that their prices have fallen because of the rise in interest rates on present securities. They will, therefore, sell them and deposit their funds with intermediaries in order to earn higher interest rates on savings deposits. In the meantime, attracted by higher interest rates, others holding idle cash balances will also deposit them with intermediaries. So when NBFIs raise the interest rates on their savings deposits, the public reduces its demand for money which, in turn, reduces the market rate of interest. Thus NBFIs make tight monetary policy less successful or effective. Similarly, NBFIs can make an expansionary monetary policy ineffective by reducing liquidity.

But unlike the Radcliffe Report, Gurley and Shaw argue that the central bank's control over NBFIs should be extended for an effective monetary policy. This is because the NBFIs create more near-money assets and thereby affect the overall liquidity which, in turn, influences aggregate demand and economic activity.

Its Criticisms

The view of Gurley and Shaw has been criticised on the following grounds:

1. Prof. Johnson does not agree with Gurley and Shaw. He observes that there seems to be no empirical case for empowering the central bank to extend its control over financial intermediaries similar to that exercised over the commercial banks. According to him, there is little reason for believing that the central bank's control is weakened by the presence of financial intermediaries. Moreover, so long as the public does not switch easily from bank deposits into indirect securities of intermediaries, the presence of intermediaries may increase the leverage of the central bank on economic activity. It implies that it is not possible for the interest rates to settle back at their old levels even by the operation of non-bank financial intermediaries. Rather, interest rates would tend to rise further. The money supply will remain tight and its influence on spending would be restrictive.

2. Further, the rapid growth of NBFIs has helped to strengthen the effectiveness of monetary policy rather than weaken it where the NBFIs have been controlled. But Gurley and Shaw do not elaborate how they should be controlled.

Conclusion

Despite the weaknesses of both Radcliffe Report and Gurley-Shaw views, they highlight the role of NBFIs in creating liquidity which affects aggregate demand and economic activity. They emphasise that the success of monetary policy depends not in controlling the money supply but general liquidity. Thus the liquidity theory of money provides a new and realistic dimension to monetary policy.

EXERCISES

1. Explain briefly the liquidity theory of money.
2. What do you mean by liquidity? Explain the Radcliffe-Sayers view about the liquidity theory of money.
3. Explain the Gurley-Shaw view about the liquidity theory of money.
4. Explain the liquidity approach to monetary policy.

PART THREE

KEYNESIAN THEORY OF INCOME OUTPUT AND EMPLOYMENT

CHAPTER 24

The Classical Theory of Income, Output and Employment

1. INTRODUCTION

John Maynard Keynes in his *General Theory of Employment, "Interest and Money* published in 1936, made a frontal attack on the classical postulates. He developed a new economics which brought about a revolution in economic thought and policy. The *General "Theory* was written against the background of the classical thought. By the ``classicists" Keynes meant ``the followers of Ricardo, those, that is to say, who adopted and perfected the theory of Ricardian economics." They included, in particular, J.S. Mill, Marshall and Pigou. Keynes repudiated traditional and orthodox economics which had been built up over a century and which dominated economic thought and policy before and during the Great Depression. Since the Keynesian Economics is based on the criticism of classical economics, it is necessary to know the latter as embodied in the theory of employment.

2. THE CLASSICAL THEORY

The classical theory assumes the existence of full employment without inflation. Given wage-price flexibility, there are automatic forces in the economic system that tend to maintain full employment, and produce output at that level. Thus full employment is regarded as a normal situation and any deviation from this level is something abnormal which automatically tends toward full employment.

Its Assumptions. The classical theory of output and employment is based on the following assumptions :

1. There is the existence of full employment without inflation.
2. There is a closed *laissez faire* capitalist economy without foreign trade.

3. There is perfect competition in labour and product markets.
4. Labour is homogeneous.
5. Total output of the economy is divided between consumption and invest-ment expenditures.
6. The quantity of money is given.
7. Wages and prices are flexible.
8. Money wages and real wages are directly related and proportional.
9. Capital stock and technological knowledge are given in the short-run.

Say's Law of Markets. Say's Law of Markets is the core of the classical theory of employment. Jean Baptiste Say, an early 19th century French Economist, enunciated the proposition that ``supply creates "its own demand." This is known as Say's Law. In Say's words, ``It is production which creates markets for goods. A product is no sooner created than it, from that instant, affords a market for other products to the full extent of its own value. Nothing is more favourable to the demand of one product, than the supply of another."[1] In its original form, the law is applicable to a barter economy where goods are ultimately sold for goods. Every good brought to the market is a demand for some other goods. According to Say, work being unpleasant no person will work to make a product unless he wants to exchange it for some other product which he desires. Therefore, the very act of supplying goods implies a demand for them. In such a situation, there cannot be general overproduction because supply of goods will not exceed demand as a whole. But a particular good may be overproduced because the producer incorrectly estimates the quantity of the product which others want. But this is a temporary phenomenon, for the excess "production of a particular product can be corrected in time by reducing "its production. Thus supply creates its own demand and there can not be general overproduction and hence general unemployment.

The existence of money does not alter the basic law. When producers obtain the various inputs (land, labour and capital) to be used in the production process, they generate the necessary income accruing to the factor-owners in the form of rent, wages and interest. This, in turn, causes demand for the goods produced. In this way, supply creates its own demand. This reasoning is based on the assumption that all income earned by the factor-owners is spent in buying commodities which they help to produce.

What is not spent is saved which is automatically invested. Thus saving must equal investment. If there is any divergence between the two, the equality is maintained through the mechanism of the rate of interest. To the classicists, interest is a reward for saving. The higher the rate of interest, the higher the saving, and vice versa. On the contrary, the lower the rate of interest, the higher the demand for investment funds, and vice versa. If at any given period, investment exceeds saving, the rate of interest will rise. Saving will increase and investment will decline till the two are equal at the full employment level. This is because saving is regarded as an increasing function of the interest rate and investment as a decreasing function of the rate of interest.

The mechanism of the equality between saving and investment is shown in Figure 1 where *SS* is the saving curve and II is the investment curve. The two curves intersect at *E* where the rate of interest is *Or* and both saving and investment are equal to *OA*. If there is an increase in investment, the investment curve shifts to the right as *I′I′* curve and at the interest rate *Or* investment *OC* is greater than *OA* saving. According to the classical economists, the saving curve *SS* remains at its original level when there is any increase in investment. So to maintain the equality between saving and investment, the rate of interest will rise. This is shown to rise to *O′* in the figure. At this interest rate, the saving curve *SS* intersects the investment curve *I′I′* at *E′*. Consequently, both saving and investment equal at *OB*.

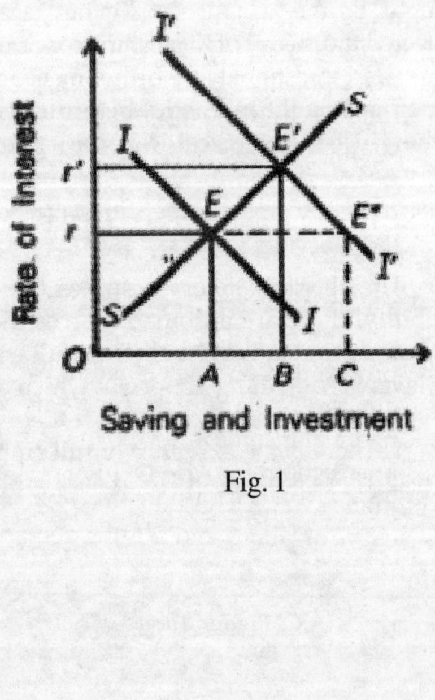

Fig. 1

The validity of Say's law in a *money economy* also depends upon the classical quantity theory of money. In the classical system,

1. J.B. Say, *Political Economy, (4th ed.)*, Vol. 7, pp. 167-170.

the main function of money is to act as a medium of exchange. It is to determine the general level of prices at which goods and services will be exchanged. This relationship between money and the price level is explained in terms of the quantity theory of money. The classical quantity theory of money states that the price level is a function of the supply of money. Algebraically, $MV=PT$ where M, V, P, and T are the supply of money, velocity of money, price level and the volume of transactions (or total output). The equation tells that the total money supply MV equals the total value of output PT in the economy. Assuming V (the velocity of money) and T (the total output) to be constant, a change in the supply of money (M) causes a proportional change in the price level (P). This is based on the assumption that money acts as a medium of exchange.

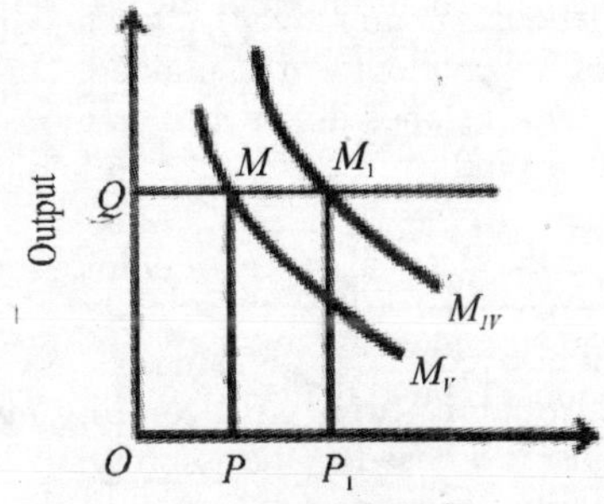

Fig. 2

The relation between quantity of money, total output and price level is depicted in Figure 2 where the price level is taken on the horizontal axis and the total output on the vertical axis. MV is the money supply curve which is a rectangular hyperbola. This is because the equation $MV=PT$ holds on all points of this curve. Given the output level OQ, there would be only one price level OP consistent with the quantity of money, as shown by point M on the MV curve. If the quantity of money increases, the MV curve will shift to the right as M_1V curve. As a result, the price level would rise from OP to OP_1, given the same level of output OQ. This rise in the price level is exactly proportional to the rise in the quantity of money, i.e.. $PP_1 = MM_1$.

If the quantity of money is doubled, the price level will also double. On the contrary, if the quantity of money is halved, the price level will also be halved. Thus money is simply a ``veil' whose main function is to determine the general level of prices at which goods and services exchange.

Pigou's Version. The classical theory of employment received its final version at the hands of Pigou who formulated Say's Law in terms of labour market. According to Pigou, under free competition the tendency of the economic system is to automatically provide full employment in the labour market. Unemployment results from rigidity in the wage structure and interferences in the working of the free market economy. When the state intervenes by recognising trade unions, passing minimum wage laws, etc., and labour adopts monopolistic behaviour, wages are pushed up and unemployment follows. If all government interferences are removed and forces of competition are allowed to work freely, the manipulation of wage rates will lead to full employment. As pointed out by Pigou, ``With perfectly free competition....there will always be at work a strong tendency for wage rates to be so related to demand that everybody is employed."[2] The Pigovian equation $N = \frac{qY}{W}$ explains the entire proposition. In this equation, N is the number of workers employed, q is the fraction of income earned as wages and salaries, Y is the national income and W is the money wage rate. N can be increased by a reduction in W. Thus the key to full employment is a reduction in money wage. This is explained in Figure 3. In panel (A), S is the supply curve of labour and D is the demand curve for labour. The intersection

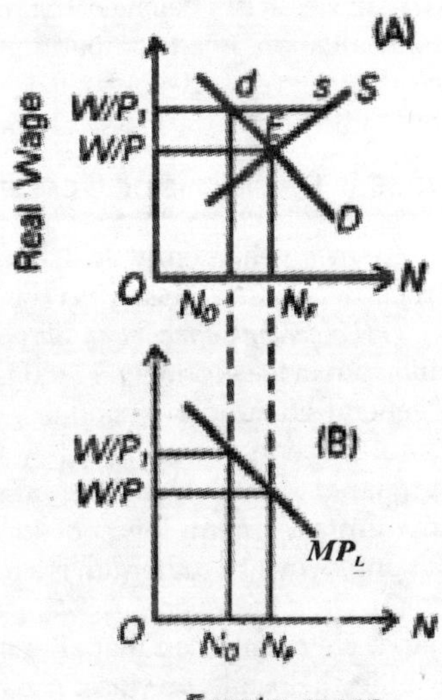

Fig. 3

2. A.C. Pigou, *Theory of Employment*, p. 252.

of the two curves at E shows the point of full employment N_F and the real wage W/P at which full employment is secured. If the real wage is maintained at a higher level W/P_1, supply exceeds the demand for labour by *sd*. N_ON_F labour is unemployed. It is only when the wage is reduced to W/P that unemployment disappears and the level of full employment is attained. This is shown in panel (B), where MP_L is the marginal product of labour curve which slopes downward as more labour is employed. Since every worker is paid wages equal to his marginal product, therefore the full employment level N_F is reached when the wage rate falls from W/P_1 to W/P.

In the classical model of employment, changes in money wages and real wages are directly related and are proportional. When there is a cut in the money wage, the real wage is also reduced to the same extent which reduces unemployment and ultimately brings full employment in the economy. This relationship is based on the assumption that prices are proportional to the quantity of money. It is argued that in a competive economy a reduction in the money wage reduces the cost of production and prices of products, thereby raising their demand. In order to meet the increased demand for the products, more workers are employed to produce them.

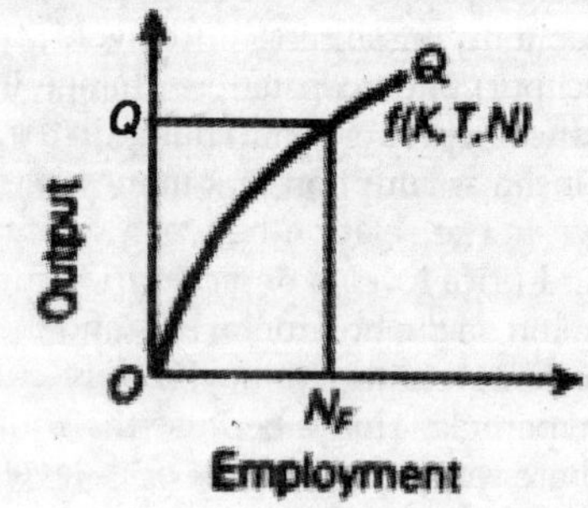

Fig. 4

As employment increases, total output also increases till full employment is reached. But when the economy is at the full employment level, total output becomes stable. Thus given the stock of capital, technological knowledge and resources, a precise relation exists between total output and the amount of employ-ment. Total output is an increasing function of the number of workers. This is shown in Figure 4 where $Q=f(K, T, N)$, that is, total output Q is a function f' of the capital stock K, of technological knowledge T, and the number of workers, N. This production function shows that in the short-run the total output is an increasing function of the number of workers, given the capital stock and technological knowledge. In the Figure, the total output OQ corresponds to the full employment level N_F (of Figure 3).

The classicists believed that under normal competitive conditions full employment will be maintained without inflation. Even competition among employers to hire more workers will not bid wages above the full employment level, and there will be no possibility of cost inflation in the economy. Hence there is full employment without inflation in the classical system.

Keynes 's Criticisms of Classical Theory

Keynes vehemently criticised the classical theory of employment for its unrealistic assumptions. He attacked the classical theory on the following counts.

(1) *Underemployment Equilibrium*. Keynes rejected the fundamental classical assumption of full employment equilibrium in the economy. He considered it as unrealistic. He regarded full employment as a special situation. The general situation in a capitalist economy is one of underemployment. This is because the capitalist society does not function according to Say's law, and supply always exceeds its demand. We find millions of workers are prepared to work at the current wage rate, and even below it, but they do not find work. Thus the existence of involuntary unemployment in capitalist economies (entirely ruled out by the classicists) proves that underemployment equilibrium is a normal situation and full employment equilibrium is abnormal and accidental.

(2) *Overproduction Possible*. Keynes refuted Say's Law of markets that supply always created its own demand. He maintained that all income earned by the factor-owners would not be spent in buying products which they helped to produce. A part of the earned income is saved and is not automatically invested because saving and investment are distinct functions. So when all earned income is not spent on consumption goods and a portion of it is saved, there results a deficiency of aggregate demand. This leads to general overproduction because all that is produced is not sold. This, in turn, leads to general unemployment. Thus Keynes invalidated Say's Law by invoking the principle that marginal propensity to consume is less than one.

(3) *Self adjustment Impossible*. Keynes did not agree with the classical view that the *laissez-faire* policy was essential for an automatic and self-adjusting process of full employment equilibrium. He pointed out that the

capitalist system was not automatic and self-adjusting because of the non- egalitarian structure of its society. There are two principal classes, the rich and the poor. The rich possess much wealth but they do not spend the whole of it on consumption. The poor lack money to purchase consumption goods. Thus there is general deficiency of aggregate demand in relation to aggregate supply which leads to overproduction and unemployment in the economy. This, in fact, led to the Great Depression. Had the capitalist system been automatic and self-adjusting this would not have occurred. Keynes, therefore, advocated state intervention for adjusting supply and demand within the economy through fiscal and monetary measures.

(4) *Equality between Saving and Investment through Income Changes*. The classicists believed that saving and investment were equal at the full employment level and in case of any divergence the equality was brought about by the mechanism of rate of interest. Keynes held that the level of saving depended upon the level of income and not on the rate of interest. Similarly investment is determined not only by rate of interest but by the marginal efficiency of capital. A low rate of interest cannot increase investment, if business expectations are low. If saving exceeds investment, it means people are spending less on consumption. As a result, demand declines. There is overproduction and fall in investment, income, employment and output. It will lead to reduction in saving and ultimately the equality between saving and investment will be attained at a lower level of income. Thus it is variations in income rather than in interest rate that bring the equality between saving and investment.

(5) *Importance of Speculative Demand for Money*. The classical economists believed that money was demanded for transactions and precautionary purposes. They did not recognise the speculative demand for money because money held for speculative purposes related to idle balances. But Keynes did not agree with this view. He emphasised the importance of speculative demand for money. He pointed out that the earning of interest from assets meant for transactions and precautionary purposes may be very small at a low rate of interest. But the speculative demand for money would be infinitely large at a low rate of interest. Thus the rate of interest will not fall below a certain minimum level, and the speculative demand for money would become perfectly interest elastic. This is Keynes `liquidity trap" which the classicists failed to analyse.

(6) *Money not Neutral*. The classical economists regarded money as neutral. Therefore, they excluded the theory of output, employment and interest rate from the monetary theory. According to them, the level of output and employment, and the equilibrium rate of interest were determined by the real forces. Keynes criticised the classical view that the monetary theory was separate from the value theory. He integrated monetary theory with value theory, and brought the theory of interest in the domain of monetary theory (by regarding the interest rate as a monetary theory phenomenon). He integrated the value theory and the monetary theory through the theory of output. This he did by forging a link between the quantity of money and the price level via the rate of interest. For instance, when the quantity of money increases, the rate of interest falls, investment increases, income and output increase, demand increases, factor costs and wages increase, relative prices increase, and ultimately the general price level rises. Thus Keynes integrated monetary and real sectors of the economy.

(7) *Refutation of Wage-Cut*. Keynes refuted the Pigovian formulation that a cut in money wage could achieve full employment in the economy. The greatest fallacy in Pigou's analysis was that he extended the argument to the economy which was applicable to a particular industry. Reduction in wage rate can increase employment in an industry by reducing costs and increasing demand. But the adoption of such a policy for the economy leads to a reduction in employment. When there is a general wage-cut, the income of the workers is reduced. As a result, aggregate demand falls leading to a decline in employment.

From the practical view point also Keynes never favoured a wage-cut policy. In modern times, workers have formed strong trade unions which resist a cut in money wages. They would resort to strikes. The consequent unrest in the economy would bring a decline in output and income. Moreover, social justice demands that wages should not be cut if profits are left untouched.

Keynes also did not accept the classical view that there was a direct proportionate relationship between money wages and real wages. According to him, there is an inverse relationship between the two. When money wages fall, real wages rise and vice versa. Therefore, a reduction in the money wage would not reduce the real wage, (as the classicists believed) rather it would increase it. This is because the money wage-cut will reduce cost of production and prices by more than the former. Thus the classical view that fall in real wages will increase employment breaks down. Keynes, however, believed that employment could be increased more easily through monetary and fiscal measures rather than by reduction in money wage. Moreover, institutional resistances to wage and price reductions are so strong that it is not possible to implement such a policy administratively.

(8)*State Intervention Essential*. Keynes did not agree with Pigou that ``frictional maladjustments alone account for failure to utilise fully our productive power." The capitalist system is such that left to itself it is incapable of using productive power fully. Therefore, state intervention is necessary. The state may directly invest to raise the level of economic activity or to supplement private investment. It may pass legislation recognising trade unions, fixing minimum wages and providing relief to workers through social security measures. ``Therefore", as observed by Dillard, ``it is bad politics even if it should be considered good economics to object to labour unions and to liberal labour legislation". So Keynes favoured state action to utilise fully the resources of the economy for attaining full employment.

(9) *Short-Run Analysis*. The classicists believed in the long-run full employment equilibrium through a self-adjusting process. Keynes had no patience to wait for the long period for he believed that ``In the long-run we are all dead". As pointed by Schumpeter, ``His philosophy of life was essentially a short- term philosophy." His analysis is confined to short-run phenomena. Unlike the classicists, he assumes tastes, habits, techniques of production, supply of labour, etc. to be constant during the short period and so neglects long-run influences on demand. Assuming consumption demand to be constant, he lays emphasis on increasing investment to remove unemployment. But the equilibrium level so reached is one of underemployment rather than of full employment.

Thus the classical theory of employment is unrealistic and is incapable of solving the present day economic problems of the capitalist world.

EXERCISES

1. State and explain Say's Law of Markets.
2. Explain the classical theory of employment. What were Keynes' criticisms of it?

CHAPTER 25

Say's Law of Markets

1. SAY'S LAW

Say's law of markets is the core of the classical theory of employment. An early 19th century French economist, J.B. Say, enunciated the proposition that ``supply creates its own demand." Therefore, there cannot be general overproduction and the problem of unemployment "in the economy. On the other hand, if there is general overproduction in the economy, then some labourers may be asked to leave their jobs. There may be the problem of unemployment in the economy for some time. In the long-run, the economy will automatically tend towards full employment.

In Say's words, ``it is production which creates markets for goods. A product is no sooner created than it, from that instant, affords a market for other products to the full extent of its own value. Nothing is more favourable to the demand of one product, than the supply of another." [1] This definition explains the following important facts about the law.

Production Creates Market (Demand) for Goods. When producers obtain the various inputs to be used in the production process, they generate the necessary income. For example, producers give wages to labourers for producing goods. The labourers will purchase the goods from the market for their own use. This, is turn, causes the demand for goods produced. In this way, supply creates its own demand.

Barter System as its Basis. In its original form, the law is applicable to a barter economy where goods are ultimately sold for goods. Therefore, whatever is produced is ultimately consumed in the economy. In other words, people produce goods for their own use to sustain their consumption levels. Say's law, in a very broad way, is, as Prof. Hansen has said, ``a description of a free-exchange economy. So conceived, it illuminates the truth that the main source of demand is the flow of factor income generated from the process of production "itself."[2] Thus, the existence of money does not alter the basic law.

General Over-production Impossible. If the production process is continued under normal conditions, then there will be no difficulty for the producers to sell their products in the market. According to Say, work being unpleasant no person will work to make a product unless he wants to exchange it for some other product which he desires. Therefore, the very act of supplying goods implies a demand for them. In such a situation, there cannot be general overproduction because supply of goods will not exceed demand as a whole. But a particular good may be over produced because the producer incorrectly estimates the quantity of the product

1. J.B. Say, *Political Economy*, 4/e, Vol. 7, pp. 167-170.
2. A.H. Hansen, *A Guide to Keynes*, p. 3.

which others want. But this is a temporary phenomenon, for the excess production of a particular product can be corrected in time by reducing its production.

J.S. Mill has supported Say's views regarding the impossibility of general overproduction and general unemployment. In his words,``Consumption is co-extensive with production and production is the cause, and the sole cause of demand. It never furnishes supply without furnishing demand, both at the same time and both to an equal extent..whatever the amount of annual demand." In other words, Say's law of markets does not consider the possibility of decrease in the demand for goods produced in the economy. By employing more factors of production, there is an increase in the level of employment and therefore profits are maximised.

Saving-Investment Equality. Income accruing to the factor-owners in the form of rent, wages and interest is not spent on consumption "but some proportion out of it, is saved which is automatically invested for further production. Therefore, investment in production is a saving which helps to create demand for goods in the market. Further, saving-investment equality is maintained to avoid general over- production.

Rate of Interest as a Determinant Factor. Say's law of market regards the rate of interest as a determinant factor in maintaining the equality between saving and investment. If there is any divergence between the two, the equality is maintained through the mechanism of the rate of interest. If at any given time, investment exceeds saving, the rate of interest will rise. To maintain the equality, saving will increase and investment will decline. This is due to the "fact that saving is regarded as an increasing function of the interest rate, and investment as a decreasing function of the rate of interest. On the contrary, when saving is more than investment, the rate of interest falls, investment increases and saving declines till the two are equal at the new interest rate.[3]

Labour Market. Prof. Pigou has formulated Say's law in terms of labour market. By giving minimum wages to labourers, according to Pigou, more labourers can be employed. In this way, there will be more demand for labour. As pointed out by Pigou, ``With perfectly free competition...there will always be at work a strong tendency for wage rates to be so related to demand that everybody is employed."[4] Unemployment results from rigidity in the wage structure and interferences in the working of the free market economy. Direct interference comes in the form of minimum wage laws passed by the state. The trade unions may be demanding higher wages, more facilities and reduction in working hours. In short, it is only under free competition that the tendency of the economic system is to provide automatically full employment in the labour market.[5]

2. PROPOSITIONS AND IMPLICATIONS OF THE LAW

Say's propositions and its implications present the true picture of the market law. These are given below.

1. *Full Employment in the Economy*. The law is based on the proposition that there is full employment in the economy. Increase in production means more employment to the factors of production. Production continues to increase until the level of full employment is reached. Under such a situation the level of production will be the maximum.

2. *Proper Utilization of Resources*. If there is full employment in the economy, idle resources will be properly utilized which will further help to produce more and also generate more income.

3. *Perfect Competition*. Say's law of market is based on the proposition of perfect competition in labour and product markets. Other conditions of perfect competition are :

(a) Size of the Market. According to Say's law, the size of the market is large enough to create demand for goods. Moreover, the size of the market is also influenced by the forces of demand and supply of various inputs.

(b) Automatic Adjustment Mechanism. The law is based on this proposition that there is automatic and self-adjusting mechanism in different markets. Disequilibrium in any market is a temporary situation. For example,

3. Give Fig. 24.1
4. A.C. Pigou, *Theory of Employment.*, p. 252.
5. Give Fig. 24.3 and Pigou's formula $N = qY/W$.

in the capital market, the equality between saving and investment is maintained by the rate of interest while in the labour market the adjustment between demand and supply of labour is maintained by the wage rate.

(c) Role of Money as Neutral. The law is based on the proposition of a barter system where goods are exchanged for goods. But it is also assumed that the role of money is neutral. Money does not affect the production process.

4. *Laissez-faire Policy*. The law assumes a closed capitalist economy which follows the policy of *laissez faire*. The policy of *laissez "faire* is essential for an automatic and self- adjusting process of full employment equilibrium.

5. *Saving as a Social Virtue*. All factor income is spent in buying goods which they help to produce. Whatever is saved is automatically invested for further production. In other words, saving is a social virtue.

3. CRITICISMS OF SAY'S LAW

J.M. Keynes in his *General Theory of Employment, Interest "and Money* published in 1936, made a frontal attack on the classical postulates and the Say's law of markets. He criticised Say's law of markets on the following grounds.

1. *Supply does not Create its Demand*. Say's law assumes that production creates market (demand) for goods. Therefore, supply creates its own demand. But this proposition is not applicable to modern economies where demand does not increase as much as production increases. It is also not possible to consume only those goods which are produced within the economy.

2. *Self-adjustment not Possible*. According to Say's law, full-employment is maintained by an automatic and self-adjustment mechanism in the long-run. But Keynes had no patience to wait for the long period for "he believed that ``In the long-run we are all dead." It is not the automatic adjustment process which removes unemployment. But unemployment can be removed by increase in the rate of investment.

3. *Money is not Neutral*. Say's law of markets is based on a barter system and ignores the role of money in the system. Say believes that money does not affect the economic activities of the markets. On the other hand, Keynes has given due importance to money. He regards money as a medium of exchange. Money is held for income and business motives. Individuals hold money for unforeseen contingencies while businessmen keep cash in reserve for future activities.

4. *Over Production is Possible*. Say's law is based on the proposition that supply creates its own demand and there cannot be general over-production. But Keynes does not agree with this proposition. According to him, "all income accruing to factors of production is not spent but some fraction out of it, is saved which is not automatically invested. Therefore, saving and investment are not always equal and they lead to the problem of overproduction and unemployment.

5. *Underemployment Situation*. Keynes regards full employment as a special case because there is underemployment in capitalist economies. This is because the capitalist economies do not function according to Say's law and supply always exceeds its demand. For example, millions of workers are prepared to work at the current wage rate, and even below it, but they do not find work.

6. *State Intervention*. Say's law is based on the existence of *laissez faire* policy. But Keynes has highlighted the need for state intervention in the case of general overproduction and mass unemployment. *Laissez faire,* in fact, led to the Great Depression. Had the capitalist system been automatic and self-adjusting, this would not have occurred. Keynes, therefore, advocated state intervention for adjusting supply and demand within the economy through fiscal and monetary measures.

7. *Equality through Income*. Keynes does not agree with the classical view that the equality between saving and investment is brought about through the mechanism of the interest rate. But in reality, it is change in income rather than the rate of interest which bring the two to equality.

8. *Wage-cut no Solution*. Pigou favoured the policy of wage-cut to solve the problem of unemployment. But Keynes opposed such a policy both from the theoretical and practical points of view. Theoretically, a wage-cut policy increases unemployment instead of removing it. Practically, workers are not prepared to accept a cut in money wage. Keynes, therefore, favoured a flexible monetary policy to a flexible wage policy to raise the

level of employment in the economy.

9. *Demand creates its own supply.* Say's law of market is based on the proposition that ``supply creates its own demand.'' Therefore, there cannot be general over production and mass unemployment. Keynes has criticised this proposition and propounded the opposite view that *demand creates its own supply.* Unemployment results from the deficiency of effective demand because people do not spend the whole of their income on consumption. Therefore, it is increase in demand which leads to more production and the supply of goods.

EXERCISES

1. ``Supply creates its own demand.'' Critically examine this statement.
2. ``General overproduction and general unemployment are impossible.'' Discuss.
3. State and explain the main propositions of Say's law. On what grounds Keynes criticised them?

Chapter 26

The Principle of Effective Demand : Aggregate Demand and Aggregate Supply

1. INTRODUCTION

The logical starting point of Keynes theory of employment is the principle of effective demand.[1] In a capitalist economy, the level of employment depends on effective demand. Thus unemployment results from a deficiency of effective demand and the level of employment can be raised by increasing the level of effective demand.

2. MEANING

In ordinary parlance, demand means desire. It becomes effective when income is spent in buying consumption goods and investment goods. Keynes used the term `effective demand' to denote the total demand for goods and services at various levels of employment. Different levels of employment represent different levels of aggregate demand. But there can be a level of employment where aggregate demand equals aggregate supply. This is the point of effective demand. In Keynes' words, ``The value of *D* (Aggregate Demand) at the point of Aggregate Demand function, where it is intersected by the Aggregate Supply function, will be called the effective demand." Thus, according to Keynes, the level of employment is determined by effective demand which, in turn, is determined by aggregate demand price and aggregate supply price.

Aggregate Demand Price

``The aggregate demand price for the output of any given amount of employment is the total sum of money of proceeds, which is expected from the sale of the output produced when that amount of labour is employed." [2] Thus the aggregate demand price is the amount of money which the entrepreneurs *expect* to get

1. D. Dillard, *The Economics of J.M. Keynes*, 1948.
2. *Ibid.*

by selling the output produced by the number of men employed. In other words, it refers to the *expected revenue* from the sale of output produced at a particular level of employment. Different aggregate demand prices relate to different levels of employment in the economy.

A statement showing the various aggregate demand prices at different levels of employment is called the aggregate demand price schedule or aggregate demand function. ``The aggregate demand function,'' according to Keynes, ``relates any given level of employment to the expected proceeds from that level of employment.''[3] Table 1 shows the aggregate demand schedule.

The Table reveals that with the increase in the level of employment *proceeds expected* (*ADP*) rise and at lower levels of employment decline. When 40 lakh people are provided employment, the aggregate demand price is Rs. 280 crores and when 25 lakh people are provided jobs, it is Rs. 250 crores. According to Keynes, the aggregate demand function is an increasing function of the level of employment and is expressed as *D=F (N)*, where *D* is the proceeds which entrepreneurs expect from the employment of *N* men.

TABLE 1 : AGGREGATE DEMAND SCHEDULE

Level of Employment (N) *(in Lakhs)*	*Aggregate Demand Price (D)* *(Rs Crores)*
0	0
25	250
30	260
35	270
40	280
40	290

The aggregate demand curve can be drawn on the basis of the above schedule. It slopes unward from left to right, because as the level of employment increases aggregate demand price also rises, shown as *AD* curve in Figure 1

Aggregate Supply Price

When an entrepreneur gives employment to certain amount of labour, it requires certain quantities of cooperant factors like land, capital, raw materials, etc. which will be paid remuneration along with labour. Thus each level of employment involves certain money costs of production including normal profits which the entrepreneur must cover. ``At any given level of employment of labour aggregate supply price is the total amount of money which all the entrepreneurs in the economy, taken together, must except to receive from the sale of the output produced by that given number of men, if it is to be just worth employing them.''[4] In brief, the aggregate supply price refers to the *proceeds "necessary* from the sale of output at a particular level of employment. Thus each level of employment in the economy is related to a particular aggregate supply price and there are different aggregate supply prices for different levels of employment.

A statement showing the various aggregate supply prices at different levels of employment is called the aggregate supply price schedule or aggregate supply function. In the words of Prof. Dillard, ``The aggregate supply function is a schedule of the minimum amounts of proceeds required to induce varying quantities of employment.''[5] Table 2 shows the aggregate supply schedule.

3. J.M. Keynes, *op. cit.*, p. 89.
4. Stonier and Hague, *A Text Book of Economic Theory*, p. 381.
5. D. Dillard, *op.cit.*, p. 31

TABLE 2 : AGGREGATE SUPPLY SCHEDULE

Level of Employment (N) (in Lakhs)	*Aggregate Supply Price (Z) (Rs Crores)*
0	0
25	240
30	255
35	270
40	285
40	300

The above table reveals that the aggregate supply price rises with the increase in the level of employment. If the entrepreneurs are to provide employment to 25 lakh workers, they must receive Rs. 240 crores from the sale of the output produced by them. It is only when they expect to receive the minimum amounts of proceeds (Rs. 255 crores, Rs. 270 crores and Rs. 270 creres) that they will provide employment to more workers (30 lakhs, 35 lakhs and 40 lakhs respectively). But when the economy reaches the level of full employment (at 40 lakh workers), the aggregate supply price (Rs. 300 crores) continues to increase but there is no further increase in employment. According to Keynes, the aggregate supply function is an increasing function of the level of employment and is expressed as $Z= F(N)$, where Z is the aggregate supply price of the output from employing N men.[6]

The aggregate supply curve can be drawn on the basis of the schedule. It slopes upward from left to right because as the necessary expected proceeds increase, the level of employment also rises. But when the economy reaches the level of full employment, the aggregate supply curve becomes vertical, shown as *AS* curve in Figure 1. Even with the increase in the aggregate supply price, it is not possible to provide more employment as the economy has attained the level of full employment (N_F).

Determination of Effective Demand

We have studied the two determinants of effective demand separately and now are in a position to analyse the process of determining the level of employment in an economy. The level of employment is determined at the point where the aggregate demand price equals the aggregate supply price. In other words, it is the point where what the entrepreneurs *expect to receive* equals what they *must receive* and their profits are maximised. This point is called the *effective "demand* and here the entrepreneurs earn normal profits. So long as the aggregate demand price is higher than the aggregate supply price, the prospects of getting additional profits are greater when more workers are provided employment. The proceeds expected (revenue) rise more than the proceeds necessary (costs). This process will continue till the aggregate demand price equals the aggregate supply price and the point of effective demand is reached. This point determines the level of employment and output in the economy. The point of effective demand is, however, not necessarily one of full employment but of *underemployment equilibrium*. If the entrepreneurs try to provide more employment after this point, the aggregate supply price exceeds the aggregate demand price indicating that the total costs are higher than the total revenue and there are losses. So the entrepreneurs will not employ workers beyond the point of effective demand till the aggregate demand price rises to meet the aggregate supply price at the new equilibrium point which may be one of full employment. If the aggregate demand price is raised still further, it will lead to inflation for no increase in employment and output is possible beyond the level of full employment.

Table 3 explains the determination of the point of effective demand.

It shows that so long as the aggregate demand price is higher than the aggregate supply price, it is profitable for the entrepreneurs to employ more workers. But when the proceeds necessary and proceeds expected equal Rs. 270 crores the level of employment rises to 35 lakhs. This is the point of effective demand.

6. J.M. Keynes, *op.cit.,* p.25.

TABLE 48.3 : SCHEDULE OF AGGREGATE DEMAND AND AGGREGATE "SUPPLY PRICES

Level of Employment (N) (in Lakhs)	*Aggregate Demand Price (D) (RS Crores)*	*AggregateSupply Price (Z) (Rs.Crores)*
0	0	0
25	250	240
30	260	255
35	270	270
40	280	285
40	290	300

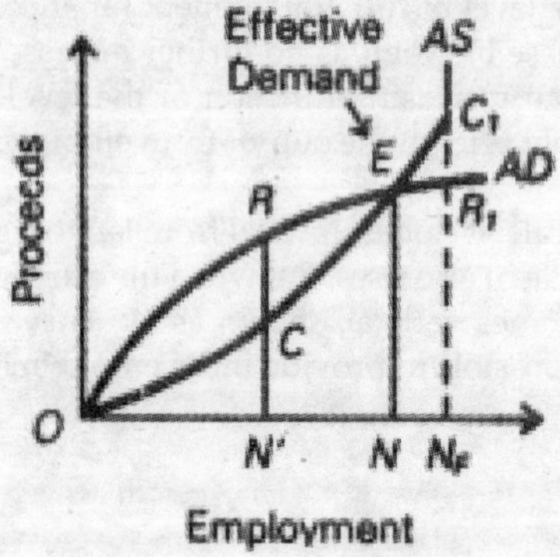

Fig. 1

Figure 1 illustrates the determination of effective demand where *AD* is the aggregate demand function and *AS* the aggregate supply function. The horizontal axis measures the level of employment in the economy and the vertical axis, the proceeds expected (revenue) and the proceeds necessary (costs). The two curves *AD* and *AS* intersect each other at point *E*. This is effective demand where *ON* workers are employed. At this point, the entrepreneurs' expectations of profits are maximised. At any point other than this, the entrepreneurs will either incur losses or earn subnormal profits. At *ON'* level of employment the proceeds expected (revenue) are more than the proceeds necessary (costs), i.e. *RN'* > *CN*. This indicates that it is profitable for the entrepreneurs to provide increasing employment to workers till *ON* level is reached where the proceeds expected and necessary equal at point *E*. It would not be, however, profitable for the entrepreneurs to increase employment beyond this to N_F level because the proceeds necessary (costs) exceed the proceeds expected (revenue), i.e., $C_1N_F > R_1N_F$ and they incur losses. Thus *E*, the point of effective demand, determines the actual level of employment in the economy which is of underemployment equilibrium.

Of the two determinants of effective demand, Keynes regards the aggregate supply function to be given because it depends on the technical conditions of production, the availability of raw materials, machines, etc. which do not change in the short-run. It is, therefore, the aggregate demand function which plays a vital role in determining the level of employment in the economy. According to Keynes, the aggregate demand function depends on the consumption function and investment function. The cause of unemployment may be a fall in either consumption expenditure or investment expenditure, or both. The level of employment can be raised by increasing either consumption expenditure or investment expenditure, or both. Thus, it is the aggregate demand function which is the ``effective'' element in the principle of effective demand. Prof. Dillard regards this as the core of the principle of effective demand.

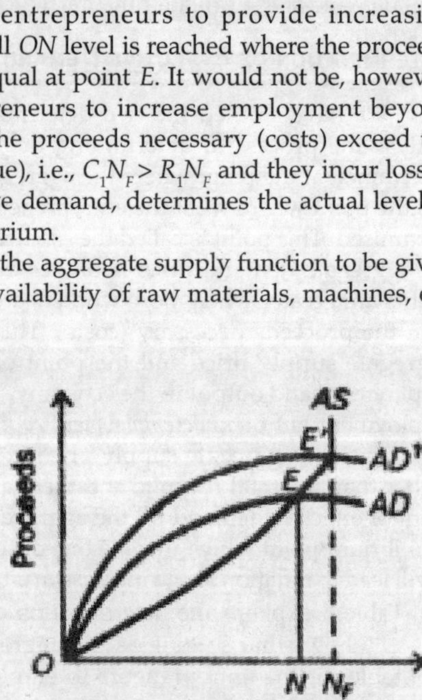

Fig. 2

It follows that to raise the economy to the level of full employment requires the raising of the point of effective demand by increasing the aggregate demand. This is illustrated in Figure 2 where *E* is the point of effective demand which determines *ON* level of employment. If ON_f is the level of full employment for the economy, it requires the raising of the point of effective demand. This is possible by raising the aggregate demand curve to *AD'* where it intersects the aggregate supply curve *AS* at *E'*. This is the new point of effective demand which provides an *optimum* level of employment ON_F to the economy. If the aggregate demand function is raised beyond this point, the economy will experience inflation because all the existing resources are fully employed and their supply cannot be increased during the short-run, as is apparent from the vertical portion of the *AS* curve in Figure 2.

3. IMPORTANCE OF EFFECTIVE DEMAND

The principle of effective demand is the most important contribution of Keynes. It is the soul of the Keynesian theory of employment. Dr. Klein attributes the Keynesian revolution solely to the development of a theory of effective demand.

(1) *Determinant of Employment.* Effective demand determines the level of employment in the economy. When effective demand increases, employment also increases, and a decline in effective demand decreases the level of employment. Thus unemployment is caused by a deficiency of effective demand. Effective demand represents the total expenditure on the total output produced at an equilibrium level of employment. It indicates the value of total output which equals national income. National income equals national expenditure. National expenditure "consists of expenditure on consumption goods and investment goods. Thus the main determinants of effective demand and the level of employment are consumption and investment. In brief, Effective Demand = Value of National Output = Volume of Employment = National Income = National Expenditure = Expenditure on Consumption Goods + Expenditure on Investment Goods.

In the Keynesian analysis of effective demand, consumption expenditure and investment expenditure relate to the private sector because Keynes considers government expenditure as autonomous. But the post-Keynesian economists include government expenditure as a component of effective demand. Thus, effective demand *(D)* = Private consumption expenditure (*C*) + Private investment (I)+Government expenditure (*G*) on both.

We may conclude that the importance of the principle of effective demand lies in pointing out the cause and remedy of unemployment. Unemployment is caused by a deficiency of effective demand and it can be removed by an increase in consumption expenditure or/and investment expenditure and in case the private expenditures are insufficient and ineffective in bringing about the required level of employment, the same can be achieved by government expenditure. Thus the principle of effective demand is the basis of the theory of employment.

(2) *Repudiation of Say's Law and Full Employment Thesis.* The principle of effective demand repudiates Say's Law of Market that supply creates its own demand and that full employment equilibrium is a normal situation in the economy. This principle points out that underemployment equilibrium is a normal situation and full employment equilibrium is accidental. In a capitalist economy, supply fails to create its own demand because the whole of the earned income is not spent on the consumption of goods and services. Moreover, the decisions to save and invest are made by different people. As a result, the existence of full employment is not a possibility and the point of effective demand at any time represents underemployment equilibrium. Thus the importance of this principle lies in repudiating Say's Law and the classical thesis of full employment equilibrium.

(3) *Repudiation of Wage-Cut.* The Pigovian view that full employment can be achieved by a reduction in money wage-cut is also repudiated by this principle. A money wage-cut will bring about a reduction in expenditure on goods and services leading to a fall in effective demand and hence in the level of employment.

(4) *Role of Investment.* The principle of effective demand highlights the significant role of investment in determining the level of employment in the economy. The two determinants of effective demand are the consumption and investment expenditures. When income increases consumption expenditure also increases but *by* less than the increase in income. Thus there arises a gap between income and consumption which leads to a decline in the volume of employment. This gap can be bridged by an increase in either consumption expenditure or investment expenditure in order to achieve full employment level of effective demand in the economy. Since the propensity to consume is stable during the short-run, it is not possible to raise the consumption expenditure. Therefore, the level of effective demand and hence of employment can be raised by

an increase in investment. In this lies the importance of investment.

(5) *The Paradox of Poverty in the Midst of Potential Plenty.* The importance of effective demand lies in explaining the paradox of poverty in the midst of potential plenty in the modern capitalism. Effective demand is mainly determined by the aggregate demand function which is composed of consumption expenditure and investment expenditure. A fundamental principle is that when income increases consumption also increases but less than proportionately (i.e., the marginal propensity to consume is less than one). This creates a gap between income and consumption which must be filled up by the required investment expenditure. If the appropriate investment is not forthcoming to fill this gap, it leads to a deficiency of effective demand resulting in unemployment.

It follows that in a poor community, the gap between income and consumption is small because the marginal propensity to consume is high. It will, therefore, have little difficulty in employing all its resources by filling the gap through small investment expenditure.

On the contrary, in a wealthy community the gap between income and consumption is very large because the marginal propensity to consume is low. It will, therefore, require large investment expenditure to fill the gap between income and consumption in order to maintain a high level of income and employment. But in a rich community, investment demand is not adequate to fill this gap and there emerges a deficiency of aggregate demand resulting in widespread unemployment. When the aggregate demand falls the potential wealthy community will be forced to reduce its actual output until it becomes so poor that the excess of output over consumption will be reduced to the actual amount of investment. Further, in such a community there is an accumulated stock of capital assets which weakens the inducement to invest because every "new investment competes with an already existing large supply of old capital assets. This inadequacy of investment demand reacts in a cumulative manner on the demand for consumption and will, in turn, lead to a further fall in employment, output and income. Thus as Keynes said, `The richer the community, the more obvious and outrageous the defects of the economic system that lead to unemployment on a mass scale in the midst of potential plenty because of the deficiency of effective demand."[7]

EXERCISES

1. What do you mean by Effective Demand? How is it determined?
2. Explain how aggregate demand and aggregate supply determine the level of income, output and employment?
3. ``The logical starting point of Keynes's theory of employment is the principle of effective demand." Discuss.
4. Explain how the principle of effective demand explains the paradox of poverty in the midst of plenty.
5. Explain the role of effective demand in Keynes's theory of employment.

7. Dillard, *op.cit.*, pp. 54-55.

CHAPTER 27

The Consumption Function

1. INTRODUCTION

One of the important tools of the Keynesian economics is the consumption function. This chapter deals with the consumption function, its technical attributes, its importance and its subjective and objective determinants along with Keynes' Psychological Law of Consumption.

2. MEANING OF CONSUMPTION FUNCTION

The consumption function or propensity to consume refers to income consumption relationship. It is a ``functional relationship between two aggregates, i.e.,total consumption and gross national income.[1]'' Symbolically, the relationship is represented as $C=f(Y)$, where C is consumption, Y is income and f is the functional relationship. Thus the consumption function indicates a functional relationship between C and Y, where C is the dependent and Y is the independent variable, i.e., C is determined by Y. This relationship is based on the *ceteris paribus* (other things being equal) assumption, as such only income consumption relationship is considered and all possible influences on consumption are held constant.

In fact, propensity to consume or consumption function is a schedule of the various amounts of consumption expenditure corresponding to different levels of income. A hypothetical consumption schedule is given in Table 1

TABLE 1 : CONSUMPTION SCHEDULE

(Rs. Crores)

Income (Y)	Consumption ($C = f(Y)$)
0	20
60	70
120	120
180	170
240	220
300	270
360	320

Table 1 shows that consumption is an increasing

1. K.K. Kurihara, *Monetary Theory and Public Policy*, p. 152.

function of income because consumption expenditure increases with increase in income. Here it is shown that when income is zero during the depression, people spend out of their past savings on consumption because they must eat in order to live. When income is generated in the economy to the extent of Rs 60 crores, it is not sufficient to meet the consumption expenditure of the community so that the consumption expenditure of Rs 70 crores is still above the income amounting to Rs 60 crores (Rs 10 crores are dis-saved). When both consumption expenditure and income equal Rs 120 crores, it is the basic consumption level. After this, income is shown to increase by Rs 60 crores and consumption by Rs 50 crores. This implies a stable consumption function during the short-run, as assumed by Keynes. Figure 1 illustrates the consumption function diagrammatically. In the diagram,[2] income is measured horizontally and consumption is measured vertically. 45° is the unity-line where at all levels income and consumption are equal. The *C* curve is a linear consumption function based on the assumption that consumption changes by the same amount (Rs 50 crores). Its upward slope to the right indicates that consumption is an increasing function of income. *B* is the break-even point where *C*=*Y* or $OY_1 = OC_1$.When income rises to OY_1, consumption also increases to OC_2, but the increase in consumption is less than the increase in income, $C_1C_2 < Y_1Y_2$. The portion of income not consumed is saved as shown by the vertical distance between 45° line and the *C* curve i.e,, *SS'* . "Thus the consumption function measures not only the amount spent on consumption but also the amount saved. This is because the propensity to save is merely the propensity not to consume. The 45° line may therefore be regarded as a zero- saving line, and the shape and position of the *C* curve indicate the division of income between consumption and saving."[3]

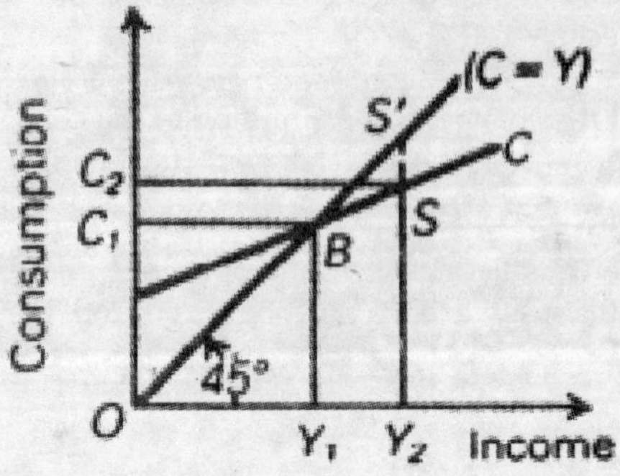

Fig. 1

3. PROPERTIES OR TECHNICAL ATTRIBUTES OF THE CONSUMPTION FUNCTION

The consumption function has two technical attributes or properties : (i) the average propensity to consume, and (ii) the marginal propensity to consume.

(1) *The Average Propensity to Consume (APC).* "The average propensity to consume may be defined as the ratio of consumption expenditure to any particular level of income."[4] It is found by dividing consumption expenditure by income, or *APC=C/Y*. It is expressed as the percentage or proportion of income consumed. The *APC* at various income levels is shown in column 3 of Table 2. The *APC* declines as income increases because the proportion of income spent on consumption decreases. But reverse is the case with *APS* (average propensity to save) which increases with increase in income (see column 4).

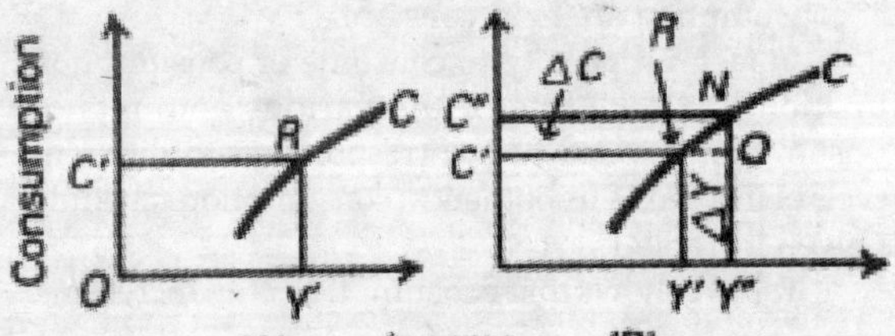

Fig. 2

2. Adapted from *Ibid.*
3. *Ibid.*, p. 153.
4. K.K. Kurihara, *Introduction to Keyncsian Dynamics.* p. 32.

Thus the *APC* also tells us about the *APS, APS*=1–*APC*.

Diagrammatically, the average propensity to consume is any one point on the C curve. In Figure 2 (A), point *R* measures the *APC* of the C curve which is OC'/OY'. The flattening of the C curve to the right shows declining *APC*.

(2) *The Marginal Propensity to Consume.* "The marginal propensity to consume may be defined as the ratio of the change in consumption to the change in income or as the rate of change in the average propensity to consume as income changes."[5] It can be found by dividing change in consumption by a change in income, or $MPC = \Delta C/\Delta Y$. The *MPC* is constant at all levels of income, as shown in column (5) of Table 2. It is 0.83 or 83 per cent because the ratio of change in consumption to change in income is $\Delta C/\Delta Y = 50/60$. The marginal propensity to save can be derived from the *MPC* by the formula 1-*MPC*. It is 0.17 in our example (see column 6).

TABLE 2

(1) Income (Y)	(2) Consumption (C)	(3) APC=C/Y	(4) APS = S/Y (I – APC)	(5) MPC= ΔC/ΔY	(6) MPS= ΔS/ΔY (I – MPC)
120	120	$\frac{120}{120}=1$ or 100%	0	—	—
180	170	$\frac{170}{180}=0.92$ or 92%	0.08	$\frac{50}{60}=0.83$	0.17
240	220	$\frac{220}{240}=0.91$ or 91%	0.09	$\frac{50}{60}=0.83$	0.17

Diagrammatically, the marginal propensity to consume is measured by the gradient or slope of the C curve. This is shown in Figure 2 (B) by *NQ/RQ* where *NQ* is the change in consumption (Δ C) and *RD* is change in income (Δ Y), or $C'C''/Y'Y''$.

SIGNIFICANCE OF MPC

The *MPC* is the rate of change in the *APC*. When income increases, the *MPC* falls but more than the *APC*. Contrariwise, when income falls, the *MPC* rises and the *APC* also rises but at a slower rate than the former. Such changes are only possible during cyclical fluctuations whereas in the short-run there is no change in the *MPC* and *MPC* < *APC*.

Keynes is concerned primarily with the *MPC*, for his analysis pertains to the short-run while the *APC* is useful in the long-run analysis. The post-Keynesian economists have come to the conclusion that over the long-run *APC* and *MPC* are equal and approximate 0.9. In the Keynesian analysis, the *MPC* is given more prominence. Its value is assumed to be positive and less than unity which means that when income increases the whole of it is not spent on consumption. On the contrary, when income falls, consumption expenditure does not decline in the same proportion and never becomes zero. The Keynesian hypothesis that the marginal propensity to consume is positive but less than unity ($O< \Delta C/\Delta Y<I$) is of great analytical and practical significance. Besides telling us that consumption is an increasing function of income and it increases by less than the increment of income, this hypothesis helps in explaining "(*a*) the theoretical possibility of general overproduction or

5. K.K. Kurihara, *Monetary Theory and Public Policy,* p. 156.

'underemployment equilibrium,' and also (*b*) the relative stability of a highly developed industrial economy.For it is implied that the gap between income and consumption at all high levels of income is too wide to be easily filled by investment with the possible consequence that the economy may fluctuate around an underemployment equilibrium."[6] Thus the economic significance of the *MPC* lies in filling the gap between income and consumption through planned investment to maintain the desired level of income. Further, its importance lies in the multiplier theory. The higher the *MPC*, the higher the multiplier and vice versa. The *MPC* is low in the case of the rich people and high in the case of the poor. This accounts for the high *MPC* in underdeveloped countries and low in advanced "countries.

4. KEYNES PSYCHOLOGICAL LAW OF CONSUMPTION

Keynes propounded the fundamental psychological law of consumption which forms the basis of the consumption function. He wrote, "Men are disposed as a rule and on the average to increase their consumption as their income increases but not by as much as the increase in their income." The law implies that there is a tendency on the part of the people to spend on consumption less than the full increment of income.

TABLE 3

(Rs. Crores)

Income (Y)	Consumption (C) ($C = f(Y)$)	Savings ($S = Y - C$)
0	20	–20
60	70	–10
120	120	0
180	170	10
240	220	20
300	270	30
360	320	40

PROPOSITIONS OF THE LAW

This law has three related propositions :

(1) When income increases, consumption expenditure also increases but by a smaller amount. The reason is that as income increases, our wants are satisfied side by side, so that the need to spend more on consumer goods diminishes. It does not mean that the consumption expenditure falls with the increase in income. In fact, the consumption expenditure increases with increase in income but less than proportionately.

(2) The increased income will be divided in some proportion between consumption expenditure and saving. This follows from the above proposition because when the whole of increased income is not spent on consumption, the remaining is saved. In this way, consumption and saving move together.

(3) Increase in income always leads to an increase in both consumption and saving. This means that increased income is unlikely to lead either to fall in consumption or saving than before. This is based on the above propositions because as income increases consumption also increases but by a smaller amount than before which leads to an increase in saving. Thus with increased income both consumption and saving increase.

The three propositions of the law can be explained with the help of Table 3.

Proposition(1) : Income increases by Rs 60 crores and the increase in consumption is by Rs 50 crores. The consumption expenditure is, however, increasing with increase in income, i.e.,"Rs. 170, 220, 270 and 320 crores against Rs 180, 240, 300 and 360 crores respectively.

Proposition (2) : The increased income of Rs 60 crores in each case is divided in some proportion between consumption and saving (i.e., Rs 50 crores and Rs 10 crores).

Proposition (3) : As income increases from Rs 120 to 180, 240, 300 and 360 crores, consumption also

6. K.K. Kurihara, *Introduction to Keynesian Dynamics*, p. 36.

increases from Rs 120 to 170, "220, 270, 320 crores, along with increase in saving from Rs 0 to 10, 20, 30 and 40 crores respectively. With increase in income neither consumption nor saving have fallen.

Diagrammaticallly, the three propositions are explained in Figure 3. Here, income is measured horizontally and consumption and saving are measured on the vertical axis. C is the consumption function curve and the 45° line represents income. Proposition (1) : When income increases from OY_0 to OY_1 consumption also increases from BY_0 to C_1Y_1 but the increase in consumption is less than the increase in income, "i.e., $C_1Y_1 < A_1Y_1$ $(=OY_1)$ by A_1C_1. Proposition (2) : When income increases to OY_1 and OY_2, it is divided in some proportion between consumption C_1Y_1 and C_2Y_2 and saving A_1C_1 and A_2C_2 respectively. Proposition (3) : Increases in income to OY_1 and OY_2 lead to increased consumption $C_2Y_2 > C_1Y_1$ and increased saving $A_2C_2 > A_1C_1$ than before. It is clear from the widening area below the C curve and the saving gap between 45° line and the C curve.

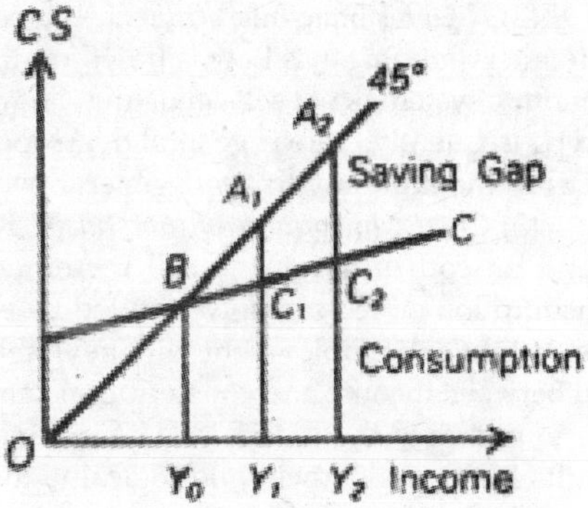

Fig. 3

ITS ASSUMPTIONS

Keynes' Law is based on the following assumptions.

(1) *It assumes a Constant Psychological and Institutional Complex.* This law is based on the assumption that the psychological and institutional complexes influencing consumption expenditure remain constant. Such complexes are income distribution, tastes, habits, social customs, price movements, population growth, etc. In the short-run, they do not change and consumption depends on income alone. The constancy of these complexes is the fundamental cause of the stable consumption function.

(2) *It assumes the Existence of Normal Conditions.* The law holds good under normal conditions. If, however, the economy is faced with abnormal and extraordinary circumstances like war, revolution or hyperinflation, the law will not operate. People may spend the whole of increased income on consumption.

(3) *It assumes the Existence of a Laissez-faire Capitalist Economy.* The law operates in a rich capitalist economy where there is no government intervention. People should be free to spend increased income. In the case of regulation of private enterprise and consumption expenditure by the state, the law breaks down. Thus the law is inoperative in socialist or state controlled and regulated economies.

Professor Kurihara opines that ``Keynes' law based on these assumptions may be regarded as a rough approximation to the actual macro-behaviour of free consumers in the normal short period."[7]

4. IMPLICATIONS OF KEYNES' LAW OR IMPORTANCE OF THE CONSUMPTION FUNCTION

Keynes' psychological law has important implications which in fact point towards the importance of the consumption function[8] because the latter is based on the former. The following are its implications :

(1) *Invalidates Say's Law.* Say's Law states that supply creates its own demand. Therefore, there cannot be general overproduction or general unemployment. Keynes' psychological law invalidates Say's Law because as income increases, consumption also increases but by a smaller amount. In other words, all that is produced (income) is not taken off the market (spent), as income increases. Thus supply fails to create its own demand.

7. K.K. Kurihara, *Monetary Theory and Public Policy,* p. 160.
8. While dealing with the importance of the Consumption Function, the students are advised to delete the word 'psychological law' and instead write the word 'Consumption Function'.

Rather, it exceeds demand and leads to general overproduction and glut of commodities in the market. As a result, producers stop production and there is mass unemployment.

(2) *Need for State Intervention*. As a corollary to the above, the psychological law highlights the need for state intervention. Say's Law is based on the existence of *laissez- faire* policy and its refutation implies that the economic system is not self-adjusting. So when consumption does not increase by the full increment of income and consequently there is gèneral overproduction and mass unemployment, the necessity of state intervention arises in the economy to avert general overproduction and unemployment through public policy.

(3) *Crucial Importance of Investment*. Keynes' psychological law stresses the vital point that people fail to spend on consumption the full increment of income. This tendency creates a gap between income and consumption which can only be filled by either increased investment or consumption. If either of them fail to rise, output and employment will inevitably fall. Since the consumption function is stable in the short-run, the gap between income and consumption can only be filled by an increase in investment. Thus the psychological law emphasises the crucial role of investment in Keynes' theory. It is the inadequacy of investment which results in unemployment and logically, the remedy to overcome unemployment is increase in investment.

(4) *Existence of Underemployment Equilibrium*. Keynes' notion of underemployment equilibrium is also based on the psychological law of consumption. The point of effective demand which determines the equilibrium level of employment is not of full employment but of underemployment because consumers do not spend the full increment of their income on consumption and there remains a deficiency in aggregate demand. Full employment equilibrium level can, however, be reached if the state increases investment to match the gap between income and consumption.

(5) *Declining Tendency of the Marginal Efficiency of Capital*. The psychological law also points towards the tendency of declining "marginal efficiency of capital in a *laissez-faire* economy. When income increases and consumption does not increase to the same extent, there is a fall in demand for consumer goods. This results in glut of commodities in the market. The producers will reduce production which will, in turn, bring a decline in the demand for capital goods and hence in the expected rate of profit and business expectations. It implies a decline in the marginal efficiency of capital. It is not possible to arrest the process of declining tendency of marginal efficiency of capital unless the propensity to consume rises. But such a possibility can exist only in the long-run when the psychological law of consumption does not hold good.

(6) *Danger of Permanent Over-saving or Under-investment Gap*. Keynes' psychological law points out that there is always a danger of an over-saving or under-investment gap appearing in the capitalist economy because as people become rich, the gap between income and consumption widens. This long-run tendency of increase in saving and fall in investment is characterised as secular stagnation. When people are rich, their propensity to consume is low and they save more. This implies low demand which leads to decline in investment. Thus the tendency is for secular stagnation in the economy.

(7) *Unique Nature of Income Propagation*. The fact that the entire increased income is not spent on consumption explains the multiplier theory. The multiplier theory or the process of income propagation "tells that when an initial injection of investment is made in the economy, it leads to smaller successive increments of income. This is due to the fact that people do not spend their full increment of income on consumption. In fact, the value of multiplier is derived from the marginal propensity to consume, i.e., Multiplier=1-1/*MPC*. The higher the *MPC*, the higher the value of the multiplier, and vice versa.

(8) *Explanation of the Turning Points of the Business Cycles*. This law explains the turning points of a business cycle. Before the economy reaches the full employment level, the downturn starts because people fail to spend the full increment of their income on consumption. This leads to fall in demand, overproduction, unemployment and decline in the marginal efficiency of capital. Figure 4 (A) shows this downturn movement. At the break-even point *B*, the level of income is OY' and consumption level OC'. When income increases above the breakeven point by Y' Y", the consumption expenditure increase by a smaller amount $C'C''$ i.e., $C'C'' < Y'Y''$. Before the economy reaches the full-employment income level Y_F, the downturn will start because the gap between the 45° line and the *C* curve continue to widen.

Conversely, the upturn in the economy starts before it reaches the stage of complete depression because when income falls, consumption also falls but by less than the fall in income. People continue to buy consumer

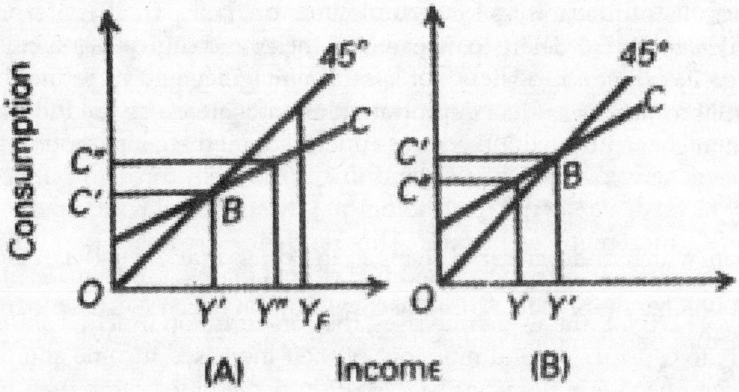

Fig. 4

goods even when their income falls. So when the excess stock of commodities is exhausted in the community during a depression, the existence of consumer expenditure on goods leads to revival. This is best explained with the help of Figure 4(B) where below the breakeven point *B*, the *C* curve is above the 45° income line and the gap between 45° line and the *C* curve becomes shorter. The fact that the consumption function curve *C* is above the income line shows that the revival will start before income falls to zero. This is because the fall in consumption *C'C''* is less than the fall in income *Y'Y*.

5. DETERMINANTS OF THE CONSUMPTION FUNCTION

Keynes mentions two principal factors which influence the consumption function and determine its slope and position. They are (i) the subjective factors, and (ii) the objective factors.

The subjective factors are endogenous or internal to the economic system. They include psychological characteristics of human nature, social practices and institutions and social arrangements. They ``are unlikely to undergo a material change over a short period of time except in abnormal or revolutionary circum- stances."[9] They, therefore, determine the slope and position of the *C* curve which is fairly stable in the short-run.

The objective factors are exogenous or external to the economic system. They may, therefore, undergo rapid changes and may cause upward or downward shifts in the consumption function (i.e.,the *C* "curve.)

1. Subjective Factors in the Consumption Function

Keynes' subjective factors basically underlie and determine the form (i.e., slope and position) of the consumption function. As already noted above, the subjective factors are the psychological characteristics of human nature, social practices and institutions, especially the behaviour patterns of business concerns with respect to wage and dividend payments and retained earnings, and social arrangement affecting the distribution of income.

Individual Motives. First, there are eight motives ``which lead individuals to refrain from spending out of their incomes." They are (i) the desire to build reserves for unforeseen contingencies; (ii) the desire to provide for anticipated future needs, i.e., old age, sickness, etc., (iii) the desire to enjoy an enlarged future "income by way of interest and appreciation; (iv) the desire to enjoy a gradually increasing expenditure in order to improve the standard of living; (v) the desire to enjoy a sense of independence and power to do things; (vi) the desire to secure a ``*masse de manoeuvre*'' to carry out speculative or business projects;(vii) the "desire to bequeath a fortune;(viii) the desire to satisfy "a pure miserly instinct.

9. J.M. Keynes, *op. cit.,* p. 91

Business Motives. The subjective factors are also influenced "by the behaviour of business corporations and governments. Keynes "lists four motives for accumulation on their part : (i) enterprise, the desire to do big things and to expand; (ii) *liquidity*, the desire to meet emergencies and difficulties successfully; (iii) *income raise*, the desire to secure large income and to show successful management; (iv) *financial prudence*, the desire to provide adequate financial resources against depreciation and obsolescence, and to discharge debt.

These factors remain constant during the short-run and keep the consumption function stable.

2. Objective Factors

The objective factors which undergo rapid changes and cause marked shifts in the consumption function are the following :

(1) *Change in the Wage Level*. If the wage rate rises, the consumption function shifts upward. The workers having a high propensity to consume, spend more out of their increased income and this tends to shift the "C curve upward. If, however, the rise in the wage rate is accompanied by a more than proportionate rise in the price level, the real wage rate will fall and it will tend to shift the C curve downward. A cut in the wage rate will also reduce the consumption function of the community due to a fall in income, employment and output. This will shift the curve downward.

(2) *Windfall Gains or Losses*. Unexpected changes in the stock market leading to gains or losses tend to shift the consumption function upward or downward. For instance, the phenomenal windfall gains due to the stock-market boom in the American economy after 1925 led to a rise in the consumption spending of the stockholders by roughly in proportion to the increased income and as a result the consumption function shifted upward. Similarly, unexpected losses in the stock market lead to the downward shifting of the C curve.

(3) *Changes in the Fiscal Policy*. Changes in fiscal policy in the form of taxation and public expenditure affect the consumption function. Heavy commodity taxation shift the consumption function downward by reducing the disposable income of the people. On the other hand, the policy of progressive taxation along with that of public expenditure on welfare programmes tends to shift the consumption function upward by altering the distribution of income.

(4) *Changes in Expectations*. Changes in future expectations also affect the propensity to consume. If a war is expected in the near future, people start hoarding durable and semi-durable commodities in anticipation of future scarcity and rising prices. As a result, people buy much in excess of their current needs and the consumption function shifts upward. On the contrary, if it is expected that prices are likely to fall in the future, people would buy only those things which are very essential. It will lead to a fall in consumption demand and to a downward shift of the consumption function.

(5) *Changes in the Rate of Interest*. Substantial changes in the market rate of interest may influence the consumption function indirectly. There are several ways in which the rate of interest may affect the consumption function. A rise in rate of interest will lead to a fall in the price of bonds, thereby tending to discourage the propensity to consume of the bond-holders. It may also have the effect of substituting one type of assets for another. People may be encouraged to save rather than invest in bonds. In case they are buying durable consumer goods like refrigerators, scooters, etc. on hire purchase system they will tend to postpone their purchases when the rate of interest rises. They will have to pay more in installments and thus "their consumption function will shift downward. Keynes wrote, ``Over a long period, substantial changes in the rate of interest probably tend to modify social habits considerably."[10]

Besides, these five factors given by Keynes, we add some of the other objective factors listed by Keynes' followers.

(6) *Financial Polices of Corporations*. Financial policies of corporations with regard to income retention, dividend payments and reinvestment tend to affect the consumption function in several ways. If corporations keep more money in the form of reserves, dividend payments to shareholders will be less. This will have the effect of reducing the income of the shareholders and the consumption function will shift downward.

(7) *Holding of Liquid Assets*. The amount of liquid assets in the form of cash balances, savings and government bonds in the hands of consumers also influence the consumption function. If people hold larger liquid assets they will have a tendency to spend more out of their current income and the propensity to

10. J.M. Keynes, *op. cit.*, p. 91

consume will move upward, and vice versa.

(8) *The Distribution of Income*. The distribution of income in the community also determines the shape of the consumption function. If there are large disparities in income distribution between the rich and the poor, the consumption function is low because the rich have a low propensity to consume and the poor with a very low income are unable to spend more on consumption. If through progressive taxation and other fiscal measures, the inequalities of income and wealth are reduced, the consumption function will shift upward because with the increase in the income of the poor their consumption expenditure will increase more than the reduction in the expenditure of the rich. "Moreover, if the distribution of income is significantly altered for political or humanitarian reasons, consumer habits themselves may undergo such changes as to cause the position or shape of the entire consumption function to vary perceptibly."[11]

(9) *Attitude toward Saving*. The consumption function is also influenced by people's attitude toward saving. If they value future consumption more than present consumption, they will tend to save more and the consumption function will shift downward. This tendency may be reinforced by the state through compulsory life insurance, provident fund and other social insurance schemes to keep the consumption function low. In a high-saving economy, the consumption function is low.

(10) *Duesenberry Hypothesis*. James Duesenberry has propounded a relative income hypothesis affecting the consumption function. The first part of this hypothesis relates to the `demonstration effect.' There is a tendency in human beings not only to keep up with the Joneses but also to surpass the Joneses, that is, the tendency is to strive constantly toward a higher consumption level and to emulate the consumption patterns of one's rich neighbours and even to surpass them. Thus consumption preferences are interdependent. The second part is the `past peak of income' hypothesis which explains the short-run fluctuations in consumption. Once the community reaches a particular income level and standard of living, it is reluctant to come down to a lower level of consumption during a recession. Consumption is sustained by the reduction in current saving and vice versa. So there is no shift in the consumption function during the short-run. There is simply an upward-downward movement on the same consumption function when income rises or falls during the short-run.

6. MEASURES TO RAISE THE PROPENSITY TO CONSUME

The propensity to consume remains stable during the short-run due to the existence of certain psychological and institutional factors in the society. But ``employment can only increase *pari passu* with an increase in investment; unless, indeed, there is a change "in the propensity to consume," as pointed out by Keynes. Therefore, it is significant to study the measures which tend to raise the propensity to consume.

(1) *Income Redistribution*. Redistribution of income in favour of the poor tends to raise the propensity to consume because the marginal propensity to consume of the low income groups is high in comparison to the rich. Therefore, the propensity to consume can be raised by transferring income and wealth from the rich to the poor. This can be done by the state through its taxation and public spending policies. By imposing progressive taxes on incomes, expenditures, estates, capital gains, etc., the state is able to mobilise larger revenues for providing more facilities to the poor. But care should be taken that such taxation should not adversely affect investment. Secondly, the state can increase the income of the poor through a judicious public expenditure programme. By starting public works, it is in a position to increase income by providing larger employment opportunities to the unemployed. The provision for free education, free mid-day meals, free health services, low-rent housing, etc. indirectly helps in increasing the income of the workers and tends to raise their consumption expenditure. Such social expenditures by the state also increase the efficiency of the workers which, in turn, leads to a rise in their wages.

(2) *Increased Wages*. If wages are raised, they will have a direct effect in shifting the consumption function upward. But a policy of high wages adversely affects the level of employment in the economy, for it is not possible to raise the marginal revenue productivity of labour in the short-run. If wages are raised in such a

11. K.K. Kurihara, *Introduction to Keynesian Dynamics*, p. 88.

situation, costs will rise in the absence of increase in the marginal revenue productivity of labour and the economy is likely to experience unemployment. Therefore, the long-run wage policy should be such that wages increase *pari passu* with increase in labour productivity. This will tend to raise the level of consumption in the economy.

(3) *Social Security Measures*. Social security measures tend to raise the consumption function in the long-run. Provisions for unemployment relief, medical facilities, old age pension, etc. remove future uncertainties and the tendency to save is reduced on the part of the people. The state should, therefore, provide larger social security measures to raise the propensity to consume of the people. Unemployment relief and old age pensions tend to maintain a high consumption expenditure even during a depression and thus help bring revival in the economy. So social security measures tend to raise the consumption function both in periods of prosperity and depression.

(4) *Credit Facilities*. Cheap and easy credit facilities help in shifting the consumption function upward. When loans are easily and cheaply available to the people, they buy more durable consumer goods like scooters, televisions, refrigerators, etc. These tend to raise the propensity to consume. To purchase these things on installment basis or on hire-purchase produces the same effect. Thus credit facilities in various ways help to raise the propensity to consume durable consumer goods.

(5) *Advertisement*. Advertisement is one of most significant ways to raise the propensity to consume in modern times. Advertisement and propaganda through the various media of radio, television, cinema, newspaper, etc. make the consumers familiar with the uses of products. The consumers are attracted toward them and they tend to buy them. These raise their propensity to consume.

(6) *Development of the Means of Transport*. Well developed means of transport also tend to shift the consumption function upward. The movement of goods from the manufacturing centres to the different parts of the country becomes easy. The size of the market expands. The prices may also fall due to the reduction of transport costs. Things are available to the people in their respective towns. All this has the tendency to raise the consumption function.

(7) *Urbanisation*. As a corollary to the above, urbanisation helps to raise the propensity to consume. When urbanisation takes place, people move from the rural to the urban areas. They are attracted enamoured by new articles and influenced by the demonstration effect. This tends to shift the consumption function upward. Thus the state should follow the policy of deliberate urbanisation for the purpose of raising the consumption function.

EXERCISES

1. What do you mean by consumption function? Explain the determinants of the levels of consumption in the short-run.
2. ``Keynes' consumption function is an epoch making tool in economic analysis." Discuss.
3. Distinguish between average propensity to consume and marginal propensity to consume.

CHAPTER 28

The Investment Function

1. MEANING OF CAPITAL AND INVESTMENT

In ordinary parlance, investment means to buy shares, stocks, bonds and securities which are already existing in stock market. But this is not real investment because it is simply a transfer of existing assets. Hence this is called financial investment which does not affect aggregate spending. In Keynesian terminology, investment refers to real investment which adds to capital equipment. It leads to increase in the levels of income and production by increasing the production and purchase of capital goods. Investment thus includes new plant and equipment, construction of public works like dams, roads, buildings, etc., net foreign investment, inventories and stocks and shares of new companies. In the words of Joan Robinson, "By investment is meant an addition to capital, such as occurs when a new house is built or a new factory is built. Investment means making an addition to the stock of goods in existence."

Capital, on the other hand, refers to real assets like factories, plants, equipment, and inventories of finished and semi-finished goods. It is any previously produced input that can be used in the production process to produce other goods. The amount of capital available in an economy is the stock of capital. Thus capital is a *stock* concept.

To be more precise, investment is the production or acquisition of real capital assets during any period of time. To illustrate, suppose the capital assets of a firm on 31 March 2004 are Rs 100 crores and it invests at the rate of Rs 10 crores during the year 2004-05. At the end of the next year (31 March 2005), its total capital will be Rs 110 crores. Symbolically, let I be investment and K be capital in year t, then $I_t = K_t - K_{t-1}$.

Capital and investment are related to each other through net investment. Gross investment is the total amount spent on new capital assets in a year. But some capital stock wears out every year and is used up for depreciation and obsolescence. Net investment is gross investment *minus* depreciation and obsolescence charges for replacement investment. This is the net addition to the existing capital stock of the economy. If gross investment equals depreciation, net investment is zero and there is no addition to the economy's capital stock. If gross investment is less than depreciation, there is disinvestment in the economy and the capital stock decreases. Thus for an increase in the real capital stock of the economy, gross investment must exceed depreciation, i.e., there should be net investment.

2. TYPES OF INVESTMENT : INDUCED VS. AUTONOMOUS

(1) Induced Investment. Real investment may be induced. Induced investment is profit or income motivated. Factors like prices, wages and interest change which affect profits and influence induced investment. Similarly, demand also influences it. When income increases, consumption demand also increases and to meet this, investment increases. In the ultimate analysis, induced investment is a function of income i.e., $I = f(Y)$. It is income elastic. It increases or decreases with the rise or fall in income, as shown in Figure 1.

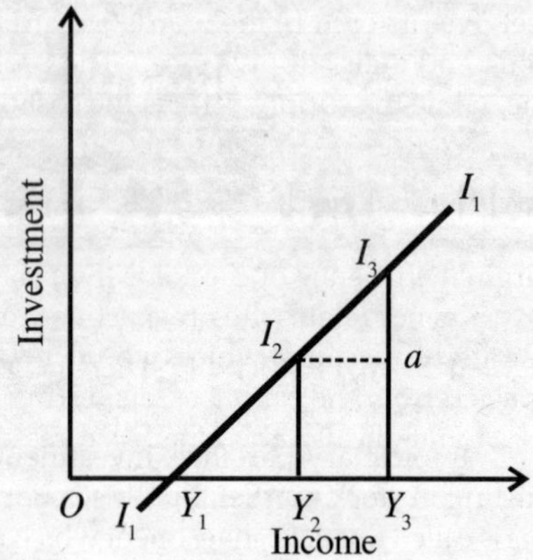

Fig. 1

I_1I_1 is the investment curve which shows induced investment at various levels of income. Induced investment is zero at OY_1 income. When income rises to OY_3, induced investment is I_3Y_3. A fall in income to OY_2 also reduces induced investment to I_2Y_2.

Induced investment may be further divided into (*i*) the average propensity to invest, and (*ii*) the marginal propensity to invest:

(*i*) *The average propensity to invest* is the ratio of investment to income, I/Y. If the income is Rs. 40 crores and investment is Rs. 4 crores, $I/Y = 4/40 = 0.1$. In terms of the above figure, the average propensity to invest at OY_3 income level is I_3Y_3 / OY_3.

(*ii*) *The marginal propensity to invest* is the ratio of change in investment to the change in income, i.e., $\Delta I/\Delta Y$. If the change in investment, ΔI=Rs 2 crores and the change in income, ΔY = Rs 10 crores, then $\Delta I/\Delta Y = 2/10 = 0.2$ In Figure 1, $\Delta I/\Delta Y = I_3a/Y_2Y_3$.

(2) Autonomous Investment. Autonomous investment is independent of the level of income and is thus income inelastic. It is influenced by exogenous factors like innovations, inventions, growth of population and labour force, researches, social and legal institutions, weather changes, war, revolution, etc. But it is not influenced by changes in demand. Rather, it influences demand. Investment in economic and social overheads whether made by the government or the private enterprise is autonomous. Such investment includes expenditures on buildings, dams, roads, canals, schools, hospitals, etc. Since investment on these projects is generally associated with public policy, autonomous investment is regarded as public investment. In the long-run, private investment of all types may be autonomous because it is influenced by exogenous factors. Diagrammatically, autonomous investment is shown as a curve parallel to the horizontal axis as I_1I' curve in Figure 2. It indicates that at all levels of income, the amount of investment OI_1 remains constant. The upward shift of the curve to I_2I'' indicates an increased steady flow of investment at a constant rate OI_2 at various levels of income. However, for purposes of income determination, the autonomous investment curve is superimposed on the C curve in a 45^0 line diagram.

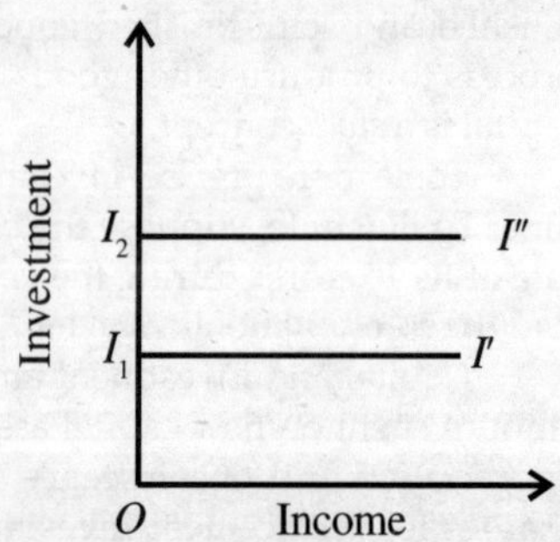

Fig. 2

3. DETERMINANTS OF THE LEVEL OF INVESTMENT

The decision to invest in a new capital asset depends on whether the expected rate of return on the new investment is equal to or greater or less than the rate of interest to be paid on the funds needed to purchase this asset. It is only when the expected rate of return is higher than the interest rate that investment will be made in acquiring new capital assets.

In reality, there are three factors that are taken into consideration while making any investment decision. They are (a) the cost of the capital asset, (b) the expected rate of return from it during its lifetime, and (c) the market rate of interest. Keynes sums up these factors in his concept of the marginal efficiency of capital (*MEC*).

MARGINAL EFFICIENCY OF CAPITAL (MEC)

The marginal efficiency of capital is the highest rate of return expected from an additional unit of a capital asset over its cost. In the words of Kurihara, "It is the ratio between the prospective yield of additional capital goods and their supply price." The prospective yield is the aggregate net return from an asset during its life time, while the supply price is the cost of producing this asset. If the supply price of a capital asset is Rs. 20,000 and its annual yield is Rs. 2,000, the marginal efficiency of this asset is $\frac{2000}{20000} \times \frac{100}{1} = 10$ per cent. Thus the marginal efficiency of capital (MEC) is the *percentage of profit expected from a given investment on a capital asset.*

Keynes relates the prospective yield of a capital asset to its supply price and defines the *MEC* as "equal to the rate of discount which would make the present value of the series of annuities given by the returns expected from the capital assets during its life just equal to its supply price."[1]

Symbolically, this can be expressed as:

$$S_p = \frac{R_1}{(1+i)^1} + \frac{R_2}{(1+i)^2} + ... + \frac{R_n}{(1+i)^n} \quad ....(1)$$

Where *Sp* is the supply price or the cost of the capital asset; R_1, R_2... and R_n are the prospective yields or the series of expected annual returns from the capital asset in the years, 1,2... and *n*; and *i* is the rate of discount which makes the capital asset exactly equal to the present value of the expected yield from it. This *i* is the *MEC* or the rate of discount which equates the two sides of the equation. If the supply price of a new capital asset is Rs 1,000 and its life is two years, it is expected to yield Rs 550 in the first year and Rs 605 in the second year. Its *MEC* is 10 per cent which equates the supply price to the expected yields of this capital asset.

Thus

$$(Sp) \text{ Rs } 1000 = \frac{550}{(1.10)} + \frac{605}{(1.10)^2} = \text{Rs. } 500 + 500$$

In equation (1), the term $\frac{R_1}{(1+i)}$ is the present value (*PV*) of the capital asset. The present value is "the value of payments to be received in the future." It depends on the rate of interest at which it is discounted.

Suppose we expect to receive Rs 100 from a machine in a year's time and the rate of interest is 5 per cent. The present value of this machine is

$$\frac{R_1}{(1+i)} = \frac{100}{(1.05)} = \text{Rs } 95.24.$$

If we expect Rs 100 from the machine after two years then its present value is $\frac{100}{(1.05)^2}$ = Rs 90.70. The present value of a capital asset is inversely related to the rate of interest. The lower the rate of interest, the higher is the present value, and vice versa. For instance, if the rate of interest is 5 per cent, *PV* of an asset of Rs 100 for one year will be Rs 95.24; at 7 per cent interest rate, it will be Rs 93.45; and at 10 per cent interest rate, it will be Rs 90.91.

The relation between the present value and the rate of interest is shown in Figure 3, where the rate of

1. J.M. Keynes, *op. cit.*, p. 135

interest is taken on the horizontal axis while the present value of the project on the vertical axis. The curve *PR* shows the inverse relation between present value and rate of interest. If the current rate of interest is I_1, the present value of the project is P_1. On the other hand, a higher rate of interest (I_2) will lead to a lower present value (P_2) and when the present value curve (*PR*) cuts the horizontal axis at point (*Z*), the net present value becomes zero.

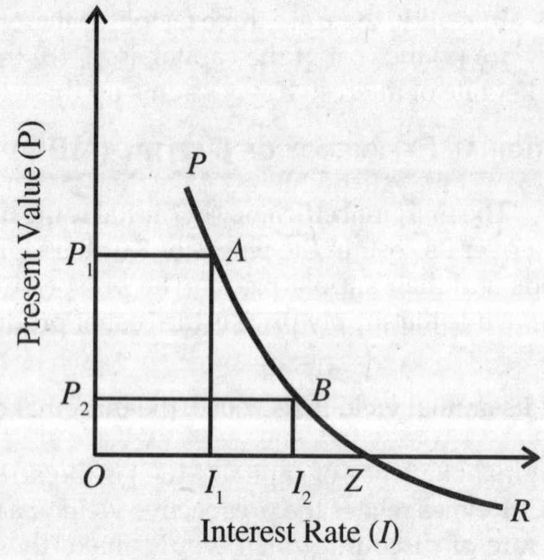

Fig. 3

As a matter of fact, the *MEC* is the expected rate of return over cost of a new capital asset. In order to find out whether it is worthwhile to purchase a capital asset, it is essential to compare the present value of the capital asset with its cost or supply price. If the present value of a capital asset exceeds its cost of buying, it pays to buy it. On the contrary, if its present value is less than its cost, it is not worthwhile investing in this capital asset.

The same results can be had by comparing the *MEC* with the market rate of interest. If the *MEC* of a capital asset is higher than the market rate of interest at which it is borrowed, it pays to purchase the capital asset, and vice versa. If the market interest rate equals the *MEC* of the capital asset, the firm is said to possess the *optimum* capital stock. If the *MEC* is higher than the rate of interest, there will be a tendency to borrow funds in order to invest in new capital assets. If the *MEC* is lower than the rate of interest, no firm will borrow to invest in capital assets. Thus the equilibrium condition for a firm to hold the optimum capital stock is where the *MEC* equals the interest rate. Any disequilibrium between the *MEC* and the rate of interest can be removed by changing the capital stock, and hence the *MEC* or by changing the rate of interest or both. Since the stock of capital changes slowly, therefore, changes in the rate of interest are more important for bringing equilibrium. The above arguments which have been applied to a firm are equally applicable to the economy.

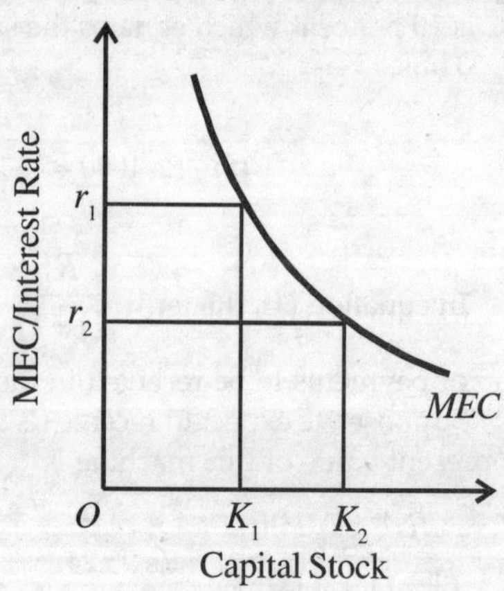

Fig. 4

Figure 4 shows the *MEC* curve of an economy. It has a negative slope (from left to right downward) which indicates that the higher the *MEC*, the smaller the capital stock. Or, as the capital stock increases, the *MEC* falls. This is because of the operation of the law of diminishing returns in production. As a result, the marginal physical productivity of capital and the marginal revenue fall. In the figure, when the capital stock is OK_1, the *MEC* is Or_1. As the capital increases from OK_1 to OK_2 the *MEC* falls from Or_1 to Or_2. The net addition to the capital stock K_1K_2 represents the net investment in the economy.

Further, to reach the optimum (desired) capital stock in the economy, the *MEC* must equal the rate of interest. If, as shown in the figure, the existing capital stock is OK_1, the *MEC* is Or_1 and the rate of interest is at Or_2. Everyone in the economy will borrow funds and invest in capital assets. This is because *MEC* (Or_1) is higher than the rate of interest (at Or_2). This will continue till the *MEC* (Or_1) comes down to the level of the interest rate (at Or_2). When the *MEC* equals the rate of interest, the economy reaches the level of optimum capital stock. The fall in the *MEC* is due to the increase in the actual capital stock from OK_1 to the optimum (desired) capital stock OK_2. The increase in the firm's capital stock by K_1K_2 is the net investment of the firm. But it is the rate of interest which determines the size of the optimum capital stock in the economy. And it is the *MEC* which relates the amount of desired capital stock to the rate of interest. Thus the negative slope of the *MEC* curve indicates that as the rate of interest falls the optimum stock of capital increases.

4. MARGINAL EFFICIENCY OF INVESTMENT (MEI)

The *MEI* is the rate of return expected from a given investment on a capital asset after covering all its costs, except the rate of interest. Like the *MEC*, it is the rate which equates the supply price of a capital asset to its prospective yield. The investment on an asset will be made depending upon the interest rate involved in getting funds from the market. If the rate of interest is high, investment is at a low level. A low rate of interest leads to an increase in investment. Thus the *MEI* relates investment to the rate of interest. The *MEI* schedule shows the amount of investment demanded at various rates of interest. That is why, it is also called the investment demand schedule or curve which has a negative slope, as shown in Fig. 5(A). At Or_1 rate of interest, investment is OI'. As the rate of interest falls to Or_2, investment increases to OI''.

To what extent the fall in the interest rate will increase investment depends upon the elasticity of the investment demand curve or the *MEI* curve. The less elastic is the *MEI* curve, the lower is the increase in investment as a result of fall in the rate of interest, and vice versa.

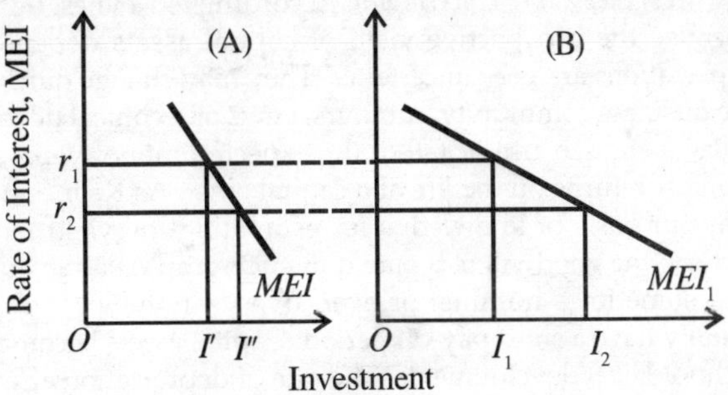

Fig. 5

In Figure 5. the vertical axis measures the interest rate and the *MEI* and the horizontal axis measures the amount of investment. The *MEI* and MEI_1 are the investment demand curves. The *MEI* curve in Panel (A) is less elastic to investment which increases by $I'I''$. This is less than the increase in investment I_1I_2 shown in Panel (B) where the MEI_1 curve is elastic. Thus given the shape and position of the *MEI* curve, a fall in the interest rate will increase the volume of investment.

On the other hand, given the rate of interest, the higher the *MEI*, the larger shall be the volume of investment. The higher marginal efficiency of investment implies that the *MEI* curve shifts to the right. When the existing capital assets wear out, they are replaced by new ones and the level of investment increases. But the amount of induced investment depends on the existing level of total purchasing. So more induced investment occurs when the total purchasing is higher. The higher total purchasing tends to shift the *MEI* to the right indicating that more inducement to investment takes place at a given level of interest rate. This is explained in Figure 6, where MEI_1 and MEI_2 curves indicate two different levels of total purchasing in the economy. Let us suppose that the MEI_1 curve indicates that at Rs 200 crores of total purchasing, OI_1 (Rs 20 crores) investment occurs at Or_1 interest rate. If total purchasing rises to Rs 500 crores, the MEI_1 curve shifts to the right as MEI_2 and the level of induced investment increases to OI_2 (Rs 50 crores) at the same interest rate Or_1.

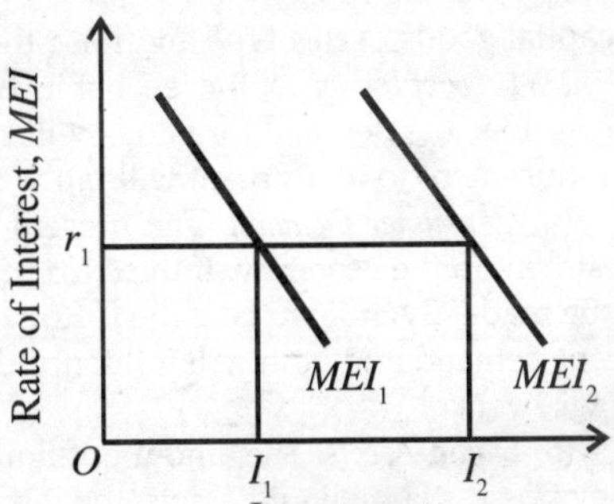

Fig. 6

5. DISTINCTION BETWEEN MEC AND MEI

Keynes did not distinguish between the marginal efficiency of capital (*MEC*) and the marginal efficiency of investment (*MEI*). But modern economists have made clear distinctions between the two concepts as follows:

The *MEC* is based on a given supply price for capital, and the *MEI* on induced changes in this price. The *MEC* shows the rate of return on all successive units of capital without regard to the existing stock of capital. On the other hand, the *MEI* shows the rate of return on only units of capital over and above the existing stock of capital. In the *MEC*, the capital stock is taken on the horizontal axis of a diagram, while in the *MEI* the amount of investment is taken horizontally on the *X*-axis. The former is a `stock' concept, and the latter is a `flow' concept. The *MEC* determines the optimum capital stock in an economy at each level of interest rate. The *MEI* determines the net investment of the economy at each interest rate, given the capital stock.

6. FACTORS OTHER THAN THE INTEREST RATE AFFECTING "INDUCEMENT TO INVEST[2]

There are a number of factors other than the rate of interest which affect the inducement to invest. They are the following :

(1) *Element of Uncertainty*. According to Keynes, the *MEC* is more volatile than the rate of interest. This is because the prospective yield of capital assets depends upon the business expectations. These business expectations are very uncertain. ``They may change quickly and drastically in response to the general mood of the business community, rumours, news of technical developments, political events, even directors' ulcers may cause a sudden rise or fall of the expected rate of yield".[3] As a result, it is difficult to calculate the expected annuals returns on the life of a capital asset. As Keynes himself wrote, "If we speak frankly we have to admit that our basis of knowledge for estimating the yield ten years hence of a railway, a copper mine, a textile factory, the goodwill of a patent medicine, an Atlantic liner, a building in the city of London amounts to little and sometimes nothing; or even five years hence."[4] Further, because of uncertainty, investment projects usually have a short pay-off period. Capital assets become obsolete earlier than their expected life due to rapid technological developments. The rate of depreciation also does not remain constant and varies much. So firms have a tendency to invest only if they are in a position to recover the capital outlay in a short period. These factors tend to bring instability in the investment function.

(2) *Existing Stock of Capital Goods*. If the existing stock of capital goods is large, it would discourage potential investors "from entering into the making of goods. Again, the induced investment will not take place if there is excess or idle capacity in the existing stock of capital assets. In case the existing stock of machines is working to its full capacity, an increase in the demand for goods manufactured by them will raise the demand for capital goods of this type and raise the inducement to invest.

(3) *Level of Income*. If the level of income rises in the economy through rise in money-wage rates and other factor prices, the demand for goods will rise which will, in turn, raise the inducement to invest. Contrariwise, the inducement to investment will fall with the lowering of income levels.

(4) *Consumer Demand*. The present and future demand for the products greatly influence the level of investment in the economy. If the current demand for consumer goods is increasing rapidly more investment will be made. Even if we take the future demand for the products, it will be considerably influenced by their current demand and both will influence the level of investment. Investment will be low if the demand is low, and vice versa.

(5) *Liquid Assets*. The amount of liquid assets with the investors also influence the inducement to invest. If they possess large liquid assets, the inducement to invest is high. This is especially the case with those firms which keep large reserve funds and undistributed profits. On the contrary, the inducement to invest is low for investors having little as liquid assets.

(6) *Inventions and Innovations*. Inventions and innovations tend to raise the inducement to invest. If inventions and technological improvements lead to more efficient methods of production with reduced costs, the *MEC* of new capital assets will rise. Higher *MEC* will induce firms to make larger investments in the new capital assets and in related ones. The absence of new technologies will mean low inducement to invest. An innovation also includes the opening of new areas. This requires the development of means of transport, the construction of housing etc., leading to new investment opportunities. Thus inducement to invest rises.

---

2. These factors also affect *MEC*. They can be divided into endogenous and exogenous, Factor 1 to 5 are endogenous and the remaining factors are exogenous.
3. F.S. Brooman, *Macroeconomics*, 4/e, 1970.
4. J.M. Keynes, *op. cit.*, p. 150.

(7) *New Products*. The nature of new products in terms of sales and costs may also influence their *MEC* and hence investment. If the sale prospects of a new product are high and the expected revenues more than the costs, the *MEC* will be high which will encourage investment in this and related industries. For example, the invention of television must have encouraged the electronics industry to invest in these capital assets and used them to produce television sets, if they had expected profits to be higher than costs. Thus lower maintenance and operating costs in the case of new products are important in increasing the inducement to invest.

(8) *Growth of Population*. A rapidly growing population means a growing market for all types of goods in the economy. To meet the demand of an increasing population in all brackets, investment will "increase in all types of consumer goods industries. On the other hand, a declining population results in a shrinking market for goods, thereby lowering the inducement to invest.

(9) *State Policy*. The economic policies of the government have an important influence on the inducement to invest in the country. If the state levies heavy progressive taxes on corporations, the inducement to invest is low, and vice versa. Heavy indirect taxation tends to raise the prices of commodities and adversely affects their demand, thereby lowering the inducement to invest, and vice versa. If the state follows the policy of nationalisation of industries, the private enterprise would be discouraged to invest. On the other hand, if the state encourages private enterprise by providing credit, power and other facilities, inducement to invest will be high.

(10) *Political Climate*. Political conditions also affect the inducement to invest. If there is political instability in the country, the inducement to invest may be affected adversely. In the struggle for power, the rival parties may create unrest through hostile trade union activities thus creating uncertainty in business. On the other hand, a stable government creates confidence in the business community, whereby the inducement to invest is raised. Similarly, the danger of a revolution or war with some other country has an adverse effect on the inducement to invest, whereas peace and prosperity tend to raise it.

EXERCISES

1. Distinguish between (1) Capital and investment, (2) Induced and autonomous investment, (3) Gross and net investment.
2. What do you mean by investment? Explain the determinants of the level of investment.
3. What do you mean by marginal efficiency of capital? How it determines the level of investment?
4. What do you mean by induced investment? Discuss the determinants of inducement to invest.
5. Distinguish between marginal efficiency of capital and marginal efficiency of investment.

CHAPTER 29

Saving and Investment Equality

1. INTRODUCTION

All economists believe in the equality of saving and investment. But they differ as to the manner in which this equality is brought about. We study the following views on this problem.

2. THE CLASSICAL VIEW

The classicists believe in the existence of a fully employed economy where saving and investment are always equal. According to them, saving and investment are a function of the rate of interest. Algebraically, $S=f(r)$ and $I=f(r)$ where r is the rate of interest. Therefore, $S=I$. In a period of less than full employment, "the inequality between the two is obvious which can be brought to equality through the mechanism of interest rate. When the rate of interest rises, saving rises and investment declines. On the other hand, with a fall in the rate of interest, saving falls and investment increases. If at any time, saving is less than investment, a rise in the rate of interest brings a decline in investment and increase in saving till saving equals investment. On the contrary, when saving is more than investment, the rate of interest falls, investment increases and saving declines till the two are equal at the new interest rate.

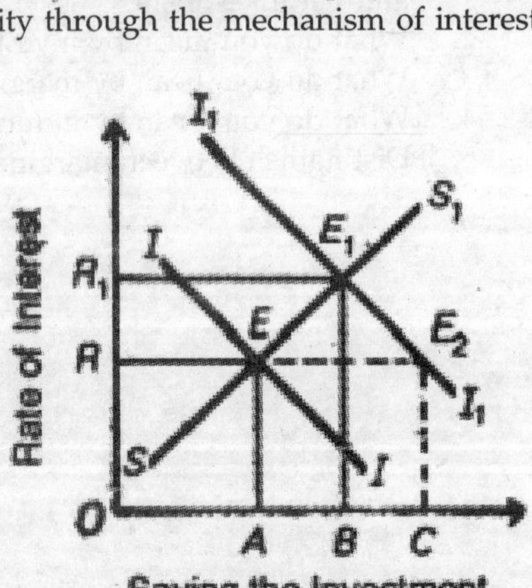

Fig.1

The mechanism of the equality between saving and investment is shown in Figure 1 where SS_1 is the saving curve and II is the investment curve. The two curves intersect at E where the rate of interest is OR and both saving and investment are equal to OA. If there is an increase in investment, the investment curve shifts to the right as I_1I_1 curve and at the interest rate OR, investment OC is greater than OA saving. According to the classical economists, the saving curve SS remains at its original level when there is any increase in investment. To maintain the equality between saving and investment, the rate of interest will rise. This is shown to rise to OR_1 in the figure. At this interest rate, the saving curve SS intersects the investment curve I_1I_1 at E_1. Consequently, both saving and investment equal at OB.

KEYNES' CRITICISMS OF THE CLASSICAL VIEW

Keynes criticises the classical view about the saving-investment equality on the following grounds.

(a) Keynes does not agree with the classical view that the equality between saving and investment is brought through the mechanism of the interest rate. According to him, it is changes in *income* "which bring the two to equality, rather than the rate of interest.

(b) He also differs with the classicists that this equality via the rate of interest shifts only the investment curve and that the saving curve does not change. Keynes' view is that whenever the investment curve changes, there is a change in the saving curve also. For instance, an increase in investment leads to a rise in income through the multiplier effect. As a result, saving also increases.

(c) Further, Keynes refutes the classical view that saving and investment are equal at the full employment level. He opines that since full employment is a rare phenomenon, saving- investment equality is found at less than full employment level.

3. THE KEYNESIAN VIEW

Keynes put forth two views with regard to the saving-investment equality. The first is the *accounting*or *definitional* equality between saving and investment which is used in national income accounting. It tells us that *actual saving and actual investment "are always equal at all times and at any level of income.* The second is the*functional* equality. In this sense, saving and investment are equal only at the equilibrium level of income. In other words, in the functional sense, saving and investment are not only *equal* but they are also in *equilibrium*. We study these views in detail below.

(1) The *Accounting* or *Definitional Equality*. Keynes "wrote in his *General Theory* that ``saving and investment are necessarily equal in amount for the community as a whole, being different aspects of the same thing." In order to show it, he defined saving and investment in such a manner as to establish their equality. Both saving and investment in the current period are defined as the excess of current income over current consumption ($Y_t - C_t$), so that they are necessarily equal. Symbolically,

$S_t = Y_t - C_t$ ....(1)

$I_t = Y_t - C_t$ ....(2)

$\because Y_t - C_t$ is common in equations (1) and (2), we have

$S_t = I_t$,

where S is saving, I is investment, Y is income, C is consumption and t is current period.

Keynes also established this equality in another way. He defined income in the current period (Y_t) as equal to current consumption (C_t) *plus* current investment (I_t); and also as current saving (S_t) plus current consumption (C_t). Thus

Thus $Y_t = C_t + I_t$....(1)

$Y_t = S_t + C_t$ ....(2)

Therefore, from equations (1) and (2), we have

$$C_t + I_t = S_t + C_t$$

or

$$I_t = S_t$$

Thus saving and investment are the same thing. They are both the difference between income and consumption. So defined, *they are always equal.*

ITS CRITICISMS

This equality or rather identity between saving and investment which Keynes established in his *General Theory* has been severely criticised.

Firstly, according to Haberler, ``If we accept these definitions, ..*S* and *I* are necessarily equal over any period of time, because they are identically defined.. It then becomes nonsensical to speak of, or to imply, differences between them." *Ohlin* has also described the relation between saving and investment as a case of equality *ex-definitiones*. Thus this identity relationship is a *truism* and lacks an adjusting mechanism.

Secondly, it is difficult to understand how this equality can take place in actuality because saving and investment decisions are taken by different groups of people. Investment decisions are taken by businessmen on the basis of the rate of interest they have to pay for capital borrowed and the return they expect from it. On the other hand, decisions to save are based on different current and future requirements for saving by millions of individual families. Thus it is not possible for total saving to equal total investment in the economy except by coincidence.

Thirdly, this accounting equality between saving and investment is a lagless analysis, which fails to explain the process of saving-investment relation. The saving-investment equality in this sense is an exercise in static analysis. Keynes failed to describe the actual dynamic process of adjustment between saving and investment.

Fourthly, according to Dr. Lutz, the Keynesian definitions do not allow us to distinguish between investment financed out of inflationary credit or dishoarding from investment financed out of current supply of voluntary savings.

Lastly, as pointed out by Ohlin, the equality between saving and investment is an ex-post equality and not an*ex-ante* one.

(2) *The Functional Equality*. The equality between saving and investment in the *functional* or *schedule* sense is brought about by the adjusting mechanism of income, as distinct from the classical view of variations in the rate of interest. In this

TABLE 1 : SAVING-INVESTMENT EQUALITY

(Rs. Crores)

Income	*Saving*	*Investment*	*Income Movements*
100	–15	10	Expansion
200	0	20	
300	15	30	
400	30	40	
500	45	50	
600	60	60	Equilibrium
700	75	70	Contraction
800	90	80	
900	105	90	

sense, saving and investment are equal only at the equilibrium level of income. Income is functionally related to saving and investment. When saving is more than investment, income falls, and when investment is more than saving, income rises. This dynamic process of changes in income, saving and investment will continue till saving and investment are not only *equal* but are also in *equilibrium*. This is illustrated in the Table 1.

The table shows that so long as investment is greater than saving income continues to increase till it reaches the equilibrium level of Rs 600 crores where saving and investment equal Rs 60 crores each. But after this point, saving exceeds investment and the equilibrium is reached when income contracts and again reaches Rs 600 crores.

The equilibrium process of saving-investment equality is shown in Figure 2. Income is measured horizontally, and saving and investment vertically. *SS* is the saving schedule and *II* the investment schedule.

When income is OY' investment is greater than saving, $I'Y' > S'Y'$. Higher investment will lead to a rise in income and saving via the multiplier process till saving and investment are equal at the equilibrium income level OY represented by the point of interaction E of II and SS curves. When income is Y'', saving is greater than investment $S''Y'' > I''Y''$. This will bring a fall in income via the reverse operation of the multiplier till saving and investment are equilibrated at OY income level. Whenever there is a gap between saving and investment, income rises or falls till the equilibrium level is reached. Thus saving and investment are *equal only in "equilibrium.*

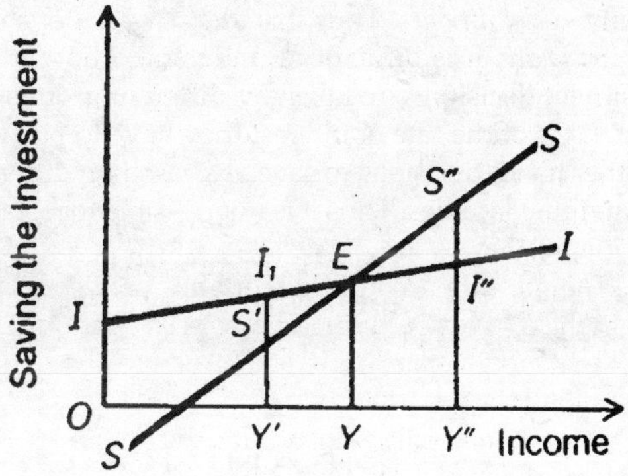

Fig. 2

Writing about the merits of this approach, Kurihara observes ``that the `Keynesian' savings and investment schedules are to general equilibrium analysis what the `Marshallian' supply and demand curves are to partial equilibrium analysis... The modern income analysis makes use of the *function* or schedule concepts of saving and investment in order to put life into dead figures, that is, to emphasize the *behaviour* of the economy as a whole instead of the *statistical result* of that behaviour."[1]

EXERCISES

1. ``Saving and investment are always equal." Saving and Investment are equal in equlibrium." Explain these statements.
2. When are saving and investment always equal and are equal in equilibrium? Explain.

1. K. Kurihara, *op. cit.*, pp. 76-77.

CHAPTER 30

The Saving Function

1. MEANING OF SAVING FUNCTION

Saving is defined as the difference between disposable income and consumption : $S=Y-C$, where S is saving, Y is income and C is consumption. Thus the level of saving depends on the level of income. This is illustrated in Table 1.

TABLE 1 : RELATION BETWEEN INCOME AND SAVING

Income (Y)	*Consumption (C)*	*Saving (S)*	*APS (S/Y)*	*MPS=* $\Delta S/\Delta Y$
(1)	(2)	(3)	3/1 = (4)	(5)
0	20	–20	—	—
60	70	–10	—	—
120	120	0	0	—
180	170	10	0.6	0.17
240	220	20	0.8	0.17

Column (3) of the Table shows that when income is zero or very low, people dissave (minus Rs 20 crores or Rs 10 crores). They have to consume even if they are not earning or their consumption expenditure (Rs 70 crores) is more than their income (Rs 60 crores). When income (Rs 20 crores) equals consumption expenditure (Rs 120 crores), savings are zero. As income increases further by Rs 60 crores, their savings increase by Rs 10 crores. It shows that as income increases savings also increase but by less than proportionately.

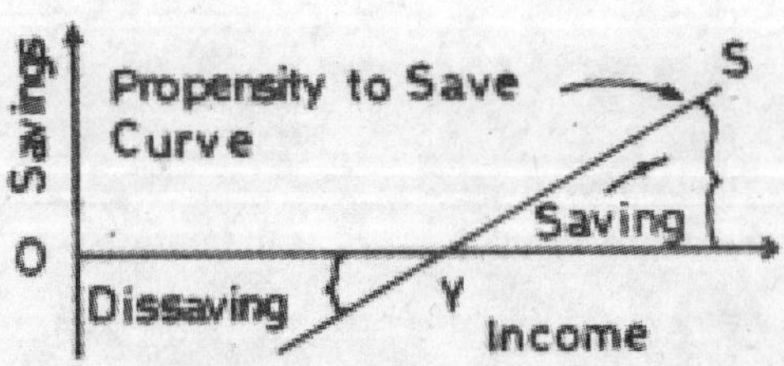

Fig. 1

This relation between saving and income is called the *propensity "to save* or the *saving function.* It is represented as S "$= f(Y)$. Thus the saving function indicates a functional relationship between S and Y, where S is the dependent and Y is the independent variable, that is, S is determined by Y. This relationship is based on the assumption ``other "things being equal" which means that all influences on savings are held constant and that income and saving increase by a constant amount, that is, income increases by Rs 60 crores and saving by Rs 10 crores, as shown in Table 1.

The propensity to save curve is shown in Fig. 1 where income is taken on the horizontal axis and saving on the vertical axis. The entire *S* curve with a definite position and slope is the propensity to save curve. The figure shows that below point *Y*, savings are negative because people dissave. At *Y*, savings are zero. Above *Y*, savings increase with the rise in income. The *S* curve is linear (straight line) because the rise in income and savings is at constant rates (Rs 60 crores and Rs 10 crores respectively).

The propensity to save is of two types : The average propensity to save and the marginal propensity to save, which we explain below.

The Average Propensity to Save (APS)

The *APS* is the ratio of saving to income. It is found by dividing saving by income, or *APS=S/Y*. It tells us about the proportion of each income level that people will save i.e., they will not spend on consumption. For example, in Table 1 at an income level of Rs 180 crores, the consumption expenditure is Rs 170 crores and the savings are Rs 10 crores. The *APS* is 0.06 which means that people save 6 per cent of their income, as shown is column (4) of the Table. It is to be noted that as income increases, the average propensity to consume (APC) decreases from 0.94 to 0.92. But *APS* increases from 0.06 to 0.08.*

Diagrammatically, the *APS* is any point on the *S* curve. In Fig. 2, point S^1 measures the *APS* of the *S* curve which is S_1Y_1/OY_1.

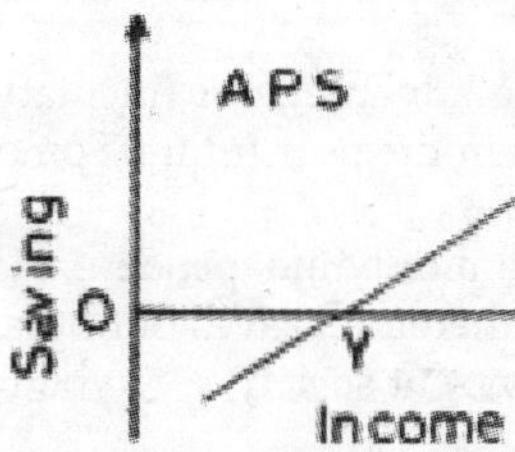

Fig. 2

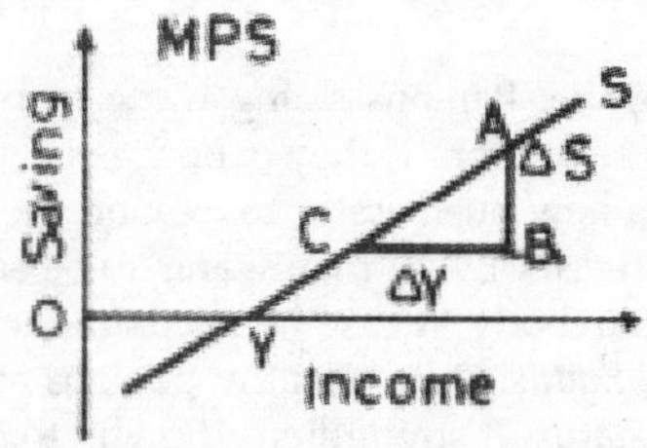

Fig. 3

The Marginal Propensity to Save (MPS)

The *MPS* is the ratio of the change in saving to the change in income. It can also be defined as the rate of change in *APS* as income changes. It can be found by dividing a change in saving by a change in income, i.e. $\Delta S/\Delta Y$. For example, in Table 1 when income increases from Rs 180 crores to Rs 240 crores, savings increase from Rs 10 crores to Rs. 20 crores so that ΔY=Rs. 60 (=240-180) crores and ΔS = Rs 10 (= 20 – 10) crores and the *MPS* =10/60=0.17. It means that 17 per cent of income is saved, as shown in column (5) of the Table. It is constant at 0.17 because $\Delta S/\Delta Y$=10/60 is constant.

Diagrammatically, the *MPS* is measured by the gradient or slope of the *S* curve at a point or over a small range. This is shown in Fig. 3 by *AB/BC* where *AB* is the change in saving (ΔS) and *BC* is the change in income (ΔY).

Thus *APS* and *MPS* are two different concepts. The *APS* relates total saving to total income. On the other hand, the *MPS* relates a *change* in saving to a change in income.

* *APC* + *APS* must equal 1.

2. DETERMINANTS OF SAVINGS

Savings depend upon the will to save, power to save and facilities to save. These three determinants of savings are discussed as under.

(A) WILL TO SAVE

A portion of the income can be saved only if a person has the will to ave. Nothing can be saved by a person, if he does not want to save. This, in turn, depends upon the following factors.

1. *Family Affection*. It is the natural love and affection for the family which makes people to save. Every person has some affection for his children and family members. To make them enjoy life and to better their future prospects, he earns more and saves more. He wants to leave more property for them. For all this, he must have the will to save.

2. *Precaution*. Need for money can arise at any time in the future and so people keep money or wealth with them. People save in order to provide for old age, disease, accident and unforeseen needs and emergencies, etc. Therefore, every person wants to save as a precaution against future unforeseen needs.

3. *Standard of Living*. A person may want to raise his standard of living which can be achieved only through savings from his present income.

4. *Farsightedness*. Future is always uncertain. A farsighted person wants to make provision for education, marriage, etc. of his children. He wants to secure his old age. All this can be done by savings in the present time.

5. *Calculating Mind*. Certain persons have a calculating mind and they want to increase their future incomes. Therefore, they save out of their present incomes so as to earn more in future by investing that saved amount.

6. *Enterprise*. Persons doing trade or business want to take advantage of fluctuations in the rate of interest. They save more if they expect a rise in the rate of interest in the near future. Sometimes, savings are done to start a new business or to expand the existing one.

7. *Independent*. Every man wants to be self-sufficient or economically independent. He does not want to borrow from anybody in case he needs money in the future. He, therefore, saves out of his present income.

8. *Social Status*. Only wealthy persons are respected in the present society. Everybody wants to enjoy a higher social status. It strengthens the will to save.

9. *Miserliness*. There are people who save without any specific purpose. Miser persons save only to satisfy their desire for wealth.

(B) POWER TO SAVE

Power to save refers to the capacity to save. It means what remains after meeting the consumption expenditure out of the present income. In spite of his willingness to save, a man cannot save, if he does not have the power to save. After providing for his consumption expenditure, if more money remains with him, his power to save will be more. Thus the power to save depends upon both the levels of income and consumption. A person can save if his income exceeds consumption. If the gap between the income and the consumption is more, the power to save will increase. The power to save can be increased only by increasing income, as there is less possibility of decreasing the consumption expenditure. Therefore, the power to save of the people in a country depends on their income or factors affecting their income. The following factors determine the power to save.

1. *Size of National Income*. Primarily, the power to save of the people depends upon the national income of the country. The higher the national income, the greater will be the power to save. The low national income is the main reason of the low power to save in India.

2. *Natural Resources*. The economic conditions and the income of a country depend upon its natural resources i.e. availability of land, water, minerals, etc. The greater use of these natural resources helps in increasing production. It increases income which further raises the power to save. But it should be noted that mere availability of natural resources does not raise the power to save, if these resources are not properly utilised. India is rich in natural resources, still its power to save is very low because we do not utilise these

resources gainfully.

3. *Trade.* Both internal and foreign trade affect income and the power to save. Income increases with the development of internal and foreign trade which, in turn, increase the power to save.

4. *Industrial Development.* Industrial development increases the power to save through the increase in income.

5. *Agricultural Development.* In countries like India where agriculture is the main occupation, power to save depends upon the development of agriculture also. Agricultural development increases income which results in an increase in the power to save.

6. *Efficiency of Labour.* An efficient labour in a country helps in increasing its production, resulting in an increase in income. It, in turn, gives rise to the power to save. A less efficient labour "proves a hindrance in the way of power to save.

7. *Distribution of Wealth and Income.* The power to save depends upon the distribution of wealth and income in the country. An unequal distribution of wealth and income contributes to an increase in the power to save. Unequal distribution concentrates wealth in a few hands who can save more after meeting their consumption requirements.

(c) Facilities to Save

Savings depend not only on the will and the power to save, they also depend upon the facility to save. These facilities are :

1. *Peace and Security.* People can save only if their life and property are secure. They will not save if there is no peace and security of life and property.

2. *Banking Facilities.* An efficient and developed banking system facilitates savings. Savings are secure and beneficial in the form of cash, if these are deposited in the banks. Lack of banking facilities diminishes savings because in the absence of banking facilities money remains in the hands of people which is readily available for spending.

3. *Taxation Policy.* The taxation policy also influences savings in the country. Progressive taxation reduces savings because tax rates increase with the rise in incomes. Similar is the case with wealth and succession taxes. People generally show a tendency to save less. They feel that most of their incomes will be taken away in the form of taxes and, therefore, they save less. On the contrary, expenditure tax encourages savings because to avoid this tax, people save more out of their income instead of spending it.

4. *Value of Money.* Facilities to save require stability in the value of money. The value of money decreases with an increase in prices. People save less for fear of fall in the money value. Stability in the price level or the value of money encourages savings.

5. *Investment Opportunities.* Investment opportunities encourage savings. Savings increase if there are sufficient opportunities to invest in trade and commerce. The development of stock and exchange markets also results in more savings. Scarce investment opportunities result in less savings.

6. *Economic Policy of Government.* Facilities to save are also influenced by the economic policy of the government. If the government wants to adopt the socialistic pattern of society, it would like to nationalise different industries and people will have a tendency to save less.

3. THE PARADOX OF THRIFT

The concept of "paradox of thrift" was first introduced by Bernard Mandeville in the *Fable of the Bees* in 1714. It was later recognised by several classical economists and became an integral part of the Keynesian economics.

Thriftiness is usually regarded as a virtue. An increase in thrift on the part of an individual leads to greater saving and wealth. It is also regarded a *public virtue* because if people consume less, then more resources can be devoted to producing capital goods which lead to increase in income, output and employment. According to Keynes, thrift is a public virtue only if the propensity to invest is equally high. Otherwise, thrift is a *public vice* if the increase in the propensity to save is unaccompanied by increase in the propensity to invest, *i.e.*(autonomous investment).

Suppose people become thrifty and decide to save more out of a given level of income, given the propensity to invest. This will lead to a lower equilibrium level of income. This situation is illust-rated in Fig. 4 where S is the saving curve and I is the income-inelastic investment curve. The equilibrium level of income is E where the two curves are equal. Suppose people become more thrifty. As a result, the saving curve shifts upward to S_1 with no change in the investment curve I. The new equilibrium point is E_1 which leads to a decline in the income level from Y to Y_1. Note that at the new equilibrium level Y_1, saving is the same as it was previously at E. (This is because both saving and investment have been taken along the vertical axis). Thus people's desire to save more has been frustrated. This is called the *paradox of thrift*.

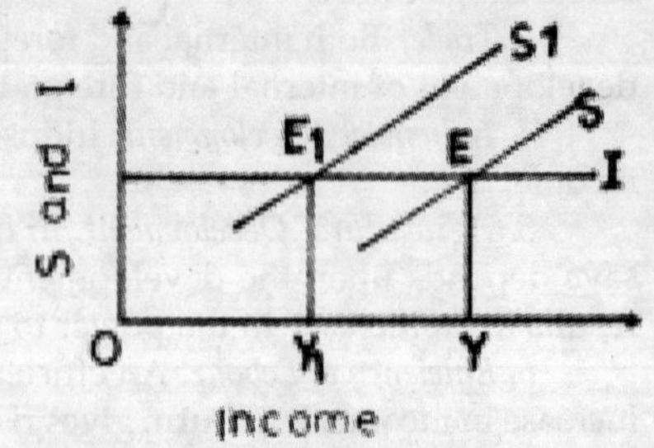

Fig. 4

The paradox of thrift can also be explained if investment is induced rather than autonomous. This is illustrated in Fig.5. The investment curve I slopes upward and intersects the S curve at point E where Y level of income is determined. Suppose people increase their savings due to thriftiness. As a result, the S curve shifts upward to S_1. It cuts the I curve at E_1 and the new equilibrium level of income is Y_1. The result is that there is reduction not only in the society's rate of saving but also in the rate of investment with the fall in income from Y to Y_1. People have tried to save more but they ended up saving less. This is the *paradox of thrift*.

Conclusion. The paradox of thrift highlights the fact that if people decide to save more, they end up saving less unless the increase in the propensity to save is offset by a higher propensity to invest, i.e.. the upward shift of the investment curve is larger than that of the saving curve. So saving is a virtue for a person or family because it leads to increase in saving and wealth. But it is a vice for the entire society because it leads to reductions in income, output and employment. Thus the paradox of thrift leads to the conclusion that saving is a private virtue and a public vice.

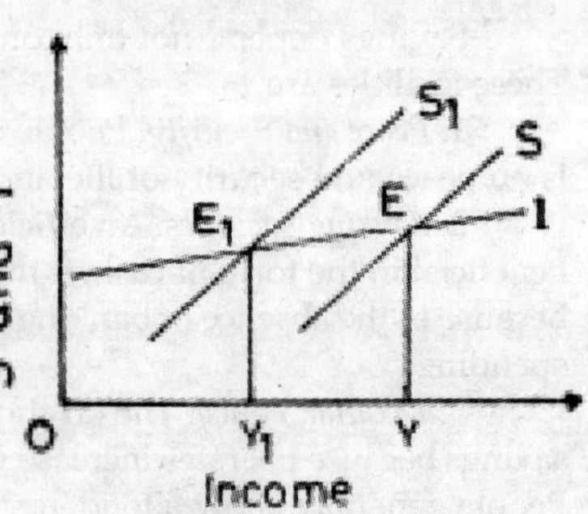

Fig. 5

EXERCISES

1. What do you mean by saving? Explain the determinants of savings.
2. Distinguish between the average propensity to save and the marginal propensity to save.
3. What do you mean by the saving function? Explain the paradox of thrift.
4. Write a note on the paradox of thrift.
5. ``Saving is a private virtue, but a public vice.'' Discuss.

Chapter 31

Pigou and Wages Price Flexibility

1. INTRODUCTION

In the chapter on the Classical Theory of Employment, it was observed that the classicists advocated a reduction in money wages to achieve full employment in the economy. Keynes was against wage-cutting and argued for increase in effective demand to remove unemployment. In this chapter, we examine in detail Pigou's views on the relationship between wages and employment and Keynes's criticism.

2. PIGOU'S VIEW

Pigou believed that there was always full employment in the economy. In case of unemployment, a general cut in money wages would take the economy to the full employment level. His argument runs as follows :

Under free competition, the tendency of the economic system is to automatically provide full employment in the labour market. Unemployment results from rigidity in the wage structure and interferences in the working of the free market economy. When the state intervenes by recognising trade unions, passing minimum wage laws, etc., and labour adopts monopolistic behaviour, wages are pushed up and unemployment results.

If all government interferences are removed and forces of competition are allowed to work freely, the manipulation of wage rates will lead to full employment. As pointed out by Pigou, ``With perfectly free competition ... there will always be at work a strong tendency for wage rates to be so related to demand that everybody is employed." The Pigouvian equation $N=qY/W$ explains the entire proposition. In this equation N is the number of workers employed, q is the fraction of income earned as wages and salaries, Y is the national income and W is money wage rate . N can be increased by a reduction in W. Thus the key to full employment is a reduction in money wage.

In a competitive economy when money wages are reduced, they lead to the reduction in cost of production and consequently to the lower prices of products. When prices fall, the demand for products will increase and the sales will be pushed up. Increased sales will necessitate the employment of more labour and ultimately full employment will be attained.

This view is based on the assumption that changes in money wages are related directly and proportionately to real wages. So when the money wage rate is reduced, the real wage is also reduced to the same extent. Consequently, unemployment is reduced and full employment prevails.

But it is at the equality of demand and supply of labour at a particular wage rate that full employment is achieved. The demand for labour is a decreasing function of the real wage rate. If *W* is the money wage rate, *P* is the price of the product, and *MP* is the marginal product of labour, we have

$W = P \times MP$

or $W/P = MP$

Since *MP* declines as employment increases, it follows that the level of employment increa-ses as the real wage (*W/P*) declines. The downward sloping demand curve for labour *D* is shown in Figure 1 (A). The supply of labour is assumed an increasing function of the real wage. This is shown by the upward sloping *S* curve in the figure. This curve indicates that the rise in real wage will induce more workers to offer themselves for employment. The interaction of the *S* and *D* curves at point *E* shows the full employment level N_F at the real wage *W/P*. If the real wage is maintained at a higher level W/P_1, there is excess supply of labour by *ds* and N_1N_F labour is unemployed. It is only when the wage rate is reduced to *W/P* that employment disappears and the level of full employment N_F is attained.

Given the stock of capital equipment, technological knowledge, and supplies of natural resources, a specific relation exists between the level of national income (or output) and employment. The national income is an increasing function of the number of workers. The relation between national income and employment is indicated by the curve *OP* in Panel (B) of the figure. The level of income Y_F corresponds to the full employment level N_F of Panel (A) of Figure 1. As employment increases, the *OP* curve flattens out which implies that the national income increases less than in proportion to the increase in employment due to the operation of the law of diminishing returns.

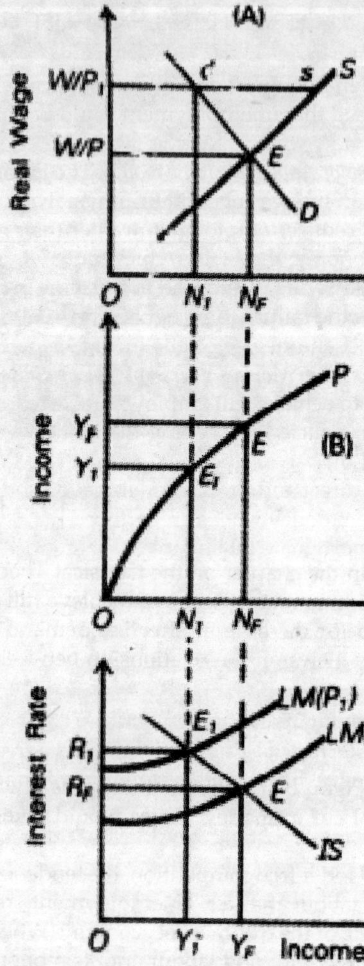

Fig.1

In Panel (C) of Figure 1, the equilibrium of the product and money markets of the economy is depicted in terms of the *IS* and *LM* curves. Taking the full employment level of income Y_F of Panel (B), the *IS* and *LM* (P_0) curves intersect at point *E* and the interest rate is R_F.

With flexible prices and wages, the price level tends to settle at P_0, thereby establishing full employment. To illustrate the mechanism by which the full employment equilibrium is attained, suppose the real wage is W/P_1 and employment N_1 in Panel (A), the level of income corresponding to this level of employment is Y_1 in Panel (B), and the price level corresponding to this income level is P_1, as represented by the *LM* (P_1) curve in Panel (C). At the real wage rate W/P_1 the supply of labour exceeds the demand for labour by *ds*. It means that N_1N_F workers are unemployed who will bid down the money wage in order to obtain employment. As the money wage falls, cost of production and prices of products fall. As wages and prices fall, the amount of money needed for transaction purposes is reduced. Thus, the supply of money exceeds the demand for money at the prevalent interest rate R_1. The excess money supply shifts the curve from *LM* (P_1) rightward to *LM* (P_0). As a result, equilibrium is established at *E* when the economy attains the level of income Y_F and interest rate R_F in Panel (C), and employment reaches the full employment level N_F at the real wage rate *W/P* in Panel (A).

3. KEYNES' CRITICISMS OF CLASSICAL VIEW

Keynes did not accept the classical view that reduction in money wages led to full employment. He emphasised that unemployment could be removed by raising the effective demand. His main objections to the classical view were as follows :

(1) *Not Applicable to Economy*. The Pigouvian view that cut in money wages tends to increase employment is based on the partial equilibrium analysis. It is applicable to an industry. But if applied to the economy as a whole, it reduces employment rather than increase it. According to Keynes, when money wages are reduced in the economy, they will reduce money incomes of the workers who will reduce their demand for products. Total outlay will fall and lead to a decline in effective demand and employment. Thus the main defect in Pigou's view was the failure to recognise the dual nature of wages—as costs and incomes. Pigou only considered the cost aspect and neglected the income aspect.

(2) *Cut in Money Wages not Essential*. Keynes did not agree with Pigou that reduction in money wages was essential to achieve full employment. According to him, full employment could be attained through monetary and fiscal policies by keeping the money wage rate constant.

(3) *Inverse Relation*. As against the Pigouvian view that the relation between money wages and real wages is direct and proportional, Keynes pointed out that the relation between the two is *inverse*. According to him, when money wages are reduced real wages rise. This is because a fall in money wages will lead to a more than proportionate fall in prices. When prices fall, real wages rise because of the increase in the value of money. Thus it is not possible for the real wage to fall with a reduction in the money wage rate. Hence the entire classical argument, based on the wrong relation between money wage and real wage, falls down and it is not possible to achieve full employment by reduction in money wages.

As a corollary to the above, since a cut in money wages will not lead to a reduction in real wages, Keynes believed that a reduction in money wages would lead to a proportionate decline in total outlay, demand and prices, leaving real wages intact.

(4) *Increase in Price Level*. Keynes agreed with Pigou that employment could be increased by a *reduction* in real wages. But the reduction in real wages was to be brought about not by a cut in money wages as Pigou believed, but by an increase in the price level. According to Keynes, an increase in aggregate demand, keeping money wages constant, would raise output, costs and prices after some time. This may happen due to three factors : (i) diminishing returns may operate in the short- run; (ii) workers may demand higher wages when their demand increase due to powerful trade unions; and (iii) "bottlenecks may appear in production in the form of non-availability of a machine, equipment, raw material, transport facilities, etc. All these factors tend to raise the cost of production and hence prices. As a result, real wages fall. Keynes, therefore, regarded ``a policy of increasing the supply of money in time of depression...preferable to cutting wages, since assuming that money wages remained constant, it would mean that members of all classes would suffer much the same change in real incomes as price rose."[1]

(5) *Workers Resist Cut in Money Wages*. Keynes further objected to a cut in money wages on practical grounds. According to him, in democratic countries where collective bargaining is permissible under the law, workers strongly resist any cut in their money wage rates.

(6) *Social Justice*. Social justice also demands that money wages of workers alone should not be reduced. A cut in the money wages of workers keeping the incomes of the other classes as unchanged, would raise the standard of living of the latter relative to the workers.

EXERCISES

1. Give the classical views on wage flexibility. On what gounds Keynes criticised it?
2. Trace the effect of a cut in money wages on the level of employment, bringing out in your answer the viewpoints of classical economists and Keynes.

---

1. A.W. Stonier and D. Hague, *A Textbook of Economic Theory*, p. 492.

Chapter 32

The Concept of Multiplier

1. INTRODUCTION

The concept of multiplier was first developed by R.F. Kahn in his article ``The Relation of Home Investment to Unemployment" in the *Economic Journal* of June 1931. Kahn's multiplier was the Employment Multiplier. Keynes took the idea from Kahn and formulated the Investment Multiplier.

2. MEANING AND DERIVATION OF INVESTMENT MULTIPLIER

Keynes considers his theory of multiplier as an integral part of his theory of employment. The multiplier, according to Keynes,``establishes a precise relationship, given the propensity to consume, between aggregate employment and income and the rate of investment. It tells us that, when there is an increment of investment, income will increase by an amount which is *K* times the increment of investment" i.e., $\Delta Y = K\Delta I$ In the words of Hansen, Keynes' investment multiplier is the coefficient relating to an increment of investment to an increment of income, i.e., K= $\Delta Y / \Delta I$, where *Y* is income, *I* is investment, Δ is change (increment or decrement) and *K* is the multiplier.

In the multiplier theory, the important element is the multiplier co-efficient, *K*which refers to the power by which any initial investment expenditure is multiplied to obtain a final increase in income. The value of the multiplier is determined by the marginal propensity to consume. The higher the marginal propensity to consume, the higher is the value of the multiplier, and vice versa. The relationship between the multiplier and the marginal propensity to consume is as follows :

$$\Delta Y = C + \Delta I$$

or $$\Delta Y = C\Delta Y + \Delta I \qquad (\because \Delta C = C\Delta Y)$$

$$\Delta Y - C\Delta Y = \Delta I$$

$$\Delta Y (1-C) = \Delta I$$

$$\Delta Y = \frac{\Delta I}{1-C}$$

$$\frac{\Delta Y}{\Delta I} = \frac{1}{1-C}$$

$$K = \frac{1}{1-C} \qquad (\because K = \frac{\Delta Y}{\Delta I})$$

Since C is the marginal propensity to consume, the multiplier K is, by definition, equal to 1–1/C. The multiplier can also be derived from the marginal propensity to save (*MPS*) and it is the reciprocal of *MPS*, *K*=1/*MPS*.

Table 1 : Derivation of The Multiplier From MPC

MPC ($\Delta C/\Delta Y$) (1)	*K*=1/1–*MPC* (2)	*MPS*($\Delta S/\Delta Y$) (3)	*K*=1/*MPS* (4)
...	...		
0	$\frac{1}{1-0}=1$	1	1
1/2	$\frac{1}{1-\frac{1}{2}}=2$	$\frac{1}{2}$	2
2/3	$\frac{1}{1-\frac{2}{3}}=3$	$\frac{1}{3}$	3
1	$\frac{1}{1-1}=\infty$	0	∞ (Infinity)

The table shows that the size of the multiplier varies directly with the *MPC*. Since the *MPC* is always greater than zero and less than one (i.e.,O < *MPC*< 1), the multiplier is always between one and infinity (i.e.,1< *K*< ∞). If the multiplier is one, it means that the whole increment of income is saved and nothing is spent because the *MPC* is zero. On the other hand, an infinite multiplier implies that *MPC* is equal to one and the entire increment of income is spent on consumption. It will soon lead to full employment in the economy and then create a limitless inflationary spiral. But these are rare phenomena. Therefore, the multiplier coefficient varies between one and infinity. The multiplier can also be derived from the marginal propensity to save (*MPS*) and it is the reciprocal of *MPS* i.e., $k = {}^{1}/_{MPS}$, as shown in columns (3) and (4) of the Table.

3. WORKING OF THE MULTIPLIER

The multiplier works both forward and backward. First, we study its forward working. The multiplier theory explains the cumulative effect of a change in investment on income via its effect on consumption expenditure.

Forward Working. We take the ``sequence analysis" which shows a ``motion picture" of the process of income propagation. An increase in investment leads to increased production which creates income and generates consumption expenditure. This process continues in dwindling series till no further increase in income and expenditure is possible. This is a lagless instantaneous process in a static framework, as explained by Keynes.

Suppose that in an economy *MPC* is 1/2 and investment in raised by Rs 100 crores. This will immediately lead to a rise in production and income by Rs 100 crores. One-half of this new income will be immediately spent on consumption goods which will lead to increase in production and income by the same amount, and so on. The process is set out in Table 3. It reveals that an increment of Rs 100 crores of investment in the primary round leads to the same increase in income. Of this, Rs 50 crores are saved and Rs 50 crores are spent on consumption which go to increase income by the same amount in the second round. This dwindling process of income generation continues in the secondary rounds till the total income generated from Rs 100 crores of investment rises to Rs 200 crores. This is also clear from the multiplier formula,

$\Delta Y = K\Delta I$ or 200 = 2× 100, where K=2 ($\because$ *MPC* =1/2) and Δ I=Rs 100 crores. This process of income propagation as a result of increase in investment is shown diagrammatically in Figure 1.

TABLE 3 : SEQUENCE MULTIPLIER

(Rs. Crores)

Round	ΔI *(Increment in investment)*	ΔY *(Increment in Income)*	$\Delta c = c\Delta Y$ $c = 0.5$	$\Delta S = (\Delta Y - \Delta S)$ *(Increment in saving)*
0				
1	100	100	50	50
2	—	50	25	25
3	—	25	12.50	12.50
4	—	12.50	6.25	6.25
5		6.25	3.12	3.12
0	—	0	0	0
Finally	100	200	100	100

The C curve has a slope of 0.5 to show that the *MPC* is equal to one-half. *C+I* is the investment curve which intersects the 45° line at E_1 so that the old equilibrium level of income is OY_1.Now there is an increase in investment of ΔI, as shown by the distance between *C+I* and *C+I+* ΔI curves. This curve intersects the 45° line at E_2 to give OY_2 as the new income. Thus the rise in income Y_1Y_2 as shown by ΔY is twice the distance between *C+I* and *C+I+* ΔI, since the *MPC* is one-half.

The same results can be obtained if *MPS* is taken so that when income increases, savings also increase to equal the new investment at a new equilibrium level of income. This is shown in Figure 2, where *S* is the saving function with a slope of 0.5 to show *MPS* of one-half. *I* is the old investment curve which cuts *S* at E_1 so that OY_1 is the old equilibrium level of income. The increase in investment ΔI is superimposed on the *I* curve in the shape of a new investment curve $I + \Delta I$ which is intersected by the *S* curve at E_2 to give OY_2 "as the new equilibrium level of income. The rise in income Y_1Y_2 is exactly double the increase in investment Δ I, as the *MPS* is one-half.

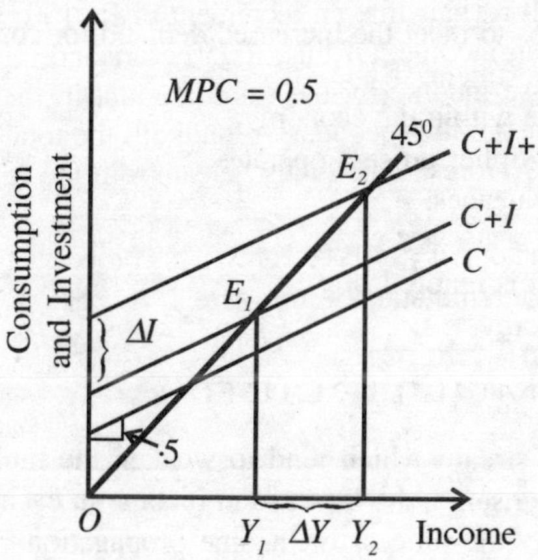

Fig. 1.

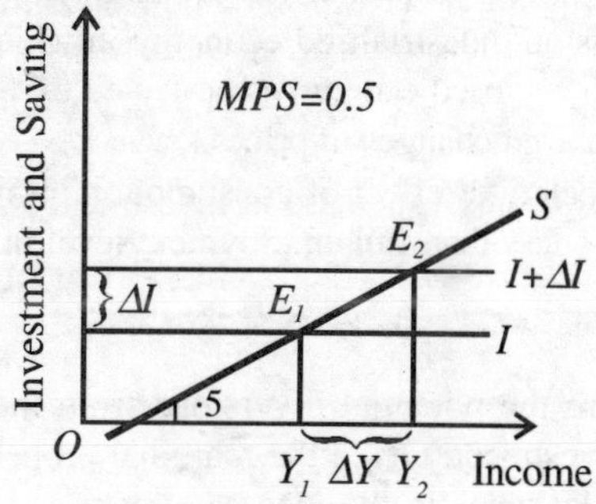

Fig. 2.

Backward Operation. The above analysis pertains to the forward operation of the multiplier. If, however, investment decreases, instead of increasing, the multiplier operates backward. A reduction in investment will lead to the contraction of income and consumption which, in turn, will lead to cumulative decline in income and consumption till the contraction in aggregate income is the multiple of the initial decrease in investment. Suppose investment decreases by Rs 100 crores. With an *MPC*= 0.5 and *K*=2, the consumption expenditure would keep on declining till aggregate income is decreased by Rs 200 crores. In terms of the multiplier formula, $-\Delta Y = K(-\Delta I)$, we get – Rs 200 = 2 (– 100)

The magnitude of contraction due to the backward operation of the multiplier depends on the value of *MPC*. The higher the *MPC*, the greater is the value of the multiplier and the greater the cumulative decline in income, and vice versa. On the contrary, the higher the *MPS*, the lower is the value of the multiplier and the smaller the cumulative decline in income, and vice versa. Thus, a community with a high propensity to consume (or low propensity to save) will be hurt more by the reverse operation of the multiplier than one with a low propensity to consume (or high propensity to save).

Diagrammatically, the reverse operation can be explained in terms of Figures 1 and 2. Taking Figure 1, when investment decreases, the investment function $C+I+\Delta I$ shifts downward to $C+I$. As a result, the equilibrium level also shifts from E_2 to E_1 and income declines form OY_2 to OY_1. The *MPC* being 0.5, the fall in income $Y_2 Y_1$ is exactly double the decline in investment, as shown by the distance between $C+I+\Delta I$ and $C+I$. Similarly, in Figure 2 when investment falls, the investment function $I + \Delta I$ shifts downward as I curve and income decreases from OY_2 to OY_1. The *MPS* being 0.5, the decrease in income Y_2Y_1 is double the decline in investment, as measured by the distance between $I + \Delta I$ and I curves.

4. ASSUMPTIONS OF MULTIPLIER

Keynes's theory of the multiplier works under certain assumptions which limit the operation of the multiplier. They are as follows :

(1) There is change in autonomous investment and that induced investment is absent.

(2) The marginal propensity to consume is constant.

(3) Consumption is a function of current income.

(4) There are no time lags in the multiplier process. An increase (decrease) in investment instantaneously leads to a multiple increase (decrease) in income.

(5) The new level of investment is maintained steadily for the completion of the multiplier process.

(6) There is net increase in investment.

(7) Consumer goods are available in response to effective demand for them.

(8) There is surplus capacity in consumer goods industries to meet the increased demand for consumer goods in response to a rise in income following increased investment.

(9) Other resources of production are also easily available within the economy.

(10) There is an industrialised economy in which the multiplier process operates.

(11) There is a closed economy unaffected by foreign influences.

(12) There are no changes in prices.

(13) The accelerator effect of consumption on investment is ignored.

(14) There is less than full employment level in the economy.

5. LEAKAGES OF MULTIPLIER

Leakages are the potential diversions from the income stream which tend to weaken the multiplier effect of new investment. Given the marginal propensity to consume, the increase in income in each round declines due to leakages in the income stream and ultimately the process of income propagation ``peters out." (see Table 3). The following are the important leakages.

(1) *Saving*. Saving is the most important leakage of the multiplier process. Since the marginal propensity to consume is less than one, the whole increment in income is not spent on consumption. A part of it is saved which peters out of the income stream and the increase in income in the next round declines. Thus the higher the marginal propensity to save, the smaller the size of the multiplier and the greater the amount of leakage out of the income stream, and vice versa. For instance, if $MPS=1/6$, the multiplier is 6, according to the formula $K=1/MPS$; and the MPS of 1/3 gives a multiplier of 3.

(2) *Strong Liquidity Preference*. If people prefer to hoard the increased income in the form of idle cash balances to satisfy a strong liquidity preference for the transaction, precautionary and speculative motives, they will act as leakages out of the income stream. As income increases, people will hoard money in inactive bank deposits and the multiplier process is checked.

(3) *Purchase of old Stocks and Securities*. If a part of the increased income is used in buying old stocks and securities instead of consumer goods, the consumption expenditure will fall and its cumulative effect on income will be less than before. In other words, the size of the multiplier will fall with a fall in consumption expenditure when people buy old stocks and shares.

(4) *Debt Cancellation*. If a part of increased income is used to repay debts to banks, instead of spending it for further consumption, that part of the income peters out of the income stream. In case, this part of the increased income is repaid to other creditors who save or hoard it, the multiplier process will be arrested.

(5) *Price Inflation*. When increased investment leads to price inflation, the multiplier effect of increased income may be dissipated on higher prices. A rise in the prices of consumption goods implies increased expenditure on them. As a result, increased income is absorbed by higher prices and the real consumption and income fall. Thus price inflation is an important leakage.

(6) *Net Imports*. If increased income is spent on the purchase of imported goods, it acts as a leakage out of the domestic income stream. Such an expenditure fails to affect the consumption of domestic goods. This argument can be extended to *net* imports when there is an excess of imports over exports, thereby causing a net outflow of funds to other countries.

(7) *Undistributed Profits*. If profits accuring to joint stock companies are not distributed to the shareholders in the form of dividend but are kept in the reserve fund, it is a leakage from the income stream. Undistributed profits with the companies tend to reduce the income and hence further expenditure on consumption goods, thereby weakening the multiplier process.

(8) *Taxation*. Taxation policy is also an important factor in weakening the multiplier process. Progressive taxes have the effect of lowering the disposable income of the taxpayers and reducing their consumption expenditure. Similarly, commodity taxation tends to raise the prices of goods, and a part of increased income may be dissipated on higher prices. Thus increased taxation reduces the income stream and lowers the size

of the multiplier.

(9) *Excess Stocks of Consumption Goods.* If the increased demand for consumption goods is met from the existing excess stocks of consumption goods there will be no further increase in output, employment and income and the multiplier process will come to a halt till the old stocks are exhausted.

(10) *Public Investment Programmes.* If the increase in income as a result of increased investment is affected by public expenditures, it may fail to induce private enterprise to spend that income for further investment due to the following reasons :

(a) Public investment programmes may raise the demand for labour and materials leading to a rise in the costs of construction so as to make the undertaking of some private projects unprofitable.

(b) Government borrowing may, if not accompanied by a sufficiently liberal credit policy on the part of the monetary authority, increase the rate of interest and thus discourage private investment.

(c) Government operations may also injure private investors' confidence by arousing animosity or fears of nationalisation.

6. CRITICISMS OF MULTIPLIER

The multiplier theory has been severely criticised by the post-Keynesian economists. Prof. Hart considers it ``a useless fifth wheel." To Stigler, it is the fuzziest part of Keynes' theory. While Hutt calls it a ``rubbish apparatus" which should be expunged from text books. Other economists have criticised the concept on the following grounds.

(1) *Merely Tautological Concept.* Prof. Haberler has criticised Keynes multiplier as tautological. It is truism which defines the multiplier as necessarily true as $K = 1/1 - \Delta C/\Delta Y$. As pointed by Professor Hansen, ``Such a coefficient "is a mere arithmetic multiplier (i.e., a truism) and not a true *behaviour* multiplier based on a *behaviour* pattern which establishes a verifiable relation between consumption and income. A mere arithmetic multiplier, $1/1 - \Delta C/\Delta Y$.

(2) *Timeless Analysis.* Keynes' logical theory of the multiplier is an instantaneous process without time lag. It is a timeless static equilibrium analysis in which the total effect of a change in investment on income is instantaneous so that consumption goods are produced simultaneously and consumption expenditure is also incurred instantaneously. But this is not borne out by facts because a time lag is always involved between the receipt of income and its expenditure on consumption goods and also in producing consumption goods. Thus ``the timeless multiplier analysis disregards the transition and deals only with the new equilibrium income level" and is therefore unrealistic.

(3) *A Worthless Theoretical Toy.* According to Hazlitt, the Keynesian multiplier ``is a strange concept about which some Keynesians make more fuss than about anything else in the Keynesian system." It is a myth, for there can never be any precise, predeterminable or mechanical relationship between investment and income. Thus he regards it as ``a worthless theoretical toy."

(4) *Acceleration Effect Ignored.* One of the weaknesses of the multiplier theory is that it studies the effects of investment on income through changes in consumption expenditure. But it ignores the effect of consumption on investment which is known as the acceleration principle. Hicks, Samuclson and others have shown that it is the interaction of the multiplier and the accelerator which helps in controlling business fluctuations.

(5) *MPC does not Remain Constant.* Gordon points out that the greatest weakness of the multiplier concept is its exclusive emphasis on consumption. He favours the use of the term `marginal propensity to spend' in place of marginal propensity to consume to make this concept more realistic. He also objects to the constancy of the marginal propensity to spend (or consume) because in a dynamic economy, it is not likely to remain constant. If it is assumed to be constant, it is not possible ``to predict with much accuracy the multiplying effects over the cycle of a given increase in private investment or public spending."

(6) *Relation between Consumption and Income*. Keynes' multiplier theory establishes a linear relation between consumption and income with the hypothesis that the *MPC* is less than one and greater than zero. Empirical studies of the behaviour of consumption in relation to income show that the relationship between the two is complicated and non-linear. As pointed out by Gardner Ackley, ``The relationship does not run simply from *current* income to *current* consumption, but rather involves some complex average of past and expected income and consumption. There are other factors than income to consider."

But despite its scathing criticisms, the multiplier principle has considerable practical applicability to economic problems as given below.

7. IMPORTANCE OF MULTIPLIER

The concept of multiplier is one of the important contributions of Keynes' to the income and employment theory. As aptly observed by Richard Goodwin, ``Lord Keynes did not discover the multiplier; that honour goes to Mr. R.F. Kahn. But he gave it the role it plays today by transforming it from an instrument for the analysis of road building into one for the analysis of income building...It set a fresh wind blowing through the structure of economic throught." Its importance lies in the following.

(1) *Investment*. The multiplier theory highlights the importance of investment in income and employment theory. Since the consumption function is stable during the short-run, fluctuations in income and employment are due to fluctuations in the rate of investment. A fall in investment leads to a cumulative decline in income and employment by the multiplier process and *vice versa*. Thus it underlines the importance of investment and explains the process of income propagation.

(2) *Trade Cycle*. As a corollary to the above, when there are fluctuations in the level of income and employment due to variations in the rate of investment, the multiplier process throws a spotlight on the different phases of the trade cycle. When there is a fall in investment, income and employment decline in a cumulative manner leading to recession and ultimately to depression. On the contrary, an increase in investment leads to revial and, if this process continues, to a boom. Thus the multiplier is regarded as an indispensable tool in trade cycles.

(3) *Saving-Investment Equality*. It also helps in bringing an equality between saving and investment. If there is a divergence between saving and investment, an increase in investment leads to a rise in income via the multiplier process by more than the increase in initial investment. As a result of the increase in income, saving also increases and equals investment.

(4) *Formulation of Economic Policies*. The multiplier is an important tool in the hands of modern states in formulating economic policies. Thus this principle pre-supposes state intervention in economic affairs.

(5) *To Achieve Full Employment*. The state decides upon the amount of investment to be injected into the economy to remove unemployment and achieve full employment. An initial increase in investment leads to the rise in income and employment by the multiplier time the increase in investment. If a single dose of investment is insufficient to bring full employment, the state can inject regular doses of investment for this purpose till the full employment level is reached.

(6) *To Control Trade Cycles*. The state can control booms and depressions in a trade cycle on the basis of the multiplier effect on income and employment. When the economy is experiencing inflationary pressure, the state can control them by a reduction in investment which leads to a cumulative decline in income and employment via the multiplier process. On the other hand, in a deflationary situation, an increase in investment can help increase the level of income and employment through the multiplier process.

(7) *Deficit Financing*. The multiplier principle highlights the importance of deficit budgeting. In a state of depression, cheap money policy of lowering the rate of interest is not helpful because the marginal efficiency of capital is so low that a low rate of interest fails to encourage private investment. In such a situation, increased public expenditure through public investment programmes by creating a budget deficit

helps in increasing income and employment by multiplier time the increase in investment.

(8) *Public Investment.* The above discussion reveals the importance of the multiplier in public investment policy. Public investment refers to the state expenditure on public works and other works meant to increase public welfare. It is autonomous and is free from profit motive. It, therefore, applies with greater force in overcoming inflationary, and deflationary pressures in the economy, and in achieving and maintaining full employment. Private investment being induced by profit motive can help only when the public investment has created a favourable situation for the former. Moreover, economic activity cannot be left to the vagaries and uncertainties of private enterprise. Hence, the importance of multiplier in public investment lies in creating or controlling income and employment. The state can have the greatest multiplier effect on income and employment by increasing public investment during a depression where the *MPC* is high (or the *MPS* is low). On the contrary, in periods of overfull employment, a decline in investment will have a serious effect on the levels of income and employment where the *MPS* is high (or *MPC* is low). The best policy is to reduce investment where the *MPC* is low (or *MPS* is high), to have gradual decline in income and employment. The important thing, however, is the timing of public investment in such a manner that the multiplier is able to work with full force and there is little scope for the income stream to peter out. Moreover, public investment should not supplant but supplement private investment so that it could be increased during depression and reduced during inflation. As a result, the forward and backward operations of the multiplier will help in two situations.

8. MULTIPLIER IN AN UNDERDEVELOPED COUNTRY

Dr. V.K.R.V. Rao has analysed the feasibility of applying the Keynesian multiplier theory and policy implications to an underdeveloped country like India.[1] According to Dr. Rao, Keynes never formulated the economic problems of underdeveloped countries nor did he discuss the relevance to these countries for either the objective or the policy that he proposed for the more developed countries. The result has been a rather "unintelligent application of Keynesian economics to the problems of "underdeveloped countries. The Keynesian concept of multiplier is based on the following four assumptions : (a) Involuntary unemployment. (b) An industrialized economy where the supply curve of output slopes upward to the right but does not become vertical till after a *substantial "interval.* (c) Excess capacity in the consumption goods industries. (d) Comparatively elastic supply of the working capital required for increased output.

Given these assumptions, if we apply the multiplier theory to underdeveloped countries, the value of the multiplier will be apparently much higher than even in a developed country. We know that the multiplier depends on the size of the marginal propensity to consume. Since in an underdeveloped country, the marginal propensity to consume is fairly high, small increments of investment are likely to induce full employment much earlier than in a rich country where the marginal propensity to consume is low. This is something paradoxical and contrary to facts. For the assumptions on which the multiplier theory is based do not hold valid in the case of an underdeveloped country. Let us test them in the light of conditions prevailing in an underdeveloped country like India.

(a) Involuntary unemployment in the Keynesian analysis is associated with a capitalist economy where the majority of workers work for wages and where production is more for exchange than for self-consumption. According to Prof. Das Gupta, the organised sector of an underdeveloped economy, with its large-scale industries and fairly well-developed banking system comes under the scope of the Keynesian economics, for it presents the features of a capitalistic economy. But involuntary unemployment in this sector is insignificant when considered in relation to the total working population of the country.[2]

In fact, in an overpopulated underdeveloped country there exists disguised unemployment. Ostensibly

1. V.K.R.V. Rao, Essays in Economic Development, Ch. 2.
2. A.K. Das Gupta, *Planning and Economic Growth,* pp. 32-33.

people are engaged in agriculture but if some of them are withdrawn from the farm, there will be no reduction in output. In an underdeveloped economy, the existence of disguised unemployment instead of involuntary unemployment hinders the working of the multiplier theory. The secondary, tertiary and other effects of the initial increment do not follow mainly because there is no labour force willing to accept employment at the current wage level. The disguised unemployed are not available at the current wage level because, *Firstly*, they are not conscious of the fact that they are unemployed and *secondly*, they are already receiving a real income which gives them at least as much satisfaction as they "would get from the current wage level. Thus the absence of involuntary unemployment and the presence of disguised unemployment in underdeveloped countries retard the operation of the multiplier towards increasing output and employment.

(b) The supply curve of output in an underdeveloped country is inelastic which renders the working of the multiplier all the more difficult. The reason is that the nature of the consumption goods industries is such that they are unable to expand output and offer more employment. The main consumption goods industry in an underdeveloped country is agriculture which is almost stagnant. The supply curve of agricultural output is backward sloping so that an increase in the value of output does not necessarily lead to an increase in the volume of output. This is because in the short-run necessary facilities are not available to the agricultural producers for increasing output. As a result, the secondary, tertiary and other increases in income, output and employment do not come about with an initial increment of investment. The primary increase in income is spent on food and its multiplier effect is lost.

(c) Since the marginal propensity to consume is high in underdeveloped countries, the increased income is spent on self-consumption of food products by the farmers which leads to a reduction of the marketable surplus of foodgrains. This, in turn, leads to a rise in the prices of foodgrains in the non-agricultural sector without a rise in the aggregate real income. The possibility of spending more by the agriculturists on non-agricultural goods is, however, limited because there is little excess capacity in industries.

(d) Output is difficult to increase due to the non-availability of sufficient raw materials, capital equipment and skilled labour. Thus, concludes Dr Rao, ``the primary increase in the investment, and therefore, increase in income and employment leads to a secondary and a tertiary increase in income, but not any noticeable increase in output or employment, either in the agricultural or in the non-agricultural sector. The multiplier principle, therefore, works with reference to money income but not with reference either to real income or employment."

Similarly, the absence of conditions (c) and (d) in an underdeveloped country renders the operation of the multiplier difficult. Absence of excess capacity in consumption goods industries coupled with a comparatively inelastic supply of working capital for increasing output prevent the required increase in the output of consumption goods industries and the resultant employment therein.

Thus the obvious conclusion is that the Keynesian principle of multiplier does not operate in an underdeveloped country like India mainly due to two reasons : *firstly*, involuntary unemployment of the Keynesian type is not to be found, and *secondly*, the supply of agricultural and non-agricultural output is inelastic due to the working of certain factors peculiar to such economies.

EXERCISES

1. What is the significance of the statement that the value of the multiplier is the reciprocal of the marginal propensity to save?
2. Discuss the concept of ``investment multiplier" and its role in the theory of income and employment.
3. ``The higher the marginal propensity to consume, the higher will be the value of the multiplier." Discuss this statement.
4. What will be the value of multiplier when *MPC* is O and 1?
5. Explain the working of the multiplier, given the value of *MPC* = 0.5.
6. Explain the relationship between *MPC* and multiplier. Derive the formula and explain diagrammatically.

CHAPTER 33

Keynes' Liquidity Preference Theory of Interest

Keynes defines the rate of interest as the reward of not hoarding but the reward for parting with liquidity for the specified period. It is not the 'price' which brings into equilibrium the demand for resources to invest with the readiness to abstain from consumption. It is the 'price' which equilibrates the desire to hold wealth in the form of cash with the available quantity of cash."[1] In other words, the rate of interest, in the Keynesian sense, is determined by the demand for and the supply of money. This theory is, therefore, characterised as the monetary theory of interest, as distinct from the real theory of the classicals.

Supply of Money. Of the two determinants of the rate of interest, the supply of money refers to the total quantity of money in the country for all purposes at any time. Though the supply of money is a function of the rate of interest to a degree, yet it is considered to be fixed by the monetary authorities, that is, the supply curve of money is taken as perfectly inelastic.

Demand for Money. For the second determinant, the demand for money, Keynes coined a new term "liquidity preference" by which his theory of interest is commonly known. Liquidity preference is the desire to hold cash. The money in cash "lulls our disquietude" and the rate of interest which is demanded in exchange for it is a "measure of the degree of out disquietude." The rate of interest, in Keynes' words, is the "premium which has to be offered to induce people to hold the wealth in some form other than hoarded money."[2] The higher the liquidity preference, the higher will be rate of interest that will have to be paid to the holders of cash to induce them to part with their liquid assets. The lower the liquidity preference, the lower will be the rate of interest that will be paid to the cash-holders.

According to Keynes, there are three motives behind the desire of the people to hold liquid cash: (1) the transaction motive, (2) the precautionary motive, and (3) the speculative motive.

Transactions Motive. The transactions motive relates to "the need of cash for the current transactions of personal and business exchanges." It is further divided into the income and business motives. The income motive is meant to bridge the interval between the receipt of income and its disbursement," and similarly, the business motive as "the interval between the time of incurring business costs and that of the receipt of the sale

---

1. J.M. Keynes, *The General Theory of Employment, Interest and Money,* p. 167.
2. Keynes in S.E. Harris (ed.), *The New Economics,* p. 187.

proceeds." If the time between incurring of expenditure and receipt of income is small, less cash will be held by the people for current transactions, and *vice versa.* There will however be changes in the transactions demand for money depending upon the expectations of the income, recipients and businessmen. They depend upon the level of income, employment and prices, the business turnover, the normal period between the receipt and disbursement of income, the amount of salary or income, and on the possibility of getting a loan.

Precautionary Motive. The precautionary motive relates to "the desire to provide for contingencies requiring sudden expenditures and for unforeseen opportunities of advantageous purchases". Both individuals and businessmen keep cash in reserve to meet unexpected needs. Individuals hold some cash to provide for illness, accidents, unemployment and other unforeseen contingencies. Similarly, businessmen keep cash in reserve to tide over unfavourable conditions or to gain from unexpected deals. "Money held under the precautionary motive is rather like water kept in reserve in a water tank." The precautionary demand for money depends upon the level of income, and business activity, opportunities for unexpected profitable deals, availability of cash, the cost of holding liquid assets in bank reserves, etc.

Keynes holds that the transactions and precautionary motives are relatively interest inelastic, but are highly income elastic. The amount of money held under these two motives (M_1) is a function (L_1) of the level of income (Y) and is expressed as $M_1=L_1 (Y)$.

Speculative Motive. Money held under the speculative motive is for "securing profit from knowing better than the market what the future will bring forth." Individuals and businessmen have fund:, after keeping enough for transactions and precautionary purposes, like to gain by investing in bonds. Money held for speculative purposes is a liquid store of value which can be invested at an opportune moment in interest-bearing bonds or securities.

Bond prices and the rate of interest are inversely related to each other. Low bond prices are indicative of high interest rates, and high bond prices reflect low interest rates. A bond carries a fixed rate of interest. For instance, if a bond of the value of Rs. 100 carries 4% interest and the market rate of interest rises to 8%, the value of this bond falls to Rs. 50 in the market. If the market rate of interest falls to 2%, the value of the bond will rise to Rs. 200 in the market. Thus individuals and businessmen can gain by buying bonds worth Rs 100 each at the market price of Rs. 50 each when the rate of interest is high (8%), and sell them again when they are dearer (Rs. 200 each) when the rate of interest falls (to 2%).

According to Keynes, it is expectations about changes in bond prices or in the current market rate of interest that determine the speculative demand for money. The speculative demand for money is a decreasing function of the rate of interest to the matter of expectations about a safe future rate of interest. The higher the rate of interest, the lower the speculative demand for money, and lower the rate of interest, the higher the speculative demand for money. Algebraically, Keynes expressed the speculative demand for money as $M_2=L_2(r)$ where L_2 is the speculative demand for money and r is the rate of interest. Geometrically, it is a smooth curve which slopes downward from left to right, as shown in Fig. 1.

But at a very low rate of interest, such as 2%, the speculative demand for money becomes perfectly elastic. This portion of the curve is known as the liquidity trap. At a very low rate of interest, people prefer to keep money in cash rather than invest in bonds because purchasing bonds will mean a definite loss.

Total Demand of Money

If the total liquid money is denoted by M, the transactions plus precautionary motive by M_1 and the speculative motive for holding by M_2, then $M=M_1+M_2$. Since $M_1=L_1(Y)$ and $M_2= L_2(r)$, the total liquidity preference function is expressed as $M=L(Y,r)$. M_1 is circulating or active money and M_2 is idle or passive money. Though M_1 is a function of income and M_2 of the rate of interest, yet they cannot be held in water-tight compartments. Even M_1 is interest elastic at high interest rates. If there is increased demand for M_1 it can be met by transferring funds from idle balances M_2. Prof. Haberler distinguishes between liquidity preference in the narrower sense and liquidity preference in the wider

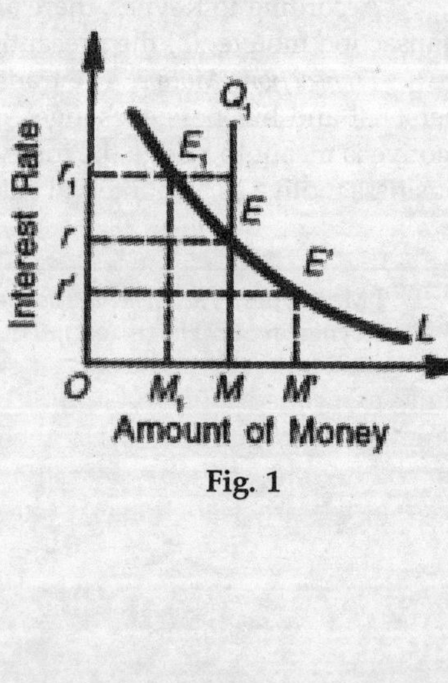

Fig. 1

sense. The former is the demand for idle balances, M_2 and is called "liquidity preference proper", and the latter is the total liquidity demand (M or M_1+M_2). Given the level of income at high interest rates, liquidity preference refers to the total demand for money (M_1+M_2), and at low interest rates the demand for speculative motive (M_2) alone."

Determination of the Rate of Interest. We have analysed the factors behind the supply and demand for money. The rate of interest, like the price of any product or service, is determined at a level where the demand for money equals the available supply of money. In Fig. 1 the vertical line Q_lM represents the supply of money and L the total demand for money curve. Both intersect at E where the *equilibrium rate* of interest r is established. If there is any deviation from this equilibrium position an adjustment will take place via the rate of interest, and the equilibrium level E is reestablished.

Thus E_1 is the position of unstable equilibrium where the supply of money OM is greater than the demand for money OM_1. Consequently, the rate of interest will start declining from r_2 till the equilibrium rate of interest r is reached. Similarly, at r' level of interest rate, the demand for money OM' is greater than the supply of money OM. As a result, the rate of interest r' will start rising till it reaches the equilibrium rate r.

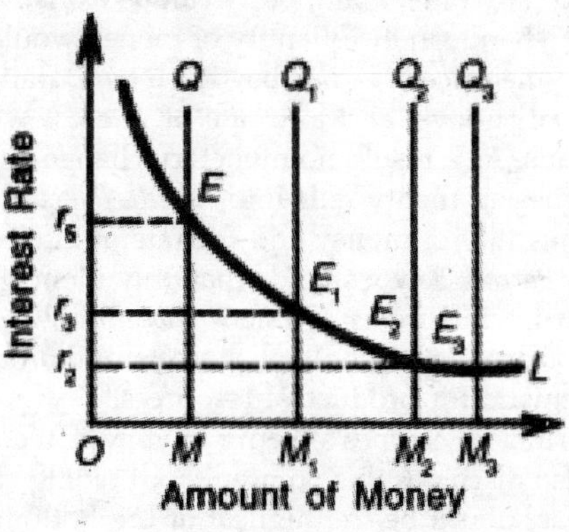

Fig. 2

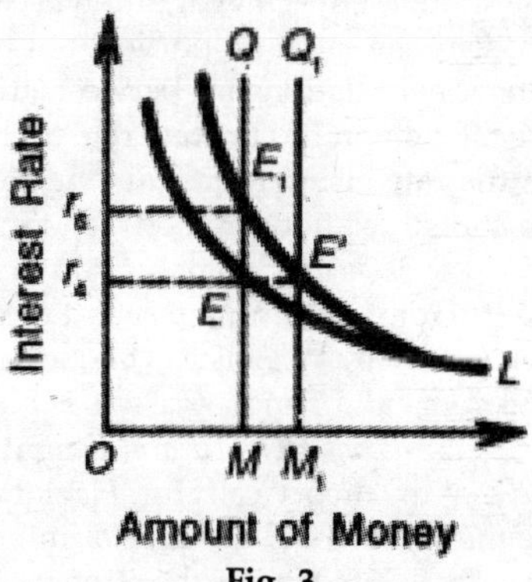

Fig. 3

If the *supply of money* is increased by the monetary authorities, but the liquidity preference curve L remains the same, the rate of interest will fall. This is illustrated in Fig. 2. Given the L curve, the supply of money curve being QM, the rate of interest is rs. With the increase in the supply of money from QM to O_lM_l and Q_2A_2, the rate of interest falls from r_3 to rr, But any further increase in the supply of money has no effect on the rate of interest because the liquidity preference curve L is perfectly elastic at r_2 rate of interest. So when the supply of money increases to Q_3M_3 the rate of interest remains stationary at r_2 corresponding to the equilibrium point E_3. This is Keynes' Liquidity Trap.

If the demand for money increases and the liquidity preference curve shifts upward, given the supply of money, the rate of interest rises. This is shown in Fig. 3. Given the supply of money curve QM, when the L curve shifts upward, the new equilibrium point is E_1 which determines r_6 interest rate. This rate of interest is higher than r_4 interest rate at the equilibrium point E. If with the increase in the liquidity preference, the supply of money also increases in the same proportion to Q_1M_1, there will be no change in the rate of interest r_4, except that the new equilibrium point is E'. Thus the theory explains that the rate of interest is determined at a point where the liquidity preference curve equals the supply of money curve.

ITS CRITICISM

The Keynesian theory of interest has been severely criticised by Hansen, Robertson, Knight, Hazlitt, Hutt and others. It has been variously characterized as "a college bursar's theory", "at best an inadequate and at worst a misleading account," and "preclassical, mercantilist, and man-in-the-sireet economics."

(1) *College Bursar's Theory.* One of the fallacies of the Keynesian analysis is that the demand for money is mainly associated with the liquidity preference for the speculative motive to which the rate of interest is brought directly into touch. The theory presumes the existence of a number of wealthy and shrewd persons who will hold more money by selling bonds when the rate of interest falls and hold less cash but more bonds in case of the rise in the interest rate. But Robertson does not regard bonds as the only alternative to money,

as a use for resources both by the individual and the entrepreneur. And a theory of money which insists on working everything through the bond market is a *College Bursar's theory* and seems to be lacking in realism and comprehensiveness.

(2) *Inadequate and Misleading Theory.* The theory tells us nothing as to what determines the normal rate and therefore, given the degree of divergence, the actual rate of interest. The actual rate of interest cannot be described consistently as measuring the cost of uncertainty of risk involved in holding-bonds rather than money. If there were no uncertainty at all, the actual rate would simply stand at a certain definite level below the normal rate. It is for these reasons that Robertson regards the liquidity preference theory "as *at best an inadequate and at worst a misleading account.*"

(3) *Falls into Methodological Fallacy.* Just as the rate of interest is explained as the price for parting with liquidity, similarly the price of eggs or any other commodity can be explained by the relative preference for them. But there is a vital difference. A change in the quantity of money would tend to change the price of the goods in the same proportion, but not the price of bonds beyond a temporary disturbance. In fact, there is no functional relationship between the price level and any rate of interest while discussing the influence of speculation on the interest rate on loans. As a result, no monetary change has any direct or permanent effect on the rate of interest. Thus the Keynesian theory falls into *"methodological fallacy"* by assuming a definite functional relationship between the quantity of money and the rate of interest.

(4) *Money as a Store of Wealth is Barren.* Keynes holds that only money held for speculative purposes is fruitful for it brings interest as a reward, while *money as a store of wealth is barren.* This is a mistaken notion. As pointed out by W.H. Hutt, "money is as productive as all other assets, and productive in exactly the same sense. The demand for money assets is a demand for productive resources."

(5) *Inconsistent Theory.* Knight criticised Keynes's theory in view of the facts which are directly contrary to what the theory calls for. Hazlitt also discusses this point without giving credit to Knight. According to the Keynesian theory, the rate of interest should be the highest at the bottom of the depression because the liquidity preference is the strongest at that time due to falling prices. A large reward will have to be paid to induce wealth-holders to part with their cash. But the facts are just the opposite. Short-term interest rates are the lowest in a depression because investment opportunities are temporarily closed and the lenders have no outlets to part with their cash. Contrariwise, the Keynesian short-term interest rates should be lowest during the peak of the boom because people would be investing their money rather than keep it in cash. The liquidity preference being the lowest, a very small reward would be required to partake with it. But in reality, the rate of interest is the highest at the peak of a boom. Thus the *theory* is inconsistent with facts.

(6) *Saving Essential for Liquidity.* Keynes regards the rate of interest as the reward for parting with liquidity and not a return merely for saving or waiting as such. Saving is necessary for obtaining funds to be invested at interest. In Viner's words: "Without saving there can be no liquidity to surrender. The rate of interest is the return for saving without liquidity."

(7) *Liquidity not Essential for Interest Rate.* Even the term liquidity preference is neither helpful nor necessary in explaining the nature of interest. It is more confusing and less illuminating. It is not only vague but is also self-contradictory. For, as pointed out by Hazlitt, "If a man is holding his funds in the form of Time deposits or short-term Treasury bills, he is being paid interest on them; therefore he is getting interest and "liquidity" too. What becomes, then, of Keynes's theory that interest is the "reward" for parting with liquidity."

(8) *Wrong Notion of Liquidity Trap.* Keynes's notion of the "Liquidity Trap" is also wrong. In reality the liquidity preference schedule may be perfectly in*elastic* rather than elastic at a low rate of interest. We know that during depression all expectations are extremely pessimistic. It is, therefore, not correct to argue that expectations with regard to the rate of interest will be that it will go up.

(9) *Ignores Real Factors.* The greatest fallacy in Keynes's analysis is that he ignores the influence of real factors in determining the interest rate. He regards the interest rate as a purely monetary phenomenon and thus merely returns "to the pre-classical assumption of the mercantilists and to what has always been the assumption of the man in the street." Knut Wicksell was the first economist to present a real-cum-monetary theory of interest which was further refined and elaborated by Irving Fisher, Ludwig Von Mises and others before Keynes wrote. Hazlitt is justified when he says that "Keynes made no new contribution. He merely muddled shallow waters and the kind of *interest* theory represented by *him* is pre-classical, mercantilistic and

man in the street economics."[3]

(10) *Indeterminate Theory.* The Keynesian theory, like the classical theory of interest, is *indeterminate.* Keynes asserts that the liquidity preference and the quantity of money determine the rate of interest. But this is not correct for a new liquidity preference curve will have to be drawn at each level of income. Therefore, unless the income level is already known, the demand and supply curves of money cannot tell us what the rate of interest will be. Thus, according to Prof. Hansen, "Keynes's criticism of the classical theory applies equally to his own theory."

(11) *Incomplete Theory.* Hicks, Somers, Lerner, Hansen and others opine that the rate of interest, alongwith the level of income is determined by four factors: *(i)* the investment demand function *MEC, (ii)* The saving function (or the consumption function), *(iii)* the liquidity preference function, and *(iv)* the quantity of money function. Though all these elements are found in the Keynesian analysis, yet Keynes does not bring them in his interest theory. He takes only the last two elements and ignores the first two, thus Keynes fails to provide an integrated and determinate theory of interest.

(12) *Confusion regarding Relation between Interest Rate and Quantity of Money.* There is confusion in Keynes's analysis about the relation between rate of interest and amount of money. On the one hand, he says that the demand for money is inversely dependent on the rate of interest, and on the other, that the equilibrium rate of interest is inversely dependent upon the amount of money. Throughout his analysis, Keynes does not make any distinction between the two propositions and often uses them in an identical manner. This is a fundamental error in Keynes's analysis for the former relation holds true for an individual and the latter for the market.

To *conclude,* the Keynesian theory of interest is not only indeterminate, but is also an inadequate explanation of the determination of the rate of interest. It treats the interest rate as a purely monetary phenomenon and by neglecting the real factors makes the theory narrow and unrealistic.

EXERCISES

1. Critically discuss the Keynesian Theory of Liquidity Preference as an explanation of interest rate.
2. Explain Keynes' Liquidity Preference Theory of Interest Rate.

3. *Op. cit.*

CHAPTER 34

IS And LM Framework : Simultaneous Determination of Interest Rate and Income Level

1. INTRODUCTION

In this chapter, we study the simultaneous determination of interest rate and level of income through the *IS* and LM framework.

The term *IS* is the shorthand expression of the equality of investment and saving, and the term *LM* is the shorthand expression of the equality of money demand (L) and money supply (*M*).

2. THE IS CURVE

This *IS* curve is a curve which explains the relationship between a family of saving schedules and investment schedules. In other words, this curve shows the equality of saving and investment at various combinations of the levels of income and the rates of interest. In Figure 1 (*A*), the saving curve *S* in relation to income is drawn in a fixed position, since the influence of interest on saving is assumed to be negligible. The saving curve shows that saving increases as income increases, *viz.*, saving is an *increasing* function of income. Investment , on the other hand, depends on the rate of interest and the level of income. Given a level of interest rates, the level of investment rises with the level of income. At a 5 per cent rate of interest, the investment curve is I_2. If the rate of interest is reduced to 4 per cent, the investment curve will shift upward to I_3 . The rate of investment will have to be raised to reduce the marginal efficiency of capital to equality with the lower rate of interest. Thus the investment curve I_3 shows more investment at every level of income. Similarly, when the interest rate is raised to 6 per cent, the investment curve will shift downward to I_1. The reduction in the rate of investment is essential to raise the marginal efficiency of capital to equality with the higher interest rate. In Figure 1. (*B*), just below Figure 1 (*A*), we derive the *IS* curve by marking the level of income at various interest rates. Each point on this *IS* curve represents a level of income at which saving equals investment at various interest rates. The rate of interest is represented on "the vertical axis and the level of income on the horizontal axis. If the rate of interest is 6 per cent, the *S* curve intersects the I_1 curve at E_1 which determines OY_1 income.

From this income level which equals Rs. 100 crores, we draw a dashed line downward to intersect the extended line from 6 per cent at point *A*. At interest rate 5 per cent, the *S* curve intersects the I_2 curve at E_2 so as to determine OY_2 income (Rs. 200 crores). In the lower Figure 1. (*B*), point *B* corresponds to 5 per cent interest rate and Rs. 200 crores income level. Similarly, the point C corresponds to the equilibrium of *S* and I_3 at 4 per cent interest rate. By connecting these points *A*, *B* and *C* with a line, we get the *IS* curve. The *IS* curve slopes *downward* from left to right because as the interest rate falls, investment increases and so does income.

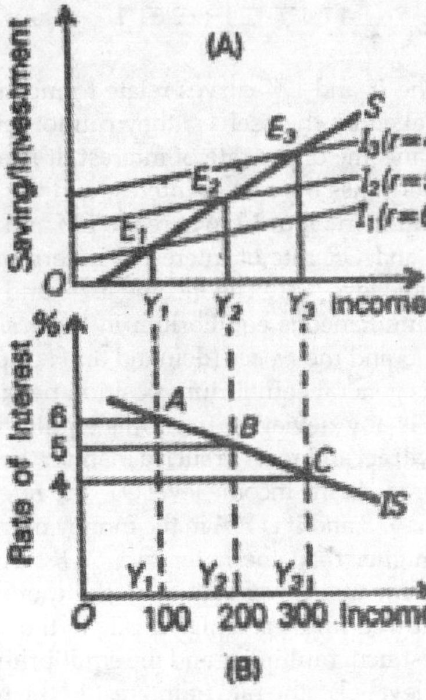

Fig. 1

3. THE LM CURVE

The *LM* curve shows all combinations of interest rates and levels of income at which the demand for and supply of money are equal. In other words, the *LM* schedule shows the combination of interest rates and the levels of income where the demand for money (*L*) and the supply of money (*M*) are equal. The *LM* curve is derived from the Keynesian formulation of liquidity preference (or demand for money) schedules and the schedule of supply of money. A family of liquidity preference curves L_1Y_1, L_2Y_2 and L_3Y_3 is drawn at income levels of Rs. 100 crores, Rs. 200 crores and Rs. 300 crores respectively, in Figure 2 (*A*). These curves together with the perfectly inelastic money supply curve *MQ* give us the *LM* curve. The *LM* curve consists of a series of points, each point representing an *interest-income* level at which the demand for money (*L*) equals the supply of money (*M*). If the income level is Y_1 (Rs. 100 crores), the demand for money (L_1Y_1) equals the money supply (*MQ*) at interest rate OR_1. At the Y_2 (Rs. 200 crores) income level, the L_2Y_2 and the *QM* curves equal at OR_2 interest rate. Similarly at the Y_3 (Rs 300 crores) income level, the L_3Y_3 and *QM* curves equal at OR_3 interest rate. The supply of money, the liquidity preference, the level of income and the rate of interest provide data for the *LM* curve shown in Figure 2. (*B*). Suppose the level of income is Y_1 (Rs. 100 crores), as marked out on the income axis in Figure 2. (B). The income of Rs. 100 crores generates a demand for money represented by the liquidity preference curve L_1Y_1. From the point E_1 where the L_1Y_1 curve intersects the *MQ* curve, extend a dashed line horizontally to the right so as to meet the line drawn upward from Y_1 at *K* in Figure 2 (B). Points *S* and *T* can also be determined in a similar manner. By connecting these points *K*, *S* and *T* with a line, we get the LM curve. This curve relates different income levels to various interest rates. The *LM* curve slopes *upward* from left to right because given the quantity of money, an increasing demand for money manifests itself in a higher rate of interest.

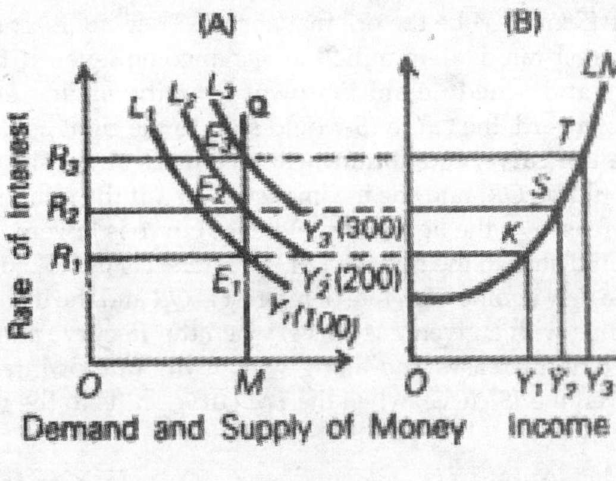

Fig. 2

4. SIMULTANEOUS DETERMINATION OF INTEREST RATE AND INCOME LEVEL

The *IS* and *LM* curves relate to income levels and interest rates. Taken by themselves, they cannot tell us either about the level of income or the rate of interest. It is only their intersection that determines the rate of interest and the level of income. This is illustrated in Figure 3, where the *LM* and *IS* curves intersect at point *E* and *OR* rate of interest is determined corresponding to the income level *OY*. The income level and the interest rate lead to the simultaneous equilibrium in the *real* (investment-saving) market *IS* and the *money* (demand and supply of money) market *LM*. This general equilibrium position persists at a point of time. If there is any deviation from this equilibrium position, certain forces will act and react in such a manner that the equilibrium will be restored. At the income level OY_1 the rate of interest in the real market is Y_1B and it is Y_1A in the money market. When the former rate is higher than the latter rate ($Y_1B > Y_1A$), the businessmen will borrow at a lower rate from the money market and invest the borrowed funds at a higher rate in the capital market. This will tend to raise the level of income to *OY* via the investment multiplier and the equilibrium level of *OR* interest rate will be reached. On the other hand, at the income level OY_2 the rate of interest in the real market is less than the interest rate in the money market ($Y_2C < Y_2D$). In this situation, the businessmen will try to discharge debts in the money market rather than invest in the capital market. As a result, investment will fall and reduce income by the multiplier to OY and the equilibrium rate of interest *OR* will be re-established.

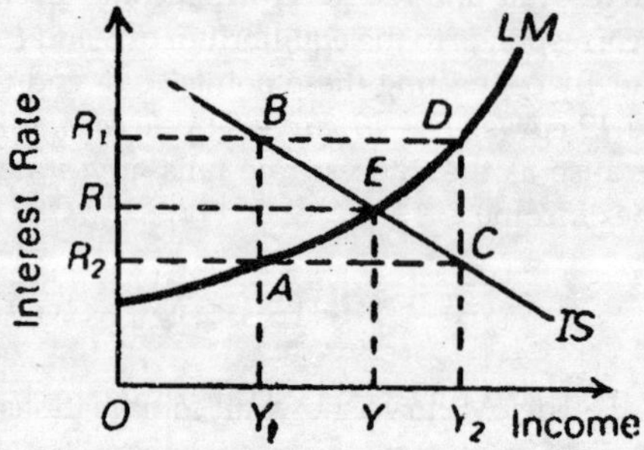

Fig. 3

Shifts or changes in the *IS* curve on the *LM* curve or in both, change the equilibrium position, and the rate of interest and income level are determined accordingly. These are illustrated in Figure 4. Let *IS* and *LM* be the original curves. They intersect at *E* where *OR* interest rate is determined at *OY* income level. If the investment demand schedule shifts upward, or the saving schedule shifts downward, the curve *IS* would shift to the right as IS_1 curve. Given the LM curve, equilibrium will take place at E_1. The rate of interest would be OR_1 and the income level OY_1. If the quantity of money is increased or the liquidity preference curve is lowered, the *LM* curve would shift to the right as LM_1. It intersects the IS_1 curve at point E_1. The new equilibrium rate of interest is *OR* and the income level is OY_2. Thus with a given *LM* curve, when the *IS* curve shifts to the right, income increases and along with it the rate of interest also rises. Given the *IS* curve, when the *LM* curve shifts to the right, income increases but the rate of interest falls.

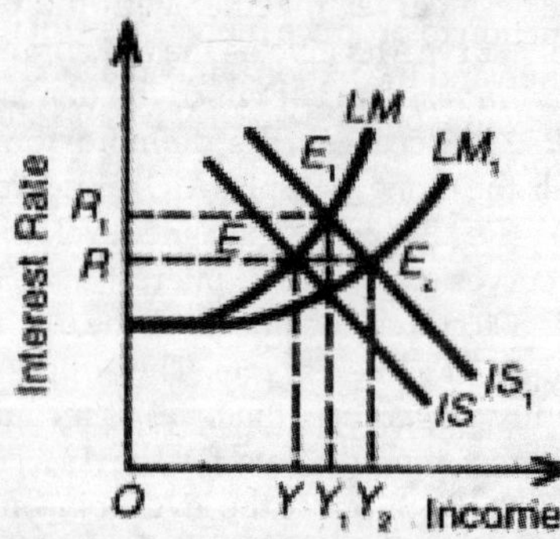

Fig. 4

EXERCISES

1. Use *IS-LM* framework to explain the joint determination of the rate of interest and the level of income.
2. Derive an *IS* and *LM* curve.
3. Use the *IS-LM* technique to determine the simultaneous equilibrium of the rate of interest and the level of income.

CHAPTER 35

Foreign Trade Multiplier

1. WORKING OF FOREIGN TRADE MULTIPLIER

The foreign trade multiplier, also known as the export multiplier, operates like the investment multiplier of Keynes. It may be defined as *the amount by which the national income of a country will be raised by a unit increase in domestic investment on exports.*

As exports increase, there is an increase in the income of all persons associated with export industries. These, in turn, create demand for goods. But this is dependent upon their marginal propensity to save (MPS) and the marginal propensity to import (MPM). The smaller these two marginal propensities are, the larger will be the value of the multiplier, and vice versa. The foreign trade multiplier process can be explained like this. Suppose the exports of the country increase. To begin with, the exporters will sell their products to foreign countries and receive more income. In order to meet the foreign demand, they will engage more factors of production to produce more. This will raise the income of the owners of factors of production. This process will continue and the national income increases by the value of the multiplier. The value of the multiplier depends on the value of MPS and MPM, there being an inverse relation between the two propensities and the export multiplier.

The foreign trade multiplier can be derived algebraically as follows :

The national income identity in an open economy is

$$Y = C + I + X - M$$

where Y is national income, C is national consumption, I is total investment, X is exports and M is imports.

The above relationship can be solved as:

$$Y - C = I + X - M$$

or

$$S = I + X - M \quad (\because S = Y - C)$$

$$S + M = I + X$$

Thus at equilibrium levels of income the sum of savings and imports (S + M) must equal the sum of investment and export (I + X).

In an open economy the investment (I) component is divided into domestic investment (I_d) and foreign investment (I_f)

$$I = S$$

$$I_d + I_f = S \qquad ...(1)$$

Foreign investment (I_f) is the difference between exports and imports of goods and services.

$$I_f = X - M \qquad ...(2)$$

Substituting (2) into (1), we have

$$I_d + X - M = S$$

or

$$I_d + X = S + M$$

which is the equilibrium condition of national income in an open economy. The foreign trade multiplier coefficient (K_f) is equal to

$$K_f = \frac{\Delta Y}{\Delta X}$$

and

$$\Delta X = \Delta S + \Delta M \qquad [\because I_d = 0]$$

Dividing both sides by ΔY, we get

$$\frac{\Delta X}{\Delta Y} = \frac{\Delta S + \Delta M}{\Delta Y}$$

or

$$\frac{\Delta Y}{\Delta X} = \frac{\Delta Y}{\Delta S + \Delta M}$$

or

$$K_f = \frac{\Delta Y}{\Delta S + \Delta M} \qquad \left(\because K_f = \frac{\Delta Y}{\Delta X}\right)$$

$\therefore$

$$K_f = \frac{1}{\frac{\Delta S}{\Delta Y} + \frac{\Delta M}{\Delta Y}} \qquad (\because \text{Dividing by } \Delta Y)$$

Hence

$$K_f = \frac{1}{MPS + MPM}$$

Let us understand it with the help of an example.

Suppose $MPS = 0.3$, $MPM = 0.2$ and ΔX (increase in exports) = Rs. 1000 crores, we get

$$K_f = \frac{\Delta Y}{\Delta X} = \frac{1}{MPS + MPM}$$

or

$$\Delta Y = \frac{1}{MPS + MPM} \Delta X$$

$$= \frac{1}{0.3 + 0.2} \times 1000 = \text{Rs. } 2000 \text{ crores}$$

It shows that an increase in exports by Rs. 1000 crores has raised national income through foreign trade multiplier by Rs. 2000 crores, given the values of *MPS* and *MPM*.

Its Assumptions

The foreign trade multiplier is based on the following assumptions :

1. There is full employment in the domestic economy.
2. There is direct link between the domestic and the foreign country in exporting and importing goods.
3. The country is small with no foreign repercussion effects.
4. It is on a fixed exchange rate system.
5. The multiplier is based on instantaneous process without time lags.
6. There is no accelerator.
7. There are no tariff barriers and exchange controls.
8. Domestic investment (I_d) remains constant.
9. Government expenditure is constant.

Diagrammatic Explanation

Given these assumptions, the equilibrium level in the economy is shown in Figure 1, where $S(Y)$ is the saving function and $(S + M)Y$ is the saving plus import function. I_d represents domestic investment and $I_d + X$ the exports plus domestic investment. The $(S + M)Y$ and $I_d + X$ functions determine the equilibrium leve of national income OY at point E, where savings equal domestic investment and exports equal imports.

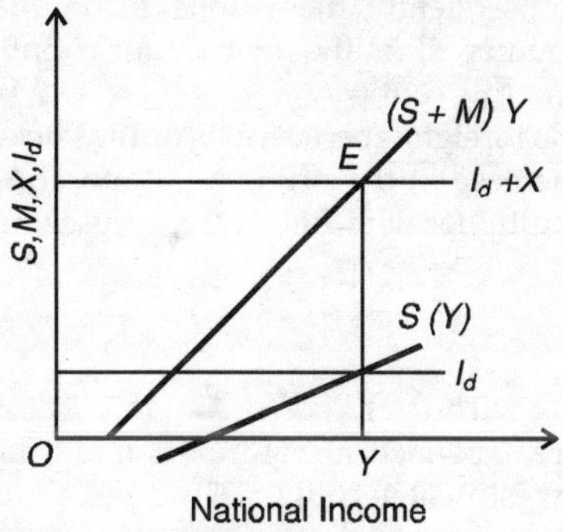

FIG. 1

If there is a shift in the $I_d + X$ function due to an increase in exports, the national income will increase from OY to OY_1, as shown in Figure 2. This increase in income is due to the multiplier effect i.e. $\Delta Y = K_f\ \Delta X$. The exports will exceed imports by sd, the amount by which savings will exceed domestic investment. The new equilibrium level of income will be OY_1. It is a case of positive foreign investment.

If there is a fall in exports, the export function will shift downward to $I_d + X_1$, as shown in Figure 3. In this case imports would exceed exports and domestic investment would exceed savings by ds. The level of national income is reduced from OY to OY_1. This is the reverse operation of the foreign trade multiplier.

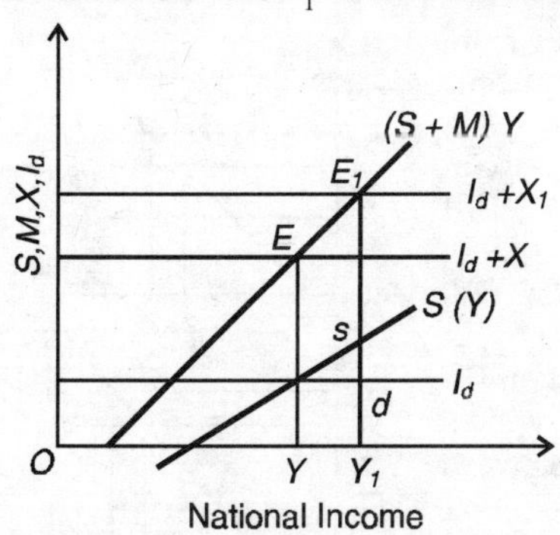

FIG. 2

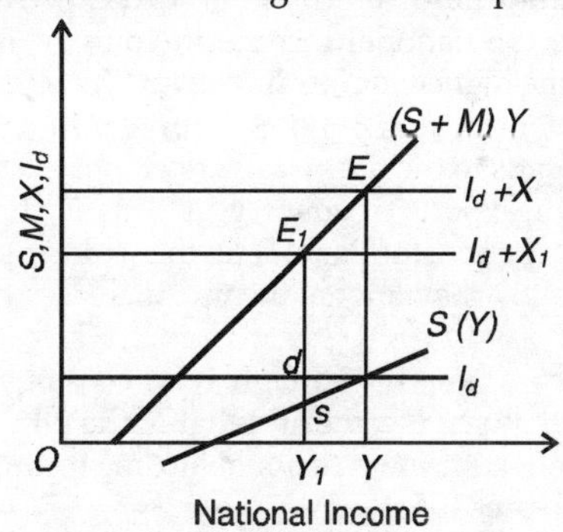

FIG. 3

Foreign Repercussion or Backwash Effect

The above analysis of the simple foreign trade multiplier has been studied in the case of one small country. But, in reality, countries are linked to each other indirectly also. A country's exports or imports affect the national income of the other country which, in turn, affects the foreign trade and national income of the first country. This is known as the *Foreign Repercussion* or *Backwash* or *Feedback Effect*. The smaller the country is in relation to other trading partner, the negligible is the foreign repercussion. But the foreign repercussion will be high in the case of a large country because a change in the national income of such a country will have significant foreign repercussions or backwash effects. Assuming two large countries A and B where A's imports are B's exports and vice versa. An increase in A's domestic investment will cause a multiplier increase in its income. This will increase its imports. This increase in A's imports will be increase in B's exports which will increase income in B through B's foreign trade multiplier. Now the increase in B's income will bring an increase in its imports from country A which will induce a second round increase in A's income, and so on. This is explained in Table 1. When autonomous domestic investment (I_d) increases in country A, its national income increases (+ Y). It induces country A to import more from country B. This increases the demand for country B's exports (X +).

Table 1

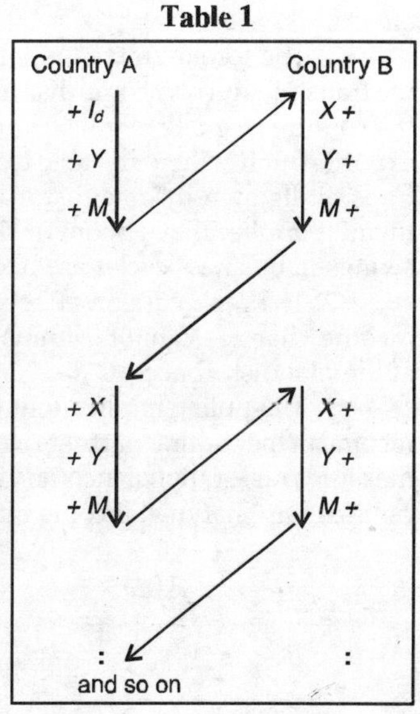

Consequently, the national income in country B increases (Y +). Now this country imports more (M +) from country A. As the demand for country A's exports increases (+ X), its national income (+ Y) increases further and this country imports more (+ M) from B country. This process will continue in smaller rounds. These are the foreign repercussions or the backwash effects for country A which will peter out and dampen the effects of increase in the original autonomous domestic investment (I_d) in country A. The formula of foreign trade multiplier with foreign repercussions for country A is

$$K_f = \frac{1 + (MPM_B / MPS_B)}{MPS_A + MPM_A + MPM_B\ (MPS_A / MPS_B)}$$

The stages of foreign repercussions shown in the above table are explained in Figure 4 Panel I, II and III. In stage I, domestic investment in country A increases from I_d to I_{d1} in Panel I. This leads to an upward shift in the $I_d + X$ curve to $I_{d1} + X$. As a result, the new equilibrium point is at E_1 which shows an increase in the national income from OY to OY_1. As the national income increases, the demand for imports from country B also increases. This means increase in the exports of country B. This is shown in Panel II when the $I_d + X$ schedule of country B shifts upwards as $I_d + X_1$. Consequently, the national income in country B increases from OY_0 to OY' at the higher equilibrium level E'. As country B's income increases, its demand for imports from country A also increases. This, in turn, leads to the backwash effect in the form of increase in the demand for exports of country A. This is shown in Panel III where the $I_{d1} + X$ curve (of Panel I) further shifts upwards to $I_{d1} + X_1$ and con-sequently the national income increases further from OY_1 to OY_2.

This shows how the foreign repercussions in one country affect its own national income and that of the other country which, in turn, again affects its own national income through the backwash effects with greater force.

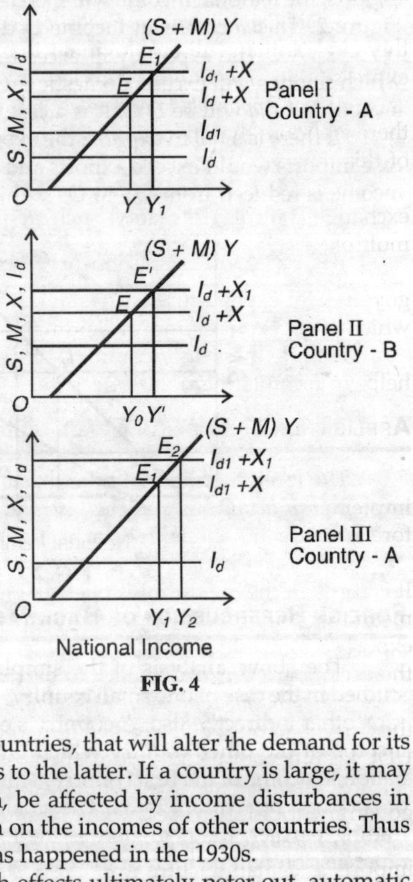

FIG. 4

Implications of Foreign Repercussion

The following are the implications of foreign repercussion effects.

1. The foreign repercussion effects suggest a mechanism for the transmission of income disturbances between trading countries. If a country is small, it will be affected by change in income of other countries, that will alter the demand for its exports. But it will not be able to transmit its own income disturbances to the latter. If a country is large, it may transmit its own income disturbances to other countries and, in turn, be affected by income disturbances in them. It implies that a boom or slump in one country has repercussion on the incomes of other countries. Thus swings in business cycles are likely to be internationally contagious, as happened in the 1930s.

2. The repercussion effects also suggest that since the backwash effects ultimately peter out, automatic income changes cannot eliminate completely the current account BOP deficit or surplus produced by an automatic disturbance.

3. The policy implications of the backwash effects suggest that export promotion policies raise national income in the trading partners at a lower rate than by an increase in domestic investment. The export promotion measures raise rational income via the simple foreign trade multiplier, whereas increase in domestic investment policies raise national income many times in multiplier rounds via the repercussion effects.

CRITICISMS OF FOREIGN TRADE MULTIPLIER

The two models of the foreign trade multiplier presented above are based on certain assumptions which make the analysis unrealistic.

1. *Exports and Investment not Independent*. The analysis of simple foreign trade multiplier is based on the assumption that exports and investment (both domestic and foreign) are independent of changes in the level of national income. But, in reality, this is not so. A rise in exports does not always lead to increase in national income. On the contrary, certain imports, of say capital goods, have the effect of increasing the national income.

2. *Lagless Analysis*. The foreign trade multiplier is assumed to be an instantaneous process whereby it supplies the final results. Thus it involves no lags and is unrealistic.

3. *Full Employment not Realistic*. The analysis is based on the assumption of a fully employed economy. But there is less than full employment in every economy. Thus the foreign trade multiplier does not find clear expression in an economy with less than full employment.

4. *Not Applicable to More than two Countries*. The whole analysis is applicable to a two-country model. If there are more than two countries, it becomes complicated to analyse and interpret the foreign repercussions of this theory.

5. *Neglects Trade Restrictions*. The foreign trade multiplier assumes that there are no tariff barriers and exchange controls. In reality, such trade restrictions exist which restrict the operations of the foreign trade multiplier.

6. *Neglects Monetary-Fiscal Measures*. This analysis is based on the unrealistic assumption that the government expenditure is constant. But governments always interfere through monetary and fiscal policies which affect exports, imports and national income.

Despite these shortcomings, the foreign trade multiplier is a powerful tool of economic analysis which helps in formulating policy measures.

APPLICATION OF FOREIGN TRADE MULTIPLIER TO UNDER-DEVELOPED COUNTRIES (UDCs)

The foreign trade multiplier has important implications for UDCs. The value of this multiplier helps in implementing various policies. It is particularly important in those economies where the contribution of foreign trade in national income is high.

1. *Basis for Export Promotion Policies*. The foreign trade multiplier supports export related policies in UDCs. It is through the export multiplier that a country can increase its national income many times. But it does not mean that imports should be reduced to increase exports. Prof. Lewis opines in this context that to make the export sector leading and developed, it is essential to adopt the policy of import substitution. In this way, both the sectors are complementary to each other.[1]

2. *Improvement in Balance of Payments*. UDCs are always faced with the BOP deficit. Under such a situation, the current account BOP can be improved by increasing exports. Moreover, by increasing domestic investment, UDCs can benefit through the repercussion or backwash effects.

3. *Incentive for Domestic Industries*. By providing incentives to domestic industries for exports, the government can increase income by multiplier times through the export multiplier.

4. *Encouragement to Foreign Investment*. Mostly goods are imported from abroad in UDCs. To cut down imports and manufacture import substitution goods, the governments of such countries encourage foreign investment. Foreign investors set up import substitution industries in UDCs which are also exported in the long run. Thus the increase in exports help in raising national income multiplier times in such countries.

EXERCISES

1. Explain the Foreign Trade Multiplier without and with foreign repercussions.
2. What is a foreign trade multiplier? How does it work? State its policy implications from the view point of under-developed economy.
3. Explain the working and limitations of foreign trade multipliers.
4. Explain the inter-relationship between national income and international trade of a country.

CHAPTER 36

The Keynesian Theory of Income, Output and Employment : A Summary

1. INTRODUCTION

Keynes restated his theory of employment in Chapter 18 of *General Theory*. We have analysed in detail the various dependent and independent variables of the Keynesian system in the foregoing chapters. Now we combine them together, as Keynes did, and present the theory of income, output and employment briefly.

2. THE KEYNESIAN THEORY OF INCOME, OUTPUT AND EMPLOYMENT

In the Keynesian theory, employment depends upon effective demand. Effective demand results in output. Output creates income. Income provides employment. Since Keynes assumes all these four quantities, viz., effective demand (*ED*), output (*Q*), income (*Y*) and employment (*N*) equal to each other, he regards employment as a function of income.

Effective demand is determined by two factors, the aggregate supply function and the aggregate demand function. The aggregate supply function depends on physical or technical conditions of production which do not change in the short-run. Since Keynes assumes the aggregate supply function to be stable, he concentrates his entire attention upon the aggregate demand function to fight depression and unemployment. Thus employment depends on aggregae demand which in turn is determined by consumption demand and investment demand.

According to Keynes, employment can be increased by increasing consumption and/or investment. Consumption depends on income *C*(*Y*) and when income rises, consumption also rises but not as much as income. In other words, as income rises, saving rises. Consumption can be increased by raising the propensity to consume in order to increase income and employment. But the propensity to consume depends upon the psychology of the people, their tastes, habits, wants and the social structure which determine the distribution of income. All these elements remain constant during the short-run. Therefore, the propensity to consume is stable. Employment thus depends on investment and it varies in the same direction as the volume of investment.

Investment, in turn, depends on the rate of interest and the marginal efficiency of capital (*MEC*). Investment can be increased by a fall in the rate of interest and/or a rise in the *MEC*. The *MEC* depends on the supply price of capital assets and their prospective yield. It can be raised when the supply price of capital assets falls or their prospective yield increases. Since the supply price of capital assets is stable in the short-run, it is difficult to lower it. The second determinant of *MEC* is the prospective yield of capital assets which depends on the expectations of yields on the part of businessmen. It is again a psychological factor which cannot be depended upon to increase the *MEC* to raise investment. Thus there is little scope for increasing investment by raising the *MEC*.

The other determinant of investment is the rate of interest. Investment and employment can be increased by lowering the rate of interest. The rate of interest is determined by the demand for money and the supply of money. On the demand side is the liquidity preference (*LP*) schedule. The higher the liquidity preference, the higher is the rate of interest that will have to be paid to cash holders to induce them to part with their liquid assets, and vice versa. People hold money (*M*) in cash for three motives: transactions, precautionary and speculative. The transactions and precautionary motives (*M*) are *income elastic*. Thus the amount held under these two motives (M_1) is a function (L_1) of the level of income (*Y*), *i.e.* $M_1=L_1(Y)$. But the money held for speculative motive (M_2) is a function of the rate of interest (*r*), *i.e.* $M_2=L_2(r)$. The higher the rate of interest, the lower the demand for money, and vice versa. Since *LP* depends on the psychological attitude to liquidity on the part of speculators with regard to future interest rates, it is not possible to lower the liquidity preference in order to bring down the rate of interest. The other determinant of interest rate is the supply of money which is assumed to be fixed by the monetary authority during the short-run.

The relation between interest rate, *MEC* and investment is shown in Figure1, where in Panels (*A*) and (*B*) the total demand for money is measured along the horizontal axis from *M* onward. The transactions (and precautionary) demand is given by the L_1 curve at OY_1 and OY_2 levels of income in Panel (A) of the figure. Thus at OY_1 income level, the transactions demand is given by OM_1 and at OY_2 level of income it is OM_2. In Panel (B), the L_2 curve represents the speculative demand for money as a function of the rate of interest. When the rate of interest is R_2, the speculative demand for money is MM_2. With the fall in the rate of interest to R_1, the speculative demand for money increases to MM_1. Panel (C) shows investment as a function of the rate of interest and the *MEC*. Given the *MEC*, when the rate of interest is R_2, the level of investment is OI_1. But when the rate of interest falls to R_1, investment increases to OI_2.

In the Keynesian analysis, the equilibrium level of employment and income is determined at the point of equality between saving and investment. Saving is a function of income, *i.e.* $S=f(Y)$. It is defined as the excess of income over consumption, $S=Y-C$, and income is equal to consumption plus investment.

Thus $\quad Y = C+I$

or $\quad Y-C = I$

$\because \quad Y-C = S$

$\therefore \quad I = S$

So the equilibrium level of income is established where saving equals investment. This is shown in Panel (D) of Figure 1 where the horizontal axis from *O* toward the right represents investment and saving, and *OY* axis represents income. *S* is the saving curve. The line I_1E_1 is the investment curve (imagine that it can be extended beyond *E* as in an *S* and *I* diagram) which touches the *S* curve at E_1* Thus OY_1 is the equilibrium level of employment and income. This is the level of underemployment equilibrium, according to Keynes. If OY_2 is assumed to be the full employment level of income then the equality between saving and investment will take place at E_2 where I_2E_2 investment equals Y_2E_2 saving.

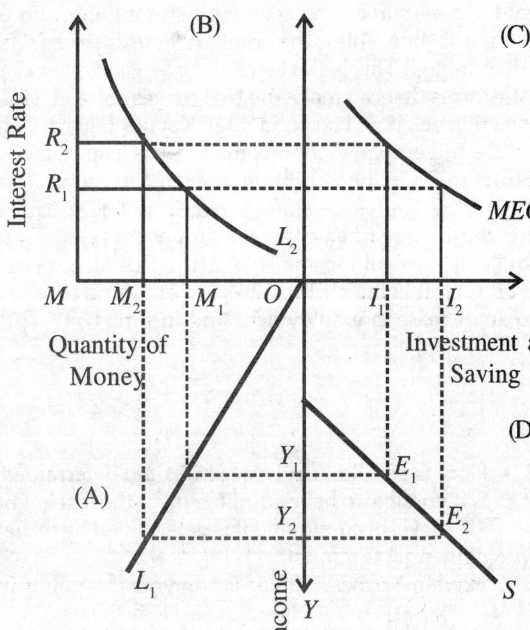

Fig. 1

* For its understanding, the reader should so hold the figure that the word INCOME is towards him.

The Keynesian theory of employment and income is also explained in terms of the equality of aggregate supply ($C+S$) and aggregate demand ($C+I$). Since unemployment results from the deficiency of aggregate demand, employment and income can be increased by increasing aggregate demand. Assuming the propensity to consume to be stable during the short-run, aggregate demand can be increased by increasing investment. Once investment increases, employment and income increase. Increased income leads to a rise in the demand for consumption goods which leads to further increase in employment and income. Once set in motion, employment and income tend to rise in a cumulative manner through the multiplier process till they reach the equilibrium level. According to Keynes, the equilibrium level of employment will be one of *under-employment equilibrium* because when income increases consumption also increases but by less than the increase in income. This behaviour of the consumption function widens the gap between income and consumption which ordinarily cannot by filled up due to the lack of required investment. The full employment income level can only be established if the volume of investment is increased to fill the income-consumption gap corresponding to full employment.

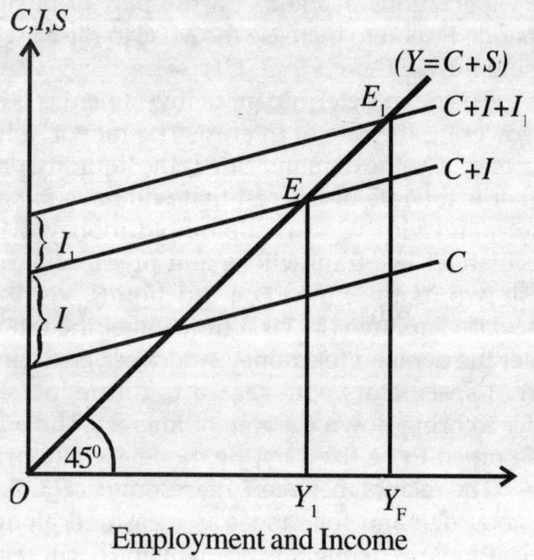

Fig. 2

The Keynesian cross model of under-employment equilibrium is explained in Figure 2 where income and employment are taken on the horizontal axis and consumption and investment on the vertical axis. Autonomous investment is taken as a first approximation. $C+I$ is the aggregate demand curve plotted by adding to consumption function C an equal amount of investment at all levels of income. The 45^0 line is the aggregate supply curve. The economy is in equilibrium at point E where the aggregate demand curve $C+I$ intersects the 45^0 line. This is the point of *effective demand* where the equilibrium level of income and employment OY_1 is determined. This is the level of *under-employment equilibrium* and not of full employment. There are no automatic forces that can make the two curves cross at a full employment income level. If it happens to be a full employment level, it will be accidental. Keynes regarded the under-employment equilibrium level as a normal case and the full employment income level as a special case.

Suppose OY_F is the full employment income level. To reach this level, autonomous investment is increased by I_1 so that the $C+I$ curve shifts upward as $C+I+I_1$ curve. This is the new aggregate demand curve which intersects the 45^0 line (the aggregate supply curve) at E_1, the higher point of effective demand corresponding to the full employment income level OY_F. This also reveals that to get a desired increase in employment and income of Y_1Y_F, it is the multiplier effect of an increase in investment by I_1 ($=I_2$ in Panel C of Figure 1) which leads to an increase in employment and income by Y_1Y_F through successive rounds of investment.

EXERCISES

1. How is equilibrium level of income determined under the Keynesian system ?
2. Is it possible to have equilibrium in the level of national income without achieving full employment?
3. "The level of employment is determined by the level of income which in turn depends upon aggregate demand." Comment.
4. Explain Keynes's under-employment equilibrium.

CHAPTER 37

National Income : Meaning and Measurement

1. INTRODUCTION

National income is an uncertain term which is used interchangeably with national dividend, national output and national expenditure. On this basis, national income has been defined in a number of ways. In common parlance, national income means the total value of goods and services produced annually in a country. In other words, the total amount of income accruing to a country from economic activities in a year's time, is known as national income. It includes payments made to all resources in the form of wages, interest, rent and profits.

2. DEFINITIONS OF NATIONAL INCOME

The definitions of national income can be grouped into two classes: *One*, the traditional definitions advanced by Marshall, Pigou and Fisher; and *two*, modern definitions.

THE MARSHALLIAN DEFINITION

According to Marshall: "The labour and capital of a country acting on its natural resources produce annually a certain net aggregate of commodities, material and immaterial including services of all kinds. ...This is the true net annual income or revenue of the country or national dividend."[1] In this definition, the word 'net' refers to deductions from the gross national income in respect of depreciation and wearing out of machines. And to this, must be added income from abroad.

Its Defects. Though the definition advanced by Marshall is simple and comprehensive, yet it suffers from a number of limitations. *First*, in the present day world, so varied and numerous are the goods and services produced that it is very difficult to have a correct estimation of them. Consequently, the national income cannot be calculated correctly. *Second*, there always exists the fear of the mistake of double counting, and hence the national income cannot be correctly estimated. Double counting means that a particular commodity or

1. A. Marshall, *Principles of Economics*, p. 434.

service like raw material or labour, etc. might get included in the national income twice or more than twice. For example, a peasant sells wheat worth Rs. 2,000 to a flour mill which sells wheat flour to the wholesaler and the wholesaler sells it to the retailer who, in turn, sells it to the customers. If each time, this wheat or its flour is taken into consideration, it will work out to Rs. 8,000, whereas, in actuality, there is only an increase of Rs. 2,000 in the national income. *Third,* it is again not possible to have a correct estimation of national income because many of the commodities produced are not marketed and the producer either keeps the produce for self-consumption or exchages it for other commodities. It generally happens in an agriculture-oriented country like India. Thus the volume of national income is underestimated.

The Pigouvian Definition

Marshall's follower, A.C. Pigou, has in his definition of national income included that income which can be measured in terms of money. In the words of Pigou, "National income is that part of objective income of the community, including of course income derived from abroad which can be measured in money."[2] This definition is better than the Marshallian definition. It has proved to be more practical also. While calculating the national income now-a-days, estimates are prepared in accordance with the two criteria laid down in this definition. *First,* avoiding double counting, the goods and services which can be measured in money are included in national income. *Second,* income received on account of investment in foreign countries is included in national income.

Its Defects. The Pigouvian definition is precise, simple and practical but it is not free from criticisms. *First,* in the light of the definition put forth by Pigou, we have unnecessarily to differentiate between commodities which can and which cannot be exchanged for money. But, in actuality, there is no difference in the fundamental forms of such commodities, no mattter they can be exchanged for money. *Second,* according to this definition when only such commodities as can be exchanged for money are included in estimation of national income, the national income cannot be correctly measured. According to Pigou, a woman's services as a nurse would be included in national income but excluded when she worked in the home to look after her children because she did not receive any salary for it. Similarly, Pigou is of the view that if a man marries his lady secretary, the national income diminishes as he has no longer to pay for her services. Thus the Pigovian definition gives rise to a number of paradoxes. *Third,* the Pigovian definition is applicable only to the developed countries where goods and services are exchanged for money in the market. According to this definition, in the backward and underdeveloped countries of the world, where a major portion of the produce is simply bartered, correct estimate of national income will not be possible, because it will always work out less than the real level. Thus the definition advanced by Pigou has a limited scope.

Fisher's Definition

Fisher adopted 'consumption' as the criterion of national income whereas Marshall and Pigou regarded it to be production. According to Fisher, "The National dividend or income consists solely of services as received by ultimate consumers, whether from their material or from the human environments. Thus, a piano, or an overcoat made for me this year is not a part of this year's income, but an addition to the capital. Only the services rendered to me during this year by these things are income."[3] Fisher's definition is considered to be better than that of Marshall or Pigou, because Fisher's definition provides an adequate concept of economic welfare which is dependent on consumption and consumption represents our standard of living.

Its Defects. But from the practical point of view, this definition is less useful, because there are certain difficulties in measuring the goods and services in terms of money. *First,* it is more difficult to estimate the money value of net consumption than that of net production. In one country there are several individuals who consume a particular good and that too at different places and, therefore, it is very difficult to estimate their total consumption in terms of money. *Second,* certain consumption goods are durable and last for many years. If we consider the example of piano or overcoat, as given by Fisher, only the services rendered to use during

2. A.C. Pigou, *The Economics of Welfare,* p. 31.
3. I. Fisher, *The Nature of Capital and Income,* p. 104.

one year by them will be included in income. If an overcoat costs Rs. 100 and lasts for ten years, Fisher will take into account only Rs. 10 as national income during one year, whereas Marshall and Pigou will include Rs. 100 in the national income for the year, when it is made. Besides, it cannot be said with certainty that the overcoat will last only for ten years. It may last longer or for a shorter period. *Third*, the durable goods generally keep changing hands leading to a change in their ownership and value too. It, therefore, becomes difficult to measure in money the service-value of these goods from the point of view of consumption. For instance, the owner of a Maruti sells it at a price higher than its real price and the purchaser after using it for a number of years, further sells it at its actual price. Now the question is as to which of its price, whether actual or black market one, should we take into account, and afterwards when it is transferred from one person to another, which of its value according to its average age should be included in national income?

But the definitions advanced by Marshall, Pigou and Fisher are not altogether flawless. However, the Marshallian and Pigovian definitions tell us of the reasons influencing economic welfare, whereas Fisher's definition helps us compare economic welfare in different years.

From the *modern point of view*, Simon Kuznets has defined national income as "the net output of commodities and services flowing during the year from the country's productive system in the hands of the ultimate consumers." On the other hand, in one of the reports of United Nations, national income has been defined on the basis of the systems of estimating national income, as net national product, as addition to the shares of different factors, and as net national expenditure in a country in a year's time. In practice, while estimating national income, any of these three definitions may be adopted, because the same national income would be derived, if different items were correctly included in the estimate.

3. CONCEPTS OF NATIONAL INCOME

There are a number of concepts pertaining to national income and methods of measurement relating to them.

(A) Gross Domestic Product (GDP)

GDP is the total value of goods and services produced within the country during a year. This is calculated at market prices and is known as *GDP* at market prices. Dernberg defines *GDP* at market price as "the market value of the output of final goods and services produced in the domestic territory of a country during an accounting year."

There are three different ways to measure *GDP* : Product Method, Income Method and Expenditure Method. These three methods of calculating *GDP* yield the same result because National Product = National Income = National Expenditure.

1. *The Product Method.* In this method, the value of all goods and services produced in different industries during the year is added up. This is also known as the Value Added Method to *GDP* or *GDP* at Factor Cost by Industry of Origin. The following items are included in India in this : agriculture and allied services; mining; manufacturing, construction, electricity, gas and water supply; transport, communication and trade; banking and insurance, real estates and ownership of dwellings and business services; and public administration and defence and other services (or government services). In other words, it is the sum of Gross Value Added.*

2. *The Income Method*. The people of a country who produce *GDP* during a year receive incomes from their work. Thus *GDP* by income method is the sum of all factor incomes : Wages and Salaries (compensation of employees) + Rent + Interest + Profit.

3. *Expenditure Method.* This method focuses on goods and services produced within the country during one year. *GDP* by expenditure method includes : (1) consumer expenditure on services and durable and non-durable goods (C),

---

* For a detailed study of this method refer to "Value Added Approach to GDP."

(2) investment in fixed capital such as residential and non-residential building, machinery, and inventories (I),

(3) government expenditure on final goods and services (G),

(4) export of goods and services produced by people of the country (X),

(5) *less* imports (M). That part of consumption, investment and government expenditure which is spent on imports is subtracted from *GDP*. Similarly, any imported component, such as raw material, which is used in the manufacture of export goods is also excluded.

Thus *GDP* by expenditure method at market prices = C+ I + G + (X – M), where (X–M) is net export which can be positive or negative.

(B) GDP at Factor Cost

GDP at factor cost is the sum of net value added by all producers within the country. Since the net value added gets distributed as income to the owners of factors of production, *GDP* is the sum of domestic factor incomes and fixed capital consumption (or depreciation).

Thus *GDP* at Factor Cost = Net value added + Depreciation.

GDP at factor cost includes : (*i*) Compensation of Employees i.e., wages, salaries, etc. (*ii*) Operating Surplus** which is the business profit of both incorporated and unincorporated firms. (*iii*) Mixed Income of Self-employed.

Conceptually, *GDP* at factor cost and *GDP* at market price must be identical. This is because the factor cost (payments to factors) of producing goods must equal the final value of goods and services at market prices. However, the market value of goods and services is different from the earnings of the factors of production. In *GDP* at market price are included indirect taxes and are excluded subsidies by the government. Therefore, in order to arrive at *GDP* at factor cost, indirect taxes are subtracted and subsidies are added to *GDP* at market price.

Thus, *GDP* at Factor Cost = *GDP* at Market Price – Indirect Taxes + Subsidies.

(C) Net Domestic Product (NDP)

NDP is the value of *net* output of the economy during the year. Some of the country's capital equipment wears out or becomes obsolete each year during the production process. The value of this capital consumption* is some percentage of gross investment which is deducted from *GDP*. Thus Net Domestic Product = *GDP* at Factor Cost – Depreciation.

(D) Nominal and Real GDP

When *GDP* is measured on the basis of *current prices*, it is called *GDP* at current prices or *nominal GDP*. On the other hand, when *GDP* is calculated on the basis of *fixed prices* in some year, it is called *GDP* at constant prices or *real GDP*.

Nominal *GDP* is the value of goods and services produced in a year and measured in terms of rupees (money) at current (market) prices. In comparing one year with another, we are faced with the problem that the rupee is not a stable measure of purchasing power. *GDP* may rise a great deal in a year, not because the economy has been growing rapidly but because of rise in prices (or inflation). On the contrary, *GDP* may increase as a result of fall in prices in a year but actually it may be less as compared to the last year. In both the cases, *GDP* does not show the real state of the economy. To rectify the underestimation and overestimation of *GDP*, we need a measure that adjusts for rising and falling prices. This can be done by measuring *GDP* at constant prices which is called *real GDP*. To find out the real *GDP*, a base year is chosen when the general price level is normal, i.e., it is neither too high nor too low. The prices are set to 100 (or 1) in the base year. Now the general price level of the year for which real *GDP* is to be calculated is related to the base year on the basis of

---

* Depreciation is called capital consumption.

** [Operating Surplus = Gross Value Added at Factor Cost—Compensation of Employees—Depreciation]

the following formula which is called the *deflator index* :

$$\text{Real } GDP = \frac{\text{GDP for the}}{\text{Current Year}} \times \frac{\text{Base Year } (=100)}{\text{Current Year Index}}$$

Suppose 1990-91 is the base year and *GDP* for 1999-2000 is Rs. 6,00,000 crores and the price index for this year is 300.

Thus, Real *GDP* for 1999-2000 = Rs. 6,00,000 ´ 100/300 = Rs. 2,00,000 crores.

(E) GDP Deflator

GDP deflator is an index of price changes of goods and services included in *GDP*. It is a price index which is calculated by dividing the nominal *GDP* in a given year by the real *GDP* for the same year and multiplying it by 100. Thus,

$$GDP \text{ Deflator} = \frac{\text{Nominal (or Current Prices) GDP}}{\text{Real (or Constant Prices) GDP}} \times 100$$

$$\text{For example, GDP Deflator in 1997-98} = \frac{\text{1426.7th. crores}}{\text{1049.2th crores at 1993-94 prices}} \times 100 = 135.9$$

It shows that at constant prices (1993-94), *GDP* in 1997-98 increased by 135.9% due to inflation (or rise in prices) from Rs. 1049.2 thousand crores in 1993-94 to Rs. 1426.7 thousand crores in 1997-98.

(F) Gross National Product (GNP)

GNP is the total measure of the flow of goods and services at market value resulting from current production during a year in a country, including net income from abroad. *GNP* includes four types of final goods and services: (1) consumers' goods and services to satisfy the immediate wants of the people; (2) gross private domestic investment in capital goods consisting of fixed capital formation, residential construction and inventories of finished and unfinished goods; (3) goods and services produced by the government; and (4) net exports of goods and services, *i.e.*, the difference between value of exports and imports of goods and services, known as net income from abroad.

In this concept of *GNP*, there are certain factors that have to be taken into consideration :

First, *GNP* is the measure of money, in which all kinds of goods and services produced in a country during one year are measured in terms of money at current prices and then added together. But in this manner, due to an increase or decrease in the prices, the *GNP* shows a rise or decline, which may not be real. To guard against erring on this account, a particular year (say for instance 1990-91) when prices be normal, is taken as the base year and the *GNP* is adjusted in accordance with the index number for that year. This will be known as *GNP* at 1990-91 prices or at constant prices.

Second, in estimating *GNP* of the economy, the market price of only the final products should be taken into account. Many of the products pass through a number of stages before they are ultimately purchased by consumers. If those products were counted at every stage, they would be included many a time in the national product. Consequently, the *GNP* would increase too much. To avoid double counting, therefore, only the final products, and not the intermediary goods should be taken into account.

Third, goods and services rendered free of charge are not included in the *GNP*, because it is not possible to have a correct estimate of their market price. For example, the bringing up of a child by the mother, imparting instructions to his son by a teacher, recitals to his friends by a musician, etc.

Fourth, the transactions which do not arise from the produce of current year or which do not contribute in any way to production, are not included in the *GNP*. The sale and purchase of old goods, and of shares, bonds and assets of existing companies are not included in *GNP* because these do not make any addition to the national product, and the goods are simply transferred. Likewise, the payments received under social security, e.g., unemployment insurance allowance, old age pension, and interest on public loans are also not included in *GNP*, because the recipients do not provide any service in lieu of them. But the depreciation of machines, plants and other capital goods is *not* deducted from *GNP*.

Fifth, the profits earned or losses incurred on account of changes in capital assets as a result of fluctuations in market prices are not included in the *GNP* if they are not responsible for current production or economic activity. For example, if the price of a house or a piece of land increases due to inflation, the profit earned by selling it will not be a part of *GNP*. But if, during the current year, a portion of a house is constructed anew, the increase in the value of the house (after subtracting the cost of the newly constructed portion) will be included in the *GNP*. Similarly, variations in the value of assets, that can be ascertained beforehand and are insured against flood or fire, are not included in the *GNP*.

Last, the income earned through illegal activities is not included in the *GNP*. Although the goods sold in the black market are priced and fulfil the needs of the people, but as they are not useful from the social point of view, the income received from their sale and purchase is always excluded from the *GNP*. There are two main reasons for this. *One*, it is not known whether these things were produced during the current year or the preceding years. *Two*, many of these goods are foreign made and smuggled and hence not included in the *GNP*.

THREE APPROACHES TO GNP

After having studied the fundamental constituents of *GNP*, it is essential to know how is it estimated. Three approaches are employed for this purpose. *One*, the income method to *GNP*; *two*, the expenditure method to *GNP*; and *three*, the value added method to *GNP*. Since gross income equals gross expenditure, *GNP* estimated by all these methods would be the same with appropriate adjustments.

1. Income Approach to GNP

The income approach to *GNP* consists of the remuneration paid in terms of money to the factors of production annually in a country. Thus *GNP* is the sum total of the following items :

(i) Wages and Salaries. Under this head fall all forms of wages and salaries earned through productive activities by workers and entrepreneurs. It includes all sums received or deposited during a year by way of all types of contributions like overtime, commission, provident fund, insurance. etc.

(ii) Rents. Total rent includes the rents of land, shop, house, factory, etc. and the estimated rents of all such assets as are used by the owners themselves.

(iii) Interest. Under interest comes the income by way of interest received by the individual of a country from different sources. To this is added, the estimated interest on that private capital which is invested and not borrowed by the businessman in his personal business. But the interest received on governmental loans has to be excluded, because it is a mere transfer of national income.

(iv) Dividends. Dividends earned by the shareholders from companies are included in the GNP.

(v) Undistributed Corporate Profits. Profits which are not distributed by companies and are retained by them are included in the *GNP*.

(vi) Mixed incomes. These include profits of unincorporated business, self-employed persons and partnerships. They form part of *GNP*.

(vii) Direct Taxes. Taxes levied on individuals, corporations and other businesses are included in the *GNP*.

(viii) Indirect Taxes. The government levies a number of indirect taxes, like excise duties and sales tax. These taxes are included in the prices of commodities. But revenue from these goes to the government treasury and not to the factors of production. Therefore, the income due to such taxes is added to the *GNP*.

(ix) Depreciation. Every corporation makes allowance for expenditure on wearing out and depreciation of machines, plants and other capital equipment. Since this sum also is not a part of the income received by the factors of production, it is, therefore, also included in the *GNP*.

(x) Net Income earned from abroad. This is the difference between the value of exports of goods and services and the value of imports of goods and services. If this difference is positive, then it is added to the *GNP* and if it is negative it is deducted from the *GNP*.

Thus *GNP* according to the Income Method = Wages and Salaries + Rents + Interest + Dividends + Undistributed Corporate Profits + Mixed Income + Direct Taxes + Indirect Taxes + Depreciation + Net Income from abroad.

2. Expenditure Approach to GNP

From the expenditure view point, *GNP* is the sum total of expenditure incurred on goods and services during one year in a country. It includes the following items.:

(i) Private Consumption Expenditure. It includes all types of expenditure on personal consumption by the individuals of a country. It comprises expenses on durable goods like watch, bicycle, radio, etc., expenditure on single-used consumers' goods like milk, bread, ghee, clothes, etc., as also the expenditure incurred on services of all kinds like fees for school, doctor, lawyer and transport. All these are taken as final goods.

(ii) Gross Domestic Private investment. Under this comes, the expenditure incurred by private enterprise on new investment and on replacement of old capital. It includes expenditure on house construction, factory-buildings, all types of machinery, plants and capital equipment. In particular, the increase or decrease in the inventory is added to or subtracted from it. The inventory includes produced but unsold manufactured and semi-manufactured goods during the year and the stocks of raw material, which have to be accounted for in *GNP*. It does not take into account the financial exchange of shares and stocks because their sale and purchase is not real investment. But depreciation is added.

(iii) Net Foreign Investment. It means the difference between exports and imports of export surplus. Every country exports to or imports from certain foreign countries. The imported goods are not produced within the country and hence cannot be included in national income, but the exported goods are manufactured within the country. Therefore, the difference of value between exports (*X*) and imports (*M*), whether positive or negative, is included in the *GNP*.

(iv) Government Expenditure on Goods and Services. The expenditure incurred by the government on goods and services is a part of the *GNP*. Central, State or Local governments spend a lot on their employees, police and army. To run the offices, the governments have also to spend on contingencies which include paper, pen, pencil and various types of stationery, cloth, furniture, cars, etc. It also includes the expenditure on government enterprises. But expenditure on transfer payments is not added, because these payments are not in exchange for goods and services produced during the current year.

Thus *GNP* according to the Expenditure Method=Private Consumption Expenditure (*C*) + Gross Domestic Private Investment (*I*) + Net Foreign Investment (*X–M*) + Government Expenditure on Goods and Services (*G*) $= C + I + (X-M) + G$.

As already pointed out above, *GNP* estimated by either the income or the expenditure method would work out to be the same, if all the items are correctly calculated.

3. Value Added Approach to GNP

Another method of measuring *GNP* is by value added. In calculating *GNP*, the money value of final goods and services produced at current prices during a year is taken into account. This is one of the ways to avoid double counting. But it is difficult to distinguish properly between a final product and an intermediate product. For instance, raw materials, semi-finished products, fuels and services, etc. are sold as inputs by one industry to the other. They may be final goods for one industry and intermediate for others. So, to avoid duplication, the value of *intermediate products* used in manufacturing final products must be subtracted from the value of total output of each industry in the economy. Thus, the difference between the value of material outputs and inputs at each stage of production is called the value added. If all such differences are added up for all industries in the economy, we arrive at the *GNP* by value added. *GNP* by value added = Gross value added + net income from abroad. Its calculation is shown in Tables 1,2 and 3.

Table 1 is constructed on the supposition that the entire economy for purposes of total production consists of three sectors. They are agriculture, manufacturing, and others, consisting of the tertiary sector. Out of the value of total output of each sector is deducted, the value of its intermediate purchases (or primary inputs) to arrive at the value added for the entire economy. Thus the value of total output of the entire economy as per Table 1 is Rs. 155 crores and the value of its primary inputs comes to Rs. 80 crores. Thus the *GDP* by value added is Rs. 75 crores (Rs. 155 minus Rs. 80 crores).

Table 1 : GDP by Value Added

(Rs. crores)

Industry	*Total Output*	*Intermediate Purchases*	*Value Added*
(1)	(2)	(3)	(4) = (2–3)
1. Agriculture	30	10	20
2. Manufacturing	70	45	25
3. Others	55	25	30
Total	155	80	75

The total value added equals the value of gross national (domestic) product of the economy. Out of this value added, the major portion goes in the form of wages and salaries, rent, interest and profits, a small portion goes to the government as indirect taxes and the remaining amount is meant for depreciation. This is shown in Table 2.

Thus we find that the total gross value added of an economy equals the value of its gross domestic product. If depreciation is deducted from the gross value added, we have *net* value added which comes to Rs. 67 crores (Rs. 75 *minus* Rs. 8 crores). This is nothing but net domestic product at market prices. Again, if indirect taxes (Rs. 7 crores) are deducted from the net domestic product of Rs. 67 crores, we get Rs. 60 crores as the net value added at factor cost which is equivalent to net domestic product at factor cost. This is illustrated in Table 3.

Thus value added at factor cost is equal to the net domestic product at factor cost, as given by the total of items 1 to 4 of Table 2 (Rs. 45+3+4+8 crores=Rs. 60 crores).

Table 2 : Gross Domestic Product

(Rs Crores)

1.	Wages and salaries	45
2.	Income from rent	3
3.	Net interest	4
4.	Profits of companies	8
5.	Indirect taxes	7
6.	Depreciation	8
Gross Domestic Product or Value added		75
7.	Net Income from abroad	5
Gross National Income		80

If we add net income received from abroad to the gross value added, this gives us gross national income. Suppose net income from abroad is Rs. 5 crores. Then the gross national income is Rs. 80 crores (Rs. 75 crores + Rs. 5 crores).

Its Importance

The value added method for measuring national income is more realistic than the product and income methods because it avoids the problem of double counting by excluding the value of intermediate products. Thus this method establishes the importance of intermediate products in the national economy. *Second,* by studying the national income accounts relating to value added, the contribution of each production sector to the value of the *GNP* can be found out. For instance, it can tell us whether agriculture is contributing more, or the share of manufacturing is falling, or of the tertiary sector

TABLE 3
VALUE ADDED AT FACTOR COST

(Rs. Crores)

1.	Market Value of output	155
2.	*Less*: cost of intermediate Goods	80
3.	Gross value added	75
4.	*Less*: depreciation	8
5.	Net value added or domestic product at market prices	67
6.	*Less*: indirect taxes	7
7.	Net value added at factor cost	60

is increasing in the current year as compared to some previous years. *Third*, this method is highly useful because "it provides a means of checking the *GNP* estimates obtained by summing the various types of commodity purchases."

ITS DIFFICULTIES

However, difficulties arise in the calculation of value added in the case of certain public services like police, military, health, education, etc. which cannot be estimated accurately in money terms. Similarly, it is difficult to estimate the contribution made to value added by profits earned on irrigation and power projects.

(G) GNP AT MARKET PRICES

When we multiply the total output produced in one year by their market prices prevalent during that year in a country, we get the Gross National Product at Market Prices. Thus *GNP* at market prices means the gross value of final goods and services produced annually in a country *plus* net income from abroad. It includes the gross value of output of all items from (1) to (4) mentioned under *GNP*.

GNP at Market Prices = *GDP* at Market Prices + Net Income from Abroad.

(H) GNP AT FACTOR COST

GNP at factor cost is the sum of the money value of the income produced by and accruing to the various factors of production in one year in a country. It includes all items mentioned above under Income Approach to *GNP less* indirect taxes. *GNP* at market prices always includes indirect taxes levied by the government on goods which raise their prices. But *GNP* at factor cost is the income which the factors of production receive in return for their services alone. It is the cost of production. Thus *GNP* at market prices is always higher than *GNP* at factor cost. Therefore, in order to arrive at *GNP* at factor cost, we deduct indirect taxes from *GNP* at market prices. Again, it often happens that the cost of production of a commodity to the producer is higher than the price of a similar commodity in the market. In order to protect such prducers, the government helps them by granting monetary help in the form of a *subsidy* equal to the difference between the market price and the cost of production of the commodity. As a result, the price of the commodity to the producer is reduced and equals the market price of a similar commodity. For example, if the market price of rice is Rs. 3 per kg but it costs the producers in certain areas Rs. 3.50, the government gives a subsidy of 50 paise per kg to them in order to meet their cost of production. Thus in order to arrive at *GNP* at factor cost, subsidies are added to *GNP* at market prices.

GNP at Factor Cost = *GNP* at Market Prices – Indirect Taxes + Subsidies.

(I) NET NATIONAL PRODUCT (NNP)

NNP includes the value of total output of consumption goods and investment goods. But the process of production uses up a certain amount of fixed capital. Some fixed equipment wears out, its other components are damaged or destroyed, and still others are rendered obsolete through technological changes. All this process is termed *depreciation or capital consumption allowance.* In order to arrive at *NNP*, we deduct depreciation from *GNP*. The word 'net' refers to the exclusion of that part of total output which represents depreciation. So *NNP* = *GNP*—Depreciation.

(J) NNP AT MARKET PRICES

Net National Product at market prices is the *net* value of final goods and services evaluated at market prices in the course of one year in a country. If we deduct depreciation from *GNP* at market prices, we get *NNP* at market prices. So *NNP* at Market Prices = *GNP* at Market Prices – Depreciation.

(K) NNP AT FACTOR COST

Net National Product at factor cost is the *net* output evaluated at factor prices. It includes income earned by factors of production through participation in the production process such as wages and salaries, rents, profits, etc. It is also called *National Income*. This measure differs from *NNP* at market prices in that indirect taxes are deducted and subsidies are added to *NNP* at market prices in order to arrive at *NNP* at factor cost.[4] Thus

NNP at Factor Cost = *NNP* at Market Prices – Indirect taxes+ Subsidies.
= *GNP* at Market Prices – Depreciation – Indirect taxes + Subsidies.
= National Income.

Normally, *NNP* at market prices is higher than *NNP* at factor cost because indirect taxes exceed government subsidies. However, *NNP* at market prices can be less than *NNP* at factor cost when government subsidies exceed indirect taxes.

(L) Domestic Income

Income generated (or earned) by factors of production within the country from its own resources is called domestic income or domestic product. Domestic income includes : (i) Wages and salaries, (ii) rents, including imputed house rents, (iii) interest, (iv) dividends, (v) undistributed corporate profits, including surpluses of public undertakings, (vi) mixed incomes consisting of profits of unincorporated firms, self-employed persons, partnerships, etc., and (vii) direct taxes.

Since domestic income does not include income earned from abroad, it can also be shown as : Domestic Income = National Income – Net Income earned from abroad. Thus the difference between national income and domestic income is the net income earned from abroad. If we add net income from abroad to domestic income, we get national income, *i.e.,* National Income = Domestic Income + Net income earned from abroad. But the net national income earned from abroad may be positive or negative. If exports exceed imports net income earned from abroad is positive. In this case, national income is greater than domestic income. On the other hand, when imports exceed exports, net income earned from abroad is negative and domestic income is greater than national income.[5]

(M) Private Income

Private income is income obtained by private individuals or firms from any source, productive or otherwise, and the retained income of corporations. It can be arrived at from *NNP* at Factor Cost by making certain additions and deductions. The additions include transfer payments such as pensions, unemployment allowances, sickness and other social security benefits, gifts and remittances from abroad, windfall gains from lotteries or from horse racing, and interest on public debt. The deductions include income from government departments as well as surpluses from public undertakings, and employees' contribution to social security schemes like provident funds, life insurance, etc.

Thus Private Income = National Income (or *NNP* at Factor Cost) + Transfer Payments + Interest on Public Debt – Social Security – Profits and Surpluses of Public Undertakings.

(N) Personal Income

Personal income is the total income received by individuals of a country from all sources *before payment of direct taxes* in one year. Personal income is never equal to the national income, because the former includes the transfer payments whereas they are not included in national income. Personal income is derived from national income by deducting undistributed corporate profits, profit taxes, and employees' contributions to social security schemes. These three components are excluded from national income because they do reach individuals. But business and government transfer payments, and transfer payments from abroad in the form of gifts and remittances, windfall gains, and interest on public debt which are a source of income for individuals are added to national income. Thus Personal Income = National Income – Undistributed Corporate Profits – Profit Taxes – Social Security Contribution + Transfer Payments + Interest on Public Debt.

---

4. In the relation between *NNP* at Market Prices and at Factor Cost, these items should be explained in detail as given under *GNP* at Factor Cost.
5. Domestic Income may be 'net' or 'gross'. If not particularly stated, it refers to *Net Domestic Product at Factor Cost* and can be distinguished from *Net Domestic Product at Market Prices as* in (K) above.

Personal income differs from *private income* in that it is less than the latter because it excludes undistributed corporate profits.

Thus Personal Income = Private Income – Undistributed Corporate Profits – Profit Taxes.

(O) Disposable Income

Disposable income or personal disposable income means the actual income which can be spent on consumption by individuals and families. The whole of the personal income cannot be spent on consumption, because it is the income that accrues before direct taxes have actually been paid. Therefore, in order to obtain disposable income, direct taxes are deducted from personal income.

Thus Disposable Income=Personal Income – Direct Taxes.

But the whole of disposable income is not spent on consumption and a part of it is saved. Therefore, disposable income is divided into consumption expenditure and savings.

Thus Disposable Income = Consumption Expenditure + Savings.

If disposable income is to be deduced from national income, we deduct indirect taxes *plus* subsidies, direct taxes on persons and on business, social security payments, undistributed corporate profits or business savings from it and *add* transfer payments and net income from abroad to it.

Thus Disposable Income = National Income – Business Savings – Indirect Taxes + Subsidies – Direct Taxes on Persons – Direct Taxes on Business – Social Security Payments + Transfer Payments + Net Income from abroad.

(P) Real Income

Real income is national income expressed in terms of a general level of prices of a particular year taken as base. National income is the value of goods and services produced, as expressed in terms of money at current prices. But it does not indicate the real state of the economy. It is possible that the net national product of goods and services this year might have been less than that of the last year, but owing to an increase in prices, the *NNP* might be higher this year. On the contrary, it is also possible that *NNP* might have increased but the price level might have fallen, as a result of which national income would appear to be less than that of the last year. In both the situations, the national income does not depict the real state of the country. To rectify such a mistake, the concept of real income has been evolved.

In order to find out the real income of a country, a particular year is taken as the base year when the general price level is neither too high nor too low and the price level for that year is assumed to be 100. Now the general level of prices of the given year for which the real national income is to be determined is assessed in accordance with the prices of the base year. For this purpose, the following formula is employed:

$$\text{Real } NNP = NNP \textit{ for the Current Year} \times \frac{\text{Base Year Index } (=100)}{\text{Current Year Index}}$$

Suppose 1990-91 is the base year and the national income for 1999-2000 is Rs. 20,000 crores and the index number for this year is 250. Hence, Real National Income for 1999-2000 will be $= 20{,}000 \times \frac{100}{250} =$ Rs. 8,000 crores. This is also known as *NI* at constant prices.

(Q) Per Capita Income

The average income of the people of a country in a particular year is called Per Capita Income for that year. This concept also refers to the measurement of income at current prices and at constant prices. For instance, in order to find out the per capita income for 2001 at current prices, the national income of a country is divided by the population of the country in that year.

$$\text{Per Capita Income for 2001} = \frac{\text{National income for 2001}}{\text{Population in 2001}}$$

Similarly, for the purpose of arriving at the Real Per Capita Income, this very formula is used.

$$\text{Real Per Capita Income for 2001} = \frac{\text{Real national income for 2001}}{\text{Population in 2001}}$$

This concept enables us to know the average income and the standard of living of the people. But it is not very reliable, because in every country due to unequal distribution of national income, a major portion of it goes to the richer sections of the society and thus income received by the common man is lower than the per capita income.

4. METHODS OF MEASURING NATIONAL INCOME

There are four methods of measuring national income. Which method is to be used depends on the availability of data in a country and the purpose in hand.

(1) *Product Method.* According to this method, the total value of final goods and services produced in a country during a year is calculated at market prices. To find out the *GNP*, the data of all productive activities, such as agricultural products, wood received from forests, minerals received from mines, commodities produced by industries, the contributions to production made by transport, communications, insurance companies, lawyers, doctors, teachers, etc. are collected and assessed at market prices. Only the final goods and services are included and the intermediary goods and services are left out.[6]

(2) *Income Method.* According to this method, the net income payments received by all citizens of a country in a particular year are added up, *i.e.*, net incomes that accrue to all factors of production by way of net rents, net wages, net interest and net profits are all added together but incomes received in the form of transfer payments are not included in it. The data pertaining to income are obtained from different sources, for instance, from income tax department in respect of high income groups and in case of workers from their wage bills.[7]

(3) *Expenditure Method.* According to this method, the total expenditure incurred by the society in a particular year is added together and includes personal consumption expenditure, net domestic investment, government expenditure on goods and services, and net foreign investment. This concept is based on the assumption that national income equals national expenditure.[8]

(4) *Value Added Method.* Another method of measuring national income is the value added by industries. The difference between the value of material outputs and inputs at each stage of production is the value added. If all such differences are added up for all industries in the economy, we arrive at the gross domestic product.[9]

5. DIFFICULTIES OR LIMITATIONS IN MEASURING NATIONAL INCOME

There are many conceptual and statistical problems involved in measuring national income by the income method, product method, and expenditure method. We discuss them separately in the light of the three methods.

6. For details refer to the first para of 'Gross National Product'.
7. For details read 'Income Approach to *GNP*' and its items.
8. For details read 'Expenditure Approach to *GNP*' and its items.
9. For details read *'GNP'* by Value Added.

(A) Problems in Income Method

The following problems arise in the computation of national income by income method.

1. *Owner-occupied Houses.* A person who rents a house to another earns rental income, but if he occupies the house himself, will the services of the house be included in national income? The services of the owner-occupied house are included in national income as if the owner sells to himself as a tenant its services. For the purpose of national income accounts, the amount of imputed rent is estimated as the sum for which the owner-occupied house could have been rented. The imputed net rent is calculated as that portion of the amount that would have accrued to the house-owner after deducing all expenses.

2. *Self-employed Persons.* Another problem arises with regard to the income of self-employed persons. In their case, it is very difficult to find out the different inputs provided by the owner himself. He might be contributing his capital, land, labour and his abilities in the business. But it is not possible to estimate the value of each factor input to production. So he gets a mixed income consisting of interest, rent, wage and profit for his factor services. This is included in national income.

3. *Goods meant for Self-consumption.* In under-developed countries like India, farmers keep a large portion of food and other goods produced on the farm for self-consumption. The problem is whether that part of the produce which is not sold in the market can be included in national income or not. If the farmer were to sell his entire produce in the market, he will have to buy what he needs for self-consumption out of his money income. If, instead, he keeps some produce for his self-consumption, it has money value which must be included in national income.

4. *Wages and Salaries paid in Kind.* Another problem arises with regard to wages and salaries paid in kind to the employees in the form of free food, lodging, dress and other amenities. Payments in kind by employers are included in national income. This is because the employees would have received money income equal to the value of free food, lodging, etc. from the employer and spent the same in paying for food, lodging, etc.

(B) Problems in Product Method

The following problems arise in the computation of national income by product method :

1. *Services of Housewives.* The estimation of the unpaid services of the housewife in national income presents a serious difficulty. A housewife renders a number of useful services like preparation of meals, serving, tailoring, mending, washing, cleaning, bringing up children, etc. She is not paid for them and her services are not included in national income. Such services performed by paid servants are included in national income. The national income is, therefore, underestimated by excluding the services of a housewife. The reason for the exclusion of her services from national income is that the love and affection of a housewife in performing her domestic work cannot be measured in monetary terms. That is why when the owner of a firm marries his lady secretary, her services are not included in national income when she stops working as a secretary and becomes a housewife. When a teacher teaches his own children, his work is also not included in national income. Similarly, there are a number of goods and services which are difficult to be assessed in money terms for the reason stated above, such as painting, singing, dancing, etc. as hobbies.

2. *Intermediate and Final Goods.* The greatest difficulty in estimating national income by product method is the failure to distinguish properly between intermediate and final goods. There is always the possibility of including a good or service more than once, whereas only final goods are included in national income estimates. This leads to the problem of double counting which leads to the overestimation of national income.

3. *Second-hand Goods and Assets.* Another problem arises with regard to the sale and purchase of second-hand goods and assets. We find that old scooters, cars, houses, machinery, etc. are transacted daily in the country. But they are not included in national income because they were counted in the national product in the year they were manufactured. If they are included every time they are bought and sold, national income would increase many times. Similarly, the sale and purchase of old stocks, shares, and bonds of companies are not included in national income because they were included in national income when the companies were started for the first time. Now they are simply financial transactions and represent claims. But the commission or fees charged by the brokers in the repurchase and resale of old shares, bonds, houses, cars or scooters, etc. are included in national income. For they are the payments they receive for their productive services during

the year.

4. *Illegal Activities*. Income earned through illegal activities like gambling, smuggling, illicit extraction of wine, etc. is not included in national income. Such activities have value and satisfy the wants of the people but they are not considered productive from the point of view of society. But in countries like Nepal and Monaco where gambling is legalised, it is included in national income. Similarly, horse-racing is a legal activity in England and is included in national income.

5. *Consumers' Services*. There are a number of persons in society who render services to consumers but they do not produce anything tangible. They are the actors, dancers, doctors, singers, teachers, musicians, lawyers, barbers, etc. The problem arises about the inclusion of their services in national income since they do not produce tangible commodities. But as they satisfy human wants and receive payments for their services, their services are included as final goods in estimating national income.

6. *Capital Gains*. The problem also arises with regard to capital gains. Capital gains arise when a capital asset such as a house, some other property, stocks or shares is sold at higher price than was paid for it at the time of purchase. Capital gains are excluded from national income because these do not arise from current economic activities. Similarly, capital losses are not taken into account while estimating national income.

7. *Inventory Changes*. All inventory changes (or changes in stocks) whether positive or negative are included in national income. The procedure is to take changes in physical units of inventories for the year valued at average current prices paid for them. The value of changes in inventories may be positive or negative which is added or subtracted from the current production of the firm. Remember, it is the change in inventories and not total inventories for the year that are taken into account in national income estimates.

8. *Depreciation*. Depreciation is deducted from *GNP* in order to arrive at *NNP*. Thus depreciation lowers the national income. But the problem is of estimating the current depreciated value of, say, a machine, whose expected life is supposed to be thirty years. Firms calculate the depreciation value on the original cost of machines for their expected life. This does not solve the problem because the prices of machines change almost every year.

9. *Price Changes*. National income by product method is measured by the value of final goods and services at current market prices. But prices do not remain stable. They rise or fall. When the price level rises, the national income also rises though the national production might have fallen. On the contrary, with the fall in the price level the national income also falls, though the national production might have increased. So price changes do not adequately measure national income. To solve this problem, economists calculate the *real* national income at a constant price level by the consumer price index.

(C) Problems in Expenditure Method

The following problems arise in the calculation of national income by expenditure method :

(1) *Government Services*. In calculating national income by expenditure method, the problem of estimating government services arises. The government provides a number of services, such as police and military services, administrative and legal services. Should expenditure on government services be included in national income ? If they are final goods, then only they would be included in national income. On the other hand, if they are used as intermediate goods, meant for further production, they would not be included in national income. There are many divergent views on this issue. One view is that if police, military, legal and administrative services protect the lives, property and liberty of the people, they are treated as final goods and hence form part of national income. If they help in the smooth functioning of the production process by maintaining peace and security, then they are like intermediate goods that do not enter into national income. In reality, it is not possible to make a clear demarcation as to which service protects the people and which protects the productive process. Therefore, all such services are regarded as final goods and are included in national income.

(2) *Transfer Payments*. There arises the problem of including transfer payments in national income. The government makes payments in the form of pensions, unemployment allowance, subsidies, interest on national debt, etc. These are government expenditures but they are not included in national income because they are paid without adding anything to the production process during the current year. For instance, pensions and unemployment allowances are paid to individuals by the government without doing any productive work during the year. Subsidies tend to lower the market price of the commodities. Interest on national or public

debt is also considered a transfer payment because it is paid by the government to individuals and firms on their past savings without any productive work.

(3) *Durable-use Consumers' Goods*. Durable-use consumers' goods also pose a problem. Such durable-use consumers' goods as scooters, cars, fans, TVs, furniture, etc. are bought in one year but they are used for a number of years. Should they be included under investment expenditure or consumption expenditure in national income estimates ? The expenditure on them is regarded as final consumption expenditure because it is not possible to measure their used up value for the subsequent years.

But there is one exception. The expenditure on a new house is regarded as investment expenditure and not consumption expenditure. This is because the rental income or the imputed rent which the houseowner gets is for making investment on the new house. However, expenditure on a car by a household is consumption expenditure. But if he spends the amount for using it as a taxi, it is investment expenditure.

(4) *Public Expenditure*. The government spends on police, military, administrative and legal services, parks, street lighting, irrigation, museums, education, public health, roads, canals, buildings, etc. The problem is to find out which item is consumption expenditure and which is investment expenditure. Expenses on education, museums, public health, police, parks, street lighting, civil and judicial administration are consumption expenditure. Expenses on roads, canals, buildings, etc. are investment expenditure. But expenses on defence equipment are treated as consumption expenditure because they are consumed during a war as they are destroyed or become obsolete. However, all such expenses including the salaries of armed personnel are included in national income.

6. IMPORTANCE OF NATIONAL INCOME ANALYSIS

The national income data have the following importance.

1. *For the Economy*. The national income data are of great importance for the economy of a country. These days the national income data are regarded as accounts of the economy, which are known as *social accounts*. These refer to net national income and net national expenditure, which ultimately equal each other. Social accounts tell us how the aggregates of a nation's income, output and product result from the income of different individuals, products of industries and transactions of international trade. Their main constituents are inter-related and each particular account can be used to verify the correctness of any other account.

2. *National Policies*. The national income data form the basis of national policies such as employment policy, because these figures enable us to know the direction in which the industrial output, investment and savings, etc. change, and proper measures can be adopted to bring the economy to the right path.

3. *Economic Planning*. In the present age of planning, the national data are of great importance. For economic planning, it is essential that the data pertaining to a country's gross income, output, saving and consumption from different sources should be available. Without these, planning is not possible.

4. *Economic Models*. The economists build short-run as well as long-run economic models or long-run investment models in which the national income data are very widely used.

5. *Research*. The national income data are also made use of by the research scholars of economics. They make use of the various data of the country's inputs, outputs, income, saving, consumption, investment, employment, etc., which are obtained from social accounts.

6. *Per Capita Income*. The national income data are significant for a country's per capita income which reflects the economic welfare of the country. The higher the per capita income, the higher the economic welfare and vice versa.

7. *Distribution of Income*. The national income statistics enable us to know about the distribution of income in the country. From the data pertaining to wages, rent, interest and profits, we learn of the disparities in the incomes of different sections of the society. Similarly, the regional distribution of income is revealed. It is only on the basis of these that the government can adopt measures to remove the inequalities in income distribution and to restore regional equilibrium. With a view to removing these personal and regional disequilibria, the decisions to levy more taxes and increase public expenditure also rest on national income statistics.

7. INTER-RELATIONSHIP AMONG DIFFERENT CONCEPTS OF NI

The inter-relationships among the various concepts of national income can be shown in the form of equations as under :

1.	Gross National Product (GNP)	=	Gross National Expenditure (GNE)
2.	Gross Domestic Product (GDP)	=	GNP – Net Income from abroad.
3.	GNP at market Prices	=	GNP at Factor cost + Indirect Taxes – Subsidies
4.	NNP at Market Prices	=	GNP at Market Prices – Depreciation or Capital Consumption Allowance
5.	Net Domestic Product (NDP) at Market Prices	=	NNP at Market Prices – Net Factor Income from abroad
6.	NNP at Factor Cost or National Income or National Product	=	NNP at Market Prices – Indirect Taxes + Subsidies
7.	NDP at Factor Cost or Domestic Income or Domestic Product	=	National Income – Net Factor Income from abroad
8.	Private Income	=	NNP at Factor Cost + Government and Business Transfer Payments + Current Transfers from abroad in the form of Gifts and Remittances + Windfall Gains + Net Factor Income from abroad + Interest on Public Debt and Consumer Interest – Social Security Contribution – Income from Government Departments and property – Profits and Surpluses of Public Corporations (or Undertakings)
			Or
		=	Income from Domestic Product accruing to Private Sector + Interest on Public Debt + Net Factor Income from abroad + Transfer Payments + Current Transfers from the rest of the world (or abroad)
9.	Income from Domestic Product accruing to Private Sector	=	NDP at Factor Cost – Income from Domestic Product accruing to Government Departments – Saving of Non-Departmental Enterprises.
10.	Personal Income	=	Private Income – Saving of Private Corporate Sector (or Undistributed Corporate Profits) – Corporation Tax (or Profit Taxes)
11.	Personal Disposable Income or Disposable Income	=	Personal Income – Direct Taxespaid by Households (or Direct Personal Taxes) and Miscellaneous Fees, Fines, etc.
			Or
		=	NDP at Factor Cost + Transfer Payments + Net Factor Income from abroad – Corporation Tax – Undistributed Corporate Profits – Social Security Payments – Direct Personal Taxes
			Or
		=	National Income at Factor Cost + Transfer Payments + Net Income from abroad – Corporate Tax – undistributed Corporate Profits – Social Security payments – Direct Personal Taxes – Indirect Taxes + Subsidies.

8. SOME SOLVED PROBLEMS

1. From the data pertaining to the Indian Economy given below, calculate (a) GNP at Factor Cost, (b) NNP at Factor Cost, (c) Net Domestic Product at Factor Cost, and (d) Net Domestic Product at market Prices.

		Rs. Crores
(i)	GNP at Market Prices	97503
(ii)	Net factor income from abroad	(–) 201
(iii)	Capital consumption allowance	5699
(iv)	Net indirect taxes	10576

Solution

(a) GNP at Market Prices = 97503

GNP at Facor Cost = GNP at Market Prices – Indirect Taxes

= 97503 – 10576 = 86927

(b) NNP at Factor Cost = GNP at Factor Cost – Depreciation

= 86927 – 5699 = 81228

(c) NDP at Factor Cost = NNP at Factor Cost – Net Factor Income from abroad

= 81228– (–201)=81429

(d) NDP at Market Prices = NDP at Factor Cost + Indirect Taxes

= 81429 + 10576 = 92005

2. On the basis of the following information relating to the Indian Economy, estimate (a) GNP at Market Prices, (b) Private Income, (c) Personal Income, and (d) Personal disposable Income.

		Rs. Crores
(i)	Net domestic product at factor cost	81,429
(ii)	Income from domestic product accruing to the Government sector	2,333
(iii)	Net factor income from abroad	(–) 201
(iv)	Indirect Taxes	12,876
(v)	Subsidies	2,300
(vi)	Interest on national debt	964
(vii)	Transfers from Government administrative departments	1,981
(viii)	Other current transfers from the rest of the world	1,271
(ix)	Corporation tax	1,251
(x)	Undistributed corporate profits	464
(xi)	Direct taxes paid by households	2,100
(xii)	Consumption of fixed capital	5,699

Solution

(a) GNP at Market Prices = Net Domestic Product at Factor Cost + Net Factor Income from abroad + Capital Consumption Allowance (or Consumption of Fixed Capital) + Indirect Taxes – Subsidies

= 81429 + (–201 + 5699 + 12876 – 2300 = 97503

(b) Private Income = NNP at Factor Cost (or NI) + Transfer Payments + Interest on Public Debt – Social Security Contributions – Income from Government Departments – Profits and Surpluses of Public Corporations.

First, calculate NNP at Factor Cost because NDP at Factor Cost is given in the illustration. So NNP at Factor Cost = NDP at Factor cost + Net Factor Income from abroad = 81429 + (–201) = 81228.

Now Private Income = 81,228 + 1,981 + 1,271 + 964 – 2,333 = 83,111

where Transfer Payments from Government

Administrative Departments	= 1,981
Other current transfers from the rest of the world	= 1,271
Interest on National Debt	= 964
Income from Government Departments	= 2,333

The remaining items in the equation are not given in our example.

Note : Items (vii) and (viii) relate to Transfer Payments.

(c) Personal Income	=	Private income – Undistributed Corporate Profit (or Savings of Private Corporate Sector) – Corporation Tax
	=	83,111 – 464 – 1,251
	=	81,396
(d) Personal Disposable Income	=	Personal Income – Direct Taxes paid by Households
	=	81,396 – 2,100
	=	79,296

3. On the basis of the following information, calculate Net National Product at Market Prices and Disposable Personal Income :

		Rs. Crores
(i)	Net domestic product at factor cost	15,480
(ii)	Income from domestic product accruing to government	140
(iii)	National debt interest	170
(iv)	Transfer payments by government	240
(v)	Net private donations from abroad	30
(vi)	Net earned income from abroad	80
(vii)	Indirect taxes	1,330
(viii)	Direct taxes	335
(ix)	Subsidies	100
(x)	Taxes on corporate profits	222
(xi)	Undistributed profits of corporations	105

Solution

First calculate NNP at Factor Cost because NDP at Factor Cost is given in the illustration. So

NDP at Factor Cost	=	15,480
+ Net earned income from abroad	=	80
∴ NNP at Factor Cost	=	15,560
NNP at Market Prices		
NNP at Factor Cost	=	15,560
+ Indirect Taxes	=	1,330
– Subsidies	=	– 100
∴ NNP at Market Prices	=	16,790

To calculate Disposable Personal Income, calculate Private Income and Personal Income.

Private Income

NNP at Factor Cost	=	15,560
+ Transfer Payments by Government	=	240
+ Net private donations from abroad	=	30
(These are transfers from the rest of the world)		
+ National debt interest	=	170
– Income from domestic product accruing to government	=	– 140
∴ Private Income		15,860

Personal Income

Private Income	=	15,860
– Taxes on corporate profits	=	– 222
– Undistributed profits of corporations	=	– 105
∴ Personal Income	=	15,533

Disposable Personal Income

Private Income	=	15,533
– Direct Taxes on persons	=	–335
Disposable Personal Income	=	15,198

EXERCISES

1. Explain the various concepts of national income. Under what circumstances does national income tend to be underestimated ?
2. Point out the difference between the following concepts of National Income and also their relationship with each other :
   (a) Gross National Product and Net National Product.
   (b) National Income at Market Prices and National Income at Factor Costs.
   (c) Net Natioal Product and Net Domestic Product.
   (d) Disposable Income and Personal Income.
3. Examine the usefulness of the concept of national income in analysing an economy's aggregate behaviour.
4. Explain the product and expenditure methods of computing national income. On what basis do they give identical results ?
5. What are the main conceptual problems involved in the estimation of *GNP*? How can they be overcome ?
6. Explain the value added method of measuring national income.

Chapter 38

Applicability of Keynes' Theory to Underdeveloped Countries

The Keynesian theory is not applicable to every socio-economic setup. It only applies to advanced democratic capitalist economies. As Schumpeter wrote, "Practical Keynesianism is a seedling which cannot be transplanted into foreign soil; it dies there and becomes poisonous before it dies. But left in English soil this seedling is a healthy thing and promises both fruit and shade. All this applies to every bit of advice that Keynes ever offered."[1] Before we study the applicability of Keynesian economics to underdeveloped countries, it is essential to analyse the assumptions of Keynesian economics *vis-a-vis* the conditions prevailing in under-developed economies.

1. KEYNESIAN ASSUMPTIONS AND UNDER-DEVELOPED COUNTRIES

The Keynesian economics is based on the following assumptions which limit its applicability to underdeveloped countries :

(1) The Keynesian theory is based on the existence of cyclical unemployment which occurs during a depression. It is caused by deficiency in effective demand. Unemployment can be removed by an increase in the level of effective demand. But the nature of unemployment in an underdeveloped country is quite different from that in a developed economy. In such economies unemployment is *chronic* rather than cyclical. It is not due to lack of effective demand but, is the result of deficiency of capital resources. Apart from chronic unemployment, underdeveloped countries suffer from disguised unemployment and the problem of economic instability. So he did not refer to disguised unemployment and its solution. The remedy for the chronic and disguised unemployment is economic development to which Keynes paid no attention at all. Thus the Keynesian assumptions of cyclical unemployment and economic instability are hardly tenable in an underdeveloped economy.

1. J.A. Schumpeter, *Ten Great Economists, op. cit.,* p. 275.

(2) The Keynesian economics is a short period analysis in which Keynes takes "as given the existing skill and quantity of available labour, the existing quantity and quality of available equipment, the existing technique, the degree of competition, the tastes and habits of the consumer, the disutility of different intensities of labour and of the activities of supervision and organisation, as well as social structure."[2] The development economics, however, is a long period analysis in which all the basic factors assumed by Keynes as given change over time.

(3) The Keynesian theory is based on the assumption of a closed economy. But underdeveloped countries are not closed economies. They are open economies in which foreign trade plays a dominant role in developing them. Such economies primarily depend on the exports of agricultural and industrial raw materials and the import of capital goods. Thus the Keynesian economics has little relevance to underdeveloped countries in this respect.

(4) The Keynesian theory assumes an excess supply of labour and other complementary resources in the economy. This analysis refers to a depression economy where "the industries, machines, managers and workers, as well as consumption habits, are all there, only waiting to resume their temporarily suspended functions and roles."[3] But in underdeveloped economies there is no temporary suspension of economic activity. Economic activity is static. Capital, skills, factor supplies and economic infrastructure are woefully lacking.

(5) Moreover, it can be inferred from the above assumption that labour and capital are unemployed simultaneously, according to the Keynesian analysis. When labour is unemployed, capital and equipment are also not fully utilised or there is excess capacity in them. But this is not so in underdeveloped countries. When labour is unemployed, there is no question of capital being unutilized because there is acute shortage of capital and equipment.

2. KEYNESIAN TOOLS AND UNDERDEVELOPED COUNTRIES

Thus the assumption on which the Keynesian theory is based are not applicable to the conditions prevailing in underdeveloped countries. We now study the principal *tools* of the Keynesian theory to test their validity to underdeveloped countries.

Effective Demand. Unemployment is caused by the deficiency of effective demand, and to get over it, Keynes suggested the stepping up of consumption and non-consumption expenditures. In an underdeveloped country, however, there is no involuntary unemployment but disguised unemployment. Unemployment is caused not by lack of complementary resources. The concept of effective demand is applicable to those economies where unemployment is due to excess savings; and in such a situation the remedy lies in stepping up the levels of consumption and investment through various monetary and fiscal measures. But in an underdeveloped economy income levels are extremely low, the propensity to consume is very high and savings are almost nil. All efforts to increase money incomes through monetary and fiscal measures will, in the absence of complementary resources, lead to price inflation. Here the problem is not one of raising the effective demand but one of raising the levels of employment and per capita income in the context of economic development. "The economic progress consists of two distinct categories: *one,* where at the given level of economic development, you move from low employment to full employment, and the *other,* where you move from full employment at a given level of economic development to full employment at the next higher level of economic development. The Keynesian thesis applies only to *the first category.*"[4]

Propensity to Consume. One of the important tools of Keynesian economics is the propensity to consume which highlights the relationship between consumption and income. When income increases, consumption also increases but by less than the increment in income. This behaviour of consumption further explains the rise in saving as income increases. In underdeveloped countries these relationships between income, consumption and saving do not hold. People are very poor and when their income increases, they spend more on consumption goods because their tendency is to meet their unfulfilled wants. The marginal propensity to consume is very high in such countries, whereas the marginal propensity to save is very low. The Keynesian economics tells us

2. J.M. Keynes, *op. cit.,* p. 245 note 1.
3. A.O. Hirschman, *The Strategy of Economic Development,* p. 54.
4. V.K.R.V. Rao, *Essays in Economic Development, op. cit.,* p. 61.

that when the *MPC* is high consumer demand, output and employment, increase at a faster rate with the increase in income. But in an underdeveloped country it is not possible to increase the production of consumer goods due to the scarcity of co-operant factors, when consumption increases with the rise in income. As a result, prices rise instead of a rise in the level of employment.

Saving. On the saving side, Keynes regarded saving as a social vice for it is excess of saving that leads to a decline in aggregate demand. Again, this idea is not applicable to underdeveloped countries because saving is the panacea for their economic backwardness. Capital formation is the key to economic development and capital formation is possible through increased saving on the part of people. Underdeveloped countries can progress by curtailing consumption and increasing saving, as opposed to the Keynesian view of raising consumption and reducing saving. To underdeveloped countries, saving is a virtue and not a vice.

Marginal Efficiency of Capital. According to Keynes, one of the important determinants of investment is the marginal efficiency of capital. There is an inverse relationship between investment and *MEC.* When investment increases, the *MEC* falls, and when investment declines, the *MEC* rises. This relationship is, however, not applicable to underdeveloped countries. In such economies, investment is at a low level and the *MEC* is also low. This paradox is due to lack of capital and other resources, small size of the market, low demand, high costs, underdeveloped capital and money markets, uncertainties, etc. All these factors keep the *MEC* (profit expectations) and investment at a low level.

Rate of Interest. The rate of interest is the second determinate of investment in the Keynesian system. It is in turn determined by liquidity preference and the supply of money. Of the motives for liquidity preference, the transaction and precautionary motives are income elastic and they do not influence the rate of interest. It is only the demand for money for the speculative motive that affects the rate of interest. In underdeveloped countries, the liquidity preference for transaction and precautionary motives is high and for the speculative motive low. Therefore, liquidity preference fails to influence the rate of interest. The other determinant of the interest rate is the supply of money. According to Keynes, increase in the supply of money lowers the interest rate and encourages investment, income and the level of employment. But in underdeveloped countries, an increase in the supply of money leads to rise in prices rather than to the fall in interest rate. As Keynes himself observed in citing India's example, "The history of India at all times has provided an example of a country impoverished by a preference for liquidity amounting to so strong a passion that even an enormous and chronic influx of the precious metals has been insufficient to bring down the rate of interest to a level which was compatible with the growth of real wealth."[5] Thus, the rate of interest in underdeveloped countries is not influenced so much by the demand for the. supply of money as by traditions, customs and institutional factors.

The Multiplier. Dr. V.K.R.V. Rao has analysed the feasibility of applying the Keynesian multiplier theory and policy implications to an underdeveloped country like India.[6] According to Dr. Rao, Keynes never formulated the economic problems of underdeveloped countries nor did he discuss the relevance to these countries for either the objective or the policy that he proposed for the more developed countries. The result has been a rather unintelligent application of Keynesian economics to the problems of underdeveloped countries. The Keynesian concept of multiplier is based on the following four assumptions: *(a)* Involuntary unemployment, *(b)* An industrialized economy where the supply curve of output slopes upward to the right but does not become vertical till after a *substantial interval, (c)* Excess capacity in the consumption goods industries, *(d)* Comparatively elastic supply of the working capital required for increased output.

Given these assumptions, if we apply the multiplier theory on underdeveloped countries, the value of the multiplier will be apparently much higher than even in a developed country. We know that the multiplier depends on the size of the marginal propensity to consume. Since in an underdeveloped country the marginal propensity to consume is fairly high. Small increments of investment are likely to induce full employment much earlier than in a rich country where the marginal propensity to consume is low. This is something paradoxical and contrary to facts. For the assumptions on which the multiplier theory is based do not hold Valid in the case of an underdeveloped country. Let us test them in the light of conditions prevailing in an underdeveloped country like India.

5. J.M. Keynes, *General Theory,* p. 337.
6. The analysis that follows is based on V.K.R.V. Rao, *op. cit.,* Ch. 2.

(a) Involuntary unemployment in the Keynesian analysis is associated with a capitalist economy where the majority of workers work for wages and where production is more for exchange than for self-consumption. According to Prof. Das Gupta, the organized sector of an underdeveloped economy, with its large-scale industries and fairly well-developed banking system-comes under the scope of Keynesian economics, for it presents the features of a capitalistic economy. But involuntary unemployment in this sector is insignificant when considered in relation to the total working population of the country." As per Prof. Das Gupta's rough estimate, involuntary unemployment in India works out to be 0.2 per cent of the total working force, on the assumption that 10 per cent of the persons employed in organized industry are involuntarily unemployed and that hardly 2 per cent of the total working population is absorbed by the organised industry.[7] In fact, in an overpopulated underdeveloped country there exists disguised unemployment. Ostensibly people are engaged in agriculture but if some of them are withdrawn from the farm, there will be no reduction in output. In an underdeveloped economy, the existence of disguised unemployment instead of involuntary unemployment hinders the working of the multiplier theory. The secondary, tertiary and other effects of the initial increment do not follow mainly because there is no labour force willing to accept employment at the current wage levei. The disguised unemployed are not available at the current wage level because, *firstly,* they are not conscious of the fact that they are unemployed and *secondly,* they are already receiving a real income which gives them at least as much satisfaction as they would get from the current wage level. Thus the absence of involuntary unemployment and the presence of disguised unemployment in underdeveloped countries retard the operation of the multiplier towards increasing output and employment.

(b) The supply curve of output in an underdeveloped country is inelastic which renders the working of the multiplier all the more difficult. The reason is that the nature of the consumption goods industries is such that they are unable to expand output and offer more employment. The main consumption goods industry in an underdeveloped country is agriculture which is almost stagnant. The supply curve of agricultural output is backward sloping so that an increase in the value of output does not necessarily lead to an increase in the volume of output. This is because in the short-run necessary facilities are not available to the agricultural producers for increasing output. As a result, the secondary, tertiary and other increases in income, output and employment do not come about with an initial increment of investment. The primary increase in income is spent on food and its multiplier effect is lost.

(c) Since the marginal propensity to consume is high in underdeveloped countries, the increased income is spent on self-consumption of food products by the farmers which leads to reduction of the marketable surplus of foodgains. This, in turn, leads to a rise in the prices of foodgrains in the non-agricultural sector without a rise in the aggregate real income. The possibility of spending more by the agriculturists on non-agricultural goods is, however, limited because there is little excess capacity in industries.

(d) Output is difficult to increase due to non-availability of sufficient raw materials, capital equipment and skilled labour. Thus, concludes Dr. Rao, "the primary increase in investment and, therefore, increase in income and employment leads to a secondary and a tertiary increase in income, but not any noticeable increase in output or employment, either in the agricultural or in the non-agricultural sector. The multiplier principle, therefore, works with reference to money income but not with reference either to real income or employment."[8]

Similarly, the absence of conditions *(c)* and *(d)* in an underdeveloped country renders the operation of the multiplier difficult. Absence of excess capacity in consumption goods industries coupled with a comparatively inelastic supply of working capital for increasing output prevent the required increase in the output of consumption goods industries and the resultant employment therein.

Thus the obvious conclusion is that the Keynesian principle of multiplier does not operate in an underdeveloped country like India mainly due to two reasons: *firstly,* involuntary unemployment of the Keynesian type is not to be found, and secondly, the supply of agricultural and non-agricultural output is inelastic due to the working of certain factors peculiar to such economies.

---

7. A.K. Dass Gupta, *Planning and Economic Growth,* pp. 32-33.
8. V.K.R.V. *Rao, op. cit.,* p. 41.

3. POLICY MEASURES

Not only this, even the Keynesian policy prescriptions are hardly tenable under the conditions prevailing in underdeveloped countries. Dr. Rao maintains that an attempt to increase investment through deficit financing leads to an inflationary rise in prices rather than to an increase in output and employment. He is, therefore, of the view that "the economic policy of deficit financing and disregard for thrift advocated by Keynes for securing full employment does not apply in the case of an underdeveloped country." But in another essay, *"Deficit Financing for Capital Formation and Price Behaviour in an Underdeveloped Economy,"*[9] he contends that deficit financing for capital formation does not lead to inflation since it is used for increasing the capacity and thereby imparting elasticity to the supply curve of output. However, a certain measure of price rise is inevitable but it is of a "self-liquidating character." He points out that the history of war finance shows that forced savings obtained through a rise in prices, when used for capital formation, are nothing but deficit financing for economic development. "The only question is the extent in which it is wise to resort to deficit financing; and the obvious answer is that deficit financing should not be resorted to beyond the point at which it becomes inflationary."

Prof. Das Gupta advocates the use of Keynesian policy of public investment to achieve a higher standard of living and to provide increasing employment opportunities in underdeveloped countries. But in the absence of adequate public savings and the flow of foreign capital, he advocates deficit financing which if not accompanied by a system of price and capital issue controls, in the transitional period, will lead to inflationary rise in prices. He, however, emphasises that "we would be deceiving ourselves if we thought that the process could function within the framework of a liberal economy, such as Keynes sought so anxiously to preserve."[10] For underdeveloped countries "the old fashioned prescription of work harder and save more still seems to hold as the medicine for economic progress"[11] than the Keynesian hypothesis that consumption and investment should be increased simultaneously. But it cannot be denied that though the Keynesian policy prescriptions do not apply *in toto* to the problems of underdeveloped countries, yet the Keynesian tools of analysis are indispensable for understanding the problems of such economies.

CONCLUSION

To conclude with Prof. Das Gupta: "Whatever the generality of the *General Theory* may be in the sense in which the term 'general' was used by Keynes, the applicability of the propositions of the *General Theory* to conditions of an underdeveloped economy is at best limited."[12].

EXERCISES

1. What assumptions has Keynes made in his *General Theory?* To what extent do you think the conditions in an underdeveloped economy affirm or refuse those assumptions?

2. Critically discass the Keynesian theory of employment and show the extent to which its main conclusions are applicable in the case of economically underdeveloped countries.

3. Point out the relevance of Keynesian economics for the developing countries.

---

9. *Ibid,* Chapter 5.
10. A.K. Das Gupta, *op. cit.,* p. 37.
11. V.K.R.V. Rao, *op. cit.*
12. A.K. Das Gupta, *op. cit.,* p. 34

CHAPTER 39

The Principle of Acceleration

1. MEANING OF THE ACCELERATION PRINCIPLE

The term "acceleration principle" itself was first introduced into economics by J.M. Clark[1] in 1917.

The principle of acceleration is based on the fact that the demand for capital goods is derived from the demand for consumer goods which the former help to produce. The acceleration principle explains the process by which an increase (or decrease) in the demand for consumption goods leads to an increase (or decrease) in investment on capital goods. According to Kurihara, "The accelerator coefficient is the ratio between induced investment and an initial change in consumption expenditure." Symbolically, $\beta = \Delta I_t / \Delta C_t$ or $\Delta I_t = \beta \Delta C_t$ where β is the accele rator coefficient, ΔI_t is net change in investment and ΔC_t is the net change in consumption expenditure in period t. If the increase in consumption expenditure of Rs 10 crores leads to an increase in investment of Rs 30 crores, the accelerator coefficient is 3. This is the original version of the acceleration principle.

This version of the acceleration principle has been more broadly interpreted by Hicks as the ratio of induced investment to changes in output it calls forth. According to Branson, "It suggests that an increase in the growth rate of output, an acceleration is needed to increase the level of investment." [2]Thus the accelerator v is equal to $\Delta I_t / \Delta Y_t$ or the capital-output ratio. It depends on the relevant change in output (ΔY_t) and the change in investment (ΔI_t). It shows that the demand for capital goods is not derived from consumer goods alone but from any *direct* demand of national output. In these two versions, the accelerator β and v are the same.

In an economy, the required stock of capital depends on the change in the demand for output. Any change in output will lead to a change in the capital stock. This change equals v times the change in output. Thus $\Delta I_t = v \Delta Y_t$ where v is the accelerator. If a machine has a value of Rs 4 lakh and produces output worth Rs 1 lakh, then the value of v is 4. An entrepreneur who wishes to increase his output by Rs 1 lakh every year must invest Rs 4 lakh on this machine. This equally applies to an economy where, if the value of the accelerator is greater than one, more capital is required per unit of output so that the increase in net investment is greater

1. J.M. Clark, "Business Acceleration and Law of Demand. A Technical Factor in Economic Cycles." *J.P.E.*, Reprinted in *Reading in Business Cycle Theory*, 1941.
2. W.H. Branson, *Macroeconomic Theory and Policy*, 3/e, 1989.

than the increase in output that causes it. Gross investment in the economy will equal replacement investment plus net investment. Assuming replacement investment(i.e.,replacement demand for machines due to obsolescence and depreciation) to be constant, gross investment will vary with the level of investment corresponding to each level of output.

In the above analysis, the investment called for by the accelerator is completed in the same period, *t*. To make the analysis realistic, economists have *lagged* the accelerator effect. This can be expressed in the form of the following equation given by Brooman.[3]

$$I_{gt} = v\ (Y_t - Y_{t-1}) + R$$
$$= v\ \Delta Y_t + R$$

where I_{gt} is gross investment in period *t*, *v* is the accelerator, Y_t is the national output in period *t*, Y_{t-1} is the national output in the previous period (t-1), and *R* is the replacement investment.

The equation tells that gross investment during period *t* depends on the change in output (*Y*) from period t–1 to period *t multiplied* by the accelerator (*v*) plus replacement investment *R*.

In order to arrive at net investment (I_n), *R* must be deducted from both sides of the equation so that net investment in period *t* is

$$I_{nt} = v\ (Y_t - Y_{t-1})$$
$$= v\ \Delta Y_t$$

This equation is nothing but $\Delta I = v\ \Delta Y$, since $\Delta Y = Y_t - Y_{t-1}$. If $Y_t > Y_{t-1}$, net investment is positive during period *t*. On the other hand, if $Y_t < Y_{t-1}$, net investment is negative or there is disinvestment in period*t*.

2. OPERATION OF THE ACCELERATION PRINCIPLE

The working of the acceleration principle is explained with the help of an hypothetical example given in Table 1

TABLE 1 : OPERATION OF THE ACCELERATIONPRINCIPLE

Period in Years	*Total output (Y)*	*Required Capital*	*Replacement Investment (R)*	*Net Investment* (I_n)	*Gross Investment* (I_g)
(1)	(2)	(3)	(4)	+ (5)	= (6)
t	100	400	40	0	40
t+1	100	400	40	0	40
t+2	105	420	40	20	60
t+3	115	460	40	40	80
t+4	130	520	40	60	100
t+5	140	560	40	40	80
t+6	145	580	40	20	60
t+7	140	560	40	—20	20
t+8	130	520	40	—40	0
t+9	125	500	40	—20	20

The Table traces changes in total output, capital stock, net investment and gross investment over ten time periods. Assuming the value of the accelerator $v = 4$, the required capital stock in each period is 4 times the

3. F.S. Brooman, *op. cit.*, p. 169.

corresponding output of that period, as shown in column (3). The replacement investment is assumed to be equal to 10 per cent of the capital stock in period *t*, shown as 40 in each time period. Net investment in Column (5) equals v times the change in output between one period and the preceding period. For example, net investment in period *t*+3 $= v\,(Y_{t+3} - Y_{t+2})$ or 40 = 4(115-105). It means that given the accelerator of 4, the increase of 10 in the demand for final output leads to an increase of 40 in the demand for capital goods (machines). Accordingly, the *total* demand for capital goods (machines) rises to 80 made up of 40 of replacement and 40 of net investment, as shown in Columns (6). Thus the table reveals that net investment depends on the change in total output, given the value of the accelerator. So long as the demand for final goods (output) rises, net investment is positive. But when it falls, net investment is negative. In the Table, total output (column 2) increases at an increasing rate from period *t*+1 to *t*+4 and so does net investment (column 4). Then it increases at a diminishing rate from period *t*+5 to *t* + 6 and net investment declines from period*t* +7 to *t* +9, total output falls, and net investment becomes negative.

The acceleration principle is illustrated diagrammatically in Figure 1 where in the upper portion, total output curve *Y* increases at an increasing rate up to *t* +4 period, then at a decreasing rate up to period *t* + 6. After this it starts diminishing. The curve I_n in the lower part of the figure shows that the rising output leads to increased net investment upto *t* + 4 period because output is increasing at an increasing rate. But when output increases at a decreasing rate between *t* + 4 and *t* + 6 periods, net investment declines. When output starts declining in period *t*+7, net investment becomes negative. The curve I_g represents gross investment of economy. Its behaviour is similar to the net investment curve. But there is one difference that gross investment is not negative and once it becomes zero in period *t* + 8, the curve I_g again starts rising. This is because despite net investment being negative, the replacement is taking place at a uniform rate.

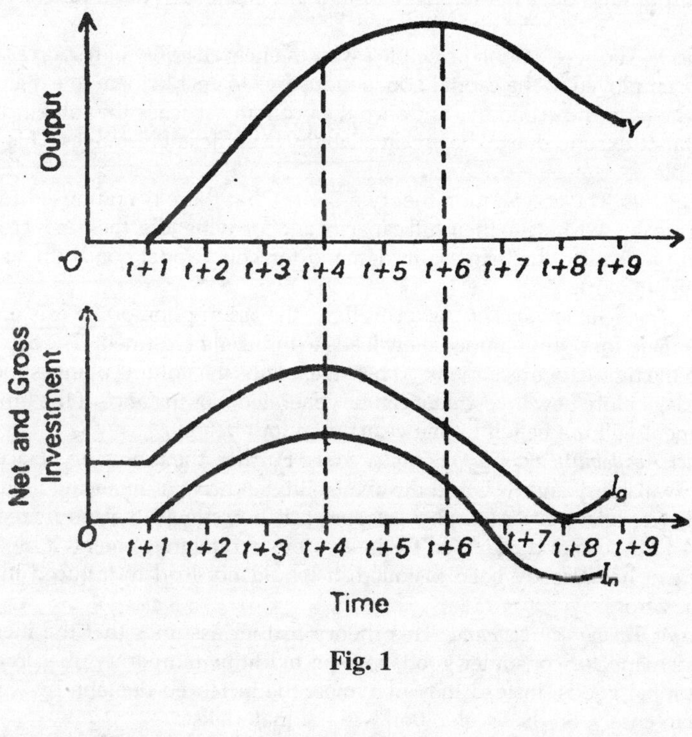

Fig. 1

3. ASSUMPTIONS OF THE ACCELERATION PRINCIPLE

The acceleration principle is based upon the following assumptions.

1. The acceleration principle assumes a constant capital-output ratio.
2. It assumes that resources are easily available.
3. The acceleration principle assumes that there is no excess or idle capacity in plants.
4. It is assumed that the increased demand is permanent.
5. The acceleration principle also assumes that there is elastic supply of credit and capital.
6. It further assumes that an increase in output immediately leads to a rise in net investment.

4. CRITICISMS OF THE ACCELERATION PRINCIPLE

The acceleration principle has been criticised by economists for its rigid assumptions which tend to limit its smooth working. The following are its limitations.

(1).*Capital-output Ratio not Constant*. The acceleration principle is based on a constant capital-output ratio. But this ratio does not remain constant in the modern dynamic world. Inventions and improvements "in techniques of production are constantly taking place which lead to increase in output per unit of capital. Or, existing capital equipment may be worked more intensively. Moreover, changes in the expectations of businessmen with regard to prices, wages, interest etc. may affect future demand and vary the capital-output ratio. Thus the capital-output ratio does not remain constant but changes in the different phases of the trade cycle.

(2) *Resources not Elastic.* The acceleration principle assumes the availability of resources. Resources should be elastic so that they are employed in the capital goods industries to enable them to expand. This is possible when there is unemployment in the economy. But once the economy reaches the full employment level, the capital goods industries fail to expand due to the non availability of sufficient resources. This limits the working of the acceleration principle.

(3) *Idle Capacity in Plants*. The acceleration theory assumes that there is no unused (or idle) capacity in plants. If some machines are not working to their full capacity and are lying idle, then an increase in the demand for consumer goods will not lead to the increase in demand for new capital goods. In such a situation, the acceleration principle will not work.

(4) *Does not Explain Timing of investment*. As a corollary, the assumption of the existence of full capacity implies that increased demand for output immediately leads to induced investment. The acceleration principle, therefore, fails to explain the timing of investment. At best it explains the volume of investment. As a matter of fact, there may be a time lag before new investment can be generated. For instance, if the time lag is four years, the effect of new investment will not be felt in one year but in four years.

(5) *Does not Consider Availability and Cost of Capital goods*. Further, the timing of the acquisition of capital goods depends on their availability and cost, and the availability and cost of financing them.

(6) *Acceleration Effect zero for installed Capital equipment*. It is assumed that no increase in demand for consumer goods had been foreseen and provided for in previous capital investment. If by anticipating future demand, capital equipment has already been installed, it would not lead to induced investment and the acceleration effect will be zero.

(7) *Does not Work for Temporary Demand*. This theory further assumes that the increased demand is permanent. In case the demand for consumer goods is expected to be temporary, the producers will refrain from investing in new capital goods. Instead they may meet the increased demand by working the existing capital equipment more intensely. So the acceleration will not materialise.

(8) *Supply of Credit not Elastic*. The acceleration principle assumes an elastic supply of credit so that when there is induced investment as a result of induced consumption, cheap credit is easily available for investment in capital goods industries. If cheap credit is not available in sufficient quantities, the rate of interest will be high

and investment in capital goods will be very low. Thus the acceleration will not work fully.

(9) *Neglects Profits as a Source of Finance.* This assumption further implies that firms resort to external sources of finance for investment purposes. But empirical evidence has shown that firms prefer internal sources of finance to external sources. The acceleration principle is weak in that it neglects profits as a source of internal finance. As a matter of fact, the level of profits is a major determinant of investment.

(10) *Neglects the Role of Expectations.* The acceleration principle neglects the role of expectations in decision-making on the part of the entrepreneur. The investment decisions are not influenced by demand alone. They are also affected by future anticipations like stock market changes, political developments, international events, economic climate, etc.

(11) *Neglects the Role of Technological Factors.* The acceleration principle is weak in that it neglects the role of technological factors in investment. Technological changes may be either capital-saving or labour-saving. They may, therefore, reduce or increase the volume of investment. Further, as pointed out by Prof. Knox, ``Capital equipment may be bulky, and the employment of additional plant is justified only when output has risen considerably. This factor is all the more important because usually what is added is a complex of machines and not a machine."[3] Thus the acceleration principle by itself is inadequate as a theory of investment, according to Knox.

CONCLUSION

Despite these limitations, the principle of acceleration makes the process of income propagation clearer and more realistic than the multiplier theory. The multiplier shows the effect of a change in investment on income via the consumption, while the acceleration shows the effect of consumption or output on investment and income. Thus the acceleration explains volatile fluctuations in income and employment as a result of fluctuations in capital goods industries. But it can explain upper turning points better than lower turning points. To conclude with Prof. Shapiro, ``The acceleration principle, however, inadequate by itself, clearly emerges as one of a number of major factors that are needed in combination with the multiplier to explain the fluctuations observed in the world of investment spending."[5]

EXERCISES

1. What do you mean by the acceleration principle? Explain its working.
2. Describe the operation of the acceleration principle. What are its limitations?

---

4. A.D. Knox, 'The Acceleration Principle and the Theory of Investment : A Survey', Reprinted in M.G. Mueller, *Readings inMacroeconomics,* 2/e, 1971.
5. Edward Shapiro, *Macroeconomic Analysis,* 4/e, 1978.

PART FOUR

INTERNATIONAL TRADE

Chapter 40

Distinguishing Features of International Trade

1. INTRODUCTION

Inter-regional trade refers to trade between regions within a country. It is what Ohlin calls inter-local trade. Thus inter-regional trade is domestic or internal trade. International trade, on the other hand, is trade between two nations or countries. A controversy has been going on among economists whether there is any difference between inter-regional or domestic trade and international trade. The classical economists held that there were certain fundamental differences between inter-regional trade and international trade. Accordingly, they propounded a separate theory of international trade which is known as the Theory of Comparative Costs. But modern economists like Bertil Ohlin and Haberler contest this view and opine that the differences between inter-regional and international trade are of degree rather than of kind.

Nevertheless, there are several reasons to believe the classical view that international trade is fundamentally different from inter-regional trade.

1. *Factor Immobility.* The classical economists advocated a separate theory of international trade on the ground that factors of production are freely mobile within each region as between places and occupations and immobile between countries entering into international trade. Thus, labour and capital are regarded as immobile between countries while they are perfectly mobile within a country. There is complete adjustment to wage differences and factor-price disparities within a country with quick and easy movement of labour and other factors from low return to high sectors. But no such movements are possible internationally. Price changes lead to movement of goods betwen countries rather than factors. The reasons for international immobility of labour are—difference in languages, customs, occupational skills, unwillingness to leave familiar surroundings, and family ties, the high travelling expenses to the foreign country, and restrictions imposed by the foreign coutnry on labour immigration. The international mobility of capital is restricted not by transport costs but by the difficulties of legal redress, political uncertainty, ignorance of the prospects of investment in a foreign country, imperfections of the banking system, instablity of foreign currencies, mistrust of the foreigners, etc.

Thus, widespread legal and other restrictions exist in the movement of labour and capital between countries. But such problems do not arise in the case of inter-regional trade.

2. *Differences in Natural Resources.* Different countries are endowed with different types of natural resources. Hence they tend to specialise in production of those commodities in which they are richly endowed and trade them with others where such resources are scarce. In Australia, land is in abundance but labour and capital are relatively scarce. On the contrary, capital is relatively abundant and cheap in England while land is scarce and dear there. Thus, commodities requiring more capital, such as manufactures, can be produced in England; while such commodities as wool, mutton, wheat, etc. requiring more land can be produced in Australia. Thus both countries can trade each other's commodities on the basis of comparative cost differences in the production of different commodities.

3. *Geographical and Climatic Differences.* Every country cannot produce all the commodities due to geographical and climatic conditions, except at possibly prohibitive costs. For instance, Brazil has favourable climate geographical conditions for the production of coffee; Bangladesh for jute; Cuba for beet sugar; etc. So countries having climatic and geographical advantages specialise in the production of particular commodities and trade them with others.

4. *Different Markets.* Internatinal markets are separated by difference in languages, usages, habits, tastes, fashions etc. Even the systems of weights and measures and pattern and styles in machinery and equipment differ from country to country. For instance, British railway engines and freight cars are basically different from those in France or in the United States. Thus goods which may be traded within regions may not be sold in other countries. That is why, in great many cases, products to be sold in foreign countries are especially designed to confirm to the national characteristics of that country. Similarly, in India right-hand driven cars are used whereas in Europe and America left-hand driven cars are used.

Moreover, a significant difference between interregional and international marketss is with regard to the manuracture and sale of goods for regional and international markets. A big firm may be producing and selling a number of products in different countries. But it may not be able to standardise its products and realise the economies of large-scale production. On the other hand, a firm which specialises in the production of only one type of product for the interregional markets may enjoy the economies of large-scale production.

5. *Different Currencies.* The principal difference between interregional and international trade lies in the use of different cur.renceis in foreign trade, but the same currency in domestic trade. Rupee is accepted throughout India from the North to the South and from the East to the West, but if we cross over to Nepal or Pakistan, we must convert our rupee into their rupee to buy goods and services there.

It is not the differences in currencies alone that are important in international trade, but changes in their relative values. Every time a change occurs in the value of one currency in terms of another, a number of economic problems arise. "Calculation and execution of monetary exchange transactions incidental to international trading constitute costs and risks of a kind that are not ordinarily involved in domestic trade."[1] Further, currencies of some countries like the American dollar, the British pound the Euro and Japanese yen, are more widely used in international transactions, while others are almost inconvertible. Such tendencies tend to create more economic problems at the international plane. Moreover, different countries follow different monetary and foreign exchange policies which affect the supply of exports or the demand for imports. "It is this difference in policies rather than the existence of different national currencies which distinguishes foreign trade from domestic trade," according to Kindleberger.[2]

6. *Problem of Balance of Payments.* Another important point which distinguishes international trade from inter-regional trade is the problem of balance of payments. The problem of balance of payments is perpetual in international trade while regions within a country have no such problem. This is because there is greater mobility of capital within regions than between countries. Further, the policies which a country chooses to correct its disequilibrium in the balance of payments may give rise to a number of other problems. If it adopts deflation or devaluation or restrictions on imports or the movement of currency, they create further problems. But such problems do not arise in the case of inter-regional trade.

1. H.B. Killough and L.W. Killough, *Economics of International Trade,* 1948.
2. C.B. Kindleberger, *International Economics,* 5/e, 1973.

7. *Transport Costs.* Trade between countries involves high transport costs as against inter-regionally within a country because of geographical distances between different countries.

8. *Different Political Groups*. A significant distinction between inter-regional and international trade is that all regions within a country belong to one political unit while different countries have different political units. Inter-regional trade is among people belonging to the same country even though they may differ on the basis of castes, creeds, religions, tastes or customs. They have a sense of belonging to one nation and their loyalty to the region is secondary. The government is also interested more in the welfare of its nationals belonging to different regions. But in international trade there is no cohension among nations and every country trades with other countries in its own interests and often to the detriment of others. As remarked by Friedrich List, "Domestic trade is among us, international trade is between us and them."

9. *Different National Policies*. Another difference between inter-regional and international trade arises from the fact that policies relating to commerce, trade, taxation, etc. are the same within a country. But in international trade there are artificial barriers in the form of quotas, import duties, tariffs, exchange controls, etc. on the movement of goods and services from one country to another. Sometimes, restrictions are more subtle. They take the form of elaborate custom procedures, packing requirements, etc. Such restrictions are not found in inter-regional trade to impede the flow of goods between regions. Under these circumstances, the internal economic policies relating to taxation, commerce, money, incomes, etc. would be different from what they would be under a policy of free trade.

Conclusion. Therefore, the classical economists asserted on the basis of the above arguments that international trade was fundamentally different from domestic or inter-regional trade. Hence, they evolved a separate theory for international trade based on the principle of comparative cost differences.

On the other hand, Bertil Ohlin shows that there is little difference between inter-regional and international trade. International values are, therefore, determined in the same way as they are determined in internal trade. According to him, "International trade is but a special case of inter-local or inter-regional trade." Therefore, he does not find any justification for a separate theory of international trade. He adduces a number of arguments in support of his answer.

Ohlin does not accept the classical argument that labour and capital are freely mobile within a country but immobile internationally. He argues that labour and capital are also immobile inter-regionally within a country. This is apparent from the fact that wage rates differ not only in different trades but also in the same trades in different regions within the same country. Similarly, interest rates vary for different purposes in different regions.

Further, labour and capital are not immobile between countries. Rather, labour and capital have moved from one country to the other. The rapid development of the USA, Australia, New Zealand, Canada and the Latin American Countries in the 19th and early 20th centuries has been due to the movement of labour and capital from England and Europe.

According to Ohlin, the basis of international trade is not much different from inter-regional trade. In both, space factor is important and goods move from places of abundant supplies to places where they are scarce. Transport costs are involved in both. Trade is carried on by firms for the purpose of maximising profits both in international and inter-regional trade.

So far as currency differences in international trade are concerned, they do not necessitate a separate theory. The rate of exchange between two countries is connected together on the basis of the purchasing power of the two currencies. Since the currency of one country is convertible into the currency of another country, there is no basic difference between international trade and inter-regional trade.

Last but not the least, Ohlin argues that the theory of comparative costs is not applicable to international trade alone but to all trade within a country. It is inherent in the principle of specialisation that an individual will devote his abilities to those pursuits for which he is best suited. For example, the manager of a firm may be able to repair his motorcar more cheaply and efficiently than a mechanic at a garage, but he does not do so because his time and energy can be more profitably employed in attending to his business.

As put by Ohlin: "Regions and nations specialise and trade with each other for the same reasons that individuals specialise and trade. Some are better fitted by temperament for one work rather than another; one is a better gardener, the other a better teacher, while the third proves an excellent doctor. The gardener would prove a poor teacher and teacher a poor doctor, and so on. Thus, the gain from specialisation is clear. Even if every individual were equally alike in ability it would pay to specialise." This fundamental principle of specialisation which permeates all walks of life, applies in exactly the same way and with the same force, to international trade. Thus, the application of the principle of comparative costs to international trade is unnecessary because it is the basis of all trade. Ohlin emphasises in this connection, "As nations are certainly the most significant of all regions, so that theory of international trade represents the chief application of the general theory of inter-regional trade."

He, therefore, believes that there is no need for a separate theory of international trade and regards international trade as "a special case of inter-local or inter-regional trade." Prices of internationally traded goods are determined in the same way as the prices of goods are determind inter-regionally. The basis of determination of prices in inter-regional trade is the general equilibrium of demand and supply which is also applicable to international trade without substantial changes. Differences existing between countries, as are based on tariff barriers, currency differences, differences of language, customs, habits, tastes, etc. are differences of degree and not differences of kind. As a matter of fact, they do not obstruct the free flow of goods and services internationally. Hence, there is practically little difference between international trade and inter-regional trade.

But we do not agree with Prof. Ohlin that there is no intrinsic difference between international and inter-rigional trade. In reality, there are sharp differences between international trade and inter-regional trade. Every country has its own currency in which its nationals can buy and sell goods freely within the country. But it is not possible to buy goods from foreign countries and to sell them because of the various restrictions imposed by each country on them. Foreign currencies are neither available freely nor convertible easily. In inter-regional trade the problem of exchange rates, balance of payments and of tariffs do not arise at all, whereas they are part and parcel of international trade. It is to solve the problems arising from the international trade that the IMF, the GATT, and the UNCTAD have been created which have no concern with inter-regional trade.

Not only this, innumerable theories and models dealing with micro and macro parts of international trade have been formulated by Hecksher, Ohlin, Samuelson, Leontief, Johnson, Bhagwati and others which are quite distinct from the theories dealing with internal trade. This proves that international trade needs a separate study and is in no way similar to inter-regional trade. As aptly put by Kindleberger, "International trade is treated as a distinct subject because of tradition, because of the urgent and important problems presented by international economic questions in the real world, because it follows different laws from domestic trade, and because its study illuminates and enriches our understanding of economics as a whole."

EXERCISES

1. Explain the fundamental differences between international trade and inter-regional trade.
2. "International trade should be regarded as a special case of inter-regional trade or perhaps rather inter-local trade." Examine this statement fully.
3. "Differences between domestic and international trade are of degrees and not of kind". Do you agree with this view or not? Give reasons. Is there any basis for a separate theory of international trade?

Chapter 41

The Theory of Comparative Costs

1. INTRODUCTION

The Classical Theory of the International Trade, also known as the Theory of Comparative Costs, was first formulated by Ricardo, and later improved by John Stuart Mill, Cairnes, and Bastable. Its best exposition is to be found in the works of Taussig and Haberler.

2. COMPARATIVE COSTS THEORY

The principle of comparative costs is based on the differences in production costs of similar commodities in different countries. Production costs differ in countries because of geographical division of labour and specialisation in production. Due to differences in climate, natural resources, geographical situation and efficiency of labour, a country can produce one commodity at a lower cost than the other . In this way, each country specialises in the production of that commodity in which its comparative cost of production is the least. Therefore, when a country enters into trade with some other country, it will export those commodities in which its comparative production costs are less, and will import those commodities in which its comparative production costs are high. This is the basis of international trade, according to Ricardo. It follows that *each country will specialise in the production of those commodities in which it has greater comparative advantage or least comparative disadvantage.* Thus a country will *export* those commodities in which its *comparative advantage is the greatest,* and *import* those commodities in which *its comparative disadvantage is the least.*

Assumptions of the Theory

The Ricardian doctrine of comparative advantage is based on the following assumptions:

(1) There are only two countries, say A and B.

(2) They produce the same two commodities, *X* and *Y*.

(3) Tastes are similar in both countries.

(4) Labour is the only factor of production.

(5) All labour units are homogeneous.

(6) The supply of labour is unchanged.

(7) Prices of the two commodities are determined by labour cost, *i.e.*, the number of labour-units employed to produce each.

(8) Commodities are produced under the law of constant costs or returns.

(9) Trade between the two countries takes place on the basis of the barter system.

(10) Technological knowledge is unchanged.

(11) Factors of production are perfectly mobile within each country but are perfectly immobile between the two countries.

(12) There is free trade between the two countries, there being no trade barriers or restrictions in the movement of commodities.

(13) No transport costs are involved in carrying trade between the two countries.

(14) All factors of production are fully employed in both the countries.

(15) The international market is perfect so that the exchange ratio for the two commodities is the same.

Cost Differences

Given these assumptions, the theory of comparative costs is explained by taking three types of differences in costs: absolute, equal and comparative.

(1) *Absolute Differences in Costs.* There may be absolute differences in costs when one country produces a commodity at an absolute lower cost of production than the other.

The absolute cost differences are illustrated in Table 1

Table 1: Absolute Differences in Costs

Country	*Commodity-X*	*Commodity-Y*
A	10	5
B	5	10

The table reveals that country A can produce 10 *X* or 5*Y* with one unit of labour and country *B* can produce 5*X* or 10*Y* with one unit of labour.

In this case, country *A* has an absolute advantage in the production of *X* (for *10 X* is greater than 5 *X*), and country B has an absolute advantage in the production of *Y* (for 10 *Y* is greater than 5 *Y*).

This can be expressed as $\frac{10X \text{ of A}}{5X \text{ of B}} > 1 > \frac{5Y \text{ of A}}{10Y \text{ of B}}$. Trade between the two countries will benefit both, as shown in Table 2.

Table 2

Country	*Production before Trade* (1)		*Production after Trade* (2)		*Gains from Trade* (2-1)	
Commodity	X	Y	X	Y	X	Y
A	10	5	20	—	+10	–5
B	5	10	—	20	–5	+10
Total Production	15	15	20	20	+5	+5

Table 2 reveals that before trade both countries produce only 15 units each of the two commodities by applying one labour-unit on each commodity. If A were to specialise in producing commodity *X* and use both units of labour on it, its total production will be 20 units of *X*. Similarly, if *B* were to specialise in the production of *Y* alone, its total production will be 20 units of *Y*. The combined gain to both countries from trade will be 5 units of *X* and *Y*.

Figure 1 illustrates absolute differences in costs with the help of production possibility curves. $Y_A X_A$ is the production possibility curve of country *A* which shows that it can produce either OX_A of commodity *X* or OY_A of commodity *Y*. Similarly, country *B* can produce OX_B of commodity *X* or OY_B of commodity *Y*. The figure also reveals that *A* has an absolute advantage in the production of commodity *X* ($OX_A > OX_B$), and country *B* has an absolute advantage in the production of commodity *Y* ($OY_B > OY_A$).

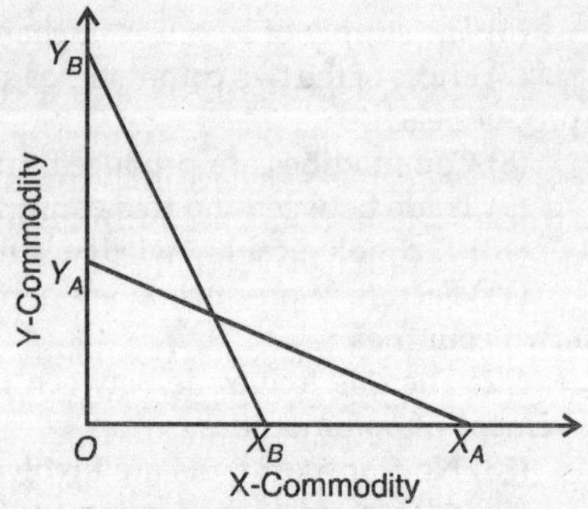

FIG. 1

Adam Smith based his theory of international trade on *absolute* differences in costs between two countries. But this basis of trade is not realistic because we find that there are many underdeveloped countries which do not possess absolute advantage in the production of commodities, and yet they have trade relations with other countries. Ricardo, therefore, emphasised comparative differences in costs.

(2) *Equal Differences in Costs*. Equal differences in cost arise when two commodities are produced in both countries at the same cost difference. Suppose country *A* can produce 10 *X* or 5*Y* and country *B* can produce 8*X* or 4 *Y*.

In this case, with one unit of labour country *A* can produce either 10 *X* or 5 *Y*, and the cost ratio between *X* and *Y* is 2:1. In country *B*, one unit of labour can produce either 8*X* or 4*Y*, and the cost ratio between the two commodities is 2:1 .

Thus the cost of producing *X* in terms of *Y* is the same in both countries. This can be expressed as

$$\frac{\text{10X of A}}{\text{8X of B}} = \frac{\text{5Y of A}}{\text{4Y of B}} = 1$$

When cost differences are equal, no country stands to gain from trade. Hence international trade is not possible.

(3) *Comparative Differences in Costs*. Comparative differences in cost occur when one country has an absolute advantage in the production of *both* commodities, but a *comparative advantage* in the production of one commodity than in the other. The comparative cost differences, are illustrated in Table 3.

The table reveals that country *A* can produce 10*X* or 10*Y*, and country *B* can produce 6*X* or 8*Y*.

In this case, country *A* has an absolute advantage in the production of both *X* and *Y*, but a comparative advantage in the production of *X*. Country *B* is at an absolute disadvantage in the production of both commodities but its least comparative disadvantage is in the production of *Y*. This can be seen from the fact that before trade the domestic cost ratio of *X* and *Y* in country *A* is 10:10 (or 1:1), while in country *B*, it is 6:8 (or 3:4). If they were to enter into trade, country *A*'s advantage over country *B* in the production of commodity *X* is $\frac{\text{10 X of A}}{\text{6 X of B}}$ or $\frac{5}{3}$, and in the production of *Y*, it is $\frac{\text{10 Y of A}}{\text{8 Y of B}}$ or $\frac{5}{4}$. Since $\frac{5}{3}$ is greater than $\frac{5}{4}$, *A*'s advantage is greater in the production of commodity *X*, *A* will find cheaper to import commodity *Y* from country *B* in exchange for its *X*.

Similarly, we can know the comparative disadvantage of country *B* in the production of both commodities. In the case of commodity *X*, country *B* 's position is $\frac{\text{6 X of B}}{\text{10 X of A}}$ or $\frac{3}{5}$. In the case of commodity *Y*, it is $\frac{\text{8Y of B}}{\text{10Y of A}}$ or $\frac{4}{5}$.

Since $\frac{4}{5}$ is greater than $\frac{3}{5}$, *B* has least comparative disadvantage in the production of *Y*. It will trade its

Y for *X* of country *A*.

In other words, country *A* has a comparative advantage in the production of commodity *X*, And *B* has *least comparative disadvantage* in the production of Y. Thus, trade is beneficial for both countries. The comparative advantage position of both countries is illustrated in Figure 2

Table 3 Comparative Differences in costs

Country	*Commodity-X*	*Commodity-Y*
A	10	10
B	6	8

Let *PQ* be the production possibility curve of country *A* and *RS* of country *B*. The curve *PQ* shows that country *A* has an absolute advantage in the production of both commodities *X* and *Y* respectively over country *B*. This is due to the fact that the production possibility curve *RS* of country *B* lies below the production possibility curve *PQ* of country *A*. Country *B* produces *OR* units of commodity Y and *OS* units of commodity X.

To show comparative advantage position in trade, draw a line *RT* parallel to line *PQ*. Now country *A* has a comparative advantage in the production of commodity *X* only because it exports *OT* (> *OS*) units relatively to country *B*. On the other hand, country *B* has a comparative disadvantage in the production of commodity *Y* only. This is because, if it gives up resources required to produce *OS* units of *X*, it would be able to produce commodity *Y* by an amount less than *OR*. Thus country *A* has a comparative advantage in the production of commodity *X*, and country *B* has a comparative disadvantage in the production of commodity *Y*.

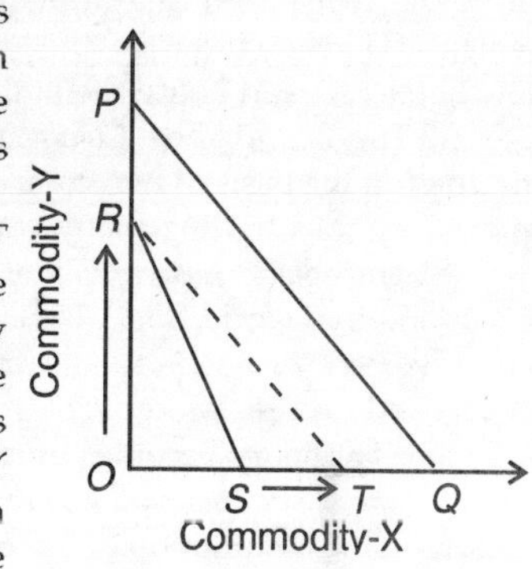

FIG. 2

3. ITS CRITICISMS

The principle of comparative advantage has been the very basis of international trade for over a century until after the First World War. Since then critics have been able only to modify and amplify it. As rightly pointed out by Professor Samuelson, "If theories, like girls, could win beauty contests, comparative advantage would certainly rate high in that it is an elegantly logical structure."[1]

But the theory is not free from some defects. In particular, it has been criticised by Bertin Ohlin and Frank D. Graham. We discuss some of the important criticisms as under.

(1) *Unrealistic Assumption of Labour Cost.* The most severe criticism of the comparative advantage doctrine is that it is based on the labour theory of value. In calculating production costs, it takes only labour costs and neglects non-labour costs involved in the production of commodities. This is highly unrealistic be- cause it is money costs and not labour costs that are the basis of national and international transactions of goods.

Further, the labour cost theory is based on the assumption of *homogeneous labour*. This is again unrealistic because labour is heterogeneous—of different kinds and grades, some specific or specialised, and other non-specific or general.

(2) *No Similar Tastes.* The assumption of similar tastes is unrealistic because tastes differ with different income brackets in a country. Moreover, they also change with the growth of an economy and with the development of its trade relations with other countries.

(3) *Static Assumption of Fixed Proportions.* The theory of comparative costs is based on the assumption that labour is used in the same fixed proportions in the production of all commodities. This is essentially a static analysis and hence unrealistic. As a matter of fact labour is used in varying proportions in the production of commodities. For instance, less labour is used per unit of capital in the production of steel than in the production of textiles. Moreover, some substitution of labour for capital is always possible in production.

(4) *Unrealistic Assumption of Constant Costs.* The theory is based on another weak assumption that an increase of output due to international specialisation is followed by constant costs. But the fact is that there are either increasing costs or diminishing costs. If the large scale of production reduces costs, the comparative

1. P.A. Samuelson, *Economics*,(8th ed.) p. 656

advantage will be increased. On the other hand, if increased output is the result of increased cost of production the comparative advantage will be reduced, and in some cases it may even disappear.

(5) *Ignores Transport Costs.* Ricardo ignores transport costs in determining comparative advantage in trade. This is highly unrealistic because transport costs play an important role in determining the pattern of world trade. Like economies of scale, it is an independent factor of production. For instance, high transport costs may nullify the comparative advantage and the gain from international trade.

(6) *Factors not Fully Mobile Internally.* The doctrine assumes that factors of production are perfectly mobile internally and wholly immobile internationally. This is not realistic because even within a country factors do not move freely from one industry to another or from one region to another.. The greater the degree of specialisation in an industry, the less is the factor mobility from one industry to another. Thus factor mobility influences costs and hence the pattern of international trade.

(7) *Two-Country Two-Commodity Model is Unrealistic.* The Ricardian model is related to trade between two countries on the basis of two commodities. This is again unrealistic because, in actuality, international trade is among countries trading many commodities.

(8) *Unrealistic Assumption of Free Trade.* Another serious weakness of the doctrine is that it assumes perfect and free world trade. But, in reality, world trade is not free. Every country applies restrictions on the free movement of goods to and from other countries. Thus tariffs and other trade restrictions affect world imports and exports. Moreover, products are not homogeneous but differentiated. By neglecting these aspects, the Ricardian theory becomes unrealistic.

(9) *Unrealistic Assumption of Full Employment.* Like all classicial theories, the theory of comparative advantage is based on the assumption of full employment. This assumption also makes the theory static. Keynes falsified the assumption of full employment and proved the existence of underemployment in an economy. Thus the assumption of full employment makes the theory unrealistic.

(10) *Self-Interest Hinders its Operation.* The doctrine does not operate if a country having a comparative disadvantage does not wish to import a commodity from the other country due to strategic, military or development considerations. Thus often self-interest stands in the operation of the theory of comparative costs.

(11) *Neglects the Role of Technology.* The theory neglects the role of technological innovations in international trade. This is unrealistic because technological changes help in increasing the supply of goods not only for the domestic market but also for the international market. World trade has gained much from innovations and research and development (R & D).

(12) *One-Sided Theory.* The Ricardian theory is one-sided because it considers only the supply side of international trade and neglects the demand side. In the words of Professor Ohlin, "It is, indeed, nothing more than an abbreviated account of the conditions of supply."[2]

(13) *Impossibility of Complete Specialisation.* Professor Frank Graham has pointed out that complete specialisation will be impossible on the basis of comparative advantage in producing commodities entering into international trade. He explains two cases in support of his argument: *one,* relating to a big country and a small country; and *two,* relating to a commodity of high value and low value.

To take the first case, suppose there are two countries which enter into trade on the basis of comparative advantage, of these, one is big and the other is small. The small country will be able to specialise completely as it can dispose of its surplus commodity to the bigger one. But the big country will not be able to specialise fully because *(a)* being big, the small country will not be in a position to meet its requirements fully, and *(b)* if it specialises completely in a particular commodity its surplus will be so large that the smaller country will not be able to import the whole of it.

In the second case of commodities having incomparable value, the country producing in high-value commodity will be able to specialise while that producing in low-value commodity will not be able to do the same. This is because the former country will be in a position to have a larger gain than the latter country. Thus, according to Graham, "The classical conclusion of complete specialisation between two countries can hold

---

2. B. Ohlin. *Interregional and International Trade,* 1933, p. 586.

ground only ... by assuming trade between two countries of equal opportunity, consumption value and between two countries of approximately equal economic performance."[3]

(14) *A Clumsy and Dangerous Tool.* Professor Ohlin has criticised the classical theory of international trade on the following grounds: *(i)* The principle of comparative advantage is not applicable to international trade alone, rather it is applicable to all trade. To Ohlin, "International trade is but a special case of inter- local or interregional trade." Thus there is little difference between internal trade and international trade, *(ii)* Factors are immobile not only internationally but also within different regions. This is proved by the fact that wages and interest rates differ in different regions of the same country. Further labour and capital can also move between countries in a limited way, as they do within a region, *(iii)* It is a two-country two-commodity model based on the labour theory of value which is sought to be applied to actual conditions involving many countries and many commodities. He, therefore, regards the theory of comparative advantage as cumbersome, unrealistic, and as a clumsy and dangerous tool of analysis. As an alternative, Ohlin has propounded a new theory which is known as the Modern theory of International Trade.

(15) *Incomplete Theory*. It is an incomplete theory. It simply explains how two countries gain from international trade. But it fails to show how the gains from trade are distributed between the two countries.

Conclusion. Despite these weaknesses, the theory has stood the test of the times. Its basic structure has remained intact, even though many refinements have been made over it. To conclude with Professor Samuelson, "Yet for all its over simplifications, the theory of comparative advantages has in it a most important glimpse of truth. Political economy has found few more pregnant principles. A nation that neglects comparative advantage may have to pay a heavy price in terms of living standards and potential rates of growth."

EXERCISES

1. Discuss critically the theory of comparative costs.
2. Discuss the doctrine of comparative costs.

---

3. F.D. Graham. *The Theory of International Values,* 1948.

CHAPTER 42

The Heckscher-Ohlin Theory

1. INTRODUCTION

Bertin Ohlin in his famous book *Inter-regional and International Trade* (1933) criticised the classical theory of international trade and formulated the General Equilibrium or Factor Endowment or Factor Proportions Theory of International Trade. It is also known as the *Modern Theory of International Trade* or the *Heckscher-Ohlin* (H.O.) *Theory.* In fact, it was Eli Heckscher, Ohlin's teacher, who first propounded the idea in 1919 that trade results from differences in factor endowments in different countries, and Ohlin carried it forward to build the modern theory of international trade.

2. THE HECKSCHER-OHLIN THEORY

The H.O. theory states that the main determinant of the pattern of production, specialisation and trade among regions is the *relative* availability of factor endowments and factor prices. Regions or countries have different factor endowments and factor prices. "Some countries have much capital, others have much labour. The theory now says that countries that are rich in capital will export capital-intensive goods and countries that have much labour will export labour-intensive goods." To Ohlin, the immediate cause of international trade always is that some commodities can be bought more cheaply from other regions, whereas in the same region their production is possible at high prices. Thus the main cause of trade between regions is the difference in prices of commodities.

ASSUMPTIONS O THE THEORY

Before analysing the theory in detail, we discuss below its assumptions:

1. It is a *two-by-two-by-two model, i.e.*, there are two countries (*A* and *B*), two commodities (*X* and *Y*), and two factors of production (capital and labour).

2. There is perfect competition in commodity as well as factor markets.

3. There is full employment of resources.

4. There are quantitative differences in factor endowments in different regions, but qualitatively they are homogeneous.

5. The production functions of the two commodities have different factor intensities, *i.e.*, labour-intensive and capital-intensive.

6. The production functions are different for different commodities, but are the same for each commodity in both countries. It means that the production function of commodity *X* is different from commodity *Y*. But the technique used to produce commodity *X* in both countries is the same, and the technique used to produce commodity *Y* in both countries is the same.

7. Factor intensities are non-reversible.

8. There is perfect mobility of factors within each region but internationally they are immobile.

9. There are no transport costs.

10. There is free and unrestricted trade between the two countries.

11. There are constant returns to scale in the production of each commodity in each region.

12. Tastes and preferences of consumers and their demand patterns are identical in both countries.

13. There is no change in technological knowledge.

Given these assumptions, Heckscher and Ohlin contend that the immediate cause of international trade is the difference in relative commodity prices caused by differences in relative demand and supply of factors (factors prices) as a result of differences in factor endowments between the two countries. Fundamentally, the relative scarcity of factors—the shortage of supply in relation to demand—is essential for trade between two regions. Commodities which use large quantities of scarce factors are imported because their prices are high while those using abundant factors are exported because their prices are low.

The H.O. theorem is explained in terms of two definitions: (1) factor abundance (or scarcity) in terms of the price criterion; and (2) factor abundance (or scarcity) in terms of physical criterion. We discuss these one by one below:

Factor Abundance in Terms of Factor Prices. Heckscher-Ohlin explain richness in factor endowment in terms of factor prices. According to their definition, country *A* is abundant in capital if $(P_C/P_L)_A < (P_C/P_L)_B$, where P_C and P_L refer to prices of capital and labour, and the subscripts *A* and *B* denote the two countries. In other words, if capital is relatively cheap in country *A*, the country is abundant in capital, and if labour is relatively cheap in country *B*, the country is abundant in labour. Thus country *A* will produce and export the capital-intensive good and import the labour-intensive good and country *B* will produce and export the labour-intensive good and import the capital-intensive good. This is illustrated in Figure 1.

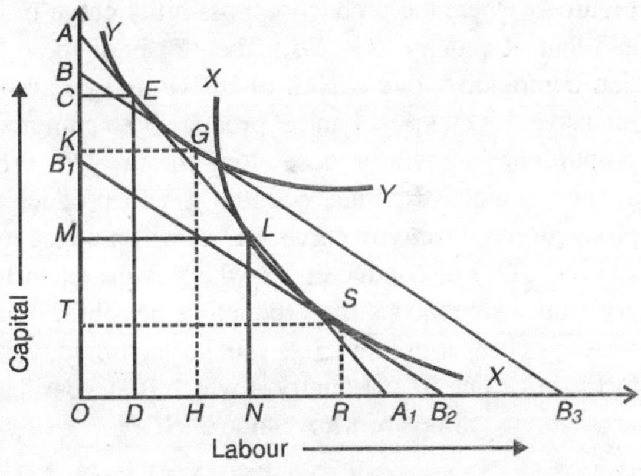

FIG. 1

Let *X* be the labour-intensive commodity taken on the horizontal axis and *Y* be the capital-intensive commodity taken on the vertical axis. *XX* is the isoquant of commodity *X* and *YY* that of commodity *Y*. They are the same for both the countries *A* and *B*. The relative factor prices in country *A* for both the commodities are given by the factor price line AA_1. Assuming that each isoquant represents one unit of the respective commodity, then 1 unit of *Y* will be produced with *OC* amount of capital and *OD* amount of labour at point *E* where the isocost line AA_1 is tangent to the isoquant *YY*. By the same reasoning, we find that the cost of producing one unit of commodity *X* in country *A* is *OM* amount of capital and *ON* amount of labour. Since capital is abundant and cheap in country *A*, it will specialise in the production of the capital-intensive commodity *Y*. This is clear from Fig. 1 where in order to produce 1 unit of *Y* it uses more amount of capital *OC* with *OD* of labour at point *E* on the isoquant *YY*. While at point *L* on the isoquant *XX*, it uses less amount of capital *OM* with more of labour *ON* in order to produce 1 unit of *X*. Hence country *A* will produce and export the relatively capital abundant and cheap commodity *Y* to the other country *B*.

In order to find the cost of producing one unit of each commodity in country *B* where labour is relatively cheap and abundant, draw a flatter factor price line BB_3 tangent to the isoquant *YY* at point *G*. A similar factor price line B_1B_2 is drawn parallel to BB_3 which is tangent to the isoquant *XX* at point *S*. Now it requires *OK* amount of capital and *OH* amount of labour to produce one unit of commodity *Y* in country *B*, and *OT* amount of capital and *OR* amount of labour to produce one unit of commodity *X* in this country. Since labour is cheap and abundant in country *B*, it will specialise in the production of labour-intensive commodity *X*. So it will produce commodity *X* at point *S* on the isoquant *XX*, which requires more amount of labour *OR* with less amount of capital *OT* than commodity *Y* which requires less amount of labour *OH* with more amount of capital *OK* at point *G* on the isoquant *YY*. Hence country *B* will export commodity *X* to country *A* in exchange for commodity *Y*.

This establishes the H.O. theorem that the capital abundant country will export the relatively cheap capital-intensive commodity, and the labour abundant country will export the relatively cheap labour-intensive commodity.

Factor Abundance in Physical Terms. Another way to explain the H.O. theorem is in physical terms of factor abundance. According to this criterion, *a country is relatively capital abundant if it is endowed with a higher proportion of capital and labour than the other country.*

If country *A* is relatively capital-abundant and country *B* is relatively labour-abundant , then measured in physical amounts $C_A/L_A > C_B/L_B$, where C_A and L_A are the total amounts of capital and labour respectively in country *A*, and C_B and L_B are the total amounts of capital and labour respectively in country *B*. This is explained in Figure 2, where the production possibility curve of country *A* is AA_1 and that of country *B* is BB_1. The slopes of these two curves show that commodity *Y* is capital intensive and commodity *X* is labour intensive. If countries *A* and *B* produce both commodities in the same proportion, they will produce along the ray *OR*. When both produce at their respective points, country *A* will produce at point *E* where the factor-price line *ST* touches the production productivity curve AA_1. It will produce more of commodity *Y* (that is *OS*) which is cheaper in it and less *(OT)* of commodity *X* which is dearer in it. Country *B* will produce at point *F* where the factor-price line *KR* touches the production possibility curve BB_1. It will produce more *(OR)* of commodity *X* which is cheaper in it and less *(OK)* of commodity *Y* which is dearer in it. This is proved by the slope of the factor-price line *ST* of country *A* which is steeper than the factor-price line *KR* of country *B* which is flatter.

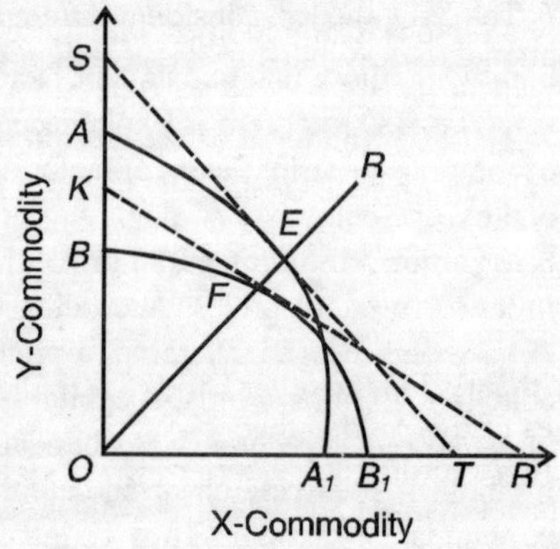

FIG. 2

Slope of *KR* > Slope of *ST*

or $$\left(\frac{P_x}{P_y}\right)_A > \left(\frac{P_x}{P_y}\right)_B$$

The difference between both factor-price lines *TR* on X-axis indicates that *OR* of commodity *X* is produced more in country *B* relatively to *OT* quantity of *X* in country *A*. Similarly, the difference between both factor price lines *KS* on *Y*-axis shows that *OS* of commodity *Y* is produced more in country *A* relatively to *OK* quantity of *Y* in country *B*. Thus the capital-abundant country *A* has a bias in favour of capital-intensive commodity *Y* from the production side, and the labour-abundant country *B* has a bias in favour of producing the labour-intensive commodity *X*.

3. ITS SUPERIORITY OVER THE CLASSICAL THEORY

The H.O. theorem is an improvement over the classical theory of international trade in many aspects.

1. The H.O. theory is superior to the classical theory in that it regards international trade as a special case of inter-regional or inter local trade as distinct from the classical theory which considers international trade totally different from domestic trade.

2. The H.O. analysis is cast within the framework of the realistic general equilibrium theory of value. It frees the classical theory from the defunct and unrealistic labour theory of value.

3. The H.O. model takes two factors—labour and capital—as against the one factor (labour) of the classical model, and is thus superior to the latter.

4. The H.O. theory is superior to the Ricardian theory in that it regards differences in factor supplies as basic for determining the pattern of international trade while the Ricardian theory takes no notice of it.

5. The H.O. model is realistic because it is based on the relative prices of *factors* which, in turn, influence the relative prices of goods, while the Ricardian theory considers the relative prices of *goods* only.

6. The H.O. theory considers differences in relative productivities of labour and capital as the basis of international trade, while the classical theory takes the productivity of labour alone. Hence the former is more realistic than the latter.

7. The H.O. model is based on differences in factor endowments in different countries as against the quality of one factor labour in the classical theory. Thus the former is superior because it lays emphasis not only on the quality but also on the quantity of factors in determining international values.

8. According to Samuelson, the Ricardian theory could not explain the causes of differences in comparative advantage. The merit of H.O. theory lies in explaining the same satisfactorily.

9. The classical theory demonstrates the *gains* from trade between the two countries. This is related to the *welfare* theory. On the other hand, the H.O. model is scientific and concentrates on the *basis* of trade. It, thus, partakes of the *positive* theory.

10. According to Haberler[2], the H.O. theory is a location theory which highlights the importance of the space factor in international trade while the classical theory regards the different countries as spaceless markets. Thus the former theory is superior to the latter.

11. The H.O. theorem is explicitly based on the assumption of production functions of the two countries. On the other hand, the classical theory is based on differences in the production of the trading countries.

12. The H.O. model is more realistic than the classical theory in that the former leads to complete specialisation in the production of one commodity by one country and of the other commodity by the second country when they enter into trade with each other. By contrast, the trade between two countries may or may not lead to complete specialisation in the classical theory.

4. ITS CRITICISMS

Ohlin's theory has been criticised on the following grounds:

1. *Two-by-two-by-two Model.* Ohlin has been criticised for presenting two-by-two-by-two model based on oversimplified assumptions. But, as Ohlin himself points out, it can be extended to many regions, many commodities and many factors. He demonstrated it in the mathematical appendix to his book.

2. *Static Theory*. Like the classical theory, the Ohlin model is static in nature. "It only gives some characteristics of an economy at a given point in time. For instance, it can give information about how to rank goods at any given moments, but it cannot give any indication about how the economy would develop if production conditions were to change."

3. *Factors not Homogeneous.* The theory assumes the existence of the homogeneous factors in the two countries which can be measured for calculating factor endowment ratios. But, in reality, no two factors are homogenous qualitatively between countries, and even one factor is of various types. For instance, labour both skilled and unskilled, is of various types. Similarly, capital goods take many forms and also perform the tasks of labour when they are labour saving.

4. *Production Techniques not Homogeneous.* Again, the Ohlin model assumes homogeneous production techniques for each commodity in the two countries. But production techniques are different for the same commodity in the two countries. For instance, textiles may be produced with handlooms which require more labour and less capital or with highly sophisticated powerlooms requiring a small number of workers. In such a situation, trade may not follow the Ohlin pattern.

5. *Tastes and Demand Patterns not Identical.* The H.O. theory is based on the assumption of identical tastes and demand patterns of consumption in both countries. This assumption implies that the tastes and demand patterns of consumers are the same for different income groups. This is unrealistic. Moreover, with inventions taking place in consumers' goods, changes in tastes and demand patterns of consumers also occur even among developed countries. Commodities which consumers demand in the United States are different from what consumers demand in Germany. Consequently, tastes are not identical in trading countries.

6. *No Constant Returns.* The assumption that there are constant returns to scale is also not realistic because a country having rich factor endowments often obtains the advantages of economies of scale through lesser production and exports. Thus there are increasing returns to scale rather than constant.

7. *Transport Costs influence Trade.* This theory does not consider transport costs in trade between two countries. Ths is an unrealistic assumption. Alongwith transport costs, loading and unloading of goods and other port charges affect the prices of produced commodities in the two countries. When transport costs are included, they lead to price differentials for the same commodity in the two countries which affect their trade relations.

8. *Unrealistic Assumptions of Full Employment and Perfect Competition.* The H.O. theory is based on the unrealistic assumptions of full employment and perfect competition because there is neither full employment nor perfect competition in any country of the world. Rather, countries do not have free trade but impose trade restrictions on a large scale.

9. *Leontief Paradox has Falsified the Theory.* Ohlin assumes that relative factor prices reflect exactly relative factor endowments. It implies that in the determination of factor prices, supply is more important than demand. If, however, the demand factors are given more importance in determining factor prices, a capital-rich country will export a labour-intensive commodity because the high demand for capital will raise the price of capital relative of labour. Prof. Leontief's[3] empirical study of the Ohlin theorem, known as the Leontief Paradox, has led to paradoxical results that the United States exports labour-intensive goods and imports capital-intensive goods, even though it is a capital-rich country.

10. *Partial Equilibrium Analysis.* Prof. Haberler criticises Ohlin for his failure to develop a comprehensive general equilibrium concept. He regards Ohlin's theory as, by and large, a partial equilibrium analysis.[4]

11. *Factor Prices do not determine Commodity Prices.* Wijanholds has criticised Ohlin for his view that commodity prices are determined by the factor prices which in turn, determine costs. He holds that the prices of commodities are determined by their utility to the consumers, and that the prices of raw materials and labour are ultimately dependent on the prices of the final commodities. He maintains that the right approach is to start with commodity prices rather than factor prices.

12. *Vague and Conditional Theory.* Ohlin's theory has been characterised as "somewhat vague and conditional.' As pointed out by Haberler, "With many factors of production, some of which are qualitatively incommensurable as between different countries, and with dissimilar production functions in different countries, no sweeping a *priori* generalisation concerning the composition of trade are possible."

Despite these criticisms, the Ohlin theory of international trade is definitely an improvement over the classical theory as it attempts to explain the basis of international trade in the general equilibrium setting.

EXERCISES

1. Discuss critically the Modern Theory of International Trade.
2. Discuss the Heckscher-Ohlin Theory of International Trade. To what extent it is superior to the classical theory of international values?
3. Critically examine the view that international trade results from differences in factor endowments in countries.
4. State and explain the Heckscher-Ohlin theory of international trade and the conditions underlying it.

CHAPTER 43

Mill's Theory of Reciprocal Demand

1. INTRODUCTION

Ricardo expounded the theory of comparative advantage without explaining the ratios at which commodities would exchange for one another. It was J.S. Mill who discussed the latter problem in detail in terms of his theory of reciprocal demand. The term 'reciprocal demand' introduced by Mill to explain the determination of the equilibrium terms of trade. It is used to indicate a country's demand for one commodity in terms of the quantities of the other commodity it is prepared to give up in exchange. It is reciprocal demand that determines the terms of trade which, in turn, determine the relative share of each country. Equilibrium would be established at that ratio of exchange between the two commodities at which quantities demanded by each country of the commodity which it imports from the other, should be exactly sufficient to pay for one another.

To explain his theory of reciprocal demand, Mill first restated the Ricardian theory of comparative costs. "Instead of taking as given the output of each commodity in two countries, with the labour costs different, he assumed a given amount of labour in each country, but differing outputs. Thus his formulation ran in terms of comparative advantage, or comparative effectiveness of labour, as contrasted with Ricardo's comparative labour cost."[2]

ASSUMPTIONS

Mill's theory of reciprocal demand is based on the following assumptions:

1. There are two countries, say, England and Germany.
2. There are two commodities, say, linen and cloth.
3. Both the commodities are produced under the law of constant returns.
4. There are no transport costs.
5. The needs of the two countries are similar.

---

1. Charles P. Kindleberger, *op. cit.*, p. 35.
2. P.T. Ellsworth and J. Clark Luth, *The International Economy*, 1975.

6. There is perfect competition.
7. There is full employment.
8. There is free trade between the two countries.
9. The principle of comparative costs is applicable in trade relations between the two countries.

2. EXPLANATION OF THE THEORY

Given these assumptions, Mill's theory of reciprocal demand can be explained with the help of Table 1.

TABLE 1. QUANTITIES OF COMMODITIES PRODUCED

Country	*Output of*	
	Linen	*Cloth*
Germany	10	10
England	6	8

Suppose Germany can produce 10 units of linen or 10 units of cloth within one man-year and England can produce 6 units of linen or 8 units of cloth with the same input of labour-time. According to Mill, "This supposition then being made, it would be in the interest of England to import linen from Germany, and of Germany to import cloth from England." This is because Germany has an absolute advantage in the production of both linen and cloth, while England has the least comparative disadvantage in the production of cloth. This can be seen from their domestic exchange ratios and international exchange ratios.

Before trade, the domestic cost ratio of linen and cloth in Germany is 1:1; and in England 3:4. If they were to enter into trade, Germany's advantage over England in the production of linen is 5:3 (or 10:6), and in the production of cloth 5:4 (or 10:8). Since 5/3 is greater than 5/4, Germany possesses greater comparative advantage in the production of linen. Thus it is in Germany's interest to export linen to England in exchange for cloth. Similarly, England's position in the production of linen is 3/5 (or 6/10) and in the production of cloth is 4/5 (or 8/10). Since 4/5 is greater than 3/5, it is in the interest of England to export cloth to Germany in exchange for linen.

Mill's theory of reciprocal demand relates to the possible terms of trade at which the two commodities will exchange for each other between the two countries. The terms of trade refer to 'the barter terms of trade' between the two countries, *i.e.*, the ratio of the quantity of imports for a given quantity of exports of a country. And "the limits to the possible barter terms of trade (the international exchange ratio) are set by the domestic exchange ratios established by the relative efficiency of labour in each country."

To take an example, in Germany 2 inputs of labour-time produce 10 units of linen and 10 units of cloth, while in England the same labour produces 6 units of linen and 8 units of cloth. The domestic exchange ratio between linen and cloth in Germany is 1:1 and 1:1.33 in England. Thus the limits of possible terms of trade are 1 linen: 1 cloth in Germany and 1 linen : 1.33 cloth in England. Thus the terms of trade between the two countries will be between 1 linen or 1 cloth or 1.33 cloth.

But the actual ratio will depend upon *reciprocal demand, i.e.* "the strength and elasticity of each country's demand for the other country's product." If Germany's demand for England's cloth is *more* intense (inelasic), then the terms of trade will be nearer 1:1. Germany will be prepared to exchange one unit of linen with one unit of cloth of England. The terms of trade will move against it and in favour of England. Consequently, Germany's gain from trade will be less than that of England. On the other hand, if Germany's demand for England's cloth is *less* intense (more elastic), then the terms of trade will be nearer 1:1.33. Germany will be prepared to exchange its one unit of linen with 1.33 units of cloth of England. The terms of trade will move in favour of Germany and against England. Consequently, Germany's gain from trade will be greater than that of England.

In short, "(1) the possible range of barter terms is given by the respective domestic terms of trade as set by comparative efficiency in each country; (2) within this range, the actual terms of trade depend on each country's demand for other country's produce; and (3) finally, only those barter terms of trade will be stable at which the exports offered by the country just suffice to pay for the imports it desires."[3]

---

3. *Ibid*, pp. 51-52.

Mill's theory of reciprocal demand is explained diagrammatically in terms of Marshall's *offer curves.*

In Fig. 1, England producing only cloth is taken on the horizontal axis and Germany producing only linen is taken on vertical axis. The curve *OE* is England's offer curve. It shows how many units of cloth England will give up for a given quantity of linen. Similarly, *OG* is the offer curve of Germany which shows how many units of linen Germany is prepared to give up in exchange for a given quantitiy of cloth. The point *T* where the two offer curves *OE* and *OG* intersect is the equilibrium point at which *OC* of cloth is traded by England of *OL* of linen of Germany. The rate at which cloth is exchanged for linen is equivalent to the slope of the ray *OT*.

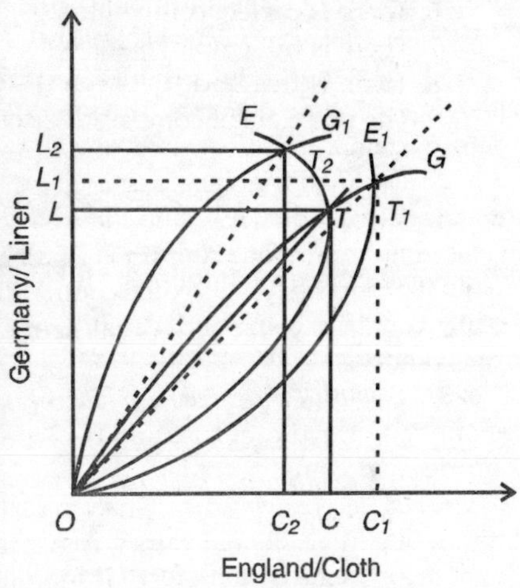

FIG. 1

A change in the demand on the part of one country for the product of the other country brings about a change in the shape of its offer curve. Suppose England's demand for Germany's linen increases. England might now be prepared to exchange more cloth for Germany's linen. Consequently, England's offer curve shifts to the right as OE_1 which intersects Germany's offer curve *OG* at T_1. Now England trades OC_1 units of cloth for OL_1 units of linen. The terms of trade, as shown by the slope of the (dotted) ray OT_1, indicate that they have deteriorated for England and improved for Germany. This is evident from the fact that England trades CC_1 units of cloth for LL_1 units of linen. CC_1 is greater than LL_1.

Similarly, if Germany's demand for England's cloth increases, Germany's offer curve shifts to the left as OG_1 which intersects England's offer curve *OE* at T_2. Now Germany exchanges OL_2 units of linen for OC_2 units of cloth. The terms of trade, as shown by the slope of the (dotted) ray OT_2, indicate that they have deteriorated for Germany and improved for England.This is clear from the fact that Germany exchanges LL_2 more linen for CC_2 less cloth, *i.e.* $LL_2 > CC_2$.

But the actual terms of trade will depend upon the elasticity of demand of the offer curve of each country. The more elastic the offer curve of a country, the more unfavourable will be terms of trade for it in relation to the other country. On the contrary, the more inelastic is its offer curve, the more favourable will be its terms of trade in relation to the other country.

3. DISTRIBUTION OF GAINS FROM TRADE

The distribution of gains from trade is explained in terms of Fig. 2 where *OE* and *OG* are the offer curves of England and Germany respectively. *Oe* and *Og* are the constant domestic cost ratios of producing both linen and cloth in the two countries respectively. The actual terms of trade are settled at *P*, the point of intersection of *OE* and *OG*. The ray *OT* represents the equilibrium terms of trade.

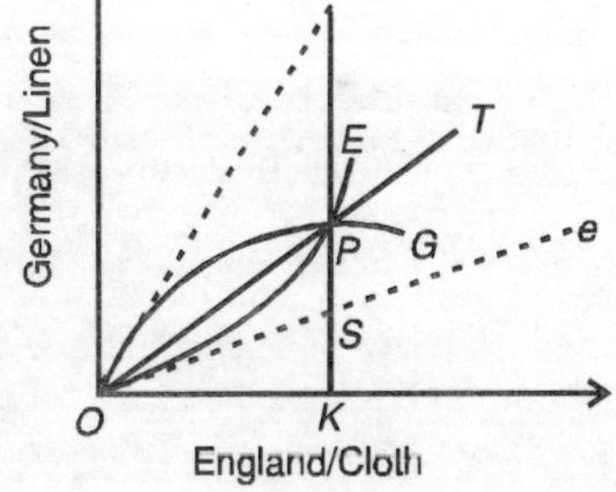

FIG. 2

The cost ratio within England is *KS* units of linen : *OK* units of cloth. But it gets *KP* units of linen through trade. *SP (= KP – KS)* units of linen is, therefore, its gain. The domestic cost ratio in Germany is *KR* units of linen: *OK* units of cloth. But it imports *OK* units of cloth from England in exchange for only *KP* units of linen. *PR (= KR – KP)* units of linen is its gain. The greater will be the gain of a country, the closer are its actual terms of trade to the other country's domestic terms of trade.

4. ITS CRITICISMS

Mill's theory of Reciprocal Demand is based on almost the same unrealistic assumptions that were adopted by Ricardo in his doctrine of comparative advantage. Thus the theory suffers from similar weaknesses.

Besides, there are some additional criticisms made by Viner, Graham, and others.

1. *Does not pay Attention to Domestic Demand*. Mill's theory of reciprocal demand does take into account the domestic demand for the product. As pointed out by Viner, each country would export its product only after satisfying its home demand. Thus the demand curve for Germany would not be below the line *Og* until the domestic demand was satisfied, and the same applies to England.

2. *Both Countries cannot be of Equal Size*. According to Graham, Mill's analysis is valid only if the two countries are of equal size and the two commodities are of equal consumption value. In the absence of these two assumptions, if one country is small and the other large, the small country gains the most on both counts: *First*, if it produced a high-value commodity, it will adopt the cost ratios of its big partner; and *Second*, the two trading countries being of unequal size, the terms of trade will be fixed at or near the comparative costs of the large country.

3. *Two-countries, Two-commodities Assumption is unrealistic*. Mill's theory is based on the unrealistic assumption of two-countries and two-commodities. Graham, therefore, favours several commodities, several countries and complex trade.[4]

4. *Neglect of Supply Side*. Graham further criticises Mill for emphasising demand and neglecting supply in determining international values. According to him, the application of the reciprocal demand makes it appear that demand alone is of interest. He maintains that production costs (supply) are also of paramount importance in international trade. He thus attacked the Law of Reciprocal Demand "as appropriate only to trade in antiques and old masters."

5. *Does not pay Attention to Fluctuations in Income in two Countries*. Another weakness of Mill's analysis of reciprocal demand is that it makes no allowance for fluctuations in incomes in the two trading countries which are bound to influence the terms of trade between them.

6. *Unrealistic and Arbitrary*. Further, the theory is based on barter of trade and relative price ratios. Thus it 'neglects all stickiness of prices and wages, all transitional inflationary and overvaluation gaps, and all balance of payments problems'. No wonder, the theory is abstract and unrealistic. Graham, therefore, regards the theory "in its essence fallacious and should be discarded."

7. *Unrealistic Assumptions*. Mill's theory is based on such unrealistic assumptions as two countries, two commodities, law of constant returns, lack of transport costs, full employment, perfect competition, etc. These make the theory unrealistic.

Conclusion. But there is little basis in the criticisms made by Graham which appear to be flimsy. As pointed out by Viner, "The terms of trade can be directly influenced by reciprocal demands and by nothing else. The reciprocal demands, in turn, are ultimately determined by the cost conditions together with the basic utility functions."[5] The real fault in Mill's analysis is that it overemphasises the basic utility functions and neglects the production costs.

EXERCISES

1. Analyse the nature and significance of the principle of reciprocal demand in the theory of comparative costs.
2. Critically discuss Mill's theory of reciprocal demand in the theory of comparative costs.

---

4. F.D. Graham, "The Theory of International Values," *Q.J.E.* XLVI, 1932.
5. J. Viner, *Studies in the Theory of International Trade*, 1937.

CHAPTER 44

Haberler's Theory of Opportunity Costs

1. INTRODUCTION

The most severe criticism of Ricardo's comparative costs theory has been that it is based on the labour theory of value. The labour theory of value states that the value of a commodity is equal to the amount of labour time involved in the production of that commodity. This means that labour is the only factor of production, labour is homogeneous and labour is used in the *same* fixed proportions in the production of all commodities. But all these assumptions are unrealistic because (*i*) labour is not the only factor of production as commodities are produced in combination with other factors, such as land, capital and other resources; (*ii*) labour is not homogeneous but is heterogeneous, of different kinds and grades divided into many non-competing groups; and (*iii*), labour is used in varying proportions in the production of different commodities, and labour is also substitutable for capital, and vice-versa.

Haberler's opportunity costs theory[1] overcomes these shortcomings and explains the doctrine of comparative costs in terms of what he calls 'the substitution curve' or what Samuelson terms 'production possibility curve' or 'transformation curve', or what Lerner calls 'production indifference curve', or production frontier.

2. THE THEORY OF OPPORTUNITY COSTS

The opportunity costs theory says that if a country can produce either commodity X or Y, the opportunity cost of commodity X is the amount of the other commodity Y that must be given up in order to get one additional unit of commodity X. Thus the exchange ratio between the two commodities is expressed in terms of their opportunity costs. The concept of opportunity costs has been illustrated in international trade theory with production possibility curves.

ASSUMPTIONS

Haberler makes the following assumptions for his theory.

1. G. Haberler, *The Theory of International Trade*, 1936.

1. There are only two countries, say *A* and *B*.
2. Each country possesses two factors of production, labour and capital.
3. Each country can produce two commodities, say *X* and *Y*.
4. There is perfect competition in both the factor and commodity markets.
5. The price of each commodity equals its marginal money costs.
6. The price of each factor equals its marginal value productivity in each employment.
7. The supply of each factor is fixed.
8. There is full employment in each country.
9. There is no change in technology.
10. Factors are immobile between the two countries.
11. Factors are completely mobile within countries.
12. Trade between the two countries is completely free and unrestricted.

EXPLANATION OF THE THEORY

Given these assumptions, a production possibility curve shows the various alternative combinations of the two commodities that a country can produce most efficiently by fully utilising its factors of production with the available technology. The slope of the production possibility curve measures the amount of one commodity that a country must give up in order to get an additional unit of the second commodity. In other words, the slope of the production possibility curve is its marginal rate of transformation (MRT).

It is the shape of the production possibility curve under different cost conditions that determines the basis and the gains from international trade under the theory of opportunity costs. If the amount of *Y* required to be given up to get additional quantity of *X* remain constant, the production possibility curve would be a straight line and it would indicate *constant* opportunity costs. If more quantity of *Y* is required to be given up in order to have an additional quantity of *X*, the production possibility curve would be concave to the origin and it would indicate *increasing* opportunity costs. Lastly, if in order to get an additional quantity of *X*, less quantity of *Y* is required to be given up, the production possibility curve would be convex to the origin, and it would indicate diminishing opportunity costs.

TRADE UNDER CONSTANT OPPORTUNITY COSTS

Under constant opportunity costs, the production possibility curve is a straight line. In figure 1, *PA* is the production possibility curve of country *A*, and *PB* of country *B*. Country *A* can produce either *OP* of *Y* or *OA* of *X*, and similarly country *B* can produce either *OP* of *Y* or *OB* of *X*. If they want to produce both commodities, then they must be on any one point of their respective production possibility curves. For instance, at point *E* country *B* can produce OX_1 of *X* and OY_1 of *Y*. Since the slope of a production possibility curve determines the relative prices of the two commodities, they are the same at all points on a straight line curve. This is because the opportunity cost of leaving a unit of one commodity in order to have an additional unit of the other is constant. Thus the cost ratio (or the relative prices) of the two commodities in country *B* is *OP*/*OB*, and in country *A*, *OP*/*OA*.

As the relative prices differ in the two countries, trade is possible between the two. Taking the two countries *A* and *B*, both can produce the same amount *OP* of *Y*, but *A* can produce a larger amount of *X*. It can produce *OA* of *X* as compared to *OB* of country *B*. So commodity *X* will be cheaper in *A* than in *B*, and *Y* will be relatively cheaper in *B* than in *A*. So *A* has a comparative advantage in the production of *X*, and *B* has a comparative advantage in the production of *Y*. Under these circumstances, country *A* will specialise in the production of commodity *X* and export it to *B*, and country *B* will specialise in the production of commodity *Y* and export it to *A*.

Suppose *B* is a smaller country than *A* and enters into trade with the latter country. Since *A* is a large country, let its internal price ratio as represented by the curve *PA* be the international price ratio for *B*. Before trade, *B* was consuming and producing at point *E* on its domestic price line *PB*. After trade, *B* can specialise in the production of only *Y*. It can move from point *E* to point *P* and produce there. It also increases its consumption from point *E* to *D* on the new international price line *PA*, where it consumes *PT* of *X* by importing it from *A* and exporting *TD* of *Y* to it at the international terms of trade represented by the line *PA*. So after entering into

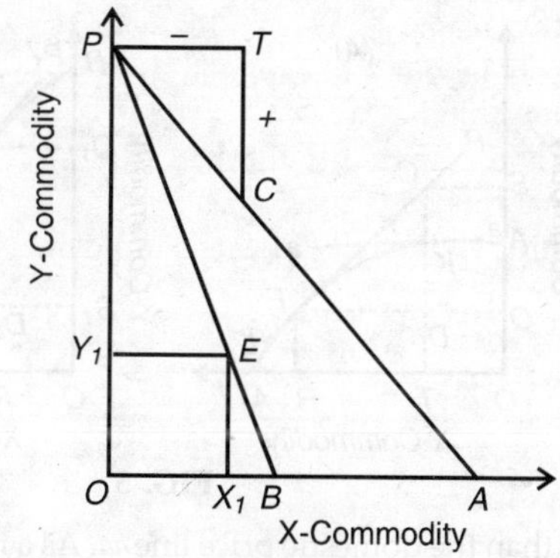

FIG. 1

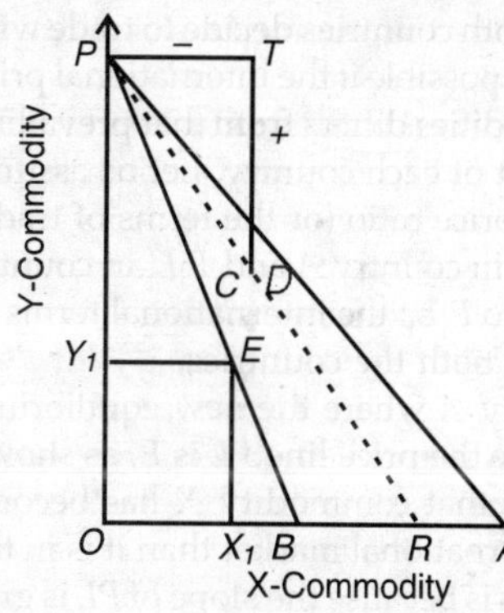

FIG. 2

trade with *A*, country *B* has definitely gained.

But country *A* has not gained from trade with *B* because the relative prices of commodities *X* and *Y* did not change in it before and after trade, as shown by the line *PA*. In reality, "the price after trade may be the same as the price before trade for one of the parties. It cannot be the same for both. Both countries must trade at the same price. Since their prices had differed before trade and are the same after trade, the price of at least one must have altered. The post-trade price can, however, differ from pre-trade price for both."

The pre-trade and post-trade situation of country *B* is now shown in Fig. 2 where *PR* is the new international price line. Before trade, it was consuming and producing both the commodities at point *E*. After trade it specialises exclusively in the production of *Y* at point *P*, and its consumption level shifts up from point *E* to *C* on the international price ratio *PR*. It will now export *TC* of *Y* to country *A* in exchange for *PT* of *X*. In this situation, country *B* will not gain as much as in the previous example, but country *A* will definitely share the gains from international trade.

Trade under Increasing Opportunity Costs

The above analysis of constant opportunity costs is based on the assumptions that factors of production are used in the same fixed proportions due to perfect substitutability for the production of both commodities, and that all units of each factor of production are homogeneous. But these assumptions are unrealistic. As a matter of fact, factors of production cannot be substituted for each other in the production of the two commodities. Moreover, some factors are more suited for the production of one commodity than for the other.

The production possibility curve under increasing opportunity costs is concave to the origin because when a country specialises in the production of one commodity, in which it possesses comparative advantage, its opportunity costs increase. In Fig. 3 Panel (*A*), AA_1 is the production possibility curve of country *A* which is concave to the origin. The slope of this curve shows that this country will specialise in the production of commodity *X*. As we move from point *A* towards point A_1 on this curve, country *A* will give up larger and larger units of commodity *Y* in order to have additional units of commodity *X*. Thus the country faces increasing opportunity costs as it produces each additional unit of commodity *X* in which it specialises.

On the other hand, Panel (*B*) of Fig. 3 shows BB_1 as the production possibility curve of country *B*. The slope of this curve reveals that it will specialise in the production of commodity *Y*. As we move upwards from point B_1 to *B* along this curve, country *B* will give up larger and larger units of *X* in order to produce additional units of commodity *Y*. Thus country *B* faces increasing opportunity costs as it produces each additional unit of commodity *Y* in which it specialises.

Suppose that in the absence of foreign trade, country *A* produces and consumes some quantities of both *X* and *Y* at point *K*, where the line *aa* is tangent to the production possibility curve AA_1. The line *aa* indicates the domestic relative commodity price of *X* and *Y* as shown in Fig. 3(*A*). Similarly, country *B* produces and consumes some quantities of the two commodities at point K_1 where its price- line *bb* is tangent to the production possibility curve BB_1, as shown in Fig. 3 (*B*).

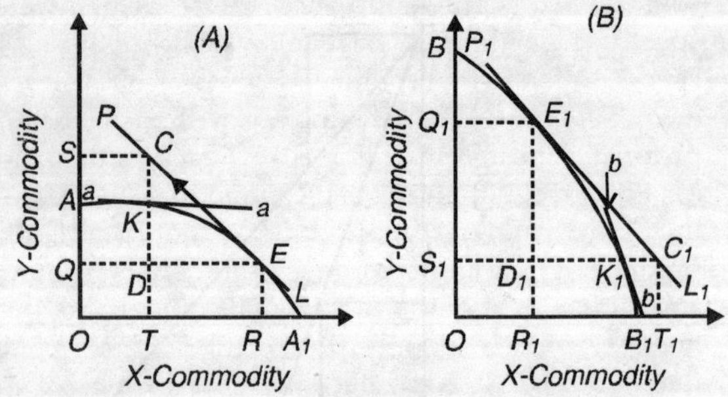

FIG. 3

Now suppose, both countries decide to trade with each other. This is only possible if the international price ratio of the two commodities differs from that prevailing in the domestic market of each country. Let us assume that the international price ratio (or the terms of trade) is given by the line *PL* in country *A* and P_1L_1 in country *B*. Since *PL* is parallel to P_1L_1, the international terms of trade are the same for both the countries.

First take country *A* where the new equilibrium point as determined by the price line *PL* is *E*, as shown in Fig. 3 (*A*). It means that commodity *X* has become more expensive in international market than it is in the domestic marktet. This is because the slope of *PL* is greater than the domestic price line *aa*. As a result, it is in the interest of country *A* to shift some of its factors of production from the production of *Y* to *X*, by moving its production level from point *K* to point *E* on the production possibility curve where the international price line *PL* is tangent. It will thus produce *OR* of *X* and *OQ* of *Y*. The consumption point for country *A* will be at *C* on the price line *PL*. It will then export *TR* of *X* and import *QS* of *Y*, and domestically consume *OT* of *X* and *OQ* of *Y*. Its export and import can also be shown by the "trade triangle" *CDE* where *DE* (= *TR*) is the export of *X* and *DC* (= *QS*) is the import of *Y*. Similarly, the consumption of *X* is *QD* (= *OT*) and of *Y* is *TD* (= *OQ*). Thus by entering into trade country *A* is able to consume more of both *X* and *Y* because point *C* is above and to the right of point *K*.

Take country *B* where the new equilibrium point, as determined by the international price line P_1L_1, is tangent to the production possibility curve BB_1 at point E_1, as shown in Fig. 3 (*B*). It means that commodity *Y* has become more expensive in the international market than in the domestic market. This is because the slope of P_1L_1 is less steep than the domestic price line *bb*. It will, therefore, be in the interest of country *B* to shift some of its resources from the production of *X* and *Y*, by moving its production level from point K_1 to E_1. It will then produce OQ_1 of *Y* and OR_1 of *X*. The consumption point of country *B* will be at C_1 on the price line P_1L_1. It will import D_1C_1 of *X* and export D_1E_1 on *Y* of the trade triangle $E_1D_1C_1$. It will domestically consume OS_1 of *Y* and OR_1 of *X*. Thus country *B* is also better off by entering into trade with country *A* because it is able to consume more of both *X* and *Y*, as the consumption point C_1 after trade is above and to the right of point K_1.

But under increasing opportunity costs specialisation is always incomplete due to decreasing returns. Hence the gains from trade are less than that under complete specialisation.

Further, the law of comparative costs is valid only under increasing opportunity costs. "In a two-goods world if one country is more efficient in producing both goods than another country, it profits by concentrating on the product in which it has a greater comparative advantage and buying the goods in which it has a comparative disadvantage. The basic criterion is that with trade it gets a higher price for its speciality or pays a lower price for the commodity in which it is relatively not so productive."

TRADE UNDER DECREASING OPPORTUNITY COSTS

When two countries experience decreasing opportunity costs, their production possibility curves are convex to the origin. Under decreasing opportunity costs, each country completely specialises in the production of only one commodity after trade. This is because there are increasing returns based on internal economies of production.

Trade under decreasing opportunity costs is illustrated in Figure 4 where AA_1 is the production possibility curve of country *A*, and BB_1 is that of country *B*. The pre-trade consumption and production point of country *A* is *K* where its domestic price line *aa* is tangent to the production possibility curve AA_1. Similarly, the pre-trade consumption and production point of country *B* is K_1 where its domestic price line *bb* is tangent to its production possibility curve BB_1. The slope of the domestic price line *aa* of country *A* shows that its comparative advantage is greater in the production of commodity *X*. Similarly, the slope of country *B*'s domestic price ratio *bb* reveals its greater comparative advantage in the production of commodity *Y*. But the points *K* and K_1 are not of stable equilibrium because of the operation of increasing returns in the production of each commodity in the respective country. Any slight disturbance in the form of increasing the price of the specialised commodity in relation to the other will lead to its complete specialisation in that country.

Suppose they enter into trade with each other and the international price ratio line in BA_1. This line BA_1 is steeper than the domestic price line *aa* of country *A*. It means that commodity *X* has become more expensive in the international market. So *A* will completely specialise in the production of *X* and accordingly shift all its resources to its production and move from point *K* to A_1. On the other hand, the international price line BA_1 is flatter than the domestic price line *bb* of country *B*. It means that commodity *Y* has become more expensive in the international market. Accordingly, *B* will shift all its resources to the production of *Y* and completely specialise in its production and move from point K_1 to *B*.

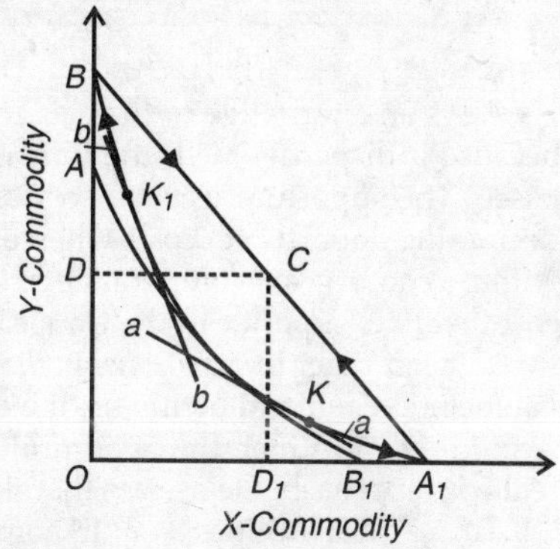

FIG. 4

Thus country *A* will completely specialise in the production of *X* at point A_1, and country *B* will completely specialise in the production of *Y* at *B*. Now each will move along the international price line *BA*, country *A* from point A_1 upward and country *B* from point *B* downward, and reach point C in consumption. *A* will export D_1A_1 of *X* to country *B* and import D_1C of *Y* from it on the trade triangle CD_1A_1 and consume OD_1 of *X* at home. Similarly, country *B* will export *DB* of *Y* to country *A* and import *DC* of *X* from it on the trade triangle *BDC*, and consume *OD* of *Y* domestically.

Trade under Decreasing and Increasing Opportunity Costs

It is not possible that both the commodities may be produced either under decreasing opportunity costs or under increasing opportunity costs. Rather, the situation may be where commodity *X* is being produced under decreasing opportunity costs and commodity *Y* under increasing oppor-tunity costs. The former commodity may be any manufactured article like cloth and the latter some agricultural crop like rice. This situation is depicted in Fig. 5 which shows *AB* as the production possibility curve of country *A*. This curve is concave in the portion *AF* showing increasing opportunity costs and is convex in the region *FB* showing decreasing opportunity costs. The point which divides the curve *AB* into these two segments is called the *point of inflection*.

First, take the region *AF* of the production possibility curve where the interna-tional terms of trade line *aa* is tangent to it at point *E* where both the commodities are being produced under increasing opportunity costs. Country *A* is producing *OX* of commodity *X* and *OY* of commodity *Y*. Its consumption point is at *C* whereby it imports *DC* of *X* and exports *DE* of *Y*. Since point *C* is outside the production possibility curve, the country is better off by trading with the other country.

Now suppose the production of *X* starts under decreasing opportunity costs due to internal economies and the production possibility curve becomes convex in the region *FB* of the *AB* curve. Consequently, as more and more commodity *X* is produced, cost of production diminishes. The country would ultimately reach point *B* where it completely specialises in the production of commodity *X*. Assuming that the international terms of trade remain the same as before, we draw *bB* parallel to *aa* so that the new consumption point is *B*. The country will now export *NB* of *X* and import *NR* of *Y*. The country gains more from trade at point *R* than at point *C*. This is possible so long as the terms of trade line *bB* is to the right of *aa*. If this line happens to be to the left of *aa*, the country would lose and it would be to its advantage not to specialise completely in the production of commodity *X* but to remain at the consumption point like *C* on the line *aa*. The same reasoning applies to country *B*.

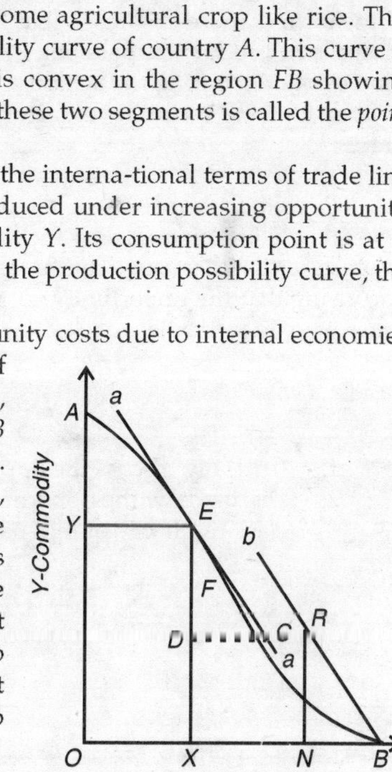

FIG. 5

3. CRITICAL APPRAISAL

As an alternative to the classical comparative cost theory, the opportunity cost theory is more realistic because it dispenses with the unrealistic assumptions of the labour theory of value on which the former is based. The opportunity cost theory analyses pre-trade and post-trade situation under constant, increasing and decreasing opportunity costs whereas the comparative cost theory is based on the constant costs of production within a country and comparative advantage and disadvantage between the two countries. Thus the opportunity cost theory is superior to the classical comparative costs theory on analytical grounds.

Jacob Viner in his *Studies in the Theory of International Trade* (1937) strongly defends the real cost theory of value and vehemently criticises the opportunity costs theory of value which is the basis of Haberler's theory. Accordingly to Viner, the opportunity costs approach is inferior as a tool of welfare evaluation of the classical real cost approach. He asserts that the doctrine of opportunity costs fails to measure real costs in the form of "sacrifices", "disutilities", or "irksomeness" involved in providing productive services. Viner further criticises this theory for the failure of the production possibility curve to take into account the preference for leisure against income.

But all these criticisms are unfounded. The real cost approach has been discarded by economists for good because it leads "into a quagmire of unreality and dubious hypothesis." Instead, the opportunity costs approach has come to stay in international trade theory in the form of a concave production possibility curve extensively used by Samuelson.

Regarding the charge that the production possibility curve does not take into account changes in factor supplies, V.C. Walsh[2] has demonstrated "changes in factor supplies occurring in response to changing commodity price ratios and factor marginal productivities" in terms of opportunity costs.

The last point of Viner's criticism that the production possibility curve cannot take into preference for leisure against income, has also been refuted by Walsh. Walsh argues that "the possibility of trading at an international price ratio normally allows a country to increase its real income. Part of this increase will be taken in the form of more leisure, so that the output of both commodities may decrease." He has demonstrated this in terms of production possibility curves on a three-dimensional figure where leisure is taken on the third dimension. According to Richard Caves, "Walsh's argument demonstrates that .... the transformation curve defined for fixed quantities of factor inputs will change in both shape and size when the preference for leisure varies."[3]

Despite these criticisms, the opportunity cost approach has been regarded as a simplified version of a general equilibrium model by Richard Caves. As pointed out by Samuelson, "The opportunity cost approach is more fertile because it can be readily extended into a general equilibrium system. It is, therefore, not surprising that the opportunity cost approach has gained more and more popularity and it is used even by those who, in principle, attack it."[4]

EXERCISES

1. Critically discuss the opportunity costs theory of international trade.
2. Discuss how the opportunity costs doctrine of international trade removes the shortcomings of the classical theory of international trade.

---

2. V.C. Walsh, "Leisure and International Trade", *Economica*, August 1956.
3. R. Caves, *Trade and Structure*, 1960.
4. P.A. Samuelson, *The Collected Scientific Papers*, Vol. II, 1960.

CHAPTER 45

The Terms of Trade

1. MEANING

The terms of trade refer to the rate at which the goods of one country exchange for the goods of another country. It is a measure of the purchasing power of exports of a country in terms of its imports, and is expressed as the relation between export prices and import prices of its goods. When the export prices of a country rise relatively to its imports prices, its terms of trade are said to have improved. The country gains from trade because it can have a larger quantity of imports in exchange for a given quantity of exports. On the other hand, when its imports prices rise relatively to its export prices, its terms of trade are said to have worsened. The country's gains from trade is reduced because it can have a smaller quantity of imports in exchange for a given quantity of exports than before.

Jacob Viner and G.M. Meier[1] have discussed many types of terms of trade which we take up one by one.

2 COMMODITY TERMS OF TRADE

The commodity or net barter terms of trade is the ratio between the price of a country's export goods and import goods. Symbolically, it can be expressed as

$$Tc = Px/Pm$$

where Tc stands for the commodity terms of trade, P for price, the subscript x for exports and m for imports.

To measure changes in the commodity terms of trade over a period, the ratio of the change in export prices to the change in import prices is taken. Then the formula for the commodity terms of trade is

$$Tc = \frac{Px_1}{Px_0} \bigg/ \frac{Pm_1}{Pm_0}$$

where the subscripts 0 and 1 indicate the base and end periods.

Taking 1971 as the base year and expressing India's both export prices and import prices as 100, if we find

1. Gerald M. Meier, *The International Economics of Development*, 1986, Ch. 3.

that by the end of 1981 its index of export prices had fallen to 90 and the index of import prices had risen to 110. The terms of trade had changed as follows :

$$Tc = \frac{90}{100} / \frac{110}{100} = 81.82$$

It implies that India's terms of trade declined by about 18 per cent in 1981 as compared with 1971, thereby showing worsening of its terms of trade.

If the index of export prices had risen to 180 and that of import prices to 150, then the terms of trade would be 120. This implies an improvement in the terms of trade by 20 per cent in 1981 over 1971.

The concept of the commodity or net barter terms of trade has been used by economists to measure the gain from international trade. The terms of trade, as determined by the offer curves in the Mill-Marshall analysis, are related to the commodity terms of trade.

Its Limitations

Despite its use as a device for measuring the direction of movement of the gains from trade, this concept has important limitations.

1. Usual problems associated with index number in terms of coverage, base year and method of calculation arise.

2. The commodity terms of trade are based on the index numbers of export and import prices. But they do not take into account changes taking place in the quality and composition of goods entering into trade between two countries. At best, a commodity terms of trade index shows changes in the relative prices of goods exported and imported in the base year. Thus the net barter terms of trade fail to account for large change in the quality of goods that are taking place in the world, as also new goods that are constantly entering in international trade.

3. Problem arises in selecting the period over which the terms of trade are studied and compared. If the period is too short, no meaningful change may be found between the base date and the present. On the other hand, if the period is too long, the structure of the country's trade might have changed and the export and import commodity content may not be comparable between the two dates.

4. Another serious difficulty in the commodity terms of trade is that it simply shows changes in export and import prices and not how such prices change. As a matter of fact, there is much qualitative difference when a change in the commodity terms of trade index is caused by a change in export prices relative to import prices as a result of changes in demand for exports abroad, and ways or productivity at home. For instance, the commodity terms of trade index may change by a rise in export prices relative to import prices due to strong demand for exports abroad and wage inflation at home. The commodity terms of trade index does not take into account the effects of such factors.

5. The concept of the commodity terms of trade throws no light on the "capacity to import" of a country. Suppose there is a fall in the commodity terms of trade in India. It means that a given quantity of Indian exports will buy a smaller quantity of imports than before. Along with this trend, the volume of Indian exports also rises, may be as a consequence of the fall in the prices of exports. Operating simultaneously, these two trends may keep India's capacity to import unchanged or even improve it. Thus the commodity terms of trade fails to take into account a country's capacity to import.

6. The commodity terms of trade also ignores a change in the productive efficiency of a country. Suppose the productive efficiency of a country increases. It will lead to a fall in the cost of production and in the prices of its export goods. The fall in the prices of export goods will be reflected in the worsening of its commodity terms of trade. But, in reality, the country will not be worse off than before. Even though a given value of exports will exchange for less imports, the country will be better off. This is because a given volume of exports can now be produced with lesser resources, and the real cost of imports, in terms of resources used in exports, remains unchanged.

Last but not the least, the concept of commodity terms of trade is valid if the balance of payments of a country includes only the export and imports of goods and services, and the balance of payments balances in the base and the given years. If the balance of payments also includes unilateral payments or unrequired exports and or/imports, such as gifts, remittances from and to the other country, *etc.*, leading to disequilibrium in the balance of payments, the commodity terms of trade is not helpful in measuring the gains from trade.

To overcome this last difficulty, Taussig[3] introduced the concept of the gross barter terms of trade.

3. GROSS BARTER TERMS OF TRADE

The gross barter terms of trade is the ratio between the quantities of a country's imports and exports. Symbolically, $Tg = Qm/Qx$, where Tg stands for the gross terms of trade, Qm for quantities of Imports and Qx for quantities of exports. The higher the ratio between quantities of imports and exports, the better the gross terms of trade. A larger quantity of imports can be had for the same volume of exports.

To measure changes in the gross barter terms of trade over a period, the index number of the quantities of imports and exports in base period and the end period are related to each other. The formula for this is :

$$Tg = \frac{Qm_1}{Qm_0} \Big/ \frac{Qx_1}{Qx_0}$$

Taking 1971 as the base year and expressing India's both quantities of imports and exports as 100, if we find that the index of quantity imports had risen to 160 and that of quantity exports to 120 in 1981, then the gross barter of trade had changed as follows:

$$Tg = \frac{160}{100} \Big/ \frac{120}{100} = 133.33$$

It implies that there was an improvement in the gross barter terms of trade of India by 33 per cent in 1981 as compared with 1971.

If the quantity of import index had risen by 130 and that of quantity exports by 180, then the gross barter terms of trade would be 72.22.

$$Tg = \frac{130}{100} \Big/ \frac{180}{100} = 72.22$$

This implies deterioration in the terms of trade by 18 per cent in 1981 over 1971.

Its Criticisms

The concept of gross barter terms of trade has been criticised for lumping together all types of goods and capital payments and receipts as one category in the index numbers of exports and imports. No units are applicable equally to rice and to steel, or to export (or import) of capital and the payment (or receipt) of a grant. It is therefore, not possible to distinguish between the various types of transactions which are lumped together in the index. Haberler, Viner and other economists have, therefore, dismissed this concept of gross barter terms of trade as unreal and impracticable as a statistical indicator. Viner uses only the concept of net barter terms of trade while other writers use only the export-import price ratio as the commodity terms of trade. So this concept has been discarded by economists.

4. INCOME TERMS OF TRADE

Dorrance[4] has improved upon the concept of the net barter terms of trade by formulating the concept of the *income terms of trade*. This index takes into account the volume of exports of a country and its export and import prices (the net barter terms of trade). It shows a country's changing import capacity in relation to changes in its exports. Thus, the income terms of trade is the net barter terms of trade of a country multiplied by its export volume index. It can be expressed as

3. F.W. Taussig, *International Trade*, 1927.
4. G.S. Dorrance, 'The Income Terms of Trade', *R.E.S.*, Vol. XVI, 1948-49.

$$Ty = Tc.Qx = \frac{Px.Qx}{Pm} = \frac{\text{Index of Export Prices} \times \text{Export Quantity}}{\text{Index of Import Prices}}$$

$$\left(\because \quad Tc = \frac{Px}{Pm}\right)$$

where Ty is the income terms of trade, Tc the commodity terms of trade and Qx the export volume index.

A.H. Imlah calculates this index by dividing the index of the value of exports by an index of the price of imports. He calls it the "Export Gain from Trade Index."[5]

A rise in the index of income terms of trade implies that a country can import more goods in exchange for its exports. A country's income terms of trade may improve but its commodity terms of trade may deteriorate. Taking the import prices to be constant, if export prices fall, there will be an increase in the sales and value of exports. Thus while the income terms of trade might have improved, the commodity terms of trade might have deteriorated.

The income terms of trade is called the *capacity to import.* In the long-run, the total value of exports of a country must equal to its total value of imports, *i.e.,* $Px.Qx = Pm.Qm$ or $Px.Qx/Pm = Qm$. Thus $Px.Qx/Pm$ determines Qm which is the total volume that a country can import. The capacity to import of a country may increase if other things remain the same (*i*) the price of exports (Px) rises, or (*ii*) the price of imports (Pm) falls, or (*iii*) the volume of its exports (Qx) rises. Thus the concept of the income terms of trade is of much practical value for developing countries having low capacity to import.

Its Criticisms

But the index of income terms of trade fails to measure precisely the gain or loss from international trade. When the capacity to import of a country increases, it simply means that it is also exporting more than before. In fact, exports include the real resources of a country which can be used domestically to improve the living standard of its people.

Moreover, the income terms of trade index is related to the export based capacity to import and not to the total capacity to import of a country which also includes its foreign exchange receipts. For example, if the income terms of trade index of a country has deteriorated but its foreign exchange receipts have risen, its capacity to import has actually increased, even though the index shows deterioration. That is why, the concept of the commodity terms of trade is usually used in preference to the income terms of trade concept for measuring the gain from international trade.

5 SINGLE FACTORAL TERMS OF TRADE

The concept of commodity terms of trade does not take account of productivity changes in export industries. Prof. Viner had developed the concept of single factoral terms of trade which allows changes in the domestic export sector. It is calculated by multiplying the commodity terms of trade index by an index of productivity changes in domestic export industries. It can be expressed as :

$$Ts = Tc.Fx = \frac{Px.Fx}{Pm} \qquad \left(\because Tc = \frac{Px}{Pm}\right)$$

where Ts is the single factoral terms of trade, Tc is the commodity terms of trade, and Fx is the productivity index of export industries.

It shows that a country's factoral terms of trade improve as productivity improves in its export industries. If the productivity of a country's exports industries increases, its factoral terms of trade may improve even though its commodity terms of trade may deteriorate. For example, the prices of its exports may fall relatively to its import prices as a result of increase in the productivity of the export industries of a country. The commodity terms of trade will deteriorate but its factoral terms of trade will show an improvement.

---

5. A.H. Imlah, 'Terms of Trade of the United Kingdom', *J.E.H.*, Nov., 1950.

Its Limitations. This index is not free from certain limitations. It is difficult to obtain the necessary data to compute a productivity index. Further, the single factoral terms of trade do not take into account the potential domestic cost of production of imports industries in the other country. To overcome this weakness, Viner formulated the double factoral terms of trade.

6. DOUBLE FACTORAL TERMS OF TRADE

The double factoral terms of trade take into account productivity changes both in the domestic export sector and the foreign export sector producing the country's imports. The index measuring the double factoral terms of trade can be expressed as

$$Td = Tc.\frac{Fx}{Fm} = \frac{Px}{Fm}.\frac{Fx}{Fm} \qquad \left(\because \quad Tc = \frac{Px}{Pm}\right)$$

where *Td* is the double factoral terms of trade, *Px/Pm* is the commodity terms of trade, *Fx* is the export productivity index, and *Fm* is the import productivity index.

It helps in measuring the change in the rate of exchange of a country as a result of the change in the productive efficiency of domestic factors manufacturing exports and that of foreign factors manufacturing imports for that country. *A* rise in the index of double factoral terms of trade of a country means that the productive efficiency of the factors producing exports has increased relatively to the factors producing imports in the other country.

Its Criticisms

In practice, however, it is not possible to calculate an index of double factoral terms of trade of a country. Prof. Devons[6] made some calculations of changes in the single factoral terms of trade of England between 1948-53. But it has not been possible to construct a double factoral terms of trade index of any country because it involves measuring and comparing productivity changes in the import industries of the other country with that of the domestic export industries.

Moreover, the important thing is the quantity of commodities that can be imported with a given quantity of exports rather than the quantity of productive factors required in a foreign country to produce its imports.

Again, if there are constant returns to scale in manufacturing and no transport costs are involved, there is no difference between the double factoral terms of trade and the commodity terms of trade of a country.

According to Kindleberger, "The single factoral terms of trade is a much more relevant concept than the double factoral. We are interested in what our factor can earn in goods, not what factor services can command in the services of foreign factors. Related to productivity abroad moreover, is a question of the quality of the goods imported."[7]

7. REAL COST TERMS OF TRADE

Viner has also developed a terms of trade index to measure the real gain from international trade. He calls it the real cost terms to trade index. This index is calculated by multiplying the single factoral terms of trade with the reciprocal of an index of the amount of disutility per unit of productive resources used in producing export commodities. It can be expressed as:

$$Tr = Ts.Rx = \frac{Px}{Pm}.Fx.Rx \qquad \left(\because \quad Ts = \frac{Px}{Pm}.Fx\right)$$

where *Tr* is the real cost terms of trade, *Ts* is the single factoral terms of trade and *Rx* is the index of the amount of disutility per unit of productive resources used in producing export commodities.

---

6. E. Devons. 'Statistics of the United Kindom Terms of Trade', *Manchester School,* Sept. 1954.
7. C.P. Kindleberger, *op. cit.,* p. 76.

A favourable real cost terms of trade index (Tr) shows that the amount of imports received is greater in terms of the real cost involved in producing export commodities. But this index fails to measure the real cost involved in the form of goods produced for export which could be used for domestic consumption to pay for imports. To overcome this problem. Viner develops the index of utility terms of trade.

8. UTILITY TERMS OF TRADE

The utility terms of trade index measures "changes in the disutility of producing a unit of exports and changes in the relative satisfactions yielded by imports, and the domestic products foregone as the result of export production." In other words, it is an index of the relative utility of imports and domestic commodities forgone to produce exports. The utility terms of trade index is calculated by multiplying the real cost terms of trade index with an index of the relative average utility of imports and of domestic commodities foregone. If we denote the average utility by u and the domestic commodities whose consumption is foregone to use resources for export production by a, then $u = \dfrac{Um_1}{Ua_1} \Big/ \dfrac{Um_0}{Ua_0}$, where u is the index of relative utility of imports and domestically foregone commodities. Thus, the utility terms of trade index can be expressed as :

$$Tu = Tr.u = \frac{Px}{Pm} . Fx.Rx.u$$

Since the real terms of trade index and utility terms of trade index involve the measurement of disutility in terms of pain, irksomeness and sacrifice, they are elusive concepts. As a matter of fact, it is not possible to measure disutility (for utility) in concrete terms.

Hence like the single and double factoral terms of trade concepts, the concepts of real and utility terms of trade are of little practical use. They are only of academic interest. That is why the concepts of the commodity terms of trade and of income terms of trade have been used in measuring the gains from international trade in developed as well as developing countries.

9. FACTORS AFFECTING TERMS OF TRADE*

The terms of trade of a country are influenced by a number of factors which are discussed as under :

1. Reciprocal Demand

The terms of trade of a country depend upon reciprocal demand, *i.e.* "the strength and elasticity of each country's demand for the other country's product". Suppose there are two countries, Germany and England, which produce linen and cloth respectively. If Germany's demand for England's cloth becomes more intense (inelastic), the price of cloth rises more than the price of linen, the commodity terms of trade will move against Germany and in favour of England. On the other hand, if England's demand for Germany's linen becomes more intense, the price of linen will rise more than the price of cloth, and the commodity terms of trade will move in favour of Germany and against England. This is explained diagrammatically in Fig. 1 where OE is England's offer curve and OG is the offer curve of Germany. The point I where the two offer curves intersect each other is the equilibrium point at which OC of cloth is traded by England for OL linen of Germany. The terms of trade are represented by the slope of the ray OT.

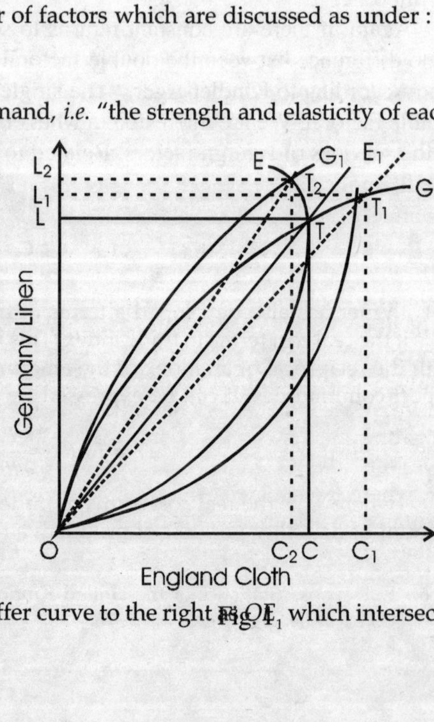

Fig. 1

Suppose England's demand for Germany's linen increases. England will be prepared to sell more cloth for Germany's linen. The increase in England's demand is shown by the shifting of its offer curve to the right to OE_1 which intersects

Germany's offer curve OG at T_1.

Now the new terms of trade are represented by the ray OT_1 whereby England exports OC_1 units of cloth for OL_1 units of linen. The terms of trade have deteriorated for England and improved for Germany. This is evident from the fact that England exports CC_1 more units of cloth in exchange for LL_1 units of linen. CC_1 is greater than LL_1.

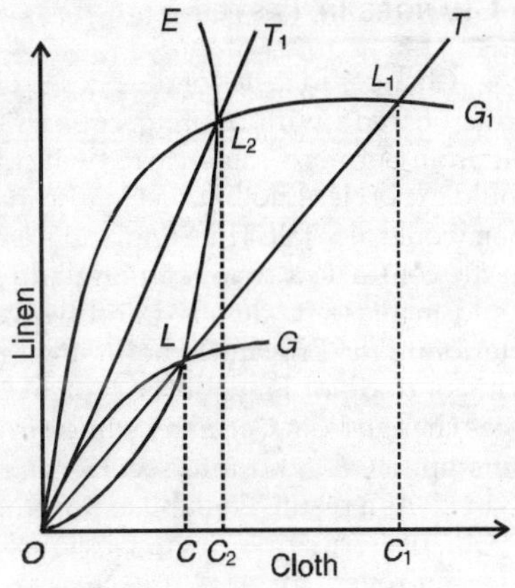

Fig. 2

Similarly, if Germany's demand for England's cloth increases, Germany's offer curve shifts to the left as OG_1 which intersects England's initial offer curve OE at T_2. Now Germany exports OL_2 units of linen for OC_2 units of cloth. The new terms of trade, as shown by the slope of ray OT_2, indicate that they have deteriorated for Germany and improved for England. This is evident from the fact that Germany exports LL_2 more linen in exchange for CC_2 less cloth.

But the terms of trade will depend upon the elasticity of demand of the offer curve of each country. The more inelastic the offer curve of a country, the more unfavourable are the terms of trade for it in relation to the other country. On the contrary, the more elastic its offer curve, the more favourable are its terms of trade in relation to the other country.

2. Changes in Factor Endowments

Changes in factor endowments of a country affect its terms of trade. Changes in factor endowments may increase exports or reduce them. With tastes remaining unchanged, they may lead to changes in the terms of trade. This is explained with the help of Fig. 2 where OE is the offer curve of England and OG is the offer curve of Germany. Before any change in factor endowments, the terms of trade of England and Germany are settled at point L where they trade OC of cloth for CL of linen. Suppose there is an increase in the supply of Germany's factors of production. As a result, the new offer curve of Germany is OG_1. At the old terms of trade OT, Germany would be at point L_1 where it would export more linen C_1L_1 and import English cloth OC_1. But England may not be willing to trade with Germany at the old terms of trade because of its inability to produce so much cloth as its factor endowments and tastes remain unchanged. Thus the terms of trade will settle on the new terms of trade line OT_1 where England's offer curve OE intersects Germany's new offer curve OG_1 at point L_2. At L_2, Germany exports C_2L_2 of linen in exchange for OC_2 of cloth from England. Thus the terms of trade have moved against Germany from L to L_2, with change in its factor endowments because it exports more linen (C_2L_2) than before (CL).

3. Changes in Technology

Technological changes also affect the terms of trade of a country. The effect of technological change on terms of trade is illustrated in Fig. 3. Suppose there is change in technology in Germany. Before technological change the terms of trade between Germany and England are settled at point L on the OT ray where Germany exports CL of linen for OC of England cloth. With technological change, Germany's new offer curve is OG_1 which cuts the terms of trade line OT at L_1. At this point, Germany would like to export less linen (C_1L_1) and import less cloth (OC_1) than England wants to exchange at the terms of trade OT. So Germany's terms of trade improve when its new offer curve OG_1 intersects England's unchanged offer curve OE at L_2 where the new terms of trade are settled on the line OT_1. At L_2, Germany is better off because it exports less linen for more of England's cloth, *i.e.* $C_2L_2 < OC_2$. Its terms of trade have improved with technological change.

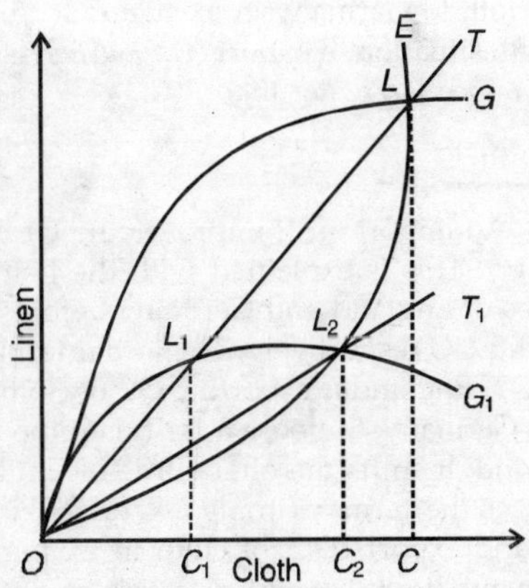

Fig. 3

4. Changes in Tastes

Changes in tastes of the people of a country also influence its terms of trade with another country. Suppose England's tastes shift from Germany's linen to its own cloth. In this situation, England would export less cloth to Germany and its demand for Germany's linen would also fall. Thus England's terms of trade would improve. On the contrary, a change in England's taste for Germany's linen would increase its demand and hence the terms of trade would deteriorate for England. The first case of an improvement in the terms of trade of England is depicted in Fig. 4. When England's tastes change from Germany's linen to its own cloth, its offer curve shifts up to OE_1, and intersect Germany's unchanged offer curve OG at L_1. As a result, England exports only OC_1 of cloth in exchange for C_1L_1 of Germany's linen. Obviously, England's terms of trade have improved for now it exchanges less cloth (OC_1) for more linen of Germany (C_1L_1) *i.e.* $OC_1 < C_1L_1$.

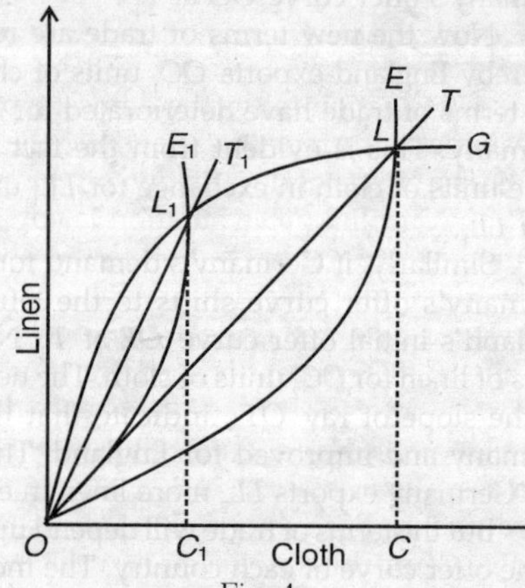

Fig. 4

5. Economic Growth

Economic growth is another important factor which affects the terms of trade. The raising of a country's national product or income over time is called economic growth. Given the tastes and technology in a country, an increase in its productive capacity may affect favourably or adversely its terms of trade. This is illustrated in Fig. 5 in terms of the production possibility curves and the community indifference curves of a country which experience economic growth. E_1E_1 is the production possibility curve of England before growth where the slope of T_1 shows its terms of trade. Before growth, it is producing at S_1 and consuming at C_1 on the community indifference curve CI_1. Thus England is exporting R_1S_1 of cloth and importing R_1C_1 of linen from Germany. When growth takes place, the production possibility curve E_1E_1 shifts outward as E_2E_2. The new terms of trade after growth, as represented by the slope of the line T_2, show an improvement when production takes place at point S_2 on the production possibility curve E_2E_2 and consumption at point C_2 of the community indifference curve CI_2. As a result of the improvement in England's terms of trade, it exports less cloth to Germany in exchange for more linen than in the pre-growth situation. It exports R_2S_2 which is less than R_1S_1 and imports R_2C_2 which is greater than R_1C_1.

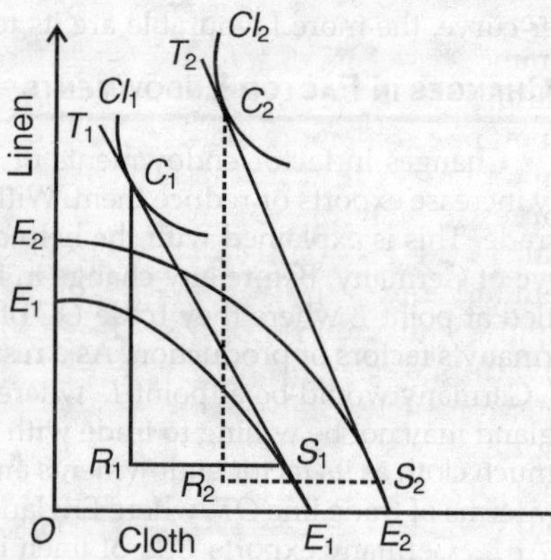

Fig. 5

6. Tariff

An import tariff improves the terms of trade of the imposing country. This is explained with the help of Fig. 6 where the offer curves of England and Germany before the imposition of tariff are OE and OG respectively. The initial terms of trade are given by the line OT. England is exporting OC of cloth and importing CL of linen from Germany. Suppose a tariff is imposed on Germany's linen by England. It shifts the offer curve of England from OE to OE_1. This changes the terms of trade OT to OT_1 in favour of England. Now England exports OC_1 of cloth in exchange for C_1L_1 of linen from Germany. It now exports CC_1 less of cloth than before and imports LL_1 less of linen. Since the quantity of exports reduced as a result of tariff by England is greater than the quantity of imports reduced by

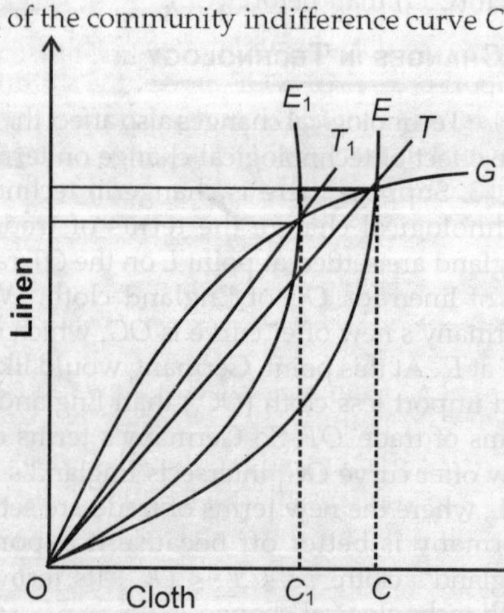

Fig. 6

Germany ($LL_1 < CC_1$), the terms of trade have definitely moved in favour of England.

7. Devaluation

Devaluation raises the domestic price of imports and reduces the foreign price of exports of a country devaluing its currency in relation to the currency of another country.

The effects of devaluation on the terms of trade have been much debated among economists. According to Prof. Machlup, "Devaluation is supposed to improve the balance of trade. A reduction in the physical volume of imports in relation to the physical volume of exports constitutes an adverse change in the gross barter terms of trade." Thus devaluation will be successful only if the gross barter term become adverse. Prof. Robertson favours the use of the concept of the commodity terms of trade to assess the effects of devaluation. To him, if this concept is used, devaluation will lead to rise in the prices of imports and fall in the prices of exports in foreign currency, and hence deteriorate the commodity terms of trade. But Prof. Hirch suggests that the right procedure should be to study price movements in exports and imports in the same currency in order to assess the true effects of devaluation. Both exports and imports prices normally rise in the home currency and fall in the foreign currency. The commodity terms of trade will deteriorate only when export prices fall more than import prices in terms of domestic currency. In reality, the elasticities of demand and supply for exports and imports of a devaluing country determine deterioration of improvement in its terms of trade. If both the foreign demand for exports and home demand for imports are highly elastic and supplies both to home exports and foreign imports are highly inelastic to price movements, devaluation leads to an improvement in the commodity terms of trade. This is explained in Fig. 7 (A) and (B).

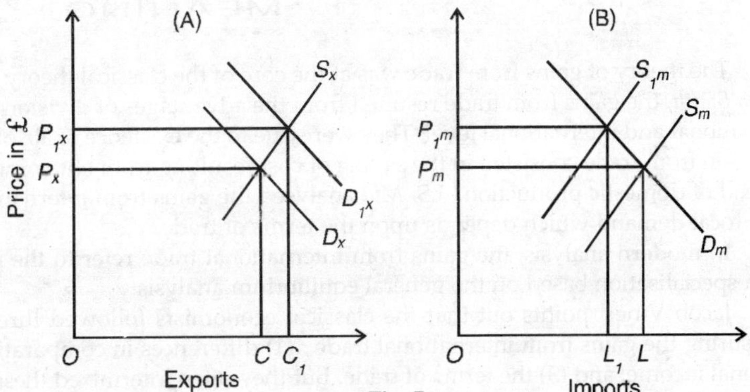

Fig. 7

Suppose English £ (pound) is devalued in relation to German Mark, and the price movements before and after devaluation are taken in pound. The pre-devaluation price of *OC* exports is *OPx* and that of *OL* imports is *OPm*. The post-devaluation export price rises to OP_1x when the demand curve shifts upward to D_1x, and the import price rises to OP_1m with the shifting of the supply curve to the left as S_1m. A comparison of Fig. 7 (A) and (B) reveals that the export price has risen more than the import price $PxP_1x > PmP_1m$, and that while exports have risen from *OC* to OC_1, imports have fallen from *OL* to OL_1. These prove that the terms of trade have improved for England after devaluation.

EXERCISES

1. Examine critically the various concepts of terms of trade.
2. Distinguish between Gross Barter Terms of Trade and Barter Terms of Trade or Income Terms of Trade and Net Barter Terms of Trade.
3. Discuss the factors which determine the terms of trade.
4. Name different kinds of terms of trade. Which of these concepts is most helpful in indicating 'gains from trade' And why?

CHAPTER 46

The Gains from Trade

1. MEANING

The theory of gains from trade was at the core of the classical theory of international trade. According to *Adam Smith*, the gains from trade resulted from the advantages of division of labour and specialisation both at the national and international level. They were due to the existence of absolute differences in costs. For *Ricardo*, 'the gain from trade consisted in the saving of cost resulting from obtaining the imported goods through trade instead of domestic production.' J.S. *Mill* analysed the gains from international trade in terms of his theory of reciprocal demand which depends upon the terms of trade.

In modern analysis, the gains from international trade refer to the gains from exchange and the gains from specialisation based on the general equilibrium analysis.

Jacob Viner[1] points out that the classical economists followed three different methods or criteria for measuring the gains from international trade : (1) differences in comparative costs; (2) increase in the level of national income; and (3) the terms of trade. But they often intermixed these methods without specifying them clearly. It is, however, the terms of trade method that has been in vogue to measure the gains from trade since Mill.

RICARDO'S APPROACH

To take Ricardo's approach first, a country will export those commodities in which its comparative production costs are less, and will import those commodities in which its comparative production costs are *high*. "The country thus economises in the use of its resources, obtaining for a given amount thereof a larger total income than if it attempted to produce everything itself."

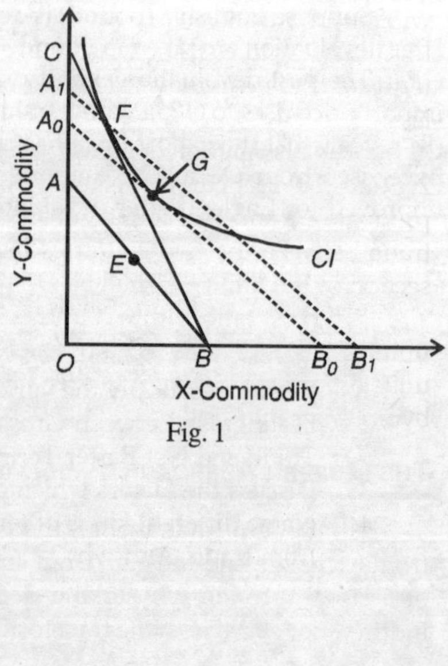

Fig. 1

Prof. Ronald Findlay in his *Trade and Specialisation* (1970) has explained Ricardo's approach to the gains from international trade in terms of Fig. 1. In the pre-trade situation, *AB* is the production possibility curve of a country which produces two commodities *X* and *Y*, given the quantity of labour input. On *AB*, the country is in equilibrium at point *E*. After it enters into trade, its international price ratio is given by the slope of the line *CB*. Suppose that it is in equilibrium at point *F*

1. Jacob Viner. *op. cit.*, pp. 436-40.

on the line CB. If the quantities of X and Y represented by the combination at F are to be produced domestically, the quantity of labour input will have to increase sufficiently to shift the domestic production possibility curve up from AB to A_1B_1. The gains from trade will thus be measured by BB_1/OB.

But Malthus criticised Ricardo for greatly over-estimating the gains from trade. In terms of Fig. 1, Malthus's view is that with the shifting of the domestic production possibility curve to A_1B_1, F would not be the equilibrium point. Relative prices along A_1B_1 would not be more favourable to the exported commodity X than along CB, so that consumer will prefer a point to the right of F on A_1B_1 rather than F itself. Hence the gains from trading along CB cannot be measured by an increase of labour input in the ratio BB_1/OB. This is because the change to the right of F on A_1B_1 is preferable to that on CB.

Prof. Ronald Findlay has modified the Ricardo measure of the gains from trade using the community indifference curve CI. If the labour input is increased sufficiently to push the production possibility curve to A_0B_0 instead of to A_1B_1, the point G on the CI curve will make each individual as better as he is at the free trade point F. The gains from trade would, therefore, be equal to BB_0/OB instead of the larger BB_1/OB. This measure satisfies Malthus's criticism of Ricardo.

Mill's Approach

J.S. Mill analysed the gains as well as the *distribution of the gains* from international trade in terms of his theory of reciprocal demand. Accroding to Mill, it is reciprocal demand that determines terms of trade which, in turn, determine the distribution of gains from trade of each country. The term 'terms of trade' refers to the barter terms of trade between the two countries *i.e.*, the ratio of the quantity of imports for a given quantity of exports of a country.

To take an example, in country A, 2 units of labour produce 10 units of X and 10 units of Y, while in country B the same labour produces $6X$ and $8Y$. The domestic exchange ratio (or domestic terms of trade) in country A is $1X = 1Y$, and in country B, $1X = 1.33Y$. This means that one unit of X can be exchanged with one unit of Y in country A or 1.33 units of Y in country B. Thus the terms of trade between the two countries will lie between $1X$ or $1Y$ or 1.33 Y.

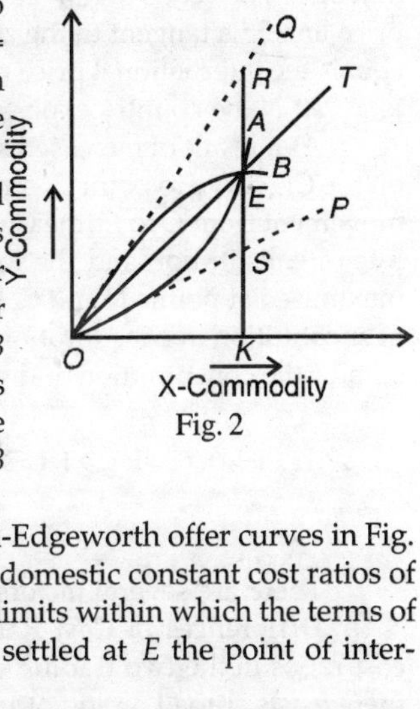

Fig. 2

However, the actual exchange ratio will depend upon reciprocal demand , *i.e.*, "the relative strength and elasticity of demand of the two trading countries for each other's product in terms of their own product." If A's demand for commodity Y is more intense (inelastic), then the terms of trade will be nearer $1X = 1Y$. The terms of trade will move in favour of B and against country A. B will gain more and A less. On the other hand, if A's demand for commodity Y is less intense (more elastic), then the terms of trade will be nearer $1X = 1.33Y$. The terms of trade will move in favour of A and against B. A will gain more and B less.

The distribution of gains from trade is explained in terms of the Marshall-Edgeworth offer curves in Fig. 2. OA is the offer curve of country A, and OB of country B. OP and OQ are the domestic constant cost ratios of producing X and Y in country A and B respectively. These rays are, in fact, the limits within which the terms of trade between the two countries lie. However, the actual terms of trade are settled at E the point of intersection of OA and OB. The line OT represents equilibrium terms of trade at E.

The cost ratio within country A is KS units of Y : OK units of X. But it gets KE units of Y through trade. SE units of Y is, therefore, its gain. The cost ratio within country B is KR units of Y : OK units of X. But it imports OK units of X from country A in exchange for only KE units of Y. ER units of Y is its gain. Thus both countries gain by entering into trade.

The Modern Approach

In modern trade theory, the gains from international trade are clearly differentiated between the gain from exchange and the gain from specialisation. The analysis is explained in terms of the general equilibrium of a closed economy by taking demand and supply. It is characterised by the tangency of a community indifference curve with the transformation curve, and the equality of the marginal rates of substitution between commodities in consumption and production with the domestic terms of trade or commodity price ratio. "The introduction of international trade permits the realisation of a gain from exchange and gain from specialisation. When equilibrium is established and these gains are maximised, the new marginal rate of transformation in production and the new marginal rate of substitution in consumption are equal to the international price ratio or terms of trade." Thus both producers and consumers gain from international trade by producing and consuming more than the pre-trade level.

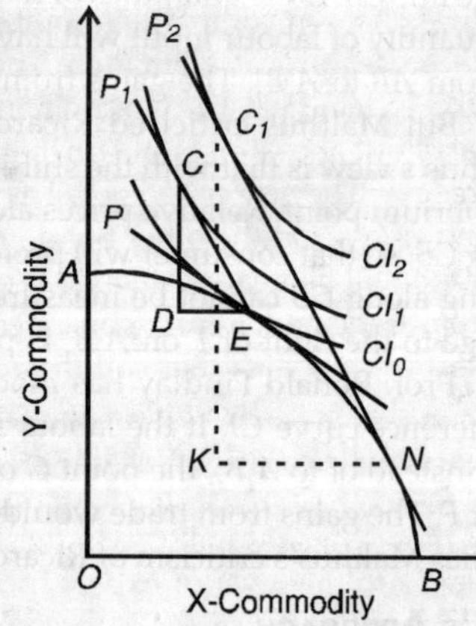

Fig. 3

Fig. 3 explains the gains from inter-national trade. *AB* is the transformation curve representing the supply side and CI_0 is the community indifference curve representing the demand side of an economy. The closed economy (no trade) equilibrium is shown by point *E* where the *AB* and CI_0 curves are tangent to each other and both equal the domestic terms of trade or commodity price ratio (line) *P*.

With the introduction of international (or free) trade, the international price ratio (terms of trade) will be different from the domestic price ratio (terms of trade). It is shown as P_1 and is steeper than the domestic price ratio *P*. It means that the price of commodity *X* has increased in relation to commodity *Y* in the world market. At the international price line P_1, the consumers move to point *C* on a higher community indifference curve CI_1 from point *E* on the CI_0 curve. This movement from *E* to *C* measures *the gain from exchange or consumption gain* with no change in production.

Since the price of *X* has increased in the world market, producers increase its production and decrease that of *Y*. This leads to movement along the transformation curve from point *E* to *N* where a new international price line P_2 is tangent to the *AB* curve. In other words, at *N* the marginal rate of transformation in production equals the international price ratio. The new world terms of trade ratio P_2 is the same as P_1 because it is parallel to P_1. At *N* the country exports *KN* of *X* in exchange for KC_1 imports of *Y*.

As a result of increased specialisation in the production of *X*, there is a shift in consumption from point *C* on the CI_1 curve to point C_1 on the CI_2 curve, where consumers consume larger quantities of both X and *Y*. This movement from *C* to C_1 measures the *gain from specialisation in production or production gain*. At C_1 the marginal rate of substitution and the international price ratio are equal. Hence the gains from international trade are maximised at points *N* and C_1 because the marginal rate of transformation in production and the marginal rate of substitution in consumption are equal to the international price ratio P_2. The total gain from free trade is the sum of the consumption and production gains and is shown as improvement in welfare from CI_0 to CI_2.

2. FACTORS DETERMINING THE GAINS FROM TRADE

There are several factors which determine the gains from international trade.

Differences in Cost Ratios. The gains from international trade depend on differences in comparative cost ratios in the two trading countries. "A country gains by foreign trade, if and when, the traders find that there exists abroad a ratio of prices very different from that to which they are accustomed at home. They buy what to them seems cheap and sell what to them seems dear. The bigger the gap between what to them seems low profits and high profits, and the more important the article affected, the greater will be the gain from trade."[1] If country *A* has a comparative advantage in the production of wheat and country *B* has a comparative advantage in the production of cotton, both countries will gain from trade. The size of the gain will depend on the cost of production of each commodity in both countries. If with increase in efficiency of labour the cost of production of wheat in country *A* falls, then country *B* shall gain more from trade. Contrary will be the case if the cost of production of cotton in country *B* falls, then country *A* will gain from trade. Thus the greater the

1. R.F. Harrod, *International Economics*, p. 34.

differences in comparative cost ratios, the larger is the gain from trade.

Reciprocal Demand. The terms of trade, in turn, depend upon reciprocal demand, *i.e.*, the relative strength and elasticity of demand of one country for the product of the other in exchange for its product. To carry out above example further, if *A*'s demand for commodity *Y* is more intense (inelastic), then the terms of trade will be nearer $1X = 1Y$. The terms of trade will move in favour of *B* and against country *A*. *B* will gain more and *A* less. On the other hand, if *A*'s demand for commodity *Y* is less intense (more elastic), then the terms of trade will be nearer $1X = 1.33Y$. The terms of trade will move in favour of *A* and against *B*. *A* will gain more from trade and *B* less. Thus a country gains the most from trade whose demand for foreign goods is highly elastic while the other country's demand for its goods is highly inelastic.

Level of Income. The level of money income of a country is another factor which determines the gains and the share of trade. A country whose goods have a constant demand in other countries will have a high level of money income. If the demand for its exports is high, it export industries will expand. Consequently, the level of money wages will rise in these industries. Competition for labour will force other industries to raise money wages to the level of export industries. Thus the overall level of money incomes will tend to be high in the country. But the prices of foreign goods being imported into the country will be low, while the money incomes of the people will be high. So people of the country will gain as consumers of cheap imported goods. On the contrary, a country having high demand for foreign goods will have low money incomes. As it will have high demand for foreign goods, their prices will be high. Consequently, its people will lose as consumers of those imported goods.

Terms of Trade. The most important factor which determines the gains from trade is the terms of trade. The terms of trade refer to the rate at which one commodity of a country is exchanged for another commodity of the other country. This refers to the barter terms of trade which *Mill* used to determine the gains as well as the distribution of the gains from international trade, as explained above in terms of Fig. 2. In the modern analysis also, it is the terms of trade that determine the gains from trade (shown by the domestic price line *P* in Fig. 3). But when international trade takes place, the terms of trade change and are different from the domestic terms of trade. It is the international terms of trade (shown by the line P_1 and P_2 in Fig. 3) that determine the gains from trade.[2]

3. GAINS FROM TRADE AND INCOME DISTRIBUTION

When a country enters into trade with another country, it gains from trade. The gain from trade leads to income distribution in the country.

The analysis that follows is based on the following assumptions :

1. There is a small country.
2. It produces two commodities *X* and *Y*.
3. There are two consumers *A* and *B*.
4. The government redistributes income between them in accordance with a defined welfare function.

Given these assumptions, the income distribution from the gains of trade is explained in terms of Fig. 4 where *A*'s utility from the consumption of commodity *X* is measured on the horizontal axis and *B*'s utility from the consumption of commodity *Y* is measured on the vertical axis. Their utility possibility frontier in the pre-trade situation is *BA*. If they consume the combination *C*, *A*'s utility is more than that of *B*'s, because *A* consumes more commodity of *X* than commodity *Y* consumed by *B*, *i.e.*, $OX > OY$. If they are at point *D*, they get equal utilities from the consumption of the two commodities, *i.e.*, $OX_1 = OY_1$.

By entering into trade, when the country gains from trade, its utility possibility frontier is B_1A_1 which touches the pre-trade utility possibility frontier at point C. Any point above C on the B_1A_1 curve such as *E* on the triangle *KDL* would make both consumers better off because they consume more of *X* and *Y* (*i.e* OX_2 and OY_2)

2. The relation between gains from trade and terms of trade should be explained in detail by drawing Fig. 2 and Fig. 3.

than in the pre-trade situation at point D (*i.e.* OX_1 and OY_1).

As a result of the gains from trade, there will be change in the distribution of income. Suppose in the trade situation, the consumers are at point P on the B_1A_1 utility possibility frontier where the consumer B is better off and A is worse off than at point D in the pre-trade situation. The government redistributes income in such a manner between the two consumers that they move along the B_1A_1 curve to point E. Point E is the optimum point where the welfare is maximised because both consumers consume more quantities of (OX_2 and OY_2) X and Y than at point D.

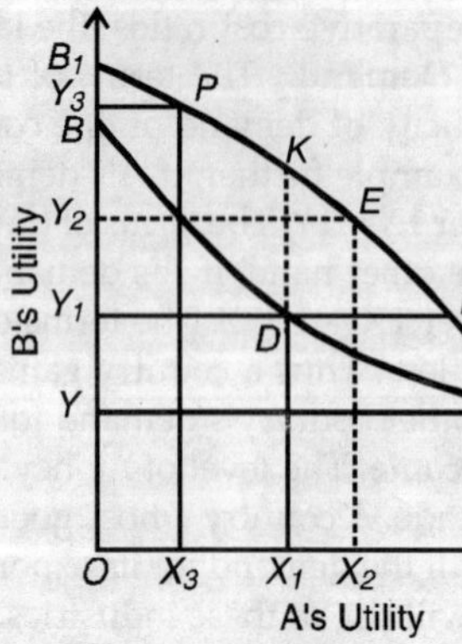

Fig. 4

EXERCISES

1. What do you mean by 'gains from trade'? Discuss the relation between 'gains from' and 'terms of trade'.
2. How is the gain from international trade determined?
3. How are the gains from trade measured? On what factors do they depend?
4. What do you mean by gains from trade? How the gains from trade lead to income distribution?

CHAPTER 47

Free Trade Versus Protection

1. FREE TRADE

MEANING

Free trade policy refers to a trade policy without any tariffs, quantitative restrictions and other devices obstructing the movement of goods between countries. Prof. Jagdish Bhagwati defines free trade policy, "as absence of tariffs, quotas, exchange restrictions, taxes and subsidies on production, factor use and consumption"[1]. This is an exhaustive definition. Prof. Lipsey gives a very simple definition. According to him, "A world of FREE TRADE would be one with no tariffs and no restrictions of any kind on importing or exporting. In such a world, a country would import all those commodities that it could buy from abroad at a delivered price lower than the cost of producing them at home." Thus the policy of free trade means simply complete freedom of international trade without any restrictions on the movement of goods between countries. However, there is an exception. Import duties can be levied for revenue and not for protection even under free trade.This can be understood with the help of an example. If the government levies a duty of 15 per cent on all imports, all foreign goods which enjoy a cost and trade will continue as usual. But if even a simple foreign good enjoys a cost advantage of less than 15 per cent, it means the end free trade and import duty is for protection and not for revenue alone. Thus a country following the free trade policy levies import duties which are lower than the cost advantage enjoyed by the lowest cost foreign good.

THE CASE FOR FREE TRADE

The classical economists were in favour of the free trade policy. Of the modern economist, Haberler[2] advanced the following arguments in favour of free trade.

1. Maximisation of Output. The case for free trade arises from the theory of comparative advantage which states that a country specialises in the production of those commodities in which it possesses greater comparative advantage or least comparative disadvantage. Therefore, under free trade a country specialises in the production of those commodities which it is relatively best suited to produce and exports them in exchange for those

1. *International Trade,* 1986, p. 10.
2. Haberler, *op. cit.,* Ch. XIV.

imports which it can obtain more cheaply. This maximises the output of all the participating countries because all gain from trade which, in turn, increases the real national income of the world economy. Thus free trade leads to the maximisation of output income and employment.

2. *Optimum Utilisation of Resources.* Free trade leads to international specialisation and geographical and territorial division of labour. Each country specialises in the production of those goods for which it has abundant supply of natural resources. As a result, the existing resources in each trading country are employed more productively and the resource allocation becomes more efficient. There is more efficient utilisation of factors within a firm or industry. Thus international trade and division of labour leads to optimum utilisation of resources.

3. *Optimisation of Consumption.* Free trade secures the optimisation of consumption. In other words, it benefits the consumers when they are able to buy a variety of commodities from abroad at the minimum possible prices. This, in turn, has the effect of raising their standard of living.

4. *Educative Value.* According to Haberler, free trade has an educative value. International competition encourages home producers to sacrifies leisure in order to increase productivity. For this, they innovate and bring improvements in organisation and methods of production.

5. *Wide Markets.* Free trade leads to wide extent of markets for goods. As the demand for goods is not confined to one country but to a number of countries, the entire world becomes the market for all types of goods. This leads to the production of quality goods at low prices because of world competition.

6. *Prevents Monopolies.* Free trade prevents the establishment of monopolies. Under free trade each country specialises in the production of a few commodities, and the firms or industries are of the optimum size so that the cost of production of each commodity is the minimum. Thus free trade ensures a lower price for exports as well as imports and the price mechanism under perfect competition prevents the formation of monopolies.

7. *Best Policy for Economic Development.* Haberler points out that "substantial free trade with marginal, insubstantial corrections and deviations is the best policy from the point of view of economic development." Besides, the direct gains of free trade noted above, free trade fosters development in the following ways : (*a*) it leads to the importation of capital goods, and raw materials; (*b*) it instills new ideas, and brings technical knowhow, skills, managerial talents and entrepreneurship to the developing countries; (*c*) it facilitates the flow of foreign capital; and *Lastly,* it fosters healthy competition and checks inefficient and exploitative monopolies.

The Case Against Free Trade

The policy of free trade, with all its advantages noted above, was abandoned after the Great Depression by the countries of the world. There are certain theoretical and practical difficulties in following the free trade policy.

1. Free trade presupposes the existence of *laissez-faire* and the working of price mechanism under prefect competition. But these conditions do not exist in the present day world. Monopoly, monopsony, cartels, imperfect labour markets and tariffs led to the abandonment of free trade.

2. Under the policy of free trade, some industries expand in which the country possesses comparative advantage but other industries are not developed. An agricultural country may develop only agriculture and neglect the industrial sector. Or, one type of industries may be developed while others may remain undeveloped. This naturally leads to the one-sided development of the economy. Hence free trade had to be abandoned.

3. There being no restrictions on the movement of goods under free trade, substandard and harmful commodities are likely to be produced and traded. This leads to diminution of social welfare. Trade restrictions on the import of such commodities become necessary.

4.Countries with better factor endowments are able to produce certain commodities cheaper than others. This led to cut-throat competition in the world market under free trade. So certain countries like Japan resorted to the policy of dumping whereby they would sell huge quantities of their products at rock-bottom prices in the foreign markets. Naturally, this policy led to the imposition of trade restrictions.

5. Free trade leads to the emergence of international monopolies and local monopolies, according to Haberler. Such monopolies developed with the spread of multinational corporation under free trade which proved harmful to the other countries and the domestic interests. This factor also led to the adoption of the

policy of protection.

6. Economists do not agree with Haberler that the free trade policy helps in the development of underdeveloped countries. Rather, this policy led to the exploitation and colonisation of countries during the 19th and early 20th centuries. It is now recognised that underdeveloped countries can develop under a policy of protection and not of free trade.

2. PROTECTION*

MEANING

The term protection refers to a policy whereby domestic industries are to be protected from foreign competition. The aim is to impose restrictions on the imports of low-priced products in order to encourage domestic industries, may be protected by imposing import duties which raise the price of foreign goods by more than the price of domestic goods. Or, they may be protected by quotas or other non-tariff restrictions which make imports of cheap foreign goods difficult or impossible. Or, the domestic industries may be paid subsides, or bounties to enable them to compete with cheap foreign goods.

ARGUMENTS FOR PROTECTION

Haberler has divided the arguments for protection into two groups: economic and non-economic. We discuss these one by one.

A. Economic Arguments. The economic arguments which are usually given in favour of protection are :

1. Terms of Trade Argument. The terms of trade argument is given to correct disequilibrium in the balance of payments of a country. It is argued that the imposition of a tariff on imports improves the rate at which the country's exports are exchanged for improts. This means that a tariff improves its terms of trade because the foreign exporter is forced to pay some part of the import duty. The extent to which a country can improve its terms of trade by imposing import duty will depend upon the relative demand and supply elasticities at home and abroad. A country which imports a large quantity of a particular commodity, whose demand is less elastic, will be in a better position to impose a tariff duty and improve its terms of trade than a country which imports a small quantity of a given commodity (i.e., demand is elastic).

However, there are certain adverse effects on the tariff imposing country, *First,* the term of trade may improve but the volume to trade of the tariff-imposing country is reduced. *Second,* the imposition of tariff increases the price of the imported commodity to the domestic consumer. *Third,* it may lead to retaliation by the other country. Thus too high a tariff leads to reduction in consumers'satisfaction, mal-allocation of domestic resources with the reduction in the volume of trade, and retaliatory tariffs harm the economies of both the countries.

2. Bargaining or Retaliation Arguments. It is argued that the imposition of tariffs is necessary to bargain in trade negotiations with other countries. Since international trade is based on reciprocal basis, tariff is used as a weapon to persuade or dissuade the other country to lower its tariff wall. Thus the fear of retaliation may induce countries to give reciprocal concessions to each other.

But the bargaining argument for protection is not sound on many counts. *First,* tariffs as a weapon for bargaining may lead to retaliation on the part of the other country, thereby harming both the countries. *Second,* vested interests may be created in the country which may be so powerful that they may not allow reduction in tariffs and reciprocal bargaining. So the bargaining argument for protection is a fallacious one.

3. Anti-dumping Argument. Protection is advocated against the practice of dumping. Dumping means selling a product in a foreign market at a lower price than in the home market, after taking into account transport and other costs of transfer. Dumping aims at flooding a foreign market with low-priced commodities. As a result, the import competing firms are ruined. To protect such firms, a high tariff is imposed. This will raise the price of the product in the importing country and removes the threat of dumping.

---

* For arguments in relation to a developing country refer to Ch. 19

4. Diversification Argument. Another argument advanced in support of protection is to diversify the domestic industries. It means that there should be a balanced growth of the economy so that all the sectors of the economy develop side by side. For this purpose, agriculture and manufacturing industries should be protected from foreign competition. This is a valid argument, for experience has shown that countries which are not developed in a balanced way are affected more by international economic disturbance, such as crop failures, depressions, inflations, wars, *etc.* Therefore, they should diversify and become self-sufficient by protecting their industries. But it is not possible to diversify completely and attain self-sufficiency even by the richest country of the world. In fact, no country has all resources for a balanced growth of the economy. It has to depend upon other countries in one way or the other. Moreover, protection is not the only means to diversify an economy.

5. Infant Industry Argument. The infant industry argument is the oldest and the most accepted argument for protection. It was formulated by Alexander Hamilton in 1790 and was popularised by Friedrich List in 1885. This argument "rests on the assumption that the country has a latent comparative advantage in the industry or group of industries to be protected." It is, therefore, argued that if industries in their infancy are not protected from established foreign producers, they must attain the optimum size so as to operate most efficiently and competitively and to produce at lower costs. Protection is also needed to facilitate the flow of resources into infant industries, even though consumers have to bear the burden of higher prices temporarily. Further, there may be "imperfection of the information flow" to infant industries in the form of difficulty to borrow funds for investment, knowledge of infrastructure facilities, labour market, *etc.* All these requires government protection to such industries. The economic justification lies in that social benefits exceed private benefits from investment in such industries. It means that the protection should be given to those infant industries which generate larger externalities than other industries not given protection. Moreover, infant industries require time to undergo the process of learning-by-doing to become competitive in the long-run. Therefore, they should be protected. Johnson regards the infant industry arguments as being explicitly dynamic arguments 'for temporary intervention of correct transient distortion.'[2] So infant industries need protection for a while so that they may grow without any threat from foreign producers. When they attain adulthood, protection can be withdrawn and then they should be left free to face foreign competition.

The case for infant industry protection is based on the argument that when a new industry is started, it cannot reap the economies of scale and its cost of production is high as compared with its foreign competitors. But if it is protected by providing all types of facilities, such as subsidies, heavy import duties on foreign goods. etc. it may expand and enjoy internal economies of scale. It may, in turn, lead to external economies for all firms within the industry in the form of lower costs of production through the availability of trained labour force, advanced production techniques, research facilities, *etc.* If infant industry protection is given to several industries simultaneously, several external economies accrue in the form of road, railway, power, technical and research facilities, *etc.* Moreover, protection to infant industry, leads to its expansion and a lowering of costs and prices which, in turn, benefits industries using the products of the protected industry. But protection results in lowering of welfare because a tariff increases production and consumption costs in the economy. Therefore, to increase social welfare, the infant industry must be protected and pass what is called *Mill's test*. This test requires that it should be protected temporarily and must grow up and be able to compete on equal terms at world market prices with foreign producers in domestic and world markets. For protection to be profitable, it should be able to pay back the losses incurred due to protection during the infancy period. After that, protection should be withdrawn. But Bastable suggested another test called *Bastable's* test which an infant industry must also pass. This test requires that the infant industry must be able to cover the costs of protection during its infancy by lowering production costs. If an industry passes these two tests, then only it should be given infant industry protection.

The infant industries argument for protection is illustrated diagrammatically in Fig. 1. The Production of commodity *X* of industry *A* is measured on the horizontal axis and the production of commodity *Y* of industry *B* on the vertical axis. The production possibility curve of the country is *BA* . Under free trade, the country

2. H.G. Johnson, "Optimal Trade Interventions in the Presence of Temporary Distortions," in R.E. Baldwin (ed.), *Trade, Growth and Balance of Payments* : Essays in Honour of G. Haberler, 1966.

produces at E where the international terms of trade line $P'P'$ is tangent to the production possibility curve. When it enters into trade, it moves from point E to C where it imports and consumes more of commodity Y. In order to protect its industry, the country introduces a prohibitive tariff on the imports of commodity Y so that the domestic terms of trade are represented by the line PP. This line is tangent to the production possibility curve BA at E'. Now the country produces and consumes commodity Y at point E'. But it consumes less goods under protection because point E' is below point C under free trade. Thus protection lowers the country's welfare.

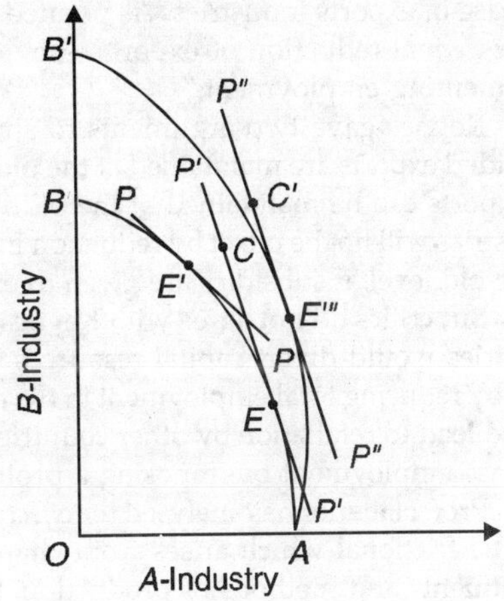

Fig. 1

But this is only a short-run situation. In the long run, protection increases the production of commodity Y when industry B experiences increasing returns so that the production possibility curve BA shifts outward to $B'A$. The country can now restart free trade. Assuming that the same international terms of trade prevail as before protection, draw a line $P''P''$ parallel to $P'P'$ which is tangent to the production possibility curve $B'A$ at E'' than before protection at E. By entering into trade, it can move to point C' which represents a higher level of social welfare than at point C. People consume more of commodity Y at C' than at C, by protecting an infant industry for some time and then reverting to free trade.

The infant industry argument for protection has been severely criticised by economists . It is difficult to decide which industry needs protection because every industry is in its infancy to begin with. In fact, it is difficult to select genuine infant industries because it requires "forecasting the potential cost structure of an industry, and its established competition." Protection is given to an infant industry with the promise that it would be withdrawn after a few years when the industry attains adulthood and is able to face foreign competition. But it is difficult to decide about this due to the lack of any reliable criteria. Once protection is granted to an industry, vested interests are created which do not want the removal of duties. Thus as pointed out by Haberler, "temporary infant-industry duties are transformed into permanent duties to preserve the industries they protect." Even if a part of the industry is able to stand upon its feet, a number of less efficient concerns are established behind the shelter of tariffs which make it difficult to remove the duties. Some of the industrialists who start making monopoly profits under protection do not want the removal of duties. They, therefore, bribe the legislators and corrupt the general politics of the country. Haberler does not agree with the view that the development of infant industries leads to internal and external economies of production. He has shown that alleged possibilities of external economies under infant industry protection are vague, muddled and doubtful "so that arguments for tariffs based upon them belong to *curiosa* of theory rather than to a practical economy theory."

6. *Socially Important or Key Industries Argument.* Protection should be given to socially important industries such as agriculture or strategically important industries as iron and steel, heavy electricals, machine making, heavy chemicals, *etc.* There is no dispute over this argument because the development of key and other socially important industries under protective tariffs is one of the principal aims of trade policy in a country.

7. *Employment Argument.* A usual argument for protection is that it is a cure for unemployment. The imposition of a tariff reduces imports and encourages employment directly in import competing industries. This, in turn, generates employment in other industries dependent upon this import-competing industry and may even spread to import-substitution industries. According to Prof. Haberler, unemployment in one single industry can be reduced by a tariff on the competing imports provided the demand for its products is *not completely elastic* and its products compete with similar imported products. But this does not mean that total unemployment will diminish.**

The critics argue that a tariff is not likely to reduce unemployment because a restriction of imports will lead to reduction of exports. While unemployment may be reduced in import-competing industries, it will increase in exports industries. As pointed by Keynes, "If a reduction of imports causes almost at once a more or less equal reduction of exports—obviously a tariff . . . would be completely futile for the purposes of argumenting employment."

Keynes gave two arguments to show that a protective tariff might lead to increase in employment, provided exports are maintained at the old level, *First,* if the tariff-imposing country lends to foreign countries, its exports can be maintained at the old level, and the increase in the employment in the import-competing industries will not be offset by reduction in employment in export industries. *Second,* exports can be maintained at the old level, if subsidies are given to export industries out of the revenue from import duties.

But critics do not agree with Keynes on the adoption of these methods. They argue that lending to other countries would divert capital resources from home investment which would reduce domestic investment, thereby reducing total employment in the country, On the other hand, the grant of subsides to export industries would lead to retaliation by other countries which would levy anti-dumping duties. Thus, it is not possible to increase employment by imposing a protective tariff.

Prof. Haberler has analysed the *effect of tariffs* on the various types of unemployment. *First,* unemployment may be frictional which arises from changes in the industrial structure as a result of the adoption of new investments and methods of production. Such technological unemployment can be removed by imposing a new tariff duty on imports only in the case of one industry, but not in the case of the entire industrial structure of the economy. Therefore, technological unemployment can be removed by protection, for it "involves the abandoning of all the fruits of technical progress, in so far as they can be enjoyed only through the medium of international division of labour." *Second,* unemployment may be due to the cyclical fluctuations of the industry. Cyclical unemployment can be reduced by a new tariff duty on one industry but not in the case of numerous industries and countries. Heavy protection in America in the 1930s failed to prevent crises and depression. As pointed out by Heberler, "Whether a country has high or low tariff has nothing to do with the acuteness of its crises and depression." *Third,* there may be permanent unemployment which can again be removed by the imposition of a new tariff duty in the case of one industry but not for the entire economy. However, only high tariffs can cure permanent unemployment if it is due to very high wages. But high tariffs lead to retaliation. Under the circumstances, it is not high tariffs but readjustment of wages are needed to cure permanent unemployment. Haberler concludes that "leaving aside a few exceptional cases, a favourable result can be expected only in the short-run, so that tariffs can be advocated on this ground only from a short-run, and indeed, short-sighted, standpoint.

8. Balance of Trade Arguments. The balance of trade argument is based on the notion that a country should impose tariffs to have a surplus of exports over imports. Such a surplus brings bullion into the country. But this is not a correct view because if all countries follow the same rule, none would gain. Moreover, a surplus of exports over imports cannot continue over the long run. An inflow of gold would raise prices and an outflow would lower prices. Thus in the long run, exports must equal imports. Moreover, the balance of trade argument in this sense is not valid these days because there are no free movements of gold among countries.

Keynes presented this argument in a different way. According to him, excess of exports over imports raises employment and income in the country through the expansion of the export sector and the decline in imports by imposing tariffs. The increase in income, in turn, increases the supply of loanable funds which reduces the interest rate and encourages investment. As a result, more employment and income are generated.

Keynes' view is not much different from the earlier view because when the export surplus increases employment and income in one country, the import surplus in the other country reduces employment and income there. Second, such a policy will lead to retaliation by the other country. Third, such a policy adversely affects the volume of world trade, and international specialisation suffers. So the balance of trade is not a valid argument.

9. Pauper Labour Argument. It is argued that goods produced by workers getting high wages in one country cannot compete with goods produced by low-wage workers in the other country. Therefore, high-wage domestic goods should be protected from low-wage imported goods by imposing tariffs.

This argument is based on two unrealistic assumption. *First,* the prices of goods are determined by wage rates alonge, and *Second,* labour is the only factor of production. But the fact is that goods are manufactured by a combination of factors. Labour is combined with land and capital. It is only in the labour-intensive goods that low-paid labour can have a cost advantage over high-paid labour. It is, therefore, fallacious to argue that a high-wage country is at a disadvantage in the production of all types of commodities.

Further, it is wrong to assume that the cost of production is high in the high-wage country. In fact, high wages may be due to high productivity. So in a country where labour productivity is high. per unit cost of production may be lower than the low-wage country. Consequently, when unit costs are low in the high-wage countries they can compete with low-wage countries.

Stopler and Samuelson have shown under some rigid assumptions that protection can support the level of wages in a country. In a country where labour is scarce, free trade will enable labour-intensive imports to enter. As a result, labour scarcity will be reduced, thereby reducing the wages of labour relative to the return on capital. So protection is justified because it will raise the wages of the scarce factor labour and reduce the return on the abundant factor capital.

The Stopler-Samuelson theorem does not support the pauper labour argument. It simply reveals that protection can lead to a redistribution of real income in favour of labour. But the real wage of labour can be increased in a better way by monetary and fiscal measures and benefits from free trade can also be enjoyed. Thus protection provides no solution to the fallacious pauper labour argument.

10. Keeping Money at Home Argument. This is also one of the fallacious arguments for protection. This argument runs as follows: "When we buy manufactured goods abroad we get the goods and the foreigner gets the money. When we buy the manufactured goods at home we get both the goods and the money." This saying by Robert Ingersoll is wrongly attributed to Abraham Lincoln. This argument is illogical because if every country were to follow this rule, there would be no international trade and the benefits of its would not accrue to any country of the world. A country buys goods from another country because the latter offers them at lower prices than the domestic manufacturers. Buying goods produced by domestic manufacturers would, therefore, mean loss to the consumers. Moreover, in international trade domestic currency cannot be used for making payments to foreigners. In fact, goods pay for goods, and payments if any are made in the international currency. Thus, as pointed out by Beveridge, this argument "has no merits; the only sensible words in it are the first eight words" in the above cited quotation.

11. Expanding Home Market Argument. This is a corollary to the above argument of keeping money at home. Accroding to this argument, protection should be given to new industries and the workers engaged in them would create a good market for other domestic products. This would expand the home market for all domestic products including agricultural commodities. This is again a fallacious argument because the home market would expand at the expense of the foreign market for exports. When imports are restricted by imposition of tariff duties, exports also decline because other countries would retaliate. Moreover, domestic producers will charge higher prices for the products of domestic industries and the consumers will be the losers.

12. Equalisation Costs of Production Argument. Protection to domestic industries is advocated for equalising costs of production or prices of domestic and foreign products. If, for example, the domestic costs are higher than foreign price by 25 per cent , an import duty of 25 per cent should be imposed on the foreign products. Thus the price of both domestic and foreign products are equalised and they can compete on equal terms. According to Taussig, this argument 'has an engaging appearance of fairness. It seems to say, no favours, no undue rates." But strictly speaking, its "apparent fairness is only skin deep," according to Ellsworth. If the domestic costs of production are high, the import duty will also be high. So it is the foreigner who suffers from such a policy. The imposition of very high import duties by all countries would lead to the destruction of international trade. Ellsworth also regards such a protection policy as discriminatory. The imposition of retaliatory tariff duties on the country's exports by other countries harms the efficient domestic export industries. Moreover, such a policy would lead to giving protection to the least efficient industries with the highest costs of production. It thus "discriminates in favour of inefficient producers; against efficient ones, and against the general body of consumers."

B. Non-Economic Arguments. There are three important non-economic arguments for protection.

1. Defence Argument. A country should adopt the policy of protecting its industries from the standpoint of national defence. If a country is dependent on other countries for its requirements of agricultural and industrial products, it will be very harmful for its national interest in times of war. The argument runs that it is no use amassing wealth and becoming richer, if the country is not in a position to defend its freedom. As aptly put by Adam Smith, "Defence is better than opulence." Therefore, a country should be self-sufficient as far as possible even if it involves an economic loss in the production of certain commodities, which are needed for national defence. In particular, protection for national defence refers to self-sufficiency in arms and ammunitions and other related industries. But complete self-sufficiency as an argument for national defence does not carry much force for it will lead to inefficiency in domestic industries and loss of the gains from international trade. Thus industries which are directly ad indirectly needed for the manufacture of arms and ammunitions and other war materials should be developed under protection.

2. *Preservation Argument.* Protection is advocated to preserve the special ethos of the nation and certain classes of the population or certain occupations. It is argued that these would tend to disappear under free trade and their preservation is desired on political and social grounds. This argument is put forth to safeguard the interests of the agriculturists. The imposition of agricultural duties on import of farm products is beneficial for the farmers who would be assured fair prices for their products. They would thus become prosperous. The prosperity of the peasantry is essential for it forms the backbone of every nation. As pointed out by Haberler "Agriculture is the wellspring from which the human race is physically and mentally regenerated. Therefore, agriculture should be protected from foreign competition at all costs to preserve the special ethos of the nation."

3. *Patriotism or Nationalism Argument.* To arouse patriotism or nationalism among the people, imports of foreign goods are restricted through high import duties so that they consume the goods manufactured within the country. This is what Gandhiji advocated in his *swadeshi* movements. For the success of such a policy, it is essential that goods produced within the country should be of high quality and available in sufficient quantities.

EXERCISES

1. State the case for and against free trade.
2. Give arguments in support of the policy of protection.
3. Examine critically the infant industry argument for protection in the context of a developing country.

CHAPTER 48

Tariffs

1. MEANING AND TYPES

A tariff is a tax levied on imports. It is synonymous with import duties or custom duties. Tariffs are used for two different purposes : for revenue and for protection. Revenue tariffs are meant to provide the state with revenue. Revenue duties are levied on luxury consumer goods. The lower the import duties, the larger is the revenue from them. This is because the rise in the price of the imported goods does not increase much with the imposition of low import duties and the consumers do not normally shift their demand to other domestically produced goods.

Protective tariffs are meant "to maintain and encourage those branches of home industry protected by the duties.[1] Now-a-days, governments levy import duties with the principal objective of discouraging imports in order to encourage domestic production of protected industry. The revenue function of an import duty is a secondary one.

"The duty which affords the maximum of protection is a prohibitive one which yields no revenue to the State. On the other hand, the revenue yielded by a duty will be the greater the less the import of the good falls off, that is to say the less the duty fulfils its protective function. This depends in turn on two things : (*a*)how demand reacts—the less demand falls off, the higher will be the revenue from the duty; and (*b*) to what extent thehome production is stimulated by the rise in price due to the duty."[2]

The following types of tariff duties are levied : ad valorem, specific, compound and sliding scale duties.

The most common type of duty is the ad valorem duty. It is levied as a percentage of the total value of the imported common duty. The import duty is a fixed percentage of the c.i.f. (cost, insurance and freight) value of the commodity. It may be 25 per cent, 50 per cent and so on.

Specific duties are levied per physical unit of the imported commodity, as Rs X per TV, as cloth per metre, as oil per litre, as fertilizers per tonne, etc.

Often, governments levy compound duties which are a combination of the ad valorem and the specific duties. In this case, units of an imported commodity are levied a percentage ad valorem duty plus a specific duty on each unit of the commodity.

Sometimes governments levy import duties which vary with the prices of commodities imported. Such duties are known as sliding scale duties which may be either ad valorem or specific. Normally, sliding scale duties are imposed on specific basis.

---

1. G. Haberler, *op. cit.*, p. 238.
2. Ibid., p. 239

2. EFFECTS OF TARIFFS

Tariffs have a variety of effects which depend upon their power to reduce imports. The effects of a tariff may be analysed from the standpoint of the economy as a whole which is known as the general equilibrium analysis. Or, they may be discussed from the point of view of a particular good or market which is known as the partial equilibrium analysis. A tariff "is likely to alter trade, prices, output, and consumption, and to reallocate resources, change factor proportions, redistribute income, change employment, and alter the balance of payments."[3]

Accordingly, Prof. Kindleberger has listed eight effects of tariffs : (1) Protective Effect; (2) Consumption Effect; (3) Revenue Effect; (4) Redistributive Effect; (5) Terms of Trade Effect; (6) Competitive Effect; (7) Income Effect; and (8) Balance of Payments Effect. All these effects are the result of the Price Effect.

The analysis of the effects of a tariff under the partical equilibrium analysis is based on the following assumptions :

1. The demand and supply curves of a commodity relate to the country which levies an import duty.
2. These curves are assumed as given and constant.
3. On the demand side, consumers' tastes, incomes and prices of other commodities are assumed to be fixed.
4. On the supply side, changes in cost conditions such as externalities, technological innovations, *etc.* do not take place.
5. There are no transport costs.
6. The foreign price of the commodity remains unchanged.

Price Effect. Given these assumptions, the price effect of a tariff is explained in terms of Fig. 1 where *D* and *S* are the domestic demand and supply curves of a commodity. *OP* represents the constant world price at which the foreign producers are prepared to sell their commodity in the domestic market. Thus the horizontal line *PB* is the supply curve of imports which is perfectly elastic at *OP* price. Thus under free trade (before the imposition of a tariff) the equilibrium market position is given by point *B* where the domestic demand curve *D* intersects the world supply curve *PB* at the price *OP*. The total demand for the commodity is OQ_3. The domestic supply is *OQ*. The difference between domestic demand and domestic supply is met by importing QQ_3 quantity at *OP* price.

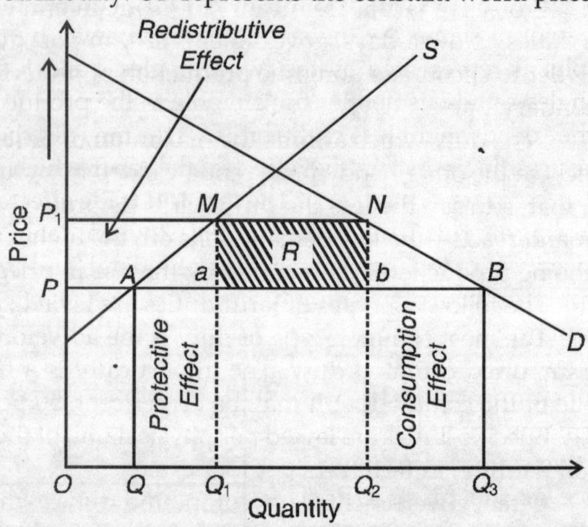

Fig. 1

Suppose a tariff of PP_1 is imposed on the import of the commodity. Given a constant foreign price, the domestic price of the commodity rises by the full amount of the tariff of OP_1. Thus the rise in the price of the commodity by PP_1 is the price effect of the tariff. As a result, the new equilibrium market position is given by point *N*. In response to the higher price, the domestic demand falls from OQ_3 to OQ_2 and the domestic supply increases from *OQ* to OQ_1. So that the total demand for the commodity is OQ_2 which is partly met by domestic supply OQ_1 and partly by importing Q_1Q_2. Thus imports have fallen from QQ_3 to Q_1Q_2 as a result of the price effect.

The protective, consumption, revenue and redistribution effects of a tariff can also be illustrated by Fig. 1.

1. *Protective Effect.* The protective effect shows how the domestic industry can be protected from foreign competition by imposing an importy duty. In Fig. 1 under free trade, OQ_3 quantity of the commodity is imported at *OP* price. With the imposition of the import duty of PP_1, imports are reduced to Q_1Q_2, while the

3. Charles P. Kindleberger, *op. cit.,* p. 107.

domestic production (supply) of the commodity increases from OQ to OQ_1. Thus the increase in the domestic production of the commodity by QQ_1 as a result of the tariff is the protective or production effect.

Prof. Ellsworth has carried this protective effect further and has analysed it as the import substitution effect. When the domestic producers face the higher price OP_1, they are able to cover the rising marginal costs of additional output, and expand production to OQ_1. This replacement of foreign production with domestic production by QQ_1 is called the import substitution effect of a tariff.

2. *Consumption Effect.* The consumption effect of the tariff is to reduce the consumption of the commodity on which the tariff is imposed, as also to reduce consumers' net satisfaction. These are illustrated in Fig. 1. Before the.imposition of a tariff, consumers were consuming OQ_3 quantity of the commodity at OP price, with the levying of an import duty of PP_1, the price of the commodity rises to OP_1. Now imports are reduced by Q_3Q_2 and the total consumption of the commodity is also reduced from OQ_3 to OQ_2. Thus Q_3Q_2 $(= OQ_3 - OQ_2)$ is the consumption effect of the tariff. This, in turn, leads to a net loss of consumers' satisfaction equal to the area PP_1NB. Prof. Kindleberger calls the combined protective and consumption effect as *trade effect*. The imposition of PP_1 tariff has the effect of reducing the total volume of trade of the country equivalent of $OQ_3 - Q_1Q_2$.

3. *Revenue Effect.* the revenue effect is the change in government receipts as a result of the tariff. In the case illustrated in Fig. 1 initially the tariff is assumed zero at price OP. So when PP_1 import duty is levied, the revenue to the government is equal to the amount of the import duty multipled by the quantity of imports. The revenue effect is, therefore, $PP_1 \times Q_1Q_2$, or the rectangular shaded area R.

4. *Redistributive Effect.* The redistribution effect results from producers receiving a higher price for their commodity after the imposition of the tariff. This is shown in Fig. 1 by the area PP_1MA. This amount is a surplus over production costs and is an economic rent which goes to producers. According to Kindleberger the redistribution effect "is an addition to producers' surplus derived by subtraction from consumers' surplus". In this sense, the net loss to consumers' satisfaction as measured by the consumption effect is PP_1NB. Out of this, the amount shown by the area R is taken away by the government as revenue, and the loss of consumers' surplus is represented by the two traingles a and b. This loss of consumers' surplus represented by the two triangles a and b is neither transferable to the producers nor to the government and is called by Kindleberger as the "deadweight loss of the tariff." This may also be called the *cost of the tariff*. Thus the quadrilateral PP_1MA measures the redistributive effect of the tariff which goes to the domestic producers of the commodity.

6. *Terms of Trade Effect.* The terms of trade effect of a tariff is that it improves the terms of trade of country imposing it. This is illustrated in Fig. 2 when Panel (*A*) shows S_1 and D_1 as the supply and demand curves respectively of the exporting country England, and Panel (*B*) shows S_2 and D_2 the supply and demand curves respectively of the importing country Germany. Before the imposition of a tariff by Germany, trade between the two countries is taking place at the price OP_1. Suppose Germany imposes tariff of P_2T amount on the imported commodity from England. This raises its price in Germany and the demand for it falls. On the other hand, its supply price in England falls with the decline in its export demand. Thus the price rises from OP_1 to OP_2 in Germany in Panel (*B*) and falls in England from OP_1 to OP' in Panel (*A*), as a result of the tariff. Of the total tariff of P_2T, a larger amount P_2P_1 is borne by the importer country Germany and P_1P' by the exporter country England. The terms of trade effect is that a tariff-imposing country improves its terms of trade by getting its imports cheaply in the sense that the exporter country is forced to pay a part of the tariff duty. "It is true that the consumer in the

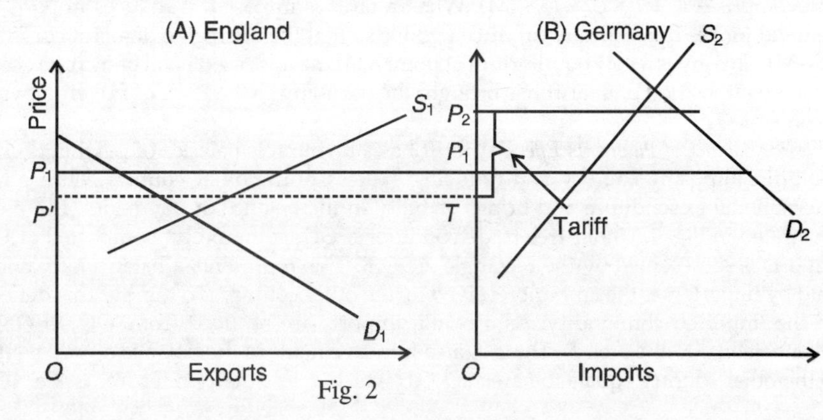

Fig. 2

importing country has to pay a higher price. But this is offset, so far as imports are concerned, by the revenue effect. If the redistribution effect can be ignorned, the revenue effect, which is the tariff times imports after the imposition of the tax, is levied partly on producers in the exporting country." If the supply is very inelastic in the exporting country and the demand fairly elastic in the importing country, the impostion of a tariff will not change the imports much, but they will be obtained much cheaply. If the suppy curve in the exporting country is perfectly elastic the imposition of a tariff cannot improve the terms of trade at all.*

7. *Competitive Effect.* The competitive effect of a tariff is to protect the domestic industry from foreign competition by imposing a tariff on the commodity imported. This effect is usually associated with the infant industry argument of protection. But the fear is expressed that an infant industry may not like to face competition even after attaining adulthood. It may develop into a monopoly and may continue to be inefficient. Prof. Kindleberger opines that "the competitive effect of a tariff is really an anti-competitive effect; competition is stimulated by tariff removal." He, therefore, favours the removal of tariff on "sluggish, fat and lazy" domestic industries in the interest of the economy.

7. *Income Effect**. The income effect refers to the effect of a tariff on the levels of income and employment of a country imposing the tariff. A tariff reduces the demand for imported goods by reducing imports, and increases the demand for home-produced goods on the assumption that there is no retaliation by the other country. It will increase the value of the export surplus $(X - M)$, thereby increasing the inflow of income from the foreign sector. The whole of the income diverted from imports will not be saved but a part of it will be spent at home. Under conditions of less than full employment, this will raise money and real incomes and employment. With full employment, however, it can raise money income, through inflation, leaving real income worsened by the altered allocation of resources. With idle resources it remains true, tariffs raise domestic spending and national income." If the tariff imposing country raises its level of income and employment at the expense of the exporting country, this is a beggar-thyneighbour policy. This is criticised because it reduces income and employment in the other country.

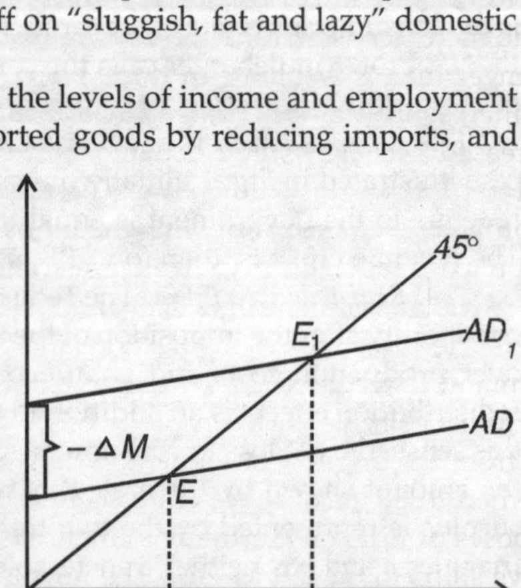

Fig. 3

The income effect of a tariff is illustrated in Fig. 3. *AD* is the total expenditure schedule of the economy at unemployment level which crosses the 45° line at *E* so that OY_1 is the equilibrium level of income. *AD* also represents the aggregate demand and comprises $C + I + G + (X - M)$. When a tariff is imposed, it reduces imports by– *DM* and increases the demand for the domestically produced goods so that the aggregate demand curve shifts to $AD_1 = [\, C + I + G + (X - M)$. This gives a new equilibrium at point E_1. If the increased level of income OY_F is one of full employment, then the imposition of a tariff has brought the economy to the level of full employment and raised the level of income of OY_F.

8. *Balance of Payments Effect.* A tariff has a favourable balance of payments effect by reducing imports in the tariff imposing country and reducing exports in the other country. Thus a tariff reduces the country's international expenditure and brings stability in the balance of payments. The balance of payments effect is illustrated in Fig. 1. Under free trade conditions, QQ_3 commodity is imported at *OP* price. The total value of imports is represented by the rectangle AQQ_3B. This represents a balance of payments deficit since the price paid by importers is the amount received by the other country. To remove this deficit, PP_1 import duty is levied on the imported commodity. As a result, imports are reduced from QQ_3 to Q_1Q_2. The government gets a revenue equal to the area *R*. There is also improvementt in the balance of payments because the amount paid to the other country equals the area aQ_1Q_2b which is less than under free trade AQQ_3B.

* C.P. Kindleberger, *op. cit.,* p. 116.

3. OPTIMUM TARIFF AND WELFARE

Usually, the imposition of a tariff improves the terms of trade of the imposing country but reduces its volume of trade. The improvement in the terms of trade increases its welfare. This is the *positive* effect of a tariff. The decrease in the volume of trade reduces its welfare. This is the *negative* effect of a tariff. It is only when the positive effect of a tariff is larger than its negative effect that there is improvement in the welfare of a country. A prohibitive tariff with a very high rate reduced welfare by decreasing the volume of trade. On the other hand, a reduction in tariff by improving the terms of trade increases welfare. Thus as long as the terms of trade effect is stronger than the volume of trade effect, welfare can be improved by increasing the tariff rate. But a tariff cannot be continuously increased because sooner or later the net gain begins to decrease and net loss begins to increase. Therefore, a country "can always improve its welfare by applying the 'right' tariff. This tariff, the tariff that maximises a country's welfare is called the optimum tariff."[4]

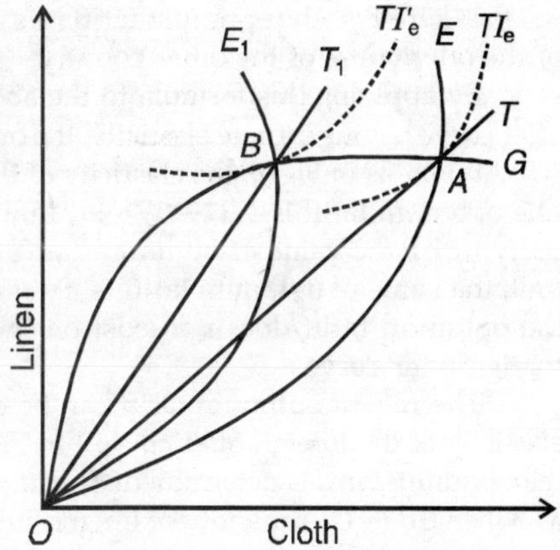

Fig. 4

The optimum tariff is explained with the help of Fig. 4, where *OE* is the offer curve of England and *OG* is the offer curve of Germany. TI_e is the indifference curve of England. Under free trade, the terms of trade between the two countries are given by the ray *OT* from the origin. Consequently, they are in equilibrium at point *A* where their offer curves intersect each other. Suppose England imposes a tariff on Germany's linen. As a result, England's offer curve shifts to the left as OE_1. The new terms of trade are given by the ray OT_1 and *B* is the new equilibrium point determined by Germany's original offer curve *OG* and England's new offer curve OE_1. This tariff which has changed England's offer curve from *OE* to OE_1 is the *optimum* tariff of this country. The point *B* where England's trade indifference curve TI_e' is tangent to Germany's offer curve *OG* is the point of optimum tariff. The welfare of people in England is greater at point *B* than at point *A*. This is because at *B* they are at the TI_e' trade indifference curve which is above the TI_e trade indifference curve at the free trade situation *A*. Thus the tariff that maximises a country's welfare is the optimum tariff. "It is the tariff that moves the country to the trade indifference curve that is tangent to the other country's offer curve."

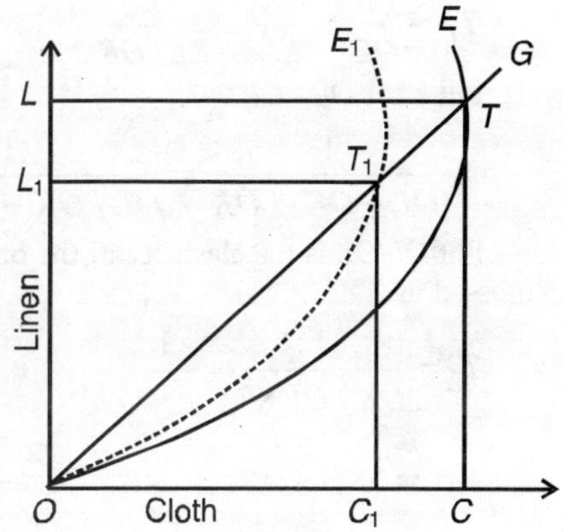

Fig. 5

The tariff imposing country can gain from the optimum tariff only if the offer curve of the other trading country is *less than perfectly elastic*. If the offer curve of the other country is perfectly or infinitely elastic, levying a tariff will not increase the welfare of the tariff-imposing country. This is illustrated in Fig. 5 where the offer curve of Germany is shown as the straight the curve *OG* and *OE* is the offer curve of England. Under free trade, the terms of trade are given by *OG* and the equilibrium is established at point *T* where the two offer curves intersect each other. When England imposes a tariff, its offer curve shifts to OE_1. The new equilibrium is set at T_1. In this case, the terms of trade remains unchanged, while the volume of trade is reduced from $OC + OL$ to $OC_1 + OL_1$. Here the *positive effect* of tariff is zero because there is no improvement in its terms of trade. And the negative effect of tariff is stronger, because of the large reduction in the volume of trade. Therefore, the optimum tariff is *zero*.

Prof. Kindleberger[6] has devised a formula to measure the rate of optimum tariff which is

4. Bo Sodersten, *op. cit.*, p. 356.
5. P.T. Ellsworth and J.K. Leith, *op. cit.*, p. 242.
6. C.P. Kindleberger, *op. cit.*, p. 482.

$$T_f = \frac{1}{e-1}$$

Where T_f is the optimum tariff rate and e is the point elasticity of the offer curve of the other country.

By applying this formula to the above case of a straight line offer curve having infinite elasticity, the optimum tariff is $1/(\infty - 1) = 0$. At point A in Fig. 6, the elasticity of the foreign offer curve is 1. The optimum tariff is $1/(1-1) = \infty$, infinity. When e is more than unity (one), the value of optimum tariff falls. When e is less than unit, the value of optimum tariff is *negative* thereby indicating that the optimum tariff does not exist on the inelastic portion of the foreign offer curve.

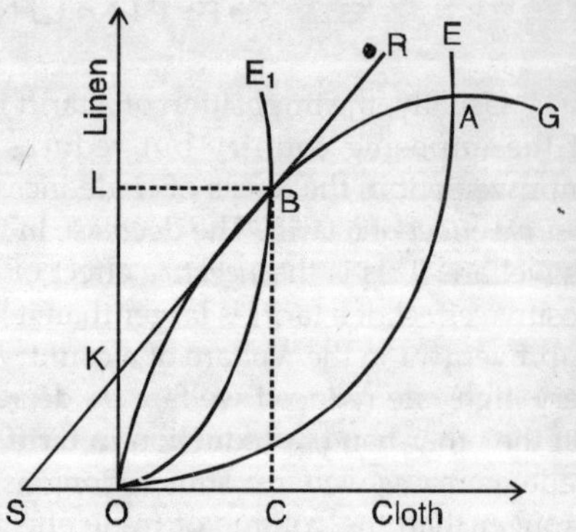

Fig. 6

The rate of optimum tariff can be calculated in terms of the elasticity of the foreign offer curve.* In Fig. 6, B is the point where the optimum tariff is determined. The import duty to the public in the tariff imposing country England is OK/KL when CB (= OL) quantity of linen is imported from Germany. Now the optimum tariff at point B is OS/OC. But $OS/OC = OS/LB$ since $OC = LB$ which, in turn, equals KO/KL by similar triangles SOK and BLK. The optimum tariff, T_f is equal to

$$T_f = \frac{OS}{OC} = \frac{OK}{KL} = \frac{1}{KL/OK}$$

But KL = $OL - OK$

$$\therefore \frac{1}{(OL-OK)/OK} = \frac{1}{OL/OK - OK/OK} = \frac{1}{OL/OK - 1}$$

But OL/OK is the elasticity of the offer curve at point B. So the optimum tariff OS/OC at point B can be expressed as

$$T_f = \frac{1}{OK/OL - 1} = \frac{1}{e-1}$$

EXERCISES

1. Explain the various types of tariffs. Show with the help of partial equilibrium diagram the price, protective, consumption, revenue and redistribution effects of a tariff.
2. What is the tariff which will maximise a country's gain, improving the terms of trade more than the volume is reduced?
3. What do you mean by optimum tariff? Under what conditions optimum tariff is likely to be high or zero?

---

* Elasticity of Offer Curve $= \frac{-(\%\text{ change in imports})}{(\%\text{ change in exports}) - (\%\text{ change in imports})} - 1$

$= \frac{(\%\text{ change in exports})}{(\%\text{ change in imports})} - 1$

Chapter 49

Import Quotas

1. MEANING

Import quota is a protectionist device to restrict the supply of a good or service from abroad. Under an import quota, a fixed amount of a commodity in volume or value is allowed to be imported into the country during a specified period of time, usually a year. For this purpose, the government may issue an import license that it may sell either to importers at a competitive price or just give it to importers on the basis of first-come first-served. Alternatively, the government may limit the value of imports by providing the importers with a limited amount of foreign exchange for the purchase of a particular commodity to be imported by them. Import quotas aim at restricting and regulating imports in order to protect domestic industries from foreign competition and to correct disequilibrium in the balance of payments. They are also used as a retaliatory device.

They are also used as a retaliatory device.

Import Quotas are of five types :

1. Tariff Quota. Under this quota system, a given quantity of a good is permitted to enter duty free or upon payment of relatively low duty. But imports in excess of that quantity are charged a relatively high rate of duty.[1]

2. Unilateral Quota. Under this system of quota, the total volume or value of the commodity to be imported is fixed by law or decree without any agreement with the other countries. The autonomously fixed quota may be either global or allocated. Under the global quota, the full amount of the quota may be imported from any one country. While under the allocated quota system, the total quantity of the quota is distributed among different countries.

3. Bilateral Quota. Under this quota system, quotas are fixed by some agreement with one or more other countries. Haberler calls them agreed quotas.

4. Mixing Quota. This system requires domestic producers in the quota fixing country to use imported raw materials in certain proportion along with domestic raw materials to produce finished products. Thus the quota of raw materials to be imported are fixed in quantity by the government. This quota system benefits the quota fixing country in two ways : *First,* It protects domestic producers of raw materials from foreign competition; and *second,* It saves the foreign exchange of the country.

5. Import Licensing. Import licensing is the system devised to administer the various types of quotas. According to this system, the amount of the commodity to be imported is first determined on the basis of the

1. G. Haberler, *op. cit.*, p. 347.

above mentioned quota systems. Then import licenses are issued by the appropriate authority to the importers for specified quantities of commodities to be imported.

2. EFFECTS OF IMPORT QUOTAS

Kindleberger has analysed eight effects of import quotas, some under partial equilibrium and others under general equilibrium analysis. First, we explain the effects of import quotas under partial equilibrium analysis.

Partial Equilibrium Analysis

Price Effect. The aim of an import quota is to limit the physical quantity of a commodity. So when an import quota is fixed, it tends to raise the price of the commodity. How much the price will rise depends upon the supply and demand conditions of the commodity within the domestic market and the extent to which the supply of the imported commodity is restricted by the quota. The price effect of an import quota is illustrated in Fig 1 where *D* and *S* are the domestic demand and supply curves respectively of a commodity. *PB* is the foreign supply curve under free trade which intersects the domestic demand curve *D* at point *B* and *OP* price is determined. Thus the total domestic demand for the commodity is OQ_3. But the domestic supply is *OQ*. So QQ_3 quantity of the commodity is being imported under free trade at *OP* price.

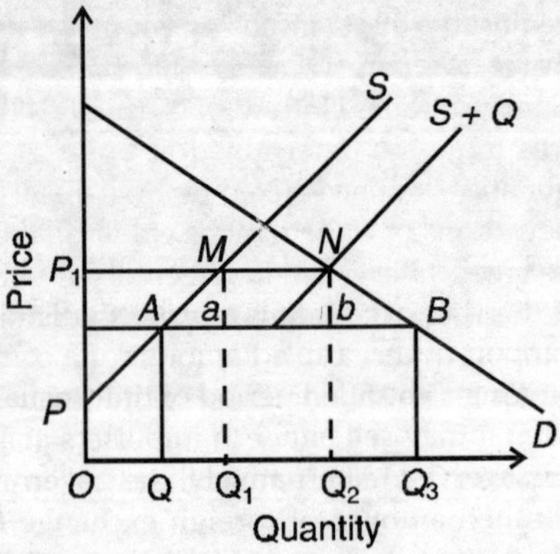

Fig. 1

Suppose the government fixes an imports quota equal to the amount Q_1Q_2. Now the total supply curve of the commodity is *S* + *Q* which consists of the domestic supply plus the quota amount. It intersects the domestic demand curve at *N* so that the quota raises the domestic price from *OP* to OP_1. Thus PP_1 is the price effect of the quota.

Protective Effect. An import quota has a protective effect when it reduces the quantity of an importable commodity and protects the domestic producers of the commodity from foreign competition. In terms of Fig. 1 when Q_1Q_2 amount of import quota is fixed, the domestic production of the commodity increases from *OQ* to OQ_1. Thus QQ_1 is the protective effect of the import quota.

Consumption Effect. When an import quota is fixed, it tends to raise the domestic price of the commodity. Consequently, the domestic consumption is reduced. This is illustrated in Fig. 1 where under free trade the total domestic consumption of the commodity is OQ_3. With the fixation of the quota of Q_1Q_2 amount, the total domestic consumption falls to OQ_2. Thus the reduction in the domestic consumption by Q_3Q_2 (= $OQ_3 - OQ_2$) is the consumption effect of the import quota.

Revenue Effect. The determination of the revenue effect of an import quota is quite complicated and difficult to determine. If the government auctions the import licenses at the price $PP_1 \times Q_1Q_2$ quantity allowed of the commodity, the revenue effect of the import quota will be equal to the area *aMNb*. This is equivalent to the import tariff. But governments do not auction import licenses these days. In that case, the revenue effect will be captured either by importers or exporter, or shared by both in the form of higher prices and profits and represents a rent for them. The revenue effect will be captured by domestic importers if they are organised and act as monopolists. On the other hand, if the foreign exporters are organised and the domestic importers are not, the revenue effect will be captured by the foreign exporters. If both domestic importers and foreign exporters are organised, there will be bilateral monopoly and the revenuc effect will be shared by both. However, the actual result will be indeterminate, as under bilateral monopoly.

Redistributive Effect. The fixation of an import quota also leads to the redistribution effect. This happens when with the rise in the price of the commodity, the domestic producers earn higher profits and the consumers' surplus from the commodity decreases. In fact, the redistribution effect is the transfer of consumers' surplus to producers resulting from the rise in the price of commodity for which the import quota is fixed. It is shown in

Fig. 1 as the quadrilateral PP_1MA.

Terms of Trade Effect. The fixation of an import quota tends to change the terms of trade of the country. The new terms of trade may be more or less favourable to the country fixing the quota. It depends upon the elasticity of the offer curve or the monopoly power of the importing country or of the exporting country. If the importing country has a monopoly in importing the commodity (or its offer curve is elastic), the terms of trade will be favourable to it. On the other hand, if the exporting country possesses monopoly in commodity on which the import quota is imposed (or its offer curve is elastic), the terms of trade will move in its favour and against the quota imposing country. The terms of trade effect is illustrated in Fig. 2 where OE is the offer curve of England and OG of Germany. England trades cloth with Germany's linen, and the terms of trade under free trade are determined at point A. Suppose an import quota of OL quantity of linen is fixed by England. The terms of trade will change. The new terms of trade may be either on the ray OT_1 or OT_2. If they are OM on the ray OT_1, the terms of trade will be favourable to England because it will be exchanging LM cloth for OL linen of Germany. On the other hand, if the terms of trade are at ON on the ray OT_2, they are unfavourable to England because it will have to exchange more cloth LN for OL linen of Germany. "As in the case of bilateral monopoly—with a monopoly buyer and a monopoly seller—the outcome is theoretically indeterminate."[2]

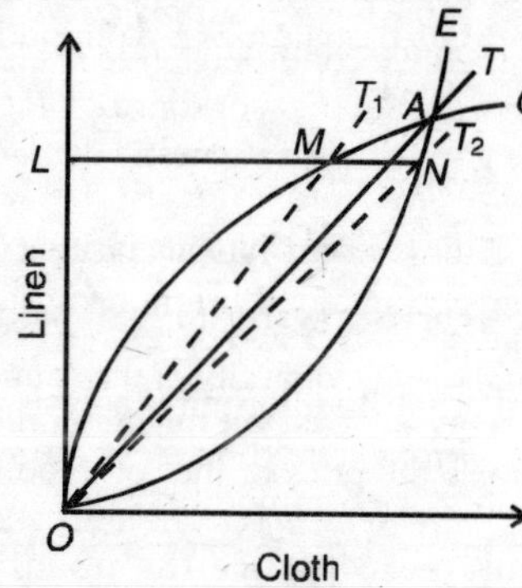

Fig. 2

Balance of Payments Effect. The balance of payments effect of an import quota is favourable to the quota imposing country. One of the objectives of fixing import quotas is to restrict imports so that they do not exceed the imports of the country. Thus import quotas tend to improve the balance of trade. Further, when imports are limited by the quota, the portion of the national income going to imports is also reduced. This is invested on domestic industries for import substitution and export promotion industries. This tends to increase the income from abroad and thereby improves the balance of payments position of the import quota imposing country. The balance of payments effect of an import quota is illustrated in Fig. 1 where under free trade QQ_3 commodity is imported at OP price. The total value of imports is represented by the rectangle AQQ_3B. This represents a balance of payments deficit because the amount paid by the importers is the amount received by the other country. To correct this balance of payments deficit, an import quota of Q_1Q_2 is fixed so that the imports are reduced to this quantity. If the government auctions this quota to importers, it receives an amount equal to the area $aMNb$. Or, if the importers are organised, they get this much amount as profits which they utilise for further investment within the country. This is also a saving on foreign exchange. There is also improvement in the balance of payments because the quota imposing country pays the amount equal to the area aQ_1Q_2b for imports which is less than what it paid under free trade AQQ_3B.

3. THE EQUIVALENCE OF TARIFFS AND QUOTAS

There is an equivalence between a tariff and a quota. Both produce similar effects in raising domestic price, protecting domestic production of the importable commodity, reducing domestic consumption and restricting the volume of imports.

The analysis of equivalence between a tariff and a quota assumes that : (*a*) there is perfect competition in the domestic market; (*b*) there is competitive foreign supply; (*c*) domestic buyers as a group face a supply curve that equals the domestic supply curve plus the fixed quota; (*d*) the quota ensures perfect competition is that it is fully used; (*e*) the tariff and the import quota are equivalent in the sense that a tariff is just high enough to make the quantity of imports equal to the amount and allowed by the quota.

Given these assumptions, the similar effects of a tariff and an import quota are illustrated in Fig. 3 where D_d and S_d are the domestic demand and supply curves of an importable commodity. OP_W is the world price and

2. C.P. Kindleberger, *op. cit.*, p. 124.

P_WS_F is the foreign supply curve under free trade which is perfectly elastic at OP_W price. Thus, under perfectly competitive conditions, free trade equilibrium is given by point B where the D_d curve intersects the supply curve P_WS_F at the world price OP_W. The total demand for the commodity is OQ_3 and the domestic supply is OQ. The gap between domestic demand and supply is met by imports of QQ_3 quantity of the commodity at OP_W price.

Price Effect. When a tariff at the rate of P_WP_T/OP_T is imposed on the imports of the commodity, it shifts the P_WS_W curve upwards to $P_T S'_F$ and raises the price to OP_T. Similarly, the direct imposition of an import quota equal to Q_1Q_2 quantity of the commodity shifts the domestic supply curve to the right as $S_d + Q$. It intersects the D_d curve at N so that the quota raises the domestic price to OP_T. Thus the price effect of a tariff and a quota is to raise the price of the commodity by an equivalent amount.

Protective Effect. The aim of both a tariff and an import quota is to reduce the quantity of the importable commodity and protect the domestic producers of the commodity from foreign competition. In terms of Fig. 3, before the imposition of a tariff, QQ_3 quantity of the commodity is imported. But with the imposition of P_WP_T/OP_T tariff, imports are reduced from QQ_3 to Q_1Q_2 and domestic production expands from OQ and OQ_1. Thus the increase in the domestic production of the commodity by QQ_1 amount is the protective or production effect of the tariff. Similarly, when Q_1Q_2 import quota is fixed, the domestic production of the commodity increases from OQ to OQ_1 thereby leading to a protective effect of QQ_1 equivalent to that under the tariff.

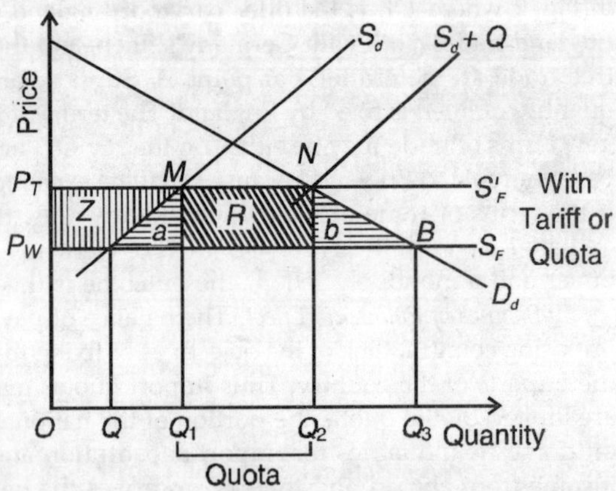

FIG. 3

Consumption Effect. A tariff and an import quota produce an equivalent consumption effect. Both tend to raise the domestic price of the commodity and reduce its domestic consumption. In Fig. 3, the domestic consumption of the commodity under free trade is OQ_3. With the imposition of P_wP_T/OP_T tariff and the rise in the price to OP_T, imports are reduced by Q_3Q_2 so that the total consumption of the commodity is also reduced from OQ_3 to OQ_2. Thus Q_3Q_2 is the consumption effect of the tariff. Similarly, when the import quota of Q_1Q_2 is fixed, the total domestic consumption falls from OQ_3 to OQ_2 so that the consumption effect of Q_3Q_2 under the quota equals that under the tariff.

Net National Loss. The net national loss from a tariff is equivalent to that of an import quota. With the increase in the domestic price of the commodity to OP_T due to a tariff, the net loss in consumers' surplus is P_TNBP_W (the area under the demand curve).

Now the area P_TNBP_W = area $Z + a + R + b$. Out of this, area R is taken away by the government as revenue. The area Z is producers' gain from the tariff. The net national loss consists of areas a and b represented by the two triangles, the former representing deadweight loss in the import quota of Q_1Q_2 brings an equivalent loss in total consumers' surplus represented by the area $Z + a + R + b$. It brings the same gain to producers and net national loss as under the tariff. And the area R is internal redistribution from consumers to holders of import licenses. This is equivalent to the revenue effect under the tariff on the presumption that the government auctions import licenses.

This equivalence of a tariff and an import quota holds only under perfectly competitive conditions. Bhagwati[3] has shown in his paper "On the Equivalence of Tariffs and Quotas" that there is *non-equivalence of tariff and quotas* if there is any monopoly power in domestic production or if there is no perfect competition among quota holders when import licenses are issued only to a few. The importer with a license can get the difference between the world price OP_W and the domestic price OP_T as amount of profit per unit. If licenses are auctioned, the importers would be prepared to pay upto P_WP_T per unit of import permitted.

3. IMPORT QUOTAS VS. TARIFFS

An import quota, like a tariff, causes a reduction in imports, a rise in prices and an increase in domestic production of a commodity on which it is imposed. Both have common price, consumption, redistributive, balance of payments and terms of trade effects. But there are important *differences* between an import quota and a tariff which are discussed as under :

The restrictive effect of an import quota is speedier and tighter than that of a tariff. While a tariff primarily influences commodity prices, an import quota determines the amount of goods imported. Unlike an import quota, a tariff does not impose any limitation on the quantity of goods imported. But if an import quota is initially meant to influence the quantity of goods imported, it may lead to scarcity of goods and steeper price rise.

As import quota fixes the maximum quantity that can be imported more rigidly than a tariff. A tariff, on the other hand, is milder because after the initial phase is over, imports tend to increase if the foreign price falls or the domestic demand or price of the protected commodity increases. An import quota is unstable because it can be changed at the discretion of the bureaucracy while a tariff is stable because any change in the tariff policy requires legislative approval.

An import quota is more discriminatory than a tariff in restricting the supply of commodities from different countries. Thus it tends to embitter international relations. Since under a tariff,the market mechanism of demand and supply operates freely, there is less scope for discrimination with other countries. But under the quota system, the basis of allocation of import quotas is not based on any one accepted principle which often leads to international discrimination.

A tariff benefits the government in the form of additional revenue earned by levying a tariff duty while an import quota brings profits to importers to holding licenses. However, the government may profit from the quota if it auctions import licenses to importers.

Import restriction by way of a tariff or an import quota attaches a scarcity value to imports which gives rise to a margin, called economic or qouta rent as a result of the difference between the domestic demand price and the foreign supply price. In the case of a tariff, the economic rent goes to the government as revenue. But in the case of an import quota, the economic rent may accrue to government, importers, foreign producers, domestic consumers or officials administering the quota system. To whom this economic rent will go depends on the domestic market conditions and organisation of an import quota. If the government merely introduces an import quota, and if domestic producers are organised, and foreign producers are not, then the domestic producers will capture the economic rent by increasing profits and prices. But if foreign producers are organised and domestic producers are not, then the foreign producers can get a substantial portion of the economic rent by increasing their prices and turning the terms of trade against the country. If the government wants to pocket the economic rent for itself, it can do so by auctioning the import licenses.[3] If there are rigid price control and rationing within the country, the economic rent will go to the consumers. If, however, some importers do not use the imported commodity themselves but sell their ration to others at a higher price, the economic rent will not accrue to the actual consumers. If the administration is lax and the officials administering the quota system possess some discretion in granting import licenses, a part of the economic rent may go to the officials by way of bribes.

An import quota eliminates foreign competition and encourages domestic monopoly more than a tariff. An import quota is worse than a tariff when it creates monopoly. A dominant domestic firm cannot get monopoly power from a non-prohibitive tariff, because it faces an elastic competing supply at the world price plus the tariff. With an import quota, however, the domestic firm knows that how high it raises its price, competing imports cannot exceed the quota. So a qsuota gives the dominant domestic firm a better chance of facing an inelastic demand curve and thus a better chance to reap monopoly profits with higher prices. So with the monopoly-creating quota, the country gets even higher prices, lower output, and greater national losses than from a tariff that would have given it the same amount of imports.[4]

---

3. Bo Sodersten, *op. cit.*, p. 368-69.
4. C.P. Kindleberger and P.H. Lindert, *International Economics, 1978.*

Import quotas and tariffs are often used to improve a country's balance of payments. But import quotas cannot lead to an improvement in the balance of payments equal to the reduction in imports. They can simply lead to a change in demand because the commodities which were being exported earlier will not be demanded by domestic consumers. Moreover, quotas make imports rigid both in the upward and downward directions by creating a large gap between the domestic and foreign price of imported goods. It is only when the foreign price rises so high or the domestic price falls so low as to fill the gap between the domestic and foreign price then imports become flexible in the downward direction. Thus to correct a deficit in the balance of payments requires large changes in prices. On the other hand, tariffs do not restrict the volume of imports and exports except under prohibitively high tariffs. Thus tariffs do not interfere in the flexibility of balance of payments mechanism.

EXERCISES

1. Consider the view that quotas are much like Tariffs in their Protective and Redistributive Effects.
2. Explain the various effects of an import quota. Discuss the similar effects of Quotas and Tariffs.
3. What is an import quota? How does it differ from a tariff?

CHAPTER 50

Exchange Control

1. MEANING

Exchange control* is one of the important devices to control international trade and payments. It aims at equilibrating foreign receipts and payments, not through such market forces or flexible exchange rates but through direct and indirect control of foreign exchange. Thus exchange control means that all foreign receipts and payments in the form of foreign currencies are controlled by the government. Prof. Haberler defines exchange control as "State regulation excluding the free play of economic forces from the foreign exchange market."[1] Prof. Ellsworth has explained it more explicitly. According to him, "Exchange control deals with the balance of payments difficulties, disregards market forces and substitutes for them the arbitrary decisions of government officials. Imports and other international payments are no longer determined solely by international price comparisons, but also by consideration of national need."[2]

2. FEATURES

The exchange control system has the following main features :

1. It involves complete government control over the foreign exchange market.
2. All foreign currencies are required to be surrendered to the central bank.
3. The central bank sanctions and allocates all foreign payments in respect of different currencies.
4. The central bank fixes the official exchange rate.
5. It regulates demand and supply so as to maintain the official exchange rate.
6. There is regulation of currency to be supplied to importers.
7. Exporters are required to surrender foreign currencies to the central bank.
8. Only specified banks and licensed dealers can deal in foreign exchange.
9. The central bank acts as a discriminating monopolist by charging low rates of exchange for the purchase of essential imports and high rates for purchasing luxury imports.

---

* For Exchange Control in India refer to the Chapter on "Reserve Bank of India".

1. G. Haberler, *op. cit.*, p. 83.
2. P.T. Ellsworth and J.K. Leith, *op. cit.*, p. 375.

3. OBJECTIVES OF EXCHANGE CONTROL

There have been varied objectives of adopting the system of exchange control by governments before, during, and after World War II. We discuss these objectives as under :

1. *Over-valuation.* Some countries resort to exchange control to keep their currencies over-valued. Under this, the foreign exchange value of the currency is fixed at a higher level than allowed by market forces. The currency is over-valued for three reasons : *first*, the country is at war and needs large quantities of imports; *second*, the country is engaged in the development process and needs raw materials and capital equipment from abroad; and *third*, the country has to repay large foreign debt. When the country overvalues its currency, its currency becomes dearer relative to other currencies. So it pays less to other countries in terms of its currency both for imported goods and for repayment of foreign debt.

2. *Under-valuation.* Some countries also exercise exchange control to keep their currency under-valued. This is done to stimulate exports and reduce imports and to raise the general price level of the country. But such a policy can succeed only in the case of a small country whose participation in world trade is insignificant. But if a large country were to adopt this policy, it will lead other countries to retaliate and follow this policy, which is highly dangerous for the world economy.

3. *Stabilisation of Exchange Rates.* Exchange control is adopted to stabilise the rate of exchange. Fluctuating exchange rates harm commerce and industry. The government, therefore, adopts exchange control measures to stabilise the exchange rates by announcing conversion at the official fixed rates of exchange.

4. *Prevention of Capital Flight.* Another objective of exchange control is to prevent the flight of capital from the country. Gold and capital funds cannot be exported without the permission of the exchange control authority. The latter may totally ban such movements or give foreign exchange in limited quantities to export capital for specific purpose. In this way, exchange control not only prevents the flight of capital but also conserves precious foreign exchange.

5. *Protection of Domestic Industries.* Exchange control is resorted to giving protection to domestic industries against foreign producers. The exchange control authority controls the import of such commodities which compete with domestic producers and thus protects them from foreign competition.

6. *Checking Non-essential Imports.* Exchange control also aims at checking imports of non-essential commodities. The exchange control authority restricts import of non-essential, luxury and harmful commodities through foreign exchange control. Licences are issued for import of essential commodities only so that foreign exchange is utilised fruitfully.

7. *Help to the Planning Process.* Exchange control helps the process of planning by controlling the non-essential and wasteful expenditure on imports and encouraging the flow of exports. The exchange control authority encourages the inflow of essential raw materials, capital goods and technical know-how by allocating scarce foreign exchange resources. Such imports are needed for the execution of plan projects.

8. *Remedying Unfavourable Balance of Payments.* Exchange control is introduced to remedy adverse balance of payments. This is achieved by checking and regulating imports and foreign exchange. With reduction in imports and control of foreign exchange, visible and invisible imports are reduced. Consequently, adverse balance of payments are corrected.

9. *Earning Revenue.* Exchange control is also used to earn revenue by the government. The central bank of the country, which is usually the exchange control authority, sells foreign currencies to traders, businessmen and individuals at rates higher than at which it buys in the international market. The difference between the selling and buying rates goes to the government as revenue.

10. *Repaying Foreign Debt.* One of the objectives of exchange control is to earn and conserve foreign exchange for the purpose of repaying the principle and interest charges on foreign debt.

11. *Retaliation.* Exchange control is used to secure bargaining power in trade with other countries and also as a retaliatory device. Exchange control gives monopoly power to a country which can get essential commodities at favourable rates from the other country. It can, thus, be used to exploit the other country. Under the circumstances, the other country can also adopt exchange control as a retaliatory measure.

4. METHODS OF EXCHANGE CONTROL

There are two methods of exchange control. One is direct and the other indirect. Crowther[3] has further divided them into a number of sub-methods which are discussed below along with those given by other economists.

DIRECT METHODS

The central bank of the country, which is the exchange control authority adopts a number of direct methods which restrict the use and quantity of foreign exchange. They are as under:

1. *Intervention.* Intervention means that "a government may intervene in the foreign exchange market to hold the value of its currency up or to hold it down." This method is known as "pegging exchange rates". If the government fixes the exchange rate of its currency at a higher level than prevailing in the foreign exchange market, it is called "pegging up". On the other hand, fixing a lower exchange rate than prevailing in the foreign exchange market is called "pegging down". Both 'pegging up' and 'pegging down' involve maintenance of fixed rates of local currency for a long period. Intervention in these two cases means selling or buying local currency in exchange for foreign currencies at fixed rates. When a country pegs up its currency, it means that the demand for its currency at the higher exchange rate is less than its supply. So the central bank must intervene to purchase local currency in exchange for foreign currencies at the fixed rate. On the other hand, in the case of pegging down of its currency, the central bank must sell the local currency in exchange for foreign currencies at the fixed rate. This is because the demand for the local currency at the lower exchange rate is more than its supply.

2. *Exchange Restriction*. Crowther defines a policy of exchange restriction as one which involves "a compulsory *reduction* by the government of *supply* of its currency coming into the market."[4] Under it, all foreign currencies are pooled with the central bank which, in turn, sanction and allocates them in accordance with the rules laid down by the government.

Exchange restrictions has many variants but we shall discuss only three.

(a) *Allocation According to Priorities*. This is the simplest method. As the foreign currencies available with the central bank are always limited in quantities, it will allocate them to finance imports and to make other foreign payments. It will do so in accordance with certain principles or priorities. All essential items of imports such as food, raw materials, capital goods, intermediate products, etc. will be accorded priorities in allocating foreign exchange over non-essential and luxury imports. This system of exchange control had been in use in England and is widely practised by developing countries. But it has the following defects:

First, allocating foreign exchange according to priorities is bound to be arbitrary because that is decided by bureaucrats.

Second, the processing and sanctioning of applications involve much time and administrative costs. *Finally,* this system leads to inequities.

(b) *Multiple Exchange Rates*. When a country establishes different exchange rates for each of several categories of imports, exports and capital transfers, it is known as the method of multiple exchange rates. This system of exchange control is operated in such a way that the foreign value of imports is reduced and the foreign value of exports is increased. The aim is to achieve balance of payments equilibrium for the country by reducing imports and increasing exports. Despite this, different exchange rates are fixed for different types of imports. For instance, the central bank may fix a low buying rate for foreign currency for the import of essential commodities and a much higher rate for the import of luxuries. On the export side, it may subsidise exports by fixing higher exchange rates. But the rates for invisibles, including capital transfers, are usually very high.

It has certain *merits:* (1) It encourages exports and discourages imports. (2) It has the same effects as a subsidy on exports and a tax on imports. (3) It helps in checking disequilibrium in the balance of payments of the country adopting this method. (4) It encourages the inflow and discourages the outflow of capital. (5) This system is better than other methods of exchange control because it restricts trade indirectly. (6) The

---

3. C. Crowther, *op. cit.*, pp. 244-70.
4. G. Crowther, *op. cit.*, p. 253.

government earns additional revenue by buying foreign exchange from exporters and selling it to importers at a high price.

But it has its *defects.* (1) It is highly discriminatory. (2) It is a complex system which requires lot of understanding and knowledge on the part of the controlling authority for an accurate fixation of exchange rates. (3) It depends much on bureaucratic decisions which are likely to be arbitrary. (4) It hinders the growth of world trade.

(c) *Blocked Accounts.* Under this system of exchange control, payments for imports are credited to blocked accounts in the name of the foreign exporters. Such accounts may be kept in the central bank of the debtor country. The creditors are prohibited for some time from drawing on them. However, they can be used in the controlling country where such accounts are located. But this system is a great hindrance to international trade and leads to corruption and black-marketing in foreign exchange.

3. *Exchange Clearing Agreements.* Under this method of exchange control two trading countries agree to establish an account in their respective central banks through which all payments for exports and imports are cleared. This method is known as bilateral clearing or clearing agreement or exchange clearing.

Under this system, if country *A* imports goods from country *B*, payments by importers are required to be made in the clearing account with its central bank in its own currency. Similarly, exporters of country *A* are paid in their own currency out of the clearing account. The same principle applies to the other trading partners. But it is not essential that exports and imports may be equal in both the countries and the clearing accounts may balance. So to balance them, the banks supply their own currency at a fixed rate of exchange against that of the other country upto a certain limit. This is known as 'swing'. For instance, the swing or limit may be fixed at $ 100. It means that exports of country *A* can exceed its imports or that of country *B* upto $ 100. Beyond this limit, any surplus or deficit is settled in terms of gold or a convertible currency acceptable to both the countries.

But this system of exchange control is also not free from certain *defects. First,* such agreements are based on agreed exchange rates between the two countries. A strong country with relatively more bargaining strength may agree to a favourable exchange rate for itself. This exchange rate may be fixed arbitrarily and to the disadvantage of the weak partner. *Second,* the size of the 'swing' may have disastrous effects on the domestic economies of the two countries. If the size of the 'swing' is too small, its limit may be reached soon and trade between the two countries may come to an end because the country may not like to lose its gold. *Third,* if a country has excess of imports over exports, more local currency will be deposited by the importers in the clearing accounts. This will lead to a decline in the monetary supply which will be deflationary. On the contrary, the excess of exports over imports will be inflationary because more currency will flow to the exporters out of the clearing account. Both situations are possible, if the clearing account reaches the limit of the 'swing'. *Fourth,* it hinders multilateral trade. *Fifth,* the central banks are overburdened under this system.

4. *Payments Agreements.* Payments agreements are another form of bilateral agreements but they are wider in scope than clearing agreements. Besides trade transactions, they include various service transactions such as shipping charges, debt services, tourism, etc. which are reflected in the balance of payments. A payments agreement is usually made for the repayment of the debt by one country to the other. Under this system of exchange control, a certain percentage of payments for imports by the creditor country is passed on to its clearing account for the repayment of its debt. The creditor country does not impose any restrictions on the imports from the debtor country. But the debtor country can restrict its imports from the creditor country so that it is in a position to repay its debt through larger exports.

Such agreements have some *defects* : (1) Such payment agreements always favour the strong partner. (2) The balances can only be used for buying goods and services from the debtor country. (3) They can only be used for payment between partners. (4) It adversely affects the balance of payments position of the debtor country. But the weak and developing countries gain from such an arrangement because their balance of payments position improves.

Indirect Methods

There are certain indirect methods of exchange control which affect the exchange rates. They are :

1. *Quantitative Restrictions.* Quantitative restrictions or commercial controls include import restrictions, import embargoes, import quotas and buying policies of state trading corporations. All these limit imports.

Quantitative import controls restrict the amount (in value or quantity) of commodity to be imported. The aim is to curtail the value of imports to correct disequilibrium in the balance of payments. The import quota is another device by which a specified quantity of a commodity is imported free of any duty, while imports above that quantity are levied on import duty. The state trading corporation or authority is given a monopoly in the import of certain commodities. It regulates the amount of commodities to be imported and distributes them within the country. The aim of these quantitative restrictions is to make the rate of exchange in favour of the country imposing them and to correct its adverse balance of payments.

2. *Export Bounties.* Similarly, a bounty on exports has the effect of raising the external value of the country giving the bounty. But export bounties are limited by the amount of funds with the government.

3. *Raising Interest Rates.* Changes in interest rates within a country also influence its foreign exchange rate. When the interest rate increases in a country, it attracts capital funds from other countries and prevents the outflow of domestic funds to other countries. Consequently, the demand for its currency rises which raises its external value and making the foreign exchange rate favourable to it. These changes in interest rates are subject to certain limitations. The rate of interest cannot be raised beyond a certain limit, otherwise it will adversely affect domestic business. Foreign countries may raise their domestic interest rates and thus offset its favourable effects on the exchange rate.

5. MERITS AND DEMERITS OF EXCHANGE CONTROL

Merits. The system of exchange control in its various forms has been used in one country or the other. It possesses the following *merits* :

1. Exchange control prevents the erratic outflow of capital.
2. By restricting imports, it helps in improving the balance of payments.
3. It makes possible the import of essential capital goods by ensuring the availability of foreign exchange for them.
4. It prevents the import of non-essential consumption goods, thereby curbing conspicuous consumption.
5. Exchange control prevents the spread of foreign companies beyond a limit, and regulates their working in national interest.
6. It is an important device to protect domestic industries from foreign competition and start import substitution and export promotion industries.
7. It helps in maintaining exchange rate stability by removing fluctuations in exchange rates.
8. With the help of exchange control, government is able to pursue a anti-deflationary policy.
9. Government employs exchange control for controlling speculation in foreign exchange.
10. It enables the government to repay foreign loans.
11. It is a source of revenue for the government when it buys foreign exchange at a low price and sells at a higher price.
12. Control over foreign exchange helps in conserving foreign exchange for strategic, defence and planning needs of the country.
13. It is a good device to enable a country to have bilateral trade relations benefitting the two countries.
14. If a country becomes hostile, the country can prevent the repatriation of funds by freezing all its assets through exchange control.

Demerits. However, there are certain *demerits* of exchange control:

1. Exchange control tends to reduce the volume and value of international trade. When one country restricts imports from other countries, the latter retaliate, and exports from the former are also restricted. This leads to the diminution of world trade which is harmful for all countries.
2. The exchange control system breeds inefficiency, red-tapism and corruption among administrators and organisers connected with this.
3. It is a very expensive system because the exchange control authority needs large number of persons to carry on the system efficiently.

4. Exchange control always creates a black market in foreign exchange. There is smuggling of foreign exchange even in a very strict and efficient exchange control system.

5. The criteria laid down for the various types of exchange control are arbitrary. They depend upon the whims of the bureaucracy which may be in the interest of some and against others.

6. The system of exchange control creates vested interests in the country for their continuance.

7. As a corollary to the above, the system of exchange control leads to inequities. Some importers profit more because there are little restrictions on their imports while the imports of others are curtailed by an import duty.

Keeping the defects in view, some of UN agencies like the IMF and GATT aim at abolishing exchange control. But they are not likely to succeed in this objective because no country wants to do away with the exchange control system.

EXERCISES

1. Explain the mechanism and objectives of Exchange Control.
2. What is Exchange Control? Briefly discuss the various methods of exchange control.
3. What do you mean by Exchange Control? Discuss its merits and demerits.

CHAPTER 51

Balance of Payments : Meaning and Components

1. MEANING AND STRUCTURE

The balance of payments of a country is a systematic record of all its economic transactions with the outside world in a given year. It is a statistical record of the character and dimensions of the country's economic relationships with the rest of the world. According to Bo Sodersten, "The balance of payments is merely a way of listing receipts and payments in international transactions for a country." It shows the country's trading position, changes in its net position as foreign lender or borrower, and changes in its official reserve holding."[1]

The balance of payments account of a country is constructed on the principle of double-entry book-keeping. Each transaction is entered on the credit and debit side of the balance sheet. But balance of payments accounting differs from business accounting in one respect. In business accounting, debits (–) are shown on the left side and credits (+) on the right side of the balance sheet. But in balance of payments accounting, the practice is to show credits on the left side and debits on the right side of the balance sheet.

When a payment is received from a foreign country, it is a credit transaction while payment to a foreign country is a debit transaction. The principal items shown on the credit side (+) are exports of goods and services, unrequited (or transfer) receipts in the form of gifts, grants, etc. from foreigners, borrowings from abroad, investments by foreigners in the country, and official *sale* of reserve assets including gold to foreign countries and international agencies. The principal items on the *Debit* side (–) include imports of goods and services, transfer (or unrequited) payments to foreigners as gifts, grants, etc., lending to foreign countries, investments by residents to foreign countries, and official *purchase* of reserve assets or gold from foreign countries and international agencies.

These credit and debit items are shown vertically in the balance of payments account of a country according to the principle of double-entry book-keeping. Horizontally, they are divided into three categories : the current account, the capital account, and the official settlements account or the official reserve assets account.

1. The *current account* of a country consists of all transactions relating to trade in goods and services and

---

1. B.J. Cohen, *Balance of Payments Policy*, 1969.

unilateral (or unrequited) transfers. Service transactions include travel and transportation, income and payments on foreing investments, etc. Transfer payments relate to gifts, foreign aid, pensions, private remittances, charitable donations etc., received from foreign individuals and governments to foreigners.

2. *The capital account* of a country consists of its transactions in financial assets in the form of short-term and long-term lendings and borrowings, and private and official investments. In other words, the capital account shows international flow of loans and investments, and represents a change in the country's foreign assets and liabilities. Long-term capital transactions relate to international capital movements with maturity of one year or more and include direct investments like building of a foreign plant, portfolio investment like the purchase of foreign bonds and stocks, and international loans. On the other hand, short-term international capital transactions are for a period ranging between three months and less than one year.

3. *The official settlements account or official* reserve assets account is, in fact, a part of the capital account. But the U.K. and U.S. balance of payments accounts show it as a separate account. "The official settlements account measures the change in nation's liquidity and non-liquid liabilities to foreign official holders and the change in a nation's official reserve assets during the year. The official reserve assets of a country include its gold stock, holdings of its convertible foreign currencies and SDRs, and its net position in the IMF."

The sum of current account and capital account is known as the basic balance .

The balance of payments account of a country is constructed in Table 1.

In the *current account,* merchandise exports and imports are the most important items. Exports are shown as a positive item and are calculated f.o.b. (free on board) which means that costs of transportation, insurance, etc. are excluded. On the other side, imports are shown as a negative item and are calculated c.i.f. which means that costs, insurance and freight are included. The difference between exports and imports of a country is its *balance of visible trade* or merchandise trade or simply *balance of trade*. If visible exports exceed visible imports, the balance of trade is favourable. In the opposite case when imports exceed exports, it is unfavourable.

It is, however, services and transfer payments or invisible items of the current account that reflect the true picture of the balance of payments account. The balance of exports and imports of services and transfer payments is called the *balance of invisible trade*. The invisible items alongwith the visible items determine the actual current account position. If exports of goods and services exceed imports of goods and services, the balance of payments is said to be *favourable*. In the opposite case, it is unfavourable.

In the current account, the exports of goods and services and the receipts of transfer payments (unrequited receipts) are entered as credits (+) because they represent receipts from foreigners. On the other hand, the imports of goods and services and grant of transfer payments to foreigners are entered as debits because they represent payments to foreigners.

There are two types of transactions in the capital account—private and government. Private transactions include all types of investment : direct, portfolio and short-term. Government transactions consist of loans to and from foreign official agencies.

Table 1. Balance of Payments Account

Credits (+) *(Receipts)*	*Debits (–)* *(Payments)*
	1. Current Account
Exports	*Imports*
(*a*) Goods	(*a*) Goods
(*b*) Services	(*b*) Services
(*c*) Transfer Payments	(*c*) Transfer Payments
	2. Capital Account
(*a*) Borrowings from Foreign Countries	(*a*) Lending to Foreign Countries

(*b*) Direct Investments by Foreign Countries	(*b*) Direct Investments in Foreign Countries
3. Official Settlements Account	
(*a*) Increase in Foreign Official Holdings	(*a*) Increase in Official Reserve of Gold and Foreign Currencies
Errors and Omissions	

In the capital account, borrowings from foreign countries and direct investment by foreign countries represent capital inflows. They are positive items or credits because these are receipts from foreigners. On the other hand, lending to foreign countries and direct investments in foreign countries represent capital outflows. They are negative items or debits because they are payments to foreigners.

The official settlements account shows transactions in country A's official reserve assets (net).

Errors and ommissions is a balancing item so that total credits and debits of the three accounts must equal in accordance with the principles of double entry book-keeping so that the balance of payments of a country always balances in the accounting sense.

"To say that the balance of payments always balances is to say that a net credit balance in one of these accounts must have a counterpart net debit balance in one of the other accounts or in a combination of the two other accounts. The algebraic sum of the net credit and debit balances of the three accounts must equal zero."

3. IS BALANCE OF PAYMENTS ALWAYS IN EQUILIBRIUM?

There exists a deficit or surplus in the balance of payments. When $B = R_f - P_f = 0$, the balance of payments is in equilibrium, where B represents the balance of payments, R_f receipts from foreigners, P_f payments made to foreigners. When $R_f - P_f > 0$, it implies receipts from foreigners exceed payments made to foreigners and there is *surplus* in the balance of payments. On the other hand, when $R_f - P_f < 0$ or $R_f < P_f$ there is *deficit* in the balance of payments as the payments made to foreigners exceed receipts from foreigners.

If net foreign lending and investment abroad are taken, a flexible exchange rate creates an excess of exports over imports. The domestic currency depreciates in terms of other currencies. The exports becomes cheaper relatively to imports. It can be shown in equation form :

$$X + B = M + I_f$$

Where X represents exports, M imports, I_f foreign investment, B foreign borrowing

or $$X - M = I_f - B$$

or $$(X - M) - (I_f - B) = 0$$

The equation shows the balance of payments in equilibrium. Any positive balance in its current account is exactly offset by negative balance on its capital account and vice versa. In the accounting sense, the balance of payments always balances. This can be shown with the help of the following equation :

$$C + S + T = C + I + G + (X - M)$$

or $$Y = C + I + G + (X - M)$$

where C represents consumption exepnditure, S domestic saving, T tax receipts, I investment expenditures, G government expenditures, X exports of goods and services, and M imports of goods and services.

In the above equation $C + S + T$ is *GNI* or national income (Y), and $C + I + G = A$, where A is called 'absorption'. In the accounting sense, total domestic expenditures $(C + I + G)$ must equal current income $(C + S + T)$ that is $A = Y$. Moreover, domestic saving (S_d) must equal domestic investment (I_d). Similarly, an export surplus on current account ($X > M$) must be offset by an excess of domestic savings over investment ($S_d > I_d$). Thus the balance of payments always balances in the accounting sense.

If the balance of payments always balances, then why does a deficit or surplus arise in the balance of payment of a country? It is only when all items in the balance of payments are included that there is no possibility of a deficit or surplus. But if some items are excluded from a country's balance of payments and then a balance is struck, it may show a deficit or surplus.

There are three ways of measuring deficit or surplus in the balance of payments. *First,* there is the *basic balance* which includes the current account balance and the long-term capital account balance. *Second,* there is the *net liquidity balance* which includes the basic balance and the short-term private non-liquid capital balance, allocation of SDRs, and errors and ommissions. *Third,* there is the *official settlements balance* which includes the total net liquid balance and short-term private liquid capital balance.

The relationship between these balances is summarised in Table 2 below.

TABLE 2

Balance		
Trade balance	a	Autonomous Items
Transfer payments balance	b	
Current Account Balance	$c\ (= a + b)$	
Long-term capital balance	d	
Basic Balance	$e\ (= c + d)$	
Short-term private non-liquid capital balance	f	Accommodating Items
Allocation of SDRs	g	
Errors and omissions	h	
Net Liquidity Balance	$i\ (= e + f + g + h)$	
Short-term private liquid capital balance	j	
Official Settlements Balance	$k\ (= i + j)$	

Each balance would give different figure of the deficit. The items that are included in a particular balance are placed 'above the line' and those excluded are put 'below the line'. Items that are put above the line are called autonomous items. Items that are placed below the line are called "settlement" or "accommodating" or "compensatory" items. On the other hand, items that are put above the liner are called "autonomous" items. In theoretical analysis, disequilibrium in the balance of payments means a balance on autonomous items. Compensating short-term capital transactions are meant to redress a disequilibrium in the autonomous items of the balance of payments.

But it is difficult to determine which item is compensatory and which is autonomous. For instance, in the table given above, the main difference in the three balances is their treatment of short-term capital movements which are responsible for deficit in the balance of payments. The basic balance places short-term private non-liquid capital movements below the line while the net liquid balance puts them above the line. Similarly, the net liquid balance places short-term private liquid capital movements below the line and the official settlements balance puts them above the line.

The above analysis is based on the assumption of fixed exchange rates. Thus a deficit (or surplus in the balance of payments is possible under a system of fixed exchange rates. But under freely floating exchange rates, there can in principle be no deficit (or surplus) in the balance of payments. The country can prevent a deficit or (surplus) by depreciating (or appreciating) its currency. Further, balance of payments always balances in an ex-post accounting sense, according to the basic principle of accounting. Lastly, such a balance of payments can be in equilibrium only if there are no compensating transactions.

3. BALANCE OF TRADE AND BALANCE OF PAYMENTS

The *balance of payments* of a country is a systematic record of its receipts and payments in international transactions in a given year. Each transaction is entered on the credit and debit side of the balance sheet (see Table 1). The principal items on the credit side are : (1) Visible exports which relate to the goods exported for which the country receives payments. (2) Invisible exports which refer to the services rendered by the country to other countries. Such services consist of banking, insurance, shipping, and other services rendered in the form of technical know-how, etc., money spent by tourists and students visiting the country for travel and education, etc. (3) Transfer receipts in the form of gifts received from foreigners. (4) Borrowings from abroad and investments by foreigners in the country. (5) The official sale of reserve assets including gold to foreign countries and international institutions.

The principal items on the debit side are : (1) Visible imports relating to goods imported for which the country makes payments to foreign countries. (2) Invisible imports in the form of payments made by the home country for services rendered by foreign countries. These include all items referred to under (2) in the above para. (3) Transfer payments to foreigners in the form of gifts, etc. (4) Loans to foreign countries, investments by residents in foreign countries, and debt repayments to foreign countries. (5) Official purchase of reserve assets or gold from foreign countries and international institutions.

If the total receipts from foreigners on the credit side exceed the total payments to foreigners on the debit side, the balance of payments is said to be *favourable*. On the other hand, if the total payments to foreigners exceed the total receipts from foreigners, the balance of payments is *unfavourable*.

The *balance of trade* is the difference between the value of goods and services exported and imported. In contains the first two items of the balance of payments account on the credit and the debit side. This is known as "balance of payment on current account." Some writers define the balance of trade as the difference between the value of merchandise exports and imports. Prof. Meade regards this way of defining the balance of trade as wrong and of minor economic significance from the point of view of the national income of the country. In equation form, the balance of payments of $Y = C + I + G + (X - M)$ which includes all transactions which give rise to or exhaust national income. In the equation, Y refers to national income, C to consumption expenditure, I to investment expenditure, G to government expenditure, X to exports of goods and services and M to imports of goods and services. The expression $(X - M)$ denotes the balance of trade. If the difference between X and M is zero, the balance of trade balances. If X is greater than M, the balance of trade is *favourable*, or there is *surplus* balance of trade. On the other hand, if X is less than M, the balance of trade is in *deficit* or is *unfavourable*.

Causes of Disequilibrium

There are many factors that may bring a deficit or surplus in its balance of payments.

First, there may be a temporary disequilibrium caused by random variations in trade, seasonal fluctuations, the effects of weather on agricultural production, etc. Deficits or surpluses arising from such temporary causes are expected to correct themselves within a short time.

Second, there are *chronic or fundamental disequilibria.* They may arise due to fundamental changes in the economic condition of a country. They may be due to changes in consumer tastes within the country or abroad thereby affecting the country's imports or exports.

Third, technological changes in methods of production or products in the domestic industries or in the industries of other countries may affect the country's ability to compete in the home or foreign markets. This may be due to changes in costs and prices and the quality of products following technological improvements.

Fourth, another cause is the change in the country's national income. If the national income of a country increases, it will lead to an increase in imports thereby creating a deficit in its balance of payments, other things remaining the same. If the country is already at full employment level, an increase in income will lead to inflationary rise in prices which may increase its imports and thus bring disequilibrium in the balance of payments.

Fifth, Inflation is another cause of disequilibrium in the balance of payments. If there is inflation in the country, prices of exports increase. As a result, exports fall. At the same time, the demand for imports increase. Thus increase in export prices leading to decline in exports and rise in imports results in adverse balance of payments.

Sixth, a country's balance of payments also depends on its stage of economic development. If a country is developing, it will have a deficit in its balance of payments because it imports raw materials, machinery, capital equipment, and services associated with the development process and exports primary products. The country has to pay more for costly imports and gets less for its cheap exports. This leads to disequilibrium in its balance of payments.

Lastly, borrowings and lendings or movements of capital by countries also result in disequilibrium in *BOP*. A country which gives loans and grants on a large scale to other countries has a deficit in its *BOP* on capital account. If it is also importing more, as is the case with the USA, it will have chronic deficit. On the other hand, a developing country borrowing large funds from other countries and international institutions may have a favourable balance of payments. But such a possibility is remote because these countries usually import huge quanties of food, raw materials, capital goods, etc. and export primary products. Such borrowings simply help in reducing balance of payments deficit.

4. ADJUSTMENT IN THE BALANCE OF PAYMENTS OR MEASURES TO CORRECT DISEQUILIBRIUM

When there is a deficit in the balance of payments of a country, adjustment is brought about automatically through price and income changes or by adopting certain policy measures like export promotion, monetary and fiscal policies, devaluation and direct controls. We study these as follows:

1. Adjustment through Exchange Depreciation (Price Effect)

Under flexible exchange rates, the disequilibrium in the balance of payments is automatically solved by the forces of demand and supply for foreign exchange. An exchange rate is the price of a currency which is determined, like any other commodity, by demand and supply. "The exchange rate varies with varying supply and demand conditions, but it is always possible to find an equilibrium exchange rate which clears the foreign exchange market and creates external equilibrium."[7] This is automatically achieved by depreciation of a country's currency in case of deficit in its balance of payments. Depreciation of a currency means that its relative value decreases. Depreciation has the effect of encouraging exports and discouraging imports. When exchange depreciation takes place, foreign prices are translated into domestic prices. Suppose the dollar depreciates in relation to the pound. It means, that the price of dollar falls in relation to the pound in the foreign exchange market. This leads to the lowering of the prices of U.S. exports in Britain and raising of the prices of British imports in the U.S. When import prices are higher in the U.S., the Americans will purchase less goods from the Britishers. On the other hand, lower prices of U.S. exports will increase exports and diminish imports, thereby bringing equilibrium in the balance of payments.

The adjustment process is explained in terms of Figure 1 where *D* is the U.S. demand curve of foreign exchange representing its demand for British imports, and *S* is the U.S. supply curve of foreign exchange representing its exports to Britain. At *P* the demand and supply of the U.S. foreign exchange is in equilibrium where the rate of exchange between U.S. dollar and British pound is *OE* and the quantity of exchange is *OQ*.

Suppose disequilibrium develops in the balance of payments of the U.S. in relation to Britain. This is shown by a shift in the demand curve from *D* to D_1 and the incipient deficit equals PP_2. This means an increase in the U.S. demand for British imports which leads to an increase in the demand for pound. This implies depreciation of the U.S. dollar and appreciation of the British pound. As a result, import prices of British goods rise in the U.S. and the prices of U.S. exports fall. This tends to bring about a new equilibrium at P_1 and a new exchange rate at OE_1 whereby the deficit in the balance of payments is eliminated. The demand for foreign exchange equals the supply of foreign exchange at OQ_1 and the balance of payments is in equilibrium.

The above analysis is based on the assumption of *relative elasticities* of demand and supply of foreign exchange. However, in order to measure the full effect of depreciation on relative prices in the two countries, it is not sufficient for demand and supply conditions to be relatively elastic. What is important is *low elasticities* of demand and supply of foreign exchange. This is illustrated in Figure 2 where the original *less elastic* demand and supply curves of foreign exchange are *D* and *S* respectively which intersect at *P* and the equilibrium exchange rate is *OE*. Now a deficit in the balance of payments develops equals to PP_2. Since the *elasticities* of demand and supply of foreign exchange are very low (inelastic), it requires a very large amount of depreciation

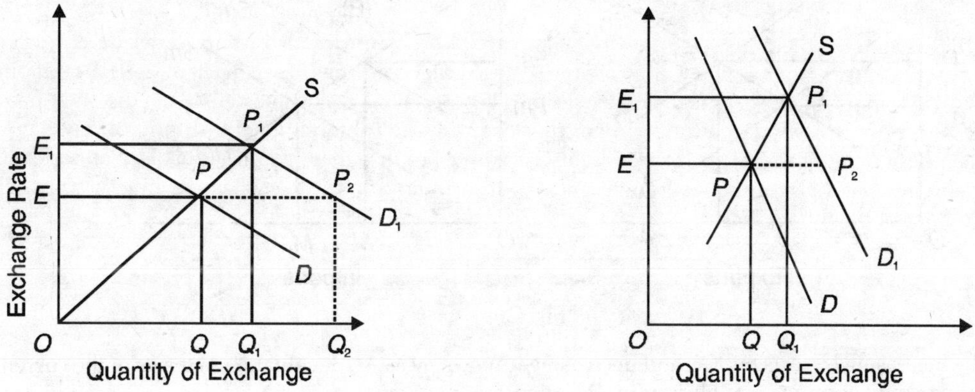

Fig. 1

of the dollar and the appreciation of the pound for the restoration of the equilibrium. The equilibrium will be established through relative price movements in the two countries, as explained above, at P_1 with a very high rate of foreign exchange OE_1. But such a high rate of depreciation would lead to very high price changes in the two countries thereby tending to disrupt their economies.

The practical use of flexible exchange rates is severely limited. *Depreciation* and *appreciation* lead to fall and rise in prices in the countries adopting them. They lead to severe depressions and inflations respectively. Further, they create insecurity and uncertainty. This is more due to speculation in foreign exchange which destabilises the economies of countries adopting flexible exchange rates. Governments, therefore, favour fixed exchange rates which require adjustments in the balance of payments by adopting policy measures.

2. Devaluation or Expenditure-Switching Policy

Devaluation raises the domestic price of imports and reduces the foreign price of exports of a country devaluing its currency in relation to the currency of another country. Devaluation is referred to as expenditure switching policy because it switches expenditure from imported to domestic goods and services. When a country devalues its currency, the price of foreign currency increases which makes imports dearer and exports cheaper. This causes expenditures to be switched from foreign to domestic goods as the country's exports rise and the country produces more to meet the domestic and foreign demand for goods with reduction in imports. Consequently, the balance of payments deficit is eliminated. In order to assess the true effects of devaluation, it is advisable to study price movements in exports and imports in the same currency. Figure 2 (A) and (B) illustrates these effects of devaluation on exports and imports respectively where *Dx* and *Sx* are the demand and supply curves of exports and *Dm* and *Sm* are the demand and supply curves of imports. Suppose the British pound (£) is devalued in relation to the U.S. dollar ($) and the price movements before and after devaluation are taken in pound. Both the demand and supply curves of exports and imports are taken as elastic. *First,* take exports and Panel (A) of the figure. Before devaluation, Britain exports *OX* quantity at OP_x price to the U.S. Devaluation of pound has no effect on the supply of exports in pound. Therefore, the supply curve of exports S_X does not change. But to the U.S. consumers of British goods, devaluation of pound means cheaper goods than before. Consequently, the demand for exports increases and the demand curve for export *Dx* shifts to the right to Dx_1. The pre-devaluation price of *OX* exports is OP_x. After devaluation of the pound, the export price rises to OPx_1 and the volume of exports increases to OX_1.

Now take the effect of devaluation on imports. Before devaluation, Britain imports OM_1 quantity at *OPm* price from the U.S. With devaluation, imports become dearer in pound and their volume is reduced than before devaluation. Therefore, the supply curve of imports *Sm* shifts to Sm_1 in Panel (B) of the figure. But the demand curve for imports *Dm* being elastic, the increase in the price of imports from *OPm* to OPm_1 reduces the quantity bought from OM_1 to *OM*.

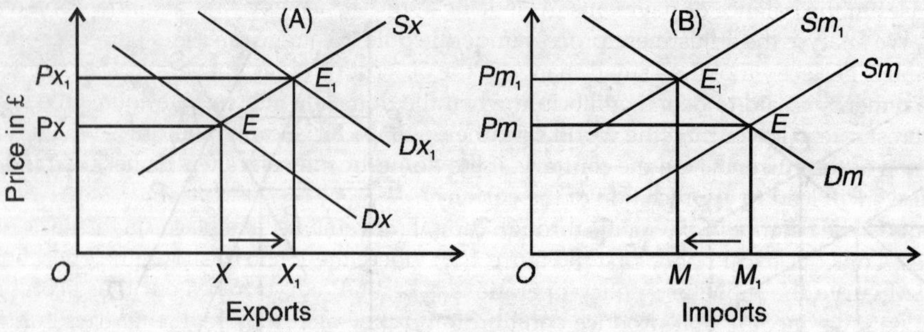

Fig. 2

Thus by increasing exports by XX_1 and decreasing imports by M_1M, devaluation in terms of the currency of the devaluing country brings equilibrium in the balance of payments.

3. Direct Controls

To correct disequilibrium in the balance of payments, government also adopts direct controls which aim at limiting the volume of imports. The government restricts the import of undesirable or unimportant items by levying heavy import duties, fixation of quotas, etc. At the same time, it may allow imports of essential goods duty free or at lower import duties, or fix liberal import quotas for them. For instance, the government may allow free entry of capital goods, but impose heavy import duties on luxuries. Import quotas are also fixed and the importers are required to take licenses from the authorities in order to import certain essential commodities in fixed quantities. In these ways, imports are reduced in order to correct an adverse balance of payments. The government also imposes exchange controls. Exchange controls have a dual purpose. They restrict imports and also control and regulate the foreign exchange. With reduction in imports and control of foreign exchange, visible and invisible imports are reduced. Consequently, an adverse balance of payment is corrected.

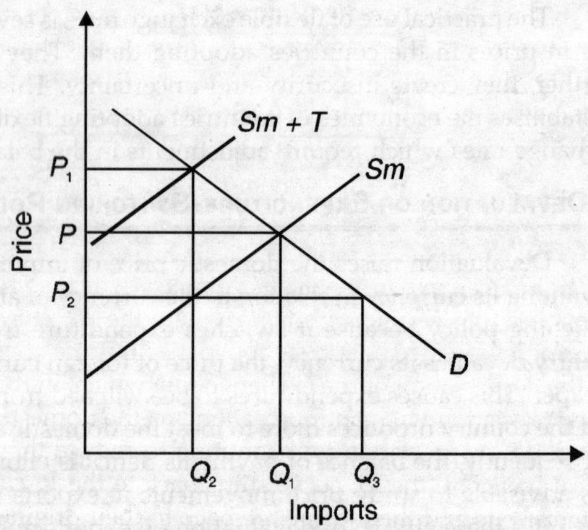

Fig. 3

We illustrate the case of a tariff In Figure 3, *D* and *Sm* are the demand and supply curves respectively. Before the imposition of tariff, OQ_1 quantity is imported at *OP* price. After the imposition of tariff P_1 *P*, the demand for imported goods decreases from OQ_1 to OQ_2 and the supply curve shifts to *Sm + T*. Although the domestic supply price will be raised to OP_1 but the supply price falls to OP_2 in the exporting country and the area P_2 P_1 goes to the government as revenue.

If the country were to maintain a low price of foreign exchange at OP_2 due to overvaluation of its domestic currency, the result is an increase in its imports from OQ_1 to OQ_3 and the deficit Q_1 Q_3 is due to excess demand of imports. Moreover, if the government were to auction this supply, the importers would be willing to pay a price OP_1 for foreign exchange. In such a case, there will be improvement in the balance of payment as the quantities of the imported goods will be reduced to OQ_2.

4. Adjustment through Capital Movements

Capital movements also bring equilibrium in the balance of payments. They can be used to finance deficits or surpluses in the balance of payments. A deficit can be financed by capital inflows and a surplus by capital outflows. We analyse the adjustment process under flexible exchange rates and perfect capital mobility.

When capital is perfectly mobile, a small change in the domestic interest rate brings large flows of capital. The balance of payments is said to be in equilibrium when the domestic interest rate equals the world rate. If the domestic interest rate is lower than the world rate, there will be large capital outflows which will produce a large depreciation of the currency. On the contrary, if the domestic interest rate is higher than the world rate large capital inflows will lead to appreciation of the currency.

Adjustments in the balance of payments through capital movements take place on the basis of fiscal and monetary policies. Consider fiscal policy first in Figure 4(A) where the *IS* curve shows the operations of fiscal policy and the *LM* curve the monetary policy operations. The BOP curve traces out those combinations of interest rate and national income that produce equilibrium in the balance of payments. The horizontal *BOP* curve reflects that capital mobility is perfect. The balance of payments is in equilibrium at only R_1 interest rate. A higher or lower interest rate than this would mean capital inflow or outflow.

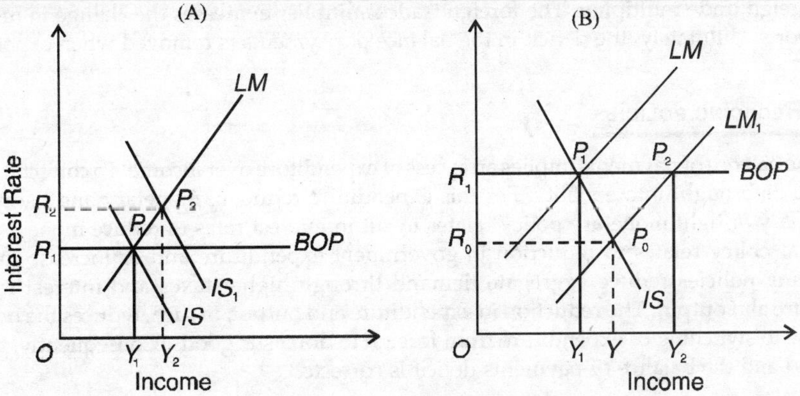

Fig. 4

Take an expansionary fiscal policy which shifts the *IS* curve to IS_1, given the *LM* curve. This brings the economy into equilibrium at P_2 where the IS_1 curve crosses the *LM* curve with OR_2 interest rate and OY_2 income level. Since point P_2 is above the *BOP* line, there is surplus in the balance of payments. This surplus leads to the appreciation of the exchange rate which, in turn, reduces the demand for domestic output. This process of appreciation will continue so long as the domestic interest rate is above the world rate and capital inflows continue. Appreciation will continue to reduce the demand for goods and offset the expansionary effect of fiscal policy till the IS_1 curve shifts back to the *IS* curve and the equilibrium is re-established at P_1 where the interest rate and the income are back to their original levels of OR_1 and OY_1. At P_1 the balance of payments is in equilibrium but there is trade deficit due to exchange appreciation which increases the prices of domestic goods for foreigners and reduces the price of imports. Consequently, exports will decline and imports will increase, thereby creating a trade deficit. The equilibrium in the balance of payments is being maintained at P_1 by financing the trade deficit through capital inflows with expansionary fiscal policy. So fiscal policy has no effect on income and employment under perfect capital mobility.

Take an expansionary monetary policy which has the effect of lowering the interest rate, increasing capital outflow and thereby bringing deficit in the balance of payments. How this deficit is removed is illustrated in Figure 4(B). Starting from P_1 an expansionary monetary policy shifts the *LM* curve to the right to LM_1 curve, given the *IS* curve. The LM_1 curve intersects the *IS* curve at P_0 which lowers the interest rate to OR_0 and raises income to *OY*. These lead to capital outflows and the consequent deficit in the balance of payments and depreciation of the exchange rate. Depreciation increases the demand for domestic goods in the foreign country, thereby increasing output and income. This moves the economy upward along the LM_1 curve till it reaches point P_2 when income rises to OY_2 and the interest rate rises to the old level OR_1. Equilibrium in the balance of payments is restored at P_2 where the increase in imports through rise in income is offset by surplus in trade balance due to depreciation.

5. Adjustment through Income Changes

An automonous increases in the value of exports causes national income to rise by an amount equal to the increases in export times the foreign trade multiplier. Thus national income increases through the operation of the foreign trade multiplier. "The foreign trade multiplier expresses the change in income causes by a change in exports or in investment in an open economy in which income spills over into imports."

6. Stimulation of Exports

A deficit in the balance of payments can also be corrected by encouraging exports. Exports can be encouraged by producing quality products, by reducing exports through increased production and productivity, and by better marketing. They can also be increased by a policy of import substitution. It means that the country produces those goods which it imports. In the beginning, imports are reduced but in the long run exports of such goods start. An increase in exports cause the national income to rise by many times through the operation of the foreign trade multiplier. The foreign trade multiplier expresses the change in income caused by a change in exports. Ultimately, the deficit in the balance of payments is removed when exports rise faster than imports.

7. Expenditure-Reducing policies

A deficit in the balance of payments implies an excess of expenditure over income. To correct it, expenditure and income should be brought into equality. For this expenditure reducing monetary and fiscal policies are used. A contractionary or tight monetary policy relates to cut in interest rates to reduce money supply and a contractionary fiscal policy relates to reduction in government expenditure and or increase in taxes. Thus expenditure reducing policies reduce aggregate demand through higher taxes and interest rates, thereby reducing expenditure and output. The reduction in expenditure and output, in turn, reduces the domestic price level. This gives rise to switching of expenditure from foreign to domestic goods. Consequently, the country's imports are reduced and the balance of payments deficit is corrected.

EXERCISES

1. Explain the concept of disequilibrium in the balance of payments. How does it arise? What are the methods available to restore equilibrium?
2. Is it correct "to view the balance of payments as a relation between the aggregate receipts and expenditure of the economy rather than as a relation between the country's credits and debits on international account"?
3. Analyse the possible income effects, and price effects associated with the adjustment in the balance of payments.
4. Why is continuing deficit in a country's balance of payments more dreaded than a continuing surplus? What are the measures to correct a deficit in a country's balance of payments?

Chapter 52

Foreign Exchange Rate

1. MEANING

The foreign exchange rate or exchange rate is the rate at which one currency is exchanged for another. It is the price of one currency in terms of another currency. It is customary to define the exchange rate as the price of one unit of the foreign currency in terms of the domestic currency. The exchange rate between the dollar and thc pound refers to the number of dollars required to purchase a pound. Thus the exchange rate between the dollar and the pound from the US viewpoint is expressed as $ 2.50 = £ 1. The Britishers would express it as the number of pounds required to get one dollar, and the above exchange rate would be shown as £ 0.40 = $ 1.

The exchange rate of $ 2.50 = £ 1 or £ 0.40 = $ 1 will be maintained in the world foreign exchange market by arbitrage. *Arbitrage refers to the purchase of a foreign currency in a market where its price is low and to sell it in some other market where its price is high.* The effect of arbitrage is to remove differences in the foreign exchange rate of currencies so that there is a single exchange rate in the world foreign exchange market. If the exchange rate is $ 2.48 in the London exchange market and $ 2.50 in the New York exchange market, foreign exchange speculators, known as arbitrageurs, will buy pounds in London and sell them in New York, thereby making a profit of 2 cents on each pound. As a result, the price of pounds in terms of dollars rises in the London market and falls in the New York market. Ultimately, it will equal in both the markets and arbitrage comes to an end. If the exchange rate betwen the dollar and the pound rises to $ 2.60 = £ 1 through time, the dollar is said to depreciate with respect to the pound, because now more dollars are needed to buy one pound. When the rate of exchange between the dollar and the pound falls to $ 2.40 = £ 1, the value of the dollar is said to appreciate because now less dollars are required to purchase one pound. If the value of the first currency depreciates that of the other appreciates, and vice versa. Thus a depreciation of the dollar against the pound is the same thing as the appreciation of the pound against the dollar, and vice versa.

2. DETERMINATION OF EQUILIBRIUM EXCHANGE RATE

The exchange rate in a free market is determined by the demand for and the supply of foreign exchange. The equilibrium exchange rate is the rate at which the demand for foreign exchange equals to supply of foreign exchange. In other words, it is the rate which clears the market for foreign exchange. Ragner Nurkse defined the equilibrium exchange rate as, "that rate which over a certain period of time, keeps the balance of payments in equilibrium." There are two ways of determining the equilibrium exchange rate. The rate of exchange between dollars and pounds can be determined either by the demand and supply of dollars with the price of dollars in pounds, or by the demand and supply of pounds with the price of pounds in dollars. Whatever method is adopted, it yields the same result. The analysis that follows is based on the dollar price in terms of pounds.

The Demand for Foreign Exchange. The demand for foreign exchange is a derived demand from pounds. It arises from import of British goods and services into the US and from capital movements from the US to Britain. In fact, the demand for pounds implies a supply of dollars. When the US businessmen buy British goods and services and make capital transfers to Britain, they create demand for British pounds in exchange for US dollars because they cannot make payments to Britain in their currency, the US dollars.

The demand curve for pounds *DD* is downward sloping from left to right in Figure 1. It implies that the lower the exchange rate on pounds, the larger will be the quantity of pounds demanded in the foreign exchange (US) market, and vice versa. This is because a lower exchange rate on pounds make British exports of goods and services cheaper in terms of dollars. The opposite happens if the exchange rate on pound is higher. It will make British goods and services dearer in terms of dollars, and the demand for pounds will fall in the foreign exchange (US) market.

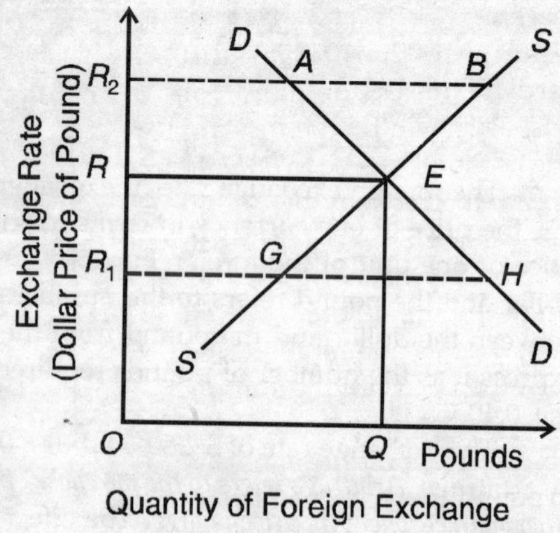

FIG. 1

But the shape of the demand curve for foreign exchange will depend on the elasticity of demand for imports. "If a country imports necessities and raw materials, we may expect the elasticity of demand for imports to be low and the quantity imported to be insensitive to price changes. If, on the other hand, the country imported luxury goods and goods for which suitable substitutes exist, demand elasticities for imports might be high.... If the country has many well-developed import competing industries, the elasticity of demand for imports most certainly is high... . In the short run, elasticity of demand for imports may not be very high. In the long run, however it is much more probable that the production pattern will alter according to price changes, and the demand for imports, therefore, will be more elastic."

The Supply of Foreign Exchange. The supply of foreign exchange in our case is the supply of pounds. It arises from the US exports of goods and services and from capital movements from the US to Britain. Pounds are offered in exchange for dollars because British holders of pounds wish to make payments in dollars. Thus the supply of foreign exchange reflects the quantities of pounds that would be supplied in the foreign exchange market at various dollars prices of pounds.

The supply curve for pounds *SS* is an upward sloping curve, as shown in Figure 1. It is a positive function of the exchange rate on pounds. As the exchange rate on pounds increases, the greater is the quantity of pounds supplied in the foreign exchange market. This is because with increase in the dollar price of pounds (lower pounds price of dollars), US goods, services and capital funds become better bargains to holders of pounds. Therefore the holders of pounds will offer larger quantities of pounds with the increase in the exchange rate.

But the shape of supply curve of foreign exchange will be determined by the elasticity of the supply curve. "As the value of the country's own currency increases, imports become relatively cheaper, and more is imported. As more is imported, more of the home currency is supplied on the foreign exchange market, provided elasticity is greater than unity. When imports become relatively cheap, new goods will start to be imported, and domestic import-competing industry will be gradually eliminated by imports. These are two important reasons why we expect the supply of foreign exchange to be quite elastic. Further, the larger the time perspective we take into account, the more elastic will be the supply."

Equilibrium Exchange Rate. Given the demand and supply curves of foreign exchange, the equilibrium exchange rate is determined where *DD*, the demand curve for pounds intersects *SS*, the supply curve of pounds. They cut each other at point *E* in Figure 1. The equilibrium rate is *OR* and *OQ* of foreign exchange is demanded, and supplied. At *OR* exchange rate the US demand for pounds equals the British supply of pounds, and the foreign exchange market is cleared. At any higher rate than this, the supply of pounds would be larger than the demand for pounds so that some people who wish to convert pounds into dollars will be unable to do so. The price of pounds will fall, less pounds will be supplied and more will be demanded. Ultimately, the equilibrium rate of exchange will be re-established. In Figure 1 when the exchange rate increases to OR_2, the supply of pounds $R_2B > R_2A$ the demand for pounds. With the fall in the price of pounds, the equilibrium exchange rate OR_2 is again established at point *E*. On the contrary, at an exchange rate lower than this, say OR_1, the demand for pounds R_1H is greater than the supply of pounds R_1G. Some people who want pounds will not be able to get them. The price of pounds will rise which will reduce the demand and increase the supply of pounds so that the equilibrium exchange rate *OR* is re-established at point *E* where the two curves *DD* and *SS* intersect.

Suppose there is a shift upward in the US demand for pounds, as shown by the upward shifting of the *DD* curve to D_1D_1 in Figure 2 (A). This may be due to increase in the US tastes for British goods, an increase in the US national income, etc. which increases the demand for imported goods in the US. With the shifting up of the demand curve to D_1D_1, the US dollar depreciates and the British pound appreciates which re-establish the new equilibrium exchange rate OR_2 at point E_2 where OQ_2 quantity of foreign exchange is demanded and supplied.

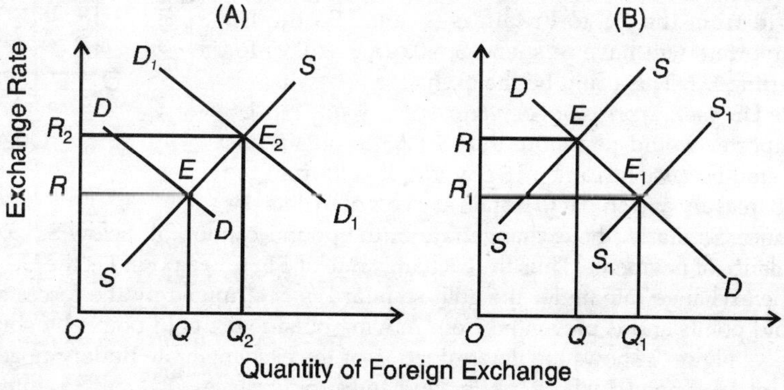

FIG. 2

On the other hand, if the supply of pounds increases and the supply curve shifts down from *SS* to S_1S_1, as shown in Figure 2 (B), the value of pounds depreciates and that of dollars appreciates. This automatically brings about a new equilibrium exchange rate OR_1 at point E_1 in Figure 2 (B) where the S_1S_1 curve intersects the *DD* curve. At the new equilibrium exchange rate OR_1, OQ_1 of foreign exchange is demanded and supplied. The supply of pounds may increase due to the increase in the tastes of Britishers for the US goods, the increase in the national income of Britain, etc.

Thus under flexible exchange rates, equilibrium rate of exchange will prevail which will clear the market and keep the balance of payments in equilibrium.

3. THEORIES OF FOREIGN EXCHANGE RATE

There are three theories of the determination of foreign exchange rate. The first is the Mint Parity Theory, the second is the Purchasing Power Parity Theory, and the third is the Balance of Payments Theory. We discuss these theories one by one.

1. The Mint Parity Theory

This theory is associated with the working of the international gold standard. Under this system, the currency in use was made of gold or was convertible into gold at a fixed rate. The value of the currency unit was defined in terms of certain weight of gold, that is, so many grains of gold to the rupee, the dollar, the pound, etc. The central bank of the country was always ready to buy and sell gold at the specified price. The rate at which the standard money of the country was convertible into gold was called the *mint price* of gold. If the official British price of gold was £6 per ounce and the US price of gold \$ 36 per ounce, they were the mint prices of gold in the respective countries. The exchange rate between the dollar and the pound would be fixed at \$ 36/£6 = \$ 6. This rate was called the mint parity or mint par of exchange because it was based on the mint price of gold. Thus under the gold standard, the normal or basic rate of exchange was equal to the ratio of their mint par values ($R = \$/£$).

But the actual rate of exchange could vary above and below the mint parity by the cost of shipping gold between the two countries. To illustrate this, suppose the US has a deficit in its balance of payments with Britain. The difference between the value of imports and exports will have to be paid in gold by US importers because the demand for pounds exceeds the supply of pounds. But the transhipment of gold involves transportation cost and other handling charges, insurance, etc. Suppose the shipping cost of gold from the US to Britain is 3 cents. So the US importers will have to spend \$ 6.03 (\$ 6 + .03*c*) for getting £ 1. This could be the exchange rate which is the US *gold export point* or *upper specie point.* No US importer would pay more than \$ 6.03 to obtain one pound because he can buy \$ 6 worth of gold from the US treasury and ship it to Britain at a cost of 3 cents per ounce. Similarly, the exchange rate of the pound cannot fall below \$ 5.97 in the case of a surplus in the US balance of payments. Thus the exchange rate of \$ 5.97 to a pound is the US *gold import point* or *lower specie point.* The exchange rate under the gold standard is determined by the forces of demand and supply between the gold points and is prevented from moving outside the gold points by shipments of gold.

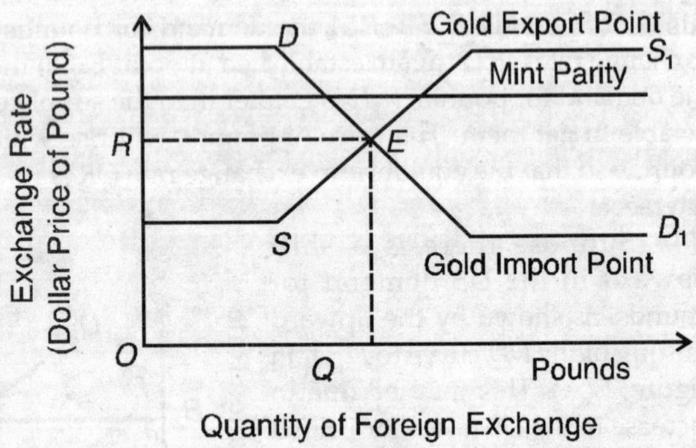

FIG. 3

Figure 3 shows the determination of the exchange rate under the gold standard. The exchange rate *OR* is set up at point *E* where the demand and supply curves DD_1 and SS_1 intersect. The exchange rate need not be at the mint parity. It can be anywhere between the gold points depending on the shape of the demand and supply curves. The mint parity is simply meant to define the US gold export point (\$ 6.03) and the US gold import point (\$ 5.97). Since the US treasury is prepared to sell any quantity of gold at a price of \$ 36 per ounce, no American would pay more than \$ 6.03 per pound, because he can get any quantity of pounds at that price by exporting gold. That is why, the US supply curve of pounds becomes perfectly elastic or horizontal at the US gold export point. This is shown by the horizontal portion S_1 of the SS_1 supply curve. Similarly, as the US treasury is prepared to buy any quantity of gold at \$ 36 per ounce, no American would sell pounds less than \$ 5.97 because he can sell any quantity of pounds at the price by gold imports. Thus the US demand curve for pounds becomes perfectly elastic at the US gold import point. This is shown by the horizontal portion D_1 of the demand curve DD_1.

The mint parity theory has long been discarded ever since the gold standard broke down. No country is on the gold standard now. There are neither free movements of gold nor gold parities. So this theory has only an academic interest.

2. The Purchasing Power Parity Theory

The purchasing power parity (PPP) theory was developed by Gustav Cassel in 1920 to determine the exchange rate between countries on inconvertible paper currencies. The theory states that equilibrium exchange rate between two inconvertible paper currencies is determined by the equality of their purchasing power. In other words, the rate of exchange between two countries is determined by their relative price levels. The theory can be explained with the help of an example.

Suppose India and England are on inconvertible paper standard and by spending Rs. 60, the same bundle of goods can be purchased in India as can be bought by spending £ 1 in England. Thus according to the purchasing power parity theory, the rate of exchange will be Rs. 60 = £ 1.

If the price levels in the two countries remain the same but the exchange rate moves to Rs. 50 = £ 1. This means that less rupees are required to buy the same bundle of goods in India as compared to £ 1 in England. It is a case of *overvaluation* of the exchange rate. This will encourage imports and discourage exports by India. As a result, the demand for pounds will increase and that of rupees will fall. This process will ultimately restore the normal exchange rate of Rs. 60 = £ 1. In the converse case, if the exchange rate moves to Rs. 70 = £ 1, the Indian currency becomes *undervalued.* As a result, exports are encouraged and imports are discouraged. The demand for rupees will rise and that for pounds will fall so that the normal exchange rate of Rs. 60 = £ 1 will be restored.

According to the theory, the exchange rate between two countries is determined at a point which expresses the equality between the respective purchasing powers of the two currencies. This is the purchasing power parity which is a moving par and not fixed par (as under the gold standard). Thus with every change in price level, the exchange rate also changes. To calculate the equilibrium exchange rate, the following formula is used :

$$R = \frac{\text{Domestic Price of a Foreign Currency} \times \text{Domestic Price Index}}{\text{Foreign Price Index}}$$

According to Cassel, the purchasing power parity is "determined by the quotients of the purchasing powers of the different currencies." This is what the formula does. Let us explain it in terms of our above example. Before the change in the price level, the exchange rate was Rs. 60 = £ 1. Suppose the domestic (Indian) price index rises to 300 and the foreign (England) price index rises to 200, thus the new equilibrium exchange rate will be

$$R = \frac{£1 \times 300}{200} = £\ 1.5$$

or $\quad$ Rs. 60 = £ 1.5

This will be the purchasing power parity between the two countries. In reality, the parity will be modified by the cost of transporting goods including duties, insurance, banking and other charges. These costs of transporting goods from one country to another are, in fact, the limits within the exchange rate can fluctuate depending upon the demand and supply of a country's currency. There is the upper limit, called the commodity export point; and the lower limit, known as the commodity import point. (These limits are not as definite as the gold points under the mint par theory).

The purchasing power parity theory is illustrated in Figure 4 where *DD* is the demand curve for foreign currency (pound in our example) and *SS* is the supply curve of currency. *OR* is the rate to exchange of rupees per £, which is determined by their intersection at point *E* so that the demand for the supply of foreign exchange equals *OQ* quantity. Suppose the price level rises in India and remains constant in England. This makes Indian exports costly in England and imports from England relatively cheaper in India. As a result, the demand for pounds increases and the supply of pounds decreases. Now the *DD* curve shifts upward to the right to D_1D_1 and the *SS* curve to the left to S_1S_1. The new equilibrium exchange rate is set at OR_1 rupees per pound, which represents the new purchasing power parity. The exchange rate rises by the same percentage as the Indian price level. The purchasing power curve

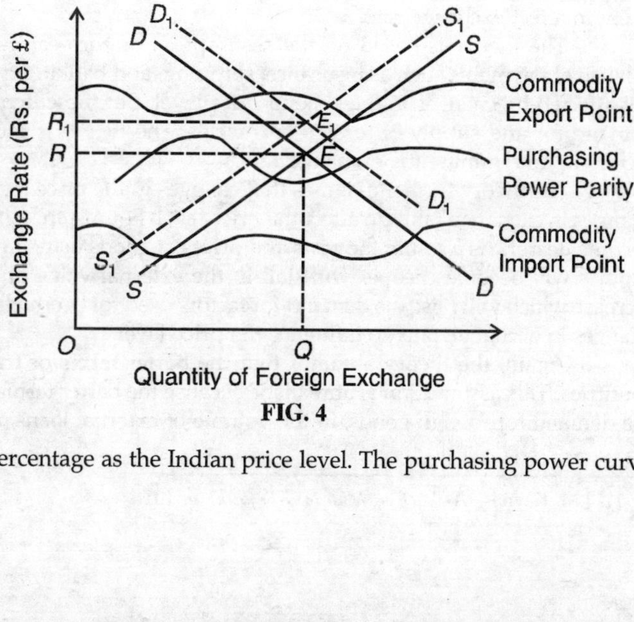

FIG. 4

shows that with relative change in the price levels, the exchange rate tends to fluctuate along this curve above or below the normal exchange rate. But there is a limit upto which the purchasing power parity curve can move up and down. The upper and lower limits are set by the commodity export point and the commodity import point respectively.

Its Criticisms. Cassell's PPP theory became very popular among economists during 1914-24 and was widely accepted as a realistic explanation of the determination of foreign exchange rate under inconvertible paper currencies. But it has been severely criticised for its weak theoretical base. Some of the criticisms are discussed as under :

1. One of the serious defects of the theory is that of calculating the price levels in the two countries. The use of index number in calculations presents many difficulties such as the base year, coverage and method of calculation. These may not be the same in both countries. The two countries may not include the same types of commodities in calculating the index numbers. Such difficulties make the index numbers only a rough guide for measuring the price levels and thus fail to give the correct purchasing power parity between the two countries.

2. According to the theory, the purchasing power parity between two countries is determined by comparing their general price levels. But the price level may be made up of internally traded plus internationally traded goods, or of the internationally traded goods. If the price level is calculated in terms of the internally traded goods, then the prices tend to equality in both countries, even allowing for the cost of transportation, tariffs, etc. Thus, according to Keynes, "confined to internationally traded commodities, the purchasing power parity becomes an empty truism."[1] On the other hand, if the price level includes both internally and internationally traded goods, then price of internally traded goods may move in the opposite direction of internationally traded goods, at least in the short period. Thus the real exchange rate may not conform to the parities.

Further, if the price level includes both types of goods, there is technical difficulty of people spending their money differently in the two countries, so that the basis for complete and accurate comparisons of price levels is lacking.

3. Another weakness of the purchasing power parity theory is that it applies to countries whose balance of payments is determined by the merchandise trade account. It is, therefore, not applicable to such countries whose exchange rate is influenced more by capital account.

4. The theory assumes the balance of payments to be in equilibrium in the base period for the determination of the new equilibrium exchange rate. This is a serious defect, because it is difficult to find the base year when the exchange rate was initially in equilibrium.

5. The theory is also based on the assumption that there have been no structural changes in the factors underlying the equilibrium in the base period. Such factors are changes in technology, resources, tastes, etc. This assumption is highly unrealistic because changes are bound to take place in these factors which, in turn, are likely to affect exchange rate.

6. The theory is based on the assumption of zero-capital movements. There are many items in the balance of payments such as insurance, shipping, and banking transactions, capital movements, etc. which are not affected by changes in the general price level. But these items affect the exchange rate by influencing the demand for and supply of foreign currencies. The theory is thus weak for it neglects the influence of these factors in determining the exchange rate.

7. The theory further assumes that changes in the price level bring about changes in exchange rates. But changes in exchange rates do affect the price level. For instance, if the external value of rupee falls, imports will become dearer. As a result, the costs and prices of goods using imported materials will rise. On the other hand, exports will become cheaper with fall in the external value of the rupee. Consequently, their demand will increase which will raise the demand for factors used for producing exports, and their prices will also rise. Thus changes in exchange rate do influence the price level.

8. Again, the theory assumes that the barter terms of trade do not change between the two trading countries. This assumption is unrealistic because the barter terms of trade constantly change due to changes in the demand for foreign goods, in the volume of external loans, in the supply of exported goods, in transport

1. J.M. Keynes, *A Tract on Monetary Reform,* p. 101

costs, etc.

9. The theory is based on the assumption of free trade and *laissez-faire* policy. But governments do not follow these policies these days. Rather, they impose a number of restrictions on the movement of goods between countries. Such trade restrictions are tariff, import quotas, customs duties and various exchange control devices which tend to reduce the volume of imports. These, in turn, cause wide deviations between the actual exchange rate and the exchange rate set by the purchasing power parity.

10. The equilibrium exchange rate may not be determined by the purchasing power parity between the two countries. Rather, a sudden increase in the demand for goods of one country may raise the demand for its currency on the part of the other country. This will lead to a rise in the exchange rate.

11. According to Keynes, one of the serious defects of this theory is that it fails to consider the elasticities of reciprocal demand. In fact, the exchange rate is determined not only by changes in relative prices, but also by the elasticities of reciprocal demand between the two trading countries.

12. Ragner Nurkse points out that the theory is one-sided in that it is based exclusively on changes in relative prices and neglects all factors that influence the demand for foreign exchange. The theory treats demand as a function of price but neglects the influence of aggregate income and expenditure on the volume and value of foreign trade, these are important factors which affect the exchange rate of a country.

Conclusion. Despite these criticisms, Haberler finds the theory useful. According to him, "While the price levels of different countries may diverge, their price systems are nevertheless interrelated and interdependent, although the relation need not be that of equality. Moreover, supporters of the theory are quite right in contending that the exchanges can always be established at any desired level of appropriate changes in the volume of money."[2]

3. The Balance of Payments Theory

According to this theory, under free exchange rates, the exchange rate of the currency of a country depends upon its balance of payments. A favourable balance of payments raises the exchange rate, while an unfavourable balance of payments reduces the exchange rate. Thus the theory implies that the exchange rate is determined by the demand for the supply of foreign exchange.

The demand for foreign exchange arises from the debit side of the balance of payments. It is equal to the value of payments made to the foreign country for goods and services purchased from it plus loans and investments made abroad. The supply of foreign exchange arises from the credit side of the balance of payments. It equals all payments made by the foreign country to our country for goods and services purchased from us plus loans disbursed and investments made in this country. The balance of payments balances if debits and credits are equal. If debits exceed credits, the balance of payments is unfavourable. On the contrary, if credits exceed debits it is favourable. When the balance of payments is unfavourable, it means that the demand for foreign currency is more than its supply. This causes the external value of the domestic currency to fall in relation to the foreign currency. Consequently, the exchange rate falls. On the other hand, in case the balance of payments is favourable, the demand for foreign currency is less than its supply at a given exchange rate. This causes the external value of the domestic currency to rise in relation to the foreign currency. Consequently, the exchange rate rises.

When the exchange rate falls below the equilibrium exchange rate in a situation of adverse balance of payments, exports increase and the adverse balance of payments is eliminated, and the equilibrium exchange rate is re-established. On the other hand, when under a favourable balance of payment situation, the exchange rate rises above the equilibrium exchange rate, exports decline, the favourable balance of payments disappears and the equilibrium exchange rate is re-established. Thus at any point of time, the rate of exchange is determined by the demand for and the supply of foreign exchange as represented by the debit and credit side of the balance of payments. "Any change in the conditions of demand or of supply reflects itself in a change in the exchange rate, and at the ruling rate the balance of payments balances from day to day or from moment to moment."

The determination of exchange rate under the balance of payments theory is illustrated in Figure 5. *DD* is the demand curve for foreign currency. It slopes downward to the left because when the rate of exchange rises, the demand for foreign currency falls, and vice versa. *SS* is the supply curve of foreign exchange which

2. G. Haberler, *op. cit.,* p. 38.

slopes upwards from left to right. This is because when the exchange rate falls, the amount of foreign currency offered for sale will be less, and *vice versa*. The two curves intersect at E where OR equilibrium exchange rate is determined. At this rate, the quantity of foreign exchange demanded and supplied equals OQ. E is also the point where the balance of payments is in equilibrium. Any exchange rate above or below OR will mean disequilibrium in the balance of payments. Suppose the exchange rate rises to OR_1. The demand for foreign exchange R_1A is less than its supply R_1B ($R_1A < R_1B$). It means that there is a favourable balance of payments. When the exchange rate is more than the equilibrium rate, exports decline and imports increase. Consequently, the demand for foreign exchange will rise and the supply will fall. Ultimately, the equilibrium exchange rate OR will be restored where demand and supply of foreign exchange equals at point E. In the opposite case, when the exchange rate falls below the equilibrium rate to OR_2, the demand for foreign exchange R_2H is greater than its supply R_2G ($R_2H > R_2G$). It implies an unfavourable balance of payments. But fall in the exchange rate leads to increase in exports and decline in imports. As a result, the demand for foreign currency starts falling and the supply starts rising till the equilibrium exchange rate OR is re-established with the equality of demand and supply of foreign exchange at point E.

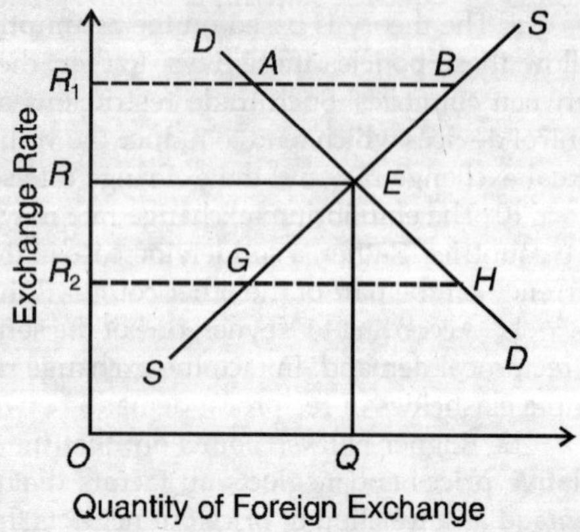

FIG. 5

Its Criticisms

The balance of payments theory has been criticised by economists on the following counts :

1. The main defect of the theory is that the balance of payments is independent of the exchange rate. In other words, the theory states that the balance of payments determines the exchange rate. This is not wholly true because it is changes in the exchange rate that bring about equilibrium in the balance of payments.

2. Another defect of the theory neglects the role of the price level in influencing the balance of payments of a country and hence its exchange rate. But the fact is that price changes do affect the balance of payments and the exchange rates between countries.

3. The theory is based on assumptions of free trade and perfect competition . This is unrealistic because free trade is not practised these days. Governments impose a number of restrictions to reduce imports and adopt measures to encourage exports. This is how they try to correct disequilibrium in the balance of payments.

4. The theory presupposes that there is an equilibrium exchange rate where balance of payments balances. This is a truism. But the equilibrium exchange rate may not be one of balance of payments equilibrium. In fact, exchange rates between countries continue to prevail under conditions of surplus or deficit in the balance of payments and there is no tendency for the balance of payments to be in equilibrium over the long run.

Despite these criticisms, the balance of payments theory is the most satisfactory explanation of the determination of exchange rate. It studies the problem of determination of exchange rate under the framework of the general equilibrium analysis in terms of demand and supply. It studies the actual forces which lie behind the demand and supply of foreign exchange, such as the current account and the capital account of the balance of payments. An important implication of the theory is that adjustments in balance of payments can be made through devaluation and revaluation of some currency in case of deficit and surplus in balance of payments respectively. That is why, it is regarded superior to the mint par and purchasing power parity theories of exchange rate.

CAUSES OF CHANGES IN THE EXCHANGE RATE

The exchange rate between countries changes due to changes in demand or supply in the foreign exchange market. The factors which cause changes in demand and supply are discussed as under :

1. *Changes in Prices.* It is changes in the relative price levels that cause changes in the exchange rate. Suppose the price level in Britain rises relative to the US price level. This will lead to the rise in the prices of British goods in terms of pound. British goods will become dearer in the US. This will lead to reduction in British exports to the US. So the supply of dollars to Britain will diminish. On the other hand, the American goods become cheaper in Britain and their imports into Britain increase. So the demand for dollars will increase. Thus the supply curve for dollars will shift to the left so that the exchange rate is established at a higher level from the point of view of the US. It implies appreciation of the value of the dollar and depreciation of the value of the pound.

2. *Changes in Exports and Imports.* The demand and supply of foreign exchange is also influenced by changes in exports and imports. If exports of the country are more than imports, the demand for its currency increases so that the rate of exchange moves in its favour. Conversely, if imports are more than exports, the demand for the foreign currency increases and the rate of exchange will move against the country.

3. *Capital Movements.* Short-term or long-term capital movements also influence the exchange rate. Capital-flows tend to appreciate the value of the currency of the capital-importing country and depreciate the value of the currency of the capital-exporting country. The exchange rate will move in favour of the capital-importing country and against the capital-exporting country. The demand for the currency of the capital-importing country will rise and its demand curve will shift upward to the right and the exchange rate will be determined at a higher level, given the supply curve of foreign exchange.

4. *Influence of Banks.* Banks also affect the exchange rate through their operation. They include the purchase and sale of bank drafts, letters of credit, arbitrage, dealing in bills of exchange, etc. These banking operations influence the demand for and supply of foreign exchange. If the commercial banks issue a large number of drafts and letter of credit on foreign banks, the demand for foreign currency rises. The bank rate also influences the exchange rate. If the bank rate rises relative to other countries, more funds will flow into the country from abroad to earn high interest rate. It will tend to raise the demand for the domestic currency and the exchange rate will move in favour of the country. Converse will be the case when the bank rate falls.

5. *Influence of Speculation.* The growth of speculative activities also influences the exchange rate. Speculation causes short-run fluctuations in the exchange rate. Uncertainty in the international money market encourages speculation in foreign exchange. If the speculators expect a fall in the value of currency in the near future, they will sell that currency and start buying the other currency they expect to appreciate in value. Consequently, the supply of the former currency will increase and its exchange rate will fall. While the demand for the other currency will rise and its exchange rate will go up.

6. *Stock Exchange Influences.* Stock exchange operations in foreign securities, debentures, stocks and shares, etc. exert significant influence on the exchange rate. If the stock exchanges help in the sale of securities, debentures, shares etc. to foreigners, the demand for the domestic currency will rise on the part of the foreigners and the exchange rate also tends to rise. The opposite will be the case if the foreigners purchase securities, debentures, shares, etc. through the domestic stock exchanges.

7. *Structural Influences.* Structural change is another important factor which influences the exchange rate of a country. Structural changes are those which bring changes in the consumer demand for commodities. They include technological changes, innovations, etc. which also affect the cost structure along with the demand for products. Such structural changes tend to increase the foreign demand for domestic products. It implies increase in exports, greater demand for domestic currency, appreciation of its value and rise in the exchanges rate.

8. *Political Conditions.* Stable political and industrial conditions and peace and security in the country have a significant influence on the exchange rate. If there is political stability and the government is stable, strong and efficient, foreigners will have tendency to invest their funds into the country. With the inflow of capital, the demand for domestic currency will rise and the exchange rate will move in favour of the country. On the

contrary, if the government is weak, inefficient and dishonest and there is no safety to life and property, capital will flow out of the country and the exchange rate will move against the country.

EXERCISES

1. What is an equilibrium rate of exchange? How is it determined?
2. How is the rate of exchange determined under gold standard?
3. Explain how foreign exchange rate is determined under inconvertible paper currencies.
4. Critically examine the Purchasing Power Parity Theory of exchange rates.
5. Discuss the Balance of Payments Theory of foreign exchange rates.
6. Examine the factors influencing the foreign exchange rates.

CHAPTER 53

Foreign Exchange Rate Policy

1. INTRODUCTION

In the previous chapter we discussed the various theories relating to the determination of exchange rate under different exchange rate regimes. The present chapter discusses the exchange rate adjustment policies that have been in vogue from time to time with the establishment of the IMF. Before we discuss them, it is instructive to have a theoretical interlude relating to fixed and fluctuating exchange rates.

2. FIXED EXCHANGE

Under fixed or pegged exchange rates all exchange transactions take place at an exchange rate that is determined by the monetary authority. It may fix the exchange rate by legislation or intervention in currency markets. It may buy or sell currencies according to the needs of the country or may take policy decision to appreciate or depreciate the national currency. The following arguments are usually advanced for and against the system of fixed exchange rates.

CASE FOR FIXED EXCHANGE RATES

Fixed exchange rates have the following advantages :

1. The case for fixed exchange rate between different countries is based on the case for a common currency within a country. A country having a common currency with a fixed value facilities trade increases production and leads to faster growth of the economy. Similarly, a country would benefit if it has a fixed value of its currency in relation to other countries. Thus fixed exchange rates encourage international trade by making prices of goods involved in trade more predictable. They promote economic integration. As pointed out by Johnson, "The case for fixed rates is part of a more general argument for national economic policies conducive to international economic integration."

2.The second argument for a system of fixed exchange rates is that it encourages long-term capital flows in an orderly and smooth manner. There is no uncertainty and risk resulting from a regime of fixed exchange rates.

3. There is no fear of currency depreciation or appreciation under a system of fixed exchange rates. For instance, it removes fear that holding large quantities of foreign currency might lead to losses, if a currency's value drops. Thus it creates confidence in the strength of the domestic currency.

4. There is no fear of any adverse effect of speculation on the exchange rate, as speculative activities are controlled and prevented by the monetary authorities under a regime of fixed exchange rates.

5. Another advantage claimed by a system of fixed exchange rates is that it serves as an 'anchor' and imposes a discipline on monetary authorities to follow responsible financial policies with countries. "Inflation will cause balance of payments deficits and reserve loss. Hence the authorities will have to take counter-measures to stop inflation. Fixed exchange rates should, therefore, impose 'discipline' on governments and stop them from pursuing inflationary policies which are out of tune with the rest of the world."

6. Johnson favours fixed exchange rates in the 'banana republics' where foreign trade plays a dominant role. Flexible exchange rates in them lead to inflation and depreciation when the exchange rate falls.[1]

Case Against Fixed Exchange Rates

The following arguments are advanced against a system of fixed exchange rates :

1. The principle defect in the operation of a system of fixed exchange rates is the sacrifice of the objectives of full employment and stable prices at the alter of stable exchange rates. For example, balance of payments adjustment under fixed exchange rates of a surplus country can take place through a rise in prices. This is bound to impose large social costs within the country.

2. Again, under this system, the effects of unexpected disturbances in the domestic economy are transmuted abroad. "While a country may be protected by fixed exchange rates from the full consequences of domestic disturbances and policy mistakes, it has to bear a share of the burden of the disturbances and mistakes of others. For to the extent that excess demand 'leaks out' of the country where it was originally created, it 'leaks in' (via a balance of payments surplus) to that country's trading partner."

3. Under it, large reserves of foreign currencies are required to be maintained. Countries with balance of payments deficits must have large reserves if they want to avoid devaluation. If countries wish to remain on the fixed exchange rate system, they must hold large reserves of foreign currencies. This also imposes a heavy burden on the monetary authorities for managing foreign exchange reserves.

4. This system requires complicated exchange control measures which lead to malallocation of the economy's resources.

5. Another problem relates to the stability of the exchange rate. The exchange rate of a country vis-a-vis another country cannot remain fixed for sufficiently long period. Balance of payments problems and fluctuations in international commodity prices often compel countries to bring changes in exchange rates. Thus it is not possible to have rigidly fixed exchange rates.

In fact, a regime of fixed exchange rates presupposes uniformity of domestic policy objectives and response of prices to fluctuations in demand. Such a system would undoubtedly run into severe difficulties in the present-day world. This is because there is a reluctance to be committed to the harmonisation of domestic policy objectives; prices respond only in a limited fashion of fluctuations in the pressures of demand, and elasticities of demand in international trade have in general turned out to be quite low, at least in the short run. For these reasons, a rigidly fixed exchange rate regime has never been advanced as serious possibility in any of the recent discussions of reform of the international monetary system.[2]

3. FLEXIBLE EXCHANGE RATES

Flexible, *floating* or *fluctuating* exchange rates are determined by market forces. The monetary authority does not intervene for the purpose of influencing the exchange rate. Under a regime of freely fluctuating exchange rates, if there is an excess supply of a currency, the value of that currency in foreign exchange markets will fall. It will lead to depreciation of the exchange rate. Consequently, equilibrium will be restored in the exchange market. On the other hand, shortage of a currency will lead to appreciation of exchange rate thereby leading to restoration of equilibrium in the exchange market. These market forces operate automatically without any intervention on the part of monetary authorities. We study below the case for and against flexible exchange rates.

---

1. Johnson uses the term 'banana republics' for small countries of Europe like UK, France, Denmark, etc. which are dependent on foreign trade.
2. Andrew Crokett, *International Money, Issues and Analysis*, 1977.

Case for Flexible Exchange rates

The following advantages are claimed for a system of flexible exchange rates:

1. A system of flexible exchange rates is simple in the operative mechanism. The exchange rate moves automatically and freely to equate supply and demand, thereby clearing the foreign exchange market. It does not allow a deficit or surplus to build up and eliminates the problem of scarcity or surplus of any one currency. It also avoids the need to induce changes in prices and incomes to maintain or restore equilibrium in the balance of payments.

2. Under it, the adjustment is continual. The adjustment in the balance of payments are smoother and painless as compared with the fixed exchange rate adjustments. In fact, flexible exchange rates avoid the aggravation of pressures on the balance of payments and the periodic crises that follow disequilibrium in the balance of payments under a system of fixed exchange rates. There is an escape from the various corrective measures that are adopted by the governments whenever the exchange rate depreciates or appreciates.

3. Under this system, autonomy of the domestic economic policies is preserved. Modern governments are committed to maintain full employment and promote stability with growth. They are not required to sacrifice these objectives of full employment and economic growth in order to remove balance of payments disequilibrium under a regime of flexible exchange rates. As pointed out by Johnson, " The fundamental argument for flexible exchange rates is that they allow countries autonomy with respect to their use of monetary, fiscal and other policy instruments, by automatically ensuring the preservation of external equilibrium."

4. Since under a system of flexible exchange rates disequilibrium in the balance of payments is automatically corrected, there is no need to accommodate gold movements and capital flows in and out of countries.

5. There is no need for foreign exchange reserves where exchange rates are moving freely. A deficit country will simply allow its currency to depreciate in relation to foreign currency instead of intervening by supplying foreign exchange reserves to the other country to maintain a stable exchange rate. According to Sohmen, [3]a system of flexible exchange rates removes the problem of international liquidity. The shortage of international liquidity is the result of pegged exchange rates and intervention by monetary authorities to prevent fluctuations beyond narrow limits. When exchange rates are flexible, speculators will supply foreign exchange to satisfy private liquidity needs. Individuals, traders, banks, governments and others would, of course, continue to hold liquid assets in the form of gold or foreign exchange, but these holdings would be working reserves for purposes other than the maintenance of a fixed external value of the country's currency.[4]

6. As a corollary to the above, when foreign exchange rates move freely, there is no need to have international institutional arrangements like the IMF for borrowing the lending short-term funds to remove disequilibrium in the balance of payments.

7. Again, according to Sohmen, the system of flexible exchange rates re-inforces the effectiveness of monetary policy. If a country wants to increase output, it will lower interest rates under a regime of flexible exchange rates, the lowering of interest rates will result in an outflow of capital, a rise in the spot rate for the currency which will, in turn, cause exports to rise and imports to fall. The increased exports will tend to rise domestic prices, or income or both. Thus a favourable trade balance will reinforce the expansionary effects of lower interest rates on domestic spending, thereby making monetary policy more effective. The above process will be reversed if the country wants to fight inflation by raising interest rates.

8. A system of flexible exchange rates does not require the introduction of complicated and expansive trade restrictions and exchange controls. Thus the cost of foreign exchange restrictions is removed.

9. Again, as a corollary to the above, the world can get rid of competitive exchange rate depreciation and tariff warfare among nations and there shall be no need of forming custom unions and currency areas which are the concomitant results of the system of fixed exchange rates.

Case Against Flexible Exchange Rates

The advocates of fixed exchange rates advance the following arguments against a system of flexible exchange rates :

1. Critics of flexible exchange rates point out that market mechanism may fail to bring about an appropriate exchange rate. The equilibrium exchange rate in the foreign exchange market at a point of time may not give

correct signals to concerned parties in the country. This may lead to wrong decisions and malallocation of resources with the country.

2. It is difficult to define a freely flexible exchange rate. It is not possible to have an exchange rate where there is absolutely no official intervention. Government may not intervene directly in the foreign exchange market, but domestic monetary and fiscal measures do influence foreign exchange rates. For instance, if domestic saving is more than domestic investment, it means that the country is a net investor abroad. The outflow of capital will bring down the exchange rate. All this may be due to the indirect impact of government policies. Further, in the absence of any understanding among governments about exchange rate manipulation, the system of flexible exchange rates might lapse into anarchy, for every country would try to establish favourable exchange rates with other countries. This may lead to retaliation among nations and result in war of exchange rates with disruptive effects on trade and capital movements. Thus some sort of understanding or agreement concerning exchange rates is implied in a regime of flexible exchange rates.

3. Another disadvantage of this system is that frequent variations in exchange rates, create exchange risks, breed uncertainty and impede international trade and capital movements. For instance, an Indian who imports from Japan and promises to pay in yen runs the risk that the rupee price of yen will rise above expected levels. And the Japanese exporter who sells for rupees runs the risk that the yen price of rupees will fall below expected levels. Similarly, exchange risks may be even more serious for long-term capital movements. This is because under a system of flexible exchange rates borrowers and lenders will be discouraged to enter into long-term contacts and the possibility of varying burden for servicing and repayment may be prohibitive.

Bo Sodersten[4] has shown how flexible exchange rates increase uncertainty for traders and have a dampening effect on the volume of foreign trade. Assume that a country is under a regime of flexible exchange rates, the general price level is stable and the balance of trade is in equilibrium. Suppose the demand for the country's exports decreases, this leads to depreciation of the country's currency which, in turn, raises import prices and brings a fall in imports. Consequently, importers will be adversely affected. At the same time, exporters will gain with the increase in the prices of export goods. But the volume of exports will decline whereby they will also be losers. Opposite will be the consequences when currency appreciates. Suppose there is an abnormal inflow of short-term capital to country *A* which tends to raise its exchange rate. This will, in turn, increase the cost of *A*'s exports in terms of foreign currencies, thereby lowering the levels of output, employment and income in its export industries. The rise of exchange rate will also lower the cost of imports, thus discouraging output and employment in *A*'s import competing industries. Thus importers and exporters will be at a disadvantage and the volume of trade will decline. This is illustrated in terms of Sodersten's diagram, shown as Figure 1. The horizontal line *S* shows stable or fixed exchange rate, and the zig-zag line *F* shows flexible exchange rate. At time t_0 the exchange rate is the same *E*, under both flexible and fixed rate systems. At t_1 the currency depreciates and the flexible exchange rate moves to *D* while the fixed exchange rate is at the same level D_1 (= *E*). Since import prices have risen, imports will be discouraged and exports will be encouraged. At time t_2 the currency appreciates and the flexible rate moves to *A* whereas the fixed rate remains at the same level A_1 (= *E*). At *A* import prices fall. Imports are encouraged and exports are discouraged. So exports will be at a disadvantage at *A* than at A_1 and importers will gain at *A* than at A_1. Similar will be at time t_3 with fixed exchange rate at C_1 and the flexible exchange rate at *C* level. Thus fluctuations of the exchange rate around a trend value will increase risks for exports and imports that will adversely affect the volume of foreign trade.

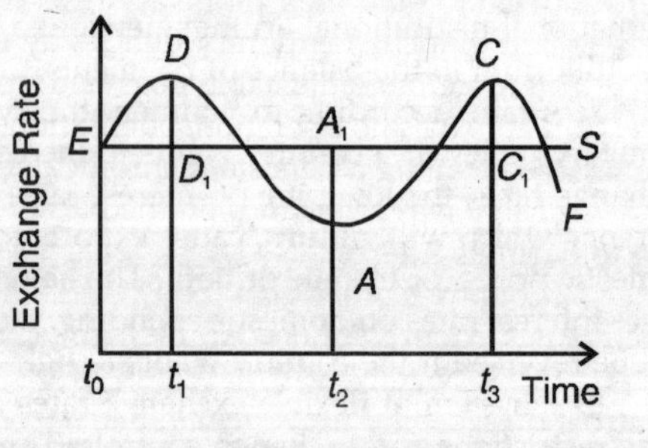

Fig. 1

4. Under this system, speculation adversely influences fluctuations in supply and demand for foreign exchange. Critics argue on the basis of empirical evidence that speculation is destabilising which means that it aggravates fluctuations in exchange rate. "It is often said that speculators see a decline in the exchange rate as a signal for further decline, and that their actions will cause the movement in the exchange rate to be larger than

4. *Ibid.*, pp. 403-4.

it would be in the absence of speculation. In such a case, speculation is destabilising.[6] Sodersten points out that "the limited experience from the 1920s seem to show that speculation at that time was destabilising. Since floating rates became common in 1973, fluctuations in exchange rates have been large. It seems that some of the excessive fluctuations have been caused by destabilising speculation." Such fluctuations increase uncertainties in trade and reduce the volume of foreign trade further.

5. Another serious drawback of a flexible exchange rate system is its inflationary bias. Critics argue that under a system of flexible exchange rates, a depreciation of the exchange rate leads to a vicious circle of inflation. Depreciation leads to a rise in import prices thereby making import goods more expensive. This leads to cost-push inflation. At the same time, export prices rise. Consequently, with the rise in the cost of living, money wages rise which, in turn, intensify inflation. But an appreciation of currency is unlikely to lead to a reduction in wages and prices when imports prices fall. This is because wages and prices are sticky downwards. This leads to an asymmetry which produces that Triffin calls *ratchet effect* that imparts an inflationary bias to the economy.

6. The main case against the system of flexible exchange rates is that it breaks up the world market. There is no one money which serves as a medium of exchange, unit of account, store of value and a standard of deferred payment. Under it, the world market for goods and capital would be divided. Resources allocation would be vastly sub-optimal. In fact, such a system clearly would not last long, according to Kindleberger.[5]

Conclusion. From the above merits and demerits of fixed and flexible exchange rates, it is difficult to conclude that either rigidly fixed or freely floating exchange rates are likely to be put into practice.

4. EXCHANGE RATE REGIMES IN PRACTICE

During the period preceding World War I almost all the major national currencies were on a system of fixed exchange rates under the international gold standard. This sytem had to be abandoned during World War I but most nations returned to pegged rates during the 1920s.

Adjustable Peg. With the establishment of the IMF under the Bretton Woods Agreement after World War II, exchange rates between countries were set or pegged in terms of gold or the US dollar at $ 35 per ounce of gold. This related to a fixed exchange rate regime with changes in the exchange rate within a band or range from 1 per cent above to 1 per cent below the par value. But this was only allowed when the country could convince the IMF authorities that there was "fundamental disequilibrium" in its balance of payments. Member countries were forbidden to impose restrictions on payments and trade, except for a transitional period. They were allowed to hold their monetary reserves partly in gold and partly in dollars and sterling. These reserves were meant to incur temporary deficits by member countries while keeping their exchange rates stable.

This system of adjustable pegs had many flaws in its working.

1. There was no operational definition of "fundamental disequilibrium." But it came to be interpreted by the IMF as meaning a persistent chronic deficit that could be ultimately corrected by devaluation.

2. There was reluctance on the part of both deficit and surplus countries to change exchange rates so as not to harm its interest.

3. Countries other than the United States wanted to increase their reserves which led to dollar holdings to a greater extent than needed by them. This was because dollar was a *numeraire* of the system.

4. This system, as it operated in the 1960s, led to destabilising speculation and consequently made controls over capital movements ineffective.

5. One basic flaw of this system of adjustable pegs was the insistence by the IMF on expenditure-reducing policies and the reluctance to use expenditure switching policies for correcting disequilibria.

Consequently, the Bretton Woods system in 1971 when the US Treasury refused to convert short-time liabilities into gold and made the dollar inconvertible.

Managed Floating. The sytem of adjustable peg continued till 14 August, 1971. Between 15 August, 1971 and the Smithsonian Agreement of 18 December, 1971, 48 countries including the United States, Japan and a large number of European countries abandoned fixed exchange rates. The 'Group of Ten' industrial countries met at the Smithsonian Institution in Washington on 18-19 December, 1971 and agreed to a new system of

5. C.P. Kindleberger, *International Money,* 1981.

stable exchange rates with *wider bands*. As a first step towards realignment of major currencies, the US devalued the dollar by 8 per cent, the Japanese revalued the yen by 17 per cent and the Germans their mark by 14 per cent. The Smithsonian Agreement widened the margin of fluctuations of the exchange rates to 2.25 per cent above or below the new parities of central rates. In 1973, the band was widened to 4.5 per cent.

Another development took place in Europe when the original six EEC member countries decided to limit the fluctuations of their currencies relative to each other to a smaller band in 1972. This came to be known as *"the snake in the tunnel"*. Under this arrangement, the EEC currencies were tied together and could fluctuate within narrow limits in relation to one another but could fluctuate in relation to other currencies within the limits set by the band proposal. But due to the lack of convergence between them and world oil crisis and high inflation around the world, this system collapsed.

The Smithsonian Agreement broke down following the US dollar devaluation of 12 February, 1973. At the beginning of March 1973 India, Canada, Japan, Switzerland, the UK and several smaller countries had floating exchange rates. However, the "joint float" of the EEC countries continued even after March 1973 and was now called the "*snake in the lake*", as there was no band within which the EEC currencies could fluctuate relative to other currencies. In March 1979 the European Monetary System (EMS) was formed which created the European Currency Unit (ECU) which is a "basket" currency of a unit of account consisting of the major European currencies. Each member of the EMS fixes the value of its currency in terms of the ECU which is a pegged system of exchange rates among members' currencies.

In the meantime, the Jamaica Agreement of January 1976 formalised the regime of floating exchange rates under the auspices of the IMF. A number of factors forced the majority of member countries of the IMF to float their currencies. There were large short-term capital movements and central banks failed to stop speculation in currencies during the regime of adjustable pegs. The oil crisis in 1973 and the increase in oil prices in 1974 led to the great recession of 1974-75 in the industrial countries of the world. As a result "the dollar went into a rapid decline, which, by late 1978, had such alarming proportions that the United States government finally decided on a policy of massive intervention in order to prevent a further fall in the value of the dollar and to head off a possible financial panic". At last, the system of floating exchange rates had come to stay by 1978.

By the Second Amendment of the IMF Charter in 1978, the member countries are not expected to maintain and establish par values with the dollar or SDRs or another denominator, cooperative arrangements to maintain the value of their currencies in relation to the value of currencies of other members, and other exchange arrangements of a member's choice. The Fund has no control over the exchange rate adjustment policies of the member countries to counter disorderly conditions in the foreign exchange markets. But it lays down principles for the guidance of members' exchange rate policies. In other words, it exercises international "surveillance" of exchange rate policies of its members.

However, the system of floating exchange rates is not one of free flexible exchange rates but of "managed floating". It has rarely operated without government intervention. Periodic intervention by governments has led the system to be called a "managed" or "dirty" floating system. In 1977, when the intervention was very heavy, it was characterised as a "filthy" float. When governments do not intervene, it is a "clean" float. But the possibilities of a clean float are very remote. Thus a system of managed floating exchange rates is evolving where the central banks are trying to control fluctuations of exchange rates around some "normal" rates even though the Second Amendment of the Fund makes no mention of normal rates.

EXERCISES

1. Give arguments for and against a system of fixed exchange rates.
2. Do you favour flexible or fixed exchange rates? Give reasons in support of your answer.
3. Explain the working of the system of adjustable peg. What led to the adoption of the system of managed floating exchange rates?

CHAPTER 54

The Foreign Exchange Market

1. INTRODUCTION

The foreign exchange market is the market in which different currencies are bought and sold for one another. For example, dollars are traded for marks, marks for francs, francs for yens or yens for dollars. Thus the national currencies of all countries are the stock-in-trade of the foreign exchange market. As such, it is the largest market to be found around the world which functions in every country.

2. THE STRUCTURE OF FOREIGN EXCHANGE MARKET

The principle participants in the foreign exchange market are banks, foreign exchange dealers, brokers, firms and central bank. For instance, in India the Reserve Bank of India authorises banks and other financial institutions to transact foreign exchange business. They are called Authorised Dealers. There are also Authorised Money Changers who are issued licences to transact foreign exchange business of issusing and encashing travellers' cheques and foreign currencies.

Banks dealing in foreign exchange are the "market makers" in the market. This means that they quote buying and selling rates of a currency (say \$) in relation to another currency (say Re) and are prepared to buy and sell it at those rates. The brokers in the foreign exchange market act as middlemen between two banks. They inform the banks about rates at which buyers and sellers are prepared to buy and sell the specific currency. The broker strikes the deal and collects his commission. But brokers do not buy or sell currencies themselves. Thus the foreign exchange rates are set in these inter-bank and bank-broker dealings. Firms need foreign exchange for making payments of imports and interest on foreign loans, conversion of exports receipts, hedging of receivables and payables, etc. They do not deal in foreign exchange like banks. The central bank intervenes in the foreign exchange market from time to time to influence the exchange rates when the country is not on a fully flexible exchange rate system. For instance, in India when the price of dollar rises above a certain level, the Reserve Bank of India intervenes by releasing a large supply of dollars so as to bring its price at that level. Even in countries with full flexible systems, the central banks do intervene to smooth out fluctuations in the exchange rate when the situation demands. This is called "dirty floating" system. The foreign exchange markets "follow the sun around the globe". In other words, they function 24 hours a day with the fastest possible communication through telephones, telexes, computers and other means of communications with the help of satellites. Some of the major foreign exchange market centres are: New York, London, Tokyo, Frankfurt, Zurich, Paris, Singapore and Hongkong.

The main functions of the foreign exchange market are : (*i*) to transfer funds through one currency of a country to another currency; (*ii*) to provide short-term credit to finance trade between countries through various credit instruments; and (*iii*) to facilitate avoidance of foreign exchange risks or hedging or speculation.

3. METHODS OF FOREIGN PAYMENTS

Foreign payments are made in the currency of the country to whom the payment is to be made. But countries mostly prefer U.S. dollars. Payment is made through the following types of credit instruments by the bank dealing in foreign exchange:

1. Demand Draft
2. Telegraphic Transfer
3. Mail Transfer
4. Banker's Cheque
5. Bills of Exchange
6. Travellers' Cheque
7. International Credit Card like the Master Card or Visa Card.

Small sums of foreign currencies can also be sent by International Money Orders.

The banks sell the required amount of foreign exchange to be remitted through the above noted credit instruments at the exchange rate prevalent at that time and also charge their commission (in Rupees in India).

All banks dealing in foreign exchange maintain abroad "Nostro Accounts" with foreign banks. So when an Indian bank draws any of the above noted credit instrument on a foreign bank (Citi Bank) with which it has a foreign currency current account, it will write the word "Nostro A/c" on it. If the payment is to be made to another bank (Bank of Tokyo) with which the Indian Bank *does not* have a "Nostro A/c", it will instruct the foreign bank (Citi Bank) with which it has its current account to credit the sum being remitted to the "Zoro A/c" of the other bank (Bank of Tokyo) and debit the same to its "Nostro A/c". If a foreign bank has to make payment to an Indian bank, its current account with the latter is called the "Nostro A/c."[1]

4. SPOT AND FORWARD EXCHANGE MARKETS

From the point of view of foreign exchange transactions, there are two types of markets : the spot exchange market and the forward exchange market.

In the spot market, the delivery of the foreign exchange has to be made 'on the spot', usually within two days of the transaction. The exchange rate at which the transaction takes place is called the "spot rate". In the forward market, the foreign exchange is bought and sold for delivery at a future date at an agreed rate today. The rate at which the forward exchange contract is agreed upon is called the "forward rate". The usual forward exchange contract and rate are for 1 month, 3 months, 6 months, 9 months and 1 year.

The spot exchange rate is determined by immediate market demand and supply of foreign exchange. On the other hand, the forward exchange rate is determined by the market demand and supply for foreign exchange to be delivered at some future time. The forward exchange rate is quoted in terms of the spot rate. If the forward rate for, say, 3 months is greater than spot rate, less of foreign currency is exchanged for a unit of domestic currency. It is called 3-month "forward premium". On the other hand, if the 3-month forward rate is less than the spot rate, more of foreign currency is exchanged for a unit of the domestic currency. This is called 3-month "forward discount". Forward premium and forward discount are expressed as percentage of the spot rate per year.

---

1. Nostro, Loro and Vostro are Latin words. The Nostro A/c means "our a/c with you"; the Loro A/c means "their a/c with you"; and the Vostro A/c means "your a/c with us".

The forward exchange rate is linked with the spot rate through the actions of hedgers, speculators and arbitrageurs. We discuss them one by one.

1. Hedging

An important factor influencing the forward rate is hedging. Hedging is the act of avoiding or covering a foreign exchange risk arising from an agreed forward rate. Usually, foreign exchange rates fluctuate continuously. Therefore, a person who has to receive or make payment in a foreign currency at a future date faces the risk of receiving less or paying more in terms of the home currency than anticipated. For instance, the exchange rate may change in the interval between an exporter shipping his goods to another country and his receiving payment. The exporter will make a gain or loss in terms of his home currency, depending on how the exchange rate between the two countries moves. He tries to avoid or cover such foreign exchange risks by hedging. Hedging involves an agreement to buy or sell the required foreign exchange at today's agreed rate on some future date, usually 3 months hence.

For example, suppose a U.S. exporter sells goods to a British firm and expects to receive $ 10,000 after 3 months. He fears that the exchange rate between dollar and pound will change during this period. In order to avoid this risk, he covers himself by hedging. He sells $ 10,000 at today's forward rate for the pound to be delivered after 3 months. He, thus, avoids the risk of the spot rate 3 months hence being much below today's rate. In this hedging operation, he has neither received nor paid any money. Out of what he actually receives after 3 months, he pays the money at the rate he had sold forward 3 months back, regardless of what the spot rate of the pound is at that time. Similarly, a U.S. importer who has to make payments to a British firm 3 months hence, can avoid exchange risk by buying $ 10,000 at today's forward rate for pound. Thus by hedging, he avoids the risk of the spot rate 3 months hence being higher than today's rate. After 3 months he pays for his goods from the dollars bought at the forward rate 3 months hence, regardless of the spot rate of the pound at that time.

Hedging also provides opportunities to people to cover risks involving other foreign exchange transactions. A Britisher who has to pay $ 10,000 three month hence, need not wait for so long to buy dollars in the future at an uncertain exchange rate. He can hedge against this dollar liability by buying dollars now at the spot rate to be able to repay after 3 months. Similarly, fluctuating exchange rates give hedgers a way of avoiding gambles on the future of exchange rates.

Hedging helps exporters and importers to concentrate on their trading exchange rate fluctuations. Further, it maintains the supply of and demand for forward exchange which depends on the volume of trade and the avoidence of risk by exporters and importers.

But hedging is possible in flexible exchange rate short-run forward market usually of 3 months. It does not function efficiently for longer periods as it fails to cover risks involving rate fluctuations.

2. Speculation

The supply of and demand for forward exchange market is also the result of speculation. Speculation means "taking of a foreign exchange risk or an open position in the hope of making profit." Speculation is based on the expectations about the future rate of the foreign currency. It takes place in the forward market and is related to the development of the future spot rate.

A speculator who excepts the spot rate of a foreign currency to increase in relation to his home currency in 3 months, he buys the foreign currency in the forward market. He sells it at the spot exchange rate after 3 months. If his expectation turns out to be correct, he earns a profit. Otherwise, he may incur a loss or break even. Suppose the forward exchange rate is $ 1.75 per pound (£). A speculator expects that the spot exchange rate will be $ 1.80 per pound (£) 3 months from now. He will buy pounds forward at $ 1.75 in the hope of selling them 3 months from now at $ 1.80 thereby earning a 5 cent profit on each pound. If the spot rate 3 months hence happens to be $ 1.70, he incurs a loss of 5 cents per pound. In case, it is $ 1.75, he breaks even.

On the contrary, if he expects the spot rate to fall in 3 months from now, he sells the currency in the forward market in order to buy at the spot rate after 3 months. If his expectation about the future spot rate is correct, he earns a profit. Otherwise, he may incur a loss or break even. In such forward transactions, transfers take place only after 3 months when the speculator sells or buys the pounds for dollars at the then spot rate.

Speculation in a foreign currency depends on domestic and foreign interest rate differentials and on expectations about future movements in the exchange rate. Suppose the interest rate in the foreign market (England) is higher than in the domestic market (U.S.). The foreign exchange traders will buy the foreign currency (pounds) in the spot market to lend in England and sell them in the forward market in order to earn from interest differentials. It will lead to the appreciation (rise in the value) of the foreign currency (pounds) due to an increased demand for it. There will also be forward discount on it because its spot rate is higher than its forward rate. The speculators will buy the foreign currency in the forward market from traders to take advantage of the forward discount. When forward contracts mature after 3 months, the foreign exchange dealers will deliver the foreign currency (pounds) to the speculator in exchange for the domestic currency. The speculators will, in turn, sell the foreign currency (pounds) on the spot market to obtain the domestic currency in order to deliver it to the traders. Selling of the foreign currency by speculators will lead to their *depreciation*.[2]

A change in expectations also affects the spot and forward exchange rates. If speculators expect the spot rate to rise, they will buy foreign exchange in the forward market. As a result, the forward rate increases. On the contrary, if they expect the spot rate to fall, they will sell foreign exchange in the forward market. Consequently, the forward rate comes down. Thus speculation leads to the movement of the spot and forward rates together.

Speculation may be stabilising or destabilising. Speculation is stabilising when speculators buy a foreign currency with a fall in its exchange rate in the expectation that it will soon rise and, thus, earn a profit. Contrariwise, when they sell a foreign currency with a rise in its exchange rate in the expectation that it will soon fall, thereby earning a profit. The effect of such speculation is to smooth out fluctuations in the exchange rate.

Speculation is *destabilising* when speculators buy a foreign currency with a rise in the exchange rate in the expectation that it will rise further. Contrariwise, when speculators sell a foreign currency with a fall in the exchange rate in the expectation that it will fall further. Thus destabilising speculation is due only to such speculators who buy foreign currency at higher than normal rates and sell at lower than normal rates. They will not make any profits and their losses will eventually force them to stop their speculative business. The effect of destabilising speculation is to increase the amplitude of exchange rate fluctuations.

3. Arbitrage

Arbitrage means the simultaneous buying and selling of a foreign currency in two markets in order to profit from the exchange rate difference between the markets. The simultaneous purchases and sales of the foreign currency by changing supply and demand in the two markets tends to smooth out different rates. Suppose the dollar-rupee exchange rate is \$ 1 = Rs. 35 in Bombay and \$ 1 = Rs. 36 in New York. Obviously, there is an opportunity to make profits out of this difference between the two market rates. Banks will buy dollars in Bombay at Rs. 35 per dollar and sell them in New York at Rs.36 per dollar and earn Re. 1 per dollar. This will increase the supply of rupees in Bombay in relation to the demand for dollars. Consequently the exchange rate moves in favour of dollars. On the other hand, the demand for rupee will increase in relation to dollars in New York market and the exchange rate will move in favour of rupee. This process will go on until the rate in India and in New York is almost the same.

Besides, there is the *interest rate arbitrage* or *interest arbitrage.* Interest arbitrage refers to buying a foreign currency spot and selling it forward to take advantage of the higher interest rate. Interest arbitrate is riskless, because it is covered by a forward sale of the foreign currency. This is also called covered interest arbitrage.

Suppose the short-term interest rate in New York is 6% per annum while it is10% per annum in London. To take advantage of the 4% per year or 1% for 3 months interest rate in London, a U.S. arbitrageur buys dollars for pounds at the current spot rate to invest them in London for 3 months and simultaneously sells an equal amount of pounds at the forward rate (including the 1% interest he will earn) for delivery in 3 months.

So far we have not taken the spot rate and the forward rate. Suppose the spot rate is \$ 2 per pound and the forward rate is \$ 2.04. If the forward rate is higher than the spot rate, there is a *forward premium* on the pound. It is expressed as a percentage of the spot rate and is calculated with the following formula :

$$\frac{\gamma_f - \gamma_s}{\gamma_s}$$

where γ_f is the forward rate and γ_s the spot rate.

In our above example, the forward premium on the pound is

$$\frac{£2.04 - £2.00}{£2.00} = \frac{£0.04}{£2.00} = 2\% \text{ per year}$$

Thus the U.S. arbitrageur will gain 1% in interest *plus* ¼ of 2% for 3 months as forward premium on his investment in London.

If the spot rate is higher than the forward rate, it is called *forward discount.* Suppose the spot rate is £2 per pound and the forward rate £1.96 per pound, the forward discount on the pound is

$$\frac{\gamma_s - \gamma_f}{\gamma_s} = \frac{£2.00 - £1.96}{£2.00} = \frac{£0.04}{£2.00} = 2\% \text{ per year.}$$

In this situation, the U.S. arbitrageur will gain 1% in interest and loose ¼ of 2% for 3 months as forward discount on his investment in London.

If the spot rate and the forward rate are equal, the arbitrageur would have riskless interest arbitrage and make a profit of interest earned from his arbitrage operations.

There is *covered interest parity* when the interest differential is positive in favour of the foreign monetary centre and equals the forward discount on the foreign currency. In such a situation, no arbitrage will take place. But arbitrage opportunities will exist so long as the interest differential between the two monetary centres exceeds the premium of discount of the forward exchange rate. When there is an interest arbitrage margin in favour of a particular centre, it will attract lenders and repel borrowers.

EXERCISES

1. What is a foreign exchange market? Explain the structure of foreign exchange market.
2. What is a foreign exchange market? Describe the methods of making foreign payments.
3. Explain the working of spot and forward exchange markets.
4. Write notes on : hedging, speculation, arbitrage.

CHAPTER 55

Business Cycles

1. INTRODUCTION

Business cycle or trade cycle is a part of the capitalist system. It refers to the phenomenon of cyclical booms and depressions. In a business cycle, there are wave-like fluctuations in aggregate employment, income, output and price level. The term business cycle has been defined in various ways by different economists. Prof. Haberler's definition is very simple: "The business cycle in the general sense may be defined as an alternation of periods of prosperity and depression of good and bad trade," Keynes' definition in his *Treatise of Money* is more explicit : "A trade cycle is composed of periods of good trade characterised by rising prices and low unemployment percentage, altering with periods of bad trade characterised by falling prices and high unemployment percentages." Gordon's definition is precise: "Business cycles consist of recurring alternation of expansion and contraction in aggregate economic activity, the alternating movements in each direction being self-reinforcing and prevading virtually, all parts of the economy." The most acceptable definition is by Estey: "Cyclical fluctuations are characterised by alternating waves of expansion and contraction. They do not have a fixed rhythm, but they are cycles in that the phases of contraction and expansion recur frequently and in fairly similar patterns."[1]

2. CHARACTERISTICS OF BUSINESS CYCLES

Business cycles possess the following characteristics :

1. Cyclical fluctuations are wave-like movements.
2. Fluctuations are recurrent in nature.
3. They are non-periodic or irregular. In other words, the peaks and troughs do not occur at regular intervals.
4. They occur in such aggregate variables as output, income, employment and prices.
5. These variables move at about the same time in the same direction but at different rates.
6. The durable goods industries experience relatively wide fluctuations in output and employment but relatively small fluctuations in prices. On the other hand, nondurable goods industries experience relatively wide fluctuations in prices but relatively small fluctuations in output and employment.
7. Business cycles are not seasonal fluctuations such as upswings in retail trade during Diwali or Christmas.

---

1. J.A. Estey, *Business Cycles*, 1956.

8. They are not secular trends such as long-run growth or decline in economic activity.
9. Upswings and downswings are cumulative in their effects.

Thus business cycles are recurrent fluctuations in aggregate employment, income, output and price level.

3. PHASES OF A BUSINESS CYCLE

A typical cycle is generally divided into four phases : (1) expansion or prosperity or the upswing; (2) recession or upper-turning point; (3) contraction or depression or downswing; and (4) revival or recovery or lower-turning point. These phases are recurrent and uniform in the case of different cycles. But no phase has definite periodicity or time interval. As pointed out by Pigou, cycles may not be twins but they are of the same family. Like families they have *common* characteristics that are capable of description. Starting at the trough or low point, a cycle passes through a recovery and prosperity phase, rises to a peak, declines through a recession and depression phase and reaches a trough. This is shown in Figure 1 where E is the equilibrium position. We describe below these characteristics of a business cycle.

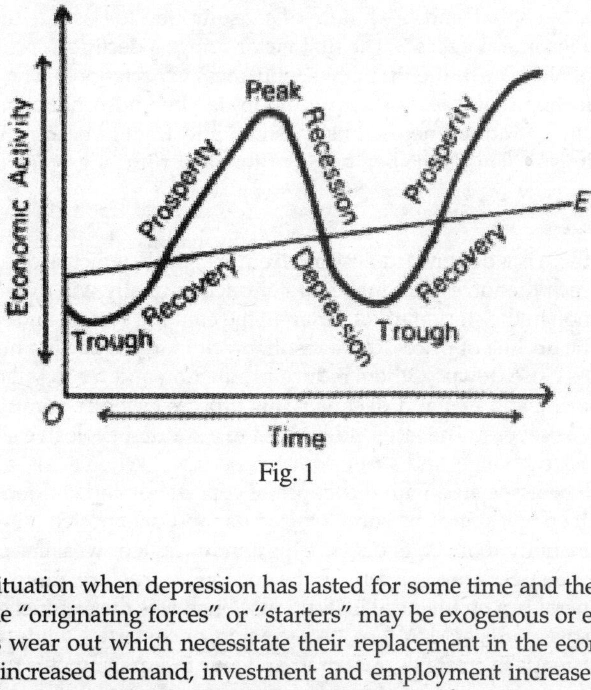

Fig. 1

RECOVERY

We start from a situation when depression has lasted for some time and the revival phase or the lower-turning point starts. The "originating forces" or "starters" may be exogenous or endogenous forces. Suppose the semi-durable goods wear out which necessitate their replacement in the economy. It leads to increased demand. To meet this increased demand, investment and employment increase. Industry begins to revive. Revival also starts in related capital goods industries. Once begun, the process of revival becomes cumulative. As a result, the levels of employment, income and output rise steadily in the economy. In the early stages of the revival phase, there is considerable *excess* or *idle* capacity in the economy so that output increases without a proportionate increase in total costs. But as time goes on, output becomes less elastic; bottlenecks appear with rising costs, deliveries are more difficult and plants may have to be expanded. Under these conditions, prices rise. Profits increase. Business expectations improve. Optimism prevails. Investment is encouraged which tends to raise the demand for bank loans. It leads to credit expansion. Thus the cumulative process of increase in investment, employment, output, income and prices feeds upon itself and becomes self-reinforcing. Ultimately, revival enters the prosperity phase.

PROSPERITY

In the prosperity phase, demand, output, employment and income are at a high level. They tend to raise prices. But wages, salaries, interest rates, rentals and taxes do not rise in proportion to the rise in prices. The gap between prices and costs increases the margin of profit. The increase of profit and the prospect of its continuance commonly cause a rapid rise in stock market values. The economy is engulfed in waves of optimism. Larger profit expectations further increase investment which is helped by liberal bank credit. Such investments are mostly in fixed capital, plant, equipment and machinery. They lead to considerable expansion in economic activity by increasing the demand for consumer goods and further raising the price level. This encourages retailers, wholesalers and manufacturers to add to inventories. In this way, the expansionary process becomes cumulative and self-reinforcing until the economy reaches a very high level of production, known as the *peak* or *boom*.

The peak or prosperity may lead the economy to over full employment and to inflationary rise in prices. It is a symptom of the end of the prosperity phase and the beginning of the recession. The seeds of recession are contained in the boom in the form of strains in the economic structure which act as brakes to the expansionary path. They are : (*i*) scarcities of labour, raw materials, etc. leading to rise in costs relative to prices; (*ii*) rise in the rate of interest due to scarcity of capital; and (*iii*) failure of consumption to rise due to rising prices and stable propensity to consume when incomes increase. The first factor brings a decline in profit margins. The second makes investments costly and along with the first, lowers business expectations. The third factor leads to the piling up of inventories indicating that sales (or consumption) lag behind production. These forces become cumulative and self-reinforcing. Entrepreneurs, businessmen and traders become over cautious and over optimism gives way to pessimism. This is the beginning of the upper turning point.

RECESSION

Recession starts when there is a downward descend from the 'peak' which is of a short duration. It marks the turning period during which the forces that make for contraction finally win over the forces of expansion. Its outward signs are liquidation in the stock market, strain in the banking system and some liquidation of bank loans, and the beginning of the decline of prices. As a result, profit margins decline further because costs start overtaking prices. Some firms close down. Others reduce production and try to sell out accumulated stocks. Investment, employment, income and demand decline. This process becomes cumulative.

Recession may be mild or severe. The latter might lead to a sudden explosive situation emanating from the banking system or the stock exchange, and a *panic* or *crisis* occurs. "When a crisis, and more particularly a panic, does occur, it seems to be associated with a collapse of confidence and sudden demands for liquidity. This crisis of nerves may itself be occasioned by some spectacular and unexpected failure. A firm or a bank, or a corporation announces its inability to meet its debts. This announcement weakens other firms and banks at a time when ominous signs of distress are appearing in the economic structure; moreover, it sets off a wave of fright that culminates in a general run on financial institutions...Such was the experience of the United States in 1873, in 1893 and in 1907." In the words of M.W. Lee, "A recession, once started, tends to build upon itself much as forest fire, once under way, tends to create its own draft and give internal impetus to its destructive ability."[2]

DEPRESSION

Recession merges into depression when there is a general decline in economic activity. There is considerable reduction in the production of goods and services, employment, income, demand and prices. The general decline in economic activity leads to a fall in bank deposits. Credit expansion stops because the business community is not willing to borrow. Bank rate falls considerably. According to Professor Estey, "This fall in active purchasing power is the fundamental background of the fall in prices, that despite the general reduction of output, characterises the depression." Thus a depression is characterised by mass unemployment;

2. M.W. Lee, Economic Fluctuations, 1955.

general fall in prices, profits, wages, interest rate, consumption, expenditure, investment, bank deposits and loans; factories close down; and construction of all types of capital goods, buildings, etc. comes to a standstill. These forces are cumulative and self-reinforcing and the economy is at the *trough.*

The trough or depression may be short-lived or it may continue at the bottom for considerable time. But sooner or later limiting forces are set in motion which ultimately tend to bring the contraction phase to end and pave the way for the revival. A cycle is thus complete.

4. CAUSES OF BUSINESS CYCLES

During the last several hundred years philosophers, economists, stock brokers and men in the street have tried to give various causes of business cycles. Some attribute them to monetary and non-monetary factors while others to psychological factors. Samuelson attributes business cycles to external and internal factors which we explain below.

1. External Factors

The external factors emphasise the causes of business cycles in the fluctuations of something outisde the economic system. Such external factors are sunspots, wars, revolutions, political events, gold discoveries, growth rate of population, migrations, discoveries and innovations. These outside factors change the level of national income by affecting either the investment or consumption component of aggregate demand. For example, a drought that destroys many crops due to sunspots may reduce the quantity of goods produced in the country and adversely affect both consumption and investment. An innovation by opening the door to new markets, raw materials, products and production processes encourages new investment in plant and equipment. Inventions of railroads, electricity, telephone, automobiles, TVs, computers, etc. have led to the burst of investments in both capital and consumer goods from time to time. Discoveries of gold, oil and natural resources have led to large scale investments. Similarly, population expansion and migrations are the causes of huge investments in both housing and other infrastructure and consumer durables. All the above noted external factors have been responsible for booms in business cycles from time to time.

Internal Factors

The internal factors relate to "mechanisms within the economic system itself which will give rise to self-generating business cycles, so that every expansion will breed recession and contraction, and every contraction will in turn breed revival and expansion, in a quasi-regular, repeating, never-ending chain."[3] Haberler divides the internal factors into monetary and non-monetary which we briefly explain.

1. Bank Credit. Hawtrey, Friedman and other monetarists regard business cycles as "a purely monetary phenomenon". According to Hawtrey, cyclical fluctuations are caused by expansion and contraction of bank credit. These in, turn, lead to changes in the demand for money on the part of producers and traders. Bank credit is the principal mean of payment. Credit is expanded or reduced by the banks by lowering or raising the rate of interest or by purchasing and selling of securities to traders. This increases or decreases the supply of money in the economy. An increase in the money supply brings about prosperity and a decrease in the money supply leads to depression.

2. Over-Saving or Under-Consumption. According to economists like Hobson, Foster and Douglas, business cycles are caused by oversaving or under-consumption. They argue that wide disparities of income and wealth lead to depression in the country. The rich people are not able to spend their entire income. So they save more and invest more in producing cnosumer goods. On the other hand, the poor people have low incomes or wages. As a result, their demand for consumer goods is low which means that there is under-consumption. According to Hobson, oversaving leads to production of consumer goods in large quantities and to a boom. But under-consumption on the part of the workers due to low wages brings a fall in the demand for consumer

3. P.A. Samuelson, *Economics,* p. 293.

goods. Stocks pile up at the current level of prices. These, in turn, lead to a fall in the prices of consumer goods and in the income of the producers. As a result, depression sets in.

3. Over-Investment. Hayek, Spiethoff, Cassel and Robertson find the root cause of business cycles in over-investment. According to Hayek, it is bank loans which lead to over-investment in capital goods industries relative to consumer goods industries that ultimately brings depression in the economy. When the total money supply exceeds the amount of voluntary savings, it leads to increase in the investment activity and ultimately to a boom. But banks cannot continue to give credit for long due to the shortage of voluntary savings. As a result, production will decline which will bring about a depression. Thus it is overinvestment in the capital goods industries which is the cause of boom and a deprssion.

4. Competition. According to Chapman, the main cause of business cycles is the existence of competition in an economy which leads to over-production and ultimately to a crises (depression). Under competitive conditions, firms produce in anticipation of demand. The profit motive attracts new firms. Production increases and boom starts. Competition and profits lead to overproduction and glunt of commodities in the market and to fall in prices. On the other hand, the race to produce more and profit more on the part of producers increases the demand for factors of production. Comptition among producers to hire more factors raises their prices. Thus costs rise which raise the prices of products. Demand falls and there is glut of commodities which eventually leads to fall in prices and to a depression.

5. Psychological Causes. According to Pigou, "The alternating waves of "over optimism" and "over pessimism" are the sole cause of the industrial fluctuations. He traces cyclical fluctuations to the tendency of businessmen to react excessively to the changing conditions of the economy. It is this tendency that causes alternating periods of over-production and under-production. Errors of optimism and pessimism are interacting forces. As soon as the business community discovers that it has made an error of optimism, it tries to correct it by making errors of pessimism. Each phase of the cycle produces a state of psychology which produces forces that bring about reversal of that psychology and in turn another reversal. These alternating waves of over-optimism (over-production) and over-pessimism (under-production), as a result of these reversals, aer the main causes of business cycles.

6. Innovations. According to Schumpeter, innovations in the structure of an economy are the source of economic fluctuations. To him, "the cause of depression is prosperity." The boom consists in the carrying out of innovation in the industrial and commercial fields. The cyclical upswing is set in motion when an innovator starts making investment in his innovation of a new product. This enables him to make profit. Soon other enrepreneurs adopts this new product in "swarm-like clusters". Innovations in one field induce innovations in related fields. There is large increase in the output of new products. Consequently, money incomes and prices rise and help to create a cumulative expansion in the economy. Overoptimism adds further to the boom. When there is glut of new products in the market, their prices fall, and profit margins of entrepreneurs are reduced. Banks ask for repayment of loans. The quantity of money is reduced and prices fall further. Some entrepreneurs cut down production and others are forced into liquidation. Thus the economy enters into depression.

7. Marginal Efficiency of Capital (MEC). According to Keynes, the cycle cnosists primarily of fluctuations in the rate of investment. And fluctuation in the rate of investment are caused mainly by fluctuations in the MEC. The MEC depends on the supply price of capital assets and their prospective yield. The supply price of capital assets being stable in the short-run, the MEC is determined by the prospective yield of capital assets being stable in the short-run, the MEC is determined by the prospective yield of capital assets. The prospective yield, in turn, depends on business expectations. Fluctuations in the rate of investment are also caused by fluctuations in the rate of interest. But it is fluctuations in the MEC which are the principal cause of cyclical fluctuations.

Conclusion. To conclude with Samuelson, business cycles are caused both by external and internal factors. The economic system responds to fluctuations in external factors according to its internal factors, and vice versa.

5. EFFECTS OF BUSINESS CYCLES

Business cycles have both good and bad effects depending upon whether the economy is passing through a phase of prosperity or depression.

In the *prosperity* phase, "the real income consumed, real income produced and the level of employment are high or rising and there are no idle or unemployed workers or very few of either." There is general increase in economic activity : aggregate output, demand, employment and income are at a high level. Prices are rising. Profits are increasing. Stock markets are rapidly reaching new heights. Investments are increasing with liberal bank credit. This entire process is cumulative and self-reinforcing.

But different sections of the society are affected differently during the prosperity phase. The landless, factory and agricultural workers and middle classes suffer because their wages and salaries are more or less fixed but the prices of commodities rise continuously. They become more poor. On the other hand, businessmen, traders, industrialists, real estate holders, speculators, landlords, shareholders and others with variable incomes gain. Thus the rich become richer and the poor poorer.

The social effects are also bad. Lured by profit, there is hoarding, black-marketing, adulteration, production of substandard goods, speculation, etc. Corruption spreads in every walk of life.

When the economy is nearing the *full employment level* of resources, the ill-effects on production start appearing. Rising prices of raw materials and increase in wages raise costs of production. As a result, profit margins decline. There is rise in interest rates due to scarcity of capital which makes investment costly. These two factors lower business expectations. Lastly, the demand for consumer goods does not rise due to inflationary rise in prices. This leads to piling up of inventories (stocks) with producers and traders. Thus sales lag behind production. There is decline is prices. Producers, businessmen and traders become pessimists and the recession starts.

During *recession,* profit margins decline further because costs start rising more than prices. Some firms close down. Others reduce production and try to sell accumulated stocks. Investment, output, employment, income, demand and prices decline further. This process becomes cumulative and recession merges into depression.

During a *depression*, there is mass unemployment. Prices, profits and wages are at their lowest levels. Demand for goods and services is the minimum. Investment, bank deposits and bank loans are negligible. Construction of all types of capital goods, buidlings, etc. is at a standstill. There is mass unemployment in the economy. The government revenues from direct and indirect taxes decline. The real burden of the debt increases. The economic development of the country suffers.

6. THEORIES OF BUSINESS CYCLES

In fact, the causes of business cycles given above are based on the theories of business cycles propounded by economists from time to time. We discuss some of the important theories as under.

1. Hawtrey's Monetary Theory

According to Prof. R.G. Hawtrey,[4] "The trade cycle is a purely monetary phenomenon." It is changes in the flow of monetary demand on the part of businessmen that lead to prosperity and depression in the economy. He opines that non-monetary factors like strikes, floods, earthquakes, droughts, wars, etc. may at best cause a partial depression, but not a general depression. In actuality, cyclical fluctuations are caused by expansion and contraction of bank credit which, in turn, lead to variations in the flow of monetary demand on the part of producers and traders. Bank credit is the principal means of payment in the present times. Credit is expanded or reduced by the banking system by lowering or raising the rate of interest or by purchasing or selling securities to merchants. This increases or decreases the flow of money in the economy and thus brings about prosperity or depression.

The expansion phase of the trade cycle starts when banks increase credit facilities. They are provided by reducing the lending rate of interest and by purchasing securities. These encourage borrowings on the part of merchants and producers. This is because they are very sensitive to changes in the rate of interest. So when credit becomes cheap, they borrow from banks in order to increase their stocks or inventories. For this, they

4. R.G. Hawtrey, *Trade and Credit, 1928; The Art of Central Banking.* 1932.

place larger orders with producers who, in turn, employ more factors of production to meet the increasing demand. Consequently, money incomes of the owners of factors of production increase, thereby increasing expenditure on goods. The merchants find their stocks being exhausted. They place more orders with producers. This leads to further increase in productive activity, income, outlay, and demand, and a further depletion of stocks of merchants. According to Hawtrey, "Increased activity means increased demand, and increased demand means increased activity. A vicious circle is set up, a cumulative expansion of productive activity."

As the cumulative process of expansion continues, producers quote higher and higher prices. Higher prices induce traders to borrow more in order to hold still larger stocks of goods so as to earn more profits. Thus optimism encourages borrowing, borrowing increases sales, and sales raise optimism.

According to Hawtrey, prosperity cannot continue limitlessly. It comes to an end when banks stop credit expansion. Banks refuse to lend further because their cash funds are depleted and the money in circulation is absorbed in the form of cash holdings by consumers. Another factor is the export of gold to other countries when imports exceed exports as a result of high prices of domestic goods. These factors force the banks to raise interest rates and refuse to lend. Rather, they ask the business community to repay their loans. This starts the recessionary phase.

In order to repay bank loans, businessmen start selling their stocks. This sets the process of falling prices. They also cancel orders with producers. The latter curtail their productive activities due to fall in demand. These, in turn, lead to reduction in the demand for factors of production. There is unemployment. Incomes fall. Falling demand, prices and incomes are the signals for depression. Unable to repay bank loans, some firms go into liquidation, thus forcing banks to contract credit further. Thus the entire process becomes cumulative and the economy is forced into depression.

According to Hawtrey, the process of recovery is very slow and halting. As depression continues, traders repay bank loans by selling their stocks at whatever prices they can. As a result, money flows into the reserves of banks and funds increase with banks. Even though the bank rate is very low, there is "credit deadlock" which prevents businessmen to borrow from banks due to pessimism in economic activity. This deadlock can be broken by following a cheap money policy by the central bank which will ultimately bring about recovery in the economy.

Its Criticisms

Monetarists like Friedman have supported Hawtrey's theory. But the majority of economists have criticised him for over-emphasising monetary factors to the neglect of non-monetary factors in explaining cyclical fluctuations. Some of the points of criticism are discussed below.

(1) Credit not the Cause of Cycle. None can deny that expansion of credit leads to the expansion of business activity. But Hawtrey believes that an expansion of credit leads to a boom. This is not correct because the former is not the cause of the latter. As pointed out by Pigou, "Variations in the bank money supply is a part of the business cycle, it is not the cause of it." At the bottom of the depression, credit is easily available. Even then, it fails to bring a revival. Similarly, contraction of credit cannot bring about a depression. At best, it can create conditions for that. Thus expansion or contraction of credit cannot originate either boom or depression in the economy.

(2) Money Supply cannot Continue a Boom or Delay a Depression. Haberler has criticised Hawtrey for "his contention that the reason for the breakdown of the boom is always a monetary one and that prosperity could be prolonged and depression stayed off indefinitely if the money suply were inexhaustible."[5] But the fact is that even if the supply of money is inexhaustible in the country, neither prosperity can be continued indefinitely nor depression can be delayed idefinitely.

(3) Traders do not Depend Only on Bank Credit. Hamberg[6] has criticised Hawtrey for the role assigned to wholesalers in his analysis. The kingpin in Hawtrey's theory is the trader or the wholesaler who gets credit from banks and starts the upturn or vice-versa. In actuality, traders do not depend exclusively on bank credit

5. G. Haberler, *Business Cycles,* pp. 27-28.
6. D. Hamberg, *Business Cycles,*1937.

but they finance business through their own accumulated funds and borrowing from private sources.

(4) Traders do not React to changes in Interest Rates. Further, Hamberg also does not agree with Hawtrey that traders react to changes in interest rates. According to Hamberg, traders are likely to react favourably to a reduction in the interest rate only if they think that the reduction is permanent. But they do not react favourably during the depression phase because traders expect a further reduction every time the interest rate is reduced. On the other hand, if traders finance their stocks with their own funds, interest rate changes will have little effect on their purchases.

(5) Factors other than Interest Rate More Important. It is an exaggeration to say that the decisions of traders regarding accumulation or depletion of stocks are solely governed by changes in interest rate. As a matter of fact, factors other than the rate of interest are more important in influencing such decisions. They are business expectations, price changes, cost of storage, etc.

(6) Inventory Investments do not Produce True Cycles. Hamberg further points out that in Hawtrey's theory cumulative movements in economic activity are the result of changes in stocks of goods. But fluctuations in inventroy investment can at best produce minor cycles which are not cycles in the true sense of the term.

(7) Does not Explain Periodicity of Cycle. The theory also fails to explain the periodicity of the cyle.

(8) Ignores Non-Monetary Factors. Hawtrey's theory is incomplete because it emphasises only monetary factors and totally ignores such non-monetary factors as innovations, capital stock, multiplier-accelerator interaction, etc.

2. Hayek's Monetary Over-Investment Theory

F.A. Hayek formulated his monetary over-investment theory of trade cycle. He explained his theory on the basis of Wicksell's distinction between the natural interest rate and the market interest rate. The natural rate of interest is that rate at which the demand for loanable funds equals the supply of voluntary savings. On the other hand, the market rate of interest is the money rate which prevails in the market and is determined by the demand and supply of money. According to Hayek, so long as the natural rate of interest equals the market rate of interest, the economy remains in the state of equilibrium and full employment . Trade cycles in the economy are caused by inequality between market and natural interest rates. When the market interest rate is less than the nautral rate, there is prosperity in the economy. On the contrary, when the market interest rate is more than the natural rate, the economy is in depression.

According to this thoery, prosperity begins when the market rate of interest is less than the natural rate of interest. In such a situation, the demand for investment funds is more than the supply of available savings. The demand for investment funds is met by the increase in the supply of money. As a result, the interest rate falls. Low interest rate induces producers to get more loans from banks. The producers get more loans to invest for the production of more capital goods. They adopt capital-intensive methods for producing more of capital goods. As a result, production costs fall and profits increase. The production process becomes very lengthy with the adoption of capital-intensive methods. This has the effect of increasing the prices of capital goods in comparison to consumer goods. There being full employment in the economy, they transfer factors of the production from consumer goods sector to capital goods sector. Consequently, the production of consumer goods falls, their prices increase and their consumption decreases. Forced savings increase with the fall in consumption which are invested for the production of capital goods. This leads to increase in their production. On the other hand, with increase in the prices of consumer goods, their producers earn more profits. Induced by high profits, they try to produce more. For this, they pay higher remuneration to factors of production in comparison with the producers of capital goods. There being competition between the two sectors, prices of factors and prices in the economy continue to rise. This leads to the atmosphere of prosperity in the country and monetary over-investment on factors spreads the boom.

According to Hayek, when the prices of factors are rising continously, the rise in production costs bring fall in profits of producers. The producers of capital goods invest less in the expectation of loss in the future. Consequently, the natural interest rate falls. Simultaneously, banks impose restrictions on giving loans to them. With low profits and reduction in loans, producers reduce the production of capital goods and adopt labour-intensive production processes. There is less investment in capital goods. Production process being small and labour-intensive, the demand for money is reduced, which increases the market interest rate which is more than the natural interest rate. Producers transfer the factors from the production of capital goods to that of consumer goods. But more factors cannot be used in the consumer goods sector as compared to the capital goods sector. This leads to fall in the prices of factors and resources become unemployed. Thus, with the continuous reduction in the prices of goods and factors in the economy, a long period of depression and unemployment begins.

According to Hayek, when the fall in prices comes to an end during depression, banks begin to raise the supply of money which reduces the market interest rate below the natural interest rate. This encourages investment and the process of revival begins in the economy.

Its Criticisms

The monetary over-investment theory of Hayek has been criticised on the following counts:

(1) Narrow Assumption of Full Employment. This theory is based on the assumption of full employment according to which capital goods are produced by reducing consumer goods. In reality, there is no full employment of resources. If resources remain unutilised, the expansion of both the capital goods sector and consumer goods sector may occur simultaneously. In such a situation, there is no need of transferring resources from one sector to the other.

(2) Unrealistic Assumption of Equilibrium. The assumption of this theory that in the beginning savings and investment are in equilibrium in the economy and the banking system destroys this equilibrium is unrealistic. This is because the equilibrium may deviate due to both internal and external reasons.

(3) Interest Rate not the only Determinant. Hayek assumes changes in the rate of interest as the cause of fluctuations in the economy. This is not correct because besides changes in the rate of interest, the expectations of profit, innovation, invention, etc. also affect trade cycles.

(4) Undue Importance to Forced Savings. Prof. Strigl has criticised this theory for giving undue importance to forced savings. According to him, when people with fixed incomes reduce their consumption with the increase in prices and the high income groups also reduce their consumption to the same extent, savings will not be forced but voluntary.

(5) Investment does not fall with Increase in Consumer Goods. Hayek argues that with the production of consumer goods and the increase in profits from them, investment falls in capital goods. This is not correct. According to Keynes, the marginal productivity of capital increases with the increase in profits of consumer goods. As a result, investment in capital goods also increases and does not fall.

(6) Incomplete Theory. Hayek's theory is incomplete because it does not explain the various phases of trade cycle.

3. Schumpeter's Innovations Theory

The innovations theory of trade cycles is associated with the name of Joseph Schumpeter.[7] According to Schumpeter, innovations in the structure of an economy are the source of economic fluctuations. Trade cycles are the outcome of economic development in a capitalist society. Schumpeter accepts Juglar's statement that "the cause of depression is prosperity," and then gives his own view about the originating cause of the cycle.

Schumpeter's approach involves the development of his model into two stages. The first stage deals with the initial impact of innovation and the second stage follows through reactions to the original impact of innovation.

The first approximation starts with the economic system in equilibrium with every factor fully employed. Every firm is in equilibrium and producing efficiently with its costs equal to its receipts. Product prices are equal to both average and marginal costs. Profits and interest rates are zero. There are no savings and investments. This equilibrium is characterised by Schumpeter as the "circular flow" which continues to repeat itself in the same manner year after year, similar to the circulation of the blood in an animal organism. In the circular flow, the same products are produced every year in the same manner.

7. J.A. Schumpeter, *Business Cycles,* 1939.

Schumpeter's theory starts with the breaking up of the circular flow by an innovation in the form of a new product by an entrepreneur for earning profit.

By innovation Schumpeter means "such changes in the production of goods as cannot be affected by infinitesimal steps or variations on the margin." An innovation may consist of : (1) the introduction of a new product; (2) the introduction of a new method of production; (3) the opening up of a new market; (4) the conquest of a new source of raw materials or semi-manufactured goods; and (5) the carrying out of the new organisations of an industry. Innovations are not inventions. According to Schumpeter, there is nothing that can explain that inventions occur in a cyclical manner. It is the introduction of a new product and the continual improvements in the existing ones that are the principal causes of business cycles.

Schumpeter assigns the role of an innovator not to the capitalist but to an entrepreneur. The entrepreneur is not a man of ordinary ability but one who introduces something entirely new. He does not provide funds but directs their use.

To perform his economic function, the entrepreneur requires two things: first, the existence of technical knowledge in order to produce new products, and second, the power of disposal over the factors of production in the form of bank credit. According to Schumpeter, a reservoir of untapped technical knowledge exists in a capitalist society which he can make use of. Therefore, credit is essential for breaking the circular flow.

The innovating entrepreneur is financed by expansion of bank credit. Since investment in an innovation is risky, he must pay interest on it. With his newly acquired funds, the innovator starts bidding away resources from other industries. Money incomes increase. Prices begin to rise, thereby stimulating further investment. The new innovation starts producing goods and there is an increased flow of goods in the economy. Consequently, supply exceeds demand. Prices and cost of production of goods start declining until recession sets in. Because of the low prices of goods, producers are not willing to expand production. During this period of recession, credit, prices and interest rate decline but total output is likely to average larger than in the preceding prosperity.

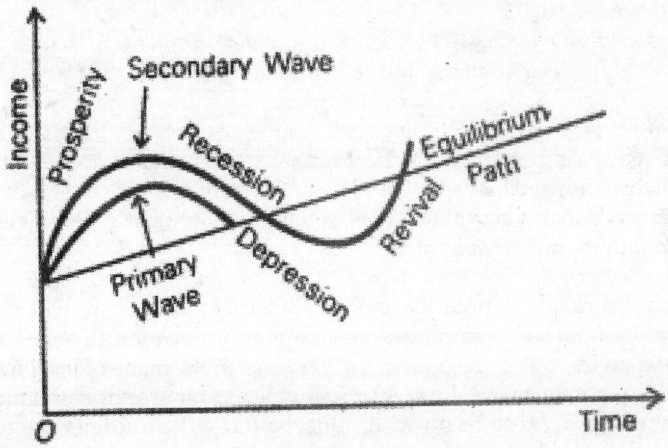

Fig. 2

Thus Schumpeter's first approximation consists of a two-phase cycle. The economy starts at the equilibrium state, rises to a peak and then starts downward into a recession and continues till the new equilibrium is reached. This new equilibrium will be at a higher level of income than the initial equilibrium because of the innovation which started the cycle. This is shown as the "Primary Wave" in Figure 2.

The second approximation of Schumpeter follows through the reaction of the impact of original innovation. Once the original innovation becomes successful and profitable, other entrepreneurs follow it in "swarm-like clusters." Innovation in one field induces innovations in related fields. Consequently, money incomes and prices rise and help to create a cumulative expansion throughout the economy. With the increase in the purchasing power of consumers, the demand for the products of old industries increases in relation to supply.

Prices rise further. Profits increase and old industries expand by borrowing from the banks. It induces a *secondary* wave of credit inflation which is superimposed on the primary wave of innovation. Overoptimism and speculation add further to the boom. After a period of gestation, the new products start appearing in the market displacing the old products and enforcing a process of liquidation, readjustment and absorption.

The demand for the old products is decreased. Their prices fall. The old firms contract output and some are even forced to run into liquidation. As the innovators start repaying bank loans out of profits, the quantity of money is decreased and prices tend to fall. Profits decline. Uncertainty and risks increase. The impulse for innovation is reduced and eventually comes to an end. Depression sets in, and the painful process of readjustment to the "point of previous neighbourhood of equilibrium" begins. Ultimately, the natural forces of recovery bring about a revival.

Schumpeter believes in the existence of Kondratieff long wave of upswings and downswings in economic activity. Each long wave upswing is brought about by an innovation which leads to abundance of goods for the masses. Once the upswing ends, the long wave downswing begins.

Thus the second approximation of Schumpeter's theory of trade cycle develops into a four phase cycle with the recession which was the second phase in the first approximation continuing downward to give the depression phase. This extension of cycle is followed by a period of revival which continues till the equilibrium level is reached. This is shown as the "Secondary Wave" in Figure 2.

Its Criticisms

Schumpeter's treatment of the different phases and turning points of the cycle is novel and different from all other economists. But it is not free from certain criticisms.

(1) Innovator not Necessary for Innovations. Schumpeter's analysis is based on the innovator. Such persons were to be found in the 18th and 19th centuries who made innovations. But now all innovations form part of the functions of joint stock companies. Innovations are regarded as the routine of industrial concerns and do not require an innovator as such.

(2) Innovations not the Only Cause of Cycles. Schumpeter's contention that cyclical fluctuations are due to innovations is not correct. As a matter of fact, trade cycles may be due to psychological, natural or financial causes.

(3) Bank Credit not the Only Source of Funds. Schumpeter gives too much importance to bank credit in his theory. Bank credit may be important in the short run when industrial concerns get credit facilities from banks. But in the long run when the need for capital funds is much greater, bank credit is insufficient. For this, business houses have to float fresh shares and debentures in the capital market. Schumpeter's theory is weak in that it does not take these factors into consideration.

(4) Innovation financed through Voluntary Savings does not produce a Cycle. Critics point out that if an innovation is financed through voluntary savings or internal funds, there will not be an inflationary rise in prices. Consequently, in an underemployed economy an innovation financed through voluntary savings might not generate a cycle.

(5) Full Employment Assumption Unrealistic. Schumpeter's analysis is based on the unrealistic assumption of full employment of resources to begin with. But the fact is that at the time of revival, the resources are unemployed. Thus the introduction of an innovation may not lead to the withdrawal of labour and other resources from old industries. Thus the competitive impact of an innovation would not increase costs and prices. Since full employment is an exception rather than the rule. Thus Schumpeter's theory is not a correct explanation of trade cycles.

4. Keynes's Theory

The Keynesian theory of the trade cycle8 is an integral part of his theory of income, output and employment. Trade cycles are periodic fluctuations of income, output and employment. Keynes regards the trade cycle as mainly due to "a cyclical change in the marginal efficiency of capital, though complicated and often aggravated by associated changes in the other significant short-period variables of the economic system."

According to Keynes, the principal cause of depression and unemployment is the lack of aggregate demand. Revival can be brought about by raising aggregate demand which, in turn, can be raised by increasing consumption and/or investment. Since consumption is stable during the short-run, revival is possible by increasing investment. Similarly, the main cause of the downturn is reduction in investment. Thus in the Keynesian explanation of the trade cycle, "the cycle consists primarily of fluctuations in the rate of investment. And fluctuations in the rate of investment are caused mainly by fluctuations in the marginal efficiency of capital."9 The MEC (marginal efficiency of capital) depends on the supply price of capital assets and their prospective yield. Since the supply price of capital assets is stable in the short-run, the MEC is determined by the perspective yield of capital assets, which, in turn, depends on business expectations. Fluctuations in the rate of investment are also caused by fluctuations in the rate of interest. But Keynes gives more importance to fluctuations in the MEC as the principal cause of cyclical fluctuations.

To explain the course of the Keynesian cycle, we start with the expansion phase. During the expansions phase, the MEC is high. Business are optimistic. There is rapid increase in the rate of investment. Consequently, output, employment and income increase. Every increase in investment leads to a multiple increase in income via the multiplier effect. This cumculative process of rising investment, income and employment continues till the boom is reached.

As the boom progresses, there is a tendency for the MEC to fall due to two reasons. First, as more capital goods are being produced steadily, the current yield on them decline. Second, at the same time the current costs of new capital goods rise due to shortage as bottlenecks of materials and labour.

During the downturn, investment falls due to a fall in the MEC and rise in the rate of interest. This leads to a cumulatie decline in employment and income via the reverse operation of the multiplier. Further, the fall in the MEC may shift the consumption function downward thereby hastening the depression. Keynes attaches more importance to the sudden collapse of the MEC than to a rise in the rate of interst as an explanation of the downturn of the cycle leading to the crises and the depression.

Unlike the sudden collapse of the economic system, the revival takes time. It depends on factors which bring about the recovery of the MEC. "The time which must elapse before recovery begins, depends partly upon the magnitude of the normal rate of growth of the economy and partly upon the length of life of capital goods. The shorter the length of life of durable assets, the shorter the depression. And also, the more rapid the rate of growth, the shorter the depression." Another factor which governs the duration of depression is the "carrying costs of surplus stocks." According to Keynes, the carrying cost of surplus stocks during the depression is seldom less than 10 per cent per annum. So for a few years disinvestment in stocks will continue till the surplus stocks are exhausted. Optimism takes the place of pessimism. The MEC increases. Fresh investment starts taking place. Revival has started.

Its Criticisms

Keynes's theory of the trade cycle is superior to the earlier theories because "it is more than a theory of the business cycle in the sense that it offers a general explanation of the level of employment, quite independently of the cyclical nature of changes in employment."10 However, critics are not lacking in pointing out its weakness.

(1) Overemphasis on the Role of Expectations. Keynes has been criticised for his analysis of business cycle based on expectations. In fact, he overemphasised the role of expectations in influencing the MEC. According to Hart, Keynes relied on "convention" for forecasting changes in business expectations. The reliance on the conventional hypothesis makes Keynes' concept of expectations superfluous and unrealistic.

(2) Psychological Theory. Keynes considers the trade cycle as mainly due to fluctations in the MEC. The MEC, in turyn, determines the rate of investment. And investment decisions, depend upon the psychology of businessmen or producers. Thus Keynes' theory is not much different from Pigou's psychological theory of the trade cycle.

(3) Explanation of Crises Wrong. Keynes attributes the downturn to the sudden collapse in the MEC. Accroding to Hazlitt, the term MEC being vague and ambiguous, "Keynes' explanation of the crises of the marginal efficiency of capital is either a useless truism or an obvious error."

(4) Incomplete Theory. Another weakness of Keynes' theory of the trade cycle is that some of its variables such as expectations, MEC and investment cannot explain the different phases of the cycle. In the words of Dillard, "It is less than a complete theory of the business cycle because it makes no attempt to give a detailed account of the various phases of the cycle."

(5) Not Based on Empirical Data. Saulnier criticises Keynes's Notes on the Trade Cycle for lacking in factual proof. According to him, Keynes makes no attempt to test any of his deductions with facts. Dillard also points toward this defect when he writes that Keynes "does not examine closely the empirical data of cyclical fluctuations."

(6) One-Sided Theory. One of the serious omissions of Keynes's theory of the trade cycle is the acceleration principle. This made his theory one-sided because his explanation centres round the principle of multiplier. As pointed out by Sir John Hicks, "The theory of acceleration and the theory of multiplier are two sides of the theory of fluctuations, just as the theory of demand and the theory of supply are the two sides of the theory of value."

7. MEASURES TO CONTROL BUSINESS CYCLES OR STABILISATION POLICIES

Various measures have been suggested and put into practice from time to time to control fluctuations in an economy. They aim at stabilising economic activity so as to avoid the ill-effects of booms and depressions. The following three measures are adopted for this purpose.

1. Monetary Policy

Monetary policy as a method to control business fluctuations is operated by the central bank of a country. The central bank adopts a number of methods to control the quantity and quality of credit. To control the expansion of money supply during a *boom*, it raises its bank rate, sells securities in the open market, raises the reserve ratio, and adopts a number of selective credit control measures such as raising margin requirements and regulating consumer credit. Thus the central bank adopts a *dear money policy*. Borrowings by business and trade become dearer, difficult and selective. Efforts are made to control excess money supply in the economy.

To control a *recession or depression*, the central bank follows an *easy* or *cheap* monetary policy by increasing the reserves of commercial banks. It reduces the bank rate and interest rates of banks. It buys securities in the open market. It lowers margin requirements on loans and encourages banks to lend more to consumers, businessmen, traders, etc.

Limitations of Monetary Policy

But monetary policy is not so effective as to control boom and depression. If the boom is due to cost-push factors, it may not be effective in controlling inflation, aggregate demand, output, income and employment. So far as depression is concerned, the experience of the Great Depression of 1930s tells us that when there is pessimism among businessmen, the success of monetary policy is practically nil. In such a situation, they do not have any inclination to borrow even when the interest rate is very low. Similarly, consumers who are faced with reduced incomes and unemployment cut down their consumption expenditure. Neither the central bank nor the commercial banks are able to induce businessmen and consumers to raise the aggregate demand. Thus the success of monetary policy to control economic fluctuations is severely limited.

2. Fiscal Policy

Monetary policy alone is not capable of controlling business cycles. It should, therefore, be supplemented by compensatory fiscal policy. Fiscal measures are highly effective for controlling excessive government expenditure, personal consumption expenditure, and private and public investment during a boom. On the other hand, they help in increasing government expenditure, personal consumption expenditure and private and public investment during a depression.

Policy during Boom. The following measures are adopted during a boom. During a boom, the government tries to *reduce unnecessary expenditure* on non-development activities in order to reduce its demand for goods and services. This also puts a check on private expenditure which is dependent on the government demand for goods and services. But it is difficult to cut government expenditure. Moreover, it is not possible to distinguish between essential and non-essential government expenditure. Therefore, this measure is supplemented by taxation.

To cut personal expenditure, the government *raises* the *rates* of personal, corporate and commodity *taxes*.

The government also follows the policy of having a *surplus budget* when the government revenues exceed expenditures. This is done by increasing the tax rates or reduction in government expenditure or both. This tends to reduce income and aggregate demand through the reverse operation of the multiplier.

Another fiscal measure which is usually adopted is to *borrow* more from the public which has the effect of reducing the money supply with the public. Further, the repayment of public debt should be stopped and postponed to some future date when the economy stabilises.

Policy during Depression. During a depression, the government increases public expenditure, reduces taxes and adopts a budget deficit policy. These measures tend to raise aggregate demand, output, income, employment and prices. An increase in public expenditure increases the aggregate demand for goods and services and leads to increase in income via the multiplier. The public expenditure is made on such public works as roads, canals, dams, parks, schools, hospitals and other construction works. They create demand for labour and the products of private construction industries and helps in reviving them. The government also increases its expenditure on such relief measures as unemployment insurance, and other social security measures in order to stimulate the demand for consumer goods industries. Borrowing by the government to finance budget deficits utilises idle money lying with the banks and financial institutions for investment purposes.

Conclusion. The effectiveness of anti-cyclical fiscal policy depends upon proper timing of policy action and the nature and volume of public works and their planning.

3. Direct Controls

The aim of direct controls is to ensure proper allocation of resources for the purpose of price stability. They are meant to affect strategic points of the economy. They affect particular consumers and producers. They are in the form of rationing, licensing, price and wage controls, export duties, exchange controls, quotas, monopoly control, etc. They are more effective in overcoming bottlenecks and shortages arising from inflationary pressures. Their success depends on the existence of an efficient and honest administration. Otherwise, they lead to black marketing, corruption, long queues, speculation, etc. Therefore, they should be resorted to only in emergencies like war, crop failures and hyper-inflation.

Conclustion

Of the various instruments of stabilisation policy, no single method is sufficient to control cyclical fluctuations. Therefore, all methods should be used simultaneously. This is because monetary policy is easy to apply but less effective while fiscal measures and direct controls are difficult to operate but are more effective. Since cyclical fluctuations are inherent in the capitalist system, they cannot be eliminated completely. Some fluctuations may be beneficial for economic growth and others may be undesirable. Stabilisation policy should, therefore, control undesirable fluctuations. We conclude with Keynes, "The right remedy for the trade cycles is not to be found in abolishing booms and thus keeping us permanently in a semi-slump; but in abolishing slumps and thus keeping us permanently in a quasi-boom."

EXERCISE

1. What do you mean by a business cycle? Explain its various phases.
2. What is a business cycle? Explain the main causes of business cycles.
3. 'The trade cycle is a purely monetary phenomenon." Discuss.

PART FIVE

INTERNATIONAL MONETARY SYSTEM

CHAPTER 56

The International Monetary Fund

1. ORIGIN OF IMF

The International Monetary Fund (IMF), also called the Fund, is an international monetary institution established by 44 nations under the Bretton Woods Agreement of July 1944. The principal aim was to avoid the economic mistakes of the 1920s and 1930s. The attempts of many countries to return to the old gold system after the First World War failed miserably. The World Depression of the thirties forced every country to abandon the gold standard. This led to the adoption of purely nationalistic policies whereby almost every country imposed trade restrictions, exchange controls and resorted to exchange depreciation in order to encourage its exports. This, further, brought a marked decline in world trade and extension of depression. It was against this background that 44 nations assembled at the United Nations Monetary and Financial Conference at Bretton Woods, New Hampshire (USA) from July 1 to July 22, 1944. Thus the IMF was established to promote economic and financial co-operation among its members in order to facilitate the expansion and balanced growth of world trade. It started functioning from March 1, 1947. In June 1996, the Fund had 181 members.

OBJECTIVES OF THE FUND

The fundamental purposes and objectives of the Fund had been laid down in Article 1 of the original Articles of Agreement and they have been upheld in the two amendments that were made in 1969 and 1978 to its basic Charter. They provide the framework within which the Fund functions. They are as under :

1. To promote international monetary co-operation through a permanent institution which provides the machinery for consumption and collaboration in international monetary problems.
2. To facilitate the expansion and balanced growth of international trade and to contribute thereby to the promotion and maintenance of high levels of employment and real income and to the development of the productive resources of all members as primary objectives of economic policy.
3. To promote exchange stability, to maintain orderly exchange arrangements among members, and to avoid competitive exchange depreciation.
4. To assist in the establishment of a multilateral system of payments in respect of current transactions

between member and in the elimination of foreign exchange restrictions which hamper the growth in the world trade.

5. To lend confidence to members by making the Fund's resources available to them under adequate safeguards, thus providing them with opportunity to correct maladjustments in their balance of payments without resorting to measures destructive of national or international prosperity.
6. In accordance with the above, to shorten the duration and lessen the degree of disequilibrium in the international balance of payments of members.

OGRANISATION AND STRUCTURE OF THE FUND

The Second Amendment of the Articles of Agreement made important changes in the organisation and structure of the Fund. As such, the structure of the Fund consists of a Board of Governors, an Executive Board, a Managing Director, a Council and a staff with its headquarters in Washington, U.S.A. There are ad hoc and standing committees appointed by the Board of Governors and the Executive Board. There is also an Interim Committee (now the International Monetary and Financial Committee—IMFC) appointed by the Board of Governors. The Board of Governors and the Executive Board are decision-making organs of the Fund. They exercise powers and take decisions that are binding on members and the Fund. The Board of Governors is at the top in the structure of the Fund. It is composed of one Governor and one alternate Governor appointed by each member. Normally, a member appoints its minister of finance or the Governor of its central bank as its Governor. The alternate Governor can participate in the meetings of the Board but has the power to vote only in the absence of the Governor.

The Board of Governors which has now 24 members, meets annually in which details of the Fund activities for the previous year are presented. The annual meeting also takes a few decisions with regard to the policies of the Fund. Special meetings can be convened by any of the five members having 25 per cent of the total voting rights. As a matter of practice, the majority of decision-making powers of the Board of Governors have been delegated to the Board of Executive Directors such a decisions on access by the members of the Fund's resources, decisions on charges and remuneration and the review of consultations between the Fund and its members.

The Executive Board has 21 members at present. Five Executive Directors are appointed by the five members (USA, UK, W. Germany, France and Japan) having the largest quotas. Saudi Arabia has appointed a sixth Executive Director by being one of the two largest contributors to the Fund. 15 Executive Directors are elected at intervals of two years by the remaining members according to the constituencies on a roughly geographical basis.

There is a *Managing Director* of the Fund who is elected by the Executive Directors. He is usually a politician or an important international official. He is the non-voting Chairman of the Executive Board. Besides acting as the Chairman of the Executive Board, the Managing Director is the head of the Fund staff and is responsible for its organisation, appointment and dismissal.

The *Executive Board* is the most powerful organ of the Fund and exercises vast powers conferred on it by the Articles of Agreement and delegated to it by the Board of Governors. So its powers relate to all Fund activities, including its regulatory, supervisory and financial activities. Any major change in the IMF procedure requires 85 per cent majority in the Executive Board. Hence the discretion lies with the US and EEC as they have 22 per cent and 27 per cent of the voting strength respectively. The Executive Board is in the continuous session and meets several times a week.

The Interim Committee (now IMFC) was established in October 1974 to advise the Board of Governors on supervising the management and adaptation of the international monetary system in order to avoid disturbances that might threaten it. It currently has 22 members.

The Development Committee was also established in October 1974 and consists of 22 members. It advises and reports to the Board of Governors on all aspects of the transfer of real resources to developing countries and makes suggestions for their implementation.

QUOTAS AND THEIR FIXATION

The Fund has General Account based on quotas allocated to its members. When a country joins the Fund, it is assigned a quota that governs the size of its subscription, its voting power, and its drawing rights. At the time of the formation of the IMF, each member was required to pay 25 per cent of its quota in gold or 10 per cent of its net official holdings of gold and US dollars whichever was less. Under the Second Amendment effective 1 April 1978, 25 per cent of a member's quota payable in gold was substituted by SDRs or usable currencies. The remaining 75 per cent of quota was to be furnished in the country's own currency. But it was kept in the country's central bank. The practice of keeping gold reserves with the Fund was discontinued from April 1978 and the Fund has been delinked from the gold since then. Now a member country is allowed to maintain the value of its currency and quota in terms of the Special Drawing Rights (SDRs).

In order to meet the financial requirements of the Fund, the quotas are reviewed every five years and are raised from time to time. But quotas can only be raised by a resolution of the majority of 85 per cent of the total voting power of the Fund's members. When the Fund started operation in March 1947, the total quotas were 7.6 billion dollars which had been increased to SDR 146 billion in April, 1994 with the Tenth General Review of Quotas. This increase was 50% of members quotas. With the Eleventh Review of Quotas effective March 1998, the quotas were raised by 45% to SDR 212 billion.

Thus a member country's quota determines its subscription to the Fund, its relative voting power, allocation of SDRs and access to Fund's resources. A member's voting power is based on one vote for each SDR 100,000 of quota in addition to the basic votes of 250 for each member. When a country becomes the member of the Fund, it is allocated a quota which raises the total resources of the IMF.

FUNCTIONS OF THE FUND

The IMF operates in such a way as to fulfil its objectives as laid down in the Bretton Woods Articles of Agreements. It is the Fund's duty to see that these provisions are observed by member countries. Some of the provisions of the original Articles such as relating to exchange rates have become obsolete due to international monetary events. Accordingly the Fund has amended its Articles of Agreement to make appropriate adjustments.

The Fund is regarded "as the guardian of good conduct" in the sphere of balance of payments. It aims at reducing tariffs and other trade restrictions by the member countries. Articles VII of the Charter provides that no member shall, without the approval of the Fund, impose restrictions on the making of payments or engage in discriminatory currency arrangements or multiple currency practices. It is the functions of the Fund to have a surveillance of the policies being adopted by the member countries.

The Fund also renders technical advice to its members on monetary and fiscal policies. It conducts research studies and publishes them. It provides technical experts to member countries having BOP difficulties. It also conducts short training courses on fiscal, monetary and balance of payments for personnel from member nations through its Central Banking Service Development, the Fiscal Affairs Department, the Bureau of Statistics and the IMF Institute.

EXCHANGE RATES

The original Fund Agreement provided that the par value of each member country was to be expressed in terms of gold of certain weight and fineness or US dollars. The underlying idea was to create a system of stable exchange rates with orderly cross rates. But the Fund was obliged to agree to changes in exchange rates which did not exceed ± 1 per cent of the initial par value. A further change of ± 1 per cent required the permission of the Fund. Since 1971, these provisions have been changed and the international monetary system has moved from fixed exhcange rates to flexible exchange rates. Under the new system, the member countries are not expected to maintain and establish par values with gold or dollar. The Fund has no control over the exchange rate adjustment policies of the member countries.

But under Article IV of the Second Amendment, effective April 1978, the Fund has laid down principles for the guidance of exchange rate policies of its members : (*a*) to avoid manipulation of exchange rates in order to gain an unfair competitive advantage over other members; (*b*) to intervene in the exchange market to counter disorderly conditions; and (*c*) to take into account in their intervention policies the interests of other members.

FUND BORROWINGS

Besides performing regulatory and consultative functions, the Fund is an important financial institution. The bulk of its financial resources comes from quota subscriptions of member countries. Besides, it increases its funds by selling gold to members. Further, it borrows from government, central banks or private institutions of industrialised countries, the Bank for International Settlements, and even from OPEC counties, like Saudi Arabia.

GENERAL ARRANGEMENTS TO BORROW (GAB)

The Fund also borrows under the General Arrangements to Borrow from its eleven industrialised members in order to forestall or cope with an impairment of the international monetary system. The GAB remained in force from October 1962 to December 1998, when its total borrowings was SDR 17 billion. Under the *New Arrangements to Borrow*, the developed countries have sanctioned $ 25 billion.

FUND LENDING

The Fund has a variety of facilities for lending its resources to member countries. Lending by the Fund is linked to temporary assistance to members in financing disequilibrium in their balance of payments on current account. If a member has less currency with the Fund than its quota, the difference is called *reserve tranche*. It can draw up to 25 per cent on its reserve tranche automatically upon representation to the Fund for its balance needs. It is not charged any interest on such drawings, but is required to repay within a period of three to five years.

CREDIT TRANCHES

A member can draw further annually from balance quota in 4 instalments upto 100% of its quota from credit tranches. Drawings from credit tranches are conditional because the members have to satisfy the Fund of adopting a viable programme to ensure financial stability. To meet the severe BOP problems, the Fund has been gradually raising the limit of borrowings by its members over the years under the credit tranche. Now members can draw up to the equivalent of 300 per cent of their new quotas on the total net use of the Fund's resources. The limits exclude drawings under CCFF, BSAF, SAF, STF and ESAF. Purchases by members are made under stand-by arrangement rather than directly. Borrowings up to this limit are allowed if a member country is making particularly strong efforts to correct its balance of payment disequilibrium and adjust its economy. Since the 1960s, the Fund has created several new credit facilities for its members. Loans from these facilities are separate from tranches and are available for a longer period. These are :

Buffer Stock Financing Facility (BSFF). It was created in 1969 for financing commodity buffer stock by member countries. The facility is equivalent to 30 per cent of the borrowing member's quota. Repurchases are made in 3¼ to 5 years. But the member is expected to cooperate with the Fund in establishing commodity prices within the country.

The Extended Fund Facility (EFF). It is another specialised facility which was created in 1974. Under EFF, the Fund provides credit to member countries to meet their balance of payments deficits for longer periods, and in amounts larger than their quotas under normal credit facilities. EFF provides credit upto a period of 10 years and loans upto 300 per cent of a member's quota are allowed. It is based on performance criteria and drawings instalments. It is availed of by developing countries.

Supplementary Financing Facility (SFF). It was established in 1977 to provide supplementary financing under extended or stand-by arrangements to member countries to meet serious balance of payments deficits that are large in relation to their economies and their quotas. The facility has been extended to low-income developing member countries of the Fund. To reduce the cost of borrowing under SFF to such countries, the Fund established Subsidy Account in 1980 through which it makes subsidy payments to borrower countries.

Structural Adjustment Facility (SAF). The Fund set up SAF in March 1986 to provide concessional adjustment to the poorer developing countries. Under it, loans are granted to them to solve balance of payments problems and to carry out medium term macro-economic and structural adjustment programmes. The SAF was created with SDR 2.7 billion of resources which come mainly from repayments on loans from the Trust Fund. Resources are made available to the poorer countries on highly concessional terms of .5 to 1 per cent interest with the principal repayable over 5½ to 10 years with a five-year grace period. Disbursements are made annually and are linked to the approval of annual arrangements with members receiving equivalent of 15 per cent of quota under the first annual arrangement, 20 per cent under the second and 15 per cent under the third.

Enhanced Structural Adjustment Facility (ESAF). The ESAF was created in December 1987 with SDR 6 billion of resources for the medium term financing needs of low income countries. The objectives, eligibility and basic programme features of this facility are similar to those of the SAF. But eligible members can receive a great deal more assistance under the ESAF than under the SAF upto 100 per cent of quota over a three-year programme period, with provision for upto 250 per cent in exceptional circumstances. Disbursements under the ESAF are semi-annual instead of annual.

Compensatory and Contingency Financing Facility (CCFF). The CCFF was created in August 1988 to provide timely compensation for temporary shortfalls or excesses in cereal import costs due to factors beyond the control of the member and contingency financing to help a member to maintain the momentum of Fund-supported adjustment programmes in the face of external shocks on account of factors beyond its control. In 1990, the Fund introduced an import element into CCFF for a temporary period upto the end of 1991 to help members overcome the Gulf War Crisis. This was within 95 per cent of quota for CCFF. The Fund also decided to expand the coverage of CCFF. Besides workers' remittances and travel receipts, shortfalls in other services such as receipts from pipelines, canals, shipping, transportation, construction and insurance have been included in the calculation of export shortfalls under compensatory financing.

Systematic Transformation Facility (STF). In April, 1993, the IMF established STF with $6 billion to help Russia and other Central Asian Republics to face balance of payments crisis.

Emergency Structural Adjustment Loans (ESAL). The Fund eastblished ESAL facility in early 1999 to help the Asian and Latin American countries inflicted with the financial crisis. Under it, such countries are given shot-term loans 3% to 5% above the Fund's normal interest rate which are to be repaid in a short period.

Contingency Credit Line (CCL). The CCL was created in April 1999 to protect fundamentally sound countries from the contagion of financial crisis occurring in other countries, rather than from domestic policy weaknesses. Only countries that over the medium term can finance BOP comfortably and enjoy healthy financial sectors and strong debtor-creditor relations are considered for CCL. So far no country has drawn from it.

Critical Appraisal of the Fund's Working

The IMF advises its member countries on various problems concerning their BOP and exchange rate problems and on monetary and fiscal issues. It sends specialists and experts to help solve BOP and exchange rate problems of member countries. They confer with local officials and suggest monetary, fiscal and other measures in their reports. The Fund has set up three departments to solve banking and fiscal problems of member countries. *First*, there is the Central Banking Service Department which helps member countries with the services of its experts to run and manage their central banks and to formulate banking legislation. Such services are especially provided to developing countries to reform their banking system. *Second*, the Fiscal Affairs Department renders advice to member countries concerning their fiscal matters. *Third*, The IMF Institute conducts short-term training courses for the officers of member countries relating to monetary, fiscal, banking, and BOP policies. Besides, the Fund's research department publishes many reports in a year containing material relating to different policy measures. These publications include IMF Annual Report and IMF Staff Papers, Finance and Development Journal, etc.

The IMF has been severely criticised in recent years for mishandling global finanacial crises in East Asia and Latin America, aggravating poverty in developing countries, encouraging bad policies by governments and financial investors and favouring the developed countries. We discuss below some points of criticism.

1. Fund Conditionalities. The Fund has developed conditionalities over the last five decades or so which a country has to fulfil for getting a loan from the Fund. Prior to the 1970s, the Fund laid stress on *expenditure reduction* for meeting disequilibrium in the balance of payments of a country. In the 1970s, the Fund conditionality included the need to take into account the *causes of balance of payments difficulties* of members requesting for Fund resources, their *economic priorities and their social and political* requirement. On March 2, 1979, a *new set of guidelines* was laid down for the use of Fund resources, besides the previous conditionality practices. These include periodic assessment of the experience of the member country with adjustment programmes financed by Fund resources. The new emphasis is on policies to increase productivity and to improve resource allocation in the programmes supported by Fund resources. They also include stringent Fund conditionalities or performance criteria such as controlling deficits, reforming the banking system, even closing down non-viable units, altering systems of administration and laws which give rise to corruption. The release of every installment requires their review.

The Fund has laid down some more conditionalities after the 1995 Mexican and the Asian financial crises. (1) to liberalise trade by removing exchange and import controls; (2) to eliminate all subsidies so that the exporters are not in an advantageous position in relation to the other trading countries; and (3) to treat foreign lenders on an equal footing with domestic lenders. Besides, the Fund insists on good governance. Thus the Fund exercises surveillance ever the exchange rates monetary, fiscal and related policies of the borrowing countries which makes a mockery of its policy of non-interfering in their internal economic affairs.

2. High Interest Rates. Besides, these hard conditionalities, the Fund charges high interest rates on loans of different types. They are a great burden on the borrowing countries. This is the reason that developing countries like India are so heavily burdened with the debt service charge that fresh borrowings are negative.

3. Secondary Role. The Fund has been playing only a secondary role rather than the central role in international monetary relations. It does not provide facilities for short-term credit arrangements. This has resulted in "swap" arrangements among the central banks of the Group of Ten of the leading developed countries. Under these arrangements, these countries exchange each other's currencies and also provide short-term credit to tide over temporary disequilibria in their balance of payments. Such swap arrangements have led to the growth of Euro-currency Market. All this has reduced the importance of the Fund.

4. Lack of Resources. The IMF has not enough resources for immediate future. But these are not sufficient to meet the future needs of its members. The need is to raise the resources of the Fund to safeguard the international financial system which is dominated by volatile capital flows. The developed countries are not willing to increase the quota of the Fund.

5. Failure to Maintain Exchange Rate Stability. The Fund has failed in its objective of promoting exchange stability and to maintain orderly exchange arrangements among members. Under the original Fund agreements, the exchange rate was permitted to fluctuate within a range of 1 per cent above to 1 per cent below the official price. This was known as the "adjustable peg" system. The exchange rate of every member country was fixed in terms of the "golden dollar". Over the years US gold stock continued to decline, the US balance of payments continued to deteriorate. Consequently, the Bretton Woods system collapsed on 15 August, 1971 when President Nixon announced that United States would no longer convert dollars into gold and that it would not intervene in foreign exchange markets to maintain exchange rate stability. Since then there has been a mixture of exchange rate systems of nationally managed floating, joint floating, and pegged exchange rates. According to Prof. Schwartz, the IMF has lost its objective.

6. Failure to Eliminate Foreign Exchange Restrictions. One of the objectives of the Fund has been to eliminate foreign exchange restrictions which hamper the growth in world trade. The Fund has not been successful in achieving this objective. The world trade is restricted by a variety of exchange controls and multiple exchange practices.

7. Discriminatory Politics. The Fund has been criticised for its discriminatory policies against the developing countries and in favour of the developed countries. It is, therefore, characterised as "Rich Countries Club". Although the majority of its members are the developing countries of Asia, Africa and Latin America, yet it is dominated by the rich countries especially the United States. The latter often adopts a rigid attitude in matters concerning increasing the Fund resources and granting loans to developing countries.

8. Responsible for Asian Crisis. The sudden and unexpected East-Asian crisis in Phillipines, South Korea, Thailand, Indonesia and Malaysia put a question mark on the working of the Fund. Friedman has put the blame on the IMF for global crisis because it has been the result of government's intervention in the market, both internationally via loans, subsidies or taxes, and externally via the IMF. With the collapse of the Bretton-Woods system in 1971 when the member countries adopted the floating exchange rate policy, the Funds role of regulating the exchange rate ended. Prior to the 1995 Mexican crisis, the objective of the Fund was to provide advice, information and loans to its members. But when it helped Mexico in a bail out package in its crisis of 1995, it acted the international lender of last resort. Under it, the Fund laid emphasis on close financial relations among banks, corporations and governments and to increase the operations of stock and bond markets so that there is greater competition between domestic and global financial institutions. This very policy led to the Asian and global financial crisis when there was successive decline in shares, bonds and currencies of these countries. The real beneficiaries of this policy were not the borrowing countries but the foreign banks and financial institutions who lend to these countries which failed to repay the loans. When due to declining exchange rates, they started withdrawing their funds, there was a crisis in the borrowing countries. A Michael Musa, the IMF Chief Economist, admitted in August 2000 that the recent financial crisis was due to high openness to international capital flows, especially short-run credit flows of countries with fragile financial systems. According to Schwartz, since the Fund lacks in high powered base money, it failed to act as an international lender of last resort. Thus the IMF has been weak in controlling financial crisis. Schwartz, therefore, suggests that it should be shut down. According to Friedman, it should be abolished as it did more harm than good.

Despite these criticisms, the IMF has shown sufficient flexibility to mould itself in keeping with the changing international economic conditions. The original Articles of Agreement were amended in 1978 to legalise flexible exchange rates, raise quotas to increase the Fund's resources and to dethrone the gold in Fund transactions. To solve the problem of international liquidity, it has created deficits, the Fund has been successively raising the limit of their borrowings which stands at 450 per cent of their quotas. The Fund has been helping the developing countries in their balance of payments and other problems through such facilities as CFF, BSFF, EFF, SFF, SAF, ESAF, CCFF, etc. Finally, the usefulness and success of the Fund lies in that its membership has risen from 44 in 1947 to 182.

2. THE ROLE OF GOLD IN THE IMF

The Fund Agreement fixed the par values of currencies of its members in terms of gold. This led economists like Williams and Halm to suggest that the Fund's gold provisions were "not just window dressing". Rather, they essentially related to a gold standard plan. On the other hand, Keynes held that the IMF had "dethroned" gold and its proposals were "the exact opposite of the gold standard". Let us analyse these views one by one.

According to the first view, the Fund incorporates all the features of the international gold standard minus its disadvantages. The par values of the currencies of its members are fixed in terms of gold. Therefore, the exchange rates of member countries are fixed in the same manner as under the gold standard. Further, gold is expressed as a common denominator for international transactions, they are like short-term capital movements under the gold standard. Member countries may buy and sell gold at the international price fixed by the Fund. The Fund may also buy gold from members at the same price. Again, the Fund mechanism has the same monetary and price effects as under the gold standard, affecting central bank reserves of member countries in precisely the same manner as the movement of gold under the gold standard. For example, when a deficit country buys foreign exchange from the Fund, the volume of international currency with its central bank is reduced which in turn reduces the reserve position of its commercial banks. They are forced to contract credit and deflation starts. In the opposite case, the volume of international currency increases in surplus country. As a result, the reserves of its commercial banks increase. They expand credit and there is inflation. Thus the Fund mechanism resembles the gold standard mechanism.

The Fund scheme differs from the gold standard in the following ways : *First,* under the gold standard all countries must adopt gold standard within their countries. Under the Fund scheme, the member countries are not required to adopt the gold standard. *Second,* the exchange rates are rigidly fixed under the gold standard. But they are flexible under the Fund scheme. They can be changed to correct fundamental disequilibrium by a member country. *Third,* the gold standard requires automatic adjustment of international prices and incomes in order to maintain rigid exchange rates. But the Fund requires adjustments in exchange rates in keeping with the internal price and income structure of the country. *Fourth,* under the Fund Charter, there is not provision for a deficit country to adopt deflationary policies. Rather, it aims at removing deflationary tendencies in member countries. *Fifth,* the supply of gold influences the value of national currency under the gold standard. But the Fund makes international currencies available to members independent of the international currencies in the "Fund pool" and loans them to deficit member countries. *Sixth,* the Fund allows temporary exchange restrictions by its member to correct their fundamental disequilibria, whereas such restrictions are not allowed under the gold standard. *Seventh,* according to Ellsworth, since the Fund Agreement "did not prescribe gold as the sole form in which reserves could be held it did not usher in a true gold standard". Thus the Fund mechanism differs fundamentally from the gold mechanism in so many way, that led Keynes to remark that it is "the exact opposite of the gold standard".

Although the Fund "dethroned" the gold standard, yet gold continued to play an important role in the Fund till the Second Amendment to the IMF Charter. The par values of currencies of member countries were expressed in terms of gold or US dollar, one dollar being equivalent to 0.888671 gram or $35 an ounce of gold. When the US devalued the dollar in May 1972, the weight of gold behind dollar was reduced to 0.818513 gram or $ 38 an ounce for gold. With the Second Amendment, a new international currency, SDR, has been introduced for all Fund transactions with member countries. This currency is no longer linked to gold but to a basket of five major currencies viz. the US Dollar, German Mark, French Franc, Japanese Yen, and British Pound. There is no official price of gold and members are required to make payments in gold to the Fund. Part of Fund's gold holdings have been sold in the market for the benefit of developing member countries. At the time of the Second Amendment, the Fund's gold holdings were equal to more than 150 million ounces or 4710 tons. It was decided to sell 50 million ounces. Accordingly, the Fund held 45 auctions from June 1976 to May 1980 amounting to 47 million ounces at gold prices prevailing in the London Market. The Fund's present gold holdings amount to 130 million ounces which can only be sold if a majority of 85 per cent in the Fund's financial transactions except that the Fund continues to value its holdings at SDR $ 35 an ounce. According to Prof. Bernstein, "All that now remains of the historic monetary role of gold is its function as reserve asset."

3. INDIA AND THE IMF

India is one of the founder members of the IMF. It signed the Fund Agreement on 27 December, 1945. Till 1970 India's quota in the Fund was the fifth and it had the power to appoint a permanent Executive Director. With the increase in the Fund quota after May 1970, the quotas of Japan, Canada and Italy increased more than that of India. Accordingly, India ceased to hold a permanent position as Executive Director of the Fund. With the Eleventh Review of Quotas, India's quota in the IMF declined from 2.09 per cent to 1.96 per cent. As a result, India's position in the Fund quota came down to 13th. However, in absolute terms, India's quota increased from SDR 3.56 billion to 4.16 billion.

The par value of the Indian rupee was fixed at 0.26801 gram of gold or 30.225 US cents when India became its member. When the rupee was devalued on September 18, 1949, its par value was reduced to 0.186621 gram of gold or 21 US cents. It was further reduced to 0.118489 gram of gold or 13.33 US cents on June 6, 1966 when the rupee was again devalued. Since the devaluation of the dollar in May 1972, its par value fell further. But with the Second Amendment of the Fund Agreement, the exchange rate of the rupee has been floating like other currencies and is linked to SDR.

India has been one of the major beneficiaries of the Fund assistance. It has been getting aid from the various Fund agencies from time to time and has been regularly repaying its debt. Between 1947 to 1955, India borrowed $100 million twice to tide over its balance of payments difficulties. India borrowed eight times between 1957 to 1975 a total sum of $1764 million. It also received loan disburse-ments at concessional terms to overcome balance of payments difficulties amounting to SDR $529 million from July 1, 1978 to February 21,

1981 under the IMF Trust Fund.

In 1979, India entered into agreement with the IMF for a loan of $5.6 billion or Rs. 5,220 crores under the EFF. It started receiving the loan in instalments for a three-year period beginning from November 9, 1981. Till April 1984, it had drawn $ 3.9 billion and intimated the Fund that it would not be drawing the remaining amount at all. After April 1984, India did not take any recourse under its modified Compensatory and Contingency Financing Facility (CCFF). In January 1991, it received $ 0.79 billion as the first credit tranche of a stand-by arrangement for three months. At the same time, India got the first credit of $ 1.09 billion under CCFF, followed by the second loan of $ 220 million in July 1991 and the third loan of $ 635 million in September 1991. On 31 October, the IMF approved a stand-by credit of $ 2.2 billion to be disbursed to India in 8 tranches over a 20-month period from November 1991 to June 1993. Normally, member countries get only 50 to 60 per cent of their quotas in loans. But India received more than 100 per cent of its quota. India's quota in the Fund was $ 3.01 billion (or SDR 2.2 billion) and its gross drawings from the Fund from January 1991 to June 1993 were $ 3.5 billion. This speaks of the Fund's confidence in the Indian economy.

Besides receiving loans to meet deficit in its balance of payments, India has benefitted in certain other respects from the membership of the Fund. By virtue of being a member of the Fund, India is also a member of the IBRD (World Bank) from which it has been receiving financial aid for its various development projects. It has been getting advisory help from the Fund under the Fund surveilance conditionality. A Fund team of four or five economists often visits India. These economists exchange views with Indian officials on India's balance of payments and exchange rate problems and suggest monetary, fiscal, and other measures to solve them. The Fund has also been providing short-term training courses to Indian personnel on monetary, fiscal, banking, exchange, and balance of payments policies through its Central Banking Service Department, the Fiscal Affairs Department, and the IMF Institute. Thus India has gained much as a member of the Fund.

4. SPECIAL DRAWING RIGHTS (SDRS)

MEANING

Special Drawing Rights (SDRs), also known as the *paper gold*, are a form of international reserves created by the IMF in 1969 to solve the problem of international liquidity. They are not paper notes or currency. They are international units of account in which the official accounts of the IMF are kept. They are allocated to the IMF members in proportion to their Fund quotas and are used to settle balance of payments deficits between them.

ORIGIN OF SDRs

SDRs were created through the First Amendment to the Fund Articles of Agreement in 1969 following persistent US deficits in balance of payments to solve the problem of international liquidity. Until December 1971, an SDR was linked to 0.88867 gram of gold and was equivalent to US $1. With the breakdown of the fixed parity system after 1973 when the US dollar and other major currencies were allowed to float, it was decided to stabilise the exchange value of the SDR. Accordingly, the value of the SDR was calculated each day on the basis of a basket of 16 most widely used currencies of the member countries of the Fund. Each country was given a weight in the basket in accordance with its importance in international trade and financial markets. After the Second Amendment to the Fund Articles of Agreement in 1978, the SDR became an international unit of account. To facilitate its valuation, the number of currencies in the "basket" were reduced to five in January 1981. They include the US dollars, the German Deutsche Mark, the British Pound, the French Franc and the Japanese Yen. The present currency composition and weighting pattern of the SDR is revised every five years beginning January 1, 1986. The revision of weights is based on both the values of the exports of goods and services and the balances of their currencies held by other members. In 1977, they were US dollar (39%), German DM (21%), UK pound and French franc (11% each) and Japanese yen (18%). The value of one SDR was equal to US $ 1.35610 on October 1, 1997.

USES OF SDRs

SDR is an international unit of account which is held in the Fund's Special Drawing Account. The quotas of all currencies in the Fund General Account are also valued in terms of the SDR. As the international monetary asset, the SDR is held in the international reserves of central banks and governments to finance their deficits or surpluses of balance of payments. All transactions by the Fund in the form of loans and their repayments, its liquid reserves, its capital, etc., are expressed in the SDR.

SDRs are used as a means of payment by Fund members to meet balance of payments deficits and their total reserve position with the Fund. They cannot be used for any other purpose. Thus SDRs act both as an international unit of account and a means of payment.

There are *three* principal uses of SDRs.

1. Transactions with Designation. Under it, Fund designates a participant in the SDR scheme who has a strong balance of payments and reserve position to provide currency in exchange for SDRs to another participant needing its currency. The currency to be exchanged for SDRs may belong to the designated participated or/ and to other participants. Participants are allowed to accept SDRs in this way as long as their holdings are less than three times their total allocations.

2. Transactions with General Account. SDRs are used in all transactions with the General Account of the Fund. Participants pay charges in SDRs to the General Account for the use of the Fund resources and also to repurchase their own currency from it.

3. Transactions by Agreement. The Fund allows sales of SDRs for currency by agreement with another participant.

In order to further widen the uses of SDRs, the Second Amendment empowered the Fund to lay down uses of SDRs not otherwise specified. Accordingly, the following additional uses of SDRs are : (*i*) in swap arrangements, (*ii*) in forward operations, (*iii*) in loans, (*iv*) in the settlement of financial objections, (*v*) as security for the performance of financial obligations, and (*vi*) in donations or grants.

The Fund also empowers certain institutions as "other holder" of SDRs. Besides the World Bank and its associates, some of the other holders of SDRs are the Bank for International Settlements, the African Development Bank. These 'other holders' acquire and use SDRs in transactions and operations by agreement under the same terms and conditions as applicable to the participants. Efforts are being made by the Fund to have a greater use of the SDR as a unit of account in private transactions and in financial markets of the world.

The Fund pays interest on all holdings of SDRs kept in the Special Drawing Account and charges interest at the same rate on allocations to participants.

ALLOCATION OF SDRs

The Fund allocates SDRs to participants in proportion to their quotas for various uses mentioned above. Initially, the Fund created SDR $ 9.3 billion over the three years 1970-72. The total holdings of SDR $ 9.3 billion continued till 1978. In 1978, the Fund decided to raise them by SDR $ 4 billion in each of the years 1979, 1980 and 1981. As a result, the total holdings of SDRs were SDR $ 13.1 billion in 1979, SDR 17.3 $ billion in 1980 and SDR $ 21.4 billion in 1981. Since 1981 no further allocation of SDRs has been made by the Fund. The quantity of SDRs is determined by members of the Fund. It can only be increased if 85% votes of its members favour their increase. The basis of allocation of SDRs among the members of IMF is their quota subscriptions. At present, about 70% of SDRs are distributed to 26 rich countries and the remaining 30% to developing countries.

MERITS OF SDRs

Despite these weaknesses, the SDRs scheme possesses the following merits:

1. SDRs are a new form of international monetary reserves which have been created to free the international monetary system from its exclusive dependence on the US dollar.
2. They have rid the world of its dependence on the supply of gold and fluctuations in gold prices.
3. They cannot be demonetised like gold or become scarce when the demand for dollar increases in the world.
4. Unlike gold, SDRs are costless to produce because production of gold requires resources to mine,

refine, transport and guard it.

5. SDRs have been created to improve international liquidity so as to correct fundamental disequilibria in balance of payments of Fund members. Under this scheme, the participants receive SDRs under *transactions with designation and transaction by agreement* unconditionally.
6. Fund members are not required to change their domestic economic policies as they are expected under the Fund aid programmes.
7. The payment and repayment of SDRs out of the Special Drawing Account is easier and more flexible than under the Fund schemes.
8. Last but not the least, SDRs act both as a unit of account and a means of payment of international monetary system.

Criticisms of SDRs

Despite these merits, the SDR scheme has been criticised on the following grounds:

1. Inequitable Distribution. It is an inequitable scheme which has tended to make unfair distribution of international liquidity. The allocation of SDRs to participating countries is proportional to their quotas. In this sense, the allocation of SDRs to developing countries is too low as compared to their needs. Low allocation of SDRs reduces the borrowing capacity of such countries.

2. Not Linked with Development Finance. SDR scheme does not link the creation of international reserves in the form of SDRs with the need for development finance on the part of developing countries. The need for liquidity on the part of developing countries is great "because of their higher costs of adjustment, limited access to private banking and higher capital markets, greater variability of exchange earnings, and opportunity cost of holding foreign exchange reserves". Under these circumstances, there is need to create more SDRs with fair distribution so that more unconditional liquidity is made available for the greater needs of developing countries.

3. High Interest Rate. The interest rate originally payable on net use of SDRs is 1.5 per cent. This has been gradually raised through time in order to make a more acceptable asset to hold. Now both users of SDRs pay and holders of SDRs receive, a market rate of interest based on interest rates prevailing in US, Britain, France, Germany and Japan which are quite high for developing countries.

4. Failure to Distribute Social Saving. Williamson and others have criticised the SDR scheme for its failure to distribute social saving of SDRs to the developing countries. The present rules for allocation distribute the social saving to a participant country in proportion to his contribution or its demand for SDRs. If the supply of SDRs equals the demand for it, there will no redistribution of resources between countries. But this is not so in the case of developing countries whose holdings of SDRs are very low as compared to the 26 developed countries. Thus the present scheme of SDRs fails to transfer social savings to the developing countries.

5. Failure to meet International Liquidity Requirements. Unfortunately, due to the rigid attitude of the United States and some other developed countries, the Fund has not been able to resume allocation of SDRs from January 1982, despite the repeated pleas of the developing countries over these years. So the Fund has failed in its objective of increasing international liquidity through SDRs. Consequently, faced with a recession, an inadequate flow of concessional aid and falling prices of commodities and raw materials, developing countries have been facing severe balance of payments and debt problems. Thus SDRs have failed to solve the problem of international liquidity.

EXERCISES

1. What were the main objectives behind the establishment of the IMF? How far the Fund has been successful in achiving these objectives?
2. Explain the objectives and functions of the IMF. Critically examine its achievements.
3. Discuss the role of gold in the scheme of the IMF.
4. Outline the objectives and functions of the IMF and explain the benefits which have flowed to India for being its member.
5. Discuss the nature and uses of Special Drawing Rights (SDRs) by the member countries of the IMF. Has their creation solved the problem of international liquidity?

CHAPTER 57

The World Bank

The International Bank for Reconstruction and Development (IBRD) or the World Bank was established in 1945 under the Bretton Woods Agreement of 1944 to assist in bringing about a smooth transition from a war-time to peace-time economy. It is a sister institution of the International Monetary Fund.

1. FUNCTIONS

The IBRD, also called the World Bank, performs the following functions :

1. To assist in the reconstruction and development of territories of its members by facilitating the investment of capital for productive purpose, and the encouragement of the development of productive facilities and resources in less development countries.

2. To promote private foreign investment by means of guarantees on particpation in loans and other investment made by private investors, and when capital is not available on reasonable terms, to supplement private investment by providing finance for productive purpose out of its own resources or from borrowed funds.

3. To promote the long-range balanced growth of international trade and the maintenance of equilibrium in the balance of payments of member countries by encouraging international investment for the development of their productive resources, thereby assisting in raising productivity, the standard of living and conditions of workers in their territories.

4. To arrange the loans made or guaranteed by it in relation to international loans through other channels so that more useful and urgent small and large projects are dealt with first.

2. MEMBERSHIP

The members of the International Monetary Fund are the members of the IBRD. It had 182 members in 2000. If a country resigns its membership, it is required to pay back all loans with interest on due dates. If the Bank incurs a financial loss in the years in which a member resigns, it is required to pay its share of the loss on demand.

3. ORGANISATION

Like the IMF, the IBRD has a three-tier structure with a President, Executive Directors and Board of Governors. The President of the World Bank Group (IBRD, IDA and IFC) is elected by the Bank's Executive

Directors whose number is 21. Of these, 5 are appointed by the five largest shareholders of the World Bank. They are the US, UK, Germany, France and Japan. The remaining 16 are elected by the Board of Governors. There are also Alternate Directors. The first five belong to the same permanent member countries to which the Executive Directors belong. But the remaining Alternate Directors are elected from among the group of countries who cast their votes to choose the 16 Executive Directors belonging to their regions.

The President of the World Bank presides over the meetings of the Board of Executive Directors regularly once a month. The Executive Directors decide about policy within the framework of the Articles of Agreement. They consider and decide on the loan and credit proposal made by the President. They also present to the Board of Governors at its annual meetings audited accounts, an administrative budget, and the Annual Report on the operations and policies of the Bank. The President has a staff of more than 6,000 persons who carry on the working of the World Bank. He is assisted by a number of Senior Vice-Presidents and Directors of various departments and regions. The Board of Governors is the supreme body. Every member country appoints one Governor and an Alternate Governor for a period of five years. The voting power of each Governor is related to the financial contribution of its government.

4. CAPITAL STRUCTURE

The IBRD started with an authorised capital of $ 10 billion divided into 1,00,000 shares of $ 1,00,000. Of this, $ 9,400 million was actually subscribed. On June 30, 1985 the authorised capital stock of the IBRD comprised 7,16,500 authorised shares of the par value of SDR 1,00,000 each. In July 1992, the total authorised Bank capital was $ 184.1 billion with a capital increase of $ 9.3 billion or 77,159 shares provided to the republics of the former Soviet Union.

5. FUNDING STRATEGY

The IBRD's funding strategy has the following four basic objectives :

The *first* is to ensure the *availability of funds* to the Bank. For this purpose, the IBRD seeks to maintain unutilised access to funds in the markets in which it borrows.

The *second* objective is to *minimise the effective cost* of those funds to its borrowers. This is done through the currency mix of its borrowings and the time of borrowings. In the former case, it tends to maximise borrowings in currencies with low nominal interest rates. The time of borrowings is manipulated in two ways : (*a*) when interest rates are expected to rise, the Bank seeks to increase its borrowigs, and (*b*) when interest rates are expected to fall, it seeks to defer borrowings.

The *third* objective is to *control volatility in net income and overall loan charges.* For this purpose, the Bank started in July 1982 a pool-based variable lending rate system that uniformly adjusts interest charges applicable to the outstanding balance on all loans made under it. The existing loans were not affected by this lending system. When the majority of loans and borrowings are incorporated into the new lending rate system in future, the volatility of interest rates will be much reduced.

The *fourth* objective of the funding strategy is to provide an appropriate degree of *maturity transformation* between its borrowing and lending. Maturity transformation refers to the Bank's capacity to lend at longer maturities than it borrows. At the same time, it provides its borrowers with a modest degree of maturity transformation.

6. BORROWING AND LENDING ACTIVITIES

The Bank borrows from the following sources :

The IBRD is a corporate institution whose capital is subscribed by its members. It finances its lending operations primarily from its own medium and long-term borrowings in the international capital markets, and currency swap agreements (CSA). Under the CSA proceeds of a borrowing country are converted into a different currency, and simultaneously, a forward exchange agreement is exectuted providing for a schedule of future exhcanges of the two currencies in order to recover the currency converted. The effect of currency swaps is to transform the cost of original borrowing to a cost which reflects the market yield of the currency obtained in the conversion.

The Bank also borrows under the Discount-Note Programme. *First,* it places bonds and notes directly with its member governments, government agencies and central banks. *Second,* it offers issues to investors and in the public markets through investing banking firms, merchant banks and commercial banks.

The IBRD has evolved two new borrowing instruments. *First,* Central Bank Facility (CBF) is a one-year, Us dollar dominated facility for borrowing from official sources, particularly central banks. It is designed to reverse the declining trend in the IBRD's borrowings from such sources since the 1970s. In 1984, the Executive Directors authorised the Bank to borrow under the Facility upto $ 750 million with a one-year maturity plus funds maturity within a month under the Facility. *Second,* borrowings in Floating Rate Notes (FRNs) is meant to help the IBRD to meet some of the objectives of its funding strategy. The FRN market enables the Bank to gain access to a set of investors like commercial banks and certain other financial institutions which have not traditionally bought IBRD notes. The FRNs carry a medium/long-term maturity. A substantial amount of its resources also comes from its retained earnings and the flow of payments on its loans.

The Bank lends to member countries in any of the following ways :

(*i*) by marketing or participating in loans out of its own funds; (*ii*) by making or participating in direct loans out of funds raised in the market of a member or otherwise borrowed by the Bank; (*iii*) by guaranteeing in whole or in part loans made by private investors through the usual investment channels.

Thc total amount outstanding of participating in loans, direct loans and guarantees should not exceed 100 per cent of its unimpaired subscribed capital, reserves and surplus. It guarantees, participates in or makes loans to its members on the following conditions :

(*i*) If it is satisfied that in the prevailing market conditions the borrower would be unable to obtain the loan under conditions which in the opinion of the Bank are reasonable to the borrower.

(*ii*) Loans are for specific projects of reconstruction or development, except in special circumstances.

(*iii*) If the member in whose territory the project is located is not itself the borrower, the member or its central bank fully guarantees the repayment of the principal, the payment of interest and other charges on the loan.

(*iv*) The project for which the loan is required has been recommended by a competent committee in the form of a written report after a carefully study of the proposal.

(*v*) The borrower or the guarantor is in a position to meet its obligations under the loan.

In 1991, the Executive Board of the Bank approved modification in IBRD repayment terms which include shifting repayment of new loans for low income countries to annuity, extension of grace period through fiscal year 1991 on new loans to middle income countries from 3 to 5 years and review of repayment terms for middle income countries within 3 years.

Development credits carry a service charge of 0.75% and generally have 35-40 year final maturities with a 10-year grace period for principal payments.

The bank provides the following facilities to member countries :

Structural Adjustment Facility (SAF). Since 1985, the IBRD has introduced SAF to borrowing countries in order to reduce their balance of payments deficits while maintaining or regaining their economic growth. SAF funds are used to finance general imports with a few agreed exceptions such as luxury and military imports. SAFs are released in two parts and are based on stiffer conditions laid down by the Bank. The Bank aims at providing support to programmes running from 5 to 7 years through a series of up to five SAFs to a borrowing country.

Enhanced Structural Adjustment Facility (ESAF). In December 1987, the Bank has set up the ESAF to increase the availability of concessional resources to low-income member countries. It provides new concessional resources totalling SDR 6 billion which will be financed by special loans and contributions from developed and OPEC countries. Like the SAF, ESAF is meant to help the borrowing countries reduce their balance of payments deficits and encourage growth. Its financial terms are similar to the SAF. The interest rate is 0.5 per cent with repayments in ten semi-annual instalments beginning after 5½ years of disbursements.

The Bank makes medium and long-term loans unusually running up to the completion of the project. Loans generally have a grace period of 5 years and repayable over 20 years or less. The interest rate charged on loans by the Bank is calculated in accordance with a guideline related to its cost of borrowing. So loans are at variable interest rates. It charges an annual commitment charge of 0.75 per cent on undistributed balance and a one-time front-end on the amount of loan.

The Bank's lending operations for two decades since its inception were concentrated heavily upon capital infrastructural projects such as power generation and distribution, railway and roads, ports, telecommunications, major irrigation works, etc. Since the 1970s, loans for infrastructural investments have come down. Instead, it has begun to finance changes in the educational system in the developing countries, to establish institutions for the financing of industrial investments and provision of technical assistance in the selection and appraisal of industrial projects, and to help in the preparation of agricultural projects. Its present development strategy lays more emphasis on investments that can directly affect the welfare of the poor people of the developing countries by increasing their productivity and standard of living. Towards this end, it has been financing projects for agriculture and rural development, education, family planning, nutrition, low-cost housing, drinking water and sewerage. The distribution of IBRD funds is made by the country-income group and by the sector to the developing countries.

Special Action Programme (SAP). The Special Action Programme (SAP) has been started in 1983 to strengthen the IBRD's ability to assist member countries in adjusting to the current economic environment. It has four major elements: (1) An expansion in lending for high-priority operations that support structural adjustment, policy changes, production for export, fuller use of existing capacity, and the maintenance of crucial infrastructure. (2) Accelerated disbursements under existing and new investment commitments to ensure timely implementation of high priority projects. (3) Expanded advisory services on the design and implementation of appropriate policies. These include reviews of state enterprises studies to strengthen development-orientation and project-implementation capabilities, studies to increase the mobilisation of domestic resources, reviews of incentives for export diversification, and exploration of ways to stengthen debt-management capabilities. (4) Enlisting familiar efforts by other donors for fast disbursing assistance in support of programmes of the Bank and IMF.

CONDITIONALITIES FOR LENDING

The World Bank conditionalities for lending are : (1) an unflinching commitment towards economic stability so as to reduce inflation and deficits; (2) an efficient regulatory mechanism ensuring transparent policies and depoliticised environment; (3) adequate risk management; (4) provision for long-term finance; and (5) increase in the share of the private sector in the country's GDP. In the Bank meeting of 1996, the Bank President declared that countries plagued by corruption would not be liable to receive Bank assistance in future.

7. OTHER ACTIVITIES

The other activities of the IBRD include training, technical assistance, inter-organisational cooperation, economic research and studies, operations evaluation, and settlement of investment disputes of its members.

Training. The Bank set up a staff college in 1956, known as the Economic Development Institute (EDI) for training senior officials of the member developing countries. It helps them to improve the management of their economies and to increase the efficiency of their investment programmes. Its training material ranges from macro-economic planning, pricing, and development policies to the management of agricultural research, rural health care, industrial policy, energy policy, railway management, etc. The EDI also organizes seminars in Washington and in different regions of the world in cooperation with regional institutes.

Technical Assistance. Technical assistance has been an integral part of the Bank operation since its inception. It consists of two broad categories : (*i*) engineering-related, such as feasibility studies, engineering design, and construction supervision; and (*ii*) institution-related, such as dignostic policy and institutional studies, management support and training. The primary way of providing technical assistance is through loans made for specific sectors and in components of loans made for capital infrastructures. Such technical assistance includes funds for supervision, implementation and engineering services, energy, power, transportation, water supply, industry, etc. To meet gaps in project preparation and for institution building, the bank advances funds to prospective buyers through Project Preparation Facility (PPF) created in 1975. The Bank also serves as executing agency for project financed by the United Nations Development Programme (UNDP). Further, it provides such technical assistance as short-term training, appointment of advisers for technology service on evaluation and monitoring panels, and demographic, economic advice on project preparation.

Inter-Organisational Cooperation. The IBRD is also engaged in inter-organisational cooperation. Cooperation between the IBRD and other international organisations is based on formal agreements such as the Co-operative Programmes between it and the FAO, the UNESCO, the WHO, the GATT, the UNCTAD, the United Nations Environment Programmes (UNEP), the UNDP, the United Nations Industrial Development Organisation (UNIDO), the International Fund for Agricultural Development (IFAD), the ILO, the African Development Bank, the Asian Development Bank, etc.

Economic and Social Research. The Bank devotes roughly 3 per cent of its administrative budget to economic and social research. In 1983, the Bank established a Research Policy Council (RPC) to provide leadership in the guidance, co-ordination, and evaluation of all bank research. A Bank Research Advisory group has been set up to advise the RPC. A small and more technically oriented Research Projects Approval Committee has been created. Research activities are undertaken by the Bank's own research staff and also in collaboration with outside researchers. The results of completed research projects appear in articles in international economic journals, books, in World Bank Staff Working Papers, and its own journal, *Finanace and Development.* It also publishes World Development Report every year. Research projects in progress are described in an annual publication, *World Bank Research Programme : Abstracts of Current Studies.* The Bank also helps strengthen indigenous research capacity in member developing countries.

Operations Evaluation. The Bank helps borrowers in the post-evaluation of their Bank assisted projects. It has set up the Operations Evaluation Department (OED) for this purpose. Projects reviewed are also subject to performance audit by the OED staff. Members of borrowers' staff visit this Department for seeking help in the preparation of project completion report. The EDI also includes a course devoted to monitoring and evaluation by borrowers which is conducted by it in collaboration with EDI staff.

Settlement of Investment Disputes. The Bank has set up the International Centre of Settlement of Investment Disputes (ICSID) between States and Nationals of other States. All members of the Bank have signed and deposited their instrument of ratification pertaining to this. The Bank has successfully mediated in solving many international investment disputes such as the River Water Dispute between the India and Pakistan, and of the Suez Canal between Egypt and the UK.

Conclusion

The Bank's overall performance must be judged not just on its lending but on its success in providing advice and technical assistance. The Bank is laying greater emphasis on developing human resources such as education, population, health and nutrition, and on environment. The Bank also provides assistance to the private sector in such areas as financial, power, telecommunications, information technology, oil and gas, and industry and mining.

In the fiscal year 2000, the World Bank disbursements totalled $ 18.5 billion.

8. CRITICAL APPRAISAL

The IBRD has been quite successful in achieving its principal objective of reconstruction and development. It helped in the reconstruction of Europe after its destruction in the Second World War. It has also been helping the developed and developing countries alike in the process of growth. Since the 1970s, it has been lending more to developing countries not only for infrastructural investment but also for raising the productivity and standard of living of the poor people. Of the total IBRD loans of $ 18.5 billion in the fiscal year 2000, member countries in Latin America and Carribean received 22 per cent, in Europe and Central Asia 16 per cent, in East Asia and Pacific 16 per cent, in Africa 12 per cent, in South Asia 11 per cent and in Middle East and North Africa 5 per cent and in others 18 per cent. Still critics are not lacking in pointing out certain criticisms of its lending policies. Some of them are discussed as under:

1. *High Interest Rate.* It is argued that the bank charges a very high rate of interest on loans, as also an

annual commitment charge on undistributed balances and a front-end fee. Recently the Bank has adopted a new procedure related to the cost of borrowing for calculating the interest rate and front-end fee. So they are no longer fixed arbitrarily at a high level. Still the interest rate continues to be high. It is 7.6 per cent now.

2. Less Aid to Developing Countries. The Bank has also been criticised for its failure to meet the financial needs of the developing countries fully. Its loans have just touched the fringes of the total capital requirements for their economic and social uplift. In order to increase the Bank funds to such countries, it established the International Development Association (IDA) in 1960. Despite this, the Bank has not been successful in raising the productivity and standard of living of their people. Its lending operations account for only a small proportion of the total net aid to developing countries. The poorest countries hardly receive 3.5 per cent of the total loans.

3. Faulty Lending Procedure. The Bank's lending procedure is faulty because it lays emphasis on the repaying capacity of the borrowing country before granting any loan. Such a condition is very harsh and discriminatory for developing countries which are poor and need financial help on a large scale. In fact, the repaying capacity of a poor country follows the utilisation of a loan. As the project is completed with the loan assistance, the repaying capacity of the borrower increases gradually.

4. Discriminatory. The Bank has been criticised for being discriminatory in its purpose-wise and region-wise assistance to its members. It is from the fiscal year 1990 that the lending policy of the Bank has been directed more towards the developing countries and for the development of agriculture and rural development, energy, transportation, communications, water supply, sewrage, human resources development, environment, etc.

5. Hard Conditionalities. The introduction of SAF and ESAF has made IBRD loans terms tighter. The borrowing country is required to follow an action programme set out in a letter of development policies such as open trade, reform in public budgeting and debt management, revision of price policies, better planning of public investment and management of public enterprises, etc. The second instalment of SAF is only released after a review of the reform programmes that are date-bound.

9. INDIA AND THE WORLD BANK

India is one of the founder members of the Bank and held a permanent seat on its Board of Executive Directors for a number of years. The Bank has been assisting India in its planned economic development by granting loans, conducting field surveys, rendering expert advice, sending missions, study teams, and training Indian personnel at the EDI. There is also a Chief of Mission of the Bank at New Delhi who represents it for monitoring and consultations on its aided projects in India. India has been the largest receiver of the World Bank assistance since August 1949. The Bank's disbursement to India during fiscal year 2000 amounted to $ 1.8 billion. The total sanctioned loans received by India till June 2000 were $ 11,071 million. Of these, outstanding loans stood at $ 7,508 million. The World Bank has been assisting India in such projects as development of ports, oil exploration including the Bombay High and gas power projects, aircrafts, coal, iron, aluminium, fertilizers, railway modernisation, technical assistance, industrial development finance corporations, etc.

The Aid India Consortium of twelve developed countries which was giving aid to India for its development plans at the instance of the World Bank has been replaced by India Development Forum since 1995. The Bank also helped India to solve amicably its river water dispute with Pakistan.

India has, thus, gained much from being the member of the World Bank for the development of agriculture, industry, energy and transport. But with reduced availability from the IDA. India will have to borrow more from the Bank in future. This will entail a heavy burden on India's resources for the terms of world Bank loans are much harder than those of the IDA credits.

EXERCISES

1. Explain the functions and activities of the International Bank for Reconstruction and Development. How far has it been successful in achieving them?
2. Explain briefly the working of the World Bank. What contributions has it made for the economic development of India?

Chapter 58

The World Bank Group

The World Bank has, at present, three affiliates : the International Development Association, the International Finance Corporation, and the Multilateral Investment Guarantee Agency. These are discussed below.

1. THE INTERNATIONAL DEVELOPMENT ASSOCIATION (IDA)

The International Development Association (IDA) is the "soft loan window" of the IBRD which was established in September 1960. It is an affiliate of the World Bank. The President of the World Bank is its head.

Its Objectives

The main objectives of the IDA are two-fold.

1. To provide assistance for poverty alleviation to the world's poorest countries.
2. To provide concessional financial assistance and macroeconomic management services to the poorest countries so as to raise their standard of living. These relate to human resource development, including population control, development of health, nutrition and education for the overall objective of removing poverty.

Its Membership

The membership of the IDA is open to all members of the World Bank. In June 2001, it had 182 members. If a country ceases to be a member of the World Bank, its membership of the IDA automatically ends. As per the Articles of Association of the IDA, its members are divided into two parts. In Part I are the developed countries which include among others Iceland, Japan, South Africa, the Russian Federation, Kuwait and UAE. It is known as G-24. Part II includes all the developing countries.

Its Organisation

The organisation of the IDA is that of the World Bank. With the exception of a few separate sections, the staff of the World Bank operates this Association. Right from the President, all the senior officers of the World Bank are its officers. Its Annual Report forms part of the World Bank Report and is submitted simultaneously.

Its Financial Resources

The resources of the IDA include the initial subscriptions from members, general replenishments from its more industrialised members, transfers from the net earnings of the World Bank, Special Funds contributions and adjustments and accumulated surpluses. The initial capital subscription from member countries at the time of its formation in 1960 was $ 757 million. A Special Fund was created in October 1982 with contributions from member countries. But its major source of funds has been the IDA replenishments for a period of three years. The IDA had 32 donor countries who provided $ 15.5 billion for the three-year IDA-9 which ended on June 30, 1993. The IDA-10 beginning July 1, 1993 had been fixed at $ 18 billion. The IDA-11 replenishment beginning July 1, 1996 had been fixed at $ 22 billion over the next three years. All contributions to capital subscription, replenishments and Special Fund are paid in convertible currencies by Part I member countries. The developing member countries of Part II make their contributions of 10 per cent in convertible currencies or gold and 90 per cent in their own currencies.

IDA Credits

The IDA loans are known as "credits" which are made to governments only. At present, countries with per capita income of less than $ 695 at 1990 prices can borrow from it. These are given for such projects for which no assistance is provided by the World Bank. Before approving a credit, the Special Committee of the IDA considers three criteria :

(a) Poverty Criterion. A country where population pressure is high and productivity is low, thereby leading to a low standard of living of the people.

(b) Performance Criterion. It relates to the past performance of the country in terms of loans received whether from the IDA or the World Bank. It must have been pursuing macroeconomic policies and executing projects satisfactorily.

(c) Project Criterion. The projects for which credits are to be utilised must yield finâncial and economic returns to justify them.

On the basis of these criteria, the IDA sanctions credits to LDCs for agriculture, education, health, nutrition, water supply, sewerage, etc. Such credits which are known as "soft loans", are given on the following terms :

(*i*) They are repayable over a period of 35-40 years; (*ii*) they have a 10-year grace period; (*iii*) the commitment fee (interest rate) which was charged from 0 to 0.5 per cent has now been waived; and (*iv*) a small administrative fee of 0.75 per cent is charged on the dibursed amount.

The gross disbursements by the IDA during the fiscal year 2000 were $ 6.8 billion.

India and IDA

Upto 1979-80, India had been the single largest beneficiary of the IDA assistance which was 40 per cent of the total credits committed to LDCs. With China becoming a member of the IDA in 1980, India's share in IDA's credits has been continuously on the decline. Between 1981-85, India received 30.5 per cent of the total assistance. From 1985 onwards, it has ranged between 15 to 20 per cent every year. During 2000, India received $ 1.2 billion interest-free IDA loan for elementary education, health, nutrition, food safety, social safety programme, environment security and supervision, etc.

Evaluation of IDA's Working

Since its inception in 1960 as the "soft window" of the World Bank, the IDA has been helping the poorest countries of the world in order to remove their poverty and raise their living standards. As a result of its assistance, the infant mortality rate in the LDCs, has been reduced to half of what it was earlier. The average life expectancy has increased by 13 per cent, and the adult literacy rate has risen to 60 per cent.

Despite these achievements, the IDA has not been able to render development assistance for the complete removal of poverty in LDCs due to lack of resources. The developed countries, especially the USA, have been the stumbling blocks in increasing the IDA replenishments. Consequently, the IDA assistance to the poorest countries had fallen from 100 per cent in 1988 to 85 per cent in 2000. According to a recent World Bank assessment, out of 350 IDA-supported projects in developing countries, only 59 per cent performed satisfactorily due to the efforts of governments of developing countries. Still, it has been successful in acting as a catalyst for their development.

2. THE INTERNATIONAL FINANCE CORPORATION (IFC)

The International Finance Corporation (IFC) is the private sector arm of the World Bank family which was established in July 1956. It is the major multilateral agency promoting productive private investment in developing countries. It helps finance private sector projects to mobilise finance for them in the international financial markets, and provides advice and technical assistance to business and governments.

Its Membership

The Articles of Agreement of the IFC are similar to that of the World Bank. A country has to be a member of the World Bank in order to join the IFC. In June 2001, it had 182 members.

Its Financial Resources

In the beginning, the authorised capital of the IFC was $ 100 million which was divided into 1,00,000 shares of $ 1000 each. At present, its authorised capital is $ 1300 million. The IFC can borrow from theWorld Bank four times its subscribed capital and surpluses. It can also borrow from the International money market.

Its Objectives

The objectives for which the IFC was set up, have been laid down in Article 1 of its Article of Agreement as under :

"The purpose of the Corporation is to further economic development by encouraging the growth of productive private enterprise in member countries, particularly in the less development areas, thus supplementing the activities of the International Bank for Reconstruction and Development. In carrying out this purpose, the Corporation shall :

(*i*) in association with private investors, assist in financing the establish-ment, improvement and expansion of productive private enterprise which would contribute to the development of its member countries by making investments, without guarantee of repayment by the member Government concerned, in cases where sufficient private investment is not available on reasonable terms;

(*ii*) seek to bring together investment opportunities, domestic and foreign private capital, and experienced management; and

(*iii*) seek to stimulate, and to help create conditions conducive to the flow of private capital, domestic and foreign, into productive investment in member countries."

Its Organisation

The IFC is an affiliate of the World Bank but it is separate from the World Bank, except for the fact that only a member of the World Bank can be its member. It has its own staff but draws upon the Bank for administrative services. Its organisational structure regarding the President, the Chairman, the Board of Governors, and Executive Directors is on the pattern of the World Bank. The World Bank President is the ex-officio Chairman of the Board of Directors of the IFC. But all the administrative powers of the IFC are vested in the Vice President of the IFC. The corporation has eight departments. Of these four relate to investment which function on geographical basis. The remaining four deparments relate to capital markets, finance and management, legal matters, and engineering which operate on functional basis.

Types of Assistance

The IFC renders assistance to a wide variety of sectors relating to large, medium and small industries which include financial services, mining, petro-chemicals, power, oil and gas exploration, telecommunications, tourism, general manufacturing and agro-based industries. The assistance to private enterprise in developing countries is in three ways : (*i*) by direct investment both in the form of loans and equity participation; (*ii*) by securing foreign and local capital; and (*iii*) by providing technical assistance.

(1) *Direct Investment.* It invests in partnership with private investors from the capital exporting country and/or from the country in which the enterprise is located. But its investments will not be more than half of the capital requirements of the enterprise. The minimum investment by the Corporation in an enterprise is $ 1 million, but there is no upper limit. The enterprise seeking loans from the IFC should be industrial, located in a developing country, and should satisfy the criteria of both economic development and reasonable commercial return. The Corporations assistance is not tied to expenditure in any particular country, but must be spent in the member countries. It is used to buy machines and other equipment and to meet foreign exchange, local costs, working capital and any other legitimate business expenses. It does not seek or accept any type of government guarantee for making investments and repayments of loans, except when it is required by law in a country. Loans and risk capital are provided at commercial rates with maturity of 7 to 12 years.

(2) *Foreign and Local Capital.* The IFC participates in promoting productive private investment in developing countries by way of equity and/or loan investment. It underwrites equity capital and helps in sponsoring and bringing together investors for new enterprises. Thus it secures the co-operation of both foreign and local enterprises. It helps them in making feasibility studies of the proposed projects.

(3) *Technical Assistance.* The IFC provides project sponsors with the necessary technical assistance so that their enterprises are potentially productive and financially sound. For this prupose, it undertakes financial studies and analysis. It also provides policy assistance to member governments so that they may develop the necessary investment climate to attract foreign and local private enterprise.

(4) *Capital Markets Development.* The Corporation has a Capital Markets Department which provides specialised resources for studying the problems and needs of the financial markets of developing countries. It provides financial support and advice for the development of financial institutions and helps in developing a legal, financial, and institutional framework which may encourage local and foreign capital in developing countries. The Corporation has been instrumental in the promotion of financial institutions, development finance companies, leasinig and venture capital companies, mutual funds, etc. by giving technical assistance to developing countries.

(5) *Help to Small Scale Industries.* The IFC also renders help to small scale industries in the form of advice for the preparation of project reports and technical assistance. It has established four such facilities for developing countries of different regions. They are the South Pacific Project Facility, the Africa Project Development Facility, the Business Advisory Service for the Caribbean and Central America, and the Polish Business Advisory Service. It has also established the African Management Services Company which provides skilled and experienced managers to small enterprises in the African region to improve their working. The IFC has a Technical Advisory Service in its Engineering Wing which gives expert advice to government institutes and small enterprises in preparing market and feasibility studies, for technical restructuring and for strategic planning. For all these services it charges a nominal fee. Finally, as in the case of medium and large scale industries, the IFC helps the small scale sector in raising funds.

In the fiscal year ending June 30, 2000, the IFC approved $ 2.6 billion in financing 264 projects in various sectors in 65 developing countries.

India and IFC

India is a founder member of the IFC. She has been receiving assistance in a variety of areas from the IFC since its inception. These include automobiles, shipping, electricity, cement, fertilisers, oil and gas, petro-chemicals, iron and steel, general manufacturing, and the financial sector. India is the second major client of IFC assistance. It has been giving about 10 per cent of total loans and equity to developing countries. The IFC invested $ 48.1 million in India, composed of loans of $ 25.4 million and an equity of $ 22.7 million, covering 11 projects which included the expansion of manufacturing facilities in computer diskettes, polyster and textiles, agribusiness exports. etc.

Its Evaluation

Over the year, the IFC has played a catalytic role in promoting productive private investment in developing countries by providing loans and equity capital, by rendering technical advice in the promotion of money and capital markets, by bringing local and foreign enterprises to co-operate in joint ventures, in starting new industrial projects in large, medium and small sectors. But its development assistance has gone more to developing countries and very little to the least developing economies.

3. THE MULTINATIONAL INVESTMENT GUARANTEE AGENCY (MIGA)

The multinational Investment Guarantee Agency (MIGA) is the newest affiliate of the World Bank family which was established in April 1988. It has been created to supplement the World Bank and the IFC to assist where the Bank and the IFC do not reach. It is joint venture with the International Finance Corporation. The MIGA has an authorised capital of $ 1.08 billion.

Its Objectives

The MIGA has the following objectives :

1. Its primary objective is to encourage the flow of direct foreign investment into developing member countries.

2. It provides insurance cover to investors against political risks.

3. The MIGA's guarantee programme protects investors against four types of non-commercial risks. They are : any danger involved in currency transfer, expropriation, war and civil disturbance, and breach of contract by governments.

4. It insures only new investments, including the expansion of existing investments, privatisation and financial restructuring.

5. It provides promotional and advisory services to the governments of developing countries to enable them to increase the attractiveness of their investment climate.

6. Another objective of the MIGA is to establish credibility among investors, and higher credit rating among global banking and financial markets of its members.

Its Working

In order to become a full-fledged member of the MIGA, a country has to ratify the convention and pay its capital subscription. By June 30, 2000, 160 countries had signed the MIGA convention. Of these, 136 countries had become its full-fledged members.

Before the investments are made, projects are to be registered with the MIGA. 90 per cent of the investment amount can be insured by the MIGA subject to a limit of $ 50 million per project. Among its eligible investments are included equity loans made or guaranteed by equity holders, and certain other types of direct investments. It covers insurance for projects for fifteen years which may be extended to 20 years in exceptional cases. It also insures eligible investments in cooperation with national insurance agencies and private insurers. All projects insured by the MIGA have to support the environmental and development objectives of the World Bank.

The MIGA provides promotional and advisory services to its developing member countries to help them attract more foreign direct investments. These services include the organisation of investment-promotion conferences, executive development programmes, foreign-investment policy, round-table conferences, and specialised advisory assistance to governments of developing member countries. It operates the Foreign

Investment Advisory Service in Policy, institutional and legal matters relating to direct foreign investment. It also gives advice on such policies and programmes which promote backward linkages between foreign investors and local investors.

Its Progress

The MIGA had signed a total or 226 contracts of guarantee for investments in 52 developing countries and its outstanding contingent liabilities were $ 2.8 billion in fiscal year 2000. It issued 68 investment guarantee contracts worth $ 862 million and the amount of insured projects of foreign investment was $ 8.4 billion. It assisted private firms from 17 different countries in making investments in 27 host countries. It launched and actively promoted "IPA-Net"—a global, Internet-based information in exchange, communications network and market-place—which facilitates the exchange of information among members of the international investment community. Thus MIGA's guarantees serve as a catalyst for multinational investments.

India and MIGA

India became the 113th country when she signed the MIGA convention on April 13, 1992. By becoming a member of the MIGA, India has entered into a commitment to provide against non-commercial risks to direct foreign investments. With the on-going process of structural adjustments and liberalisation of the Indian economy, the insurance guarantee of the MIGA to direct foreign investments and the help rendered by its advisory services, are bound to benefit its programmes for industrial development.

EXERCIESES

1. What are the objectives of the International Development Association? To what extent it has been successful in helping the developing countries?
2. Examine the working of the International Finance Corporation.
3. What is Multinational Investment Guarantee Agency (MIGA)? Explain its objectives and working.

Chapter 59

International Monetary System

1. MEANING

International monetary system refers to the system prevailing in world foreign exchange markets through which international trade and capital movements are financed and exchange rates are determined. We discuss below the international monetary system since the end of the World War II.

2. THE BRETTON WOODS SYSTEM

During the period preceding World War I almost all the major national currencies were on a system of fixed exchange rates under the international gold standard. This system had to be abandoned during World War I. There were fluctuating exchange rates from the end of the War to 1925. Efforts were made to return to the gold standard from 1925. But it collapsed with the coming of the Great Depression. Many countries resorted to protectionism and competitive devaluations—with the result that world trade was reduced to almost half. But depression completely disappeared during World War II.

In July 1944, the allied countries met at Bretton Woods in the USA to avoid the rigidity of the gold standard and the chaos of the 1930s in international trade and finance and to encourage free trade. The new system was the present International Monetary Fund (IMF) which worked out an *adjustable peg system.*

Under the Bretton Woods system exchange rates between countries were set or pegged in terms of gold or the US dollar at $ 35 per ounce of gold. This related to a fixed exchange rate regime with changes in the exchange within a band or range from 1 per cent above to 1 per cent below the par value. But these adjustments were not available to US which had to maintain the gold value of dollar. If the exchange rate hit either of the bands, the monetary authorities were obliged to buy or sell dollars against their currencies. Large adjustments could be made where there were "fundamental disequilibrium" (i.e. persistent and large deficits or surpluses) in BOP with the approval of the IMF and other countries. Member countries were forbidden to impose restrictions on payments and trade, except for a transitional period. They were allowed to hold foreign reserves partly in gold and partly in dollars. These reserves were meant to incur temporary deficits or surpluses by member countries, while keeping their exchange rates stable. In case of a BOP deficit, there was a *reserve outflow* by selling dollar and *reserve inflow* in case of a BOP surplus.

Reserve outflows were a matter of concern under the Bretton Woods system. So the IMF insisted on expenditure reducing policies and devaluation to correct BOP deficit. Temporary BOP deficits were also met by borrowing from the Fund for a period of 3 to 5 years. A country could borrow from the Fund on the basis of the size of its quota with it. The loans made by the IMF were in convertible currencies.

The first 25 per cent of its quota was in *gold tranche* which was automatic and the remaining under the *credit tranches* which carried high interest rates. To provide long-term loans the World Bank (or IBRD) was set up in 1946 and subsequently its two affiliates, the International Finance Corporation (IFC) in 1956 and International Development Association (IDA), in 1960. For the removal of trade restrictions, the *General Agreement on Tariffs and Trade* (GATT) came into force from January 1948. To supplement its resources, the Fund started borrowing from the ten industrialised countries in order to meet the requirements of the international monetary system under General Agreements to Borrow (GAB) from October 1962. Further, it created special Drawing Rights (SDRs) is January 1970 to supplement international reserves to meet the liquidity requirements of its members. The Bretton Woods system worked smoothly from 1950s to mid 1960s. During this period world output increased and with the reduction of tariffs under the GATT, world trade also rose.

3. THE BREAKDOWN OF THE BRETTON WOODS SYSTEM

The following are the principal causes and sequences of the breakdown of the Bretton Woods system.

1. *Built-in Instability.* The Bretton Woods System had a built-in instability that ultimately led to its breakdown. It was an adjustable peg system within plus or minus 1 per cent of the par value of $ 35. In case of fundamental disequilibrium, a country could devalue its currency with the approval of the IMF. But countries were reluctant to devalue their currencies because they had to export more goods in order to pay for dearer imports from other countries. This led countries to rely on deflation in order to cure BOP deficits through expenditure-reducing monetary-fiscal policies. The UK often restored to deflation such as in 1949, 1957 and 1967.

2. *The Triffin Dilemma.* Since the dollar acted as a medium of exchange, a unit of account and a store of value of the IMF system, every country wanted to increase its reserves of dollar which led to dollar holdings to a greater extent than needed. Consequently, the US gold stock continued to decline and the US balance of payments continued to deteriorate. Robert Triffin warned in 1960 that the demand for world liquidity was growing faster than the supply because the incremental supply of gold was increasing little. Since the dollar was convertible into gold, the supply of US dollars would be inadequate in relation to the liquidity needs of countries. This would force the US to abandon its commitment to convert dollars into gold. This is the Triffin Dilemma which actually led to the collapse of the Bretton Woods System in August 1971.

3. *Lack of International Liquidity.* There was a growing lack of international liquidity due to increasing demand for the dollar in world monetary markets. With the expansion of world trade, BOP deficits (and surpluses) of countries increased. This necessitated the supply of gold and of the dollar. But the production of gold in Africa was increasing very little. This led to larger demand and holdings of the dollar. Countries also wanted to have more dollar holdings because they earned interest. As the supply of dollars was inadequate in relation to the liquidity needs of countries, the US printed more dollars to pay for its deficits which other countries accepted as reserves.

4. *Mistakes in US Policies.* The BOP deficits of the US became steadily worse in the 1960s. To overcome them, the policies adopted by the US government ultimately led to the world crises. Rising US government expenditure in the Vietnam War, the financing of US space programme and the establishment of the "Great Society" (social welfare) programme in the 1960s led to large outflow of dollar from the US. But the US monetary authority (FED) did not devalue the dollar. Rather, it adopted monetary and fiscal measures to cut its BOP deficit.

5. *Destabilising Speculation.* Since countries with "fundamental disequilibrium" in BOP were reluctant to devalue their currencies and also took time to get the approval of the IMF, it provided speculators an opportunity to resort to speculation in dollars. When devaluations were actually made, there were large doses of devaluation than originally anticipated. This was due to destabilising speculation which made controls over capital flows even through monetary-fiscal measures ineffective. This was the immediate reason for the UK to devalue the pound in 1967.

6. *Crisis of Confidence and Collapse.* The immediate cause of the collapse of the Bretton Woods System was the eruption of a crisis of confidence in the US dollar. The pound had been devalued in November 1967. There was no control over the world gold market with the appearance of a separate price in the open market. The immediate cause for the collapse of the Bretton Woods System was the rumour in March 1971 that the US would devalue the dollar. This led to a huge outflow of capital from the US. On 15 August 1971, the US suspended the conversion of dollars into gold when some small European central banks wanted to convert their dollar reserves into gold at the US. It refused to intervene in the foreign exchange markets to maintain exchange rate stability and imposed a 10% import surcharge. Thus the main cause of breakdown of the Bretton Woods System was the problems of liquidity, adjustment and confidence. The increase in liquidity (international reserves) was in the form of dollars arising from BOP deficits of the US. But as the US was unable to adjust its deficits and excessive dollars accumulated in foreign countries, there was a *crisis* of *confidence* in the dollar and the Bretton Woods System brokedown.

Between 15 August 1971 and the Smithsonian Agreement of 18 December 1971, 48 countries including the United States, Japan and a large number of European countries abandoned fixed exchange rates. The 'Group of Ten' industrial countries met at the Smithsonian Institution in Washington on 18-19 December, 1971 and agreed to a new system of stable exchange rate with *wider bands.* As a first step towards realignment of major currencies, the US, devalued the dollar by 8 per cent, the Japanese revalued the yen by 17 per cent and the Germans their mark by 14 per cent. *The Smithsonian Agreement* widened the margin of fluctuations of the exchange rates to 2.25 per cent above or below the new parities of central rates. It officially devalued the dollar against gold from $ 35 to $ 38 per ounce. In 1973, the band was widened to 4.5 per cent. The Smithsonian Agreement broke down following the devaluation of the US dollar by 10% in February, 1973.

Another development took place in Europe when the EEC countries decided to limit the fluctuation of their currencies relative to each other to a smaller band. This came to be known as *"the snake in the tunnel"*. Under this arrangement, the EEC currencies were tied together and could fluctuate within narrow limits in relation to one another but could fluctuate in relation to other currencies within the limits set by the band proposals.

4. THE PRESENT INTERNATIONAL MONETARY SYSTEM

At the beginning of March 1973 India, Canada, Japan, Switzerland, the UK and several smaller countries had floating exchange rates. However, the *"joint float"* of the EEC countries continued even after March 1973 and was now called the *"snake in the lake"*, as there was no band within which the EEC currencies could fluctuate relative to other currencies. In March, 1979 the European Monetary System (EMS) was formed which created the European Currency Unit (ECU) which is a "basket" currency of a unit of account consisting of the major European currencies. The EMS limits the internal exchange rate movement of the member countries to not more than 2.25 per cent from the "central rates" with the exception of Italy whose lira can fluctuate up to 6 per cent.

In the meantime, the *Jamaica Agreement* of January 1976 (ratified in April 1978) formalised the regime of floating exchange rates under the auspices of the IMF. A number of factors forced the majority of member countries of the IMF to float their currencies. There were large short-term capital movements and central banks failed to stop speculation in currencies during the regime of adjustable pegs. The oil crisis in 1973 and the increase in oil prices in 1974 led to the great recession of 1974-75 in the industrial countries of the world. As a result "the dollar went into a rapid decline, which, by late 1978, had such alarming proportions that the United States government finally decided on a policy of massive intervention in order to prevent a further fall in the value of the dollar". At last, the system of managed floating exchange rates had come to stay by 1978. By the *Second Amendment of the IMF Charter* in 1978, the member countries are not expected to maintain and establish par values with gold or dollar. The Fund has no control over the exchange rate adjustment policies of the member countries. But it exercises international "surveillance" of exchange rate policies of its members.

The Second Amendment has reduced the position of gold in the global monetary system in the following ways by : (*a*) abolishing the official price of gold; (*b*) delinking it with the dollar in exchange arrangements; (*c*) eliminating the obligations of the Fund and its members to transfer or receive gold; and (*d*) selling a part of Fund's gold holdings.

The Second Amendment has also made SDRs as the chief reserve assets of the global monetary system whose value is expressed in currencies and not gold. It is now a unit of account, a currency peg and medium of transactions.

The present international monetary system of floating exchange rates is not one of free flexible exchange rates but of "managed floating". It has rarely operated without government intervention. Periodic intervention by governments has led the system to be called a "managed" or "dirty" floating system. In 1977, when the intervention was very heavy, it was characterised as a "filthy" float. When Governments do not intervene, it is a "clean" float. But the possibilities of a clean float are very remote. Thus a system of managed floating exchange rates is evolving where the central banks are trying to control fluctuations of exchange rates around some "normal" rates even though the Second Amendment of the Fund makes no mention of normal rates.

"*The present international monetary system* has also evolved in a number of important ways, including new allocation of SDRs, increased nations' quota in the IMF, renewal of the General Agreements to Borrow (GAB), the abolishment of the official gold price, and the formation of the European Monetary System (EMS) and the Euro Currency."[1]

The US is the major country which has been influencing the global monetary system. It has permitted the dollar to float in realtion to other currencies with occasional interventions when the dollar has reached extreme highs or lows. When the dollar was extremely high (appreciating), the G-5 (US, UK, Germany, Japan and France) agreed to intervene to bring the dollar down by the *Plaza Accord* in September 1985. Subsequently, the dollar depreciated substantially i.e. by more than 50% relative to the yen. By early 1987, the dollar had become undervalued and by the *Louvre Accord,* the G-7 countries (G-5 plus Canada and Italy) agreed to cooperate in keeping their exchange rates around their current levels at that time. "The Louvre Accord was successful in stabilising exchange rates for the rest of the year. Since then there seems to have been a consensus that exchange rates should be broadly stabilised, but there is little overt cooperation *among countries*."

Its Problems

The present international monetary system is faced with excessive fluctuations and large disequilibria in exchange rates. Often countries, both developed and developing, have been faced with either excessive appreciation or depreciation of their currencies in relation to the dollar which continues to dominate the world monetary system. Even the newly created Euro of the EU which was supposed to be a strong currency has been depreciating considerably since its inception against the dollar. This has adversely affected the world trade.

Reform of the Present International Monetary System

Economists have suggested a number of measures in order to avoid the excessive fluctuations and large disequilibria in exchange rates for reforming the present world monetary system.

1. *Coordination and Cooperation of Policies.* A few economists, and McKinnon in particular, suggested international co-operation and co-ordination of policies among the leading developed countries for exchange rate stability. According to McKinnon[2], the US, Germany and Japan should have the optimal degree of exchange rate stability by fixing the exchange rates among their currencies at the equilibrium level based on the purchasing power parity. Thus they would co-ordinate their monetary policies for exchange rate stability.

2. *Establishing Target Zones.* Williamson called for the establishment of target zones within which fluctuations in exchange rates of major currencies may be permitted. According to him, the forces of demand and supply should determine the equilibrium exchange rate. There should be an upper target zone of 10% above the

1. D. Salvatore, *Theories and Problems of International Economics,* 3/e, 1990. Italics added.
2. R.I. McKinnon, "The Rules of the Game : International Money in Historical Perspective", *J.E.L.*, 31, 1993.

equilibrium rate and a lower target zone of 10% below the equilibrium exchange rate. The exchange rate should not be allowed to move outside the two target zones by official intervention. In February 1987, the leading five developed countries agreed under the Louvre Agreement to have some sort of target zones for the stability of exchange rates among their currencies. Despite official intervention by these countries, the exchange rates continued to fluctuate within wide margins than agreed upon at Louvre. Thus Williamson's proposal has since been discarded being impracticable.

3. *Improving Global Liquidity.* The reform package of the present world monetary system should improve global liquidity. As a *first* step, both BOP deficit and surplus countries should take steps to reduce a persistent imbalance through exchange rate changes via internal policy measures. *Second,* they should also cooperate in curbing large flows of "hot money" that destabilise their currencies. *Third,* they should be willing to settle their BOP imbalances through SDRs rather than through gold or dollar as reserve assets. *Fourth,* there should be increasing flow of resources to the developing countries.

4. *Leaning Against the Wind.* To reduce the fluctuations in exchange rates, the IMF *Guidelines for the Management of Floating Exchange Rates,* 1974 suggested the idea of leaning against the wind. It means that the central banks should intervene to reduce short-term fluctuations in exchange rates but leave the long-term fluctuations to be adjusted by the market forces.

5. Richard Cooper suggests a global central bank with a global currency which should be a global lender of last resort.

6. Jaffrey Sachs proposes the creation of an international bankruptcy court which should deal with countries.

7. George Soros opines that the IMF should set ceilings for external finance for each country beyond which access to private capital need not be insured. But there should be mandatory insurance by an international credit insurance corporation.

8. Paul Krugman suggests reintroduction of capital controls as a "least bad response" to an international crisis.

9. *Objective Indicators.* To iron out exchange rate fluctuations, the IMF Interim Committee suggested the adoption of such objective indicators as inflation-unemployment, growth of money supply, growth of GNP, fiscal balance, balance of trade and international reserves. The variations in these indicators require the adoption of restrictive monetary-fiscal measures to bring stability in exchange rates.

Conclusion. The various suggestions to reform the present monetary system are closely inter-linked. But there is lack of unanimity over the various proposals among the nations. Given the differences of opinion between the developing and developed countries and among the developed countries themselves, there is no hope that any concrete proposal to reform the global monetary system would be acceptable to nations. So the present system of managed floating exchange rate is likely to stay on.

EXERCISES

1. Explain briefly the working of the Bretton Woods System. What led to its breakdown?
2. What were the causes for the collapse of Bretton Woods System? Explain briefly the present international monetary system.
3. What are the main problems of the present international monetary system. Give suggestions to remove these problems.
4. Explain the present international monetary system. What suggestions have been made to reform it.

CHAPTER 60

International Liquidity

1. MEANING

International liquidity is defined as the aggregate stock of internally acceptable assets held by the central bank to settle a deficit in a country's balance of payments. In other words, international liquidity provides a measure of a country's ability to finance its deficit in balance of payments without resorting to adjustment measures. Shortage of liquidity hampers the expansion of global trade and its surplus leads to global inflationary pressures.

International liquidity is generally used as a synonym for international reserves. Such reserves include a country's official gold stock holdings, its convertible foreign currencies, SDRs, and its net reserve position in the IMF. Economists like Heller and McKinnon use a broader definition of international liquidity to include international borrowings, commercial credit operations, and the international financial structure in a country's reserves. This definition implies international availability of liquidity and the possibility of obtaining credit from financial institutions operating in international financial markets. Thus, in the broader sense, international liquidity includes private as well as official holdings of international liquidity assets.

In the literature on international liquidity distinction is made between owned and borrowed reserves, and between conditional and unconditional reserves. Foreign exchange surplus, after meeting all current and capital account obligations of the country with the rest of the world, are *"owned" reserves*. Similarly, the official gold stock of a country constitutes its owned reserves. Capital imports in the form of borrowings from abroad and direct investments by foreign countries constitute *borrowed reserves*. Both owned and borrowed reserves are the source of international liquidity.

Unconditional international liquidity consists of a country's official gold stock, holdings of its foreign currencies and SDRs, its net position in the IMF, and private holding of international assets. In all such cases, liquidity assets are available to the country without any conditions or restrictions on their use. But in the case of borrowed reserves, the lender country may impose conditions or restrictions on the use of liquid assets by the borrowing country. Many international financial institutions provide funds on conditional basis for specific projects and on specified repayment provisions. All these are cases of *conditional liquidity*. This is done to avoid the misue of liquidity by the borrowing country.

2. NEED AND PROBLEM OF INTERNATIONAL LIQUIDITY

The (need or) problem of international liquidity arises because the demand for internatonal liquidity is rising more than its supply, thereby implying shortage of international liquidity. The principal causes for the shortatge of international liquidity are the following:

1. *BOP Deficits.* There have been increasing BOP deficits of the majority of countries in the world. In particular, after the opening of LDCs to world markets, these countries have been facing persistent BOP deficits. Too much dependence on exports has exposed these economies to international fluctuations in the demand for and prices of their products. They have become unstable due to international cyclical instability. On the other hand, their import requirements have been on the increase in order to develop. As a result, they are faced with foreign exchange constraints. This has necessitated larger inflow of aid and foreign investment. Consequently, debt serving and interest on debt have risen and payments of dividends, profits and royalties on private direct foreign investment have grown, thereby leading to decline in the net inflow of foreign capital. All these have led to further shortage of foreign exchange reserves.

2. *High Tariff Barriers.* The exports of LDCs to developed countries have not been increasing, thereby adversely affecting their export earnings. One of the reasons for the non-expansion of their exports has been high tariff barriers imposed by the developed countries on their exports, especially by their regional groups like the EEC. At the same time, the LDCs are trying to cut down their essential imports from the developed countries by means of exchange controls, high tariffs, import quotas and similar protectionist devices in order to conserve foreign exchange. This has adversely affected their development process.

3. *Attitude of Developed Countries.* The majority of developed countries have surplus in their balance of payments. They are creditors of LDCs and do not take any interest in getting rid of their surplus so as to increase international liquidity.

4. Unequal Distribution of International Reserves. The distribution of international reserves is biased and favours the developed countries. It is primarily based on the their quotas in the IMF. Whenever the IMF quotas are revised, the larger share goes to the developed countries. It is the developing countries whose need for international liquidity is far greater which suffer from its shortage.

MEASURES TO SOLVE THE PROBLEM OF INTERNATIONAL LIQUIDITY

The following measures have been suggested to solve the problem of international liquidity.

1. *Promoting Export Expansion.* Developing countries should reduce BOP deficit by promoting export expansion. The choice lies in concentrating the expansion of primary or secondary products or both. The expansion of secondary products requires import substitution for export expansion. These policies will earn them foreign exchange.

2. *Limiting Exports.* They should ban non-essential consumer goods, and limit imports of specific goods by selective tariffs, physical quotas, etc. This policy will enable them to conserve foreign exchange.

3. *Changing Official Echange Rate.* A developing country can change its official exchange rate by devaluing its currency so that its export prices are lowered and import prices are increased. This will help in earning foreign exchange.

4. *Restrictive Monetary-Fiscal Policies.* By following restrictive monetary and fiscal policies, a developing country can reduce domestic demand for products which will lower import prices, reduce inflationary pressures and BOP deficit.

5. *Reduction in BOP Surplus.* The majority of developed countries have BOP surplus which they should reduce by (*a*) accepting the national currencies of developing countries for payments; (*b*) removal of trade barriers to the products of developing countries; and (*c*) accepting products of developing countries in exchange for their products, as was done by the earstwhile USSR.

6. *Expanding International Reserves.* The IMF should expand international reserves by fresh allocation of larger quotas to member countries. In particular, all new issues of SDRs should be distributed to developing countries so that they may pay then to developed countries to solve their foreign exchange problem.

3. INTERNATIONAL RESERVES

The main features of international reserves or international liquidity have been :

1. Gold reserves of the countries of the world increased from $ 33.9 billion in 1951 to SDR 224.1 billion in 1997.
2. Marked increase in the share of foreign exchange reserves from $13.7 billion in 1951 to SDR 1078.2 billion in 1997.
3. Increase in reserve position in the IMF from $ 1.7 billion in 1951 to SDR 36.2 billion in 1997.
4. Emergence of SDRs since 1972 which increased from SDR 8.7 billion to SDR 18.7 billion in 1997.

Thus the total international reserves comprising the above four items increased from $ 49.3 billion to SDR 1357.2 billion in 1997.

No doubt, international reserves have been on the increase but they have not been rising as much as the increase in the volume and value of world trade. More so in the case of LDCs whose needs are greater and more urgent than that of developed countries.

4. IMF AND INTERNATIONAL LIQUIDITY*

There was no problem of international liquidity prior to 1970. This was because under the Bretton Woods Agreement the exchange rates of countries were fixed in terms of gold or the US dollar at $ 35 per ounce of gold. Member countries were forbidden to impose restrictions on payments and trade, except for a transitional period. They were allowed to hold their monetary reserves partly gold and partly in dollars and sterling. These reserves were meant to incur temporary deficits by member countries while keeping their exchange rates stable. The IMF insisted on expenditure reducing policies and devaluation to correct deficit in balance of payments. "Therefore, apart from ad hoc loans made by the IMF, the growth in liquidity needed to finance the expansion of world trade had to be found in liquidity needed to finance the expansion of world trade had to be found in the expansion of gold and the supply of dollar and sterling. But the physical supply of gold is virtually limited to the output of the mines in South Africa and the Soviet Union." Since the dollar acted as a medium of exchange, a unit of account and a store of value of the IMF system, every country wanted to increase its reserves of dollar which led to dollar holdings to a greater extent than needed. Consequently, the US gold stock continued to decline and the US balance of payments continued to deteriorate. Robert Triffin warned in 1959 that the demand for world liquidity was growing faster than the supply because the incremental supply of gold was increasing little. Since the dollar was convertible into gold, the supply of US dollars would be inadequate in relation to the liquidity needs of countries. This might introduce trade barriers by countries in order to have balance of payments surpluses and build up reserves. Thus, according to Triffin, a growing liquidity shortage would generate strong contractionary forces that would threaten the expansion of the world economy and lead to a world recession of the 1931 type.

A crisis of confidence had already erupted. The pound had been devalued in November 1967. There was no control over the world gold market with the appearance of a spearate price in the open market. On 15 August, 1970, the United States suspended the conversion of dollars into gold and refused to intervene in the foreign exchange markets to maintain exchange rate stability. The 'Group of Ten' industrial countries met at the Smithsonian Institute in Washington in December 1971 and agreed to the realignment of major currencies by devaluing the dollar by 10 per cent and revaluing their currencies. The Smithsonian Agreement broke down following the US dollar devaluation of February 1973 again and in March 1973 a number of countries had floating exchange rates and the EEC countries had a "joint float" of their currencies. The Jamaica Agreement of January 1976 formalised the regime of floating exchange rates. By the Second Amendment of the IMF Charter in 1978, the member countries are not expected to maintain and establish par values with gold or dollar. The Fund has no control over the exchange rate adjustment policies of the member countries. The system of flexible exchange rates has tended to reduce the need for more reserves.

5. ROLE OF THE IMF IN INCREASING WORLD LIQUIDITY

The IMF is an international monetary institution which is the principal source of supply of world liquidity to its 182 members. Over the years, it has adopted the following measures to increase international liquidity.

SDRs. In early 1970, it introduced a scheme for the creation and issue of Special Drawing Rights (SDRs) as unconditional reserve assets to influence the level of world reserves and to solve the problem of international liquidity. There are SDR 146 billion in the Fund's General Account. The Fund also creates SDRs and allocates them to members in proportion of their quotas. For this purpose, the Fund has established the Special Drawing Account. As the international monetary asset, SDRs are held in the international reserves of central banks and governments to finance improve international liquidity so as to correct fundamental disequilibria in the balance of payments of Fund members. The participants in the SDR scheme receive SDRs under "transactions with designation" and "transactions by agreement" unconditionally. The IMF acts as a clearing house in these transactions. Since 1981 there are 21.4 billion SDRs in the Fund.

Quotas. The bulk of Fund's financial resources comes from quota subscriptions of member countries. To meet the global demand for liquidity, it has been increasing quotas of members every four years under the General Review of Quotas. As a result, it increased the member quotas from 7.6 billion in 1947 to SDR 212 billion in 1998.

Selling Gold. It increases its funds by selling gold to members.

Borrowings. It borrows from governments, central banks or private institutions of industrialised countries, the Bank for International Settlements, and even from OPEC countries, like Saudi Arabia.

Reserve Tranche. The Fund has a variety of facilities for lending its resources to member countries. Lending by the Fund is linked to temporary assistance to member in financing disequilibrium in their balance of payments on current account. If a member has less currency with the Fund than its quota, the difference is called gold or reserve tranche. It can draw upto 25 per cent on its reserve tranche automatically upon representation to the Fund for its balance of payments needs. It is not charged any interest on such drawings, but is required to repay within a period of three to five years.

Credit Tranche. A member can draw further from balance quota in 4 instal-ments upon 100 per cent of its quota from credit tranche annually. Drawings from credit tranche are conditional because the members have to satisfy the Fund of adopting a viable programme to ensure financial stability. To meet the severe balance of payments problems, the Fund has been gradually raising the limit of borrowings by its members over the years under the credit tranche. Now members can draw upto the equivalent of 300 per cent of their new quotas on the total net use of the Fund's resources. The limits exclude drawings from CCFF, BSAF, SAF, STF and ESAF. The purchases are made under *stand-by arrangements* rather than directly.

New Credit Facilities. Since the 1960s, the Fund has created several new credit facilities for its members. Loans from these facilities are separate from tranches and are available for a longer period. These are : BSFF (Buffer Stock Financing Facility), EFF (Extended Fund Facility), SFF (Supplementary Financing Facility), SAF (Structural Adjustment Facility), ESAF (Enhanced Structural Adjustment Facility), CCFF (Compensatory and Contingency Financing Facility), STF (Systematic Transformation Facility), ESAL (Emergency Structural Adjustment Loans) and CCL (Contingency Credit Line).[1] These facilities provide for members annual access to Fund resources up to 150% of their quotas or up to 450% over a three year period.

IDA Replenishments. Another important source for increasing world liquidity is the IDA Replenishments to the poor developing countries for three years by the developing countries. In recent years, IDA-9 Replenishment gave $ 15.55 billion in 1990, IDA-10 gave $ 18 billion in 1993, and IDA-11 gave 22 billion in 1996 for three years.

6. ITS CRITICISMS

The various Fund schemes for increasing global liquidity have been criticised for favouring the developed countries. They are inequitable which have tended to mark unfair distribution of international liquidity. For instance, the allocation of SDRs to participating countries is proportional to their quotas. In this sense, the allocation of SDRs to developing countries is too low as compared to their needs. Low allocation of SDRs reduces the borrowing capacity of such countries.

Moreover, the SDR scheme does not link the creation of international reserves in the form of SDRs with the need for development finance on the part of developing countries. The need for liquidity on the part of developing country is great. Therefore, there is need to create more SDRs with fair distribution so that more unconditional liquidity is made available for the greater needs of developing countries.

Unfortunately, due to the rigid attitude of the United States and some other developed countries, the Fund has not been able to resume allocation of SDRs from January 1982, despite the repeated pleas of the developing countries over these years. So the Fund has failed in its objective of increasing international liquidity through SDRs. Consequently, faced with a recession, an inadequate flow of concessional aid and falling prices of commodities and raw materials, developing countries have been facing severe balance of payments and debt problems. To solve this problem, there is urgent need for fresh allocation of SDRs which should be distributed only to developing countries.

EXERCISES

1. What is meant by international liquidity? Comment upon the efforts made by the International Monetary Fund to solve this problem.
2. Write an essay on the problems and solution of international liquidity.
3. What do you mean by international liquidity? Discuss the causes and measures adopted to solve this problem.

Chapter 61

The Euro-Dollar Market

1. MEANING

The Euro-dollar market is the largest market in the international monetary system. It has been playing a central role in international finance.

Euro-dollar is not a different currency from the US dollar. But it is the American dollar which stands deposited with banks, known as Eurobanks (European banks), outside the United States. Quite often, they are deposited with a bank in London, or in Paris, Frankfurt, Amsterdam or Zurich. The term Euro-dollar market is now a misnomer because quite a large number of US dollars have accumulated in banks outside Europe such as in Japan, Canada, Hongkong, Singapore, and other countries. Moreover, Eurobanks have also been dealing in other currencies, such as the British sterling, German marks, Swiss francs, Dutch guilders[1], etc. So it is no longer a Euro-dollar market but a *Euro-currency market.*

2. ORIGIN AND GROWTH

The origin of the Euro-dollar market can be traced back to the 1920s when the US dollars were deposited in the European banks which converted them into their local currencies for lending purposes. But the real growth of the Euro-dollar market began after the Second World War. The following factors led to its growth:

1. *Flow of US Aid*. The United States emerged as the most powerful nation in the post-war period which spent huge sums of money on the rehabilitation of Europe both in terms of economic and military aid. This led to the transfer of a large number of dollars in Eurobanks.

2. *Cold War*. The cold war which started in the 1950s led the Soviet Union and the East European government to transfer their dollar deposits from America to Eurobanks for fear that they might be blocked by the American Government.

3. *Decline in the Importance of Sterling*. In the post-war period Britain emerged as a debtor country. Consequently, the British sterling which had dominated the international financial market in the pre-war era gave place to the dollar in the post-war period. The importance of sterling further fell when the British Government placed severe restrictions on the grant of sterling to central banks outside the sterling area under the British Exchange Control Act in the early post-war period.

4. *Regulation-Q*. Regulation-Q of the US Federal Reserve System had been a major factor which gave rise to the Euro-dollar market in the late 1960s. Under the Regulation-Q, a ceiling was imposed on the interest rate payable on time deposits with the US banks and it prohibited the payment of any interest at all on deposits upto

30 days. This encouraged the US banks to open branches in Europe and attract dollar deposits to be used for financing international trade. In particular, this happened in 1968 and 1969 and again from 1979 onwards when the Regulation-Q ceiling kept low interest rates on time deposits. Consequently, both the US citizens and foreigners having dollars in excess of their transactions requirements transferred them in Eurobanks because they paid higher interest rate than the US banks. This also encouraged European lenders and borrowers to trade in dollars in London and other European financial markets rather than in New York.

5. *Other US Measures*. There were some other measures which hampered the capacity of US banks to compete for international business including curbs on the release of taxes on profits earned by foreigners in the United States, the introduction of the Interest Equalisation Tax in 1964, controls over the US direct investment abroad, and tight monetary policy to control inflationary pressures. These led to heavy borrowing by US banks from the Euro-dollar market to meet the demand for dollars in the US.

6. *BOP Deficits in US*. There have been large and persistent BOP deficits in the US thereby leading to the outflow of the US dollars to the Eurobanks in countries having surplus with it.

7. *Petro-dollars*. The increase in the oil prices since 1973 has resulted in the tremendous increase in the incomes of the oil producing countries of the world which are known as petro-dollars. These are deposited in Eurobanks. These have further expanded the Eurodollar market.

8. *Innovative Banking*. Because of special circumstances that were present in the 1950s, there came into being a banking system distinct from but supplementary to the banking system of Europe. Like any other banking system, its elements consisted of reserves, deposits and loans, all in US dollars and recorded in Eurobanks. Consequently, the Euro-dollar market has grown rapidly, in which deposits are received and loans made in currencies other than that of the country in which the market is situated. Now Eurocurrency market dominates international transactions and traditional foreign banking accounts for only 11 per cent of international banking.

3. HOW DOES IT FUNCTION?

The Euro-dollar market is very extensive and complex. It is a means of transferring short-term and medium-term funds from one country to another. Euro-dollar deposits and loans expand whenever funds flow into the Eurobanks as deposits from (*i*) commercial banks or residents of the United States; (*ii*) transfers by commercial banks or residents of other countries; and (*iii*) central banks, either directly or through the Bank for International Settlements. The first type of flow from the United States can be caused by one or more of the following factors : (1) a fall in US interest rates relative to Euro-dollars rates; (2) an increased desire for asset diversification; (3) a fall in covered yield of foreign assets; or (4) an expected appreciation of the US dollar.

The flow of Euro-dollar from commercial banks or residents outside the United States involve a portfolio shift out of domestic currency assets into US dollars. Moreover, many central banks also redeposit a substantial proportion of their reserve gains in the Euromarket.

The Euromarket is connected closely to the foreign exchange market because banks are able to manage their foreign currency positions in two ways : (1) They can buy and sell currencies outright in the spot and forward exchange markets. (2) They can borrow and lend currencies in the interbank market. However, many Euro-currency loans are made to non-bank borrowers also. Let us analyse the functioning of the Euromarket. Suppose that a bank in London acquires dollar-deposits on a New York bank. If the London bank simply keeps these deposits, no Euro-dollars are created. But if this bank lends these dollars to some individual at interest rate, it creates dollar deposit claims against itself. These claims are Euro-dollars which the bank in London has created in excess of what it holds on a New York bank. Thus the ultimate increase in Euromarket aggregates will not be identical to initial deposit inflows because there are always subsequent flows induced by interest differentials and portfolio adjustments.

The above process of credit creation in the Euromarket has led economists to use the credit-multiplier analysis to explain its behaviour. Given the initial levels of US and foreign interest rates, this multiplier is always less than 1. This is because an initial deposit inflow of, say, $ 100 will encourage dollar rates to fall relative to foreign rates. This will, in turn, lead to a leakage in the original inflow. Moreover, the Euromarket is very vast and unregulated. Therefore, it does not operate like the ordinary banking system. Last but not the least, the multiplier analysis is essentially a tool for examining a credit creation in a closed economy, whereas the Euromarket is an open market. This fact severely limits the usefulness of the credit multiplier as a method for expanding the growth of the Euro-dollar market.

4. ROLE IN INTERNATIONAL FINANCIAL SYSTEM

The Euro-dollar market has been playing an important role in international financial system. Investing and borrowing US dollars is the core function of the Euro-currency market. It transfers short and medium terms funds throughout the world, thereby increasing international capital mobility. It not only enables individual banks to improve their portfolio allocation, but also provides important services to the non-bank private sector. The Euro-currency market attracts funds because it offers higher interest rates, greater flexibility of maturities, and a wider range of investment qualities than other short-term capital markets. It attracts borrowers because it lends funds at relatively low interest rates. It is competitive in the interest rates it charges and receives, both because of the economies of scale afforded by concentrating on wholesale transactions, and because the Eurobanks are not subject to the regulations which tend to raise costs in domestic banking.[1]

Commercial banks, central banks, government treasuries, international banks like the Bank of International Settlement, and multinational corporations are the borrowers and lenders in the Euro-currency market. Private firms are often engaged in hedging or arbitrage operation in Euro-dollars in order to earn profits from interest differentials.

The expansion of the Euro-dollar market has greatly increased international capital mobility. It has helped in integrating international capital markets. It has played an effective role in recycling funds from countries having surplus balance of payments to those having deficit balance of payments. Again, international flows of Euro-dollars have improved economic efficiency by reducing interest differential among nations.

The Euro-dollar market has also resolved the problems of countries whose policy objectives aim at controlling international capital movements. For instance, when deposits are transferred from a US bank to a Eurobank, there is an outflow of capital which increases a US deficit in balance ofpayments or reduces a surplus. In the opposite case, there is an inflow of capital when the transfer is from a Eurobank to a US bank. If theEurobank is the central bank of a country which transfers some of its dollar holdings into Euro-dollar deposits, or viceversa, transfer does not affect the US deficit or surplus, but helps to finance it, because the transfer consists of official foreign exchange.[3]

However, these flows of Euro-dollars have three adverse effects :

First, when the monetary authority of a country is trying to curb inflation through a restrictive monetary policy, an inflow of short-term capital defeats such a policy. Again when there is an outflow of capital and the country is following an easy monetary policy to combat unemployment, such a policy again becomes ineffective.

Second, Euro-dollars provide an enoromous fund of liquid resources which are used for speculative capital movements. These expose the economies of the concerned countries to severe strains of sudden and large withdrawals of credits. Such financial upheavals and disturbances also affect the international monetary system as a whole, especially when the countries involved are not protected by exchange controls or trade barriers. Despite the fact that the developing countries resort to exchange controls and trade barriers on a large scale, their economies are adversely affected by such financial disturbances more than the developed countries. This is because the former are more dependent on the major international financial centres like the Euromarket.

EXERCISES

1. What is Euro-currency market? How does it function? What role does it play in the international financial system?
2. What is Euro-dollar market? Explain its working and economic consequences.

---

2. Andrew Crockette, *International Money,* 1977.
3. P.T. Ellsworth and J.C. Leith, *op. cit.,* p. 465.

CHAPTER 62

The European Economic Community (EEC)

1. INTRODUCTION

The European Economic Community (EEC) or European Community (EC) was founded in 1957, under the Treaty of Rome, by France, Germany, Italy, Belgium, Luxemburg, and the Netherlands. The community of the original six members was enlarged as from January 1, 1973 with the inclusion of Ireland, Denmark and the United Kingdom. Greece became its member in 1981, followed by Portugal and Spain in 1984. The Community has now fifteen members. Since 1995, it is called the European Union (EU).

2. HISTORY

The forerunner of the EC was the European Coal and Steel Community (ECSC) Treaty which was ratified by the original six members in 1952. It removed all import duties and quota restrictions on coal, iron ore, steel and scrap on intra-community trade. The aim was to have economies of scale in these industries in order to compete effectively with the US and other foreign producers.

This partial integration by the six members of the ECSC was enlarged by the Treaty of Rome in 1957, for the establishment of a common market for all commodities and for the development of atomic power.

3. OBJECTIVES

The EC consists of three organisations based on their separate treaties originally signed by the six member states : *first*, the ECSC set up by the Treaty of Paris in 1951, valid for 50 years; *second*, the EEC by the Treaty of Rome in 1957 of unlimited duration; and *third*, the European Atomic Energy Community (Euratom) by the Second Treaty of Rome in 1957, also of unlimited duration. The first treaty was already in operation from July 1952 and the other two came into force from January 1958. The Single European Act of 1986 led to the formation of a single internal market in the EC. The objectives of the Community include :

(*a*) the elimination, as between Member States, of custom duties and of quantitative restrictions in regard to the import of and export of goods, as well as all other measures having equivalent effect;

(*b*) the establishment of a common customs tariff and of a common commercial policy towards third countries.

(*c*) the abolition, as between Member States, of obstacles to freedom of movement for persons, services and capital;

(*d*) the establishment of a common policy in the sphere of agriculture;

(*e*) the adoption of a common policy in the sphere of transport;

(*f*) the establishment of a system ensuring that competition in the common market is not distorted;

(*g*) the application of procedures by which the economic policies of Member States can be co-ordinated and disequilibrium in their balance of payments can be remedied;

(*h*) the approximation of the laws of Member States to the extent required for proper functioning of the common market;

(*i*) the creation of a European Social Fund in order to improve the possibilities of employment of workers and to contribute to the raising of their standard of living;

(*j*) the establishment of a European Investment Bank to facilitate the economic expansion of the Community by opening up fresh resources; and

(*k*) the association of overseas countries and territories with a view to increasing trade and to promoting jointly economic and social development.

Thus the principle objectives of the EC are the elimination of all obstacles to the free movement of goods, services, capital and labour between the member countries, and the establishment of common policies in the spheres of agriculture and transport, and a common external commercial policy. To make the common market effective, a variety of national policies relate to competition, fiscal matter and regional aids.

4. ORGANISATION

The principal administrative body of the EEC is the European Council which consists of one minister from each member country. Its decisions are taken by unanimous or majority voting. The Presidency of the Council is held by each member country by rotation for a six-monthly period. The Council has its own secretariat with the Committee of Permanent Representatives (Coreper) as a most important body. Members of Coreper are officials of ambassadorial rank who are assisted by a number of specialist and subordinate committees. All major policy-making decisions of the Community, ranging from early discussions to decision taking by the Council, are made by Coreper. It is also an essential link between the EEC and member governments. Thus the Council "is the executive agent of the Community making daily decisions, formulating rules of conduct, preparing new legislation, and providing members to carry out the provisions of the Treaty."

The Council is assisted in its work by the European Commission. This consists of 20 Commissioners, two each from the 5 large countries and one each from the small. This is the executive body of the EC whose members are appointed for periods of four years with renewable appointments. The President and Vice-Presidents are chosen from its members by governments for a two-year renewable period. The Commission has its own staff of over ten thousand civil servants, including translators and interpretors. It administers existing treaties and their subsequent rules and proposes new policies.

The Court of Justice adjudicates disputes relating to agriculture, competition policy and social security for migrants among the member countries. It also decides about cases brought by the Commission against member states or against the Council or Commission or by a firm or person against a Community decision. It also interprets the Treaty and other regulations, and levies penalties for infringements. Member states are bound by the Treaty of Rome to comply with the judgement of the Court.

By an amerndment to the Treaty of Rome, the Court of Auditors was appointed as an integral part of the organisational structure of the EEC. It audits the Community budget, monitors its expenditure thoroughly and lays down better procedures for the collection of duties and levies.

There is also the European Parliament whose first international election took place in June 1979. Its role is of a general consultative and informative nature. But it has the power to approve or reject the draft budget prepared by the Commission. It can also dismiss the Commission. It must be consulted by the Council before a final decision is taken. The Parliament usually acts through the main Parliamentary Committee.

Advisory institutions include the Economic and Social Committee, the Monetary Committee and the Consultative Committee on coal and steel industry. The Economic and Social Committee represents the various categories of economic and social activity such as employers, unions, farmers, retail trade and liberal professions, as well as general public. Its members are appointed by the Council from member states, each member being appointed for four years. The Monetary Commitee examines disturbing developments in monetary affairs and in balance of payments of the EEC, and recommends remedies. The Consultative Committee is confined to the problems of coal and steel industry.

5. WORKING AND ACHIEVEMENTS

The principle objective of the EC was the creation of a customs union. To achieve this, the Treaty of Rome provided 12 years for the elimation of internal tariffs and other trade barriers, and the adoption of a common external tariff for industrial goods. Both these goals were achieved on 1 July, 1968 and full *customs union* became a reality.

Common Agricultural Policy (CAP). The CAP machinery varies from product to product, but the basic features are the same. The agricultural support prices for different products are fixed by the Council in Units of Account. For each member country there is a "Green Rate" at which the support prices are converted into national prices. Farmers in all member countries are free to produce as much as they like at the support prices. There are no trade barriers on the movements of agricultural products from one member country to another. Imports from the outside world are allowed only if there is excess demand over domestic production of farm products. To keep imports under check, a variable import levy is used that can be raised or lowered thereby completely offsetting any price advantage enjoyed by importers. In the case of those farm products whose production exceeds the community requirements, subsidies are provided to finance their exports or additional consumption within the community.

With the adoption of the CAP, the Community has become self-sufficient in agriculture and another step towards customs union has been achieved. But it has its failures. *First,* the CAP has not been able to encourage farmers to seek alternative occupations, as per the objectives of the Treaty of Rome. *Second,* it has made the rich farmers richer but has failed to do anything for the poorer farmers. *Third,* it has failed to provide farm products to consumers at reasonable and stable prices because the support prices have been set at high levels. *Finally,* the CAP has led to huge surpluses in the form of "the butter and beef mountains; the wine lakes; earlier on, the grain and sugar surpluses; and more recently the milk lake." The EEC sells them at world market prices.

Common Fisheries Policy. It covers marketing of fresh frozen and preserved fish. It applies common market standards and facilitates trading between member countries. It provides equal access to fishing areas for all EEC nationals, with provisions for certain kinds of offshore fishing. But this policy has been far from common because it has been based on ad hoc compromises and concessions for individual member nations.

Factor Mobility. Workers and their families can move from one member country to another without a permit, and they have the same rights to work and social security and are subject to the same taxation as nationals of the concerned country. So far as capital mobility is concerned, it has been obstructed by international monetary disturbances. Consequently, capital mobility has not taken place smoothy and easily.

Regional Development Policy. The regional policy of the EC has been mainly concerned with providing financial help to the backward areas of member countries. It provides regional aid through the European Investment Bank (EIB), the European Social Fund (ESF), and the European Regional Development Fund (ERDF). The EIB is a non-profit making institution which performs three important functions. *First,* it gives loans and guarantees to improve basic common facilities in the underdeveloped regions of the member countries and associated countries. *Second,* it provides financial aid to projects for modernisation, conversion or development that are too large to be handled by individual member states. *Third,* it helps finance projects in which member countries have a common interest. The ESB assists financially the reemployment of workers thrown out of work as a result of EC policies. The ERDF lends and grants money for the development of the backward regions of the EC. It makes supplementary grants to help investment in the industrial and service sectors. It makes investments in infrastructure that create new jobs or safeguard existing jobs, and in infrastructure in backward rural area.

Despite these measures, the Community's regional development policy has failed to iron out income disparities. Rather, the disparities between the economies of member countries have been widening.

Common Transport Policy. The Treaty of Rome laid down the adoption of a common transport policy which includes : (*a*) the elimination of obstacles which transport may put in the way of the establishment of the common market as a whole; (*b*) integration of transport on the community level in the form of free movement of transport services within the member countries; and (*c*) general organisation of the transport within the communitiy. Except for the first objective, little progress has been made in achieving the other two objectives towards a common transport policy. This has been due to the complex problems involved in infrastructure pricing, entry controls and rate controls of the individual member states relating to the hauling of goods by rail and road transport.

Monopoly and Restrictive Practice Policy. This policy applies primarily to companies operating in more than one member state. It prohibits agreements between firms which adversely affect competition in trade between member states.

Harmonisation of Taxation. Goods can move from one member states to another without any border control. But VAT is the standard form of tax which is charged in the country of destination when goods cross from one EU country to another. They are exempt from VAT in the country where they are produced. However, there are differences in VAT rates between member states. But there is no harmonisation of other indirect taxes and direct taxes.

Common Social Policy. This relates to laws relating to employment, health and safety at work, equal pay for men and women for the same work, and collective bargaining rights. Till the adoption of the Social Charter in 1989, little progress had been made in this direction. The Social Charter established 12 principles relating to workers' rights and social justice. Of these, the following have been adopted by the member states:

(1) Right of citizens of one state to live and work in another state for the same wages and under the same working conditions;

(2) passing of various types of equal opportunities legislation such as child care for working parents;

(3) a maximum working week of 48 hours, one day off per week, and four weeks' minimum annual holiday;

(4) Protection of pension and other social security rights of workers moving from one state to another;

(5) health and safety measures in the workplace;

(6) creation of European Employment Service; and

(7) European information network for vacancies.

Economic and Monetary Union (EMU). The Treaty of Rome did not specifically mention about a European Monetary Union. But the monetary upheavals of 1970 prompted the Community Ministers at the Hague to agree to the establishment of an economic and monetary Union. Accordingly, the Werner Report recommended the establishment of the European Monetary Union by stages and the achievement of complete monetary integration by 1980. The member countries were asked to join the "European current snake" procedure for the control of exchange rates. But it was by the Bremen Declaration of July 1978 that the European Council decided to establish the European Monetary System (EMS). The EMS was started in March 1979. It had four main features : (*i*) the Exchange Rate Mechanism (ERM), (*ii*) the European Currency Unit (ECU), (*iii*) the European Monetary Cooperation Fund (EMCF), and (*iv*) financing facilities. The ERM and EMS worked smoothly and were very successful in bringing monetary cooperation among member states. The success of the ERM encouraged the EC countries to have a single currency which led to the *Maastricht Treaty.*

The Euro. In February 1992, the 15-member countries signed a treaty for the European Monetary Union at Maastricht in Netherlands. But only 11 EU countries[1] have confirmed the Treaty. The time table for EMU has been divided into three stages.

In the *first stage,* the European Central Bank (ECB) was established on June 30, 1998 at Frankfurt for a smooth changeover of the currencies of member nations to the Euro. The main functions of the Bank till the circulation of Euro coins and bank notes from July 1, 2002 are to control inflation and to create confidence of the global financial markets in the Euro. In the *second stage* beginning January 1, 1999, the Central banks of the EU countries adopted the Euro as a single monetary unit. In the *third stage* beginning July 1, 2002, Euro coins and bank notes will be put into circulation and the currencies of the EMU countries will stop to be legal tender.

With the advent of Euro bank notes and coins in 2002, 300 million European citizens will have the benefits of a single currency. They will have little need to change money or pay exchange fees. The costs of money transactions will be reduced, competition will increase in the global capital and money markets and the European financial market will expand and become stronger.

However, the success of EMU depends upon the *convergence* of *EU economies*. This means that these nations should achieve similar levels of growth, inflation, BOP, budget deficits as a percentage of GDP, etc. As the working of the EMU so far has shown, there has been very little convergence of these economies. The Euro has been on the decline and interest rates, budget deficits, rates of inflation, etc. have diverged.

Single or Common Market. Till the 1980s, the EU was a customs union having the above noted features. But it was not a common market where all sorts of non-tariff barriers existed. The Single European Act of 1986 proposed to remove these barriers by December 31, 1992. On January 1, 1993, the EU emerged as a single frontier-free market of 345 million people which became fully operational from January 1, 1995. The main features of the single market are : (1) Free movement of goods, capital, services and persons inside the EU; (2) restrictions on imports imposed by member states replaced by a Community tariff system; (3) the right for everyone to live in another member state; (4) recognition of vocational qualifications in other member states; (5) right of accountants, engineers, medical practitioners, teachers and other professionals to practice throughout the Union; (6) common commercial laws; acceptance of the Principle of Mutual Recognition whereby one country's rules and recognitions must apply through the Union. In case of any conflict, individuals and firms are free to choose which rules and regulations to obey; and (7) acceptance of the Principle of Majority Voting relating to harmonisation of rules and regulations. In all there were 282 proposals in the Single European Act which have been adopted throughout the Union. Thus EU is not only a customs union but also a common market.

CRITICAL APPRAISAL

The EU has achieved some of its major objectives relating to the removal of all obstacles to the free movement of goods, services, capital and labour between the member countries, and the establishment of common policies in the sphere of agriculture and common external commercial policy. Consequently, a vast common market has been created and trade has expanded considerably. Over the years member nations have enjoyed high rates of investment and growth in income. It has been successful in creating the Economic and Monetary Union (EMU) as a bulwark against the hegemony of the dollar. The balance of payments position of the member countries has become stronger. The Community has been able to levy duties at standard rates on products from the United States, Japan and Canada. It has even withstood American threats over the issues without making any compromises. Encouraged by the success of the EU in various fields, parleys are going on in the European Commission to expand the Community by including of East European countries by mid-2004.

Despite all these achievements, the EC has not been successful in achieving a complete economic and political union. It has failed to evolve a common transport policy. There has been no harmonisation of monetary and fiscal measures. Regional disparities within member countries persist. The EC is emerging as a "disunited states of Europe" with significant policy differences between states policy. Empirical studies have revealed that some trade diversion effects have occurred. But trade creation effects have been much stronger so that the total trade of the Community with the outside world has increased manifold.

6. EEC AND DEVELOPING COUNTRIES

The European EC's relations with the developing countries go back to the Treaty of Rome in 1957. The original six signatories to the Treaty agreed to associate the EC to those non-European countries and territories which had special relations with France, Belgium, Italy and the Netherlands. The exports and imports of the "associated members" are treated at par with the Community members. With the entry of the UK into the EC in 1973, a large number of her former colonies became associated members of the EC. Initially, separate agreements were signed with such developing countries who became associated members of the Community. But in 1975, a sigle agreement was signed under the Lome Convention with 45 African, Caribbean and Pacific

(ACP) countries. At present, there are 12 countries in Mediterranean region, and 66 ACP countries that have signed the third Lome Convention. The Lome accord includes the relaxation of some non-tariff barriers, less stringent enforcement of some trade regulations, and exemptions from certain bilateral trade agreements such as the MFA (Multi-Fibre Arrangement). But it is subject to regulations which severely limit free access for the exports of beneficiaries, including a safeguard clause which allows the EC to suspend any concessions unilaterally. Although the ACP countries as a group have been receiving preferential tariff rates and exemption from the MFA, empirical evidence reveals that there has been actually a decrease in trade between ACP countries and the EC. But some trade-creating effects have occurred in the form of diversification of exports from the ACP countries in the form of manufactures, and processed agricultural and temperate agricultural products.

So far as the other developing countries of South East Asia, Latin America and the Gulf and Southern Mediterranean are concerned, a link between them and the EC was provided by the Generalised System of Preferences (GSP) in July 1971. The GSP allowed free entry of certain manufactured goods exported by developing countries to the EC and helped them to industrialise. The GSP was phased out in January 1998. Now developing countries have signed individually commercial and co-operation ageements wiht the EC. Leaving aside those developing countries that are associated members of the Community, the other developing countries have not benefited much from the GSP. They continue to suffer from rising protectionism in their trade relations with the EC. At the same time, budgetary constraints prevent the community from increasing its financial aid to developing countries. By remaining outside the UNCTAD, the EC has failed to help such countries much. However, the announcement in March 2001 by the EU Trade Commission for zero-tariff, zero-duty trade package for the world's poorest nations is a major contribution of the community towards the developing countries.

The EC is the largest textiles market in the world. It has negotiated bilateral trade agreements with the South Asian and Latin American countries and other low-wage textile exporting countries under the provisions of the GATT Multi Fibre Arrangement.(MFA). The EC has agreed to a gradual phasing out of the MFA in three stages by January 1, 2005 under the GATT Uruguay Round talks. Until then, the bilateral agreements would continue to be extended for the benefit of developing countries.

The EC helps developing countries in developing tele-communication, science and technology, energy, and human resource development. It carries on Joint research projects in developing countries which include biotechnology, health, environment, material sciences, energy, agriculture and food technology. It aids such countries in trade promotion, stabilisation of export earnings, and enoucrages regional integration among them. The EC funded development projects are mostly in rural areas. They include rural electrification, irrigation, primary education, and community development.

The EC has been playing a major role in international drugs control. It launched a special programme to curb drug abuse in 1987 with emphasis on backing the efforts of developing countries to reduce demand for and production of narcotics. The EC finances projects for education, detoxification, rehabilitation, and cutting back the consumption and production of drugs in Asia, Latin America, Africa and Caribbean.

The European Community launched in 1988 the EC Investment Partners (ECIP) in order to boose economic development in Asia, Latin America and the developing Mediterranean countries. The scheme provides financial help to EC companies willing to undertake direct investment in developing countries. The ECIP promotes joint investment projects so as to encourage transfers of capital and technology and help create jobs in new industrial sectors. It also helps those companies which want to operate in developing countries through licensing and technical assistance agreements. The emphasis is on promoting small and medium enterprises. It covers all sectors of the economy, including industry, services, agriculture and mining. It operates through financial institutions, both in the EC and the developing countries. The act as ECs agents. They analyse projects, recommend whether to accept or reject joint ventures, draft contracts and make payments. The ECIP provides funds for projects identification studies, for human resources development, and for equity participation in joint ventures. It operates on a first come first served basis and no quotas are fixed for individual developing countries.

7. INDIA AND THE EC

India has entered into a commercial and economic cooperation agreement with the 15-nation EC. She is represented by an ambassador at the Indo-EC Joint Commission. The EC's share in Indian foreign trade has not changed much over the years. In 1970-71, India's exports to the Community were 18.4 per cent of the total exports of India which increased to 26 per cent in 1998-99. But the share of imports has increased more. It was 19.6 per cent in 1970-71 which increased to 23.6 per cent in 1998-99. In absolute terms, India's trade deficit has been widening. Even though Indian exports to the EC have increased, yet these amount to less than 0.6 per cent of imports of the Community. The reasons for India's sluggish exports over the years to the EC are not far to seek. About 60 per cent of Indian exports are subjected to non-tariff barriers of various kinds by the Community. In fact, rising protectionism has been largely responsible for the decline in Indian exports, in particular agricultural and marine products, chemicals, garments and engineering products. Under GSP, India had been getting duty free entry for its exports of semi-manufactured and manufactured goods which was phased out in January 1998. Despite this, with almost 400 million people and per capita GDP of about $ 19,900, there is large scope for India to increase its exports of consumer and manufactured goods to the EC.

There have been two main elements in the Community's relations with India. *First*, trade co-operation, and *second*, development aid. Under the former, it has entered into a commercial agreement with India for the import of textiles under the MFA (Multi Fibre Agreement). Under it, India exports textiles and clothing to EC. India is the largest source to the Community. In December 1992, the EC extended its bilateral agreement with India for textiles and clothing exports for a two-year period with a possibility of extending it further for one year. With the phasing out of MFA in stages by January 2005 under the GATT Uruguay Round of talks, India's exports of clothing and textiles are expected to increase in the years to come.

Development aid includes cooperation in science and technology, energy and human resources. An important element of aid to India is food aid in the form of skimmed milk powder (SMP) and butter oil for Operation Flood, and financial aid for the purchase of fertilisers. The counterpart funds generated by the sale of SMP and butter-oil are used to finance rural development projects. They include rural electrification, irrigation, and primary education. The Community has also funded a number of training programmes, and programmes for trade promotion of Indian products. The aim is to help Indian industry improve its technology, produce to standards acceptable to European buyers, reduce production costs, and acquire greater familiarity with European business culture. The European Commission is also promoting wide ranging contacts in a variety of new sectors such as engineering goods, machine tools and medical and surgical equipment.

The EC has been helping India in its environmental programmes and energy management and planning. An EC-India Energy Management Centre has been set up with EC funds in 1989. Its main aim is to encourage the transfer to reliable EC energy technology. Besides, to prevent drug abuse, projects sanctioned by the EC include the setting up of detoxification centres in New Delhi and Bombay and pilot programme for anti-drug education in Bombay schools.

The process of liberalisation of Indian economy has led to a greater emphasis on direct contact and cooperation between economic operators, particularly in the private sector, in both EC and India. This has received further encouragement under the ECIP scheme which provides financial assistance to EC companies to set up joint ventures in developing countries. India has been receiving capital and technical assistance through its agents the Exim Bank of India, ICICI and IDBI. The recently set up Indo-EC Business Forum enables businessmen and industrialists in both the EC and India to be in close contact with each other on mutual business issues.

On the official level, an Indo-EC Co-operation Agreement on Partnership and Development has been signed in December 1992. India is the first country with which the EC has entered into such an agreement. The agreement stipulates that trade relations between the EC and India will continue on an MFN basis. But market access will be increased to the highest possible level by removing nontariff barriers and resolving disputes, including anti-dumping. There will be greater cooperation in frontiers of technology, such as bio-technology, new materials, informatics, energy, etc. The agreement will help improve India's economic and business climate.

The EC has passed a legislation whereby exports of food, food products, drugs and pharmaceuticals, and most durable consumer goods, including electrical equipment, are required to meet EC standards and certification. The Indian companies which are adopting ISO 9000 as the basis for quality management system are also required to meet the corresponding EC, standard EN 29000. Manufacturers whose products do not conform to these standards will be barred from entering the EC, thereby creating problems for them. To overcome them, Indian experts at the ISI are being trained in European testing laboratories while EC experts are visiting India to advise manufacturers as well as testing laboratories. A modernisation programme is also being undertaken to help Indian laboratories to come up to the EC standards. The EC also support sector development at the national, state and district level. It funds operational research at the national level aimed at promoting attitude changes and managerial skills. At the state level, it contributes to consensus building on primary health system reform within the context of reproductive and child health. At the district level, it supports organising and implementing the decentralised process. All these funds are being provided in grant form. India is the largest single beneficiary of EC development assistance.

EXERCISES

1. Discuss the achievements of the European Community in the light of its objectives.
2. Discuss the working and achievements of the European Community. To what extent it has been successful in achieving the objectives of a common market?
3. Explain briefly the objectives of the European Community. What is its role in helping developing countries? Explain in particular its relations with India.
4. Write notes on Economic and Monetary Union (EMU), EC and India, EC and Developing Countries.

CHAPTER 63

The General Agreement on Tariffs and Trade (GATT)

1. INTRODUCTION

The General Aggreement on Tariffs and Trade (GATT) emerged from the "ashes of the Havana Charter". The world had experienced the rigours and problems of an extensive pattern of trade barriers in the 1930s and during the Second World War. So the Allied Powers thought of having a liberal world trading system after World War II. For this purpose, the International Conference on Trade and Employment was held in Havana in the winter of 1947-48. Fifty-three nations drew up and signed a charter for establishing an International Trade Organisation (ITO). But the US Congress did not ratify the Havana Charter with the result that the ITO never came into existence. Simultaneously, twenty-three nations agreed to continue extensive tariff negotiations for trade concessions at Geneva which were incorporated in General Agreement on Tariffs and Trade. This was signed on October 30, 1947 and came into force from January 1, 1948 when other nations had also signed it. On January 1, 1995, the GATT disappeared and passed into history when it was merged in the World Trade Organisation (WTO).

2. WHAT IS GATT?

The GATT was a multilateral treaty which had been signed by 96 governments known as "contracting parties". Thirtyone other countries had applied GATT rules de facto. The GATT was neither an organisation nor a court of justice. It was simply a multinational treaty which covered 80 per cent of world trade. It was a decision making body with a code of rules for the conduct of international trade, and a mechanism for trade liberalisation. It was a forum where the contracting parties met from time to time to discuss and solve their trade problems, and also negotiated to enlarge their trade. The GATT rules provided for the settlement of trade disputes, called for consultations, waived trade obligations, and even authorised retaliatory measures.

The GATT was a permanent international organisation having a permanent Council of Representatives with headquarters at Geneva. Its function was to call international conferences to decide on trade liberalisation on a multilateral basis.

3. OBJECTIVES OF GATT

The objectives of the GATT were based on a few fundamental principles contained in the Code of International Trade Conduct.

1. To follow unconditional most favoured-nation (MFN) principle.
2. To carry on trade on the principle of non-discrimination, reciprocity and transparency.
3. To grant protection to domestic industry through tariffs only.
4. To liberalise tariff and non-tariff measures through multilateral negotiations.

To achieve these objectives, the Agreement provided for : (*a*) multilateral trade negotiations; (*b*) consultation, conciliation and settlement of disputes; and (*c*) waivers to be granted in exceptional cases.

The ultimate aim of establishing liberal world trading system was to raise living standard, ensure full employment through a steadily growing effective demand and real income, develop fully the resources of the world, and expand the production and exchange of goods on global level.

4. PROVISIONS OF GATT

The objectives and basic principles of the GATT could be viewed from its various articles which are discussed as under :

1. Most Favoured Nation Clause

To ensure non-discrimination, Article I dealt with unconditional most favoured nation (MFN) clause for all import and export duties. The principle of MFN implies that tariff preferences accorded by a country to another are extended to all others with which it has trade relations. It also forbade the contracting parties from granting any new preferences.

2. Schedules of Tariff Concessions

The most fundamental component of GATT was a negotiated balance of mutual tariff concessions among contracting parties. The contracting parties committed themselves not to raise import tariffs above the negotiated rates "bound" in the schedules of concessions, as incorporated in Article II of the Agreement. The bound tariff rates negotiated were generalised to all contracting parties through the MFN principles. Thus the GATT emphasised reciprocal and mutually advantageous arrangements among contracting parties.

3. General Elimination of Quantitative Restrictions

Article XI of the Agreement prohibited or restricted the use of quantitative trade restrictions to trade. GATT encouraged countries to fix a ceiling on their import duties at the lowest possible level.

4. Emergency Safeguard Code

Article XIX of the GATT provided emergency safeguard code. Under this, a country could impose a tariff or quota to restrain imports which "caused or threaten serious injury" to domestic producers.

5. Exceptions

Articles XX and XXI provided "General" and "Security" exceptions towards the prohibitions of import quotas by contracting parties. They were not directly related to the need to afford protection to local industries. The six important exceptions were : *One*, a country in balance of payments difficulties could introduce temporary quantitative restrictions, but under MFN rule these must apply equally to imports from all sources. However, they must be limited to the extent necessary to stop a serious decline, forestall a threatened decline in reserves, or achieve a reasonable increase in abnormally low reserves. *Two*, underdeveloped countries were allowed to apply quantitative restrictions to further their economic development, but only under procedures approved by the GATT. *Three,* quantitative restrictions could also be applied to agricultural or fishery products if domestic production of these articles was subject to equally restrictive production or marketing controls. *Four,* the GATT allowed a country to take action if products of other countries were imported at artificial low (dumped) or subsidised prices. *Five,* it also allowed a country to introduce temporary "safeguard" increases in protection when industries were injured by sudden increase in imports. *Six,* Article XXIV permitted countries to form customs or free trade areas among themselves, provided they were formed to facilitate trade between the constituent territories and not to raise barriers to the trade of other contracting parties.

6. Rules on Subsidies and Countervailing Duties

The rules on subsidies and countervailing duties were incorporated in a separate code negotiated in the Tokyo round of the 1970s. Under these rules export duties on manufactured products were banned except for developing countries. Export subsidies for primary products were restricted only by the condition that they could not lead to acquisition or more than an equitable share of world export trade. The Agreement also contained provisions that authorised importing countries to take compensating action against trading partners found to be dumping goods in their markets or increasing rates through exports subsidies. In the event of dumping, the importing country could impose anti-dumping or countervailing duties whenever and to the extent that the sale of imported goods took place in the importing country's market at less than its "normal value" and resulted in mateial injury to the domestic industry. Similary, the Agreement authorised an importing country to impose offsetting countervailing duties on goods benefitting from production or export subsidies in the exporting country, when these resulted in material injury to the domestic industry. But such anti-dumping or countervailing duties should not result in net additional protection of the affected industry in the importing country. In other words, these duties could not be imposed at rates higher than were necessary to offset the margins of dumping or subsidisation.

7. Settlement of Disputes

Under the GATT dispute settlement procedures complaints could be brought against actions that violated the rules or impeded the objectives of the General Agreement. The GATT relied on panels of three or five independent experts which made findings and recommendations for adoption by the GATT Council. This procedure which blended elements of third party adjudication and negotiation had successfully resolved disputes among contracting parties.

5. GATT "ROUNDS" OF GLOBAL TRADE NEGOTIATIONS

Since 1947, seven "rounds" (conferences) of global trade negotiations under the GATT had taken place, and the eighth, the Punta Del Este (Uruguay) started in September 1986 and concluded on April 15, 1994.

The first conference on trade negotiations was held at Geneva in 1947, the second at Annecy (France) in 1949, the third at Torquay (England) in 1950-51, the fourth at Geneva (Switzerland) in 1955-56, the fifth at Geneva between 1954-62 (Dillon Round), the sixth at Geneva between 1963-67 (Kennedy Round), and the seventh at Tokyo (Japan), between 1973-79. These conferences led to reduction or stabilisation of more than 60000 tariff rates, and to a number of non-tariff agreements among contracting parties having 80 per cent of the world trade.

However, we shall briefly discuss the Kennedy, the Tokyo and the Uruguay conferences.

The Kennedy Round

Since the formation of GATT, five tariff reduction conferences had been held under the auspices of the GATT. They had been conducted bilaterally on commodity-by-commodity basis. This was a cumbersome procedure and the progress had been slow. The United States had been put at a disadvantage in its trade relations with the formation of the EEC. As a reaction to this, the US Congress passed the Trade Expansion Act in October 1962 which authorised the Kennedy administration to make a 50 per cent tariff reduction on all commodities. This paved the way for the opening of the Kennedy Round of trade negotiations at Geneva in May 1964 which were to be completed by 30 June 1967. The results of negotiations were incorporated in the schedules to the Geneva Protocol to the General Agreement on Trade (1967).

Thirty-seven countries joined in making tariff reductions covering approximately $ 40 billion or four-fifths of world trade. The major industrial countries in this group applied these cuts about as widely as the United States to 64 per cent of their dutiable imports. Average reductions ranged in depth from 38 per cent in the case of Britain to 30 per cent in the case of Japan and 24 per cent in the case of Canada. They left US and European tariff on the manufactured goods in the range of 5 to 15 per cent. These tariff concessions were limited to manufactured goods by developed countries. With agricultural products, the negotiators had less success. They agreed on an average duty reduction of 25 per cent on agricultural items/products.[1] Non-tariff obstacles to trade remained untouched and scant attention was paid to the problems of developing countries.

An IMF study revealed that by the end of the Kennedy Round, the weighted average tariff for the major trading nations had been reduced to 7.7 per cent on all industrial products, 9.8 per cent on finished manufactured products, 8 per cent on semi-finished products, and 2 per cent on raw materials. Thus trade in industrial products after the completion of the Kennedy Round was substantially free of restrictions.

The Tokyo Round

The Seventh Round of Multilateral Trade Negotiations (MTN) was launched in September 1973 under the auspices of GATT. Its objectives were laid down in the Tokyo declaration. The declaration set out a far-reaching programme for the negotiators in six areas: tariff reductions; reduction or elimination of non-tariff barriers; coordinated reduction of all trade barriers in selected sectors; discussion on the multilateral safeguard system; trade liberalisation in the agricultural sector taking into account the special characteristics and problems in this sector; and special treatment of tropical products. The Tokyo declaration also emphasised that the MTN must take into account the special interests and problems of developing countries.

At the end of the Tokyo Round on 12 April 1979, a number of agreements on specific non-tariff measures and on agricultural products were reached which came into force from 1 January, 1980.

1. *The Agreement on Subsidies and Countervailling Duties.* It covered industrial, agricultural, fisheries, and forestry products, and procedure for the settlement of disputes between contracting parties.

2. *The Agreement on Customs Valuation.* It provided for a fair, uniform and natural system for the valuation of goods for customs purposes.

3. *The Agreement on Government Procurement.* It aimed at securing a greater international competition and thus more effective use of tax revenues and other public funds through the application of commercial considerations when governments purchase for their own use. It laid down principles of nondiscrimi-nation and national treatment.

4. *The Agreement on Technical Barriers to Trade.* It provided for removing unnecessary barriers to trade existing in the form of technical standards and specifying rules of a legally binding character between governments to complain and obtain redress in the course of violation of the Code of Technical Standards by the signatories.

5. *The Agreement on Import Licensing Procedures.* It is related to automatic grant of approval of application on the inflow of goods, non-automatic import licensing in the case of quotas arid other types of import restrictions and institutions and procedures for consultation and settlement of disputes.

6. *The Agreement on Dairy Products.* It was initially for three years beginning 1 January 1980 with provision for further three years extensions. It provided for the setting up of International Dairy Products Council which was expected to meet twice a year. This agreement related to the provision for dairy products as food aid to developing countries, and three Protocols regarding skimmed, whole, and butter milk powders, anhydrous milk fat, and cheese.

7. *The Agreement on Bovine Meat.* It covered beef, veal and live cattle. It was also for three years commencing 1 January 1980 with provision for further three-year extensions. It provided for the establishment of International Meat Council which would meet twice a year.

---

1. P.T. Ellsworth and J.C. Leith, *op. cit.,* p. 533.

8. *The Agreement on Trade in Civil Aircraft.* It included all civil aircraft, their engines, parts and components, and all ground flight simulators and their parts and components. It provided for elimination of all customs, duties and similar charges on the importation of above mentioned items and repairs on civil aircrafts. It established a Committee on Trade in Civil Aircraft which was to meet once a year.

Though the Tokyo Round had extended its scope to non-tariff matters, yet the legal position in each of these Agreements was specifically devised to meet the objectives set by the US, EEC, and other developed countries. Special provisions were, however, incorporated in some of them for those developing countries which wished to subscribe to them.

The Uruguay Round

The Eighth Round of GATT negotiations which began at Punta Del Esta in Uruguay in September 1986 ought to have been concluded by the end of 1990. But at the ministerial meeting in Brussels in December, 1990, an impasse was reached over the area of agriculture and the talks broke down.

The talks were restarted in February 1991 and continued till August 1991. On December 20, 1991, Aurthur Dunkel, the then Director-General of GATT tabled a Draft Final Act of the Uruguay Round, known as the Dunkel Draft Text. This was a "take-it-or-leave-it" document which was hotly discussed at various fora in the member countries through 1992 till July 1993 when the then Director-General, Sutherland relaunched the negotiations in Geneva. On August 31, 1993, the Trade Negotiations Committee (TNC) passed a resolution to conclude the Uruguay Round by 15 December. On December 15, 1993 at the final session, chairman Sutherland declared that seven year of Uruguay Round negotiations had come to an end. Finally, on April 15, 1994, 123 Ministers of member countries ratified the results of the Uruguay Round at Marrakesh (Morocco) and the GATT disappeared and passed into history and it was absorbed by the World Trade Organisation (WTO) on January 1, 1995.

The Uruguay Round of trade negotiations undertaken by the GATT since its establishment in 1947 had a wide agenda. The GATT originally covered international trade rules in the goods sector only. Domestic policies were outside the GATT purview and it operated only at international border. In the Uruguay Round, the GATT extended to three new areas, *viz.*, intellectual property rights, services and investment. It also covered agriculture and textiles which were outside the GATT jurisdiction.

The Final Act embodying the results of the Uruguay Round of Multilateral Trade Negotiations comprises 28 Agreements. It had two components : the WTO Agreements and the Ministerial decisions and declarations. The WTO Agreement covers the formation of the organisation and the rules governing its working. Its Annexures contain the Agreements covering trade in goods, services, intellectual property rights, plurilateral trade, GATT Rules 1994, disputes settlements rules and trade policy review.

The Uruguay Round was concerned with the two aspects of trade in goods and services. The *First* related to increasing market access by reducing or eliminating trade barriers. This was met by reductions in tariffs, reductions in non-tariff support in agriculture, the elimination of bilateral quantitative restrictions, and reductions in barriers to trade in services. The *second* related to increasing the legal security of the new levels of market access by strengthening and expanding rules and procedures and institutions.

Gains from Uruguay Round

The GATT Secretariat estimated the following gains as the result of the Uruguay Round agreements and their implementation:

1. Income and Trade. The estimated gains are :

(1) $ 510 billion increase in annual world income by 2005;

(2) World trade in *goods* higher by $ 745 billion in the year 2005;

(3) Largest increase in world trade in goods by 60% in clothing, 20% in agriculture, forestry and fishery products, and 19% in processed food and beverages; and

(4) Increase in the exports and imports of the developing and transition (the erstwhile Communist East European and U.S.S.R.) economies as a group by 50 % above the average increase for the world trade as a whole.

2. Tariff Reduction. In the Uruguay Round developed and developing countries abandoned several of their restrictive and discretionary trade and industrial policy tools. As a result, there have been higher levels of tariff "bindings". Binding means that they have ended the freedom to use the protectionist instruments of the past.

Tariff reductions and bindings had been as under :

(1) Tariff bindings in developed countries on industrial products increased from 78% to 99% and from 22% to 72% in developing countries.

(2) In agriculture, the bindings of the developed countries increased from 81% to 100% and of the developing countries from 22% to 100%.

(3) Tariffs on industrial goods in developed countries reduced from 6.3 to 3.9%.

(4) Progress in reducing tariff escalation which would benefit developing countries seeking to export more processed primary products.

(5) Above average tariff cuts for many products of export interest to developing countries.

3. Market Access. There were several areas in the Uruguay Round that related to market access. The important ones were tariffs, textiles and garments, and agriculture.

(1) *Tariffs.* In developed countries, industrial tariffs were reduced on an average to 4%. They are no longer significant barriers to trade. Developing countries also reduced their tariffs considerably. The overall tariff reductions in the Uruguay Round were an average of one-third. The value of industrial products which enter the developed countries duty free under MFN increased from 20% to 44%. The proportion of imports into developed countries from all sources with tariffs above 15%, declined from 7 to 5% and from 9 to 5% for imports from developing countries. The market access also increased through higher levels of tariff bindings on industrial products from 78% to 99% in developed countries and from 22% to 72% in developing countries.

(2) *Textiles and Clothing.* The Textiles and Clothing Agreement also forms part of market access. A major achievement of the Uruguay Round was the commitment to integrate this sector into a multilateral framework. The integration of this sector into the GATT Rules, 1994 would take place in four phases by January 1, 2005 when all products would be integrated. All MFA (Multi-Fibre Agreement) restrictions existing on December 31, 1994 were carried over to the WTO Agreement and would be removed when the products are gradually integrated into the GATT by January 1, 2005. As a result, the exports of textiles and clothing from developing countries would increase manifold, provided they are competitive.

(3) *Agriculture.* The Agriculture Agreement contained minimum market access commitment on agricultural products. It sought : (*i*) to open national markets to world competition by replacing non-tariff barriers with normal customs duties; (*ii*) to check overproduction in progressively reducing government aids, and (*iii*) to reduce subsidies alongwith the volume of subsidised exports.

First the estimates by the GATT Secretariat revealed that the minimum market access commitments on agricultural products subject to tariffication would create vast market opportunities for among such important products as 1.8 m. tons of course grain, 1.1 m. tons of rice, 0.8 m. tons of wheat, and 0.7 m. tons of dairy products. *Second,* a 36% reduction in export subsidies and an 18% decline in domestic support to agricultural producers would further increase market access. Lastly, the increase of tariff bindings from 81% to 100% in developed countries and from 22% to 100% in developing countries, and no non-tariff barriers on agricultural products would further enhance market access in these products. Thus the reductions in tariffs on farm products and of subsidies to agriculture by the developed countries would make the exports of developing countries more profitable. The terms of trade would, in turn, be in favour of agriculture.

4. Rules and Disciplines*. The Uruguay Round also strengthened multilateral rules and disciplines. The most important of these related to subsidies and countervailing measures, antidumping, safeguards and disputes settlement. Rules concerning dispute settlement have been made time bound, automatic and judicial in approach under the W.T.O.

5. TRIMs.** Trade Related Investment Measures (TRIMs) prohibit investment measures that are inconsistent with national treatment or general elimination of quantitative restrictions. Developing countries have been given 5 years to phase out inconsisternt TRIMs and developed countries 2 years. The TRIMs Agreement does not impose any obligation to provide access to any particular sector for foreign investment.

6. GATS. The achievement of the Uruguay Round was the General Agreement on Trade in Servics which is the first set of multilaterally agreed and legally enforceable rules and disciplines relating to international trade in services. Services include financial, telecommunications and services of natural persons. The GATS requires non-discrimination by governments on the basis of Most Favoured Nation (MFN) clause and transparency in the form of publication of all relevant laws and regulations relating to service trade.

7. TRIPs. The Uruguay Round also contained the Agreement on Trade Related Intellectual Property Rights. It provides norms and standards for copyrights and related rights, trademarks, geographical indications, industrial designs, patents, layout designs of integrated circuits, trade secrets and protection of undisclosed information. The Agreement allowed one year for developed countries, 5 years for developing and 11 years for least developed countries to change their laws for the implementation of TRIPs.

The TRIPs Agreement on patents would be able to tap the generic market in the USA and is expected to generate new business worth billions of dollars by the turn of the century and similar opportunities in the EEC for developing countries like India. They would also gain from the inflow of better technology and create a better climate for research and development in agriculture and pharmaceuticals. As a result, the quality of products available in the market will improve. For instance, if the farmers can get better quality seeds from multinationals even at higher prices and improve and increase their produce substantially, they stand to gain. Similar will be the case with national drug manufacturers in developing countries when they establish strategic linkages for development of their new discoveries in drugs.*

6. GATT AND DEVELOPING COUNTRIES

Before the Kennedy Round (1964-67), developing countries gained very little from the GATT except that they could use quantitative restrictions to correct disequilibrium in balance of payments and benefitted from tariff reduction by developed countries. But the principle of reciprocity for trade concessions went against the developing countries, because they were unable to provide equivalent benefits to the developed countries. For instance, tariffs on total manufactured imports by developed countries averaged 11 per cent but were 17 per cent on those from developing countries. Moreover, GATT did not take any initiative on trade barriers on agricultural and tropical products of developing countries.

The concept of "special and preferential" treatment for developing countries was formally introduced into the General Ageement in 1957. Under it, negotiations would take in account their needs for a more flexible use of tariff protection to assist their economic development and the special needs of these countries to maintain tariffs for revenue purposes. On the recommendations of the Haberler Report, the GATT started an action programme in 1958 which recommended that the developed countries should reduce taxation and trade barriers on industrial and primary products of developing countries.

In 1963, the contracting parties agreed on a more flexible attitude towards them. Accordingly, tariffs on some tropical products like tea and timber were reduced or eliminated by developed countries.

In 1965, a new Part IV on Trade and Development was incorporated into the General Agreement dealing with the principle on non-reciprocity for developing countries.

The Kennedy Round (1964-67) bestowed some benefits on developing countries when thirty-seven developed countries reduced tariffs on manufactured goods. But little attention was paid to the problems of developing countries.

In 1970, the Generalised System of Preferences (GSP) was introduced which permitted developed countries to grant unilateral tariff preference to developing countries. In June 1971, GATT waived the MFN treatment obligation for developed countries for a period of ten years to the extent needed to grant preferential treatment under the GSP which has since been extended further.

It was, however, in the Tokyo Round (1973-79) that a number of agreements on subsidies and countervailing duties covering agricultural, fisheries and forestry products; on customs valuation; on government procurement; on technical barriers to trade; on import licensing; on dairy products; on bovine meat; and on civil aircraft were reached. It was a triumph for developing countries for these agreements contained special provisions for developing countries. The Tokyo Round also led to trade concessions to the exports of raw, processed, and semi-processed tropical products of developing countries by developed countries.

However, trade in textiles and clothing has been subjected to special restrictions for nearly four decades by developed countries outside the GATT rules. Developing countries, being the principal exporters of these goods, have been at a disadvantage in this respect. The early 1960s witnessed the advent of the Short-term Arrangement on Cotton Textiles in 1961-62 and the Long-term Arrangement from 1962-73 restricted trade in cotton textiles on the plea that developed countries which are the principal importers, need special protection against "market disruption" by lower-cost developing country suppliers. The market disruption is claimed by developed countries under Article XIX of GATT. In 1974 the first Multifibre Arrangement (MFA I) was negotiated between the developed and developing countries for a period of four years which was renewed in 1978 (MFA II) and in 1982 (MFA III). MFA IV was renewed in 1986 for a period of five years. The renewed MFA was potentially more restrictive than the previous ones. It contained the right of the developed importing country to cut imports of specific products from particular developing countries on a selective basis when it was feared that too many imports capable of market disruption of local products might occur. The most significant change in MFA IV was that it extended its coverage from cotton, wool and man-made fibres to all vegetable fibres as well as silk mixed with cotton, wool or man-made fibres. For the first time, a return to GATT rules was written into the MFA. But it made no mention of phasing out the MFA or setting a time limit within which the final objective of application of GATT rules to trade in textiles would be attained. Under the Uruguay Round, textiles and clothing would be integrated into a multilateral framework. The integration of this sector into the GATT Rules 1994 would take place in four phases by January 1, 2005, when all products would be integrated. As a result, all MFA restrictions would be removed by that date. For other benefits to developing countries under the Uruguay Round refer to the previous section on Uruguay Round.

Despite special and preferential treatment for developing countries provided in the GATT rules, they are being discriminated under the "escape clauses" and "safeguard" rules of the GATT. Moreover, the multiplication of trade restrictions outside the GATT rules, such as "voluntary export restraints", and "orderly marketing agreements" go against the interest of developing countries and undermine the utility of the General Agreement under the Uruguay Round.

7. CRITICISMS OF GATT

There had been large scale evasion of GATT rules[1] by contracting parties over the years which made a mockery of the GATT.

1. From the beginning of the GATT, agriculture was treated as a special case where GATT rules hardly applied. Almost every developed country followed such agricultural trade policies which were inconsistent with the GATT rules. It was only at the Kennedy Round and the Tokyo Round that a few agreements were arrived at relating to agricultural and dairy products. But trade liberalisation for agricultural products has much less than for manufactures. Producers of agricultural products have been resorting to domestic support policies leading to surplus production that can be exported only with the help of heavy subsidies. For example, European countries have been exporting subsidised wheat, while the US has placed import restrictions on dairy products.

2. No doubt, developed countries have removed the majority of tariff barriers, yet they have been reluctant to abolish others. Rather, they have devised new trade restrictions under the garb of "voluntary export restraints", "low-cost suppliers", "market disruption" etc. which are outside the GATT rules. They are applied against developing and state trading countries and Japan. For instance, such restrictions affect over 50 per cent of the French imports and 45 per cent of the United States.

3. The GATT's role was being undermined by concluding bilateral, discriminatory and restrictive arrangements outside the GATT rules. The EEC and the US have placed many import restrictions on innumerable products from Brazil, HongKong, Korea, and a host of other developing countries, besides Japan, after bilateral negotiations. At present, over 100 MFA type bilateral agreements are in force in the world which restrict exports of developing countries to the developed ones.

4. The increasing use of subsidies had been another important factor in side-tracking the GATT. This is because GATT's rule on subsidies are not explicit. The GATT rules permitted domestic subsidies but they led to retaliation if they damaged the trade interests of other countries. The result has been further worsening of

open trade.

5. The "safeguard" rules under Article XIX of the GATT allowed the contracting parties to grant protection in case of need, such as injurious dumped or subsidised imports, or in severe balance of payments difficulties. But all temporary restrictions permitted under the escape clause have become permanent features of the world trading system.

6. The GATT rules in Article XXIV which permitted the formation of customs unions and free-trade areas had been distorted and abused. These rules left many ambiguities which seriously weakened the GATT. "They had set a dangerous precedent for further special deals, fragmentation of the trading system, and damage of the trading interests of non-participants." As a result, the benefits of MFN rule failed to spread uniformly among the contracting parties.

7. The GATT being a mandatory body did not possess any mechanism to get its rules implemented by contracting parties. The procedure for dispute settlement consisted of a panel of three to five independent experts whose recommendations had no legal binding. This was a serious weakness of the GATT.

It was perhaps due to these inherent loopholes in the working of GATT that as much as 80 per cent of world trade was being conducted outside the GATT rules.

Despite these criticisms, 125 countries operated under the GATT rules, while the remaining countries of the world benefitted from them under the umbrella of the MFN rule.

EXERCISES

1. Examine the principles underlying the GATT from the point of view of an underdeveloped country.
2. How far the GATT was able to achieve its objectives? Discuss critically.
3. Discuss critically the objectives and achievements of GATT.
4. What did the GATT do for the developing countries? Examine critically.
5. Discuss the achievements of the Uruguay Round of the GATT.

CHAPTER 64

The World Trade Organisation (WTO)

1. INTRODUCTION

The Uruguay Round of GATT negotiations concluded on April 15, 1994 at Marrakesh, Morocco. India, alongwith 123 Ministers besides the EC countries signed the Final Act incorporating the Eighth round of multilateral trade negotiations. The Final Act consists of : (1) the WTO Agreement which covers the formation of the organisation and the rules governing its working; and (2) the Ministerial decisions and declarations which contain the important agreements covering trade in goods, services, intellectual property and plurilateral trade. They also contain the dispute settlement rules and trade policy review system. The WTO Agreement is in fact the Uruguay Round agreements whereby the original GATT is now a part of the WTO Agreement which came into force from January 1, 1995.

2. THE WTO

The WTO is the successor to the GATT. The GATT was a forum where the member countries met from time to time to discuss and solve world trade problems. But the WTO is a properly established permanent world trade organisation. It has a legal status and enjoys privileges and immunities on the same footing as the IMF and the World Bank. It includes : (1) the GATT, as modified by the Uruguay Round; (2) all agreements and arrangements concluded under the GATT; and (3) the complete results of the Uruguay Round.

There were 77 member countries of the WTO on January 1, 1995 which had increased to 128 by 2001. India is one of the founder members.

3. DIFFERENCE BETWEEN GATT AND WTO

The WTO is not an extension of the GATT but successor to the GATT. It completely replaces GATT and has a very different character. The major differences between the two are the following :

1. The GATT had no legal status whereas the WTO has a legal status. It has been created by international treaty ratified by the governments and legislatures of member states. It has a global status similar to that of the IMF and the World Bank. But unlike them, it is not an agency of the UN, although it has a 'cooperative relationship' with the UN.

2. The GATT was a set of rules and procedures relating to multilateral agreements of a selective nature. There were separate agreements on separate issues which were not binding on members. Any member could stay out of an agreement. Only those who signed the agreement could be penalised on default. The agreements which form part of the WTO are permanent and binding on all members. Action can be taken against any defaulting member by all the member states.

3. The GATT dispute settlement system was dilatory and not binding on the parties to the dispute. The WTO dispute settlement mechanism is automatic, faster and binding on the parties. The Dispute Settlement Board of the WTO in its first decision brought the mighty US to accept its verdict. Thus the WTO has teeth whereas the GATT was toothless.

4. The GATT was a forum where the member countries met once in a decade to discuss and solve world trade problems. There used to be long, protracted negotiating rounds which took decades to complete. The WTO, on the other hand, is a properly established rule-based world trade organisation where decisions on agreements are time bound. The dateline can be extended only by consensus.

5. The GATT rules applied to trade in goods. Trade in services was included in Uruguay Round but no agreement was arrived at. The WTO covers not only trade in goods and services but also trade-related aspects of intellectual property rights and a number of other agreements.

6. The GATT had a small secretariat managed by a Director General. But the WTO has a large secretariat and a huge organisational set-up.

4. ITS STRUCTURE

The structure or organisation of the WTO is headed by the *Ministerial Conference* composed of representatives of all the members which meet at least once every two years. It carries out the functions of the WTO and takes actions necessary to this effect. It takes decisions on all matters under any of the Multilateral Trade Agreements. The Ministerial Conference is the supreme authority of the WTO.

There is the *General Council* composed of representatives of all the members to oversee the operation of the WTO Agreement and ministerial decisions on a regular basis. It also acts as a Dispute Settlement Body (DSB) and a Trade Policy Review Body (TPRB), each having its own Chairman. The General Council sits in Geneva on an average of once a month.

There is the Council for Trade in Goods, the Council for Trade in Services and the Council for Trade-Related Aspects of Intellectual Property Rights (TRIPs) which operate under the General Council. These Councils, in turn, have their subsidiary bodies. The Councils and subsidiary bodies meet as necessary to carry out their respective functions.

There is the Committee on Trade and Development, the Committee on Balance of Payments Restrictions and the Committee on Budget, Finance and Administration which carry out the functions assigned to them by the WTO Agreement, the Multilateral Trade Agreements and any additional function assigned to them by the General Council.

The *Secretariat* of the WTO is headed by the Director General. The Ministerial Conference appoints the Director General and sets out his powers, duties, conditions of service and terms of office. The Director General is appointed for a four-year term. He has four deputies from different member states.

The Director General appoints the members of staff of the Secretariat and determines their duties and conditions of service in accordance with the regulations adopted by the Ministerial Conference.

The Director General presents to the Committee on Budget, Finance and Administration, the annual budget estimates and financial statement of the WTO. The Committee, in turn, reviews the annual budget estimates and the financial statement and makes recommendations to the General Council for final approval. The General Council adopts the annual budget estimates and financial statements by a two-third majority comprising more than half the members of the WTO. The financial regulations relating to the scale of contributions and the budget are based on the rules and practices of the GATT.

The WTO continues the practice of decision-making by consensus, as followed under the GATT 1947. Where a decision cannot be arrived at by consensus, the matter at issue is decided by 2/3rd majority voting on the basis of "one country, one vote". But in the case of interpretation of the provisions of the agreements and waiver of a member's obligations, the majority required is 3/4th of the members. However, amendments relating to general principles, such as MFN treatment must be approved by all members.

5. ITS OBJECTIVES

In its Preamble, the Agreement establishing the WTO lays down the following objectives of the WTO:

1. Its relations in the field of trade and economic endeavour shall be conducted with a view to raising standards of living, ensuring full employment and large and steadily growing volume of real income and effective demand, and expanding the production and trade in goods and services.

2. To allow for the optimal use of the world's resources in accordance with the objectives of sustainable development, seeking both (*a*) to protect and preserve the environment, and (*b*) to enhance the means for doing so in a manner consistent with respective needs and concerns at different levels of economic development.

3. To make positive efforts designed to ensure that developing countries, especially the least developed among them, secure a share in the growth in international trade commensurate with the needs of their economic development.

4. To achieve these objectives by entering into reciprocal and mutually advantageous arrangements directed towards substantial reduction of tariffs and other barriers to trade and the elimination of discriminatory treatment in international trade relations.

5. To develop an integrated, more viable and durable multilateral trading system encompassing the GATT, the results of past liberalisation efforts, and all the results of the Uruguay Round of multilateral trade negotiations.

6. To ensure linkages between trade policies, environmental policies and sustainable development.

6. ITS FUNCTIONS

The following are the functions of the WTO:

1. It facilitates the implementation, administration and operation of the objectives of the Agreement and of the Multilateral Trade Agreements.

2. It provides the framework for the implementation, administration and operation of the Plurilateral Trade Agreements relating to trade in civil aircraft, government procurement, trade in dairy products and bovine meat.

3. It provides the forum for negotiations among its members concerning their multilateral trade relations in matters relating to the agreements and framework for the implemenation of the results of such negotiations, as decided by the Ministerial Conference.

4. It administers the Understanding on Rules and Procedures governing the Settlement of Disputes of the Agreement.

5. It co-operates with the IMF and the World Bank and its affiliated agencies with a view to achieving greater coherence in global economic policy-making.

7. WTO AGREEMENT

The Agreement establishing the WTO consists of the following which embody the results of the Uruguay Round of the Multilateral Trade Negotiations:

1. Multilateral Agreements on Trade in Goods : GATT Rules 1994.
2. General Agreements on Trade in Services.
3. Agreement on Trade-Related Aspects of Intellectual Property Rights (TRIPs).
4. Understanding on Rules and Procedures governing the Settlement of Disputes.
5. Plurilateral Trade Agreements.
6. Trade Policy Review Mechanism.

They are discussed as under :

1. Multilateral Agreements on Trade in Goods

The general agreement on trade in goods defines the GATT 1994 and includes various agreements dealing with different aspects related to trade in goods.

(1) GATT 1994

The GATT 1994 includes GATT 1947 as amended up to January 1, 1995 when the WTO Agreement came into force. It also includes the provisions of specified legal instruments, the Marrakesh Protocol to GATT 1994 and the following understandings :

(*a*) *Article II : 1(b) of GATT 1994*. To ensure transparency of the legal rights and obligations, the nature and level of any "other duties or charges" levied on bound tariff items in the Schedules of concessions continue with effect from April 15, 1995.

(*b*) *Article XVII of GATT*. To ensure transparency of the activities of state trading enterprises, members are required to notify such enterprises to the Council for Trade in Goods for review by the working party atleast once a year and report to the Council.

(*c*) *Understanding on Balance of Payment Provisions of GATT*. Members imposing restrictions for purposes of balance should do so in the least disruptive manner. They should give preference to price-based measures like import surcharges, import deposits or measures which affect the price of imported goods. They should avoid the imposition of "new" quantitative restrictions and should publicly announce "as soon as possible" time schedules for the removal of restrictive import measures for purposes of balance of payments. The Committee on Balance of Payments Restrictions carries out consultations in order to review all restrictive import measures taken for balance of payments purposes.

(*d*) *Article XXIV of GATT 1994*. The Agreement on Customs Unions and Free Trade Areas clarifies and reinforces the criteria and procedures for the review of new or enlarged customs unions or free trade areas and for the evaluation of their effects on third parties. The Agreement also clarifies the procedure for any compensatory adjustment in the event of contracting parties forming a customs union seeking to increase a bound tariff.

(*e*) *Understanding on the Interpretation of Article XXVIII*. Article XXVIII covers modification of GATT Schedules. It lays down new procedures for the negotiation of compensation when tariff bindings are modified or withdrawn.

(2) Agreement on Agriculture

The Agreement on Agriculture relates to domestic subsidies, export subsidies (including volume of subsidised exports), minimum market access commitment, domestic support, sanitary and phytosanitary and food aid operations.

The Agreement seeks to open national markets to international competition by replacing non-tariff measures with normal customs duties that would be progressively reduced. Second, it seeks to check overproduction by progressively reducing government aids that encourage overproduction and hence surpluses which are either disposed of through export subsidies or destroyed. Third, it seeks new disciplines on export competition and reduction in subsidies alongwith the volume of subsidised exports.

(*i*) *Domestic Subsidies*. Domestic subsidies fall into two categories : (*a*) *non-product specific subsidies* given for all crops which include subsidies given for fertilisers, water, electricity, seeds and credit; and (*b*) *product-specific subsidies* given for specific crops, as in India in the form of minimum support price for some agricultural crops.

For the purpose of calculating total subsidies given to farmers, known as the Total Aggregate Measurement of Support or *Total AMS,* both types of subsidies mentioned above must be totalled together. Such total in any year, called the *Current Total AMS,* should not exceed 10 per cent of the value of total agricultural production in that year in the case of a developing country to be exempt from any obligation to reduce its subsidies. The subsidy is to be calculated at the international price for the commodity.

(*ii*) *Export Subsidies*. WTO members are required to reduce the value of *direct export subsidies* to a level of 36 per cent below the 1986-90 base period level over the *six-year* implementation period, and the quantity of subsidised exports by 21 per cent over the same period. In the case of developing countries, the reductions are 2/3rd those of developed countries over a *ten-year* period. But no reductions apply to the least developed countries.

(iii) Minimum Market Access Commitment. The minimum market access commitment applies to those countries that maintain restriction of various types on agricultural imports, and are, therefore, required to convert those restrictions into tariffs and reduce those tariffs by 36 per cent over the six-year period. Such countries are also required to allow a minimum market access opportunity of 3 per cent of their domestic consumption for foreign agricultural consumption for six years which will rise to 5 per cent after that period. These commitments apply only if a country is obliged to render its import controls in terms of tariffs. In the case of developing countries, tariffs on agricultural products are to be reduced by 24 per cent over a period of *ten years*. Least developed countries are not required to reduce their tariffs.

(iv) Domestic Support. Domestic support measures that have a minimum impact on trade, known as *green box* policies are excluded from reduction commitments. Such policies include general government services, such as in the areas of research, disease control, infrastructure and food security. It includes direct payments to producers in the form of income support, structural adjustment assistance, direct payments under environmental programmes and under regional assistance programmes.

In addition, there are other policies which are not to be included in the *Total Average Measurement of Support (Total AMS)* reduction commitments. They are direct payments under production limiting programmes, certain government assistance measures to encourage agricultural and rural development in developing countries and other support measures. These should make up only 10 per cent of the value of production of individual products or of the total agricultural production in the case of developed countries and 5 per cent in the case of developed countries.

(v) Sanitary and Phytosanitary Measures. The application of sanitary and phytosanitary measures concern food safety, and animal and plant health measures. The agreement recognises that governments have the right to take sanitary and phytosanitary measures in order to protect human, animal or plant life or health. But they should not arbitrarily or unjustifiably discriminate between members where identical or similar conditions prevail. The agreement seeks to ensure that animal and plant health and safety measures do not serve as unwarranted trade barriers. The agreement lays down procedures and criteria for the assessment of risk and determination of appropriate levels of sanitary or phytosanitary protection.

(vi) Food Stocking and Food Aid. The agreement recognises that during the interim period least developed and net food-importing developing countries may experience negative effects with respect to supplies of food imports. It, therefore, sets out objectives with regard to the provision of food aid and basic foodstuffs in full grant form and aid for agricultural development. It also refers to the possibility of short-term financing of commercial food imports by the IMF and the World Bank.

A Committee on Agriculture has been established to monitor and review the implementation of the provision of the Agriculture Agreement.

(3) Agreement on Textiles and Clothing

The objective of this Agreement is to secure the integration of the textiles and clothing sector into the GATT 1994. The integration of this sector would take place in four phases. *First*, on January 1, 1995 each party was integrated into GATT products from the specific list in the Agreement which accounted for not less than 16 per cent of its total volume of imports in 1990. In the *second* phase beginning January 1, 1998, products which accounted for not less than 17 per cent of 1990 imports would be integrated. In the *third* phase beginning January 1, 2002, products which accounted for not less than 18 per cent of 1990 imports would be integrated. All remaining products would be integrated at the end of the transition period on January 1, 2005 in the *fourth* phase. Integration means that trade in *tops* and yarns, fabrics, made-up textiles products, and clothing will be governed by the General Rules of GATT. All MFA (Multi-Fibre Agreement) restrictions existing on December 31, 1994 have been carried over into the new Agreement and would be maintained until such time as the restrictions are removed or the products integrated into the GATT. In the case of non-MFA restrictions maintained by some members, they would also be brought within the purview of the GATT 1994 within one year of the coming of the Agreement into force or phased out progressively by 2005.

There is a specific transitional safeguard mechanism for products not yet integrated into the GATT 1994 at any phase. Action can be taken against an individual exporting country if it is found by the importing country that overall imports of a product were entering the country in such large quantities as to cause serious damage to the relevant domestic industry. Action under the safeguard mechanism can be taken either by mutual agreement following consultations or unilaterally but subject to the review of the Textile Monitoring Body. Safeguard restraints can be in operation for up to three years without extension or until the product is integrated into the GATT.

As part of the integration process, all members shall take such actions in the area of textiles and clothing as may be necessary so as to follow GATT Rules and improve market access and ensure the application of policies relating to fair and equitable trading conditions and avoid discrimination against imports.

(4) Agreement on Technical Barriers to Trade

This Agreement extends and clarifies the Agreement on Technical Barriers to Trade reached in the Tokyo Round. It seeks to ensure that technical negotiations and standards, and testing and certification procedures do not create unnecessary obstacles to trade. However, it recognises that countries have the right to establish protection on human, animal or plant life or health or the environment. A Code of Good Practice for the Preparation, Adoption and Application of Standards by standardising bodies has been included into the Agreement.

(5) Agreement on Trade Related Aspects of Investment Measures (TRIMs)

It calls for the removal of all trade related investment measures within a period of five years. These measures are confined to quantitative restrictions and national treatment. In particular, they relate to such measures as investment in identified areas, level of foreign investment for treating foreign companies at par with national companies, export obligations, and use of local raw materials. It prevents the imposition of any performance clauses on foreign investors in respect of earnings of foreign exchange, foreign equity participation, and transfer to technology. It requires foreign investment companies to be treated at par with national companies. It prevents the imposition of restrictions on areas of investment. It requires free import of raw materials, components and intermediates.

The Agreement recognises that certain investment measures restrict and distort trade. It, therefore, requires mandatory notification of all non-confirming TRIMs and their removal within two years for developed countries, within five years for developing countries and within seven years for least developed countries. It establishes a Committee on TRIMs which will monitor the implementation of these commitments and report to the Council of Trade in Goods annually.

(6) Agreement on Anti-Dumping

Article VI of the GATT provides for the right of contracting parties to apply anti-dumping measures if dumped imports cause injury to a domestic industry in the importing member country. The revised Agreement is an improvement over the Tokyo Round Agreement. It provides greater clarity, more detailed rules and the criteria to be taken into account for determining injury caused by dumped imports to domestic industry, the procedure to be followed in initiating and conducting anti-dumping investigations, and the implementation and duration of anti-dumping measures, and dispute settlement relating to anti-dumping actions taken by domestic authorities. Under the new rules, an anti-dumping investigation should be immediately terminated if the "margin of dumping" is less than 2 per cent of the export price or the volume of dumped imports from a particular country is less than 3 per cent of the total imports of that product subject to a ceiling of 7 per cent of all such dumped imports.

The Multilateral Agreement on Trade in Goods also includes agreements on Customs Valuation, Pre-shipment Inspection, Rules of Origin, Import Licensing Procedures and Safeguards.

2. General Agreements on Trade in Services (GATS)

This Agreement covers all internationally traded services. Foreign services and service suppliers would be treated on equal national footing with domestic services and service suppliers. However, governments may indicate specific Most-Favoured Nation (MFN) exemptions which will be reviewed after 5 years, with a normal limitation of 10 years. It requires transparency which includes the publication of all relevant laws and regulations relating to services trade. International payments and transfers relating to trade in services shall not be restricted, except in the event of balance of payments difficulties where such restrictions will be temporary, limited and subject to conditions. Any liberalisation of trade in services would be progressive in character. It would be through negotiations at five-year intervals in order to reduce or remove the adverse effects of measures on trade in services and to increase the general level of specific commitments by governments.

The Agreement sets out special conditions relating to individual sectors. So far as the *movement of natural persons* is concerned, it permits the governments to negotiate specific commitments applicable to the temporary stay of people for the purpose of providing a service. It does not apply to persons seeking permanent employment or residence in a country.

In *financial* services, it establishes the right of goverments to take appropriate measures for the protection of investors, depositors and policy holders, and to ensure the integrity and stability of the financial system. They came into effect 6 months after WTO came into force.

In *telecommunications*, the Agreement requires a Member to establish, construct, acquire, lease, operate or supply telecommunications transport networks and services and make it available to the public. However, a developing country may place reasonable conditions on access to and use of public telecommunica-tions, transport networks and services to strengthen its domestic telecommunica-tions infrastructure and service capacity and to increase its participation in international trade in telecommunications services in co-operation with the International Telecommunication Union and the International Organisation for Standardisation.

The GATS will also apply to *aircraft* repair and maintenance services, marketing of air transport services and computer reservation services.

The governments have agreed to set up working parties on : (1) Trade in services and environment to examine and report, with recommendations, on the relationship between services trade and environment, including the issue of sustainable development. (2) Professional services to examine and report, with recommendations, on the disciplines necessary to ensure that measures relating to qualifications requirements and procedure, technical standards and licensing requirements in the field of professional services do not constitute unnecessary barriers to trade.

The GATS also contains consultations and dispute settlement and the establishment of a Council on Services.

3. Agreement on Trade-Related Aspects of Intellectual Property Rights (TRIPs)

The TRIPs Agreement covers seven categories of intellectual property : (1) copyright and related rights; (2) trademarks; (3) geographical indications; (4) industrial designs; (5) patents which also include micro-organisms and plant varieties; (6) integrated circuits; and (7) trade secrets. We discuss them briefly as under :

(1) *Copyright and Related Rights*. The parties are required to comply with the Berne Convention for the protection of literary and artistic works. Computer programmes are included in literary works. Authors of computers programmes, performers on a phonogram, producers of phonograms (sound recordings) and broadcasting organisations are to be given the right to authorise or prohibit the commercial rental of their works to the public. A similar exclusive right applies to films. The protection for performers and producers of sound recordings are to be for no less than 50 years and for broadcasting organisations for atleast 20 years.

(2) *Trademarks*. Any sign, or any combination of signs, capable of distinguishing the goods or services of one undertaking from those of other udertakings constitutes a trade mark. Such signs, in particular words including personal names, letters, numerals, figurative elements and combinations of colours as well as combinations of such signs are eligible for registration as trademarks. The owner of a registered trademark has the exclusive right to prevent all third parties not having the owner's consent from using in the course of trade identical or similar signs for goods or services. Initial registration, and each renewal of registration, of a trademark is for a term of no less than seven years. The registration of a trade mark is renewable indefinitely.

(3) *Ccographical Indications*. Geographical indications refer to the indentity of a good as originating in the territory of a Member, or a region or locality in that territory where a given quality or reputation of the good is essentially attributed to its geographical origin. Members are required to provide the legal means for interested parties to prevent the use of any indication which misleads the consumer as to the origin of goods and any use which would constitute an act of unfair competition. Additional production is applied for geographical indications for wines and spirits.

(4) *Industrial Designs*. Industrial designs are protected for a period of 10 years. Owners of protected designs would be able to prevent the manufacture, sale or importation of articles bearing or embodying a design which is a copy of the protected design for commercial purposes. The duration of protections available

shall be for at least 10 years.

(5) *Patents.* Patents shall be available for any inventions, whether products or processes, in all fields of technology, provided they are new, involve an inventive step and are capable of industrial application. Patent owners shall have the right to assign, or transfer by succession, the patent and to conclude licensing contracts. The Agreement requires 20-year patent protection.

Inventions may be excluded from patentability if their commercial exploitation is prohibited for reasons of public order or morality. Further, diagnostic, therapeutic and surgical methods for the treatment of humans or animals, plants and animals other than micro-organisms, and essentially biological processes for the production of plants or animals other than non-biological and microbiological processes may be excluded from patentability. However, members shall provide for the protection of plant varieties either by patents or by an effective *sui generis* system (breeder's rights) or by any combination thereof. These provisions shall be reviewed 4 years after January 1, 1995.

(6) *Integrated Circuits.* The TRIPs Agreement provides protection to the layout-designs (topographies) of integrated circuits for a period of 10 years. But the protection shall lapse 15 years after the creation of the layout-design.

(7) *Trade Secrets.* Trade secrets and know-how having commercial value shall be protected against breach of confidence and other acts. Test data submitted to governments in order to obtain marketing approval for pharmaceuticals or agricultural chemicals shall be protected against unfair commercial use.

Lastly, this Agreement refers to the controls of anti-competitive practices in contractual licenses pertaining to intellectual property rights. It provides for consultations between governments in order to protect intellectual property rights from being absued.

The Agreement requires a one-year transition period for developed countries to bring their legislation and practices into conformity for the implementation of TRIPs. Developing countries and the erstwhile East-European and U.S.S.R. countries would have a 5-year transition period and the least developed countries 11 years. Those developing countries which do not provide product patent protection have been given 10 years.

The Agreement also envisages the establishment of a Council for Trade-Related Aspects of Intellectual Property Rights to monitor the operations of the Agreements and Governments' compliance with it.

4. Dispute Settlement System

The Understanding on Rules and Procedures Governing the Settlement of Disputes shall apply to consultations and the settlement of disputes between Members concerning their rights and obligations under the provisions of the Agreement establishing the WTO. For this purpose, a Dispute Settlement Body (DSB) will be established. The first stage in the settlement of disputes is the holding of consultations between the members concerned. If consultations fail and if both parties agree, the Director General of WTO offers good offices, conciliations and mediation. The complainant member can ask the DSB to establish a panel of three experts within 30 days. There is also the provision of the appellate review by a standing Appellate Body of seven members to be established by the DSB who will report to the DSB between 60-90 days. The DSB will adopt the report within 30 days which will be unconditionally accepted by the parties to the dispute.

5. Plurilateral Trade Agreements (PTA)

The Plurilateral Trade Agreements consist of the Agreement on Trade in Civil Aircraft, Agreement on Government Procurement, International Dairy Agreement and International Bovine Meat Agreement. The first Agreement was done at Geneva in April 1979, as subsequently modified, rectified or amended. The latter three Agreements were done at Marrakesh on April 15, 1994.

6. Trade Policy Review Mechanism (TPRM)

The TPRM aims to carry out reviews of the trade policies and practices under the Multilateral Trade Agreements and the Plurilateral Trade Agreements for the smoother functioning of the multilateral trading system. For this purpose, it envisages the establishment of the Trade Policy Review Body (TPRB). In order to achieve full transparency, each member shall report regularly to the TPRB about the trade policies and practices pursued by it. An annual overview of developments in the international trading environment having an impact on the multilateral trading system shall also be undertaken by the TPRB. The overview shall be assisted by an Annual Report by the Director General setting out major activities of the WTO and highlighting significant policy issues affecting the multilateral trading system.

8. CRITICAL APPRAISAL OF URUGUAY ROUND AND WTO AGREEMENT

The Uruguay Round took eight long years of negotiations by the contracting countries. The legal document comprising the Final Act of the results of the Uruguay Round of Multilateral Trade Negotiations contains 28 Agreements.

The Uruguay Round was larger in scope and coverage than the earlier Rounds and for the first time covered areas like services, agriculture, intellectual property rights and investments. It also emphasised linkages between trade policies, environmental policies and sustainable development through the WTO. The replacement of the GATT, as a discussion forum by the WTO, as a permanent world trade organisation, was a spectacular achievement of the Uruguay Round. The WTO contains not only the original GATT as amended by the Uruguay Round but also a number of new Agreements discussed above.[1] These Agreements are likely to benefit the developing and least developed countries in the long-run, provided they receive full cooperation from the developed countries in their efforts towards globalisation. However, there are many loopholes in these Agreements which are likely to be to the disadvantage of the developing countries. We discuss them briefly in the case of each Agreement.[2]

1. Agriculture. The Agreement on agriculture would harm the interests of farmers in developing countries. It makes no distinction between subsidies to promote food security and self-reliance, and those meant to increase exports of farm products. As it allows *subsidy* only up to 10% of the value of production, it would become almost impossible for the governments of developing countries to provide price support to particular agricultural commodities. This is also the case of input subsidies which are allowed only to low income farmers. Thus all subsidies on such imports as fuel, electricity, fertilisers, transportations, seeds, etc. to farmers, and consumer subsidy in the form of public distribution system would have to be abolished. The reduction and removal of subsidies unaccompanied by a rational price policy would hit farmers in developing countries.

Again, the *free market access* and the removal of all restrictions on imports would adversely affect the farming community. Cheap imports of agricultural products would push farmers out of production. Prices of farm products in international markets are not determined by competition but by the corprorations of the developed countries which procure and sell them. Moreover, they would increase foreign debt and worsen the balance of payments problem.

The Agreement lays down the application of sanitary and phytosanitary measures against the farm products of developing countries. These would be based on regulations established by such international organisations as the Codex Alimentarius which is not subjected to any democratic process. This agency might declare as "safe" products of developed countries and as "unsafe" of developing countries.

These free trade and market-based agricultural systems cannot solve the problems of developing countries. The persistence of high domestic support to agriculture in many developed countries has been encouraging over production at high cost to them. The export subsidies are used to dispose of excess supplies in these countries which artificially lower the prices of such commodities in the global markets.

Further, the opening up of markets since the WTO Agreement has been in the developing countries while there has been little success in getting market access in developed countries. For instance, the share of agricultural exports from developing countries to Western Europe declined from 30.5% in 1990 to 28% in 1998. Market access to developing countries continues to be restricted by continuous protection by tariff and other barriers such as Sanitary and Physiosanitary standards. To safeguard the interest of farmers in developing countries, certain degree of protection in terms of moderately high tariffs and special safeguard clause are required to be added in the Agricultural Agreement for sustainable agricultural development in these countries.

Despite these, the agricultural sector in developing countries is expected to gain much from this Agreement by generating export surpluses after meeting the growing domestic demand. They may gain from higher prices of such crops as foodgrains, cotton, etc. and by diversifying in the areas of horticulture, floriculture, dairy products and other allied activities with the increase in the tariff bindings to 100% in agricultural products. Further, the reduction of subsidies to agriculture by the developed countries are expected to make the exports of developing countries more profitable.

2. Textiles and Clothing. This Agreement would benefit most developing countries during the transitional period. But the gains to them are likely to be delayed because of the long period of phasing out of the MFA due to two reasons. *First,* when a developed country takes certain types of textiles and clothing out of the MFA, it will apply on a non-discriminatory MFN (Most-Favoured Nation)basis to all exporting countries. *Second,* only 49% of all products would be integrated into the GATT on the last day of the 10-year transition period. This phasing out period is very long and the WTO may be pressurised to extend the transition period.

Further, the "product coverage" for the phasing out is so large that all items of textiles and clothing which are not covered by quotas are included in it. Thus there will be little phasing out of quota items till the end of the 10-year phasing out period.

Recently, the US has announced a four-stage quota-phaseout programme ending January 2005 under which 90 per cent of the restrictions on Indian apparel exports would actually remain till 2005. Till then, the Indian apparel exports will suffer. In the EU phaseout programme, one-sixth of Indian apparel exports would continue to face restriction till 2005.

3. TRIMs. The Agreement on TRIMs is a weak one. Article IV of the Agreement lays down that developing countries can deviate from the above provisions temporarily. The extent and manner of deviation would depend upon the interpretation of the contracting parties. Under this 'escape' clause, the right to regulate foreign companies and trade-balancing measures have in no way been curtailed if there are valid reasons such as adverse balance of payments.

These safeguards apart, the TRIMs agreement would remove restrictions on foreign investments. Though foreign direct investment is not mentioned, yet it is feared that MNCs would try to control high priority areas in developing countries.

Further, the TRIMs mentioned are those that are applied in a discriminatory manner on foreign owned enterprises when the same requirements are not applicable to the national enterprises. The Agreement also deals with discriminatory imports restrictions.

On the whole, the TRIMs Agreement has reduced the decision-making powers of national governments. For instance, they cannot specify local contents in domestic manufacturing and cannot restrict the percentage of imported inputs in its exported products or the export of a particular product.

4. GATT Rules. The GATT Rules 1994 pertaining to the phasing out of the *quantitative restrictions* (QRs) and preferences are vague. The use of QRs by developing countries to overcome their balance of payments difficulties has been rendered ineffective by providing it only for the least developed countries. In the case of developing countries, QRs would be eliminated and replaced by price-based measures. Only the least developing countries would impose QRs, but these would be viewed as temporary. Countries which impose such QRs would publicly announce as soon as possible, time schedules for their removal. But the developing countries have the right to use different duty rates for different goods so that they can discourage excessive imports of non-essential goods. This would enable developing countries to facilitate the import of essential inputs and capital goods while restricting the import of non-essential goods.

One developing country provides tariff preferences to another under the *Global System of Tariff Preferences* (GSTP). Similarly, a developed country offers tariff preferences to a developing country under the Generalised System of Preferences (GSP). These tariff reductions are over and above the tariff preferences provided to countries under the Most Favoured Nation (MFN) obligations of the WTO. As a result, for developing countries in general, preferential margins will totally disappear in some sectors. The OECD has estimated that Africa will lose by an average of 30 per cent through the erosion of their preferences by 2002. Exports of tropical products from the African, Caribbean and Pacific (ACP) countries will suffer to the extent of 51 per cent.

Under the Uruguay Round Agreement, the developing countries have committed themselves to "bind" their industrial tariff lines by 72 per cent and 100 per cent for agricultural products. In the Subsidies Agreement, the developing countries have committed to eliminate subsidies having an impact on export prices with the result that they will be giving up the policy of export-led growth.

The GATT Rules on anti-dumping leave so much at the discretion of national governments that very few actions would actually qualify as their violations. Thus partly due to the GATT Rules and partly due to economic circumstances, anti-dumping and countervailing duties are being used for restricting trade by the USA, EEC and other developed countries.

Further, the non-technical barriers to trade like the environmental, health, and sanitary considerations can also act as non-tariff barriers in the case of developing countries. For instance, the US has tried to block shrimp exports from India by insisting that they should be caught with devices which do not net turtles. Obviously, Indian fishermen do not have the means to use such devices.

5. GATS. The GATS goes against the interests of the developing countries. It emphasises on the liberalisation of only those services such as financial, shipping, transport and communications, health, educational, professional and media services, in which the developing countries have a distinct advantage. By liberalising trade in services, the developed countries aim at seeking control over the production and use of services in developing countries.

The services sector in developing countries would have to face unequal competition from the vast resources which the firms of developed countries possess. Many developing countries have a comparative advantage in skilled and unskilled labour. But their free movement is controlled by stringent immigration laws of developed countries. But nothing has been proposed on this aspect of the services sector because the developed countries stand to gain from the selective brain drain of developing countries.

6. TRIPs. The TRIPs agreement is patently discriminatory. It would favour the developed countries and go against the interest of developing countries for the following reasons:

It would increase the area of coverage under the patent system such as drugs, agriculture, plants and animals, etc. As developed countries and their MNCs have vast resources and facilities for R & D, they would be at an advantage to invest and patented processes and products. In all such cases, developing countries would have to pay royalties. The domestic prices of such goods, especially of drugs and medicines would increase and burden the consumers. There would be larger imports of patented raw materials and products by developing countries. Exports would receive a setback. Consequently, there would be worsening of the balance of payments.

Even the developed countries will be affected by TRIPs. According to an estimate, 90 per cent of the world's population would suffer on account of skyrocketing prices of pharmaceutical products if the TRIPs Agreement is implemented in full.

Many developing countries like India are engaged in R & D programmes in such critical areas as drugs, farm products, chemical, etc. which would come to a standstill. This is because after the transitional period of ten years, the patent law would change.

The acceptance of TRIPs agreement would necessitate wide-ranging amendments in the patents laws of developing countries.

A change in the patent laws of developing countries in accordance with the TRIPs agreement would further lead to brain drain which would prove costly for such countries.

The increase in the patent right to 20 years would again be detrimental to the interests of developing countries. It is only in the developed countries that patent rights are of 20 years duration. Of course, developing countries would be given 10 years to change their existing laws. But the TRIPs agreement takes away this concession through the "classical pipeline protection" clause. According to this clause, patent applications for pharmaceutical and agricultural products would be accepted by the concerned authorities even after the agreement came into force from January 1, 1995, irrespective of whether the national law provided for the grant of product patents or not. For instance, in the case of a pharmaceutical product normally it takes 10 years from the date of filing a patent to market it. Consequently, patent protection to such a product would only be necessary from the year 2005 onwards. When the patent would be valid for only 20 years, nobody would make investments on new products.

Again, the Agreement provides for the grant of "exclusive marketing rights" in another country to an applicant for a maximum period of 5 years. The information concerning such innovation would be kept secret even without the grant of a patent. This provisioin is inimical to the interests of developing countries because it grants the patentee the right to prevent the use of his patent product or process being used for the export market. Thus the patented technology might be provided by an MNC for the exploitation of the local market of a developing country.

In the case of the working of a patent, the patentee would be given the freedom to import the product instead of setting up the product unit in the other country. The developed countries and their MNCs would not be under any obligation to transfer their technologies to the developing countries to satisfy the requirement of "working". Rather, they would be used as markets for their products.

The inclusion of the clause "reversal of the burdern of proof" is against all canons of justice. It would be for the producers of new products and processes to prove the non-infringement of their patent rights. It thus relieves the patentee from producing proof of the infringement of his process or product patent. This is arbitrary.

The TRIPs rules are also self-contradictory. They do not provide specific mechanism to achieve the objectives of sustainable development and environmental protection. The link between intellectual property rights and environment arises because some protected technologies directly affected the environment in a positive or negative manner. In fact, for technologies affecting environment, exclusion from patentability or a ban on their use or commercial exploitation would appear to be *prima facie* necessary. The TRIPs Agreement does not clarify whether members can ban the commercial exploitation of environmentally-injurious technologies while granting patent protection or whether this can give rise to non-violation type complaints.

According to Dr. Deepak Nayyar, the implications of the TRIPs agreement for the absorption, diffusion and adaptation of technologies, let alone innovation, in developing countries are far reaching. Much needed technologies may no longer be available at affordable costs. The emergence of domestic technologies may be pre-empted. Transfer of technology may slow down. The incidence of restrictive business practices by MNCs may increase. The implications and consequences of the TRIPs agreement suggest that the emerging international system for the protection of intellectual property rights is bound to be inequitable and inimical for the developing countries.

7. Dispute Settlement. The dispute settlement system of the WTO provides for adjudication of issues pertaining to the internal policies of the member countries. Such a measure poses a threat to the sovereignty of countries. For instance, if a request is made to the WTO for establishing a panel in case of a dispute, the WTO secretariat has been authorised to propose nominations on the panel. But the parties to the dispute shall not oppose nominations. In such a situation, the parties to the dispute shall have no say in decision-making. This tantamounts to interference in their sovereign rights. Moreover, the powerful developed countries like the US adopt cross-retaliatory measures under the guise of the dispute settlement mechanism which may go against the developing countries.

Further, there is the US Trade Law Section 301 which allows individual enterprises to compel the US government to investigate foreign trade practices that restrict or harm their trade interests. It is doubtful if the WTO dispute settlement system can resolve complaints arising out of the use of this law.

Conclusion. Despite these criticisms, the formation of the WTO and GATT Rules provide greater transparency, predictability and security in international trade relations to developing countries.*

9. WORKING OF WTO

The first biennial Ministerial Meeting of the WTO was held at Suntec City in Singapore from December 9 to 13, 1996. The ministers of member countries adopted a consensus declaration reaffirming their faith in the multilateral trading system as the means to promote free world trade. In the declaration, they renewed their commitment to : (1) a fair, equitable and more open rule-based system; (2) progressive liberalisation and elimination of tariff and non-tariff barriers to trade in goods; (3) progressive liberalisation of trade in services; (4) rejection of all forms of protectionism; (5) elimination of discriminatory treatment in international trade relations; (6) integration of developing and least developed countries and economies in transition into the multilateral system; and (7) the maximum possible level of transparency.

The Ministers discussed some new issues of trade such as competition policy, labour standards, multilateral investment agreement and government procurement. In their declaration, they rejected the use of labour standards for protectionist purpose, agreed to establish separate working groups to examine the relationship between trade and investment, to study issues pertaining to the interaction between trade and competition, including anti-competitive practices, and to conduct a study on transparency in government procurement practices. They admitted that progress in negotiations on liberalising world markets in financial services, maritime services and basic telecommunications had been unsatisfactory which would be completed by the end of 1997.

The only positive side of the Meeting was the launching of the Information Technology Agreement signed by 28 countries which aims at slashing tariffs on items of information technology to zero by the year 2000. It was agreed to start negotiations in Geneva in January 1997 and the Agreement would come into effect by July 1997. The second phase of tariff cuts would be in January 1998, the third phase in January 1999, and the final cut to zero by the beginning of 2000. The Agreement will cover a wide range of items including computers and software, semi-conductors, fibre-optic cables, photo-copiers and capacitors.

The first Ministerial Meeting was severely criticised for the manner in which its decisions were arrived at. There was a facade of consensus because most developing countries were marginalised in the decision-making process. Most countries were not invited to participate in the informal consultations, as in the case of the Information Tehnology Agreement. This Agreement which is of most benefit to developed countries has been arrived at with some armtwisting, whereas those aspects of the Uruguay Round Agreement having potential benefit for developing countries, such as the Textiles and Agriculture Agreements were not discussed at the meeting.

The second Ministerial Conference was held at Seattle (US) from November 30, to December 3, 1999. The Conference was marred by many controversies between the developed and developing countries. A large number of member countries emphasised on a comprehensive round of negotiations covering a wide range of subjects like investment issues, competition policy, transparency in government procurement, trade facilitations, trade and labour standards, trade and environment, industrial tariff reduction, etc. The inclusion of non-trade issues like labour standards in the WTO agenda was vehemently opposed by the developing countries. The conference also highlighted the differences between the US and EEC on issues like environment, trade and labour, anti-dumping. As no concensus based conclusions could be reached on most of the issues, the Conference failed to kick off a new round of trade talks. The Conference failed due to large disagreements among the groups of developed and developing countries on certain disputed issues like textiles, agriculture and anti-dumping.

The critics point out that outcome of the Singapore and Seattle meetings confirmed the image of the WTO as a "rich men's club", like the earlier GATT where the WTO was viewed as an instrument of domination by the developed countries over the developing countries.

Apart from the Ministerial Meetings, the Dispute Settlement Board (DSB) of the WTO has been actively functioning. So far more than 100 disputes have been brought to it and many have been settled by it. All member countries have praised the WTO for its transparent dispute settlement process and procedures without any pressure from the "big" powers.

EXERCISES

1. What is World Trade Organisation? Explain its objectives and functions.
2. Explain the main features of the Trade Related Intellectual Property Rights (TRIPs) Agreement under the Uruguay Round. What will be its effects on the developing countries?
3. Write notes on any two of the following agreements with their effects on developing countries under the Uruguay Round: Agreement on Agriculture; Agreement on Textiles and Clothing; General Agreement on Trade in Services (GATS).
4. Explain the main features of the World Trade Organisation. How does it differ from the GATT?
5. Discuss the WTO Agreement embodying the results of the GATT Uruguay Round.

CHAPTER 65

The UN Conference on Trade and Development (UNCTAD)

1. ORIGIN

The United Nations Conference on Trade and Development (UNCTAD) was established in 1964 following the growing dissatisfaction with the operation of such international institutions as the IMF and the GATT. These institutions favoured the developed countries and failed to tackle the special trade and development problems of the LDCs. The GATT, in particular, being committed to free trade, reduction of tariffs and abolition of preferences and import restrictions, did not pay any attention to proposals to stabilise commodity prices and give preferential treatment to LDCs in trade with developed countries.[1]

The first step towards the creation of UNCTAD was taken when the UN General Assembly declared the 1960s as the United Nations Development Decade in December 1961. By so doing, it recognised the need for adopting measures by developed countries to bridge the gap between the rich and poor nations through trade and aid. It was on the recommendations of the UN Economic and Social Council in July 1963 for convening a conference on trade and development that the UN General Assembly convened the first UNCTAD at Geneva in 1964.

Accordingly, the UNCTAD I was held at Geneva in 1964. Since then such conferences have been held normally every four years : UNCTAD II at New Delhi, 1968; UNCTAD III at Santiago, 1972; UNCTAD IV at Nairobi, 1976; UNCTAD V at Manila, 1979; UNCTAD VI at Belgrade, 1983; UNCTAD VII at Geneva, 1987; UNCTAD VIII at Cartagena (Columbia), 1992; and UNCTAD IX at Midrand (South Africa), 1996.

2. ORGANISATION

The UNCTAD is a permanent organ of the UN General Assembly with its headquarters at Geneva. It has a Secretariat. UNCTAD VIII agreed upon a new organisational structure for the UNCTAD which has been in operation since April 1992. It includes the following :

Conference. The (UNCTAD) Conference consisted of 188 members as on April 1996.

1. LDCs refer to less developed or developing countries.

Secretariat. The UNCTAD is run by a secretariat under the Secretary-General who is elected by the members. The organisational entities of the secretariat are the executive direction and management, the administrative service and inter-governmental support services. Other organisational institutions of the secretariat are detailed below.

Trade and Development Board. An executive body known as the Trade and Development Board which meets twice a year in Regular Session and in Special Session as required. It takes policy decisions when the Conference is not in session. It is composed of 55 members elected from among the Conference Members on the basis of equitable geographical distribution.

Executive Committee. There is an Executive Committee of the Board which is composed of the permanent representatives of member states deputed to the UNCTAD in Geneva. It meets periodically, usually every month.

Standing Committees. The Board is assisted in its functions by four new standing committees relating to commodities, poverty alleviation, economic co-operation among developing countries, and services. These Committees make studies and prepare reports from time to time, especially for the Conference to be held.

Special Committee. There is a Special Committee on Preferences.

Divisions. In response to the new orientation for working, resulting from UNCTAD IX, the UNCTAD secretariat has been reorganised to make it more performance-driven and to improve its quality of service. The secretariat now consists of four divisions (or groups) instead of nine previously. They are : (1) Division on Globalisation and Development Strategies ((DGDS); (2) Division on International Trade in Goods and Services and Commodities (DITGSC); (3) Division on Investment, Enterprise Development and Technology (DIEDT); and (4) Division on Services Infrastructure for Development and Trade Efficiency (DSIDTE). These divisions are responsible for helping the developing countries reap the benefits of globalisation to attain sustainable development.

In addition, the Secretary-General of the UNCTAD has established an office of the Special Coordinator for least developed, landlocked and island developing countries. Its aim is to prevent further marginalism of least developed countries in the world economy and to solve their specific problems.

The various committees and divisions have fixed terms. The divisions can bring in national experts so that their deliberations are enriched with national experience and empirical evidence. Non-governmental experts are also invited to participate both in the divisions and in the public sessions of the Board. They can also act in an advisory capacity to the Committees.

The Secretariat publishes an annual report based on the studies made by the Committees.

3. FUNCTIONS OF UNCTAD

The UNCTAD is expected to perform the following functions as laid down by the UN General Assembly :

1. To promote international trade between countries with different socio-economic systems, especially for accelerating the economic development of LDCs.

2. To formulate principles and policies of international trade and related problems of economic development.

3. To make proposals for putting the said principles and policies into effect, and to take such steps which may be relevant towards this end.

4. Generally, to review and facilitate the co-ordination of activities of other institutions within the UN system in the field of international trade and related problems of economic development.

5. To be available as a centre for harmonious trade related development policies of government, and regional economic groupings.

4. OBJECTIVES AND ACHIEVEMENTS OF UNCTAD

UNCTAD is supposed to fulfil the following objectives which have been evolved gradually of the various conferences : (1) trade in primary commodities, (2) trade in manufactured goods, (3) development financing, (4) technology transfer, and (5) economic co-operation among developing countries. We discuss below the extent to which UNCTAD has been successful in achieving these objectives.

1. Trade in Primary Commodities

The UNCTAD has been active in the international commodity arrangements since its inception. LDCs want to expand the market for their traditional exports of primary commodities. Developed countries place restrictions on the exports of the latter in such forms as licensing, quotas, tariffs, health and packaging regulations, etc. and provide subsidies to domestic producers. Such trade restrictions tend to be higher for processed products than for unprocessed. Besides, exports from LDCs have been subject to wide fluctuations. Consequently, there has been a continual deterioration in the terms of trade of primary products of the LDCs in relation to the export of manufactured products from the developed countries.

Since UNCTAD II, the LDCs have been insisting on International Commodity Agreements (ICA) to stabilise the prices and markets for their exports of primary products. These agreements seek: (1) to stabilise the price of the commodity concerned so as to reduce price fluctuations and the resulting instability in the economies of the producing LDCs; and (2) to increase its price to compensate for the fast worsening in the terms of trade of the LDCs.

At UNCTAD IV (Nairobi), in 1976 it was proposed to have an Integrated Programme for Commodities (IPC), and to create a common fund for buffer stock financing. The proposal was to negotiate international commodity ageements to stabilise the prices of 18 commodities, ten of which were to be included in the initial buffer stock scheme. This programme led to the international commodity agreements on only cocoa (1981) and rubber (1980). UNCTAD VI (Belgrade) in 1983 also emphasised the importance of negotiating ICAs for ten commodities. Of the five agreements on commodities—coffee, cocoa, sugar, tin and rubber—only that for rubber is still in operation.

UNCTAD VII had a Subsidiary Committee on Commodities and UNCTAD VIII set up a Standing Committee on Commodities for making recommendations to the TDB.

The UNCTAD IV proposed for a $6 billion Common Fund in 1976 to create and finance international buffer stock of ten storable commodities. It was at UNCTAD VII (Geneva) that a Common Fund for commodities under the IPC became operational after a number of countries ratified it or expressed their intentions to do so. New pledges announced at UNCTAD VII raised its total pledged capital to 66.9 per cent $ 4.7 billion fund, allowing it to become operational.

2. Trade in Manufactured Goods (GSP)

LDCs have strongly urged the developed countries to give them tariff preferences on their manufactured and semi-manufactured goods. At UNCTAD I, the G-77 urged the developed countries to grant a *Generalised System of Preferences* (GSP) to the exports of such goods to the developed countries. It was at UNCTAD II (New Delhi) in 1968 that all members unanimously agreed for the early establishment of a mutually acceptable system of generalised, non-reciprocal and non-discriminatory preferences. The objectives specified for the GSP were : (*a*) to increase the export earnings of LDCs; (*b*) to promote their industrialisation; and (*c*) to accelerate their growth rates. Thus the main aim of the GSP was to create a trade mechanism to enable LDCs to export without any tariff or other barriers to the developed countries and enable their products to compete on those markets with local production and thus encourage industrialisation and investment in the LDCs.

In June 1971, the GATT approved a waiver to MFN *(Most Favoured Nation)* clause which permitted developed countries to accord more favourable tariff treatment to goods imported from LDCs for a period of ten years. The EEC, Japan and Norway were the first to implement the GSP in 1971, followed by Denmark,

Finland, New Zealand, Sweden, Switzerland and Austria in 1972, by Australia and Canada in 1974, and finally by the United States in 1976. At the conclusion of GATT's Tokyo round in 1979, the GSP was given legal status in the trading system through the 'enabling clause', allowing developed countries to give such tariff and other concessions favouring the LDCs. The UNCTAD undertook a general review of GSP in 1980 and agreed that the objectives had not been fully achieved and that the system should be continued beyond its initial period. Accordingly, the scheme of GSP was renewed for a second term of 10 years in 1981. The GSP still continues. But a number of developed countries have unilaterally made changes into their trade laws which favour them.

The UNCTAD IX held at Midrant (SA) in May 1996 urged the developed countries to adopt a non-discriminatory and universal GSP for developing countries and it should be continued after the post-Uruguay round. It should be strengthened and procedures simplified and product coverage increased to cover more items of export of developing countries.

Under the GSP, most manufactured and semi-manufactured goods from LDCs to developed countries enjoy tariff reductions or exemptions from custom duties. A majority of developed countries grant duty free treatment for all or most products eligible for GSP. The United States, Sweden, Norway and Finland give completely duty free treatment under the GSP schemes. Japan and Switzerland allow generally duty free treatment with varying rates of duty upto 50 per cent lower than under MFN for individual products from LDCs. The EEC also gives duty free treatment for all industrial products eligible for GSP.

During the 1970s, constant efforts were made to expand the coverage of the GSP. But in the wake of global recession, rising protectionism and other obstacles in the way of increased access to international markets, the LDCs experienced a severe setback in their exports of manufactured and semi-manufactured products during 1980-82. Again during 1983-84, slower growth in developed countries and in world trade reduced the growth rate of exports of LDCs due to fall in international commodity prices. However, there has been a moderate recovery in export prices of manufactures of LDCs since 1985.

In 1993, about 50 per cent of products actually received preferential treatment, according to UNCTAD's 1993 review of the GSP. Within this total, the three major importing countries—the EC, Japan and US—accounted for more than 90 per cent. There were 14 GSP schemes in operation in 29 preference giving countries, including the 15 members of the EC.

In April 1996, India extended for the first time tariff preferences to eight developing countries under the Global System of Tariff Preferences (GSTP). GSTP differs from GSP in that the former are provided by one developing country to another, while the latter are provided by a developed country to a developing one. They are over and above the tariff preferences provided to countries under the MFN obligations of the WTO. India had provided tariff preferences to 22 products and received preferences for 32 products from developing countries under the GSTP.

Limitations of GSP. There are, however, certain limitations of the scheme of GSP.

1. Despite efforts made to expand the coverage of the GSP, such important items as textiles, clothing, leather and leather products, and steel and footwear are excluded by a number of developed countries. These are the products in which the more industrialised developing countries have been specialising.

2. Many developed countries have evolved their own schemes which subject the preferences to a variety of restrictions. Some give preferential tariff treatment to those LDCs that abide by 'voluntary export restraint'. Others offer GSP treatment in the form of a tariff quota whereby a limit is set on a certain volume of imports which enters duty free into the developed country. But any volume in excess of this is subject to MFN duty. There are also limits on the value of imports that can receive preference treatment.

3. There is no long-term guarantee in the case of GSP concessions which can be altered or withdrawn at short notice. For example, the EEC and the USA withdrew GSP concessions from a number of more industrialised developing countries in 1981 on the plea that they no longer needed preferential treatments.

4. Among the LDCs, the benefits of GSP have been consistently concentrated among few of the more advanced developing countries. In 1980, eleven advanced developing countries accounted for 80 per cent of the total products of all LDCs. The position does not seem to have changed since then because the products covered by the GSP correspond to those actually by the eleven for export.

5. LDCs cannot become actual GSP beneficiaries until they have notified to the respective developed country the names of the bodies or authorities which are empowered to issue origin certificates. This prerequisite

has not been fulfilled by a large number of LDCs. As a result, a significant number of preferential opportunities remain untapped for essentially administrative reasons.

Lastly, the scope for the extension of GSP is quite limited as product-producers in LDCs have a strong competitive position in the world markets.

3. Development Finance

Right from the UNCTAD III LDCs have been voicing their concern over the growing problems of their balance of payments deficits and indebtedness. The UNCTAD III held at Santigo in May 1972 passed a resolution asking the IMF to work out a scheme for the link-up of Special Drawing Rights (SDRs) with development finance. This was essential because the SDRs had been linked with individual members' quotas in the IMF. Since the quotas of LDCs were small, they received a very small share of SDRs. By another resolution, the UNCTAD III asked the IMF to set up a Committee for Monetary Reform which should have as many members from LDCs as there were from the developed countries. The UNCTAD III was also called upon to provide for a close examination of the relationship between indebtedness and development and to recommend appropriate remedial measures. Moreover, the LDCs proposed at UNCTAD III that the one per cent target of development assistance agreed upon by the developed countries as part of the international development strategy should not include components distinct from assistance, such as private investment, and credits by suppliers and purchasers, and that it should be not of reverse flows of interest payments. But UNCTAD III failed to achieve anything on all these issues.

The UNCTAD IV held at Nairobi in May 1976 also failed to solve the debt and development finance problems of LDCs. It passed three resolutions in this connection. The first dealt with the debt problems of LDCs and asked the developed countries to convert ODA debt into grants and establish a framework within which future debt problems could be solved. The second related to an effective system to international financial cooperation which suggested a number of measures to improve the working of the IMF in relation to LDCs. The third resolution concerned the establishment of multilateral guarantee facility. The Conference also appealed to developed countries to achieve 0.7 per cent target of development of LDCs. They should announce in advance ODA assistance which should be in the form of grants to the least developing countries, and larger concessional aid to other LDCs.

The UNCTAD V held at Manila in May-June 1979 passed a number of resolutions concerning finance and debt problems of LDCs. *First*, it asked the IMF to examine the overall size of its quotas in relation to the magnitude of world trade and balance of payments deficits of its members and to increase the quota share of LDCs. *Second*, the IMF was asked to apply conditionality in a flexible and appropriate manner taking into account the domestic social and political objectives and economic priorities of the borrowing LDC so as to encourage timely recourse to Fund's facilities, and a higher rate of utilization of its resources. *Third*, it stressed the IMF to find out ways to improve the terms and use of extended facility of LDCs. *Fourth*, it emphasized the IMF to improve and liberalise the existing compensatory facility. *Fifth*, it asked the IMF to consider an interest subsidy account for LDCs in order to make use of the supplementary financing facility. The Conference also set up an ad hoc inter-governmental group of experts to suggest reforms in the international monetary system to help LDCs to tide over their debt problems. Earlier, the developed countries had rejected the proposal of the G-77 to establish an International Debt Commission.

The UNCTAD VI held at Belgrade in June 1983 again passed resolutions relating to development finance, debt rescheduling, conversion of loans into grants of the least developing countries, and raising the official ODA assistance to 0.7 per cent by developed countries. It again stressed the need to bring structural reforms in the IMF and World Bank in the interest of LDCs.

UNCTAD VII held at Geneva in 1987 emphasised the need for providing more development finance, debt rescheduling and conversion of loans into grants for the LDCs.

UNCTAD VIII held at Cartagena in February 1992 had on its agenda "resources for development." It appointed ad hoc working groups to deal with investment and capital flows, non-debt creating finance for development, and new mechanism for increasing investment and financial flows to developing countries. These working groups would prepare reports and submit them to the TDB.

The UNCTAD IX (May 1996) called upon the developed countries to provide debt relief to LDCs undertaking economic reforms.

Over the years, the various UNCTAD meetings have failed to solve the problems of debt and development aid of LDCs. At best, they have been forums for exchanging ideas and passing resolutions rather than getting the issues solved. As observed by *The Economist*, London, UNCTAD has lost the initiative on debt to the IMF and on development to the World Bank. The debt issue has been taken over by the IMF because it acts as a bank itself and has the confidence of western bankers and governments. Unlike UNCTAD, the World Bank has both money and effective advice to dispense to promote development.

4. Technology Transfer

It was at the UNCTAD at Nairobi in 1976 that the meeting pressed for measures which would strengthen the technology capability of LDCs. It was pointed out that better research facilities, training programmes and establishment of local and regional centres for technology transfer would serve the purpose. The Conference also set up a group of experts to draft a code of conduct of technology transfer. Besides it urged the revision of international patent system.

The UNCTAD VI held at Belgrade in June 1983 emphasised the need for transfer of technology to LDCs in order to promote their speedy and self-reliant development. The Conference discussed and approved a policy paper, "A Strategy for the Technological Transformation of Developed Countries" prepared by the UNCTAD secretariat. The study noted that during the post-World War II era many LDCs attained political independence but it has been severely constrained by their economic and technological dependence on the developed countries. The LDCs are weak partners in an unequal world. Despite considerable progress in LDCs during the past three decades, technological gap between them and the developed countries has widened. The study emphasised the need to attain technological transformation of LDCs by reducing their external technological dependence and strengthening their national capacity for autonomous technological development. This requires reduction in its dependence on the agricultural sector and on primary production in general. The spearhead of the strategy for technological transformation has to be an accelerated tempo of industrialisation. Processing of primary products, before marketing them will widen industrialisation through diversification. Since technology is embodied both in capital goods and human skills, technological transformation requires the rapid enlargement of the domestic ability to produce the required capital goods and skilled manpower.

Policy formulation related with the transfer and development of technology vary from country to country. Therefore, an international code of conduct on the transfer of technology has been under negotiations in UNCTAD. The code of conduct will provide important elements for the design and development of national policies for technology transfers.

UNCTAD VII passed a resolution relating to the transfer of technology to LDCs on the lines of the Policy Paper approved at UNCTAD VI. UNCTAD VIII set up an ad hoc working group relating to inter-relationships between "investment and technology transfer" which was to submit its report to the TDB within two years.

The UNCTAD IX (May 1996) urged the developed countries to give developing countries access to high technology crucial to their development.

The UNCTAD has simply laid down the broad principles for transfer of publicly funded technologies at the inter-governmental level. It may facilitate the process of technology transfer by freer access to sources of information, cutting down barriers to freer flow of technology, etc. No doubt governmental policies have a significant role to play in this direction, but the fact remains that technology transfer will have to be at industry levels. This is because much of the technology in developed countries is closely held by MNCs.

5. Economic Cooperation among LDCs

UNCTAD II held at New Delhi in 1968 emphasised for the first time the need for promoting international co-operation and self-reliance among the LDCs. UNCTAD VI held at Belgrade in June 1983 again emphasised the need for co-operative efforts among LDCs through widening the scope of preferential trading arrangements, harmonising industrial development programmes through infrastructural facilities, particularly in respect of shipping services and simple payment mechanism under common clearing system.

The first step towards economic co-operation among LDCs was taken at the ministerial meeting of G-77 held at New York in October 1982 when it was decided to launch the Global System of Tariff Preferences (GSTP). In 1984, the UNCTAD organised two meetings where intensive technical level discussions were held in drafting the ground rules procedures for GSTP negotiations. Another ministerial conference held at New Delhi in July 1985 decided to conclude the first round of GSTP negotiations in May 1987, on the eve of UNCTAD VII. GSTP is a major initiative of developing countries to expand mutual trade through grant of tariff and non-tariff concessions and other measures such as long-term contracts under the UNCTAD.

Besides increasing trade, UNCTAD VI recommended the initiation or strengthening of a number of cooperative measures in the fields of research and development, design and engineering among LDCs. Harmonisation of LDCs policies, rules, regulations, laws and practices governing technology in all its aspects, training and exchange of personnel, including cooperative exchange of skills, establishment of preferential arrangements for the transfer and development of technology, technological cooperation in specific areas and sectors of critical importance. The possibilities of cooperation of technological transfer among LDCs exist for particularly the following four sectors: capital goods, human skills, energy, and food production and processing. However, possibilities in other sectors of their economies cannot be ruled out.

The UNCTAD V held at Manila in May-June 1979 passed a resolution relating to liner shipping. Among other things, the resolution included provisions aimed at enhancing the position of LDCs as both providers and users of liner shipping. It urged the LDCs to cooperate among themselves in pooling information regionally on cargo movements and service requirements, and to ensure the establishments or strengthening of national and regional shippers' organisations. The Belgrade Conference (UNCTAD VI) entrusted the UNCTAD secretariat with the task of carrying out studies on ship and port finance, structure of the global shipping industry, policies and practices of governments in respect of investment in and support of shipping etc.

UNCTAD VI also hinted at a simpler payments mechanism under a common clearing system. This is another area which can provide considerable encouragement to co-operation among LDCs. Further, the developed countries insist that the existing international institutions like the IMF and World Bank should be strengthened financially so that they may provide larger aid to LDCs to tide over their balance of payments and debt problems. But the LDCs call for the setting up of a new financial institution which should exclusively cater to their special financial requirements in fields such as joint ventures, development projects, export credit, commodity price stabilisation, and regional payments support, and long-term investment to expand trade in food and primary products, and for storage, processing and transport. So far no progress has been made in this direction.

UNCTAD VII also stressed the importance of economic co-operation among developing countries on the lines of the previous conference. It was UNCTAD VIII which set up a new Standing Committee on Economic Co-operation among developing countries to study and report on all facets of cooperation to the TDB.

There are many factors which stand in the way of economic co-operation among the LDCs. The economies of LDCs are highly competitive in nature. They have limited import capacity, inadequate credit facilities, chronic foreign exchange shortage, and prejudice against the goods traded among themselves. Consequently they prefer to trade with developed countries even though goods manufactured by LDCs are cheaper and of high quality. However, some of the LDCs suffer from other limitations which prevent them from entering into trade with other LDCs. These are technological backwardness, shortage of key inputs, high cost of production, lack of competitive strength and weak marketing structure. The various problems listed above can be overcome by mutual help and trust among LDCs of region and working in close cooperation among themselves. UNCTAD is a forum where they can meet, discuss and formulate plans for regional economic co-operation.

6. New Issues

During the late 1980s, a large number of developing countries changed their economic policies to a market orientation, and began the process of structural adjustments involving exchange rate alignments and outward-looking liberalisation of their economies. In the early 1990s, socialist countries of Eastern Europe and the Soviet Union had disintegrated and adopted the market-oriented reforms. It was against this background that UNCTAD VIII met at Cartagena in February 1992. The proceedings at UNCTAD VIII emphasised global cooperation rather than confrontation, the need for negotiations and promotion of knowledge-based policies.

UNCTAD VIII had five key areas on the agenda : resources for development, international trade, technology, services, and commodities. In order to evolve consensus on these issues, the conference decided that the focus should be on their analysis rather on negotiations. It was, therefore, agreed that the UNCTAD should have a new structure on the lines of the OECD secretariat so that it could devote itself to the analysis of issues which was set up in April 1992, as detailed above. Thus UNCTAD VIII focussed on new issues such as services and sustainable development and on its new organisational structure.

The UNCTAD IX held at Midrand (S.A.) in May 1996 urged its members to provide more resources for sustainable development and debt relief to developing countries and to carry on the issues relating to technology, services and commodities in the light of the WTO Agreement 1994 of the GATT.

5. AN APPRAISAL OF UNCTAD

The UNCTAD was set up in 1964 as an international forum to discuss and analyse trade related development issues which might lead to negotiations between the developed countries and LDCs. Since the UNCTAD is a conference, it added a group approach to negotiations. Till UNCTAD VII, there were four groups : Group A of the developed countries, the Group of 77 of developing countries (G-77), Group C of China, and Group D of the socialist countries of Eastern Europe. These groups were pitted against each other in a giant conference invariably every four years. Now there are only two groups—the developing and developed countries.

During the 1970s, with the breakdown of the Bretton Woods system, oil crisis, inflationary pressure and accumulation of debt by many LDCs, the UNCTAD became a large debating forum between the North and the South.

During the 1980s some of the newly industrialised developing countries had impressive growth rates, while others had disappointingly low growth rates. The developing countries experienced declines in their commodity prices and terms of trade. Their debts mounted and international aid flows were inadequate. On the other hand, many developed countries faced recessionary tendencies. Consequently, there was nothing but hot air at the UNCTAD conferences. There was disillusionment among the developing countries because of the hardening attitude of the developed countries towards almost every issue raised by the former at the conferences. As pointed out by *The Economist*, London, the UNCTAD was "a political circus". So each UNCTAD was a non-event that led to its failure to come to any agreement.

Despite long debates and disagreements at each conference, the UNCTAD has played a key role in the emergence of GSP, a maritime shipping code, commodity agreements to stabilise the volatile prices of primary product exporters, special international programmes to help the developing countries, and international aid targets.

Conclusion

The UNCTAD secretariat has been doing yeoman's service to LDCs through its annual and other reports which highlight their trade, finance and debt problems vis-a-vis developed countries. In fact, the detailed reports prepared by it before each conference have created a new climate of thought with regard to the problems and needs of LDCs. These are again discussed at other international forums such as the IMF, World Bank, OECD, EEC, NAM, etc. Often, positive measures follow such as larger aid by the World Bank and OECD, giving more trade concessions by EEC to LDCs, etc. As such the UNCTAD reflects the sentiments, hopes and aspirations of LDCs in a world still dominated by the developed countries, both politically and economically.

EXERCISES

1. Discuss briefly the aims and objectives of UNCTAD. To what extent have these conferences been successful in promoting trade and development of the developing countries?
2. Explain the functions of UNCTAD. To what extent it has been able to achieve its objectives of promoting trade and development of the less developed countries.
3. What is the generalised system of preferences (GSP)? How far it has been successful in achieving its objectives?

Chapter 66

New International Economic Order (NIEO)

1. ORIGIN

The demand for a New International Economic Order (NIEO) by developing countries goes back to the first session of the UNCTAD in 1964. The various resolutions adopted in the subsequent sessions of the UNCTAD contain a systematic account of the various elements of an NIEO. At the root of the call for an NIEO lies the dissatisfaction of LDCs with regard to trading, financial, technological and other policies pursued by the developed countries towards the LDCs. The developed countries have oppressed the LDCs, discriminated against them, drained their income and denied them access to advanced technology. Such policies have obstructed their development efforts, perpetuated inequalities in wealth and incomes and increased unemployment and poverty in them. But there were three phenomena that gave an immediate impetus to the demand for an NIEO in the early 1970s. They were : (*a*) a severe energy crisis; (*b*) the breakdown of the Bretton Woods System in 1973; (*c*) the disappointment with development aid which was much below the UN target of 0.7% of GNP of developed countries; (*d*) the formation of the OPEC (Organisation of Petroleum Exporting Countries) in 1973 and its success in raising oil prices; and (*e*) the existence of unusual high rates of inflation and unemployment in LDCs.

Specific proposals for an NIEO were put forward at the Summit Conference of Non-Aligned Nations held in Algiers in September 1973. The success of OPEC led the developing countries to call the Sixth Session of the UN General Assembly in April 1974. This session adopted, without a vote, a declaration and a Programme of Action on the Establishment of New International Economic Order "based on equity, sovereign equality, interdependence, common interest and cooperation among all states, irrespective of their economic and social systems which shall correct inequalities and redress existing injustices, make it possible to eliminate the widening gap between the developed and the developing countries and ensure steadily accelerating economic and social development and peace and justice for present and future generations." In December 1974, the UN General Assembly approved the "Charter of Economic Rights and Duties of States". All these three Resolutions constitute the documents of NIEO.

2. OBJECTIVES (OR FEATURES) OF NIEO

The following are the most important objectives of an NIEO based on the proposals of the UN Resolutions:

1. *International Trade.* The NIEO lays emphasis on a greater role of LDCs in international trade by

adopting the following measures which aim at improving the terms of trade of LDCs and to remove their chronic trade deficits: (*i*) establishment of LDC sovereignty over natural and especially mineral resources for export; (*ii*) promoting the processing of raw materials for exports; (*iii*) increase in the relative prices of the exports of LDCs through integrated programme for commodities, compensatory financing, establishment of international buffer stocks and creation of a common fund to finance stocks, and formation of producers' associations; (*iv*) providing proper framework for stabilising prices of raw materials and primary products so as to stabilise export income earnings; (*v*) indexation of LDC export prices to rising import prices of manufactured exports of developed countries; (*vi*) increase in the production of manufactured goods; and (*vii*) improved access to markets in developed countries through progressive removal of tariff and non-tariff barriers and restrictive trade practices.

2. *Technology Transfer.* The NIEO proposals stress the establishment of mechanism for the transfer of technology to LDCs based on the needs and conditions prevalent in them. In this context, particular emphasis is on the : (*i*) establishment of a legally binding international code regulating technology transfers; (*ii*) establishment of fair terms and prices for the licensing and sale of technology; (*iii*) expansion of assistance to LDCs in research and development of technologies and in creation of indigenous technology; and (*iv*) adoption of commercial practices governing transfer of technology to the requirements of LDCs.

3. Regulation and Control of the Activities of MNCs. The NIEO declaration also emphasises on the formulation, adoption and implementation of an international code of conduct for MNCs (multinational or transnational corporations) based on the following : (*i*) to regulate their activities in host countries so as to remove restrictive business practices in LDCs; (*ii*) to bring about assistance, transfer of technology and management skills to LDCs on equitable and favourable terms; (*iii*) to regulate the repatriation of their profits; (*iv*) to promote reinvestment of their profits in LDCs.

4. *Reforming the International Monetary System and Special Aid Programme.* The NIEO declaration proposes to reform the international monetary system on the following lines : (*i*) elimination of instability in the international monetary system due to uncertainty of the exchange rates; (*ii*) maintenance of the real value of the currency reserves of LDCs as a result of inflation and exchange rate depreciation; (*iii*) full and effective participation by LDCs in the decisions of the IMF and the World Bank; (*iv*) linkage of development aid with the creation of additional SDRs; (*v*) attainment of the target of 0.7% of GNP of developed countries for development assistance to LDCs; (*vi*) debt re-negotiation on a case-by-case basis with a view to concluding agreements on debt-cancellation, moratorium or rescheduling; (*vii*) deferred payments for all or parts of essential products; (*viii*) commodity assistance, including food aid, on a grant basis without adversely affecting the exports of LDCs; (*ix*) long-term suppliers' credit on easy terms; (*x*) long-term financial assistance on concessionary terms; (*xi*) provision on more favourable terms of capital goods and technical assistance to accelerate the industrialisation of LDCs; and (*xii*) investment in industrial and development projects on favourable terms.

5. *Interdependence and Cooperation.* Above all, the NIEO declaration lays emphasis on more efficient and equitable management of interdependence of the world economy. It brings into sharp focus the realisation that there is close interrelationship and interdependence between the prosperity of developed countries and the growth and development of LDCs. For this, there is need to create an external economic environment conducive to accelerated social and economic development of LDCs. Further, it requires the strengthening of mutual economic, trade, financial and technical cooperation among LDCs, mainly on preferential basis.

3. IMPLEMENTATION OF NIEO PROGRAMME

LDCs have been striving hard to get the NIEO programme implemented at the various international fora in cooperation with the developed countries. But they have been successful in only limited fields.

1. *Trade.* In the package of proposals to readjust international trade, no wothwhile progress has been made. The implementation of integrated programme for commodities (IPCs) has been extremely slow. The principal element of this programme is the creation of a Common Fund for financing international buffer stocks. After several years of negotiations at the various UNCTAD meetings, a Common Fund for commodities of $ 4.7 billion has been created with a total pledged capital of 66.9 per cent at the UNCTAD VII in 1987, allowing it to become operational. Whether this Fund will succeed in providing adequate price support to commodities of LDCs in markets dominated by developed countries is highly uncertain.

As regards international commodity agreements, the NIEO proposals relate to 18 commodities, ten of which were to be initially included in the buffer stock scheme. Of these, five agreements on coffee, cocoa, sugar, tin and rubber were negotiated. But only the agreement on rubber is still in operation.

Little has been done in providing a suitable framework for stabilising prices of raw materials, and processed primary products to stabilise the export earnings of LDCs. Similarly, no steps have been taken up to implement the proposal of indexation of export prices of LDCs to rising import prices of manufactured goods of developed countries.

No doubt, exports of manufactured goods from LDCs have increased rapidly, yet their share in world trade is still very small. The developed countries have agreed to give tariff preferences on the manufactured and semi-manufactured goods of LDCs under GSP (Generalised System of Preferences). GSP schemes are in operation in 29 preference-giving countries including the 15 members of the EC.

So far as tariff cuts on primary and other products from LDCs are concerned, there are apparently no significant barriers to trade after the Uruguay Rounds. Products of LDCs enter the developed countries duty free under MFN (Most Favoured Nation). But in the case of many agricultural products of LDCs which compete with those of developed countries, tariff reductions have been nominal. Developed countries which produce agricultural products have been resorting to subsidisation of their products, while others place restrictions on imports from LDCs. Developed countries have devised new trade restrictions on the products of LDCs such as VER (Voluntary Export Restraint), OMA (Orderly Marketing Agreements), low-cost suppliers, market disruption, etc. Moreover, in the garb of non-technical barriers to trade like environmental, health and sanitary conditions, the developed countries are restricting the exports of LDCs.

As regards non-tariff barriers, agreements have been reached under the GATT Rules for codes on subsidies, countervailing duties, customs valuation, technical barriers to trade, etc. But LDCs are being discriminated under the "escape clauses" and "safeguard rules".

2. *Transfer of Technology.* In the area of technology transfer, UNCTAD-IV at Nairobi in 1976 approved a policy paper on the Code of Conduct on Transfer of Technology. The draft code prohibits restricted business practices. There are clauses forbidding LDCs which are the recipients of a particular technology to manufacture export-oriented goods, to introduce on its own changes in that technology, to apply it for purposes other than those specified in the agreement, etc. Such clauses prohibit the use of technologies in their own interests. The policy paper renounces the practice of transferring technology in the form of "single packages" of plants, equipments, materials and managerial services, etc. It also provides criteria for determining "just prices" of technologies.

Subsequent UNCTAD meetings have been simply passing resolutions for the adoption of this policy paper with slight modifications which have been rejected by LDCs. Even the setting up of an ad hoc working group relating to "Investment and Technology Transfer" at UNCTAD-VIII in 1992 has failed to come out with a code of conduct acceptable to LDCs. UNCTAD-IX in 1996 also urged to the developed countries to give LDCs access to high technology crucial to their development. But no progress has been made to evolve a code of conduct for technology transfer by the developed countries. However, an agreement was reached in 1979 for the establishment of a UN Financing System for Science and Technology for Development. To begin with, an Interim Fund had been proposed to supplement the financial resources of LDCs. But nothing has materialised so far.

3. *MNCs.* The only significant development in the case of MNCs has been the efforts made by the UN Commission on Transnational Corporations in drawing up a code of conduct for the operations of MNCs. It sets out comprehensive standards of behaviour of these corporations and of their treatment by home and host governments. Besides, negotiations have been going on the code of conduct for technology transfer for establishing a general and universal legal framework for transfer and development of scientific and technological capabilities of LDCs.

4. *International Monetary System and Development Aid.* After the collapse of the Bretton Woods System, the present international monetary system has not failed to protect the interests of LDCs. The excessive reliance on market forces coupled with excessive exchange rate fluctuations have been responsible for financial crises in some Asian and Latin American developing countries. The IMF has failed to increase the allocation of SDRs with the result that the volume of international liquidity does not meet the requirements of LDCs. The only positive gain has been the 10th and 11th quota reviews enlarging the IMF's quotas to SDR $ 212 billion. The establishment of *Emergency Structural Adjustment Loans* in early 1999 to help the Asian and Latin American

countries inflicted with the financial crisis, and *Contingency Credit Line* in April 1999 to protect other LDCs from the contagion of crisis are welcome measures by the IMF. Despite these, the management of international monetary system by the IMF, World Bank and its affiliates continues to be guided by ad hocism.

Over the years, the various UNCTAD meetings have failed to solve the problems of debt and development aid to LDCs. At best, they have been fora for exchanging ideas and passing resolutions rather than getting issues solved. As regards the flow of official development assistance to LDCs by developed countries, it continues to be nearly half of 0.7% of their GNP target. The IMF and the World Bank have been trying to solve the debt problem of LDCs but with little success because of the paucity of funds with them and strict conditionalities. However, some European banks have been rescheduling debts and a few governments have started debt cancellations. The emphasis continues on tied aid or programme assistance. Several donor countries continue to use aid increasingly as an instrument of promoting their exports to LDCs.

5. *Interdependence and Cooperation.* The first step towards economic cooperation among LDCs was taken at the Ministerial meeting of G-77 held at New York in October 1982 when it decided to launch the Global System of Tariff Preferences (GSTP). GSTP is a major initiative undertaken in 1987 by developing countries to expand mutual trade through grant of tariff and non-tariff concessions and other measures. This is being achieved by the ASIAN, SAARC and NAFTA countries.

Besides increasing trade, UNCTAD-VI recommended the initiation or strengthening of a number of cooperative measures in the fields of research and development, design and engineering among LDCs. The possibilities of cooperation for technological transfer among LDCs exist for particularly the following four sectors : capital goods, human skills, energy, and food production and processing. The developing countries are helping the least developed countries in these areas.

It also proposed a simpler payments unechanism under a *common clearing system.* This is another area which provides considerable encouragement to cooperation among LDCs. Further, the developed countries insist that the existing international institutions like the IMF and World Bank should be strengthened financially so that they may provide larger aid to LDCs to tide over their balance of payments and debt problems. But the LDCs call for the setting up of a new financial institution which should exclusively cater to their special financial requirements in fields such as joint ventures, development projects, export credit, commodity price stabilisation, and regional payments support, and long-term investment to expand trade in food and primary products, and for storage, processing and transport. So far no progress has been made in this direction.

UNCTAD-VIII set up a new Standing Committee on Economic Cooperation among developing countries to study report on all facets of co-operation. But nothing has come out of it.

There are many factors which stand in the way of economic cooperation among the LDCs. The economies of LDCs are highly competitive in nature. They have limited import capacity, inadequate credit facilities, chronic foreign exchange shortage, and prejudice against the goods traded among themselves. Consequently, they prefer to trade with developed countries even though goods manufactured by LDCs are cheaper and of high quality. However, some LDCs suffer from other limitations which prevent them from entering into trade with other LDCs. These are technological backwardness, shortage of key inputs, high cost of production, lack of competitive strength, and weak marketing structure. The various problems listed above can be overcome by mutual help and trust among LDCs of a region and working in close cooperation among themselves.

Conclusion. Besides the lack of economic cooperation among the LDCs, the developed countries have explicitly and implicitly tried to oppose NIEO programmes. This is apparent from the "trade" and "escape" clauses, phasing out of concessions to LDCs and other agreements forced upon LDCs under the GATT Rules and WTO Agreement at the Uruguay Round. To overcome the opposition of developed countries, LDCs require greater unity and solidarity and broader use of all types of cooperation in their struggle for NIEO at all international fora.

EXERCISES

1. What do you mean by New International Economic Order? Explain its objectives and to what extent they have been achieved?
2. What is the need for New International Economic Order? What objectives should be fulfilled to achieve it? Explain them.
3. Explain the origin and objectives of New International Economic Order.

Chapter 67

The Asian Development Bank

1. ORIGIN

During the 1950s, it was strongly felt that there should be a bank for Asia like the World Bank to meet the development needs of this region. This view was suggested for the first time at the Ministerial Conference on Asian Cooperation held at Manila in December 1963. The Conference constituted a working group of experts which submitted its report to the UN Economic Commission for Asia and Far East (ECAFE) at its session held at Wellington in March 1965. It was on the basis of this report that an Agreement Eastablishing the Asian Development Bank was drafted and adopted at the Second Ministerial Conference on Asian Economic Cooperation at Manila in November-December 1965. By January 1966, 33 countries had signed its Charter and the Asian Development Bank was set up on December 19, 1966 with its headquarters at Manila in the Philippines.

2. ITS OBJECTIVES

The aim for the establishment of ADB was to supplement the work of the World Bank in Asia. Its objectives are :

1. To promote public and private investment for economic development in the ECAFE region.
2. To utilise the available resources for financing of economic development. To achieve this, it gives priority to those regional and sub-regional and national projects and programmes which contribute more effectively to the harmonious growth of the entire region, especially of the smaller and less developed members of the region.
3. To help the regional members in the coordination of their plans and policies for economic development to enable them to achieve a better utilisation of their resources.
4. To provide technical assistance for the preparation, financing and implementation of projects and programmes for economic development, including the formulation of specific projects.
5. To co-operate with the United Nations and its organs and subsidiaries, including, in particular, the ECAFE and other international institutions and organisations and national entities in the investment of development funds in the region.
6. To undertake all such activities and provide such services which may fulfil the above objectives.

3. ITS MEMBERSHIP

The membership of ADB is open to the following : (1) Members of the ECAFE; (2) associate members of ECAFE; (3) other countries of the ECAFE region which are the members of the United Nations or any of its specialised agencies; and (4) developed countries outside the ECAFE region which are the members of the UN or any of its specialised agencies. It has a membership of 56 countries at present. Any country can become its member when two-third members of the Board of Governors cast their vote in its favour.

4. ITS MANAGEMENT

The ADB is manged by a President, Vice-President, and a Board of Governors alongwith an administrative staff. The President is the administrative head of the Bank. The Vice-President performs the duties of the President in his absence. Each member country nominates a Governor and an Alternate Governor to the Board of Governors. Atleast one meeting of the Board of Governors is held every year. The Board of Governors has delegated its executive powers to the Board of Directors. The Board of Directors consists of ten members of whom seven belong to regional countries and three to non-regional countries. The Board of Directors takes all decisions relating to the Bank, passes its annual budget and presents the accounts of the Bank to the Board of Governors for approval. There are certain functions which only the Board of Governors has to perform. They are : (*a*) entry of new members; (*b*) change in the authorised capital of the Bank; (*c*) election of the President and administrators; and (*d*) amendment in the Charter of the bank.

5. ITS FINANCIAL RESOURCES

The Bank started its operations with an authorised capital of $ 2.9 billion which was raised to $ 25 billion in 1992. Out of this, 50 per cent had been contributed by Japan and the remaining by member countries. To increase its resources, the Bank issues debentures and accepts deposits from its special funds. To augment its resources further, the Bank borrows from the capital markets of the world.

6. ITS FUNCTIONS

The ADB performs the following functions :

FINANCIAL ASSISTANCE

The Bank provides financial assistance in the form of grants and loans. It gives three types of loans : project loans, sector loans, and programme loans. Project loans are tied to specific projects. Sector loans are given to a number of related projects in a given sector. Programme loans cover more than one sector and relate to the implementation of a policy or programme for bringing about certain changes.

The Bank advances loans out of its Ordinary Funds Reserve and Special Funds Reserve. The Ordinary Funds Reserve refers to the Bank's ordinary capital resources OCRs out of which direct loans are given for development projects or specific projects. These consist of the financing of foreign exchange or local currency component of the cost of specific projects. The Bank also lends to development banks of member countries for relending to specific projects. All direct loans are "hard loans" for a period of 20 years repayable with in 15 years with a five-year grace period. The interest rate is determined in accordance with ADB's poolbased variable lending rate system for US dollar loans.

For sector lending, the Bank has established Special Funds such as the Asian Development Fund, Multipurpose Special Funds and Agriculture Special Fund. Loans out of these funds are given for projects of high development priority for longer periods and at lower rates of interest than for ordinary loans. These are called "soft loans". The Special Funds are different from the Bank's ordinary capital resources. The Bank contributes 10 per cent of its paid-in capital to these funds and the remaining amount comes as donations from its members countries such as America, Britain, Germany, Canada, Switzerland, Denmark, India, Pakistan, China, etc. For lending out of Special Funds, the sanction by two-thirds of the total number of Governors of the Bank is required.

In short, the ADB sanctions for the following types of loans : (1) To development finance institutions on the guarantee of the government : (2) to small and medium enterprises on the government's guarantee; (3) to private enterprises in the form of equity and loans without government guarantee; (4) to strengthen financial institutions and capital market; and (5) to public sector enterprises for privatisation without government guarantee.

The ADB grants loans on the basis of certain *criteria*. At the time of evaluating projects that it proposes to finance, the Bank considers their economic, technical and financial feasibility, their effects on the general activity of the concerned country, their contributions to the removal of economic bottlenecks, and their capacity to repay the loans. In granting loans to the various types of projects, the ADB Charter does not impose any restrictions. Even the minimum and maximum limits of loans are left open to be decided by the Bank on merits and viability of the projects. Since July 1990, it charges 6.53% interest rate annually on dollar loans.

Technial Assistance

The ADB also provides technical assistance to member countries out of the Technical Assistance Special Fund. The technical assistance is provided to the members in ECAFE region through their governments, agencies, regional institutions and private firms. It may be in the form of grants or loans or both. The Bank's technical assistance has two main objectives : *first*, to prepare and finance and implement specific national and/or regional development plans and projects; and *second*, to help in the working of existing institutions and/or the creation of new institutions on a national or regional basis in such areas as agriculture, industry, public administration, etc. The Bank also provides advisory services under its technical assistance programme. It sends its own experts and even hires consultants from other institutions on short and long missions for setting up or reorganising institutions for project implementation in member countries.

Surveys and Research

One of the functions of ADB is to conduct surveys and research in order to formulate policies for the future and to promote regional economic integration. It brings out an annual report in which it highlights the achievements, prospects and failures relating to the economic development of the member countries of the ECAFE region and also suggests measures to solve their problems.

Poverty Reduction

Since the 1990s, Bank's greater emphasis has been to promote employment and reduce poverty through improved efficiency, sustainable pro-poor economic growth and better development opportunities for the poor. In promoting economic growth, the Bank stresses the importance of increasing productivity. Productivity improvement depends on new investments, the efficiency with which new and existing capital are used and incorporation of technological changes. The Bank encourages domestic resource mobilisation to finance new investments, private sector development and public sector reform to improve efficiency. The Bank targets resources where private sector provision is inadequate and seeks to involve the private sector in services formerly left to the public sector. The ADB now pays more attention to human resource development, poverty reduction, social infrastructure development, urban environmental improvement and development, comprehensive economic and structural reforms, etc.

7. ITS PROGRESS

The ADB was set up in 1966. For the first time, it sanctioned loans amounting to $ 41.6 million in 1968. The Bank has been providing assistance in the fields of agriculture and agro-based industries, energy, industry and non-fuel minerals, development banking, transport and communications, water supply, urban development, education, health and population planning.

The ADB commenced lending to India in 1986, though it has been a founder member of the Bank. In the earlier period, loans to India were mainly for infrastructure sectors such as power, roads, ports, etc. In recent years, the emphasis has shifted to public resource management programme, urban environmental improvement and development, health and nutrition, and housing finance to reduce poverty. Since 1966, India had received 65 loans amounting to $ 5.8 billion at the end of 2000 for infrastructure, energy and financial sectors.

9. ITS EVALUATION

The ADB has been playing an important role in providing finance in the form of loans and grants to its member developing countries for their development. There have been two factors for the increase in the Bank's lending operations. *First*, at the time of its establishment, India had agreed not to get loans from the Bank so that smaller developing member countries might be given larger aid. But when China became its member and started getting assistance from the Bank, India followed it. This has led to increase in the Bank's lending operations. The *second* factor has been the introduction of non-project loans through the Bank's concessional window, the Asian Development Fund (ADF). China and India do not receive 'soft' loans from it which carry a nominal rate of interest.

SOME WEAKNESSES

Even though the bank has made long strides in providing assistance for the economic development of its ECAFE member countries, yet it is dogged by a number of problems : (1) its financial resources are limited because the regional member countries are mostly poor. Developed member countries which include Japan, Britain, America and others are not prepared to contribute much. (2) There have been negative transfer to the Bank during the last few years from such countries as Fiji, Malaysia and Philippines. (3) No doubt, loan sanctions have increased from the Asian Development Fund, but their disbursements have been less. The Bank should undertake such measures whereby the loan-absorption capacity of the recipients may increase. (4) It provides assistance for mega projects and does not consider cheap community-based alternative projects.

Despite these weaknesses, the ADB's contribution to the economic development of the developing member countries of the region has been creditable.

EXERCISES

1. Discuss the working and achievements of the Asian Development Bank.
2. Discuss the functions of the Asian Development Bank. What has been its contribution to the regional development of Asia?

PART SIX

MONEY AND BANKING IN INDIA

CHAPTER 68

Present Monetary System of India

1. INTRODUCTION

This chapter studies the present monetary system of India and narrates a brief history of the Indian currency in the pre-independence and post-independence periods.

2. INDIA'S PRESENT MONETARY SYSTEM

The monetary system is related to the control and regulation of the supply of money in a country. According to Prof. Shapiro, "The monetary system of a nation involves the overall set of laws and practices that control the quantity and quality of money in an economy." Every country has its own monetary system which consists of the country's unit of money (Rupee in the case of India), the types of coins and notes in circulation, the system of note issue, the monetary standard and the relation of the country's currency with other countries. As such, the monetary system of a country is divided into two parts: internal and external. The internal aspect consists of the internal problems of the monetary system such as the nature of money, system of issue, monetary standard and money supply. The external aspect consists of the relation of the country's currency with foreign currencies, foreign exchange, exchange control etc.

We study below the internal and external features of India's present monetary (or currency) system.

A. Internal Features of India's Present Monetary System

The following are the features of present monetary system of India:

1. *Unit of Money.* The unit of money in India is the rupee, it is not only a medium of exchange but also a unit of value which facilitates accounting. As a unit of account, the rupee helps in the estimation of costs and prices and revenues of firms and projects, and the gross national product.

2. *Monetary Standard.* The present monetary standard of India is *the managed paper currency standard.* According to this, the paper currency is in circulation which is non-convertible into gold. It is managed paper

standard because the issue of notes and coins is managed by the Reserve Bank of India.

3. *Types of Coins and Notes (or Currency).* The following types of coins and notes are included in India's present monetary system:

(i) *Coins.* The Rupee-coin in India is a standard token coin whose intrinsic value of the metal is less than its face value. If the Rupee-coin is melted, its metal will not be sold worth one rupee. The Rupee-coin is an unlimited legal tender in which payment of any amount can be made. There are also 2-Rupee coins and 5-Rupee coins in circulation since 1990.

(ii) *Subsidiary Coins.* There are also subsidiary coins in India to assist the token money. At present, coins of the denomination of 50 paisa are in circulation. The 50-paise coin like the Indian rupee-coin is unlimited legal tender.

(iii) *Notes or Paper Currency.* Paper currency in India consists of notes of various denominations which are issued by the Reserve Bank of India and the Government of India. The *one-rupee note* is issued by the Ministry of Finance of the Government of India and bears the signature of the Secretary. It is inconvertible paper money which is also known as fiat money or representative or token money. But it is unlimited legal tender. The other notes of the denominations of Rs. 2, 5, 10, 20, 50, 100, 500 and 1000 are issued by the Reserve Bank of India.[1] They are inconvertible into gold but are unlimited legal tender. They are convertible into coins and notes. They are *fiduciary* money.

(iv) *System of Note Issue.* The present system of note issue in India is the *Minimum Reserve System.* Under this system, the RBI is authorised to issue notes up to any extent but it must keep a statutory minimum reserve of gold and foreign securities. Accordingly, the RBI is required to keep a minimum reserve cf Rs. 200 crores. Of this, Rs. 115 crores must be in gold and Rs. 85 crores in foreign securities.

4. *Money Supply.* In India, the money supply consists .of both narrow money (M_1) and broad money (M_3). M_1 consists of currency notes and coins with the public, demand deposits with commercial and co-operative banks and other deposits with RBI. M_3 consists of M_1 plus time deposits with banks and is also known as aggregate monetary resources.

B. External Features of India's Monetary System

The external features of India's present monetary system are the following:

1. *Foreign Exchange Rate.* Since January 1976 with the signing of Jamaica Agreement, India is following the policy of floating exchange rates. According to this, the external value of Indian rupee is linked to a 'basket' of currencies of those countries with which India has large trade. This is the Nominal Effective Exchange Rate (NEER) of the rupee which is a weighted average of exchange rates *vis-a-vis* the currencies of India's major trading partners. Upto February 1993, India followed a *dual* exchange rate regime. According to it, the RBI fixed the exchange rates in terms of the various currencies such as dollar, pound, mark, yen, franc, rouble, etc. from time to time and all legal exchange transactions took place at the announced official rates. In March 1993, India moved to a single market-determined exchange rate system. Under it, there is no officially fixed exchange rate of the rupee. Instead, the exchange rate is determined by the demand and supply conditions in the foreign exchange market. But the RBI intervenes only to maintain orderly market conditions and to curb excessive speculation.

2. *Exchange Control.* In order to conserve foreign exchange, the RBI controls all foreign receipts and payments in the form of foreign currencies. It has an Exchange Control Department for this purpose. Foreign currencies coming into India are required to be sold and exchanged for the rupee either direct to the RBI or to its authorised dealers (ADs). Its authorised dealers include certain commercial banks, hotels, firms, shops, etc. which deal in foreign currencies and foreign travellers' cheques. They are also authorised to lend and borrow foreign currency among themselves in the inter-bank market locally. The actual lending limit for each AD is fixed by the RBI depending upon the size of its operations and other relevant factors.

In March 1992, the RBI introduced the *partial* convertibility of the rupee in 60:40 ratio. This was the Liberalised Exchange Rate Management System (LERMS). Under this system, all foreign exchange receipts on

---

1. Printing of Rs 1, 2 and 5 notes has been stopped.

current account transactions (i.e. exports, remittances, etc.) were required to be surrendered to the authorised dealers (ADs) in full. The rate of exchange for these transactions was the free market rate quoted by the ADs. The ADs, in turn, surrendered to the RBI 40 per cent of their purchase of foreign currencies at the exchange rate announced by the RBI. They were free to sell the balance of 60 per cent of foreign exchange in the free market. All importers of goods and services and persons travelling abroad bought foreign exchange at market-determined rates from the ADs subject to liberalised exchange control rules.

In March 1994, *full convertibility* of the rupee on the entire current account transactions was introduced. Consequently, the RBI announced further relaxations in the exchange control regulations upto a specified limit relating to: (a) exchange earners foreign currency accounts; (b) basic travel quota; (c) studies abroad; (d) gift remittances; (e) donations; (f) 100% export oriented units; and (g) payments of certain services rendered by foreign parties. Further relaxations in them are made from time to time in keeping with the foreign exchange position of the country.

3. *Foreign Exchange Reserves*. Foreign exchange reserves with the RBI show the quantity of foreign currencies which can be utilised by the country for trade and other foreign transactions. The variations in foreign exchange reserves also show the balance of payments position of the country.

3. BRIEF HISTORY OF INDIAN CURRENCY SYSTEM

Prior to the Indian Currency Act of 1835 about 994 multiple types of gold and silver coins were in circulation in India. This Act brought uniformity in the Indian currency system by issuing silver coins of 180 grains. Thus one-rupee silver coin was legal tender and the country was on the Silver Standard.

With increase in the supply of silver in 1871, its value in terms of gold decreased considerably. This adversely affected India's foreign trade. This led to the appointment of the Herchell Committee, on whose recommendations the silver standard was given up in 1893. With the Indian Currency Act of 1893, paper notes and gold coins were put into circulation and the Indian currency was related to the British pound. The exchange rate of rupee was fixed at 1 shilling 4 pence. Free coinage of silver was also stopped. On the recommendations of the Fowler Committee, the Indian Currency Act of 1899 was passed which led to the establishment of the Gold Exchange Standard. The circulation of gold coins was stopped. The currency consisted of paper notes and token coins of silver and other metals. These were not convertible into gold coins or bullion. The rupee coins were converted into gold at the fixed exchange rate of 1s-4d per rupee only to make payments to Britain. On the recommendations of the Babington Committee in 1920, the rupee was revalued to 2s-10d.

The recommendations of the Hilton Young Commission led to the passing of the Indian Currency Act of 1929 which devalued the rupee to 1s-6d. The Gold Exchange Standard was replaced by the Gold Bullion Standard. According to this rupee notes were convertible into gold bars of 40 tolas at the rate of Rs 27-7 annas - 10 pies per tola. (These weights and currency were prevalent in those times). But a purchaser was required to buy 1065 tolas of gold at a time. Gold was freely exported and imported.

The Great Depression of 1929 and some other factors led to the abandonment of the gold standard by England on 21 September 1932. The rupee was delinked from gold and linked with pound at the rate of ls-6d under the Sterling Exchange Standard. According to it, rupee was inconvertible into bullion and currency consisted of paper notes and metallic coins. With the establishment of the Reserve Bank of India in 1935, it was given the sole right to issue notes. It issued notes on the basis of the Proportional Reserve System, whereby it was required to keep 40 per cent of the total value of notes issued in the form of gold.

The Sterling Exchange Standard continued during the 2nd World War (1939 to 1948), when India adopted the Gold Parity Standard after the establishment of the International Monetary Fund (IMF). In this standard, the rupee was linked with gold or US dollar at $ 35 per ounce of gold. In January 1976, the IMF gave up the Gold Parity Standard and allowed the Managed Floating Exchange System. Under this system which is in operation at present, India is not expected to maintain and establish par values with gold or dollar. The rupee is allowed to adjust itself to the different currencies on the basis of their demand and supply in the market. But the system of floating exchange rates is not one of *free* flexible exchange rates but of *managed* floating. In case the exchange rate changes beyond a certain level, the Reserve Bank of India often intervenes to bring stability in the exchange rate.

EXERCISES

1. Discuss the present monetary system of India.
2. Discuss the present currency system of Indian.
3. Give a brief history of the Indian Currency System.

CHAPTER 69

Indian Capital Market

The capital market comprises the various institutions and mechanisms through which medium-term and long-term funds are pooled and lent to individuals, businesses and the governments. It includes various types of securities which are bought and sold to serve the requirements of investors and borrowers of funds.

1. FEATURES OF INDIAN CAPITAL MARKET

The capital market in India consists of unorganised and organised markets. The unorganised sector, also known as the informal sector, comprises indigenous bankers, moneylenders, etc. who operate in the small industry sector, in trade and agriculture. A large part of private savings are invested by people in their own businesses. Many people invest in the enterprises of their relatives and friends. Large chunks of black money and wealth flow freely between the unorganised and organised sectors. Thus the unorganised capital market in India is unsystematic with no uniform policy relating to interest rate charged, maturity of financial assets, etc. It is free from any regulation and control though efforts have been made towards this direction by the Government of India and the Reserve Bank. On the other hand, the organised capital market comprises a variety of financial institutions which mobilise private savings in various ways and provide long-term funds to the capital market. They are: UTI, IFCI, ICICI, IDBI, IRBI, LIC, GIC, SIDBI, State Financial Corporations, State Industrial Development Corporations, commercial banks, merchant bankers, leasing companies, venture capital companies, mutual funds, housing finance banks, Stock Holding Corporation of India, and Discount and Finance House of India. The organised sector of the Indian capital market is regulated by the Securities and Exchange Board of India (SEBI).

CAPITAL MARKET INSTRUMENTS

The Indian capital market deals in a variety of securities or instruments to serve the requirements of borrowers and investors of funds. These differ in nature, maturity, interest rate, dividend, liability, ownership, voting'right, etc. The various capital market instruments are the following:

(1) Corporate securities which include preference, bonus and rights issue shares, stocks, bonds, convertible and nonconvertible debentures, etc., and PSULs (public sector undertaking) bonds.

(2) Shares issued by mutual funds under their income, growth and tax planning schemes such as UTI Master Shares, UTI Master Growth, Canshare, Cangrowth, SBI Magnums, GIC Growth Plus, Goldshare, Starshare, etc.

(3) Government bonds and securities issued by the Central and State Governments and local bodies. They are also known as gilt-edged securities. Recently, a variety of innovative and hybrid instruments have been introduced to attract more investors for new issues like warrants attached to convertible and non-convertible debentures, secured premium notes attached with warrants, deep discount bonds, accident insurance attached with warrants and non-convertible debentures.with sale of *khokhas* to banks, zero-coupon bonds, zero-interest bonds, etc.

Security Market

On the basis of instruments or securities, the capital market in India is divided into the gilt-edged market and industrial security market.

(1) *Gilt-edged Market.* It is the market for Government securities. Central and State Governments and local bodies sell long-term bonds or securities to the public, banks and financial institutions. These bonds are backed by the Reserve Bank. They carry lower interest rates than bonds issued by companies. But they attract more investors because they carry a variety of tax incentives and rebates on income tax and wealth tax. They are less risky, more safer and more liquid than industrial securities.

(2) *Indian Security Market.* This market deals in a variety of new and old shares and debentures of commercial, financial and industrial concerns. It is divided into the primary market and the secondary market.

(a) *The Primary or New Issues Market.* The primary capital market is for new issues by public limited companies in the form of new capital issues directly to the public in the form of shares, fully convertible debentures, non-convertible debentures, preferential issues of shares and debentures, and rights issues at par or at a premium. Capital is also raised by companies in the primary market by private placement whereby shares are sold to specific group of investors such as relatives, friends, and holders of shares of the same industrial group or house. Merchant bankers, mutual funds, commercial banks and other financial institutions operate as underwriters and lead managers. They help in mobilising the savings of the public in new issues market and channelising them into productive uses by trade and industry.

(b) The Secondary Market. It is the market which deals in shares and debentures at the stock exchanges. Such a market is also known as the stock market where various types of shares and debentures are actively traded by brokers, mutual funds and NBFIs like the UTI, GCI, etc. Presently, there are 22 recognised stock exchanges operating in the secondary market in India.

2. WORKING OF INDIAN CAPITAL MARKET

Introduction

India is one of the few countries among the developing nations where the Bombay Stock Exchange began to function as early as in 1874, where the Government securities and bonds issued by Port Trust Municipal Corporation, etc. were traded. At the time of partition in 1947, there were nine stock exchanges on the Indian side at Mumbai, Kolkata, Chennai, Ahmedabad, Delhi, Kanpur, Hyderabad and Bangalore. They traded in ordinary and preference shares of the British Managing Agency houses and of Indian companies such as the Tata Iron and Steel Company, in addition to Government securities.

In the early 1950s, the capital market in India helped to mobilise financial resources for the corporate sector. But with the nationalisation of insurance companies in 1956, the State Bank of India in 1955, the establishment of development banks like IDBI, ICICI, IFCI, etc., and the nationalisation of 14 commercial banks in 1969, the capital market suffered a setback, because subsidised credit was available to trade and industry from these institutions. Consequently, companies had to issue equities at a discount substantially below market value.

With the amendment of the Foreign Exchange Regulation Act (FERA), the expansion of foreign owned and controlled companies was limited. Accordingly, the FERA companies were required to dilute their capital by issuing new capital either at par or at an approved premium to the Indian shareholders. This led to the issue of 40 per cent of their shares at low prices to Indians. The capital market continued to grow substantially during the 1980s as various measures were taken to stimulate both demand and supply in the capital market. The Government gave a number of incentives to equity and debenture issues such as reducing the corporate tax rate for listed companies and allowing higher interest rate for debentures above that for fixed deposits but below that for bank loans. Besides, the companies were authorised to use cumulative and convertible preference shares and equity-linked debentures, and investors were given tax incentives in new issues. Thus the Indian capital market was undeveloped till the 1970s. For instance, during the Fifth Plan (1974-79), Rs. 551 crores were raised from the primary market. The secondary market was also very small with only 8 stock exchanges, 1203 listed companies, Rs. 2600 crores of market capitalisation which was 7.6 per cent of GDP and with less than one million investors. Since the 1980s both the primary and secondary capital markets have been showing remarkable growth. In 1995-96, 1704 companies raised Rs. 22,918 crores from the primary market. The secondary market had a phenomenal growth. At present there are 22 stock exchanges in India with over 6,500 listed companies, thus putting India a little behind the United States. There are 15 million shareholders, the second largest in the world after the United States. The total market capitalisation of the Indian stock market is $ 138.6 billion. The Indian capital market has thus emerged as one of the important markets in the world. It has been identified as the primary source of finance for the private and public sectors in the Tenth Five-Year Plan, in which it was estimated to raise Rs 50,000 crores.

Despite the rapid growth of the capital market in the 1980s, a number of abuses existed such as insider trading, price rigging, inadequate, vague and misleading prospectuses of companies, delays in share allocation and in issuing refund orders and manipulation of prices in stock exchanges. The capital market was less liquid and lacked in transparency thereby providing little protection to investors.

CAPITAL MARKET REFORMS

On the recommendations of the Narasimham Committee and other committees and groups appointed by the Government of India from time to time, a number of measures have been taken up to reform the Indian capital market. These are listed below :

(A) Securities and Exchange Board of India (SEBI). On 31 March 1992, the Securities and Exchange Board of India was established as an autonomous and statutory body. With the repeal of the Capital Issues Control Act, 1947 in May 1992, the office of the Controller of Issues was abolished from 29 May 1992. The SEBI is the regulatory authority to oversee the new issues, protect the interests of investors, promote the development of the capital market and to regulate the working of stock exchanges. It has initiated a number of measures in these directions such as registration of intermediaries, strict disclosure norms, regulations on insider trading and inspection of the functioning of the stock exchanges and mutual funds, etc.

These and other measures explained below are likely to impart confidence in investors.

(B) Primary Market Reforms. The following measures have been taken up to reform the primary or new issues capital market in order to remove the inadequacies and deficiencies in the issue procedures.

(1) The control over price and premium of shares has been removed. Companies are now free to fix the price and premia of shares and debentures after clearance from the SEBI. Vetting of offer documents is not done by the SEBI.

(2) Companies issuing shares and debentures in the primary market are required to disclose all material facts and specific risk factors associated with their projects. They are also required to disclose the basis of calculation of premium on equity issues.

(3) The minimum percentage of securities to be issued to the public has been fixed at 25 per cent.

(4) Minimum subscription for public issue has been fixed at Rs. 2000 in the case of an individual w.e.f. 1.11.1996.

(5) The SEBI has ensured through an advertisement code that advertisements do not contain such statements which may mislead the investors.

(6) The allotment procedure requires that shares are allotted on a prorata basis and mutual funds and foreign institutional investors (FIIs) are allowed firm allotment in public issues.

(7) A SEBI representative supervises the allotment process in the case of oversubscribed public issues.

(8) Bonds of Public Sector Undertakings (PSUs) have been brought under the regulatory authority of the SEBI.

(9) NRIs and overseas companies are free to invest in the Indian capital market without the prior approval of the RBI.

(10) FIIs have been allowed to invest in the capital market on registration with the SEBI and foreign brokers are allowed to assist them on the same condition.

(11) The stock exchanges have been directed by the SEBI to collect from companies making public issues a deposit of one per cent of the issue amount which is liable to forfeiture in case the companies do not comply with the listing agreement, and do not despatch the refund orders and share certificates by registered post within 3 months of allotment.

(12) The company is required to complete the allotment of shares within 30 days of the closure of the issue. Thereafter it is required to pay interest at the rate of 15 per cent per annum.

(13) Banks have been permitted to operate in the secondary market since November 1996.

(C) Secondary Market Reforms. The SEBI has also introduced a number of regulatory and supervisory measures for intermediaries in the secondary market. Specific rules and regulations have been laid down for intermediaries in the secondary market. They are the merchant bankers, portfolio managers, underwriters, registrars, brokers and sub-brokers, and share transfer agents. They are required to adhere to specific capital adequacy norms, meet certain eligibility criteria and follow a code of conduct towards investors. They also provide for action by the SEBI in case of default. Some of these are as under:

(1) All brokers are required to register themselves with the stock exchange in which they wish to operate.

(2) The capital adequacy norms laid down by the SEBI for stock brokers are: 3 per cent for individual brokers and 6 per cent for corporate members.

(3) Stock Exchanges have been directed to ensure that contract notes are issued by brokers to clients within 24 hours of dealings. Time limit has been laid down for payment of sale proceeds and deliveries by brokers and payment of margins by clients to brokers. Penalties have been provided for default.

(4) To control rigging of prices and other malpractices in the stock exchanges, the SEBI has introduced such measures as penal margin on net undelivered portion at the end of the settlement, special margin for buyers in case of rise in share prices, joint suspension of trading by stock exchanges in case of price stipulation, etc.

(5) To bring greater transparency in transactions, Brokers are required to maintain separate accounts for clients and for themselves. The contract notes issued to clients must contain the transaction price and brokerage separately.

(6) Share jobbers have been introduced in the stock exchanges who simultaneously display buying-selling rates of scrips in which they are doing jobbing.

(7) Stock brokers are required to have their books audited, and audit reports are required to be filed with the SEBI every year.

(8) The SEBI has broad-based the governing boards of the stock exchanges and has changed the composition of their arbitration, default and disciplinary committees.

(9) The SEBI has started the inspection of the working of stock exchanges.

(10) The trading in the stock exchanges has been fixed for three hours instead of the earlier two-and-a-half hours.

(11) Failure to comply with the instructions issued by the SEBI on the working of stock exchanges, will invite penalties including fines and suspension from trading.

(12) Screen-based on-line trading has been introduced by NSE, OTCEI, and major stock exchanges like Mumbai, Delhi, etc.

(13) Efforts are being made to revamp the operations of stock exchanges in India. The lead has been given by the Bombay Stock Exchange which has introduced several changes to revamp its operations such as making the BOLT system operational for all the scrips, regrouping of shares, and introduction of weekly settlements for *A* and *B* group shares, dealing in odd lot shares, etc.

(D) Institutional and Market Development. Besides the establishment of SEBI, the Government has initiated the following steps for institutional and market development.

(*i*) *Market Makers.* Steps have been taken to promote the emergence of market makers. Since in the stock exchanges not more than 20 per cent of the scrips are actively traded, the holders of ihe majority of other scrips do not find sufficient liquidity. The institution of market makers is meant to rectify this lacuna. The market maker is required to make a market for a minimum of, say, five scrips (equity shares) which are not included in group A traded shares at a stock exchange. Market makers are required to offer two-way quotes for a minimum period of 18 months from the date on which the securities (shares) are admitted for dealing. The minimum quantity offered or bid for at any price has to be three times the market lot (either 50 or 100). Moreover, the bid-ask spread (difference between quotations for sale and purchase) cannot exceed 10 per cent. Unlisted companies planning public issues below Rs 5 crores are required to appoint market makers on all stock exchanges where the share is proposed to be listed. To ensure that market makers are able to impart liquidity to scrips and reduce volatile movements in share prices, the RBI issued guidelines on 5 August, 1993 regarding bank financing of their operations. Market makers require financial support from banks like other traders. Banks have been permitted by the RBI to exercise their commercial judgement in determining the working capital requirements of market makers which are different from those laid down for traders. Market makers are approved by the SEBI on the recommendations of the stock exchanges.

(ii) Foreign Institutional Investors (FIIs). FIIs such as pension funds, mutual funds, asset management companies, investment trusts, nominee companies, and incorporated or institutional portfolio managers have been allowed to operate in the Indian capital market. The SEBI has simplified the common application forms for registration with it by FIIs. Foreign brokers have also been allowed to assist FIIs and operate on their behalf to buy and sell scrips in the Indian stock exchanges. They have been permitted to open bank and custodial accounts. Foreign firms have also been allowed to set up joint ventures in the financial sector. Portfolio investments by FIIs are subject to a ceiling of 24 per cent of issued share capital for the total holdings of all registered FIIs in one company. To attract FIIs to participate in the Indian capital market, a number of concessions have been provided to them. They have the right of repatriation of capital, capital gains, dividends, and income received by way of interest. They have been given tax concessions at a flat rate of 20 per cent on dividend and tax rate of 10 per cent on capital gains. The cumulative net FII investment was more than 47 billion on 31 March, 2003

(iii) Selling in Global Markets. There has been globalisation of Indian equity with the selling of scrips by Indian companies in the international capital markets. During 2002-03, Indian companies had raised Rs. $ 600 million by issuing foreign currency convertible bonds and shares through the global depository receipts (GDRs) mechanism. The selling of scrips in global markets and the entry of FIIs in the Indian capital market reflect the confidence of international business community in India's sound financial system.

(*iv*) *Over-the-Counter Exchange of India* (OTCEI). Over-the-counter exchange of India has been promoted jointly by ICICI, UTI, IDBI, IFCI, GIC, L1C, SB1 Capital Markets, and Canbank Financial Services. It has been registered as a stock exchange with the SEBI and has commenced its operations from 6 October, 1992. Its main aim is to provide small and medium companies an access to capital market in order to raise capital in a cost effective manner. It is also meant to provide a convenient and efficient avenue for investors in the capital market. OTCEI is a ringless, electronic and national exchange which trades in selected scrips and debt instruments. It is a regulatory body which supervises, monitors and controls the trading activity at OTC (over-the-counter). It is a national stock exchange in the sense that all the scrips listed with the OTCEI are traded over its counter throughout the country. No separate listing at different places is needed unlike the regular stock exchange. Companies can make public offer in two ways. In the case of a new issue, a company can offer its shares directly to the public through a sponsor. But in the case of a secondary issue, the company may first offer its shares to the sponsor who can make a public offer later on at a convenient time. This is the "indirect offer" where the pricing of the shares is done by the sponsor as per SEBI guidelines. The OTCEI listed share-issue application forms are similar to the normal public issue forms of companies. But it has the name of the sponsor who is solely responsible for appraising the company, to its listing and to trading. In the event of under-subscription, he is responsible for putting in the required money. The OTCEI approves the allotment of shares with the Registrar to the issue and takes it for listing with itself. All refund / allotment letters are issued to subscribers within 28 days of the closing of the issue. All share certificates remain with the Registrar and are not sent to the shareholders. The shareholders are issued Counter Receipt (CR) which is a tradeable document. The shareholder wanting to sell his shares has to give the CR and the transfer deed at the OTC. He receives in exchange a sales confirmation slip. After verification from the Registrar, the seller receives the sale note and the cheque from the OTC. The OTCEI operates at Bombay with regional windows at other metropolitai cities and representative offices in a few major cities. The OTC scan screens display selling and buying prices of OTCEI listed shares and debentures at which market makers are willing to buy and sell. The exact transaction price is displayed at the OTC computer. The Infrastructure Leasing and Financial Services (ILFS) is the compulsory market maker for debt instruments in which the OTCEI deals in. For scrips, there are separate market makers appointed by it.

(*v*) *National Stock Exchange of India* (NSEI). The NSEI has been jointly promoted by IDBI, ICICI, IFCI, GIC, LIC, SBI Capital Markets, SHCIL (Stock Holding Corporation of India Limited) and ILFS as a limited company. It has been recognised by the Government of India from 26 April, 1993. Its main objective is to have a comprehensive nationwide trading facility in scrips, debentures and PSUs bonds to investors through electronic screen-based trading, post-trade clearing and settlement. It is an order-driven system where there are neither jobbers nor market makers. It operates in two segments: in wholesale debt instruments and in capital market instruments. In the first segment are included such instruments as Government securities, PSUs bonds. Units 64 of UTI, CDs, CPs by banks, institutions and brokerage houses, etc. The second segment includes equity and corporate debt instruments traded by the financial companies and individuals. The capital market segment follows a weekly settlement cycle with all settlements completed within seven days of the last trading day of the cycle. The NSEI is an on-line, screen-based and scripless trading exchange which enables buyers and sellers to operate from anywhere in India. In its effort to further improve the settlement system and minimise risks associated therein, the NSEI has set up a subsidiary, the National Securities Clearing Corporation (NSCC). It guarantees settlement of trades executed and settled through it.

(*vi*) *National Securities Depository Ltd.* (NSDL). On 8 November, 1996, India's first depository, the National Securities Depository Ltd. (NSDL) was started. It has been jointly promoted by the IDBI, UTI and NSEI. Initially, it will start dematerialising the shares of ten companies. They are ACC, BPCL, Cnsil, LML. HDFC, ICICI, L&T, RIL, TISCO and Siemens. The depository participants of the NSDL are SCHIL, NSCC, IDBI, ILFS, Global Trust Bank, HDFC Bank, IIT Trust Corporate Services, Citibank, Morgan Stanley Custodial, SBI, and Standard Chartered Bank.

A depository is a bank for share certificates. The investor operates his account in the depository in the same way as a bank account. Shareholders have the choice of continuing with the share certificates or opt for the depository mode. Those opting for the latter will send the share certificates through the "participants" which will be "dematerialised" and the names of the owners would be registered in the electronically operated registers of the depository or participants. The NSDL will enable investors to settle "paperless" transactions through electronic book entry adjustment. It will, thus provide an alternative to the paper-based system of settling of shares. It will do away with risks associated with paper-based settlements such as delays in transfers, loss or theft of shares in transit and fear of certificates tearing or catching fire. The transfer of ownership of shares through the depository will be exempt from payment of stamp duty. The companies, investors, transfer agents and brokers will be able to save on space in the depository system because there will be no need to store share certificates. It will take 15 days for the registrar to dematerialise the shares before they can be sold whereas it takes 40 days at present. The Depository will charge a.nominal custodial fee for holding the share certificates. Thus in the paperless depository system, settlement problems will be simplified, trading costs will be reduced, and the volume of trade and returns will improve. Morevoer, it will encourage FIIs to participate more in the Indian capital market.

3. DEFECTS OF INDIAN CAPITAL MARKET

Despite these reforms, there are many defects in the working of the Indian capital market which are discussed as under :

1. *Poor Liquidity.* The Indian capital market does not possess sufficient liquidity. A recent study shows that only 20 per cent of the scrips are traded everyday arid that too of Group "A". Another 20 per cent are traded 2 to 3 times a week and 10 per cent once in a fortnight. Thus 50 per cent scrips listed on the Bombay Stock

Exchange, the biggest in the country, have very poor liquidity. At other stock exchanges two-thirds of the scrips listed are not traded at all.

2. *Delay in Delivery.* There is unusual delay in the delivery of scrips and settlement or payment of transactions. The delivery of scrips usually takes 3 to 4 months and payments range between 2 to 3 months. Bad deliveries mainly due to the verification of signatures of sellers further lengthen the period and complicate the problem. There are also delays in payments which usually range between 1 to 2 months. Often delays in payments and deliveries lead to suspension of stock exchange operations.

3. *Insider Trading.* The Indian capital market has been plagued with fluctuations due to insider trading. Persons working inside a company often buy or sell shares on the basis of the expected profitability or losses of the company. This brings about price fluctuations in the scrips of the company thereby adversely affecting the interests of the small investors. Some big industrial houses also resort to transactions in the shares of group companies thereby accentuating this problem of insider trading to the detriment of ordinary shareholders.

4. *Inadequate Market Instruments.* The capital market instruments in India are confined primarily to shares and debentures which are inadequate for the proper functioning of a capital market. The newly introduced warrants, zero-coupon bonds, etc. are not yet popular with the investors.

5. *Inefficient Banking and Postal Services.* Banking and postal services are inefficient which add to the woes of the small investors. Refunds, dividend warrants and interest payments are sent by companies to the small clients by ordinary post which often do not reach them. Some dishonest postal and bank employees often collaborate and pocket such cheques through fraudulent means and dupe the small investors.

6. *Stockinvest not Popular.* The stockinvest instrument has been virtually cornered by big investors. The non-availability of stockinvests of small denominations, procedural difficulties and high bank charges have kept the small investors away from this instrument.

7. *Existence of Grey Market.* The unofficial unregulated market before the listing of shares, called the grey market, attracts and misleads gullible investors. They are also led to invest in new shares by financial analysts who are neither fair nor objective in their analysis. They often mislead investors at the instance of companies. Consequently, the small investors suffer the most.

8. *Vague Prospectus.* Despite SEBI's guidelines, the prospectuses issued by individual companies do not contain all the information and are vague. Free pricing norms laid down by the SEBI are not strictly followed. Premium fixing is also not fair. As a result, many companies dupe the investors outright and close down without any trace.

9. *Stock Broking System Defective.* The system of stock broking continues to be defective. The brokers have their sub-brokers and sub-brokers, in turn, have their own sub-sub-brokers who manipulate prices and cheat the sellers and buyers of shares and debentures in the secondary market.

10. *Lacks Transparency.* Trading transactions in stock exchanges still lack transparency. Buyers and sellers of scrips are at the mercy of brokers and sub-brokers who often quote the lowest traded rate of a scrip to the sellers and the highest to the buyers. Thus they pocket the maximum fraudulent gain on both the transactions besides their brokerage. There is also no uniformity in charging brokerage from clients by them. They do not maintain proper accounts and manipulate them.

11. *Inadequate Protection to Investors.* The protection given to clients in case of default by brokers and sub-brokers is inadequate. The protection given to an individual shareholder under the Consumers' Protection Fund set up at each stock exchange is limited to Rs. 40,000 in case of a defaulting broker. This limit is very low because it may be the cost of one lot of a high priced share.

12. *Odd Lot Shares Problem.* Despite SEBI's instructions regarding the non-issuing of odd lot shares by the companies, bonus shares and rights issue shares are being allotted in odd lots. Nothing has also been done for small investors who already hold odd lot shares issued prior to the instructions of the SEBI. The holders of odd lots have to pay brokerage upto 15 per cent while buying and selling odd lot shares. The efforts of the BSE, UTI and GIC to buy and sell odd lots at fair brokerage are limited only to selective and good scrips.

13. *Defective Operations of Stock Exchanges.* The stock exchanges in India continue to be defective in their operations. They do not have proper infrastructure. They lack adequate space for the stock brokers to operate efficiently. They do not possess adequate telecommunication and computerisation facilities. Old trading practices are still followed. All these defects deter trading of listed shares in the majority of stock exchanges in India. This

has led to great rush at the Bombay Stock Exchange with its consequent delays in transactions, deliveries and payments.

14. *Inadequate Stock Exchanges.* With the phenomenal increase in the number of companies being listed every month and in the number of shareholders, the existing stock exchanges numbering 22 with Mumbai having three, are inadequate. This has resulted in the mushrooming of unauthorised and unregistered private stock exchanges all over the South. These share trading "houses" and "associations" indulge in speculative transactions.

15. *Fragmented Market.* The secondary capital market is fragmented into the *ring operated* stock exchanges and *ringless* OTCEI. It has further fragmented with the operation of the on–line, screen-based and scripless NSEI. All this has confused the ordinary buyers and sellers of scrips with the multiplicity of brokers and sub-brokers already duping them. This has the effect of reducing liquidity.

4. SOME SUGGESTIONS FOR IMPROVEMENT

In the light of the defects noted above and the reform measures already adopted by the Government to streamline the working of stock exchanges and to rectify the defects of the Indian capital market, the following suggestions are made to improve upon them :

1. *Improving Liquidity.* The distinction between Group A and Group B shares should be removed in order to enhance liquidity in the capital market. There should be limited carry-forward of shares and all sales should be for delivery.

2. *Streamlining the Working of Stock Exchanges.* For removing delays in transactions, delivery of scrips and transfer of shares, to increase liquidity further, and to improve the working of stock exchanges, a number of suggestions have been made. *First,* there should be computerisation at all stock exchanges so that trading becomes automatic and transparent. This step will also help in removing other defects of stock exchanges and streamlining their operations. *Second,* the transfer of scrips and debentures should be done through book entry without the movement of share/debenture certificates. *Third,* the shareholders should be issued Counter Receipts (CR) in lieu of share certificates, as has been done by the OTCEI. The share certificates should remain with the Registrars. *Fourth,* to eliminate trading by illegal trading houses, registration of spot transactions should be made compulsory.

3. *Controlling Insider Trading.* To control insider trading and manipulation of prices, strict regulatory and punitive measures should be adopted by the SEBI and stock exchanges. Companies and brokers engaged in unlawful activities should be severely punished by fines and legal actions.

4. *Devising New Market Instruments.* New market instruments should be devised to mobilise larger capital resources. They should have liquidity, safety and fair return. They should attract rural investors, be of small lots, be able to buy goods and services, and banks and post offices should deal in them. Besides, such instruments as convertible cumulative preference shares, non-voting shares for NRIs, risk-free instruments by banks and merchant bankers, etc. should be introduced. The recently introduced new instruments like warrants of a variety of types, deep discount bonds, zero-interest bonds, etc. should be made popular for investors by highlighting their merits in comparison to traditional instruments.

5. *Banning Grey Market Operations.* To stop operations in the unofficial and unregulated grey market, the publication of unofficial quotations in newspapers and magazines should be declared illegal and the sale of shares before acquisition by buyers should be banned. The SEBI should also lay down guidelines and a code of conduct for financial analysts.

6. *Transparency in Prospectus.* Companies which do not follow the guidelines in supplying the required information in their prospectuses at the time of public issue should be penalised through legal action against them. There should be full transparency in the prospectus for the benefit of investors before the SEBI gives *its* permission for the public issue.

7. *Streamlining the Stock Broking System.* 'The system of appointing sub-brokers should be dispensed with. But this is not possible till the offices of brokers and stock exchanges are fully computerised and automatic trading is introduced, till then, the activities of sub-brokers should also be regulated by the SEBI and the stock

exchanges should be authorised to deal with them as in the case of brokers. The operation of illegal trading houses should be declared illegal.

8. *Protecting Investors and Brokers.* To protect the interests of small investors from the fraudulent devices of some dishonest postal and bank employees, the SEBI has already instructed the companies to ask for the bank account numbers of the share/debenture holders to be indicated on the refund orders, dividends and interest warrants. The companies should be instructed to strictly adhere to them. The best course would be for the companies to direct the Registrars to deposit the amount direct into the bank accounts of investors under intimation to them. This will also discourage benami or bogus deals. The maximum limit of Rs. 40,000 to be paid to an individual client in the case of a defaulting broker out of the Customers' Protection Fund at the stock exchanges should be raised to Rs. 1 lakh. A similar fund should be created for the brokers when some clients default by not making payments for deals to brokers.

9. *Disposal of Odd Lots.* A separate trust should be formed to dispose off odd lots held by millions of shareholders in India. It should purchase odd lot shares from holders, get them converted into marketable lots from the companies and then sell them in the market at a profit. To solve the problem of odd lots permanently, companies should be instructed by the SEBI not to issue rights and bonus shares to small shareholders in odd lots but compensate them by offering cash incentives.

10. *Opening More Stock Exchanges.* Keeping in view of the large number of listed shares and listing of fresh shares every month at the stock exchanges, their number should be increased in the country. This is essential to deal with a large number of operators in stock trading and to enhance liquidity in the capital market. This will also eliminate to some extent the mushroom growth of illegal trading houses.

11. *Regulating the Activities of Intermediaries.* For the proper functioning of the secondary capital market, the operations of such intermediaries as sub-brokers, underwriters, registrars, transfer agents, portfolio managers, merchant bankers and other intermediaries should be regulated by the SEBI. It should lay down rules for their proper functioning in the capital market.

12. *Coordinating the Activities of Stock Exchanges.* To avoid confusion among the investors, there should be proper coordination among the three types of stock exchanges in India, viz. the traditional stock exchanges, the OTCEI and the NSEI. There should not be any overlapping in their areas of operations.

13. *Giving Tax Concessions.* To encourage the market, more tax concessions shculd be given to investors by abolishing double tax on dividends and by increasing the minimum tax-free levels of dividends and capital gains.

Conclusion

Thus the SEBI should address itself to such reforms as paperless settlement, futures and options markets, free issuing pricing and more transparency and greater competition.

EXERCISES

1. What is meant by capital market? Describe the main features of the Indian capital market.
2. Explain the working of the Indian capital market.
3. Explain the main defects in the capital market. Describe the measures that have been adopted in recent years to rectify them.
4. Explain the weaknesses of the Indian capital market. Suggest measures for its improvement.
5. Write notes on:
   New Issues Market; Secondary Capital Market; Over-the-Counter Exchange of India; National Stock Exchange of India; National Securities Depository.

Chapter 70

Indian Money Market

1. MEANING

The money market is not a market in the usual sense of the term. It does not mean a single trading place or trading organisation dealing in money. But "it is a collective name given to the various forms and institutions that deal with the various grades of near money".[1] It is a market in short-term funds in which the lenders of money meet the borrowers of money. The lenders of money are the Reserve Bank of India, all scheduled commercial banks, co-operative banks, financial institutions like the LIC, UTI, GIC, foreign exchange banks, and indigenous bankers, moneylenders, etc. The borrowers of money are the Central Government, State Governments, local bodies, traders, merchants, businessmen, exporters, importers, companies, farmers, and the public. Thus the money market is a market for monetary assets in which the short-term requirements of the borrowers are met in order to provide liquidity or cash to the lenders.

2. NATURE OF INDIAN MONEY MARKET

The structure of money market in India comprises of both organised and unorganised markets.

The organised money market consists of the Reserve Bank of India, all scheduled commercial banks, cooperative banks, and financial institutions like Life Insurance Corporation, General Insurance Corporation and Unit Trust of India and foreign exchange banks, and DFHI.

The unorganised money market includes indigenous bankers, moneylenders, both professional and non-professional traders, merchants, landlords, pawn brokers, nidhis, and chit funds. Nidhis are mutual loan associations and chit funds are voluntary loan associations for mobilising savings.

CHARACTERISTICS OF THE UNORGANISED MONEY MARKET IN INDIA

The main characteristics of the unorganised money market in India are:

1. *Personal Touch.* The moneylenders have a personal touch with the borrowers. The moneylender knows every borrower personally in the village because the latter resides there.

---

1. G. Crowther, *op. cit.*, p 66.

2. *Informality.* The moneylenders have considerable amount of informality in dealing with their borrowers.

3. *Flexibility in Loans.* There is no rigidity in loan transactions. The borrower can have more or less amount of loan according to his requirements depending upon the nature of security or his goodwill with the moneylender.

4. *Multiplicity of Lending Activities.* Mostly peopie do not specialise in moneylending alone. They combine moneylending with other economic activities. A moneylender may supply goods on loan instead of money in cash.

5. *Varied Interest Rates.* There is multiplicity of interest rates. Interest rates are much higher than rates in the developed sector of the money market. The interest rates are not even uniform. The rate depends on the need of the borrower, the amount of loan, the time for which it is required and the nature of security. The greater the urgency, the higher will be the interest rate.

6. *Defective System of Accounting.* In the unorganised sector of the money market, the system of maintaining accounts is highly defective. Proper accounts are never maintained. Formal receipts are not issued for the interest charged and the principal repaid by the borrowers. Besides, there is utmost secrecy in maintaining accounts and lending procedures. The accounts of the moneylenders are not liable to checking by any higher authority.

7. *Absence of Link with the Developed Money Market.* The undeveloped sector is not linked with the developed sector of the money market. The former works independently of the latter and is also not under the control of the developed market. This has the effect of reducing the volume of monetary transactions and savings, and prevents their use in productive investments.

3. FUNCTIONS OF INDIAN MONEY MARKET*

The money market performs a number of functions in the Indian economy.

1. It provides short-term funds to public and private institutions needing such financing for their working capital requirements. It is done by discounting trade bills through commercial banks, discount houses, brokers and acceptance houses. Thus the money market helps the development of commerce, industry and trade within and outside the country.

2. It provides an opportunity to banks and other institutions to use their surplus funds profitably for a short period. These institutions include not only commercial banks and other financial institutions but also large non-financial business corporations, states and local governments.

3. The money market removes the necessity of borrowing by the commercial banks from the Reserve Bank of India. If the former find their reserves short of cash requirements they can call in some of their loans from the money market.

The commercial banks prefer to recall their loans rather than borrow from the central bank at a higher rate of interest.

4. The money market helps the government in borrowing short-term funds at low interest rate on the basis of treasury bills. On the other hand, if the government were to issue paper money or borrow from the Reserve Bank of India, it would lead to inflationary pressures in the economy.

5. The money market helps in the successful implementation of the monetary policies of the central bank. It is through the money market that the Reserve Bank of India is in a position to control the banking system and thereby influence commerce and industry.

6. By facilitating the transfer of funds from one sector to another, the money market helps in financial mobility. Mobility in the flow of funds is essential for the development of commerce and industry in an economy.

7. One of the important functions of the money market, is thai it promotes liquidity and safety of financial assets. It thus encourages savings and investment.

---

* This also relates to the Importance of Money Market.

8. The money market brings equilibrium between the demand and supply of loanable funds. This it does by allocating savings into investment channels. In this way, it also helps in rational allocation of resources.

9. As the money market deals in near-money assets and not money proper it helps in economising the use of cash. It thus provides a convenient and safe way of transferring funds, from one place to another, thereby immensely helping commerce and industry.

4. CONSTITUENTS OF INDIAN MONEY MARKET

The constituents of the organised sector of the Indian money market consist of DFHI, STCI, call money market, treasury bills, commercial bills, intercorporate funds, certificates of deposits, commercial paper and Repos. We explain these constituents (or *instruments)* of the Indian money market as under :

1. Call Money Market

The call money market or the inter-bank call money market is an important constitutent of the organised money market and it functions as an immediate source of short-term funds. The major suppliers of the funds in the call money market are SBI, LIC, GIC, UTI, IDBI and NABARD and the major borrowers are the scheduled commercial banks. As the participants are mostly banks, it is called inter-bank call money market. The commercial banks use their unused or surplus cash to lend for very short periods to bill brokers. The bill brokers, in turn, use them to discount or purchase bills. Such funds are borrowed at the "call-rate" which varies with the volume of funds lent by the banks. When the brokers are asked to pay off loans immediately, then they borrow from SBI, LIC, GIC, UTI, etc.

Of the total market for short-term funds, the public sector banks account for about 80 per cent of the borrowings. The foreign banks and private sector banks account for the remaining 20 per cent. While some banks operate both as lenders and borrowers, others are either only borrowers or lenders in this market. Non-bank financial institutions such as IDBI, LIC, GIC, etc., participate only as lenders. DFHI and STCI operate as borrowers and lenders in this market. All call money transactions have a maturity of one day to a fortnight.

The call money rate is determined by demand and supply of short-term funds in the call money market The variations in it depend upon busy and slack seasons and the credit policy of the RBI. When the demand for credit increases in the money market and the RBI does not take any action, the call money rates rise. On the contrary, if the RBI influences the money market by reducing CRR or / and Bank Rate or / and through additional money supply, the call money rates decline.

2. Commercial Bills Market

The commercial bills market in India is underdeveloped. There is nc proper market for bills of exchange. The Reserve Bank of India introduced the bill market scheme in 1952. Its aim was to provide finance against bills of exchange and promissory notes for 90 days. The scheduled commercial banks were allowed to convert a part of their advances, loans, cash credits or overdrafts into usance promissory notes for 90 days for lodging as collateral (security) for advances from the RBI. Since this scheme was primarily meant to accommodate banks, it did not help in developing a bill market.

On the recommendations of the Narsimham Committee, the RBI introduced the Bill Rediscounting Scheme on November 1, 1970. Under this scheme, all licensed scheduled commercial banks are eligible to rediscount with RBI genuine trade bills arising out of sale or despatch of goods. Apart from scheduled commercial banks, certain other financial institutions like LIC, GIC, UTI, IDBI, ICICI, IRBI, IFCI, ECGC, NABARD, NHB, EXIMBANK, SCICI, Tourism Development Finance Corporation, SBI and CANBANK Mutual Funds and select urban cooperative banks are included in the scheme. The DFHI participates actively in this market and provides bid rates on daily basis. With the introduction in October 1988 of the usance promissory note for the purposes of rediscounting of bills, banks could draw a derivative usance promissory note for suitable sums with maturity period upto 90 days on the basis of bonafide commercial or trade bills discounted at their branches. In August 1989, the Government remitted the stamp duty on usance bills and thereby removed a major administrative constraint in the use of bill system.

3. Inter-Bank Participation (IBP)

The Reserve Bank of India has introduced a new instrument called Inter-Bank Participations with a view to facilitate the adjustment of short-term liquidity within the banking system. These participations are of two types—one on risk sharing basis and the other without risk sharing. IBPs on risk sharing basis can be for 91-180 days at an interest rate to be determined between the issuing bank and the participating bank. IBP without risk taking can have a tenure not exceeding 90 days at an interest rate to be determined between the concerned banks. IBPs without risk taking are treated as a part of the demand and time liabilities of the borrowing bank and subject to reserve requirements.

4. Certificates of Deposit (CD)

In March 1989, the Reserve Bank of India introduced the certificates of deposit in order to widen the range of money market instruments and give investors greater flexibility in the deployment of their short-term surplus funds. The minimum size of the issue of CDs to a single investor is Rs. 5 lakh in multiple of Rs. 1 lakh at present. There is no bank-wise limit for issue of CDs and banks are free to issue CDs depending upon their requirements. The CD can be issued at a discount on face value and the discount rate can be freely determined. The maturity period of CDs is between 3 months and one year. The CDs can be freely transferable by endorsement and delivery but only after 15 days from the date of issue. CDs are subject to the reserve requirements. Banks are also required to maintain CRR and SLR on the issue price of CDs. The DFHI also operates in the secondary market for CDs. Six all India financial institutions, viz., IDBI, ICICI, IFCI, IRBI, SIDBI and EXIM Bank have also been permitted to issue CDs with maturity of more than one year and upto 3 years. The interest rates on CDs with a maturity of 3 months have been less than that for one year and more upto 3 years, as is the case with term deposits.

5. Commercial Paper (CP)

The commercial paper is a short-term money market instrument. It is in the nature of an unsecured promissory note. It can be either sold directly by the issuer to the investors or placed by an intermediary bank or securities dealer. It is not tied to any specific transaction. It attracts stamp duty. It does not carry any collateral security. In brief, the aim of CP is to enable high-rated corporate borrowers to diversify their sources of short-term borrowings and to provide an additional instrument to investors to deploy their short-term surplus funds.

The RBI issued detailed guidelines for the issue of CP on 4 January, 1990. As amended, they are as under : (1) The tangible network of a company should be at least Rs. 5 crores. (2) It should enjoy a fund-based working capital limit of Rs. 5 crores and above. (3) If should obtain a P2 + rating from the Credit Rating and Information Services of India Ltd. (CRISIL) which should not be more than 2 months old at the time of issue. (4) It should have Health Code No. 1 rating from the company's bankers. (5) Its shares should be listed on at least one stock exchange. (6) The minimum size of a CP issue is Rs. 50 lakhs and the face value of each CP should be Rs 10 lakhs. (7) The maturity period of each CP is 3 months to 1 year without any grace period. (8) The company has to get the permission of RBI every time it issues CP and the RBI will operate a queue system to regulate the CP market. (9) Non-resident Indians can invest in CP only on a non-repatriable basis and such CP will also be non-transferable. (10) Now closely held companies are also permitted to issue CPs even though their shares are not listed on a stock exchange. (11) CP cannot be purchased by any individual, firm or corporate body. The DFHI is the- market maker for this instrument and provides daily bid rates. When short-term surplus funds shrink with banks and interest rates are rising, there is a decline in the outstanding amount of CP and *vice versa.* Commercial banks are significant holders of CPs.

6. Treasury Bills Market

The treasury bills are short-term monetary instruments issued by the Government of India at a discount and for a fixed period. There are treasury bills of varied maturities. There are : 14-day and 28-day Treasury Bills, that are auctioned on a weekly basis. 182-day Treasury Bills are auctioned on a fortnightly basis and 364-day

Treasury Bills on a monthly basis. These Treasury Bills provide investors with financial instruments of varying short-term maturities and facilitate the cash management requirements of various segments of the economy.

7. Repurchase Auctions (Repos)

The RBI introduced the Repurchase Agreements Auctions (Repos) in the Central Government dated securities on 10 December, 1992 to even out interest rates in the call money market. Repos are repurchase agreements for the sale and subsequent repurchase of Government Securities. They allow the holder of the security to raise cash using the security as collateral. Under repos transactions, a part of one kind of asset is liquidated in order to buy it back. In the case of banks, repos result in the substitution of either cash or RBI balance for securities. The RBI indirectly intervenes in the money market through *reverse repo operations* to undo pressure on overnight call money rates. Initially, repos/reverse repo auctions were conducted on a daily basis (Monday through Friday) and with one-day maturity (except on Fridays/days preceding holidays) were introduced. Subsequently, multiple repo/reverse repo auctions with 3-7 days maturity period were introduced in August 2000. Interest rates in respect of both repo and reverse repos are the cut-off yields which arise from auctions conducted on a uniform price basis. The transactions of repos are conducted through SCL (Subsidiary Central Ledger) of the RBI.

Inter-Bank Repos. The RBI has also allowed repo transactions among banks and in select bonds of public sector undertaking (PSUs) and in private corporate debt securities. These provide liquidity support to the debt market. In July 1999, non-bank participants in the money market were also permitted to access short-term liquidity through repos on par with banks and PDs (primary dealers), thereby providing them facility to manage their cash.

8. Discount and Finance House of India (DFHI)

The Discount and Finance House of India Limited (DFHI) was set up on 25 April, 1988 with its own resources of Rs. 100 crores and the financial support of RBI. Its aims are (i) to bring into the fold of the Indian money market the entire financial system comprising the scheduled commercial banks, public sector banks, foreign banks and private sector banks, cooperative banks, state cooperative banks, scheduled urban cooperative banks, all-India financial institutions, and non-banks in the public and private sectors, and (ii) to equilibrate short-term surpluses and deficits of these instruments at market related rates through inter-bank transactions in the case of banks, and through money market instruments in the case of banks and others. It deals in call funds (including notice funds), Treasury bills, commercial bills, certificates of deposit, commercial paper, term deposits and Central Government dated securities. The DFHI aims at increasing the liquidity of these money market instruments. It operates both as a borrower and a lender. It aims at stabilising the call money market rates by building up a large turnover, while retaining for itself only a small spread between the borrowing and lending rates. Since June 1996 the RBI has extended liquidity support to DFHI in the form of "reverse repos facility" in Government dated securities to stabilise call money rates. Now the DFHI has also become operational as primary dealer in Government securities.

9. Securities Trading Corporation or India (STCI)

The STCI was set up in May 1994 with a fully issued paid-up capital of Rs 100 crores. It started operating from June 1994. It aims at developing secondary market in Government securities and Treasury Bills. It undertakes ready forward transactions in Treasury Bills and Government dated securities. These transactions take place in Mumbai and are routed through the SGL accounts maintained by the RBI. Like the DFHI, it borrows and lends in the call/notice money market. It receives liquidity support from the RBI in the form of "reverse Repos facility" and in Government dated securities and Treasury Bills. It has also become a primary dealer in Government securities.

10. Primary Dealers (PDs)

Besides the DFHI and the STCI, there are 13 more primary dealers who are operating in Government securities. They are the ICICI Securities, the SBI Gilts Ltd., the PNB Gilts Ltd., the Gilt Securities Trading Corporation Ltd., etc. Like the DFHI and the STCI, they receive liquidity support from the RBI in the form of reverse Repos facility in Government dated securities and Treasury Bills. The RBI pays to PDs commission for underwriting Government of India dated securities and Treasury Bills. PDs are provided advances against the security of their holdings of Government dated securities and Treasury Bills in Subsidiary General Ledger (SGL) Accounts of the RBI.

11. Satellite Dealers (SDs)

The RBI has also set up SDs in Government securities market. They act as second tier in trading and distribution of Government securities. It has registered nine financial institutions and two banks (Bank of America and Bank of Madura) as SDs. They have been provided ready forward transaction facility in Government securities market. They can get loans by issuing short period commercial papers which cannot be of less than Rs. 25 lakh in multiples of Rs. 5 lakh. Like PDs, satellite dealers can get advances from the RBI on the basis of Government dated securities and Treasury Bills.

12. Money Market Mutual Funds (MMMFs)

The RBI allowed scheduled commercial banks and public financial institutions to set up MMMFs in April 1992. They invest their resources mobilised from the public in such money market instruments as Treasury Bills, Government dated securities and rated corporate bonds and debentures with a maturity upto one year, call/notice money, commercial paper, accepted or coaccepted commercial bills by banks, and certificates of deposit. MMMFs have not made any progress in the money market because their number has come down to three from eight.

Conclusion

The foregoing analysis of the constituents of the money market in India shows that there have been significant changes in their structure and growth in recent years which have strengthened it. The setting up of DFHI has imparted greater liquidity to money market instruments and has helped in developing an active secondary market in them.

5. DEFECTS OF INDIAN MONEY MARKET

The Indian money market is not well developed. Compared to the growth in the economy, the growth of the money market has been slow and the influence of the money market in the economy has been quite limited. This can be traced to the following deficiencies in the Indian money market :

1. *Dual Character.* The Indian economy has dichotomic money markets with an organised sector and an unorganised sector. The organised sector consists of specialised banking and financial institutions like the RBI, SBI, commercial banks, cooperative banks, LIC, UTI, GIC, etc. which operate in the money market in accordance with rules laid down. On the other hand, the unorganised sector includes indigenous bankers, moneylenders, traders, merchants, landlords, brokers, nidhis, chit funds, etc. which do not follow any set rules in loan operations. The two sectors do not have any contact with each other and lack coordination or cooperation. In fact, the unorganised sector reduces the effectiveness of monetary policy measures because it does not fall under the jurisdiction of the RBI.

2. *Captive Market.* The Indian money market is captive. It is governed by a few institutions which participate in it. The participants in the organised money market are limited to banks and a few all-India financial institutions like UTI, GIC, LIC, etc., while in the unorganised market the principal participants are moneylenders and indigenous bankers.

3. *Narrow Based.* The Indian money market is narrow based and is functioning with limited number of

instruments. The main instruments are inter-bank call money, treasury bills, commercial bills, inter-corporate funds, certificates of deposit and commercial paper. The last two have just been started and others have made little impact on the working of the money market. In fact, only few instruments are being used in practice and others remain only in paper. Moreover, these instruments do not serve those institutions which can deal in the money market whenever they have excess funds or paucity of funds.

4. *Small Geographical Area.* The Indian money market is confined to a small geographical area comprising four capital cities of India, viz., Delhi, Mumbai, Kolkata and Chennai. This inhibits the growth of the money market. A large segment of rural, semi-urban, and urban India is out of the purview of the organised money market.

5. *Slow Rate of Monetisation.* The slow rate of monetisation is another factor which has kept the Indian money market under-developed. There are still large backward areas in rural India in which monetisation is taking place at a very slow pace. They fall in the unorganised sector of the money market and get loans from the merchant-moneylenders.

6. *Shortage of Capital.* There is shortage of capital in the Indian money market which fails to meet the requirements of the trade and industry. The main reasons for the insufficiency of funds are: (i) low saving capacity of the people due to low levels of income; *(ii)* inadequate banking facilities in the rural areas; *(iii)* preferences of savers to invest in physical assets like land, real estate, gold, etc. than in financial savings.

7. *Defects in the Call Money Market.* The Call Money Market is highly skewed with a few predominant lenders and a large number of borrowers. The entry of participants in the market is strictly regulated. Until 1 May, 1989, the interest rate was also regulated. It was 10 per cent. But the banks often violated the guidelines relating to this ceiling rate. From 1 May, 1989 the interest rate has been freed and is determined by market forces with the result that there have been wide variations in the interest rate which fell to as low as 4 per cent and rose to as high as 72 per cent within one year. In fact, such frequent and wide changes in the interest rate affect the profitability of banks and also create conditions inimical to the growth of a healthy money market.

8. *Defects in the Bill Market.* Despite the introduction of the Bill Market Scheme in 1952 and the Bill Rediscounting Scheme in 1970, the bill market in India continues to remain underdeveloped. In fact, bill culture has not been developed properly because preference for cash credit type of financing still continues. The bill rediscounting business constitutes a very small part of the total lending activities of the banks in India. Several factors are responsible for the non-development of the bill market: *(i)* reluctance of industry and trade, and Government departments and undertakings to move towards bill culture; *(ii)* absence of specialised credit information agency; *(iii)* absence of an active secondary market; *(iv)* lack of first class commercial bills; *(v)* administrative problems like physical scrutiny of invoices accompanying bills to ensure that they are related to trade, physical presentation of bills for repayment, requirement of physical endorsement, and endorsement of bills at the time of rediscount; *(vi)* no proper market for bills; and *(vii)* absence of strict discipline on the part of industry, trade and Government departments.

9. *Large Unorganised Sector.* A major defect of the Indian money market is the existence of a large unorganised sector. This sector is dominated by indigenous bankers and moneylenders. They are neither under the control of the RBI nor are they influenced by market rates of interest. There is also no clear demarcating line for short-term and long-term finance in this sector.

10. *No Relation between Organised and Unorganised Sectors.* In India the organised and the unorganised sector of the money market do not have any relation with each other. The moneylenders and indigenous bankers work independently and they fail to get funds from commercial banks except like other customers. Rather, they prefer to borrow from each other because the commercial banks insist on observance of formal rules and procedures.

6. SUGGESTIONS TO IMPROVE THE INDIAN MONEY MARKET

To remove the defects of the Indian money market and to develop it on sound lines, the Reserve Bank of India appointed the Chakravarty Committee and the Veghul Committee which submitted their respective Reports in 1985 and 1987. It was on the basis of their recommendations that the RBI has taken a number of measures to develop the money market. We have already discussed them in detail under the Constituents of Indian Money Market. To recapitulate they are: *(i)* introduction of 182-Days Treasury Bills on an auction basis with flexible interest rates; *(ii)* lowering of the bill discount rate to encourage the bill market; *(iii)* setting up the DFHI; *(iv)* introduction of Inter-Bank participations, Certificates of Deposit, and Commercial Paper; and *(v)* total freeing of interest rates on call and notice money, inter-bank term money, rediscounting of commercial bills, and on Inter-Bank Participation without risk.

Despite the introduction of the above noted instruments and adoption of new measures, the Indian money market is still not developed properly and continues to suffer from certain serious defects as outlined above.

The following suggestions are made to further improve the Indian money markets :

1. *Control over Indigenous Bankers.* After nationalisation of banks in 1969, banking facilities have considerably expanded in rural India under the branch expansion scheme of commercial banks, lead bank scheme, regional rural banks, cooperative banks, etc. But the hold of the indigenous bankers still continues over the majority of villagers. As recommended by the Banking Commission, 1972, the activities of the indigenous bankers should be controlled through the commercial banks and they should encourage the former to transform themselves into corporate bodies. The RBI should lay down guidelines for commercial banks in dealing with indigenous bankers.

2. *Control Over Chit Funds.* To control the activities of chit funds which exploit and cheat their members of their hard-earned savings, the Banking Commission suggested that there should be a uniform legislation for chit funds throughout the country and that only public limited companies with a minimum paid-up capital should be allowed to run chit funds.

3. *Standard Forms of Hundis.* In the unorganised sector of the money market, large transactions are performed by discounting *hundis* by indigenous bankers. But these hundis are not accepted by commercial banks. In order to bring these hundis within the purview of the organised money market, the Banking Commission recommended that standard forms of *Darshni* (sight) and *Muddati* (usance) hundis should be prescribed and the Negotiable Instruments Act be made applicable to these hundis.

4. *Development of Bill Market.* In the organised sector of the money market, a properly developed bill market is essential for the growth of money market in India. For this purpose, the Government should direct departmental undertakings and public sector organisations that payments for all credit purchases should be in the form of bills which should be strictly honoured on due dates. A similar procedure should be adopted in respect of CAS parties. The procedure for rediscounting of bills should be simplified. Further, rediscounting by the institutions should be freely permitted. The need is to develop bill culture in the country.

5. *Growth of Money Market in Other Centres.* The money market is restricted to four major cities in India. To expand the money market in other cities, banking and clearing house facilities should be provided on a larger scale. Discount houses and acceptance houses should be established. Cheap remittance facilities should be extended throughout the country to increase the mobility of funds. These measures will go a long way in the growth of the money market in other cities.

6. *Creation of Secondary Market.* For the smooth functioning and growth of the money market, an active secondary market should be created by establishing new sets of institutions which should impart sufficient liquidity in the Indian money market.

EXERCISES

1. Explain the various constituents of Indian money market.
2. Point out the main defects of the Indian money market. Suggest suitable measures to remove them.
3. Write notes on : Bill Market in India, Inter-Bank Call Money Market, Treasury Bills Market.
4. Explain the nature of Indian money market. What are its functions?
5. Explain the main features of the unorganised money market in India.
6. Write notes on : Discount and Finance House of India, Certificates of Deposit, Commercial Paper.

CHAPTER 71

Moneylenders and Indigenous Bankers

The moneylenders and indigenous bankets ate the two main organs of the unorganised sector of the Indian money market: We discuss below their working and importance.

1. MONEYLENDERS

Moneylenders are those whose primary business is moneylending. They are classified into two categories: (a) professional, and *(b)* non-professional. The professional moneylenders are those whose primary business is moneylending. On the other hand, the non-professional moneylenders are those who are engaged in some other profession but whose side business is moneylending. They include landlords, agriculturists, merchants, traders, rich widows, pensioners, advocates, teachers, or any other person who has got surplus money. The professional and non-professional money lenders operate both in rural and urban areas. But this division is not water-tight because an urban merchant may also lend to a farmer whose produce he buys.

1. Working of Moneylenders

The functions pf moneylenders are:

(1) The main function of moneylenders is to give short-term loans. Loans may be given for consumption purposes, to meet social and religious obligations *or* the needs of farmers for seeds, cattle, fertilisers, etc.

(2) Loans are generally given on the personal security of borrowers. However, grant of loans on the security of costly things in urban areas and against land or crop in rural areas; is also common.

(3) They have personal contacts with the borrowers who approach them directly and informally,

(4) The moneylenders normally lend their own funds.

(5) The non-professional moneylenders prefer to lend in kind.

(6) Since the moneylenders have a personal knowledge about the creditworthines of borrowers they adopt rigid or flexible attitude while lending, charging interest, and recovery of loans.

(7) They charge excessively high rates of interest.

(8) The moneylenders in rural areas are quite influential persons who adopt pressure tactics in the recovery of loans, such as forcible occupation of the cultivator's land, caste disapproval, pressure from panchayats, etc.

(9) The moneylenders also resort to some malpractices in rural areas which are: manipulating accounts

deducting interest in advance, demanding presents, exacting free services from the borrower, demanding donations, obtaining thumb impression of borrower on blank paper, non-issue of receipts for payment of interest and principal, keeping the deed of land or house of the borrower as a security, forcing the borrower-farmer to sell his produce in advance at a price lower than the market, etc.

2. Importance of Moneylenders

The importance of moneylenders is immense in rural India because of the inadequacy of institutional financing agencies like commercial banks and cooperative banks. They meet the short-term monetary requirements of farmers, landless agricultural workers, marginal farmers, rural artisans, and petty shopkeepers and traders. They give loans for consumption needs, for social and religious ceremonies, and for such productive purposes as seeds, fertilisers, cattle etc. The professional moneylender is more useful because he also provides articles of daily requirements. There being personal contact with the moneylender, the borrowers approach him directly and informally. Generally they get loans on personal security. As the moneylender is known to every borrower personally, the former is in a position to get the loan easily. A moneylender is often regarded as the friend, guide, and helper of the people in rural areas.

The importance of moneylenders can be assessed from the All India Rural Credit Survey Committee's findings that in 1950-51 professional and agricultural moneylenders accounted for nearly 70 per cent of the total borrowings of cultivators, and only 7.3 per cent was contributed by the organised institutions like commercial banks and cooperatives. The All India Investment and Rural Debt Survey estimated that in 1960-61 the moneylenders accounted for 49 per cent of the total borrowings by farmers.

During the British rule in India, a number of Provinces passed Acts in 1938 to restrain some of the objectionable practices of moneylenders, such as provisions for registration, licensing, and regulation of their activities. But these Acts remained on paper.

However, after nationalisation of 14 banks and with branch expansion and opening of rural banks, and strengthening of cooperative banks, the hold of moneylenders on rural credit has become weak.

2. INDIGENOUS BANKERS

The indigenous bankers are those who accept deposits and deal in *hundis.* An indigenous banker may also combine banking and business, but banking is his main function. As such, indigenous bankers are of two types: *(a)* Professionals, such as Shroffs of Gujarat, Sahukars of U.P. Chettiars of the South, etc. who function as bankers, and *(b)* non-professionals, such as Marwaris, Multanis, wholesale and retail traders, etc.

1. Functions of Indigenous Bankers

The indigenous bankers perform a number of banking and non-banking functions which are explained as under:

1. *Accepting Deposits.* The indigenous bankers accept deposits from the public which are of current account and for a fixed period. Higher interest rate is paid on fixed account than on current account. Entries relating to deposits received, amount withdrawn and interest paid are made in the pass books issued to the clients. The indigenous bankers also get funds from the commercial banks, friends, relatives and even from each other.

2. *Advancing Loans.* The indigenous bankers advance loans against security of land, jewellery, crops, goods, etc. Loans are given to known parties on the basis of the promissory notes. Loans given on the security of land and buildings are based on mortgages registered with the Registrar of the area.

3. *Discounting Hundis.* Discounting of hundis is an important function of indigenous bankers. They write, buy and sell hundis which are bills of exchange.

Hundis are of two types:

(a) Darshni or sight hundi which is payable on demand, and

(b) Muddati or time hundi which is payable after the period mentioned on the face of. the hundi.

4. *Remittance Facilities.* The indigenous bankers also provide remittance facilities to their clients. This is

done by writing a finance bill to their branches, if they have at other place, or to some other indigenous banker, with whom they have such arrangements.

5. *Financing Inland Trade.* They finance both wholesale and retail traders within the country and thus help in buying, selling, and movement of goods to different trading centres.

6. *Speculative Activities.* They indulge in speculation of food and non-food crops, and other articles of consumption.

7. *Commission Agents.* They act as commission agents to firms.

8. *Run Firms.* Some of the non-professional indigenous bankers run their own manufacturing, processing or service firms, and on the strength of that they provide expertise and working capital to small industrialists.

9. *Subscribe to Shares and Debentures.* They provide long-term finance by subscribing to the shares and debentures of large companies.

2. Importance of Indigenous Bankers

The indigenous bankers have been playing a significant role in the economic life of India. When commercial banking had not developed, they were the main source of finance for agriculturists, traders, businessmen, small industrialists, etc. After nationalisation of commercial banks and the spread of banking in urban and rural areas, the activities of indigenous bankers have declined, but their importance has not become less because of the difficulties still faced by the borrowers in getting loans from the banks. The borrowers approach them directly and informally and get loans promptly and easily. They do not have any fixed banking hours and do not enter into formalities and procedures followed by commercial banks in advancing loans. That is why they are still popular with traders, businessmen, agriculturists, and ordinary people. They give loans mostly for productive purposes to meet the immediate and short-term needs of the borrowers.

Indigenous bankers provide finance and remittance facilities to traders and small industrialists by advancing loans; writing, buying and selling hundis; writing finance bills and trade bills. Thus they help not only in financing internal trade but also in expanding it. In particular, they help in the movement of agricultural products from rural areas to markets, and of industrial products to different parts of the country.

Those indigenous bankers who combine banking with trading and agriculture help the farmers by lifting their produce from the farms, paying them in cash on the spot, and also giving them loans.

The indigenous bankers act as commission agents when they purchase agricultural products on behalf of firms, mills, and trading houses. In this way, they again help in the development of internal trade.

The importance of indigenous bankers has increased further with the development of capital market in India. They now provide long-term credit to companies by subscribing to their shares and debentures.

3. Defects of Indigenous Banking

The following defects are associated with the majority of indigenous bankers:

(1) They are a *hindrance* in the development of an organised money market in India. The Reserve Bank of India has no control over them.

(2) They follow *old methods of business* which are based on secrecy of accounts and activities. Accounts are mostly maintained in vernacular. They are neither audited nor published.

(3) They also provide loans for *unproductive* purposes.

(4) They combine *banking with other activities* which bring them more profits such as speculation, trading, brokerage, etc.

(5) They charge very *high rates of interest.*

(6) They also indulge in some *undesirable practices,* such as manipulating accounts, deducting interest in advance, non-issue of receipts for payment of interest and principal, etc.

(7) They are *unorganised* except at a few places like Mumbai and Kolkata. This has hindered the mobility of funds.

(8) They do not work in co-operation with the commercial and cooperative banks. This has kept *dichotomy* in the Indian money market.

(9) They are *unable to mobilise savings* because they prefer giving loans than accepting deposits.

(10) Except in big towns, they *have failed to develop the hundi* (bill market) in trade and business. They do

business in cash.

(11) They are *not able to meet the financial needs* of borrowers because they operate with insufficient capital.

4. Suggestions to Reform Indigenous Banking

From time to time suggestions have been made to reform the working of indigenous bankers by certain committees, commissions, and organisations, such as the Indian Central Banking Enquiry Committee, 1931, the Banking Commission, 1971, etc. We summarise these suggestions as under:

(1) The indigenous bankers should do only banking business and not any other activity.

(2) They should maintain proper account books in a prescribed and recognised form and get them audited.

(3) They should be registered with the, Reserve Bank o£ India and licence should be issued to them.

(4) For this purpose, every indigenous banker should have a minimum capital requirement.

(5) The indigenous bankers should be linked with commercial banks and their hundis should be discounted by commercial banks like other bills of exchange.

(6) The indigenous bankers registered with the RBI should be provided remittance facilities by all commercial banks.

(7) They should also be allowed to collect cheques, drafts, etc. like other banks.

(8) The indigenous bankers should form an association at all India level and become its members.

(9) They should develop the hundi in a proper format duly approved, by the RBI so that it may be accepted like other bills by the commercial banks.

(10) They should be encouraged to develop the business of bill-broking like the bill-brokers of the London Money Markets.

(11) The benefit of the Bankers' Book Evidence Act should also be extended to the indigenous bankers.

These suggestions have failed to elicit any response from the indigenous bankers who are not prepared to give up their non-banking functions, to publish their audited accounts, and to register themselves with the RBI. The Reserve Bank of India is also not prepared to relax its conditions and provide facilities to them like commercial banks. The best course is to link the indigenous bankers with commercial banks, as suggested by the Banking Commission. The Reserve Bank of India should lay down guidelines for this purpose.

3. DISTINCTION BETWEEN INDIGENOUS BANKERS AND MONEYLENDERS

The indigenous bankers are distinguished from moneylenders in the following ways:

(1) Banking is the main function of an indigenous banker while that of a moneylender is moneylending.

(2) The indigenous bankers accept deposits and deal in hundis but the moneylenders do not perform these functions.

(3) The scale of operations of indigenous bankers is larger than that of moneylenders. They combine banking with trading, speculation, commission agent, etc., while the moneylenders combine moneylending with petty shopkeeping.

(4) The indigenous bankers have larger funds at their disposal than the moneylenders. They accept deposits from the public, borrow from each other and also from commercial banks. On the other hand, the moneylenders operate with small funds of their own and also borrow from their relatives and friends.

(5) The indigenous bankers finance trade, industry and agriculture, while the moneylenders finance the common man, small farmers, landless workers, and petty shopkeepers.

(6) The indigenous bankers give productive loans, while the moneylenders mostly give unproductive loans.

(7) The financial transactions of indigenous bankers are based on hundis, while those of moneylenders are in cash and promissory notes.

(8) The indigenous bankers operate in a business-like manner from properly maintained offices, while

the moneylenders operate from their residences or shops.

(9) The indigenous bankers maintain proper accounts and issue receipt against deposits and for payments received from their clients. The moneylenders neither maintain proper accounts nor issue receipts for payments received from the borrowers.

(10) As the operations of indigenous bankers are more systematic and on a larger scale, they charge lower rates of interest than the moneylenders.

(11) The indigenous bankers work in cooperation with one-another, while the moneylenders function in isolation and compete with each other.

(12) The indigenous bankers have links with the commercial banks from whom they borrow and also keep their deposits. On the other hand, the moneylenders do not have any link with the commercial banks.

4. DISTINCTION BETWEEN INDIGENOUS BANKERS AND COMMERCIAL BANKS

There are marked differences between indigenous banking and commercial banking which are discussed as under:

(1) The indigenous bankers perform banking as well as non-banking functions, such as trading, speculation, etc. while the commercial banks perform only banking functions.

(2) The indigenous bankers work as individual proprietors, while the commercial banks work as joint stock companies with a number of shareholders as their owners.

(3) The financial resources of indigenous bankers are limited whereas those of commercial banks are very vast. The former can get funds from relatives, friends, and even from commercial banks but only in limited quantity, while the latter have their own large resources from the shareholders and also get funds from the Reserve Bank of India.

(4) The indigenous bankers deal in cash, whereas the commercial banks deal both in cash and cheques.

(5) The indigenous bankers operate at one place. Very few indigenous bankers have a branch at some other place. But the commercial banks have a network of branches throughout the country.

(6) The lending policy of the indigenous bankers is very liberal. They advance money even on personal security and bear high risk. But the commercial banks lend money on the basis of a security and under the rules framed by the Reserve Bank of India.

(7) The indigenous bankers give short-term, medium-term and long-term loans, whereas the commercial banks give only short-term loans.

(8j The indigenous bankers operate only within the country, whereas the commercial banks also operate outside the country and do foreign exchange business.

(9) The indigenous bankers do not have a proper accounting system. They operate under a veil of secrecy. On the other hand, the commercial banks operate under the modern accounting system by publishing and submitting their balance sheets to the RBI.

(10) The indigenous bankers are not under the jurisdiction of the RBI or any other authority, whereas the commercial banks are under the RBI and operate as per the guidelines issued by the former from time to time.

(11) The indigenous bankers form part of the unorganised sector of the Indian money market. On the other hand, the commercial banks are an important constituent of the organised Indian money market.

EXERCISES

1. Examine the role of indigenous bankers in the Indian economy.
2. What is an indigenous banker? What is his importance in our economy?
3. Give the defects of the working of indigenous bankers. Suggest remedies to improve their working.
4. Distinguish between a moneylender and an indigenous banker.
5. Discuss the working and importance of moneylenders in India.
6. Write notes on: Importance of Moneylenders, Functions of Indigenous Bankers.
7. How do indigenous bankers differ from commercial banks?

CHAPTER 72

Cooperative Banks in India

The organisational set up of the cooperative banking system in India is based on the credit needs of agriculturists. It consists of three tiers for the short-term and medium-term credit: (1) Primary Agricultural Cooperative Credit Societies at the village level; (2) Central Cooperative Banks at the district level; and (3) State Cooperative Banks at the state level. For meeting the long-term credit needs, there are the Land Development Banks. We discuss below the functions, organisational set up, progress and weaknesses of these institutions.

1. PRIMARY AGRICULTURAL CREDIT SOCIETIES (PACSs)

Primary Agricultural Credit Societies, also known as Agricultural Cooperative Societies, are meant to develop the spirit of mutual help and cooperation among their members, besides meeting their credit and other needs. The main features of PACSs are as under:

OBJECTIVES

The main objectives of PACSs are: *(i)* to provide short-term and medium-term credit; *(ii)* to foster the habit of saving; *(iii)* to distribute fertilisers and seeds; *(iv)* to provide help in milk production, egg production, sugar production or any other product depending upon the resources of the area; and *(v)* to distribute consumer goods to their members.

MEMBERSHIP

The membership of a PACS is confined to persons belonging to a village or a group of villages where every person is known to other person. Ten or more persons of a locality can form a PACS. Any person can become its member by purchasing a minimum number of shares. The liability of members is unlimited which means that each member is fully responsible for the loss in the event of failure of the society.

MANAGEMENT

The management of PACSs is on democratic lines. Each member has the right to cast only one vote, irrespective of the number of shares held by him. All members form the General Body which, in turn, elects the Managing Committee annually. It consists of the President or Chairman, Secretary and members. Except the

Secretary who is paid some remuneration, all others work in a honorary capacity.

FUNDS

The working funds of PACSs consist of share capital, membership fee, reserve fund (which is 25% of profits), deposits of members and non-members, and loan from the Central Cooperative Bank. They also accept grants, gifts and charities.

LOANS

The PACSs grant short-term loans for meeting productive as well as unproductive needs of their member only. The medium-term loans are granted up to a certain limit and in special cases. Loans are given against personal security and security of land or crop. The rate of interest charged is lower than the rate in the organised money market. Loans are repayable in instalments.

PROGRESS

In terms of membership, PACSs have spread widely in the country. There were 98,247 PACSs having about 10 crore members as on 31 March, 2002. Their deposits increased from Rs. 4 crores in 1950-51 to Rs. 6,518 crores in 1998-99. Total loans issued in 1998-99 amounted to Rs 16,081 crores as against Rs. 24 crores in 1950-51. Total loans outstanding increased from Rs. 6 crores in 1950-51 to Rs. 34,522 crores in 2000-01.

DRAWBACKS

The performance of PACSs in the issue of loans has no doubt been commendable, but they suffer from some serious weaknesses. They are: (1) They have failed to mobilise deposits. (2) The recovery of loans advanced has been disappointing. (3) Majority of them are non-viable, and the States of Maharashtra, Gujarat and J & K have not taken steps to reorganise them. (4) PACSs take very long time in granting loans. (5) The share capital of many PACSs is very small. (6) There is lack of properly trained staff. Majority of them do not have full-time paid secretaries. (7) PACSs have failed to meet the credit needs of small farmers and tenants. (8) PACSs do not possess adequate finance.

MEASURES TO REMOVE WEAKNESSES

The Agricultural Credit Review Committee (ACRC) of the RBI in its Report (1989) made a number of recommendations to remove the weaknesses of PACSs, and to strengthen them so as to enable them to carry out their functions effectively. They are grouped as under:

(1) *Viability.* The minimum criterion of viability of a PACS can be summed up as its ability to *(i)* appoint a full-time paid secretary; *(ii)* set up a regular office in a building; *(iii)* contribute to statutory and other reserves on the scales considered necessary; and *(iv)* pay a reasonable dividend. Non-viable PACSs should be reorganised as per the guidelines laid down by the RBI.

(2) *Strengthening of Share Capital.* The share capital of PACSs in many cases needs strengthening. For this: (a) The NABARD should provide the minimum essential requirement of share capital loan to State Governments in the light of the action programme irrespective of overdues level. *(b)* The ratio of share linking at the Central Cooperative Bank level for PACSs should be fixed at 5% so that they are able to retain with them a part of the share capital received from their members, *(c)* The ratio of share linking in respect of cash credit to PACSs should be reduced from 2.5% to 1%.

(3) *Deposit Mobilisation.* Deposit mobilisation is absolutely vital for the future growth and strength of PACSs. For this: *(i)* The PACSs should preferably mobilise low cost deposits such as savings bank deposits, *(ii)* They should maintain 15% of deposits with Central Cooperative Banks in a special account. *(iii)* To provide insurance cover to the deposits of PACSs the State Cooperative Banks in coordination with their State Governments should formulate suitable schemes.

(4) *Improving Lending Policies and Procedures for Crop Loans.* Crop loans are granted for a period not exceeding 12 months. The Committee has recommended that: *(a)* The cash credit system should be introduced in areas where perennial irrigation is available and multiple cropping is practised. *(b)* The credit statements for fixing individual crop loans limits by PACSs should be prepared once in three years, instead of every year,

except in cases where crop acreages are changed, (c) In areas where fertiliser / pesticide use is well-established, the PACSs should not insist on disbursing the input part of the loan in kind, *(d)* Where due to shortage of resources it becomes necessary to reduce the quantum of crop loans fixed, the larger farmers should be given less and smaller ones their full credit requirements.

(5) *Management.* To improve the quality of management of PACSs, a full-time trained secretary should be provided to every PACS. The Committee suggested a two-part salary structure for the secretary: one, a reasonable fixed salary in a scale of pay; and *two,* a variable payment based on increased performance, such as recovery, deposits, additional loan, business generated, and additional non-credit business undertaken. It should be in terms of additional remuneration by way of percentage of salary. Further, the Managing Committee of a PACS should be provided training through orientation and educational programmes.

(6) *Office Premises and Godowns.* All PACSs should have proper office premises and godown space to conduct their activities as multipurpose societies.

(7) *Loans for Non-productive Purposes.* PACSs should be allowed to give loans out of their resources for non-productive purposes such as consumption loans, upto certain prescribed limits, but against tangible security only. They may also be allowed to grant loans upto 20% of their deposits against the security of gold and silver ornaments at a rate of interest higher than that on crop loans. This will provide added viability to PACSs.

(8) *Audit.* The audit of PACSs should be done free of cost or at a nominal fee only.

2. CENTRAL COOPERATIVE BANKS (CCBs)

The Central Cooperative Banks are federations of primary agricultural credit societies in a particular district. That is why they are also known as District Central Cooperative Banks (DCCBs). They are of two types : *One,* whose membership is confined to PACSs. This type is known as Banking Union and such banking unions exist in Kerala, Orissa, Punjab, Haryana and Rajasthan. *Two,* those having mixed membership, consisting of both PACSs and individuals. Such banks exist in the majority of States in India.

Functions

The CCBs perform the following functions: (1) They give credit to PACSs without any security. (2) They also give credit to individual customers on the security of gold, etc. (3) They foster the habit of thrift and saving among their clients by accepting deposits and paying higher rate of interest than commercial banks. (4) They also provide remittance facilities to their customers. (5) They help in solving the problems of PACSs. (6) They also control and rupervise the working of PACSs especially where the recovery of loans is slow. (7) They help in maintaining a balance among the PACSs under their jurisdiction by transferring funds from a surplus society to a deficit society. (8) They help in the proper utilisation of the reserve fund of PACS lying with them.

Management

The CCBs are managed by a Board of Directors who are elected on the principle of one member one vote. Its members vary between 10 and 20. The Board appoints trained staff like manager, accountant, etc. for proper functioning of the bank.

Funds

The working capital of CCBs consists of : *(i)* the share capital which they get by selling their shares to individuals and PACSs under their jurisdiction; *(ii)* reserve fund of PACSs and owned funds; *(iii)* deposits of members and non-members; *(iv)* borrowings from the State Cooperative Bank, commercial banks, and the State Government; and *(v)* deposits of local bodies and even of educational institutions.

Loans

CCBs give loans to their PACSs to meet their financial needs. Short-term loans are provided far agricultural operations for a period not exceeding 12 months. The medium-term loans are given for the purchase of cattle, for installing pumps, and for the repair of wells or sinking of well for a period ranging from 1 to 5 years. Loans arc given to societies on their promissory notes.

Progress

The number of CCBs-decreased from 509 in 1950-51 to 343 in 2003 as a policy of amalgamation of having one CCB for every district. Deposits with them increased from Rs 38 crores in 1950-51 to Rs 72,983 crores in 2002-03, and loans advanced from Rs 106 crores in 1950-51 to Rs 50,482 crores in 2002-03.

Drawbacks

The CCBs suffer from a number of weaknesses: *(i)* There is lack of coordination between PACSs and CCBs. *(ii)* There are political considerations in granting loans. *(iii)* They lack efficient and sufficient staff to examine the credit-worthiness of PACSs. *(iv)* They lack funds, *(v)* There is undue delay in grant of loans, *(vi)* They hesitate to grant medium-term loans because of the lack of proper planning, *(vii)* They charge very high interest rates, *(viii)* The majority of CCBs have low level of deposits and high level of overdues which adversely affect their working. During 1998-99, the percentage of their overdues to demand was 70%. Consequently, they are week. *(ix)* They are not allowed to lend to individuals and non-cooperative institutions with the result that they are not in a position to earn more by way of interest.

Suggestions

The various committees appointed by the Reserve Bank of India from time to time suggested measures to remove the drawbacks of CCBs and to improve their functioning. Some of them are: (1) They should make efforts to mobilise more deposits from individuals and non-cooperative institutions. (2) They should open more branches in a district. (3) They should provide more banking facilities to the people. (4) As recommended by the Agricultural Credit Review Committee (1989), CCBs should be permitted to lend to non-members whether individuals or institutions, to the extent of not more than 20 per cent of their deposits. (5) The programme of improving the working of weak CCBs was launched by the RBI in 1971. But it has not made any impact and the number of such banks has been on the increase. For this the ACRC recommended a multi-ironged attempt at providing finance adequately to eligible borrowers, intensive deposit mobilisation, recovery of overdues and current dues, strengthening of PACSs etc.

3. STATE CO-OPERATIVE BANKS (SCBs)

The State Cooperative Banks are federations of District Central Cooperative Banks. They are Apex Banks in the three tier cooperative structure in India. Each State has one SCB.

Functions

The SCBs perform the following functions: (1) They coordinate the activities of PACSs and CCBs in the State. (2) They arrange funds for the entire credit structure of the State. (3) They control the activities of the CCBs. (4) They act as an important link between the Indian money market and the cooperative sector. (5) They help in maintaining a balance among the CCBs by transferring funds from surplus CCBs to deficit CCBs within a State. (6) In case there is no CCB in a district, it provides credit facilities direct to PACSs in that district. (7) It also functions as a commercial bank.

Management

A SCB is managed by a General Body which holds its meeting once a year. It is formed by. the representatives of PACs, CCBs and individuals. But it is governed by a Board of Directors whose number varies between 10 and 30 which also appoints the staff.

Funds

The working capital of a SCB consists of: *(i)* the share capital which it gets by selling its share to PACSs,

CCBs, and individuals; *(ii)* reserve fund which comprises 25% of its profits; *(iii)* deposits from members and non-members; and *(iv)* borrowings from the Reserve Bank of India, State Government, commercial banks and inter-bank borrowings.

Loans

SCBs lend to CCBs for short-term to meet the needs of PACSs. They do not lend direct to PACSs except in those cases where there is no CCB in a district. Loans are given on the basis of promissory note.

Progress

The number of SCBs increased from 16 in 1950-51 to 29 in 2002-03 with total deposits rising from Rs. 21 crores to Rs 37,439 crores over the period. Total loans advanced by them increased from Rs. 55 crores in 1950-51 to Rs. 38,318 crores in 2002-03 and loans outstanding were 34,864 crores.

Drawbacks

There are a number of drawbacks in the working of SCBs, which are: *(i)* They lack sufficient funds to meet the needs of the farm sector, *(ii)* They are more involved in commercial banking operations, *(iii)* There is no proper planning in granting loans to farmers through the DCCBs. *(iv)* They do not have adequate and trained staff to supervise and help in the efficient working of CCBs. *(v)* They are influenced by political considerations in sanctioning loans than by the genuine needs of agriculturists, *(vi)* They have failed to recover overdues. *(vi)* The Board of Directors is not properly managed, and its members are not experienced.

Suggestions

The All India Rural Credit Survey Committee and the Agricultural Credit Review Committee made a number of suggestions to improve the working of banks. Some of them are: (1) The membership of SCBs should be restricted only to PACSs and DCCBs. (2) They should try to increase their share capital, mobilise more deposits from the urban sector, and keep.the reserve funds of PACSs and DCCBs with them in order to have larger funds as working capital. (3) They should meet the farm needs of agriculturists rather than function as commercial banks. (4) Not more than 33 per cent of the members should be nominated by the State Government on the Board of Directors and one of them must be the Registrar of Cooperative Societies, (5) Each SCB should set up a technical cell with trained staff to formulate schemes for financing and helping DCCBs in credit planning and project formulation. Besides, expertise should be developed at the SCBs' level to advise DCCBs on better financial management and investment/portfolio management. (6) For an efficient working of SCBs, the staff should be recruited in the same manner as is being done in the case of Regional Rural Banks and commercial banks through Banking Commission of the respective-region. (7) The Government of India along with the State Governments should chalk out a concrete long-term policy to recover overdues and take firm steps in respect of wilful defaulters. (8) The politicisation of agricultural credit system should be stopped, loan 'melas' should be discouraged, and loans should be given to needy farmers.

4. LAND DEVELOPMENT BANKS (LDBs)

The Land Development Banks, which were earlier known as Land Mortgage Banks are meant to meet the long-term credit needs of agriculturists. Their structure is not uniform in the country. It is unitary in some States, while in some others it is federal, and in Himachal Pradesh and West Bengal, it is both unitary and federal. Under the federal structure, there is the Central Land Development Bank at the State level, and the Primary Land Development Banks (PLDBs) at the district level. The Central Land Development Bank lends to agriculturists through the PLDBs. They are now known as State Cooperative Agriculture and Rural Development Banks (SCARDBs).

Functions

The LDBs provide long-term loans to agriculturists for a period ranging from 5 to 25 years, for the following purposes: *(i)* to make improvements on the land; *(ii)* to repay old debts; *(iii)* to free the mortgaged land; and *(iv)* to buy new land. In recent years, they have also started lending for non-agricultural purposes such as, to the rural cottage industries and small enterprises in rural areas.

Management

The LDBs are registered under the Cooperative Societies Act. A Land Development Bank is managed by a Board of Directors consisting of 15 to 20 members duly elected by the members of PLDBs, and nominated members by the State Government, and the Registrar of Cooperative Societies.

Funds

The financial resources of LDBs consist of: *(i)* the share capital contributed by borrowing and non-borrowing members; *(ii)* deposits from the public; and *(iii)* by issuing debentures. Debentures are of three types: *First,* ordinary debentures purchased by institutions and individuals. *Second,* rural debentures issued to farmers at the time of harvesting for 7 years and 15 years. *Third,* special development debentures issued for land development or improvement which are purchased by NABARD, the concerned State Government and the Central Government.

Loans

The LDBs give loans to their members on the security of their lands which are generally limited to 50% of the value of land mortgaged. Loans are given for a maximum period of 25 years. They are meant to meet the long-term needs of the agriculturists such as land development, land reclamation, buying new land, for minor irrigation works like buying pump sets, digging wells and tubewells or tanks, for related agricultural activities like dairy, poultry farming, bee-keeping, sericulture, biogas, etc. LDBs also give credit to non-agriculturists such as village, household and handicraft industries in rural areas.

Progress

The number of LDBs increased from 6 in 1950-51 to 20 in 2002-03. Loans advanced increased from Rs 2.5 crores in 1950-51 to Rs. 2,631 crores in 2002-03. Their loans outstanding rose from Rs. 8 crores to Rs. 13,870 crores.

Drawbacks

The LDBs have been facing a number of problems which hinder their proper functioning. Some of their problems are:

(1) *Overdues.* The LDBs have not been able to recover past loans with the result that their overdues have been rising which affect their smooth working. During 2000-01 the percentage of their overdues was 58 per cent of the demand.

(2) *Restricted Lending Eligibility.* Due to the lack of working capital, the lending eligibility of PLDBs and of the branches of LDBs have restricted lending eligibility. There are hardly one-third of them which have unrestricted lending eligibility.

(3) *Non-viable.* Due to the restricted lending eligibility, 30% of the total PLDBs and the branches of LDBs are not viable.

(4) *Falling Profits.* Due to their non-viability, there is deterioration in their profitability.

(5) *Debentures.* People are reluctant to buy their debentures and the cost of raising even ordinary debentures is very high.

(6) *Delay.* There is delay in the grant of loans.

(7) *High Margin.* The LDBs keep a high margin of 50% of the value of land mortgaged for the grant of loans.

(8) *Discharge of Past Debts.* More loans are granted to repay past debts and less for productive purposes.

(9) *Benefits to Rich Farmers.* Rich farmers are able to get more benefits as they have more land than the other farmers having less land.

(10) *Interference.* There is much external interference and government intervention in the management

of LDBs.

(11) *Inefficient Working.* The LDBs are not working properly due to lack of adequate and trained staff. There is no definite policy in regard to recruitment, appointment, promotion and training of staff. The Chief Executives are either IAS or PCS officers or from the cooperative departments.

Suggestions

The various committees appointed by the Reserve Bank of India have made a number of suggestions to remove the defects and improve the working of LDBs in the country. Some of the suggestions made by the Agricultural Credit Review Committee (1989) are:

(1) Effective steps should be taken by the LDBs to recover overdues in order to make theni viable.

(2) For LDBs to work as viable units, every effort should be made to increase their volume of business with such diversification of activities as may be feasible.

(3) The LDBs should adopt viability criterion in place of eligibility criteria in order to obtain adequate funds from the NABARD.

(4) The NABARD should provide adequate interim finance for issue of loans before debentures are floated at concessional rates.

(5) The State Governments and institutions should support the programme of issuing of ordinary debentures. So far as the flotation of special development debentures is concerned, the NABARD should provide refinance by way of term loans instead of by contribution to special development debentures.

(6) Politicisation of loans should be stopped and loans should be primarily given for productive purposes.

(7) LDBs should have a definite policy for recruitment, appointment, career planning and development of the staff. They should have their own staff and taking of government staff on deputation should be resorted to only in exceptional cases. There should be no government interference in the management of LDBs.

(8) Loans should be granted without unnecessary delay.

(9) The keeping of high margins for the grant of loans should be relaxed for the benefit of farmers.

5. STRENGTHENING THE CO-OPERATIVE STRUCTURE

The Agricultural Credit Review Committee (ACRC) had made comprehensive recommendations for improving the cooperative credit structure in the country.[1] The Government of India has implemented a number of recommendations which are discussed as under :

1. Reorganisation of PACSs

The process of reorganisation of PACSs has been started on the model laid down by the NABARD. It envisages an area of. operation of 5 km radius and a potential loan business of Rs. 13.50 lakhs for the reorganised society. Except in Maharashtra and the Kashmir region of J&K, the process of reorganisation of PACSs has been completed. However, the majority of states have not achieved the norms laid down by the NABARD though they have completed the reorganisation work.

2. Business Development Plans (BDPs) for PACSs

In view of the poor financial position of PACSs, the Government of India has launched a business-oriented development programme for PACs. The programme envisages preparation of BDPs for selected PACSs for implementation in a phased manner. Its aim is to develop selected societies in certain States into viable units to serve all socio-economic groups in their areas of operation through economically viable activities. It is expected to cover, in phases, all PACSs in the country.

1. These have already been enumerated above under "Suggestions" in different sections.

3. Deposit Insurance Scheme for PACSs

The main thrust of BDPs is on deposit mobilisation by PACSs. But the absence of deposit insurance has been the major constraint in deposit mobilisation at the PACS level. To overcome this, the Government of India has formulated a model deposit insurance scheme for PACSs to create a sense of security in the depositors. The scheme would be applicable only to viable PACSs which are implementing BDPs. The scheme lays down the following conditions: (a) the PACSs covered under the scheme should have deposits of maturity period of more than 6 months; (*b*) such deposits should be at least Rs. 25,000 per society; (c) the accounts of the society should be maintained regularly.

4. Kisan Credit Card (KCC) Scheme

This scheme was introduced in 1998-99 with a view to facilitating the flow of timely and adequate short-term credit to farmers. The KCC scheme is an on-going scheme which is meant to gradually replace the traditional system and procedures in the short-term crop, loans. Loans disbursed under the scheme have also been brought under the Krishi BimaYojna of the General Insurance Corporation. KCCs are issued to eligible farmers for even amounts below Rs. 5,000 per card by cooperative banks, Regional Rural Banks and commercial banks in rural areas.

5. Institutional Strengthening Programme (ISP)

The ISP aims at making non-solvent banks such as SCBs, DCCBs, State LDBs and PLDBs as viable units within a period of 3 to 5 years. The programme includes investigation of overdues, measures for their recovery, rationalising loans policies and procedures, expansion and diversification of loan portfolio, mobilisation of resources, revitalisation of primary cooperative societies, reduction in management costs, and redeployment of manpower and resources, etc. The programme also requires administrative support and financial assistance from Central and State Governments, RBI and NABARD. The banks which fail to become viable within 3 to 5 years would not be given refinance facility by the NABARD and alternative arrangements would be made to maintain credit flow in these banks.

6. The Model Cooperative Societies Act

The Planning Commission appointed a committee to review the status of cooperative laws which submitted its report on the Model Cooperative Societies Act in May 1991. The main thrust of the Act is to impart a federal character to cooperatives, facilitate self-reliance and to minimise Government control and interference. The State Governments have been asked by the Planning Commission to incorporate the amendments to the Model Act in a phased manner. So far, only Orissa State has accepted it fully and implemented it. Some States have yet to initiate legislative action while others are in the process of taking action.

7. Integrated Cooperative Development Projects (ICDPs)

The National Cooperative Development Corporation launched a scheme during the Seventh Plan for Integrated Cooperative Development Projects for selected districts. The scheme aims at strengthening and developing cooperative infrastructure in order to cater to the overall needs of the rural community in selected areas of districts.

EXERCISES

1. Describe the organisation, structure, working and progress of Primary Agricultural Credit Societies.
2. Why have Primary Agricultural Credit Societies been not successful? Suggest measures to improve their working.
3. Describe the functions, working and progress of Land Development Banks.
4. Explain the defects found in the agricultural cooperative societies. What measures have been taken to improve them?

CHAPTER 73

Regional Rural Banks and NABARD

1. RURAL BANKS

In India four sets of cooperative credit institutions have been providing farm credit. These have been the Primary Agricultural Societies and other primary level farm credit societies and Land Development Banks which deal directly with the farmer-borrowers. There are also State Cooperative banks and Central Cooperative Banks which extend only indirect finance. Both before and after Independence, these institutions failed to meet the farm credit requirements, and the farmers had to depend primarily on the moneylenders. The involvement of commercial banks in rural banking began with the nationalisation of Imperial Bank of India into the State Bank of India in 1955. The SBI started providing finance to agriculture through cooperative banks, land mortgage banks and cooperative processing and marketing societies in 1956.

With the adoption of the New Agricultural Strategy in 1968, it was felt that the cooperative institutions helped by the SBI would not be able to meet the credit requirements of the expanding farm sector by themselves. Accordingly, the government accepted the principle of Multi-Agency Approach to farm credit with the entry of commercial banks in the sphere of agricultural finance. This led to nationalisation of 14 commercial banks in 1969. It was only after this that commercial banks as a class began to enter the rural sector in a big way. There was remarkable expansion of branches of commercial banks in rural areas. But they failed to meet the credit needs of the farmers except that of the rich farmers and landlords. Instead of supplementing cooperative credit, they weakened cooperative societies by mobilising the savings of rich farmers and channelising them into urban areas for earning profits. Moreover, commercial banks experienced that working in rural areas was very costly and not viable, and secondly, the urban staff was unable to understand the needs and problems of rural finance.

It was against this background that the Banking Commission in its report published in 1972 recommended the establishment of a chain *of Rural Banks* in one of the three ways: (1) Conversion of primary agricultural credit societies into rural cooperative banks providing all the banking services; (2) restructuring sound agricultural credit societies as subsidiaries of commercial banks to be called 'rural subsidiary banks'; and (3) establishing special type of 'rural banks' sponsored by commercial banks with local participation in capital and management; if suitable primary credit societies are not available.

The Banking Commission laid down the following functions for the rural banks to accept deposits; to advance loans to provide ancillary banking services; to supply farm inputs and equipment to farmers; to help in the marketing of farm output; to maintain godowns; and to help in the overall development of villages in the area of operations. It emphasised that rural banks would meet the farm needs of the marginal, small and medium farmers and rural artisans.

The Banking Cojnmission observed that in a country like India any single type of financial institution was incapable of meeting the credit needs of the rural sector. It, therefore, recommended a multi-pronged programme where cooperative credit societies, commercial banks, SBI, and sponsored rural banks had to play an important role.

But the Government of India did not give any thought to the recommendations of the Banking Commission to start a chain of rural banks in the country till 1975, when five Regional Rural Banks were started in five selected districts in the country.

2. REGIONAL RURAL BANKS (RRBs)

The idea of establishing Regional Rural Banks was mooted in the Twenty Point Economic Programme of July 1975 to cater to the credit needs of rural people. The Government of India appointed Narasimham Committee in July 1975 to set up the new institution in order *(i)* to provide employment to the rural educated youth; and *(ii)* to bring down the cost of rural banks by recruiting their staff on the same scale of pay and allowances as for the employees of State Government/local bodiss. It was on the recommendations that the first five RRBs were set up on 2 October, 1975 under an Ordinance promulgated on 26 September, 1975 which was replaced by the Regional Rural Banks Act of 1976.

Objectives

The major objectives of the RRBs are to develop the rural economy by providing credit and other facilities for agriculture, trade, commerce, industry and other productive activities in the rural areas, particularly to the small and marginal farmers, agricultural labourers, artisans and small entrepreneurs.

Organisational Structure of Regional Rural Banks

A Regional Rural Bank is sponsored by a commercial bank. For this purpose, the sponsor bank requests the Central Government, which issues a notification after consulting the concerned State Government. Normally, a RRB covers one district but it is also permitted to open its branches in other districts. So far the maximum coverage has been eight districts, as in the case of Manipur Regional Rural Bank which covers the entire State of Manipur.

The authorised capital of an RRB at present is Rs. 5 crcres. The issued share capital is Rs. 1 crore now and is subscribed by the Central Government, the sponsor bank and the concerned State Government in the ratio of 50:35:15. The Government of India raised the issued share capital of 27 RRBs from Rs. 50 to 75 lakh and of 42 RRBs from Rs. 75 lakh to Rs. 1 crore during 1994-95. This has raised the number of RRBs having issued capital of Rs. 1 crore to 62 and those having issued capital of Rs. 75 to 122 lakh.

The RRB is governed by a Board of Directors who exercises all the powers and discharges all the functions of RRB. It consists of a Chairman appointed by the Central Government for five years, three directors nominated by the Central Government, two directors nominated by the concerned State Government, and three directors nominated by the sponsor bank. Usually the Chairman of the RRB belongs to the sponsor bank, though hc is nominated by the Central Government.

The NABARD is vested with powers of inspection of RRBs and to call for any data from them. For opening of new branches, applications are routed through NABARD to Reserve Bank of India for issue of licences. The responsibility of overseeing the overall functioning of RRBs rests on NABARD. NABARD also provides refinance at concessional interest rate to RRBs.

Functions of Regional Rural Banks

The main functions (or objectives) of the RRBs are:

1. To grant loans and advances to the weaker sections of the rural population, especially to the small and

marginal farmers, agricultural labourers, artisans and small entrepreneurs who are engaged in agriculture, trade, commerce, industry and other productive activities.

2. To grant loans and advances to cooperative societies, including marketing societies, agricultural processing societies, cooperative farming societies, primary agricultural credit societies or farmers' service societies for agricultural purposes.

3. To take banking services to the doorsteps of the rural masses, particularly in hitherto unbanked rural areas.

4. To mobilise rural savings by accepting deposits and channelise them for productive activities in the rural areas.

5. To create a supplementary channel for flow of credit from the urban money market to the rural areas through refinance.

6. To generate employment opportunities in rural areas.

7. To bring down the cost of supplying credit in rural areas.

In recent years, the RRBs have been permitted to extend advances for purchase of durable consumer goods and loans for various purposes against the security of gold ornaments, National Savings Certificates, Indira Vikas Patras to both target and non-target groups up to 10 per cent of their fresh lending within the over ceiling of 60 per cent of fresh loans to non-target group lending.

They have also been allowed to issue guarantees on behalf of their customers without any limition 100 per cent cash margin and upto Rs. 20 lakh on Rs. 40 lakh cash margin plus collateral security of more than 50 per cent.

The limits for purchase of demand drafts and cheque have been raised per customer and per branch to Rs. 25,000 and Rs. 1 lakh respectively. The RRBs can issue travellers' cheques as agents of their sponsor banks and also provide locker facilities.

The RRBs can invest their surpluses in UTI listed schemes, fixed deposits of profit making term lending institutions, bonds of nationalised banks and other public sector undertakings, non-convertible debentures of blue chip companies and in credit portfolios of their sponsor banks-subject to a maximum of 15 per cent of their fresh lending during the year. Effective 8 January, 1997, RRBs have been allowed to invest in corporate shares and debentures and units of mutual funds. But these investments cannot exceed 5 per cent of the RRBs' incremental deposits. They have also been allowed to buy corporate shares and debentures from the secondary market. They are also free to fix their lending and deposit rates.

Achievements (or Progress) of Regional Rural Banks

The RRBs have carried banking to the doorsteps of rural masses. They have opened branches in remote and isolated villages which had no banking facilities. Initially starting with five RRBs at Moradabad and Gorakhpur in Uttar Pradesh, Jaipur in Rajasthan, Bhiwani in Haryana and Malda in West Bengal on 2 October, 1975, the RRBs have achieved a phenomenal growth over the years. As on June 30, 2003, they numbered 196, covering 451 districts, with a network of 14,522 branches.

The aggregate outstanding deposits of 196 RRBs in 2002-03 were Rs. 48,346 crores. Their aggregate direct and indirect outstanding advances stood at Rs.. 15,944 crores in 2002-03. The credit-deposit ratio increased from 43 per cent as at the end of March, 1999 to 45 per cent in March, 2003. Investment-deposit ratio increased from 19.7 per cent in 1998-99 to 25.9 per cent in March 2003.

The loans and advances disbursed by RRBs for agriculture accounted for 46.3 per cent and the share of non-agricultural advances was 53.7 per cent. Out of 196 RRBs, the number of profit making banks stood at 156 in 2002-03 as compared with 170 out of 196 in 2000-01. Their operating profit fell by 7.7 per cent and net profit by -13.7 per cent over the period. The RRBs showed significant improvement in terms of reduction in their NPAs (non-performing assets). The share of NPAs in total assets declined from 18.8 percent to 16.1 per cent in 2002-03.

During 2002-03, the NABARD sanctioned Rs. 1,406 crores as short-term credit limits for seasonal and non-seasonal agricultural operations to RRBs. It sanctioned medium-term loans to RRBs amounting to Rs. 3 crores.

Thus, the RRBs have been highly successful in mobilising rural savings. In advancing loans, they have been concentrating on target groups viz., small and marginal farmers, landless labourers, rural artisans, self-employed persons, etc. They have also been playing a vital role in implementing the IRD Programme. Mostly, they have employed local persons. Clerical staff is recruited from within the area of operation of the RBBs from adjoining districts, whereas the officer staff is from the concerned State.

Problems of Regional Rural Banks

Despite the important role played by RRBs in providing credit to the weaker sections of society in rural areas, they are faced with serious problems which have led critics to question their very existence. The Dantwala Committee (1978), the Kelkar Committee (1986) and the Khusro Committee (1989) have pointed towards some of the weaknesses in the working of RRBs which are as follows:

1. *Haphazard Branch Expansion.* A large network of branches has been opened at a fast pace which has not contributed to substantial increase in business. It has added to overhead costs without contributing to profits.

Moreover, major variations persist among States in the coverage of districts/ branches by the RRBs. In some States, backward areas still remain uncovered by these banks. In many districts, the RRBs do not have link branches at the Taluka/ Block headquarters for meeting the cash requirements and to overcome other operational problems. In some of the places where branches are essential, it is difficult to get suitable accommodation for housing the branches.

2. *Defective Recruitment Policy.* Being rural oriented, the RRBs are expected to recruit staff locally. With the transfer of recruitments in RRBs to the Banking Service Recruitment Boards, the candidates outside the area of operations of RRBs are also made eligible for recruitment into RRBs. This is against the concept of RRBs where the 'local feel and familiarity' of the staff is essential for the successful working of the RRBs.

3. *Rigid Norms.* The norms laid down for the selection of beneficiaries in RRBs are rigid and based on an all India income level. The poverty line available in Haryana is not the poverty line obtained in Andhra Pradesh. The village, its people, their occupations and economic status differ widely in Andhra Pradesh with that of All India average. But to apply the same norms to all the States leave out many persons who are in need of credit from the RRBs.

4. *Weak Capital Base.* The capital base of each RRB is weak. Initially, the issued capital was Rs. 50 lakh which has been raised to Rs. 75 lakh and Rs. 1 crore in the case of selected RRBs. But the State Governments failed to contribute their share. In view of its enormous credit obligation in rural areas, this limit is on the lower side. The working of many RRBs reveals thai they have eroded their capital base on account of continuous losses.

5. *Constraints in Deposit Mobilisation.* As the RRBs supply credit only to the weaker sections of the rural population, they have been unable to mobilise sufficient deposits. The weaker sections who are the main beneficiaries are poor and do not save so much as to deposit in the RRBs. The middle classes and the rural elite are not interested to deposit their saving in the RRBs. They deposit them in commercial banks from whom they get credit facilities.

6. *Erosion of Profitability.* The RRBs have not been able to operate on a viable basis. The major factors which have contributed to the erosion of their profitability have been their lending exclusively to the weaker sections, low interest margins and high operating cost involved in handling small loans. During 1999-2000 there were 33 loss making RRBs which incurred a net loss of Rs. 109 crores.

7. *Poor Recoveries.* The recover of loans due has been very poor. The estimate of the Khusro Committee revealed that as on June 1986, the recoverv of RRBs was 49 per cent. During 1999, the recovery level was below 30 per cent. The main factors have been wilful defaults, misuse of loans, lack of follow-up, wrong identification of borrowers, extension of benami loans, staff agitations, etc.

8. *Defective Credit Deployment.* In many districts, the credit deployment has not been proper., The loaning activities are mainly confined to crop loans and the schemes sponsored by the State Governments. The schematic approach towards lending is lacking in many cases. Activities allied to agriculture, cottage and rural industries, rural artisans/craftsmen and other self-employed programmes have not been given due importance in the loaning activities of the RRBs.

9. *High Loan Transaction Cost.* With parity in pay scales between the RRBs and commercial banks, the loan transaction costs in RRBs are many times higher than in rural branches of commercial banks.

Conclusion. Notwithstanding the constraints under which the RRBs are operating, they constitute one of the effective instruments for bringing about faster rural development with social justice.

Suggestions to Improve the Working of RRBs

To improve the working of the RRBs, the Dantawala Committee (1978), the Kelkar Committee (1986) and the Khusro Committee (1989) have made a number of suggestions. Some of these are enumerated below:

1. To improve the *viability* of RRBs, the Khusro Committee recommended that the RRBs should be merged with the commercial banks. The merger would solve the problems of accumulated losses, of insolvency, and of the in-built non-viability of the majority of RRBs. But it is wrong to presume that after merger with sponsor banks, the RRBs will be viable because many branches of commercial banks are incurring huge losses. Therefore, the suggestions made by the Kelkar Committee should be implemented. They are the bifurcation of unwieldy RRBs, and the amalgamation of small RRBs.

2. In order to strengthen the capital structure of RRBs, the Kelkar Committee recommended the raising of issued capital of RRBs from Rs. 25 to 100 lakhs and the authorised capital from Rs. 1 to 5 crore.

3. As the very purpose of establishing RRBs is to transfer funds from urban money market to rural centres, the State Governments should permit the Panchayats and other quasi-government bodies functioning in rural areas to keep their funds with the RRB branches functioning within their area of operations.

4. The State Governments should either reorganise agricultural credit societies or establish new Farmers' Service Societies through which RRBs can provide production credit on a large scale and thereby the cost of servicing will be reduced considerably.

5. The sponsor banks should play a more active role in advising and helping their RRBs in managing their funds, in appraising loan schemes, in making proper end-use of credit, and in providing staff for internal audit of RRBs.

6. The sponsor banks should charge a lower interest rate on the refinance to RRBs and involve themselves less in RRBs short-term and non-schematic loans.

7. The sponsor banks should invest the deposits of RRBs in long-term Government securities which are being kept in non-interest earning current accounts.

8. To increase the profit margin, the RRBs should extend credit facilities to non-target groups subject to a ceiling of 25 percent of their total outstanding advances. The State Government should help the RRBs in recovering dues by creating a proper climate for recovery and in taking action against wilful defaulters.

9. The RRBs should have their own recovery system with adequate trained staff and organise recovery camps involving the Government officials, local leaders and branch staff.

10. The business of rural branches of commercial banks should be handed over to RRBs.

11. There should be uniform scales of pay for all the RRBs staff.

12. The RRBs should devise suitable strategies to develop banking habits and practices among the rural folk by imbibing banking education and awareness.

13. The RRBs should widen their sphere of activity. Instead of concentrating mainly on lending, they should provide rural consultancy services, phased credit programmes, create better avenues for employment, and take over the work of farmers' service societies.

14. Since RRB is an area specific and target specific bank, its working hours should be suitably amended to enable the customers to make full use of its facilities. It is inconsistent to have the usual office hours between 10 AM and 5 PM in a village where the customers are busy in the fields at that time., Therefore, the working hours of RRBs should be fixed according to the needs of the area.

15. New RRBs should be opened in areas where SC/ST population predominates.

16. The entire recruitment process in the RRBs should be streamlined. Local people should be preferred and training should be given on the problems of rural life which are peculiar to the RRBs.

Restructuring of RRBs

These suggestions apart, keeping in view that only 29 RRBs were profit making in 1991-92, the Government of India had been considering a number of options which include the merger of RRBs with the sponsor banks as suggested by the RBI or making them rural subsidiaries of sponsor banks as suggested by the Narasimhan Committee or their amalgamation with the proposed National Rural Bank of India. As the RRBs became non-viable, the Government's interest in supporting them financially declined. The budgetary support for RRBs was Rs. 11 crores in 1992-93 which declined to Rs. 5 crores in 1993-94. There was no provision for them in the budget for 1994-95 though it was announced by the Finance Minister that 50 select RRBs would be taken up for revival and restructuring. Accordingly, the Government appointed the Bhandari Committee on Restructuring of RRBs which has since submitted its report. Based on its recommendations, action has been taken on the managerial, operational and organisational restructuring of RRBs including cleansing up their balance sheets and infusing fresh capital. In the first phase, 49 RRBs were taken up for selective restructuring. These RRBs drew up their Development Action Plans in consultation with NABARD and sponsor banks and Mou were entered between them and sponsor banks. The Government of India contributed Rs. 180 crores as its share of 50 per cent during 1994-95. During 1995-96, a sum of Rs. 223.57 crores was further released by the Government for capital restructuring of select RRBs. The Budget for 1996-97 made, a further provision for the same purpose in the second phase.

In June 1995, the Reserve Bank set up an Expert Group under Dr Thingalaya to examine the major policy issues concerning the managerial and financial restructuring of RRBs undertaken during 1994-95 and to monitor their progress on an ongoing basis. Another Committee headed by K. Basu was set up by the NABARD to look into the norms afresh and for revamping the RRBs. It recommended the selection of 68 RRBs for comprehensive restructuring in the second phase.

In order to impart durability to the restructuring process, the RRBs have been advised by the Reserve Bank to adopt income recognition, asset classification and exposure norms from 1995-96 and provisioning norms from 1996-97 onwards. As a result of these restructuring measures the number of profit making RRBs stood at 156 in 2002-03

3. NATIONAL BANK FOR AGRICULTURE AND RURAL DEVELOPMENT (NABARD)

The National Bank for Agriculture and Rural Development (NABARD) was established on 12 July, 1982 by Government of India by merging the Agricultural Credit Department of the RBI, the Agricultural Refinance and Development Corporation, the National Agricultural Credit (Long Term Operations) Fund and the National Agricultural Credit (Stabilisation) Fund of the RBI.

Objectives of NABARD

The NABARD is an apex development bank which provides help for agricultural and rural development. It has been established with the following objectives:

1. To give undivided attention and purposeful direction to integrated rural development.
2. To act as a centre piece for the entire rural credit system at the national level.
3. To act as a provider of supplemental funding to rural credit institutions.
4. To arrange for investment credit to small industries, village and cottage industries, handicrafts and other rural crafts, artisans, and farmers.
5. To improve the credit distribution system by institution building, rehabilitation of credit institutions and training of bank personnel.
6. To provide refinance facilities to SLDBs, SCBs, RRBs and commercial banks for development purposes in rural areas.
7. To coordinate the working of different agencies engaged in development work in rural areas at the regional level, and to have liaison with Government of India, RBI, State Governments and other policy-making institutions at the national level.
8. To inspect, monitor and evaluate projects getting refinance from the NABARD.

Functions of NABARD

The functions of NABARD have been divided into three categories: *(a)* Credit Distribution; *(b)* Development, and *(c)* Regulatory.

These are discussed as under:

(a) Credit Distribution

The NABARD provides refinance of various types to the following institutions :

(1) *Short Term Credit.* It provides short term credit to State Cooperative Banks (SCBs), Regional Rural Banks (RRBs), and other financial institutions approved by the RBI for the following purposes: *(i)* seasonal agricultural operations; *(ii)* marketing of agricultural produce; *(iii)* marketing and distribution of such inputs as pesticides, fertilisers, etc.; *(iv)* other activities related to rural/agriculture sector; *(v)* real commercial trade activities; *(vi)* production and marketing of the following activities: handicrafts, small industries, village and cottage industries, artisans, silk industry, etc. The duration of short term loans for the above purposes is up to 15 months.

(2) *Medium Term Credit.* The NABARD provides medium term credit to SCBs, LDBs, RRBs, and other approved institutions for a period ranging from 18 months to 7 years. The medium term loans are given for investment schemes relating to agriculture and rural sector.

(3) *Long Term Credit.* The NABARD provides long term credit to State Land Development Banks, RRBs, commercial banks, SCBs, and to any approved financial institution. It provides refinance for investment in the following activities: minor irrigation, land development, soil conservation; dairy development, sheep rearing, poultry farming, pig rearing, farm mechanisation, afforestation, fish farming, storage and market yard, agricultural operations through aeroplane, biogas and other alternative sources of energy, silk production, beekeeping, cattle and cattle driven carts, compost equipment, pump set, and other agricultural and related activities. The duration of the loan is for a period of 25 years.

(4) *Facilities for Changes and Rearrangement.* The NABARD provides refinance facilities to SCBs and RRBs in the event of changes and rearrangement of credits when there is drought, famine or other natural calamities, army operations, enemy operations, etc. Such facilities are also provided to loans given to artisans, small industries, etc. The duration of such refinance facilities is not more than 7 years.

(5) *Refinancing of Industries in Rural Areas.* The NABARD provides refinancing facilities to all small, village and cottage industries in rural areas.

(b) Developmental Functions

The NABARD performs the following developmental functions: *(i)* coordinates the rural credit institutions; *(ii)* takes measures towards institution building to improve the capacity of credit delivery system; *(iii)* develops specialisation to solve problems relating to agriculture and villages; *(iv)* helps the Government, **RBI**, and other institutions in their rural development efforts; *(v)* acts as an agent of the Government and RBI for monitoring work in agricultural related areas; *(vi)* provides facilities for research and training to the staff of RRBs, SCBs, LDBs, .etc. and promotes research in agricultural and rural development activities out of its R&D (Research and Development) Fund. To provide training facilities in the fields of rural banking, and agriculture and rural development, the NABARD has the Banker Rural Development Institute -and National Bank Staff Colleges at Lucknow, Bolpur and Manglore, and College of Agriculture Banking (CAB) at Pune; *(vii)* spreads information regarding rural banking and development; *(viii)* helps the State Governments so that they may subscribe to the share capital of State Cooperative Banks; *(ix)* provides direct credit in cases approved by the Central Government connected with agriculture and rural development; and *(x)* maintains an Easy Credit Aid Fund out of its profits so that entrepreneurs getting refinance facilities for village, cottage and very small industries may be provided margin money. This help is given interest-free and is recovered in yearly instalments after the loan is repaid.

(c) Regulatory Functions

The NABARD also performs the following regulatory functions: *(i)* It inspects the working of RRBs and cooperative banks of all types except the primary cooperative banks, *(ii)* It also inspects apex cooperative marketing federations, state handloom weaving societies, etc. which are financed on voluntary basis, (iii) All applications for opening of a branch by the RRB or a cooperative bank, other than a primary cooperative society, are required to be submitted to the RBI through the NABARD. *(iv)* All RRBs and cooperative banks submitting returns to the RBI are required to furnish a copy of returns to the NABARD. *(v)* It is empowered to obtain any information or statement from the RRBs and cooperative banks.

(*d*) Recent Additions to Its Functions

For the last few years a number of additions have been made the functions of NABARD relating to farm and non-farm sectors in order to make it more broad-based. They are:

(i) *Farm Sector.* The National Bank has been engaged in reorienting its policies relating to the farm sector in tune with emerging needs. Accordingly, it has taken some major initiatives for promoting agriculture and rural development. These include: (1) refinement and updating of Potential Linked Credit Plans (PLCPs) and their synthesis with Service Area Plans (SAPs); (2) introduction of full refinance scheme in those districts where such synthesis has taken place; (3) rationalization and liberalisation of eligibility criteria for refinance of term credit; (4) introduction of Self Help Groups Scheme for providing institutional credit to weaker sections; (5) rationalisation of interest rate structure for ultimate borrowers; (6) issuance of guidelines to banks on new/ innovative schemes for diversification of lending under agriculture; and (7) creation of a Cooperative Development Fund to promote institutional strengthening activities.

(ii) *Non-Farm Sector.* For accelerating the development of non-farm sector, NABARD has taken the following initiatives: (1) introduction of Small Road Transport Scheme for automatic refinance to all banks for financing transport vehicles to carry farm produce and products of village industries for marketing; (2) project finance for commercial banks for financing non-agro small industry units; (3) assisting Khadi and Village Industries Centres in modifying their schemes so as to conform them to banking norms and bringing them under automatic refinance facility; (4) formation of an Advisory Committee for the* non-farm sector in its office to guide in the formulation of policies to promote non-farm sector and to introduce innovative schemes; (5) appointment of technical experts in non-farm sector at its offices in order to identify, formulate and appraise schemes and conduct surveys for estimating industrial potential; (6) formulation of District Rural Industries Project; and (7) setting up of Agriculture and Rural Enterprises Incubation Fund.

Its Resources

The authorised capital of NABARD has been raised from Rs. 500 crores to Rs. 5,000 crores effective 1 February, 2001 with equal contributions by the RBI and Government of India. Besides share capital contribution, the RBI has been providing the NABARD a General Line of Credit (GLC) I and II to meet the short-term credit requirements of cooperatives and RRBs. Its other resources consist of National Rural Credit Funds, reserves and surplus, deposits and borrowings. In addition, the Union Government provides funds received from the World Bank Group, IFAD, EU and other countries. The aggregate resources mobilised by NABARD through various sources amounted to Rs. 5,786 crores during 2002-03.

Its Organisation

The NABARD is managed by a 15-member Board of Directors consisting of Chairman, Managing Director, two experts of rural economies, three experts from cooperative and commercial banks, three directors from the current directors of the RBI, three directors from the Government of India, and two directors representing the State Governments.

Achievements of NABARD

The NABARD is an apex institution in the organised rural credit structure. It plays an important role in reducing regional disparities and helps small farmers, marginal farmers and the weaker sections of the society. It channelises its refinance facilities for agricultural and rural development in the country through major financial intermediaries like SCBs, SLDBs, RRBs, commercial banks, etc.

1. *Short Term Credit.* During 2002-03, it sanctioned Rs. 8,764 crores as short term credit to SCBs and RRBs

for financing seasonal agricultural operations, marketing of crops, purchase and distribution of fertilisers, and working capital requirements of cooperative sugar factories.

2. *Medium Term Credit.* The NABARD sanctioned Rs. 496 crores in 2002-03 as medium term credit to SCBs and RRBs for approved agricultural purposes.

3. *Long Term Credit.* The NABARD provides long term loans not exceeding 20 years to State Governments to enable them to contribute to the share capital of the cooperative credit institutions. In 2002-03 it sanctioned Rs. 62 crores to State Governments for this purposes.

4. *Schematic Lending.* The NABARD provides refinance facilities relating to minor irrigation, land development, farm mechanisation, plantation, horticulture, poultry, sheep breeding, piggery, fisheries, dairy development, storage, market yards, IRDP, etc.

5. *Assistance to Non-Farm Sector.* The NABARD provides financial assistance to the non-farm sector. The ceiling on individual loans under Composite Loan Scheme is Rs. 50,000 and under Integrated Loan Scheme Rs. 7.5 lakhs to enable the financing banks to meet the credit requirements of entrepreneurs for setting up cottage, tiny, village and small scale industries. Further, State Cooperative Banks have been permitted to get refinance on an automatic basis from the NABARD through CCBs for financing industrial cooperative societies upto Rs. 7.5 lakhs. The Integrated Loan Scheme has also been extended to Land Development Banks for financing non-farm activities upto Rs. 7.5 lakhs. SCBs have been permitted to draw refinance on automatic basis for loans to industrial cooperative Societies for modernisation of existing units upto Rs. 7.5 lakhs. With the introduction of Swarnajayanti Gram Swarozgar Yojna from April 1999 in rural areas, the NABARD provides refinance to commercial banks for loans extended by them under the scheme. A wide spectrum of activities covering agricultural allied activities, industries, services and business that are bankable and viable are eligible for refinance.

6. *Other Types of Assistance.* The NABARD has started the following types of assistance recently:

(a) It undertakes on a modest scale cofinancing/direct financing of hi-tech and other special projects.

(b) Beginning 1995-96, it has started sanctioning a separate Short Term (Seasonal Agricultural Operations) Credit limit to each of the SCBs/RRBs operating in the 114 identified districts in the country.

(c) To step up credit flow to weaker sections including SCs/STs, the NABARD has earmarked a sum of Rs. 150 crores for refinance under the "SC/ST Action Plan" for allocation among commercial and cooperative banks. The level of refinance is 100 per cent.

7. *Institutional Development.* One of its important function is institutional development. In addition to inspection of cooperative banks and RRBs, it helps in their rehabilitation, reorganisation and re-establishment.

8. *Cooperative Development Fund (CDF).* NABARD set up CDF in 1993 for strengthening the cooperative credit institutions in the areas of organisational structure, human resource development, resource mobilisation, recovery position, etc. The assistance is provided to SCBs, CCBs, etc. by way of a grant or a soft loan or both. At the end of March 2003, cumulative loans sanctioned from CDF amounted to Rs.. 65 crores.

9. *Rural Infrastructure Development Fund (RIDF).* KIDF-I was set up in 1995-96 with a corpus of Rs. 2,000 crores for providing funds to State Governments and State owned corporations to enable them to complete various types of rural infrastructure projects. This scheme had been continued in subsequent years as RIDP-II with Rs. 2,500 crores in 1996-97, RIDF-III with Rs. 2,500 crores in 1997-98, RIDF-IV with Rs. 3,000 crores in 1998-99, RIDF-V with Rs. 3,500 crores in 1999-2000, RIDF-VI with Rs. 4,500 crores in 2000-01, RIDf-VII with Rs. 5,000 crores in 2001-02, RIDF-VIII with Rs. 5,500 crores in 2002-03 and RIDF-IX with Rs. 5,500 crores in 2003-04. The amount mobilised under various RIDF schemes amounted to Rs. 16,145 crores as at ending March 2002. The cumulative sanctions of loans under RIDF were Rs. 29,475 crores as at 31 March, 2003.

10. *Memorandum of Understandings (MOUs).* The NABARD signs MOUs with the' Cooperative banks and the concerned State Government for revamping and improving the cooperative credit structure. Similar MOUs exist between tthe RRBs and the sponsor banks.

11. *Research and Development.* It has been providing financial assistance for research and training to the staff of rural banking structure out of its R&D Fund and for strengthening the technical, monitoring, and evaluation cells of RRBs. Its three staff colleges, CAB, and Banker Rural Development Institute have been providing research and training facilities in rural credit and development to the staff of banks.

Despite its manifold achievements, NABARD has yet to become an apex regulator and development bank for farm lending.

VIEWS OF THE KHUSRO COMMITTEE

The ACRS or Khusro Committee in its Report published in January 1989 pointed out certain weaknesses and made suggestions to improve the working of NABARD. Some of these are as under:

1. NABARD's activities in institutional development are primarily reactive rather than proactive in nature. It should therefore undertake a more effective role in institutional development, particularly with regard to cooperative development. Its role should be one of policy planning and review, besides extension of necessary financial assistance.

2. The inspection function of NABARD is not integrated with refinancing and institutional development function. It should redefine the purpose and objectives of inspections to facilitate such integration.

3. The training of NABARD's staff should be separated from that of client banks.

4. R&D Fund should be used much more aggressively and imaginatively to identify, evaluate, develop and promote new and practical initiatives in rural development.

5. It has to find resources to meet its client banks' demand for investment loans which it will have to provide in an increasing measure in the next 10-12 years. If NABARD has to expand its operations, either its equity base should be strengthened or low cost borrowings should be resorted to at a concessional rate of 5.5 per ceni from GOI/RBI.

6. There is lack of control over NABARD's member institutions. It should be rectified with the help of and in coordination with RBI.

The Khusro Committee observed, "If NABARD has to emerge as a strong development bank of rural regeneration, it has to take certain fresh initiatives. It should concentrate more on building up of the cooperatives, improve its functional capabilities in project identification, preparation, appraisal, and monitoring, forge a better linkage between inspection and function, pay greater attention to-the non-farm sector and staff training and extend its network to the district level. NABARD will have to play its part in open market borrowing also, so that it could meet its refinance commitments."

CONCLUSION

The Government has not implemented the recommendations of the Khusro Committee, except raising the issued capital of the NABARD to Rs. 5,000 crores. Mere increasing its capital base is not enough. What is important is that it should be allowed to keep its surpluses which are to be transferred to the Central Government and the RBI after 1997.

EXERCISES

1. Describe the objectives and working of Regional Rural Banks.
2. Discuss the working of Regional Rural Banks. Critically examine their achievements.
3. To what extent Regional Rural Banks have achieved their objectives? Suggest measures to improve their operations.
4. Describe the objectives and achievements of NABARD.
5. Explain the functions of NABARD.
6. Discuss the achievements of NABARD. Give suggestions for making improvement in its working.

CHAPTER 74

Exchange Banks

1. FUNCTIONS OF EXCHANGE BANKS

Exchange banks perform the following functions in India:

1. *Financing Exports.* The exchange banks facilitate the payment of goods exported. This is done through Document Against Acceptance (D.A.) Bill which the Indian exporter draws against the importer. This bill is sent to the importer through the exchange bank. The importer returns it to the exporter after acceptance and the latter discounts it from his exchange bank.

2. *Financing Imports.* The exchange banks also facilitate the financing of imports. When an Indian importer imports goods, he receives through the exchange bank on the basis of the Document Against Payment (D.P.) Bill drawn by the foreign exporter.

3. *Financing Internal Trade.* The exchange banks finance the internal trade of the country. They finance the movement of goods from one commercial centre to another. They advance loans to traders and discount their bills of exchange.

4. *General Banking Functions.* The exchange banks perform general banking functions like Indian banks such as accepting deposits, advancing loans, agency services, credit remittance facility, locker facility, stock invest facility, card facility, etc.

5. *Encourage Foreign Investments.* The exchange banks encourage the flow of foreign investments into India. Foreign investors usually rely on their banker's judgement for overseas investment. Exchange banks are an important medium for projecting the country's image abroad. They provide Indian corporations access to foreign collaborators as well as introduce foreign companies to Indian corporations.

6. *Access to International Capital Markets.* The exchange banks help in providing Indian corporations and government agencies access to international capital markets.

7. *Develop Expertise and Innovations.* The exchange banks help in developing expertise and innovations in several areas such as trade, finance, payment systems, currency and interest rate risk management and financial engineering. To the extent these help in improving the efficiency of Indian banks, competitiveness improves.

8. *Mobilising Funds from Non-Resident Indians.* The exchange banks help in mobilising deposits from non-resident Indians (NRI) abroad through their network of branches located in foreign countries.

9. *Canalising Agent.* The exchange banks play the role of canalising agents for foreign currency credits for major projects. For example, Grindlays helped in arranging credits for the HBJ gas pipeline.

10. *Revival of Sick Industries.* The exchange banks help in the revival of Indian sick industries by putting their Indian clients in touch with NRIs who might be willing to invest in the equity of firms in question, and also facilitate the transfer of technology.

11. *Cover the Risks of Exchange Rate.* The exchange banks cover the risks of exchange rate movements by booking forward contracts.

12. *Some Innovative Schemes.* Some exchange banks in India have started a number of new schemes for their clients which are as follows:

(a) General Purpose Loan. Some exchange banks offer the Freedom Finance Scheme whereby the client can avail of loan facility from Rs. 10,000 to 50,000 for expenditure like a marriage, a holiday or even an admission to an institute for higher studies.

(b) Fixed Deposits. The exchange banks have introduced an innovation in fixed deposits which they call under different names to attract customers. The Citibank has Unfixed Deposit, the Grindlays has an Easy Access Deposit and a High Performance Saving Account, and the Hongkong Bank the Smart Money Account. These banks provide the facility of withdrawing up to 75 per cent of the deposit to a depositor while paying 2 per cent interest during the withdrawal period over the overall interest earned for the deposit period.

(c) *Global Banking Systems (GBS).* GBS is the Bank of America's standard computer system which operates worldwide in Europe, Asia and America. GBS enables the BOA to provide its customers speedy and efficient service throughout the world. Banking services like funds transfers or letters of credit involving any of its branches worldwide are automatically transmitted through BOA global network of telecommunication.

(d) Finance Against Securities in Time. The Standard Chartered Bank has started Finance Against Securities in Time (FAST) facility which provides loans to all individuals who have invested in shares and other securities.

(e) Non-Fund Business. The exchange banks undertake non-fund business on a fairly substantial scale. It includes letters of credit for imports, advising of letters of credit to exporters, execution of overseas contracts, syndication of international loans, and public flotation of equities and debentures.

(f) Mutual Funds and Technology Funds. Several exchange banks have opened divisions like mutual funds and technology funds which provide venture capital for new and existing companies to expand, modernise and diversify.

(g) Merchant Banking. They are engaged in merchant banking, equipment leasing, housing finance, car finance, venture capital, factoring, etc.

2. WORKING OF EXCHANGE BANKS OF INDIA

The number of exchange banks, better known as foreign banks, operating in India at present is 36. They have a network of 204 branches. Among the biggest foreign banks in India are: Citi Bank, ANZ Grindlays Bank, Standard Chartered Bank, Hong Kong Bank, American Express Bank, Bank of America, British Bank of Mideast, Bank of Tokyo, and Deutsche Bank.

For operating in India, every foreign bank is required to obtain a licence from the RBI. The licence is given with the condition that there should not be any discrimination against any Indian bank operating in that country to which the foreign bank belongs. A foreign bank is required to bring in $ 10 million for the first branch it sets up, $ 10 million for the second and $ 5 million for the third. It is also required to deposit with the RBI either in cash or in the form of unencumbered approved securities or both an amount equal to the amount specified above.

Every foreign bank operating in India is also required to deposit with the RBI at the end of each calendar year 20 per cent of its profits earned in India. Every foreign bank is further required to keep 12 per cent of the total of its time and demand liabilities with the RBI as CRR (Cash Reserve Ratio) which is interest free. In addition to the CRR, it is required to maintain in cash, gold or unencumbered securities, known as Statutory Liquidity Ratio (SLR) upto the level of its outstanding net demand and time liabilities equal to 25 per cent with effect from 13 April, 1996. Every foreign bank is required to maintain its assets equivalent to not less than 85 per cent of its demand and time liabilities in India at the close of business on the last Friday of every quarter.

Foreign banks operating in India are required to comply with the capital adequacy norm of 8 per cent from 1 April, 1993 which they have achieved.

The foreign banks operating in India are required to provide a minimum of 32 per cent of their net outstanding advances to the priority sector in India every year. It is inclusive of the sub-targets of 10 per cent each in respect of credit for exports and small scale industries, the shortfall, if any, in the overall target as well as sub-targets has to be made good by placing deposits with the Small Industries Development Bank of India (SIDBI) at a rate of 8 per cent with effect from March 1995.

For opening a new branch or to change the location of an existing branch, a foreign bank is required to take prior permission of the RBI. With effect from 22 April, 1992, they have been permitted to expand branches on considerations of national advantage from the viewpoint of facilitating exports and investment, with no change in other conditions.

They are also required to submit the various statements of their assets, liabilities, investments and advances, etc. to the RBI as per the RBI guidelines. Besides, the RBI is empowered to inspect their books and accounts whenever it deems essential from time to time.

The performance of 36 foreign banks in India during 2002-03 showed decrease in their income by 7.10 per cent over 2001-02, operating profits by 6.10 per cent, net profits by 22.25 per cent and total assets by 2.72 per cent.

The foreign banks have an edge over Indian banks in the spheres of customer service and technology back-up.[1]

3. DEFECTS IN THE WORKING OF EXCHANGE BANKS

Despite better and efficient working of exchange banks, these banks have certain defects in their working from the Indian viewpoint. These arise from the liberal attitude of the Reserve Bank of India towards them. Some of the defects are :

1. *Vast Funds in Non-Costing Deposits.* The exchange banks hold vast funds in their non-costing current accounts. They are able to invest out of them at prescribed rates of interest so that their margin of profits on these no-cost funds increases. In the case of nationalised banks the share of non-costing current Accounts in total deposits is IS per cent whereas in the case of exchange banks it is 21 per cent. Thus their deposits cost them less as compared to Indian banks. As a result, they earn more profits than Indian banks.

2. *Large Non-Fund Business.* The exchange banks undertake non-fund business on a fairly large scale. The combined average ratio of non-fund income of exchange banks is 13 per cent against 9.0 per cent in the case of nationalised banks, except the State Bank of India. Consequently, they are able to earn more profits than Indian banks. This is because of their monopolistic position in foreign business.

3. *Ignore Term Advances.* The exchange banks ignore such advances as term loans, hypothecation advances and other short term advances, But they engage themselves in bill business for very short periods of 30 to 90 days with the result that their current account funds increase. They are able to invest these funds for short periods in the inter-bank call, money market ancl earn interest

4. *Ignore Priority Sectors.* They are required to lend 32 per cent of net bank credit to priority sectors including 10 per cent for exports. But in 1999-2000, they lent 22.5 per cent for exports and 10.2 per cent to SSIs and ignored all other priority sectors.

5. *Operate Funds Management Schemes.* Due to the liberal policy of RBI, the exchange banks accept funds under the funds management schemes. These funds are not considered deposits. They are treated as non-statutory because the banks are not required to maintain the prescribed Cash Reserve Ratio (CRR) and Statutory Liquidity- Ratio (SLR) on these Funds. These banks are making a profit of about Rs. 200 crores annually from these funds.

6. *Discriminate against Indian Firms.* The exchange banks discriminate against Indian trading firms. They offer D.P. Bills to Indian importers whereby they are required to make full payment in order to get possession of goods. On the other hand, the Indian exporters are required to export goods against D.A. Bills whereby they receive deferred payments.

7. *Encourage Foreign Shipping and Insurance Companies.* These banks generally force Indian exporters and importers to get the services of foreign shipping and insurance companies. This goes against the interests of Indians.

8. *Unhealthy Competition with Indian Banks.* Due to their superior management techniques, larger funds and RBI's liberal policy towards them, the exchange banks have been able to provide better services and higher

---

1. We have not studied Indian banks operating abroad as Exchange banks as they operate as foreign banks in other countries. However, for the information of readers, there are 8 nationalised Indian banks and one private scheduled bank with 93 branches and 17 representative offices operating abroad in 25 countries.

interest rates to their customers. This has led to unhealthy competition with Indian banks. As a result, their profits have been rising at a much higher rate than those of Indian banks.

9. *Foreign Links.* The exchange banks being foreign banks have links in foreign countries where they have their head offices. Their directors, shareholders and management are entirely foreign. So their main interest is to earn higher profits, part of which are taken away.

10. *Hindrance to Bill Market.* They are a hindrance to the development of Indian Bill Market because they discount the export bills in London Bill Market while the import bills are fully paid before the delivery of goods.

11. *Help Transfer Illegal Money.* The exchange banks help transfer the i! illegal money kept abroad into Foreign Currency Non-Resident (FCNR) deposits of their branches. Thus they encourage black money within the country.

4. SUGGESTIONS FOR IMPROVEMENT

A number of suggestions have been made to improve the working of exchange banks in India so that they may be more helpful to the economy. Some of the suggestions are:

1. *No Preferential Treatment.* The exchange banks operating in India should be treated at par with Indian commercial banks.

2. *Restriction on Branch Expansion.* RBI should not allow exchange banks to open more branches in the country so that their activities are confined to port cities and big commercial centres. RBI has done well in asking the exchange banks to bring in an initial capital of Rs. 15 crore in foreign exchange to open a branch.

3. *Restriction on Non-Costing Deposits.* The exchange banks encourage the opening of current accounts by multinational corporations and big industrial houses because they bring them more profits without payinp interest. They do not welcome small depositors. RBI should direct them to accept small saving deposits and place a limit on non-costing deposits.

4. *Restriction on Funds Management Schemes.* The exchange banks are earning huge profits by accepting money under the funds management schemes which are not considered deposits. RBI should place restrictions on such schemes by asking these banks to maintain the prescribed Cash Reserve Ratio and the Statutory Liquidity Ratio on these funds as applicable to Indian banks.

5. *Regulation of Lending Activities.* The exchange banks are allowed to undertake lending, advancing and investment activities without much restriction. RBI should regulate such activities. They should be directed to give more advances for long term and invest in Indian companies rather in multinationals operating in India.

6. *Participate in Social Banking.* The exchange banks participate less in social banking. RBI should direct them to lend more to small scale industry sector, retail trade, self-employed persons, etc.

7. *Limit on Repatriation of Profits.* As exchange banks in Indian earn huge profits, they also repatriate huge sums to their head offices abroad, even after keeping 20 per cent of their annual profits with RBI. Recently, RBI has asked these banks to keep another 20 per cent of their profits in the Indian books. This is not enough. They should be asked to keep at least 50 per cent of their profits in India.

8. *Removal of Discrimination against Indian Importers.* The exchange banks should remove discrimination against Indian importers by offering them D.A. Bills, as is the practice in advanced countries.

9. *Indians in Management.* All exchange banks operating in India should be directed to have at least one Indian on the Management working in India.

10. *No Mergers.* The exchange banks operating in India should not be allowed to merge their branches without the permission of the Reserve Bank.

11. *No Control over Indian Banks.* The exchange banks should not be allowed to have any type of direct or indirect control over Indian banks. They should not be permitted to acquire the shares of Indian banks.

12. *No Association.* The exchange banks operating in India should not be allowed to form any association without the permission of RBI.

5. PARTICIPATION OF INDIAN BANKS IN FINANCING FOREIGN TRADE

There were 93 branches, including off-share branches and mobile agencies of 8 public sector banks and one Indian private sector bank, operating in foreign countries as on September 2002. These branches are spread over 25 countries and located in major international centres like London, New York, etc. They specialise in various areas of international banking including financing of foreign trade. Besides these branches, they are having 17 representative offices and also 15 wholly owned subsidiaries and 5 joint ventures in various countries of the world.

The commercial banks help in receiving payments from the overseas importers and to make payments to overseas exporters. But Indian banks mostly finance export trade. They meet the credit needs of the exporters both at the preshiptnent and post-shipment stages. The exporter requires pre-shipment credit in order to manufacture or assemble the goods meant for export. The exporter can also obtain pre-shipment finance from his bank in two ways: *(i)* By asking the overseas buyer to open in his favour an anticipatory letter of credit; and *(ii)* By applying for an export packing credit to his bank. It is granted by the bank against goods earmarked for export by lodging the letter of credit covering the export order to the bank.

The commercial banks in India also grant medium term advances ranging trom 6 months to 5 years against the deferred instalments receivable from importers. The exporter furnishes to his bank the promissory note executed by him or a guarantee from the importer's bank covering the deferred payment receivable.

In November 1992, all scheduled commercial banks were asked to reach an export credit target of 10 per cent of each bank's net bank credit by June 1993. The RBI stated that failure to achieve the stipulated target of export credit and/or failure to achieve this would invite raising of reserve requirements and withdrawal of refinance facilities. In April 1993, the rediscounting of export bills abroad was allowed at rates linked to international rates. The RBI also fixes interest rate structure for advances of scheduled commercial banks for exports. It is for pre-shipment credit, post-shipment credit, usance bills and deferred credit for the period beyond 180 days. The interest rates usually range between 13 to 15 per cent. Besides, the RBI provides export credit rupee refinance to scheduled commercial banks to the extent of 60 per cent of increase in outstanding export credit. The refinance facility provided against post-shipment export credit in US dollars is equivalent to 100 per cent of outstanding credit.

Prior to 1982, the refinance, facility for financing foreign trade was being provided by the Reserve Bank. But with the establishment of the Export-Import (Exim) Bank of India on 1 January, 1982, the refinance business has also been entrusted to this Bank. The main objective of the bank is to provide financial assistance to exporters and importers, and to function as the principal financial institution for coordinating the working of institutions engaged in financing export and import of goods and services with a view to promoting the country's international trade. Thus the Exim bank extends direct and indirect financial assistance in the short, medium and long-term for the promotion of international trade, and acts as an apex body for coordinating the activities of institutions engaged in similar business. The Exim Bank is empowered for the purpose of export and import to extend loans and advances to banks or financial institutions, to provide refinance facilities, render international merchant banking services, extend buyer's credit and lines of credit to parties, including foreign governments and financial institutions, outside India, finance Indian joint ventures abroad, deal in foreign exchange, and undertake and finance technical consultancy services.

Presently, the Exim Bank refinances only the export trade of India and the financing of imports has been left entirely to foreign banks, the ICICI (Industrial Credit and Investment Corporation of India), the World Bank, etc. The short term requirements of exporters are largely met by the commercial banks. The Exim Bank concentrates mainly on medium and long term credit for export of goods and services on deferred terms. It offers credit on liberal terms to enable Indian exporters to compete in international markets. It extends financial assistance to foreign buyers for the purchase of Indian goods. It also gives financial assistance to Indian promoters towards their equity participation in joint ventures abroad.

Thus, the participation of Indian banks in financing foreign trade is limited only to exports and the financing of imports is done by exchange banks, the ICICI, the World Bank, etc.

EXERCISES

1. Explain the functions of exchange banks.
2. In what ways the exchange banks are harmful to Indian interest? What measures do you suggest to remove these defects?
3. To what extent Indian banks participate in financing India's foreign trade?
4. Write a note on the participation of Indian banks in financing foreign trade of India.

CHAPTER 75

Commercial Bank in India

The joint stock banks in India are the most important segment of the Indian banking system. They are the major source of institutional credit in India. They are commercial banks registered under the Indian Companies Act, 1936 and are also governed by the Indian Banking Regulation Act, 1949.

1. CLASSIFICATION OF COMMERCIAL BANKS

Indian joint stock banks or commercial banks are classified on statutory and ownership basis.

On the statutory basis, they are further classified into scheduled banks and non-scheduled banks.

A *scheduled bank* is one which has been included in the second schedule of the Reserve Bank of India Act, 1934. To be a scheduled bank, it must be financially and economically sound and satisfy the following three conditions: (i) it must have a paid-up capital and reserves of an aggregate value of not less than Rs 5 lakhs; (ii) its affairs are not being or likely to be conducted in a manner detrimental to the interests of its depositors; (iii) it must be a joint stock company and not a sole trader or partnership firm. Besides, it is required to keep a certain percentage of its cash reserves with the RBI and submit periodical returns to the latter under the Banking Regulation Act, 1949. In return, the scheduled bank receives concessional remittance and borrowing facilities from the RBI or its agents.

On the other hand, a non-scheduled bank is that which has not been included in the second schedule of the RBI Act, 1934. But is subject to the statutory cash reserve requirements which it is required to keep with itself and not with the RBI. It is not entitled to concessional remittance and borrowing facilities from the RBI. There were 95 scheduled commercial banks in India having 5 1.970 branches as on 30 June 2003. Of these, 8 were State Bank of India and its associate banks with 13.499 branches: 19 nationalised banks with 32,643 branches; 32 Indian private sector banks (23 old + 9 new) with 5.624 branches; and 36 foreign banks with 204 branches. There are also 196 Regional Rural Bank which are sponsored by scheduled commercial banks But they are considered as rural banks even though they perform as commercial banks also. There is no non-scheduled bank in India.

On the *basis of ownership*, banks are classified into public sector banks and private sector banks. A public sector bank is a Government of India undertaking and a private sector bank is owned by the shareholders. Both types of banks perform the same functions, pay and charge the same rates of interest, and also pay the same salary and allowances to their staff, except the non-scheduled banks. The first public sector bank was established in India on 1 July, 1955 with the nationalisation of Imperial Bank of India as State Bank of India. It had seven subsidiaries which were nationalised in 1959. These seven associate banks are State Bank of Hyderabad, State Bank of Jaipur and Bikaner, State Bank of Travancore, State Bank of Mysore, State Bank of Patiala, State Bank of Indore, and State Bank of Saurashtra.

On 19 July 1969, fourteen major scheduled banks were nationalised. They are: Allahabad Bank, Bank of Baroda, Bank of India, Bank of Maharashtra, Canara Bank, Central Bank of India, Dena Bank, Indian Bank, Indian Overseas Bank, Punjab National Bank, Syndicate Bank, Union Bank of India, United Bank of India, and United Commercial Bank. Six more scheduled banks were nationalised on 15 April 1980. They are Andhra Bank, Corporation Bank, New Bank of India, Oriental Bank of Commerce, Punjab and Sind Bank and Vijaya Bank. New Bank of India was merged with Punjab National Bank with effect from 4 September 1993.

The regional rural banks which have been sponsored by the nationalised banks are also public sector banks which at present number 196. Thus the total public sector banks in India are 223 comprising State Bank of India and its 7 subsidiaries, 19 nationalised banks and 196 regional rural banks.

2. FUNCTIONS OF INDIAN COMMERCIAL BANKS

The Indian joint stock banks are in fact commercial banks which perform a number of functions and render a variety of ancillary services. The Banking Regulation Act, 1949 lists them as under:

(1) the borrowing, raising or taking of deposits of money;

(2) the lending or advancing of money either with or without security;

(3) the drawing, making, accepting, discounting, buying, selling, collecting and dealing with bills of exchange, hundis, promissory notes, coupons, drafts, bills of lading, railway receipts, warrants, debentures, certificates, scrips and other securities whether transferable or negotiable or not;

(4) the granting and issuing of letters of credit, travellers' cheques and circular notes;

(5) the buying, selling and dealing in bullion and species;

(6) the buying and selling of foreign exchange, including foreign bank notes;

(7) the acquiring, holding, issuing on commission, underwriting and dealing in stocks, funds, shares, debentures, stock, bonds, obligations, securities and investments of all kinds;

(8) the purchasing and selling of bonds, scrips or other forms of securities on behalf of constituents or others;

(9) the negotiation of loans and advances;

(10) the receiving of all kinds of bonds, scrips or valuables on deposit or for safe custody or otherwise;

(11) the providing of safe deposit vaults for custody of valuables of customers;

(12) the collecting and transmitting of money and securities;

(13) the acting of agents for any government or local authority or any other person or persons, but not as managing agent or secretary and treasury of a company;

(14) the contracting of private and public loans and negotiating and issuing them;

(15) the insuring, guaranteeing, underwriting, participating in managing and carrying out of any issue of loans or securities made by state, municipality, company, corporation or any other association, and also lending for the purpose;

(16) the carrying on and transacting every kind of guarantee and indemnity business;

(17) the managing, selling and realising any property which may come into its possession in satisfaction of its claims;

(18) the acquiring, holding and dealing with any property or any right, title or interest therein which forms the security for any loans or advances sanctioned;

(19) the undertaking and executing of trusts, as also administering estates as executor, trustee or otherwise;

(20) the establishing and supporting or aiding in the establishment of associations, institutions, funds, trusts and conveniences for the benefit of its present and past employees and their dependents, and granting or guaranteeing moneys for charitable purposes;

(21) the acquiring, constructing, maintaining and altering of any building or works necessary for its purposes;

(22) the selling, improving, managing, developing, exchanging, leasing, mortgaging, disposing of or otherwise dealing with any of its properties and rights;

(23) the taking over and undertaking the whole or any part of the business of any person or company

when such business is of a nature described above;

(24) the doing of all such other things as are incidental or conducive to the promotion and advancement of its business, such as giving an opinion as to its customer's financial standing as a referee; and

(25) the engaging in any other form of business which the Central Government specifies to be lawful.

Besides, the Indian joint stock banks have started performing a number of other functions in recent years, such as issuing credit cards, setting of mutual funds, engaging in merchant banking, giving advances to priority sectors like agriculture, small scale industries, retail trade, small business, professional and self-employed persons, consumption loans, education loans, housing loans, etc.[1]

3. WORKING RESULTS OF SCHEDULED COMMERCIAL BANKS

The total deposits of scheduled commercial banks accounted for 79.8 per cent of their total liabilities and their loans and advances 43.6 per cent of their total assets as on 31 March 2003. The total income of 95 scheduled commercial banks was 10.1 per cent, total expenditure 9.1 per cent, operating profit 2.4 per cent and net profit 1.0 per cent of their total assets in 2002-03. The credit-deposit ratio of these banks was 59.4 per cent, cash balance-deposit ratio 6.35 per cent and investment-deposit ratio 51.17 per cent during this year. The ratio of net non-performing assets (NPAs) to net advances was 4.4 per cent and the total assets 1.9. per cent as on 31 March 2003.

EXERCISES

1. Give the classification of Joint Stock Banks in India.
2. Distinguish between a scheduled bank and non-scheduled bank
3. Describe the functions of Indian scheduled commercial banks.
4. Describe the working of scheduled commercial banks in India. Point out their defects.

1. For their defects, refer to section 5 of the Chapter "Recent Trends in the Indian Banking System".

CHAPTER 76

Banking Legislation in India

Banks deal with the money of a large number of depositors who do not have any say in their working. Banking legislation is enacted to safeguard the interest of the depositors and the shareholders of banks.

The first attempt at banking legislation in India was the passing of the Indian Companies (Amendment) Act, 1936 which contained special provisions relating to banking companies. Prior to that they were governed by the general provisions of the Indian Companies Act, 1913. The Indian Companies (Amendment) Act, 1936 was subsequently amended in 1942 to incorporate a few more provisions concerning banks. But the years following this amendment led to a mushroom growth of banking companies in India which ultimately led the Government alter Independence to pass a comprehensive law exclusively for their regulation and control under the name of Banking Companies Act, 1949 which was renamed as the Banking Regulation Act, 1949.

This Act has been amended a number of times to suit the needs of changing circumstances and to plug the loopholes found in its provisions. Its two important amendments have been: (1) the Banking Companies (Acquisition and Transfer of Undertakings) Act, 1970 whereby the Government nationalised 14 banks, and the Banking Companies (Acquisition and Transfer of Undertakings) Act, 1980 nationalising 6 more scheduled banks; and (2) the Banking Laws (Amendment) Act, 1983 which amended the following banking legislation: Bankers' Book Evidence Act, 1891; Reserve Bank of India Act, 1934; Banking Regulation Act, 1949; State Bank of India Act, 1955; State Bank of India (Subsidiary Banks) Act, 1959; Deposit Insurance and Credit Guarantee Corporation Act, 1961; Banking Companies (Acquisition and Transfer of Undertakings) Act, 1970; Regional Rural Banks Act, 1976; Banking Companies (Transfer and Acquisition of Undertakings) Act, 1980; and Banking Companies (Acquisition and Transfer of Undertakings) Amendment Act, 1994.

Another important banking legislation has been the Banking Laws (Application to Cooperative Societies) Act, 1966 which brought the cooperative societies under the RBI's statutory control by including the State Cooperative Banks in the Second Schedule of the RBI.

1. BANKING REGULATION ACT, 1949

The Banking Regulation Act, 1949 as amended up-to-date contains the following five parts:

Part I: Preliminary (Sections 1 to 5A).

Part II: Business of Banking Companies (Sections 6 to 36A).

Part IIA: Control and Management (Sections 6 to 36A).

Part IIB: Prohibition of Certain Activities in Relation to Banking Companies (Section 36AD).

Part IIC: Acquisition of the Undertakings of Banking Companies in Certain Cases (Sections 36AE to 36AJ).

Part III: Suspension of Business and Winding up of Banking Companies (Sections 36 to 45).

Part IIIA: Special Provision of Speedy Disposal of Winding up Proceedings (Sections 45A to 45X).

Part IIIB: Provisions relating to Certain Operations of Banking Companies (Sections 45Y to 45ZF).

Part IV: Miscellaneous (Sections 46 to 55).

Part V: Main Provisions as Applicable to Cooperative Banks (Section 56).

The above details reveal that the Act contains 56 sections, Parts I, II, IIA, IIB, and IIIB are important because they relate to a banking company as a going concern. The last Section 56 relates to cooperative banks.

We give below some of the important provisions of the Act.

1. *Definition of a Banking Company.* The Act defines the term 'Banking' as "accepting, for the purpose of lending or investment, of deposits of money from the public, repayable on demand or otherwise, and withdrawable by cheque, draft, order, or otherwise". It also defines a banking company as "any company which transacts the business of banking in India". As such, it performs the functions of accepting deposits and lending or investing the same.

2. *Minimum Capital Requirements.* The Act prescribes minimum capital requirement for banking companies. A banking company incorporated *outside* India (i.e. foreign bank) is required to have its paid-up capital and reserves of the aggregate value of not less than Rs. 15 lakhs, but if it has a place or places of business in the city of Mumbai or Kolkata, or both, Rs. 20 lakhs. It is also required to deposit with the RBI either in cash or in the form of unencumbered approved securities or both an amount equal to the minimum capital specified above (i.e. Rs. 15 lakhs or Rs. 20 lakhs). The Act also requires a foreign banking company to deposit with the RBI at the end of each calendar year 20 per cent of its profit earned in India. On the other hand, a banking company incorporated within India is required to have paid-up capital and reserves of an aggregate value of not less than Rs. 5 lakh. If it has business in more than one State, and if any such place is situated in the city of Bombay, or Calcutta, or both, Rs. 10 lakhs. The subscribed capital of a banking company should not be less than *one half* of its authorised capital, and the paid-up capital should not be less than *one half of* the subscribed capital.

3. *Reserve Fund.* Every banking company incorporated *within* India is required to create a Reserve Fund and to transfer to such Fund, before any dividend is declared, 20 per cent of its profit.

4. *Cash Reserve.* Every scheduled bank is required to keep 3 per cent of the total of its time and demand liabilities with the RBI as cash reserve which is interest-free. But a non-scheduled bank is permitted to maintain its cash reserve either (i) with itself; or (ii) in current account opened with the RBI or the State Bank of India, or any other bank notified by the Central Government for the purpose; or *(iii)* partly in cash with itself or partly in such account or accounts. The cash reserve ratio (CRR) can be raised up to 15 per cent. The CRR is 15 per cent with effect from 1 July, 1989.

5. *Maintenance of Liquid Assets.* Maintenance of adequate liquid assets is essential for sound banking. The Act requires every bank to maintain in cash, gold or unencumbered approved securities not less than 25 per cent of the total of its demand and time liabilities in India. The RBI is empowered to step up the Statutory Liquidity Ratio (SLR) to 40 per cent. Since 4 April, 1992, the SLR has been fixed at 30 per cent. The SLR is in addition to the CRR which a bank is required to maintain with the RBI.

6. *Maintenance of Assets in India.* Every bank is required to maintain its assets equivalent to not less than 75 per cent of its demand and time liabilities in India at the close of business on the last Friday of every quarter.

7. *Management of Banking Companies.* The Act has also tried to tone up the administration and management of banks. It lays down that no banking company can employ or be managed by a managing agent, or any person who has been declared an insolvent, or has been convicted by a criminal court of an offence involving moral turpitude, or who takes a commission or a share in the profits of the company, or is a director of any other company, or engaged in any other business or vocation, or has a contract with the company for a period exceeding five years at a time, or whose remuneration is excessive in the opinion of the RBI.

8. *Prohibitions and Restrictions on Banking Companies.* To safeguard the interests of depositors, the Act provides for a number of prohibitions and restrictions on the banking companies. They are as under:

(*i*) The Act prohibits a banking company from engaging directly or indirectly in trading activities and undertaking trade risks.

(ii) It prohibits a banking company from holding any immovable property, howsoever acquired, except for its own use, for a period exceeding 7 years from its acquisition.

(iii) A banking company cannot form any subsidiary company.

(iv) It cannot hold shares in any company exceeding 30 per cent of the paid-up share capital of that company, or its own capital and reserves, whichever is less.

(v) It cannot grant any loan or advance on the security of its own shares, or on behalf of or to any of its directors, any firm in which any of its directors is interested as partner, manager, employee or guarantor, or any company in which any of its directors has substantial interest of any kind, or to any individual, in whom any of its directors is a partner or guarantor.

(vi) A banking company cannot create a charge upon its unpaid capital. It cannot create a floating charge on the company or any of its property or any of its parts unless the RBI certifies that the creation of such floating charge shall not be detrimental to the interests of its depositors.

(vii) A banking company is prohibited from payment of dividend until all its capitalised expenses have been completely written off.

(viii) A director of a banking company, other than the chairman or the whole time director, cannot be continued for more than eight years.

(ix) The Act prohibits violent demonstrations by bank employees or by others within the premises of a banking company.

9. *Powers of the Reserve Bank of India.* The Act confers wide powers on the RBI to control and regulate the working of banking companies. Some of these are as under:

(i) No banking company can operate in India without getting a licence from the RBI. The Reserve Bank issues a licence, if it is satisfied that the banking company is or will be in a position to pay its present or future depositors in full; that its operations are not detrimental to the interests of its depositors; that it has adequate capital structure and earning prospect; that public interest will be served by it; and that it would not be prejudicial to the operation and consolidation of the banking system. If the banking company is incorporated *outside* India, then an additional condition for the grant of licence is that there should not be any discrimination against Indian banking companies operating in that country to which the foreign bank belongs.

(ii) The Act requires every banking company, Indian as well as foreign, to take prior permission of the RBI for opening a new branch or to change the location of an existing branch in India.

(iii) Every banking company is required to submit the following return/statements: monthly return of liquid assets and liabilities; quarterly return of assets and liabilities; return of unclaimed deposits; and half-yearly returns regarding the investments of a banking company and the classification of its advances in respect of industry, commerce, and agriculture.

(iv) The RBI is empowered to inspect any banking company and its books and accounts.

(v) The Act confers powers on the RBI to issue directions from time to time to banking companies generally or to any banking company in particular in the public interest or in the interest of banking policy or in the interest of depositors, or to secure the proper management of any banking company.

(vi) The RBI has been given wide powers to issue directions to the banking companies to control advances. The directions may relate to: *(a)* the purpose for which advances may or may not be made; *(b)* the margins to be maintained in respect of secured advances; *(c)* the maximum amount of advance to any one company, firm, individual, or association of persons; *(d)* the maximum amount up to which guarantees may be given by the banking company on behalf of any one company, firm etc., and *(e)* the rate of interest and other terms and conditions on which advances or guarantees may be given.

(vii) No bank can remit, without the prior approval of the RBI any debt due to it by any of its directors, or by any firm, company or individual in which any of its directors may be interested.

(viii) It is empowered to inspect a bank thoroughly and without previous notice and to order the bank to rectify actions which it considers unsound, unsafe of antisocial.

(ix) Every bank has to obtain the prior consent of the RBI for all advances of Rs.. 5 crores and over to any one borrower.

(x) The Act requires every banking company to take prior approval of the RBI for the appointment, reappointment or termination of chairman, managing or wholetime director, manager or chief executive

officer.

(xi) It empowers the RBI to appoint one or more additional directors of a banking company but not exceeding 5 or one-third of the maximum strength of the Board of Directors, whichever is less.

(xii) The RBI is empowered to acquire the undertaking of any banking company, or to approve its merger with any other bank.

(xiii) The RBI is authorised to publish any information relating to banking companies in such consolidated form as it thinks fit, and as such brings out many reports and brochures relating to the trend and progress of banking in India.

Conclusion

The Banking Regulation Act, 1949 as amended up-to-date is a very comprehensive piece of legislation which has played an important role in establishing the banking system on sound lines throughout the country and providing stability and flexibility to the Indian monetary system in keeping with the overall objective of growth and stability.

2. BANKING AMENDMENT ACT, 1994

The Banking Companies (Acquisition and Transfer of Undertakings) Amendment Act, 1994 amends the Banking Companies Acts of 1970 and 1980 whereby 14 and 6 scheduled commercial banks were nationalised respectively. The present Act provides for partial privatisation of these banks which are 19 at present with the merger of New Bank of India with the Punjab National Bank in 1993. The main features of the amendments are:

(1) The authorised capital of every nationalised bank has been set at Rs. 1,500 crores divided into Rs. 150 crores fully paid up shares of Rs. 10 each.

(2) The Centre may, after consultation with the RBI and by notification in t:ie official gazette, increase or reduce the authorised capital subject of the condition that the authorised capital shall not exceed Rs. 3,000 crores or be less than Rs. 1,500 crores.

(3) The Central Government shall retain 51 per cent of the share in these banks and private individuals and companies, including NRIs shall hold upto 49 per cent of their shares.[1]

(4) However, the holdings of NRIs, including companies not registered in India, shall not be more than 20 per cent of the 49 per cent private shares.

(5) The shares not held by the Central Government shall be freely transferable.

(6) No shareholder other than the Union Government shall be entitled to exercise voting rights in respect of any shares held by them in excess of one per cent of the total voting rights of all shareholders of the bank.

(7) Each bank shall have 15 Directors on the Board, out of which 9 shall be nominated by the Central Government, and the other six shall be non-official nominees. There shall be one Director from among the workmen of the bank and one from other employees.'

(8) Every bank shall ensure that its total capital equals at least 8 per cent of its risk weighted assets by 31 March, 1996.

EXERCISES

1. Explain the provisions of the Banking Regulation Act, 1949.
2. Discuss the main powers of the Reserve Bank of India under the Banking Regulation Act, 1949.
3. Discuss the main,provisions of the Banking Regulation Act, 1949 with regard to: (i) Requirement as to minimum paid-up Capital and Reserve, *(ii)* Restrictions on Loans and Advances, *(iii)* Cash and Liquid Asset Reserves.
4. Write a note on Banking Companies (Acquisition and Transfer) Amendment Act of 1994.

---

1. By an amendment to the 1994 Act in 2000 the Government has reduced its minimum shareholding in nationalised banks from 51 to 33 per cent.

Chapter 77

Nationalisation of Commercial Banks

1. INTRODUCTION

Prior to 1949, commercial banks in India were exclusively owned, controlled and managed by private entrepreneurs and shareholders. The process of nationalisation of banks began when the Reserve Bank of India was nationalised on 1 January, 1949 with the passing of the Reserve Bank (Transfer of Public Ownership) Act, 1948. It was essential to nationalise the RBI as the central bank of the country in order to ensure greater coordination of monetary, economic and fiscal policies in independent India which was to embark itself on the path to planned economic development.

But the first step towards the nationalisation of commercial banks was taken with the nationalisation of the Imperial Bank of India as the State Bank of India on 1 July, 1955. The second step was taken when 7 State-associated banks were nationalised as subsidiaries of the State Bank of India in 1959. These seven associate banks are: the State Bank of Hyderabad, the State Bank of Jaipur and Bikaner, the State Bank of Travancore, the State Bank of Mysore, the State Bank of Patiala, the State Bank of Indore, and the State Bank of Saurashtra.

The third major step was the nationalisation of 14 major commercial banks with deposits exceeding Rs. 50 crores each on 19 July 1969. They are: Allahabad Bank, Bank of Baroda, Bank of India, Bank of Maharashtra, Canara Bank, Central Bank of India, Dena Bank, Indian Bank, Indian Overseas Bank, Punjab National Bank, Syndicate Bank, Union Bank of India, United Bank of India, and United Commercial Bank.

The last step was the nationalisation of 6 more commercial banks on 15 April 1980. They were: Andhra Bank, Corporation Bank, New Bank of India, Oriental Bank of Commerce, Punjab and Sind Bank, and Vijaya Bank. At the time of nationalisation, each one of these had crossed the deposit mark of Rs. 200 crores, though at the time of nationalisation of 14 banks their individual deposits were below Rs. 50 crores.

In June 1996, there were 19 nationalised banks, New Bank of India was merged with Punjab National Bank in 1993.

We discuss below the justification, objectives, achievements and failures of nationalisation of commercial banks in India. As nationalisation of major commercial banks is an established fact now, the case against nationalisation is uncalled for and hence of purely academic interest.

2. JUSTIFICATION FOR NATIONALISATION OF COMMERCIAL BANKS

The nationalisation of the commercial banks in India was a very controversial issue till the nationalisation of 14 major banks in July, 1969. A number of arguments were advanced by economists, political leaders, bankers, workers, and the public in support of nationalisation of banks which are enumerated below:

1. *Neglect of Priority Sectors.* A major charge against banks in India was that they advanced loans to large scale industries, and neglected the priority sectors such as agriculture, small scale industries, etc. The banks advanced 60% of the total bank credit to big industries and 19% to trade in March 1968. On the other hand, the share of agriculture was 2.2%, of small industries 6.9%, and of retail trade less than 2% in the total bank credit. It would be possible to direct bank credit on a large scale through bank nationalisation.

2. *Neglect of Plan Priorities.* Another charge was that commercial banks neglected plan priorities and diverted credit into less important channels. Bank nationalisation would help the Government in directing bank credit in accordance with plan priorities.

3. *High Profits.* It was alleged, that banks earned huge profits which were disproportionate to the capital invested in the banks. The ratio of profits of scheduled banks before tax to the paid-up capital and reserve increased from 12.2% to 42.5% in 1968. In other words, they earned Rs. 42.5 crores annually. On the other hand, their capital base was declining. The ratio of paid-up capital and reserves to deposits fell from 9.7% in 1951 to 2.6% in 1968. This was in contravention of RBI's directives to banks to keep at least 6% of their deposit liabilities in reserve. Whereas the banks earned huge profits and used them for their interests, the shareholders earned almost nothing because they had hardly more than 1% of deposits as share capital. This was one of the arguments advanced by the Government for bank nationalisation.

4. *Funds for Plans.* By nationalising the banks, these huge profits of the banks would be available to the Government for financing plans and achieving the plan objectives.

5. *Concentration of Economic Power.* It was alleged that commercial banks had led to the concentration of wealth and economic power in the hands of a few big business houses and industrialists. For instance, the Central Bank of India Ltd. was being controlled by the Tatas, the Bank of India Ltd. by the Mafatlals, the Punjab National Bank Ltd. by the Dalmias, the United Commercial Bank Ltd. by the Birlas, etc. These big business houses, in turn, controlled a number of industries, thereby enjoying a virtual monopoly in their business.

Moreover, about 90% members of the Board of Directors of banks consisted of industrialists and big businessmen. A single director of a bank was a common director of many other industrial concerns and with his control over the bank he was able to turn the bank for the benefit of his industrial house. This interlocking of directorship in banks led to unusually high amount of credit to big business houses. Bank nationalisation was, therefore, essential to stop the misuse of the resources of the banks for the benefit of directors and their concerns, and to reduce the concentration of economic power and wealth in a few hands.

6. *Socialist Arguments.* It was argued that bank nationalisation,was essential for the attainment of a socialist society in India. Such a step would not only reduce concentration of economic power and wealth but also give the State, control over the resources of the banks to be utilised for the masses.

7. *Regional Imbalances.* It was alleged that commercial banks were increasing regional imbalances. Banking was concentrated in big cities, urban centres and a few States. The Gadgil Study Group of the National Credit Council (1969) vividly brought out the imbalances in banking in the country. It pointed out that till December 1967, out of 5,64,000 villages in India, not even 1% were served by commercial banks. In 13 districts of the country, there was not a single commercial bank office. More than 600 towns did not have commercial banking facilities. There were 63 districts in which per capita credit was less than one rupee, in another 13 districts, credit was not extended even to a single individual, although deposits were mobilised from there. The two metropolitan cities of Mumbai and Kolkata accounted for one-third of total deposits and one-half of total credit disbursed by banks. The ratio of credit to deposits was more than 100% in the metropolitan cities, which means that deposits mobilised in smaller centres were diverted to these cities for financing the activities of big business. It was argued that bank nationalisation would remove these imbalances, ensure even distribution of banking facilities, and spread banking to rural unbanked and under-banked areas.

8. *Ignored RBI Directives.* Big banks with strong financial background often ign6red the Reserve Bank's directives under the Banking Regulation Act, 1949. This, in turn, adversely affected the RBI's monetary policy. By nationalising such banks, the RBI would be in an advantageous position to implement its monetary policy more effectively.

9. *Protection to Depositors.* It was argued that bank nationalisation would remove the fear of bank failures from the mind of public, thereby protecting the interests of depositors. This, in turn, would inculcate banking habits among the people, especially in the rural non-monetised sector of the economy.

10. *Check of Undesirable Activities.* The commercial banks often indulged in anti-social and undesirable activities. They advanced credit for such activities which encouraged speculation, profiteering, black marketing, etc. which led to accumulation of black money in bank accounts. All such activities would be stopped when banks were nationalised.

11. *Encouraged Inflation.* It was alleged that commercial banks encouraged inflation by increasing the supply of money without due regard to the directives of the RBI. Banks often used their resources to the discretion of their directors for their own interest and that of their business friends. So, they did not follow the guidelines issued by the RBI for credit restriction. This led to inflation. Thus nationalisation of banks was considered to be the only remedy.

12. *Increase in Efficiency.* It was argued that bank nationalisation would improve the efficiency of banks and the quality of service to the customers because the employees would have a greater sense of security. The efficiency of banks would also increase due to the standardisation of banking operations throughout the country.

13. *Better Management.* With the nationalisation of banks, the Government would be in a position to develop and provide adequate training and modern managerial techniques to the staff. This would lead to greater efficiency in bank operations.

14. *Better Service Conditions.* It was hoped that bank nationalisation would provide better service conditions for the employees. They would have the satisfaction of being Government employees. This would also improve employer-employee relations and pave the way for a smooth working of the banking system in the country.

15. *Success in Other Countries.* The protagonists of bank nationalisation argued that in a number of developed and developing countries where commercial banking was in the hands of State, it had been highly successful in helping the masses and mobilising resources for development. For example, 90% of commercial banking was in the public sector in Italy, 80% in France and 70% in Germany. Among the developing countries, Egypt, Myanmar, Indonesia, and Srilanka had been successfully operating nationalised banks.

Conclusion

Out of the above only a few arguments seemed to have weighed with the Government in nationalising 14 major commercial banks on 19 July, 1969 and 6 more commercial banks on 15 April, 1980. This becomes clear from the objectives of bank nationalisation outlined by the Government in the Parliament.

3. OBJECTIVES OF BANK NATIONALISATION

The Banking Companies (Acquisition and Transfer of Undertakings) Act, 1970 under which 14 banks were nationalised with effect from 19 July, 1969 spelt the main objective as "to serve better the needs of development of the economy in conformity with national policy and objectives and for matters connected therewith or incidental thereto". The specific objectives which the nationalised banks were expected to pursue were outlined by the then Prime Minister Mrs. Indira Gandhi in her statement to the Parliament on 21 July, 1969. These objectives included:

(1) To mobilise the savings of the people to the largest possible extent and to utilise them for productive purposes in accordance with our plans and priorities;

(2) To ensure the operations of the banking system for a larger social purpose and to subject them to close public regulation;

(3) To meet the legitimate credit needs of private sector industry and trade, big or small;

(4) To meet in an increasing manner the needs of productive sectors of the economy and in particular those of farmers, small scale industrialists and self-employed professional groups;

(5) To actively foster the growth of the new and progressive entrepreneurs and credit fresh opportunities for hitherto neglected and backward areas in different parts of the country;

(6) To curb the use of bank credit for speculative and other unproductive purposes;

(7) To develop adequate professional management and modern managerial techniques and practices in the banking field;

(8) To provide adequate training and reasonable terms of service to bank staff;

(9) To considerably expand the branch network of banks in all parts of the country, and

(10) To reduce regional and sectoral imbalance in banking and through that in economic development.

4. A CRITICAL APPRAISAL OF THE FUNCTIONING OF NATIONALISED BANKS IN INDIA

With study the extent to which bank nationalisation has been able to achieve its objectives.

ACHIEVEMENTS

The nationalisation of 14 commercial banks on 19 July, 1969 was a watershed in the history of Indian banking. Together with the State Bank of India and its 7 associates which were brought under public ownership in the 1950s, the nationalisation of 20 commercial banks thereafter resulted in bringing about 90% of banking business under the direct control, ownership and management of the public sector. We enumerate below some of the achievements of nationalisation:

1. *Branch Expansion.* There has been a sea-change in the banking landscape, both geographically and functionally. The objective of creating an infrastructure for banking activity has, by and large, been achieved. From 6,596 branches and offices in June 1969, their number increased to 32,643 in June 2003.

2. *Deposit Growth.* Besides, there has been functional diversification in the form of growth in bank deposits. The deposits of these banks in June 1969 were Rs. 3,897 crores which increased to Rs. 6,88,361 crores in March 2003 and grew by 11.47 per cent during 2002-03 over 2001-02.

3. *Credit Expansion.* There has been an impressive record of the nationalised banks in the realm of credit expansion. The amount advanced by them increased from Rs. 3,035 crores in June 1969 to Rs. 3,60,147 crores in March, 2003 and grew by 14.12 per cent during 2002-03 over 2001-02.

4. *Priority Sector Lending.* These banks have undergone a major transformation from 'wholesale' banking to 'retail' banking. In other words, there has been greater emphasis on disbursing credit to the priority sector comprising agriculture, small scale industry, transport operators, retail trade, professional and self-employed persons, and education. The priority sector lending by the nationalised banks increased from Rs. 441 crores in June 1969 to Rs. 2,03,095 crores in March 2003. As percentage to net bank credit, the same increased from 14.6% to 42.5 during the above period. Agricultural advances increased from 5.4% to 15.3%, the share of credit to SSI units increased from 8.5% to 11.1 and the share of other priority sectors in overall net bank credit increased from 0.7% to 15% during the same period.

5. *Spread of Banking in Rural Areas.* Since nationalisation, the spread of banking has increased considerably in rural areas. As a result of the deliberate policy of opening a large number of branches in rural areas, 63.1% of the branches of the 19 nationalised banks were operating in rural and semi-urban areas in June 2003 as against 22% on the eve of nationalisation in June 1969.

6. *Reduction in Regional Disparities.* Regional imbalances in the availability of banking facilities have been considerably reduced. The majority of these branches have been opened in unbanked areas. In June 1969, there were 74 bank branches in Assam, 172 in Haryana, 42 in Himachal Pradesh and only 2 in Nagaland. In June, 2003 their number had increased to 1,212; 1,580; 784 and 70 respectively. 35% of branches had been opened in those States where banking facilities were less. Consequently, the average population per bank office declined to 16,000 in June 2003 against 65,000 in June 1969.

7. *Some New Schemes.* Public sector banks have been departing from their traditional role and introducing some new schemes. Besides launching a range of new savings and other innovative schemes, these banks have taken up merchant banking and leasing, and have also been floating mutual funds and venture capital funds. A number of other steps have been taken up to improve customer service. Courier services have been introduced to expedite collection of outstation credit instruments. Nomination facilities have been extended to the depositors to avoid hardship to the legal heirs of deceased account holders. Customer service centres have been set up in all major cities. Customer relations programmes are organised periodically. The system of personal hearing of the grievances of customers has been introduced at appropriate levels to serve the customer better. Nine nationalised banks have opened offices in foreign countries thereby opening new vistas in international trade and finance.

FAILURES

Despite the above enumerated achievements, the public sector banks suffer from a number of weaknesses which are discussed as under:

1. *Deterioration in Customer Service.* One of the important drawbacks of nationalisation of banks has been deteriorating customer service. The evils connected with public sector undertakings have crept in these banks thereby resulting in red-tapism, inordinate delays and lack of responsibility. Despite the directives of the RBI for improving the quality of customer service, little has been done to implement it at the branch level. For instance, there are delays in opening of the counters and sometimes counters are closed for short periods on flimsy grounds causing inconvenience to customers. The branch managers are helpless to control the staff due to the spread of unionism. Complaint boxes are not maintained in many branches nor are the addresses of regional/zonal managers displayed to help customers who want to appeal to higher officers. Facilities like automatic credit of outstation cheques of Rs. 5000 and above and crediting of interest at savings bank rate in case of collection of outstation cheques being delayed beyond three weeks are not being extended to customers. Moreover, most bank branches give demand drafts against cash to businessmen towards the end of the day.

2. *Political Interference.* There has been much political interference in granting of loans by public sector banks which has destroyed the sanctity of banking norms. This defeats the very purpose of social banking and leads to malpractices. An important instance is politically organised loan melas.

3. *Social Banking Inadequate.* Social banking in the form of flow of credit to the priority sector is inadequate. It is less than the total advances of public sector banks. Even today these banks mainly cater to the needs of the corporate sector.

4. *Window-dressing of Balance Sheets.* Some of the public sector banks have been resorting to window-dressing of their balance sheets so that their balance sheets do not reveal the actual state of affairs. They artificially step up their deposits in the last week of the fiscal year. This has been possible because auditing in the banks is incomplete and partial.

5. *Large Scale Irregularities.* A number of public sector banks have been resorting to large scale irregularities in their operations. Some of these are:

(i) Indulging in Share Speculation. A few banks have started Mutual Funds and subsidiary financial companies and instances have been found of their involvement in share speculation. For instance, Bob Fiscal, a subsidiary of the Bank of Baroda arranged for funds for the Reliance Company in order to corner the shares of Larsen & Toubro. The securities scam involving Harshad Mehta and others revealed the involvement of the SBI and a number of other banks.

(ii) Favouritism in Granting Loans. Some of the banks are guilty of favouring certain companies in granting loans. For instance, Vijaya Bank advanced large loans to a certain big industrial house and its group companies in small tranches so as to avoid clearance under the credit authorisation scheme.

(iii) Bad Quality of Loan Portfolios. Despite the bad quality of loan portfolios, the banks have been advancing loans under extraneous pressures. Some of the banks have been extending letters of credit and guarantee limits as a routine affair without adopting normal commercial procedure in granting loans. The non-performing assets (NPAs) of banks reflect the quality of their loan portfolios. NPAs include sub-standard assets, doubtful assets, loss assets, etc. During 1999-2000, the gross NPAs of public sector banks were Rs. 53,294 crores, constituting 14.0 per cent of their gross advances.

(iv) Irregularities in Accounts. Some of the public sector banks have been resorting to large scale irregularities in operating their accounts. In certain cases, .bad accounts have been taken over by one bank from the other without proper scrutiny and judgement.

(v) Large Bad Debts. These banks have accumulated large amounts of bad debts. As on 31 December 1999, there were 3,185 cases of frauds involving Rs. 640 crores of public sector banks.

6. *Declining Profitability.* The most important problem of the nationalised banks has been their declining profitability. Irregularities and corruption in lending operations, misappropriation, fraud, rising operating cost, deterioration in customer services, etc. have led to declining profitability of these banks. The ratio of net profit to total assets was (-) 1.15% in 1993-94 which improved to onlv 0.96 per cent in 2002-03.

7. *Sŏme Banks as Sick Units.* In October 1990, the Reserve Bark of India in a survey found all the nationalised banks in a bad shape and identified eight banks as 'sick'. The 'sick' included: New Bank of India, Punjab and Sind Bank, Bank of India, UCO Bank, Vijaya Bank of India, Syndicate Bank, Bank of Maharashtra, and United Bank of India. Some of these banks had eroded their reserves and paid-up capital and there had been erosion of their deposit base. To this 'sick-list* were added: Central Bank, Indian Overseas Bank, Allahabad Bank, Andhra Bank, and Dena Bank, in 1992.93. New Bank of India became so sick that the Government merged it with Punjab National Bank effective 4 September 1993. During 1999-2000, three nationalised banks had been identified as weak. To adjust the losses of weak banks, the Government had contributed Rs. 20,466 crores towards their recapitalisation by 31 March 1999. But no amount was provided during 1999-2000. However, it provided Rs. 297 crores towards writing down of the investments of Vijaya Bank for adjustment of its losses.

8. *Low Capital Adequacy Ratio.* Every bank is required to achieve minimum capital to risk assets ratio, known as capital adequacy ratio (CAR) of at least 9 per cent. Out of 27 public sector banks, two banks had not achieved it during 2002-03.

Conclusion. In a confidential report, the World Bank came out with trenchant criticism of the Indian banking system and called for urgent reforms. Since nationalised banks account for more than 90% of the assets of the entire banking in India. The World Bank's criticisms was directed against the sloppy management of these banks. The Report noted that these "banks were uncompetitive, overstretched, overstaffed and often provide poor service". It suggested a number of urgent reforms like cutting subsidised loans to targeted socially backward areas by half, making rates more flexible and rational, and giving commercial banks a measure of operational autonomy.

The fault also lies with the Government which has placed these banks under the Banking Department of the Ministry of Finance with the result that the RBI cannot regulate the working of these banks independently instead of sharing the responsibility with a parallel controlling authority. This dyarchy must go. There must be a thorough review of the working of these banks. The secrecy clause must be scrapped and the banking business made open and accountable. The defaulters must be identified. The machinery for the grant and recovery of toans should be streamlined and the entire procedure should be closely monitored.

Keeping these in view, the Finance Ministry and RBI took a series of measures to improve the performance and profitability of public sector banks. These included augmentation of capital, higher coupon rates on Government securities and higher return on cash balances. The banks were advised to draw up Action Plans to improve their operational efficiency.[1]

EXERCISES

1. What led the Government of India to nationalise commercial banks in India? What have been the achievements of these banks since 1969?
2. Discuss the achievements and failures of nationalised banks in India.
3. Give a critical appraisal of the functioning of nationalised banks in India.
4. What were the objectives of nationalisation of banks in India? How far these objectives have been achieved?

---

1. For details refer to the "Recent Bank Reforms" in the Chapter "Recent Trends In the Banking System".

CHAPTER 78

The Reserve Bank of India (RBI)

1. ITS CONSTITUTION

The origin of the Reserve Bank of India in 1935 was the culmination of a long series of efforts. The earliest effort to set up a central bank dates back to January 1773 when Warren Hastings, the Governor of Bengal, recommended the establishment of a "General Bank in Bengal and Bihar". The next attempt was made in 1807-08 when Robert Richards, a member of the Bombay Government submitted a scheme for a "General Bank". But the Governor-General was not impressed. The name of John Maynard Keynes also figures in the events leading to the establishment of the RBI. As a member of the Royal Commission on liidian Finance and Currency of 1931, Keynes submitted a memorandum entitled "Proposals for the Establishment of a State Bank in India". The State Bank proposed by Keynes was to perform both central banking and commercial banking functions. However, the scheme could not be implemented due to the outbreak of the First World War.

The first major step was taken in 1921 when the three Presidency Banks were amalgamated to form the Imperial Bank of India. It was primarily a commercial bank but it also performed certain central banking functions, such as acting as banker to the Government and to some extent as bankers' bank. But the regulation of note issue and management of foreign exchange were the diiect responsibility of the Central Government.

In 1926, the Hilton Young Commission recommended that the dichotomy of functions and division of responsibility should be ended. It suggested the establishment of a central bank to be called the "Reserve Bank of India". Accordingly, the Gold Standard and Reserye Bank of India Bill was introduced in the Legislative Assembly in January 1927 but was dropped on account of sharp differences of opinion on the bank's ownership and the composition of its Board of Directors. The Indian Constitutional Reforms in 1933 made it obligatory that the transfer of responsibility from the British Government in India to Indian hands was dependent on the establishment of a Reserve Bank free from political influence and its successful operation. These events led to the introduction of a fresh bill in the Indian Legislative Assembly on 8 September, 1933; which was passed by it on 22 December, 1933 and by the Council of States on 16 February, 1934. It received the Governor-General's assent on 6 March, 1934. The Reserve Bank of India was constituted in accordance with the provisions of the Act containing 58 Sections and was inaugurated on 1 April, 1935.

The RBI was constituted as a shareholders' bank with a fully paid-up capital of Rs. 5 crores divided into shares of Rs. 100 each. Of these 5 lakh shares, 2200 shares were subscribed by the Directors of the Bank and the remaining by private shareholders.

In view of the need for close integration between the Bank's policies and those of the Government, the question of State ownership of the Bank was raised from time to time. But it was only after Independence that the decision to nationalise the Bank was taken. In terms of the Reserve Bank (Transfer to Public Ownership) Act, 1948, its entire paid-up capital was transferred to the Central Government on 1 January 1949 when it became a State-owned institution.

2. ITS ORGANISATIONAL STRUCTURE AND MANAGEMENT

The organisational structure of the RBI consists of the Central Board and the Local Boards.

The RBI is managed by the Central Board of Directors comprising 20 members. There is one Governor who is the executive head of the Bank. He is assisted by four Deputy Governors. They are appointed by the Government of India for a period of five years. Four Directors are nominated by the Central Government, one each from the four Local Boards situated at "Mumbai, Kolkata, Chennai and Delhi. In addition, the Central Government nominates ten Directors who are experts from various fields. They are appointed for four years. The 20th member of the Board is one Government official who is usually the Secretary, Ministry of Finance nominated by the Central Government. The government official and the four Deputy Governors do not have the right to vote at the meetings of the Board. All powers of the Bank are vested in the Central Board of Directors. It must hold at least six meetings in a year and at least one in three months. However, the Governor is empowered to call a meeting of the Board whenever he likes. The Governor and Deputy Governors are whole-time paid officers of the Bank while the other Directors are part-time officers who receive T.A. and other allowances prescribed for them when they attend the meetings of the Board.

There are four Local Boards with headquarters at Mumbai, Kolkata, Chennai and Delhi representing the Western, Eastern, Southern and Northern regions respectively. The Central Government nominates five members on each Local Board for a four-year term. The Chairman is elected from among the members and the Manager of the RBI office in a region acts as the ex-officio Secretary of the Local Board.

The RBI is managed by the Central Board of Directors with the Governor as its Chairman. The Governor is the chief executive of the Bank who exercises wide powers of supervision and issues directions on behalf of the Board. He is assisted by four Deputy Governors and four Executive Directors.

The Head Office of the RBI at Mumbai, which has sixteen departments such as the Banking, Issue, Currency Management, Exchange Control, Industrial Credit, Agricultural Credit, etc. The bank has 15 offices and 2 branches in different parts of the country. Where the RBI has no office or branch, the State Bank of India and its 7 associates act as its agents or sub-agents.

3. OBJECTIVES OF RESERVE BANK OF INDIA

The broad objectives of the Reserve Bank of India as spelt out in the preamble to the RBI Act, 1934 are "to regulate the issue of Bank notes and the keeping of reserves with a view to securing monetary stability in India and generally to operate the currency and credit system of the country to its advantage". What was implied in the objectives stated was more concretely stated in the First Five-Year Plan: "It would have to take on a direct and active role, *firstly*, in creating and helping to create the machinery needed for financing developmental activities all over the country, and *secondly*, ensuring that the finance available flows in the directions intended". Thus the main objectives of the RBI have been:

1. To promote monetisation and monetary integration of the economy.
2. To manage currency and regulate foreign exchange.
3. To institutionalise savings through promotion of banking habit.
4. To build up a sound and adequate banking and credit structure.
5. To evolve a well-differentiated structure of institutions purveying credit for agriculture and allied activities.
6. To set up or promote several specialised financial institutions at the all-India level and regional levels

to widen facilities for term finance to industry.

7. To lend support to planning authorities and governments in their efforts to accelerate the pace of economic development with stability and social justice.

The extent to which the RBI has been able to fulfil these objectives shall be discussed in the last section of this chapter entitled "A Critical Appraisal of the Functioning of Reserve Bank of India".

4. FUNCTIONS OF RESERVE BANK OF INDIA

The Reserve Bank of India performs all the traditional functions of a central bank. At the same time, it also undertakes active promotional and developmental functions. Thus, we divide the functions of the RBI into two parts:

(1) Traditional Functions, and (2) Promotional and Developmental Functions, These are discussed as under:

1. Traditional Functions

The RBI performs the following traditional functions:

(1) *Issue of Currency.* The RBI acts as the currency authority. As such, it has the monopoly of issuing currency of all denominations except one rupee notes and coins, and small coins which are issued by the Ministry of Finance of the Government of India. At present, the RBI is issuing notes of the denominations of Rs. 10, 20, 50, 100, 500 and 1000.[1] These notes are printed and issued by its Issue Department. Rs. 1, 2 and 5 coins, issued by the Ministry of Finance are also distributed by the Issue Department. For the distribution of notes and coins of all denominations to the public and banks, the Issue Department maintains currency chests at its 15 offices and 2 branches and elsewhere keeps them with the State Bank of India, and its 7 associates, some public sector banks, and State Government treasuries and sub-treasuries. The RBI issues currency on the basis of minimum of Rs. 200 crores of gold and foreign exchange reserves, of which at least Rs. 115 crores worth of gold must be there.

(2) *Banker to Government.* The RBI acts as banker to the Central Government and the State Governments. As such, it renders the following services to them:

(i) It maintains and operates the cash balances of the Central and State Governments in the current account deposit on which it pays no interest.

(ii) It receives and makes payments on behalf of the Central and State Governments.

(iii) It carries out exchange, remittance and other banking operations on behalf of these Governments.

(iv) It buys and sells Government securities in the market.

(v) It manages the public debt by issuing Government loans and paying interest and principal.

(vi) It also sells treasury bills through tender on behalf of the Government.

(vii) It makes ways and means advances to the Central and State Governments by purchasing treasury bills from them for a period not exceeding 91 days.

(viii) It advises the Governments on all banking and financial matters, such as financing of five year plans and resource mobilisation, balance of payments, etc.

(ix) It acts as the agent of the Central and State Governments in their dealings with the International Monetary Fund, the World Bank, International Financial Corporation, IDA, Exim Bank, and other financial institutions.

(3) *Bankers' Bank. Firstly,* The RBI acts as banker to the scheduled commercial banks in India. As such, it keeps a part of the cash reserves of these banks and provides them with remittance facilities. Under the Banking Regulation Act, 1949, every bank is required to keep between 3% to 15% of the total of its time and demand liabilities with the RBI as cash reserve ratio which is interest-free. The CRR which was reduced to 14 per cent effective 15 May, 1993 was again raised to 15 per cent effective 6 August, 1994. Besides, every bank is

1. Printing of Rs 1, 2 and 5 notes has been stopped.

required to maintain with the RBI between 25% to 40% of its net time and demand liabilities as the Statutory Liquidity Ratio (SLR). It had been reduced from 34.75 per cent to 33.75 per cent effective 16 May 1994. The incremental SLR continues to be 25 per cent. *Secondly*, the RBI supervises, regulates and controls the working of banks in India. These powers relate to issue of licence for opening and branch expansion, calling of returns/ statements, inspection of books and accounts, issue of directions concerning terms and conditions of advances, giving approval for the appointment of chairman and directors, and to acquire or approve the merger of any bank. *Thirdly*, the RBI acts as a clearing house for banks. It has clearing houses at its 17 offices/branches and at other places the State Bank of India and its associates provide clearing and remittance facilities on its behalf. *Fourthly*, the RBI provides refinance facilities to commercial banks for export credit, against 364-Day Treasury Bills, standby refinance limits against the collateral of approved securities (that is for those banks having excess SLR) and discretionary refinance including limits under the facility to draw without prior approval from the RBI.

(4) *Exchange Management and Control.* The RBI manages and controls the country's foreign exchange reserves and external value of the rupee. Under the Foreign Exchange Regulation Act, 1973, the RBI controls the receipts and payments of foreign currencies. Foreign currencies coming into India are required to be sold and exchanged for the rupee either direct to the RBI or to major commercial banks authorised by it. Similarly, foreign currencies are allowed to persons travelling abroad and to importers by the RBI as per rules laid down by it. All such transactions of foreign currencies are made at rates fixed by the RBI from time to time.

The RBI determines the external value of the rupee in relation to the weighted basket of India's major trading partners with pound-sterling as the intervention currency. Since the exchange value of these currencies keeps on changing in the international market, the RBI also changes the exchange rate of the rupee in relation to other currencies such as dollar, mark, yen, sterling, etc. Effective 1 March, 1994, the RBI introduced full convertibility of rupee to the entire current account transactions.

(5) *Control of Credit.* The RBI controls the money supply and credit to ensure price stability and meet the varying economic conditions of the country. It estimates the credit needs of the economy in relation to the targets laid down in the five-year plans and ensures the supply of credit to different sectors. For this purpose, it uses various credit control measures such as variations in interest rates, open market operations, changes in CRR and SLR, selective credit controls, etc.

(6) *Collection and Publication of Data and Reports.* The RBI has a Division of Reports, Reviews, and Publications under its Department of Economic Analysis and Policy which collects data on economic matters such as money, credit, finance, agricultural and industrial production, balance of payments, prices, etc. and publishes them in various publications. Some of its important publications are the Reserve Bank of India Bulletin (monthly) and its Weekly Statistical Supplements, Annual Report on Currency and Finance, and Report on Trend and Progress on Banking in India, etc. Besides, it brings out Occasional Papers by its experts, and conducts surveys and publishes reports on them.

(7) *Training Facilities.* The RBI has set up a number of training colleges and centres to provide training to the banking personnel at different levels. They are:

(i) Bankers Training College (BTC). The BTC is located at Mumbai. It provides training to senior officers of the Bank in the areas of application of statistical methods, negotiating skills, counselling, import-export financing. Service Area Approach, etc.

(ii) Reserve Bank Staff College (RBSC). The RBSC is located at Chennai. It conducts training programmes for officers of the Bank on areas of investment and fund management, financial services, housing finance, customer service, etc. Officials of foreign banks also participate.

(iii) College of Agricultural Banking (CAB). The CAB is located at Pune and it caters to the training needs of personnel of co-operative banks, commercial banks, regional rural banks, NABARD, RBI, Deposit Insurance and Credit Guarantee Corporation, Government officials, and also officials from South Asian and African countries. It conducts training programmes in the field of agricultural finance, rural banking and allied subjects.

(iv) Zonal Training Centres (ZTCs). The ZTCs are situated in Mumbai, Kolkata, Chennai and New Delhi. They provide training to class III and class IV staff of the Bank. These centres also conduct training programmes on computer and customer service. The RBI has also introduced training in commercial banking for the banks' officers at these Zonal centres.

(v) Indira Gandhi Institute of Development Research. This was set up by the RBI in 1987. It conducts research on projects and arranges workshop, conferences and seminars.

(vi) Training in Computer Technology. The RBI set up the Department of Computer Technology in 1995 for efficient and quick use of new technologies. This Department provides incentives to the Bank's staff to acquire qualifications in computer technology.

2. Promotional and Developmental Functions

The RBI has been taking a direct and active role, *firstly*, in creating or helping to create the machinery needed for financing development activities all over the country, and *secondly*, ensuring that the finance available flows in socially desired directions. In order to achieve these two objectives the RBI has been financing agriculture, industry and exports. It has also been instrumental in the development and regulation of the banking system and the bill market. We refer to these activities of the RBI briefly. They are discussed in detail in subsequent sections.

(1) *Agricultural Finance.* The RBI has been extending advice and financial assistance to the co-operative credit institutions for the development of agriculture and allied rural activities since its inception in 1935. For this purpose it set up an Agricultural Credit Department and separate funds for providing medium-term and long-term finance. Since 1982, the functions of this Department and those of the funds have been passed on to the National Bank for Agriculture and Rural Development (NABARD).

(2) *Industrial Finance.* The RBI set up an Industrial Credit Department in 1957 to advise and help the bank in providing financial assistance to industries and in setting up financial institutions like State Financial Institutions, IFCI, IDBI, ICICI, etc. It also established the National Industrial Credit (Long-Term Operations) Fund in 1964 to provide financial assistance to large scale industries.

(3) *Export Credit.* The RBI provides concessional credit, refinance facilities and guarantee to commercial banks for exporters. It has also set up the Export-Import Bank of India to finance export trade.

(4) *Credit to Priority Sector and Weaker Sections.* Under its Differential Rate of Interest Scheme, the RBI provides concessional finance to priority sectors and weaker sections of the society at 4 per cent interest rate.

(5) *Bill Market Scheme.* The RBI has been instrumental in developing a well-organised bill market scheme in order to provide rediscounting facilities to commercial banks from the Bank and other financial institutions.

(6) *Development and Regulation of Banking System.* The RBI has played an important role in the development and promotion of banking in the country. It has spread banking to the remotest corners of India through its Lead Bank Scheme, SAA, and Regional Rural Banks. It has helped in promoting development banking by establishing such financial institutions as IDBI, IFCI, ICICI, SIDBI, etc. Further, the RBI has strengthened the banking system in India and placed it on a sound footing through a judicious policy of regulation and control of banks.

3. Other Functions

The RBI also performs the following banking functions also :

(a) It issues demand drafts made payable at its own offices or agencies, and makes, issues and circulates bank post-bills.

(b) It can borrow money from a scheduled bank in India or from central banks in other countries.

(c) It is authorised to open an account or make an agency agreement with central banks in other countries and act as their agent and invest funds in their shares.

(d) It purchases and sells gold and bullion.

4. Prohibitory Functions

The RBI Act prohibits the Bank to perform certain functions so that it may not compete with other banks and may keep its assets in liquid form to meet any eventuality. Some of its prohibited functions are: *(a)* It cannot participate in any business, trade or industry, *(b)* It cannot buy its own shares or those of any other banking company or of any corporation. Nor can it give loan on the security of shares, *(c)* It cannot give loans against immovable property, *(d)* It cannot purchase immovable property except for its offices, *(e)* It cannot accept bills not payable on demand. *(f)* It cannot give interest on deposits held by it.

5. RBI AND AGRICULTURAL FINANCE

Since its inception in 1935, the Reserve Bank of India has been entrusted with the task of formulating agricultural credit policy, developing an infrastructure for implementing it, giving advice on these matters to the State and Central Governments, and providing credit for agricultural and allied activities. The RBI has been performing these tasks in the following ways:

AGRICULTURAL CREDIT DEPARTMENT (ACD)

Alongwith the RBI, a separate Agricultural Credit Department was set up in 1935 to study the problems of agricultural credit, to develop cooperative credit movement, and to provide necessary advice, guidance and financial assistance. Its main functions were: *(a)* to maintain an expert staff to study all problems of agricultural credit and provide consultation to the Central and State Governments, State Cooperative Banks, and other banking organisations; and *(b)* to coordinate the operations of the RBI relating to agricultural credit with those State Cooperative Banks and other organisations engaged in the supply of agricultural credit. The ACD was engaged in the collection of statistics and research in rural credit. It was only with the beginning of the planning era that this Department became more active and it was entrusted with an additional function: to finance the processing, marketing, and other agricultural operations through State Cooperative Banks and other agencies of rural credit. The ACD has been merged with NABARD effective July, 1982.

ALL INDIA RURAL CREDIT SURVEY COMMITTEE

The RBI appointed an All India Rural Credit Survey Committee in 1951 which submitted its report in 1954. The Committee observed that the contribution of co-operatives in providing rural finance was only 3 per cent in total rural credit. It, therefore, made a number of recommendations for strengthening co-operative credit movement and to provide more funds for agricultural and allied activities. On the recommendations of the Committee, the Reserve Bank made the following changes to develop co-operative credit movement and to provide agricultural finance:

(1) *Integrated Scheme of Rural Credit.* The RBI Act was amended to implement the integrated scheme of rural credit. The main features of the scheme were: *(a)* State partnership in co-operative credit institutions between credit societies with marketing and processing activities; and *(b)* administration through adequately trained and efficient personnel responsive to the needs of the rural population. The RBI was required to play an active role in the development of co-operative credit, co-ordinating credit with marketing, processing end ware housing activities, and training of co-operative personnel. As a result of the implementation of this scheme, it was revealed by the All India Rural Debt and Investment Survey conducted by the RBI (1961-62) that the share of co-operatives in rural credit increased from 3.1 per cent in 1951-52 to 25.8 per cent in 1961-62.

(2) *State Bank of India.* It was on the recommendations of the Committee that the Imperial Bank of India was nationalised in 1955 and renamed the State Bank of India. The RBI became its major shareholder. The SBI has been entrusted with the task of financing agricultural operations.

(3) *Agricultural Credit Board (ACB).* Though the Committee recommended the formation of a Statutory Agricultural Credit Board, the RBI constituted a Standing Advisory Committee on Agricultural Credit in 1956. Lateron it was changed into the Standing Advisory Committee on Rural and Co-operative Credit. It was again reconstituted in 1970 as the Agricultural Credit Board. It formulated policies relating to agricultural finance and co-ordinated the activities of co-operative credit institutions, the RBI, and commercial banks in providing refinance facilities. The NABARD has taken over the activities of the Board since July 1982.

(4) *Rural Credit Funds.* On the recommendations of the Committee, the RBI established in February 1956 the National Agricultural Credit (Long-Term Operations) Fund to grant long-term loans to State Governments and Land Development Banks to enable them to subscribe to the share capital of co-operative banks and co-operative societies. The RBI also established the National Agricultural (Stabilisation) Fund in June 1956 for

converting short term agricultural loans into medium-term loans by the State Co-operative Banks to enable co-operative societies to repay loans in case of default by borrowers as a result of drought, famins or other natural calamities. These funds have been transferred to the NABARD since July 1982 and renamed as National Rural Credit (Long Term Operations) Fund and National Rural Credit (Stabilisation) Fund.

ESTABLISHMENT OF OTHER ORGANISATIONS

With a view to provide larger credit facilities to the rural sector, the RBI has also been instrumental in the establishment of the following organisations:

(1) *Nationalisation of Banks.* In 1969, 14 scheduled banks were nationalised and 6 more commercial banks were nationalised in 1980 in order to spread a network of their branches in rural areas so as to provide larger credit facilities for agricultural and allied activities.

(2) *Agricultural Refinance and Development Corporation (ARDC).* The RBI set up the Agricultural Refinance Corporation in July 1963 which was subsequently renamed as Agricultural Refinance and Development Corporation. The main objectives of the Corporation were to provide medium and long-term refinance to Central Land Mortgage Banks, State Co-operative Banks and commercial banks; and to subscribe to the debentures of Central Land Mortgage Banks and State Co-operative Banks. Since its inception in 1963 to June 1982, it sanctioned 19,601 schemes and disbursed Rs. 2,808 crores. With the establishment of the NABARD in July 1982, the ARDC was merged with it.

(3) *Regional Rural Banks (RRBs).* The RBI was instrumental in establishing RRBs in 1975. The RBI issues licences to sponsoring commercial banks for opening branches of RRBs which are routed through the NABARD after July 1982. The RBI has vested the work of financing and supervision of the RRBs to the NABARD. The principal objective of the RRBs is to grant loans and advances to the weaker sections of the rural population and to co-operatives.

(4) *National Bank for Agriculture and Rural Development (NABARD).* The NABARD was established in July 1982 as an apex rural development bank by merging ACD of the RBI, ARDC, and the NRC (LTO) Fund and NRC (Stabilisation) Fund of the RBI. The RBI lends to the NABARD.under the General Line of Credit (GLC) for short periods, and also contributes annually to the NRC (LTO) Fund and NRC (Stabilisation) Fund of the NABARD. The National Bank provides credit, refinance and institutional building facilities fo integrated rural development. The RBI sanctioned Rs. 3,750 crores to NAB ARD in 1992-93 under general line of credit.

(5) *Service Area Approach (SAA).* The RBI introduced the SAA scheme from April 1989 whereby the service area of the branch of a commercial hank, a co-operative bank, and a RRB covers 15 to 25 villages. Every branch in the service area prepares a credit plan relating to agricultural and allied activities for the target groups and for lending to the priority sector categories of borrowers in particular.

HELP TO CO-OPERATIVES

The RBI inspects and audits the accounts of co-operative societies. It provides cheap remittance facilities to them. It renders them advice about making adjustments of their loans and assets. It also runs the College of Agricultural Banking at Pune where it conducts training programmes in the field of agricultural finance, rural banking and allied subjects for the personnel of co-operative and other banks.

FINANCIAL ASSISTANCE

The RBI dos not provide direct finance to agriculturists but through the State Co-operative Banks and NABARD. It provides short-term, medium-term and long-term financial assistance to meet the needs of rural and allied activities.

(1) *Short-Term Advances.* The RBI grants short-term loans and advances to State Co-operative Banks for the purpose of general banking business against the pledge of Government and other approved securities. The RBI also lends to NABARD under the GLC for short-term lending operations for agricultural and other purposes. The NABARD, in turn, makes short-term advances to State Co-operative Banks for agricultural operations, marketing of crops, purchase and distribution of chemical fertilisers, financing of cottage and small scale industries, working capital requirements of co-operative sugar factories, etc. Short-term advances of the

RBI/NABARD to the State Co-operative Banks amounted to Rs, 7,358 crores in 2002-03.

(2) *Medium-Term Advances.* Medium-term loans and advances are granted by the RBI to the State Co-operative Banks for the purpose of general banking business against the pledge of Government and other approved securities for a period of 15 months to 5 years at an interest rate below the bank rate. The NABARD also gives medium term loans from NRC (Stabilisation) Fund for conversion of short term into medium-term loans, and from the NRC (LTO) Fund for approved agricultural purposes and purchase of shares in co-operative processing societies by farmer members of PACs. The medium-term loans and advances by RBI/ NABARD to the State Co-operative Banks amounted to Rs. 493 crores in 2002-03.

(3) *Long-Term Advances.* The RBI provides long-term advances for agricultural and allied activities to the State Governments to enable them to contribute to the share capital of co-operatives and the NRC (LTO) Fund and NRC (Stabilisation) Fund. During 1990-91, the RBI contributed Rs. 375 crores to the NRC (LTO) Fund and Rs. 10 crores to the NRC (Stabilisation) Fund. The RBI/NABARD sanctioned long-term credit limits amounting to Rs. 61 crores to State Governments for contribution to the share capital of co-operative credit institutions during 2002-03.

Conclusion

The Reserve Bank's role in rural finance is confined to the following areas: advisory, training, supervision, strengthening of rural credit institutions, formulating rural credit policy and providing refinance facilities. The RBI has been successful in creating a number of institutions like the RRBs, NABARD, etc., and strengthening of co-operative banking in rural areas in order to provide credit facilities for agricultural and allied activities.

6. RBI AND INDUSTRIAL FINANCE

The Reserve Bank has been playing an important role in providing finance indirectly to large, medium and small scale industries. Towards this end, it has been instrumental in setting up a number of financial corporations at the Centre and in the States. The RBI provides long-term loans as well as medium/short-term credit facilities to these financial institutions.

RBI Assistance to Financial Institutions

To provide credit facilities to industries, the RBI has helped in the establishment of the following financial institutions:

(1) *Industrial Finance Corporation of India (IFCI).* The IFCI was set up in 1948 by the RBI with the objective of providing medium and long-term financial assistance to the industrial sector. The RBI subscribed 40 per cent of the issued capital of the Corporation. It also subscribed to the debentures of the Corporation. In 1964, it was made a subsidiary of the Industrial Development Bank of India. The RBI provides medium/short-term credit limits to the IFCI against the security of eligible usance bills rediscounted by it. During 1990-91, the RBI sanctioned Rs. 60 crores as credit limits to the Corporation. No amount had been sanctioned after this.

(2) *National Industrial Credit (Long-Term Operations) Fund.* The RBI created the NIC (LTO) Fund in 1964 for providing long term credit limits to the leading financial institutions such as IDBI, IRBI, etc.

(3) *Industrial Development Bank of India (IDBI).* The RBI established in 1964 the IDBI as the principal financial institution for industrial finance in the country. It is a wholly owned subsidiary of the RBI. It provides direct assistance to medium and large industrial concerns by purchasing/underwriting their shares and debentures. It also provides refinance facilities to other term lending institutions in the large, medium and small scale sectors. During 1992-93, the RBI sanctioned a special refinance facility of Rs. 400 crores to IDBI. It did not sanction any amount after this.

(4) *Industrial Credit and Investment Corporation of India (ICICI).* The ICICI was established in 1955 as a public limited company at the initiative of the World Bank. The RBI played an indirect role in its formation. The 1CICI provides assistance for industrial development and investment, by way of rupee and foreign currency loans, underwriting and direct participation to shares, debentures and guarantees. The RBI provides medium/short-term credit limits to the ICICI against the security of eligible usance bills rediscounted by it. It sanctioned Rs.

33 crores to the ICICI as credit limits for the year 1990-91. No amount was sanationed after this.

(5) *Industrial Reconstruction Bank of India (IRBI).* The IRBI was established in 1985 after reconstituting the erstwhile Industrial Reconstruction Corporation of India. It is the principal credit and reconstruction agency for rehabilitation of sick and closed industrial units. It assists industrial concerns by grant of term loans and advances, underwriting of stocks, shares, bonds and debentures, and guarantees for loans/deferred payments. During 1990-91, the RBI sanctioned Rs. 35 crores to the IRBI as long-term assistance from the NIC (LTO) Fund. No amount had been sanctioned after this.

(6) *State Financial Corporations (SFCs).* SFCs are the state-level development banks set up under the SFCs Act, 1951 for the development of medium and small scale industries in their respective States. At present there are 18 SFCs which provide financial assistance to industries by way of term loans, direct subscription to equity/ debentures, discounting of bills of exchange and guarantees. Most of the IDBI schemes for assistance to small and medium sectors are operated through SFCs. During 1999-2000, the RBI sanctioned fresh adhoc borrowing limits aggregating to Rs. 152.5 crores to 15 SFCs.

(7) *Small Industries Development Bank of India (SIDBI).* The SIDBI was set up as a wholly-owned subsidiary of IDBI on 2 April, 1990. It aims at ensuring larger flow of financial and non-financial assistance to smill scale industrial sector. Its major activities relate to refinance of loans and advances, discounting and rediscounting of bills, extension of seed capital/soft loans, granting direct assistance and refinancing of loans, providing services like factoring, leasing, etc., and extending financial support to Small Industries Development Corporations. During 1995-96, the RBI sanctioned long-term credit assistance to SIDBI amounting to Rs. 224 crores. It made no sanction after this.

(8) *Export-Import Bank of India (Exim Bank).* The Exim Bank was set up in January 1982 as a statutory corporation of the Central Government. It provides financial assistance to promote Indian exports through direct financial assistance, overseas investment, finance, term finance for export production and export development, preshipment credit, buyers' credit, lines of credit, relending facility, export bills rediscounting, refinance to commercial banks, finance for computer software exports, finance for export marketing and bulk import finance to commercial banks. It also extends non-fund facility to Indian exporters in the form of guarantees. The lending programme of the Exim Bank covers various stages of export such as from the developmentof export markets to expansion of production capacity for exports production for exports and post-shipment financing. Its focus is on export of manufactured goods, project exports, exports of technology services, export of manufactured goods and export of computer software. The RBI sanctioned Rs. 120 crores as long-term assistance to the Exim Bank out of NIC (LTO) Fund in 1990-91. It made no sanction after this.

(9) *National Housing Bank (NHB).* The NHB was set up in 1988 to meet the requirements of housing finance. Its paid-up capital of Rs. 250 crores is fully subscribed by the RBI. The bank is providing assistance through Home Loan Account Scheme, liberalised lending by commercial banks and refinance facilities. Refinance is for land development and shelter programmes of public/private agencies and co-operatives. During 1992-93 the RBI sanctioned a loan of Rs. 1 crore to NHB out of the National Housing Credit (Long-Term Operations) Fund set up by the RBI. No amount was sanctioned after this.

CREDIT GUARANTEE SCHEMES

The RBI established in 1971 the Credit Guarantee Corporation of India in order to encourage greater flow of bank credit to small borrowers. In 1978, this Corporation was merged with the Deposit Insurance Corporation and renamed as Deposit Insurance and Credit Guarantee Corporation (DICGC). This Corporation guarantees support for the entire priority sector advances by banks and other approved financial institutions to small borrowers and small scale industries. At present, the DICGC is operating three credit guarantee schemes. The RBI does not lend to the Corporation and has simply helped in its formation.

INDUSTRIAL CREDIT DEPARTMENT

Earlier, the RBI had established the Industrial Credit Department in 1957 to solve the problems of industrial finance. It was this Department which administered the Credit Guarantee Scheme for SSI introduced in July 1960. With the formation of DICGC, this department was wound up by the RBI in 1981.

Credit Monitoring Arrangement (CMA)

The RBI introduced the CMA in place of the Credit Authorisation Scheme (CAS) in October 1988 whereby it delegated authority to banks to sanction credit proposals of large borrowers and thereafter submit the same for post-sanction scrutiny to the RBI. These credit limits relate to working capital (of Rs. 5 crores and above), term finance (of Rs. 2 crores and above), sale of machinery on deferred payments, etc. in case of large scale industries. The CMA has made possible prompt and easy availability of credit to large industries with post-sanction by the RBI.

From 1992-93, the working capital credit limit has been raised from Rs. 5 to 10 crores. The CMA has also been extended to the export sector. The RBI has advised banks to meet the additional credit needs of exporters in full even if sanction of additional credit exceeds maximum permissible bank finance (MPBF), provided exporters have firm orders or confirmed letters of credit. This facility has been extended to exports by small scale industries where the working capital limit from banks is less than Rs. 1 crore, provided their exports are not less than 25 per cent of their total turnover during the previous accounting year. Further, this facility has been given to companies/organisations engaged in the marketing/trading of the products of village, tiny and small scale industrial units.

Conclusion

The RBI has done a remarkable job in creating a number of financial institutions aiid evolving credit guarantee schemes to help finance large, medium and small industries, and small borrowers. It provides direct long-term assistance from the NIC (LTO) Fund and medium/short-term assistance to financial institutions. It also changes its credit policy from time to time to help the industrial sector to get larger financial assistance from banks.

7. RBI AND BILL MARKET SCHEME

The RBI pioneered the development of the bill market scheme for trade and industry in 1952. Its aim was to induce banks to provide finance against bills of exchange and promissory notes for 90 days. The scheduled commercial banks were allowed to convert a part of their advances, loans, cash credits or overdrafts into usance promissory notes for 90 days for lodging as collateral (security) for advances from the RBI. Since this scheme was primarily meant to accommodate the banks, it did not help in developing a bill market.

In November 1970, the RBI introduced the Bill Rediscounting Scheme with several new features. Under this scheme, all licensed scheduled commercial banks were made eligible to rediscount with the RBI genuine trade bills arising out of sale or despatch of goods. But this did not lead to the development of bill culture as preference for cash credit type of financing continued in the country: Several difficulties were cited by trade and industry in developing the bill market: *(a)* non-availability of stamp paper of required denomination, *(b)* the need to affix stamp on each bill and payment of stamp duty, *(c)* reluctance of industry, trade and Government Departments to accept bills, *(d)* absence of specialised credit information agencies, *(e)* absence of any active secondary market for bills as rediscounting is permitted only with the apex level financial institutions, and *(f)* administrative work involved in handling invoices/documents of title to goods.

The Committee to Review the working of the Monetary System (1985) and the Working Group on the Money Market (1986) set up by the RBI made a number of recommendations which have sir.ce been accepted and implemented by the RBI as under:

1. The RBI has developed the treasury bills or Government Securities market in 14-day Treasury Bills, 91-day Treasury Bills, 182-day Treasury Bills and 364-day Treasury Bills.

2. In order to augment the facilities for rediscounting and to provide liquidity to the bills, the RBI has been progressively permitting a larger number of financial institutions eligible for rediscounting bills. Apart from all scheduled commercial banks and selected urban co-operative banks, 21 other financial institutions like LIC, UTI, GIC, NABARD, all development banks; all mutual funds, etc., are included in the scheme.

3. The RBI has set up the Discount and Finance House of India (DFHI) as a major financial institution to

rediscount commercial bills, treasury bills and Government dated securities which it has been doing since its inception on 15 April 1988.

4. In May 1994, the RBI set up the Securities Trading Corporation of India (STCI) to develop secondary market in Government securities and Treasury bills. The STCI undertakes ready forward transactions in Treasury Bills and Government dated securities. From March 1996, it has become a primary dealer in Government securities.

5. Besides, the DFHI and the STCI, the RBI has granted permission to ICICI Securities, SBI Gilts Ltd., PNB Gilts Ltd. and Gilt Securities Trading Corporation Ltd. to operate as primary dealers in Government securities. The RBI also provides liquidity support to them in the form of reverse Repos in Government dated securities and 91-Day Treasury Bills.

6. Upto September 1988 under the bill rediscounting procedure, the bills had to be endorsed and lodged with the rediscounting banks or institutions. But preference for cash-credit type of financing continued because certain administrative difficulties, were faced by banks in following this procedure. In October, 1988, the RBI introduced the scheme of *derivative usance promissory note* for the purpose of rediscounting of bills whereby banks could draw a derivative usance promissory note for suitable sums with maturity upto 90 days on the basis of bona-fide commercial or trade bills discounted at their branches. Since August, 1989, the derivative promissory note has been exempted from stamp duty. Thus a major administrative constraint in the use of the bill system has been removed.

7. To encourage the development of bill finance and bill culture, the RBI had fixed a discount rate equivalent to an effective interest rate of 15.5 per cent. Further, to stimulate the supply of funds in the rediscount market, the RBI had fixed the ceiling on rediscount rate at 12.5 per cent. But this rediscount rate was not applicable when banks and financial houses rediscounted bills with DFHI which could fix its own discount rates for bills. With effect from 1 May, 1989, the bill rediscounting rate has been totally freed.

8. The Working Group on the Money Market (1986) made recommendations for developing bill financing in relation to cash credit system and developing the bill culture. In pursuance of the recommendations, the RBI advised banks to fix for the Credit Authorisation Scheme (CAS) now covered by the Credit Monitoring Scheme since October 1988, to attain a ratio of bill acceptance to their inland credit purchases of 25 per cent and a bill discounting limit of the same order.

9. To secure finance from banks against bills accepted by the large scale units for prompt payment to small scale units, the RBI has introduced a Drawee Bill Scheme.

10. The RBI advised commercial banks in July, 1992 that *(a)* they should be cautious in discounting bills drawn by finance companies set up by large industrial houses on other group companies; *(b)* they should not rediscount the bills discounted by non-bank financial companies and thus desist from providing any rediscount facility to finance companies; and *(c)* they should ensure that the overall credit limit provided to finance companies and to hire-purchase and equipment leasing companies should not exceed three times the net worth of such companies.

11. Recognising the need to derive the benefit of internationally competitive rates, the RBI decided to allow with effect from 7 April, 1993 authorised dealers in India to rediscount export bills abroad at rates linked to international interest rates.

DEFECTS

Despite these measures, the RBI has failed to develop bill finance and bill culture in the country. Bill financing hardly covers about 4 per cent of the total credit covered by banks today. There are many reasons for this: *(a)* The Government, public sector undertakings, and large industries do not accept bills as a basis for financing business, *(b)* The bill market is primarily confined to derivative usance promissory notes rather than to genuine trade bills, *(c)* Indigenous bills of exchange, known as *hundis,* which finance a large segment of commerce and trade in India are not recognised by the RBI. For a faster growth of bill financing and bill culture, the RBI should try to remove these drawbacks of the bill market.

8. EXCHANGE CONTROL MANAGEMENT BY RBI

The RBI manages and controls the country's foreign exchange reserves and the external value of the rupee. Foreign exchange is managed and controlled in order to overcome the deficit in balance of payments. The RBI controls and manages the inflow and outflow of foreign currencies under the Foreign Exchange Regulation Act, 1973 and Foreign Exchange Regulation (Amendment) Act, 1993.

Foreign currencies coming into India are required to be sold and exchanged for the rupee either direct to the RBI or to its authorised dealers. Its authorised dealers include certain commercial banks, hotels, firms, shops, etc. which deal in foreign currencies and foreign travellers' cheques. They are also authorised to lend and borrow foreign currency among themselves in the inter-bank market locally. The actual lending limit for each authorised dealer is fixed by the RBI depending upon the size of its operations and other relevant factors. Authorised dealers are permitted to maintain with overseas branches and correspondents, balances in foreign currencies at levels which are commensurate with normal needs of their business, such as payments towards imports or maturing deliveries under forward contracts. They are also permitted to transfer foreign currency funds rendered surplus over normal anticipated needs of their business on a day-to-day basis to special interest bearing accounts.

The blanket foreign exchange permits are issued to exporters in lump sums. Exporters are allowed to receive export proceeds through normal banking channels. The payments for imports against foreign currency loans / credits extended by foreign governments / financial institutions are made either under the Direct Payment Method, also known as Letter of Commitment Method or Reimbursement Method.

Since 1991 significant changes have been made in the exchange rate system by the RBI. In July, 1991, the rupee was devalued by about 20 per cent with respect to US dollar in two stages. Simultaneously, the Exim Scrip Scheme was introduced under which certain imports were permitted only against export entitlement. This was followed by partial convertibility of rupee in 60:40 ratio with effect from 1 March, 1992. This was the Liberalised Exchange Rate Management System (LERMS). Under this system, all foreign exchange receipts on current account transactions (i.e. exports, remittances etc.) were required to be surrendered to the authorised dealers (ADs) in full. The rate of exchange for these transactions was the free market rate quoted by the ADs. The ADs, in turn, surrendered to the RBI 40 per cent of their purchase of foreign currencies at the exchange rate announced by the RBI. They were free to sell the balance of 60 per cent of foreign exchange in the free market. All importers of goods and services and persons travelling abroad bought foreign exchange at market-determined rates from the ADs subject to liberalised exchange control rules.

The RBI issued instructions to authorised dealers to sell foreign exchange without prior approval for business visits overseas sponsored by firms / companies / organisations, visits by self-employed professionals and by journalists on short-term assignments, for medical treatment abroad, persons proceeding abroad for employment / emigration and on the hospitality of the overseas organisation, to exporters by way of agency commission and settlement of quality claims, for sundry personal and commercial remittances, etc. In all such cases, except exporters, the sale of foreign exchange limit had been raised between $ 100 to $ 500.

Under LERMS, the Reserve Bank provides foreign exchange at the official exchange rate in the following cases: *(a)* For import of crude, diesel and kerosene by the Indian Oil Corporation, *(b)* For import of fertilisers by MMTC. *(c)* For discharge of financing arrangements like payments under Banker's Acceptance Facility and Suppliers' Credit in respect of items *(a)* and *(b)* above by IOC and MMTC respectively, *(d)* For import of goods by Ministries and Departments of Government of India on a certification from the Financial Adviser / Internal Finance Wing of the Ministry concerned that the import of such goods is as per authorisation of the Foreign Exchange Budget of the Department of Economic Affairs, *(e)* For import of Life-saving Drugs and Equipment. *(f)* For meeting 40 per cent of foreign exchange requirements of Advance Licences, Imprest Licence and import for replenishment of raw materials for Gem and Jewellery exports.

With effect from 2 March, 1993, the dual exchange rate system was replaced by the Unified Exchange Rate System (UERS) under which the 60:40 ratio was extended to 100 per cent conversion. The UERS was introduced to rectify the anomally of the LERMS under which exporters and other earners of foreign exchange indirectly subsidised certain imports. Under this system, the exchange rate was fully determined by market forces of relative demand and supply. The RBI had been announcing its buying and selling rates at the ongoing market rates for transactions with ADs. This system permitted 100 per cent conversion of the rupee for all exports and imports of goods. But the official RBI exchange rate continued for the conversion of items not permitted under the UERS. These included more than half-a-dozen invisible items of current account and all capital account payments. Further, various exchange control norms of the RBI remained in operation with a few relaxations.

As a result of the operation of the UERS, the exchange rate remained more or less steady at the level of Rs. 31.37 per dollar. With stability in the exchange rate and the large inflow of resources following liberalisation of foreign investment policy and removal of industrial and trade restrictions, there had been substantial improvement in the current account deficit. This led to the *current account convertibility* of the rupee effective 1 March, 1994. The RBI announced further relaxations in the exchange control regulations on a number of invisible items as part of the *current account* convertibility of the rupee. The final step towards current account convertibility was taken in August 1994 by further liberalisation of invisibles payments and acceptance of the obligations under Article VIII of the IMF. Under it, India is committed to forsake the use of exchange restrictions on current international transactions. There is no officially fixed exchange rate of the rupee. Instead, the rate is determined by the demand and supply conditions in the foreign exchange market. The RBI intervenes to maintain orderly market conditions and to curb excessive speculation in foreign exchange.

Foreign exchange is released by authorised dealers (ADs) for various purposes like foreign travel, medical treatment, gifts, services, studies, etc. Release of foreign exchange by ADs for the above purposes was initially governed by limits laid down by the RBI. Beyond the specified limits foreign exchange could be obtained after seeking prior approval of the RBI. Effective July 1995, the RBI has permitted ADs to provide exchange facilities to their customers for the above mentioned purposes beyond the indicative limit without its prior approval, provided they are satisfied about the bonafides of the application. But, they are required to report such transactions to the RBI.

The process of liberalisation towards current account convertibility has been continued by delegating more powers to ADs. (1) They have been permitted to export their surplus stocks of *foreign currency notes* and coins for realisation of proceeds to private money changers abroad, in addition to their overseas branches and correspondents. (2) They have been permitted to allow EEFC (Exchange Earners Foreign Currency) account holders to utilise funds held in such accounts for making remittances in foreign exchange connected with their trade and business related transactions which are of current account nature. (3) The RBI has set up *Inter-Bank Forex Clearing House* where foreign exchange transactions by ADs are cleared. (4) The RBI has set up a *Market Intelligence Cell* to study and closely monitor the developments in the Indian foreign exchange market. The Cell receives from the ADs on a daily basis information on forex transactions which are critically analysed and followed up.

9. CRITICAL APPRAISAL OF THE FUNCTIONING OF RBI

From a rudimentary beginning in 1935, the Reserve Bank of India has developed into a major central banking institution after it became a state-owned bank in January, 1949. Besides, it has been performing a variety of promotional and development functions.

ITS ACHIEVEMENTS

Some of the principal achievements of the RBI are as follows: 1. *Regulator of Credit.* The bank has been successfully regulating credit in the economy to meet the requirements of trade, industry and agriculture during periods of recession and inflation. For this purpose, it followed a cheap money policy in the early phase of development planning and after that a policy of controlled monetary expansion to meet the requirements of a growing economy.

2. *Banker to the Government.* As banker to the Government, the RBI has been admirably managing the

public debt. It has successfully floated loans on behalf of the Central and State Governments at low interest rates. It has also provided ways and means advances to the State Governments through the sale of treasury bills. It has been rendering advice to the Government on economic matters in general and on financial matters in particular.

3. *Development of Sound Banking System.* Another achievement of the Bank has been that it has developed and promoted sound banking practices in the country. In exercise of the powers vested in it by the Banking Regulation Act, it has been keeping a constant vigil over the banks, trying to remove their defects, and strengthening them. Consequently, this has inspired public confidence in the banking system as a whole.

4. *Institutionalisation of Savings.* The RBI has been successfully promoting the institutionalisation of savings by promoting banking habits, by large scale extension of banking facilities in rural and urban areas, and promoting and establishing new specialised financial agencies.

5. *In the Field of Co-operative Credit.* The RBI has successfully promoted co-operative credit. It has strengthened co-operatives by setting up NRC (LTO) Fund and NRC (Stabilisation) Fund and NABARD which now administers these Funds. It also finances the State Co-operative Banks. It has been due to the efforts of the RBI that the co-operative movement has been placed on a sound footing.

6. *In the Field of Rural Credit.* The Bank has been admirably engaged in the task of promoting rural credit since its inception. It runs a separate department to render advice to the Government on rural credit. By adopting the multi-agency approach (viz. the commercial banks, the co-operative banks, the RRBs, and NABARD), it has been successful in providing credit for the development of agriculture, trade, commerce, industry, and other productive activities in the rural areas.

7. *In the Sphere of Industrial Finance.* In the sphere of industrial credit, the RBI has played a pioneering role by promoting a wide range of institutions for providing medium and long-term credit such as IDBI, IFCI, ICICI, IFC, UTI, etc. It also provides medium/short-term credit limits to these institutions by rediscounting their usance bills and long-term assistance from the NIC (LTO) Fund.

8. *In the Field of Export Finance.* Another achievement of the bank has been in providing credit facilities to exporters. It has been providing concessional credit, refinance facilities, and guarantee to commercial banks for exporters. It has been instrumental in establishing the Export-Import Bank to provide credit and other facilities to exporters.

9. *Guardian of Banking System.* As the guardian of banking system, the RBI has been providing deposit insurance and credit guarantee facilities to the banks. For this purpose it has set up the Deposit Insurance and Credit Guarantee Corporation (DICGC).

10. *Promotion of Social Banking.* The RBI has played a vital role in the promotion of social banking in the country. It has progressively directed the banking system since 1969 towards national social economic objectives, including rural development and uplift of the weaker sections of the society. It has converted banks in India as instruments of social uplift instead of simply profit-making institutions.

11. *Change in the Pattern of Lending.* The Reserve Bank has been successful in changing the pattern of bank lending. *Firstly,* banks have been directed to lend 40 per cent of their total advances to the priority sectors. *Secondly,* they have been asked to ensure that 60 per cent of their deposits raised from rural and semi-urban centres are deployed as credit in those very areas. *Thirdly,* under the DRI scheme, the public sector banks have to ensure that one per cent of the previous year's advance is earmarked each year to be lent to certain specified weaker sections at a low rate of interest of 4 per cent.

12. *Development of Bill Market.* The RBI has been successful to a considerable extent in developing bill market in India. For this purpose, it has set up the Discount and Finance House of India (DFHI) and the Securities Trading Corporation of India (STCI) as major financial institutions to rediscount commercial bills. It has introduced a number of schemes such as 364-Day Treasury Bills, primary dealers in securities, etc.

13. *Providing Information and Research.* The Reserve Bank has been doing an excellent job in providing information and data on the different sectors of the economy through its weekly and monthly journals and annual reports. Its Department of Economic Analysis and Policy conducts highly useful surveys and carries on research on economic matters and publishes reports on them.

14. *Clearing House Facilities.* The Bank has been successfully rendering clearing house facilities at its 15 branches and 2 offices and at other places in the country through the SBI and its associates. It has introduced

Electronic Clearing System. This has helped in the use of cheques and inter-bank transactions.

15. *Exchange Management and Control.* Another achievement of the RBI has been its admirable management and control of the foreign exchange. It has gradually and successfully led the Indian economy to current account convertibility of the rupee.

16. *Representation at International Fora.* The Bank has been successfully representing the country at the international monetary forum such as the IMF and the World Bank.

17. *Human Resource Development.* One of the principal achievements of the RBI has been the setting up of a number of training centres and colleges to impart training to the staff of co-operative banks, commercial banks, RRBs, NABARD etc. Thus it has played a major role in human resource development in the field of banking.

18. *Computerisation.* To modernise the functioning of the RBI, its Department of Information Technology (DIT) has introduced advanced computer technology for inter-office communication and Internet technology for information collection and sharing. It has also encouraged computerisation of branches of commercial banks.

FAILURES OF THE RBI

Despite the above achievements, there are certain fields in which the RBI has not been able to function successfully. They are as under:

1. *Failure to Control Unorganised Money Market.* The Bank has not been able to control the unorganised sector of the money market. The indigenous bankers function independently of the policies of the RBI. The latter has failed to bring them under its control and supervision.

2. *Multiplicity of Interest Rates.* As there is a large unorganised monetary sector which is not under the RBI, there is no uniformity in the bank rate and other money market rates. Even the money market rates charged by banks and non-bank financial intermediaries differ widely.

3. *Failure to Check Inflationary Pressures.* Despite following the policy of controlled monetary expansion, the RBI has failed to control and contain inflationary pressure within the economy.

4. *Falling Profitability of Banks.* The RBI's policy of credit squeeze has led to the decline in the profitability of banks. With total deposits of banks blocked by reserves upto about 54 per cent, only 46 per cent are left with them for lending. Out of this 40 per cent is required to be given to the priority sector. On the other hand, the deposits of banks are on the decline due to the growing number of alternative saving instruments. All these measures by RBI have led to decline in the profitability of banks.

5. *Failure to Develop Bill Culture.* Despite its best efforts, the RBI has failed to develop an organised bill market to provide rediscounting facilities to banks. In fact, it has not been able to develop bill culture so that commerce, trade and industry may deal in bills of exchange. Further, it has not done anything to systematise and recognise *hundis* as bills of exchange.

6. *Failure to Provide Sufficient Rural Credit.* No doubt, the RBI has done a lot in providing rural credit through multiple agencies, but it is insufficient keeping in view the credit needs of the rural population. Consequently, it has not been able to free the ruralites from the hold of the indigenous bankers and money-lenders.

7. *Failure to Develop Exchange Banks.* The Bank has failed to develop Indian exchange banks with the result that foreign banks operating in the country continue to pocket a major portion of the foreign exchange business. The State Bank of India and a few public sector banks which deal in foreign exchange business and have their offices in foreign countries have not been able to achieve much in this direction because of the lack of clear policy guidelines by the RBI

8. *Deterioration of Customer Service.* Since the nationalisation of 20 banks, the customer service in these banks has deteriorated. The RBI has recently adopted a few measures in this direction, but customer service in public sector still lags behind private and foreign banks.

9. *Failure to Control Black Money.* The RBI has failed to check the growth of black money in the country. In fact, its credit squeeze policy has encouraged black money because traders and businessmen are able to get credit from the black money.

CONCLUSION

Despite these failures, the RBI has ushered in a new era of social banking. It has carried banking to the remotest corners of the country. It has created sound credit and monetary policies in keeping with the development efforts of the country. It has brought stability to the banking system. It has been instrumental in providing credit facilities to agriculturists, industrialists, exporters, and to ordinary persons engaged in different vocations. It is thus one of the prime movers in the development process.

EXERCISES

1. Describe the constitution and organisational structure of the Reserve Bank of India.
2. What are the functions of the Reserve Bank of India? How far has it succeeded as the Central Bank of the country?
3. Discuss the achievements and failures of the Reserve Bank of India.
4. What has the Reserve Bank of India done to develop and regulate banking in India?
5. Explain the role of Reserve Bank of India in developing Bill Market.
6. Explain how the Reserve Bank of India manages the exchange control system.
7. What role the Reserve Bank of India has been playing with regard to the financing of agriculture?
8. Discuss the policy of the Reserve Bank of India in financing industries in the country.
9. Give a critical appraisal of the functioning of Reserve Bank of India.
10. Write notes on : Bill Market Scheme, Exchange Control Management, Social Banking, Regulation of Banking in India by the Reserve Bank.

CHAPTER 79

Monetary Policy of Reserve Bank of India*

1. INTRODUCTION

Monetary policy in India is an adjunct of economic policy. As such, the objectives of monetary policy are not different from the objectives of economic policy. The three major objectives of economic policy in India have been growth, social justice, and price stability. The Government of India tries to manipulate its monetary policy through the Reserve Bank of India which is the monetary authority in the country. The monetary (or credit control) policy of the Reserve Bank has been characterised as one of controlled monetary expansion. It aims at controlling inflation by restraining the secondary expansion of credit and regulating the supply of money in order to meet the requirements of different sectors of the economy to accelerate the pace of economic growth.

ITS OBJECTIVES

Broadly speaking, the following are the objectives of monetary policy wrich the Reserve Bank has been trying to achieve:

1. *Price Stability.* The RBI tries to achieve price stability by controlling inflationary pressures in the area of aggregate demand through controlled monetary expansion and by facilitating allocation and effective utilisation of credit in relatively more productive channels.

2. *Reduce Deficit.* It tries to reduce the monetised deficit (net RBI credit to the Government) in order to bring down Government's gross fiscal deficit.

3. *Encourage Exports.* It boosts exports in order to solve the problem of balance of payments deficit.

4. *Growth.* It promotes growth through appropriate credit policy by promoting savings, mobilisation of resources and encouraging the requirements of different sectors of the economy according to plan priorities.

5. *Social Justice.* It supports programmes of social justice (i.e. more equitable distribution of income) by influencing the cost, volume and direction of credit to priority sectors of the economy.

Of these objectives, price stability is the dominant one. It is price stability which provides the appropriate

1. This also relates to Management of Credit and Currency.

environment in which growth can take place and social justice can be ensured. Price stability is also required to augment our exports and to service our external debt. In the context of economic growth, price stability does not mean no increase in prices. In fact, price stability refers to controlling inflation or keeping the general price level from rising by more than four per cent per year, as suggested by the RBI Chakravarty Committee (1985). For this the Committee advocated "monetary targeting with feed back" in order to keep the growth of money supply in step with the demand for it. The monetary target is not fixed but may be revised on a mid-year assessment of the price situation.

2. METHODS OF CREDIT CONTROL

To achieve these objectives, the RBI follows the following methods of credit control:[1]

1. Open Market Operations

Open market operations refer to the sale and purchase of gold related securities and other securities, bills and bonds of Government by the RBI from and to the public and financial institutions. To control inflation and tackle the problem of excess liquidity due to foreign exchange inflows, the RBI sells Government securities. As a result, there is reduction in the cash balances of banks and other deposits of banks held by the RBI. The opposite happens when the RBI purchases securities from the open market. In Government securities, there were adhoc Treasury Bills which were replaced by Ways and Means Advances from April 1997. They are meant to serve as a means of meeting temporary mismatches between the receipts and expenditure of the Central Government rather than a source of financing fiscal deficit. This has provided more flexibility to the RBI in operating its monetary policy. Besides, to control fluctuations in call money market rates repos/reverse repo auctions, first on daily basis then with 3-7 day maturity, were introduced under full-fledged liquidity, Adjustment Facility (LAF) effective August 2000. Besides, weekly auctions of 14-day Treasury Bills and 28-days Treasury Bills; fortnightly auctions of 182-day Treasury Bills; and monthly auctions of 364-day Treasury Bills were started from 1997-98.

The RBI has been resorting to open market operations in order to reduce the lending power of commercial banks because its sale of securities have normally exceeded its purchases. But the effectiveness of open market operations as an instrument of credit control in India is limited by a number of factors. *First,* except for the gilt-edged market in India, there is the absence of other first class securities. *Second,* the market for Government securities is a 'captive' market over which the RBI has almost a monopoly and some institutional investors like LIC, UTI, GIC, and commercial banks, etc. are required to invest in them. *Third,* open market operations are being used as an instrument of debt-management rather than to influence the cost and availability of credit. As such, open market operations have not been a success in India.

1. Bank Rate Policy

The bank rate is the rate fixed by the central bank at which it rediscounts first class bills of exchange and government securities held by commercial banks. But in India, the bank rate policy is limited to give advances to commercial banks against first class bills of exchange by the RBI. The latter include Government securities and genuine trade bills. Under the Bill Rediscounting Scheme introduced in November 1970, all licensed scheduled commercial banks are eligible to rediscount with the RBI genuine trade bills arising out of sale or despatch of goods.

The objectives of the RBI's bank rate policy are to influence the availability and cost of credit. The RBI has been unsuccessful in achieving these objectives. From its establishment in 1935 up to 14 November. 1951, the bank rate was stable at 3 per cent. It was cheap monetary policy which led to an unlimited expansion of credit. Consequently, speculative activities received encouragement and the deficit in balance of payments increased. For the first time, the bank rate was raised to 3.5 per cent in November 1951. It was raised to 4 per cent in May 1957, to 4.5 per cent in January 1963, to 5 per cent in September 1964, to 6 per cent in January 1971 and to 7 per

1. We have given a detailed explanation which may be confined to the latest measures without loss in continuity.

cent in May 1973. With an unprecedented rise in prices, the RBI resorted to a policy of dear money in July 1974 and raised the bank rate to 9 per cent in 1977, to 10 per cent in July 1981, to 11 per cent in July 1991 and to 12 per cent in October 1991. To overcome recession in the economy, the RBI started following cheap money policy by reducing the bank rate to 11 per cent in April 1997 and subsequently by stages to 6 per cent on April 29, 2003.

Thus the bank rate had not been used as an instrument of credit control till 1973. It is only in the 1980s and 1990s that its proper use has been made in the form of cheap or dear monetary policy.

3. Interest Rate Policy

Interest rate adjustment is a flexible and potent tool of credit policy. It reinforces restrictive/liberal impact of credit policy. In order to supplement the bank rate policy, the RBI has been following the policy of changing the interest rate structure for different sectors of the economy in the light of evolving economic trends.

(i) *Deposit Rates.* Since November 1975, the RBI has been following the policy of administered interest rates. This policy has the twin objectives of mobilising savings and providing funds for productive activities in the priority sectors of the economy at concessional rates of interest. The interest rates on all saving instruments including bank deposits are sometimes reduced to prevent banks from getting locked into longer period maturities. At other times, they are raised to assist the banks in deposit mobilisation and to offer a better rate of savings. Upto 21 April, 1992, the term deposit rates of scheduled commercial banks were prescribed in three slabs of maturities and rates. Effective 22 April, 1992, the banks were given freedom to determine the term deposits of three maturity slabs of their chbice, subject to a choice of interest rate 'not exceeding 13 per cent*. With the fall in inflation rate, the ceiling rate was gradually reduced to 'not exceeding 10 per cent' by 2 September 1993. When the inflation rate started rising, the ceiling rate was gradually raised to 'not exceeding 12 per cent' effective 18 April, 1995 for 46 days to 3 years and above.

To augment the resources of banks and to impart greater flexibility to term deposit rate structure, the banks have been allowed freedom to fix their own interest rates on domestic term deposits of all categories. The minimum period of term deposits has been gradually reduced from 46 days to 30 days; and subsequently to 15 days. Effective May 2001, the banks had been permitted to pay higher interest rates to senior citizens on their term deposits by 0.5 to 1.0 per cent.

The savings deposit rate has been lowered from to 4.0 per cent to 3.0 per cent effective March 1, 2003.

Term deposit rates on NRE accounts were also rationalised in accordance with the domestic rates. With a view to maintaining the differential between the interest rates on term deposits and NRE Rupee term deposits, banks were permitted to offer differential rates of interest on NRE deposits on size-group basis subject to the overall ceiling rate effective 27 April, 2000. Effective 4 April, 1996, interest rates on NRE term deposits of over two years had been freed for banks.

(ii) Lending Rates. The lending rate structure prescribed for banks since their nationalisation in 1969 had been cumbersome and complicated. It was characterised by a multiplicity of rates relating, to numerous criteria, such as size of loan, priority of a sector, location of activity, specific programmes, income of borrowers, etc. In September 1990, the RBI rationalised the lending rate structure of commercial banks. It is linked to the size of loan granted by the commercial banks.

When the inflation rates were high, upward revisions were made in the lending rates of commercial banks. The first upward revision was made on 13 April, 1991, when the minimum rate on advances above Rs. 2 lakh was raised from 16 per cent to 17 per cent effective 13 April, 1991 and gradually to 20 per cent on 9 October, 1991. As the inflation rate declined and the macroeconomic situation improved, the lending rate was reduced gradually from 20 per cent to 14 per cent effective 1 March, 1994. Effective 18 October, 1994, the prescription of a *minimum* lending rate has been abolished and banks have been given freedom to fix the prime lending rate (PLR) for all advances above Rs. 2 lakh. Each bank is required to declare its PLR and made uniformly applicable to all its branches.

In keeping with its policy of rationalisation of the lending rate structure according to the size of credit limit, the RBI reduced the number of categories from six to three by April 1993. The three categories with interest rates effective 18 October, 1994 were: *(a)* Upto Rs. 25,000 at 12 per cent (fixed); *(b)* Over Rs. 25,000 and upto Rs. 2 lakh at 13 per cent (fixed); and *(c)* Over Rs. 2 lakh freed.

Under the DIR (Differential Interest Rate) scheme, term loans are provided to small and water transport operators, professionals and self-employeds in the priority sector at the concessional rate of 4 per cent by both the commercial banks and urban co-operative banks. They are required to lend 40 per cent of their total advances to the priority sector.

Alongwith the above measures, interest rates on export credit are reviewed from time to time with a view to providing an incentive to exporters for repatriating the proceeds as well as discouraging them from delaying repatriation of export proceeds. On *preshipment* export credit, banks have been allowed to charge 10 per cent interest upto 180 days and 13 per cent beyond 180 days to 270 days since 1 April, 1999. On *post-shipment* export credit upto 90 days, the interest rate has been 10 per cent since 1 April, 1999, beyond 90 days to 6 months, and beyond six months the banks are free to charge interest rates decided by them.

4. Changes in Variable Reserve Ratio

The variable reserve ratio is a very effective instrument of monetary control with the RBI. In India, the variable reserve ratio is of the following types:

(i) Cash Reserve Ratio (CRR). Since the establishment of RBI till 1956, the commercial banks were required to keep 2 per cent of their time deposits and 5 per cent of their demand deposits with the RBI in the form of reserves. Thus this tool of monetary policy was not used for more than 20 years in India. With the RBI Amendment Act, 1956, the RBI was empowered to raise the time deposits of commercial banks from 2 to 8 per cent and the demand deposits from 5 to 20 per cent. By the RBI Amendment Act, 1962 the distinction between time and demand deposits was abolished and the provision was made to keep the CRR between 3 to 15 per cent. After this, the RBI had been making changes in the CRR in keeping with the monetary and economic conditions.

Effective 1 July, 1989, instead of separate ratios for different types of liabilities, there is a uniform CRR of 15 per cent of the entire net demand and time liabilities (NDTL) of banks, including FCNR and NRE accounts. The CRR was reduced to 14 per cent effective 15 May, 1993 and again raised to 15 per cent effective 6 August, 1994. This was to meet monetary pressure arising from large capital inflows. For the same reason, the CRR on FCNR accounts was raised to 15 per cent and on NRNR deposits to 7.5 per cent. When these conditions reversed and money growth slowed, the CRR was reduced from 15 per cent to 14 per cent effective 9 December 1995 and that on FCRR and NRNR deposited removed. To augment the lendable resources of banks, the CRR was further reduced from 14 per cent to 13 per cent effective 11 May, 1996, and to 12 per cent effective 6 July, 1996 and in subsequent years gradually to 8 per cent on 1 April, 2000 and to7.5 per cent on 14 May, 2001 .The reduction in CRR to 7.5 per cent has been done to enable banks to reduce their PLR and to release more liquidity into the monetary system. As a policy measure, the variations in CRR has been more successful in controlling credit than open market operations and bank rate policy.

(ii) Statutory Liquidity Ratio (SLR). Another important tool of monetary policy with the RBI is the Statutory Liquidity Ratio (SLR) which supplements the CRR. Under the Banking Regulation Act, 1949, the commercial banks are required to keep 20 per cent of their net demand and time liabilities (NDTL) deposits with them in the form of liquidity ratio. In this liquidity ratio are included excess reserves, current account balances of the commercial banks with the RBI and other banks, gold and unencumbered approved securities. But whenever the RBI raised the CRR, the commercial banks would make this unsuccessful by increasing their liquidity power through the sale of government securities. In order to overcome this weakness, the SLR was raised to 25 per cent by the Banking Amendment Act of 1962. But the cash reserves kept with the RBI were not included in this ratio. In order to contain the liquidity growth in the banking system and consequent monetary expansion, the SLR was raised to 30 per cent in November 1972. Since then it had been revised upward regularly so that with effect from 22 September, 1990 it had been 38.5 per cent. To make more funds available for. commercial bank lending, the *base* SLR on NDTL was reduced gradually and by the end of 1996, it was brought down to 25 per cent as per the recommendations of the Narasimhan Committee. The incremental SLR is 25 per cent. This refers to the ratio, the banks are required to keep if there NDTL increase over the base SLR. The advantages of SLR are that by implementing it along with CRR, it controls the liquidity of banks and thereby limits their power to make advances to trade and industry. Thus the quantitative monetary policy is successful in reducing inflationary pressures. Second, more financial resources are available to the government for its use.

5. Selective Credit Controls

Selective credit controls are meant to regulate and control the supply of credit. They aim at channelising the flow of bank credit from speculative and other undesirable purposes to socially desirable and economically useful uses. Thus they help in curtailing the rise in prices of commodities.

The method of selective credit controls was introduced in India by the RBI in May 1956. Under this: *(i)* it fixes minimum margins for advances against securities for banks. These margins are from 20 to 100 per cent; *(ii)* it fixes ceilings on maximum advances against stocks of certain commodities to traders; *(iii)* it fixes minimum discriminatory rates of interest for certain kinds of advances by banks; *(iv)* it prohibits advances for financing hoarding of certain commodities; and *(v)* prohibits the discounting of bills of exchange relating to the sale of some selected commodities.

Selective credit controls relate to such commodities as cotton, wheat, paddy/rice, pulses, oilseeds, vegetable oils, sugar, gur and khandsari, man-made fibres and cloth. The rate of interest charged on advances by banks against the security of such commodities is higher than on other securities. If the RBI wants to control speculation on the prices of such commodities, it raises the minimum margins. In case it wants to liberalise credit facilities for them, it lowers the minimum margins. It does so in keeping with changing market conditions.

For instance, to curb inflationary pressures, the RBI had fixed the ceiling of 45 per cent on the incremental net non-food credit deposit ratio for banks from October 1989. Further, restrictions had been placed on loans for purchase of consumer durables and other non-priority sector personal loans. The minimum margin for loans against shares and debentures/bonds was fixed at 75 per cent. When in early 1992, the inflation rate started declining, the banks were advised to support the revival of productive activity. At the same time, effective 22 April, 1992, all restrictions on credit or purchase of consumer durables, other non-priority sector personal loans and stipulation on net non-food credit-deposit ratio were removed. Effective 21 October, 1996, selective credit controls on pulses, coarse grains, oil seeds, vanaspati, sugar, gur, khandsari, cotton, kapas had been abolished, except buffer stocks. Banks were given freedom to fix margins on advances against sensitive commodities, except unreleased stocks of sugar for which 15 per cent margin had been fixed. Effective 2 December, 1996, the banks were granted freedom to advance loans against shares/debentures with the maximum limit of Rs. 10 lakh. It has since been raised to Rs. 20 lakh.

Credit Monitoring Arrangement (CMA). With effect from 10 October 1988, the RBI dispensed with the Credit Authorisation Scheme (CAS) and introduced the Credit Monitoring Arrangement (CMA) for bank lending for working capital purposes. Under the revised scheme effective 30 October, 1996 all sanctions/renewals of credit limits to borrowers enjoying fund-based working capital limits of Rs. 10 crores and above and term loans in excess of Rs. 5 crores were required to be reported by the banks to the RBI for post-sanction scrutiny. All sanctions/renewals of credit limits were required to be reported to the RBI. In this way, the RBI regulated the sanctioning of loans by banks through CMA. The CMA was discontinued from 8 December, 1997.

In recent years, the Reserve Bank has announced several steps to facilitate the flow of credit to the commercial sector, particularly for exports, information technology, infrastructure, agriculture, small scale industries, etc. The coverage of the priority sector credit has been widened considerably. Bank credit to NBFCs (non-bank financial companies) for on-lending to small road and water transport operators, software industry having credit limit up to Rs. 1 crore, to the food and agro-based sector, to NBFCs and financial institutions for on-lending to the tiny sector, and to both public and private sector undertaking for financing infrastructure projects is now being treated as priority sector lending. Besides, bank lending to sensitive sectors comprising capital market, real estate (housing) and commodities is regulated in keeping with the trends in the economy.

Their Effectiveness. Selective credit controls have been more effective in controlling credit than the quantitative methods. They have been instrumental in channelising the flow of credit from speculative and other undesirable purposes to socially desirable and economically useful purposes. They have helped in restricting the demand for money by laying down certain conditions for borrowers by fixing minimum margin requirements and other limits. Thus they have been successful in regulating credit for different uses in various sectors of the economy according to plan priorities.

Despite all these successes, selective credit controls have failed to control the demand for and supply of money in the country. They have, therefore, failed to control inflationary pressures.

With the introduction of commercial paper by the large organised sector, the RBI's control over credit through the CMA had become less effective. Now large industries can raise money directly from the market at cheaper rates than bank credit.

Moreover, trade and industry can get funds from non-bank financial institutions, mutual fund's, etc. which have made selective credit controls less effective.

Above all, selective credit controls alone are not effective in controlling credit. They must be combined with general (or quantitative) control measures like bank rate, open market operation, CRR, SLR, etc.

6. Direct Action

The Banking Companies Act, 1949 empowers the RBI to caution or prohibit banks generally or any individual bank in particular, from entering into any particular transaction or class of transactions. The RBI has also the power to inspect any bank and its books accounts. On a report from the RBI, the Central Government may prohibit any bank from receiving fresh deposits or direct the RBI to order for the winding up of the bank or its merger with some other bank.

7. Moral Suasion

Besides, the above noted quantitative and qualitative measures of credit control, the RBI also follows the method of moral suasion. By this method of persuasion, suggestion and advice, the RBI asks the banks to follow its declared monetary policy from time to time. By sending circular letters or calling meetings of directors of banks, it persuades them not to give credit for speculative activities and/or to give more credit facilities to priority sectors of the economy. Before the nationalisation of 20 banks in India, the method of moral suasion was not successful but now all banks follow the RBI guidelines. As a matter of fact, the RBI is so powerful that no bank dares to ignore its circulars and suggestions.

3. CRITICAL APPRAISAL OF MONETARY POLICY

The main aim of India's monetary policy which is regulated by the RBI, is to have growth with stability. It is also known as the policy of controlled monetary (or credit) expansion. In pursuance of this policy, the RBI affects the quantity, availability and cost of credit by adopting both the quantitative and qualitative methods of credit control. It increases the quantity of money and credit to meet the growing requirements of the developing economy, and at the same time imposes restrictions on the use of credit for non-essential and unproductive activities. In periods of recession, it follows the policy of easy credit or cheap money, and to control inflationary pressures, it follows the policy of credit squeeze or tight money. It is contributing to the economic development of the economy in an important way by giving cheap and easy credit to the priority sector consisting of marginal and small farmers, artisans, unemployeds, small traders, village and small industries etc. At the same time, it also provides credit to large industries and to exporters to meet their expanding credit requirements so that production may increase and exports expand.

4. CAUSES OF FAILURE OF MONETARY POLICY

Despite these achievements, the monetary policy of RBI has not been a success in bringing stability to the economy. Some of the reasons are:

(1) *Inflationary Pressures.* During the plans, the average growth rate of money supply has been 15 per cent per annum with the average growth rate of domestic product of 5 per cent per annum. The disproportionate and persistent increase in liquidity has been a significant factor contributing to inflationary pressures in the economy.

(2) *Excessive Government Borrowing and Budgetary Deficits.* Another reason for the failure of monetary policy in India has been the impact of large and growing Government borrowing and budgetary deficits over the plans. The budgetary deficits have been virtually monetised (i.e. financed) by the RBI through the creation of ad hoc treasury bills. Besides, the RBI has been providing support to the Government's market borrowing programmes. Consequently, this has led to the phenomenal increase in reserve money contributed (i.e. created) by RBI credit to the Government. This has led to inflationary pressure in the economy.

(3) *High CRR and SLR.* In order to contain the inflationary impact of monetisation of the budget deficits, the RBI has been continuously increasing the CRR and SLR. The reserve ratios in India are quite high being 45 per cent of the deposits, leaving 55 per cent for lending. Out of these, 40 per cent go to priority sector advances at low rates of interest. Thus, only a small portion of funds is available for deployment in non-food and trading activities at commercial rates of interest. This has tended to reduce the profitability of banks.

(4) *Defective Interest Rate Policy.* The RBI has been following a policy of administered interest rates. The structure of these rates is complex and cumbersome. It conceals an element of arbitrariness. It fails to take into account the risk involved, the maturity period or the liquidity factor on individual instruments of credit. The interest rate structure is also not separate for the captive market and the borrowing public.

(5) *Organised Sector Uninfluenced by Bank Credit.* With the introduction of commercial paper by the large organised sector, industries can raise money directly from the market at cheaper rates than bank credit. This has blunted the edge of monetary policy in controlling the activities of the organised sector.

(6) *Other Sources for Banks.* Besides getting funds from NBFIs, commercial banks are able to maintain enough liquidity with them from the call money market, mutual funds and similar other sources. As a result, the RBI is not in a position to control the lending activities of the banks.

(7) Little Co-ordination between Monetary and Fiscal Policies. There is little co-ordination between monetary and fiscal policies being pursued by the RBI and the Government. There is no co-ordination between the expansion in RBI credit to the Government and Central Government's budgetary deficits. With increasing budgetary deficits from year to year, the RBI has to monetise them. Consequently, its power to regulate the volume of money is limited. This has made monetary policy less effective in India.

(8) *Existence of Parallel Economy.* There is a large sector of unaccounted black money which is beyond the jurisdiction of RBI. The existence of this parallel economy makes a mockery of the credit policy of the RBI because individuals, traders and businessmen borrow, lend and spend money at their will.

(9) *Government Policy.* There are some more weaknesses of monetary policy of the RBI due to Government policies. These are: *(i)* the government depends more on the public for borrowing outside the captive market, and *(ii)* yields on the Government securities are not fixed independently of the conditions in the capital market.

Conclusion. We have seen above that one of the principal reasons for the failure of monetary policy in controlling inflationary pressures in India has been the growing budgetary deficits. Monetary policy at best can control the secondary effects of excessive budget deficits. It is, therefore, essential that monetary and fiscal policies should move in tandem.

EXERCISES

1. Explain critically monetary policy in India.
2. Explain India's monetary policy. To what extent it has been successful in its objectives?
3. Discuss critically the monetary policy of the Reserve Bank of India.
4. What are the instruments of selective credit control employed by the Reserve Bank of India? Discuss their effectiveness.
5. Explain how the Bank Rale Policy is operated by the Reserve Bank of India.

CHAPTER 80

The State Bank of India (SBI)

1. ITS CONSTITUTION

The original name of the State Bank of India was Imperial Bank of India. The Imperial Bank of India was formed in 1921 by amalgamating the three Presidency banks of Bengal, Bombay and Madras. Prior to Independence, the Imperial Bank was handling the entire business and banking transactions of the Government. Though the Reserve Bank of India had been established in 1935, it was undertaking only central banking functions. Therefore, the Imperial Bank continued to handle Government transactions.

On the recommendations of the All India Rural Credit Survey Committee (1954), the Government of India nationalised the Imperial Bank of India and renamed it as the State Bank of India with effect from 1 July, 1955. Further, eight banks of the former princely States were brought under the SBI as its subsidiaries in 1959. They were State Bank of Bikaner, State Bank of Jaipur, State Bank of Patiala, State Bank of Saurashtra, State Bank of Indore, State Bank of Hyderabad, State Bank of Mysore, and State Bank of Travancore. In 1963, State Bank of Bikaner and State Bank of Jaipur were merged as State Bank of Bikaner and Jaipur.

2. ITS ORGANISATIONAL STRUCTURE

The SBI is not a bank wholly owned by the Government. It is a corporate body with an authorised share capital, of Rs. 1000 crore and paid-up capital of Rs. 526 crores of shares of Rs. 10 each as on 31 March, 1998. The apex body in the organisational structure of the SBI is the Central Board of Directors, which consists of a Chairman, two Managing Directors and 17 Directors appointed/elected under Section 19(1) of the State Bank of India Act, 1955. The Chairman and the Managing Directors are appointed by the Central Government in consultation with the RBI for a period not exceeding five years. Out of 17 Directors 6 are ex-officio representing different organisations, 4 are elected by the shareholders, 6 are nominated by the Central Government and one is nominated by the RBI. To manage the different Departments of the Bank, there is a Central Management Committee which has ten members consisting of the Chairman, two Managing Directors and seven Deputy Managing Directors. The Chairman is the ex-officio member of the Committee. All the Deputy Managing Directors function under the overall charge of the Managing Directors. During 1995-96, several organisational changes have been carried out in the areas of structure, systems and strategies of the SBI. Large integrated top management now consists of the Chairman, group executives for National Banking Group, Corporate Banking Group, International Banking Group and Associates and Subsidiaries Group and four staff functionaries in charge of financial, credit, human resources and technology management, and inspection and audit.

Three Strategic Business Units (SBUs) have been set up under the Corporate Banking Group to focus attention on very large corporate customers, lease finance and project finance. They are the Corporate Accounts Group, Leasing Group and Project Finance Group. Each SBU has been given profit responsibility.

A committee approach has been adopted, both at the apex and circle levels for sanctioning large advances. For this purpose, Central Office Credit Committee and Circle Credit Committees have been set up. They have been delegated higher financial powers to ensure faster decision-making of credit disposals. At the circle level, Commercial and Development and Personal Banking Networks have been created under the charge of General Managers to cater to the client-specific banking needs.

3. ITS OBJECTIVES

The State Bank of India was established with the following specific objectives:

1. To have a strong commercial bank under the control and supervision of the Government.

2. To spread banking facilities in rural, semi-urban and metropolitan areas by opening 400 branches within five years of its establishment. This policy of branch expansion has since been continued.

3. To help spread banking in rural areas for the purpose of encouraging and mobilising savings among the ruralists and to provide credit to them.

4. To subscribe to the debentures of State Land Development Banks and to advance loans on their security.

5. To strengthen co-operative societies, help in the establishment of licensed warehouses arid co-operative marketing societies.

6. To provide financial assistance to small, cottage and village industries.

7. To help other banks and strengthen the banking system.

8. To help the RBI in implementing its monetary and credit policies.

4. ITS FUNCTIONS

The State Bank performs the following functions:

1. *Central Banking Functions.* The SBI performs a number of functions on behalf of the Reserve Bank of India.

(a) It acts as the agent of the RBI where the latter has no branch, *(b)* It receives money on behalf of the Central and State Governments and makes payments on their behalf, *(c)* It buys and sells securities on behalf of the Government and manages the public debt, *(d)* It receives deposits from commercial banks and state co-operative banks and in turn lends to them, *(e)* It provides remittance facilities to these banks. *(f)* It rediscounts their bills of exchange, *(g)* It acts as a clearing house at places where the RBI has no office.

2. *Accepts Deposits.* The State Bank accepts deposits of all kinds from the Indian public and NRIs in rupees and foreign currencies.

3. *Gives Loans and Advances.* It gives loans and advances against an eligible security including goods, bills of exchange, promissory notes, fully paid shares and debentures or other securities of a civil authority, etc.

4. *Invests and Borrows.* The SBI invests in Government securities and borrows from the Reserve Bank.

5. *Deals in Bills of Exchange.* The State Bank draws, accepts, discounts, buys and sells bills of exchange and deals in letters of credit payable in and outside India.

6. *Deals in Gold and Silver.* The SBI buys and sells gold and silver. In June and July 1991, it sold gold to the Swiss Bank and pledged gold to the Bank of England on behalf of the Reserve Bank.

7. *Deals in Foreign Currencies.* The SBI is an authorised agent for dealing in foreign currencies. As such, it exchanges foreign currencies in Indian rupees and rupees into foreign currencies.

8. *Acts as Agent.* It acts as the agent of any registered co-operative bank.

9. *Business on Commission.* The State Bank transacts pecuniary business on commission.

10. *Underwrites Issues.* It underwrites issues of stocks, shares, debentures and other securities in which it is authorised to invest.

11. *Capital Stock of Banking Company.* It can subscribe to, buy, acquire, hold and sell any shares in the capital stock of any banking company.

12. *Form Subsidiary.* It can form any banking company as its subsidiary or take over any banking company on the direction of the Reserve Bank.

13. *Hire Purchase Companies.* It is authorised to make loans and advances to firms and companies engaged in the financing of hire purchase transactions on the security of book debts, etc. subject to the approval of the Central Board.

14. *Housing Schemes.* The State Bank is authorised to act as an agent of the Central Government, a State Government or any corporation in implementing schemes for financing the construction of houses and manage the funds placed at its disposal for this purpose.

15. *Finances Foreign Trade.* The SBI finances the foreign trade of the country.

5. WORKING OR ACHIEVEMENTS OF STATE BANK OF INDIA

The State Bank of India is the biggest commercial bank in the country with the largest number of branches and offices in India and abroad. Since its nationalisation in 1955, its working reveals that it has made tremendous progress in deposits, advances, rural credit, industrial finance, priority sectors, merchant banking, mutual fund, housing finance, factoring etc. We discuss below its role and importance as the leading commercial bank of the country.

A. Banking Trends

1. *Paid-up Capital and Reserves.* There has been a phenomenal growth in the paid-up capital and reserves of the State Bank over the years. From mere Rs. 12 crores in 1955 and Rs. 20 crores in 1969, they had risen to Rs. 9,608 crores as at the end of March 1998.

2. *Deposits Growth.* The SBI has made great efforts towards deposit mobilisation. In absolute terms, they increased from Rs. 226 crores in 1955 to Rs. 131,091 crores in 1998.

3. *Credit Expansion.* The Bank has expanded much its policy of giving loans and advances for food and non-food purposes. The overall amount of advances increased from Rs. 106 crores in 1955 to Rs. 841 crores in 1969 to Rs. 74,237 crores as on March 1998.

4. *Investments.* Its investments in Government securities also show considerable growth. In absolute amount, they increased from Rs. 117 crores in 1955 to Rs. 350 crores in 1969 and to Rs. 54,982 crores in March 1998.

5. *Branch Expansion.* Since its nationalisation in 1955, the SBI has been successfully carrying on its policy of branch expansion. Its number of offices including foreign offices increased from 497 in 1955 to 8,979 in June 2003. Alongwith branch expansion, the number of employees also increased from 14,682 to 2,33,000 over the period.

6. *Other Highlights.* Its credit-deposit ratio was 47 per cent in 1995 which increased to 62 per cent in 1996. Its capital adequacy ratio was 13.50 per cent in 2002-03 well above the stipulated 9 per cent.

B. State Bank of India and Agricultural Finance

The State Bank of India is a pioneer in the field of agricultural finance. In fact, it has been a pace setter for other banks in rural banking. It has been helping in providing rural finance in the following ways:

1. *Branch Expansion.* At the time of nationalisation, the State Bank was required to open not less than 400 branches within five years of its inception mainly in rural and semi-urban areas. In fact, it opened 416 branches during the stipulated period. Since then it has kept up the tempo of branch expansion with the result that at the

end of June 2003, it had 4,098 branches in rural areas which formed about 46 per cent of its total branches in the country.

2. *Remittance Facilities.* With the spread of a network of branches in rural areas, the SBI has been providing cheap remittance facilities to State and Central Co-operative Banks, Land Development Banks, farmers and traders.

3. *Help to Co-operative Banks.* The SBI has been of great help to co-operative and land development banks engaged in providing rural credit. It grants short-term credit to the State and Central Co-operative Banks against Government securities at a concessional rate. It also grants advances to these banks for financing marketing of agricultural produce, distribution of fertilisers, and procurement of foodgrains.

4. *Help to Land Development Banks.* The State helps the Land Development Banks which provide long-term credit to agriculturists in the following ways: The SBI subscribes to the debentures of LDBs and grants them loans and advances on the security of such debentures. It also gives advances to them for a short-term on the guarantee of the State Government, pending flotation of debentures by them.

5. *Credit to Co-operative Marketing and Processing. Societies.* It provides direct credit to co-operative marketing and processing societies for working capital requirements. This help is given when they are unable to get financial assistance from Central / State Co-operative Banks. The marketing societies are given advances against the pledge of their goods / produce to the SBI till they sell the produce in the market. Similarly, the Bank grants loans to co-operative processing societies engaged in the processing of sugar, jute, cotton, etc.

6. *Production Finance.* The SBI provides short-term credit to individual farmers for raising of crops.

7. *Finance for Irrigation.* The Bank has been extending assistance by way of term loans to various minor irrigation projects, command area development schemes, dugwell and tubewell sinking projects, etc. Besides, under the Special Project Agriculture sponsored by the Rural Electrification Corporation for energisation of pumpsets. The Bank has also been financing *drip irrigation scheme* which involves application of adequate water to the plant root at definite intervals, thereby ensuring efficient management of limited water resources.

8. *Modernisation of Farm Practices.* The SBI provides finance to farmers from raising agricultural productivity through modernisation of farm practices.

9. *Wasteland Development.* The Bank extends credit facilities to farmers for reclaiming wastelands under social forestry schemes, for raising nurseries and planting trees to meet the raw material requirements of fuel and fodder. It also provides credit for setting up plantations in order to meet the raw material requirements of user industries, joint sector undertaking, companies, co-operatives and individual entrepreneurs.

10. *Financing of Warehouses.* The establishment of warehouses helps in the marketing of agricultural produce by farmers. The SBI has been associated with development of warehouses in a number of States. It also gives advances to farmers against warehouse receipts thereby preventing distress sales on the part of growers and provides a cushion against violent fluctuations in the prices of farm produce. Warehouses help in storing farm products and prevent their wastage.

11. *Financing of Fisheries.* The SBI finances fisheries schemes for increasing fish production to meet the domestic demand and export potential.

12. *Financing of Other Activities.* The SBI also provides financing assistance to special agricultural activities such as animal husbandry, cattle breeding, dairy farming, piggery, poultry farming, horticulture, sericulture, vermi-culture, tissue-culture and mushroom cultivation and high-tech agriculture. During 1995-96, the Bank's advances to agriculture and allied activities amounted to Rs. 6,749 crores.

13. *Service Area Approach.* Under the Service Area Approach introduced from 1 April, 1989, 86 per cent of the Bank's branches had implemented village credit plans in 1,12,064 villages allotted under SAA. The Bank's branches had also to finance 'non-target' group of borrowers in 54,353 villages allotted to branches of Regional Rural Banks sponsored by the RBI, but falling outside the service areas of the branches of the Bank. Under the activity-wise Special Credit Plan, the Bank disbursed Rs. 2,706 crores during 1995-96.

14. *Integrated Area Approach.* Since 1971, the SBI has been laying emphasis on an integrated area approach with developing compact areas where economic growth could be accelerated with the Bank's support, preference being given to areas which are backward and where special schemes of the Government have been taken up. In keeping with this approach, the SBI has started the *Village Adoption Scheme.* Under this scheme, the Bank adopts a village, fixes a target and meets the entire financial needs of the village including its farmers, artisans

and others.[1]

15. *ADBs and ABDs.* The State Bank has Agricultural Development Branches (ADBs) and Agricultural Banking Divisions (ABDs) in selective areas particularly included in IRDP, HYVP and IAAP areas. The aim is to finance allround development of agriculture. The Bank works in close co-operation with NABARD.

16. *RRBs.* The Bank also finances rural activities through the Regional Rural Banks. It has sponsored 30 RRBs in 14 States covering 76 districts with a network of 2,385 branches. Under the first phase of restructuring, 8 SBI-sponsored RRBs were covered. In the second phase, 9 RRBs have been covered.

Conclusion. The State Bank has been a pioneer in agricultural finance in the country. It has been providing direct as well as indirect credit facilities to farmers, artisans, marginal farmers, and weaker sections of rural India.

C. State Bank of India and Industrial Finance

The State Bank of India occupies the premier position in providing finance to large/medium, and small scale industries. The type of financial assistance being rendered to them is as under:

1. Financing Large/Medium Scale Industries

The Bank has been financing medium/large scale industries on a selective basis. On the one hand, it has been financing new ventures of industrial groups with a good track record and on the other, new generation entrepreneurs with viable ventures. During 1995-96, the Bank's industrial advances were Rs. 8,298 crores. The Bank has been making loans and advances to such industrial groups as iron and steel, coal, electricity generation, chemicals, cement, petroleum, engineering, cotton textiles, food processing, gem and jewellery, paper products, etc.

Industrial Finance Branches (IFBs). To strengthen infrastructure for catering 'to medium/large industries, it has set up 9 IFBs at important centres.

Monitoring of Credit. The Bank has been making special efforts for monitoring of credit by exposing the officials to different training programmes, including on-the-job training at the apex level.

Industrial Rehabilitation. The SBI set up a separate Department of Industrial Rehabilitation in 1990-91 to deal with sick and financially weak units and to rehabilitate them. Its main thrust towards this direction has been to extend nursing assistance to the sick units, mainly under the aegis of the Board for Industrial and Financial Reconstruction (BIFR). At the same time, speedy disposal of cases which are not amenable to nursing has been achieved through compromises, recoveries, write-offs and mergers with healthy companies. So far, 101 out of the 351 rehabilitation packages drawn up for assisted units under the direction of BIFR have been put in operation, and 51 companies ordered to be wound up during the year.

Infrastructure Development. For financing infrastructure projects, the Bank assisted 9 independent power projects envisaging Rs. 2,276 crores. The Bank also sanctioned Bid Bond guarantees to enable 8 companies bid for Basic and Cellular services during 1995-96.

2. Financing of Small Scale Industries

The State Bank has been meeting the growing needs of the small scale sector by providing credit facilities on liberal terms. Its financial assistance covers all stages of manufacturing, viz. working capital, purchase of raw materials, marketing, entrepreneurial assistance, etc. It also covers expansion and modernisation of plants and equipment. Smaller units predominate the Bank's portfolio of small scale industries and about 66 per cent of the small industrial units financed by the Bank have limits below Rs. 25,000. The Bank's outstanding advances to small scale units stood at Rs. 7,790 crores at the end of March 1996 and the number of units financed was 10 lakh.

---

1. Assistance to Weaker Sections of Society under Other Achievements of SBI given below should also be mentioned here.

Equity Fund. To provide equity support to small scale units, the Bank operates its Equity Fund Scheme. Under this scheme, it provides interest free loans, repayable over a period of 5-7 years with an initial starting period. Equity support is provided up to Rs. 1 lakh to deserving entrepreneurs setting up new small scale units and upto Rs. 50,000 to professionals and self-employed persons.

Entrepreneur Scheme. Under this scheme, the Bank finances technically qualified persons and experienced craftsmen up to Rs. 10 lakhs for starting new projects. Assistance up to Rs. 2 lakhs is made available free of margin. Where project cost exceeds Rs. 2 lakhs, margins ranging from 5 to 12.5 per cent are required to be contributed by the entrepreneur.

Consultancy Cells. The Bank has Consultancy Cells which provide management consultancy support to small scale units and technical guidance to operating staff. These Cells are also actively engaged in the work relating to technology upgradation. Officials of the Cell are trained to act as nodal points for collecting and making available necessary information relating to the industry, including techno-economic aspects.

Entrepreneurial Development Programme. The Bank conducts entrepreneurial development programmes in the backward districts and its lead districts to motivate first generation entrepreneurs to set up risk-bearing ventures.

Rehabilitation of Sick Units. Under the guidance of its Department of Industrial Rehabilitation, the Bank identifies sick small units and formulates expeditious nursing programmes for the viable units. So far about 90 per cent of the total viable small scale sick units in the Bank's books have been placed under suitable rehabilitation programmes. The Bank has also initiated steps for upgradation of technology of selected groups of small scale industries to make them more competitive.

Technology Upgradation. The Bank has a separate Department of Systems aiid Technology which set up the Industrial Technology Group (known as UPTECH Group) in 1988. This Group directs and guides programmes aimed at facilitating technology upgradation in the small scale industrial sectors. For this purpose, the Bank has set apart Rs. 2 crores to form a Technology Data and Information Services Centre Fund. The UPTECH group has taken up location and industry-specific programmes. Upgradation of products and processes are attempted in these programmes to bring about quality control, increased productivity and efficiency. The Bank offers packages of assistance to units which wish to implement the technological upgradation programmes.

Small Business Finance. The Bank also provides finances to small business enterprises which include retail traders, transport operators, professionals and others. The main objective of the Bank has been to increase opportunities for self-employment in the tertiary sector. The Bank's advances to small business units amounted to Rs. 2,414 crores covering 25 lakh accounts at the end of March 1996.

Conclusion. The above analysis reveals that the State Bank has been playing a vital role in financing large scale industries. But its contribution in supplying loans and advances, in providing equity funds, in modernisation, in helping to supply inputs, in marketing, etc., to small scale industries and small business has been immense. No other commercial bank in the country is in a position to compete with it.

D. Other Achievements of the State Bank of India

Other achievements of the State Bank spread to a wide range of activities which are discussed as under:

1. Assistance to Weaker Sections of Society

The Bank has been carrying out a number of schemes to assist the weaker sections of society so that they are provided gainful employment opportunities and are able to raise their income levels. Some of the schemes are:

Integrated Rural Development Programme. The Bank is actively engaged in alleviating rural poverty under the Government sponsored IRDP. It assists the rural poor in acquiring income-generating assets. Since the inception of the Programme in 1980 the cumulative disbursement of the Bank upto March 1996 amounted to Rs. 2,195 crores covering 61.55 lakh beneficiaries. .

Differential Rate of Interest (DRI) Scheme. Under this scheme, the Bank has been providing financial assistance at a concessional rate of interest of 4 per cent to persons belonging to the weaker sections of society who are engaged in productive activities. At the end of March 1996, the Bank's DRI advances stood at Rs. 1,443 crores. Over 60 per cent of the Bank's DRI advances were made to SC/ST and women beneficiaries, exceeding the stipulation of 40 per cent laid down by the Government involving Rs. 248 crores.

Twenty-Point Programme. The Bank has achieved considerable progress under the restructured Twenty-Point Programme which mainly aims at raising agricultural productivity, eradication of rural poverty and ensuring justice to the underprivileged sections of the society. As at the end of March 1996, the Bank's aggregate loans under the Programme stood at Rs. 4,142 crores covering 95 lakh borrowal accounts. The major chunk of Bank's assistance has been in the spheres of attack on poverty, needs of SC/ST borrowers, strategy for rainfed agriculture, better use of irrigation water, bigger harvests, energy for villages, etc.

Scheme for Urban Micro Enterprises. The Scheme which is a component of the Jawahar Rozgar Yojana, was introduced in 1990. The scheme aims at encouraging the unemployed and underemployed urban poor living below the poverty line in metropolitan areas, cities and towns with population exceeding 10,000, to take up self-employment ventures with the help of Bank loans and Government subsidy.

Prime Minister's Rozgar Yojana. The Prime Minister's Rozgar Yojana was launched on 2 October, 1993 to help educated unemployed youth in establishing self-employment ventures. The Bank financed 68,889 beneficiaries to the tune of Rs. 375 crores during 1995-96.

Total Assistance to Weaker Sections. At the end of March 1996, the Bank's total advances to weaker sections such as SC/ST, small and marginal farmers, landless labourers, including beneficiaries under IRDP and DRI Schemes amounted to Rs. 3,886 crores.

2. Community Services Programmes

The Bank has a number of Community Services Programmes which aim at closer identification with various strata of society, especially the weaker ones, such as women, slum-dwellers, physically handicapped, victims of natural calamities, ex-prisoners, orphans, ex-defence personnel etc. Financial assistance is provided under these Programmes for self-employment and rehabilitation of the beneficiaries. As at the end of March 1996, aggregate financial assistance rendered by the Bank under various community services programmes amounted to Rs. 317 crores spread over 11 lakh beneficiaries. Under the 15-Point Programme on minorities welfare, the Bank disbursed Rs. 372 crores to 5 lakh beneficiaries in 41 identified districts.

3. Area Development

The State Bank has been successfully carrying out its responsibility of the development of districts under the Lead Bank Scheme. As on March 1996, the Bank had lead responsibility in 113 districts in different parts of the country where it had been acting as a catalyst agent of banking and rural development. Under the Annual Action Plans for 1995-96, the Bank had extended Rs. 464 crores as credit and under the Annual Action Plans for non-lead districts, the credit extended amounted to Rs. 3,052 crores.

4. Development of Backward Areas

The Bank lays special emphasis on the balanced development of different regions, with greater emphasis on the development of backward districts. More than 46 per cent of the Bank's direct agricultural advances are in backward districts, covering over 51 per cent of the borrow accounts. The Bank has also been assisting in the creation of self-employment opportunities as well as industrial development of backward districts in the country. About 50 per cent of the small scale industrial units and 55 per cent of the transport operators assisted by the Bank are in the backward districts. Of the small business units financed by the Bank, 50 per cent are in backward areas, amounting for 48 per cent of the total quantum of assistance provided to the small business sphere. Out of the 187 Entrepreneurial Development Programmes organised by the Bank so far, 118 have been conducted in the backward districts.

5. Export Finance

The Bank has been providing larger credit facilities to exporters and also promotional and development support to them at the national level. The total export credit provided by the Bank amounted to Rs. 6,955 crores as at the end of March 1996. The share of export credit in Bank's total credit was 12.4 per cent which was higher than the export credit target of 10 per cent laid down for banks by the RBI.

Among the promotional measures taken by the Bank was the creation of an Export Promotion Fund, with an allocation of Rs. 1 crore out of the Bank's profits in 1987. The Bank has been actively associated with a number of Export Promotion Councils relating to different commodities and with the Ministry of Commerce, Government of India in streamlining the procedures and to render speedy and smooth service to exporters. Further, the State Bank is the sole commercial bank nominated by the Government of India for implementing financial transactions under the lines of credit extended by the Government of India to various countries. The Bank also administers Gold and Silver Jewellery Export Promotion Schemes as a canalising agency on behalf of the Government of India.

6. Merchant Banking

The State Bank has been rendering merchant banking services to its customers since 1972. But it was with the setting up of SBI Capital Markets Ltd. in 1986, SBI Mutual Fund in 1987, SBI Home Finance Ltd. and SBI Funds Management Ltd. that its merchant banking activities have spread considerably. These subsidiaries promote merchant banking, equipment leasing, venture capital finance, portfolio management services, hire-purchase activity, housing finance activities, etc. In fact, the Bank is a pioneer in the field of merchant banking and house finance.

7. Development of Debt Market

With a view to further develop the debt market in India, the Bank has set up a subsidiary called the SBI Gilts Ltd., to act as a Primary Dealer in Government securities. During 1995-96, the Bank acquired controlling interest in Discourt and Finance House of India Ltd.

8. Factors and Commercial Services

The Bank launched the SBI Factors and Commercial Services Pvt Ltd. (FACS) on 30 July, 1991 as a new subsidiary. The SBI has 54 per cent share holding in the subsidiary, the Small Industries Development Bank of India 20 per cent, Union Bank of India 10 per cent, State Bank of Indore 6 per cent and State Bank of Saurashtra 10 per cent. The SBI has been allotted the west zone for factoring. The SBI FACS performs the function of discounting the bills of its customers by buying invoices on a continuing basis. The customer prepays upto 80 per cent of the value of the invoices immediately. The SBI FACS maintains the sales ledger and performs the function of realising the invoices purchased. All types of business organisations engaged in either manufacturing or trading are eligible for factoring.

9. Human Resources Development (HRD)

The State Bank has been a pioneer in the field of HRD. As such, it has been focusing attention on development of job knowledge, skills and appropriate attitudes of its employees. Manpower Planning, Performance Appraisal System, Career Planning and Development, Organisation Development, and Training and Research are the various tools used in the process of development of human resources.

The Bank lays more emphasis on training its employees at all levels and prepares them to meet the growing needs of the Bank in the context of changing market scenario and environment. For this purpose, the Bank has two training Staff Colleges at Hyderabad and Gurgaon, and the Institute of Rural Development, Hyderabad and 55 Staff Training Centres. In February 1990, it started the Institute of Information and Communication Management in Hyderabad to spread computer education and information, and communication management skills. In addition to the above institutional training system, the Bank also has in-branch training arrangements in the form of visiting faculty and on-site training.

10. Customer Services

It has been the constant endeavour of the Bank to improve its service to the satisfaction of customers. It has Customer Service Committees and Customer Councils at almost all branches in important towns and cities. The 'Speedline' system introduced in 1986 now covers 209 centres. It expedites collection, remittances and transfer of accounts of customers. The Bank operates eight Customer Service Centres in different parts of the country which receive and dispose customer complaints pertaining to all public sector banks at the centres.

Tele-Service has been introduced at select branches to enable customers to obtain information over telephone.

11. New Schemes for Customers

The Bank has been a pace setter in introducing several new schemes for the benefit of its customers. There are a number of schemes for grant of loans to purchase consumer durables such as Big Buy, SCO-OM and Computer Loan. The State Bank Card and the High Value Card Scheme have created a place in the market. There is the Travelcash Scheme for granting loans to individuals for meeting travelling expenses. Under the 'Cash-key' Scheme, individuals making deposits in the form of Term/Special Term Deposits, Cash Certificates, Recurring Deposits with the Bank and in Magnum Certificates of SBICAP can be granted simultaneous overdraft facility for drawing up to 75 per cent of the amount of such deposit. In order to cover investment counselling and portfolio management activities under a 'single window service', Personal Investment Cells have been established in a number of metropolitan and urban branches. On 4 May, 1992, the SBI launched the Stock-invest Scheme. SBINET facility has been extended to all main branches, zonal offices and regional offices of the Bank. 72 branches have been connected by SWIFT. A fast cheque collection scheme has been introduced at major centres. ATM has been installed at Mumbai, New Delhi, Kolkata, Bangalore, Patna and Jamshedpur.

12. Overseas Operations

The SBI is the foremost Indian bank with overseas operations and international network. Its international network comprises 50 offices spread over 34 countries. The Bank has established correspondent relations with several established banks in six republics of CIS to increase trade relations between India and CIS. In December 1992, the Bank set up the SBI Europlan Bank Limited in London to exploit opportunities and meet the challenges arising out of integration of markets in the European Community. This subsidiary is engaged in wholesale banking. The Bank's other branches advance loans to both the private and public corporate sector in order to finance commodity and raw material imports into India. To serve the NRIs better, the Bank has exclusive NRI centres in Flushing (New York) and in Melbourne. The Bank operates the SWIFT network in its ten foreign branches. The Bank is empanelled as a consultant with the World Bank, the Commonwealth Fund for Technical Co-operation, UK, the Food and Agricultural Organisation (FAO) and the European Bank for Reconstruction and Development.

Conclusion. The State Bank has been highly successful in its objectives in opening a network of branches in rural and semi-urban areas. It has established itself as the largest commercial bank of the country. Further, it has helped in developing agriculture, small industry and business, and uplifting the weaker sections and priority sectors through liberal credit facilities. Besides, it operates a number of customer oriented services, engages in export promotion and successfully carries out overseas operations.

EXERCISES

1. Explain the functions, objects and organisational structure of the State Bank of India.
2. Discuss the achievements of the State Bank of India.
3. Give the objectives of the State Bank of India. Has it succeeded in achieving its objectives?
4. Explain the role of the State Bank of India in agricultural finance.
5. Explain the role of the State Bank of India in financing industries.

Chapter 81

Recent Trends in the Banking System

1. INTRODUCTION

The Indian banking system after independence has passed through distinct phases of development. During the first phase stretching upto the nationalisation of 14 banks in 1969, Indian banks followed almost traditional banking with small time innovations. During the second phase beginning from July 1969, the emphasis had been on the diversification of the banking system in terms of expansion of branches, deposits and advances on the one hand, and on the other hand on social banking. This phase is still continuing. Simultaneously the third phase of innovative banking has started which consists of merchant banking, leasing, mutual funds, venture capital, factoring, housing finance, deposit insurance etc. We will study in this chapter the second and third phase.

2. SOCIAL BANKING

During the post-nationalisation period Indian banks have been assigned the role of catalyst agents for achieving rapid economic growth accompanied by higher income and removal of poverty. The first step towards realisation of this objective was the change in the style of banking operations from "wholesale" or "elitist" banking to "retail" or "mass" banking. The phenomenal expansion of bank branches, lead bank scheme, service area approach, advance to priority sectors, etc. are some of the programmes which try to fulfil the goal of social banking. We will study these programmes in detail.

1. Branch Expansion

In the post-nationalisation period, commercial banks have made tremendous progress in the field of branch expansion. The branch expansion policy of banks has two main objectives: *first*, to narrow down regional imbalances; and *second*, to provide more banking facilities in rural and semi-urban areas. The RBI formulates branch licensing and branch expansion policy for the commercial banks, generally for three years. In June 2003 there were 66,514 bank branches in the country of which 49 per cent were in rural areas as compared with 32.5 per cent in June 1969. As a result of the rapid pace of branch expansion since 1969, the average population served per branch office was 65,000 at the time of bank nationalisation which came down to 16,000 as at end of June 2003. But there are still some inter-State disparities in the spread of banking, particularly in the Eastern, North-Eastern and Central Regions.

2. The Lead Bank Scheme

The Lead Bask Scheme was introduced by the Reserve Bank in December 1969 as an adjunct to the branch expansion programme of commercial banks. Its main objective was to ensure the flow of bank credit to priority sector and to coordinate the activities of the various agencies, such as banks and developmental agencies of Government at various levels. It was the first attempt towards 'Area Approach'.

Initially, a Study Group of the National Credit Council under Prof. D.R. Gadgil recommended in October 1969 the adoption of an Area Approach by commercial banks to identify and study local problems and evolve an integrated credit plan in rural areas of the country's districts. The Nariman Committee appointed by the RBI also recommended in November 1969 that banks should be allotted specific districts where they should take 'the lead' in surveying the potential of banking development, in extending branch expansion and expanding credit facilities. The RBI accepted its recommendations and introduced the Lead Bank Scheme in December 1969.

Under the Scheme, the major public sector banks were allotted all the 388 districts at that time in the country. A particular bank was made responsible for a particular district to develop banking and credit in that district. All other agencies operating in the district were also to be involved. The bank so selected was designated as the Lead Bank for that district. It was expected to act as a consortium leader for coordinating the efforts of all credit institutions in the allotted district for branch expansion and for meeting the credit needs of the rural economy.

Functions of a Lead Bank. A Lead Bank is expected to perform the following functions:

(1) To survey the resources and potential for banking development in its district

(2) To identify unbanked growth centres for branch opening on the basis of a phased programme.

(3) To survey the number of commercial units and other establishments not having banking accounts or which were dependent primarily on moneylenders.

(4) To examine the facilities for the marketing of agricultural produce and industrial production, storage and warehousing space and the linking of credit with marketing in the district.

(5) To survey the facilities for the stocking of fertilizers and other agricultural inputs and for the repair and servicing of equipment.

(6) To recruit and train staff for offering advice to small borrowers and farmers and for the follow-up and the inspection of end-use loans.

(7) To assist other primary lending agencies.

(8) To maintain contacts and laison residually with Government and semi-Government agencies.

Working of Lead Bank Scheme. The Lead Bank Scheme initially consisted of two phases. The first was the survey of districts to identify institutional and credit gaps, and the second was the preparation and implementation of District Credit Plans (DCPs). Both the phases were completed by July 1978. But there was no uniformity in the DCPs. So the RBI advised the lead banks to terminate them. Instead, it issues fresh guidelines from time to time for the preparation of new DCPs, accompanied by separate Annual Action Plans (AAPs). The DCP is the perspective plan and the AAP is its yearly phasing. The RBI constituted the High Power Committee on Lead Bank Scheme which issues guidelines for the preparation of DCPs for specified periods, the last being for the period January 1988 to December 1990.

The Lead Bank Scheme has been successful in bringing about a phenomenal growth in branch expansion and providing larger credit facilities in rural areas. It extended banking facilities to the under-banked and unbanked rural and semi-urban areas from 5,175 branches in June 1969 to 47,216 in June 2003 and increased the share of public sector banks' priority sector advances from 14.6 per cent to 42.5 per cent over the period. Upto the end of June 2003, it covered 575 districts in the country. Despite these merits, the Lead Bank Scheme suffers from certain weaknesses. *First,* there has been the lack of coordination and cooperation among various agencies such as commercial banks, cooperatives, State Governments and others. *Second,* the designation of a particular bank as the lead bank does not make it a leader automatically. But it dilutes the enthusiasm of other banks for the scheme. The scheme is considered to be the scheme of the lead bank and the other agencies feel like being only spectators. *Third,* the attitude of Government agencies at the block level in the preparation of DCPs has been one of indifference. There has been absence of blockwise monitoring. There has been no awareness of targets and no conscious implementation of these targets. *Fourth,* under broad sectoral heads, agriculture and small industries lag far behind the targets whereas the service sector exceeds the target to a considerable extent. This phenomenon is almost common for all the districts. *Fifth,* the degree of cohesion at the block and village level where the AAPs are implemented, has been much wanting, reflecting the failure to realise the consortium approach. *Sixth,* the scheme is based on the principle of voluntary team work which is lacking, and therefore fails to produce the desired results. This is because the lead bank staff and officers do not take interest.

In order to have a certain uniformity and homogeneity in the operations of commercial banks, the Service Area Approach under the overall lead bank scheme has been started since April 1989.

3. The Service Area Approach (SAA)

The Lead Bank Scheme introduced by the Reserve Bank in December 1969 fulfilled only the quantitative aspects of branch expansion and priority sector advances. But it failed to touch the qualitative aspects like identification of needy people and extension of timely credit to them. To assess the impact of credit from banks on the overall economic development of the rural sector in general and agricultural productivity and production in particular, the RBI asked the Chief Executives of the public sector banks to carry out field visits in rural areas of different districts all over the country. They visited 88 districts in 21 States in November 1987. They discussed the findings of these visits in a seminar convened by the RBI in January 1988 and recommended that the time was opportune to adopt a system in which each bank could concentrate in a specified area to develop productive lending. Therefore, the RBI set up a Committee under the chairmanship of its Deputy Governor, Dr. P.D. Ojha, to examine the operational aspects involved in implementing this approach. The RBI accepted the Ojha Committee recommendations. Subsequently, the 1988-89 Budget announced the 'Service Area Approach'. The RBI instructed all commercial banks including the Regional Rural Banks to start implementation of SAA under the overall Lead Bank Scheme with effect from 1 April, 1989.

The SAA involves five distinct stages in its implementation which are discussed as under:

1. *Allocation of Service Area.* There is the allocation of specific villages to all the rural and semi-urban bank branches including RRB branches for providing credit for all-round development. Each branch on an average is allocated 15 to 25 villages under the area of its operation known as Service Area. There are at least five States, viz., Himachal Pradesh, Arunachal Pradesh, Manipur, Meghalaya, Orissa and one Union Territory Andaman where the average number of villages allocated per branch exceeds 25 villages. Similarly, the average number of kms to be covered by each branch is more than 100 sq kms for at least nine States and one Union Territory.

2. *Survey of Villages.* After fixation of the service area, each branch is to undertake village-wise surveys in respect of their allotted villages and prepare village profiles in a proforma prescribed by the RBI. The village profile has to be updated periodically taking into account the development changes which may have taken place in the intervening period. The branch managers are expected to periodically visit the villages in their service area to have a continuous contact with extension and developmental agencies.

3. *Preparation of Credit Plans.* Each branch is required to prepare an annual credit plan for its service area on an ongoing basis. *First,* the credit plan is prepared for each village and then the village credit plans are aggregated into service area credit plan. The annual credit plan should reflect the potentialities, and needs of the people of the area on the basis of survey reports. The Lead Bank Officer plays a crucial role in this regard and is expected to provide necessary support to all the branch managers in the district. The RRB branches prepare credit plans for the target group only and for the non-target group the designated bank prepares the credit plan.

4. *Coordination.* A Block Level Bankers' Committee (BLBC) has to be formed to coordinate the activity of the banks and Government agencies. The Lead Bank Officer is the convenor-chairman of BLBC and all the bank branch managers located in the block, including cooperative banks, BDO and his extension officers in the block are its members. The officers of the RBI and NABARD can also attend the BLBC meetings. The BLBC finalises the branch credit plans and these plans are aggregated to block credit plans.

5. *Monitoring.* The BLBC holds periodical meetings at least once in a quarter to review the progress of implementation of the branch credit plans and sort out operational problems.

Working of SAA. The SAA was introduced as part of the Lead Bank Scheme for improving the quality of rural lending by commercial banks including RRBs. It came into operation from 1 April, 1989 covering 6,18,216 villages which had been allocated to 42,158 branches of the various banks. The survey of villages and preparation of credit plans had been completed by March 1989. The RBI asked the public sector banks to conduct a second round of field studies in December 1989 with a view to ascertaining the manner of implementation of the SAA in rural branches, the problems encountered in effective implementation and steps needed for improving the operational aspects of the Scheme. Following these studies, it was felt that the Scheme held the promise of improving the productivity of rural credit and efforts should be made towards stabilising it at the earliest. It was also decided that the relaxations already granted to bank branches to lend to their old clients residing in the service area of other bank branches may continue for some time more, so that the credit flow does not get disrupted. Further, cooperative banks were advised to prepare credit plans and their staff would be given training in this direction. The RBI issues fresh guidelines for the preparation of branch credit plans for each year keeping in view the deficiencies observed in the credit plans prepared for the previous years in order to remove their shortcomings. To plan, co-ordinate and effectively monitor the credit plans prepared by bank branches and improve upon them, the NABARD has been setting up district level offices in a phased manner so as to cover all the districts in the country within the next 3 or 4 years. These offices also transmit potential linked credit plans to rural and semi-urban branches of banks to help them prepare their credit plans. The RBI issues revised guidelines on credit planning and monitoring from time to time to make the SAA more effective. The following modifications have been introduced recently: *(i)* SA branches may be grouped block-wise without disturbing their SA identities or their obligation to prepare village level/service area plans so that the borrowers have the flexibility to approach other branches within the block to meet their credit requirement adequately; *(ii)* satellite/mobile offices be opened in Service Areas which are very large and are located in tribal/hilly and inaccessible areas; *(iii)* the area of operations of the specialised branches such as agricultural development branches, agricultural banking division and *gram vikas kendras* may be enlarged to use their infrastructure to the maximum; *(iv)* realigning the sacred service areas; and *(v)* exemptions from the SAA in respect of large projects covering several districts/ States.

Under the SAA, Annual Credit Plan is prepared by the concerned commercial bank under the Lead Bank Scheme. During 1999-2000, the all-India sector-wise targets were : Rs. 39,168 crores for agriculture and allied activities; Rs. 12,773 crores for SSIs and Rs. 12,945 crores for services. These figures reveal that the quality of delivery system in rural lending has definitely improved under the SAA. These figures reveal that the quality of delivery system in rural banking has definitely improved under the SAA.

4. Local Area Banks (LABs)

The Finance Minister in his budget speech for 1996-97 announced the Local Area Banks scheme. The LAB scheme owes its origin to the complaints of many State governments that public sector banks were extorting the rural areas of all their money. States like Punjab, Haryana, Uttar Pradesh, Kerala are much below the national average in their credit-deposit ratios. They have been complaining that the public sector banks are taking away their resources to lend them in other States. These banks are expected to remedy these defects by concentrating their operations in rural areas. Unlike the RRBs, these banks will be set up in the private sector and registered and licensed as scheduled banks. The RBI issued the following guidelines on setting up of the LABs on 24 August, 1996.

Object. The aim is to set up LABs in the private sector in district towns to cater to the credit needs of the local people and to provide efficient and competitive financial intermediation services in their area of operation. These banks will promote rural savings and provide credit to viable economic activities in local areas. They are expected to bridge the gaps in credit availability and enhance the institutional credit framework in rural and semi-urban areas.

Functions. Since the LABs will be located in district towns, their activities will be focussed on the local customers. They will promofe and mobilise savings. They will lend to agriculture and allied activities, SSI, agro-industrial units, trading units and the non-farm sector in their area of operation. These will observe the priority sector lending target of 40 per cent of net bank credit, as applicable to other commercial banks. Within this target, they will lend at least 25 per cent or 10 per cent of net bank credit to the weaker sections.

Capital. The minimum paid-up capital for starting an LAB shall be Rs. 5 crores. The promoters' contribution shall be at least Rs. 2 crores. The promoters may comprise individuals, corporations, trusts or societies.

Area of Operation. The area of operation of such a bank shall be a maximum of three geographically contiguous districts. Its Head / Registered Office will be located at a centre within its area of operation. The Bank shall be allowed to open branches only in its area of operation. In regard to branch licensing, it shall be governed by the existing policy.

Prudential Norms. Such a bank shall be subject to prudential norms, accounting policies and other policies as are laid down by the RBI. The SLR and CRR to these banks will be the same as that for RRBs. So will be the deposit rates and lending rates. The .bank will have to achieve capital adequacy ratio of 8 per cent from the very beginning. Similarly, norms for income recognition, asset classification and provisioning will be applicable from day one.

Critical Appraisal. Academicians and bankers have questioned the wisdom of the Government and RBI in adding another institution to the plethora of financial institutions and agencies for providing credit to the rural areas. If the existing large number of institutions have failed to deliver the goods, the introduction of one more may be a futile exercise. What is ths guarantee that the LABs will be a success, given the attitudes and approaches of the people and the banking staff? However, it is hoped that the LABs will be successful where the RRBs have failed. Presently, eight 'in-principle' approvals have been given for setting up Local Area Banks, of which three have been registered.

5. Financing of Priority Sectors

The concept of 'Priority Sector Advances' was formulated in 1968 with the introduction of social control over banks. The National Credit Council pointed out that those sectors of the economy which did not have adequate access to bank finance but which due to their economic importance deserved due recognition from the banking system should be treated as 'Priority Sectors'. Therefore, there should be a conscious and deliberate effort to ensure that these sectors obtained adequate credit from the banking system. At that time, the priority sectors consisted of agriculture, small scale industry and exports. With the nationalisation of 14 commercial banks in 1969, the term 'Priority Sectors' was enlarged to include 'hitherto neglected sectors' comprising of small road and water transport operators, retail trade including petty shopkeepers and self-employed persons such as artisans, craftsmen, etc. and indigent students receiving education. A Working Group set up by the RBI under the Chairmanship of Dr K.S. Krishnaswamy introduced the concept of 'weaker sections' within the priority sectors. Consequently, at present the priority sector advances as redefined on 13 June 1995 include:

1. Agriculture, both direct and indirect
2. Small scale industries.
3. Other priority sectors which comprise of:
   (*a*) road and water transport operators;
   (*b*) retail trade and small business:
   (c) setting of industrial estate;
   (*d*) professional and self-employed persons;
   (*e*) education;
   (*f*) financial assistance to ex-servicemen; and
   (*g*) SUME—Scheme of Urban Micro Enterprises.
4. Weaker sections consisting of: (*i*) small and marginal farmers with land holdings upto 5 acres, landless labourers, tenant fanners and share croppers; (*ii*) artisans, village and cottage industries enjoying credit limits upto Rs. 25,000; (*iii*) IRDP beneficiaries; (*iv*) beneficiaries belonging to scheduled castes / scheduled tribes; (*v*) beneficiaries under the DRI and SUME schemes, as also those under the Scheme for Liberation and Rehabilitation of Scavengers (SLRS); and (*vi*) Self Help Groups under NABARD's Pilot Projects.

Both the Government and the RBI have laid down the fallowing targets for lending to priority sectors. The banks are expected to ensure that 40 per cent of the total credit is extended to priority sectors. With the overall target of 40 per cent, the following sub-targets have been laid down: (*i*) 18 per cent of the bank credit to the agricultural sector; (*ii*) 50 per cent of the direct lending to agriculture for small and marginal farmers and agricultural labourers; (*iii*) 12.5 per cent of the total credit advanced to small scale industries reserved for artisans, village craftsmen and cottage industries; (*iv*) advances to the weaker sections to the level of 25 per cent of priority sector advances or 10 per cent of the total bank credit outstandings; and (*v*) 1 per cent of aggregate advances under DRI scheme.

During 1993-94, the RBI made certain changes in the composition of priority sector targets within its overall 40 per cent target for commercial banks. Banks have been allowed to combine direct and indirect advances to agriculture within the 18 per cent target. Their indirect lending to agriculture has been limited to one-fourth of the total agricultural lending. Within the SSI credit limit, 40 per cent has been earmarked for khadi, village, cottage and tiny units. Effective 1 July, 1993, the priority sector target for foreign banks has been raised to 32 per cent. They have been allowed to include credit of 10 per cent for loans to the export sector and SSI units each in the overall target of 32 per cent. If they fail to achieve the targets, they are required to deposit the deficit with the SIDBI. The SIDBI pays the foreign banks 10 per cent interest on the deposited amount.

In the case of other banks, the shortfall in lending to agriculture (18 per cent) is required to be deposited with the NABARD for making funds available to the Rural Infrastructure Development Fund (RIDF) from 1996. These deposits with the NABARD are subject to a maximum of 1.5 per cent of the bank's net credit. The NABARD pays such a bank 0.5 per cent above the ceiling rate of interest on deposits.

Effective 6 July, 1996, the private sector banks which fail to reach the required target of 40 per cent are directed to deposit 50 per cent of the shortfall for one year either with the NABARD or SIDBI. The rate of interest on such deposits is 8 per cent.

The priority sector advances under major categories are discussed briefly as under:

1. Priority sector advances of *public sector banks* increased from 14.6 per cent as at the end of June 1969 to 42.5 per cent as at the end of March 2003. Within the priority sectors, the share of advances to agriculture increased from 5.4 per cent in June 1969 to 15.3 per cent in March 2003. Of this, direct finance to agriculture increased from 1.3 per cent to 10.8 per cent. The share of SSI increased from 8.5 per cent in June 1969 to 11.1 per cent in March 2003, and other priority sector advances increased from 0.7 per cent to 15.0 per cent.

2. The proportion of priority sector advances by *foreign banks* to their net bank credit was well above the target of 32 per cent as at the end of March 2003. It was 33.9 per cent with credit to export constituting 18.7 per cent and SSI 8.7 per cent.

3. Priority sector advances by *private sector* commercial banks were 44.4 per cent as at the end of March 2003 against the target of 40 per cent.

4. The advances to *weaker sections* within the priority sectors constituted 6.76 per cent of the net bank credit of public sector banks ending March 2003 as against the target of 10 per cent.

3. INNOVATIVE BANKING

Public sector banks in India in recent years have been engaged in innovative banking. The RBI has given them freedom to innovate in the promotion of a variety of financial services such as merchant banking, leasing, venture capital, mutual funds, factoring, housing, etc. We will explain these services briefly here.

1. Merchant Banking

Merchant banking includes such services as management of public issues, loan syndication, financial and management consultancy, project counselling, mergers and acquisitions, management of non-resident investments, etc. The credit for starting merchant banking in India goes to foreign banks like Grindlays Bank, Citibank, etc. At present, a number of public sector banks are performing merchant banking services which are the subsidiaries of banks. Some of these are SBI Capital Markets Limited, Bank of Baroda Merchant Bank Division, Canbank Financial Services Ltd., Allbank Finance Ltd., Union Bank of India Merchant Bank Division, PNB Capital Services Ltd., BOI Finance Ltd., etc.

2. Leasing

Leasing is an instrument of corporate finance whereby industries enter into a contractual arrangement with a leasing company to use an asset (i.e. plant, equipment, transportation facilities or any other services) in return for rent for an agreed period of time. Leasing companies also provide finance to industries. Equipment leasing and financial leasing in India have been in the hands of private companies since 1973. It is only recently with the establishment of merchant banking subsidiaries that public sector banks have made their entry into the leasing business. As at the end of June 1991, there were nine equipment leasing-cum-merchant banking subsidiaries set up by Indian banks. But they have yet to make a niche for themselves in a very competitive leasing market where about 400 private leasing companies are operating.

3. Venture Capital

Venture capital relates to finance provided to small/medium business units promoted by firms or individuals having sound project ideas. These projects involve new technology or products but the promoter lacks financial resources to promote his project. Venture capital provided by banks or financial institutions imply equity investment in the initial stages of the company. Financial institutions like ICICI, IDBI, UTI and IFCI have been the pioneers in promoting venture capital finance in India. Of the banks, SBI Capital Markets Limited has been in the forefront in providing assistance to industries under its Equity Support and Venture Capital Schemes.

4. Mutual Funds

Mutual funds mobilise savings from the public and invest them in different types of securities in the stock markets and thus help both the investor and the industry. Mutual funds earn interest, dividend and capital gains from such investments and distribute them to small investors as return. Thus they provide safety, liquidity and growth to investors. They provide stability to share prices by buying them when they are falling and selling them when they are rising. They provide safety and income to investors and resources to entrepreneurs for the growth of industry. The UTI was the first mutual fund set up in India in 1964. In recent years a number of public sector banks have set up mutual funds as their subsidiaries. These banks are Indian Bank, Bank of India, SBI, Canara Bank, Bank of Baroda, PNB, etc. The SBI group also launched the India Magnum Fund in 1989, a maiden offshore fund which was privately placed with institutional investors and others primarily in the USA.

5. Factoring

A 'Factor' is a commission agent who besides offering funds to its clients, undertakes management of accounts receivables, collection of debts and safety against risk of default. Factoring agencies ensure smooth of cash flows. The factor undertakes collection of a client's (say a small scale unit) debts and finances it on the basis of accounts receivables. In fact, debts are assigned to the factor which are collected in due course. The factor, in turn, receives the service charge by way of discount or rebate deducted from the bills. In short, factoring is a collection and finance service designed to improve the cash flow of small firms by turning their sales invoices into ready cash.

The Vaghul Committee recommended the introduction of factoring services with a view to undertaking the collection of dues on behalf of suppliers in the small scale sector. The Kalyanasundaram Committee examined the feasibility of factoring services and recommended their introduction in India. The Banking Regulation Act was amended in July 1990 for this purpose and the RBI directed that factoring be done by banks through separate subsidiaries. Accordingly, the State Bank of India launched a new subsidiary called the SBI Factors and Commercial Services Ltd on 30 July, 1991. The aim is to render factoring services to the industrial and commercial units in Western India, covering the States of Maharashtra, Gujarat, Goa, Madhya Pradesh and the Union Territories of Daman, Diu, Dadra and Nagar Haveli. Similarly, the Canara Bank launched its factoring subsidiary, the Canbank Factoring Ltd. on 24 August, 1991 to serve units in Southern India and the Punjab National Bank and Allahabad Bank have come forward to set up factoring agencies in Northern India and Eastern India respectively.

Its Working. Factoring in India involves the following procedure:

The factoring service buys invoices on a continuing basis, prepays upto 80 per cent of the value of the invoices immediately, performs the accounting function of sales ledger maintenance and the collection function of realising invoices purchased. The suppliers invoice their customers in the usual way but only add that the debt due on the invoice must be paid to the Factor. The suppliers offer the assigned invoices to the Factor with a schedule of offer, accompanied by a copy of the receipted delivery of the challan. The Factor provides prepayment up to 80 per cent of the value of each invoice. When the Factor collects the debts, the supplier receives an official notification and personalised statement of accounts from the former. When the supplier settles the invoice, the Factor pays, the supplier the remaining 20 per cent of the invoice value. To keep the supplier informed of the factored invoices, the Factor sends monthly statements of accounts.

The Factor charges discount on the prepayment drawn by its client. The discount rate which is comparable to bank lending rate is collected monthly on actual drawings, in the prepayment account. In addition, there is a service charge (or fee) which varies between one and five per cent depending on the services availed of and the volume of transactions made.

Its Benefits. Factoring benefits the supplier, his banker and his customer. The supplier converts his invoice into instant cash up to 80 per cent of its value, without having to wait for the usual 30 or more credit days. His bank can leave the post-sale finance to the factor and concentrate only on inventory finance. The factor need not accept a bill of exchange. He has just to abide by a notice on the invoice to pay money direct to the Factor.

But it will take some time before full factoring is started in India where the risk is entirely borne by the Factor. For the present, there is recourse factoring where, in case of default, the risk ultimately devolves on the supplier.

6. HOUSING

Habitat banking is fast catching up in India. For meeting the requirements of housing finance, a National Housing Bank (NHB) was established as an apex institution in 1988. It has been providing assistance through a number of schemes. These include: Home Loan Account Scheme, liberalised lending by commercial banks, and refinance facilities. Besides, the banking sector has been involved substantially in housing finance in recent years. Commercial banks provide finance to low and middle income groups to purchase or construct houses or flats. Interest rates are fixed by the RBI and NHB for the loans advanced by commercial banks and housing finance institutions. Effective 5 June, 1991, banks were allowed to provide housing finance to builders by way of term loans for periods ranging from 3 to 5 years, linked to specific projects for development of plots together with construction of flats/houses under the refinance scheme of the NHB. A number of public sector and private sector banks have promoted housing finance companies such as SBI, Bank of Baroda, Andhra Bank, Central Bank of India, Vijaya Bank etc.

7. NEW TECHNOLOGY IN BANKING MECHANISATION

Another innovation in Indian banking has been the use of new technology in banking mechanisation. Majority of Indian banks, have provided Electronic Accounting Machines and Advance Ledger Posting Machines in their branches. Banks have taken up the project of total computerisation of operations of their branches. About 260 offices of banks have been hooked through BANKNET, a data communication network for the Reserve Bank and public sector banks at Mumbai, New Delhi, Chennai, Kolkata, Bangalore, Hyderabad and Nagpur. Banks have been asked to introduce Magnetic Ink Character Recognition (MICR) cheques. The RBI is providing MICR-based cheque clearing facilities at Mumbai, Chennai, Kolkata, New Delhi and Nagpur. Several banks are using SWIFT (Society for Worldwide Inter-bank Financial Telecommunications) network and have installed hardware and software required for connecting to SWIFT. With a view to further improving the communication network in regard to speed, dependability and security, a number of banks have installed satellite disk antennae at their offices in many cities. When fully operational, these would form part of the Remote Area Business Message Network (RABMN) and would be used to transmit messages including SWIFT messages, between bank offices in India and abroad. A number of banks have started Electronic Clearing Service which is being used by several corporate bodies to effect dividend/interest to their shareholders/ customers.

8. Customer Service

Improvement in the level of customer satisfaction has been another innovation of banking services. To ensure efficient customer service, banks collect feedback on a regular basis through visits of senior officials from controlling offices to their branches. To elicit customer reactions about the quality of service rendered, the system of holding Customer Meets at regular intervals at branches has been evolved. Some banks have formed Customer Service Committees and Customer Councils. Banks have put up 'Complaints and Suggestions' boxes at all branches which are dealt with promptly. Some of the banks have also introduced courier system to expedite collections, remittances and transfer of accounts of customers.

9. Banking Ombudsman

For expeditious and inexpensive settlement of customer complaints against deficiency in banking services, including non-observance of the RBI directives on loans and advances, etc., the Banking Ombudsman has been appointed on a full time basis each at Mumbai, Delhi, Bhopal, Chandigarh, Hyderabad, Patna, Jaipur, etc. The scheme covers all scheduled commercial banks, except RRBs and PCBs.

10. Credit Cards

The credit card is now a days an integral part of better customer service. Under the credit scheme, card holders are allowed credit facilities for a specified period of time without obtaining any security from them. The card holders can purchase commodities and pay for services such as hotel bills, railway and airways tickets, etc. without making cash payments. The bank issuing the credit card is able to make increased earnings by way of commission from dealers and interest from cardholders. The credit card system has become an aggressive area of business for Indian banks. Major public sector and private sector banks have come out with their credit cards. Some of them have been permitted by the RBI to have tie-up arrangements with other banks in India and abroad. This has facilitated wider use of cards nationally and internationally.

11. Installation of ATMs

Several banks have installed Automated Teller Machines (ATMs) at licensed branches and extension counters where clients can withdraw cash 24 hours a day upto a certain limit.

12. Hire-Purchase Business

On the recommendations of the Reserve Bank, the Government of India notified on 7 September, 1990 hire-purchase as a permissible form of business for banks to engage in. Accordingly, Canara Bank, State Bank of India, Punjab National Bank and Indian Bank have been permitted to engage in hire-purchase business through their respective merchant banking subsidiaries.

13. Consumer Credit

Consumer credit is also developing as a profitable area of business for banks in India. Banks help the middle class customers to purchase durable consumer goods such as motor vehicles, refrigerators, TVs, etc. The banks earn interest on such credits. The consumer goods industry gets a boost in its sales which in turn help in increasing employment opportunities.

4. Deposit Insurance Corporation

The Deposit Insurance Corporation (DIC) was established on 1 January, 1962 under the Deposit Insurance Corporation Act, 1961 passed by the Parliament. The failure of the Palai Central Bank and the Laxmi Bank in 1960 shook the confidence of the depositors in the banking system. The DIC aimed at providing protection to small depositors by insuring their deposits in banks. In case an insured bank failed, the Corporation was to pay depositors upto a specified limit. Originally the limit was Rs 1,500 per depositor in respect of all deposits held by him in an insured bank. The limit was raised to Rs. 5,000 in 1968, to Rs. 10,000 in 1970, to Rs. 20,000 in 1976 and to Rs. 30,000 in July 1980. The premium rate paid by the banks to the Corporation quarterly was reduced from 5 paise to 4 paise per Rs. 100 per annum in October 1971. The DIC has authorised and paid-up capital of Rs 2 crores. It could also borrow from the Reserve Bank upto Rs. 5 crores. It maintained a Deposit Insurance Fund (DIF) in which all premia collected from the registered bankers was deposited and out of which deposit insuranced claims were paid. It also maintained a General Fund made up of its capital, reserves and income from investments by the DIC.

Originally only commercial banks were eligible for insurance cover. But in 1968, the DIC Act was amended to provide insurance cover to cooperative banks having paid-up capital and reserves of Rs 1 lakh and above. But the co-operative banks were eligible for insurance provided the State Government concerned enacted legislation. It was only from 1971 that cooperative banks in a few States were registered with the DIC. Not all State Governments have enacted such a legislation till now.

Credit Guarantee Corporation of India (CGCI)

To examine the problem of insurance of advances of commercial banks and cooperative banks to small borrowers in the priority sector, the Department of Banking of the Government of India appointed a Working Group which submitted its report in November 1969. It recommended a centralized credit guarantee scheme for various segments of priority sector under the DIC. But the Government decided to set up a separate organization to extend guarantee to commercial banks in respect of their advances to small and neglected borrowers. Accordingly the Credit Guarantee Corporation of India came into existence as a Government company in January, 1971. Its main function was to administer the scheme of guarantees in respect of advances granted by the credit institutions and to indemnify them in respect of such advances.

Deposit Insurance and Credit Guarantee Corporation (DICGC)

On 15 July, 1978, the Deposit Insurance Corporation took over the Credit Guarantee Corporation of India and it was named the Deposit Insurance and Credit Guarantee Corporation. The DICGC has a paid-up capital of Rs. 50 crores which is entirely issued and subscribed by the RBI. It has two main functions. *First,* to insure the deposits of the small depositors in banks. For this purpose, it operates the Deposit Insurance Scheme which was earlier operated by the DIC. *Second,* to provide guarantee support to eligible credit institutions for the priority sector advances to small borrowers and small scale industries. The DICGC had been operating six credit guarantee schemes. Out of these, the Corporation terminated three schemes with effect from 1 April, 1992 on account of either nil or negligible guaranteed advances and continued default in payment of guarantee fee, etc. by participating institutions. The three schemes were Small Loans (Financial Corporations) Guarantee Scheme, 1971, Service Cooperative Societies Guarantee Scheme, 1971, and Small Loans (Cooperative Credit Societies) Guarantee Scheme, 1992.

At present, the DICGC provides insurance cover to depositors in banks through its Deposit Insurance Scheme and guarantees coyer to eligible credit institutions through its three credit guarantee schemes—two for small borrowers and one for SSIs.The limit of insurance cover is Rs 1 lakh per bank and the premium payable by insured banks on their assessable deposits is at 5 paise per Rs 100 per annum. To reform the deposit insurance system, the Reserve Bank appointed a Working Group which submitted its Report in October 1999. It recommended : *(i)* raising the capital of DICGC to Rs 500 crores; *(ii)* withdrawing the function of credit guarantee on loans from it; and *(iii)* risk-based pricing of the deposit-insurance premium in place of the flat rate system. These recommendations are in the process of being implemented.

5. DEFECTS OF INDIAN BANKING SYSTEM

Despite the tremendous progress made by Indian commercial banks during the last two decades, they are still faced with a number of problems which are as under:

1. *Low Profitability.* Banks in India have low profitability. Irregularities and corruption in lending operations,

misappropriation, frauds, rising operating costs, etc. have led to decline in their profitability. During 1992-93 and 1993-94, scheduled commercial banks incurred a net loss of Rs. 4,150 crores and Rs 3,625 crores respectively. But in 2002-03 they earned a net profit of Rs 17,077 crores.

2. *Growing Non-performing Assets.* The non-performing assets of Indian commercial banks have been growing rapidly. Non-performing assets consist of *(i)* debts recalled, *(ii)* suit-filed accounts i.e. where legal action or recovery proceedings have been initiated, *(iii)* decreed debts i.e. where suits have been filed and decrees obtained; and (iv) debts classified as bad and doubtful. In the case of public sector banks ending March 2003 non-performing assets accounted for 9.36 per cent of their gross advances.

3. *Low Capital Base.* The capital base of Indian banks in India was very low and not uniform. In the case of 28 public sector banks, the capital base was the same as at the time of their nationalisation. For rivate sector banks, the required capital was linked to their geographical location while foreign banks operating in India were required to have foreign funds equivalent to 3.5 per cent of the deposits deployed in Indian business as at the end of each year. As a measure of capital adequacy, there was no weighted risk-asset ratio system for banks in India till March, 1993. There were 2 commercial banks with a ratio of less than 9% in 2002 - 03.

4. *Window-dressing of Balance Sheets.* Despite compulsory audit of banks, many banks indulge in window-dressing of their balance sheets. They artificially, increase their deposits in the last week of the fiscal year.

5. *Favouritism in Advancing Loans.* Some banks favour certain companies in advancing loans. This is not only in the case of public sector banks. Often such loans turn into bad debts, thereby weakening the financial position of the concerned banks.

6. *Bad Quality of Loan Portfolios.* The quality of loan portfolios of a number of banks is very bad. Often, they advance loans under extraneous (or political) pressures. They extend letters of credit and guarantee limits as a routine affair without adopting commercial procedure in granting loans.

7. *Indulge in Share Speculation.* Many banks indulge in share speculation, thereby misutilising public deposits. A number of public sector banks and their subsidiaries in the form of mutual funds have been found to be involved in share speculation. The recent securities scam involving Harshad Mehta and other brokers revealed the role of a number of public and private sector banks in the entire episode.

8. *Irregularities in Maintaining Accounts.* Many banks resort to large scale irregularities in operating their accounts. Often, bad accounts of one bank have been taken over by the other bank without proper scrutiny.

9. *Banks as Sick Units.* As a corollary to the above, many banks operate as sick units. Consequently, they are amalgamated, dissolved or liquidated. During 1985-91, ten banks were amalgamated. As on 30 June, 1991, three banks were dissolved. New Bank of India became so sick that it was merged with Punjab National Bank in 1993. Even during 1999-2000, three nationalised banks were sick.

10. *Social Banking Inadequate.* Despite the fact that a number of schemes have been in operation to help the weaker sections of Indian society, banks mainly cater to the needs of the corporate sector. For instance, bank credit to medium and large scale industry was 33.7 per cent in 1999-2000 to agriculture 9.5 per cent, to small scale industries 8.7 per cent and to trade 5.7 per cent.

11. *Dual Control.* The Indian banking system suffers from dual control of the Government and Reserve Bank. It is over-regulated and over-administered. The credit decisions in individual cases and matters pertaining to internal management have been subjected to excessive administrative and political pressures and interferences. The investing and lending programmes are directed from above. So are the appointments of chief executives and directors.

Conclusion. All this shows that Indian commercial banks are not operating properly, their management is sloppy, they are uncompetitive, overstretched, overstaffed and provide poor service.

6. SUGGESTIONS TO IMPROVE WORKING: NARASIMHAM COMMITTEE REPORT

From time to time, a number of committees have suggested measures to improve the working of the Indian banking system. However, we give a summary of the recommendations of the Narasimham Committee of 1991.

1. Structure of the banking sector should be revamped so as to have 3 or 4 large banks which could become international in character.

2. Eight to ten national banks with a network of branches throughout the country should be engaged in universal banking.

3. Local bank operations should be confined to a specific region.

4. Rural banks, including RRBs, should operate only in rural areas and their business should be predominantly to engage in financing of agriculture and allied activities, but based on profitability considerations.

5. One or more rural banking subsidiaries by each public sector bank should be set up to take overall its rural branches.

6. RRBs should be allowed to engage in all types of banking business.

7. Abolition of branch licensing and opening or closing of branches should be left to the individual banks.

8. Foreign banks should be permitted to open offices in India as branches or as subsidiaries.

9. Foreign banks should be subject to the same requirements as applicable to Indian banks.

10. Foreign operations of Indian banks should be rationalised.

11. Computerisation of bank operations needs to be stepped up.

12. No need to set up a banking commission.

13. Individual banks should be permitted to recruit officers.

14. Inspection by supervisory staff should be based on the internal audit and internal inspection reports.

15. Duality of control over the banking system between the RBI and the Banking Division of the Ministry of Finance should end, and the RBI should be the primary agency for regulation of the banking system.

16. To perform supervisory function over the banks and other financial institutions, there should be a separate authority to operate as a quasi-autonomous body under the aegis of the Reserve Bank.

17. Appointment of chief executives of the banks and directors should be depoliticised.

18. SLR requirements of banks should be brought down to 25 per cent over a period of five years.

19. CRR should be progressively reduced.

20. Directed credit programmes should be phased out.

21. The priority sector should be redefined.

22. There should be deregulation of interest rate so as to reflect emerging market trends.

23. The commercial banks should achieve a minimum 4 per cent capital adequacy ratio in relation to risk weighted assets by March 1993.

24. Banks should adopt uniform accounting practices

25. They should impart transparency to balance sheets and make full disclosure in them.

26. Government should set up Special Tribunals to speed up the process of recovery of loans.

27. An Assets Reconstruction Fund (ARF) should be established to take over from basks and financial institutions a portion of their bad and doubtful debts at a discount

The recommendations of the Narasimham Committee would have far reaching implications on the working of the banking system. They have not yet been implemented except in the case of reduction of SLR.*

7. RECENT BANKING REFORMS

Since nationalisation of 14 commercial banks in 1969, the Indian banking system has made tremendous progress both in terms of deposit mobilisation and branch expansion. Aggregate deposits of all banks rose from about 15 per cent in 1969 to 79.8 per cent in 2003. The total number of bank branches went up from 8,262 to 66,514 over the period. Of these, about 50 per cent were in rural areas in 2003 as against less man 25 per cent in 1969. Besides performing ordinary banking services, Indian Banks also started innovative banking thereby diversifying their activities in new directions.

Despite all this, they failed to provide reliable, efficient and low-cost services. Both productivity and profitability of banks declined and especially, the public sector banks became a burden on the exchequer. To overcome the defects of the Indian banking system, the Narasimham Committee made a number of suggestions.

---

* Recommendations relating to the financial system have not been given in the above paras.

Some of these have been implemented from 1991-92 onwards. They are enumerated as under:

1. *Capital Adequacy Norms.* To avoid risk, the RBI laid down capital adequacy norms in April 1992 to be complied by banks by March 1996. All banks in India were required to achieve a risk-weighted capital adequacy ratio of 4 per cent by 31 March 1993 and of 8 per cent by 31 March, 1996. Foreign banks operating in India and Indian banks with branches abroad were to attain 8 per cent by March, 1993. This has been raised to 9 per cent from March 2000 for all banks

2. *Recapitalisation.* In order to enable the public sector banks to meet the prescribed capital adequacy ratio, the Government of India has been contributing to the capital of such banks. During 1993-94, the Government provided Rs. 5,700 crores towards recapitalisation of 19 nationalised banks; during 1994-95 Rs. 5,293 crores to 13 banks; Rs. 850 crores to 6 banks; during 1995-96 and Rs. 909 crores to 4 banks during 1996-97; and Rs 297 crores to one bank in 1999-2000.

3. *Partial Privatisation of Public Sector Banks.* But recapitalisation is not a permanent solution of the problem. As the Government resources are limited, banks have been allowed to mobilise equity resources from the public. First, the State Bank of India Act was amended to enable the Bank to have access to the capital market. The RBI shareholding in SBI has been reduced to 67 per cent. Similarly, by the Banking Companies (Acquisition and Transfer of Undertakings) Amendment Act, 1994, the Government's share in the paid-up capital of public sector banks had been reduced to 51 per cent. With another amendment in 2000, it has been reduced to 33 per cent.

4. *Prudential Accounting Norms.* The RBI has introduced prudential accounting norms for banks since 1992-93. A credit facility is required to be treated as non-performing asset (NPA) if interest or instalment of principal are in arrears for *any* two quarters in the accounting year. Provisioning requirement for NPAs with balances of less than Rs 25,000 was increased to 10 per cent of the aggregate amount outstanding for the year ended March, 1995 from 7.5 per cent a year ago. For substandard and doubtful advances of Rs 25,000 and above, they are required to make 100 per cent provision with regard to loss assets.

5. *Recovery of Debts.* Indian banks suffer from large debt arrears which adversely affect their current cash flow position and reduce profits. To recover bad debts, a new Act known as the "Recovery of Debts due to Banks and Financial Institutions Act, 1993" has been passed to set up Debt Recovery Tribunals. Such tribunals have been set up at major centres.

6. *Freedom about Bank Branches.* Banks have been given freedom to open new branches and upgrade extension counters on attaining capital adequacy norm of 8 per cent, net profits for last 3 consecutive years, NPAs of less than 15 per cent and minimum owned funds of Rs 110 crores. They are also permitted to close non-viable branches except in rural and semi-urban areas.

7. *Entry of Private Sector Banks.*To introduce greater competition in banking so as to improve banking services to customers, private banks have been allowed entry as per RBI guidelines. Approval has been given to a few proposals for setting up new private sector banks. Private banks have been allowed to raise capital from institutional investors upto 20 per cent and from NRIs upto 40 per cent. Ten new private sector banks have been established since 1994. It has also been made clear by the RBI that existing private sector banks will be allowed to expand without fear of nationalisation.

8. *Department of Supervision.* A Department of Supervision has been set up in the RBI with effect from 22 December 1993 to supervise the working of commercial banks. It undertakes inspection, surveillance and special investigations including those connected with frauds, and appointment of statutory auditors.

9. *Board for Financial Supervision (BFS).* The BFS has been set up within the RBI in November 1994. The Board ensures implementation of regulations in the areas of credit management, asset classification, income recognition, provisioning, capital adequacy and treasury operations.

10. *Disclosure on Defaulting Borrowers.* To enforce payments discipline among borrowers, a scheme for disclosure of information regarding defaulting borrowers of banks with outstandings aggregating to Rs. 1 crore and above as on 31 March and 30 September every year has been in operation since April 1994.

11. *Banking Ombudsman Scheme.* The Banking Ombudsman Scheme has been started from June 1995 for speedy and inexpensive settlement of customer complaints about the deficiencies in banking services. Ten Ombudsmen are functioning at important centres in the country.

12. *Central Board of Bank Frauds (CBBF).* The Finance Ministry has set up the CBBF in January 1997 to

advise it on the merits of the cases being pursued by the CBI against bank officials up to the level of the general manager. The Board is to scrutinise banking transactions referred to it and give its opinion within 3 months as to whether there is sufficient basis for proceeding with criminal investigations against the officials.

13. *Consortium Arrangements.* To encourage competition and slow-down disintermediation, lending restrictions on banks have been reduced. Large borrowers above a specified credit limit have been allowed to borrow through a consortium of scheduled commercial banks headed by a lead bank. The threshold limit for such consortium arrangement was raised from Rs 5 crores to Rs 50 crores from October 1993. The number of borrower accounts subject to this procedure had been fixed at 76. Borrowers beyond this limit are permitted to induct new banks into a consortium. Banks have been permitted to leave the consortium after two years of joining it.

14. *Lending Norms Liberalised.* Bank lending norms have been liberalised subject to the observance of prescribed prudential norms and quarterly reporting requirements, as laid down by the RBI. They are free to decide levels of holding of individual items of inventory and receivables to be permitted to borrowers. They are also free to decide about the quantum and period of adhoc credit limits without charging additional interest.

15. *Measures to Streamline Working of Banks.* A number of measures have been adopted by the RBI to improve the quality of performance and management of banks. These include: management information systems and the internal audit and control mechanisms; computerisation of banking operations; prudential norms for income recognition assets, etc.

16. *Liberal Credit Control Measures.* A number of steps have been taken to reduce controls and distortions in the working of banks. Statutory Liquidity Ratio (SLR) on incremental net demand and time liabilities (NDTL) has been reduced to 25 per cent. SLR on total NDTL has been brought down to 25 per cent by 1996. The banks have been allowed freedom to fix their deposit and lending rates. They can invest in corporate shares, debentures and units of mutual funds, not exceeding 5 per cent of their outstanding advances effective March 2001. They can also buy shares and debentures of companies from the secondary market.

17. *Entry of New Private Banks.* The RBI issued in January 2001 guidelines for the entry of new private sector banks other than 10 previous banks. They are : *(i)* minimum paid-up capital of Rs. 200 crores to be raised to Rs 300 crores within three years of opening; *(ii)* promoters' contribution of minimum 40 per cent; *(iii)* NRI contribution in primary equity 40 per cent; *(iv)* no large industrial house can promote a new bank but individual companies can contribute up to 10 per cent equity; *(v)* NBFCs with AAA rating and 12 per cent capital adequacy can become private sector banks; *(vi)* 10 per cent capital adequacy ratio to be maintained by the new bank; *(vii)* 40 per cent of net bank credit for priority sector lending, and *(viii)* 25 per cent branches in rural/semi-urban areas.

18. *Entry of Banks into Insurance.* All banks have been allowed to enter insurance business subject to having a minimum net worth of Rs. 500 crores and satisfying other criteria in regard to capital adequacy, profitability, etc.

EXERCISES

1. Explain briefly recent trends in the Indian Banking System.
2. Write notes on: *(i)* Lead Bank Scheme, *(ii)* Service Area Approach, *(iii)* Financing of Priority Sector, *(iv)* Factoring, *(v)* Deposit Insurance and Credit Guarantee Corporation.
3. Explain the main features of Innovative Banking in India.
4. What are the principal defects in the Indian Banking System? Give suggestions to remove them.
5. Give the main recommendations of the Narasimham Committee relating to the Indian Banking System.

CHAPTER 82

Development Banking in India

1. INTRODUCTION

Development banking is a post-World War II financial innovation. However, the first development bank was the Industrial Development Bank of Japan established in 1902. Initially, it provided ship mortgage loans. After 1927, it started financing small scale industries. But it was after the Second World War that it started functioning as a development bank in the modern sense of the term. Development banks were also started in a number of developed countries in the post-war era such as the Industrial Bank of Canada (1944), the Finance Corporation for Industry Ltd. and the Commercial Finance Corporation Ltd. of Great Britain (1945), the Industrial Finance Department of the Commonwealth Bank of Australia (1946), the Dutch Herstel Bank (1949), the Industriekredit Bank of Germany (1949), etc. Development banks were also established in many developing countries like India, Pakistan, Sri Lanka, Iran, Chile, Ghana, Malaysia, Thailand, Nigeria, etc. These banks were mostly sponsored by the World Bank. The World Bank itself had its affiliates like the IFC and IDA. In 1959 was established the Inter-American Development Bank with the participation of 19 Latin American countries. The Asian Development Bank came into existence in 1967. The first development bank in India was the IFC established in 1946.

2. MEANING

Development banks are those financial institutions which provide term finance, promote entrepreneurship, enhance organisational effectiveness and upgrade know-how and do-how. They provide either loan or equity capital or both, as also advisory, promotional and entrepreneurial services. Thus development banks administer a blend of financial and developmental services. Boskey defines a development bank as "a financial intermediary supplying medium and long-term funds to bankable economic development projects and providing related services".

3. FUNCTIONS OF DEVELOPMENT BANKS

Development banks have certain distinct characteristics which distinguish them from commercial banks and other financial institutions. *First,* unlike commercial banks, they do not accept deposits from the public. *Second,* they provide medium and long-term finance, whereas commercial banks provide long-term finance. *Third,* they do not perform ordinary banking functions but perform promotional, developmental and innovative functions. *Fourth,* they are motivated by social profit, while commercial banks are motivated by commercial profit.

We enumerate some of the functions of development banks below:

1. They provide risk capital.
2. They grant medium and long-term loans or advances.
3. They subscribe to the issue of stocks, shares, bonds and debentures of industrial concerns.
4. They underwrite the issue of stocks, shares, bonds and debentures of industrial concerns.
5. They guarantee loans raised from within and outside the country.
6. They guarantee deferred payment of loans in connection with the purchase of capital goods or machinery within and outside the country.
7. They develop capital market by trying to broaden ownership and by other devices.
8. They provide assistance for setting up new industrial projects.
9. They provide assistance for the expansion of existing units.
10. They provide assistance for modification, renovation and modernisation of existing plants and machinery.
11. They arrange for general industrial surveys and feasibility studies for specific projects.
12. They formulate specific proposals for new enterprises.
13. They assist in finding technical and entrepreneurial partners for local clients or for foreign investors.
14. They provide consultancy assistance in respect of technical know-how and market information to new entrepreneurs.
15. They provide necessary guidance, training and other facilities like project identification, project formulation, project implementation, etc. to new entrepreneurs.
16. They sponsor programmes for the upgradation of managerial skills and professionalism of management.
17. They help in the dispersal of industries and development of backward areas.

4. IMPORTANCE OF DEVELOPMENT BANKS

Development banks have unique importance in the development process of a country. In fact, they are a catalyst agent for development. We enumerate their role as active engines of growth.

1. *Engines of Development.* Development banks are engines of development. By providing expertise, arranging for feasibility studies and finance, they act as active agents of growth.

2. *Spirit of Development Finance.* The importance of development banks lies in spreading the spirit of development finance whereby entrepreneurs learn to invest in real fixed assets.

3. *Creation and Promotion of Enterprise.* Development banks are the instruments for the creation, promotion and spread of enterprise and initiative.

4. *Promotion of Balanced Regional Development.* Development banks are important in that they help in decentralisation and diversification by financing small, medium and large entrepreneurs in backward regions of the country. They are thus the promoters of balanced regional development.

5. *Increasing Productivity of Investment.* They help increase productivity of investment by bringing professionalism in management and providing consultancy and extension services to the tiny, small and new entrepreneurs.

6. *Upgradation of Skills.* By providing appropriate training and upgradation of managerial skills, they help in skill formation among small entrepreneurs.

7. *Upgradation of Technology.* With their technical, advisory and R&D departments, development banks

give advice and training in new technology and also help in the upgradation of indigenous technology.

8. *Research.* Development banks undertake market and investment research and surveys as also technical and economic studies related to development of industries.

9. *Gap-Filling.* They help in filling gaps in the industrial structure of the economy by providing and developing industries.

10. *Coordination.* To avoid haphazard growth of financial institutions, development banks coordinate the working of other financial term lending institutions engaged in financing, promoting and developing industries.

11. *Institution Building.* Development banks are the instruments of institution building. They assist in the creation and promotion of term lending institutions. For instance, the Risk Capital and Technology Finance Corporation has been sponsored by the IFCI.

12. *Assist in Purveying Foreign Capital.* It is development banks which acquire foreign capital and allocate it to varied industrial sectors in keeping with national priorities. They get finance from the World Bank, IDA, etc. and allocate it to different industrial projects.

5. DEVELOPMENT BANKS IN INDIA

There are three types of development banks in India: *First,* there are development banks for agriculture at local, state and national level. They are Primary Land Development Banks, State / Central Land Development Banks, and NABARD. *Second,* there are development banks for industry at the national and State level. At the national level are included Industrial Development Bank of India (IDBI), Industrial Finance Corporation of India (IFCI), Industrial Credit and Investment Corporation of India (ICICI), Small Industries Development Bank of India (SIDBI), Industrial Reconstruction Bank of India (IRBI), Risk Capital and Technology Finance Corporation (RCTF), Technology Development and Information Company of India (TDICI), Shipping Credit and Investment Corporation of India (SCICI), and Tourism Finance Corporation of India (TFCI). At the same level are State Financial Corporations (SFCs) and State Industrial Development Corporations (SIDCs). *Third,* there is the Export-Import (EXIM) Bank of India for the foreign sector.

We shall confine our study to some of the important financial institutions as development banks.

1. Industrial Finance Corporation of India (IFCI)

The IFCI was the first development bank established in India in 1948. It has been converted into a public limited company with effect from 1 July, 1993. Its main objective is to make medium and long term credit to industrial concerns in the private, public, joint and co-operative sectors in India. It is a subsidiary of the IDBI which holds 50 per cent of its share capital and the remaining 50 per cent is held by banks, insurance companies, and co-operative banks. It augments its resources by borrowing from the Government of India, RBI, IDBI, UTI, LIC and by issuing its bonds and debentures in the market, and by borrowing in foreign currency from the World Bank and other foreign organisations.

Its Functions

The IFCI performs the dual function of a financier and promoter. These functions reveal its multifaceted activities :

(1) *As a Financier.* As a financier, the IFCI performs the following functions:

(a) It grants loans and advances both in rupee and foreign currencies to individual concerns which are repayable within a period of 25 years.

(b) It subscribes to the issue of shares, bonds and debentures by industrial concerns.

(c) It underwrites the issue of shares, bonds and debentures by industrial concerns which must be disposed by the IFCI within seven years of their acquisition.

(d) It guarantees loans both in rupee and foreign currencies and deferred payments in connection with machinery imported from abroad or purchased within India.

(e) It provides financial assistance for setting up new industrial projects, expansion of existing units, and

modernisation, renovation and modification of existing units.

(f) It can convert in full or part its rupee loan into equity capital of the industrial concern assisted by it. But it cannot acquire more than 40 per cent of the share capital except in case of persistent default of repayment of loan when its shareholding may go up to 51 per cent or more. But this conversion clause is not applicable to loans sanctioned in foreign currency, to co-operative banks and for modernisation and rehabilitation of sick units, etc.

(g) As part of its financial services, it provides equipment financing, equipment leasing, equipment procurement, suppliers' credit, buyers' credit, merchant banking and hire-purchase services to industrial concerns.

(h) It also provides financial support to other financial concerns.

(i) It has introduced Instalment Credit Scheme in November 1991.

(j) It has entered into a Memorandum of Understanding (MoU) with Housing and Urban Development Corporation Ltd (HUDCO) for joint financing of infrastructure projects.

(2) *As a Promoter. (a)* The promotional activities of the IFCI cover funds supplied for technical consultancy, risk capital, venture capital, technical development, tourism, housing, development of securities market, entrepreneurship development and subsidy support to help entrepreneurs and enterprises in the village and small industries sector.

(b) It sanctions assistance to industrial units in backward areas for balanced regional development.

(c) The IFCI sponsored the *Risk Capital and Technology Finance Corporation* (RCTC) in January 1988 after reconstituting the Risk Capital Foundation set up by it in 1975. The RCTC operates two schemes viz. first, Risk Capital Schene, and second, Technology Finance and Development Scheme. Under these schemes, assistance is available to first generation entrepreneurs, particularly technocrats and professionals who have proposals for technology oriented ventures. Assistance is available for funding innovative technologies, technological upgradation, energy conservation processes, systems, environment protection, infrastructural support for advanced/complex technologies, setting up of pilot plants, etc. Assistance is provided on soft terms by way of conventional loans on predetermined interest rates, grace period, repayment period, etc.

(d) It set up a credit rating agency known as the Investment-Information and Credit Rating Agency of India (IICRA) in January 1991, as a public limited company with an authorised capital of Rs 10 crores.

(e) It established the Merchant Banking and Allied Services Department (MB&AD) in 1986 which handles merchant banking assignments relating to public issue management.

(f) It has recently promoted three subsidiary companies, viz., IFCI Financial Services Ltd., IFCI Investors Services Ltd., and IFCI Custodial Services Ltd.

Its Working

During 2002-03, the IFCI sanctioned financial assistance under its various schemes amounting to Rs 2,031 crores. Component-wise, sanctions of rupee loans amounted to Rs 16.38 crores. Sanctions by way of underwriting and direct subscriptions amounted to Rs 394 crores and others nil.

The IFCI is required to achieve 9 per cent capital adequacy norm since 2000 which it has been maintaining on an average of more than 8 per cent.

, Thus the IFCI has helped in industrial development through financial and promotional assistance and through diversification of industries in backward areas and states. The criticisms levelled against it for delay in sanctioning loans, favour shown to big industrial houses and neglect of backward regions and industries are unwarranted.

2. Industrial Development Bank of India (IDBI)

The IDBI was established in July 1964 as a wholly owned subsidiary of the Reserve Bank but was made an autonomous institution in February 1976. At the time of its formation, it took over the Refinance Corporation for Industry which was set up in June 1958. At present, the IFCI, UTI and Small Industries Development Bank of India (SIDBI) are its subsidiaries. Since 1986, the authorised capital of IDBI has been raised to Rs 1,000 crores which can be further increased to Rs. 2,000 crores. It mobilises funds through borrowings from the Government of India, the RBI, by way of bonds/debentures, by selling capital bonds, through investment deposit account scheme, foreign currency borrowings, etc.

Its Functions

The IDBI is an apex institution in the sphere of development banking in India which performs financing, coordination and promotional functions. It renders assistance to small, medium and large scale industries in public, private, joint and co-operative sectors.

(1) **As a Financier.** As a financier, the IDBI renders direct and indirect assistance to all types of industrial concerns :

(a) Schemes of Direct Assistance. It extends direct assistance to industry under its Project Finance Scheme and the Technical Development Fund Scheme. The Project Finance Scheme also covers assistance under the Textile Modernisation Fund, Venture Capital Fund, Technology Upgradation, Energy Audit Subsidy, and Equipment Finance for Energy Conservation Schemes. The Project Finance Scheme of the IDBI mainly covers project loans to industries, underwriting and direct subscriptions to shares and bonds or debentures of industrial concerns, guarantees for loans/deferred payments due from industrial concerns, and equipment finance, asset credit, and equipment leasing.

(b) Schemes of Indirect Assistance. The IDBI renders the following types of indirect assistance to industrial concerns.

(i) Refinance of Industrial Loans. It renders indirect assistance by refinancing ine term loans extended by SFCs, SIDCs, commercial/cooperative banks and RRBs to industrial concerns.

(ii) Bills Rediscounting Scheme. This scheme is meant to help the use of indigenous machinery by industrial concerns. Under this scheme, the purchaser draws the bill in favour of the manufacturer of machinery who discounts it with his banker who in turn gets it rediscounted from the IDBI. This facility is provided mainly to sugar, jute, cotton textiles, cement and engineering industries.

(iii) Seed Capital Scheme. Under this scheme, financial assistance is available to new entrepreneurs for meeting the gap in promoters' contribution as well as equity where no issue of public shares is done.

(iv) Assistance to Leasing Companies. Financial assistance is also sanctioned to leasing companies for refinancing their hire-purchase and leasing schemes.

(v) Resources Support to Other Institutions. The IDBI provides resource support to other financial institutions by subscribing to their shares and bonds/debentures such as IFCI, ICICI, SFCs, SIDCs, NSIC, TCOs, etc.

(vi) Merchant Banking. It carries out merchant banking activities and helps the industry in raising capital from the market and renders advice.

(vii) Commercial Banking. It has set up the IDBI Bank Ltd. since 1995 as a private commercial bank.

(2) **As a Coordinator.** The primary objective of the IDBI is to act as a coordinator. As such, it coordinates the activities and operations of other term lending institutions engaged in financing, promoting or developing industries. Coordination is achieved through the inter-institutional meetings and uniform policies and code of conduct in formulation of policies. This has led to the emergence of consortium financing.

(3) **As a Promoter.** This is an important function of the IDBI which includes planning, promoting and developing industries to fill the gaps in the industrial structure of the country. For this purpose, it provides technical and administiative assistance, undertakes market and investment research and surveys, and also technical and economic studies related to development of industry. We discuss its following promotional activities.

(a) Development of Backward Areas. The IDBI conducts surveys of backward areas for assessing their industrial growth potential and publishes reports. It then identifies projects which can be implemented in specific backward areas. It gives both direct and indirect financial assistance for the implementation of such projects in backward areas. The IDBI also undertakes follow-up of those projects on a selective basis.

(b) Promotion of Institutions for SSI. The IDBI promoted the Small Industries Development Fund (SIDF) and National Equity Fund (NEF) for assistance to the small scale sector. In 1990, the IDBI created the Small Industries Development Bank of India (SIDBI) as its wholly owned subsidiary. From April 1990 the SIDBI took over the operations of the two Funds.

(c) The IDBI has sponsored credit rating agency CARE.

(d) It has entered into corporate trusteeship by accepting assignments as mortgage trustee and trustee

to odd-lot shareholders.

(e) It has also started stock broking.

(f) It has set up a mutual fund.

(g) Establishment of Technical Consultancy Organisations (TCOs). The IDBI has set up a network of TCOs in collaboration with State level financial and development institutions and commercial banks to provide inexpensive consultancy services to small and new entrepreneurs in the country. The activities of TCOs include preparing project profiles and feasibility studies, undertaking industrial potential surveys, conducting entrepreneurship development programmes and rendering technical and administrative assistance. They also provide consultancy services for modernisation and rehabilitation of industrial units, transfer of technology, design and engineering services, management and export consultancy, rural industrial development, retainer consultancy services, turnkey assignments, and energy and conservation services.

(h) In association with other all-India financial institutions and the Department of Biotechnology of the Government of India, it has set up the Bio-tech Consortium India Ltd. to help commercialisation of processes and products in the field of biotechnology developed in the research institutes of the country. It aims at the transfer of technology, product development, feedback from market, minimisation of investment risk, and to supplement the efforts of existing research and development institutes in the field of biotechnology.

Its Working

During 2002-03, the IDBI sanctioned financial assistance to industrial concerns amounting to Rs 3,889 crores. Out of this, Rs. 2,924 crores were disbursed. Of the total financial assistance disbursed, rupee loans, foreign currency loans and guarantees amounted to Rs 7,853 crores; underwriting and direct subscriptions Rs. 140 crores and others Rs. 117 crores. The IDBI is required to achieve 9 per cent capital adequacy norm which it has been maintaining on an average of 11 per cent. The IDBI has been merged with IDBI Bank in 2004.

Critical Appraisal of its Working. The IDBI is an apex development bank in the country. Its performance has been quite impressive in terms of the range and pattern of assistance rendered by it. Despite the fact that it has to work under the prevailing economic policy and environment, it has certain flaws.[1]

1. Its emphasis has been on providing project loans. It has therefore been giving less importance to underwriting of shares and debentures of industrial concerns. It has thus failed to develop the capital market.
2. The IDBI's assistance to industries has been mainly of the financial type. As a result, it has paid less attention to promotional and consultancy services.
3. The major portion of its financial assistance has gone to the large scale industries and hardly 28 per cent of the total assistance has gone to the small scale industries.
4. The major portion of its assistance has gone to the already developed states and that too only to a few states. It has thus failed to foster balanced development of all states.
5. Its financial assistance to backward areas has been hardly 42 per cent and that has also been provided to such areas mostly in developed states. This has not been a healthy trend.
6. The major portion of its financial assistance has gone to the private sector which already has access to a variety of sources. It has, therefore, neglected the other sectors, especially the cooperative.

In fact, there is not much weight in these criticisms[1] because the assistance to be provided by the IDBI to different industries, areas, and purposes depends upon the criteria laid down by it. Therefore, those who meet these criteria are sanctioned assistance.

3. Industrial Credit and Investment Corporation of India (ICICI)

The ICICI was established in January 1955 as a public limited company. It is a private sector development bank in India. The World Bank played a key role in its formation. Its authorised capital is Rs 100 crores. About 11 per cent of its share capital is held by the World Bank and other foreign financial institutions, and the remaining by Indian Banks, UTI, GIC, LIC, etc. During 1990-91 for the first time, ICICI entered the capital market with a public issue and raised Rs 100 crores.

1. The points of criticism *inter alia* apply to all Development Banks.

Its Objectives

The ICICI was established to fulfil the following main objectives: *(a)* to finance the foreign exchange component of industrial projects; *(b)* to provide assistance in the creation, expansion and modernisation of industrial enterprises; *(c)* to encourage and promote industrial development and investment; and *(d)* to expand capital markets in the country.

Its Functions

The ICICI renders both financial and promotional assistance to private, joint, public and cooperative sector industrial concerns.

(1) **Financial Assistance.** The ICICI provides financial assistance of the following types:

(a) Project Finance. Assistance for project finance is by way of rupee and foreign currency loans, underwriting and direct subscriptions to shares and debentures, and guarantees.

(b) Financial Services. Assistance by way of financial services to industry includes assistance under schemes of deferred credit since 1982-83, equipment leasing since 1983-84, venture capital during 1986-87 to 1987-88, instalment sale since 1988-89 and asset credit facility since 1989-90.

(c) Merchant Banking. The ICICI also renders merchant banking services.

(d) Commercial Banking. It has set up the ICICI Banking Corporation as a commercial bank since 1994.

(2) **Promotional Assistance.** The ICICI renders the following promotional assistance to industrial concerns:

(a) Assistance to Backward Areas. It provides project finance assistance on concessional terms to industries in backward areas. It also gives loans on soft terms to suitable rural development schemes sponsored by corporate bodies. It extends financial assistance in the form of seed money/margin money or interest rate subsidy in backward areas.

(b) Project Assistance. The ICICI provides assistance to new projects and to expansion/diversification projects. It renders assistance for modernisation/rehabilitation/balancing equipment projects. Further, it provides supplementary assistance to industrial concerns which includes equipment finance and finance for meeting cost overrun and for various other purposes like energy conservation, pollution control, etc.

(c) Technology Upgradation. The ICICI has promoted a number of institutions for technology upgradation. It has promoted TCQs in a number of states in collaboration with IDBI, IFCI and state level institutions. It provides assistance to Indo-US collaboration projects under the US-aided Programme for the Advancement of Commercial Technology (PACT) for development of innovative products and processes in such areas as informatics, biotechnology, engineering, etc. It also renders assistance for R&D projects under the Programme for Acceleration of Commercial Energy Research (PACER) funded by USAID with a grant of $ 20 million. In July 1988, the ICICI established the Technology Development and Information Company of India (TDICI) to finance technology-intensive development activities, including commercial R&D schemes. During 1992-93, the ICICI introduced two new projects with the help of USAID: *First*, Agricultural Commercialisation and Enterprise (ACE) Project, and *second*. Trade in Environmental Services and Technologies (TEST) Programme with grants of S 20 million and $ 25 million respectively.

(d) Venture Capital. The venture capital operations of the ICICI have been taken over by the TDICI since July 1988. However, in association with UTI ard corporate sector, the ICICI floated a second Venture Capital Fund (VECAUS-II) of Rs. 100 crores in April 1990.

(e) It has promoted a new company for providing share registry and transfer services to investors.

(f) It has promoted a mutual fund.

Its Working

Financial assistance sanctioned and disbursed by the ICICI during 2001-02 amounted to Rs. 36,229 crores and 25,831 crores respectively. Of the total disbursed amount, rupee loans, foreign currency loans and guarantiees amounted to Rs. 14,475 crores; underwriting and direct subscriptions Rs 3,348 crores; and others Rs 8,009 crores. The ICICI is required to achieve 9 per cent capital adequacy norm which it has been maintaining on an average of 13 per cent. The ICICI has been merged with the ICICI Bank in April 2002.

4. Industrial Investment Bank of India (IIBI)

Earlier the IIBI was known as the Industrial Reconstruction Corporation of India and renamed as Industrial Investment Bank of India from March 27, 1997. It is the principal credit and reconstruction institution for rehabilitation of sick and closed industrial units in the public, joint and cooperative sectors and those units in the private sector whose management has been taken over under the Industrial (Development & Regulation) Act. It mobilises funds for its use from: *(a)* external sources which include borrowings from the Government of India, RBI and by way of subscription of bonds and debentures of Industrial concerns; and *(b)* internal sources which include repayments by borrowers, and interest and dividend received. Its total financial assets in 1980-81 were Rs 924 crores which increased to Rs 4,526 crores in 2002-03.

Its Functions

The IIBI Performs the following functions :

1. It grants term loans and advances to sick industrial concerns tor modernisation/rehabilitation/balancing equipment.

2. It provides supplementary assistance for *(a)* meeting cost overrun, *(b)* correcting imbalances, and *(c)* other purposes.

3. It underwrites stocks, shares, bonds and debentures and gives guarantees for loans/deferred payments of such industrial concerns.

4. It provides infrastructural facilities, consultancy, managerial and merchant banking facilities.

5. It makes available machinery and other equipment on lease and hire-purchase basis.

Its Working

Sanctions and disbursements by the IIBI during 2002-03 aggregated to Rs 1,207 crores and Rs 1,045 crores respectively. Of the total sanctioned amount, term loans amounted to Rs 163 crores, underwriting and direct subscriptions Rs 1,043 crores.

The IIBI is required to achieve capital adequacy ratio of 9 per cent per annum since 2,000 which it has been maintaining at a higher level.

5. Small Industries Development Bank of India (SIDBI)

The SIDBI was established in April 1990 as a wholly owned subsidiary of the IDBI. The authorised capital of the Bank is Rs 250 crores which can be increased up to Rs 1,000 crores. The Small Industries Development Fund (SIDF) and National Equity Fund (NEF) were taken over by it. Apart from these funds and its share capital, its other sources of funds comprise loans from the IDBI, short-term and long-term funds from the RBI, loans from the Government of India, etc.

Its Functions

The SIDBI performs the following functions:

(i) It is the principal financial institution for the promotion, financing and development of small scale industries.

(ii) It coordinates the functioning of existing institutions engaged in similar activities.

(iii) It renders assistance to small scale industries through refinance of loans and advances, bills finance, seed capital/soft loans, direct assistance, providing services like factoring, leasing, etc.

(iv) It refinances National Industries Development Corporation, State Industrial Development Corporations, State Small Industries Corporations, scheduled banks, state cooperative banks, etc.

(v) It subscribes or purchases stocks, shares, bonds or debentures of State Financial Corporations, State Industrial Development Corporations, etc.

(vi) It renders assistance to small scale industries by way of resource support to NSIC and SSIDCs for their hire purchase, raw material supply and marketing support schemes.

(vii) It initiates steps for technological upgradation and modernisation of existing units.

(viii) It expands channels for marketing products of SSI sector in domestic and overseas markets.

(ix) It promotes employment-oriented industries, especially in semi-urban areas, to create more employment opportunities and thereby check migration of population to urban and metropolitan areas.

Since 1991-92, the SIDBI has introduced the following new schemes:

(1) a scheme of direct assistance to widen the supply base of small-scale ancillary units;

(2) a scheme to provide resource support to factoring companies against factored debts of SSIs;

(3) a refinance scheme for acquisition of computers including their accessories;

(4) a scheme for refinancing assistance to qualified professionals for setting up their ewn business enterprises;

(5) an equipment financing scheme to assist existing small-scale units;

(6) a refinance scheme to resettle voluntarily retired workers of National Textile Corporation (NTC) and to help them in purchasing upto four looms at the maximum;

(7) a venture capital fund was created with an initial corpus of Rs 10 crores;

(8) a special Self-Employment Scheme for Ex-servicemen;

(9) Mahila Udyam Nidhi Scheme to help women entrepreneurs;

(10) it is enrolled as member of the Over-The-Counter Exchange of India (OTCEI) to help SSIs to get access to capital market through SIDBI.

(11) Under the Single Window Scheme (SWS) in operation since the inception of SIDBI, the limit of refinance against cash credit sanctioned by banks has been raised to 75 per cent. The limit of term loans under the Automatic Refinance Scheme (ARS) has been raised to Rs. 50 lakh and the limit of refinance to 90 per cent.

(12) During 1993-94, SIDBI took new initiatives such as the extension of foreign currency loans to Export Oriented Units (EOUs) and support to Non-Government Organisations (NGOs) for promoting self-help by the rural poor.

(13) It has signed MoUs with 5 public sector banks for jointly extending direct assistance to SSI units.

(14) The SIDBI has started a venture capital fund with a corpus of Rs 20 crores.

(15) During 1994-95, it introduced new schemes such as direct equity investment in SSIs and financial assistance to enable well-run EOUs to acquire ISO-9000 series certification.

(16) It has set up a Technology Bureau for SSI units in New Delhi in collaboration with Asia Pacific Centre for Transfer of Technology.

Its Working

The SIDBI sanctioned and disbursed Rs 10,904 crores and Rs 6,789 crores respectively during 2002-03. Of the total disbursed amount, term loans amounted to Rs 6,789 crores; underwriting and direct subscriptions; and others nil.

6. Export-Import Bank of India (EXIM Bank)

The Export-Import Bank of India *was* established in January 1982 as a statutory corporation wholly owned by the Government of India.

Its Objectives : The main objectives of the Exim Bank are:

1. To ensure an integrated arid coordinated approach to solve the problems of exporters;
2. To provide special attention to the export of capital goods;
3. To encourage project exports;
4. To finance Indian joint ventures abroad;
5. To undertake and finance the export of technical consultancy services;
6. To deal in foreign exchange;
7. To render international merchant banking services;
8. To provide refinance facilities;
9. To extend buyers credit and lines of credit to parties outside India; and
10. To tap domestic and overseas markets for resources for undertaking developmental and financing activities in the sphere of exports.

Its Functions

The Exim Bank performs the following promotional and developmental functions:

1. To undertake and finance research, surveys, techno-economic or any other study in connection with the promotion and development of international trade;
2. To provide technical, administrative and financial assistance of any kind for export or import;
3. To plan, promote, develop and finance export-oriented concerns; and
4. To collect, compile and disseminate market and credit information in respect of international trade.

Its Resources

The authorised capital of the Exim Bank is Rs. 200 crores which can be raised to Rs 500 crores. Its paid-up capital is Rs 75 crores. The Central Government sanctioned a loan of Rs 20 crores repayable in equal annual instalments, commencing on the expiry of fifteen years from the date of receipt of loan. The Exim Bank can also raise resources by issuing and selling bonds and debentures, borrowing from the Reserve Bank, Government of India, and domestic and international markets.

The Exim Bank maintains three funds: the Export Development Fund (EDF), the General Fund, and the Export Marketing Fund (EMF).

The EDF is a special fund in which the following can be credited: *(a)* all amounts received by way of loans, gifts, grants, donations from the Government or any other source in or outside India; *(b)* repayments or recoveries in respect of loans, advances or facilities granted the Fund; *(c)* income or profits from investments made from the Fund; and *(d)* income accruing or arising to the Fund by way of interest or otherwise.

The General Fund is used for the grant of loans or advances for its export development activities. All receipts of the Exim Bank, except those which are credited to the EDF, are credited to the General Fund, and all payments, other than those which are debited to the EDF are made out of the General Fund.

The Exim Bank set up the EMF in June 1986. It consists of a component of World Bank loan to India which is managed by the Bank on behalf of the Government of India. This Fund provides grants and loans for the promotion of select group of engineering products for export to developed countries.

Its Working

The Exim Bank provides both funded and non-funded assistance to promote Indian exports. It provides funded assistance in the following forms: direct financial assistance, export credit refinance, buyers' credit, lines of credit, overseas investment finance, finance for export oriented units, finance for computer software exports, agency credit lines, pre-shipment credit, export bills rediscounting, small scale industry export bills rediscounting, bulk import finance, etc. During 1999-2000, sanctions of funded assistance under various programmes amounted to Rs 2831.8 crores.

New Export Promotion Programmes. The Exim Bank has recently introduced a number of programmes and schemes for export promotion. They are: *(i)* Africa Project Development Facility (APDF) which is meant to promote private sector investment in Africa through financial support for consultancy studies. It has started generating business for Indian consultants in African countries. *(ii)* Project Preparatory Services Overseas Programme (PPSOP) provides finance for feasibility studies in other countries for Indians. *(iii)* Financing Market Entry Costs Programme which provides assistance to Indian exporters to cover the costs of entry into new markets abroad, *(iv)* Pre-shipment Export Credit Scheme Denominated in Foreign Currency which provides exporters access to imports of raw material components, *(v)* Post-shipment Export Credit Denominated in Foreign Currency Scheme which enables exporters to avail of this scheme and pay interest at rates applicable to foreign currency concerned, *(vi)* Production Equipment Finance Programme which ensures rupee term finance to eligible export-oriented units for acquiring equipment, *(vii)* European Community International Investment Partners (ECIIP) which aims at promoting and financing joint ventures in India with private sector small and medium enterprises in the EC. *(viii)* Forfeiting is meant to provide to Indian exporters facilities for discounting of their medium and long term export receivables with forfeiting international agencies, *(ix)* Business Advisory and Technical Assistance (BATA) programme which provides services of Indian exports to the International Finance Corporation (IFC) sponsored BATA programme for the Caribbean, Central America, South Pacific, and East European countries, *(x)* Export Marketing Finance programme which provides financial assistance to Indian manufacturing companies to undertake strategic export marketing activities with industrialised country markets, *(xi)* Export Vendor Development Finance (EVDF) programme which provides integrated financing packages to manufacturer/exporters and export/trading houses to implement strategic vendor development schemes.

Thus, the Exim Bank's programmes cover various stages of exports from the development of export markets to expansion of production capacity for exports, production **for** exports, consultancy and feasibility studies for exports and pre and post-shipment financing.

7. State Financial Corporations (SFCs)

SFCs are the state-level development banks for the development of small and medium scale industries in 18 States of India. They aim at bringing about balanced regional development by wider dispersal of industries, promoting greater investment and generating larger employment opportunities. Besides their paid-up capital, SFCs augment their funds by borrowings from the Governments, RBI, IDBI, banks and by way of bonds/ debentures, by accepting deposits and sale of investment in shares and debentures of industrial concerns.

Their Functions

SFCs perform the following functions:

(i) They provide financial assistance to industries by way of term loans, direct subscription to equity/ debentures, discounting of bills of exchange and guarantees.

(ii) They meet the term loan requirements of small and medium scale industries for acquisition of fixed assets like land, building, machinery and equipment.

(iii) They provide loans for setting up new industrial units as well as for expansion and modernisation of the existing units.

(iv) They also promote the development of medium and small scale industries in backward areas of the country.

(v) Under the Special Capital Scheme, SFCs provide equity type support of upto Rs 4 lakhs on soft terms to entrepreneurs for bridging the gap in equity or promoters' contribution. Entrepreneurs with viable projects but lacking adequate own funds are assisted under the scheme.

(vi) SFCs operate a number of schemes on behalf of the IDBI. These include composite loan scheme, schemes for women entrepreneurs, modernisation scheme, equipment finance scheme, schemes for hospitals and nursing homes, scheme for ex-servicemen, single window scheme, and special capital and seed capital schemes.

Their Working

SFCSs sanctioned an amount of Rs 2,210 crores in 2001-02 and their disbursements amounted to Rs 1,750 crores. Top four SFCs in terms of annual sanctions were Gujarat, Uttar Pradesh, Maharashtra, and Karnataka. These four SFCs together accounted for about 50 per cent of the totai sanctions by all SFCs up to the end of March 1999. Industry-wise five industries were viz. services, food products, textiles, chemicals and chemical products, and metal products together accounted for more than 54 per cent of the cumulative sanctions of all SFCs to industries. Cumulative sanctions to backward areas by SFCs accounted for more than 51 per cent of total sanctions. Small scale sector accounted for more than 76 per cent of cumulative sanctions. New projects claimed the bulk of sanctions from SFCs and accounted for about 84 per cent of total sanctions, followed by expansion/diversification, supplementary assistance, and modernisation/rehabilitation/balancing equipment.

8. State Industrial Development Corporations (SIDCs)

SIDCs were set up during the sixties and early seventies as wholly-owned State Government undertakings for the promotion and development of medium and large scale industries. Their main objective is to act as catalytic agents for the development of industries in their respective States. There are at present 26 SIDCs in the country. Nine of them also function as SFCs and provide assistance to small scale units and act as promotional agencies in their respective areas of operation. Seven SIDCs are also involved in infrastructure development and other extension services for promotion of small sector.

Besides increase in paid-up capital, SIDCs borrow funds from the Government, IDBI, banks and other financial institutions. They also borrow by way of bonds, by accepting deposits, sale of investments in shares and debentures of industrial concerns, and repayments by borrowers.

Their Functions

SIDCs perform the following functions:

(i) They provide financial assistance to industrial units by way of term loans, underwriting and direct subscriptions to shares/debentures and guarantees.

(ii) They undertake a variety of promotional activities like preparation of feasibility reports, industrial potential surveys, entrepreneurship development programmes and developing industrial areas/estates.

(iii) They are engaged in setting up of medium and large industrial projects in joint sector in collaboration with private entrepreneurs or as wholly-owned subsidiaries.

(iv) Some SIDCs also administer the incentive schemes of Central/State Governments and participate in risk capital.

(v) Some SIDCs extend assistance by way of interest free sales tax/unsecured loans on behalf of respective State Governments.

(vi) SIDCs are agents of IDBI for operating its seed capital scheme. Under the scheme, equity type assistance is provided to deserving first generation entrepreneurs who possess necessary skills but lack adequate resources required towards promoter contribution.

Their Working

Assistance sanctioned by SIDCs (excluding sales tax, loans) amounted to Rs 1,594 crores during 2001-02. Out of this, Rs 1,718 crores were disbursed. Component-wise, term loans accounted for 96.63 per cent of total disbursements of SIDCs during 2001-02. Assistance by way of underwriting/direct subscriptions, others constituted 3.37 per cent of total disbursements. Cumulatively, seven SIDCs in the States of Uttar Pradesh, Maharashtra, Gujarat, Karnataka, Andhra Pradesh, Punjab and Tamil Nadu together constituted nearly 66 per cent of the total sanctions of all SIDCs. In the industry-wise cumulative assistance, chemicals and chemical products, textiles, food products, basic metals and services together accounted for 48 per cent of total sanctions by SIDCs. Assistance sanctioned to backward areas accounted for a share of 62 per cent in the cumulative sanctions of SIDCs up to the end of March 1999. Of the sector-wise assistance, private sector accounted for 79.5 per cent of the cumulative sanctions of SIDCs followed by joint sector, public sector and cooperative sector (0.5 per cent). Under the purpose-wise assistance, new projects constituted about 70 per cent of the cumulative sanctions followed by expansion/diversification, modernisation/rehabilitation/balancing equipment and supplementary assistance.

Appraisal of Development Banking in India

The study of various development banks in India reveals that they have been playing a crucial role in setting, promoting and developing industrial units in the small, medium and large scale sectors of the Indian economy. They have helped in the dispersal of industries in backward regions/areas. They have been providing necessary know-how, technical, expertise, machinery and equipment for the modernisation of industrial units. In fact, they have been acting as catalytic agents of industrial growth in India.

Despite these achievements, they suffer from certain weaknesses. *First,* the main sources of funds of development banks are borrowings from the Government of India, RBI, banks and other financial institutions and foreign sources. But they do not raise funds from the public. They do not sell their shares, bonds or debentures in the market. These borrowings by development banks have encouraged high debt-equity ratios and since they borrow at low rate of interest, it has led to high capital intensity in industry because the latter is able to procure term loans at low rates in turn. *Second,* the majority of financial assistance is provided by development banks in the form of term loans to industrial units. This has led to large defaults on loans by companies which have become weak units. *Third,* the development banks do not encourage lending on the basis of loans/debentures of industrial units. They have, therefore, failed to develop a corporate bond market.

Fourth, these development banks have provided more financial assistance to the private sector than to the public, joint and cooperative sectors. They also provide soft loans to them at concessional rates at the cost of public exchequer with the result that the State's revenue from them is insufficient. It has led to highly capital-intensive technology and has failed to absorb the growing labour force of the country thereby leading to more unemployment. *Fifth,* they have not been successful in achieving balanced regional development of industries. More assistance has flowed to the already developed States and to backward areas of these States. *Sixth,* their role as promotional agencies has been weak. *Seventh,* there are unnecessary delays in sanctioning and disbursing assistance due to red-tapism. *Eighth,* their overdues to industries have been mounting and the problem of industrial sickness is on the increase. *Ninth,* they have failed to develop adequate human resources with the result that their personnel lack in proper managerial, administrative and technical skills which are essential for the rapid growth of industries.

EXERCISES

1. Discuss the importance of development banking in India.
2. What is a development bank? Explain its functions.
3. Discuss the functions and working of Industrial Finance Corporation of India.
4. Discuss critically the functions and working of the Industrial Development Bank of India.
5. Write notes on: (1) Industrial Credit and Investment Corporation of India; (2) Industrial Reconstruction Bank of India; (3) Small Industries Development Bank of India; (4) Exim Bank.
6. Define a development bank. Give its functions. Critically examine development banking in India.

CHAPTER 83

Non-Bank Financial Intermediaries in India

1. INTRODUCTION

In India Non-bank financial intermediaries (NBFIs) are of two types: organised and unorganised. Organised NBFIs are all development banks which include IDBI, IFCI, ICICI, SIDBI, SFCs, NABARD, Land Development Banks, etc. They raise funds from various sources and provide medium and long-term advances. Besides these, there are the UTI, GIC and LIC. The UTI is a pure NBFI while the later two are insurance companies which raise funds from the insurance premia and lend to individuals and companies. There are also provident funds and pension funds which mobilise savings and invest them in Government and other approved securities. Lastly, post offices mobilise small savings of the public which go to the Government for investment purposes. All organised NBFIs are in the public sector. They follow rules and regulations laid down by the Government.

2. NON-BANKING FINANCIAL COMPANIES (NBFCs)

NBFIs in the unorganised sector are called Non-Banking Financial Companies (NBFCs) in India. They are equipment leasing companies, hire-purchase finance companies, loan (or finance) companies, investment companies, mutual benefit financial companies, chit funds, miscellaneous non-banking companies (nidhis), residuary non-banking companies, non-banking non-financial companies, and housing finance companies.

REGULATION OF NBFCs

NBFCs were registered under the Indian Companies Act and not the Banking Regulation Act. So the RBI had no control over them. In recent years, they have grown in number and volume of business by entering into those areas where banks were not allowed to enter due to regulatory restrictions. In view of their increasing role in the financial intermediation process, the Narasimham Committee recognised the need for integrating them within the mainstream of the financial system. Accordingly, the RBI constituted a Working Group under Dr. A.C. Shah in May 1992 to set out a programme of reform for financial companies.

On the basis of its recommendations, the RBI introduced a scheme of registration of NBFCs on 12 April, 1993. All NBFCs having Net Owned Fund (NOF) of Rs. 50 lakhs and above were required to register with the Reserve Bank. On 13 June, 1994, it issued prudential norms relating to income recognition, accounting standards, assets classification, provisioning for bad and doubtful debts, capital adequacy and concentration of credit/investments for registered NBFCs. The RBI also specified compulsory credit rating for them in a phased manner. They were required to achieve a minimum capital adequacy norm of 8%. Besides, they were required to get themselves rated by any one of the credit rating agencies at least once a year. Credit rating provides objective information to depositors and creditors and helps in protecting their interest. The RBI directions brought all public deposits and inter-corporate deposits of NBFCs within the discipline of its regulations. Further, the interest rates payable on deposits by NBFCs were also laid down. They were also required to attain a minimum liquid asset ratio to deposits. These measures had no statutory backing because the RBI Act, 1934 did not confer such'powers to the Reserve Bank.

By the January 9, 1997 Ordinance, the RBI has been given greater control over the activities of NBFCs. This ordinance was replaced by the RBI (Amendment) Act in March 1997. The conditions under which NBFCs can operate have been laid down by the RBI through several amendments to NBFCs regulations upto 2001.

(1) Entry point norm of Rs. 25 lakhs as minimum NOF which can be raised to Rs. 2 crores;

(2) compulsory registration with the RBI;

(3) maintenance of certain percentage of liquid funds in the form of unencumbered approved securities;

(4) creation of reserve funds in which 20% of the net profit to be transferred every year;

(5) issuing of directions for prudential norms by the RBI;

(6) prohibition of NBFCs from accepting public deposits;

(7) filing of winding-up positions for violation of RBI directions;

(8) empowering the Company Law Board to direct a defaulting NBFC to repay deposits; and

(9) stringent penal provisions in the form of pecuniary penalties for violation of RBI directions.

The various steps taken up by the RBI to consolidate the functioning of NBFCs failed to streamline their working. It, therefore, instituted a new regulatory framework for the operation of NBFCs. Consequently, NBFCs were classified into the following three categories for purposes of regulation:

(a) those accepting public deposits;

(b) those not accepting public deposits but engaged in financial business; and

(c) core investment companies holding atleast 90% of their assets as investments in the securities of group/holding/subsidiary companies.

While NBFCs accepting public deposits are subject to all types of regulations, those not accepting public deposits are regulated in a limited manner.

We will discuss each category briefly.

(a) Regulations over NBFCs Accepting Public Deposits

These regulations are applicable to equipment leasing/hire purchase (EL/HP) and loan companies/investment companies (LC/IC).

(1) For old NBFCs, the minimum NOF remains at Rs. 25 lakhs. But those seeking registration with the RBI and commencing business on or after April 21, 1999, the minimum NOF is Rs. 2 crores. NBFCs with NOF of below 25 lakhs cannot accept deposits. Companies with Rs. 25 lakhs and above NOF can have public deposits not exceeding 1.5 times of NOF or Rs. 10 crores whichever is less.

(2) The period of deposits should not be less than 12 months but not exceed 60 months.

(3) The rate of interest payable on such deposits should not be more than 16 per cent per annum.

(4) The brokerage fees and other expenses should not exceed 2% and 0.5% of the deposits respectively.

(5) The capital adequacy ratio has been fixed at 12% and above, in accordance with the eligibility criteria for accepting deposits.

(6) An EL/HP finance company accepting deposits is required to disclose in its advertisement and application form that it is an unrated company having capital adequacy ratio of not less than 15% and within the RBI regulations mentioned above.

(7) Restrictions have been placed on NBFCs to invest in real estate, except for their own use, upto 10% of

their NOF for EL/HP finance companies and 20% of NOF for LC/IC companies.

(8) NBFCs which fail to repay matured deposits cannot create assets in any manner, including giving loans or making investment, until the default is rectified. Depositors can also lodge their complaints to the Company Law Board.

(9) NBFCs are required to maintain liquid assets of not less than 15% of their public deposits effective April 1,1999. In case of default in maintaining approved securities of requisite value, the RBI imposes penalties.

(10) The liquid assets of NBFCs are required to be deposited in scheduled commercial banks appointed by the RBI so that the securities are not utilised otherwise, except for repayment to depositors. They are also permitted to keep their liquid securities with the Stock Holding Corporation of India.

(11) The RBI has introduced certain regulations in respect of opening and closing of branches. For instance, for closing a branch 3 months' public notice prior to the date of closure has to be given in at least one national newspaper.

(12) The RBI has also instituted a comprehensive supervisory mechanism over NBFCs. This includes on-site inspection, external auditing and off-site surveillance system regarding submission of various returns at quarterly/half-yearly/annual intervals irrespective of the size of their NOF.

(13) An independent Department of Non-Banking Supervision has been opened in the RBI to supervise the operations of NBFCs with its 16 regional offices at different centres of the country.

(14) NBFCs are required to follow a uniform accounting year of March 31 every year effective March 31, 2001.

(15) Any NBFC with NOF of Rs. 2 crores has been permitted to undertake insurance business as agent on fee basis without any risk participation since July 2000. But those NBFCs which have NOF of not less than Rs. 500 crores with good trackrecord in terms of net profits, subsidiaries, net NPA of not less 5%, etc. can set up joint venture company or insurance business with risk participation.

(16) The RBI has also allowed an NBFC to become a private sector bank effective March 31, 2001. For this it has laid down: *(a)* The NBFC should have a minimum net worth of Rs. 200 crores as per its' latest balance sheet which would increase to Rs. 300 crores within three years of the date of conversion, *(b)* It should not have been promoted by a large industrial house or by local, state or central public authority, *(c)* It should have a *triple A* credit rating in the previous year, *(d)* It should have capital adequacy of not less than 12% and its net NPA should be below 5%.

(17) Effective April 2001, the RBI has permitted foreign direct investment (FDI) in the NBFC sector. Foreign NBFCs can set up wholly-owned operating subsidiaries subject to bringing in $ 50 million. Joint venture operating NBFCs having 75% or less foreign investment have been allowed to set up subsidiaries, provided they comply with the applicable minimum capital'inflow of $ 50 million.

(b) Other NBFCs

Since January 2000, NBFCs engaged in *(a)* micro-financing activities; *(b)* not accepting public deposits; and *(c)* mutual benefit companies, have been exempted from the purview of registration, maintenance of liquid assets, creation of reserve funds, etc. Similarly, core investment companies, not accepting public deposits have been exempted from all prudential norms except registration and creation of reserve fund.

Operations of NBFCs

Prior to the RBI (Amendment) Act of 1997, there were over 40,000 NBFCs in the organised and unorganised sectors. With the implementation of various regulations by the RBI from time to time, there were 13,849 NBFCs in June 2003. Of these, only 918 NBFCs were registered with the RBI and only 710 NBFCs were accepting public deposits. The total assets of 910 reporting NBFCs as on March 31, 2002 were Rs 50,290 crores, with NOFs of Rs 4,383 crores and public deposits amounting to Rs 18,822 crores.

Critical Appraisal

NBFCs have been performing a vital function in economic development by mobilising savings and making investments, advancing loans, providing equipment leasing and hire-purchase facilities. But their operations leave much to be desired. However, the RBI (Amendment) Act, 1997 has empowered the RBI with greater controlling powers over the activities of NBFCs of both the incorporated and unincorporated varieties. Now there is a compulsory registration for all NBFCs. The RBI is empowered to issue directions to them on such matters as deposits, NOF, recognition, asset classification, capital adequacy, loan and investment, interest payment, credit rating, accounting standards, etc. Giving more statutory powers to the RBI has been felt long ago because the NBFCs have been openly flouting rules. They lack transparency with regard to the sources of income, bad debts and non-recuring income. There has been no provision in the RBI Act to force an NBFC to refund the depositor his amount.

Still, there is dichotomy in control and regulation of NBFCs. The RBI is to control and regulate the activities of NBFCs. The Company Law Board (CLB) is the agency to redress the grievances of depositors.

With the changing national scenario in the financial markets, most of the NBFCs face difficulties in getting lower-cost funds, stiff competition from large NBFCs and subsidiaries of foreign NBFCs and joint venture foreign companies with the result that their business is dwindling. Even though the RBI has opened more avenues in the form of entry into insurance business and private sector banks, they are only for larger NBFCs. The smaller NBFCs are trying to spread to rural and semi-urban areas. A few NBFCs have started new lines of business, such as financing vehicles, working as agents of larger NBFCs and foreign banks, etc.

EXERCISE

1. Explain the working of non-bank financial companies in India. What has been done to control and regulate them? Explain briefly.

PART SEVEN

PUBLIC FINANCE

CHAPTER 84

Meaning, Scope and Importance of Public Finance

1. MEANING

Public finance means the study of income and expenditure of central, state and local governments and the principles underlying them. However, economists have defined it in a narrow and wide sense. According to **Bastable**, "Public finance deals with expenditure and income of public authorities of the states and their mutual relation and also with the financial administration and control."[1] **Findlay Shirras** defines it as "the study of the principles underlying the spending and raising of funds by public authorities."[2] Prof. **Dalton** also defines public finance in the same manner: "Public finance is concerned with the income and expenditure of public authorities, and with the adjustment of the one to the other. The 'Principles of Public Finance' are the general principles which may be laid down with regard to these matters."[3]

All these definitions are narrow because they do not include the major divisions of public finance and its main functions. **Harold Groves** defines public finance as "a field of inquiry that treats of the income and expenditure of Government. In modern times, this includes four major divisions : public revenue, public expenditure, public debt and certain problems of the fiscal system as a whole such as fiscal administration and fiscal policy."[4] Mrs. Ursula Hicks gives a more comprehensive definition. She writes, 'The main content of Public Finance consists of the examination and appraisal of the methods by which Government bodies provide for the collective satisfaction of wants and secure the necessary funds to carry on their purposes."[5] Thus *public finance studies the income and expenditure of central, state and local governments for the collective satisfaction of wants*

1. Charles F. Bastable, *Public Finance*, 1903.
2. Findlay Shirras, *The Science of Finance*, 1936.
3. H. Dalton, *The Principles of Public Finance*, 1951.
4. Harold Groves, *Financing Government*, 1964.
5. U.K. Hicks, *Public Finance*, 1948.

and the principles which govern income and expenditure.

2. NATURE OF PUBLIC FINANCE

Public finance is a *social science* which is concerned with the problems of raising of funds and their allocation for the collective satisfaction of wants. Its methods of study are based both on the study of the principles and theories or laws of public finance and on a descriptive and statistical study of the actual operations of government finances. Its principles are in the nature of generalisations which state the cause and effect relationships of different variables like public revenue, expenditure, debt and financial administration. These also form the subject matter of public finance.

Public finance cannot undertake controlled experiments to test the validity of its deductions which are done in pure sciences. But it depends on actual case studies such as how to collect more revenues, how to allocate finances among different departments or ministries, how to share the tax burden among the people, why the governments have a deficit budget, and so on. In a federation, there are central and state government which require finances for administrative and developmental purposes. They are faced with the problems of how and where from to get finances and how to allocate then. These are solved by the principles of federal finance.

Public finance is also an *art*. It is concerned with fiscal policies which influence economic policies and economic structure of the country. All governments aim at bringing social justice through an equitable financial system.

3. SCOPE OF PUBLIC FINANCE

Prof. Dalton divides the scope of public finance into four categories: Public Income; Public Expenditure; Public Debt; and Financial Administration. We discuss them as under.

1. *Public Income or Revenue.* Public income is called public revenue. The main sources of public revenue are taxes, fees, fines, special assessments and commercial revenues from public undertakings. In public income, we study the canons and principles of taxation, the various direct and indirect taxes and their impact and incidence, the effects of taxation, the problems of tax evasion and avoidance and the measures to solve these problems so as to raise public revenues.

2. *Public Expenditure.* Public expenditure is the beginning and end of the collection of revenues by the government. As pointed out by Plehn, "Public expenditure is the end and aim of collection of revenues and of other financial activities of the statesman."[6] Under public expenditure we study its classification, the canons or principles which govern it, and its effects on production, employment, income distribution, stability and growth. We also study the reasons for increase in public expenditure and changes in the pattern.

3. *Public Debt.* When public revenue falls short of public expenditure, the government borrows from the public to meet the gap. This is public debt. Under public debt, we study the reasons, methods and sources of public debt, its effects on production, consumption, income distribution and economy, the burden of public debt, and the methods of debt redemption.

4. *Financial Administration.* The aim of financial administration is to control processes and operations of public revenue, public expenditure and public debt. The scope of financial administration includes the collection, custody and disbursement of public money; the coordination of expenditure according to a well-formulated plan; the management of public debt; and the general control of the financial operations of the state. It also includes the preparation of the budget, its execution, and above all auditing the finances of the state.

4. DIFFERENCES BETWEEN PUBLIC AND PRIVATE FINANCE

Public finance is the study of income, expenditure, borrowing and financial administration of the government. On the other hand, private finance is the study of income, expenditure, borrowing and financial administration of individuals or private companies. There are, therefore, no fundamental differences between public finance and private finance. However, there are certain basic differences between the two. We examine below both the views.

SIMILARITIES

The following are the similarities between public and private finance.

1. *Objective.* Both public and private finance aim at the satisfaction of human wants. The objective of public finance is to satisfy social wants and that of private finance to satisfy individual wants.

2. *Principles.* Both government and individuals follows similar principles. The government follows the principle of maximum social benefit while spending its income. Similarly, an individual follows the principle of maximum satisfaction when spending out of his given income.

3. *Income, Expenditure and Borrowing.* Both government and individual have similar but limited sources of income. Both earn their incomes. Both can spend in anticipation of receiving incomes. If their incomes are insufficient to meet their expenditures, both borrow. Both have also to repay the borrowed money.

4. *Policies.* Both government and private companies (and even individuals) follow sound or unsound (rational or irrational) financial policies. If the government follows sound financial policies, it maximises social welfare. Similarly, an individual maximises his welfare. The opposite happens in the case of unsound financial policies.

5. *Administration.* Both government and private companies require efficient administration for their success. If the government administration is corrupt and inefficient, it will lead to misuse and wastage of finances. Similar is the case with a private company.

DIFFERENCES OR DISSIMILARITIES

The following are the main points of differences or dissimilarities between public and private finance.

1. *Adjustment between Income and Expenditure.* An individual determines his expenditure on the basis of his income. He prepares his family budget on his expected income during the month. On the other hand, the government first estimates about its expenditure and then finds out means to raise the necessary income. As pointed out by Bastable, "The individual says, 'I can spend so much', the Finance Minister says, 'I have to raise so much".

But this difference between private and public finance is not always rigid. The opposite may happen under certain circumstances. For example, an individual adjusts his income to expenditure when he marries and then has children. He works harder inorder to increase his income. Similarly, the government adjusts its expenditure to income during recession. It cuts down its expenditure on various programmes and projects when its income falls.

2. *Elasticity.* There is greater elasticity in public finance than in private finance. The government has more resources of income whereas the resources of an individual are limited. The government "has the whole wealth of the community on which to draw, in addition to the possibility of raising external loans." It has many resources such as taxes, fees, assessments, internal and external forrowings, and printing notes. On the other, the income of an individual is limited to his current income, past savings and borrowings.

3. *Motives.* There are also differences in motives between private and public finance. An individual or a firm has the profit motive whereas the government has the welfare motive. An individual always tries to save and a firm to earn profit. But there are no such considerations on the part of the government, except the public welfare. However, there are some public enterprises which are run on profits that are utilised for public welfare.

4. *Expenditure.* There are differences in the nature of expenditure between the two. An individual's expenditure is governed by his habits, customs, fashions, etc. On the other hand, the government expenditure depends on its economic and social policies, like removing unemployment and poverty, reducing income inequalities, providing infrastructure facilities, etc.

5. *Compulsion.* There is compulsion in public finance. People have to pay taxes. If they do not pay, they are punished by fine and imprisonment. But an individual or firm cannot force any body to pay him money. He can file a suit in the court. But even then he may not receive his money back. The same is the case with loans.

The government can force the people to lend it during war or emergency. But an individual cannot compel any person to lend him money.

6. Law of Equimarginal Utility. An individual spends his limited income on various goods and services in such a manner that the MUs of these expenditures are equal. The government also tries to maximise social welfare based on the law of equimarginal utility. But often the government cannot follow this principle because a large volume of government expenditure is of a fixed nature which cannot be changed to equalise marginal utilities. Further, the government expenditure may be influenced by non-economic considerations such as political pulls and pressures that do not maximise social welfare.

7. Present Vs Future. An individual is more concerned with his present needs and tries to satisfy them. Life being uncertain and short, he has his immediate gain or profit in view. On the other hand, government is a permanent organisation. Only the ruling party changes. It is concerned not only with the welfare of present generation but also with future generations. If, therefore, undertakes and spends on those activities which also benefit future generations.

8. Budgeting. The duration and nature of private and public budgets also differ. An individual may have a weekly or monthly budget. On the other hand, a public budget is for one fiscal year. An individual tries to have a surplus budget in order to save same money for the future. He can have a deficit budget occasionally by borrowing from some body. But a government can have a surplus, deficit or balanced budget. Further, the government budget is passed by the parliament. But the budget of an individual or firm is a private affair without any controlling authority.

9. Secrecy Vs Openness. There is secrecy in private finance, No individual wants to reveal his income and saving, so does a firm about its accounts. On the contrary, the government budget is an open public document which is commented, debated and publicised at various fora.

10. Bankrupt. An individual or firm can be bankrupt. But a government cannot go bankrupt because it can borrow from international agencies and also print notes. It can only face a financial crisis.

11. Print Notes. The government has the power and authority to print notes to meet its financial requirements during war, emergency, etc. and for economic development. But an individual cannot raise his income by creating money.

Thus there are many differences between public finance and private finance and very few similarities.

5. IMPORTANCE OF PUBLIC FINANCE

Public finance plays an important role in the economy of a country whether it is developed or developing in the following ways.

1. In a Developed Country

The importance of public finance in an advanced country is to *stabilise* its *growth rate*. For this, the government changes its expenditure and taxation policies to produce good effects and avoid bad effects on national income, production, employment and prices. When the prices are falling in a recession, private investment falls. To compensate for the lack in investment and to raise effective demand, output, employment and income, the government increases its expenditure on public works and social security programmes through budget deficits, debt repayment, and reduction in taxes. On the other hand, when there are inflationary tendencies and boom starts, the government reduces its expenditure on public works. It reduces effective demand through a budget surplus, public borrowings, and raising taxes. Thus the government controls deflationary (recessionary) and inflationary (boom) pressures by an appropriate combination of expenditure, borrowing and taxation policies.

2. In a Developing Country

Public finance plays a dynamic role in a developing country. It is indispensable for its economic development. According to Prof. Nurkse, "Public finance assumes a new significance in the face of the problem of capital formation in underdeveloped countries." The per capita incomes and savings are extremely low in such countries. The few rich waste large portions of their savings in property, jewellery, gold, speculation, etc. and in conspicuous consumption. Fiscal policy diverts them into productive channels through taxation, borrowing and expenditure. Fiscal policy promotes economic development by increasing the rate of investment, encouraging investment in social and economic infrastructure, increasing employment opportunities, reducing balance of payments disequilibrium, counteracting inflation, reducing inequalities of income and wealth, and increasing national income.

By a judicions policy of *taxation*, the government reduces private consumption and transfers resources to the government for investment, increases the incentive to save and invest, reduces economic inequalities and mobilises economic surplus.

Public borrowing is an anti-inflationary measure by mobilising surplus money in the hands of the people in a developing country. It is a useful tool of economic development by diverting resources from such unproductive uses as property, jewellery, gold, etc. to productive uses. Public borrowing is resorted to for specific development projects like power generation, irrigation works, roads, etc.

The role of *public expenditure* in economic development lies in increasing the growth rate of the economy, providing more employment opportunities, raising incomes and standard of living, reducing inequalities of income and wealth, encouraging private initiative and enterprise and bringing about regional balance in the economy. Al these are achieved by spending on public works, agriculture, industry, transport and communications, power, financial and banking institutions, social services, etc. The government is able to increase public expenditure through a budget deficit.

EXERCISES

1. What do you understand by public finance ? Explain its scope.
2. Explain the differences between public finance and private finance.
3. Give the importance of public finance.
4. What is the role of public finance in the economic development of a country?

CHAPTER 85

The Principle of Maximum Social Advantage

1. MEANING

The theory of maximum social advantage is the fundamental principle of public finance. According to Prof. **Dalton**, this principle lies "at the root of public finance." Prof. **Pigou** calls it the principle of maximum aggregate welfare. This principle states that public finance leads to economic welfare when public expenditure and taxation are carried to that point where the benefit derived from the MU (marginal utility) of expenditure is equal to the marginal disutility of sacrifice imposed by taxation. In other words, maximum social advantage or aggregate welfare is the result of two contradictory and opposite forces. One which tries to increase it through public expenditure and the other which tries to decrease it through taxation. Thus social advantage is the maximum when the benefits flowing from public expenditure are maximised and the sacrifices imposed by taxation are minimised so that both are equalised.

2. MAXIMISATION OF SOCIAL ADVANTAGE

According to Dalton, public expenditure in every direction should be carried just so far that the advantage to the community of a further small increase in any direction is just counter-balanced by the disadvantage of a corresponding small increase in taxation. This process of transferring revenue from taxation to public expenditure by the state should continue up to the point where the marginal benefit from expenditure to the people is equal to the marginal sacrifice from taxation for the people. In other words, public expenditure and taxation should be so matched that the MU of expenditure incurred is equal to the marginal disability from taxation. Any expenditure incurred beyond this point could lead to a smaller gain in utility than the sacrifice undergone by taxation. On the contrary, in an expenditure less than this point, the gain in utility would be greater than the sacrifice from taxation. But the social advantage will not be maximised till the expenditure is increased to the point where the MU from a given public expenditure equals the marginal sacrifice from taxation.

This principle of maximum social advantage is explained graphically in Fig. 1 in terms of Prof. Musgrave's diagram. Amounts of public expenditure and taxation are measured along the horizontal axis, the marginal social benefit is measured on the vertical axis from *O* upwards and the marginal social sacrifice is measured below O on the vertical axis. The curve EE_1 measures marginal social benefit to the society from public expenditure. The curve TT_1 shows the marginal sacrifice of the society for paying taxes to the government. The difference between EE_1 and TT_1 is the *net social advantage* to society because EE_1 is the gain to society from public expenditure and TT_1 is the cost to society in the form of taxes paid. The net social advantage is shown by the NN_1 curve. The marginal social benefit and the marginal sacrifice are equal at point M where MB up to point M, the social gain from public expenditure is greater than the social sacrifice or loses from taxes MS. But beyond M, the sacrifice from taxes is greater than the gain from public expenditure. Hence point M is of maximum social advantage where the gain from public expenditure is equal to the loss from taxes to the society. It is depicted by the shaded area OMN in the figure.

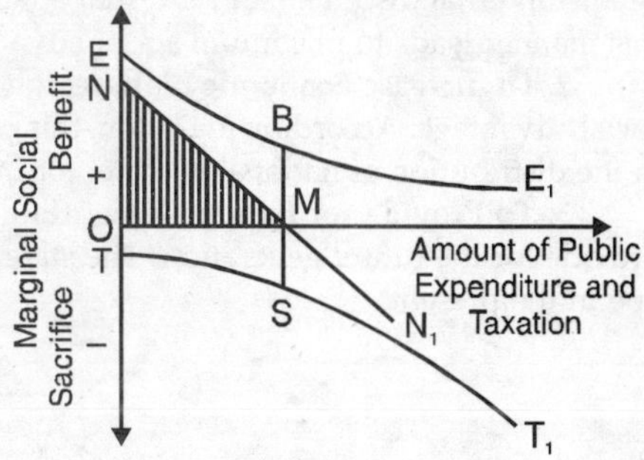

Fig. 1

3. LIMITATIONS OF MAXIMUM SOCIAL ADVANTAGE PRINCIPLE

The principle of maximum social advantage possesses the following limitations:

1. Different Areas. It is not be possible to compare the marginal benefits accruing to people in one area from a given public expenditure with the marginal sacrifice undergone by persons who are taxed in some other area.

2. Different Projects. It is not possible to compare the marginal benefits by spending the same amount by the state on two different projects, say on constructing a bridge and a college building.

3. Differences in Standard of Living. It is also not possible to calculate the marginal sacrifice of the same amount of tax paid by two persons, having different living standards, say a shopkeeper and a government employee.

4. Vague and Abstract. The terms "benefit" and "sacrifice" are vague and abstract. It is not possible to quantify them and find out their exact implications.

5. Simultaneous Calculations not Possible. This principle requires simultaneous calculations and equating marginal social benefits from public expenditure and of sacrifices from taxation which is not easy. As put by Prof. Buchanan, "To match them is a function for the 'fiscal brain' or computer."

6. Different Periods. There is the problem of calculating social benefits from public expenditure on short period and long period projects. It requires equalising the marginal benefits of expenditures over projects relating to different time periods. This is not an easy task.

7. Lack of Divisibility. In order to equate the marginal benefit from public expenditure with the marginal sacrifice from taxation, the resources are required to be divided into smaller units. But it is not possible because of the lack of divisibility of public expenditure and taxes in small units.

8. Ignores Non-Tax Revenues. This principle takes into consideration the sacrifice on the part of direct tax payers and ignores non-tax revenues. Non-tax revenues like fines, fees, market borrowings, profits of public undertakings, etc. are equally important as sources of revenue and in their effects on social benefit.

Despite these limitations, the principle of maximum social advantage is "the best system of public finance", according to Dalton.

4. OBJECTIVE TESTS OF SOCIAL ADVANTAGE

Due to the above noted limitations of the principle of social advantage, it is not possible to put it into practice. But Dalton has given the following three objective tests which can lead to maximum social advantage.

1. To Preserve the Community. According to Dalton, the first test is the need to preserve the community against internal disorders and external attacks. The financial operations of the state to preserve the society in this manner leads to maximum social advantage.

2. To Increase Economic Welfare. Increasing the economic welfare of the community leads to maximum social advantage. According to Dalton, this can be achieved by improvements in production and improvements in the distribution of national product (or income) through state's financial operations.

3. To Provide for Future Generation. According to Dalton, the financial operations of the state should provide for the future generation. The state should prefer a larger social advantage in the future to a smaller one in the present.

EXERCISES

1. Explain the principle of Maximum Social Advantage, Give its limitations.
2. Explain the meaning of Maximum Social Advantage. How can it be achieved? What are the difficulties in its application?
3. Explain critically the principle of Maximum Social Advantage. What objective tests are required to achieve this principle in practice?

CHAPTER 86

Taxes

1. INTRODUCTION

Dr. Dalton makes a distinction between public receipts and public revenue. Public income, in the broad sense, is referred to as public receipts. Income received by the government from all sources is known as public receipts. Public income, in the narrow sense, is called public revenue which excludes "receipts from public borrowings and from the sale of public assets, such as war stores."

The main surces of public revenue are taxes and prices, while public recepts also include receipts from public enterprises, receipts from special assessments, income from the issue of paper money (i.e., deficit financing), and voluntary gifts. We discuss the sources of public income as under.

TAXES

Taxes are the most important source of government income. Dr **Dalton** defined a tax as "a compulsory contribution imposed by a public authority, irrespective of the exact amount of service rendered to the taxpayer in return."[1] According to Prof. **Seligman**, a tax is "a compulsory contribution from a person to the government to defray the expenses incurred in the common interest of all, without reference to special benefits conferred."[2]

These definitions point towards three characteristics of a tax.

First, it is a compulsory contribution imposed by the government on the people residing in the country. Since it is a compulsory payment, a person who refuses to pay a tax is liable to punishment. But a tax is to be paid only by those who come under its jurisdiction. Similarly, persons who buy a commodity which carries a tax on it, pay the tax while others do not.

Second, a tax is a payment made by the taxpayers which is used by the government for the benefit of all the citizens. The state uses the revenue collected from taxes for providing hospitals, schools, public utility services, etc. which benefit all people.

Third, a tax is not levied in return for any specific service rendered by the government to the taxpayer. An individual cannot ask for any special benefit from the state in return for the tax paid by him. In the words of Prof. **Taussig**, "The essence of a tax... is the absence of a direct *quid pro quo* between the taxpayer and the public

1. H. Dalton, *Principles of Public Finance, 4th Ed.*, 1954, p. 23.
2. E.A.R. Seligman, *Essays in Taxation*, p. 432.

authority." It implies that the taxpayer cannot claim something equivalent to the tax paid *(quid pro quo)* from the government.

Revenue from Public Enterprises

Revenues received by the government from public enterprises are also an important source of public income. The Union and State Governments, and local bodies operate commercial enterprises and public utilities. The surpluses obtained by selling their goods and services are called 'prices' by Dalton, and 'commercial revenues' by Taylor. Such enterprises may be run on monopolistic or/and competitive basis. If the state has a monopoly of water, electricity, or city transport, the price charged in excess of normal cost of production is like a tax. In case of competitive selling, whatever public undertakings earn above normal profits are surpluses which do not have any element of compulsion on the part of buyers of those goods and services.

Special Assessments

According to **Seligman,** "A special assessment is a compulsory contribution, levied in proportion to the special benefits, derived to defray the cost of a specific improvement to property undertaken in the public interest." When a public authority provides certain facilities like drainage, street lighting, parks, roads, etc. in a particular area, the people benefit. At the same time, the rents or values of properties in the area also go up. In lieu of these benefits, the government may levy a special assessment on the property-owners. Similarly, farmers benefiting from a canal adjoining their farms are charged a betterment levy to partially cover the cost of construction of the canal. "A special assessment resembles a tax in that it is a compulsory payment but differs form it in that the payer has received a definite and direct *quid pro quo*. In the latter respect it resembles a price, but differs from it in that the payment is not voluntary."

Fees

Seligman defines a fee as "a payment to defray the cost of each recurring service undertaken by the government, primarily in the public interest, but conferring a measurable special advantage on the fee payer." A person who wants to benefit from a particular service rendered by the public authority is charged a fee. The service may be legal for which a person has to pay a court-fee, registration fee of property or marriage, payment of fee for a competitive examination, etc. Like prices, there is an element of *quid pro quo* in the payment of fees. But if the cost of performing a service is less than the fee charged, the excess is in the nature of a tax.

A *licence fee* is different from a fee. A fee is paid for some service actually rendered while a licence fee is charged by a public authority to grant permission to a person to perform service by himself. The aim is to exercise state control or regulation over the various activities. Persons wishing to open chemist shops and wine shops, to drive a scooter or any other vehicle, and to keep a gun or a revolver have to obtain a licence from an appropriate authority.

Fines

Fines and penalties are not imposed to collect revenue but to punish the people for the infringement of state laws. They, therefore, resemble taxes only in that they are compulsory payments without any *quid pro quo*.

Receipts from the Use of the Printing Press

Dalton refers to the use of the printing press for the purpose of meeting public expenditure by the issue of new paper money. This is one of the important sources of public income which is known as deficit financing. To bridge the gap between public expenditure and public revenue, the state may borrow from within the country or from abroad. But it may not succeed in bridging the gap completely, and in addition, it may burden the people with loans and their repayment. But when the state uses the printing press, the cost of printing notes is much less than the value of notes. Moreover, when the government spends the additional money created by printing more notes, it raises the demand for consumer goods which leads to the rise in prices because of the failure of supplies to meet the increased demand. In this way, the government purchases a part of the resources from the market with created money which is just like taxing them away.

GIFTS AND GRANTS

Gifts and voluntary contributions are made by individuals and societies to the government for relief work in the event of an earthquake, flood, famine, or war. So they are not in the nature of a tax.

Grants are given by the federal government to the state or provincial governments to meet the cost of specific projects or schemes in public interest, such as the provision for drinking water, drainage, irrigation, roads, etc. Besides, there are unconditional grants which can be utilised by the recipient authority in any manner it likes for purposes of development.

Grants are also made by one country to another at governmental level. They are for reconstruction, for development, or for war. European countries received American aid for reconstructing their war-shattered economies after the Second World War. Underdeveloped countries are receiving grants for economic development from the developed nations of the world. But all grants are voluntary gifts and are thus very uncertain source of revenue for the government.

2. CHARACTERISTICS OF A GOOD TAX SYSTEM

Public expenditure has been continuously increasing with the expansion of the functions of modern governments. Since the tax revenue is the easiest and the most convenient and productive source of income, governments are inclined to use more of this rather than the non-tax revenue. It is, therefore, instructive to study the characteristics of a good tax system.

(1) Equitable. The tax system should meet the canon of equity. Every person should be taxed according to his ability, that is, the rich should pay more and the poor less so that taxes should be progressive in nature.

(2) Certain. A good tax system should be based on the cannon of certainty. "The time of payment, the manner of payment, the quantity to be paid, ought all to be clear and plain to the contributor and to every other person." The tax which every individual is required to pay should be certain and not arbitrary so that he is not left to the whims of the tax officials

(3) Convenient. The tax system should satisfy the canon of convenience, *i.e.,*the time and mode of payment of the tax should be so fixed that it is not inconvenient for the taxpayer.

(4) Economical. A good tax system should be economical to the government in the sense that the cost of collection of taxes should be small in proportion to the revenue from them.

(5) Productive. The tax system should be such as to bring in sufficient revenue in the exchequer. In other words, it should be productive.

(6) Elastic. A good tax system should be sufficiently elastic so that the tax revenue may be increased or decreased according to the requirements of the state.

(7) Simple. The tax system should be simple to understand and administer.

(8) Multiple Taxes. A good tax system should have multiple taxes rather than a single tax. According to Dalton, "It is best to rely on a few substantial taxes for the bulk of the tax revenue."

(9) Income-Elastic. It should be income-elastic. As national income increases, the share of taxation in national income should rise more than proportionately.

(10) Least Bad Economic Effects. According to Dalton. "The best system of taxation from the economic point of view is that which has the best, or the least bad, economic effects." It should not adversely affect production through effects on ability and desire to work, save and invest.

(11) Reduce Inequalities. According to Wagner, a good tax system should reduce the inequality of incomes.

(12) Balanced. The tax system should be a balanced one in which progressive, proportional, direct and indirect taxes should be properly distributed.

Conclusion. The major problem is to find a sufficient number of taxes that may satisfy these criteria. But treasury officials can no more find one tax that pre-eminently meets all requirements than an automobile engineer can design a car that is simultaneously fastest, safest and cheapest.

3. PROGRESSIVE, PROPORTIONAL AND REGRESSIVE TAXES

Taxes are levied by the government on the basis of three major classes of tax rates. They are progressive, proportional and regressive. In order to understand them, it is essential to know how these three types of tax rates differ from each other on the basis of the *tax base.* The base is the item to be taxed. It is the income being taxed in the case of income tax, the value of property in the case of a property tax, and the value of goods sold in the case of a sales tax.

TABLE 1: PROPORTIONAL TAX

TAX BASE	*TAX Rate (%)*	*Amount of Tax (Rs)*
100000	30	30000
200000	30	60000
300000	30	90000
400000	30	120000
500000	30	150000

PROPORTIONAL TAX

A proportional tax is one whose percentage rate remains the same as the tax base increases. As a result, the amount of tax paid is proportional to the tax base. If the tax rate is constant at 30%, every person shall have to pay income tax at this rate as his/her income increases. Table 1 explains this in the case of an income tax. The Table shows that a person with an income of Rs 1 lakh pays Rs 30000 as the tax at the rate of 30%. The person with double the income of Rs 2 lakhs pays double the amount of tax i.e. Rs 60000. Thus as the income increases, the amount of tax also increases in the same proportion, and so on. The tax rate being 30%, the tax takes away the same percentage of income from low as well as high income persons.

Fig 1 illustrates the proportional taxation. Persons with Rs1 lakh income are charged the same tax rate of 30% as persons with Rs 2 lakhs, Rs 3 lakhs and so on. The resultant tax curve T is horizontal.

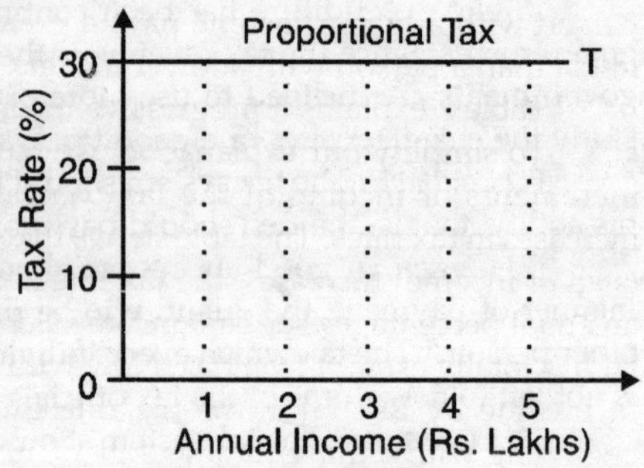

FIG. 1

Its Merits

The proportional tax system has the following merits.

1. *Simple.* It is very simple and every person can understand it without any difficulty. It can be easily administered because there are no complicated tax slabs. As *J.B.Say* said, "There is no necessity to define proportional tax. It is the simple rule of three".

2. *Easy.* It is easy for every person to calculate the amount of tax he is required to pay.

3. *No Change in Income Distribution.* It does not affect the pattern of income distribution in the country because every person pays the same rate of tax.

4. *Neutralising Effects.* Proportional taxation has neutralising effects on savings and incentives.

5. *Non-disturbing.* This tax system disturbs the economy as little as possible because every person contributes as nearly as possible in proportion to his ability to pay, according to *Adam smith.*

Its Demerits

Despite these advantages, the proportional tax system possesses the following demerits.

1. *Inequitable.* This tax system is inequitable because it adversely affects the low income groups and favours the high income groups. This is because with the increase in the income of a person, the marginal utility *(MU)* of income diminishes for him. As such, the *MU* of money for low income groups is high and low for high income groups. So when both income groups are taxed at the same rate, persons belonging to the low income groups make a greater sacrifice than those in the high income groups. Thus the proportional tax system is

inequitable.

2. *Increases Inequalities.* It increases inequalities of income and wealth instead of reducing them because the gap between the high income and low income groups widens. This is the result of the same tax rate for the two income groups.

3. *Less Productive.* This tax system is not sufficiently productive in the sense that it does not bring enough revenue into the public exchequer due to a constant tax rate.

4. *Against the Principle of Taxable Capacity.* The proportional tax system goes against the principle of taxable capacity because the lower income groups are required to sacrifice more than the higher income groups.

5. *Bad Effects on the Economy.* By taxing the high and low income groups at the same rate, this tax system proportionately takes away a larger percentage of the income of low income groups. As a result, the consumption standard of such groups falls, thereby leading to their weak health and consequently to low productivity. This adversely affects the country's productive resources.

Conclusion. It is due to the above demerits of proportional taxation that no country follows it in the case of *direct taxes* like income and corporation taxes. However, it is practised in the case of *indirect taxes* like sales tax, excise duties, etc.

PROGRESSIVE TAX

A progressive tax is one whose percentage rate increases as the tax base increases. In other words, as the income of a person increases, the tax rate also increases gradually, and vice versa. A progressive tax is graduated so that a person with a higher income pays a greater percentage in tax than a person with a lower income.

Table 2 explains a progressive income tax system. To simplify our explanation, we have taken equal increments of income of the tax base and also equal increases in tax rates. The table shows that as the tax base (slab of income) increases, the tax rate also increases by an equal percentage. The first income slab of Rs 0 to Rs1 lakh is totally exempt from tax. Now with every increase in income by Rs1 lakh, the tax rate increases by 5% beginning with a minimum tax rate of 10%. The tax takes a larger percentage of income from people in higher income slabs than those in lower income slabs. A person in Rs 1 lakh to Rs 2 lakhs income slab pays Rs 10000 as tax and a person in Rs 2 lakhs to Rs 3 lakhs slab pays Rs 25000 (= Rs 10000 + Rs 15000) as tax, and so on.

Table 2 is illustrated in Fig 2 which shows that the tax line *T* rises upward from left to right, as the tax rate increases with the rise in income.

TABLE 2 : PROGRESSIVE TAX

TAX BASE	*TAX Rate (%)*	*Amount of Tax (Rs)*
0-100000		Exempt
100001-200000	10	10000
200001-300000	15	10000 +15000
300001-400000	20	25000+20000
400001-500000	25	45000+25000

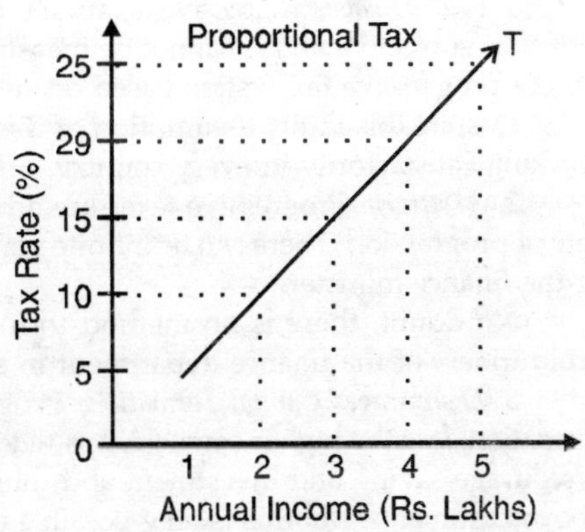

FIG. 2

MERITS OF PROGRESSIVE TAXES

During the 18th and 19th centuries, the proportional tax system was in vogue. It was only in the early 20th century that the progressive tax system was started in Great Britain for the first time and later on it spread to other countries of Europe. At present, progressive tax system is prevalent in every country because it possesses the following advantages:

1. *Ability to Pay.* Progressive taxes are based on the principle of ability to pay. According to the progressive tax system, as a person's income increases, he is required to pay more tax. This is because the *MU* of income

falls as income increases. Therefore, the rich should pay more because their ability to pay increases with the rise in their incomes. But for a person with low income, the *MU* of income increases as his income rises because he needs more money to satisfy his unsatisfied wants. By levying high tax rates on higher incomes and low tax rates on lower incomes, the progressive tax system satisfies the principle of ability to pay.

2. *Productive.* Progressive taxation is highly productive because it yields more revenue to the government. The government can increase its income by substantially raising the tax rate to meet its increasing expenditure now-a-days.

3. *Elastic.* This tax system is elastic because the government can change the tax rates whenever it needs extra revenue or wants to give relief to low income groups.

4. *Economical.* Progressive taxation is economical because the cost of collection of taxes does not increase when the tax rates are increased. It is occasionally that the cost of collection rises less than the revenue from the tax as the tax rate is increased, depending on the nature of the tax, as in the case of sales tax.

5. *Income Equality.* It brings equality of income and wealth in the country when the rich are taxed at higher rates and the low income groups at lower rates or even are exempted.

6. *Social Justice.* As a corollary to the above, when the rich are taxed heavily and the low income groups are exempted from paying taxes, progressive taxation promotes social justice in the country.

7. *Equitable.* Progressive taxes are equitable. They require proportional sacrifice on the part of taxpayers. The high income groups bear the heaviest burden and the low income groups low burden of such taxes.

8. *Economic Stability.* Progressive taxation helps economic stability in the country. By reducing the tax rates during a recession or depression, the government provides relief to the taxpayers so that they may increase their demand for goods. As a result, investment is encouraged. On the other hand, by raising the tax rates during a boom, the government reduces the purchasing power of the taxpayers. Consequently, the demand for goods and investment are discouraged. Thus this tax system helps in bringing economic stability in the economy.

9. *Better Use of Resources.* Progressive taxation helps in making better use of a country's productive resources. The high income groups mostly indulge in conspicuous consumption and thus waste their incomes. By taxing luxury goods and the incomes of the rich heavily, the government can prevent them from wasteful expenditures and make better use of the country's productive resources.

Demerits of Progressive Taxation

Despite these merits, the progressive tax system has the following disadvantages which are refuted by economists side by side.[3]

1. *Faulty Basis.* Progressive taxation is based on the principle of diminishing *MU* of income which is faulty. Utility is subjective and it cannot be measured and compared in terms of money. Therefore, it is not right to have a progressive tax system based on subjective utility.

Despite this faulty assumption of diminishing marginal utility of income, the progressive tax system is working satisfactorily in every country.

2. *Arbitrary.* Progressive taxes are arbitrary because there is no scientific or standard method to fix the rate of progression. There can be infinite scales of progression depending on the whims of the finance secretary or the finance minister.

No doubt, there is no method to fix the rate of progression. But there are legislators to check the arbitrariness of the finance department in every country.

3. *Discourages Capital Formation.* Progressive taxation adversely affects saving, investment and capital formation. It is the high income groups who are the main source of savings in a country. Heavy taxes on them discourage saving and investment and thus hamper trade and industry in the country. There is truth in the above arguments. But this is only possible if the rate of progression is very high. No wise government would try to retard capital formation by adopting a very high tax rate structure in the economy.

3. The second para of each point is meant only for a discussion on proportional and progressive taxation. Students may leave the second para in case of a question on only merits and demerits.

4. *Unjustified.* Critics point out that progressive taxation is an unjustified method. People become rich through thrift and hard work. Those who are extravagant and lazy remain poor. Taxing the high income groups at high rates is unjustified.

But this criticism is not valid because it is not only through thrift and hard work that people become rich. There are other factors like entreprenurial ability, favourable economic environment, etc. that make people wealthy. Similarly, extra- vagance and laziness do not make people poor. Poverty may be the result of economic and social factors.

5. *Tax Evasion.* Progressive taxation leads to tax evasion and avoidance. People who are taxed heavily, try to evade taxes by maintaining false accounts and submitting false statements to income authorities. They also try to avoid taxes by finding loopholes in the tax laws.

This is no valid argument because all types of taxes can be avoided and evaded. Payment of taxes depends on the social and tax consciousness of the people.

Conclusion. Despite the above mentioned weaknesses of progressive taxation, this system is in practice in every country of the world because it confirms to the canons of productivity, elasticity and economy. It is socially and economically desirable because it removes inequalities of income and wealth distribution.

TABLE 3 : REGRESSIVE TAX

Tax Base (Rs)	*Tax Rate (%)*	*Amount of Tax (Rs)*
100000	60	60000
200000	50	100000
300000	40	120000
400000	30	120000
500000	20	100000
600000	10	60000

REGRESSIVE TAX

A regressive tax is one whose percentage rate decreases as the tax base increases. In other words, as the income of a person rises, the tax rate decreases. A high-income person pays less tax than a low-income person in proportion to his income. Thus regressive taxation is just the opposite of progressive taxation.

Table 3 explains a regressive income tax.

Table shows that as the income increases from Rs 1 lakh to Rs 6 lakhs, the tax rate decreases from 60% to 10%. Consequently, a person with an income of Rs1 Lakh pays Rs60000 as tax. As income doubles from Rs1 lakh to Rs2 lakhs. he pays Rs1 lakh as tax which is less than proportionate to the increase in income, and so on.

This is illustrated in Fig. 3 when the income is Rs1 lakh the tax rate is 60% as at point A. As income increases to Rs 2 lakhs, the tax rate declines to 50% and so on. Thus the tax curve *T* of a regressive tax slopes downward from left to right.

No country in the world has a regressive income and corporate tax system. It is only the indirect taxes like the sales tax that are regressive in nature. They are like proportional taxes. For instance, a 10% sales tax is uniform for all consumers whether their income is high or low. But low-income consumers spend a larger proportion of their income on the commodity than the high-income consumers.

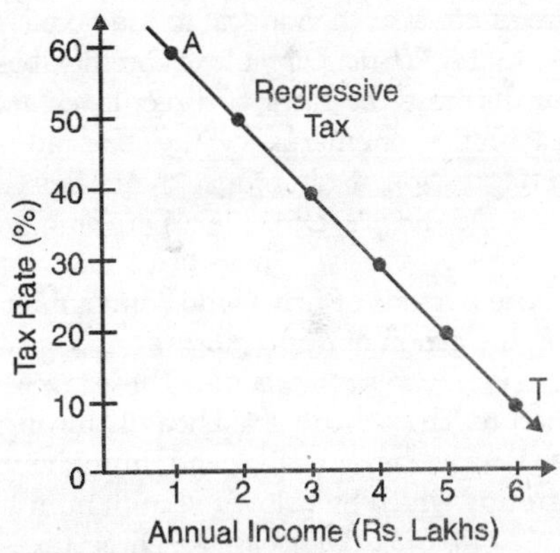

FIG. 3

4. DIRECT AND INDIRECT TAXES

MEANING

Direct and indirect taxes are usually defined on the basis of the effects and expectations or intentions. According to Dr. **Dalton**, "A direct tax is really paid by the person on whom it is legally imposed, while an indirect tax is imposed on one person, but paid partly or wholly by another, owing to a consequential change in the terms of some contract or bargain between them. Thus an indirect tax is conceived as one which can be shifted or passed on; a direct tax as one which cannot be shifted or passed on. Disregarding incidence, . . .

indirect taxes are those levied on the sale or purchase of any goods or services other than personal services and that all other taxes are direct." This distinction is based on the basis of the results of a tax.

John Stuart Mill defined a direct tax as one which is "demanded from the very person who its is intended or desired should pay it." On the other hand, an indirect tax is defined as one which is "demanded from one person in the expectation and intention that he shall indemnify himself at the expense of another." This is the administrator's or government's viewpoint which may create confusion. The government imposes a commodity tax which is an indirect tax in the *expectation* that it will be shifted. But if the producer is unable to shift the tax on to the sellers, it is a direct tax.

It is, therefore, convenient and better to discard the administrator's viewpoint on the distinction between direct and indirect taxes and follow the economist's viewpoint as given by Dr. Dalton.[4] Accordingly, income tax, corporation tax, wealth tax, gift tax, death duties, expenditure tax, etc. are direct taxes. On the other hand, excise duties, import and export duties, sales tax, entertainment tax, passenger tax, etc. are indirect taxes. We study below the merits and demerits of direct and indirect taxes.

Merits of Direct Taxes

Direct taxes possess the following merits :

(1) Equitable. Direct taxes are based on the canon of equity. Their burden is equitably distributed as they are progressive in nature. As the income of a person increases, the rate of income tax also increases. so all direct taxes fall heavily on the people whose income and wealth increase. The poor are not affected by such taxes.

(2) Certain. Direct taxes satisfy the canon of certainty. The taxpayer is certain as to the time and manner of payment, and the amount to be paid in the case of these taxes. Similarly, the government is also certain as to the amount of money it shall receive from these taxes.

(3) Economical. These taxes also satisfy the canon of economy. The cost of collection of direct taxes is low. In the case of income tax, it is deducted at the source from the salaried persons. The assessments of wealth, incomes, inheritances, gifts, etc. can be made by the same officers. No separate staff is needed for each. Such taxes are also economical to the taxpayers who make payments direct into the treasury.

(4) Elastic. Direct taxes are flexible and thus satisfy the canon of elasticity. The government can increase or decrease the rates of direct taxes according to the requirements of the economy. In case of war, natural calamities, or emergency, the state can raise the rates of these taxes in order to have larger tax revenue. During a depression, it can reduce their rates considerably.

(5) Simple. Direct taxes are simple and easy to understand.

(6) Desirable. These taxes do not involve general opposition from the public because they are paid by those persons or firms who come under the jurisdiction of income tax or corporation tax. Thus they are based on the canon of desirability.

(7) Reduce Inequalities. These taxes help reduce income and wealth inequalities because of their progressive nature. The rich are taxed heavily through income tax, wealth tax, expenditure tax, excess profit tax, gift tax, etc. so long as they are alive; and through inheritance taxes or death duties when they die. The poor and the income groups which lie below the minimum tax limit are exempted from these taxes.

(8) Civic Consciousness. Direct taxes inculcate civic consciousness among the taxpayers. They are conscious that they are paying taxes to the government and take interest in the activities of the state as to whether public expenditure is incurred on public welfare or not. Such civic consciousness puts a check on the wastage of public expenditure in a democratic country.

Demerits of Direct Taxes

Direct taxes have the following demerits:

(1) Unpopular. Direct taxes pinch the taxpayers because they have to pay them directly out of their incomes or salaries. They are, therefore, unpopular.

4. P.E. Tayor in his *The Economics of Public Finance,* 3rd Ed., 1968, p. 307, F.N. 1, also writes that direct and indirect taxes "are finally distinguishable in meaning only in terms of shiftability. Direct taxes are not shifted, while indirect taxes are."

(2) Inconvenient. These taxes are inconvenient in nature because traders, businessmen, producers, etc. have to comply with a number of formalities relating to their sources of income and expenditure incurred in earning that income. Often the details are incomplete and the various sections of the Acts so complicated that the taxpayers have to take the help of income tax experts by making them payments. Moreover, these taxes are payable in advance and in lump sum, except in the case of salaried persons. Hence they are inconvenient.

(3) Arbitrary. Direct taxes possess an element of arbitrariness in them. They leave much to the discretion of the taxation authorities in fixing the rates of taxation and in interpreting them.

(4) Evasion. Since direct taxes pinch every taxpayer, he tries to evade them by filling wrong returns and even takes the help of income tax experts. Thus such taxes cultivate dishonesty and there is loss of revenue tc the state.

(5) Not Imposed on All. Direct taxes are not imposed on all income groups. Low income groups do not come under the purview of these taxes. Such groups, therefore, do not contribute anything to the state exchequer through direct taxation.

(6) Discourage Saving and Investment. Direct taxes adversely affect saving and investment. When people know that with the increase in their incomes and wealth, they will have to pay a large portion in the form of taxes, they are reluctant to save and invest more. This adversely affects the will to work, save and invest.

(7) Discourage Production. Corporation taxes discourage those industries and firms which produce essential goods.

MERITS OF INDIRECT TAXES

Indirect taxes possess the following merits:

(1) Convenient. Indirect taxes are less inconvenient and less burdensome. They are paid only when a commodity or a service is bought. So they are paid in small amounts rather than in lump sum. Since these taxes are included in the prices of commodities, buyers do not feel the burden of these taxes. Such taxes are like sugar-coated pills.

(2) Wide Coverage. These taxes reach the pockets of all income groups—low, middle and high. They are levied on necessaries, comforts, and luxuries. Thus they have a wide coverage, and every consumer pays to the state exchequer according to his *ability* to pay. Thus they are equitable.

(3) Elastic. Indirect taxes are also elastic in nature. The government can reduce or increase the rates of, say, excise duties, or custom duties according to its requirements. But care should be taken in not imposing high rates on necessaries which are mostly consumed by the poor.

(4) Economical. These taxes are economical in the sense that they involve little cost of collection because the producers and sellers themselves deposit them with the government.

(5) Diversity. Indirect taxes satisfy the canon of diversity. They can be levied on a variety of commodities and services. So the government can be sure of a continuous and sufficient revenue, even if it is required to reduce the rates of taxes on certain commodities due to the fall in their demand.

(6) Less Evasion. There is less possibility of evasion in the case of indirect taxes because they are included in the prices of commodities. As these taxes are shiftable on the ultimate consumers, the producers, the wholesalers, and the retailers do not mind paying them. The consumers can evade them only if they decide not to buy the taxed commodities. However, these taxes are generally evaded by producers when they sell their products to the wholesalers and the retailers without entering the goods in their stocks and without issuing a bill/cash receipt for the same.

(7) Check the Consumption of Harmful Goods. Indirect taxes have the great merit of checking the consumption of harmful goods like wine, cigarettes and other intoxicants. The state levies heavy duties on such articles of consumption which are injurious to health and efficiency of the people. As a result, their prices rise and their consumption is reduced. The state also earns substantial revenue.

(8) Powerful Tool of Economic Policies. Indirect taxes can be used as a powerful tool for implementing economic policies by the government. If the government wants to protect domestic industries from foreign competition, it can levy heavy import duties. This will help develop domestic industries. If the government wants to encourage one industry on priority basis, it may not levy any taxes on its products but continue the taxes imposed on other industries. The government may do so in order to encourage a particular technology

or employment in a particular industry.

DEMERITS OF INDIRECT TAXES

The following are the demerits of indirect taxes:

(1) Uncertain Revenue. The revenue from indirect taxes is uncertain because it is not possible to accurately estimate the effect of such taxes on the demand for products. If a heavy excise duty is levied on some luxury article, its price will rise. Since the demand for a luxury good is elastic, its sales may be adversely affected by a fall in demand and the state revenue may actually decline.

(2) Regressive. Indirect taxes on necessaries, which are consumed by the poor, are regressive in nature. The rich and the poor are required to pay the same amount of tax on such commodities as matches, kerosene, toilet soap, washing soap, tooth paste, blades, shoes, etc. But the burden is heavier on the poor than on the rich. Thus they do not satisfy the canon of *equity*.

(3) Uneconomical. These taxes are uneconomical in that the cost of collection to the state is heavy. The state has to appoint inspectors to check the accounts and stocks of producers, wholesalers, and retailers in order to find out whether they are paying taxes or not. Thus they are more expensive than direct taxes.

(4) Bad Effect on Production and Employment. Sometimes, these taxes adversely affect production of commodities, and even employment. When the price of a commodity increases with the levy of a tax, its demand falls (if it happens to be a commodity with elastic demand). As a result, its production falls, and so does employment.

(5) Feed Inflation. Another demerit of indirect taxes is that they feed inflation. Imposition of these taxes tends to raise the prices of commodities, thereby leading to higher costs, to higher wages, and again to higher prices. Thus price-wage-cost spiral sets in the economy.

(6) Lack of Civic Consciousness. A person who buys a commodity does not know that he is paying a tax to the government in the price of the commodity. Therefore, such taxes do not inculcate civic consciousness among the majority of taxpayers who are ignorant of the fact that they are contributing something to the state exchequer.

CONCLUSION

We have discussed above the merits and demerits of direct and indirect taxes but it is difficult to say whether direct taxes are superior to indirect taxes, or vice versa. As a source of revenue, both direct and indirect taxes are regarded as essential by modern governments. **Gladstone** regarded it a sign of financial virtue to 'keep a balance' between direct and indirect taxation, and likened these two sources of revenue to 'two attractive sisters', as between whom the state should be 'perfectly impartial.'

5. CANONS OF TAXATION

Adam Smith was the first economist who laid down four important canons of taxation to which were added few more by subsequent economists. We discuss these below.

1. THE CANON OF EQUALITY

The canon of equality, equity or justice is the most important canon of taxation. **Smith** explained it thus: "The subjects of every state ought to contribute towards the support of the government, as nearly as possible, in proportion to their respective abilities, that is, in proportion to the revenue which they respectively enjoy under the protection of the State." It means that every person should pay the tax according to his ability and not the same amount. It also means that everybody should not pay at the same rate. Rather, every taxpayer should pay the tax in proportion to his income. The rich should pay more and at a higher rate than the other person whose income is less. Thus this canon implies equality of sacrifice or ability to pay the tax in proportion to the income of the taxpayer.

2. The Canon of Certainty

According to **Smith**, there should be certainty in taxation because uncertainty breeds corruption. By the canon of certainty he means that "the tax which each individual is bound to pay ought to be certain, and not arbitrary. The time of payment, the manner of payment, the quantity to be paid ought all to be clear and plain to the contributor and to every other person." Thus this canon requires that there should be no element of arbitrariness in a tax. It should be clear to every taxpayer as to what, when, and where the tax is to be paid. Nothing should be left to the discretion of the income tax department. Certainty also means that the state should also be certain about the amount of tax revenue and the time when it is expected to flow in the exchequer.

3. The Canon of Convenience

This canon lays down that both the time and manner of payment should be convenient to the taxpayer. In the words of **Smith**, "Every tax ought to be levied at the time or in the manner in which it is most likely to be convenient for the contributor to pay." In India, the payment of land revenue is in keeping with this canon because it is to be paid after harvesting. Similarly, the payment of sales tax and excise duty by the consumer is also convenient because he pays these taxes when he buys commodities and at a time when he has the means to buy. The manner of payment is very convenient to him because these taxes are included in the prices of commodities.

4. The Canon of Economy

Every tax should satisfy the canon of economy in two ways. First, it should be economical for the state to collect it. If the cost of collection in the form of salaries of tax officials is more than what the tax brings as revenue, such a tax is uneconomical, and hence it should not be levied. Second, it should be economical to the taxpayer. It means that he should have sufficient money left with him after paying the tax. A very heavy tax on incomes will discourage saving and investment, and thus adversely affect the productive capacity of the community. **Smith** states this canon in these words: "Every tax ought to be so contrived as both to take out and to keep out of the pockets of the people as little as possible, over and above what it brings into the public treasury of the state."

5. The Canon of Productivity

According to this canon, a tax should be productive in the sense that it should bring large revenue which should be adequate for the government. But it does not mean that in its efforts to raise more revenue, the government should tax the people heavily. Such an effort would adversely affect the productive capacity of the economy. Further, this canon implies that one tax which brings large revenue is better than a number of taxes which bring small revenue. Many taxes may not be productive. They may also be uneconomical.

6. The Canon of Elasticity

This canon is closely related to that of productivity. The canon of elasticity requires that the government should be able to raise the rates of taxes when it is in need of more revenue. In other words, taxes should be elastic. The best example is excise duties. They can be levied on any number of commodities and their rates can be increased every year in order to raise more revenue. But care has to be taken that the rates of excise duties should not be so raised that they may encourage inflationary pressures in the economy.

7. The Canon of Flexibility

Flexibility in taxation is different from elasticity. Flexibility means that there should be no rigidity in taxation. The tax system can be changed to meet the revenue requirements of the state. On the other hand, elasticity in taxation means that the revenues can be increased under the prevailing tax system. But there cannot be any elasticity in taxation without flexibility because some change is required in the rates and structure of taxes if the state wants to increase revenue.

8. The Canon of Simplicity

The tax system should be simple, plain and intelligible to the common taxpayer. The tax system should not be complicated. It should be simple to understand as to how is it to be calculated and how much is it to be paid. The form/forms to be filled up for calculation and payment of a tax should be simple and intelligible to the taxpayer. This canon is essential in order to avoid corruption and oppression on the part of the tax department.

9. The Canon of Diversity

There should be diversity or variety in taxation. A single or a few taxes would neither meet the revenue requirements of the state nor satisfy the canon of equity. There should, therefore, be a variety of taxes so that all citizens should contribute towards the state revenues according to their ability to pay. There should be a variety of direct and indirect taxes. But a large multiplicity of taxes will be difficult to administer and hence uneconomical.

EXERCISES

1. Give the various sources of public revenue.
2. Define a 'tax'. Give the characteristics of a good tax system.
3. Distinguish between a tax, a special assessment and a fee.
4. Distinguish between progressive and proportional taxes. Which one would you prefer and why?
5. Explain a progressive tax. Give its merits and demerits.
6. Write notes on : progressive, proportional and regressive taxes.
7. Distinguish between direct and indirect taxes. How do they differ in their equity effects.
8. Give the merits and demerits of direct taxes and indirect taxes.
9. Discuss the various canons of taxation.

CHAPTER 87

Incidence and Effects of Taxes

1. INCIDENCE OF COMMODITY TAXATION

The problem of incidence of taxation is related to the important question : who ultimately pays a tax? Or, who bears the *money burden* of a tax? *The incidence of a tax involves the process of transfer from the person on whom the tax is imposed initially to the ultimate taxpayer who bears the money burden of the tax. The process of transfer of a tax is known as the shifting of the tax, while the settlement of the burden on the ultimate taxpayer is called the incidence of the tax.*

Suppose the government imposes an excise duty on tea. The tea company which grows, blends and packs the tea has to pay the tax to the government in the first instance. This is called the *impact* of the tax. The tea manufacturer includes the tax in the price of tea and transfers it to the wholesaler, who, in turn, transfers it to the retailer, and the retailer, in turn, transfers it to the ultimate consumer. This process of transferring the tax is known as *tax-shifting*. The *incidence* of the tax is on the consumer who ultimately bears the money burden of the tax.

FORWARD AND BACKWARD SHIFTING

A tax may be shifted either *forward* or *backward*. A tax is shifted *forward* when the producer of a commodity transfers the money burden of the tax on the wholesaler, the wholesaler on the retailer, and the retailer on the consumer. On the other hand, *backward shifting* occurs when the producer shifts the money burden of the tax on the suppliers of factors of production by forcing them to accept lower prices for their services, such as reducing the wages of the labourers.

But the tax may be shifted either wholly or partly depending upon the extent of the rise in the price of the taxed commodity. If the price of the commodity rises equal to the amount of the tax, the entire money burden (incidence) of the tax is shifted from the producer to the consumer. If the price of the commodity does not rise by the *full* amount of the tax, the consumer pays a part of the tax which is equal to the difference between the new price and the pre-tax price of the commodity. In this situation, the incidence of the tax falls partly on the producer and partly on the consumer. If the price does not rise at all, either the incidence of the tax remains with the producer or it has been shifted backward. But it is rare that a tax may be entirely shifted either backward or forward.

Incidence vs. Effects

Distinction may be made *between the incidence and effects of a tax*. When a tax is imposed on a commodity, it produces certain effects on the producer, the consumer, and the economy. Suppose the government levies excise duty on tea, it will raise the price of tea, which will reduce the disposable income of the consumers of tea who will, in turn, reduce its consumption. If the tea companies are not able to shift the full amount of the excise duty to the consumers (for fear of reduction in sales), their cost of production rises and the profit-margins are reduced. This will adversely affect investment and production. If they are not able to shift the incidence of the tax backward on the suppliers of factors of production, investment will again be adversely affected. These are the effects of a tax which may, in the long run, adversely affect production, employment, income, saving and investment in the economy.[1]

Dalton has distinguished the incidence and effects of a tax in terms of its direct and indirect money and real burdens. The incidence of a tax is its *direct money burden* which is equal to the total tax collections going to the treasury. Sometimes, a taxpayer has to incur more expenses than the amount of the tax, such as payment of fee to a tax-consultant for filling up the tax return, and on conveyance for depositing the amount of tax in the treasury or for submitting the tax return to the taxation officer. This is the *indirect money burden* of the tax.

The *effects* of a tax refer to its *real burden* which may be direct or indirect. The *direct real burden* is in the form of sacrifice of economic welfare on the part of the taxpayers as a result of the imposition of a tax When a person has to pay a tax whereby his income is reduced, it relates to the direct real burden of the tax. When the imposition of a tax reduces the consumption of a commodity, it is the *indirect real burden* of the tax.

Mrs Hicks calls the direct money burden of the tax as *formal incidence* and the effects of a tax as *effective incidence*.

From the above, some points of distinction may be made between the incidence and effects of a tax.

(1) The incidence of a tax relates to the money burden of the tax, while the effects of a tax relate to its real burden.

(2) It is the incidence of a tax that leads to its effects and not the other way.

(3) The incidence of a tax can be shifted but the effects of a tax cannot be passed on to some other person.

I. Factors Determining the Incidence of a Commodity Tax under Perfect Competition

The incidence of a tax levied on a commodity is shifted by the producer through a rise in the price of the commodity. But the price may be raised either by reduction in supply or increase in demand. Thus the incidence of a tax depends upon the forces of supply and demand. But the supply and demand conditions of the taxed commodity influence the incidence of the tax according to the nature of the elasticities of supply and demand, and the cost conditions under which the taxed commodity is produced. First, we analyse the incidence of commodity taxation in terms of elasticities of supply and demand, and then in terms of the cost conditions.

(A) Elasticities of Supply and Demand Analysis

According to Dalton, the incidence of commodity taxation is shared between the buyers and sellers in the ratio of the elasticity of supply of the taxed commodity to the elasticity of demand for it, $\frac{E_s}{E_d} = \frac{\textit{Incidence on Buyers}}{\textit{Incidence on Sellers}}$. This is explained diagrammatically in Figure 1.

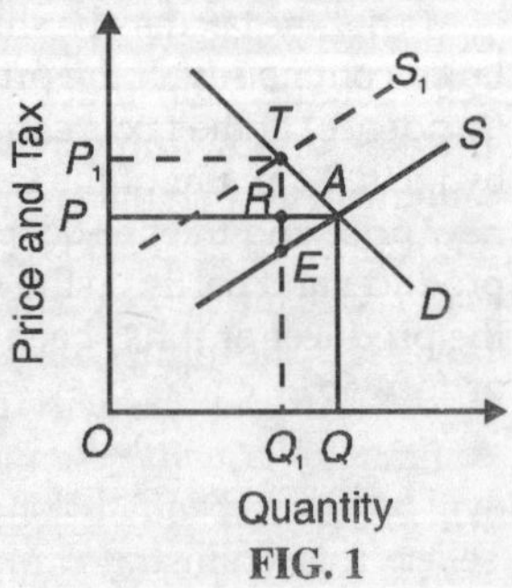

FIG. 1

Let D be the demand curve and S be the supply curve of the commodity before the tax is levied. OQ quantity of the commodity is sold and bought at QA ($=OP$) price. Suppose an excise duty equivalent to ET is imposed on per unit of the commodity, which is collected from the sellers. As a result, the supply curve shifts

1. For a detailed discussion on Effects of Taxation, see section 2.

upward as S_1 and the price of the commodity rises to Q_1T (=OP_1). But the per unit increase in price is *RT*, the difference between the new price (Q_1T) and the pre-tax price (*QA*). Thus the *RT* portion of the tax is borne by the buyers and *ER* portion by the sellers, $ET = ER + RT$. This division of tax-incidence between buyers and sellers can be explained algebraically in terms of the usual formulae of elasticity of demand and elasticity of supply.

$$E_s = \frac{\textit{Proportionate change in supply}}{\textit{Proportionate change in price}} = \frac{QQ_1}{OQ} \bigg/ \frac{ER}{QA}$$

$$\text{Similarly, } E_d = \frac{\textit{Proportionate change in demand}}{\textit{Proportionate change in price}} = \frac{QQ_1}{OQ} \bigg/ \frac{RT}{QA}$$

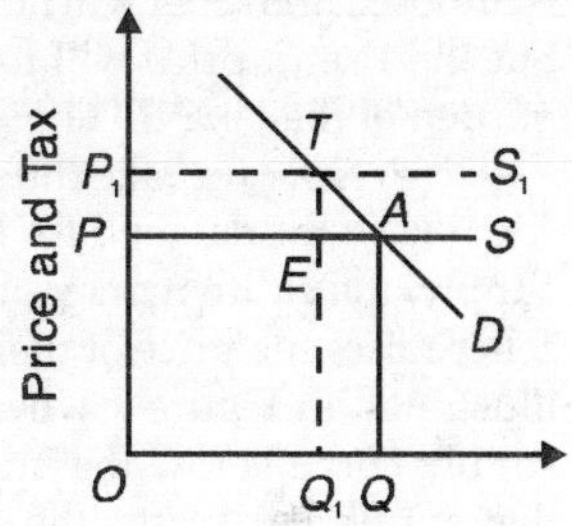

FIG. 2

$$\text{Thus, } \frac{E_s}{E_d} = \left(\frac{QQ_1}{OQ} \bigg/ \frac{ER}{QA}\right) \bigg/ \left(\frac{QQ_1}{OQ} \bigg/ \frac{RT}{QA}\right)$$

$$= \left(\frac{QQ_1}{OQ} \times \frac{QA}{ER}\right) \bigg/ \left(\frac{QQ_1}{OQ} \times \frac{QA}{RT}\right)$$

$$= \left(\frac{QQ_1}{OQ} \times \frac{QA}{ER}\right) \times \left(\frac{OQ}{QQ_1} \times \frac{RT}{QA}\right) = \frac{RT}{ER} = \frac{\text{Incidence on Buyers}}{\text{Incidence on Sellers}}$$

The same result will follow if the tax of the equivalent amount is imposed on the buyers with the only difference that the demand curve will shift downward to the left.

On the basis of this general principle of incidence of commodity taxation, Dalton stated two propositions : (1) Other things being equal, *the more elastic* the *demand* for the taxed commodity, the more will be the incidence of the tax upon *the seller*; and (2) other things being equal, the more elastic the supply of the taxed commodity, the more will be the incidence of the tax upon the buyer.

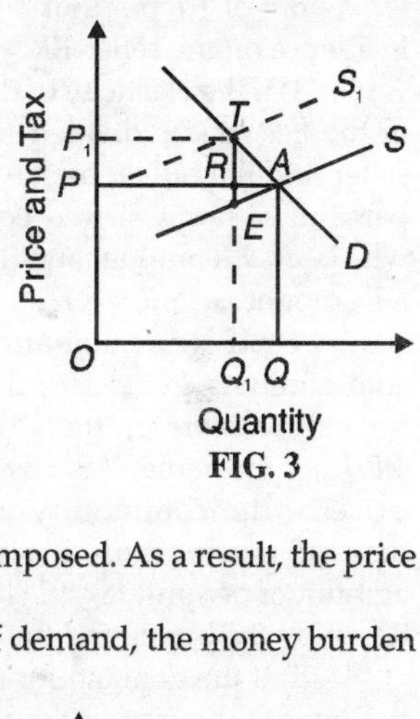

FIG. 3

From these propositions we can derive *ten* cases of incidence of taxation based on different elasticities of supply and demand .

(a) First we take different *elasticities* of *supply*, given the elasticity of demand for the commodity.

(1) If the supply of a commodity is *perfectly elastic,* given its elasticity of demand, the entire money burden (incidence) of the tax will be upon the buyer. This is illustrated in Figure 2. *S* is the supply curve and *D* is the demand curve. *QA* is the price before the imposition of the tax. Now a tax equivalent to *ET* per unit is imposed. As a result, the price rises by the full amount of the tax, *i.e., ET* which the seller shifts to the buyer.

(2) If the supply of a taxed commodity is *highly elastic,* given the elasticity of demand, the money burden of the tax will be *more* on the buyer and *less* on the seller, Figure 3 illustrates this case where *QA* is the price before the imposition of the tax. When *ET* amount of tax per unit is imposed, the supply curve shifts upward as S_1 and the new equilibrium price is Q_1T. The incidence on the seller is *ER*, and on the buyer *RT*. The former is less than the latter, $ER<RT$.

(3) If the elasticity of supply of the taxed commodity is *unity,* the money burden of the tax will be divided equally between the buyer and the seller. This is illustrated in Figure 4 where *ET* per unit tax is divided in equal proportions between the buyers and the seller. *ER,* the incidence on the

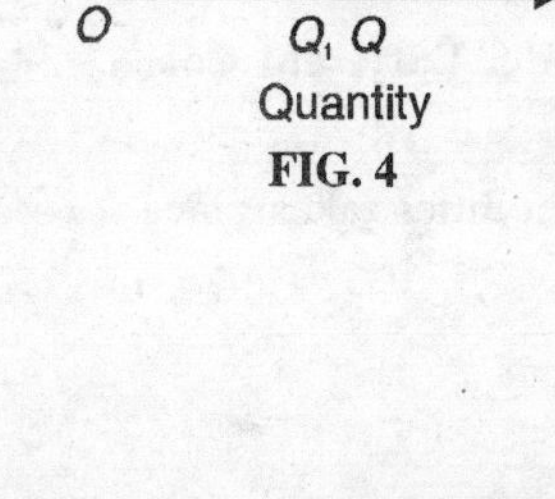

FIG. 4

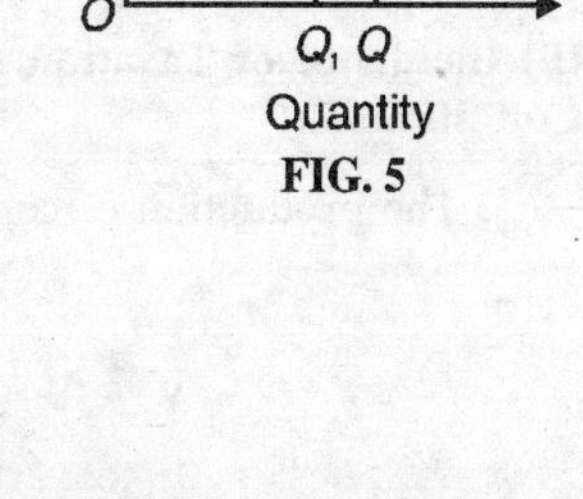

FIG. 5

seller exactly equals the incidence on the buyer *RT i.e.* $ER = RT$.

(4) If the elasticity of supply of the commodity is *less elastic*, given the elasticity of demand, the burden of the tax will be more on the seller and less on the buyer, as shown in Figure 5 Out of *ET* amount of per unit tax, the larger portion *ER* is borne by the seller, and the smaller portion *RT* by the buyer *i.e.* $ER>RT$.

(5) If the supply of a taxed commodity is *perfectly inelastic*, the entire money burden of the tax will be upon the seller. *S* is the perfectly inelastic supply curve in Figure 6 where *QT* is the original price before the tax. When a tax equal to *ET* is imposed, the seller will not raise the price because his supply is perfectly inelastic but the rise in price will lower the demand. He will, therefore, bear the entire burden of the tax*n ET* himself by keeping the price at the old level, *QT*.

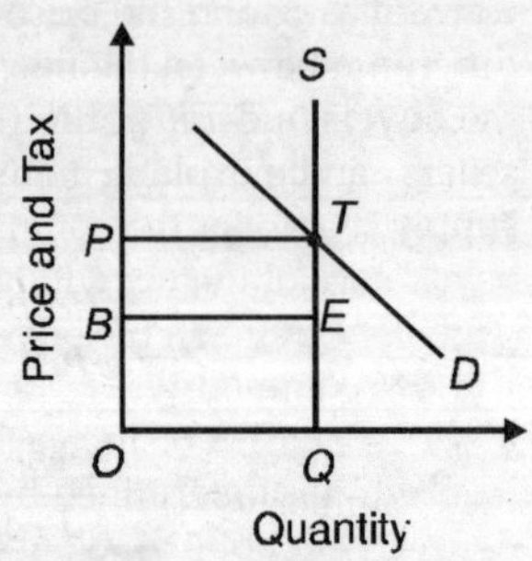

FIG. 6

(b) Now we take different *elasticities of demand*, given the elasticity of supply of the commodity.

(1) If the demand for the commodity is *perfectly elastic*, given its elasticity of supply, the entire money burden of the tax will be upon the seller because if the seller raises the price of the commodity its demand will fall considerably. This is illustrated in Figure 7 where *D* is the perfectly elastic demand curve. *S* is the supply curve before the imposition of the tax. *QA* is the pre-tax price. S_1 is the new supply curve after the imposition of *ET* per unit of tax which is entirely borne by the seller because the new price Q_1T equals the old price *QA*.

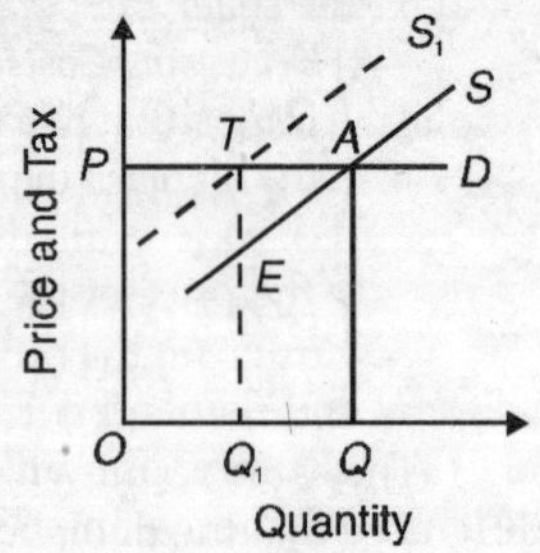

FIG. 7

(2) If the demand for the taxed commodity is *highly elastic*, the incidence of the tax will be more on the *seller* and *less* on the *buyer*. Figure 8 illustrates this case where out of *ET* per unit tax, the seller bears *ER* and the buyer *RT* amount. The incidence on the seller $ER > RT$, the incidence on the buyer.

(3) If the elasticity of demand for the commodity is *unity*, the money burden of the tax will be divided *equally* between the seller and the buyer, as shown in Figure 9. *ET* per unit of tax is shared equally by the seller who bears *ER* amount and the buyer who bears *RT* amount *i.e.*, $ER = RT$.

(4) If the demand for the taxed commodity is *less elastic*, the incidence of the tax will be more on the *buyer* and less on the *seller*. As the demand is less elastic, a rise in the price of the commodity will not affect the demand much. Figure 10 shows that out of *ET* amount of per unit tax, the larger amount *RT* is borne by the buyer and the smaller amount *ER* is borne by the seller i.e., $RT>ER$.

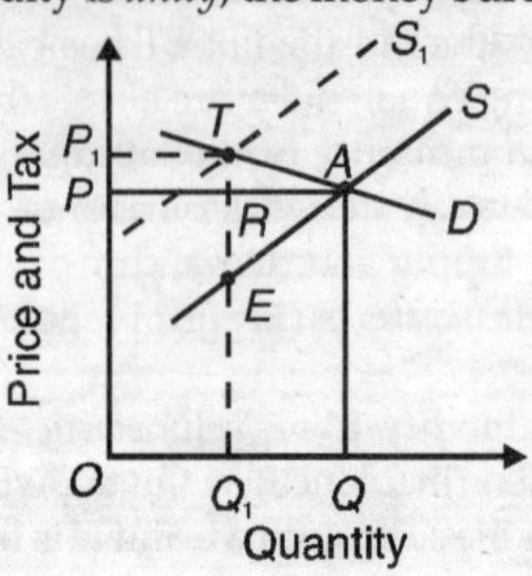

FIG. 8

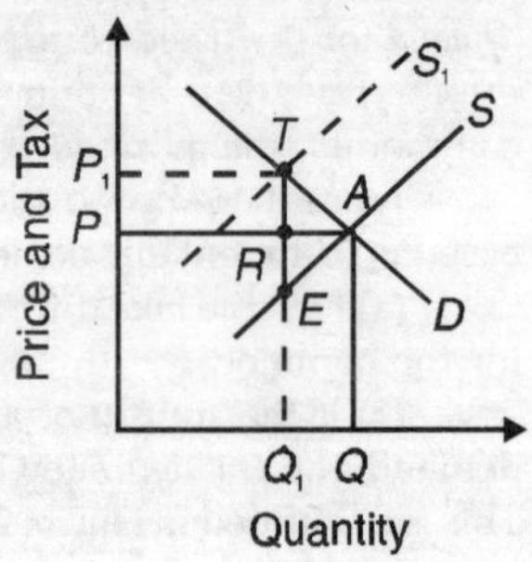

FIG. 9

(5) If the demand for the commodity is *perfectly inelastic*, the entire money burden of the tax is borne by the buyer. The rise in the price of the commodity even by the full amount of tax by the seller will not reduce the demand because the demand is perfectly inelastic. This is illustrated in Figure 11 where *QE* (= *OP*) is the pre-tax price. When *ET* per unit of tax is imposed on the commodity, the supply curve shift upward as S_1 and the price rises to $QT(= OP_1)$ and the entire tax burden *ET* is borne by the buyer.

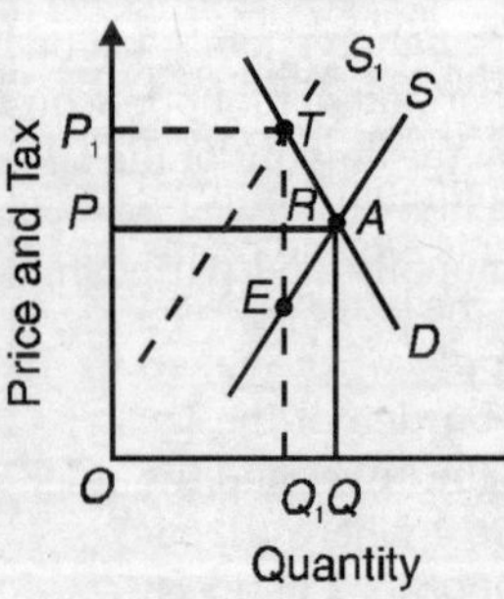

FIG. 10

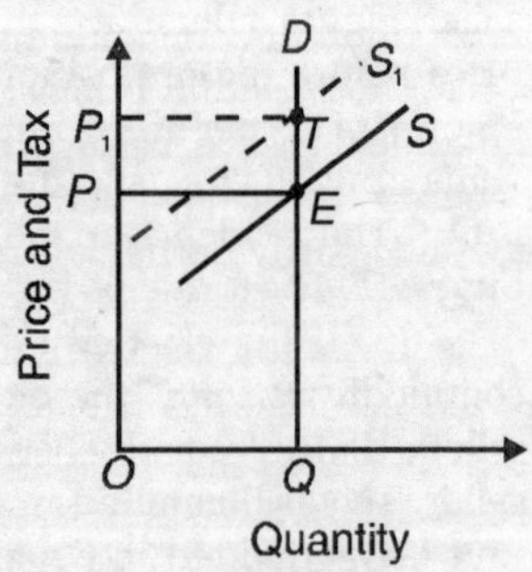

FIG. 11

(B) Incidence of Taxation under Different Cost Conditions

The production of commodities takes place

under the three laws of production which affect their costs of production. They are the laws of increasing costs, decreasing costs, and constant costs. The incidence of commodity taxation is, therefore, also influenced by these laws.

(1) *Increasing Costs.* If a commodity is produced under the law of increasing costs or diminishing returns, the imposition of a tax on such a commodity will *raise the price* of the commodity *by less than the amount of the tax*. As a result, the incidence of the tax will be partly on the seller and partly on the buyer. Whether it will be more on the buyer or the seller will depend upon the elasticity of supply of the commodity.[2]

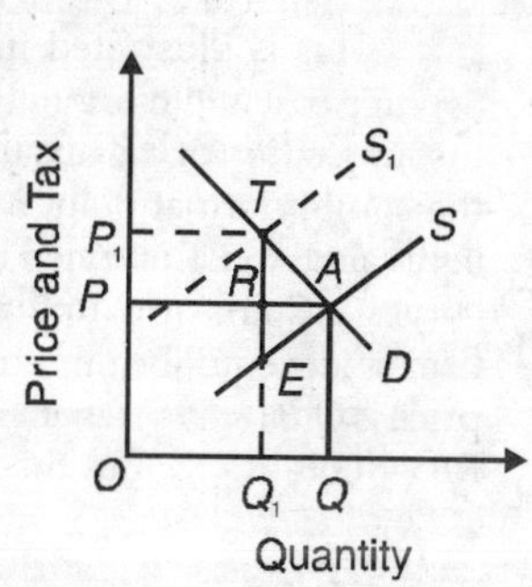

FIG. 12

The case of increasing costs is illustrated in Figure 12 where the pre-tax price *QA* is determined by the interaction of the supply curve *S* and the demand curve *D* at point *A*. Now *ET* per unit tax is imposed on the commodity and the supply curve shifts upward as S_1. The new equilibrium is set at *T* where S_1 intersects the demand curve *D*. The imposition of the tax raises the price by *RT* (= PP_1) but by less than the tax *ET*. The incidence on the buyer is *RT* and on the seller *ER*.

(2) *Decreasing Costs.* If a commodity is produced under the law of decreasing costs, the imposition of a tax on it will raise its price by *more than* the amount of the tax. With the increase in price, the quantity demanded will fall and the supply will be reduced. As a result, the per unit cost of production will increase[3] and the seller will raise the price of the commodity by more than the tax and pass on its entire money burden on the buyer. This is illustrated in Figure 13 where *S* and *D* are the supply and demand curves before the imposition of the tax. The pre-tax price is *QA* (= *OP*). Suppose *ET* per unit tax is levied on the commodity, shown as the difference between *S* and S_1 curves. As a result, the price rises to Q_1T (= OP_1). The difference between the new price and the old price is $RT=(Q_1T-Q_1R)$.* The rise in the price of the commodity by *RT* is more than the tax *ET* *i.e.*, *RT* > *ET*. The entire incidence of the tax *ET* has been shifted by the seller upon the buyer.

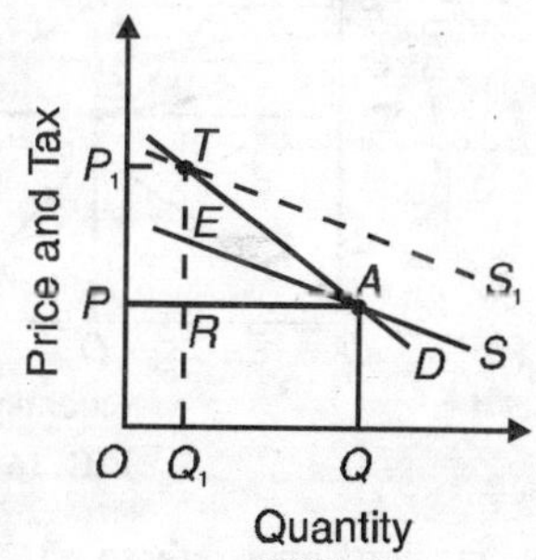

FIG. 13

(3) *Constant Costs.* If the commodity is produced under the law of constant costs or constant returns, the supply curve is horizontal to the *X*-axis and the price *rises* by the full *amount* of the tax. The seller shifts the entire money burden of the tax on the buyer. This is illustrated in Figure 14 where *QA* (= *OP*) is the pre-tax price arrived at by the intersection of the supply curve *S* and the demand curve *D* at point *A*. Suppose *ET* tax per unit is imposed on the commodity and the new price is set at Q_1T (= OP_1). The price has risen by $ET=(Q_1T-Q_1E)$** which is also the tax imposed on the commodity. The entire tax amount is shifted by the seller upon the buyer.

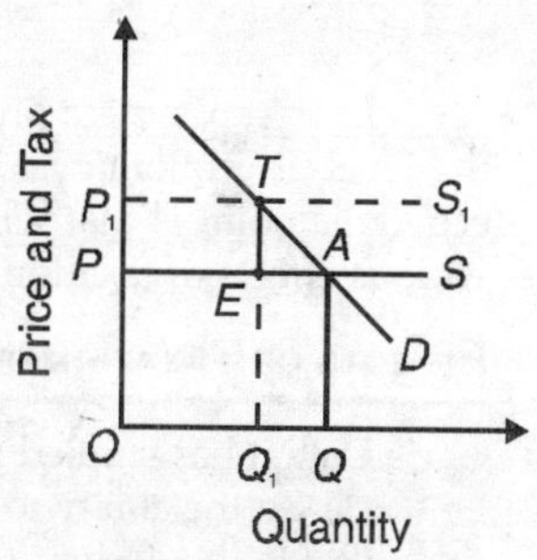

FIG. 14

II. Incidence of Taxation under Monopoly

A monopolist fixes the price of his commodity by equating his marginal cost of production with the marginal revenue. A tax on the monopoly firm may be either specific or lumpsum.

A *specific tax* is levied on per unit of monopoly output. This has the effect of shifting both the average and marginal cost curves upward by the amount of the tax. The monopoly price will *not* rise by the full amount of the tax. It will, however, depend upon the elasticity of demand of the taxed commodity. The incidence of the tax will be partly borne by the monopolist and partly shifted on the buyers.

2. See Figures 3 to 5.
3. Under this law of decreasing costs, when production increases, per unit cost falls. The opposite will happen when production falls.

* $Q_1R = QA$.

** $Q_1E = QA$.

This is illustrated in Figure 15 where AC and MC are the average cost and marginal cost curves of the monopoly firm before the imposition of the tax. It sells OQ output at QA (= OP) price with the equilibrium at point e where MC=MR. Suppose a specific tax equivalent to ET is levied by the government which shifts the cost curves AC and MC upwards to AC_1 and MC_1 respectively. The firm's new equilibrium point is e_1 where MC_1 equals MR. The new price is Q_1B (= OP_1) which is higher than the old price QA(= Q_1R) by RB (= $Q_1B - Q_1R$). But the rise in the price of the commodity (RB) after the imposition of the tax (ET) is less than the tax *i.e.*, $RB < ET$. The monopolist shifts this portion (RB) of the money burden of the tax on the buyers.

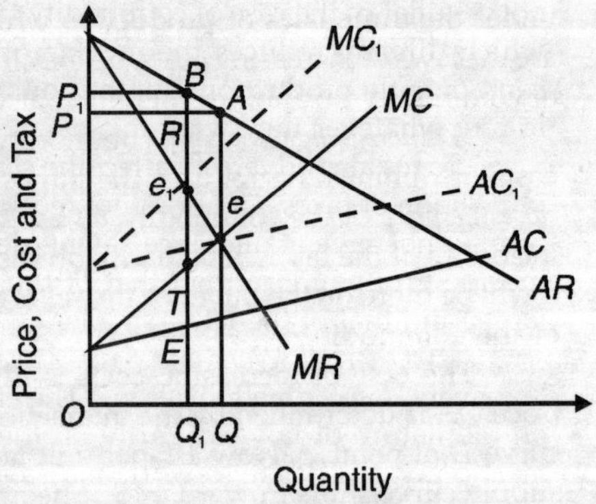

FIG. 15

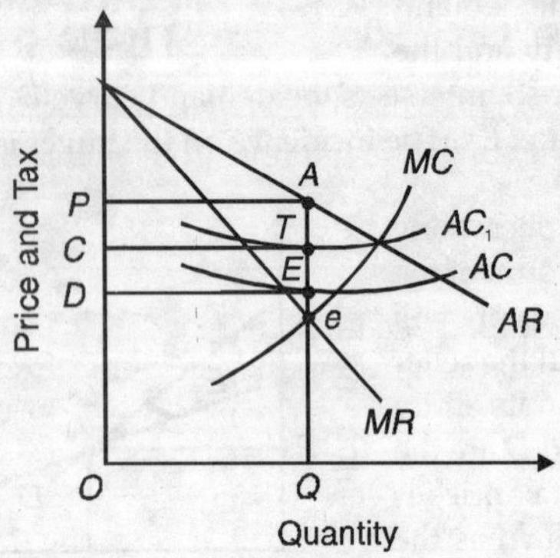

FIG. 16

If the government imposes a *lumpsum tax*[4] on the monopoly profit, the monopolist cannot shift it on the buyers and he will have to bear the entire money burden of the tax himself. This is illustrated in Figure 16 where AC and MC are the average and marginal cost curves before the imposition of the tax. The firm is selling OQ output at QA price and earning $PAED$ monopoly profit. The imposition of a lumpsum tax is a fixed cost to the monopoly firm because it is independent of output. It, therefore, raises the average cost by the amount of the tax ET, so that the AC curve shifts upward as AC_1, but the marginal cost curve remains unaffected. As a result, the monopoly profit is reduced from $PAED$ to $PATC$. The entire money burden of the tax is borne by the monopolist himself because there is no change in his price-output combination.

2. EFFECTS OF TAXATION

Every tax system produces various types of consequences on production, distribution, consumption and the level of economic activity. The effects may be good or bad, but "the best system of taxation from the economic point is that which has the best, or the least bad, economic effects," according to Dr Dalton. The various effects of taxation are studied below.

Effects of Taxation on Production

Dalton has studied the effects of taxation on production under three categories:
(1) On the ability to work and save.
(2) On the desire to work and save.
(3) On the composition and pattern of production.

Let us analyse how taxation affects production through these three factors.

(1) *Ability to Work and Save.* Taxes which lower the efficiency of the taxpayers adversely affect their *ability to work* and hence production. When taxes are levied, they reduce the purchasing power of the people who are forced to cut down expenditures on necessaries, comforts and luxuries. This effect is more pronounced in the case of the lower and middle income groups than on the upper income groups. People in the lower and middle income groups reduce expenditure on necessaries of efficiency (such as milk) when taxes are imposed on necessaries of life. Similarly, taxes on conventional necessaries like cigarettes also force people to reduce expenditure on necessaries of efficiency, and even on medical facilities and education of children. This effect is

4. This is not a commodity tax.

not peculiar in the case of commodity taxation alone. It is also to be found in the case of progressive income tax which directly reduces the income of the taxpayers and thus adversely affects their ability to work, and consequently production. But the ability to work of the rich is not affected by taxation because they can afford to buy whatever they want to.

Taxes also adversely affect the *ability to save.* If a taxpayer maintains the same standard of living after the imposition of taxes, and does not reduce his consumption expenditure on goods accordingly, he will save less or may not save at all. Since saving depends upon income, all taxes reduce the ability to save of the higher income groups more than that of the lower income groups because the saving-margins of the former are larger and that of the latter smaller.

(2) *Desire to Work and Save.* Taxes also affect production through the desire to work and save of the taxpayers. According to Dalton, "The effects of any particular tax upon desire to work and save depend partly on the nature of tax and partly on the nature of individual reaction to taxation." We analyse the effects of taxation on the desire to work and save in terms of these two factors.

The Nature of Taxes. Moderate commodity taxes do not adversely affect the incentive to work and save and even the production of taxed commodities. But if heavy commodity taxes are imposed, they will raise the prices of commodities, reduce their demand, and bring a fall in their production.

On the other hand, some direct taxes do not have any effect on the desire to work and save, and hence on production. Such taxes are on windfalls, monopoly profits, and on expenditure. Windfalls or unexpected gains from war profits, inflation, increase in land values, or from inheritances are unearned incomes. Taxes on them are not felt by the recipients of such gains. Hence they do not adversely affect the desire to work and save. Similarly, a tax on monopoly profit does not reduce the willingness to work, save, and produce on the part of the monopolist. His interest lies in maximising his profit. So he will continue to work, save, invest, and produce so long as he earns some profit. Further, an expenditure tax discourages expenditure rather than the desire to work, save, and produce. In fact, the latter is encouraged.

But highly progressive income tax, corporation tax, and wealth tax will discourage the willingness to work, save and invest. These adversely affect business and production. If the inputs are also taxed heavily, the cost of production and prices of commodities will increase, thereby adversely affecting their demand and production. On the other hand, moderate rates of taxes on income, corporate profit, wealth, and on factors of production (which can be easily passed on to the consumers by the producers) have little adverse effect on the incentives to work and save and hence on production.

The Nature of Individual Reaction. The immediate reaction of a taxpayer to the announcement of tax proposals in a budget is to adversely affect his willingness to work and save. This is what Pigou called *the announcement effect of taxation*. But this effect is not uniform on all taxpayers. "Any person's reaction to taxation is governed by the elasticity of his demand for income," according to Dr Dalton.

The *elasticity of demand for income* refers to the intensity of desire for obtaining a particular income on the part of a person. A person's demand for income is *elastic* when he is not anxious to maintain a certain minimum level of income. Accordingly, he is not prepared to work more or save more to maintain that level. Suppose a person's salary is Rs 15000 per month and he is required to pay Rs 150 per month in the form of income tax. His demand for income is said to be elastic if he is not prepared to do some extra work in order to compensate for the reduction in his income to the tune of Rs 150 paid as the tax. The demand for his income is said to be *inelastic* if he works to earn at least this much so as to maintain his income at Rs 15000 per month.

Thus the imposition of a tax will retard the desire to work and save if a person's demand for income is elastic. On the other hand, if the demand for income is *inelastic,* the desire to work and save will be encouraged. In the former case, production will be adversely affected and in the latter case it will be favourably affected.

The elasticity of demand for income differs with individuals depending upon their circumstances. But generally the elasticity of demand for income is *inelastic.* This is because people like to maintain a minimum standard of living, have strong desire to save for the future, or for running a business of their own, or for acquiring power, prestige and distinction, or for deriving satisfaction from having more income and wealth than others. In the case of such persons, whenever the rates of taxation are raised there is greater effort on their part to increase their incomes.

(3) *The Composition and Pattern of Production.* Taxation affects the composition and pattern of production through the diversion of resources between different industries and places. Such diversions may be beneficial or harmful.

Taxes on luxury goods and intoxicants raise their prices, reduce their demand and hence their production. As a result, factors of production engaged in manufacturing such socially undesirable commodities shift to the production of other socially useful commodities.

In regions where tax concessions and exemptions are granted to industries, resources flow into them from those regions where the rates of taxation are high. Such diversions take place in the form of establishment of new industries. This leads to the opening up and development of new regions which provide larger employment opportunities to the people, and increase production and income.

Similarly, when protection is granted to certain domestic industries in the form of grants, bounties, import duties, tax concessions and exemptions, etc., there is diversion of resources from *non-priority* industries to the protected industries. This will lead to increased production within the country.

These may be called the beneficial effects of diversion of resources.

On the other hand, there may be the harmful effects of diversion of resources if heavy taxes are imposed on necessaries. Prices of such articles will rise, their demand will be reduced and production will be adversely affected. This will lead to the diversion of resources to other non-essential articles having low rates of taxation.

Again, heavy taxation in the country which leaves little for the investors will lead to the flight of capital to foreign countries. This will adversely affect local industries whose production will fall due to the lack of capital.

So taxation affects the composition and pattern of production in a country through the diversion of resources.

EFFECTS OF TAXATION ON DISTRIBUTION

One of the important objectives of taxation is to reduce the gap between the rich and the poor. Taxes levied with this motive are known as *redistributive taxes*. The effects of taxation on distribution depend upon the nature of taxation and the types of taxes

The Nature of Taxation. Taxes which are regressive or proportional in character increase inequalities of income and wealth. A regressive tax is one which falls more heavily on smaller incomes, such as poll tax, sales tax, tax on necessaries, etc. A proportional tax is one which is imposed on all incomes at a flat rate. Such taxes adversely affect the lower income groups and favour the high income groups. Thus from the point of view of distribution, the best taxes are those which are progressive in nature. The rates of progressive taxes increase with the increase in the income and wealth of the people. Accordingly, the rich are required to pay more and the lower income groups less, while people below the minimum taxable limit are totally exempted from taxation.

Types of Taxes. Types of taxes—direct and indirect—also affect the distribution of income and wealth.

Indirect taxes on necessaries, such as sales tax and excise duties, are regressive in nature because the lower incomes groups spend a larger percentage of their incomes on such articles while the higher income groups spend a smaller percentage on them. Thus taxes on necessaries raise the prices of such commodities and reduce their consumption on the part of the masses and thus increase inequalities.

On the other hand, taxation of luxuries with differentiation in rates affect the rich the most. This means that higher-priced goods may be taxed at higher rates so that there is a broad element of progression. Thus high rates on luxuries and low rates on articles of common consumption have beneficial redistributive effects. Similar is the case with heavy import duties on luxury articles.

Highly progressive direct taxation of income and wealth has the effect of reducing the accumulation of income and wealth by the rich. Progressive taxation of income, gifts, inheritances, property or wealth will reduce the concentration of income and wealth in the hands of the few rich. But such taxes should be so levied as not to adversely affect productive investment.

EXERCISES

1. What is the 'incidence' of a tax? Discuss the factors that determine the incidence of a commodity tax.
2. Distinguish between the 'impact' and 'incidence' of a commodity tax. Trace the incidence of a tax on a monopoly firm.
3. Discuss the effects of taxes on production and distribution.

CHAPTER 88

Taxable Capacity

1. MEANING

Taxable capacity refers to the extent of tax burden which the people can bear in a country. It is a level up to which taxes can be imposed without harming the interest of individuals in a community. Economists differ over its definition. Sir **Josiah Stamp** defines taxable capacity as "the total production minus the amount required to maintain the population at the subsistence level." He also defines it "as the maximum amount which the citizens of a country contribute towards the expenses of public authorities without having a really unhappy and downtrodden existence and without dislocating the economic organisation too much."[1] These two definitions by Lord Stamp do not convey a clear idea about the concept of taxable capacity. In the first definition, the "subsistence (or consumption) level" is vague which connot be accurately measured. It depends on the standard of living of the people which differs with individuals, places, circumstances and time. In the second definition, the words "unhappy and downtrodden existence" and "dislocating the economic organisation too much" create confusion. It is not possible to ascertain whether by paying taxes people are unhappy and taxes are dislocating the economic organisation.

Findlay Shirras defines taxable capacity as "the limit of squeezability. It is the total surplus of production over the minimum of consumption required to produce that volume of production, the standard of living remaining intact."[2] This definition is also vague because it is not possible statistically to measure the "limit of squeezability" and the "minimum of consumption". Shirras maintains that the standard of living remains unchanged. But standard of living does not remain constant but changes from person to person and from time to time. Moreover, this definition is confusing. A person can be squeezed upto his last rupee and for a country it might include the entire income of the people. Moreover, both this definitions do not take into account public expenditure.

ABSOLUTE AND RELATIVE TAXABLE CAPACITY

Taxable capacity is of two types : absolute and relative taxable capacity. The above definitios of Stamp and Shirras relate to absolute capacity. Relative taxable capacity refers to the impact of taxation on two or more

1. Josiah Stamp, *Wealth and Taxable Capacity, 1921.*
2. Findlay Shirras, *The Science of Public Finance, 1936.*
3. Hugh Dalton, *Principles of Public Finance*, 1943. Italics mine.

communities sharing a common expenditure. Dalton favours the concept of relative capacity because it is easy to find out the impact of taxation on different sections of the community. According to him, "My general conclusion is that relative capacity is a reality..., while absolute capacity is a myth." He, therefore advocates "that the phrase *absolute* taxable capacity' should be banished,"[3] because absolute taxable capacity cannot be measured. Moreover, whatever is left with people after consumption is taken away by the state through taxation. But in the case of relative taxable capacity, people are taxed according to their relative capacities. This concept is of much use in a federal country where each state contributes towards the common expenditure of the federal government according to its ability to pay. Thus the concept of relative taxable capacity is simpler and realistic than that of absolute capacity.

2. FACTORS DETERMINING TAXABLE CAPACITY

The taxable capacity of a country depends on the following factors.

1. *Size of National Income.* Taxable capacity depends on the size of national income or wealth or natural resources of a country and the extent to which they are developed. The higher the national income, the higher the taxable capacity of a country, and vice versa.

2. *Distribution of National Income.* In a country where there is inequality of income, taxable capacity is high because the few rich can be taxed heavily. On the other hand, if there is equality of income, the taxable capacity is relatively low because the government expenditure to uplift the poor will be less.

3. *Stability of Income.* In developed countries, the incomes of individuals are stable, the taxable capacity is high. But where incomes are subject to fluctuations and are unstable, as in underdeveloped countries, the taxable capacity is low.

4. *Size and Growth of Population.* If the size and growth rate of population are high, the per capita income will be low. So the taxable capacity will also be low, and vice versa.

5. *Standard of Living.* If the standard of living of the people is high, it means that people are spending more on comforts and luxuries. So their capacity to pay taxes is also high, and vice versa.

6. *Tax System.* The type of tax system affects the taxable capacity. A progressive tax system has a higher taxable capacity because it falls on higher income groups, as in the case of direct taxes on incomes. On the other hand, regressive indirect taxes which fall heavily on low income groups have low taxable capacity.

7. *Sources of Revenue.* Taxable capacity depends on the number of sources of revenue available to the government. The greater the number of revenue sources that are productive, the higher the taxable capacity, and vice versa.

8. *Public Expenditure.* If public expenditure is meant to increase the welfare of the people, people do not mind paying taxes. If the government spends money on unnecessary and unproductive projects, people will not be willing to pay taxes. Thus taxable capacity is high for productive public expenditure which increases national income, and vice versa.

9. *Taxing and Spending Income.* Taxable capacity depends on the manner and timing of both taxing and spending income by the government. This involves compensatory spending and compensatory taxation. Compensatory spending compensates for the fall in private investment and increases output, employment and income. Compensatory taxation compensates for the fall in private expenditure, compensates for the fall in private expenditure, saving or investment by taxing the people. Both tend to increase economic activity and national income thereby raising the taxable capacity.

10. *Price Situation.* Taxable capacity is determined by the price situation in the country. If prices are rising, the real income of the people falls and their taxable capacity declines. The converse is the case when prices are falling.

11. *Organisation of the Economy.* If the economy is primarily agricultural, the taxable capacity will be low because the income from agricultural operations is uncertain. On the other hand, an industrial economy has high taxable capacity because the industrial sector generates larger income than the agricultural sector.

12. *Psychology of the People.* Taxable capacity also depends upon the psychology of the people. People are prepared to more pay taxes honestly and willingly during a war and natural calamities like floods, earthquakes,

etc. As pointed out by Findlay Shirras, "The psychology of the people has much to do with the extent of taxable capacity. People are often willing to bear heavier taxation on patriotic or sentimental grounds. On the other hand, adverse psychology of the people towards the payment of taxes lowers down the taxable capacity."

13. Political Conditions. What should be the level of taxation is a political factor these days. A country which has political stability, its taxable capacity will be high. If there is political instability or the government is unsympathetic and repressive, the taxable capacity will be low.

Conclusion. Thus the taxable capacity of a country depends upon a number factors. These factors change from time to time and so does the taxable capacity.

3. MEASUREMENT OR LIMIT OF TAXABLE CAPACITY

Colin Clark gives a limit of taxable capacity of a country. According to him, "The safe upper limit of taxation is 25 per cent of national production." Thus he takes it to be 25 per cent of national income. If the level of taxation exceeds this limit, it will adversely affect production and incentive to work, save and invest. Further, a high level of taxation will lead to increase in wages and to a rise in prices. All these factors will reduce national income. Colin Clark places this limit for advanced countries.

But Kaldor does not agree with Colin Clark. He suggests a different limit for different types of taxes. According to him, a particular tax upto 10 per cent of national income may be a heavy burden on people and another tax of 25 per cent may not be a burden. For instance, an income tax upto 10 per cent of national income may adversely affect incentive to work, save and invest. On the other hand, an expenditure tax of 10 per cent or more will increase production rather than retard it. People will not spend extravagantly. They will reduce wasteful expenditures. They will save and invest and production will not be adversely affected.

However, most governments have accepted Clark's 25 per cent limit of taxable capacity. But the followers of Kaldor persist that 25 per cent should not be the limit for taxes on incomes.

EXERCISES

1. What do you man by taxable capacity ? On what factors taxable capacity depends?
2. Distinguish between absolute and relative taxable capacity. What is the limit of taxable capacity?

CHAPTER 89

Canons, Effects and Growth of Public Expenditure

1. CANONS OF PUBLIC EXPENDITURE

The canons or principles of public expenditure have been enunciated by Findlay Shirras and Dalton. We discuss these canons as follows :

1. The Canon of Benefit

The canon of benefit is also known as the canon of maximum social advantage or benefit. According to this canon, public expenditure should be so incurred on various items that it provides maximum benefit to the society as a whole. Nicholson says that the maximum social welfare is achieved when the public utility of marginal expenditure in each case is equal. Shirras points out that no public expenditure should be incurred for the benefit of individual or society unless it satisfies three conditions. First, the amount of expenditure should be small. Second, a claim for the amount should be enforced in a court of law. Third, the expenditure should be incurred in pursuance of a recognised policy or custom. This canon is fulfilled if these three conditions are satisfied.

2. The Canon of Economy

By the canon of economy is meant that public expenditure should be so incurred as to avoid the waste of public money. It should avoid all extravagance and useless expenditure. The word 'economy' can be interpreted both in the narrow and wide sense. In its narrow sense, it means that there is no extravagance in public expenditure. In its wide sense, it means that if a particular public expenditure is not incurred on a particular item or use, it will not lead to the maximum social welfare. In this sense, it simply means application of the canon of maximum social benefit. According to Shirras, the word 'economy' means protecting the interest of the taxpayer not merely in affecting economies in expenditure but also in developing revenue. In this interpretation, economy refers to expenditure as well as revenue. But this is not a correct view because in this interpretation of economy, the canon of economy in public expenditure is intermingled with the canon of economy in taxation.

3. The Canon of Sanction

This canon states that no public expenditure should be incurred without the sanction of proper authority. Public expenditure cannot be incurred by any public officer because it will lead to misuse or malallocation of funds. These should be a competent authority to sanction all public expenditures which may allocate them according to the requirements of the country. It is the finance ministry that sanctions all expenditure to the heads of departments. The finance ministry, in turn, gets power to spend funds from parliament. Shirras observes in this connection that no expenditure should be sanctioned by an authority which at a latter date is likely to involve expenditure beyond its powers of sanction. Even the authority should sanction that much amount which is in its competence, otherwise the subordinate authority will be meeting obligations more than the sanctioned amount and the purpose of this canon will be defeated.

4. The Canon of Surplus

The cannon of surplus means that the public authority must earn its living and pay its way like ordinary citizens. Balanced budgets, as in private expenditure, should be the order of the day. The above definition by Shirras points towards a balanced budget. The government revenue should be more than its expenditure. But it again becomes a canon both of public income and public expenditure, and is thus not a canon of expenditure alone. Moreover, the state cannot be expected to behave like an individual. It has to spend sometimes more and at other times less than its revenue. This entirely depends on the prevailing economic conditions of the country. If there are inflationary pressures, the government will spend less than its revenues. On the other hand, when there are deflationary pressures, more will be spent than the revenue. Thus this canon is not satisfied.

5. The Canon of Elasticity

By the canon of elasticity is meant that public expenditure should change according to the needs and requirements of the economy. It should be quite flexible so that it can be increased during depression and reduced during inflation. In other words, public expenditure should be sufficiently elastic.

6. Canon of Equitable Distribution

According to this canon, public expenditure should be incurred in such a manner that it helps in reducing the inequalities of income and wealth. The pattern of public expenditure should be such that the poor and weaker sections receive the maximum benefits in the form of free education, medical facilities, old age pension housing, etc.

7. Canon of Productivity

This canon requires that public expenditure should help in increasing productivity. Public expenditure should increase such infrastructure facilities as roads, bridges, railways, transport, communications, power, etc.

8. The Canon of Neutrality

The canon of neutrality implies that public expenditure should be incurred in such a manner that it neutralises all adverse effects on production and distribution. Rather, it should have a healthy influence on both production and distribution in the country. It should encourage productive activity and at the same time reduce inequalities of income and wealth. But it is not always possible that public expenditure should have neutral effects. At the most, the adverse effects of public expenditure can be minimised.

2. EFFECTS OF PUBLIC EXPENDITURE

Public expenditure has far reaching effects on production, employment and distribution in a country. We discuss these effects as under :

1. Effects of Public Expenditure on Production

According to Dalton, production and employment in a country depend on three factors : (a) ability of the people to work, save, and invest; (b) willingness to work, save and invest; and (c) diversion of economic resources as between different uses and localities. Public expenditure influences these factors in a number of ways and thus helps in increasing production and employment within the country. The ability and willingness to work, save and invest depend on the nature of expenditure. The former increase with the increase in the efficiency of workers which, in turn, raises production and employment.

(1) On Social Insurance. Public expenditure on social insurance benefits such as unemployment, sickness, maternity, old age pensions, etc. tends to increase the purchasing power of workers indirectly. When these facilities are provided by the state, the workers are not required to spend on them, thereby increase their real purchasing power. The money so saved is spent by them on other articles. It means an increase in their standard of living which raises their efficiency and production.

If, on the other hand, the workers spend the money so saved on gambling, drinking, etc. their ability and willingness to save fall which adversely affect their ability to work, thereby reducing production.

(2) On Basic Facilities. Public expenditure on basic facilities also tends to raise efficiency and ability to work. When the state provides such basic facilities as cheap ration, low-rent houses, mid-day meals to children, cheap milk, etc., the ability to save increases. This, in turn, tends to raise their ability to work, thereby increasing production.

(3) On Education and Public Health. Public expenditure on education and public health has direct welfare effects on society. Expenditure on education is regarded as investment in human capital because it helps in skill formation and thus raises the ability to work and produce more. Similarly, public health is also another form of investment in human capital. Healthy workers, who are free from diseases, work more and raise production.

(4) On Economic Overheads, Basic Industries, etc. Public expenditure on economic overheads, basic industries, etc. also helps in increasing the productive capacity of the economy. Public expenditure on power, transport, communications, irrigation, soil erosion, land reclamation, etc. tends to increase the supply of resources for production over a long period. Moreover, expenditure on roads, railways, and other means of transport also affects the mobility of men and materials, which, in turn help in increasing the productive capacity. Further, the development of basic industries like iron and steel, engineering, heavy chemicals, fertilisers, etc. is very helpful in the development of other industries. Again, public expenditure on river valley projects helps in providing larger employment opportunities. It provides protection against floods and drought, thereby avoiding loss of resources.

(5) On Credit and Banking Facilities. Public expenditure in providing credit and banking facilities also helps in increasing the productive capacity of the economy. It is through bank nationalisation and/or through state and cooperative banks and opening of a network of branches throughout the country that the state can provide cheap and better credit and banking facilities to agriculture, industry and trade, and thus help in increasing their productivity.

(6) On Backward Regions and Areas. Public expenditure on the development of backward regions and depressed areas helps in providing employment through basic facilities. The private enterprise is shy to invest in these areas. It is only the state which by providing all types of basic facilities like roads, railways, power, industries, etc. develops such areas whereby the people get jobs and the productive power of the area increases.

(7) In the Form of Grants and Subsidies. Public expenditure in the form of grants and subsidies to farmers, firms and industries is highly productive. When there is a bumper crop, the prices of farm products fall considerably. The state can save them from disaster through price support. It can purchase their surplus stocks at fixed minimum prices. In order to encourage higher production, the state can provide such inputs as fertilisers, seeds, pump sets, etc. at subsidised prices. Similarly, the state can help develop industries by providing

them subsidies. Some of the industries have high costs in the initial stage of production. As a result, the prices of their products are high and they are not in a position to compete in the market, and thus they meet an early death. To save such industries, public expenditure in the form of subsidies may enable them to develop without charging high prices from its customers.

(8) On Information. Public expenditure on providing information in the form of such publicity media as TV, commercial broadcast, etc. helps private and public enterprises in getting their products publicised. As a result, their sales and production increase. Similarly, public expenditure on employment news, bureaux and exchanges helps in placing the right man at the right job and in this way provides larger employment opportunities and tends to increase productivity.

2. Effects of Public Expenditure on Diversion of Resources

Public expenditure affects the pattern of production through the diversion of resources from existing uses to more productive uses. In fact, government expenditure in itself is a diversion of resources from private to public uses. Public expenditure induces people to divert their resources to more productive uses in the following ways :

(1) On Infrastructure. Public expenditure on the development of roads and railways helps in diverting resources to more productive uses when the market for products becomes large. Again, public expenditure on generation of power supply and irrigation facilities helps in the diversion of resources to large industries and agriculture. Further, public expenditure on providing research, technical education, etc. tends to divert resources to more productive uses. In fact, public expenditure on infrastructure is essential to divert economic resources in order to create conditions of economic stability. Further, when public expenditure is made on such long-run infrastructural facilities as roads, railways, power, irrigation, etc., it is trying to divert resources from their present to future uses which are more productive.

(2) On Backward Areas. Public expenditure on the development of backward regions or areas brings diversion of resources from more developed to less developed areas. Such diversion takes place when the government incurs more expenditure in the form of transport, power, and on the establishment of public enterprises in a backward region. Grants made by the government for the development of such areas helps in diverting natural and human resources from the developed to backward areas.

(3) To Private Enterprise. Public expenditure in the form of loans and subsidies to private enterprise helps in the diversion of resources into productive channels. Sometimes loans and subsidies are made conditional. They are dependent on the quality of the product. In such cases, diversion of resources leads to the production of better quality products as against inferior goods.

(4) On Defence. Public expenditure on defence or war leads to the greatest diversion of resources. Such expenditure diverts resources from peaceful uses to war uses. It is normally regarded as the wastage of human and material resources which can otherwise be used for social benefits. But to defend a country is the foremost duty of a government. It provides security to life and property and saves the nation from foreign domination. All expenditure on defence is not wasteful rather it is productive indirectly. Defence expenditure on the construction of roads, bridges, aerodromes, shipyards, and on other means of transport and communications helps in building infrastructure in the country which are ultimately used by the civilian population. It also provides employment to people engaged in their construction. Moreover, public expenditure incurred in maintaining the armed forces in the form of supplies of food, clothing and other materials increases their demand and production and helps in increasing employment opportunities manifold. No doubt, when resources are diverted from their private uses to war, their supplies to the masses are reduced which adversely affect their standard of living. But this is only a temporary phase so long as the war continues.

3. Effects of Public Expenditure on Income Distribution

Public expenditure by increasing social welfare helps in reducing inequalities of income and wealth. According to Dalton, it is only progressive expenditure that tends to reduce inequalities. A progressive expenditure is one when a person with lower income receives larger benefit as compared to a person with higher income. Public expenditure for purposes of income distribution is of two types : transfer expenditure and exhaustive expenditure. In the case of *transfer expenditure,* low income groups are given cash benefits in the form of unemployment, sickness, disablement, dependents, and maternity benefits, and old age pensions. All such expenditures by the state help the poor and middle income groups in raising their incomes indirectly. *Exhaustive public expenditure* also tends to reduce income inequalities and it is in the form of free and cheap services of commodities, such as free education, free medical facilities, free milk or meals to school children, free transport for school children and for workers, subsidised rations, subsidised lunch to workers, rent-free quarters, etc.

There are also intangible benefits such as providing rent and recreation centres, public parks, reading rooms and libraries, etc. which tend to raise the efficiency of workers indirectly. Such non-monetary benefits increase the real income and standard of living of the workers and masses. Public expenditure of both transfer and exhaustive types helps in the redistribution of income. On the other hand, if such benefits reduce the desire to work and save, they will tend to reduce the incomes of the beneficiaries. Consequently, the inequalities are not reduced. To conclude with Dalton, "That system of public expenditure is best which has the strongest tendency to reduce the inequalities of incomes."

4. Effects of Public Expenditure on Economic Stability

Increase in public expenditure tends to raise national income, employment, output, and prices. An increase in public expenditure during deflation increases the aggregate demand for goods and services and leads to a large increase in income via the multiplier process. It has the effect of raising disposable income, thereby increasing consumption and investment expenditures of the people. The public expenditure includes expenditure on such public works as roads, canals, dams, parks, schools, hospitals and other buildings, etc. and on such relief measures as unemployment insurance, pensions, etc. Expenditure on public works creates demand for the products of private construction industries and helps in reviving them, while expenditure on relief measures stimulates the demand for consumer goods industries. But the effectiveness of public expenditure primarily depends upn the public works programme, its importance in the economic system, the volume and nature of public works and their planning and timing.

5. Effects of Public Expenditure on Economic Development

The effects of public expenditure on economic development lie in increasing the growth rate of the economy, providing more employment opportunities, raising incomes and standard of living, reducing inequalities of income and wealth, encouraging private initiative and enterprise, and bringing about regional balance in the economy.

1. Rise in Growth Rate of the Economy. Public expenditure on the establishment of heavy and basic goods industries in the initial periods increases the growth rate of the economy. But investment in the capital goods sector may increase production in the long run. Therefore, public expenditure should also be directed towards meeting the immediate needs of the economy, so as to raise agricultural and industrial production, and to increase the production of essential consumer goods.

2. Increase in Employment, Income and Production. Public expenditure on economic and social overheads provides larger employment opportunities, raises incomes and, above all, the productive capacity of the economy.

3. Increase in Revenue and Profit. To increase the production of certain essential commodities, to end private monopoly in various spheres, and to control the "commanding heights" of the economy, the state starts public enterprises. These bring revenue to the government and profits.

4. Reduction in Inequalities. Public expenditure tends to lessen inequalities of income and wealth by raising the earning capacity of the people. This is done by providing educational facilities and through skill formation.

5. Help to Private Enteprise. Public expenditure helps in encouraging private enterprise by establishing state-owned financial and banking institutions to provide cheap credit.

6. Regional Balance. Public expenditure helps in bringing about regional balance in the economy by diversifying industries in backward and less developed areas of the country. Thus public expenditure is one of the important instruments for economic development.

3. GROWTH OF PUBLIC EXPENDITURE

There has been a phenomenal increase in public (centre, state and civic bodies) expenditure over the years. The following reasons are given for this.

1. *Expansion of State Activities.* Adolph Wagner, a German economist, writing in 1883 propounded the *Law of Ever-increasing State Activity*. According to Wagner, public expenditure increases in response to the law of increasing expansion of public activities. He maintained that there is a persistent tendency both toward an intensive and expensive increase of state functions and activities. New duties are being continuously undertaken and old ones are being performed on a large scale. As a result, public expenditure is increasing steadily.

2. *Internal Security.* Wagner also referred to the maintenance of internal security as an important factor for the increase in government expenditure. Enforcement of law and order for maintaining peace and security has led to the expansion of legal and administrative systems and police force. These have led to the increase in public expenditure.

3. *Defence.* Every country pays greater attention to its defence preparedness against foreign attacks. As a result, public expenditure on equipping its armed forces with the latest armaments has increased. As Adam Smith said long ago, "Defence is better than opulence." So public expenditure on defence is essential.

4. *Welfare Activities.* Wagner wrote about the increase is public expenditure due to the expansion of cultural and welfare activities of the state. Modern states are welfare states which provide free education, medical facilities, social security measures, maintain historical monuments, museums and public libraries, and encourage cultural, sports and health programmes. Consequently, public expenditure has tended to increase.

5. *Population Increase.* The increase in population on account of better health and medical facilities leading to reduction in death rates has resulted in increasing public expenditure on the people. The state has to spend more on roads, railways, schools, colleges, hospitals, houses, etc.

6. *Urbanisation.* With the growth of population, there is migration of population from rural to urban areas in search of employment. Existing cities expand and new cities come up. These require huge public expenditure in providing civic amenities like water, street lighting, sewerage, roads, transport, schools, parks, zoos, houses, etc. Simultaneously, the expenditure on civil administration also increases.

7. *Price Rise.* In modern times, prices have a tendency to rise continuously with the increase in the growth rate of the economy. As a result, the government expenditure on goods and services increases. The rise in the cost of living further increases government expenditure by way of higher salaries and enhanced D.A. to its employees in various civil and military departments.

8. *Economic Development.* Modern governments are engaged in the development of their economies. They spend large sums on infrastructural facilities, on research and development in various fields, on the development of agriculture and industry, on the development of public sector, etc. This has led to the increase in public expenditure.

9. *Public Debt.* The state borrows both internally and externally to meet its ever increasing public expenditure. This further raises public expenditure in the form of repayment of loans and interest charges.

10. *Burden of Democracy.* Modern governments are democratic in nature. Countries are run on a multi-party system with elections after four or five years. Often governments fail due to lack of majority in the parliament. This necessitates frequent elections. This tends to increase public expenditure. Further, there are "pressure groups" and "interest groups" within the parliament which want allocation of government funds for providing public services in their constituencies. Moreover, according to the World Bank, wide spread corruption in democratic countries has increased public expenditure manifold.

4. DEVELOPMENT EXPENDITURE OF DEVELOPING ECONOMIES

Development expenditure refers to public (government) expenditure for developing the economy. The development expenditure of modern developing economies consists of expenditure on :

(1) *Social services* like education, health, social security and others;

(2) *Economic services* like agriculture, industries, minerals, fuel and power, transport and communications and others; and

(3) *Community services* such as roads and bridges, sanitation and others.

On the other hand, the non-development expenditure of modern developing economies includes : (1) expenditure on *general services* such as defence, justice, police and general administration; (2) expenditure on unallocable and other purposes such as interest on public debt.

But in these countries, these two types of expenditure cannot be placed in water-tight compartments. This is because without expenditure on defence, police, etc., it is not possible to keep up the pace of development if there is aggression from outside and unrest from within the country. Unless there is peace on the boarders and protection of life and property within the country, economic development is not possible. Similarly, interest on public debt may also be regarded as development expenditure. This is because governments of developing countries borrow both internally and externally mainly for development purposes.

Role of Development Expenditure in a Developing Economy

The role of development expenditure in a country lies in increasing the growth rate of the economy, providing more employment opportunities, raising incomes and standard of living, reducing inequalities of income and wealth, encouraging private initiative and enterprise, and bringing about regional balance in the economy.

1. Heavy and Basic Goods Industries. Development expenditure on the establishment of heavy and basic goods industries in the initial period increases the growth rate of the economy. But investment in the capital goods sector increases production in the long run.

2. Consumer Goods and Raw Materials. To meet the immediate needs of the economy, development expenditure should be directed towards increasing agricultural productivity to meet the growing demand for goods and raw materials, and increasing the supply of consumer goods by encouraging the establishment and expansion of the small industries sector which may also provide sufficient employment opportunities. The growth rate of the economy can be increased only when public expenditure fulfils the short-term and long-term objectives of the development plan. Moreover, to prevent inflationary tendencies within the economy, the public expenditure should secure a balance between demand and supply of goods.

3. Economic Overheads. Economic overheads are such public works as roads, railways, canals, power projects, etc. When the government spends on such projects, it provides employment to millions of unemployed people in underdeveloped countries. The provision for such services helps to increase production, trade and commerce. As a result, employment and incomes increase.

4. Social Overheads. Development expenditure on social overheads like education, public health, cheap housing, etc., makes the people healthier and efficient. It is the state which can create the "critical skills" needed for rapid development by investing in human capital.

5. Allocation of Resources. Development expenditure helps in improving the allocation of resources towards desired channels. In order to remove scarcities of food products, the state opens fair price shops and may even subsidise food for the working classes to maintain their health and efficiency. It may fix minimum prices for foodgrains, and through state trading and creation of buffer stocks encourage farmers to produce more.

6. Public Enterprises. To increase the production of certain essential commodities to end private monopoly in various spheres of production, and to supplement private enterprise, the state may start public enterprises. The development expenditure may, therefore, be directed to provide public utility services, to develop and conserve natural resources, to establish basic and key industries like heavy electricals, chemicals, fertilisers, machine tools, defence production, etc., to undertake state trading, etc.

7. To Stimulate Private Enterprise. Development expenditure helps in stimulating private enterprise through the establishment of state-owned financial and banking institutions to provide cheap credit to farmers, small and large industries, traders, etc. Development expenditure also encourages the agricultural and industrial sectors of the economy by means of grants, subsidies, tax exemptions, etc. Moreover, when the state spends on the creation of economic and social overheads like power, transport, education, etc., they pave the way for the establishment and expansion of the private sector. The creation of the infrastructure leads to external economies that are reaped by the private sector.

8. To Remove Inequalities. Developing countries are characterised by extreme inequalities of income and wealth. Development expenditure tends to lessen them. Expenditure on education, public health and medical facilities helps in human capital formation. As a result, the earning power of the working population is enhanced. As economic development proceeds rapidly through rising public expenditure, the barriers to upward mobility are removed. Occupations expand and spread, providing more jobs to the people. With the acquisition of skills, the level of wages tends to rise within the economy. Moreover, industrialisation increases the share of wages and decreases the share of profits in national income in the long run, and the gap between higher and lower incomes is narrowed.

9. To Remove Regional Imbalance. Development expenditure helps to remove regional imbalance in the economy. If things were left to market forces, commerce, banking, industries and almost all the main activities would be localised in a few selected regions, and the rest of the economy may be in a state of perpetual backwardness, as was the case under the British rule in India. It is through development expenditure that less developed areas and backward regions can be developed by starting certain projects like building a dam, digging a canal, starting new industries, etc. Such projects will not only promote but also secure larger employment opportunities, thereby increasing per capita output and income of such areas in developing countries.

EXERCISES

1. Explain the reasons for the increase in public expenditure in recent years.
2. Discuss the various canons of public expenditure.
3. Discuss the effects of public expenditure on production and distribution.

Chapter 90

Public Debt

1. MEANING OF PUBLIC DEBT

Public debt is one of the means to finance government revenue. When the government expenditure exceeds its receipts, it borrows from the public. Thus borrowing or taking loans from the public is called public debt. **Findlay Shirras** defines it thus: "National Debt is a debt which a state owes to its own subjects or to the nationals of other countries." Public debt as a source of government revenue is different from other sources of public revenue such as taxes, fees, etc. In the case of public debt, the government has to pay interest and repay the principal to the public. But nothing is required to be paid by the government in the case of other sources of revenue.

2. DIFFERENCE BETWEEN PUBLIC DEBT AND PRIVATE DEBT

There are some similarities and dissimilarities between internal public debt and private debt.

Similarities

1. The government and the private borrowers are on the same footing and so are the holders of government bonds and private lenders.
2. The government borrows for consumption and/or investment purpose. So does the private borrower.
3. The government has to repay the principal and pay interest to the lender like a private borrower.

Dissimilarities

The following are the points of dissimilarities between public debt and private debt.

1. Compulsion. The government can compel the people to lend money to it in case of war, economic crises or any other emergency. Defiance may invite legal action. But this is not possible in the case of private debt where the borrower cannot force the lender to pay him debt.

2. Repudiation. The government can repudiate (cancel) the repayment of public debt under exceptional circumstances. But a private borrower cannot refuse to pay back the debt without inviting legal action. This is, however, possible only if there is a legal contract between the borrower and lender. Otherwise, the borrower can refuse to repay the debt.

3. *Durability.* The government can borrow from the public for longer periods because it is a permanent institution and people have faith in it. But a private person can borrow for shorter periods due to the risks involved on the part of the lender.

4. *Interest Rate.* The government can borrows at a lower interest rate because of its high credit-worthiness and no risk. This is not so in the case of a private borrower who has to pay a higher interest rate because risk is involved for the lender.

5. *Reduction in Interest Rate.* The government can unilaterally reduce the interest rate on public loans in case of a financial crises. But a private borrower cannot do so as he has entered into a legal contract with the lender to repay the loan at a fixed rate of interest.

6. *Mode of Repayment.* The repayment of public debt is done by taxing the people. But in the case of private debt, the borrower may repay out of his savings, or accumulated assets or by borrowing from others.

7. *Sources.* The government can borrow both from foreign governments, and international institutions and internally. But a private person can borrow only from within the country. However, private corporations are also able to borrow from external sources now-a-days.

8. *Productive.* The government borrows only for productive purposes. On the other hand, the private debt is for both productive and unproductive purposes. A person may borrow for the marriage of his daughter which is an unproductive loan. But when he borrows for his business, it is a productive loan. Note that public debt taken for war is productive because as put by Adam Smith, "Defence is better than opulence." If the country is defeated in war what is the use of being a rich nation.

9. *Welfare.* The government borrows to spend an development schemes and projects in order to promote welfare of the people. But the private debt is for personal motives or to maximise profit.

10. *Effects on the Economy.* Public borrowing does not adversely affect consumption and investment. But it has an expansionary effect on the economy when the government spends the borrowed money on public works. This is likely to lead to inflationary conditions in the economy with their consequent adverse effects. But there is no adverse effect of private borrowings on the economy. Rather, they help in increasing production, employment and income if used for productive purposes.

3. PUBLIC LOANS VS TAXES

Taxes and public loans are the two main sources of revenue of a government. But they differ from each other in the following ways.

1. Taxes are a compulsory payment whether they are direct or indirect.Direct taxes on income, wealth, etc. are paid by those persons who come within the lower limits of such taxes. Indirect taxes are paid by all persons who consume the commodities on which such taxes are levied. But public loans are voluntary and not compulsory except when they are raised during emergencies like war.

2. Taxes cannot be raised beyond the optimum taxable capacity of the people. There is no such limit for public loans.

3. Taxes are charged on the current income of tax payers but people buy government bonds out of their present and past savings.

4. Taxes reduce the current purchasing power of the tax payers while loans reduce the future purchasing power of the lenders.

5. Taxes are a once-for-all payments. they are not to be paid back by the government. But loans are repayable with interest by the government. The government imposes and/or raises taxes at the time of repayment of a loan. Thus public loans are a burden on future generations.

6. The burden of taxes is spread over a short period. But the burden of a public loan is spread over a long period because interest is to be paid every year and the principal after the duration of the loan.

7. Taxes reduce the savings power of the people while loans induce them to save more to earn interest.

4. TYPES OF PUBLIC DEBT

Public debt is of various kinds which are explained as under.

1. Voluntary Debt and Compulsory Debt. Voluntary debt is that debt which is taken by the government without any force or coercion. People lend to the government voluntarily. In fact, all public loans are voluntary. However, sometimes the government compels the people to buy government bonds in case of a war or national emergency. According to **Dalton**, "A compulsory or forced loan is a rarity in modern public finance since it combines the disadvantages, while lacking the advantage of both a tax and voluntary loan."

2. Funded Debt and Unfunded Debt. Funded debt is a long term debt for a definite period. The interest rate to be paid, with terms and conditions of repayment are clearly stated in the debt instrument (certificate). In order to repay the debt, a debt fund is created in which some money is deposited every year by the government. The debt is repaid out of this fund on maturity. According to **Findlay Shirras**," Funded debt is a debt which is repayable at a distant date and for the payment of interest on which regular provision is made." On the other hand, unfunded debt is for a short period of less than a year. The government does not create any separate fund to repay the debt. Such a debt is repaid out of its current receipts, often by floating additional bonds in the market. Thus it is also called floating debt.

3. Productive Debt and Unproductive Debt. According to **Findlay Shirras**, "Productive or reproductive loans are debts which are fully covered by assets of equal or greater value and the source of the interest is the income from the ownership of these, such as railways and irrigation works." Thus a debt is productive when its amount is spent to finance a project which in the long run brings revenue to the government out of which interest is paid on the debt. That is why it is called productive debt. Unproductive debt does not increase the productive capacity of the economy because it is not backed by any existing assets. Loans taken by the government for covering the budget deficit or to help the war or earthquake or famine or flood victims, etc. are unproductive debts. They do not bring any revenue to the government and are, therefore, called dead weight debts. According to **Findlay Shirras**," Dead weight or unproductive debts are those which have no existing assets."

4. Redeemable Debt and Irredeemable Debt. Redeemable debt is that which is repayable by the government after a fixed period of time. The interest on this loan is paid by the government regularly half-yearly or annually. When the debt matures, the government pays back the principal amount to the lenders. For the repayment of the principal, either the government creates a fund in which a fixed amount is deposited every year or it raises the amount through taxation. Irredeemable debt is that whose principal amount is not refunded by the government. However interest is paid regularly on such a debt for the period of its duration. Debt incurred during a war may be non-redeemable by the government.

5. Internal Debt and External Debt. Internal debt is that debt which is raised by the government from individuals, institutions, etc. within the country. According to **Dalton**, "A loan is internal if subscribed by persons or institutions within the area controlled by the public authority which raises the loan." Internal sources are purchase of public bonds by non-banking financial institutions like insurance companies, investment trusts, mutual funds, etc. individual corporations, commercial banks and central bank. In the case of external debt, the government borrows from persons or institutions outside the country. Such loans are subscribed by foreign governments, private foreign institutions, foreign individuals, and international organizations like IDA, IMF, IBRD, IFC, ADB, etc.

5. NEED FOR PUBLIC DEBT[1]

In recent times, governments have been borrowing huge sums both internally and externally for the following seasons.

1. Deficit Budget. The government borrows when there is budget deficit, that is, its expenditure is greater than its revenue. The deficit can be met by raising the tax rates and levying new taxes. But tax collection takes

1. This also relates to the reasons for increase in public debt and its importance.

long time. But by giving a particular date for the subscription of a loan, the government can meet its requirement immediately. That is why modern governments prefer public debt to other sources of revenue.

2. *War.* The government borrows from the public when it is involved in a war. During a war the government's expenditure increases manifold on armaments and forces. This can be met by raising public loans on a large scale rather than through taxation.

3. *Natural Calamities.* Natural calamities like earthquakes, floods, famines, etc. tend to increase government expenditure in order to provide relief to the victims. This necessitates large public borrowings by the government.

4. *Economic Development.* Both developed and developing countries borrow for their economic development. Developing countries do not have sufficient resources to finance their development plans because they are poor. They, therefore, borrow not only from within the country but also from foreign sources for the development of agriculture, industry, power, transport and communications, etc. Developed countries also borrow to modernize their infrastructure facilities like roads, railways, power, etc.

5. *Public Enterprises and Utilities.* Every country whether a socialist or capitalist or mixed economy runs certain public enterprises and utilities like railways, post and telegraphs, power works, etc. which require large funds. The government can meet them only through public borrowing rather than by taxation.

6. *Economic Stability.* Government borrows to stabilise the economy. To control inflationary conditions, the government borrows to take away excess money supply from the public. Since public borrowing is voluntary, this is a better method than raising taxes because loans from the public do not increase the costs of production. Public borrowing also helps to lift the economy from a depression. During a depression idle funds are lying with the banks which the government borrows in order to spend on public works programme.

6. SOURCES OF PUBLIC BORROWINGS

There are two major sources of public borrowings internal and external. According to Dalton, "A loan is internal if subscribed by persons or institutions within the area controlled by the public authority which raises the loan." Thus the government may borrow internally from individuals, banks and non-banking financial institutions like insurance companies, investment trusts, mutual funds, etc., individual corporations, commercial banks and central bank.

On the other hand, external borrowings, are generally voluntary. The government borrows from persons or institutions outside the country. Such loans are subscribed by foreign governments, private foreign institutions, foreign individuals, and international organizations like IDA, IMF, IBRD, IFC, ADB, etc.

These sources of public borrowing are explained in detail as under :

INTERNAL SOURCES

The following are the sources of internal borrowing by the government :

(1) Borrowing from Individuals. The government borrows from individuals by selling bonds, national saving certificates, etc. When an individual purchases government bonds, he makes some adjustment in his consumption pattern or in the use of his accumulated savings. When government bonds are sold to individuals, there is little direct effect in curtailing either consumption or business investment. The government bonds are bought largely from funds that would have been kept to buy other securities and partly from idle cash balances.

(2) Borrowing from Non-Banking Financial Institutions. Another sources of government borrowing is borrowing from non-banking financial institutions, investment trusts, mutual savings banks, etc. purchase government bonds in order to reduce their idle cash balances. These institutions prefer to invest their funds in government bonds because these bonds are free from credit-risk and also due to their high negotiability and liquidity.

(3) Borrowing from Commercial Banks. Government also borrows from commercial banks when the latter buy government bonds. Unlike individuals and non-banking financial institutions that purchase government bonds out of their own cash funds, commercial banks do so by creating additional purchasing power. Commercial banks can make additional loans upto an amount determined by the credit multiplier which is

determined by their excess cash reserves and the required reserve ratio.

(4) Borrowing from Central Bank. The central bank of the country subscribes to government loans by supporting these loans in the money and capital markets. By purchasing government bonds, the central bank credits the account of the government. The government pays to its creditors by drawing cheques on its account maintained with the central bank. Those who receive cheques from the government deposit these cheques with their banks. As a result, these banks have large cash reserves which are used for additional loans and advances.

External Sources

Externally, the government borrows in the form of foreign capital which can enter a country as private capital and / or public capital. Private foreign capital may take the form of direct and indirect investments in the borrowing country.

Direct investments may take many forms: The formation in the borrowing country of a subsidiary of a company of the investing country; the formation of a concern in which a company of the investing country has a majority holding; the formation in the borrowing country of a company financed exclusively by the present concern situated in the investing country; setting up a corporation in the investing country for the specific purpose of operating in the other country; or the creation of fixed assets in the borrowing country by the nationals of the investing country. Such companies or concerns are known as transnational corporations (TNCs) or multinational corporations (MNCs).

Indirect investment better known as 'portfolio' or 'rentier' investment consists mainly of the holding of transferable securities (issued or guaranteed by the government of the borrowing country), shares or debentures of the companies of borrowing country by the nationals of some other country.

Public foreign capital may consist of : (a) 'Bilateral hard loans' i.e., giving of loans by the British Government in pounds sterling to the Indian Government; (b) Bilateral soft loans' i.e., sale of food grains and other farm products to India by the United States under PL 480*; and (c) 'Multilateral loans' by a number of countries. Under this category are also included loans made available by the various agencies of the United Nations like World Bank, IMF, IFC, IDA, ADB, UNDP, etc., and (d) intergovernmental grants.

7. EFFECTS OF PUBLIC DEBT

When the government borrows, it transfers money from one type of people to another. Money flows from the people to the government, and further to those on whom the government spends the borrowed money. These lead to expenditure effects of public debt. When the government pays the interest and repays the loan, money is again transferred from those who are taxed (by the government in order to pay the interest and principal) to those who hold government bonds. These lead to *revenue effects* of public debt. These transferences of money from one set of people to the other through public debt affect consumption, production, distribution and business activity on the whole, as explained below.

1. Effects of Public Debt on Consumption

When people buy government bonds out of their past idle savings, their present consumption remains unaffected because the current expenditure is not affected. If they buy bonds by reducing their present expenditure, their consumption is reduced. In case, people are forced to buy government bonds, their will reduce their consumption expenditure.

When the government levies new taxes and / or raises the tax rates to repay the debt, the consumption of the people and of bondholders is reduced.

If the government spends the borrowed funds on public works like roads, canals, power, etc., the incomes of the recipients of their benefits increase who tend to increase their consumption. Similarly, if public debt is used to increase production of goods, it will increase consumption if there were shortages of these

* Under the US agricultural Trade Development Assistance Act popularly known as Public Law 480, agricultural surpluses are sold for payment in local currency.

goods.

Income Effect. When the government starts paying interest to the bond holders, their income increases which leads to rise in consumption. This is the income effect of public debt. Again, when the entire principal amount of bonds is received, the bond holders raise their consumption expenditure.

Asset Effect. According to Pigou, lenders consider government bonds to be an addition to their wealth. They, therefore, feel themselves to be richer than before and spend more on consumption. This is called the asset effect of debt. If however, the market rate of interest rises, the value of bonds will fall.[2] The bond holders will feel that their wealth has been reduced. They will, therefore, reduce their consumption. This is called the negative asset effect of debt. These effects will be on future consumption.

2. Effects of Public Debt on Production

Public debt affects production in three ways : *first,* through public expenditure; *second,* through ability to work, save and invest; and *third,* diversion of resources. We discuss these as under.

(i) If the government spends the borrowed money on public works and other development projects, it increases the productive capacity of the economy and production. When the government levies more taxes and/or increases tax rates for servicing the debt, productivity is adversely affected. But it depends on the types of taxes. Taxes which fall heavily on business and companies adversely affect investment and production. So do indirect taxes which tend to raise the prices of consumer goods thereby adversely affecting workers.

Another adverse affect of public debt may be through the payment of interest to bond holders. The bond holders receive an income without any effort on their part. Thus a new rentier class comes up which enjoys a fixed income in the form of interest without any work. They will, therefore, have no incentive to work and not contribute to production.

(ii) Public debt affects production through the ability to work, save, and invest. If the borrowed money is spent by the government on productive works, the willingness and ability of the people to work and save more increase which raise their productive capacity. Again, if it is spent in such a way as to raise the incomes of the poor, it raises their efficiency and ability to work thereby increasing their productivity.

Other effects on production are the result of taxes which are levied to service the debt. If the loans are "productive" in the sense that the borrowed funds generate revenue out of which interest and principal are paid, then there are no adverse affects on the ability of the people to work and save, and hence on production. But if taxes are levied to service the debt, it adversely affects the ability to work and save. Heavy taxes on high profits and incomes of corporations and business people will adversely affect incentives to work and invest. As a result, production will suffer. Similarly, taxes on low income groups will reduce both their willingness and ability to work. Consequently, production will be adversely affected. But public debt does not always adversely affect production for the following reasons. First, government bonds are safe which encourage low income groups to save and invest in them. Income from them will induce them to buy durable consumer goods which will their further production. Second,many businessmen and companies invest in government bonds for the purpose of getting regular interest which they utilise for further production. Third, on the maturity of loans, they invest their funds for further production.

(iii) Public debt also affects production through the diversion of resources from their present uses to new more useful uses. When the government spends the borrowed money to encourage agriculture and industry, it increases production via diversion of resources. Similarly, if it is spent on public utilities like railways, power, irrigation, post and telegraph, etc., it again leads to diversion of resources to more useful uses which tend to increase the productive capacity of the economy. But if the government spends the borrowed money on unproductive schemes such as war, there is the diversion of resources from their present productive to unproductive uses.

We may conclude that if the government spends public loans on development projects, productivity increases. If they are used in raising the incomes of the poor, they tend to raise their ability to work and hence

2. Bonds carry a fixed rate of interest. Their value is inversely related to the market rate of interest. When the market rate of interest rises, the price of bonds falls, and vice versa.

productivity. But if taxation is levied to repay the debt, production may be adversely affected.

3. Effects of Public Debt on Distribution

Public debt leads to the transference of money from one set of people to the other. Mostly the rich people buy government bonds. But the burden of taxes for servicing the debt falls on the people, the majority of whom are not bond holders. Thus income distribution is likely to be unequal in the country. If public debt is subscribed by small savers, it tends to reduce income inequalities. But this is not a possibility because small investors are always very small in number.

If the bond holders are the only tax payers and the amount of interest •received and the amount of tax paid are the same, there will not be any affect on income distribution. But this never happens. In reality, there are persons other than the bond holders who also pay direct and indirect taxes. According to Dalton, it is the common man who bears the real burden of the tax because he pays tax when he buys goods and services. This leads to the widening of income inequalities. So far as direct taxes are concerned, persons who do not hold bonds are left with a small disposable income. But the bond holders pay less taxes than the amount of interest received. Often government bonds are tax- free. Under the circumstances, income inequalities •increase even in the case of tax payers.

Distribution of income also depends upon the manner in which borrowed money is spent by the government. If it is spent on benefiting the lower income groups in the form of social security, public works, development schemes, etc. public debt reduces income inequalities.

4. Effects of Public Debt on Prices or Economic Activity

According to Prof. Lerner, one of the most important objectives of public debt is to affect economic activity in the country. The government affects economic activity through the supply of money. When the government borrows, money flows from the people to the government. It reduces the quantity of money with the people and their purchasing power is reduced. This has a deflationary effect on the economy. Thus public debt acts as an antinflationary device.

On the other hand, if the borrowed money is spent on public works, it leads to greater economic activity in terms of high employment, income, production and price level. In particular, this happens when the government borrows from banks. Banks create more credit on the basis of government bonds. This increases the purchasing power of the people which leads to increase in economic activity.

5. Effects of Public Debt on Private Sector

When the government spends the borrowed money in buying goods and services from the private sector, the demand for them increases and the private sector expends. If the government raises the salaries of its staff, it increases the demand for goods and services of the private sector which again leads to the expansion of the private sector. Further, if the government spends the borrowed funds in providing cheap power and other infractructural facilities to the private sector industries, it would reduce their cost of production and lead to their expansion.

8. BURDEN OF PUBLIC DEBT

Public debt is required to be paid back along with interest from whom the government borrows. This is done by levying taxes on the people. This involves hardships on the tax payers which is the burden of public debt. The burden of debt, both internal and external, may be direct money burden, indirect money burden, direct real burden and indirect real burden. We discuss them as under.

Burden of Internal Debt

When the government raises a loan from within the country, it is internal debt. The internal debt imposes burdens on the society in the following ways.

1. Direct Money Burden. Direct money burden is the amount of tax which the people have to pay to the government for the repayment of principal and interest. If the tax payers and bond holders are the same persons, there is no direct money burden. There is only transfer of money within the community. If the tax payers and bond holders are different persons, there will be changes in the distribution of income between different groups of people within the country. If lower income groups contribute more towards taxes to be paid to rich bond holders, the money burden of debt is heavier on the former. As a result, there is redistribution of income in favour of the rich bond holders.

(2) Direct Real Burden. The direct real burden is in the form of reduction in economic welfare and the strains and stresses undergone by the tax payers. If the tax payers are the bond holders and each tax payer contributes exactly the amount equal to the interest received from the government, the direct real burden would consist of the strains and stresses in filling forms, making tax payments, etc. If the tax payers and bond holders are different persons, the real burden will depend upon the persons who pay taxes and who hold bonds. If bonds are held by the rich and the taxes are raised from the poor, the real burden of the tax is on the latter in the form of loss in their economic welfare. If the bond holders belong to the lower income group and taxes are levied on the rich to repay the debt, the real burden will be on the latter. But this is not possible for bonds are mostly held by the wealthier classes. The direct real burden of public debt is also felt in another way. The bond holders are comparatively old people, while the taxpayers are mostly young. Thus the real burden of debt falls on the young. This leads to the argument that the burden of debt passes from the active to inactive users. The younger person are engaged in active professions while older persons are inactive, depending upon their past savings and pensions. So money is transferred from the active to inactive users of wealth. The burden of public debt falls on young persons.

The direct real burden is also affected by the rise and fall in the price level. When prices rise, the value of money falls and the direct real burden of the debt also falls. People pay less in real terms in taxes. When prices fall, the value of money rises and people pay more in real terms in taxes. Thus the real burden of the debt increases.

Indirect Money Burden. The indirect money burden is felt through its effects on production. If the loans have been utilised for productive purposes, the indirect money burden will not be heavy. For a large portion of the debt will be repaid out of the monetary benefits flowing from the projects. If the government reduces its expenditure on public works in order to finance a part of the public debt, the indirect money burden will be more on the people who are affected by the reduction in public expenditure. But in the case of an unproductive debt such as to finance a war, its repayment after the war involves a heavy indirect money burden. This is because at the end of the war there is fall in production and mass unemployment.

Indirect Real Burden. The indirect real burden of a debt is also felt through its ultimate effects on production. When the government levies taxes to pay the interest and repay loans, it discourages the willingness of tax payers to work and save more. It will, therefore, adversely affect production in the country. The indirect real burden of the tax will be heavy.

Conclusion. It may be concluded that the direct money burden is not much but the indirect money burden and the direct real burden of public debt are heavier.

BURDEN OF EXTERNAL DEBT

The external debt is what a country borrows from foreign countries and institutions. It involves direct and indirect money burden and direct and indirect real burden on the people and its economy. We discuss them as under.

Direct Money Burden. The direct money burden of an external debt is the amount which a debtor country pays to the foreign creditor country in the form of interest and principal. The repayment of loan and payment of interest to the foreign country is made in foreign currency. This imposes a direct money burden on the borrower country.

Direct Real Burden. The direct real burden of an external debt is the loss of economic welfare of the people of the debtor country when they make payments to foreign creditors. In order to pay the interest and loan, the debtor country exports more to earn foreign exchange or pays the debt to the external creditor in the form of exports of goods and services. As a result, the people are deprived of these goods and services. This is the direct real burden of the external debt.

The direct real burden of an external debt will also depend upon the section of the community which is taxed. If indirect taxes are imposed on articles of mass consumption, the burden will be heavier on low income groups. If progressive taxes are imposed on the higher income groups, the direct real burden will be less than it would be on the low income groups.

Indirect Money Burden. If the external debt is utilised for productive purposes such as on building roads, channels, power projects, etc. and establishing industries, this will increase employment, income and production. Its monetary burden will not be heavy because the payment of the principal and interest will be more than compensated by the benefits flowing from productive projects. According to Prof. Domar, if the interest payments on external borrowings rise, the tax burden on the people will also increase which will lead to a reduction in the net income of the country. This imposes a heavy indirect money burden on the economy.

Indirect Real Burden. The imposition of more indirect taxes on commodities in order to pay interest and principal on external loans puts heavy burden on the people. This is because their capacity to work and save declines. This leads to a fall in production. If the interest on external debt consumes a large part of national income, the government is forced to reduce social and development expenditures. The burden of debt will be more. The indirect real burden is again very heavy if the external loans are used in unproductive channels like a war. For it will be a dead weight debt on the people.

Conclusion. Thus it is clear from the above discussion that the direct real burden and indirect real and money burden of an external debt are more than its direct money burden.

Debt Burden and Future Generations

Many economists argue that when the government incurs long-term debt, it burdens future generations with the cost of its present policies. Cost means the sacrifice undergone by the people. When the government finances development projects by public borrowing, the present generation escapes the cost. The burden of debt is shifted to the future generations which pay the principal and interest and also benefit from the projects. But this is not a correct view. The real burden is borne in the period in which the government expenditure is incurred. Therefore, when the government borrows, it diverts private savings to public use. The payment of interest on bonds is made through taxation. So there is no burden on the future generations.

Again, if the debt is incurred during a period of unemployment or recession, there is no burden either on the present generation which incurs the debt or on future generations. In fact, the present generation benefits from increase in output, employment and income. Further, the future generations will benefit from that portion of the nation's capital stock, they will inherit. This argument equally applies to public debt for economic development.

But the situation is different when the debt is incurred to finance a war. People who live during the war bear the heaviest burden by sacrificing consumption of goods. For the government produces war materials instead of civilian goods. The burden is on the present generation. If the nation is also starved of capital goods, there will indirect burden on the future generation. It will have to sacrifice consumption in order to save and invest more to produce capital goods. After the war (and this applies to peace time also) certain young persons (who were children and those unborn at the time of incurring the debt) will be taxed to pay interest and principal. This will be a burden on the future generations. At the same time, some taxpayers who inherit bonds from their fathers and grandfathers, do not bear any debt burden. For this is only transfer of money by the same person. But it is not possible that the amount of tax paid and interest received will exactly equal. If the former is more than the latter, the burden is there. In the opposite case, there is no burden.

But there is the burden of external debt on future generations. Future generations have to pay interest and principal to foreign creditors without receiving corresponding benefits in return. For the foreign bond holders will spend the sums received in their own countries. If the foreigners are to be paid in goods, the burden will be greater on future generations in the form of more sacrifices on the part of the debtor country. However, there is an exception if the borrowed funds were used for capital projects, such as roads, railways, bridges, industries, dams, etc., the burden on future generations can be less. The increase in output, employment and income may be large enough to cover most of interest and principal payments on the debt.

9. MANAGEMENT OF PUBLIC DEBT

MEANING

Debt management is often referred to the amount, composition and refunding of the national debt. But, in actuality, it is related to the composition (the types of securities sold) and the refunding of the debt held by the public within a country. So far as the amount of new securities sold by the government is concerned, it falls within the jurisdiction of fiscal policy. The amount of securities bought and sold by the central bank is a monetary policy decision. Thus debt management is defined as all actions of the government, including both the treasury and central bank, which affect the composition and retirement of the debt held by the public.

OBJECTIVES OF DEBT MANAGEMENT

The main objectives of debt management are the following

1. To minimise the interest cost of servicing the debt to the taxpayer.
2. To employ it contracyclically as a stabilization weapon to supplement monetary and fiscal policy.

TECHNIQUES OR METHODS OF DEBT MANAGEMENT

Many techniques have been suggested by economists to achieve the objectives of debt management. We discuss below a few practical and important techniques.

1. Lowering the Interest Cost. The most important objective of debt management is that the interest cost of the public debt to the government should be low so that the burden of servicing the debt should be the minimum to the taxpayers. The government repays the debt by raising revenues from taxation. The higher the cost of servicing the debt, the higher would be the level of taxation and the greater the burden on taxpayers. The government should so work out the pattern of interest rates that it conforms to the preference pattern of security holders. The lower the interest rates on government securities, the smaller will be the transference of resources from the taxpayers to bond holders.

Minimizing the interest cost means that during a recession, interest rates are low. The government should exchange its maturing securities with new long-term securities carrying low interest rates so that their interest cost is less in the future. On the other hand, when interest rates are high during a boom, the government should exchange its maturing securities with short-term securities which carry low interest rates so that it has not to pay high rates when the interest rates fall to normal levels.

In practice, most governments keep very low interest rates on short-term securities and gradually increase the interest rates as the maturity period of the debt lengthens. This method gives rise to wide spreads between the short-term and long-term interest rates. This induces bond holders to switch over from short-term securities thereby increasing the debt burden of the government and imposing a higher tax burden on the taxpayers.

2. Changing the Maturity Structure. One of the techniques of debt management is to change the maturity structure of the debt as a device for economic stabilisation. This is done by "swapping operations" by the central bank. During boom periods the central bank sells more long-term government securities in the open market and purchases a corresponding amount of short-term government securities with the same amount of money. This lengthens the average maturity structure of the existing public debt which tends to raise the interest rate. The rise in the long-term interest rate would curb private spending by reducing the availability of credit. The value of outstanding assets of financial institutions is also reduced with the increase in interest rate. Thus the reduction in the availability of credit and holding of more short-term securities will have a tendency to control a boom.

During a recession, the central bank sells short-term government securities and purchases long-term government securities. This tends to bring a sharp fall in the long-term interest rate and a mild fall in the short-term interest rate. Thus the fall in the interest rates would increase investment spending. Thus debt management requires the manipulation of the term structure of the debt to bring about economic stability.

3. *Advance Refunding.* Another method of lengthening the public debt is advance refunding. The central bank offers the holders of a particular long-term government security, which still has some years to mature, to exchange the securities for a new security with a longer maturity. The new security carries a little higher yield and the holders of the old security do not realise any capital loss or gain. This technique has the advantage over the other techniques described above in that the central bank is not required to resort to open market operations for managing the public debt.

4. *Coordination with Monetary-Fiscal Policies.* Debt management requires coordination with monetary and fiscal policies. The central bank, as the controller of monetary policy, should be ready to purchase or sell government securities in the open market in order to bring upward or downward pressure on interest rates for economic stabilisation and to minimise the interest cost of the debt to the government.

Similarly, the government should resort to fiscal policy so as to manage the public debt effectively. A budget surplus is used as a fiscal devise during a boom and a budget deficit during a recession.

Coordination between monetary and fiscal policies is essential on a regular basis because of the frequent debt refunding operations of the central bank. When government securities mature, it is the central bank which is required to refund them on behalf of the government. At the same time, the government has to follow a surplus budgetary policy to retire the public debt. But this policy is deflationary in nature and requires to be controlled by an appropriate antideflationary monetary policy. If the government adopts a deficit budgetary policy for debt retirement, it would be inflationary in nature which is again required to be controlled by an appropriate anti-inflationary monetary policy. Thus for an effective debt management, there should be a close coordination between monetary, fiscal and debt management policies.

10. REDEMPTION OF PUBLIC DEBT

Debt redemption means payment of interest and repayment of principal by the government. There are various methods of debt redemption which are discussed as under.

1. *Out of Revenues.* Generally, the government pays the debt out of its revenues through a surplus budget. It makes a provision in the budget as to the amount to be paid during the year.

2. *Sinking Fund.* Under this method, the government creates a fund for the repayment of debt, known as the sinking fund. The government deposits a fixed sum of money out of its revenues each year for the period of the loan. After the end of the period, the entire loan is paid back. The second type of sinking fund is in which the government deposits a small or large amount depending upon the availability of surplus revenues. Still another type of fund is related to a service. When the government borrows for providing a particular service to the people, such as a bridge, it creates a fund and at the same time levies a tax and collects in that fund. The debt is repaid out of this fund after the completion of the project. Now-a-days governments do not create such funds. Even if they create, they utilise it for other purposes whenever they are in need of funds.

3. *Serial Bond Redemption.* In this method, whenever a debt is floated, the date of maturity of certain bonds is fixed before hand on the basis of their serial numbers. When the time for maturity comes bonds bearing those serial numbers are paid back.

4. *Lottery Method.* According to this method, bonds which are to mature in a particular period are drawn on the basis of the lottery system. Only those bond holders whose bond numbers come out are paid back while the payments of others are deferred to the other lottery date. Such a method creates uncertainty among the bondholders.

5. *Debt Conversion.* In this method, the debt with high interest rate is converted into a new debt when the market rate of interest falls. The government borrows at low rate of interest and repays the past debt even before it matures. The lender is free to take his money back or get his loan converted into a fresh one.

6. *Capital Levy.* Capital levy is a "once for all" tax to redeem a public debt. It is levied on capital assets on a progressive scale just after a war or an emergency when the burden of the debt is very heavy. The following arguments are put forward in favour of a capital levy.

(1) Heavy debt incurred by the government during the war can be paid back quickly.

(2) The poor are not burdened at all.

(3) It is levied on producers, businessmen and speculators who have earned a lot during the war.

(4) The higher income groups are mostly bondholders. So they are not burdened by the capital levy. They receive back from the government from debt redemption almost the same amount which they pay as capital levy.

Prof. Hicks, Shirras and others have criticised capital levy on the following grounds.

1. According to Hicks, the initial effect of a levy is expected to be deflationary because of the disturbances to the business programmes and capital markets.
2. It is not easy to evaluate capital assets.
3. It is not possible that all bondholders may be rich and have capital assets.
4. It tends to adversely affect saving, investment and production.
5. Even though capital levy is said to be once-for-all, the government may repeat in future.
6. It is against the canon of equity because it spares those who do not have capital assets.

Prof. Hicks concludes: "In practice the levy imposed may not have the desired effect but rather the opposite This was certainly the experience of almost all the countries which attempted levies in the twenties."

7. *Debt Repudiation.* It means cancellation of the debt altogether. The government refuses to repay the debt. This method of debt redemption is not practicable because the government's reputation may be at stake. Its very existence may be in danger. But this method is generally followed in the case of external debt. Russia did so in 1917.

10. ROLE OF PUBLIC DEBT IN ECONOMIC DEVELOPMENT

Public debt plays an important role in the economic development of a country in the following ways.

1. Capital Formation

Borrowing from the public can be another important source of capital formation in underdeveloped countries. this device is better than taxation. Taxation means forced saving; borrowing is voluntary. The tax payer is never happy in paying a tax, for he does not expect to get his money back. A lender, on the other hand, gives his money on loan of his own accord to receive it back along with interest after a stipulated period. Unlike taxation, borrowing does not adversely affect incentives to save and invest. The lure of interest is always there to increase the incentives instead.

2. Anti-Inflationary

Public borrowing acts as an anti- inflationary measure by mobilizing surplus money in the hands of the people in a developing economy. A successful public borrowing programme can be a useful tool of economic development by diverting resources from unproductive channels, i.e., real estates, jewellery, gold, etc., to productive channels. Public borrowing is resorted to for specific development projects like power generation, irrigation works, roads, railways, etc. Thus it is a useful method of financing development projects.

3. Compulsory Savings

If sufficient funds are not forthcoming in the form of voluntary loans, the government may have to resort to compulsory borrowing for the mobilization of resources for capital formation. Compulsory public borrowing is, therefore, justified in those underdeveloped countries where taxation and voluntary borrowing fail to bring adequate funds for development to the exchequer. Certain sections of the society who waste a larger portion of their income in unproductive channels or derive special benefits from particular development projects may be forced to subscribe to government bonds. Nurkse justifies the use of compulsory borrowing. But it is not advisable for an underdeveloped country to rely on this method of forced savings except for specific development projects and for a short period. Ultimately governments will have to depend on voluntary borrowings. The government of India's voluntary borrowing programme has been a great success.

EXERCISES

1. Distinguish between (a) public debt and private debt (b) public loans and taxes
2. Distinguish between : (i) voluntary and compulsory debt; (ii) funded and unfunded debt; (iii) productive and unproductive debt; (iv) redeemable and irredeemable debt; (v) internal and external debt; (vi) sources of public borrowing.
3. Explain the main causes for the increase in public debt.
4. Discuss the effects of public debt on comsumption, production and distribution.
5. Explain the direct and indirect money and real burden of an internal debt. How it affects the future generation?
6. Discuss the burden of an external debt. How does it affect future generation?
7. What is debt management? Explain the various methods of debt management.
8. What is debt redemption? Explain the methods usually adopted by a government to redeem public debt.
9. Explain the role of public debt in the economic development of a country.

CHAPTER 91

Public Goods, Private Goods and Market Failure

1. PUBLIC GOODS

Public goods are those goods and services which are jointly and equally consumed by many people at the same time, and its consumption by one person does not alter its availability for another person. These goods may not be produced through the free market pricing mechanism because those persons who do not want to pay the price can not be prevented from the consumption of these goods and services. The examples of public goods and services may be public roads, dams, defence and education services, etc. According to **J. Sloman,** Public good refers to "a good or service which has the features of non-rivalry and non-excludability and as a result would not be provided by the free market."

Thus, public goods have the following characteristics.

(1) They are non-rivalrous i.e. no one has an exclusive right over the consumption of the good. The quantity that a person consumes does not affect the quantity that others can consume.

(2) They are non-excludable i.e., if one person consumes the good, it is not possible to prevent others from consuming it.

(3) These goods are of collective consumption.

(4) These goods may not be produced through the free-market pricing mechanism.

(5) They are indivisible.

(6) The consumption of a public good is always joint and equal. Thus public goods are produced and supplied by the society to meet its collective wants for increasing social welfare.

(7) Public goods create externalities or divergences between social and private benefits.

Prof. **R.A. Musgrave** has classified public goods into two categories : (1) Social wants, and (2) Merit wants.

1. Social Wants. According to Musgrave, "Social wants are those wants which are satisfied by services that must be consumed in equal amounts by all." The goods and services meant for satisfying these wants are neither excludable nor rivalrous. These wants may not be satisfied through the free market pricing mechanism. But they are provided by the government whether an individual pays for them or not. Examples are city parks, defence, judicial, education, and other services. The government provides them out of the general budget.

2. Merit Wants. Merit wants are those wants which are satisfied by the government on merit through the general budget. When the government feels that people are not consuming goods and services in sufficient quantities in the society, it provides them free or subsidises them. The government encourages and supports the use of such goods and services which are called **merit goods.** Thus merit goods are goods which the society, operating through the government, feels the individuals should be encouraged to consume. Such goods are housing, education, health care, etc. The government may also seek to protect individuals through laws prohibiting the use of harmful drugs like cocaine, heroin, etc. and preseribe laws for the installation and use of car seat belts. These involve interference in the free choices of consumers. They are called **non-merit** or **demerit goods** whose use and consumption should be discouraged.

Differences between Social Wants and Merit Wants

There are important differences between social wants and merit wants :

(1) The satisfaction of social wants provides benefit to all while the satisfaction of merit wants involves interference with consumer preferences.

(2) Social wants are subject to the conditions of non-rivalry and non-excludability, but merit wants may or may not be subject to these conditions.

(3) Merit wants may have a substantial element of social wants. The provision of merit wants will confer immediate benefits on those who are in immediate need of, say, free education and health care but the community as a whole also benefits because it becomes more healthier and educated.

1. Optimum Level of Production of Public Goods

Now of the questions are : how much public goods should the government produce and what constitutes optimum resource allocation in the case of public goods?

In the case of a public good, a certain quantity is consumed by everyone. Therefore, the demand for any quantity of that public good is the sum of the prices that each individual consumer is willing to pay for that quantity. In this way, the community's demand curve, for a public good is the vertical summation of the demand curves of the individual consumers which represents the sum of the marginal benefits received by all the consumers. Each demand curve implies the marginal benefit that the consumer gets from consuming every level of production. The optimum level of production of a public good is determined by equating the sum of the marginal benefits to the marginal cost of production.

In other words, the optimum quantity is that quantity for which the marginal cost of the last unit is equal to the sum of the prices that all consumers are willing to pay for that unit.

This is illustrated in Fig. 1. Suppose that there is a community of two persons. *D* is the demand curve of the community which is the vertical summation of two individual demand curves, D_1 and D_2 Suppose the first consumer is willing to pay Rs. 1,000 for 200 units of a public good, whereas the second consumer is willing to pay Rs. 2,000 for the same quantity. Thus the community is ready to pay Rs. 3,000 for 200 units which is shown by the community demand curve, *D*. Here, the optimum level of production of the public good under consideration is 200 units where the marginal cost curve MC intersects the community demand curve, *D*. In this way, the society's resources are optimally allocated when social marginal cost equals its marginal benefits.

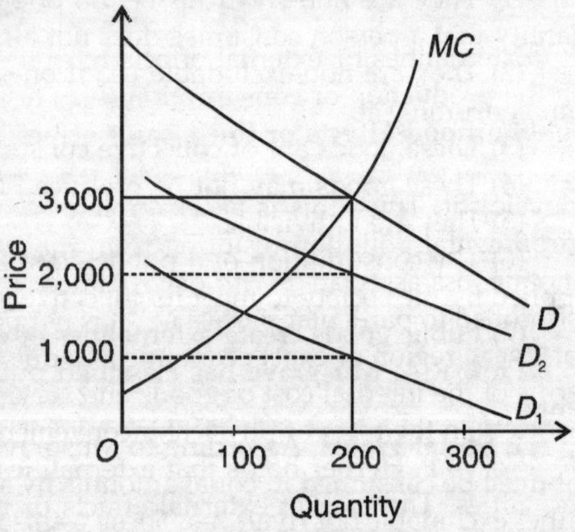

FIG. 1

2. PRIVATE GOODS

Private goods are those goods and services which satisfy individual wants and have the characteristics of rivalry and exclusiveness. These goods can be produced by the free market pricing mechanism. Private goods are rival in consumption i.e., their consumption by a person reduces the amount available to others. Moreover, all those who want to pay the market price for them will consume them and those who do not want to pay will be excluded from their use. In this way, private goods are subject to the *principle of exclusion.* These relate to food, clothing, shelter, transportation and communication, etc.

Private goods have the following characteristics :

1. Private goods are rivalrous in consumption.
2. These goods are subject to the exclusion principle.
3. These goods satisfy individual wants.
4. These can be produced through free market pricing mechanism.
5. Private goods are divisible in so far as their use is concerned.
6. Marginal cost of providing a private good to an extra consumer is always positive.

3. DIFFERENCE BETWEEN PUBLIC AND PRIVATE GOODS

There are some important differences between public goods and private goods.

1. Public goods satisfy social wants or merit wants while private goods satisfy individual wants.
2. Public goods are non-rival in consumption while private goods are rivalrous.
3. Public goods are nonexclusive whereas private goods permit exclusion.
4. Public goods can not be provided by the free market pricing mechanism while private goods are priced in the market.
5. The marginal cost of providing a private good to an extra consumer is positive while in the case of a public goods, it is zero.
6. The efficient level of production of a private good is achieved when the marginal benefit and the marginal cost are equal. But with a public good, we must ask how much each person values an additional unit of output and how to add them. Then we equate them to the marginal cost of production.

4. NOTE ON EXTERNALITIES

Externalities or external effects refer to the favourable and unfavourable effects which are associated with the production or consumption (use) of goods. Such economic effects are also called **spill-over effects, neighbourhood effects or third party effects.** These externalities may be either economic gain or economic loss to other parties or economic units. For example, the setting up of a factory in a backward region will help to develop it. Thus, this is an example of economic gain associated with externalities. On the other hand, environmental pollution resulting from the establishment of a paper mill in an area may be an example of economic loss associated with externalities. This economic gain or loss can not be priced in the market and apportioned to particular parties i.e., it is not possible to find out how much is the benefit of a factory set up in a backward region or exact economic loss due to air and water pollution of a paper mill. Market price is fixed interms of the internal cost of goods and services, whereas social cost of some goods and services is borne by the society in the form of physical inconvenience and diseases.

Prof. **B.P. Herber** holds that externalities are of two types : (i) market externalities, and (ii) non-market externalities. The market external effects or market externalities are those effects which can be valued in money and expressed in terms of price in the market as determined by the forces of demand and supply. On the other hand, non-market externalities are those which can not be expressed in terms of price in the market and can not be made part of the cost of production.

5. MARKET FAILURE AND ROLE OF GOVERNMENT

Market failure refers to the circumstances under which market fails to allocate resources efficiently. Market failure may occur due to externalities and public goods. They are explained as under :

1. Externalities

The presence of externalities in production and consumption lead to market failure. Externalities are market imperfections where the market offers no price for service or disservice. These externalities lead to malallocation of resources and cause consumption or production to fall short of an optimum level. They do not lead to maximum social welfare. Externalities, also lead to the divergence of social cost from private cost, and of social benefits from private benefits. When social and private costs and social and private benefits diverge, perfect competition will not achieve maximum social welfare. This is because under perfect competition private marginal cost (PMC) is equated to private marginal benefit (PMB) (i.e. the price of the product), i.e. PMC = PMB. We discuss below how external economic and diseconomies of consumption and production affect adversely the allocation of resources and lead to market failure.

External Economies of Production. These economies accrue to other firms in the industry with the expansion of a firm. Whenever external economies exist, social marginal benefit (SMB) will exceed private marginal benefit (PMB), SMB > PMB and private marginal cost (PMC) will exceed social marginal cost (SMC), PMC > SMC. So when under perfect competition, private marginal cost is equated to price which is also private marginal benefit, social marginal benefit will be higher than social marginal cost because of external economies of production. The firms will produce less than the socially optimum level of output. This is illustrated in Fig. 2 where PMC is the private marginal cost curve of firms. SMC is the social marginal cost curve. *D* is the demand curve which intersects the PMC curve at point *E* and determines the competitive price *OP* and output *OQ*. But the socially optimum output is OQ_1 and price is OP_1, as determined by the intersection of the SMC curve and the *D* curve at Point E_1. Thus the industry is producing Q_1Q less than the socially optimum output OQ_1. Since for every unit of output between Q_1 and Q, social marginal cost (SMC) is less than the competitive market price *OP*, its production involves a social gain. Thus there is market failure.

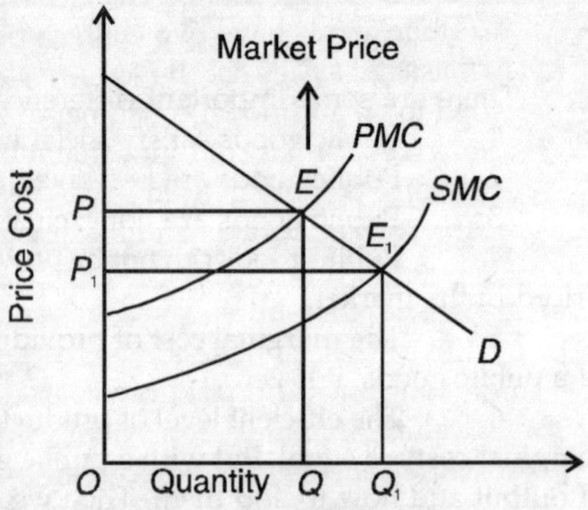

FIG. 2

External Diseconomies of Production. When there are external diseconomies of production, social marginal cost is higher than social marginal benefit. SMC > SMB. Firms will produce more than the socially optimal level of output. A factory situated in a residential area emits smoke which affects adversely health and household articles of the residents. In this case, the factory benefits at the expense of residents who have to incur extra expenses to keep themselves healthy and their households clean. These are social marginal costs because of harmful externalities which are higher than private marginal cost and also social marginal benefit.

This is illustrated in Fig. 3 where the SMC curve is above the PMC curve which intersects the *D* curve at point *E* and determines the competitive price *OP* and output *OQ*. But the socially optimum output is OQ_1 and price is OP_1, as determined by the intersection of SMC and *D* curves at point E_1. Thus the firms are producing Q_1Q more than the social optimal output OQ_1. In this case, for every unit between Q_1 and Q_2 social marginal cost (SMC) is more than the competitive market price *OP*. Thus its production involves a social loss. This is again market failure.

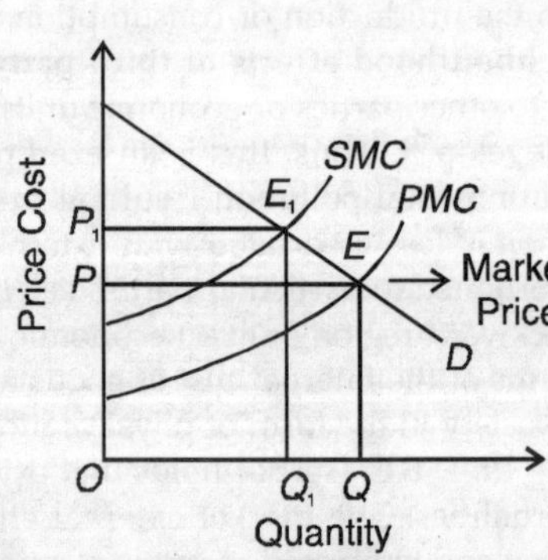

FIG. 3

Externalities in Consumption. They lead to non-attainment of maximum social welfare. In the case of external economies in consumption, the consumption of a good or service leads to increase in utility (or welfare or satisfaction) of other consumers. When an individual installs a TV set, the satisfaction of his neighbours increases because they can watch TV programmes free at his place. Here social benefit is larger and social cost is lower than private benefit and cost. But the TV owner is likely to use his TV set to a smaller extent than the interests of society require because of the inconvenience and nuisance caused by his neighbours to him.

External Diseconomies of Consumption. They arise when the consumption of a good or service by one consumer leads to reduced utility (or dissatisfaction or loss of welfare) of other consumers. Consumption diseconomies arise in the case of dress, fashions and articles of conspicuous consumption which reduce their utility to some consumers. Smokers cause disutility to non-smokers, and noise nuisance from stereo systems to neighbours are other examples. Such diseconomies of consumption prevent the attainment of maximum social welfare.

2. Public Goods

Another cause of market failure is the existence of public goods. A public goods is one whose consumption or use by one individual does not reduce the amount available for others. Examples are city parks, defence, police, ocean or lake fishing, etc.

Public goods have two characteristics : non-excludable and non-rivalrous. A good is *non-excludable* if it *can be consumed by any one.* It is *non-rivalrous* if *no one has an exclusive right over its consumption.* Its benefit can be provided to an additional consumer at zero marginal cost. Thus public goods being both non-excludable and non-rivalrous are not sold in a free market like private goods. They lead to market failure in the following ways.

The consumption of a public good is always *joint and equal.* The maximum social welfare condition for a public good is that its marginal social benefit should equal its marginal social cost (MSB = MSC). But the characteristics of a public good are such that the economy will not reach an optimum point in a perfectly competitive market. Public goods create externalities. The externality starts when the marginal cost of consuming or producing an additional unit of a public good is zero, but a price above zero is being charged. This violates social welfare maximisation criterion of equating marginal social cost and marginal social benefit. This is because the benefits of a public good must be provided at a zero marginal social cost.

Again, public goods are not subject to the "exclusion principle" which means that their benefits are available to every body, whether a person pays for them or not. But in the case of some public goods, exclusion is practised. Take the example of a bridge as the public good whose use is restricted to those who pay a toll tax. This does not lead to maximisation of social welfare because the toll tax restricts the services of the bridge to only those who pay the toll tax. For social welfare maximisation, its services should be available to every consumer at a zero price.

In the case of some public goods where exclusion cannot be practised, all payments for their services are purely voluntary. In such a situation, many users have the tendency to avoid paying for their services when they know their benefits can be obtained free. All such users are known as "free riders". Therefore, when such a public good is produced, much less than the optimum quantity would be available to its users. The use of TV signals by TV owners with their own "dish" antennas is an example of free riders because they do not pay anything for signals whereas the cable operators pay.

The market failure in the case of public goods is explained in Fig. 4. Suppose there are two individuals *A* and *B* and two goods *X* and *Y* with *X* being a public good in the economy. D_A and D_B are the demand curves of two individuals *A* and *B* respectively. MC_X is the marginal cost curve of the public good. The curve ΣD is the vertical summation of D_A and D_B curves. The curves MC_X and ΣD intersect at point *E* which determine *OP* price and *OQ* quantity of public good. The two consumers are charged the price $OP = OP_A + OP_B$. But each consumer is being charged a different price. This is a case of price discrimination because $OP_A > OP_B$. Hence there is market failure.

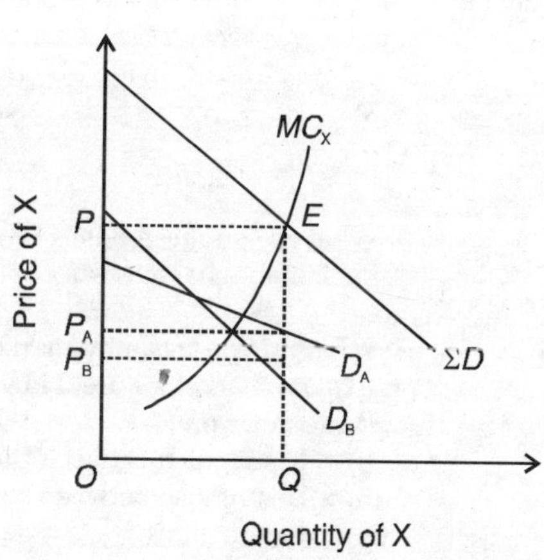

FIG. 4

MEASURES TO CORRECT MARKET FAILURE

To correct market failure, economists have suggested the following measures which may be adopted by the government.

1. Externalities

To achieve optimal allocation of resources in the face of externalities, Pigou suggested social control measures and the use of taxes and subsidies. The state can interfere in all cases of external diseconomies of production to remove the divergence between private and social costs and benefits. For instance, it can ask the factory owner to move out of the residential area by providing appropriate facilities to the smoke emitting factory. In the case of external diseconomies of consumption, the state can put an end to noise nuisance by banning the use of loud speakers except for special occasions during specific hours with prior permission.

Pigou further suggested that the state should encourage production of goods with positive externalities by the grant of subsidy on per unit of commodity to the producer. It can help consumers in maximising their satisfactions by tax concessions so that they consume more commodities. In the case of negative externalities, it should discourage their consumption and production by leving taxes. For instance, the state can levy a tax on every family in the area and pay the sum so collected to the smoke emitting factory to move away. Thus taxes and subsidies help to bridge the gap between private and social costs and benefits.

2. Internalisation

Another measure commonly suggested is *internalisation* or *unitisation* of externalities in production. For example, firms that are engaged in oil operations in the same field lead to inefficient over-drilling and over-pumping. When the government permits unitisation or merger of firms, oil is produced most efficiently without diseconomies of production.

3. Public Goods

Because public goods are non-excludable and non-rivalrous, they are not sold in a free market like private goods. Therefore, they cannot be provided by private firms. In this situation, they can be provided by some public authority. As the benefits of public goods are indivisible, the state should make people share the costs of public goods so that every one is made better off. One way to pay for a public good is to charge each person the same proportion of the maximum amount he or she would be prepared to pay rather than go without the good, while fixing that proportion so as to cover the total costs of production.

In the case of some public goods such as materials for defence, the government can either itself produce them or it can pay private firms to produce them.

So far as the *free rider problem* is concerned whereby such services as defence, police, etc. are provided free to every user, they can be provided by the government out of tax revenues.

EXERCISES

1. What are public goods? How do they differ from private goods?
2. Explain the characteristics of a public good. How would you explain the optimum level of a public good?
3. What do you mean by market failure? How market failure occurs?
4. Explain market failure. How market failure can be corrected by the government?
5. Write notes on :
   (i) Distinguish between public goods and private goods
   (ii) Distinguish between social wants and merit wants.
   (iii) Externalities

CHAPTER 92

Theories of Taxation

1. INTRODUCTION

Every tax is an additional compulsory burden on the taxpayer. Therefore, the problem of equity in taxation is very important in the study of public finance. The burden of tax should be divided fairly and appropriately. Taxation is not only an instrument of raising revenue for the government, but also a tool for administering social justice. Even a small burden of tax may prove too heavy to bear if it is not well distributed. So, the tax burden should be distributed equitably on all persons.

There are various theories of equity in taxation or of *just distribution of tax burden*. We discuss a few main theories here.

2. COST OF SERVICE THEORY

According to the cost of service theory, the cost incurred by the government in providing certain services to the people must collectively be met by the people who are the ultimate receivers of the services. This theory believes that tax is similar to price. So if a person does not utilise the services of the state, he should not be charged any tax. In the words of *Buehler*, "The taxes should be prices or rates paid for the services rendered to each person by governments according to the cost incurred."[1] Hence, the basis of taxation should be the cost of the different services rendered by the government to the taxpayers.

Its Criticisms

This theory has no place in the modern tax system because it has the following defects:

1. *Restrictions on Government Services*. The objective of the government is to provide welfare to the poor. If this theory is applied, the state will not undertake welfare activities e.g. free education, medical aid, etc. The relief to a cyclone hit area can not be provided because the people are unable to repay the cost in the form of taxes. The Government will also not be concerned with the problems of income distribution, cyclical fluctuations or social security.

2. *Measurement of Cost is Difficult*. It will be very difficult to compute cost per head of the various services provided by the state. Most of the government services, such as roads, parks, dams, defence, justice, etc. are for

---

1. A.G. Buehler, *Public Finance*, p. 377.

the people as a whole and not for any individual or a group of individuals. Moreover, the identification of proper beneficiaries of any service is also a problem.

3. *Incorrect Assumption.* This theory is against the accepted definition of the tax. A tax is imposed to meet the government expenditure, and not to meet the necessity of a particular individual or a group, as this theory assumes.

4. *Tax is not an Optional Payment.* Tax is not an optional payment but is an obligatory payment. It is to be given even by the person who does not make the slightest use of government services.

5. *False Theory.* This is a false theory because it believes in voluntary membership of the state, while state membership is compulsory.

6. *Basis of Taxation is Misleading.* Some of the state services have externalities that appear in the form of social benefits and costs. In such a case, if the state confines its attention to only the commercial costs as the private entrepreneurs do, it will be dangerous on the part of the state and will disrupt the working of the economy.

3. THE BENEFIT THEORY

This theory is a modified form of cost of service theory. According to this theory, the burden of taxation should fall on the people according to the benefit received by them from the state. In other words, the collective amount of taxes should not be more than the aggregate benefit secured by the tax payers. Whatever services the government confers on the people, they provide some benefit to them. So the people should share the burden of taxation in proportion to the benefits received by them. According to J. S. Mill, the relationship between the tax-payer and the state runs in *quid pro quo* terms. Adam Smith writes, "The subjects of every state ought to contribute towards the support of the government as nearly as possible in proportion to the revenue which they respectively enjoy under the protection of the state.". This makes taxation justified.

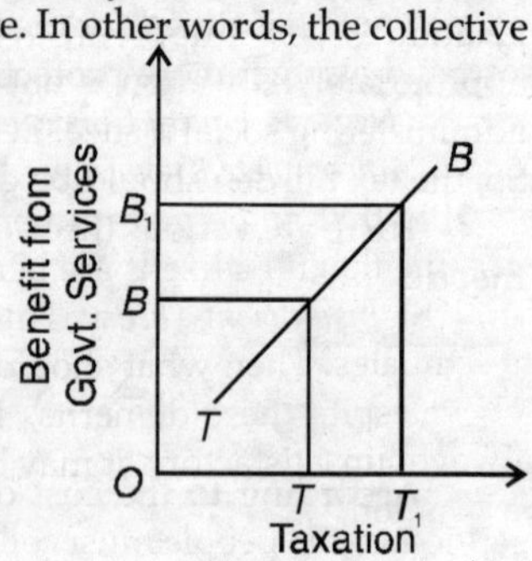

FIG. 1

This theory is illustrated in Fig. 1. In Fig. 1, TB is the tax-benefit line which shows that for OB aggregate benefit received from government services, OT tax has been levied by the government. When aggregate benefit increases from OB to OB_1, the tax also increases in the same proportion from OT to OT_1. It implies that tax should be imposed in proportion to the benefit received by a person from the expenditure made by the government.

ITS MERITS

The benefit theory has the following merits :

1. *Incentive.* This Theory may be used as an incentive to produce more and more by providing benefits to those who are the tax payers.

2. *Just Basis.* This theory is based on the assumption that the benefits received by the government services justify the imposition of taxes to pay for them.

3. *Helpful in Price Determination.* It may be helpful in determining the prices of certain government services such as, railways, airways, etc.

4. *Vast Applicability.* The benefit theory is highly applicable specially where the benefit received by individuals can be measured. Petrol tax, and motor tax on the users of roads, tax for fire protection and sewage services to finance local public works are its examples.

5. *Local Tax.* This theory can be used by the local governments in determining special taxes on certain local services such as electricity, roads, etc. The services rendered by the local bodies can be measured properly and taxed accordingly.

ITS DEMERITS

In spite of the above mentioned merits, this theory has also some drawbacks:

1. *Benefit is not Quantitative.* Benefit cannot be expressed in quantity, but in quality. It is a subjective thing and cannot be measured directly.

2. *Unrealistic Assumption.* The assumption of this theory that varied and complex activities of the government can and should be calculated and assessed against each person on the basis of the individual benefit derived, is highly unrealistic.

3. *Unrealistic Theory.* This is an unrealistic theory. It assumes a *quid pro quo* relation between the state and the tax-payers, while no such relation exists in modern times, governments have to undertake various administrative and social welfare activities also.

4. *Difficult in Application.* The government functions not for any particular individual, but for the whole society. So it is difficult to know how much benefit an individual is receiving and how much tax he should pay in return.

5. *Limitation in Government Services.* This theory cannot be applied to social services such as free education, medical aid, mid-day meals in schools, etc. The relief to a cyclone hit area cannot be provided because the people are unable to repay the benefit in the form of taxes.

6. *Taxes are not the only Source.* The government collects its funds not only from taxes but from other sources also, so prices can only partially be considered as taxation.

7. *Unjust Theory.* Since income is subject to the law of diminishing marginal utility, the equal amount of tax may not be justified for the same benefit received by the poor and the rich people. In fact, the poor people need and also get more protection from the state. It is not just that they should pay more tax than the rich.

8. *Neglects Equity Concept.* This theory does not recognise the objective of equity in taxation.

9. *Incomplete Knowledge.* Many people lack the knowledge of various government programmes. It is also possible that some government services are more beneficial to certain sections of the community. So to presume that all citizens are benefitted equally and so should be taxed equally is incorrect.

10. *Insufficient Theory.* This theory becomes silent when the revenue collected through taxes falls short of its estimates. Then what should the government do?

Despite these demerits, **Buehler** writes, "It must be concluded therefore, that the benefit principle, however unsatisfactory, it may be as a standard by which to apportion taxes, does have an important influence on taxation."

4. ABILITY TO PAY THEORY

The ability to pay principle of taxation is just, equitable and the most accepted theory of taxation. This theory proposes that those who possess income or wealth should contribute to the support of public functions according to their relative ability to pay. In brief, the burden of tax should be according to the ability of the tax-payers. Those who have means to pay should pay and those who have not, need not to pay. According to **Adam Smith,** "The subjects of every state ought to contribute towards the support of the government, as nearly as possible in proportion to their respective abilities." **William Petty** and **Adam Smith** actually combined the ability theory with the benefit theory. **J.S. Mill** was also among the main supporters of this theory.

MEASUREMENT OF ABILITY TO PAY

Now the problem is how to measure the ability to pay of a tax payer? There may be two approaches to this problem: (*i*) subjective approach, and (*ii*) objective approach.

1. Subjective Approach

This approach is based on the psychological state of a tax-payer. Payment of every tax involves a certain burden or sacrifice upon the taxpayer. Hence the essence of the subjective approach is what feelings come in the mind of the tax-payer or how much sacrifice has been undergone by him when he bears the burden of tax.

Since payment of every tax is a sacrifice of the tax payer, we discuss the measurement of ability to pay of a tax payer in terms of equity or welfare. The equity or equal sacrifice approach proposes that each tax payer should be made to undergo the same or equal amount of sacrifice irrespective of his income.

Its Assumptions.

The equity or equal sacrifice approach has the following assumptions.

1. There is no difficulty in identifying or correlating units of income with units of utility or satisfaction.
2. The utility curve for income has a downward slope, i.e., the marginal utility of income varies inversely with income.
3. The income utility function of everyone has exactly the same characteristics.

There are three interpretations of the equity approach or equal sacrifice which are given below.

1. Equal Absolute Sacrifice

This approach implies that the total loss of utility as a result of tax should be equal for all tax-payers. Since marginal utility of income falls as income rises, equal absolute sacrifice dictates that the rich should be taxed more heavily than the poor. But, how much more depends on the slope of the marginal utility curve. The steeper the marginal utility curve, the more progressive will be the tax.

In other words, the difference between the aggregate utility from income before tax and the utility of income after tax should be the same for every tax-payer. This approach received the greatest support at one time because of its apparent fairness.

2. Equal Proportional Sacrifice

Equal proportional sacrifice implies that the loss of utility as the result of a tax should be proportional to the total income of tax-payers. Here again the person with higher income will pay higher than a person having lower income. In other words, the direct real burden of the tax-payer would be proportionate to the economic welfare which he derives from his income.

Suppose that there are two tax payers, A and B. This approach may be expressed mathematically as :

$$\text{Burden of Tax} = \frac{\text{Sacrifice made by A}}{\text{Total Income of A}} = \frac{\text{Sacrifice made by B}}{\text{Total Income of B}}$$

Here, progressive taxation is possible because the marginal utility of income falls with the increase in the income of the people.

3. Equal Marginal Sacrifice or Least (Minimum) Aggregate Sacrifice

This approach implies that the burden of tax would be distributed among different tax payers in such a way that the marginal utility of income left after the payment of tax by an individual would be the same for all individual tax payers so that the aggregate sacrifice of all the people would be the least. This would create maximum welfare to all. In the words of **Prof. Pigou**, "The principle of least aggregate sacrifice is that which makes the marginal not the total sacrifice borne by all the members of the community equal."[1]

This principle is based on the Law of Diminishing Marginal Utility. Since the marginal utility of higher income is low as compare to that of low income, the person with higher income will be expected to bear the most burden. In this principle all income above the minimum necessary will have to be taxed away. **Edgeworth, Carver** and **Pigou** have emphasised particularly on the welfare of the community.

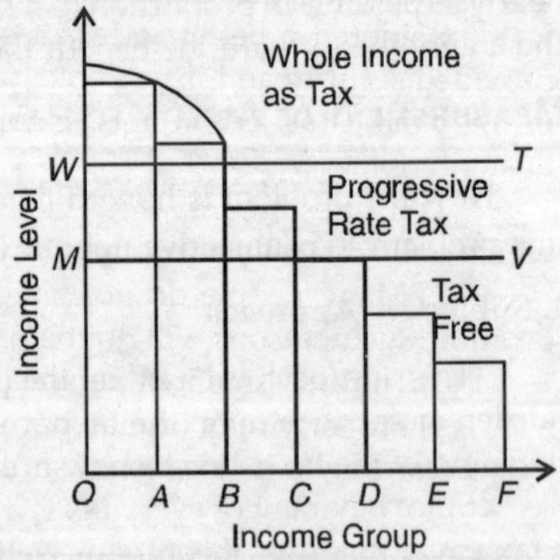

Fig.2

This is the most progressive tax system. **Pigou** indicates it as, "Ropping off the tops of all incomes above the minimum income and leaving everybody, after taxation, with equal incomes."

This means that every individual should not be taxes and only persons with incomes higher them the minimum income level should be levied progressive tax. This is because with the increase in income, itts marginal utility to individuals declines. So when a portion of this increase in incomeis taken away as tax, the person has to sacrifice less satisfaction. This principle is illustrated in Fig. 2 where income level is taken on the vertical axis and income groups on the horizontalaxis. **First,** persons in income groups D, E and F below My income level are tax free. **Second,** person, in income groups *A* and *B*, their entire income above *WT* level is taxed. **Third,** persons with incomes in between My and WT levels are taxed at progressive rates.

Thus, this theory of taxation is better than many other theories. **Pigou** has called it the "final principle of taxation." However, it is also necessary to take into account the effects on output due to a highly progressive tax structure. **Dalton** regards it as controversial when he writes: "Equity is anillusive mistress,whom perhaps it isonly worth the while of philosophers to pursue ardently and of politicians to watch warily."

Limitations of the Subjective Approach

The subjective approach of ability to pay suffers from the following limitations.

1. *Measurement of Sacrifice.* It is not possible to measure utility quantitatively. In other words, since sacrifice is subjective in nature, the tax assessing authorities cannot calculate its amount.

2. *Inter-personal Comparisons of Utility.* Interpersonal comparisons of utility are not possible. Even when different persons have the same income and tax liability, they may not undergo the same amount of sacrifice. This is because of differences in their psychology, tastes, outlook, size of the family, temperament and attitude to pay tax.

3. *Applicability of Diminishing Marginal Utility.* It is difficult to measure the diminishing rate of marginal utility with increase in income. It is seen that people acquire new tastes and preferences along with increase in income.

4. *Source of Income.* The subjective approach does not differentiate between the sources of income and their nature. A tax on the income earned through the inherited property or unearned sources will involve less sacrifice than a tax on an income earned by an individual through hard labour.

5. *Neglects Long-term Economic Growth.* Though after tax equality may maximise total utility in the short-run, it may reduce total utility over time. Therefore, it is essential to know how much of the progressive tax system should be accepted in order to increase the rate of growth over time. This approach is silent over this.

Despite these criticisms, we may conclude that a shift towards equality in income distribution would maximise the aggregate satisfaction of the community.

Objective Approach

It is clear from the above discussion that the subjective approach is not practicable because it mainly emphasizes on the emotions and feelings of the tax payers which are really difficult to measure. Therefore, many economists have adopted the objective approach for determining the ability to pay taxes.

According to this approach, the criteria for determining the ability to pay of an individual tax payer are property, income and expenditure.* They are discussed as under :

1. *Property or Wealth.* According to this criterion, a person with a large property should pay more tax in comparison to the person who possesses less property. This approach proposes that the presence of property is an indication of economic power and a person who is economically powerful should pay more taxes. Wealth was considered a better index of ability than income because in addition to being a source of income, it provided security and insurance against risk. Now, it is considered that property may not be a satisfactory or primary indicator. Rather, it is a supplementary indicater of ability to pay. The following are the weaknesses of this criterion:

(1) If taxes are imposed on an individual's property, people would be discouraged to save and invest, which will adversely affect the growth and capital accumulation in the economy.

(2) Many people do not have much property but earn huge income. If only property is the basis of taxation, such persons will not be paying any tax although their tax paying capacity is high.

(3) The assessment of personal property is not an easy job. So, the tax based on property will not be just.

(4) Property may or may not yield an income in any particular year. It may not be continuous and may vary according to its location, use, etc.

---

* These are the factors which affect the ability to pay of a tax payer.

(5) Income from property may not be the same in all cases. Some properties may yield more income than others and some may not yield any income at all.

(6) A tax on property is levied on its capital value. But, if it does not yield any income, the tax may be unjust.

In spite of these weaknesses, property certainly indicates the tax paying capacity of an individual. Though it can not be relied upon as the main or sole source of taxation, it can certainly be considered as a supplementary and important index of ability to pay.

2. *Income.* An another widely accepted criterion for determining the ability to pay tax is the income of an individual. According to this criterion, a person should be taxed in proportion to his income, from whatever source it may have come. People with low income need not pay any tax and the rate of tax should gradually increase with every increase in income. It is true that wealthier people spend more on luxury goods. So, income is generally regarded as the best indicator of a person's ability to pay. It can not be considered as the main index but a supplementary index of ability to pay.

This criterion has the following difficulties :

Firstly, income has two parts : earned and unearned. **Earned** income includes wages, salaries, etc., whereas unearned sources of income are capital gains, windfall income, etc. The taxation will be unjust if unearned income does not fall under heavier taxation.

Secondly, two persons having similar incomes may not have similar tax paying capacity due to differences in the size of the family, their financial responsibilities and consumption patterns.

Thirdly, People generally become dishonest by concealing their real income in order to escape tax burden.

Despite these weaknesses, income is still regarded as a more accepted index of ability to pay tax. **Adam Smith** also accepted income as a proper measure of ability to pay tax.

3. *Consumption Expenditure.* Consumption expenditure of an individual is another basis for determining ability to pay tax. This basis was approved by **Hobbes, Mill, Fisher, Kaldor,** etc. This criterion suggests that the persons spending more should be taxed heavily, while persons spending less should not be taxed. In other words, people with low consumption expenditure need not pay any tax. But after a certain level, the rate of tax should gradually increase with every increase in expenditure.

This criterion is criticised on the following grounds :

First, it is not essential that a person spending more should pay more tax because the expenditure of a person depends on the size of the family.

Second, tax on consumption expenditure of the people will reduce their consumption. As a result, their efficiency and production will be affected adversely.

Third, there is no sense in taking consumption expenditure as an index of ability to pay and ignore saving and investment expenditure.

Thus, a tax on consumption expenditure should be adopted alongwith other forms of taxes.

EXERCISES

1. What is the cost of service theory of taxation? Discuss.
2. Critically examine the benefit principle of taxation.
3. Explain the ability to pay theory of taxation? How is ability to pay of a taxpayer affected?
4. What are the subjective and objective approaches to measure the ability to pay? Explain.
5. What do you mean by ability to pay tax? How can ability to pay be measured? Discuss.

CHAPTER 93

Trends in Tax Revenue and Expenditure of Centre and State Governments in India

This chapter analyses the trends in tax revenue and expenditure of the Government of India (Centre) and of State Governments.

1. TRENDS IN TAX REVENUE OF THE CENTRE

Tax revenue of the Union Government has been divided into direct and indirect taxes. We discuss below the trends in these components of tax revenue.

1. Tax Revenue. The tax revenue of the Central Government has been rising very Fast over the years on accounts of more taxes, tax rationalisation and inflation.

Table 1 shows that tax revenue rose at a fast pace from Rs. 357 crores in 1950-51 to Rs. 1,64,177 crores in 2002-03. But its share in total revenue receipts declined from 88% in 1950-51 to 69% in 2002-03 because of the increase in non-tax revenue of the Government mainly from rise in dividends and profits of public sector undertaking.

TABLE 1. TOTAL REVENUE RECEIPTS

(Rs. Crores)

	1950-51	*1980-81*	*1990-91*	*2002-03*
Net Tax Revenue	357	9,390	42,980	1,64,177
As % of Total Revenue Receipts	88	73	75	69
Total Revenue Receipts	406	12,830	57,650	2,36,936

2. *Low Tax-GDP Ratio.* The tax-GDP ratio has been low in India. It was 97% in 1980-81, rose to 10.1% in 1990-91 and since then it has been on the decline, being 9% in 2002-03. This decline is closely related to the structural change in GDP by industry of origin. Between 1990-91 and 2002-03, the *share* of *industrial sector* dropped by 6.6 percentage points. The tax revenue from the agricultural sector being negligible, the industrial sector is the principal tax source for the economy. Despite the substantial increase in the share of *services sector* in GDP by 12 percentage points over the period, its contribution to the exchequer is not significant. Another cause of low tax-GDP ratio has been the lowering of *customs tariff.*

3. *Decline in Buoyancy of Taxes.* The low tax revenue collection is reflected in the decline in tax buoyancy. Between the Eighth and Ninth Plan periods, the buoyancy of Central taxes declined from 0.9 to 0.8. But the buoyancy in direct tax collections was maintained at 1.3 between these periods, while the buoyancy in indirect taxes declined from 0.7 to 0.6. This decline in buoyancy was mainly in the customs revenue from 0.9 to 0.1. The reasons for this decline were scaling down of the tax rate, reduction in the number of slabs, etc.

4. *Direct and Indirect Tax Revenue as Proportion of GDP.* Direct tax revenue of the Centre as a proportion of GDP increased from 1.9% in 1990-91 to 3.5% in 2002-03. On the other hand, indirect taxes as a proportion of GDP declined from 7.9% in 1990-91 to 5.7% in 2002-03.

5. *Compositional Shift in Tax Structure.* There has been a compositional shift in the tax structure with the share of indirect taxes in gross tax revenue declining from 78% in 1990-91 and to 60% in 2002-03, and that of direct taxes rising from 19% to 39% over the period. Within direct taxes, the share of income tax almost doubled from 9.3% in 1990-91 to 18% in 2002-03 and that of corporation tax increased by 12 percentage points. As far as indirect taxes are concerned, the share of customs duties declined from 36% to 19% and that of excise duties from 43% to 39% over the period. These structural shifts show that direct taxes are dependent more on the industrial performance and rise in personal incomes while commodity taxes depend on excise duties.

6. *Rationalisation of Tax Structure.* There has been simplification and rationalisation of tax structure with the introduction of structural reforms since 1991. As a result, the tax structure has been modified. Unproductive taxes have been dropped and new taxes introduced. The *expenditure tax* was abolished. It was reintroduced in 1998 and is now applicable on expenditure incurred in a hotel for room charges of Rs. 3,000 or more per day. The *gift tax* was abolished in 1998-99. The *capital gains tax* and the *wealth tax* have also been modified.

The *informal sector* consisting of small traders, retailers and small road transporters has been brought under the tax-net with the introduction of *Lumpsum Presumptive Tax* of Rs. 1,400 per year.

Further, *taxation of services* has been introduced since 1994-95. It has been extended to 51 services over the years.

There has also been rationalisation of the commodity tax structure. *Customs duties* have been considerably reduced both on consumer and capital goods.

The *MODVAT* was introduced in 1986-87 on a number of commodities in place of excise duties. This has been replaced by the CENVAT (Central VAT) in 2000-01.

7. *Lowering of Tax Rates.* Another trend in Central tax structure has been the reduction in tax rates. The rates of income tax, corporate tax and customs duties were very high in India which have been gradually reduced. The maximum rate of basic income tax was 50% in 1990-91 which has been brought down to 30% since 1997-98, of corporate tax from 40% to 35% and of customs duties from 200% to 25% in 2003-04 budget.

8. *Increase in Share of States in Taxes.* The share of States in income tax and excise duties levied by the Centre has been on the increase. These taxes are divided among the States on the basis of the recommendations made by the Finance Commissions every five years. In 1951-52, the States' share was Rs. 51 crores which had increased to Rs. 61,235 crores in 2002-03.

2. EXPENDITURE TRENDS OF THE CENTRE

The expenditure of Government of India is divided into Plan expenditure and Non-Plan expenditure. The Plan expenditure includes Central Plan outlays on various Projects, schemes and programmes and assistance for Plans of the States and Union Territories. Non-Plan expenditure includes all expenditures by the Centre which are not included in the Plan. It includes both development and non-development expenditures such as interest payments, expenditure on defence, subsidies, pensions, grants to States and general services. These

Plan and Non-Plan expenditures are based on Revenue Account and Capital Account. Expenditure on Revenue Account is incurred out of proceeds of taxes and other revenue receipts. On the other hand, Expenditure on Capital Account is met out recoveries of loans and advances, net market borrowings, other capital receipts, like provident funds, small savings, and net external assistance.[1]

The following are the trends in expenditure of the Centre.

1. Increase in Size. The size of public expenditure has grown on a massive scale.

TABLE 2 EXPENDITURE OF CENTRAL GOVERNMENT

(Rs crores)

Year	*Revenue Expenditure*	*Capital Expenditure*	*Total Expenditure*
1950-51	350	180	530
1980-81	14,540	9,630	24,170
1990-91	76,210	31,780	1,07,990
2002-03	3,41,648	62,365	4,04,013

Table 2 shows the phenomenal increase in the total expenditure of the Centre from a small amount of Rs. 530 crores in 1950-51 to Rs. 1,07,990 crores in 1990-91 to Rs. 4,04,013 crores in 2002-03. In particular, the revenue expenditure has grown much faster than the capital expenditure. From Rs. 76,210 crores in 1990-91, the revenue expenditure grew to Rs., 3,41,648 crores in 2002-03 But capital expenditure which in essential for asset creation rose from Rs. 31,780 crores in 1990-91 to Rs. 62, 365 crores in 2002-03.

2. Decline in Plan Expenditure. There has been a decline in the ratio of Plan expenditure to total revenue expenditure in recent years. During the eighties and nineties, the Plan expenditure steadily rose to 45% of the total revenue expenditure. But it fell to 21% in 2002-03.

3. Rise in Non-Plan Expenditure. The non-Plan expenditure has been increasing rapidly in recent years. It rose from Rs. 76,933 crores in 1990-91 to Rs. 2,96,809 crores in 2002-03. But there are three main items in the non-Plan revenue expenditure which have been on the increase over the years, as shown in Table 3.

TABLE 3 NON-PLAN REVENUE EXPENDITURE

(Rs. crores)

Items	*1990-91*	*2002-03*
1.Interest Payments	21,500	1,17,390
2. Defence	10,870	43,589
3. Subsidies	12,160	39,801

(i) *Interest Payments.* There has been a phenomental increase in interest payments from Rs. 21,500 crores in 1990-91 to Rs. 1,17,390 in 2002-03. This is the result of ever-growing public debt and other liabilities of the Government.

(ii) *Defence Expenditure.* The defence expenditure has also been growing due to the ever-present threat from Pakistan and the spread of terrorism in Kashmir. It rose from Rs. 10,870 crores in 1990-91 to Rs. 43,589 crores in 2002-03.

(iii) *Subsidies.* Another reason for the ballooning of non-Plan revenue expenditure is the uncontrolled expansion of subsidies on food, fertilisers and exports. They increased from Rs. 12,160 crores in 1990-91 to Rs. 89,801 crores in 2002-03.

These there items accounted for 74% of the total non-Plan revenue expenditure of the Centre in 2002-03.

4. Increasing Government Debt. The Government has been borrowing on a large scale both within the

1. Students may leave this para. It is meant for understanding.

country and externally for economic development. In recent years outstanding external debt as percentage of GDP has declined from 5.5 percent in 1990-91 to 2.8% in 2002-03. But internal debt as percentage of GDP has been on the increase. It rose from 49.8% in 1990-91 to 58.6% in 2002-03. This has led to increase in public expenditure in the form of interest and principal payments.

3. TRENDS IN REVENUE AND EXPENDITURE OF STATE GOVERNMENTS

The State Governments in India prepare their own budgets of revenue and expenditure like the Central Government. The trends of their consolidated tax revenues and expenditures are discussed as under.

Trends in Revenues of State Governments

State revenues from taxes come from (i) States' own taxes, and (ii) share of taxes received from the Central Government. The taxes levied by the States are (i) taxes on agricultural income; (ii) profession tax; (iii) taxes on property and capital transactions; and taxes on commodities and services.

The trends in tax revenues of States are analysed on the above basis.

1. Increase in Tax Revenues. Revenues of States from their own taxes increased rapidly since 1951-52. From a small sum of Rs. 280 crores in 1951-52, they increased to Rs. 1,49,358 crores in 2002-03. This phenomenal increase has been due to the revision in the rates of oid taxes and imposition of new taxes to meet the growing responsibilities of rising population in the States.

2. Taxes on Income. Taxes on income by States include agricultural income tax and profession tax. Revenue from these sources was very insignificant in 1951-52, being Rs. 4 crores, because only a few States had levied profession tax and income from agricultural income tax was also very low on account of backward agriculture. But with the growth of agricultural production over the years and rise in the income levels of the people, the revenue from State taxes on income had increased to Rs. 5,793 crores in 2002-03.

3. Taxes on Property and Capital Transactions. The State Governments receive income from land revenue, stamp duties and registration fees and tax on urban immovable property. These sources of tax revenue had increased considerably from Rs. 76 crores in 1951-52 to Rs. 16,688 crores in 2002-03.

4. Taxes on Commodities and Services. The State Governments levy commodity and service taxes in the form of excise duties, general sales tax, motor vehicles tax, electricity duty, entertainment tax, etc. The revenue from these items had increased from Rs. 150 crores in 1951-52 to Rs. 1,26, 878 crores in 2002-03. During 1951-52, these taxes accounted for 47% of the revenue from States' taxes which had gone up to 85% in 2002-03. This has led to the increase in the burden of these taxes on lower and middle income groups.

5. States' Share in Central Taxes. The share of States in Central income tax and union excise duties was very insignificant in 1951-52, being Rs. 54 crores (Rs. 53 crores + Rs. 1 crore). This had increased to Rs. 62,459 crores in 2002-03 due to rise in the share of the States on the basis of the recommendations of Finance Commissions and the collection of the absolute amounts of these Central taxes over the years.

Expenditure Trends of State Governments

The expenditure of State Government is divided into revenue account and capital account. Expenditure on revenue account has three components: (i) Development expenditure, (ii) non-development expenditure, and (iii) contribution to local bodies. *Development expenditure* is incurred on social services like education, medical and public health, etc. and economic services like forests, agriculture, soil conservation, dairy development, roads, bridges, irrigation, multipurpose river valley projects. Non-development expenditure consists of debt servicing charges, expenditure on administrative services, etc. Expenditure on capital accounts includes capital outlay, repayment of internal debt, loans of the Union Government and of other State Governments, etc.

The following have been the trends in expenditure of the States in India.

1. Increase in Expenditure. There has been rapid and phenomenal increase in the aggregate expenditure of State Governments. It increased from Rs. 392 crores in 1951-52 to Rs. 4,42,609 crores in 2002-03. The revenue expenditure was 62% of the total expenditure and the remaining was on account of capital expenditure in 2002-03. Component-wise, development expenditure was 56% of the total expenditure while non-development expenditure was 36%.

2. *Growth of Expenditure more then Receipts.* The rate of growth of expenditure has been higher than that of receipts in State finances. The resources gap (deficit) was Rs. 897 crores in 1980-81. It windened during the mid-nineties and was Rs. 5,317 crores in 2002-03. This resources gap has been primarily due to deficit on revenue account to the tune of Rs. 61,302 crores in 2002-03. This has led to the diversion of capital receipts towards current expenditure with the result that expenditure on investment programmes has been reduced.

3. *Pattern of Revenue Expenditure.* Of the total revenue expenditure, the State Governments have been spending more on social services as compared to economic services. In 2002-03, they incurred 36% of the total revenue expenditure on social services and 29% on economic services. Of the economic services, they spent 52% on education, and the remaining on medical and public health, water supply and sanitation, and on natural calamities.

4. *Rise in Non-Development Expenditure.* The Non-development expenditure of the States on revenue account has also increased considerable over the years from Rs. 196 crores in 1951-52 to Rs. 1,57,0146 crores in 2002-03. This rise has seen due to the increase in State expenses on administration, law and order, revision of salaries and D.A. and pensions of employees.

5. *Increase in Capital Expenditure.* The expenditure of States on capital projects like roads, irrigation, power, etc. has been on the increase. It was Rs. 119 crores in 1951-52 which rose to Rs. 87,439 crores in 2002-03.

6. *Rise in Debt and Market Borrowings.* The large and increasing gross fiscal deficit of States has led to a steady rise in the outstanding debt of State governments. In terms of GDP, the debt Stock of states rose from 19.4% in 1990-91 to 28.1% in 2002-03. This has led to increase in market borrowings, loans from financial institutions, funds, etc., basides loans from the Central Government. Market borrowings (net) increased from Rs. 2,556 crores in 1990-91 to Rs. 23,264 crores in 2002-03 and loans from financial institutions and funds, etc. from Rs. 6,253 crores in 1990-91 to Rs. 35,463 crores in 2002-03. So far as the Centre is concerned, the loans from it have been on the decline over the years, particularly capital transfers in the form of loans and advances.

EXERCISES

1. Explain the trends in tax revenue and expenditure of the Government of India.
2. Explain the main trends in tax revenues and expenditure of State Governments in India.

Index

B

C

E

G

Q

R